DICCIONARIO
INGLÉS–ESPAÑOL · ESPAÑOL–INGLÉS
ENGLISH–SPANISH · SPANISH–ENGLISH
DICTIONARY

LAROUSSE

© Larousse, 2010
21, rue du Montparnasse
75283 Paris Cedex 06, France

Original Edition / Edición original

Project management / Dirección de la obra: Sharon J. Hunter

Editors / Redacción: Dileri Borunda Johnston,
Claudia Brovetto, Clio E. Bugel, Talia Bugel,
Magdalena Coll, Antonio Fortin,
José A. Gálvez, Rebecca K. Phillips y Carol Styles Carvajal

Publishing manager / Dirección editorial: Janice McNeillie

Design / Diseño : Sophie Compagne

Illustrations / Ilustraciones: Jean-Pierre Lamerand,
Laurent Blondel y Agathe Bouton

Spanish edition / Edición española

Publishing manager / Dirección editorial: Núria Lucena Cayuela

Project management / Dirección de la obra: Eladio Pascual Foronda

Coordination / Coordinación editorial: Isabel Aparici Turrado

Editors / Redacción: Lidia Bayona Mons,
Encarna Martínez Montoya y Mark Waudby

Typesetting / Realización: dos + dos, serveis editorials, s.c.c. l.

Published in the United States of America and Canada by:
Publicado en Estados Unidos y Canadá por:
Éditions LAROUSSE
21 rue du Montparnasse
75283 Paris Cedex 06, France
www.larousse.fr

ISBN 978 2 03 541014 6

Sales / Distribución: Houghton Mifflin Harcourt, Boston
Library of Congress CIP Data has been applied for

Imprimé en Italie par «La Tipografica Varese S.p.A.»
Dépôt légal : Septembre 2010
541014 -11026754/03 - Décembre 2013

Introduction

The *School* dictionary is a completely new reference book for students in their first two years of learning Spanish. The concept is simple: each different sense of a word has a translation and an example. The two-colour layout ensures that each entry stands out clearly, as well as its different senses and the translations. Words and senses have been carefully selected to meet the needs of young learners. The wordlist is complemented by instructive notes containing lots of useful information on false friends, usage and essential grammar points. As learning a language involves not only learning words, but also learning about a different way of life, the dictionary includes boxed notes on Spanish and Latin American culture. Last but not least this dictionary aims to teach through pictures: themed colour illustrations allow the learner to associate an image with a word or phrase.

Prólogo

El diccionario *School* es una obra totalmente nueva, destinada a los jóvenes de los últimos cursos de primaria y los primeros de secundaria que estudian inglés. Se basa en un concepto pedagógico simple: a cada palabra, o a cada significado de una palabra, se asocian una traducción y un ejemplo. Este concepto se refleja en una presentación a dos colores donde las palabras, los sentidos y las traducciones aparecen claramente identificados. Además, dichas palabras y sus sentidos han sido cuidadosamente seleccionados atendiendo a las necesidades de los jóvenes alumnos. Para completar el léxico, hemos añadido una serie de notas pedagógicas con información acerca de los falsos amigos, el uso de las palabras y los aspectos gramaticales más difíciles. Asimismo, como creemos que el aprendizaje de una lengua no se limita a las palabras, sino que es también importante conocer la cultura, hemos dedicado cuadros especiales a aspectos culturales de los países de habla inglesa. Finalmente, este nuevo diccionario utiliza la imagen como método pedagógico: las ilustraciones en color, agrupadas en láminas temáticas, permiten asociar una imagen a una palabra o expresión.

How to use the dictionary

Cómo usar este diccionario

Entries
Entries are in alphabetical order and are highlighted.

bear [beə^r] *(noun & verb)*
■ *noun*
el **oso**: a polar bear un oso polar
■ *verb (past tense* bore, *past participle* borne*)*
soportar: I can't bear her no la soporto; I can't bear to see him go no puedo soportar que se vaya.

Grammatical categories
The grammatical category of each word is shown in full. Some words have more than one grammatical category. Each new category is preceded by a yellow square.

Pronunciation
Phonetics show the pronunciation of a word.

cap [kæp] *noun*
1. la **gorra**: he wears his cap backwards usa su gorra con la visera hacia atrás
2. el **tapón**: take the cap off the bottle sácale el tapón a la botella.

Senses
If a word has more than one sense and more than one translation, each new sense is numbered.

Translation
The translation of the entry is given on a new line. The gender of Spanish nouns is shown by the article.

frog [frɒg] *noun* ■ la **rana**
to have a frog in one's throat tener carraspera.

Phrases
Important phrases are shown at the end of the entry preceded by a yellow arrow.

add [æd] *verb*
1. **agregar**: add some sugar to the mixture agregar un poco de azúcar a la mezcla
2. **sumar**: she added the numbers together sumó los números

Examples
Examples illustrate the meaning of a word and help with choosing the right translation.

add up *phrasal verb* ■ **sumar**: add the numbers up sumar los números.

Subentries
Words bordered in yellow are subentries and show a different form of the main entry. Phrasal verbs are given in alphabetical order as subentries.

mineral water ['mɪnərəl'wɔːtə^r] *noun* ■ el **agua mineral**

Feminine noun that takes un or el in the singular.

Notes
Grammatical difficulties are explained in the yellow boxes. Boxes preceded by a warning symbol point out false friends and boxes preceded by a book symbol explain certain cultural aspects.

Irregular forms
Irregular forms appear as entries with a cross-reference to the main form.

ridden ['rɪdn] *past participle* ➤ ride.

UK and US
Words that are only used in the United Kingdom are marked *UK*. Words that are only used in the United States are marked *US*.

rumour *UK*, **rumor** *US* ['ruːmə^r] *noun* ■ el **rumour** *(plural* los **rumores**)*:* it's just a rumor sólo es un rumor.

Cómo usar este diccionario

Entrada
Las entradas aparecen por orden alfabético, sobre un fondo amarillo.

el **cómic** ■ comic: me encanta leer cómics I love reading comics.

Traducciones
Cada traducción aparece ilustrada con un ejemplo.

abrigar [12] *verbo*
1. **to wrap up: abriga bien al niño** wrap the baby up warm
2. **to be warm: esta cazadora abriga demasiado** this jacket is too warm.

Conjugación
Los números de conjugación remiten a las tablas de verbos que se encuentran al final del diccionario.

Sentidos
Cuando una entrada tiene varias traducciones, éstas aparecen precedidas de un número.

fumar [1] *verbo* ■ **to smoke: fumar en pipa** to smoke a pipe
prohibido fumar no smoking.

Locuciones
Las locuciones, los compuestos y las frases hechas aparecen agrupadas al final de cada categoría gramatical, precedidas de una flecha amarilla.

calzar [10] *verbo* ■ **to put shoes on: los niños están descalzos, cálzalos** the children are barefoot, put their shoes on
¿qué número calzas? what size shoe do you take?

Subartículo
En un cuadro amarillo sobre fondo blanco aparecen las formas diferentes de algunas entradas.

calzarse *verbo pronominal* ■ **to put one's shoes on: cálzate, que vamos a salir** put your shoes on, we're going out.

Categoría gramatical
La categoría gramatical aparece sin abreviar. En el caso de los sustantivos, la categoría viene determinada por el artículo

fabric ['fæbrɪk] *noun* ■ el **tela**, el **tejido: cotton fabric** tela de algodón

⚠ Fabric es un falso amigo, no significa "fábrica".

Dificultades lingüísticas
Los recuadros precedidos de un signo de peligro avisan sobre la existencia de un falso amigo y los recuadros de fondo amarillo aclaran dificultades gramaticales.

soccer ['sɒkəʳ] *noun* ■ el **fútbol: I play soccer every Saturday** juego al fútbol todos los sábados
a soccer player un jugador de fútbol

SOCCER

Soccer es la palabra que se utiliza en Estados Unidos para referirse al deporte mundialmente conocido como fútbol. Ha ganado mucha popularidad en años recientes y hoy en día muchos niños y niñas estadounidenses practican este deporte.

Notas culturales
Los recuadros precedidos del dibujo de un libro explican algunos aspectos de la vida y la cultura británica o estadounidense.

phonetic transcription   transcripción fonética

English vowels

[ɪ]	pit, big, rid	[ə]	mother, suppose
[e]	pet, tend	[iː]	bean, weed
[æ]	pat, bag, mad	[ɑː]	barn, car, laugh
[ʌ]	run, cut	[ɔː]	born, lawn
[ɒ]	pot, log	[uː]	loop, loose
[ʊ]	put, full	[ɜː]	burn, learn, bird

Vocales españolas

[a]	pata, amigo	[o]	bola, otro
[e]	tila, eso	[u]	luz, una
[i]	piso, imagen		

English diphthongs

[eɪ]	bay, late, great	[aʊ]	now, shout, town
[aɪ]	buy, light, aisle	[ɪə]	peer, fierce, idea
[ɔɪ]	boy, foil	[eə]	pair, bear, share
[əʊ]	no, road, blow	[ʊə]	poor, sure, tour

Diptongos españoles

[ei]	ley, peine	[au]	causa, aula
[ai]	aire, caiga	[eu]	Europa, deuda
[oi]	soy, boina		

English semi-vowels

[j]	you, spaniel	[w]	wet, why, twin

Semivocales españolas

[j]	hierba, miedo	[w]	agua, hueso

English consonants

[p]	pop, people	[ð]	this, with
[b]	bottle, bib	[s]	seal, peace
[t]	train, tip	[z]	zip, his
[d]	dog, did	[ʃ]	sheep, machine
[k]	come, kitchen	[ʒ]	usual, measure
[g]	gag, great	[h]	how, perhaps
[tʃ]	chain, wretched	[m]	metal, comb
[dʒ]	jet, fridge	[n]	night, dinner
[f]	fib, physical	[ŋ]	sung, parking
[v]	vine, livid	[l]	little, help
[θ]	think, fifth	[r]	right, carry

Consonantes españolas

[p]	papá, campo	[s]	solo, paso
[b]	vaca, bomba	[z]	alpinismo
[β]	curvo, caballo	[x]	gemir, jamón
[t]	toro, pato	[m]	madre, cama
[d]	donde, caldo	[n]	no, pena
[k]	que, cosa	[ŋ]	banca, encanto
[g]	grande, guerra	[ɲ]	caña
[ɣ]	aguijón, iglesia	[l]	ala, luz
[tʃ]	ocho, chusma	[r]	atar, paro
[f]	fui, afán	[r]	perro, rosa
[θ]	cera, paz	[ʎ]	llave, collar
[ð]	cada, pardo		

The symbol ['] indicates that the following syllable carries primary stress and the symbol [ˌ] that the following syllable carries secondary stress.

El símbolo ['] indica que la sílaba siguiente lleva el acento primario y el símbolo [ˌ], que la sílaba siguiente lleva el acento secundario.

The symbol [ʳ] in English phonetics indicates that the final r is pronounced only when followed by a word beginning with a vowel. Note that it is nearly always pronounced in American English.

En fonética inglesa, el símbolo [ʳ] indica que la r final sólo se pronuncia cuando va seguida de una palabra que empieza por vocal. Sin embargo, hay que tener en cuenta que casi siempre se pronuncia en inglés americano.

Words considered to be trademarks have been designated in this dictionary by the symbol ®. However, neither the presence nor the absence of such designation should be regarded as affecting the legal status of any trademark.

En este diccionario, las palabras que se consideran como marca registrada llevan asociado el símbolo ®. No obstante, ni la presencia ni la ausencia de este signo afecta al estatus legal de cualquier marca registrada.

English-Spanish
Inglés-Español

a [eɪ, ə] *indefinite article* (**an** [ən] *antes de una vocal)*

1. **un** *(masculine)*, **una** *(feminine)*: **is it a bird or a plane?** ¿es un pájaro o un avión?; **it's an ostrich** es una avestruz
2. *when talking about somebody's job*

> The indefinite article is not translated in Spanish when you say what somebody's profession or trade is:

> **he's an architect** es arquitecto; **she's a doctor** es doctora

3. *when talking about prices, quantities and rates* **It costs 2 pounds a kilo** cuesta 2 libras el kilo; **50 miles an hour** 50 millas por hora; **20 euros an hour** 20 euros la hora; **7 dollars a head** 7 dólares por persona; **twice a week** dos veces a la semana.

abbey ['æbɪ] *noun* ■ la **abadía**.

abbreviation [ə,briːvɪ'eɪʃn] *noun* ■ la **abreviatura**.

abdomen ['æbdəmən] *noun* ■ el **abdomen** *(plural* los **abdómenes**).

ability [ə'bɪlətɪ] *(plural* abilities) *noun* ■ la **habilidad**: **children of different abilities** niños con diferentes habilidades.

able ['eɪbl] *adjective*

> **to be able to do something**
1. **poder hacer algo**: **I'm sure I'll be able to come** estoy seguro de que voy a poder venir

2. **saber hacer algo**: **I'd like to be able to swim** me gustaría saber nadar.

aboard [ə'bɔːrd] *(preposition & adverb)*

■ *preposition*

a bordo de: **there are 42 passengers aboard the train** hay 42 pasajeros a bordo del tren

■ *adverb*

a bordo: **is everyone aboard?** ¿están todos a bordo?

about [ə'baʊt] *(preposition & adverb)*

■ *preposition*

1. **por**: **his parents worry about him** sus padres se preocupan por él
2. **sobre**: **I'm reading a book about magic** estoy leyendo un libro sobre magia

■ *adverb*

1. **alrededor de**: **there were about 50 people** había alrededor de 50 personas; **they'll get here about 5 o'clock** van a llegar aquí alrededor de las 5
2. **de**: **what are you talking about?** ¿de qué estás hablando?

> **just about** casi: **I'm just about ready** estoy casi listo
> **to be about to do something** estar a punto de hacer algo: **he was about to leave when the phone rang** estaba a punto de irse cuando sonó el teléfono
> **how about...?** OR **what about...?** ¿qué tal si...?
> **how about going to the beach?** ¿qué tal si vamos a la playa?

above [ə'bʌv] *(preposition & adverb)*

■ *preposition*

1. **encima de**: **the bathroom is above the kitchen** el baño está encima de la cocina
2. **por encima de**: **we flew above the clouds** volamos por encima de las nubes

> **temperatures above 90 degrees** temperaturas de más de 90 grados

■ *adverb*

1. **de arriba**: **put it on the shelf above** ponlo en el estante de arriba
2. **más**: **you can win with a score of 70 or above** puedes ganar con una puntuación de 70 o más

above all sobre todo: **above all, remember to drive on the right!** ¡sobre todo, recuerda conducir por la derecha!

abroad [ə'brɔːd] *adverb* ■ **en el extranjero**: **Mary spent a year abroad** Mary pasó un año en el extranjero

to **go abroad** irse al extranjero: **she went abroad** se fue al extranjero.

absent ['æbsənt] *adjective*

to **be absent from something** faltar a algo: **Fred was absent from school** Fred faltó a clase.

absolutely ['æbsə'luːtlɪ] *adverb* ■ **absolutamente**: **it's absolutely forbidden** está absolutamente prohibido

she's absolutely right tiene toda la razón.

accelerate [ək'seləreɪt] *verb* ■ **acelerar**: **the train is accelerating** el tren está acelerando.

accent ['æksent] *noun* ■ **el acento**: **she has an English accent** tiene acento inglés.

accept [ək'sept] *verb* ■ **aceptar**: **I accept your offer** acepto tu oferta.

access ['ækses] *noun* ■ **el acceso**

to **have access to something** tener acceso a algo: **the bedroom has access to a balcony** el dormitorio tiene acceso a un balcón.

accessory [ək'sesərɪ] *(plural* accessories*) noun* ■ **el accesorio**

fashion accessories accesorios.

accident ['æksɪdənt] *noun* ■ **el accidente**: **he had an accident** tuvo un accidente

by accident

1. **por casualidad**: **I met her by accident** la conocí por casualidad

2. **sin querer**: **I broke the cup by accident** rompí la taza sin querer.

accommodation UK [ə,kɒmə'deɪʃn] *uncountable noun*, **accommodations** US [ə,kɒmə'deɪʃns] *plural noun* ■ **el alojamiento**: **our travel agent found us accommodation for our trip** nuestro agente de viajes nos encontró alojamiento para el viaje.

according to [ə'kɔːdɪŋtuː] *preposition* ■ **según**: **according to her** según ella

everything went according to plan todo salió según lo planeado.

accordion [ə'kɔːrdiən] *noun* ■ **el acordeón** *(plural* los **acordeones**).

account [ə'kaʊnt] *noun*

1. la **cuenta**: **a bank account** una cuenta bancaria

2. el **relato**: **he gave us an account of his adventures** nos hizo un relato de sus aventuras

to **take something into account** tener en cuenta algo.

accountant [ə'kaʊntənt] *noun* ■ **el/la contable**: **Tanya's father is an accountant** el padre de Tanya es contable.

accurate ['ækjʊrət] *adjective* ■ **exacto**: **it's an accurate description** es una descripción exacta.

accuse [ə'kjuːz] *verb* ■ **acusar**: **she accused him of lying** lo acusó de mentir.

ace [eɪs] *noun* ■ **el as**: **the ace of clubs** el as de trébol.

ache [eɪk] *(noun & verb)*

■ *noun*

el **dolor**: **aches and pains** dolores

■ *verb*

my head aches me duele la cabeza.

achieve [ə'tʃiːv] *verb* ■ **lograr**: **he achieved his objectives** logró sus objetivos.

achievement [ə'tʃiːvmənt] *noun* ■ **el logro**: **it's a real achievement** es un verdadero logro.

acid ['æsɪd] *noun* ■ **el ácido**.

acne ['æknɪ] *uncountable noun* ■ **el acné**: **Molly has acne** Molly tiene acné.

acorn ['eɪkɔːn] *noun* ■ **la bellota**.

acquainted [ə'kweɪntɪd] *adjective*

to **be acquainted with somebody** conocer a alguien: **are you acquainted with Bob?** ¿conoces a Bob?

acrobat ['ækrəbæt] *noun* ■ **el/la acróbata**.

across [ə'krɒs] *(preposition & adverb)*

■ *preposition*

there's a bridge across the river hay un puente que atraviesa el río

> When **across** is used with a verb of movement (to walk across, to run across), you can use a verb alone in Spanish to translate it:

I walked across the street crucé la calle; **don't run across the road** no cruces la calle corriendo

■ *adverb*

the river is 1 mile across el río tiene una 1 milla de ancho.

act [ækt] *(noun & verb)*

■ *noun*

1. **el acto**: **the ghost appears in the second act** el fantasma aparece en el segundo acto
2. **el número**: **a circus act** un número de circo

■ *verb*

actuar: **we must act quickly** debemos actuar rápidamente; **have you ever acted in a play?** ¿has actuado alguna vez en una obra de teatro?

action ['ækʃn] *noun* ■ **la acción** *(plural* las **acciones)*: **the film has a lot of action** la película tiene mucha acción

> **we must take action** debemos actuar

> **an action film** *UK*, **an action movie** *US* una película de acción.

active ['æktɪv] *adjective* ■ **activo**: **he's very active** es muy activo

> **an active volcano** un volcán en actividad.

activity [æk'tɪvətɪ] *(plural* activities) *noun* ■ **la actividad**: **the club offers many outdoor activities** el club ofrece muchas actividades al aire libre.

actor ['æktə'] *noun* ■ **el actor**: **he's an actor** es actor.

actress ['æktrɪs] *noun* ■ **la actriz** *(plural* las **actrices)*: **she's an actress** es actriz.

actual ['æktʃʊəl] *adjective* ■ **verdadero**: **what are your actual reasons?** ¿cuáles son tus verdaderas razones?

> **the actual ceremony starts at 10** la ceremonia misma comienza a las 10

 La palabra inglesa **actual** es un falso amigo, no significa "actual".

actually ['æktʃʊəlɪ] *adverb*

1. **en realidad**: **it's not actually raining** en realidad no está lloviendo
2. **de hecho**: **actually, I do know the answer** de hecho, conozco la respuesta

⚠ La palabra inglesa **actually** es un falso amigo, no significa "actualmente".

acute [ə'kju:t] *adjective* ■ **agudo**: **an acute pain** un dolor agudo.

ad [æd] *(abbreviation of* advertisement) *noun* ■ *informal* **el anuncio**: **I'm calling about the ad in the paper** llamo por el anuncio en el diario

> **the classified ads** los anuncios por palabras, los anuncios clasificados

A.D. [eɪdi:] *(abbreviation of* Anno Domini) **d. de C.** *(abreviatura de* **después de Cristo)** **in 2000 A.D.** en el 2000 d. de C.

adapt [ə'dæpt] *verb* ■ **adaptarse**: **he has adapted well to his new school** se ha adaptado bien a su nuevo colegio.

add [æd] *verb*

1. **agregar**: **add some sugar to the mixture** agregar un poco de azúcar a la mezcla
2. **sumar**: **she added the numbers together** sumó los números

add up *phrasal verb* ■ **sumar**: **add the numbers up** sumad los números.

addict ['ædɪkt] *noun* ■ **el adicto, la adicta**: **a therapy for all sorts of addicts** una terapia para toda clase de adictos

> **he's a drug addict** es drogadicto

> **I'm a TV addict** soy un fanático de la tele.

addicted [ə'dɪktɪd] *adjective* ■ **adicto**

> **to be addicted to something** ser adicto a algo: **she's addicted to cigarettes** es adicta al tabaco.

addition [ə'dɪʃn] *noun* ■ **la suma**

> **in addition** además: **in addition, they offer an English course** además, ofrecen un curso de inglés

in addition to además de: **there will be a disco in addition to the band** habrá una discoteca además de la banda.

address [ə'dres] *noun* ■ la **dirección** *(plural* las **direcciones***)*: **what's your address?** ¿cuál es tu dirección?

▷ **an address book** una libreta de direcciones.

adjective ['ædʒɪktɪv] *noun* ■ el **adjetivo**: **"happy" and "sad" are adjectives** "alegre" y "triste" son adjetivos.

adjust [ə'dʒʌst] *verb*

1. **regular**: **he adjusted the volume** reguló el volumen

2. **ajustar**: **he adjusted the mirror** ajustó el retrovisor

3. **adaptarse**: **I adjusted to the new situation** me adapté a la nueva situación.

administration [əd,mɪnɪ'streɪʃn] *noun* ■ la **administración** *(plural* las **administraciones***)*: **the administration of a company** la administración de una compañía

▷ **the Clinton administration** el gobierno Clinton.

admire [əd'maɪəʳ] *verb* ■ **admirar**: **he admires his teacher** admira a su profesora.

admission [əd'mɪʃn] *noun* ■ la **entrada**: **admission to the museum is free** la entrada al museo es libre.

admit [əd'mɪt] *verb* ■ **reconocer**: **I admit that I'm wrong** reconozco que estoy equivocada

▷ **to admit to doing something** admitir haber hecho algo: **he admitted to stealing the car** admitió haber robado el coche

▷ **he was admitted to the hospital** lo ingresaron en el hospital.

adopt [ə'dɒpt] *verb* ■ **adoptar**: **Ed was adopted as a baby** Ed fue adoptado cuando era bebé.

adore [ə'dɔːʳ] *verb* ■ **adorar**: **she adores her cat** adora a su gato

▷ **I just adore chocolate** me encanta el chocolate.

adult ['ædʌlt] *noun* ■ el **adulto,** la **adulta**: **he's 21 — he's an adult** tiene 21 años –es un adulto.

advance [əd'væns] *(noun & verb)*

■ *noun*

el **adelanto**: **there have been great advances in technology** ha habido grandes adelantos en la tecnología

▷ **the enemy's advance** el avance del enemigo

▷ **in advance** con anterioridad: **we reserved our seats in advance** reservamos nuestros asientos con anterioridad

■ *verb*

avanzar: **the soldiers are advancing** los soldados están avanzando.

advanced [əd'vænst] *adjective* ■ **avanzado**: **she's in the advanced maths class** está en la clase de matemáticas avanzadas.

advantage [əd'væntɪdʒ] *noun* ■ la **ventaja**: **what are the advantages of this method?** ¿cuáles son las ventajas de este método?

▷ **to take advantage of something**

1. **aprovechar algo**: **she took advantage of the opportunity** aprovechó la oportunidad

2. **aprovecharse de algo**: **he took advantage of her ignorance** se aprovechó de su ignorancia.

adventure [əd'ventʃəʳ] *noun* ■ la **aventura**: **they had an exciting adventure in Africa** vivieron una emocionante aventura en África

▷ **an adventure playground** *UK* el parque infantil.

adverb ['ædvɜːb] *noun* ■ el **adverbio**: **"quickly" is an adverb** "rápidamente" es un adverbio

Los adverbios en inglés terminan por lo general en "ly", lo que facilita su reconocimiento.

advert ['ædvɜːt] *UK noun* ■ *informal* el **anuncio**: **he put an advert in the newspaper** puso un anuncio en el periódico.

advertise ['ædvətaɪz] *verb* ■ **anunciar**: **a lot of companies advertise their products on the Internet** muchas empresas anuncian sus productos en Internet.

advertisement [UK əd'vɜːtɪsmənt, US ædvər'taɪzmənt] *noun* ■ el **anuncio**: an advertisement for a new brand of cosmetics un anuncio para una nueva marca de cosméticos.

advice [əd'vaɪs] *uncountable noun* ■ **a piece of advice** un consejo; it was a good piece of advice fue un buen consejo
I asked him for advice le pedí consejo
can you give me some advice? ¿me puedes aconsejar?

advise [əd'vaɪz] *verb* ■ **aconsejar**: he advised me to wait a while me aconsejó que esperara un rato

When using **aconsejar que** remember to put the following verb in the subjunctive.

aerobics [eə'rəʊbɪks] *noun* ■ el **aerobic**: I'm going to my aerobics class voy a la clase de aerobic.

aerosol ['eərəsɒl] *noun* ■ el **aerosol**: an aerosol spray un aerosol.

affect [ə'fekt] *verb* ■ **afectar**: this problem affects a lot of people este problema afecta a mucha gente

affectionate [ə'fekʃənət] *adjective* ■ cariñoso.

afford [ə'fɔːd] *verb*
I can't afford a new car no tengo dinero para comprarme un coche nuevo
we can't afford to go on holiday no podemos permitirnos el lujo de ir de vacaciones.

afraid [ə'freɪd] *adjective*
to be afraid of something tenerle miedo a algo: she's afraid of the dark tiene miedo a la oscuridad
I'm afraid I can't come to your party me temo que no puedo ir a tu fiesta
I'm afraid so me temo que sí.

Africa ['æfrɪkə] *noun* ■ **África**

Feminine noun that takes **el** or **un**.

African ['æfrɪkən] *(adjective & noun)*
■ *adjective*
africano

Remember not to use a capital letter for the adjective in Spanish.

■ *noun*
el **africano**, la **africana**

In Spanish, a capital letter is not used for the inhabitants of a country or region.

after [UK 'ɑːftər, US 'æftər] *(preposition, conjunction & adverb)*
■ *preposition*
después de: after you! ¡después de usted!; we'll leave after breakfast nos iremos después del desayuno
it's twenty after three *US* son las tres y veinte
■ *conjunction*
después de: after I had spoken to him I left me fui después de hablar con él
■ *adverb*
después: the day after el día después
after all después de todo: it doesn't really matter after all la verdad es que después de todo no tiene importancia.

afternoon [UK ,ɑːftə'nuːn, US ,æftə'nuːn] *noun* ■ la **tarde**: I have lessons in the afternoon tengo clases en la tarde
I'll see you on Tuesday afternoon te veo el martes en la tarde
good afternoon! ¡buenas tardes!

afterwards UK ['æftəwədz] , **afterwards** US ['æftərwərd] *adverb* ■ **después**: they went home afterwards se fueron a su casa después.

again [ə'gen] *adverb* ■ **otra vez**: try calling him again prueba a llamarlo otra vez; I'd like to see you again me gustaría verte otra vez
again and again una y otra vez: he tried again and again probó una y otra vez
to do something again volver a hacer algo: he did the exercise again volvió a hacer el ejercicio.

against [ə'genst] *(preposition & adverb)*
■ *preposition*
contra: she was leaning against the wall estaba apoyada contra la pared

■ *adverb*

2. en contra: they voted against votaron en contra; we're against animal testing estamos en contra de los experimentos con animales.

age [eɪdʒ] *noun* ■ la **edad:** he started school at the age of five empezó la escuela a los cinco años de edad

> it took ages to download tardó muchísimo en bajar

> I haven't seen him for ages hace siglos que no lo veo.

agency ['eɪdʒənsɪ] *(plural* agencies*) noun* ■ la **agencia**

> a travel agency una agencia de viajes

> an employment agency una agencia de empleo.

aggressive [ə'gresɪv] *adjective* ■ **agresivo:** city dwellers tend to be very aggressive la gente que vive en ciudades tiende a ser muy agresiva.

ago [ə'gəʊ] *adverb*

> a long time ago hace mucho tiempo

> she left three years ago se fue hace tres años

> how long ago did he die? ¿cuánto hace que murió?

agree [ə'griː] *verb*

1. estar de acuerdo: Jim agrees with me Jim está de acuerdo conmigo

2. aceptar: Gabriel agreed to go with them Gabriel aceptó ir con ellos

3. acordar: they agreed on a date acordaron una fecha

> to agree to do something quedar en hacer algo: I agreed to meet him at the cinema quedé en encontrarme con él en el cine.

agreement [ə'griːmənt] *noun* ■ el **acuerdo:** we've reached an agreement hemos llegado a un acuerdo.

ahead [ə'hed] *adverb*

1. delante: look straight ahead mira hacia delante

2. adelantado: the work is ahead of schedule el trabajo está adelantado respecto de lo previsto.

aid [eɪd] *noun* ■ la **ayuda:** the refugees received aid from the government los refugiados recibieron ayuda del gobierno.

AIDS , **Aids** , [eɪdz] *(abbreviation of* acquired immune deficiency syndrome*)* ■ *noun* el **sida.**

aim [eɪm] *(noun & verb)*

■ *noun*

el **propósito:** I did it with the aim of saving him lo hice con el propósito de salvarlo

> to take aim apuntar

■ *verb*

1. apuntar: she aimed her gun at the tiger apuntó al tigre con su pistola

2. proponerse: I aim to help him me propongo ayudarlo.

air [eər] *noun* ■ el **aire:** he threw the ball into the air tiró la pelota al aire; I'm going outside for some fresh air voy a salir a tomar el aire

> travelling by air is the fastest way viajar en avión es más rápido

> the air force el Ejército del Aire

> an air raid un ataque aéreo

> an air terminal una terminal aérea.

air conditioning [eər'kən'dɪʃnɪŋ] *noun* ■ el **aire acondicionado.**

airline ['eəlaɪn] *noun* ■ la **línea aérea:** I've never flown with this airline before nunca había viajado en esta línea aérea.

airmail ['eəmeɪl] *noun* ■ el **correo aéreo:** she sent the package by airmail mandó el paquete por correo aéreo.

airplane *US* ['eəpleɪn] *noun* ■ el **avión** *(plural* los **aviones***).*

airport ['eəpɔːt] *noun* ■ el **aeropuerto:** they met me at the airport me fueron a buscar al aeropuerto.

aisle [aɪl] *noun* ■ el **pasillo:** the cereal is in aisle five los cereales están en el pasillo cinco.

alarm [ə'lɑːm] *noun* ■ la **alarma:** the fire alarm went off sonó la alarma contra incendios

> an alarm clock un despertador: I'll set the alarm for 7 a.m. voy a poner el despertador a las 7 de la mañana.

album ['ælbəm] *noun* ■ el **álbum**: Garbage's new album el nuevo álbum de Garbage.

alcohol ['ælkəhɒl] *noun* ■ el **alcohol**.

alien ['eɪljən] *noun*
1. el/la **extraterrestre**
2. el **extranjero**, la **extranjera**: illegal alien inmigrante ilegal.

alike [ə'laɪk] *adverb*
> to be alike ser parecidos: they're very much alike son muy parecidos
> to look alike parecerse: they really look alike de verdad se parecen.

alive [ə'laɪv] *adjective* ■ **vivo**: is he still alive? ¿aún está vivo?

all [ɔːl] *(adjective, pronoun & adverb)*
■ *adjective & pronoun*
todo: they danced all night bailaron toda la noche; he lost all his money perdió todo su dinero; all of the girls were laughing todas las chicas se reían; I've invited all of them los invité a todos; tell me all about it cuéntamelo todo
■ *adverb*
todo: he was all wet estaba todo mojado
> all alone completamente solo: the boys are all alone los chicos están completamente solos
> not at all nada: I didn't like the play at all no me gustó nada el juego
> all over por todas partes: we looked all over for the perfect dress buscamos por todas partes el vestido perfecto
> the score is two all van empatados a dos.

allergic [ə'lɜːdʒɪk] *adjective* ■ **alérgico**: he's allergic to cats es alérgico a los gatos.

allergy ['ælədʒɪ] *(plural* allergies) *noun* ■ la **alergia**.

alley ['ælɪ] *noun* ■ el **callejón** *(plural* los callejones).

alligator ['ælɪgeɪtər] *noun* ■ el **caimán** *(plural* los caimanes).

allow [ə'laʊ] *verb* ■ **permitir**
> to allow someone to do something permitirle a alguien hacer algo: are you allowed to go out alone? ¿te permiten salir solo?

allowance [ə'laʊəns] *noun* ■ las **dietas**
> travel allowances dietas de viaje
> family allowance subvención familiar.

all right ['ɔːlraɪt] *adverb*
1. **bien**: it's working all right está funcionando bien; are you all right? ¿estás bien?; she had an accident but she's all right tuvo un accidente, pero está bien
2. **vale**: do you want to go? —all right! ¿quieres ir? —¡vale!
3. **no estar mal**: did you like the film? —it was all right ¿te gustó la película? —no estuvo mal

Aunque mucha gente usa en el lenguaje escrito alright, se considera más correcto all right.

almond ['ɑːmənd] *noun* ■ la **almendra**.

almost ['ɔːlməʊst] *adverb* ■ **casi**: I've almost finished this book casi he terminado este libro; I almost missed the train casi pierdo el tren.

alone [ə'ləʊn] *adjective & adverb* ■ **solo**: he's all alone está completamente solo; she went out alone salió sola
> leave me alone! ¡déjame en paz!
> leave my computer alone! ¡no toques mi ordenador!

along [ə'lɒŋ] *(adverb & preposition)*
■ *adverb*
please move along por favor, muévanse; can I come along with you? ¿puedo ir contigo?
> all along desde el principio: he was lying to me all along me mintió desde el principio
■ *preposition*
por: I walked along the beach caminé por la playa.

aloud [ə'laʊd] *adverb* ■ **en voz alta**: he was reading aloud estaba leyendo en voz alta.

alphabet ['ælfəbet] *noun* ■ el **alfabeto**.

alphabetical [ˌælfə'betɪkl] *adjective* ■ **alfabético**: they're in alphabetical order están en orden alfabético.

already [ɔːl'redɪ] *adverb* ■ **ya**: he has already left ya se ha ido.

alright ['ɔːlraɪt] *adverb* ➤ all right.

also ['ɔːlsəʊ] *adverb* ■ **también**: he also speaks French también habla francés.

alternate [UK 'ɔːltɜːnət, US 'ɔːltərnət] *adjective* ■ **they come on alternate days** vienen un día sí y otro no.

alternative [ɔːl'tɜːnətɪv] (*adjective & noun*)
■ adjective
otro: there's an alternative route hay otra ruta
➤ **alternative medicine** la medicina alternativa
■ noun
la **alternativa**: I have no alternative no me queda otra alternativa.

although [ɔːl'ðəʊ] *conjunction* ■ **aunque**: she went to school although she was ill fue al colegio aunque estaba enferma.

altogether [,ɔːltə'geðər] *adverb*
1. **del todo**: that's not altogether true eso no es del todo cierto
2. **en total**: we spent 80 dollars altogether gastamos 80 dólares en total.

aluminium UK [,æljʊ'mɪnɪəm], **aluminum** US [ə'luːmɪnəm] *noun* ■ el **aluminio**
➤ aluminium foil el papel de aluminio.

always ['ɔːlweɪz] *adverb* ■ **siempre**: she's always late siempre llega tarde.

am [æm] ➤ be.

a.m. [eɪem] **de la mañana**
➤ at 8 a.m. a las 8 de la mañana.

amazed [ə'meɪzd] *adjective* ■ **asombrado**: I was amazed to see her me quedé asombrado al verla.

amazing [ə'meɪzɪŋ] *adjective* ■ **increíble**: it's an amazing story es una historia increíble.

amber ['æmbər] *noun* ■ el **ámbar**.

ambition [æm'bɪʃn] *noun* ■ la **ambición** (*plural* las **ambiciones**): her ambition is to be an astronaut su ambición es ser astronauta.

ambitious [æm'bɪʃəs] *adjective* ■ **ambicioso**: John is very ambitious John es muy ambicioso.

ambulance ['æmbjʊləns] *noun* ■ la **ambulancia**.

America [ə'merɪkə] *noun*
1. **América**: America is a continent América es un continente
2. los **Estados Unidos**: I'm going to America voy a los Estados Unidos.

American [ə'merɪkn] (*adjective & noun*)
■ adjective

Remember not to use a capital letter for the adjective in Spanish:

1. *of America* **americano**: the American continent el continente americano
2. *of the US* **estadounidense**: he has an American accent tiene acento estadounidense
➤ **The American Revolution** la guerra de independencia norteamericana
■ noun

In Spanish, a capital letter is not used for the inhabitants of a country or region:

1. *of America* el/la **americano**
2. *of the US* el/la **estadounidense**

AMERICAN FOOTBALL

La versión estadounidense del fútbol es más bien una adaptación del rugby. Generalmente se le llama **football** a secas y es uno de los deportes más populares en Estados Unidos. Todas las escuelas secundarias y universidades tienen equipo de fútbol y los partidos son acontecimientos muy concurridos.

THE AMERICAN REVOLUTION

Así se llama a la guerra en que los habitantes de lo que serían los Estados Unidos se enfrentaron a los ingleses entre 1775 y 1783. Los americanos querían independizarse, sobre todo para no tener que seguir pagando impuestos a Inglaterra. El 4 de julio de 1776, el futuro presidente Thomas Jefferson firmó la Declaración de Independencia. Inglaterra se negó a reconocerla y la guerra continuó. George Washington, con la ayuda de soldados franceses, encabezó las tropas rebeldes y en 1783 se firmó el convenio de paz: habían nacido los Estados Unidos de América.

among [ə'mʌŋ] *preposition* ■ **entre**: there are children among the crowd hay niños entre la multitud.

amount [ə'maʊnt] *noun* ■ la **cantidad**: there was a large amount of cream in the dessert el postre tenía una gran cantidad de nata.

amp [æmp] *noun*

1. el **amplificador**: unplug the amp! ¡desenchufa el amplificador!

2. el **amperio**: the amp is the unit of electric current el amperio es la unidad de la corriente eléctrica.

amuse [ə'mjuːz] *verb*

1. **hacerle gracia a**: the joke amused Peter el chiste le hizo gracia a Peter

2. **entretener**: the children were very amused by the clown el payaso entretuvo mucho a los niños; she knows how to keep them amused sabe entretenerlos
she amused herself by reading se entretuvo leyendo.

amusement arcade *UK* [ə'mjuːzmənt-ɑːk'keɪd] *noun* ■ el **salón recreativo**.

amusement park [ə'mjuːzməntpɑːk] *noun* ■ el **parque de atracciones**.

an [ən] *article* ➤ a.

anaesthetic *UK*, **anesthetic** *US* [,ænɪs'θetɪk] *noun* ■ la **anestesia**.

analyze *UK*, **analyze** *US* ['ænəlaɪz] *verb* ■ **analizar**.

ancestor ['ænsestəʳ] *noun* ■ el **antepasado**, la **antepasada**: my ancestors came from Cuba mis antepasados eran de Cuba.

anchor ['æŋkəʳ] *noun* ■ el **ancla** *(feminine)*: they dropped anchor echaron el ancla

Feminine noun that takes **un** or **el** in the singular.

ancient ['eɪnʃənt] *adjective* ■ **antiguo**: it's an ancient monument es un monumento antiguo.

and [ænd, ənd] *conjunction* ■ **y**: your father and mother tu padre y tu madre; six and a half years seis años y medio

come and see who's here! ¡ven a ver quién está aquí!
he's getting taller and taller está cada vez más alto.

anesthetic *US noun* ➤ anaesthetic.

angel ['eɪndʒəl] *noun* ■ el **ángel**.

anger ['æŋgəʳ] *noun* ■ la **rabia**: he was shaking with anger temblaba de rabia.

angle ['æŋgl] *noun* ■ el **ángulo**: a triangle has three angles un triángulo tiene tres ángulos.

angry ['æŋgrɪ] *adjective* ■ **enfadado**
to be angry with somebody estar enfadado con alguien: Peggy is angry with me Peggy está enfadada conmigo
to get angry enfadarse: Mrs. Smith got very angry la señora Smith se enfadó mucho.

animal ['ænɪml] *noun* ■ el **animal**: wild animals los animales salvajes.

ankle ['æŋkl] *noun* ■ el **tobillo**: he sprained his ankle se torció un tobillo.

anniversary [,ænɪ'vɜːsərɪ] *(plural anniversaries) noun* ■ el **aniversario**
wedding anniversary el aniversario de bodas.

announce [ə'naʊns] *verb* ■ **anunciar**: they announced the news anunciaron la noticia.

announcement [ə'naʊnsmənt] *noun* ■ el **anuncio**: the president made an announcement el presidente hizo un anuncio.

annoy [ə'nɔɪ] *verb* ■ **molestar**: you're annoying me! ¡me estás molestando!

annoyed [ə'nɔɪd] *adjective* ■ **molesto**: he's annoyed with me está molesto conmigo; I got annoyed with her me enfadé con ella.

annoying [ə'nɔɪɪŋ] *adjective* ■ **molesto**: trying to park here is so annoying tratar de aparcar aquí es tan molesto.

annual ['ænjʊəl] *adjective* ■ **anual**: the group is having its annual dinner el grupo tiene su cena anual.

anonymous [ə'nɒnɪməs] *adjective* ■ anónimo: she got an anonymous letter ha recibido una carta anónima.

another [ə'nʌðəʳ] *adjective & pronoun* ■ otro: would you like another drink? ¿quieres otra bebida?; he's looking for another job está buscando otro trabajo

> one another el uno al otro: they love one another se aman el uno al otro.

answer ['ænsəʳ] *(noun & verb)*

■ *noun*

1. la respuesta: I'm waiting for an answer estoy esperando una respuesta

2. la solución *(plural* las soluciones*)*: there's no easy answer to this problem no hay una solución fácil a este problema

■ *verb*

contestar: she didn't answer no contestó

> to answer the door abrir la puerta.

answering machine [US 'ɑːnsərɪŋ məˈʃiːn, US 'ænsərɪŋ məˈʃiːn] *noun* ■ el contestador automático.

ant [ænt] *noun* ■ la hormiga.

anthem ['ænθəm] *noun* ■ el himno: the national anthem el himno nacional.

antibiotic [ˌæntɪbaɪ'ɒtɪk] *noun* ■ el antibiótico: the doctor gave me an antibiotic for my ear infection el médico me dio un antibiótico para la infección de oído.

anticlockwise UK [ˌæntɪ'klɒkwaɪz] *adjective & adverb* ■ en sentido contrario a las agujas del reloj.

antique [æn'tiːk] *adjective* ■ la antigüedad: the house is full of antiques la casa está llena de antigüedades.

antiseptic [ˌæntɪ'septɪk] *noun* ■ el antiséptico.

anxious ['æŋkʃəs] *adjective* ■ preocupado: she was very anxious about her Spanish test estaba muy preocupada por su examen de español

> to be anxious to do something estar ansioso por hacer algo: I'm anxious to meet him estoy ansiosa por encontrarme con él.

any ['enɪ] *(adjective, pronoun & adverb)*

■ *adjective*

1.

In questions, negative and conditional sentences any is usually not translated:

have you got any bread? ¿tienes pan?; are there any famous people here? ¿hay gente famosa aquí?; I don't have any money no tengo dinero; call me if you need any help llámame si necesitas ayuda

2.

In questions and negative sentences any can be translated as algún/alguna or ningún/ninguna:

do you have any friends called Peter? ¿tienes algún amigo que se llama Peter?; do you have any questions? tienes alguna pregunta?; I don't have any friends no tengo ningún amigo; there aren't any oranges left no queda ninguna naranja

3.

In affirmative sentences when any means whichever it's translated by cualquier:

you can listen to any station you like puedes escuchar cualquier emisora de radio que quieras

■ *pronoun*

1.

In questions when any refers to a countable noun, it's translated by alguno/alguna, when it refers to an uncountable noun, it's not translated:

I need a clip, are there any left? necesito un clip ¿queda alguno?; we're short of bread, did you buy any nos falta pan ¿has comprado?

2.

In negative sentences, when any refers to a countable noun, it's translated by ninguno/ninguna, when it refers to an uncountable noun, it's not translated:

I don't want any of them no quiero ninguno; there isn't any milk no hay leche

■ *adverb*

Any is not always translated in Spanish:

is he any better ? ¿está mejor?; I can't go any faster no puedo ir más rápido

> any more más: do you want any more? ¿quieres más?; I don't want any more no quiero más.

anybody ['enɪ,bɒdɪ], **anyone** ['enɪwʌn] *pronoun*

1. **alguien:** is anybody home? ¿hay alguien en casa?
2. **nadie:** I can't see anybody no veo a nadie
3. **cualquiera:** anybody can do it cualquiera puede hacerlo.

anyhow *adverb* ➤ anyway.

anymore ['enɪmɔːʳ] *adverb*
she doesn't live here anymore ya no vive aquí.

anyone *pronoun* ➤ anybody.

anyplace *UK adverb* ➤ anywhere.

anything ['enɪθɪŋ] *pronoun*

1. **algo:** can I do anything? ¿puedo hacer algo?
2. **nada:** I can't see anything no veo nada
3. **cualquier cosa:** anything can happen puede suceder cualquier cosa.

anyway ['enɪweɪ], **anyhow** ['enɪhaʊ] *adverb* ■ **de todos modos:** I don't want to go, and anyway it's too late no quiero ir y de todos modos ya es demasiado tarde.

anywhere ['enɪweəʳ], **anyplace** *US* ['enɪpleɪs] *adverb*

1. **en alguna parte:** have you seen John anywhere? ¿has visto a John en alguna parte?
2. **en ninguna parte:** I can't find him anywhere no lo encuentro en ninguna parte
3. **en cualquier parte:** put it down anywhere déjalo en cualquier parte.

apart [ə'pɑːt] *adverb*
they are two feet apart hay 67 centímetros entre uno y otro

> apart from aparte de: apart from that, you're right aparte de eso, tienes razón.

apartment [ə'pɑːtmənt] *noun* ■ **el piso, el apartamento:** she lives in an apartment vive en un piso

> an apartment building un edificio de apartamentos.

apologize , apologise *UK* [ə'pɒlədʒaɪz] *verb* ■ **disculparse:** she apologized for being late se disculpó por llegar tarde.

apology [ə'pɒlədʒɪ] *(plural apologies)* *noun* ■ **la disculpa:** she owes me an apology me debe una disculpa.

apostrophe [ə'pɒstrəfɪ] *noun* ■ **el apóstrofo.**

apparently [ə'pærəntlɪ] *adverb* ■ **por lo visto:** apparently she doesn't live here anymore por lo visto, ya no vive aquí.

appeal [ə'piːl] *verb*

1. **atraer:** to appeal to somebody atraerle a alguien; this colour appeals to me este color me atrae
2. **hacer un llamamiento:** they appealed for help hicieron un llamamiento pidiendo ayuda.

appear [ə'pɪəʳ] *verb*

1. **aparecer:** he suddenly appeared apareció de repente
2. **parecer:** she appears to be sleeping parece que está durmiendo.

appearance [ə'pɪərəns] *noun* ■ **la apariencia:** don't judge by appearances no juzgues por las apariencias.

appetite ['æpɪtaɪt] *noun* ■ **el apetito:** David has a big appetite David tiene mucho apetito.

applaud [ə'plɔːd] *verb* ■ **aplaudir:** everyone applauded todos aplaudieron.

applause [ə'plɔːz] *uncountable noun* ■ **los aplausos:** the singer was greeted by loud applause recibieron al cantante con fuertes aplausos.

apple ['æpl] *noun* ■ **la manzana**
> an apple pie una tarta de manzana
> an apple tree un manzano.

appliance [ə'plaɪəns] *noun* ■ **el aparato**
> domestic appliances los electrodomésticos.

application [,æplɪ'keɪʃn] *noun* ■ **la solicitud:** you have to fill out a job application tiene que rellenar una solicitud de empleo. ■

apply [ə'plaɪ] *verb*

1. **solicitar**: I applied for a job solicité un empleo
2. **aplicarse**: this rule applies to everybody esta norma se aplica a todo el mundo
3. **aplicar**: apply the cream with your fingers aplicar la crema con los dedos.

appointment [ə'pɔɪntmənt] *noun* ■ la **cita**: he has an appointment with the dentist tiene cita con el dentista.

approach [ə'prəʊtʃ] *verb*

1. **acercarse**: the enemy is approaching el enemigo se acerca; we approached the summit nos acercamos a la cumbre
2. **abordar**: we must approach the problem in a different way tenemos que abordar el problema de otra manera.

appropriate [ə'prəʊprɪət] *adjective* ■ **apropiado**: these shoes aren't appropriate for hiking estos zapatos no son apropiados para el excursionismo.

approve [ə'pruːv] *verb* ■ **aprobar**: our project was approved aprobaron nuestro proyecto

> I don't approve of his ideas no estoy de acuerdo con sus ideas

> they don't approve of me going out every night no les parece bien que yo salga cada noche.

approximately [ə'prɒksɪmətlɪ] *adverb* ■ **aproximadamente**: it costs approximately 20 euros cuesta aproximadamente 20 euros.

apricot ['eɪprɪkɒt] *noun* ■ el **albaricoque**.

April ['eɪprəl] *noun*

In Spanish the months of the year do not start with a capital letter:

abril *(masculine)*: in April en abril; on April 17th el 17 de abril; next April el próximo abril; last April el pasado abril

> April Fools' Day el día de los Inocentes

APRIL FOOL'S DAY

Tanto en Gran Bretaña como en Estados Unidos, el uno de abril es el día en que la gente se gasta bromas, es decir, el equivalente de nuestro día de los Inocentes. Sin embargo, no existe la tradición de colgar monigotes de papel en la espalda y no se permiten más bromas después del mediodía.

apron ['eɪprən] *noun* ■ el **delantal**: the cook is wearing an apron el cocinero lleva puesto un delantal.

aquarium [ə'kweərɪəm] *noun* ■ el **acuario**.

archaeologist *UK*, **archeologist** *US* [ˌɑːkɪ'ɒlədʒɪst] *noun* ■ el **arqueólogo**, la **arqueóloga**: Paul is an archeologist Paul es arqueólogo.

archaeology *UK*, **archeology** *US* [ˌɑːkɪ'ɒlədʒɪ] *noun* ■ la **arqueología**.

architect ['ɑːkɪtekt] *noun* ■ el **arquitecto**, la **arquitecta**: Sandra is an architect Sandra es arquitecta.

architecture ['ɑːkɪtektʃər] *noun* ■ la **arquitectura**.

are [ər, ɑːr] ➤ be.

area ['eərɪə] *noun*

1. el **área**: he lives in the London area vive en el área de Londres
2. la **zona**: I like this area of town me gusta esta zona de la ciudad
3. la **superficie**: the room has an area of 200 square feet la habitación tiene una superficie de 20 metros cuadrados

> area code el prefijo: the area code for Madrid is 91 el prefijo de Madrid es el 91.

aren't [ɑːnt] = are not.

Argentina [ˌɑːdʒən'tiːnə] *noun* ■ **Argentina**.

Argentinian [ˌɑːdʒən'tiːnɪən] *(adjective & noun)*

■ *adjective*

Remember not to use a capital letter for the adjective in Spanish:

argentino: I like Argentinian beef me gusta la carne argentina

■ *noun*

In Spanish, a capital letter is not used for the inhabitants of a country or region:

el **argentino,** la **argentina:** he married an Argentinian se casó con una argentina.

argue ['ɑːgjuː] *verb* ■ **discutir:** they're always arguing siempre están discutiendo.

argument ['ɑːgjʊmənt] *noun* ■ **la discusión** *(plural* las **discusiones)*:* they had an argument tuvieron una discusión.

arm [ɑːm] *noun* ■ **el brazo:** he broke his arm se rompió el brazo.

armchair ['ɑːmtʃeəʳ] *noun* ■ **el sillón** *(plural* los **sillones).**

armour *UK,* **armor** *US* ['ɑːməʳ] *noun* ■ **la armadura:** a knight in armour un caballero con armadura.

armpit ['ɑːmpɪt] *noun* ■ **la axila.**

army ['ɑːmɪ] *(plural* armies*) noun* ■ **el ejército:** he's in the army está en el ejército.

around [ə'raʊnd] *(preposition & adverb)*

■ *preposition*

1. **alrededor de:** they walked around the lake caminaron alrededor del lago

2. **por:** we were driving around town all afternoon anduvimos en coche por la ciudad toda la tarde

■ *adverb*

1. **alrededor de:** I'll see you around 9 o'clock te veré alrededor de las 9

2. **alrededor:** a garden with a fence all around it un jardín con una valla a su alrededor

3. **por:** he lives around here vive por aquí

4. **por ahí:** she left her clothes lying around everywhere dejó su ropa tirada por todas partes.

arrange [ə'reɪndʒ] *verb*

1. **colocar:** she arranged the chairs around the table colocó las sillas alrededor de la mesa

2. **organizar:** they've arranged a meeting for Monday han organizado una reunión para el lunes

> to arrange to do something quedar en hacer algo: we've arranged to meet at the park quedamos en encontrarnos en el parque.

arrangements [ə'reɪndʒmənts] *plural noun*

1. **los planes:** we made arrangements to get a babysitter hicimos planes para conseguir una canguro

2. **los preparativos:** they made the arrangements for me to travel hicieron los preparativos para mi viaje.

arrest [ə'rest] *(noun & verb)*

■ *noun*

la **detención,** el **arresto:** they made several arrests hicieron varias detenciones

> you're under arrest queda detenido

■ *verb*

detener, arrestar: the police arrested the thief la policía detuvo al ladrón.

arrival [ə'raɪvl] *noun* ■ **la llegada:** what's the arrival time? ¿cuál es la hora de llegada?

arrive [ə'raɪv] *verb* ■ **llegar:** Uncle Tony just arrived el tío Tony acaba de llegar.

arrow ['ærəʊ] *noun* ■ **la flecha:** a bow and arrow un arco y flecha.

art [ɑːt] *noun* ■ **el arte:** modern art el arte moderno; a work of art una obra de arte.

artichoke ['ɑːtɪtʃəʊk] *noun* ■ **la alcachofa.**

article ['ɑːtɪkl] *noun* ■ **el artículo.**

artificial [ˌɑːtɪ'fɪʃl] *adjective* ■ **artificial:** it's an artificial lake es un lago artificial.

artist ['ɑːtɪst] *noun* ■ **el/la artista:** Teresa is an artist Teresa es artista.

as [əz, æz] *conjunction & adverb*

1. **cuando:** as he walked into the room everyone started clapping cuando entró en la habitación, todos empezaron a aplaudir

2. **como:** as you can see, I'm very busy como puedes ver, estoy muy ocupada; he's late as usual llega tarde, como siempre

> as … as tan … como: he's as tall as his father es tan alto como su padre

as much as tanto como: she doesn't earn as much as I do ella no gana tanto como yo

you can have as many as you like puedes tener tantos como quieras

as soon as possible lo antes posible: I'll come as soon as possible vendré lo antes posible

as if OR as though como si: he acted as if nothing had happened él actuó como si nada hubiera sucedido.

a.s.a.p. [eɪeseɪpiː] *(abbreviation of* as soon as possible*)* ■ lo antes posible.

ash [æʃ] *noun* ■ la ceniza.

ashamed [əˈʃeɪmd] *adjective*

to be ashamed of something estar avergonzado de algo: he was ashamed of his behaviour estaba avergonzado de su comportamiento

you should be ashamed of yourself! ¡debería darte vergüenza!

ashtray [ˈæʃtreɪ] *noun* ■ el cenicero.

Asia [ˈeɪʒə] *noun* ■ Asia: Asia is a continent Asia es un continente; Indonesia is in Asia Indonesia está en Asia.

Asian [ˈeɪʒn] *(adjective & noun)*

■ *adjective*

Remember not to use a capital letter for the adjective in Spanish:

asiático: an Asian country un país asiático

■ *noun*

In Spanish, a capital letter is not used for the inhabitants of a country or region:

el asiático, la asiática.

aside [əˈsaɪd] *adverb*

1. a un lado: can you stand aside? ¿puedes ponerte a un lado?

2. en reserva

I've got some money set aside tengo un poco de dinero ahorrado.

ask [æsk] *verb*

1. preguntar: I'd like to ask something quisiera preguntar algo

2. invitar: he asked me to the party me invitó a la fiesta

3. pedir: Fran asked her teacher for help Fran le pidió ayuda a su profesor

to ask somebody to do something pedirle a alguien que haga algo: I asked her to wait le pedí que esperara.

asleep [əˈsliːp] *adjective* ■ dormido: he's already asleep ya está dormido

to fall asleep quedarse dormido: she fell asleep se quedó dormida.

asparagus [əˈspærəgəs] *uncountable noun* ■ el espárrago, los espárragos.

aspirin® [ˈæsprɪn] *noun* ■ la aspirina.

asset [ˈæset] *noun*

Fred is an asset to the team Fred es muy valioso para el equipo.

assignment [əˈsaɪnmənt] *noun* ■ el trabajo, la tarea: he handed in his assignment entregó su trabajo.

assistant [əˈsɪstənt] *noun* ■ el/la ayudante: my assistant will call you tomorrow mi ayudante le llamará mañana

personal assistant la secretaria de dirección.

assume [əˈsuːm] *verb* ■ suponer: I assume you're coming too supongo que tú también vienes.

assure [əˈʃʊəʳ] *verb* ■ asegurar: I assure you I'm not lying te aseguro que no estoy mintiendo.

asterisk [ˈæstərɪsk] *noun* ■ el asterisco.

asthma [*UK* ˈæsmə, *US* ˈæzmə] *noun* ■ el asma *(feminine)*

Feminine noun that takes un or el in the singular.

astonished [əˈstɒnɪʃt] *adjective* ■ pasmado: I was astonished to hear the news me quedé pasmado al escuchar las noticias.

astrology [əˈstrɒlədʒɪ] *noun* ■ la astrología.

astronaut [ˈæstrənɔːt] *noun* ■ el/la astronauta.

astronomy [əˈstrɒnəmɪ] *noun* ■ la astronomía.

at [ət, æt] *preposition*

1. *indicating a place* en: the kids are at school los niños están en la escuela; he's at the office está en la oficina; I was at home last night anoche estaba en casa
2. *indicating a time or a speed* a: the film starts at 8 o'clock la película empieza a las 8; she was driving at 100 kilometres an hour iba conduciendo a 100 kilómetros por hora

➤ at night de noche: owls hunt at night los búhos cazan de noche

➤ at Christmas en Navidad

➤ at the weekend *UK* el fin de semana.

ate [eɪt] *past tense* ➤ eat.

Atlantic [ət'læntɪk] *(adjective & noun)*

■ *adjective*

atlántico: the Atlantic coast la costa atlántica

■ *noun*

the Atlantic el Atlántico.

athlete ['æθliːt] *noun* ■ el/la atleta.

atlas ['ætləs] *noun* ■ el atlas *(plural los atlas)*: a world atlas un atlas del mundo.

ATM *(abbreviation of* Automated Teller Machine) [eɪtiː'em] *noun* ■ el cajero automático: I'll get some money from the ATM voy a sacar dinero del cajero automático.

atmosphere ['ætmə,sfɪə'] *noun*

1. la atmósfera: the earth's atmosphere la atmósfera de la Tierra
2. el ambiente: there's a good atmosphere in this class hay un buen ambiente en esta clase.

atom ['ætəm] *noun* ■ el átomo

➤ the atom bomb la bomba atómica.

atomic [ə'tɒmɪk] *adjective* ■ atómico

➤ atomic energy energía atómica.

attach [ə'tætʃ] *verb*

1. poner: he attached the label to his suitcase le puso la etiqueta a la maleta; a notice was attached to the window habían puesto un aviso en la ventana
2. adjuntar: I've attached a file to this e-mail he adjuntado un archivo a este correo electrónico

➤ to be attached to someone OR something tenerle cariño a alguien o a algo: she's very attached to her aunt le tiene mucho cariño a su tía.

attack [ə'tæk] *(noun & verb)*

■ *noun*

el ataque: the enemy attack came at dawn el ataque enemigo ocurrió al amanecer

➤ a heart attack un ataque al corazón

■ *verb*

atacar: the army attacked the fort el ejército atacó el fuerte; her letter attacks the mayor's plan su carta ataca el plan del alcalde.

attempt [ə'tempt] *(noun & verb)*

■ *noun*

el intento: her last attempt was successful su último intento tuvo éxito

■ *verb*

tratar

➤ to attempt to do something tratar de hacer algo: they attempted to steal the diamond trataron de robar el diamante.

attend [ə'tend] *verb* ■ asistir a: over 100 people attended the meeting unas 100 personas asistieron a la reunión.

attention [ə'tenʃn] *noun* ■ la atención *(plural* las atenciones): I was trying to catch her attention estaba tratando de atraer su atención

➤ pay attention! ¡prestad atención!

attic ['ætɪk] *noun* ■ el desván *(plural los desvanes)*: the attic is full of old junk el desván está lleno de cachivaches viejos.

attitude [*UK* 'ætɪtjuːd, *US* 'ætɪtuːd] *noun* ■ la actitud: I don't like her attitude no me gusta su actitud.

attorney *US* [ə'tɜːnɪ] *noun* ■ el abogado, la abogada: my attorney will contact you mi abogado se pondrá en contacto con usted.

attract [ə'trækt] *verb* ■ atraer: magnets attract iron los imanes atraen el hierro

➤ he's attracted to brunettes le atraen las morenas.

attraction [ə'trækʃn] *noun* ■ la atracción *(plural* las atracciones): a tourist attraction una atracción turística

I don't see the attraction of video games no le veo el atractivo a los videojuegos.

attractive [əˈtræktɪv] *adjective* ■ **atractivo**: she's a very attractive girl es una chica muy atractiva.

aubergine *UK* [ˈəbəʒiːn] *noun* ■ la **berenjena**.

audience [ˈɔːdjəns] *uncountable noun* ■ el **público**: the audience started clapping el público empezó a aplaudir.

August [ˈɔːgəst] *noun*

In Spanish the months of the year do not start with a capital letter:

agosto *(masculine)*: in August en agosto; on August 17th el 17 de agosto; next August el próximo agosto; last August el pasado agosto.

aunt [*UK* ˈɑːnt, *US* ˈænt] *noun* ■ la **tía**: aunt Helen la tía Helen.

Australia [ɒˈstreɪljə] *noun* ■ **Australia**.

Australian [ɒˈstreɪljən] *(adjective & noun)*
■ *adjective*

Remember not to use a capital letter for the adjective in Spanish:

australiano: the Australian bush el bosque australiano
■ *noun*

In Spanish, a capital letter is not used for the inhabitants of a country or region:

el **australiano** la **australiana**: the singer is an Australian el cantante es australiano.

author [ˈɔːθəʳ] *noun* ■ el **autor**, la **autora**: J.K. Rowling is my favourite author J.K. Rowling es mi autora favorita.

autograph [*UK* ˈɔːtəgrɑːf, *US* ˈɔːtəgræf] *noun* ■ el **autógrafo**: she collects film stars' autographs colecciona autógrafos de estrellas de cine.

automatic [ˌɔːtəˈmætɪk] *adjective* ■ **automático**.

automatically [ˌɔːtəˈmætɪklɪ] *adverb* ■ **automáticamente**: the door opens automatically la puerta se abre automáticamente.

automobile *US* [ˈɔːtəməbiːl] *noun* ■ el **coche**.

autumn [ˈɔːtəm] *noun* ■ el **otoño**.

available [əˈveɪləbl] *adjective* ■ **disponible**: he's available on Mondays and Wednesdays está disponible los lunes y los miércoles.

avalanche [*UK* ˈævəlɑːnʃ, *US* ˈævəlæntʃ] *noun* ■ la **avalancha**.

avenue [*UK* ˈævənjuː, *US* ˈævənuː] *noun* ■ la **avenida**.

average [ˈævərɪdʒ] *(adjective & noun)*
■ *adjective*
medio: that's the average price ése es el precio medio
■ *noun*
el **promedio**: they study an average eight hours per week estudian un promedio de ocho horas a la semana
on average de media: on average, how much TV do you watch every day? de media, ¿cuántas horas al día ves la tele?

avocado [ˌævəˈkɑːdəʊ] *noun* ■ el **aguacate**.

avoid [əˈvɔɪd] *verb* ■ **evitar**: let's try to avoid rush hour traffic tratemos de evitar el tráfico de la hora punta.

awake [əˈweɪk] *adjective* ■ **despierto**: he's wide awake está completamente despierto.

award [əˈwɔːd] *noun* ■ el **premio**: her film won an award su película ganó un premio.

aware [əˈweəʳ] *adjective*
to be aware of something ser consciente de algo: he wasn't aware of the danger no era consciente del peligro.

away [əˈweɪ] *adverb* ■ **fuera**: I'll be away for two weeks voy a estar fuera dos semanas
is the beach far away ¿queda muy lejos la playa?
it's two miles away queda a dos millas
tell him to go away dile que se vaya.

awful [ˈɔːfʊl] *adjective* ■ **horrible**: the weather has been awful ha hecho un tiempo horrible an awful lot of un montón de: the were an awful lot of people there allí había un montón de gente.

awfully [ˈɔːflɪ] *adverb*

it's awfully cold today hoy hace un frío horrible

the book is awfully boring el libro es aburridísimo.

awkward [ˈɔːkwəd] *adjective*

1. **torpe:** he's a slightly awkward child es un niño un tanto torpe

2. **Incómodo:** I felt awkward me sentí Incómodo; there was an awkward pause in the conversation hubo una pausa incómoda en la conversación

3. **delicado:** the situation is a bit awkward la situación es un poco delicada.

axe *UK*, **ax** *US* [æks] *noun* ■ **el hacha** *(feminine)*

Feminine noun that takes **un** or **el** in the singular.

baby [ˈbeɪbɪ] *(plural* babies*) noun* ■ **el/la bebé**

a baby boy un niño

a baby girl una niña.

babysit [ˈbeɪbɪsɪt] *verb* ■ **cuidar niños:** I'll get my neighbour to babysit llamaré a mi vecina para cuide a los niños.

babysitter [ˈbeɪbɪˌsɪtəʳ] *noun* ■ **el/la canguro** *(plural* los/las **canguros***).*

bachelor [ˈbætʃələʳ] *noun*

1. **el soltero:** he's a bachelor está soltero

2. **el licenciado la licenciada.**

back [bæk] *(noun, adjective, adverb & verb)*

■ *noun*

la **espalda:** my back hurts me duele la espalda

the back of the car la parte de atrás del coche

he's lying on his back está tendido de espaldas

the sweater was at the back of the cupboard el suéter estaba en el fondo del armario

the back of a chair el respaldo de una silla

■ *adjective*

de **atrás:** the map is on the back seat el mapa está en el asiento de atrás; the back door was locked la puerta de atrás estaba cerrada con llave

■ *adverb*

she took a step back dio un paso hacia atrás

I'll be back at 8 voy a estar de vuelta a las 8

to get back volver: we got back very late volvimos muy tarde

to go back volver: I went back to the shop volví a la tienda

to give back devolver: I have to give this book back tengo que devolver este libro

to put back volver a poner: she put the bottle back in the fridge volvió a poner la botella en la nevera

back and forth para atrás y para adelante

back up *phrasal verb*

1. **respaldar:** I'll back you up yo te voy a respaldar

2. **hacer una copia de seguridad:** it's a good idea to back up your files sería una buena idea que hicieras un copia de seguridad de tus archivos.

backache [ˈbækeɪk] *noun* ■ **el dolor de espalda.**

backbone [ˈbækbəʊn] *noun* ■ **la columna vertebral.**

background [ˈbækgraʊnd] *noun*

1. **el fondo:** you can see the mountains in the background puedes ver las montañas al fondo

2. el **entorno:** the family background is very important el entorno familiar es muy importante

> he comes from a modest background es de origen modesto.

backpack ['bækpæk] *noun* ■ la **mochila.**

backwards *UK* ['bækwərdz], **backward** *US* ['bækwərd] *adverb*

1. **atrás:** I took a step backwards di un paso atrás

2. **hacia atrás:** move backwards moveos hacia atrás

3. **al revés:** you've got your sweater on backwards llevas puesto el suéter al revés

> can you count backwards? ¿puedes contar de atrás hacia adelante?

backyard *US* [ˌbækˈjɑːd] *noun* ■ el **patio trasero.**

bacon ['beɪkən] *noun* ■ el **tocino,** el **beicon,** la **panceta:** bacon and eggs huevos con beicon.

bacteria [bækˈtɪərɪə] *plural noun* ■ las **bacterias.**

bad [bæd] *(comparative* **worse,** *superlative* **worst)** *adjective*

1. **malo**

Malo changes to **mal** before a masculine noun:

he's a very bad driver es muy mal conductor; he's a bad boy es un niño malo; did you hear the bad news? ¿te ha enterado de las malas noticias?; I'm bad at maths soy malo para las matemáticas

2. **fuerte:** I was home with a bad cold estaba en casa con un fuerte resfriado

> to go bad echarse a perder: the meat will go bad if it's not in the fridge la carne se va a echar a perder si no está en el frigorífico.

badge [bædʒ] *noun*

1. *of a school* la **insignia**

2. *of metal* la **chapa**

3. *of a policeman* la **placa.**

badly ['bædlɪ] *(comparative* **worse,** *superlative* **worst)** *adverb*

1. **mal:** he plays very badly toca muy mal

2. **gravemente:** he was badly wounded resultó gravemente herido.

badminton ['bædmɪntən] *noun* ■ el **bádminton:** to play badminton jugar a bádminton.

bag [bæg] *noun*

1. la **bolsa:** a paper bag una bolsa de papel

2. la **maleta:** I'm packing my bags estoy haciendo las maletas.

baggage ['bægɪdʒ] *uncountable noun* ■ el **equipaje:** do you have a lot of baggage? ¿tienes mucho equipaje?

baggy ['bægɪ] *adjective* ■ **ancho:** she wore a baggy old sweatshirt llevaba una sudadera ancha y vieja.

bake [beɪk] *verb*

1. **hacer al horno:** are you going to bake it? ¿lo vas a hacer al horno?

2. **hornear:** I'm baking a cake estoy haciendo un pastel

> a baked potato una patata asada.

baker ['beɪkər] *noun* ■ el **panadero,** la **panadera**

> the baker's shop la panadería.

bakery ['beɪkərɪ] *(plural* **bakeries)** *noun* ■ la **panadería.**

balance ['bæləns] *(noun & verb)*

■ *noun*

el **equilibrio:** I lost my balance perdí el equilibrio

■ *verb*

hacer equilibrio: he is balancing on one foot está haciendo equilibrio en un pie.

balcony ['bælkənɪ] *(plural* **balconies)** *noun* ■ el **balcón** *(plural* los **balcones).**

bald [bɔːld] *adjective* ■ **calvo:** he's going bald se está quedando calvo.

ball [bɔːl] *noun*

1. la **pelota:** a tennis ball una pelota de tenis

2. el **balón** *(plural* los **balones):** the player kicked the ball el jugador chutó el balón

3. el **ovillo:** a ball of yarn un ovillo de hilo

4. el **baile:** Cinderella went to the ball Cenicienta fue al baile.

ballerina [ˌbælə'riːnə] *noun* ■ la **bailarina**: she's a ballerina es bailarina.

ballet ['bæleɪ] *noun* ■ el **ballet** (los ballets): we went to a ballet fuimos a ver un ballet

➤ a ballet dancer un bailarín de ballet (feminine una bailarina de ballet)

balloon [bə'luːn] *noun* ■ el **globo**: the children are blowing up the balloons los niños están inflando los globos.

 La palabra inglesa **balloon** es un falso amigo, no siginifica "halón"

ballpoint pen ['bɔːlpɔɪntpen] *noun* ■ el **bolígrafo**.

ban [bæn] *verb* ■ **prohibir**: they want to ban smoking in restaurants quieren prohibir que se fume en los restaurantes.

banana [UK bə'nɑːnə, US bə'nænə] *noun* ■ el **plátano**: a bunch of bananas un racimo de plátanos.

band [bænd] *noun*
1. la **banda**: I used to play in a rock band yo tocaba en una banda de rock
2. la **cinta**: there was a band of paper around the flowers había una cinta de papel alrededor de las flores.

bandage ['bændɪdʒ] *noun* ■ la **venda**: he has a bandage on his head tiene una venda en la cabeza.

Band-Aid® US ['bændeɪd] *noun* ■ la **tirita®**.

bang [bæŋ] *(noun & verb)*
■ *noun*
1. la **explosión** (plural las **explosiones**): I heard a bang oí una explosión
2. el **golpe**: she got a bang on her head recibió un golpe en la cabeza
■ *verb*
1. **golpear**: somebody's banging on the door alguien está golpeando la puerta
2. **golpearse**: I banged my head me golpeé la cabeza.

bangs US [bæŋz] *plural noun* ■ el **flequillo**.

bank [bæŋk] *(noun & verb)*
■ *noun*
1. el **banco**: she has money in the bank tiene dinero en el banco
2. la **orilla**: we walked on the bank of the river caminamos por la orilla del río
➤ a bank account una cuenta bancaria
➤ a bank holiday UK el día festivo
➤ a bank note el billete de banco
■ *verb*
tener una cuenta: I've been banking here for years tengo una cuenta aquí desde hace años.

banker ['bæŋkəʳ] *noun* ■ el **banquero** la **banquera**: he's a banker es banquero.

banner ['bænəʳ] *noun* ■ la **pancarta**: the demonstrators were carrying banners los manifestantes llevaban pancartas.

baptize , baptise UK ['bæptaɪz] *verb* ■ **bautizar**: she was baptized at St. Peter's la bautizaron en la iglesia de San Pedro.

bar [bɑːʳ] *noun*
1. el **barrote**: there were bars on the windows había barrotes en las ventanas
2. el **bar**: we'll meet in the bar at 5 nos encontramos en el bar a las 5
3. la **barra**: they sat at the bar se sentaron en la barra
➤ a bar of soap una pastilla de jabón
➤ a bar of chocolate una tableta de chocolate.

barbecue ['bɑːbɪkjuː] *noun* ■ la **barbacoa**: we're having a barbecue estamos haciendo una barbacoa.

barbed wire UK ['bɑːʳbdwaɪəʳ], **barbwire** US ['bɑːʳbwaɪəʳ] *noun* ■ el **alambre de espino**.

barber ['bɑːbəʳ] *noun* ■ el **peluquero**
➤ a barber's shop una barbería.

bare [beəʳ] *adjective*
1. **descalzo**: his feet were bare tenía los pies descalzos
2. **desnudo**: the walls were bare and white las paredes eran blancas y estaban desnudas.

barefoot [ˌbeə'fʊt] (adjective & adverb)

■ *adjective*

descalzo: she was barefoot estaba descalza

■ *adverb*

he was walking barefoot iba descalzo.

barely ['beəlɪ] *adverb* ■ **apenas: I barely had time to eat** apenas tuve tiempo para comer.

bargain ['bɑːgɪn] *noun* ■ **la ganga: it's a real bargain** es una verdadera ganga.

bark [bɑːk] (noun & verb)

■ *noun*

la corteza: the bark of a tree la corteza de un árbol

■ *verb*

ladrar: the dog barked at the boy el perro ladró al niño.

barmaid ['bɑːmeɪd] *noun* ■ **la camarera.**

barman *UK* ['bɑːmən] (plural **barmen** ['bɑːmən]) *noun* ■ **el camarero.**

barn [bɑːn] *noun* ■ **el granero.**

bartender *US* ['bɑːtendəʳ] *noun* ■ **el camarero, la camarera: she's a bartender** es camarera.

base [beɪs] (noun & verb)

■ *noun*

la base: the base of the pyramid la base de la pirámide; **they have their base in London** tienen su base en Londres

■ *verb*

basar: I base my opinions on hard facts baso mis opiniones en datos concretos

> **the book is based on his life** el libro se basa en su vida

> **the company is based in Detroit** la compañía tiene su sede en Detroit.

baseball ['beɪsbɔːl] *noun* ■ **el béisbol: he plays baseball** juega al béisbol

> **a baseball cap** una gorra de béisbol.

basement ['beɪsmənt] *noun* ■ **el sótano: she went down to the basement** bajó al sótano.

basic ['beɪsɪk] *adjective*

1. **elemental: I have a basic knowledge of French** tengo nociones elementales de francés

2. **sencillo: the food is quite basic** la comida es bastante sencilla.

basil ['bæzl] *noun* ■ **la albahaca.**

basis ['beɪsɪs] (plural **bases** ['beɪsiːz]) *noun*

1. **la base: on the basis of the student performance** sobre la base del rendimiento del estudiante

2. **el fundamento: what is the basis of your theory?** ¿cuál es el fundamento de tu teoría?

> **on a monthly basis** mensualmente

> **on a regular basis** regularmente.

basket ['bɑːskɪt] *noun*

1. **el cesto, la cesta: a shopping basket** la cesta de la compra

2. **la canasta**

> **he scored a basket** metió una canasta.

basketball ['bɑːskɪtbɔːl] *noun* ■ **el baloncesto: they're playing basketball** están jugando al baloncesto.

bass [beɪs] *noun* ■ **el bajo: a bass guitar** un bajo eléctrico; **a double bass** un contrabajo.

bat [bæt] (noun & verb)

■ *noun*

1. **el bate: a baseball bat** un bate de béisbol

2. **el murciélago: bats come out at night** los murciélagos salen de noche

■ *verb (past tense & past participle* **batted,** *present participle* **batting)**

batear: dad is teaching me to bat papá me está enseñando a batear.

bath [*UK* bɑːθ, *US* bæθ] *noun*

1. **el baño: to have a bath** bañarse; **I'm going to have a bath** voy a bañarme

2. **la bañera**

> **a bath towel** una toalla de baño.

bathing suit ['beɪðɪŋsuːt] *noun* ■ **el bañador.**

bathrobe [*UK* 'bɑːθrəʊb, *US* 'bæθrəʊb] *noun* ■ **el albornoz.**

bathroom [*UK* 'bɑːθrʊm, *US* 'bæθrʊm] *noun*

1. **el baño: he was having a shave in the the bathroom** se estaba afeitando en el baño

2. *US* **los servicios.**

bathtub [UK 'bɑːθtʌb, US 'bæθtʌb] *noun* ■ la bañera.

battery ['bætərɪ] *(plural* batteries*) noun*

1. la pila: this radio runs on batteries esta radio funciona con pilas

2. la batería: a car battery una batería de coche.

battle ['bætl] *noun*

1. la batalla: a bloody battle una batalla sangrienta

2. la lucha: the battle against cancer la lucha contra el cáncer.

bay [beɪ] *noun* ■ la bahía: San Francisco bay la bahía de San Francisco.

B.C. [biː'siː] *(abbreviation of* before Christ*)* a. de C.: in 200 B.C. en el año 200 a. de C.

be [biː] *(past tense* was OR were, *past participle* been*) verb*

As a general rule, when be is followed by an adjective, it can be translated into Spanish by ser when it's used to describe permanent or inherent states or by estar when it's used to describe temporary states:

they're happy children son niños felices; I'm very happy in my new school estoy muy contento en mi nuevo colegio; he's handsome es guapo; Anne is French Anne es francesa; the soup is cold la sopa está fría; we are alone estamos solos

2.

Use ser when talking about dates and time:

it's April the first today hoy es el primero de abril; it's one o'clock es la una

3.

Use estar when describing where something or someone is:

my school is near the church mi colegio está cerca de la iglesia; where is Alice? ¿dónde está Alice?; they are in Seville están en Sevilla

4.

With certain adjectives that describe how you feel, like "cold", "hot", "hungry" or "thirsty", use the verb tener:

I'm cold tengo frío; my hands are cold tengo las manos frías; I'm too hot tengo mucho calor; are you hungry? ¿tienes hambre?

5.

Use tener to say how old somebody is:

how old are you? ¿cuántos años tienes?; I'm thirteen years old tengo trece años

6.

Use hacer to talk about the weather:

it's cold today hace frío hoy; it was very hot hacía mucho calor

7.

Use estar to talk about health and to say how somebody is:

how are you? ¿cómo estás?; I'm very well, thank you estoy muy bien, gracias; Sam is much better Sam está mucho mejor; she's ill está enferma

8.

Use estar in the continuous tense:

I'm working estoy trabajando; what are you doing? ¿qué estás haciendo?; it's raining está lloviendo; I was reading when you phoned estaba leyendo cuando llamaste

The present continuous can also be translated by the simple present tense in Spanish, especially with verbs of movement:

where are you going? ¿adónde vas?; she's leaving se va

9.

The passive is formed in the same way in Spanish and in English: ser + past participle . Remember that in Spanish the past participle must agree in gender (masculine & feminine) and number (singular & plural) with the subject of the verb and is not as common as it is in English. The active construction or a verb with se is preferred:

the soldier was kidnapped el soldado fue secuestrado; this method is used by many people muchas personas utilizan este método; I was told to leave me dijeron que me fuera; red wine is produced in Spain el vino tinto se produce en España ➤ been.

beach [biːtʃ] *noun* ■ **la playa: they're playing on the beach** están jugando en la playa; **let's go to the beach** vamos a la playa.

bead [biːd] *noun* ■ **la cuenta: a necklace made of glass beads** un collar de cuentas de vidrio.

beak [biːk] *noun* ■ **el pico: the pelican has a big beak** el pelícano tiene un pico grande.

beam [biːm] *noun*
1. **el rayo: a laser beam** un rayo láser
2. **la viga: wooden beams** vigas de madera.

bean [biːn] *noun* ■ **la alubia**
> **green beans** las judías verdes
> **kidney beans** alubias rojas.

bear [beəʳ] *(noun & verb)*
■ *noun*
el oso: a polar bear un oso polar
■ *verb (past tense* bore, *past participle* borne)*
soportar: I can't bear her no la soporto; **I can't bear to see him go** no puedo soportar que se vaya.

beard [bɪəd] *noun* ■ **la barba: my uncle has a beard** mi tío tiene barba.

beat [biːt] *(noun & verb)*
■ *noun*
el ritmo: this music has a strong beat esta música tiene un ritmo marcado
■ *verb (past tense* beat, *past participle* beaten)*
ganarle a: we beat the third year ganamos a los de tercero; **our team beat them 4-2** nuestro equipo les ganó 4 a 2
> **she beat the world record** batió el récord mundial

beat up *phrasal verb* ■ **darle una paliza a: he was beaten up** le dieron una paliza.

beaten ['biːtn] *past participle* ➤ beat.

beautiful ['bjuːtɪfʊl] *adjective* ■ **precioso: he has beautiful eyes** tiene unos ojos preciosos
a beautiful woman una mujer preciosa.

beauty ['bjuːtɪ] *noun* ■ **la belleza**
> **a beauty salon** un salón de belleza.

became [bɪ'keɪm] *past tense* ➤ become.

because [bɪ'kɒz] *conjunction* ■ **porque: he went to bed early because he has to get up at 6** se ha acostado temprano porque tiene que levantarse a las 6
> **because of** por: **I can't sleep because of the noise** no puedo dormir por el ruido.

become [bɪ'kʌm] *(past tense* became, *past participle* become)* *verb* ■ **hacerse: we've become great friends** nos hemos hecho muy amigos
> **it's become fashionable** se ha puesto de moda
> **he's becoming more like his father** se parece cada vez más a su padre.

bed [bed] *noun* ■ **la cama: he's in bed** está en cama
> **to go to bed** acostarse: **I'm going to bed** me voy a acostar
> **to get out of bed** levantarse: **I got out of bed very early today** hoy me he levantado muy temprano
> **a bed and breakfast** una casa de huéspedes

> BED AND BREAKFAST

La mayoría de los establecimientos conocidos como **bed and breakfast** son casas particulares que reciben huéspedes. Además del tradicional desayuno casero, algunos ofrecen cenas. Muchos están ubicados en zonas turísticas costeras pero se encuentran tanto en las grandes ciudades como en remotos parajes campestres. En Gran Bretaña, los **bed and breakfast** son más baratos que los hoteles; en Estados Unidos, suelen ser más caros y modernos.

bedroom ['bedrʊm] *noun* ■ **el dormitorio: the house has three bedrooms** la casa tiene tres dormitorios.

bee [biː] *noun* ■ **la abeja.**

beef [biːf] *noun* ■ **la carne de vaca**
> **roast beef** el rosbif.

been [bɪn] *past participle* ➤ be
I have been in this country for three years he estado tres años en este país; **he has always been clever** siempre ha sido inteligente

When "has been" or "have been" is used as a past participle of **go**, use a conjugated form of **estar** to translate it:

have you ever been to Boston? ¿has estado alguna vez en Boston?

beer [bɪəʳ] *noun* ■ la **cerveza**.

beet *US* [biːt] *noun* ■ la **remolacha**.

beetle ['biːtl] *noun* ■ el **escarabajo**.

before [bɪ'fɔːʳ] *(preposition, adverb & conjunction)*

■ *preposition*

1. antes de: **I'll be back before midnight** voy a volver antes de la medianoche
2. antes que: **I arrived before him** llegué antes que él; **i comes before e in "believe"** la i viene antes que la e en "believe"
3. ante: **he was brought before the judge** lo llevaron ante el juez

■ *adverb*

antes: **it has never happened to me before** no me había pasado nunca antes; **I think I've met him before** creo que ya lo conocía de antes

■ *conjunction*

antes de que: **I'll cook dinner before they arrive** preparé la cena antes de que lleguen.

beg [beg] *(past tense & past participle* begged, *present participle* begging) *verb* ■ **mendigar**: **he was begging in the street** estaba mendigando en la calle

▷ **to beg somebody to do something** rogarle a alguien que haga algo

▷ **I beg you not to tell him** te ruego que no se lo digas

▷ **I beg your pardon?** ¿perdón?

began [bɪ'gæn] *past tense* ➤ begin.

beggar ['begəʳ] *noun* ■ el **mendigo**, la **mendiga**.

begin [bɪ'gɪn] *(past tense* began, *past participle* begun, *present participle* beginning) *verb* ■ **empezar**: **my next class begins at noon** mi próxima clase empieza al mediodía

▷ **to begin to do something** empezar a hacer algo: **the band began to play** la banda empezó a tocar.

beginner [bɪ'gɪnəʳ] *noun* ■ el/la **principiante**.

beginning [bɪ'gɪnɪŋ] *noun* ■ el **principio**: **in the beginning** al principio.

begun [bɪ'gʌn] *past participle* ➤ begin.

behalf [bɪ'hæf] *noun*

▷ **on behalf of somebody** en nombre de alguien: **I'm speaking on behalf of the class** hablo en nombre de toda la clase

▷ **he called on behalf of a friend** llamó de parte de un amigo.

behave [bɪ'heɪv] *verb* ■ **portarse**: **he behaves badly** se porta mal; **the children are behaving themselves** los niños se están portando bien.

behaviour *UK*, **behavior** *US* [bɪ'heɪvjəʳ] *noun* ■ el **comportamiento**: **his behaviour has improved in the new school** su comportamiento en el colegio nuevo ha mejorado.

behind [bɪ'haɪnd] *(preposition & adverb)*

■ *preposition*

detrás de: **he's behind you** está detrás de ti; **the switch is behind the door** el interruptor de la luz está detrás de la puerta

■ *adverb*

▷ **he's behind with his work** va retrasado con su trabajo

▷ **to leave something behind** olvidar algo: **I left my umbrella behind** se me olvidó el paraguas.

being ['biːɪŋ] *noun* ■ el **ser**: **we are human beings** somos seres humanos.

believe [bɪ'liːv] *verb* ■ **creer**: **I believe you** te creo

▷ **to believe in something** creer en algo: **do you believe in ghosts?** ¿crees en fantasmas?

bell [bel] *noun*

1. el **timbre**: **somebody rang the bell** alguien tocó el timbre
2. la **campana**: **the church bells are ringing** las campanas de la iglesia están sonando.

belly ['belɪ] *(plural* bellies) *noun* ■ la **barriga**

▷ **belly button** el ombligo.

belong [bɪ'lɒŋ] *verb*

- to belong to someone pertenecer a alguien: all this belonged to the same family todo esto pertenecía a una misma familia
- does this pen belong to you? ¿este bolígrafo es tuyo?
- he belongs to the tennis club es socio del club de tenis
- put it back where it belongs vuélvelo a poner en su lugar.

belongings [bɪ'lɒŋɪŋz] *plural noun* ■ **las pertenencias**: I'll just get my belongings together voy a juntar mis pertenencias.

below [bɪ'ləʊ] *(preposition & adverb)*

■ *preposition*

1. **debajo de**: her dress came to below the knee el vestido le llegaba debajo de la rodilla
2. **bajo**: it's 10 below zero estamos a 10 grados bajo cero

■ *adverb*

de abajo: they live on the floor below viven en el piso de abajo.

belt [belt] *noun* ■ **el cinturón** *(plural* los **cinturones)**: he's wearing a belt lleva puesto un cinturón

- fasten your seat belts abróchense sus cinturones de seguridad.

bench [bentʃ] *noun* ■ **el banco**: she sat on a bench in the park se sentó en un banco del parque.

bend [bend] *(noun & verb)*

■ *noun*

la curva: there's a bend in the road la calle tiene una curva

■ *verb (past tense & past participle* bent*)*

doblar: I can't bend my arm no puedo doblar el brazo; I bent the wire doblé el cable

bend down *phrasal verb* ■ **agacharse**: he bent down to pick up his book se agachó para recoger el libro

bend over *phrasal verb* ■ **inclinarse**: she bent over to have a closer look se inclinó para mirar más de cerca.

bent [bent] *(adjective & verb form)*

■ *adjective*

doblado: a bent nail un clavo doblado

■ *past tense & past participle*

➤ **bend.**

berry ['berɪ] *(plural* berries*) noun* ■ **la baya**: holly has red berries el acebo tiene bayas rojas.

beside [bɪ'saɪd] *preposition* ■ **al lado de**: come and sit beside Bob ven a sentarte al lado de Bob

- she's beside herself with joy está fuera de sí de alegría.

besides [bɪ'saɪdz] *(adverb & preposition)*

■ *adverb*

además: besides, I think you're wrong además, creo que estás equivocado

■ *preposition*

además de: besides this book I bought two others además de este libro, me compré dos más.

best [best] *(adjective, adverb & noun)*

■ *adjective (superlative of* good*)*

mejor: she's my best friend ella es mi mejor amiga

- the best man el padrino de boda

■ *adverb (superlative of* well*)*

- which one do you like best? ¿cuál es el que más te gusta?

■ *noun*

- the best el mejor, la mejor: of all the players I know, you're the best de todos los jugadores que conozco, tu eres el mejor
- to do one's best hacer todo lo posible: I'll do my best voy a hacer todo lo posible

BEST MAN

En los países anglosajones existe una tradición que consiste en que el padrino de boda entrega el anillo al novio y luego, durante el banquete nupcial, pronuncia un breve discurso. En esa alocución, suele incluir algún chascarrillo o comentario burlón sobre el novio.

bestseller [best'selə'] *noun* ■ **un best seller.**

bet [bet] *(noun & verb)*

■ *noun*

la apuesta: let's make a bet hagamos una apuesta

verb *(past tense & past participle* bet, *present participle* betting)*

apostar: I bet you can't do it apuesto a que no puedes hacerlo.

better ['betər] *(adjective & adverb)*

adjective *(comparative of* good)*

mejor: this method is better than the other este método es mejor que el otro

adverb *(comparative of* well)*

mejor: she sings better than I do ella canta mejor que yo; I feel much better now ahora me siento mucho mejor

to get better

1. **mejorar:** the weather is getting better el tiempo está mejorando

2. **mejorarse:** I hope you get better soon espero que te mejores pronto

I'd better go home tengo que irme a casa.

between [bɪ'twiːn] *(preposition & adverb)*

preposition

entre: he's sitting between Paul and Anne está sentado entre Paul y Anne; we can split the work between us podemos dividirnos el trabajo entre los dos

adverb

in between en medio: John's sitting in between John se ha sentado en medio.

beware [bɪ'weər] *verb* ■ **tener cuidado:** beware of pickpockets on the underground tengan cuidado con los carteristas en el metro; "beware of the dog!" "¡cuidado con el perro!"

beyond [bɪ'jɒnd] *preposition* ■ **más allá de:** don't go beyond the gate no vayas más allá de la puerta

> it's beyond me! ¡no lo puedo entender!

bicycle ['baɪsɪkl] *noun* ■ **la bicicleta:** can you ride a bicycle? ¿sabes montar en bicicleta?

> a bicycle lane un carril para bicicletas

> a bicycle pump una bomba de bicicleta.

big [bɪg] *(comparative* bigger, *superlative* biggest) adjective*

1. **mayor:** my big brother mi hermano mayor

2. **grande:** a big book un libro grande

Grande changes to gran before singular nouns:

there was a big fire hubo un gran incendio

bike [baɪk] *noun* ■ **la bici:** she rides her bike to work va en bici al trabajo.

bikini [bɪ'kiːnɪ] *noun* ■ **el bikini:** she's wearing a bikini lleva puesto un bikini.

bilingual [baɪ'lɪŋgwəl] *adjective* ■ **bilingüe:** a bilingual dictionary un diccionario bilingüe.

bill [bɪl] *noun* ■

1. *UK* **la cuenta:** can I have the bill please? ¿me trae la cuenta, por favor?

2. **la factura:** the electricity bill la factura de la luz

3. *US* **el billete:** a dollar bill un billete de dólar.

billboard *US* ['bɪlbɔːd] *noun* ■ **la valla publicitaria.**

billiards ['bɪljədz] *noun* ■ **el billar.**

billion ['bɪljə] *noun*

1. **mil millones:** three billion dollars tres mil millones de dólares

2. *UK* **el billón.**

bin *UK* [bɪn] *noun* ■ **la papelera.**

binoculars [bɪ'nɒkjʊləz] *plural noun* ■ **los prismáticos:** a pair of binoculars unos prismáticos.

biology [baɪ'ɒlədʒɪ] *noun* ■ **la biología.**

bird [bɜːd] *noun* ■ **el pájaro:** the birds sing at dawn los pájaros cantan al amanecer

> a bird of prey un ave de rapiña.

birth [bɜːθ] *noun* ■ **el nacimiento:** what's your date of birth? ¿cuál es tu fecha de nacimiento?

> to give birth to dar a luz a: she gave birth to a girl dio a luz a una niña

> a birth certificate una partida de nacimiento.

birthday ['bɜːθdeɪ] *noun* ■ **el cumpleaños** *(plural* los **cumpleaños**): Gary's birthday is on February 6th el cumpleaños de Gary es el 6 de febrero

> happy birthday! ¡feliz cumpleaños!

bishop ['bɪʃəp] *noun* ■ **el obispo.**

bison ['baɪsn] *noun* ■ el **bisonte**.

bit [bɪt] *(noun & verb form)*
■ *noun*
el **pedazo**: a bit of cheese un pedazo de queso
- a bit un poco: I'm a bit tired estoy un poco cansada
- a bit of un poco de: he has a bit of money tiene un poco de dinero
- bit by bit poco a poco
- for a bit por un momento
■ *past tense* ➤ bite.

bite [baɪt] *(noun & verb)*
■ *noun*
1. la **picadura**: an insect bite una picadura de insecto
2. el **mordisco**: he took a bite of my apple le dio un mordisco a mi manzana
■ *verb (past tense* bit, *past participle* bitten)
1. **morder**: the dog bit me el perro me mordió
2. **picar**: I've been bitten by mosquitoes me han picado los mosquitos
- to bite one's nails morderse las uñas: he bites his nails se muerde las uñas.

bitten ['bɪtn] *past participle* ➤ bite.

bitter ['bɪtər] *adjective*
1. **amargo**: it has a bitter taste tiene un sabor amargo
2. **glacial**: there's a bitter wind blowing sopla un viento glacial.

black [blæk] *adjective* ■ **negro**: he wore a black hat llevaba puesto un sombrero negro; a black man un hombre negro
- I drink my coffee black tomo el café negro
- a black eye un ojo morado
- black and white blanco y negro: a black and white photo una foto en blanco y negro.

blackberry ['blækbərɪ] *(plural* blackberries) *noun* ■ la **mora**.

blackbird ['blækbɜːd] *noun* ■ el **mirlo**.

blackboard ['blækbɔːd] *noun* ■ la **pizarra**: the teacher is writing on the blackboard el profesor está escribiendo en la pizarra.

blade [bleɪd] *noun* ■ la **hoja**: a razor blade una hoja de afeitar.

blame [bleɪm] *verb*
- to blame somebody for something culpar a alguien de algo: he blames me for his problems me culpa a mí de sus problemas
- who's to blame? ¿quién tiene la culpa?: he's to blame él tiene la culpa.

blank [blæŋk] *adjective* ■ **en blanco**: a blank sheet of paper una hoja de papel en blanco
- a blank tape una cinta virgen
- my mind went blank me quedé en blanco.

blanket ['blæŋkɪt] *noun* ■ la **manta**: she put a blanket on the bed puso una manta en la cama.

blast [blɑːst] *noun* ■ el **estallido**: a bomb blast el estallido de una bomba.

bleach [bliːtʃ] *noun* ■ la **lejía**.

bled [bled] *past tense & past participle* ➤ bleed.

bleed [bliːd] *(past tense & past participle* bled [bled]) *verb* ■ **sangrar**: my nose is bleeding me sangra la nariz.

blender ['blendər] *noun* ■ la **batidora**: mix the sauce in the blender mezcle la salsa en la batidora.

bless [bles] *(past tense & past participle* blessed) *verb* ■ **bendecir**: the priest blessed him el sacerdote lo bendijo
- bless you! ¡salud!

blew [bluː] *past tense* ➤ blow.

blind [blaɪnd] *(adjective & noun)*
■ *adjective*
ciego: he's been blind since birth es ciego de nacimiento
■ *noun*
la **persiana**: pull down the blind baja la persiana.

blindfold ['blaɪndfəʊld] *(noun & verb)*
■ *noun*
la **venda sobre los ojos**: they put a blindfold on me me pusieron una venda sobre los ojos
■ *verb*
vendarle los ojos a: they blindfolded the man vendaron los ojos al hombre.

blink [blɪŋk] verb ■ **parpadear:** she blinked when the light came on parpadeó cuando se encendió la luz.

blister ['blɪstər] noun ■ **la ampolla:** I have a blister on my heel tengo una ampolla en el talón.

block [blɒk] (noun & verb)
■ noun
1. el **bloque:** a block of ice un bloque de hielo
2. la **manzana:** I'll walk around the block voy a dar la vuelta a la manzana
   it's five blocks from here queda a cinco manzanas de aquí
■ verb
1. **bloquear:** a fallen tree was blocking the road un árbol caído bloqueaba el camino
2. **atascar:** something is blocking the sink algo está atascando el fregadero
   my nose is blocked tengo la nariz tapada.

blond [blɒnd] adjective ■ **rubio:** he has blond hair tiene el pelo rubio.

blonde [blɒnd] noun ■ **la rubia:** a stunning blonde una rubia despampanante
Anne is a blonde Ana es rubia.

blood [blʌd] noun ■ **la sangre:** he was covered in blood estaba cubierto de sangre
blood group el grupo sanguíneo
blood pressure la presión sanguínea.

blouse [blaʊs] noun ■ **la blusa:** she's wearing a pretty blouse lleva una blusa muy bonita.

blow [bləʊ] (past tense blew, past participle blown) verb ■ **soplar:** the wind was blowing soplaba el viento
to blow a whistle tocar un silbato: the referee blew his whistle el árbitro tocó el silbato
to blow one's nose sonarse la nariz

blow out phrasal verb ■ **apagar:** she blew out the candles on the cake apagó las velas del pastel

blow up phrasal verb
1. **inflar:** I'm going to blow up some balloons for the party voy a inflar unos globos para la fiesta

2. **explotar:** two bombs blew up explotaron dos bombas
3. **hacer volar:** they blew up the bridge hicieron volar el puente
   the whole building blew up todo el edificio voló.

blown [bləʊn] past participle ➤ blow.

blue [bluː] adjective ■ **azul:** Cathy has blue eyes Cathy tiene los ojos azules; she's wearing a blue dress lleva puesto un vestido azul
navy blue azul marino
sky blue azul celeste.

blueberry ['bluːbərɪ] (plural blueberries) noun ■ el **arándano:** a blueberry pie una tarta de arándanos.

blunt [blʌnt] adjective
1. **desafilado:** the knife is blunt el cuchillo está desafilado
2. **franco:** he's very blunt es muy franco.

blurred [blɜːrd] adjective ■ **borroso:** the photo is blurred la foto está borrosa.

blush [blʌʃ] verb ■ **sonrojarse:** you're blushing te estás poniendo colorado; she blushed when I said his name se puso colorada cuando dije su nombre.

board [bɔːrd] (noun & verb)
■ noun
1. la **tabla:** a bread board una tabla de cortar el pan
2. la **pizarra:** write the sentence on the board escribe la oración en la pizarra
3. el **tablón de anuncios** (plural los **tablones de anuncios**): there are a lot of notices on the board hay muchos avisos en el tablón de anuncios
4. el **tablero:** put the pieces on the board coloca las piezas en el tablero
5. la **junta:** Mr. Owen is on the board of directors el señor Owen está en la junta directiva
   board games juegos de mesa
   on board a bordo: how many passengers are on board? ¿cuántos pasajeros hay a bordo?
■ verb
embarcar: we'll start boarding in five minutes empezaremos a embarcar en cinco minutos.

boarding card ['bɔːdɪŋkɑːd] *noun* ■ la **tarjeta de embarque.**

boarding school ['bɔːdɪŋskuːl] *noun* ■ el **internado:** he goes to boarding school va a un internado.

boast [bəʊst] *verb* ■ **alardear:** she's boasting about her marks alardea de sus notas.

boat [bəʊt] *noun*
1. el **barco:** we went to France by boat fuimos a Francia en barco
2. *smaller* la **lancha:** we're taking the boat out on the lake today hoy vamos a llevar la lancha al lago.

body ['bɒdɪ] *(plural* bodies*) noun* ■ el **cuerpo:** the human body el cuerpo humano.

bodyguard ['bɒdɪgɑːd] *noun* ■ el/la **guardaespaldas** *(plural* los/las **guardaespaldas***):* he's the president's bodyguard es el guardaespaldas del presidente.

boil [bɔɪl] *verb* ■ **hervir:** the water is boiling el agua está hirviendo
➤ I boiled some potatoes he cocido unas patatas.

boiler ['bɔɪləʳ] *noun* ■ la **caldera.**

boiling ['bɔɪlɪŋ] *adjective* ■ it's boiling hot today hoy hace un calor espantoso.

bold [bəʊld] *adjective* ■ **osado:** it was a bold move for her to change jobs fue muy osado por su parte cambiar de trabajo
➤ bold type la negrita.

bolt [bəʊlt] *(noun & verb)*
■ *noun*
1. el **tornillo:** nuts and bolts tuercas y tornillos
2. el **cerrojo:** there's a bolt on the door hay un cerrojo en la puerta
■ *verb*
echarle el cerrojo a: have you bolted the door? ¿has echado el cerrojo a la puerta?

bomb [bɒm] *(noun & verb)*
■ *noun*
la **bomba:** a bomb scare una amenaza de bomba
■ *verb*
bombardear: the city was bombed continuously bombardearon continuamente la ciudad.

bone [bəʊn] *noun*
1. el **hueso:** he gave the dog a bone le dio un hueso al perro
2. la **espina:** a fish bone una espina de pescado.

bonfire ['bɒn,faɪəʳ] *noun* ■ la **hoguera:** we sat around the bonfire nos sentamos alrededor de la hoguera.

Bonfire Night *UK* ['bɒn,faɪəʳnaɪt] *noun* ■ *fiesta que se celebra el 5 de noviembre en Gran Bretaña con lanzamiento de petardos y fuegos artificiales.*
➤ Guy Fawkes' Night.

bonnet ['bɒnɪt] *noun*
1. *UK* el **capó**
2. el **gorro.**

boo [buː] *(noun & verb)*
■ *noun*
el **abucheo:** a chorus of boos came from the audience el público lanzó un fuerte abucheo
➤ boo! ¡uuh!
■ *verb*
abuchear: the audience booed him el público le abucheó.

book [bʊk] *(noun & verb)*
■ *noun*
el **libro:** Brian is reading a book Brian está leyendo un libro
➤ a book of tickets un taco de entradas
■ *verb*
reservar: I booked two tickets to Buenos Aires he reservado dos billetes para Buenos Aires.

bookcase ['bʊkkeɪs] *noun* ■ la **estantería:** there's a bookcase in the office hay una estantería en la oficina.

booklet ['bʊklɪt] *noun* ■ el **folleto:** an instruction booklet un folleto de instrucciones.

bookmark ['bʊkmɑːk] *noun* ■ el **marcador de libro.**

bookshelf ['bʊkʃelf] *(plural* bookshelves ['bʊkʃelvz]*) noun* ■ el **estante.**

bookshop *UK* ['bʊkʃɒp], **bookstore** *US* ['bʊkstɔːʳ] *noun* ■ la **librería:** this is my favourite bookshop esta es mi librería favorita.

boot [bu:t] *noun*

1. la **bota**: she was wearing red boots llevaba puestas botas rojas; football boots botas de fútbol
2. *UK* el **maletero**.

booth [bu:ð] *noun* ■ la **cabina**: a telephone booth una cabina telefónica.

border ['bɔ:dəʳ] *noun* ■ la **frontera**: the border between Spain and Portugal la frontera entre España y Portugal.

bore [bɔ:ʳ] *(verb & past tense)*

■ *verb*

aburrir: this really bores me esto me aburre muchísimo
➤ the film bored me to death me aburrí como una ostra con la película

■ *past tense*
➤ bear.

bored [bɔ:d] *adjective*
➤ to be bored estar aburrido: I was so bored in that class estaba tan aburrido en esa clase

boring ['bɔ:rɪŋ] *adjective*
➤ to be boring ser aburrido: this is such a boring book este libro es muy aburrido.

born [bɔ:n] *adjective*
➤ to be born nacer: where were you born? ¿dónde naciste?; I was born in 1990 nací en 1990.

borne [bɔ:n] *past participle* ➤ bear.

borrow ['bɒrəʊ] *verb* ■ **pedir prestado**: he borrowed some money from a friend le pidió dinero prestado a su amigo
➤ can I borrow your pen? ¿me prestas tu bolígrafo?
➤ I had to borrow the book from the library tuve que sacar el libro de la biblioteca.

boss [bɒs] *noun* ■ el **jefe**, la **jefa**: she's my boss es mi jefa.

bossy ['bɒsɪ] *adjective* ■ **mandón** *(feminine* **mandona**, *plural* **mandones***)*: his sister is very bossy su hermana es muy mandona.

both [bəʊθ] *adjective & pronoun* ■ **ambos, ambas, los/las dos**: both of the girls are Spanish las dos chicas son españolas; both of them are coming los dos vienen.

bother ['bɒðəʳ] *verb*

1. **molestar**: I'm sorry to bother you siento molestarte
2. **preocupar**: something is bothering her algo le preocupa
3. **molestarse**
➤ to bother to do something molestarse en hacer algo: he didn't bother to get up no se molestó en ponerse de pie
➤ why bother? ¿para qué preocuparse?
➤ don't bother! ¡no te preocupes!
➤ I can't be bothered no tengo ganas.

bottle ['bɒtl] *noun* ■ la **botella**: a bottle of milk una botella de leche.

bottle-opener ['bɒtl'əʊpnəʳ] *noun* ■ el **abrebotellas** *(plural* los **abrebotellas***)*.

bottom ['bɒtəm] *(noun & adjective)*

■ *noun*

1. el **final**: at the bottom of the page al final de la página
2. el **fondo**: it was at the bottom of the lake estaba en el fondo del lago
3. el **pie**: at the bottom of the hill al pie de la colina
4. el **trasero**: she patted his bottom le dio una palmada en el trasero
➤ she's the bottom of her class es la última de su clase
➤ they're the bottom of the league van los últimos en la liga

■ *adjective*

inferior: it's on the bottom shelf está en el estante inferior
➤ he got the bottom grade se sacó la nota más baja.

bought [bɔ:t] *past tense & past participle* ➤ buy.

bounce [baʊns] *verb*

1. **botar, rebotar**: the ball bounced twice la pelota botó dos veces
2. **hacer rebotar, hacer botar**: she bounced the ball against the wall hizo rebotar la pelota contra la pared.

bound [baʊnd] *adjective* ■ **seguro**: he's bound to win seguro que gana.

bow *(noun & verb)*
■ *noun* [bəʊ]
1. el **arco**: a bow and arrows un arco y flechas
2. el **lazo**: she tied the ribbon in a bow hizo un lazo con la cinta
> a bow tie una pajarita
■ *verb* [baʊ]
  hacer una reverencia: the actors bowed los actores hicieron una reverencia.

bowl [bəʊl] *noun* ■ el **tazón** *(plural* los tazones), el **bol**: a bowl of milk un tazón de leche
> a salad bowl un bol para ensalada.

bowling ['bəʊlɪŋ] *uncountable noun* ■ los **bolos**: bowling is an interesting sport los bolos son un deporte interesante
> to go bowling jugar a los bolos: he often goes bowling with his friends a menudo juega a los bolos con sus amigos
> a bowling alley una bolera.

box [bɒks] *noun* ■ la **caja**.

boxer ['bɒksəʳ] *noun* ■ el **boxeador**, la **boxeadora**: he's a boxer es boxeador.

boxer shorts ['bɒksəʳʃɔːts] *plural noun* ■ los **calzoncillos**: a pair of boxer shorts unos calzoncillos.

boxing ['bɒksɪŋ] *uncountable noun* ■ el **boxeo**: he likes to watch boxing le gusta ver boxeo
> a boxing match un combate de boxeo
> a boxing ring un cuadrilátero.

Boxing Day UK ['bɒksɪŋdeɪ] *noun* ■ el **26 de diciembre**.

> BOXING DAY
>
> El 26 de diciembre, día festivo en Gran Bretaña, se llama **Boxing Day**. La palabra viene de la **Christmas box** (la caja de Navidad), pequeño detalle o aguinaldo que los señores de la casa regalaban a sus sirvientes. Hoy en día, en esas fechas, se mantiene la tradición de dar un aguinaldo al cartero, al repartidor de leche o al basurero.

boy [bɔɪ] *noun* ■ el **niño**: a good boy un niño bueno.

boyfriend ['bɔɪfrend] *noun* ■ el **novio**.

bra [brɑː] *noun* ■ el **sostén** *(plural* los sostenes).

brace UK [breɪs], **braces** US [breɪsɪz] *noun* ■ el **aparato dental**: he has a brace on his teeth tiene un aparato en los dientes.

bracelet ['breɪslɪt] *noun* ■ la **pulsera**.

brag [bræg] *(past tense & past participle* bragged, *present participle* bragging) *verb* ■ **presumir**: stop bragging! ¡deja de presumir!
> he's always bragging about his rich father siempre está presumiendo de tener un padre rico.

brain [breɪn] *noun* ■ el **cerebro**
> he's got brains es inteligente.

brainy ['breɪnɪ] *adjective* ■ **inteligente**.

brake [breɪk] *(noun & verb)*
■ *noun*
  el **freno**: the brakes failed fallaron los frenos
■ *verb*
  frenar: he braked suddenly frenó de repente.

branch [UK brɑːntʃ, UK bræntʃ] *noun*
1. la **rama**: the boy was hanging from a branch el niño estaba colgado de una rama
2. la **sucursal**: the bank has a branch in New York el banco tiene una sucursal en Nueva York.

brand [brænd] *noun* ■ la **marca**: it's a well-known brand of clothing es una marca de ropa muy conocida.

brand-new [brændnjuː] *adjective* ■ **flamante**: I've bought a brand-new computer me he comprado un flamante ordenador.

brass [brɑːs] *noun* ■ el **latón**: it's made of brass está hecho de latón.

brave [breɪv] *adjective* ■ **valiente**.

Brazil [brəˈzɪl] *noun* ■ **Brasil**.

Brazilian [brəˈzɪljən] *(adjective & noun)*
■ *adjective*
  Remember not to use a capital letter for the adjective in Spanish:

brasileño: I like Brazilian music me gusta la música brasileña

■ *noun*

In Spanish, a capital letter is not used for the inhabitants of a country or region:

el **brasileño** la **brasileña:** a Brazilian sings that song un brasileño canta esa canción.

bread [bred] *uncountable noun* ■ el **pan**
➤ a loaf of bread una barra de pan
➤ bread bun el panecillo.

break [breɪk] *(noun & verb)*

■ *noun*

el **descanso:** they took a break se tomaron un descanso

■ *verb (past tense* broke, *past participle* broken*)*

1. **romper:** I've broken the radio he roto la radio
2. **romperse:** she has broken her leg se ha roto la pierna; the glass has broken se ha roto el cristal
➤ to break the law violar la ley: she broke the law violó la ley
➤ to break a promise romper una promesa: Tom broke his promise Tom rompió su promesa
➤ to break a record batir un récord: he broke the world record batió el récord mundial

break down *phrasal verb*

1. **averiarse:** their car broke down se les ha averiado el coche
2. **echar abajo:** the police broke the door down la policía tiró la puerta abajo

break in *phrasal verb* ■ **entrar:** a burglar broke in through the window un ladrón entró por la ventana

break up *phrasal verb*

1. **partir:** they broke it up into five pieces lo partieron en cinco pedazos
2. **romper:** he broke up with his girlfriend rompió con su novia
3. **terminar:** the meeting broke up at three la reunión terminó a las tres.

breakdown ['breɪkdaʊn] *noun* ■ la **avería:** we had a breakdown on the motorway tuvimos una avería en la autopista
➤ a nervous breakdown una crisis nerviosa.

breakfast ['brekfəst] *noun* ■ el **desayuno**
➤ to have breakfast desayunar.

breast [brest] *noun* ■ el **pecho**
➤ a chicken breast una pechuga de pollo.

breaststroke ['breststrəʊk] *noun* ■ la **braza:** she's learning the breaststroke está aprendiendo el estilo braza
➤ he's swimming breaststroke está nadando en estilo braza.

breath [breθ] *noun* ■ el **aliento:** I need to get my breath back necesito recobrar el aliento
➤ he took a deep breath respiró hondo
➤ hold your breath contén la respiración
➤ out of breath sin aliento: I'm out of breath me he quedado sin aliento
➤ bad breath el mal aliento.

breathe [briːð] *verb* ■ **respirar:** breathe deeply respira hondo

breathe in *phrasal verb* ■ **inspirar**

breathe out *phrasal verb* ■ **espirar.**

breed [briːd] *(verb & noun)*

■ *verb (past tense & past participle* bred*)*

1. **criar:** he breeds ostriches cría avestruces
2. **reproducirse:** rabbits breed very fast los conejos se reproducen muy rápido

■ *noun*

la **raza:** what breed is that dog? ¿de qué raza es ese perro?

bred [bred] *past tense & past participle*
➤ breed.

breeze [briːz] *noun* ■ la **brisa.**

brick [brɪk] *noun* ■ el **ladrillo.**

bride [braɪd] *noun* ■ la **novia:** the bride looked really beautiful la novia estaba muy guapa
➤ the bride and groom los novios.

bridegroom ['braɪdgrʊm] *noun* ■ el **novio.**

bridesmaid ['braɪdzmeɪd] *noun* ■ la **dama de honor.**

bridge [brɪdʒ] noun ■ el **puente: she walked across the bridge** atravesó el puente.

brief [briːf] adjective ■ **breve: his speech was very brief** su discurso fue muy breve.

briefcase ['briːfkeɪs] noun ■ el **maletín** (plural los **maletines**), el **portafolios** (plural los **portafolios**).

bright [braɪt] adjective
1. **brillante: I like bright colours** me gustan los colores brillantes
2. **luminoso: the room is very bright** la habitación es muy luminosa
3. **inteligente: she's very bright** es muy inteligente.

brilliant ['brɪljənt] adjective
1. **brillante: he's a brilliant student** es un estudiante brillante
2. UK informal **genial: the film was brilliant** la película fue genial.

bring [brɪŋ] (past tense & past participle brought) verb ■ **traer: I've brought you some flowers** te he traído flores; **you can bring a friend** puedes traer a un amigo

bring back phrasal verb
1. **devolver: I'll bring your things back tomorrow** te voy a devolver tus cosas mañana
2. **traer: he brought a T-shirt back from Barcelona** trajo una camiseta de Barcelona
3. **llevar: she brought him back home** lo llevó de vuelta a su casa

bring up phrasal verb
1. **criar: he was brought up by his grandparents** lo criaron sus abuelos
2. **plantear: he brought the matter up at the meeting** planteó la cuestión en la reunión.

Britain ['brɪtn] noun ■ **Gran Bretaña: I'm going to Britain** voy a Gran Bretaña; **she lives in Britain** vive en Gran Bretaña
➤ Great Britain.

British ['brɪtɪʃ] (adjective & noun)
■ adjective

The Spanish adjective does not start with a capital letter:

británico: he's a British actor es un actor británico
■ noun

In Spanish, a capital letter is not used for the inhabitants of a country or region:

➤ **the British** los británicos
➤ **the British Isles** las Islas Británicas.

broad [brɔːd] adjective ■ **ancho: he has broad shoulders** es ancho de espaldas
➤ **in broad daylight** a plena luz del día.

broadcast ['brɔːdkɑːst] (noun & verb)
■ noun
el **programa: a live TV broadcast** un programa de televisión en directo
■ verb (past tense & past participle broadcast)
emitir: the programme is broadcast on the radio emiten el programa por la radio.

Broadway ['brɔːdweɪ] noun ■ nombre de una calle de Nueva York.

broccoli ['brɒkəlɪ] uncountable noun ■ el **brócoli**.

broke [brəʊk] (adjective & verb form)
■ adjective
informal **sin blanca: he's broke** está sin blanca
■ past tense
➤ break.

broken ['brəʊkn] (adjective & verb form)
■ adjective
roto: the cup is broken la taza está rota
➤ **he has a broken bone in his foot** tiene un hueso del pie roto
■ past participle
➤ break.

bronze [brɒnz] noun ■ el **bronce: bronze has many different uses** el bronce tiene usos muy variados
➤ **the Bronze Age** la Edad de Bronce
➤ **he won the bronze medal** ganó la medalla de bronce.

brooch [brəʊtʃ] noun ■ el **broche**.

broom [bruːm] noun ■ la **escoba**.

brother ['brʌðəʳ] noun ■ el **hermano: she has two brothers** tiene dos hermanos.

brother-in-law [ˈbrʌðəˈɪnlɔː] *(plural* brothers-in-law) *noun* ■ el **cuñado.**

brought [brɔːt] *past tense & past participle* ➤ bring.

brown [braʊn] *adjective*
1. **marrón** *(feminine* **marrón** *plural* **marrones**)*: brown shoes zapatos marrones
2. **castaño:** he has brown hair tiene el pelo castaño
3. **moreno:** he was very brown after his holiday estaba muy moreno después de sus vacaciones
➤ brown bread el pan integral
➤ brown sugar el azúcar moreno.

brownie [ˈbraʊnɪ] *noun* ■ el **bizcocho de chocolate y nueces.**

browse [braʊz] *verb*
1. **mirar:** he likes browsing in that shop le gusta mirar en esa tienda
2. **hojear:** he's browsing through a magazine está hojeando una revista
3. **navegar:** she's browsing the Internet está navegando por Internet.

browser [ˈbraʊzəˈ] *noun* ■ el **navegador:** an Internet browser un navegador de Internet.

bruise [bruːz] *(noun & verb)*
■ *noun*
el **moretón** *(plural* los **moretones**)*: he's covered in bruises está lleno de moretones
■ *verb*
he bruised his knee se hizo un moretón en la rodilla.

brush [brʌʃ] *(noun & verb)*
■ *noun*
1. el **cepillo:** pass me the brush please pásame el cepillo, por favor
2. el **pincel:** the brush was stiff with dry paint el pincel estaba duro con la pintura seca
■ *verb*
1. **cepillar:** she's brushing her hair se está cepillando el pelo; don't forget to brush your teeth! no olvides cepillarte los dientes
2. **pasar rozando:** she brushed against the table pasó rozando la mesa.

bubble [ˈbʌbl] *(noun & verb)*
■ *noun*
1. la **burbuja:** the bubbles rose to the surface of the lake las burbujas subían a la superficie del lago
2. la **pompa:** the girl was playing with soap bubbles la niña estaba jugando con las pompas de jabón
➤ bubble plastic plástico de burbuja
■ *verb*
burbujear: the oil was bubbling in the pan el aceite burbujeaba en la sartén.

buck [bʌk] *noun* ■ *informal* el **dólar:** it costs ten bucks cuesta diez dólares.

bucket [ˈbʌkɪt] *noun* ■ el **cubo.**

buckle [ˈbʌkl] *noun* ■ la **hebilla:** my belt buckle is broken la hebilla de mi cinturón está rota.

buddy *US* [ˈbʌdɪ] *(plural* buddies) *noun* ■ *informal* el **amigo,** la **amiga.**

buffalo [ˈbʌfələʊ] *noun* ■ el **búfalo.**

bug [bʌg] *(noun & verb)*
■ *noun*
1. el **bicho:** a bug flew in through the window entró un bicho volando por la ventana
2. el **virus:** he's caught a bug ha pillado un virus
3. el **error:** there's a bug in the program hay un error el programa
■ *verb (past tense & past participle* bugged, *present participle* bugging) *informal*
fastidiar: stop bugging me! ¡deja de fastidiarme!

build [bɪld] *(past tense & past participle* built) *verb* ■ **construir:** they're building houses near the school están construyendo casas cerca de la escuela.

building [ˈbɪldɪŋ] *noun* ■ el **edificio**
➤ a building site una obra.

built [bɪlt] *past tense & past participle* ➤ build.

bulb [bʌlb] *noun* ■ la **bombilla.**

bull [bʊl] *noun* ■ el **toro.**

bullet [ˈbʊlɪt] *noun* ■ la **bala.**

bullfight [ˈbʊlfaɪt] *noun* ■ la **corrida de toros.**

bull's-eye ['bolzaı] *noun* ■ el **blanco**: she hit the bull's-eye! ¡dio en el blanco!

bully ['bolı] *(noun & verb)*
■ *noun (plural* bullies*)*
el **matón** *(plural* los **matones***)*: he's a real bully es un verdadero matón
■ *verb*
amedrentar: she bullies the whole class ella amedrenta a toda la clase.

bump [bʌmp] *(noun & verb)*
■ *noun*
1. el **chichón** *(plural* los chichones*)*: I have a bump on my forehead tengo un chichón en la frente
2. el **golpe**: they felt a bump as the car went over the pothole sintieron un golpe cuando el coche pasó por el bache
■ *verb*
golpear: I bumped my head me golpeé la cabeza

bump into *phrasal verb*
1. **darse contra**: they bumped into the wall me di contra la pared
2. **tropezarse**: I bumped into my old teacher me tropecé con una antigua profesora mía.

bumper ['bʌmpəʳ] *noun* ■ el **parachoques** *(plural* los parachoques*)*.

bumpy ['bʌmpı] *adjective*
1. **desigual**: it has a bumpy surface tiene una superficie desigual
2. **lleno de baches**: the road is bumpy la calle está llena de baches
3. **agitado**: we had a bumpy flight tuvimos un vuelo agitado.

bun [bʌn] *noun*
1. el **bollo**
2. el **panecillo**
3. el **moño**: Susie wears her hair in a bun Susie lleva el pelo recogido en un moño.

bunch [bʌntʃ] *noun*
1. el **ramo**: a bunch of flowers un ramo de flores
2. el **racimo**: a bunch of grapes un racimo de uvas
3. el **manojo**: a bunch of keys un manojo de llaves.

bunk beds ['bʌŋ'bedz] *plural noun* ■ la **litera**.

burger ['bɜːgəʳ] *noun* ■ la **hamburguesa**.

burglar ['bɜːgləʳ] *noun* ■ el **ladrón** *(plural* los **ladrones***)*, la **ladrona**
➤ a burglar alarm una alarma antirrobo.

buried ['berıd] *past tense & past participle* ➤ bury.

burn [bɜːn] *(verb & noun)*
■ *noun*
la **quemadura**: she has a burn on her arm tiene una quemadura en el brazo
■ *verb (past tense & past participle* burnt OR burned*)*
1. **arder**: the house is burning la casa está ardiendo
2. **quemar**: I burned myself me quemé; I've burned my hand me he quemado la mano.

burnt [bɜːnt] *past tense & past participle* ➤ burn.

burp [bɜːp] *verb* ■ *informal* **eructar**.

burst [bɜːst] *(past tense & past participle* burst*)* *verb*
1. **estallar**: the bubble burst la burbuja estalló
2. **reventarse**: the balloon burst el globo se reventó
3. **reventar**: he burst the balloon el reventó el globo
➤ to burst into tears romper a llorar: the little boy burst into tears el niño rompió a llorar
➤ to burst out laughing echarse a reír: they all burst out laughing todos se echaron a reír.

bury ['berı] *(past tense & past participle* buried*)* *verb* ■ **enterrar**: my grandmother is buried in Glasgow mi abuela está enterrada en Glasgow.

bus [bʌs] *noun* ■ el **autobús**: we took the bus into town tomamos el autobús al centro
➤ a bus stop una parada de autobús.

bush [boʃ] *noun* ■ el **arbusto**.

business ['bıznıs] *(plural* businesses*) noun*
1. los **negocios**: she's good at business es buena para los negocios
2. la **empresa**: he has a small business tiene una pequeña empresa
➤ business meeting la reunión de negocios

mind your own business! ¡no te metas en lo que no te importa!

businessman [ˈbɪznɪsmæn] (plural businessmen [ˈbɪznɪsmen]) noun ■ el **empresario.**

businesswoman [ˈbɪznɪsˌwʊmən] (plural businesswomen [ˈbɪznɪsˌwɪmɪn]) noun ■ la **empresaria.**

busy [ˈbɪzɪ] adjective
1. **ocupado:** I'm very busy estoy muy ocupado
2. **ajetreado:** I have a busy week tengo una semana ajetreada
3. **de mucho movimiento:** New York is a busy city Nueva York es una ciudad de mucho movimiento.

but [bʌt] conjunction
1. **pero:** I called him but he wasn't there lo llamé, pero no estaba
2. **sino:** she wasn't sad but angry no estaba triste sino enfadada

Sino is used to express a contradiction of a previous negative statement.

butcher [ˈbʊtʃər] noun ■ el **carnicero,** la **carnicera**
the butcher's shop la carnicería.

butter [ˈbʌtər] uncountable noun ■ la **mantequilla.**

butterfly [ˈbʌtəflaɪ] (plural butterflies) noun ■ la **mariposa.**

buttocks [ˈbʌtəks] plural noun ■ las **nalgas.**

button [ˈbʌtn] noun ■ el **botón:** he lost a button from his shirt perdió un botón de la camisa; click on the left mouse button presiona el botón izquierdo del ratón.

buy [baɪ] (past tense & past participle bought) verb ■ **comprar:** I'm going to buy some bread voy a comprar pan; she bought him a present le compró un regalo.

buzzer [ˈbʌzər] noun ■ el **timbre.**

by [baɪ] preposition
1. **por:** this temple was built by the Romans este templo fue construido por los romanos
2. **de:** a book by Tolkien un libro de Tolkien

3. **en:** we went by bus fuimos en autobús
4. **junto a:** he was sitting by the fire estaba sentado junto al fuego
5. **para:** I want to be home by 8 quiero estar en casa para las 8
   by oneself solo: I did it all by myself lo hice yo solo
   by the way a propósito: by the way, are you coming tonight? a propósito, ¿vienes esta noche?

bye [baɪ], **bye-bye** [bəˈbaɪ] exclamation ■ **adiós.**

cab [kæb] noun ■ el **taxi:** I'll take a cab tomaré un taxi.

cabbage [ˈkæbɪdʒ] noun ■ el **repollo,** la **col.**

cabin [ˈkæbɪn] noun
1. el **camarote:** her cabin is on the top deck su camarote está en la cubierta de arriba
2. la **cabaña:** he lives in a log cabin vive en una cabaña de madera.

cabinet [ˈkæbɪnɪt] noun
1. el **armario:** a bathroom cabinet un armario de baño
2. el **gabinete:** he was in the president's cabinet estuvo en el gabinete del presidente
   a medicine cabinet un botiquín.

cable [ˈkeɪbl] noun ■ el **cable**
cable television OR cable TV televisión por cable: we have cable television tenemos televisión por cable.

cafe , café ['kæfeɪ] *noun* ■ el **café: we had ice-cream in a café** tomamos helado en un café.

cafeteria [ˌkæfɪ'tɪərɪə] *noun* ■ la **cafetería.**

cage [keɪdʒ] *noun* ■ la **jaula.**

cake [keɪk] *noun* ■ el **pastel: she's making a chocolate cake** está haciendo un pastel de chocolate

➤ **a cake shop** una pastelería.

calculator ['kælkjʊleɪtər] *noun* ■ la **calculadora.**

calendar ['kælɪndər] *noun* ■ el **calendario.**

calf [kɑːf] *(plural* calves [kɑːvz]) *noun*
1. el **ternero: a cow and her calf** una vaca y su ternero
2. la **pantorrilla: I've got a pain in my calf** tengo un dolor en la pantorrilla.

call [kɔːl] *(noun & verb)*
■ *noun*
la **llamada: I have to make a call** tengo que hacer una llamada
➤ **I'll give you a call** te voy a llamar
■ *verb*
llamar: we called the police llamamos a la policía; **everyone calls her Peggy** todos la llaman Peggy; **he called me a liar** me llamó mentiroso
to be called llamarse: **what is he called?** ¿cómo se llama?
➤ **what's this called?** ¿cómo se llama esto?
➤ **who's calling?** ¿de parte de quién?

call back *phrasal verb* ■ **volver a llamar: I'll call back later** volveré a llamar más tarde

call off *phrasal verb* ■ **cancelar: they called off the meeting** cancelaron la reunión

call on *phrasal verb* ■ **pasar a ver: they called on us yesterday** ayer nos pasaron a ver.

calm [kɑːm] *(adjective & verb)*
■ *adjective*
tranquilo, en calma: the sea is calm el mar está en calma

➤ **keep calm!** ¡tranquilo!
■ *verb*
calmar, tranquilizar: she tried to calm him ella intentó calmarle

calm down *phrasal verb* ■ **calmarse, tranquilizarse: calm down!** ¡cálmate!

calves [kɑːvz] *plural* ➤ calf.

camcorder ['kæmˌkɔːdər] *noun* ■ la **videocámara.**

came [keɪm] *past tense* ➤ come.

camel ['kæml] *noun* ■ el **camello.**

camera ['kæmərə] *noun* ■ la **cámara.**

camp [kæmp] *(noun & verb)*
■ *noun*
el **campamento: we set up camp near the river** levantamos el campamento cerca del río
■ *verb*
acampar: we camped on the beach acampamos en la playa.

camper ['kæmpər] *noun* ■ el/la **campista: there are campers near the river** hay campistas cerca del río.

camping ['kæmpɪŋ] *uncountable noun*
➤ **to go camping** ir de camping: **we go camping every spring** nos vamos de camping cada primavera
➤ **camping is not allowed in that park** no está permitido acampar en ese parque.

campus ['kæmpəs] *noun* ■ el **campus.**

can *(verb & noun)*
■ *verb* [kən, kæn] *(negative* can't OR cannot*)*
1. **poder: can I help you with anything?** ¿puedo ayudarte en algo?; **Peter can't come on Friday** Peter no puede venir el viernes; **can I speak to Rachel, please?** ¿puedo hablar con Rachel, por favor?

When can is used with a verb of perception (like see, hear, feel, understand) it is not translated at all:

I can't see no veo; **can you hear me?** ¿me oyes?; **I can't feel anything** no siento nada;

he can't understand what you are saying no entiende lo que dices

2.

When **can** means "know how to":

saber: can you swim? ¿sabes nadar?; **I can't drive** no sé conducir
■ *noun* [kæn]
la **lata: a can of beer** una lata de cerveza
➤ **a can opener** un abrelatas.

Canada ['kænədə] *noun* ■ el **Canadá**.

Canadian [kəˈneɪdjən] *(adjective & noun)*
■ *adjective*

Remember not to use a capital letter for the adjective in Spanish:

canadiense: there is a maple leaf on the Canadian flag la bandera canadiense tiene una hoja de arce
■ *noun*

In Spanish, a capital letter is not used for the inhabitants of a country or region:

el/la canadiense: many Canadians are bilingual muchos canadienses son bilingües.

canal [kəˈnæl] *noun* ■ el **canal: Amsterdam is famous for its canals** Amsterdam es famosa por sus canales.

cancel ['kænsl] *(past tense & past participle UK* cancelled, *US* canceled, *present participle UK* cancelling, *US* canceling) *verb* ■ **cancelar: they cancelled the meeting** cancelaron la reunión.

cancer ['kænsəʳ] *noun* ■ el **cáncer.**

candidate ['kændɪdeɪt] *noun* ■ el **candidato,** la **candidata.**

candle ['kændl] *noun* ■ la **vela.**

candy *US* ['kændɪ] *(plural* candies) *noun* ■ la **golosina: he wants a piece of candy** quiere una golosina
➤ **a candy store** una tienda de golosinas.

canned [kænd] *adjective* ■ **enlatado: canned sardines** sardinas enlatadas.

cannot ['kænɒt] *negative* ➤ can.

canoe [kəˈnuː] *noun* ■ la **canoa.**

canoeing [kəˈnuːɪŋ] *uncountable noun* ■ el **piragüismo: she enjoys canoeing** le gusta el piragüismo
➤ **to go canoeing** hacer piragüismo: **he goes canoeing every weekend** hace piragüismo todos los fines de semana.

can't [*UK* kɑːnt, *UK* kænt] = cannot.

canvas ['kænvəs] *noun*
1. la **lona: canvas shoes** zapatillas de lona
2. el **lienzo.**

cap [kæp] *noun*
1. la **gorra: he wears his cap backwards** usa su gorra con la visera hacia atrás
2. el **tapón: take the cap off the bottle** sácale el tapón a la botella.

capable ['keɪpəbl] *adjective* ■ **capaz.**

capital ['kæpɪtl] *noun*
1. la **capital: London is the capital of England** Londres es la capital de Inglaterra
2. la **mayúscula: write your name in capitals** escriba su nombre en mayúsculas
➤ **a capital city** una capital.

captain ['kæptɪn] *noun* ■ el **capitán** *(plural* los **capitanes),** la **capitana.**

car [kɑːʳ] *noun*
1. el **coche: he bought a red car** se compró un coche rojo; **we're going by car** vamos en coche
2. *US* el **vagón** *(plural* los **vagones): this train has ten cars** este tren tiene diez vagones
➤ **a car crash** un accidente de coche.

card [kɑːd] *noun*
1. la **tarjeta: a birthday card** una tarjeta de cumpleaños
2. la **carta: they're playing cards** están jugando a las cartas.

cardboard ['kɑːdbɔːd] *noun* ■ el **cartón** *(plural* los **cartones): a cardboard box** una caja de cartón.

care [keə^r] *(noun & verb)*

■ *uncountable noun*

el **cuidado**: skin care cuidado de la piel

➤ to take care of cuidar: Jack takes care of the children Jack cuida a los niños

➤ take care! ¡cuídate!

■ *verb*

preocuparse

➤ who cares? ¿y a mí qué?

➤ I don't care no me importa

care about *phrasal verb* ■ **importar**: she doesn't care about her appearance no le importa su aspecto

care for *phrasal verb*

1. **cuidar**: she cares for her elderly parents ella cuida a sus padres ancianos

2. **gustar**: I don't care for his new friends no me gustan sus nuevos amigos.

career [kə'rɪə^r] *noun* ■ la **carrera**: Muriel made a career for herself as a journalist Muriel se forjó una carrera como periodista.

careful ['keəfʊl] *adjective* ■ **cuidadoso**: he's always very careful siempre es muy cuidadoso

➤ be careful! ¡ten cuidado!

carefully ['keəfəlɪ] *adverb*

1. **con cuidado**: he drives carefully conduce con cuidado

2. **con esmero**: she did the work carefully hizo el trabajo con esmero.

careless ['keəlɪs] *adjective*

1. **descuidado**: Mary is very careless Mary es muy descuidada

2. **poco cuidado**: his work is careless su trabajo es poco cuidado

➤ a careless mistake un descuido.

Caribbean [kə'rɪbɪən] *(noun & adjective)*

■ *noun*

the Caribbean el Caribe

■ *adjective*

Remember not to use a capital letter for the adjective in Spanish:

caribeño: I like Caribbean music me gusta la música caribeña

➤ the Caribbean Sea el mar Caribe.

carnival ['kɑːnɪvl] *noun* ■ el **carnaval**.

carol ['kærəl] *noun*

a Christmas carol un villancico.

carpet ['kɑːpɪt] *noun*

1. la **alfombra**: a Persian carpet una alfombra persa

2. la **moqueta**: a wall-to-wall carpet una moqueta.

carried ['kærɪd] *past tense & past participle*

➤ carry.

carrot ['kærət] *noun* ■ la **zanahoria**.

carry ['kærɪ] *(past tense & past participle carried) verb*

1. **llevar**: she's carrying a large bag lleva una bolsa grande

2. **transportar**: the bus can carry up to 50 passengers el autobús puede transportar hasta 50 pasajeros

carry on *phrasal verb* ■ **seguir**: he carried on working siguió trabajando.

cart ['kɑːt] *noun*

1. el **carro**: the horse was pulling the cart el caballo estaba tirando el carro

➤ a shopping cart *US* un carro de la compra.

carton ['kɑːtn] *noun* ■ el **cartón**: a carton of cigarettes un cartón de tabaco; a carton of milk un cartón de leche.

cartoon [kɑː'tuːn] *noun*

1. el **chiste**: she likes the cartoons in the newspapers le gustan los chistes de los periódicos

2. los **dibujos animados**: he likes to watch cartoons in the afternoon le gusta ver dibujos animados por la tarde

➤ a cartoon strip una tira cómica.

carve [kɑːv] *verb*

1. **tallar**: he carved a statue out of wood talló una estatua de madera

2. **grabar**: Kevin carved his name on the bench Kevin grabó su nombre en el banco

3. cortar: she's carving the chicken está cortando el pollo.

case [keɪs] *noun*

1. la **maleta**: I've packed my case he hecho mi maleta

2. el **estuche**: she put her glasses in their case puso sus gafas en el estuche

3. el **caso**: a case of chickenpox un caso de varicela; in that case I'm not coming en ese caso, no voy

▷ in any case en cualquier caso

▷ in case por si

▷ take your coat in case it rains coge el abrigo por si llueve.

cash [kæʃ] *uncountable noun* ■ el **dinero en efectivo**: I have no cash on me no tengo dinero en efectivo

▷ to pay cash pagar al contado.

cashier [kæ'ʃɪəʳ] *noun* ■ el **cajero**, la **cajera**.

cash machine ['kæʃməˌʃiːn] *noun* ■ el **cajero automático**.

cash register ['kæʃˌredʒɪstəʳ] *noun* ■ la **caja registradora**.

casserole ['kæsərəʊl] *noun*

1. el **guiso**

2. la **cazuela**.

cassette [kæ'set] *noun* ■ el/la **casete**, la **cinta**

▷ a cassette player un magnetófono.

castle ['kɑːsl] *noun* ■ el **castillo**.

casual ['kæʒʊəl] *adjective*

1. informal: they were wearing casual clothes llevaban ropa informal

2. descuidado: he's very casual about things es muy descuidado con las cosas

⚠ La palabra inglesa **casual** es un falso amigo, no significa "casual".

casualty ['kæʒjʊəltɪ] *(plural* casualties) *noun*

1. la **víctima**

2. urgencias: I was taken to casualty me llevaron a urgencias.

cat [kæt] *noun* ■ el **gato**.

catalogue *UK,* **catalog** *US* ['kætəlɒg] *noun* ■ el **catálogo**.

catch [kætʃ] *(past tense & past participle* caught) *verb*

1. agarrar: he caught me by the arm me agarró del brazo

2. pescar: he caught a very big fish pescó un pez muy grande

3. resfriarse: she caught a cold the other day el otro día se resfrió

4. coger: Fred is catching the 6 o'clock bus Fred va a coger el autobús de las 6

5. pillar: I caught him smoking lo pillé fumando; I caught my finger in the door me pillé el dedo en la puerta

6. oír: I didn't catch what you said no oí lo que dijiste

catch up *phrasal verb*

1. ponerse al día: I was away yesterday so I'll have to catch up ayer no estuve, así que tendré que ponerme al día

2. alcanzar: you go ahead, I'll catch you up adelántate, yo te alcanzo.

category ['kætəgərɪ] *(plural* categories) *noun* ■ la **categoría**.

caterpillar ['kætəpɪləʳ] *noun* ■ la **oruga**.

cathedral [kə'θiːdrəl] *noun* ■ la **catedral**.

Catholic ['kæθlɪk] *adjective & noun* ■ católico: he's a Catholic es católico.

cattle ['kætl] *plural noun* ■ el **ganado**.

caught [kɔːt] *past tense & past participle* ➤ catch.

cauliflower ['kɒlɪˌflaʊəʳ] *noun* ■ la **coliflor**.

cause [kɔːz] *(noun & verb)*

■ *noun*

la **causa**: we don't know the cause of the accident no conocemos la causa del accidente

■ *verb*

causar: the storm caused a lot of damage la tormenta causó muchos daños.

cautious ['kɔːʃəs] *adjective* ■ **cauteloso**.

cave [keɪv] *noun* ■ la **cueva**.

CD [ˌsiːˈdiː] *(abbreviation of* compact disc*)* *noun* ■ el **CD**
▷ a CD player un reproductor de CD.

CD-ROM [ˌsiːdiːˈrɒm] *(abbreviation of* compact disc read only memory*)* *noun* ■ el **CD-ROM**.

ceiling ['siːlɪŋ] *noun* ■ el **techo**
▷ a ceiling lamp una lámpara de techo.

celebrate ['selɪbreɪt] *verb* ■ **celebrar**: we're going to celebrate my birthday vamos a celebrar mi cumpleaños; people are celebrating in the streets la gente está de fiesta en las calles.

celebrity [sɪˈlebrətɪ] *(plural* celebrities*)* *noun* ■ la **celebridad**.

celery ['selərɪ] *uncountable noun* ■ el **apio**: a stick of celery una penca de apio.

cell [sel] *noun*
1. la **celda**: the prisoner is in his cell el prisionero está en su celda
2. la **célula**: we have many cells in our bodies tenemos muchas células en el cuerpo.

cellar ['selər] *noun* ■ el **sótano**.

cello ['tʃeləʊ] *noun* ■ el **violonchelo**.

cemetery ['semɪtrɪ] *(plural* cemeteries*)* *noun* ■ el **cementerio**.

cent [sent] *noun*
1. el **centavo**: that's 5 dollars and 20 cents son 5 dólares y 20 centavos
2. el **céntimo**: that's 3 euros and 5 cents son 3 euros y 5 céntimos.

center *US noun* ➤ **centre**.

centigrade ['sentɪɡreɪd] *adjective* ■ **centígrado**: it's 20 degrees centigrade estamos a 20 grados centígrados.

centimetre *UK,* **centimeter** *US* ['sentɪˌmiːtər] *noun* ■ el **centímetro**.

central ['sentrəl] *adjective* ■ **central**.

centre *UK,* **center** *US* [sentr] *noun* ■ el **centro**
▷ in the centre of town en el centro.

century ['sentʃʊrɪ] *(plural* centuries*)* *noun* ■ el **siglo**: in the 20th century en el siglo XX.

cereal ['sɪərɪəl] *noun* ■ el **cereal**, los cereales.

ceremony ['serɪmənɪ] *(plural* ceremonies*)* *noun* ■ la **ceremonia**.

certain ['sɜːtn] *adjective*
1. **seguro**: I'm certain that it's her estoy seguro de que es ella
2. **cierto**: certain people think he's guilty ciertas personas creen que es culpable
▷ to make certain of something asegurarse de algo: he made certain the window was closed se aseguró de que la ventana estuviera cerrada.

certainly ['sɜːtnlɪ] *adverb* ■ **por supuesto**: certainly not! ¡por supuesto que no!; I will certainly come por supuesto que vendré.

certificate [səˈtɪfɪkət] *noun* ■ el **certificado**.

chain [tʃeɪn] *noun* ■ la **cadena**.

chair [tʃeər] *noun* ■ la **silla**: a table and chairs una mesa y sillas.

chairman ['tʃeəmən] *(plural* chairmen ['tʃeəmən]) *noun* ■ el **presidente**.

chairperson ['tʃeəˌpɜːsn] *(plural* chairpersons*)* *noun* ■ el **presidente**, la **presidenta**.

chairwoman ['tʃeəˌwʊmən] *(plural* chairwomen ['tʃeəˌwɪmɪn]) *noun* ■ la **presidenta**.

chalk [tʃɔːk] *uncountable noun* ■ la **tiza**: a piece of chalk una tiza.

challenge ['tʃælɪndʒ] *(noun & verb)*

■ *noun*
el **reto**

■ *verb*

retar: he challenged me to a game of tennis me retó a jugar un partido de tenis.

champagne [ˌʃæmˈpeɪn] *noun* ■ el **champán.**

champion [ˈtʃæmpjən] *noun* ■ el **campeón,** la **campeona:** she's the world champion es la campeona mundial.

championship [ˈtʃæmpjənʃɪp] *noun* ■ el **campeonato.**

chance [tʃɑːns] *noun*

1. la **posibilidad:** he has a good chance of winning hay muchas posibilidades de que gane
2. la **oportunidad:** it gave me a chance to explore the city me dio la oportunidad de explorar la ciudad
3. la **casualidad:** I met him by chance lo encontré por casualidad

> to take a chance **arriesgarse:** he took a chance and succeeded se arriesgó y tuvo éxito.

change [tʃeɪndʒ] *(noun & verb)*

■ *noun*

el **cambio:** there's been a change of plan ha habido un cambio de planes; do you have any change? ¿tienes algo de cambio?

> a change of clothes un cambio de ropa
> for a change para variar: he's watching TV, for a change está viendo la tele, para variar

■ *verb*

1. **cambiar:** he really has changed ha cambiado muchísimo; I want to change 200 dollars into euros quiero cambiar 200 dólares a euros; she changed before going out se cambió antes de salir
2. **cambiar de:** we have to change buses tenemos que cambiar de autobús; he changed into another pair of trousers se cambió los pantalones

> to change one's mind cambiar de idea: Richard changed his mind Richard cambió de idea
> to get changed cambiarse: I'm going to get changed me voy a cambiar

changing room *UK* [ˈtʃeɪndʒɪŋˌruːm] *noun*

1. el **probador**
2. el **vestuario.**

channel [ˈtʃænl] *noun* ■ el **canal:** could you change the channel? ¿podrías cambiar de canal?

> the Channel OR the English Channel el Canal de la Mancha
> the Channel Tunnel el Túnel del Canal de la Mancha.

chapter [ˈtʃæptər] *noun* ■ el **capítulo:** the hero dies in chapter three el héroe muere en el capítulo tres.

character [ˈkærəktər] *noun*

1. el **carácter:** Jennifer has a very gentle character Jennifer tiene un carácter muy dulce
2. el **personaje:** I like the character played by Johnny Depp me gusta el personaje que interpreta Johnny Depp.

charge [tʃɑːdʒ] *(noun & verb)*

■ *noun*

1. el **coste:** there's a delivery charge hay costes de envío
2. el **cargo:** he denies the charges niega los cargos

> it's free of charge es gratuito
> to be in charge estar a cargo: I'm in charge of the department estoy a cargo de la sección

■ *verb*

1. **cobrar:** they charged me 5 dollars me cobraron 5 dólares
2. **acusar:** he has been charged with murder ha sido acusado de asesinato.

charity [ˈtʃærətɪ] *(plural* charities*) noun*

1. la **organización benéfica** *(plural* las **organizaciones benéficas***)*: Oxfam is a charity Oxfam es una organización benéfica
2. la **caridad:** I helped him out of charity lo ayudé por caridad

> for charity para una obra benéfica: we raised 100 dollars for charity recaudamos 100 dólares para una obra benéfica.

charm [tʃɑːm] *noun* ■ el **encanto:** he has a lot of charm tiene mucho encanto.

charming ['tʃɑːmɪŋ] *adjective* ■ **encantador.**

chart [tʃɑːt] *noun* ■ el **gráfico:** the chart shows average temperatures el gráfico muestra las temperaturas medias

➤ the charts la lista de éxitos: her new song is number two in the charts su nueva canción es la número dos en la lista de éxitos.

chase [tʃeɪs] *(noun & verb)*

■ *noun*

la **persecución** *(plural* las **persecuciones***)*: a car chase una persecución en coche

■ *verb*

perseguir: somebody is chasing me alguien me está persiguiendo

chase after *phrasal verb* ■ **perseguir:** the dog was chasing after me el perro me perseguía.

chat [tʃæt] *(noun & verb)*

■ *noun*

1. la **charla,** la **conversación:** we had a long chat tuvimos una larga charla

2. **chat**

➤ a chat room sala de chat

■ *verb (past tense & past participle* chatted, *present participle* chatting*)*

1. **charlar:** he was chatting with a friend estaba charlando con un amigo

2. **chatear:** he likes to chat on the Internet le gusta chatear en Internet.

cheap [tʃiːp] *adjective* ■ **barato:** it's a cheap dress es un vestido barato.

cheat [tʃiːt] *(noun & verb)*

■ *noun*

el **tramposo,** la **tramposa:** he's a cheat es un tramposo

■ *verb*

hacer trampa: he cheats at cards hace trampas jugando a las cartas.

cheater *US* ['tʃiːtər] *noun* ➤ cheat.

check [tʃek] *(noun & verb)*

■ *noun*

1. el **control:** an identity check un control de identidad

2. *US* la **cuenta:** can I have the check, please? la cuenta, por favor

3. *US* el **cheque:** he paid by check pagó con un cheque

■ *verb*

1. **comprobar:** the accountant checked the figures el contable comprobó los números

2. **revisar:** they checked our passports revisaron nuestros pasaportes

check in *phrasal verb*

1. **facturar el equipaje:** they checked in for their flight facturaron su equipaje para el vuelo

2. **registrarse:** we checked in at the hotel nos registramos en el hotel

check out *phrasal verb*

1. **dejar:** they checked out from the hotel dejaron el hotel

2. *informal* **mirar:** check this out! ¡mira esto!

checkbook *US noun* ➤ chequebook *UK.*

checked [tʃekt] *adjective* ■ **a cuadros:** a checked shirt una camisa a cuadros.

checkers *US* ['tʃekəz] *noun* ■ las **damas:** they're playing checkers están jugando a las damas.

check-in [tʃekɪn] *noun* ■ la **facturación de equipajes:** check-in is at 6 o'clock la facturación de equipajes es a las 6.

checkout ['tʃekaʊt] *noun* ■ la **caja:** please pay at the checkout por favor, paguen en caja.

checkup ['tʃekʌp] *noun* ■ el **chequeo:** he's going to the dentist for a checkup va al dentista para un chequeo.

cheek [tʃiːk] *noun* ■ la **mejilla:** she kissed him on the cheek le besó en la mejilla

➤ what a cheek! ¡qué cara!

cheeky ['tʃiːkɪ] *adjective* ■ **descarado.**

cheer [tʃɪəʳ] (noun & verb)

■ noun

la **ovación** (plural las **ovaciones**): there were cheers when he came on stage hubo una ovación cuando subió al escenario

➤ three cheers for Donald! ¡viva Donald!

➤ cheers! ¡salud!

■ verb

gritar entusiasmadamente: everyone was cheering todos estaban gritando entusiasmadamente

cheer up phrasal verb

1. **levantar el ánimo**: I tried to cheer him up traté de levantarle el ánimo

2. **animarse**: he cheered up when his friends came to see him se animó cuando sus amigos vinieron a verlo; cheer up! ¡anímate!

cheerful [ˈtʃɪəfʊl] adjective ■ **alegre**.

cheerleader [ˈtʃɪəliːdəʳ] noun ■ el **animador**, la **animadora**.

cheese [tʃiːz] noun ■ el **queso**: a cheese sandwich un bocadillo de queso.

cheeseburger [ˈtʃiːzˌbɜːgəʳ] noun ■ la **hamburguesa con queso**.

cheesecake [ˈtʃiːzkeɪk] noun ■ el **pastel de queso**.

chef [ʃef] noun ■ el **chef**.

chemical [ˈkemɪkl] noun ■ la **sustancia química**.

chemist [ˈkemɪst] noun

1. el **químico**, la **química**

2. UK el **farmacéutico**, la **farmacéutica**

➤ a chemist's shop una farmacia.

chemistry [ˈkemɪstri] noun ■ la **química**: a chemistry lesson una clase de química.

cheque UK, **check** US [tʃek] el **cheque**, el **talón**: can I pay by cheque? ¿puedo pagar con un cheque?

chequebook UK, **checkbook** US [ˈtʃekbʊk] noun ■ el **talonario**.

cherry [ˈtʃeri] (plural cherries) noun ■ la **cereza**

➤ a cherry tree un cerezo.

chess [tʃes] noun ■ el **ajedrez**: they're playing chess están jugando al ajedrez.

chest [tʃest] noun

1. el **pecho**: he has a pain in his chest tiene un dolor en el pecho

2. el **baúl**: there's a big chest in the attic hay un baúl grande en el desván

➤ a chest of drawers una cómoda.

chestnut [ˈtʃesnʌt] noun ■ la **castaña**

➤ a chestnut tree un castaño.

chew [tʃuː] verb ■ **masticar**.

chewing gum [ˈtʃuːɪŋgʌm] noun ■ el **chicle**.

chicken [ˈtʃɪkɪn] noun ■ el **pollo**: a roast chicken un pollo asado.

chickenpox [ˈtʃɪkɪnpɒks] noun ■ la **varicela**: he has chickenpox tiene varicela.

chief [tʃiːf] (noun & adjective)

■ noun

el **jefe**, la **jefa**: he's the chief of an African tribe es el jefe de una tribu africana

■ adjective

principal: that's the chief problem ése es el problema principal.

child [tʃaɪld] (plural children [ˈtʃɪldrən]) noun ■ el **niño**, la **niña**: she acts like a child se comporta como una niña.

childhood [ˈtʃaɪldhʊd] noun ■ la **infancia**.

children [ˈtʃɪldrən] plural ➤ child.

Chile [ˈtʃɪli] noun ■ **Chile**.

Chilean [ˈtʃɪliən] (adjective & noun)

■ adjective

Remember not to use a capital letter for the adjective in Spanish:

chileno: Isabel Allende is a famous Chilean writer Isabel Allende es una famosa escritora chilena

■ *noun*

> In Spanish, a capital letter is not used for the inhabitants of a country or region:

el **chileno,** la **chilena: the Chileans export various agricultural products** los chilenos exportan varios productos agrícolas.

chill [tʃɪl] *(noun & verb)*

■ *noun*

1. el **resfriado: she caught a chill** pescó un resfriado
2. **fresco: there's a chill in the air** hace fresco

■ *verb*

enfriar: you should chill the champagne deberías enfriar el champán.

chilli , **chili** [ˈtʃɪlɪ] *(plural* chillies OR chilies) *noun* ■ el **chile.**

chilly [ˈtʃɪlɪ] *adjective* ■ **frío: I feel chilly** tengo frío; **it's chilly** hace frío.

chimney [ˈtʃɪmnɪ] *noun* ■ la **chimenea.**

chimpanzee [tʃɪmpənˈziː] *noun* ■ el/la **chimpancé.**

chin [tʃɪn] *noun* ■ la **barbilla.**

china [ˈtʃaɪnə] *uncountable noun* ■ la **porcelana: a china cup** una taza de porcelana.

China [ˈtʃaɪnə] *noun* ■ **China.**

Chinese [ˌtʃaɪniːz] *(adjective & noun)*

■ *adjective*

> Remember not to use a capital letter for the adjective in Spanish:

chino: Chinese medicine la medicina china

■ *noun*

> In Spanish, a capital letter is not used for the inhabitants of a country or region:

el **chino: she speaks Chinese** habla chino the **Chinese** los chinos.

chip [tʃɪp] *noun* ■

1. UK la **patata frita: egg and chips** un huevo con patatas

2. US la **patata frita de bolsa**
3. el **chip** *(plural* los **chips***): a computer chip* un chip de ordenador.

chocolate [ˈtʃɒkələt] *noun* ■ el **chocolate**

▶ **a chocolate bar** una tableta de chocolate
▶ **a chocolate cake** una tarta de chocolate.

choice [tʃɔɪs] *noun* ■ la **elección** *(plural* las **elecciones***): it was a good choice* fue una buena elección.

choir [ˈkwaɪər] *noun* ■ el **coro.**

choke [tʃəʊk] *verb*

1. **ahogarse: he's choking** se está ahogando
2. **ahogar: you're choking me!** ¡me estás ahogando!

choose [tʃuːz] *(past tense* chose, *past participle* chosen) *verb* ■ **elegir: she will choose between the two** va a elegir entre los dos.

chop [tʃɒp] *(noun & verb)*

■ *noun*

la **chuleta: a pork chop** una chuleta de cerdo

■ *verb (past tense & past participle* chopped, *present participle* chopping)

1. **cortar: he's chopping wood** está cortando madera
2. **picar: you have to chop the vegetables** tienes que picar las verduras

chop down *phrasal verb* ■ **talar: they chopped the tree down** talaron el árbol.

chopsticks [ˈtʃɒpstɪks] *plural noun* ■ los **palillos: can you eat with chopsticks?** ¿sabes comer con palillos?

chose [tʃəʊz] *past tense* ➤ choose.

chosen [ˈtʃəʊzn] *past participle* ➤ choose.

christening [ˈkrɪsnɪŋ] *noun* ■ el **bautismo.**

Christian [ˈkrɪstʃən] *adjective & noun* ■ **cristiano: she's a Christian** es cristiana.

Christmas [ˈkrɪsməs] *noun* ■ la **Navidad: what are you doing at Christmas?** ¿qué vas a hacer en Navidad?

> Merry Christmas! ¡Feliz Navidad!
> a Christmas card una tarjeta de Navidad
> Christmas Day el día de Navidad
> Christmas Eve la Nochebuena
> a Christmas tree un árbol de Navidad
> Christmas pudding *pudin de frutas confitadas, que se toma en Navidad.*

chunk [tʃʌŋk] *noun* ■ el **pedazo**: a chunk of cheese un pedazo de queso.

church [tʃɜːtʃ] *noun* ■ la **iglesia**: we go to church on Sundays los domingos vamos a misa.

cigar [sɪˈgɑːʳ] *noun* ■ el **cigarro**.

cigarette [ˌsɪgəˈret] *noun* ■ el **cigarrillo**: she's smoking a cigarette está fumando un cigarrillo.

cinnamon [ˈsɪnəmən] *noun* ■ la **canela**.

circle [ˈsɜːkl] *noun* ■ el **círculo**.

circulate [ˈsɜːkjʊleɪt] *verb* ■ **circular**: blood circulates around the body la sangre circula por el cuerpo.

circumstances [ˈsɜːkəmstənsɪz] *plural noun* ■ las **circunstancias**: under the circumstances dadas las circunstancias.

circus [ˈsɜːkəs] *noun* ■ el **circo**.

citizen [ˈsɪtɪzɪn] *noun* ■ el **ciudadano, la ciudadana**: he's a British citizen es ciudadano británico.

city [ˈsɪtɪ] *(plural cities) noun* ■ la **ciudad**
the city centre el centro de la ciudad
city hall el ayuntamiento

civil war [ˈsɪvlwɔːʳ] *noun* ■ la **guerra civil**
> the American Civil War la Guerra de Secesión

claim [kleɪm] *(verb & noun)*
■ *verb*
1. **afirmar**: he claims to be famous afirma que es famoso
2. **exigir**: he claimed compensation exigió una indemnización
3. **cobrar**: she claims unemployment benefits cobra subsidio por desempleo
■ *noun*
la **demanda**: a wage claim una demanda de aumento salarial

clap [klæp] *(past tense & past participle* clapped, *present participle* clapping*) verb* ■ **aplaudir**: everyone clapped todos aplaudieron.

clapping [ˈklæpɪŋ] *uncountable noun* ■ los **aplausos**: the clapping was loud los aplausos eran fuertes.

clarinet [ˌklærəˈnet] *noun* ■ el **clarinete**.

clash [klæʃ] *verb*
1. **enfrentarse**: the boss often clashed with his employees el jefe a menudo se enfrentaba con sus empleados
2. **desentonar**: those pink shoes clash with the yellow trousers esos zapatos rosas desentonan con los pantalones amarillos.

class [klɑːs] *noun* ■ la **clase**: we travelled first class viajamos en primera clase; I have a Spanish class at 11 o'clock tengo una clase de español a las 11.

classic [ˈklæsɪk] *(adjective & noun)*
■ *adjective*
clásico: it's a classic design es un diseño clásico
■ *noun*
el **clásico**: this film is a classic esta película es un clásico.

classical [ˈklæsɪkl] *adjective* ■ **clásico:** classical music la música clásica.

classroom [ˈklɑːsrʊm] *noun* ■ la **clase.**

claw [klɔː] *noun*

1. la **garra:** lions have sharp claws los leones tienen garras afiladas
2. la **uña:** the cat's claws las uñas del gato
3. la **pinza:** the crab's claws las pinzas del cangrejo.

clean [kliːn] *(adjective & verb)*

■ *adjective*

limpio: my hands are clean tengo las manos limpias

■ *verb*

1. **limpiar:** clean the table before you set it limpia la mesa antes de poner los cubiertos
2. **lavar:** he's cleaning the car está lavando el coche

clean up *phrasal verb* ■ **limpiar:** don't forget to clean up before you go no te olvides de limpiar antes de irte.

cleaner [ˈkliːnəʳ] *noun* ■ el **hombre de la limpieza,** la **mujer de la limpieza:** the cleaner comes twice a week la mujer de la limpieza viene dos veces a la semana

➤ she's a cleaner trabaja haciendo limpieza.

cleaning [ˈkliːnɪŋ] *uncountable noun* ■ la **limpieza:** she's doing the cleaning está haciendo la limpieza.

clear [klɪəʳ] *(adjective & verb)*

■ *adjective*

1. **claro:** the instructions are clear las instrucciones son claras; it's clear he has made a mistake está claro que cometió un error
2. **transparente:** it's clear glass es cristal transparente
3. **despejado:** the road is clear la calle está despejada

■ *verb*

1. **despejar:** they're clearing the road están despejando la calle
2. **quitar:** can you clear the table? ¿puedes quitar la mesa?
3. **disiparse:** the fog is beginning to clear la niebla está empezando a disiparse

clear out *phrasal verb* ■ **ordenar:** I'm going to clear out the cupboards voy a ordenar los armarios

clear up *phrasal verb*

1. **resolver:** he cleared up the problem resolvió el problema
2. **ordenar:** he cleared up the house after the party ordenó la casa después de la fiesta
3. **despejar:** it's clearing up outside está despejando.

clearly [ˈklɪəlɪ] *adverb* ■ **claramente:** you've explained it clearly lo has explicado claramente

➤ he's clearly wrong está claro que está equivocado.

clerk [klɜːrk] *noun*

1. *UK* el/la **oficinista:** he's an office clerk es oficinista
2. *US* el **empleado,** la **empleada:** he's a clerk in the toy department es un empleado de la sección de juguetes
➤ a hotel clerk *US* un/una recepcionista.

clever [ˈklevəʳ] *adjective*

1. **inteligente:** Stephen's a clever boy Stephen es un chico inteligente
2. **hábil:** he's clever with his hands es hábil con las manos.

click [klɪk] *verb* ■ **hacer clic:** click on the icon haz clic en el icono.

client [ˈklaɪənt] *noun* ■ el **cliente,** la **clienta.**

cliff [klɪf] *noun* ■ el **acantilado.**

climate [ˈklaɪmɪt] *noun* ■ el **clima.**

climb [klaɪm] *verb*

1. **subir:** she climbed the stairs subió las escaleras
2. **escalar:** they climbed Everest escalaron el Everest
3. **trepar a:** the boy climbed the tree el chico trepó al árbol

climb down *phrasal verb* ■ **bajarse de:** he climbed down the ladder se bajó de la escalera

climb over *phrasal verb* ■ **trepar por:** he climbed over the fence trepó por la valla.

climbing ['klaɪmɪŋ] *uncountable noun* ■ **el montañismo:** climbing is an adventure sport el montañismo es un deporte de aventura

➤ **to go climbing** hacer montañismo: they went climbing in the Alps fueron a hacer montañismo a los Alpes.

cling [klɪŋ] *(past tense & past participle* clung*)* *verb* ■ **agarrarse a:** she was clinging to the rope se agarraba a la soga.

clip [klɪp] *noun*

1. **el clip:** I need a clip for these papers necesito un clip para estos papeles
2. **la horquilla:** she's looking for a clip for her hair está buscando una horquilla para el pelo.

cloakroom ['kləʊkrʊm] *noun* ■ **el guardarropa.**

clock [klɒk] *noun* ■ **el reloj:** the clock on my desk is fast el reloj de mi escritorio va adelantado

➤ **an alarm clock** un despertador
➤ **around the clock** las veinticuatro horas: this supermarket is open around the clock este supermercado está abierto las veinticuatro horas.

clockwise ['klɒkwaɪz] *adverb* ■ **en el sentido de las agujas del reloj.**

close *(verb, adjective & adverb)*

■ *verb* [kləʊz]

1. **cerrar:** he closed his eyes cerró los ojos; the shops close at 6 o'clock las tiendas cierran a las 6
2. **cerrarse:** the door closed behind him la puerta se cerró detrás de él

■ *adjective* [kləʊs]

1. **cerca:** the school's close to the station el colegio queda cerca de la estación
2. **unido:** she's very close to her brother está muy unida a su hermano
3. **reñido:** it's a close contest es un concurso muy reñido

■ *adverb* [kləʊs]

➤ **de cerca:** I looked at it close up lo miré de cerca
➤ **close by** cerca: they live close by viven cerca
➤ **close to** junto a: I live close to the park vivo junto al parque
➤ **come closer!** ¡acércate!

closed [kləʊzd] *adjective* ■ **cerrado.**

closely ['kləʊslɪ] *adverb* ■ **detenidamente:** he looked at it closely lo miró detenidamente.

closet *US* ['klɒzɪt] *noun* ■ **el armario.**

cloth [klɒθ] *noun*

1. **el trapo:** she wiped the table with a cloth limpió la mesa con un trapo
2. **la tela:** I like this cloth me gusta esta tela.

clothes [kləʊðz] *plural noun* ■ **la ropa.**

clothes-peg *UK* [kləʊðzpeg], **clothes-pin** *US* ['kləʊðzpɪn] *noun* ■ **la pinza.**

cloud [klaʊd] *noun* ■ **la nube.**

cloudy ['klaʊdɪ] *adjective* ■ **nublado:** it's cloudy today hoy está nublado.

clown [klaʊn] *noun* ■ **el payaso.**

club [klʌb] *noun*

1. **el club:** she's a member of the chess club es socia del club de ajedrez
2. **la discoteca:** we went to a club last night anoche fuimos a la discoteca
3. **el palo:** he hit him with a club le pegó con un palo
➤ **a golf club** un palo de golf.

clue [kluː] *noun* ■ **la pista:** the police are looking for clues la policía está buscando pistas
➤ **give me a clue!** dame una pista
➤ **I don't have a clue** no tengo ni la menor idea.

clumsy ['klʌmzɪ] *adjective* ■ **torpe.**

clung [klʌŋ] *past tense & past participle* ➤ cling.

cm *(abbreviation of* centimetre*) noun* ■ el **cm.**

coach [kəʊtʃ] *noun*
1. el **entrenador,** la **entrenadora:** the team needs a new coach el equipo necesita un nuevo entrenador
2. el **vagón:** the train has ten coaches el tren tiene diez vagones
3. el **carruaje**
4. UK el **autocar:** we went by coach fuimos en autocar.

coal [kəʊl] *noun* ■ el **carbón.**

coast [kəʊst] *noun* ■ la **costa:** Plymouth is on the coast Plymouth está en la costa.

coastguard [ˈkəʊstgɑːd] *noun* ■ el **guardacostas** *(plural* los **guardacostas***)*.

coat [kəʊt] *noun*
1. el **abrigo:** put your coat on ponte el abrigo
2. la **capa:** a coat of paint una capa de pintura
➤ a coat hanger una percha: your jacket's on the coat hanger tu chaqueta está en la percha.

cobweb [ˈkɒbweb] *noun* ■ la **telaraña.**

Coca-Cola® [ˌkəʊkəˈkəʊlə], **Coke®** [kəʊk] *noun* ■ la **Coca-Cola®:** a can of Coke® una lata de Coca-Cola®.

cockroach [ˈkɒkrəʊtʃ] *noun* ■ la **cucaracha.**

cocoa [ˈkəʊkəʊ] *noun* ■ el **cacao**
➤ a cup of cocoa una taza de cacao.

coconut [ˈkəʊkənʌt] *noun* ■ el **coco.**

cod [kɒd] *(plural* cod*) noun* ■ el **bacalao.**

code [kəʊd] *noun* ■ el **código:** a secret code un código secreto; the message is in code el mensaje está en código.

coffee [ˈkɒfɪ] *noun* ■ el **café:** a cup of coffee una taza de café
➤ a coffee pot una cafetera
➤ a coffee shop una cafetería.

coffin [ˈkɒfɪn] *noun* ■ el **ataúd.**

coin [kɔɪn] *noun* ■ la **moneda:** a 1-euro coin una moneda de 1 euro; a 50-cent coin una moneda de 50 céntimos.

cold [kəʊld] *(adjective & noun)*
■ *adjective*
frío
➤ to be cold tener frío: I'm cold tengo frío; my hands are cold tengo las manos frías
➤ it's cold outside fuera hace frío
■ *noun*
1. el **resfriado:** he caught a cold pescó un resfriado
2. el **frío:** I don't like the cold no me gusta el frío.

collapse [kəˈlæps] *verb* ■ **venirse abajo, derrumbarse:** the whole building collapsed todo el edificio se vino abajo.

collar [ˈkɒləʳ] *noun*
1. el **cuello:** his shirt collar is dirty tiene el cuello de la camisa sucio
2. el **collar:** the dog is wearing a collar el perro tiene puesto un collar.

collect [kəˈlekt] *verb*
1. **recoger:** she collected the children from school recogió a los niños del colegio; they're collecting seashells están recogiendo conchas de mar
2. **coleccionar:** he collects stamps colecciona sellos
➤ a collect call US una llamada a cobro revertido: I'd like to make a collect call quisiera hacer una llamada a cobro revertido.

collection [kəˈlekʃn] *noun*
1. la **colección** *(plural* las **colecciones***):* his stamp collection su colección de sellos
2. la **colecta:** they made a collection for the refugees hicieron una colecta para los refugiados.

college [ˈkɒlɪdʒ] *noun*
1. UK el **instituto de enseñanza técnica**
2. US la **universidad:** she's in college está en la universidad ➤ school.

collide [kəˈlaɪd] *verb* ■ **chocar:** the cab collided with a truck el taxi chocó con un camión.

Colombia [kə'lɒmbɪə] *noun* ■ **Colombia.**

Colombian [kə'lɒmbɪən] *(adjective & noun)*
■ *adjective*

Remember not to use a capital letter for the adjective in Spanish:

colombiano: I like Colombian coffee me gusta el café colombiano
■ *noun*

In Spanish, a capital letter is not used for the inhabitants of a country or region:

el **colombiano**, la **colombiana: many Colombians live in the capital** muchos colombianos viven en la capital.

colon ['kəʊlən] *noun* ■ **los dos puntos: you use a colon to introduce a list** para introducir una lista, hay que usar dos puntos.

colonel ['kɜːnl] *noun* ■ **el/la coronel.**

colour *UK,* **color** *US* ['kʌlər] *noun* ■ **el color: what colour is it?** ¿de qué color es?

a **colour photo** una foto en color

a **colour television** una televisión en color.

colourful *UK,* **colorful** *US* ['kʌləfʊl] *adjective* ■ **de colores muy vivos: a very colourful sweater** un suéter de colores muy vivos.

column ['kɒləm] *noun* ■ **la columna: the columns of a Greek temple** las columnas de un templo griego; **the sports column in the newspaper** la columna de deportes del periódico.

comb [kəʊm] *(noun & verb)*
■ *noun*
el peine
■ *verb*
peinarse: he combed his hair se peinó.

come [kʌm] *(past tense* came, *past participle* come) *verb*

1. **venir: he's coming to the game with us** viene al partido con nosotros; **the bus is coming** viene el autobús; **we came by taxi** vinimos en taxi; **Donald came to see me** Donald vino a verme

2.

To say in Spanish what place a person comes from, use **ser de** followed by the name of the place:

ser de: where do you come from? ¿de dónde eres?; **I come from Atlanta** soy de Atlanta
come on! ¡venga!
to come true hacerse realidad: **her dream came true** su sueño se hizo realidad
I'm coming ya voy

come back *phrasal verb* ■ **volver: I'll come back later** volveré más tarde

come down *phrasal verb* ■ **bajar: prices have come down** han bajado los precios
come down from there! ¡bájate de ahí!

come in *phrasal verb* ■ **entrar: come in!** ¡entra!; **she came in through the kitchen window** entró por la ventana de la cocina

come off *phrasal verb* ■ **caerse: one of my buttons has come off** se me ha caído un botón

come over *phrasal verb* ■ **venir: come over this evening** ven esta noche

come out *phrasal verb* ■ **salir: come out with your hands up!** ¡sal con las manos en alto!; **their new album is coming out in May** su nuevo álbum va a salir en mayo; **this stain won't come out** esta mancha no se va a quitar

come round *UK,* **come around** *US phrasal verb*

1. **venir: Janet is coming round tonight** Janet vendrá a casa esta noche

2. **volver en sí: he's starting to come round** está volviendo en sí

come up *phrasal verb*

1. **subirse: come up here!** ¡sube aquí!

2. **salir: the sun has come up** ha salido el sol

3. **surgir: the problem came up in class** el problema surgió en la clase

come up to *phrasal verb*

1. **llegar a: the mud came up to our knees** el barro nos llegaba a las rodillas

2. acercarse: he came up to me and shook my hand se me acercó y me dio la mano.

comedian [kə'miːdjən] *noun* ■ el/la humorista.

comedy ['kɒmədɪ] *(plural* comedies*) noun* ■ la comedia.

comfort ['kʌmfət] *(noun & verb)*
■ *noun*
1. la comodidad: he likes comfort le gusta la comodidad
2. el consuelo: you've been a great comfort to me has sido un gran consuelo para mí
■ *verb*
consolar: the policeman comforted the crying girl el policía consoló a la niña que lloraba.

comfortable ['kʌmftəbl] *adjective* ■ cómodo: it's a very comfortable bed es una cama muy cómoda; are you comfortable? ¿estás cómodo?; make yourself comfortable ponte cómodo.

comic ['kɒmɪk] *noun* ■ el cómic
> comic strip la tira cómica.

comma ['kɒmə] *noun* ■ la coma.

command [kə'mɑːnd] *(noun & verb)*
■ *noun*
la orden *(plural* las órdenes*)*: the captain gave a command el capitán dio una orden
■ *verb*
ordenar: the king commanded him to leave el rey le ordenó marcharse.

comment ['kɒment] *(noun & verb)*
■ noun
el comentario: he made some comments on my work hizo algunos comentarios sobre mi trabajo
■ *verb*
hacer comentarios: she commented on the news hizo comentarios sobre la noticia.

commercial [kə'mɜːʃl] *adjective & noun)*
■ *adjective*
comercial: the film is a commercial success la película es un éxito comercial
■ *noun*
el anuncio, el aviso: he doesn't like TV commercials no le gustan los anuncios de la tele.

commit [kə'mɪt] *verb* ■ cometer: he has committed many crimes ha cometido muchos crímenes
> to commit suicide suicidarse.

committee [kə'mɪtɪ] *noun* ■ el comité.

common ['kɒmən] *adjective* ■ común *(plural* comunes*)*: it's a common expression es una expresión común; the English and the Americans share a common language los ingleses y los americanos tienen un idioma común
> in common en común: we have a lot in common tenemos mucho en común
> common sense el sentido común: she has a lot of common sense tiene mucho sentido común
> the Commons *UK* la Cámara de los Comunes.

communicate [kə'mjuːnɪkeɪt] *verb* ■ comunicarse: we communicate by e-mail nos comunicamos por correo electrónico.

communication [kə,mjuːnɪ'keɪʃn] *noun* ■ la comunicación *(plural* las comunicaciones*)*.

community [kə'mjuːnətɪ] *(plural* communities*) noun* ■ la comunidad: there is a large Spanish community in London hay una gran comunidad española en London.

compact disc [,kɒmpækt'dɪsk] *noun* ■ el disco compacto.

companion [kəm'pænjən] *noun* ■ el acompañante, la acompañante.

company ['kʌmpənɪ] *(plural* companies*) noun* ■ la compañía: she works for an Irish company trabaja para una empresa irlandesa
> an insurance company una compañía de seguros
> to keep somebody company hacerle compañía a alguien: her dog keeps her company su perro le hace compañía.

compare [kəm'peəʳ] *verb* ■ comparar
> you can't compare them, they're too different no puedes compararlos, son demasiado diferentes

> **compared with** OR **compared to** comparado con: **she's very smart compared to her brother** comparada con su hermano, ella es muy inteligente.

comparison [kəm'pærɪsn] *noun* ■ la **comparación** *(plural* las **comparaciones***)*: **Spain is small in comparison with Australia** España es pequeña en comparación con Australia.

compass ['kʌmpəs] *noun*
1. la **brújula**
2. el **compás.**

compete [kəm'piːt] *verb* ■ **competir**: **there are ten runners competing in the race** hay diez corredores compitiendo en la carrera

> **to compete against somebody** competir contra alguien: **she will compete against her brother** va a competir contra su hermano

> **to compete for something** competir por algo: **they're competing for the gold medal** están compitiendo por la medalla de oro.

competition [ˌkɒmpɪ'tɪʃn] *noun*
1. el **concurso**: **she entered a beauty competition** se presentó a un concurso de belleza
2. la **competencia**: **the competition is strong in this field** la competencia es fuerte en este campo.

competitor [kəm'petɪtəʳ] *noun* ■ el **competidor**, la **competidora.**

complain [kəm'pleɪn] *verb*
1. **quejarse**: **he complained about the cold** se quejó del frío; **don't complain!** ¡no te quejes!
2. **reclamar**: **if you don't like it you can complain** si no te gusta puedes reclamar; **I'll complain to the manager** voy a reclamarle al director.

complaint [kəm'pleɪnt] *noun* ■ la **queja**: **they received a lot of complaints** recibieron muchas quejas

> **to make a complaint** presentar una queja: **she made a complaint** ella presentó una queja.

complete [kəm'pliːt] *(adjective & verb)*
■ *adjective*
1. **completo**: **the complete works of Shakespeare** las obras completas de Shakespeare
2. **total**: **there's been a complete change** ha habido un cambio total
3. **terminado**: **work on the building is complete** el trabajo en el edificio está terminado
4. **verdadero**: **I feel like a complete idiot** me siento como un verdadero idiota
■ *verb*
1. **completar**: **can you complete this sentence?** ¿puedes completar esta oración?
2. **terminar**: **I've completed my work** he terminado mi trabajo.

completely [kəm'pliːtlɪ] *adverb* ■ **completamente.**

complexion [kəm'plekʃn] *noun*
1. el **cutis**: **she has a very good complexion** tiene muy buen cutis
2. la **tez**: **he has a very light complexion** tiene la tez muy clara.

complicated ['kɒmplɪkeɪtɪd] *adjective* ■ **complicado.**

compliment ['kɒmplɪmənt] *noun* ■ el **cumplido**: **she paid me a compliment** me hizo un cumplido.

composer [kəm'pəuzəʳ] *noun* ■ el **compositor**, la **compositora**: **Elgar is a famous British composer** Elgar es un famoso compositor británico.

compulsory [kəm'pʌlsərɪ] *adjective* ■ **obligatorio.**

computer [kəm'pjuːtəʳ] *noun* ■ el **ordenador**

> **a laptop computer** un ordenador portátil
> **computer games** videojuegos
> **computer science** la informática.

computing [kəm'pjuːtɪŋ] *uncountable noun* ■ la **informática**: **he works in computing** trabaja en informática.

concentrate ['kɒnsəntreɪt] *verb* ■ **concentrarse**: **I can't concentrate** no me puedo concentrar.

concentration [ˌkɒnsən'treɪʃn] noun ■ la **concentración**: it needs a lot of concentration necesita mucha concentración.

concern [kən'sɜːn] verb ■ **concernir**: this concerns us all esto nos concierne a todos

➤ as far as I'm concerned en lo que a mí respecta

➤ to be concerned estar preocupado: I'm concerned about him estoy preocupado por él.

concert ['kɒnsət] noun ■ el **concierto**: they're going to a concert van a ir a un concierto.

concrete ['kɒŋkriːt] noun ■ el **hormigón**.

condition [kən'dɪʃn] noun

1. la **condición** (plural las **condiciones**): he will come with us, but on one condition vendrá con nosotros, pero con una condición

2. el **estado**: it's in good condition está en buen estado.

conditioner [kən'dɪʃnəʳ] noun ■ el **acondicionador para el cabello**.

condom ['kɒndəm] noun ■ el **condón** (plural los **condones**).

conductor [kən'dʌktəʳ] noun

1. el **director**, la **directora**: an orchestra conductor un director de orquesta

2. el **cobrador**, la **cobradora**: a conductor of a train un cobrador de un tren

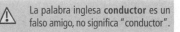 ⚠ La palabra inglesa **conductor** es un falso amigo, no significa "conductor".

cone [kəʊn] noun ■ el **cono**
➤ an ice-cream cone un cucurucho.

confess [kən'fes] verb ■ **confesar**: he confessed to the murder confesó haber cometido el asesinato.

confidence ['kɒnfɪdəns] noun ■ la **confianza**: he has no confidence no tiene confianza; I have confidence in you tengo confianza en ti.

confident ['kɒnfɪdənt] adjective
➤ I'm confident you'll win confío en que vas a ganar
➤ she's very confident está muy segura de sí misma.

confirm [kən'fɜːm] verb ■ **confirmar**: you must confirm your flight debe confirmar su vuelo.

confuse [kən'fjuːz] verb ■ **confundir**: don't confuse me! ¡no me confundas!; he confused me with my brother me confundió con mi hermano.

confused [kən'fjuːzd] adjective ■ **confundido**: I'm confused, can you say all that again? estoy confundido, ¿puedes decir todo eso de nuevo?

confusing [kən'fjuːzɪŋ] adjective ■ **confuso**: it's very confusing es muy confuso.

confusion [kən'fjuːʒn] noun ■ la **confusión**: there's some confusion over the dates hay un poco de confusión con las fechas.

congratulate [kən'grætʃʊleɪt] verb ■ **felicitar**: they congratulated me on winning the prize me felicitaron por ganar el premio.

congratulations [kənˌgrætʃʊ'leɪʃənz] plural noun ■ la **enhorabuena**, las **felicitaciones**: congratulations on your success! ¡enhorabuena por tu éxito!

congress ['kɒŋgres] noun ■ el **congreso**
➤ Congress US el Congreso.

connect [kə'nekt] verb

1. **conectar**: the bridge connects the two parts of the town el puente conecta las dos partes del pueblo

2. **conectarse**: I can't connect to the Internet no puedo conectarme a Internet.

connection [kə'nekʃn] noun

1. la **conexión** (plural las **conexiones**): I don't want to miss my connection no quiero perder mi conexión; an Internet connection una conexión a Internet

2. la relación (plural las **relaciones**): there's no connection between the two events no hay ninguna relación entre ambos acontecimientos.

conscience ['kɒnʃəns] noun ■ la **conciencia**: he has a guilty conscience le remuerde la conciencia.

conscious ['kɒnʃəs] adjective ■ **consciente**: I wasn't conscious of what I was doing no era consciente de lo que estaba haciendo.

consciousness ['kɒnʃəsnɪs] noun ■ el **conocimiento**: he lost consciousness perdió el conocimiento.

conservative [kən'sɜːvətɪv] adjective & noun ■ **conservador**

> the Conservative Party UK el Partido Conservador.

consider [kən'sɪdər] verb

1. considerar: I consider him my friend lo considero mi amigo

2. tener en cuenta: you must consider the risks debes tener en cuenta los riesgos

3. pensar: she's considering leaving her job está pensando en dejar su trabajo.

considerate [kən'sɪdərət] adjective ■ **considerado.**

consideration [kən,sɪdə'reɪʃn] noun ■ la **consideración** (plural las **consideraciones**): he has no consideration for others no tiene ninguna consideración por los demás

> to take something into consideration tener algo en cuenta: I'll take that into consideration lo tendré en cuenta.

consist [kən'sɪst] verb

1. consistir: our job consists in helping others nuestro trabajo consiste en ayudar a los demás

2. estar formado por: our team consists of ten players el equipo está formado por diez jugadores

> to consist of consistir en: her luggage consisted of a bag and a rucksack su equipaje consistía en una bolsa y una mochila.

consonant ['kɒnsənənt] noun ■ la **consonante.**

constant ['kɒnstənt] adjective ■ **constante**: constant criticism críticas constantes.

constantly ['kɒnstəntlɪ] adverb ■ **constantemente.**

constipated ['kɒnstɪpeɪtɪd] adjective ■ **estreñido**: he's constipated está estreñido.

constitution [,kɒnstɪ'tjuːʃn] noun ■ la **constitución** (plural las **constituciones**): the Spanish Constitution la Constitución española.

consumer [kən'sjuːmər] noun ■ el **consumidor,** la **consumidora.**

contact ['kɒntækt] (noun & verb)

■ noun

el **contacto**: we've lost contact with her perdimos contacto con ella

> contact lenses lentes de contacto

■ verb

ponerse en contacto con: I couldn't contact him no pude ponerme en contacto con él.

contain [kən'tɪn] verb ■ **contener**: milk contains calcium la leche contiene calcio.

container [kən'tɪnə'] noun ■ el **recipiente**: I need a bigger container necesito un recipiente más grande.

contents ['kɒntɒnts] plural noun

1. el **contenido**: he emptied the contents of the box onto the floor vació el contenido de la caja en el suelo

2. el **índice**: the contents are at the front of the book el índice está en la parte de adelante del libro.

contest ['kɒntest] noun ■ el **concurso**: a beauty contest un concurso de belleza.

contestant [kɒn'tesənt] noun ■ el/la **concursante.**

continent ['kɒntɪnənt] noun ■ el **continente**: there are five continents hay cinco continentes

> the Continent UK el continente europeo.

continue [kən'tɪnjuː] *verb* ■ **continuar:** they continued playing continuaron jugando.

contraceptive [ˌkɒntrə'septɪv] *noun* ■ el **anticonceptivo.**

contract ['kɒntrækt] *noun* ■ el **contrato:** he signed the contract firmó el contrato.

contrary ['kɒntrərɪ] *noun* on the contrary al contrario.

contrast ['kɒntrɑːst] *noun* ■ el **contraste.**

contribute [kən'trɪbjuːt] *verb*
1. **contribuir:** he contributed to the success of the project contribuyó al éxito del proyecto
2. **contribuir con:** he contributed a lot of money contribuyó con mucho dinero.

control [kən'trəʊl] *(noun & verb)*
■ *noun*
el **control:** she lost control of her car OR her car went out of control perdió el control del coche
> we're in control of the situation controlamos la situación
> everything's under control todo está bajo control
■ *verb (past tense & past participle* controlled, *present participle* controlling*)*
controlar: who controls the company? ¿quién controla la compañía?; the police can't control the crowd la policía es incapaz de controlar a la muchedumbre
to control oneself controlarse: control yourself! ¡contrólate!

convenient [kən'viːnjənt] *adjective* ■ **adecuado:** it's a convenient place to meet es un lugar adecuado para encontrarse
> the hotel is convenient for the shops el hotel está bien ubicado respecto a las tiendas
> is Monday convenient for you? ¿te viene bien el lunes?

conversation [ˌkɒnvə'seɪʃn] *noun* ■ la **conversación** *(plural* las **conversaciones***):* I had a long conversation with her tuve una larga conversación con ella.

convince [kən'vɪns] *verb* ■ **convencer:** he convinced me to wait me convenció para que esperara.

cook [kʊk] *(noun & verb)*
■ *noun*
el **cocinero,** la **cocinera:** he's a good cook es buen cocinero
■ *verb*
1. **cocinar:** ¿can you cook? ¿sabes cocinar?
2. **preparar:** I'm cooking breakfast estoy preparando el desayuno
3. **cocer:** cook the potatoes for 15 minutes cueza las patatas durante 15 minutos
> the vegetables are cooked las verduras están cocidas.

cookbook US ['kʊkˌbʊk] *noun* ■ el **libro de cocina.**

cooker UK ['kʊkər] *noun* ■ la **cocina:** an electric cooker una cocina eléctrica.

cookery ['kʊkərɪ] *noun* ■ la **cocina:** a cookery book UK un libro de cocina.

cookie US ['kʊkɪ] *noun* ■ la **galleta.**

cooking ['kʊkɪŋ] *uncountable noun* ■ la **cocina:** I like Spanish cooking me gusta la cocina española
> I do the cooking yo cocino.

cool [kuːl] *(adjective & verb)*
■ *adjective*
1. **fresco:** the water's cool el agua está fresca; it's cool tonight hace fresco esta noche
2. *informal* **guay:** my Spanish teacher is really cool mi profesora de español es muy guay
> what a cool computer! ¡qué ordenador más genial!
> he stayed cool no perdió la calma
■ *verb*
enfriar: leave it to cool déjelo enfriar

cool down *phrasal verb*
1. **enfriarse:** the water has cooled down el agua se ha enfriado
2. **refrescar:** this drink will cool you down esta bebida te refrescará.

cope [kəʊp] *verb* ■ **arreglárselas:** I can cope on my own puedo arreglármelas solo

> I can't cope with so much work no puedo con tanto trabajo
> he has to cope with lots of problems tiene que hacer frente a muchos problemas.

copied ['kɒpɪd] *past tense & past participle*
➤ copy.

copper ['kɒpəʳ] *noun* ■ el **cobre.**

copy ['kɒpɪ] *(noun & verb)*
■ *noun (plural* **copies)**
1. la **copia:** make a copy of the disc haz una copia del disco
2. el **ejemplar:** they've sold a thousand copies of the book han vendido mil ejemplares del libro
■ *verb (past tense & past participle* **copied)**
copiar: he copied the poem from the book copió el poema del libro
> to copy and paste copiar y pegar: he copied and pasted the text copió y pegó el texto.

corn [kɔːn] *uncountable noun*
1. *UK* el **trigo**
2. *US* el **maíz**
> corn on the cob la mazorca de maíz.

corner ['kɔːnəʳ] *noun*
1. el **rincón** *(plural* los **rincones):** Ron is sitting in a corner Ron está sentado en un rincón
2. la **esquina:** there is a shop on the corner hay una tienda en la esquina
3. el **saque de esquina:** Beckham took a corner Beckham lanzó un saque de esquina
4. la **curva:** the car took the corner too quickly el coche tomó la curva muy rápido
> around the corner a la vuelta de la esquina: the bank's just around the corner el banco está justo a la vuelta de la esquina.

corpse [kɔːps] *noun* ■ el **cadáver.**

correct [kə'rekt] *(adjective & verb)*
■ *adjective*
correcto: that's the correct answer esa es la respuesta correcta; you've made the correct decision has tomado la decisión correcta
> you're completely correct tienes toda la razón

■ *verb*
corregir: I corrected the mistake corregí el error.

correction [kə'rekʃn] *noun* ■ la **corrección** *(plural* las **correcciones).**

corridor ['kɒrɪdɔːʳ] *noun* ■ el **pasillo.**

cosmetics [kɒz'metɪks] *plural noun* ■ los **cosméticos.**

cost [kɒst] *(verb & noun)*
■ *verb (past tense & past participle* cost)
costar: how much does it cost? ¿cuánto cuesta?; it costs 20 dollars cuesta 20 dólares
■ *noun*
el **coste:** the cost of living el coste de vida.

Costa Rica [ˌkɒstə'riːkə] *noun* ■ **Costa Rica.**

Costa Rican [ˌkɒstə'riːkən] *(adjective & noun)*
■ *adjective*

Remember not to use a capital letter for the adjective in Spanish:

costarricense: the Costa Rican landscape is beautiful el paisaje costarricense es precioso
■ *noun*

In Spanish, a capital letter is not used for the inhabitants of a country or region:

el/la costarricense: the Costa Ricans are relatively prosperous los costarricenses son relativamente prósperos.

costume [*UK* 'kɒstjuːm, *US* 'kɒstuːm] *noun* ■ el **traje:** national costume traje nacional
> swimming costume *UK* traje de baño.

cosy *UK,* **cozy** *US* ['kəʊzɪ] *adjective* ■ **acogedor:** a cosy bedroom un dormitorio acogedor; it's cosy in here qué bien se está aquí dentro.

cottage ['kɒtɪdʒ] *noun* ■ casa pequeña, *generalmente en el campo.*

cotton ['kɒtn] *uncountable noun* ■ el **algodón**
> cotton candy *US* algodón de azúcar
> cotton wool *UK* algodón hidrófilo.

couch [kaʊtʃ] *(plural* couches [ˈkaʊtʃɪz])
noun ■ el **sofá.**

cough [kɒf] *(noun & verb)*
■ *noun*
la **tos**
> to have a cough tener tos: I have a cough
tengo tos
■ *verb*
toser: she's coughing because of the
smoke tose por el humo.

could [kʊd] *verb (negative* couldn't *OR* could
not*)*
1. **poder:** he couldn't come to the party no
pudo venir a la fiesta; they couldn't stay for
dinner no pudieron quedarse a cenar

> When you make a polite request, an offer or a
suggestion, "could" is translated by the Spanish
verb **poder** in the conditional tense:

could I speak to Scott please? ¿podría
hablar con Scott, por favor?; you could wait
for him podría esperarlo; could you help
me, please? ¿podría ayudarme, por favor?;
don't touch it, it could be dangerous no lo
toque, podría ser peligroso

> When "could" is used with a verb of perception
(see, hear, feel, understand) it is not translated
at all:

I couldn't see anything no vi nada; she
couldn't hear me no me oyó; we could understand what they were saying entendi-
mos lo que estaban diciendo
2. *when "could" means "knew how to"* **saber:** she couldn't swim no sabía nadar;
they couldn't speak English no sabían hablar inglés.

couldn't [ˈkʊdnt] = could not.

could've [ˈkʊdəv] = could have.

council [ˈkaʊnsl] *noun*
1. el **consejo**
2. el **ayuntamiento**
> a council house *UK* una casa de protección
oficial.

count [kaʊnt] *verb* ■ **contar:** he counted
sheep to get to sleep contó ovejas para
quedarse dormido
> to count on somebody contar con alguien:
you can count on me puedes contar conmigo.

counter [ˈkaʊntər] *noun*
1. el **mostrador:** the barman is behind the
counter el camarero está detrás del mostrador
2. la **ficha:** each player has ten counters cada
jugador tiene diez fichas.

counterclockwise *US* [ˌkaʊntəˈklɒk-
waɪz] *adverb* ■ **en sentido contrario a las
agujas del reloj.**

country [ˈkʌntrɪ] *(plural* countries) *noun*
1. el **país:** it's interesting to visit foreign countries es interesante visitar países extranjeros
2. el **campo:** we live in the country vivimos
en el campo.

county [ˈkaʊntɪ] *(plural* counties) *noun* ■
el **condado.**

couple [ˈkʌpl] *noun* ■ la **pareja:** a young
couple una pareja joven
> a couple of un par de: I waited a couple of
hours esperé un par de horas.

courage [ˈkʌrɪdʒ] *noun* ■ el **valor:** he
got up the courage to go in se armó de val-
or para entrar.

courgette *UK* [kɔːrˈʒet] *noun* ■ el **calabacín.**

course [kɔːs] *noun*
1. el **curso:** he's taking a Spanish course está
haciendo un curso de español
2. el **plato:** the main course of the meal el
plato principal de la comida; a five-course
meal una comida de cinco platos
3. el **campo:** a golf course un campo de golf
> of course por supuesto
> of course not por supuesto que no.

court [kɔːt] *noun*
1. el **tribunal:** he appeared in court compare-
ció ante el tribunal
2. la **pista:** a tennis court una pista de tenis.

courthouse US ['kɔ:thaʊs] *noun* ■ el **juzgado**.

courtyard ['kɔ:tjɑ:d] *noun* ■ el **patio**.

cousin ['kʌzn] *noun* ■ el **primo**, la **prima**.

cover ['kʌvə'] *(noun & verb)*
■ *noun*
1. la **tapa**: put the cover on the saucepan ponle la tapa a la olla
2. la **cubierta**: there's a dragon on the cover of the book hay un dragón en la cubierta del libro
3. la **manta**: she put two covers on the bed puso dos mantas en la cama
➤ to take cover ponerse a cubierto: they're coming, let's take cover ya vienen, pongámonos a cubierto
■ *verb*
cubrir: she covered the chair with a sheet cubrió la silla con una sábana
➤ Tom was covered with bruises Tom estaba lleno de moretones.

cow [kaʊ] *noun* ■ la **vaca**.

coward ['kaʊəd] *noun* ■ el/la **cobarde**.

cowboy ['kaʊbɔɪ] *noun* ■ el **vaquero**.

cozy US ['kəʊzɪ] *adjective* ➤ cosy UK.

crab [kræb] *noun* ■ el **cangrejo**.

crack [kræk] *(noun & verb)*
■ *noun*
1. la **raja**: there's a crack in the glass hay una raja en el vaso
2. la **grieta**: there are cracks in the wall hay grietas en la pared
■ *verb*
1. **rajar**: I've cracked the glass he rajado el vaso
2. **romper**: you have to crack the egg first tienes que romper el huevo primero
3. **rajarse**: the mirror cracked el espejo se rajó
➤ to crack a code descifrar un código: they managed to crack the code consiguieron descifrar el código
➤ to crack a joke contar un chiste: Lynn cracked a joke Lynn contó un chiste.

cracked [krækt] *adjective* ■ **rajado**: the glass is cracked but not broken el vaso está rajado pero no está roto.

cracker ['krækə'] *noun* ■ la **galleta salada**: he's eating a cracker él está comiendo una galleta salada.

craftsman [UK 'krɑːftsmən, US 'kræftsmən] *(plural* craftsmen [UK 'krɑːftsmən, US 'kræftsmən] *noun* ■ el **artesano**.

cranberry ['krænbərɪ] *(plural- cranberries)* *adjective* ■ el **arándano**: cranberry sauce salsa de arándanos ➤ Thanksgiving.

crane [kreɪn] *noun* ■ la **grúa**: there's a crane on the building site hay una grúa en la obra.

crash [kræʃ] *(noun & verb)*
■ *noun*
1. el **accidente**: he was injured in a car crash resultó herido en un accidente de coche
2. el **estruendo**: I heard a loud crash escuché un gran estruendo
➤ a crash helmet un casco: the motorcyclist is wearing a crash helmet el motociclista lleva casco
■ *verb*
1. **chocar**: I'm driving carefully, I don't want to crash estoy conduciendo con cuidado, no quiero chocar
2. **estrellarse**: the plane crashed el avión se estrelló
3. **colgarse**: my computer crashed se me ha colgado el ordenador
➤ to crash into something estrellarse contra algo: they crashed into a wall se estrellaron contra una pared.

crawl [krɔːl] *verb & noun)*
■ *verb*
gatear: the baby is crawling el bebé está gateando
■ *noun*
el **crol**: he's doing the crawl está nadando crol.

crayon ['kreɪɒn] *noun* ■ el **lápiz de colores**.

crazy [ˈkreɪzɪ] *adjective* ■ *informal* **loco:** you're completely crazy! ¡estás completamente loco!; that noise is driving me crazy ese ruido me está volviendo loco.

cream [kriːm] *noun*
1. la **nata: strawberries and cream** fresas con nata
2. la **crema: a hand cream** una crema de manos; **a cream of carrot soup** una crema de zanahorias.

crease [kriːs] *(noun & verb)*
■ *noun*
la **arruga: there's a crease in the paper** hay una arruga en el papel
■ *verb*
arrugar: try not to crease my dress trata de no arrugarme el vestido.

create [kriːˈeɪt] *verb* ■ **crear: he created a new company** creó una nueva compañía; **to create a file** crear un fichero.

creature [ˈkriːtʃər] *noun* ■ **ser: creatures from outer space** seres del espacio exterior.

credit [ˈkredɪt] *noun* ■ el **crédito**
> **a credit card** una tarjeta de crédito.

creep [kriːp] *(past tense & past participle* crept) *verb* ■ **entrar sigilosamente: he crept into the room** entró sigilosamente en la habitación.

creeps [kriːps] *plural noun*
> **to give somebody the creeps** darle escalofríos a alguien: the graveyard gives me the creeps el cementerio me da escalofríos.

crept [krept] *past tense & past participle* > creep.

crew [kruː] *noun*
1. la **tripulación** *(plural* las **tripulaciones):** **the ship's crew** la tripulación del barco
2. el **equipo: a film crew** el equipo de rodaje.

cricket [ˈkrɪkɪt] *noun*
1. el **grillo: I can hear the crickets** puedo oír a los grillos
2. **cricket: they're playing cricket** están jugando al cricket.

cried [kraɪd] *past tense & past participle* > cry.

crime [kraɪm] *noun*
1. el **delito: theft is a crime** robar es un delito
2. el **crimen: a crime against humanity** un crimen contra la humanidad
3. la **delincuencia: crime is on the increase** la delincuencia va en aumento.

criminal [ˈkrɪmɪnl] *noun* ■ el/la **delincuente**
> **to have a criminal record** tener antecedentes penales.

crisis [ˈkraɪsɪs] *(plural* crises [ˈkraɪsiːz]) *noun* ■ la **crisis** *(plural* las **crisis).**

crisp [krɪsp] *(noun & adjective)*
■ *noun*
UK la **patata frita: a packet of crisps** una bolsa de patatas fritas
■ *adjective*
crujiente.

critic [ˈkrɪtɪk] *noun* ■ el **crítico,** la **crítica: he's a film critic** es crítico de cine.

criticism [ˈkrɪtɪsɪzm] *noun* ■ la **crítica.**

criticize , criticise *UK* [ˈkrɪtɪsaɪz] *verb* ■ **criticar: she's always criticizing me** siempre me está criticando.

crocodile [ˈkrɒkədaɪl] *noun* ■ el **cocodrilo.**

crook [krʊk] *noun* ■ el/la **sinvergüenza.**

crooked [ˈkrʊkɪd] *adjective* ■ **torcido: the picture's crooked** el cuadro está torcido; **he has a crooked nose** tiene la nariz torcida.

crop [krɒp] *noun*
1. el **cultivo: they grow many different crops in this region** producen una gran variedad de cultivos en esta región
2. la **cosecha: we had a good crop of cherries this year** tuvimos una buena cosecha de cerezas este año.

cross [krɒs] *(adjective, noun & verb)*
■ *adjective*
enfadado: he's very cross with you está muy enfadado contigo

■ *noun*

la **cruz**: there is a cross by the altar hay una cruz junto al altar; the hotel's marked with a cross on the map el hotel está marcado con una cruz en el mapa

■ *verb*

cruzar: he crossed the road cruzó la calle; she crossed her legs cruzó las piernas

> cross your fingers! ¡deséame suerte!

cross off *phrasal verb* ■ **tachar**: he crossed my name off the list tachó mi nombre de la lista

cross out *phrasal verb* ■ **tachar**: she crossed out the word tachó la palabra

cross over *phrasal verb* ■ **cruzar**: I crossed over the road crucé la calle.

crossroads ['krɒsrəʊdz] *(plural cross-roads)* *noun* ■ el **cruce**: turn left at the crossroads doble a la izquierda en el cruce.

crosswalk *US* ['krɒswɔːk] *noun* ■ el **paso de peatones**.

crossword puzzle ['krɒswɜːd'pʌzl] *noun* ■ el **crucigrama**: he's doing a crossword puzzle está haciendo un crucigrama.

crow [krəʊ] *noun* ■ el **cuervo**.

crowd [kraʊd] *noun* ■ la **muchedumbre**: there's a huge crowd hay una enorme muchedumbre.

crowded ['kraʊdɪd] *adjective* ■ **abarrotado de gente**: the train is crowded el tren está abarrotado de gente.

crown [kraʊn] *noun* ■ la **corona**: the Queen is wearing a crown la Reina lleva una corona.

cruel [krʊəl] *adjective* ■ **cruel**.

cruise [kruːz] *noun* ■ el **crucero**: she's going on a Caribbean cruise va a hacer un crucero por el Caribe.

crumb [krʌm] *noun* ■ la **miga**.

crush [krʌʃ] *(verb & noun)*

■ *verb*

aplastar: he crushed a fly aplastó una mosca

■ *noun informal*

> to have a **crush** on somebody estar colado por alguien: he's got a crush on my sister está colado por mi hermana.

cry [kraɪ] *(noun & verb)*

■ *noun*

el **grito**: he let out a cry dejó escapar un grito

■ *verb (past tense & past participle* cried*)*

1. **llorar**: don't cry! ¡no llores!
2. **gritar**: "help!" she cried "¡socorro!", gritó

cry out *phrasal verb* ■ **gritar**: he cried out in pain gritaba de dolor.

Cuba ['kjuːbə] *noun* ■ **Cuba**.

Cuban ['kjuːbən] *(adjective & noun)*

■ *adjective*

Remember not to use a capital letter for the adjective in Spanish:

cubano: I enjoy Cuban music me gusta la música cubana

■ *noun*

In Spanish, a capital letter is not used for the inhabitants of a country or region:

el **cubano**, la **cubana**: there are many Cubans in Miami hay muchos cubanos en Miami.

cube [kjuːb] *noun* ■ el **cubo**: a dice is a cube un dado es un cubo.

cuckoo ['kʊkuː] *noun* ■ el **cuco**.

cucumber ['kjuːkʌmbəʳ] *noun* ■ el **pepino**.

cuddle ['kʌdl] *(noun & verb)*

■ *noun*

el **abrazo**: she gave him a cuddle le dio un abrazo

■ *verb*

hacer mimos: she's cuddling the baby le está haciendo mimos al bebé.

cuddly toy ['kʌdlɪtɔɪ] *noun* ■ el **muñeco de peluche**.

culprit ['kʌlprɪt] *noun* ■ el/la **culpable**: who is the culprit? ¿quién es el culpable?

culture ['kʌltʃəʳ] *noun* ■ la **cultura**.

cunning [ˈkʌnɪŋ] *adjective* ■ **astuto:** he's very cunning es muy astuto.

cup [kʌp] *noun*
1. la **taza:** she's drinking a cup of coffee está tomando una taza de café
2. la **copa:** Brazil won the cup last year Brasil ganó la copa el año pasado.

curb US [kɜːb] *noun* ■ el **bordillo de la acera.**

cure [kjʊəʳ] *(noun & verb)*
■ *noun*
la **cura:** there is no cure for that illness esa enfermedad no tiene cura
■ *verb*
curar: the doctor cured him el doctor lo curó.

curious [ˈkjʊərɪəs] *adjective* ■ **curioso:** that's a curious story esa es una historia curiosa
> **to be curious about something** tener curiosidad por algo: he's very curious about what's in the box tiene mucha curiosidad por lo que hay en la caja.

curly [ˈkɜːlɪ] *adjective* ■ **rizado:** she has long curly hair tiene el pelo largo y rizado.

currant [ˈkʌrənt] *noun* ■ la **pasa de Corinto.**

currency [ˈkʌrənsɪ] *(plural* currencies*)* *noun* ■ la **moneda:** the pound is the currency of the United Kingdom la libra es la moneda del Reino Unido.

current [ˈkʌrənt] *(adjective & noun)*
■ *adjective*
actual: the current fashion la moda actual
> **current affairs** temas de actualidad: he is interested in current affairs está interesado en los temas de actualidad
■ *noun*
la **corriente:** an electric current una corriente eléctrica; he was swimming against the current estaba nadando contra la corriente.

curry [ˈkʌrɪ] *(plural* curries*)* *noun* ■ **curry:** a chicken curry un pollo al curry.

cursor [ˈkɜːsəʳ] *noun* ■ el **cursor:** move the cursor down baja el cursor.

curtain [ˈkɜːtn] *noun* ■ la **cortina:** draw the curtains, it's getting dark corre las cortinas, está oscureciendo.

curve [kɜːv] *noun* ■ la **curva:** there's a curve in the river el río traza una curva.

cushion [ˈkʊʃn] *noun* ■ el **cojín** *(plural* los cojines*)*.

custard [ˈkʌstəd] *noun* ■ las **natillas.**

custom [ˈkʌstəm] *noun* ■ la **costumbre:** it's an old English custom es una vieja costumbre inglesa.

customer [ˈkʌstəməʳ] *noun* ■ el **cliente,** la **clienta.**

customs [ˈkʌstəmz] *plural noun* ■ la **aduana:** we went through customs pasamos por la aduana.

cut [kʌt] *(noun & verb)*
■ *noun*
1. el **corte:** I've got a cut on my arm tengo un corte en el brazo
2. el **corte de pelo:** a cut and blow-dry cortar y secar
3. la **reducción** *(plural* las **reducciones***):* a cut in prices una reducción en los precios
■ *verb (past tense & past participle* cut*)*
cortar: he cut the cake into four slices cortó la tarta en cuatro trozos
> he cut his finger se ha cortado el dedo

cut off *phrasal verb* ■ **cortar:** he cut off another slice cortó otro trozo; his phone has been cut off le cortaron el teléfono
> we were cut off se cortó la comunicación

cut out *phrasal verb* ■ **recortar:** I cut out the article recorté el artículo.

cute [kjuːt] *adjective* ■ **mono:** the baby's really cute el bebé es realmente mono.

cyberspace [ˈsaɪbəspeɪs] *noun* ■ el **ciberespacio.**

cycle [ˈsaɪkl] *(noun & verb)*
■ *noun*
1. el **ciclo:** the cycle of the seasons el ciclo de las estaciones

2. la **bicicleta**
a cycle lane un carril-bici
■ *verb*
ir en bicicleta: they cycle to school van al colegio en bicicleta.

cycling ['saɪklɪŋ] *noun* ■ el **ciclismo:** cycling is a popular sport el ciclismo es un deporte popular
to go cycling ir (de paseo) en bicicleta: we go cycling on Sundays vamos en bicicleta los domingos.

cyclist ['saɪklɪst] *noun* ■ el/la **ciclista.**

cymbals ['sɪmblz] *plural noun* ■ los **platillos:** she plays the cymbals toca los platillos.

dad [dæd], **daddy** ['dædɪ] *noun* ■ el **papá.**

daffodil ['dæfədɪl] *noun* ■ el **narciso.**

daily ['deɪlɪ] *(adjective & adverb)*
■ *adjective*
diario: it's her daily walk es su paseo diario
a daily newspaper un diario
■ *adverb*
todos los días: open daily from 8 till 6 abierto todos los días de 8 a 6.

dairy ['deərɪ] *adjective* ■ **lácteo:** dairy products productos lácteos.

daisy ['deɪzɪ] *(plural daisies) noun* ■ la **margarita.**

dam [dæm] *noun* ■ la **presa:** there's a dam across the river hay una presa en el río.

damage ['dæmɪdʒ] *(uncountable noun & verb)*
■ *uncountable noun*
el **daño:** the rain caused a lot of damage la lluvia causó muchos daños
■ *verb*
1. dañar: the building was seriously damaged by fire el edificio fue seriamente dañado por el incendio
2. estropear: you'll damage the car vas a estropear el coche.

damp [dæmp] *adjective* ■ **húmedo.**

dance [dɑːns] *(noun & verb)*
■ *noun*
el **baile:** the rumba is a Cuban dance la rumba es un baile cubano; he invited her to the dance la invitó al baile
■ *verb*
bailar: can you dance? ¿sabes bailar?

dancer ['dɑːnsər] *noun* ■ el **bailarín** *(plural* los **bailarines),** la **bailarina.**

dancing ['dɑːnsɪŋ] *uncountable noun* ■ el **baile:** he has dancing lessons tiene clases de baile
to go dancing ir a bailar: he goes dancing every Tuesday va a bailar todos los martes.

dandruff ['dændrʌf] *uncountable noun* ■ la **caspa:** she has dandruff tiene caspa.

danger ['deɪndʒər] *noun* ■ el **peligro:** we're in danger estamos en peligro; you're out of danger now estás fuera de peligro ahora
to be in danger of doing something correr el riesgo de hacer algo: he's in danger of losing all his money corre el riesgo de perder todo su dinero.

dangerous ['deɪndʒərəs] *adjective* ■ **peligroso:** skydiving can be dangerous saltar en caída libre puede ser peligroso.

dare [deər] *verb*
1. atreverse: I daren't tell him no me atrevo a decírselo; I didn't dare to do it OR I didn't dare do it no me atreví a hacerlo

2. desafiar: **I dare you to jump** te desafío a saltar.

daring ['deərɪŋ] *adjective* ■ **audaz** *(plural* audaces*)*.

dark [dɑːk] *(adjective & noun)*

■ *adjective*
oscuro: it's dark in here está oscuro aquí dentro; **he has dark hair** tiene pelo oscuro; **dark blue trousers** pantalones azul oscuro

■ *noun*
➢ **the dark** la **oscuridad; she is afraid of the dark** le tiene miedo a la oscuridad
➢ **it's getting dark** está oscureciendo
➢ **it's dark outside** está oscuro afuera
➢ **after dark** de noche: **he never goes out after dark** nunca sale de noche.

darling ['dɑːlɪŋ] *noun* ■ **querido: hello, darling!** ¡hola, querido!

dart [dɑːt] *noun* ■ **el dardo: he's playing darts** está jugando a los dardos.

dash [dæʃ] *verb*
➢ **he dashed into the room** entró corriendo al cuarto.

data ['deɪtə] *uncountable noun* ■ **los datos: the data is stored on computer** los datos están almacenados en el ordenador.

database ['deɪtəbeɪs] *noun* ■ **la base de datos.**

date [deɪt] *noun*
1. la **fecha: what's your date of birth?** ¿cuál es tu fecha de nacimiento?; **what's the date today?** ¿qué fecha es hoy?
2. la **cita: let's make a date for lunch** quedemos para ir a comer
3. el **dátil: I like dates** me gustan los dátiles
➢ **a blind date** una cita a ciegas
➢ **to have a date with somebody** salir con alguien: **she has a date with Ken tonight** va a salir con Ken esta noche.

daughter ['dɔːtər] *noun* ■ la **hija: they have two daughters** tienen dos hijas.

daughter-in-law ['dɔːtərɪnlɔː] *(plural* daughters-in-law) *noun* ■ la **nuera.**

dawn [dɔːn] *noun* ■ el **amanecer: I got up at dawn** me levanté al amanecer.

day [deɪ] *noun* ■ el **día: he took two days off** se tomó dos días libres; **she comes to see him every day** viene a verlo todos los días
➢ **the day before** el día anterior
➢ **the day after** el día después
➢ **the day before yesterday** anteayer
➢ **the day after tomorrow** pasado mañana.

daylight ['deɪlaɪt] *noun*
➢ **it's daylight** es de día.

daytime ['deɪtaɪm] *noun* ■ el **día: it happened in the daytime** sucedió de día.

dead [ded] *(adjective & adverb)*
■ *adjective*
muerto: he's dead está muerto
■ *adverb*
➢ **I'm dead set against it** estoy totalmente en contra de eso
➢ **to stop dead** pararse en seco: **she stopped dead** se paró en seco.

deaf [def] *adjective* ■ **sordo.**

deal [diːl] *(noun & verb)*
■ *noun*
el trato: I'll make a deal with you haré un trato contigo; **it's a deal!** ¡trato hecho!
➢ **a good deal** OR **a great deal** mucho: **I don't have a great deal of time** no tengo mucho tiempo
■ *verb (past tense & past participle* dealt*)*
repartir: he deals the cards él reparte las cartas

deal with *phrasal verb*
1. ocuparse de: **I'll deal with it** me ocuparé de eso
2. tratar: **we'll deal with that subject in the next chapter** trataremos ese tema en el próximo capítulo.

dealt [delt] *past tense & past participle* ➢ **deal.**

dear [dɪər] *(adjective & exclamation)*
■ *adjective*
querido: he's a very dear friend es un amigo muy querido; **Dear Mr Jones** Querido señor Jones

■ *exclamation*
oh dear! I've left my homework at home
¡ay, Dios! me he dejado los deberes en
casa.

death [deθ] *noun* ■ la **muerte:** it's the
tenth anniversary of his death es el décimo
aniversario de su muerte

> I was bored to death me aburrí como una
ostra

> I'm scared to death casi me muero del susto.

debate [dɪ'beɪt] *noun* ■ el **debate.**

debt [det] *noun* ■ la **deuda:** to pay a
debt pagar una deuda

> they are in debt están endeudados.

decade ['dekeɪd] *noun* ■ la **década.**

deceive [dɪ'siːv] *verb* ■ **engañar:** he de-
ceived his family engañó a su familia.

December [dɪ'sembər] *noun*

In Spanish the months of the year do not start
with a capital letter:

diciembre *(masculine)*: in December en diciembre; next December el próximo diciembre; last December el pasado diciembre.

decent ['diːsnt] *adjective*

1. **decente:** put on something more decent
ponte algo más decente

2. **bueno:** they gave us a decent meal nos
dieron una comida bastante buena

3. **honrado:** he's a decent man es un hombre
honrado.

deception [dɪ'sepʃən] *noun* ■ el **engaño**

⚠ La palabra inglesa **deception** es un
falso amigo, no significa "decepción".

decide [dɪ'saɪd] *verb*

1. **decidir:** I decided to help him decidí ayudarle; she decided not to go decidió no ir

2. **decidirse:** I can't decide no me puedo decidir.

decimal ['desɪml] *adjective* ■ **decimal:**
the decimal system el sistema decimal

> a decimal point la coma decimal: don't for-
get the decimal point when you write the
sum no te olvides de la coma decimal cuando
escribas el total.

decision [dɪ'sɪʒn] *noun* ■ la **decisión** *(plural* las **decisiones)**: I've made a decision he
tomado una decisión.

deck [dek] *noun*

1. la **cubierta:** they were on the deck of the
ship estaban en la cubierta del barco

2. la **baraja:** he bought a deck of cards compró una baraja.

deckchair ['dektʃeər] *noun* ■ la
hamaca: he was sitting in a deckchair estaba sentado en una hamaca.

declare [dɪ'kleər] *verb* ■ **declarar:** do
you have anything to declare? ¿tiene algo
que declarar?

decorate ['dekəreɪt] *verb*

1. **decorar:** they decorated the Christmas
tree decoraron el árbol de Navidad

2. *UK* **pintar:** we are decorating the kitchen
estamos pintando la cocina.

decoration [ˌdekə'reɪʃn] *noun* ■ el
adorno: they are putting up the Christmas
decorations están colocando los adornos de
Navidad.

decrease *(noun & verb)*

■ *noun* ['diːkriːs]
la **disminución** *(plural* las **disminuciones)**:
there's been a decrease in sales ha habido
una disminución de las ventas

■ *verb* [dɪ'kriːs]
disminuir: the number of students has decreased el número de estudiantes ha disminuido.

deep [diːp] *adjective*

1. **profundo:** the hole is deep el agujero es
profundo

2. **grave:** he has a deep voice tiene una voz
grave

> how deep is the river? ¿qué profundidad
tiene el río?

deeply ['diːplɪ] *adverb* ■ **profundamente.**

deer [dɪəʳ] *(plural* deer*) noun* ■ el **ciervo.**

defeat [dɪˈfiːt] *(noun & verb)*

■ *noun*

la **derrota: the team suffered a defeat** el equipo sufrió una derrota

■ *verb*

derrotar: our team was defeated by two goals to nil nuestro equipo fue derrotado por dos a cero.

defence *UK,* **defense** *US* [dɪˈfens] *noun* ■ **defensa: he came to my defence** salió en mi defensa.

defend [dɪˈfend] *verb* ■ **defender: she tried to defend herself** trató de defenderse.

defense *US noun* ➤ **defence** *UK.*

definite [ˈdefɪnɪt] *adjective*

1. **seguro: is it definite that he's coming?** ¿es seguro que viene?; **she was quite definite about it** estaba bastante segura de eso

2. **definitivo: we want a definite answer** queremos una respuesta definitiva

3. **concreto: I haven't made any definite plans** no tengo planes concretos

4. **claro: there's a definite improvement** hay una clara mejoría.

definitely [ˈdefɪnɪtlɪ] *adverb* ■ **sin duda: he's definitely the smartest** es sin duda el más inteligente

➤ **I will definitely come** es seguro que voy

➤ **definitely not!** ¡de ninguna manera!

degree [dɪˈgriː] *noun*

1. **el grado: it's 30 degrees in the shade** estamos a 30 grados a la sombra

2. **el título: she wants to get a university degree** quiere tener un título universitario

➤ **she has a degree in English** es licenciada en filología inglesa

➤ **to a certain degree** hasta cierto punto.

delay [dɪˈleɪ] *(noun & verb)*

■ *noun*

el **retraso: there's a two-hour delay** hay un retraso de dos horas

➤ **without delay** inmediatamente, sin demora

■ *verb*

retrasar: he delayed his departure retrasó su partida.

delete [dɪˈliːt] *verb* ■ **borrar: I deleted the file** borré el archivo; **the delete key** la tecla de supresión.

deliberate [dɪˈlɪbərət] *adjective* ■ **intencionado: that was deliberate!** ¡eso fue intencionado!

deliberately [dɪˈlɪbərətlɪ] *adverb* ■ **adrede: he did it deliberately** lo hizo adrede

➤ **the fire was started deliberately** el fuego fue intencionado.

delicate [ˈdelɪkət] *adjective* ■ **delicado.**

delicatessen [ˌdelɪkɪˈtesn] *noun* ■ la **tienda de alimentación de alta calidad.**

delicious [dɪˈlɪʃəs] *adjective* ■ **delicioso: this soup is delicious** esta sopa es deliciosa.

delighted [dɪˈlaɪtɪd] *adjective* ■ **encantado: I'm delighted to see you** estoy encantada de verte.

deliver [dɪˈlɪvəʳ] *verb* ■ **entregar: when can you deliver the order?** ¿cuándo puede entregar el pedido?

➤ **to deliver a speech** pronunciar un discurso.

delivery [dɪˈlɪvərɪ] *(plural* deliveries*) noun*

1. la **entrega: allow sixty days for delivery** el plazo de entrega es de sesenta días

2. el **reparto: free home delivery** reparto gratuito a domicilio

3. el **parto: the midwife assisted the delivery** la comadrona atendió el parto

➤ **they do free deliveries** hacen entregas a domicilio gratis.

demand [dɪˈmɑːnd] *(verb & noun)*

■ *verb*

exigir: I demand an explanation exijo una explicación

■ *noun*

1. la **exigencia: they won't meet their demands** no van a satisfacer sus exigencias

2. la demanda: there's a lot of demand for organic produce hay mucha demanda de productos ecológicos.

democracy [dɪ'mɒkrəsɪ] *(plural* democracies) *noun* ■ la **democracia: Spain is a democracy** España es una democracia.

Democrat ['deməkræt] *noun* ■ el/la **demócrata** ➤ Political parties.

democratic [ˌdeməˈkrætɪk] *adjective* ■ **democrático** ➤ Political parties
➤ the Democratic Party el Partido Demócrata.

demonstrate ['demənstreɪt] *verb*

1. manifestarse: students are demonstrating in the street los estudiantes se están manifestando en la calle

2. hacer una demostración de: he demonstrated how to use the vacuum cleaner hizo una demostración de cómo usar la aspiradora.

demonstration [demən'streɪʃn] *noun*

1. la manifestación *(plural* las manifestaciones)*: she went on an anti-war demonstration participó en una manifestación contra la guerra

2. la demostración *(plural* las demostraciones)*: he gave us a demonstration of the computer's functions nos hizo una demostración de las funciones del ordenador.

denied [dɪ'naɪd] *past tense & past participle* ➤ deny.

dense [dens] *adjective* ■ **denso: a dense forest** un bosque denso; **a dense fog** una niebla densa.

dentist ['dentɪst] *noun* ■ el/la **dentista.**

deny [dɪ'naɪ] *(past tense & past participle* denied) *verb* ■ **negar: don't deny it!** no lo niegues; **he denied taking the money** negó haber cogido el dinero.

deodorant [diː'əʊdərənt] *noun* ■ el **desodorante.**

depart [dɪ'pɑːt] *verb* ■ **salir: the train is now departing** el tren está saliendo ahora.

department [dɪ'pɑːtmənt] *noun*

1. la sección *(plural* las secciones)*: the toy department la sección de juguetes

2. el departamento: the Spanish department at the university el departamento de español de la universidad
➤ a department store unos grandes almacenes.

departure [dɪ'pɑːtʃəʳ] *noun* ■ la **salida: the train's departure was delayed** se retrasó la salida del tren.

depend [dɪ'pend] *verb* ■ **depender: it depends on you** depende de ti; **it all depends** todo depende.

deposit [dɪ'pɒzɪt] *noun*

1. el depósito: you will get your deposit back when you return the keys recuperarás tu depósito cuando devuelvas las llaves

2. la señal: you pay a deposit now and the rest later paga ahora una señal y el resto lo paga después
➤ to make a deposit efectuar un depósito: he made a deposit at the bank efectuó un depósito en el banco.

depressed [dɪ'prest] *adjective* ■ **deprimido.**

depression [dɪ'preʃn] *noun* ■ la **depresión** *(plural* las depresiones)*.*

depth [depθ] *noun* ■ la **profundidad: what is the depth of the river?** ¿qué profundidad tiene el río?
➤ I'm out of my depth no entiendo nada.

deputy ['depʊtɪ] *adjective* ■ **adjunto**
➤ deputy manager director adjunto
➤ deputy mayor teniente de alcalde.

describe [dɪ'skraɪb] *verb* ■ **describir: describe your room** describe tu habitación.

description [dɪ'skrɪpʃn] *noun* ■ la **descripción** *(plural* las descripciones)*.*

desert ['dezət] *noun* ■ el **desierto**
➤ a desert island una isla desierta.

deserve [dɪ'zɜːv] *verb* ■ **merecer: they didn't deserve to win** no merecían ganar
➤ he got what he deserved se llevó su merecido.

design [dɪ'zaɪn] *(noun & verb)*
■ *noun*
1. el **diseño**: it's a car with a completely new design es un coche con un diseño completamente nuevo
2. el **plano**: I like the designs for the new house me gustan los planos de la nueva casa
3. el **motivo**: a carpet with a floral design una alfombra con un motivo floral
■ *verb*
   diseñar: he designed this bicycle for young children diseñó esta bicicleta para niños pequeños; she designs jewellery diseña joyas.

designer [dɪ'zaɪnə'] *noun* ■ el **diseñador**, la **diseñadora**: he's a big fashion designer es un gran diseñador de moda
> designer clothes la ropa de diseño.

desk [desk] *noun*
1. el **escritorio**: he's sitting at his desk está sentado en su escritorio
2. el **mostrador**: leave your key at the desk in the lobby deje su llave en el mostrador del vestíbulo.

desktop ['desk,tɒp] *noun* ■ el **escritorio**: the icon is on the desktop of the computer el icono está en el escritorio del ordenador
> a desktop computer un ordenador de mesa.

desperate ['desprət] *adjective* ■ **desesperado**
> the situation is desperate la situación es desesperada
   to be desperate to do something no ver la hora de hacer algo: I was desperate to leave no veía la hora de irme.

despite [dɪ'spaɪt] *preposition* ■ **a pesar de**: despite the rain he went out salió a pesar de la lluvia.

dessert [dɪ'zɜːt] *noun* ■ el **postre**: what's for dessert? ¿qué hay de postre?

destroy [dɪ'strɔɪ] *verb* ■ **destruir**: the tsunami destroyed the village el tsunami destruyó el pueblo.

detached house *UK* [dɪ'tætʃthaʊs] *noun* ■ **la vivienda unifamiliar**.

detail ['diːteɪl] *noun* ■ el **detalle**: the details aren't important los detalles no son importantes
> in detail detalladamente: he described the island in detail describió la isla detalladamente.

detective [dɪ'tektɪv] *noun* ■ el/la **detective**: the detective in charge of the investigation el detective a cargo de la investigación
> a detective story una novela policíaca
> a private detective un detective privado.

determined [dɪ'tɜːmɪnd] *adjective* ■ **decidido**: he's determined to go back to England está decidido a volver a Inglaterra.

develop [dɪ'veləp] *verb*
1. **ampliar**: they're trying to develop the business están tratando de ampliar el negocio
2. **revelar**: they developed my photos quickly revelaron mis fotos rápidamente
3. **desarrollarse**: babies develop very fast los bebés se desarrollan muy rápido
> to develop into convertirse en: he developed into a charming young man se convirtió en un joven encantador.

devil ['devl] *noun* ■ el **diablo**.

devote [dɪ'vəʊt] *verb* ■ **dedicar**: he devoted himself to his studies se dedicó a sus estudios.

diagram ['daɪəgræm] *noun* ■ el **diagrama**.

dial ['daɪəl] *(verb & noun)*
= *verb (past tense & past participle UK* dialled, *US* dialed, *present participle UK* dialling, *US* dialing)
   marcar: she dialled the number marcó el número
■ *noun*
   la **esfera**: a watch with a luminous dial un reloj con una esfera luminosa.

dial tone *US noun* ➤ dialling tone *UK*.

dialling code *UK* ['daɪəlɪŋkəʊd] *noun* ■ el **prefijo**: what's the dialling code for Manchester? ¿cuál es el prefijo de Manchester?

dialling tone *UK* ['daɪəlɪŋtəʊn], **dial tone** *US* ['daɪəltəʊn] *noun* ■ el **tono de**

marcar: there's no dialling tone no hay tono de marcar.

dialogue UK, **dialog** US ['daɪəlɒg] noun ■ el **diálogo**: the dialogue box el cuadro de diálogo.

diamond ['daɪəmənd] noun ■ el **diamante**: a diamond ring un anillo de diamantes; the ace of diamonds el as de diamantes.

diaper US ['daɪəpəʳ] noun ■ el **pañal.**

diary ['daɪərɪ] (plural diaries) noun
1. el **diario**: she keeps a diary escribe un diario
2. la **agenda**: he wrote down my birthday in his diary anotó mi cumpleaños en su agenda.

dice [daɪs] (plural dice) noun ■ el **dado**: he rolled the dice tiró los dados.

dictation [dɪk'teɪʃn] noun ■ el **dictado.**

dictionary ['dɪkʃənrɪ] (plural dictionaries) noun ■ el **diccionario**: look it up in the dictionary búscalo en el diccionario.

did [dɪd] past tense ➤ do.

didn't ['dɪdnt] = did not: didn't do it yo no lo hice.

die [daɪ] (present participle dying) verb ■ **morir**: he died last year murió el año pasado
to be dying to do something morirse de ganas de hacer algo: I'm dying to see you me muero de ganas de verte
to be dying for something morirse por algo: I'm dying for a cool drink me muero por una bebida fresca.

diet ['daɪət] noun ■ la **dieta**: it is important to have a balanced diet es importante llevar una dieta equilibrada
on a diet a dieta: she's on a diet está a dieta; he went on a diet se puso a dieta.

difference ['dɪfrəns] noun ■ la **diferencia**: there's a big difference between the two of them hay una gran diferencia entre los dos
it makes no difference da lo mismo.

different ['dɪfrənt] adjective ■ **diferente, distinto**: London is different from New York Londres es diferente de Nueva York

you look different se te ve diferente.

difficult ['dɪfɪkəlt] adjective ■ **difícil**: it's a difficult problem es un problema difícil; it's difficult to say es difícil decirlo.

difficulty ['dɪfɪkəltɪ] (plural difficulties) noun ■ la **dificultad**: she did it without any difficulty lo hizo sin ninguna dificultad
to have difficulty doing something tener problemas para hacer algo: I had difficulty persuading him tuve problemas para convencerlo.

dig [dɪg] (past tense & past participle dug, present participle digging) verb
1. **cavar**: he's digging a hole está cavando un hoyo
2. **clavar**: he accidentally dug his nails into her arm le clavó las uñas sin querer en el brazo
dig up phrasal verb ■ **desenterrar**: the dog dug some bones up el perro desenterró unos huesos.

digital ['dɪdʒɪtl] adjective ■ **digital**
a digital camera una cámara digital
digital television la televisión digital
a digital watch un reloj digital.

dilute ['daɪluːt] verb ■ **diluir**: you dilute the juice with water diluye el zumo con agua.

dim [dɪm] adjective ■ **tenue, débil**: the light's a little dim la luz es un poco tenue.

dime US [daɪm] noun ■ la **moneda de diez centavos**: he put a dime in the machine puso una moneda de diez centavos en la máquina.

diner US ['daɪnəʳ] noun ■ el **restaurante de carretera.**

dinghy ['dɪŋgɪ] (plural dinghies) noun ■ la **barca, el bote**
a sailing dinghy una barca de vela
a rubber dinghy una lancha neumática.

dining room ['daɪnɪŋruːm] noun ■ el **comedor.**

dinner ['dɪnəʳ] noun ■ la **cena**: he's cooking dinner está preparando la cena
Christmas dinner la cena de Navidad.

dinnertime ['dɪnətaɪm] noun ■ la **hora de la cena.**

dinosaur ['daɪnəsɔːʳ] noun ■ el **dinosaurio.**

dip [dɪp] (past tense & past participle dipped, present participle dipping) verb ■ **mojar:** she dipped her bread into the soup mojó el pan en la sopa.

diploma [dɪ'pləʊmə] noun ■ el **diploma:** he has a diploma in computing tiene un diploma en informática.

direct [dɪ'rekt] (adjective & verb)
■ adjective
directo: a direct flight between Paris and Athens un vuelo directo entre París y Atenas
■ verb
1. **dirigir:** he directs the company dirige la compañía; Spielberg directed that film Spielberg dirigió esa película
2. **indicarle el camino a:** he directed me to the station me indicó el camino para llegar a la estación.

direction [dɪ'rekʃn] noun ■ la **dirección** (plural las **direcciones**): we're going in the wrong direction vamos en la dirección equivocada
> to ask for directions preguntar cómo llegar: she asked me for directions me preguntó cómo llegar
> directions for use modo de empleo: read the directions lea el modo de empleo.

directly [dɪ'rektlɪ] adverb
1. **directamente:** I went directly to the station fui directamente a la estación
2. **justo:** he was directly behind me estaba justo detrás de mí.

director [dɪ'rektəʳ] noun ■ el **director,** la **directora:** she's the director of a big firm es directora de una gran compañía; who's the director of this film? ¿quién es el director de esta película?

directory [dɪ'rektərɪ] (plural directories) noun
1. la **guía:** the telephone directory la guía telefónica

2. el **directorio:** save it in that directory guárdalo en ese directorio
> directory enquiries UK información telefónica.

dirt [dɜːt] uncountable noun
1. la **suciedad:** it's covered in dirt está cubierto de suciedad
2. US la **tierra:** put some dirt in the flower pot coloca un poco de tierra en la maceta.

dirty ['dɜːtɪ] adjective ■ **sucio:** my jeans are dirty mis vaqueros están sucios
> to get something dirty ensuciar algo: I got my shoes dirty me ensucié los zapatos.

disabled [dɪs'eɪbld] adjective ■ **discapacitado:** she's disabled es discapacitada.

disadvantage [ˌdɪsəd'vɑːntɪdʒ] noun ■ el **inconveniente:** its main disadvantage is the price su mayor inconveniente es el precio.

disagree [ˌdɪsə'griː] verb ■ **no estar de acuerdo:** I disagree with you no estoy de acuerdo contigo.

disappear [ˌdɪsə'pɪəʳ] verb ■ **desaparecer:** the fox disappeared el zorro desapareció.

disappoint [ˌdɪsə'pɔɪnt] verb ■ **decepcionar:** he really disappointed me realmente me decepcionó.

disappointed [ˌdɪsə'pɔɪntɪd] adjective ■ **decepcionado:** I was disappointed with the film quedé decepcionado con la película.

disappointment [ˌdɪsə'pɔɪntmənt] noun ■ la **decepción** (plural las **decepciones**): what a disappointment! ¡qué decepción!

disapprove [ˌdɪsə'pruːv] verb
> she disapproves of smoking está en contra del tabaco
> they disapprove of my friends a ellos no les gustan mis amigos.

disaster [dɪ'zɑːstəʳ] noun ■ el **desastre:** a natural disaster un desastre natural; the meeting was a disaster la reunión fue un desastre.

disc UK, **disk** US [dɪsk] noun ■ el **disco**
> a compact disc un disco compacto
> a disc jockey un pinchadiscos.

discipline ['dɪsɪplɪn] noun ■ la **disciplina**.

disco ['dɪskəʊ] (abbreviation of discotheque) noun ■ la **disco**: they go to a disco on Saturdays van a una disco todos los sábados.

discount ['dɪskaʊnt] noun ■ el **descuento**: I got a 20% discount on it me hicieron un 20 por ciento de descuento.

discover [dɪ'skʌvəʳ] verb ■ **descubrir**: she discovered a new chemical element descubrió un nuevo elemento químico.

discovery [dɪ'skʌvərɪ] (plural discoveries) noun ■ el **descubrimiento**.

discrimination [dɪˌskrɪmɪ'neɪʃn] noun ■ la **discriminación**: racial discrimination la discriminación racial.

discuss [dɪ'skʌs] verb
1. **discutir**: she discussed the problem with him discutió el problema con él
2. **hablar de**: we discussed the book in class hablamos del libro en clase.

discussion [dɪ'skʌʃn] noun ■ la **discusión** (plural las **discusiones**): they had a long discussion on the subject tuvieron una larga discusión sobre el tema
➤ we had a discussion about the book in class hablamos del libro en clase.

disease [dɪ'ziːz] noun ■ la **enfermedad**: she caught a rare disease se contagió de una enfermedad poco común.

disguise [dɪs'gaɪz] (verb & noun)
■ verb
disfrazar: she disguised herself as a witch se disfrazó de bruja
■ noun
el **disfraz** (plural los **disfraces**)
➤ in disguise disfrazado: everyone was in disguise todos estaban disfrazados.

disgusted [dɪs'gʌstɪd] adjective ■ **indignado**: she was disgusted because of her boyfriend's behaviour estaba indignada por el comportamiento de su novio

 La palabra inglesa **disgusted** es un falso amigo, no significa "disgustado".

disgusting [dɪs'gʌstɪŋ] adjective ■ **repugnante**: that smell is disgusting ese olor es repugnante.

dish [dɪʃ] noun ■ el **plato**: paella is a Spanish dish la paella es un plato español
➤ the dishes los platos: he's doing the dishes OR he's washing the dishes está lavando los platos.

dishonest [dɪs'ɒnɪst] adjective ■ **deshonesto**.

dishwasher ['dɪʃˌwɒʃəʳ] noun ■ el **lavavajillas** (plural los **lavavajillas**).

disinfectant [ˌdɪsɪn'fektənt] noun ■ el **desinfectante**.

disk [dɪsk] noun
1. el **disco**: the hard disk is full el disco duro está lleno
2. US ➤ disc UK.
➤ floppy disk disquete: save the file on a floppy disk guarda el archivo en un disquete.

diskette [dɪs'ket] noun ■ el **disquete**.

dismiss [dɪs'mɪs] verb ■ **despedir**: they dismissed her from her job la despidieron de su trabajo.

disorganized , disorganised UK [dɪs'ɔːgənaɪzd] adjective ■ **desorganizado**: they are very disorganized son muy desorganizados.

display [dɪ'spleɪ] (noun & verb)
■ noun
1. la **exposición** (plural las **exposiciones**): an art display una exposición de arte
2. la **exhibición** (plural las **exhibiciones**): an acrobatic display una exhibición de acrobacias
➤ on display expuesto: his paintings are on display sus pinturas están expuestas
■ verb
1. **demostrar**: he displayed great courage demostró un gran coraje
2. **aparecer**: the information is displayed on the screen la información aparece en la pantalla.

disposable [dɪ'spəʊzəbl] adjective ■ **desechable**

a **disposable camera** una cámara de fotos desechable.

distance ['dɪstəns] *noun* ■ la **distancia: what's the distance between the two towns?** ¿qué distancia hay entre las dos ciudades?

▷ **in the distance** a lo lejos: **I could see her in the distance** la veía a lo lejos

it's within walking distance se puede ir andando.

distant ['dɪstənt] *adjective* ■ **lejano: in the distant future** en un futuro lejano.

distinguish [dɪ'stɪŋgwɪʃ] *verb* ■ **distinguir: he can't distinguish between red and green** no distingue entre el verde y el rojo.

distort [dɪ'stɔːt] *verb* ■ **distorsionar: this mirror distorts your face** este espejo distorsiona la cara.

distract [dɪ'strakt] *verb* ■ **distraer: you're distracting me from my work** me distraes de mi trabajo.

distribute [dɪ'strɪbjuːt] *verb* ■ **distribuir: students were distributing flyers** los estudiantes estaban distribuyendo hojas de propaganda.

district ['dɪstrɪkt] *noun* ■ el **distrito: the financial district of London** el distrito financiero de Londres.

disturb [dɪ'stɜːb] *verb* ■ **molestar: sorry to disturb you** perdone que le moleste.

dive [daɪv] *(past tense* dived OR dove *US, past participle* dived*) verb* ■ **zambullirse: he dived into the water** se zambulló en el agua.

diver ['daɪvər] *noun* ■ el **buceador,** la **buceadora.**

divide [dɪ'vaɪd] *verb*

1. **dividir: she divided the cake into three equal parts** dividió el pastel en tres partes iguales; **14 divided by 2 is 7** 14 dividido entre 2 es igual a 7

2. **repartir: they divided the money between them** se repartieron el dinero entre ellos.

diving ['daɪvɪŋ] *noun* ■ el **buceo: he goes diving near the coral reef** hace buceo cerca del arrecife de coral

▷ a **diving board** un trampolín.

divorced [dɪ'vɔːst] *adjective* ■ **divorciado: his parents are divorced** sus padres están divorciados

▷ **to get divorced** divorciarse: **they're getting divorced** se van a divorciar.

DIY *UK* [diːaɪ'waɪ] *(abbreviation of* do-it-yourself*) noun* ■ el **bricolaje: a DIY shop** una tienda de bricolaje.

dizzy ['dɪzɪ] *adjective*

▷ **to feel dizzy** sentirse mareado: **I'm feeling a bit dizzy** me siento un poco mareado.

DJ ['dɪdʒeɪ] *(abbreviation of* disc jockey*) noun* ■ el/la **pinchadiscos** *(plural* los/las **pinchadiscos***)*.

do [duː] *(past tense* did, *past participle* done*) verb*

1. **hacer: what are you doing?** ¿qué estás haciendo?; **I'm doing my homework** estoy haciendo los deberes; **I've got a lot to do** tengo mucho que hacer; **do as you're told!** ¡haz lo que te digan!

2. **bastar: will 10 dollars do?** ¿bastará con 10 dólares?; **that'll do now!** ¡ya basta!

3. **servir: what does this switch do?** ¿para qué sirve este interruptor?; **this box is too small, the other one will do** esta caja es muy pequeña, la otra me servirá

4.

Followed by **well** or **badly:**

I'm doing well me va bien; **he's doing well at school** le va bien en el colegio; **she did badly in the exam** le fue mal en el examen

5.

Do is not translated when it is used to form a question:

do you speak English? ¿hablas inglés?; **how did you meet Isabela?** ¿cómo conociste a Isabela?; **does your mother have the keys?** ¿tiene las llaves tu madre?; **did Tom call?** ¿llamó Tom?

6.

In negative constructions **do** is not translated, just put **no** before the verb:

I don't want to come no quiero ir; he doesn't eat meat no come carne; we didn't go out last night no salimos anoche

7.

In short answers **do** is not translated when it is used to take the place of another verb:

I like reggae — so do I me gusta el reggae –a mí también; do you know how to ski? — no, I don't ¿sabes esquiar? –no, no sé

8.

In question tags use ¿**no**? or ¿**verdad**? as a translation:

you know Fran, don't you? conoces a Fran, ¿no?; he doesn't like garlic, does he? no le gusta el ajo, ¿verdad?

9. *in emphatic sentences* I DO like him, but I don't want to marry him me gusta, sí, pero no quiero casarme con él; I DO want to go sí que quiero ir

10. *in polite requests* do sit down siéntese, por favor; do help yourselves sírvanse, por favor

▸ how are you doing? ¿cómo te va?

▸ how do you do? mucho gusto

▸ what does your father do? ¿a qué se dedica tu padre?

▸ to do one's hair arreglarse el pelo

do up *phrasal verb*

1. abrocharse: he did up his jacket se abrochó la chaqueta

2. atarse: do your laces up átate los cordones

3. subir la cremallera: do up your zip súbete la cremallera

4. reformar: they're doing up an old farmhouse están reformando una vieja casa de campo

do without *phrasal verb* ■ arreglárselas sin: they did without bread se las arreglaron sin pan.

doctor ['dɒktəʳ] *noun* ■ el **médico**, la **médica**: I went to the doctor fui al médico; she's a doctor es médica.

document ['dɒkjʊmənt] *noun* ■ el **documento**.

documentary [ˌdɒkjʊ'mentərɪ] *(plural documentaries) noun* ■ el **documental**: there's a documentary about sharks on TV hay un documental sobre tiburones en la tele.

does [dəz, dʌz] ➤do.

doesn't ['dʌznt] – does not.

dog [dɒg] *noun* ■ el **perro**, la **perra**: my dog's name is Lassie mi perra se llama Lassie.

doll [dɒl] *noun* ■ la **muñeca**: she collects dolls colecciona muñecas.

dollar ['dɒləʳ] *noun* ■ el **dólar**: it costs 20 dollars cuesta 20 dólares

▸ a dollar bill un billete de un dólar.

dolphin ['dɒlfɪn] *noun* ■ el **delfín** *(plural* los **delfines***)*.

Dominican [də'mɪnɪkən] *(adjective & noun)*

■ *adjective*

Remember not to use a capital letter for the adjective in Spanish:

dominicano: Dominican cuisine is different from Mexican cuisine la cocina dominicana es diferente de la mexicana

■ *noun*

In Spanish, a capital letter is not used for the inhabitants of a country or region:

el **dominicano**, la **dominicana**: the Dominicans are usually friendly to tourists los dominicanos suelen ser amables con los turistas.

Dominican Republic [də'mɪnɪkən rɪ'pʌblɪk] *noun* ■ la **República Dominicana**.

dominoes ['dɒmɪnəʊz] *noun* ■ el **dominó**: they're playing dominoes están jugando al dominó.

donate [də'neɪt] *verb* ■ **donar**: he donated a thousand dollars to charity donó mil dólares para obras de caridad

▸ to donate blood donar sangre.

done [dʌn] *(adjective & verb form)*

■ *adjective*

cocido: the potatoes aren't done las patatas no están cocidas

➤ **are you done with this** ¿has terminado con esto?

➤ **I'm nearly done** ya casi he terminado

■ *past participle*

➤ do: **I haven't done it yet** todavía no lo he hecho.

donkey ['dɒŋkɪ] *noun* ■ el **burro.**

don't [dəʊnt] = do not.

donut *US noun* ➤ doughnut.

door [dɔːʳ] *noun* ■ la **puerta: close the door** cierra la puerta; **the car door is dented** la puerta del coche está abollada.

doorbell ['dɔːbel] *noun* ■ el **timbre**

➤ **to ring the doorbell** tocar el timbre: **somebody rang the doorbell** alguien tocó el timbre.

doormat ['dɔːmæt] *noun* ■ el **felpudo: leave the keys under the doormat** deja las llaves debajo del felpudo.

doorstep ['dɔːstep] *noun* ■ el **peldaño de la puerta.**

dormitory ['dɔːmətrɪ] *(plural* dormitories*) noun* ■ la **residencia de estudiantes.**

dot [dɒt] *noun* ■ el **punto: don't forget the dot on the "i"** no olvides ponerle el punto a la "i"

➤ **on the dot** en punto: **at 6 o'clock on the dot** a las 6 en punto.

double ['dʌbl] *(adjective, adverb, noun & verb)*

■ *adjective*

1. **doble: she had a double helping of ice cream** se sirvió una porción doble de helado

2. **dos: "address" is spelt with a double "d"** "address" se escribe con dos des

3. *in phone numbers* **double two three five** dos, dos tres cinco

➤ **a double bass** un contrabajo

➤ **a double bed** una cama de matrimonio

➤ **a double room** una habitación doble

■ *adverb*

1. **el doble: these tickets cost double** estas entradas cuestan el doble

2. **doble: he was seeing double** estaba viendo doble

■ *noun*

1. **el doble: the men's doubles** (partido de) dobles masculinos

2. **el/la doble: she's my double** es mi doble

■ *verb*

duplicarse: prices have doubled los precios se han duplicado.

double-click ['dʌblklɪk] *verb* ■ hacer **doble clic: double-click on the icon** haz doble clic en el icono.

double-decker *UK* ['dʌbl'dekəʳ] *noun* ■ el **autobús de dos pisos.**

doubt [daʊt] *(noun & verb)*

■ *noun*

la **duda: there is no doubt about it** no hay duda acerca de eso

➤ **without doubt** sin duda: **he's without doubt the champion** es, sin duda, el campeón

➤ **to be in doubt** dudar: **if you're in doubt ask your parents** si dudas, pregúntale a tus padres

■ *verb*

dudar: I doubt it lo dudo; **I doubt he'll come** dudo que venga

Use the subjunctive after **dudar que.**

dough [dəʊ] *uncountable noun* ■ la **masa: bread is made from dough** el pan se hace con masa.

doughnut , donut *US* ['dəʊnʌt] *noun* ■ el **donut®.**

dove *(noun & verb form)*

■ *noun* [dʌv]

la **paloma: the dove is a symbol of peace** la paloma es un símbolo de paz

■ *past tense* [dəʊv]

➤ dive *US.*

down [daʊn] *(adverb, preposition & adjective)*

■ *adverb*

1. *with a verb of movement*

When "down" is used with a verb of movement in English (to come down, to go down, etc.), you often use a verb alone in Spanish to translate it:

are you coming down? ¿bajas?; **prices have come down** los precios han bajado; **I fell down the stairs** me caí por las escaleras

2. **abajo:** she's down in the street está abajo en la calle; **she cycled all the way down** llegó hasta abajo en bicicleta
➤ **he threw the book down** tiró el libro al suelo
➤ **down below** abajo
➤ **down there** allá abajo: **can you see that man down there?** ¿ves a ese hombre allá abajo?
■ preposition
I. *in a prepositional phrase*

When 'down' is used with a verb of movement in English, even when being used in a prepositional phrase, you often use a verb alone in Spanish to translate it:

we walked down the street caminamos por la calle; **they ran down the hill** bajaron la colina corriendo

2. **abajo:** the bathroom is down the stairs el baño está abajo
➤ **further down** más abajo: **they live further down the street** viven más abajo en esta calle
■ adjective
informal **deprimido:** I feel a bit down estoy un poco deprimido.

Downing Street ['daonıŋstriːt] *noun* ■ nombre de una calle de Londres

---

DOWNING STREET

La residencia oficial del Primer ministro británico está en el número 10 de esta calle. El ministro de Economía y Hacienda vive en el 11. En los medios de comunicación, muchas veces se emplea el término **Downing Street** para designar al Primer ministro o al gobierno británico.

---

download [,daon'ləod] *verb* ■ **descargar:** he downloaded the attached file descargó el archivo adjunto.

downstairs [,daon'steəz] *(adjective & adverb)*
■ adjective
de abajo: our downstairs neighbours nuestros vecinos de abajo
■ adverb
abajo: wait for me downstairs espérame abajo

➤ **to come downstairs** OR **to go downstairs** bajar: he went downstairs to answer the phone bajó a contestar el teléfono
➤ **she ran downstairs** bajó corriendo las escaleras.

downtown *US* [,daon'taon] *adverb* ■ **al centro:** tomorrow we're going downtown mañana vamos al centro
➤ **they live in downtown Chicago** viven en el centro de Chicago.

downwards ['daonwədz] *adverb* ■ **hacia abajo:** he looked downwards miró hacia abajo.

dozen ['dʌzn] *noun* ■ **la docena:** they cost 50 cents a dozen cuestan 50 centavos la docena; she bought a dozen eggs compró una docena de huevos.

Dr *(abbreviation of* Doctor*)* el **Dr.,** la **Dra.**

draft *US noun* ➤ draught.

drafty *US adjective* ➤ draughty.

drag [dræg] *(past tense & past participle* dragged, *present participle* dragging*) verb* ■ **arrastrar:** he dragged his bag along the ground arrastró la bolsa por el suelo.

dragon ['drægən] *noun* ■ el **dragón** *(plural* los **dragones***)*.

drain [dreın] *(noun & verb)*
■ noun
el **desagüe:** the drains are blocked los desagües están obstruidos
■ verb
escurrir: you have to drain the vegetables first tienes que escurrir las verduras primero.

draining board ['dreınıŋbɔːrd] *UK,*
drainboard *US* ['dreınbɔːrd] *noun* ■ el **escurreplatos:** put the glasses on the draining board pon los vasos en el escurreplatos.

drama ['drɑːmə] *noun*
I. el **teatro:** he teaches drama enseña teatro
2. el **drama:** the play is a drama la obra es un drama.

dramatic [drə'mætık] *adjective* ■ **espectacular:** the end of the film is very dramatic el final de la película es muy espectacular.

drank [dræŋk] *past tense* ➤ drink.

draught *UK* [drɑːft], **draft** *US* [dræft] *noun* ■ la **corriente**: there's a draught from the window entra corriente por la ventana.

draughts *UK* [drɑːfts] *plural noun* ■ las **damas**: they're playing draughts están jugando a las damas.

draughty *UK* [drɑːftɪ], **drafty** *US* [dræftɪ] *adjective*
➤ this room is draughty hay mucha corriente en esta habitación.

draw [drɔː] *(verb & noun)*
■ *verb (past tense* drew, *past participle* drawn*)*
1. **dibujar**: she drew a tree dibujó un árbol; he drew a picture of a dinosaur hizo un dibujo de un dinosaurio
2. **correr**: she drew the curtains corrió las cortinas
3. **atraer**: we tried to draw his attention tratamos de atraer su atención
4. **empatar**: the two teams drew los dos equipos empataron
■ *noun*
1. el **empate**: the game ended in a draw el partido terminó en empate
2. el **sorteo**: the lottery draw is tonight el sorteo de la lotería es esta noche.

drawer [drɔːʳ] *noun* ■ el **cajón** *(plural* los **cajones***)*: she took the knife out of the drawer sacó el cuchillo del cajón.

drawing [ˈdrɔːɪŋ] *noun* ■ el **dibujo**: she did a drawing of a whale hizo un dibujo de una ballena.

drawn [drɔːn] *past participle* ➤ draw.

dreadful [ˈdredfʊl] *adjective* ■ **horrible**: the weather is dreadful hace un tiempo horrible
➤ to feel dreadful sentirse fatal: I feel dreadful me siento fatal
➤ to look dreadful estar horrible: you look dreadful in that hat estás horrible con ese sombrero
➤ you look dreadful, you should go and lie down for a while tienes muy mala cara, deberías echarte un rato.

dream [driːm] *(noun & verb)*
■ *noun* .
el **sueño**: I had a strange dream tuve un sueño raro
■ *verb (past tense & past participle* dreamed OR dreamt*)*
soñar: I dreamt about you last night anoche soñé contigo.

dreamt [dremt] *past tense & past participle* ➤ dream.

drenched [drentʃ] *adjective* ■ **estar empapado**: I'm completely drenched estoy completamente empapado.

dress [dres] *(noun & verb)*
■ *noun*
el **vestido**
■ *verb*
1. **vestirse**: she dresses very elegantly se viste con elegancia
2. **vestir**: she's dressing the children está vistiendo a los niños
➤ they were dressed in black iban vestidos de negro
➤ to get dressed vestirse: I got dressed and went out me vestí y salí

dress up *phrasal verb*
1. **disfrazarse**: she dressed up as a witch se disfrazó de bruja
2. **ponerse elegante**: she always dresses up to go out siempre se pone elegante para salir.

dresser [ˈdresəʳ] *noun* ■ la **cómoda**.

dressing gown [ˈdresɪŋgaʊn] *noun* ■ la **bata**.

dressing table [ˈdresɪŋˈteɪbl] *noun* ■ el **tocador**: she keeps her perfume on her dressing table tiene el perfume encima del tocador.

drew [druː] *past tense* ➤ draw.

dried [draɪd] *(adjective & verb form)*
■ *adjective*
seco: dried flowers flores secas
■ *past tense & past participle*
➤ dry.

drill [drɪl] *(noun & verb)*
■ *noun*
el **taladro**

■ *verb*
taladrar
➤ he's drilling a hole está haciendo un agujero con un taladro.

drink [drɪŋk] *(noun & verb)*
■ *noun*
la **bebida**: a cold drink una bebida fría
➤ we went out for a drink salimos a tomar algo
➤ would you like a drink? ¿quieres tomar algo?
■ *verb (past tense* drank, *past participle* drunk*)*
beber: he's drinking coffee está bebiendo café; they've been drinking han estado bebiendo.

drinking water ['drɪŋkɪŋ'wɔːtəʳ] *noun*
■ el **agua potable**

Feminine noun that takes **un** and **el** in the singular.

drive [draɪv] *(noun & verb)*
■ *noun*
1. una **vuelta en coche**: we went for a drive fuimos a dar una vuelta en coche
2. el **viaje en coche**: it's a long drive es un largo viaje en coche
3. el **camino de entrada**: we walked up the drive to the house fuimos andando por el camino de entrada a la casa
➤ the disk drive la unidad de disco
■ *verb (past tense* drove, *past participle* driven*)*
1. **conducir**: can you drive? ¿sabes conducir?; he was driving a sports car conducía un coche deportivo; I don't want to drive, I'll take the train no quiero conducir, voy a coger el tren; they drive on the left in the UK en el Reino Unido conducen por la izquierda
2. **llevar en coche**: she drives me to school every day me lleva al colegio en coche todos los días
➤ to drive somebody crazy volver loco a alguien: you're driving me crazy! ¡me estás volviendo loca!

driven ['drɪvn] *past participle* ➤ drive.

driver ['draɪvəʳ] *noun* ■ el **conductor**, la **conductora**, el **chófer**: he's a bus driver es chófer de autobús
➤ she's a good driver conduce muy bien
➤ he's a taxi driver es taxista
➤ a driver's license *US* un carné de conducir.

driving ['draɪvɪŋ] *noun*
➤ what do you think about John's driving? ¿cómo crees que conduce John?
➤ a driving lesson una clase de conducir
➤ a driving licence *UK* un carné de conducir: he has a driving licence tiene carné de conducir
➤ a driving test un examen de conducir: he passed his driving test aprobó el examen de conducir.

drop [drɒp] *(noun & verb)*
■ *noun*
1. la **gota**: a few drops of water unas pocas gotas de agua
2. el **descenso**: there's been a drop in the temperature ha habido un descenso de la temperatura
■ *verb (past tense & past participle* dropped, *present participle* dropping*)*
1. **caerse**: he dropped the plate se le cayó el plato
2. **dejar**: can you drop me off at the station? ¿puedes dejarme en la estación?
3. **bajar**: temperatures have dropped han bajado las temperaturas

drop by *phrasal verb* ■ **pasar**: can you drop by tomorrow? ¿por qué no pasas por casa mañana?

drought [draʊt] *noun* ■ la **sequía**.

drove [drəʊv] *past tense* ➤ drive.

drown [draʊn] *verb* ■ **ahogarse**: he drowned in the lake se ahogó en el lago.

drug [drʌg] *noun*
1. el **medicamento**: the doctor prescribed drugs el médico le recetó medicamentos
2. la **droga**: opium is a drug el opio es una droga
➤ a drug addict un drogadicto.

druggist *US* ['drʌgist] *noun* ■ el **farmacéutico**, la **farmacéutica**.

drugstore ['drʌgstɔːʳ] *noun*
1. *tienda que vende una gran variedad de artículos como medicamentos, cosméticos, periódicos, comida rápida, etc*
2. *US* la **farmacia**.

drum [drʌm] *noun* ■ el **tambor: he's beating a drum** está tocando un tambor ➤ the **drums** la batería: **she plays the drums** toca la batería.

drummer ['drʌmə^r] *noun* ■ el/la **batería.**

drunk [drʌŋk] *(adjective & verb form)*
■ *adjective*
borracho: you're drunk estás borracho ➤ to get **drunk** emborracharse: **he got drunk** se emborrachó
■ *past participle*
➤ drink.

dry [draɪ] *(adjective & verb)*
■ *adjective*
seco: the ink is dry la tinta está seca ➤ it'll be **dry tomorrow** no va a llover mañana ➤ the **dry cleaner's** la tintorería
■ *verb (past tense & past participle* dried*)*
1. **secarse: dry yourself** sécate; **she dried her hair** se secó el pelo
2. **secar: he's drying the dishes** está secando los platos; **we need to dry the clothes** tenemos que secar la ropa.

dryer ['draɪə^r] *noun* ■ la **secadora: put the clothes in the dryer** pon la ropa en la secadora.

dubbed [dʌbd] *adjective* ■ **doblado: the film is dubbed into English** la película está doblada al inglés.

duck [dʌk] *(noun & verb)*
■ *noun*
el **pato: there are some ducks on the river** hay algunos patos en el río
■ *verb*
agacharse: he ducked as he went through the door al pasar por la puerta, se agachó.

due [*UK* djuː, *US* duː] *adjective*
➤ **what time is the train due?** ¿a qué hora llega el tren?
➤ **she's due back soon** va a regresar pronto
➤ **due to** debido a: **he arrived late due to the bad weather** llegó tarde debido al mal tiempo.

dug [dʌg] *past tense & past participle* ➤ dig.

dull [dʌl] *adjective*
1. **aburrido: the film is very dull** la película es muy aburrida
2. **gris: it's a dull day** hace un día gris.

dumb [dʌm] *adjective*
1. **mudo: he was struck dumb** se quedó mudo
2. *US* **idiota: that guy's really dumb** este tipo es realmente idiota
➤ **that was a dumb thing to do** eso fue una tontería.

dump [dʌmp] *noun* ■ el **basurero: we took the rubbish to the dump** llevamos la basura al basurero.

during [*UK* 'djʊərɪŋ, *US* 'dʊərɪŋ] *preposition* ■ **durante: it happened during the night** sucedió durante la noche.

dusk [dʌsk] *noun* ■ el **atardecer: we went home at dusk** volvimos a casa al atardecer.

dust [dʌst] *(noun & verb)*
■ *noun*
el **polvo: there's a layer of dust on the table** hay una capa de polvo en la mesa
■ *verb*
quitarle el polvo a: he dusted the shelf le quitó el polvo a la repisa.

dustbin *UK* ['dʌstbɪn] *noun* ■ el **cubo de la basura: they've emptied the dustbin** han vaciado el cubo de la basura.

duster ['dʌstə^r] *noun* ■ el **trapo del polvo.**

dustman *UK* ['dʌstmən] *(plural* dustmen ['dʌstmən]*) noun* ■ el **basurero,** la **basurera.**

dusty ['dʌstɪ] *adjective*
1. **polvoriento: a dusty road** un camino polvoriento
2. **lleno de polvo: the furniture is all dusty** los muebles están todos llenos de polvo.

duty [*UK* 'djuːtɪ, *US* 'duːtɪ] *(plural* duties*) noun* ■ el **deber: he's doing his duty** cumple con su deber
➤ **on duty**
1. **de guardia: Dr Jones is on duty** el doctor Jones está de guardia
2. **de servicio: go and get the police officer on duty** ve a buscar al policía que está de servicio.

DVD [di:vi:'di:] *(abbreviation of* Digital Video Disc OR Digital Versatile Disc*) noun* ■ el DVD: **I watched the film on DVD** vi la película en DVD.

dwarf [dwɔ:f] *(plural* dwarfs OR dwarves [dwɔɪvz]*) noun* ■ el **enano**, la **enana**.

dye [daɪ] *(noun & verb)*
■ *noun*
el **tinte**
■ *verb*
teñir: I'm going to dye my jeans voy a teñir mis vaqueros
➤ **to dye one's hair** teñirse el pelo: **she dyed her hair pink** se tiñó el pelo de rosa.

dying ['daɪɪŋ] *present participle* ➤ die.

each [i:tʃ] *(adjective & pronoun)*
■ *adjective*
cada: each time I see that film, I cry cada vez que veo esa película, lloro; **each child has their own computer** cada niño tiene su propio ordenador
■ *pronoun*
cada uno *(feminine* **cada una***):* **they each have their own room** cada uno tiene su propio cuarto; **each of us had a dessert** cada uno de nosotros comió un postre; **melons cost 1 euro each** los melones cuestan 1 euro cada uno
➤ **each other**

A reflexive pronoun **se** or **nos** is normally used in Spanish to translate "each other":

they love each other se quieren; **do you know each other?** ¿os conocéis?; **we write to each other** nos escribimos.

eager ['i:gəʳ] *adjective*
➤ **to be eager to do something** estar impaciente por hacer algo
➤ **she's eager to learn Spanish** está impaciente por aprender español.

eagle ['i:gl] *noun* ■ el **águila** *(feminine)*

Feminine noun that takes **un** and **el** in the singular.

ear [ɪəʳ] *noun* ■ la **oreja**.

earache ['ɪəreɪk] *noun* ■ el **dolor de oídos**
➤ **to have earache** UK OR **to have an earache** US tener dolor de oídos.

earlier ['ɜ:lɪəʳ] *(comparative of* early*) (adverb & adjective)*
■ *adverb*
1. **más temprano: I got up earlier than usual** me he levantado más temprano de lo usual
2. **antes: I saw them earlier** los vi antes
■ *adjective*
anterior: I took an earlier train cogí un tren anterior.

earliest ['ɜ:lɪəst] *(superlative of* early*) (adjective&noun)*
■ *adjective*
primero: what is the earliest delivery date? ¿cuál es la primera fecha de entrega?
■ *noun*
➤ **at the earliest** como muy pronto: **I can come at 7 o'clock at the earliest** puedo llegar a las 7 como muy pronto.

early ['ɜ:lɪ] *(adverb & adjective)*
■ *adverb*
temprano: I got up early me levanté temprano; **you're early** llegas temprano
➤ **he's 10 minutes early** llega con 10 minutos de antelación
■ *adjective*
➤ **we had an early night** nos acostamos temprano
➤ **she made an early start** salió temprano
➤ **in early spring** a principios de primavera.

earn [ɜ:n] *verb* ■ **ganar: she earns 40 dollars an hour** gana 40 dólares por hora.

earphones [ˈɪəfəʊnz] *plural noun* ■ los **auriculares**.

earring [ˈɪərɪŋ] *noun* ■ el **pendiente**.

earth [ɜːθ] *noun*

1. la **Tierra**: the moon goes around the earth la luna gira alrededor de la Tierra

> In Spanish, **Tierra** is written with a capital when it means the planet earth.

2. la **tierra**: the box was covered with earth la caja estaba cubierta de tierra
> **what on earth is that?** ¿qué diablos es eso?

earthquake [ˈɜːθkweɪk] *noun* ■ el **terremoto**.

ease [iːz] *(noun & verb)*

■ *uncountable noun*

la **facilidad**

> **with ease** con facilidad: he passed the exam with ease aprobó el examen con facilidad
> **at ease** a gusto: she felt at ease with them se sintió a gusto con ellos

■ *verb*

aliviar: this ointment will ease the pain esta pomada te aliviará el dolor.

easier *(comparative of* easy*) adjective* ➤ **easy**.

easiest *(superlative of* easy*) adjective* ➤ **easy**.

easily [ˈiːzɪlɪ] *adverb*

1. **fácilmente**: I'll easily finish it tonight lo terminaré fácilmente esta noche

2. **con mucho**: that's easily the best film I've ever seen ésa es con mucho la mejor película que he visto.

east [iːst] *(noun, adjective & adverb)*

■ *noun*

el **este**: the sun rises in the east el sol sale por el este

■ *adjective*

este: Norfolk is on the east coast of England Norfolk está en la costa este de Inglaterra

■ *adverb*

hacia el este: we went east fuimos hacia el este

> **east of** al este de: Manchester is east of Liverpool Manchester está al este de Liverpool
> **the East End** *barrio obrero del este de Londres.*

Easter [ˈiːstər] *noun* ■ la **Semana Santa**: I went to see her at Easter fui a visitarla en Semana Santa

> **an Easter egg** un huevo de Pascua

EASTER

La Pascua o Semana Santa es una de las festividades religiosas más importantes en Gran Bretaña y Estados Unidos. Tanto el Viernes Santo como el Lunes de Pascua son fiestas nacionales. En Estados Unidos, existe la tradición del **Easter Bunny** (conejito de Pascua), personaje imaginario que llega la madrugada del Domingo de Resurrección y esconde cestitas o huevos de Pascua (elaborados con chocolate) por toda la casa, el jardín o el patio para que los niños jueguen a buscarlos. En Nueva York, en esas fechas se celebran unos desfiles espectaculares.

eastern [ˈiːstən] *adjective* ■ **oriental**: Eastern Europe Europa Oriental.

easy [ˈiːzɪ] *(comparative* easier [ˈiːzɪər]*, superlative* easiest [ˈiːzɪəst]*) adjective* ■ **fácil**: an easy job un trabajo fácil; it's easy to install this software es fácil instalar este software

> **as easy as pie** pan comido.

eat [iːt] *(past tense* ate*, past participle* eaten*) verb* ■ **comer**: she's eating a sandwich está comiendo un bocadillo; there's nothing to eat no hay nada para comer.

eaten [ˈiːtn] *past participle* ➤ **eat**.

echo [ˈekəʊ] *(plural* echoes*) noun* ■ el **eco**.

eclipse [ɪˈklɪps] *noun* ■ el **eclipse**: there was an eclipse of the sun hubo un eclipse de sol.

ecological [ˌiːkəˈlɒdʒɪkl] *adjective* ■ **ecológico**.

ecology [ɪˈkɒlədʒɪ] *noun* ■ la **ecología**.

economic [ˌiːkəˈnɒmɪk] *adjective* ■ **económico**: an economic crisis una crisis económica.

economical [ˌiːkəˈnɒmɪkl] *adjective* ■ **económico**: this car is very economical este coche es muy económico.

economics [ˌiːkə'nɒmɪks] *uncountable noun* ■ la **economía: she's** studying economics estudia economía.

economy [ɪ'kɒnəmɪ] *(plural* economies*)* *noun* ■ la **economía: the** country's economy is strong la economía del país es fuerte.

Ecuador ['ekwədɔːr] *noun* ■ **Ecuador.**

Ecuadorian [ˌekwə'dɔːrən] *(adjective & noun)*
■ *adjective*

Remember not to use a capital letter for the adjective in Spanish:

ecuatoriano: the Ecuadorian landscape is beautiful el paisaje ecuatoriano es precioso
■ *noun*

In Spanish, a capital letter is not used for the inhabitants of a country or region:

el **ecuatoriano,** la **ecuatoriana: some Ecuadorians live in jungle areas** algunos ecuatorianos viven en regiones selváticas.

edge [edʒ] *noun* ■ el **borde: he's** standing on the edge of the cliff está de pie al borde del acantilado.

edition [ɪ'dɪʃn] *noun* ■ la **edición** *(plural* las ediciones*)*: **a new edition of the** dictionary una nueva edición del diccionario.

educated [ˌedʒʊ'keɪtɪd] *adjective* ■ **culto: he's** not very well educated no es muy culto.

education [ˌedʒʊ'keɪʃn] *noun* ■ la **educación: education is important in early childhood development** la educación es importante durante la primera infancia; **she works in education** trabaja en educación.

effect [ɪ'fekt] *noun* ■ el **efecto: the drug** had no effect on him el medicamento no le hizo ningún efecto
▷ **special effects** los efectos especiales.

effective [ɪ'fektɪv] *adjective* ■ **eficaz** *(plural* eficaces*)*: **the treatment is very effective** el tratamiento es muy eficaz.

efficient [ɪ'fɪʃənt] *adjective* ■ **eficiente: our secretary is very efficient** nuestra secretaria es muy eficiente.

effort ['efət] *noun* ■ el **esfuerzo: make an effort!** ¡haz un esfuerzo!

egg [eg] *noun* ■ el **huevo: fried eggs** huevos fritos; **a boiled egg** un huevo pasado por agua; **egg yolk** yema de huevo.

eggplant *US* ['egplænt] *noun* ■ la **berenjena.**

eight [eɪt] *number* ■ **ocho: there are eight boys in the group** hay ocho muchachos en el grupo; **she's eight** tiene ocho años; **the film starts at eight** la película empieza a las ocho.

eighteen [ˌeɪ'tiːn] *number* ■ **dieciocho: she's eighteen** tiene dieciocho años.

eighteenth [ˌeɪ'tiːnθ] *number* ■ **decimoctavo**
▷ **it's her eighteenth birthday** cumple dieciocho años
▷ **it's the eighteenth of May** *UK* OR **it's May eighteenth** *US* estamos a dieciocho de mayo.

eighth [eɪtθ] *number* ■ **octavo: on the eighth floor** en el octavo piso
▷ **it's the eighth of November** *UK* OR **it's November eighth** *US* estamos a ocho de noviembre.

eighty ['eɪtɪ] *number* ■ **ochenta: she's eighty** tiene ochenta años
▷ **eighty-one** ochenta y uno
▷ **eighty-two** ochenta y dos.

either ['aɪðər, 'iːðər] *(adverb, adjective & pronoun)*
■ *adverb*

tampoco: I don't want to go and he doesn't either yo no quiero ir y él tampoco; **I haven't had anything to eat — I haven't either** no he comido nada –yo tampoco
■ *adjective*

cualquiera de los dos: either team could win cualquiera de los dos equipos podría ganar
▷ **there are trees on either side of the road** hay árboles a cada lado de la calle

■ *pronoun*
1. **cualquiera de los dos:** you can have either, but not both puedes quedarte con cualquiera de los dos, pero no con ambos
2. **ninguno:** I don't like either no me gusta ninguna
> does either of them play the guitar ¿alguno de los dos toca la guitarra?
> either... or... o... o...: you can pay in either euros or dollars puede pagar o en euros o en dólares; either you be quiet, or I'll go home o te quedas callado, o me voy a casa.

elastic [ɪ'læstɪk] *adjective* ■ el **elástico.**

elbow ['elbəʊ] *noun* ■ el **codo.**

elder ['eldə^r] *adjective* ■ **mayor:** he's my elder brother es mi hermano mayor.

elderly ['eldəlɪ] *adjective* ■ **anciano:** she looks after her elderly parents cuida a sus padres ancianos.

eldest ['eldɪst] *adjective* ■ **mayor:** she's my eldest sister es la mayor de mis hermanas.

elect [ɪ'lekt] *verb* ■ **elegir:** he was elected president lo eligieron presidente.

election [ɪ'lekʃn] *noun* ■ la **elección** *(plural* las **elecciones):** he won the election ganó la elección.

electric [ɪ'lektrɪk] *adjective* ■ **eléctrico:** an electric light una luz eléctrica
> an electric blanket una manta eléctrica
> an electric shock una descarga eléctrica: I got an electric shock me dio una descarga eléctrica.

electrical [ɪ'lektrɪkl] *adjective* ■ **eléctrico:** an electrical appliance un aparato eléctrico.

electrician [ˌɪlek'trɪʃn] *noun* ■ el/la **electricista:** he's an electrician es electricista.

electricity [ˌɪlek'trɪsətɪ] *noun* ■ la **electricidad.**

electronic [ˌɪlek'trɒnɪk] *adjective* ■ **electrónico:** electronic mail correo electrónico.

elegant ['elɪgənt] *adjective* ■ **elegante.**

elementary school US [ˌelɪ'mentərɪskuːl] *noun* ■ la **escuela primaria.**

elephant ['elɪfənt] *noun* ■ el **elefante.**

elevator US ['elɪveɪtə^r] *noun* ■ el **ascensor.**

eleven [ɪ'levn] *number* ■ **once:** there are eleven glasses hay once vasos; he's eleven tiene once años; I went out at eleven salí a las once.

eleventh [ɪ'levnθ] *number* ■ **onceavo**
> it's his eleventh birthday cumple once años
> it's the eleventh of January UK OR it's January eleventh US es el once de enero.

El Salvador [ˌel'sælvədɔː^r] *noun* ■ **El Salvador.**

else [els] *adverb* ■ **más:** what else? ¿qué más?; anyone else? ¿alguien más?; nothing else nada más; nobody else nadie más; I don't want anything else no quiero nada más
> everyone else todos los demás: everyone else had left todos los demás se habían ido
> someone else otra persona
> something else otra cosa
> or else de lo contrario: hurry up or else we'll be late date prisa o de lo contrario vamos a llegar tarde.

e-mail , email ['iːmeɪl] *(noun & verb)*
■ *noun*
el **correo electrónico:** you can read your e-mails on my computer puedes leer tu correo electrónico en mi ordenador
— *verb*
enviar
> to e-mail somebody enviarle un correo electrónico a alguien: he e-mailed me me envió un correo electrónico
> to e-mail something enviar algo por correo electrónico: he e-mailed the file to me me envió el fichero por correo electrónico
> an e-mail address una dirección de correo electrónico.

embarrassed [ɪm'bærəst] *adjective* ■ **avergonzado:** Laura's very embarrassed Laura está muy avergonzada

⚠ La palabra inglesa **embarrassed** es un falso amigo, no significa "embarazada".

embarrassing [ɪm'bærəsɪŋ] *adjective* ■ **embarazoso**: it's very embarrassing es muy embarazoso.

embassy ['embəsɪ] *(plural* embassies*)* *noun* ■ la **embajada**: the British embassy la embajada británica.

emerald ['emərəld] *noun* ■ la **esmeralda**.

emergency [ɪ'mɜːdʒənsɪ] *(plural* emergencies*) (noun & adjective)*
■ *noun*
la **emergencia**: this is an emergency! ¡es una emergencia!
in an emergency en caso de emergencia: in an emergency call the police en caso de emergencia, llame a la policía
■ *adjective*
urgencia: the emergency services los servicios de urgencia
an emergency exit una salida de emergencia.

emotion [ɪ'məʊʃn] *noun* ■ la **emoción** *(plural* las emociones*)*.

emotional [ɪ'məʊʃənl] *adjective* ■ **emotivo**: she tends to be an emotional person tiende a ser emotiva.

emperor ['empərəʳ] *noun* ■ el **emperador**: Augustus was a Roman emperor Augusto fue un emperador romano.

emphasize , **emphasise** *UK* ['emfəsaɪz] *verb* ■ **hacer hincapié en**: he emphasized the importance of physical exercise hizo hincapié en la importancia del ejercicio físico.

empire ['empaɪəʳ] *noun* ■ el **imperio**: the Roman empire el imperio romano.

employ [ɪm'plɔɪ] *verb* ■ **emplear**: the firm employs 100 people la empresa emplea a 100 personas.

employee [ɪm'plɔɪiː] *noun* ■ el **empleado**, la **empleada**.

employer [ɪm'plɔɪəʳ] *noun* ■ el **empleador**, la **empleadora**.

employment [ɪm'plɔɪmənt] *noun* ■ el **empleo**.

empty ['emptɪ] *(adjective & verb)*
■ *adjective*
vacío: the bottle is empty la botella está vacía
■ *verb (past tense & past participle* emptied*)*
vaciar: she emptied the drawers vació los cajones
he emptied his pockets se vació los bolsillos.

encourage [ɪn'kʌrɪdʒ] *verb* ■ **animar**
to encourage somebody to do something animar a alguien a hacer algo: he encouraged me to work harder me animó a trabajar más duro.

encyclopedia , **encyclopaedia** *UK* [ɪn,saɪklə'piːdjə] *noun* ■ la **enciclopedia**: look it up in the encyclopedia búscalo en la enciclopedia.

end [end] *(noun & verb)*
■ *noun*
el **final**: she dies at the end of the film se muere al final de la película; the shop's at the end of the street la tienda está al final de la calle
in the end al final: in the end she said yes al final dijo que sí
■ *verb*
1. **terminar**: the show ends at 11 o'clock el espectáculo termina a las 11; how does the story end? ¿cómo termina la historia?
2. **terminar con**: this ended our friendship eso terminó con nuestra amistad

end up *phrasal verb* ■ **terminar**: he ended up doing all the work himself terminó haciendo todo el trabajo; he ended up in Spain terminó en España.

ending ['endɪŋ] *noun* ■ el **final**: the film has a happy ending la película tiene un final feliz.

enemy ['enɪmɪ] *(plural* enemies*) noun* ■ el **enemigo**, la **enemiga**.

energetic [,enə'dʒetɪk] *adjective*
1. **lleno de energía**: a very energetic person una persona llena de energía
2. **enérgico**: a very energetic exercise un ejercicio muy enérgico.

energy ['enədʒɪ] *uncountable noun*
1. la **energía**: water is a source of energy el agua es una fuente de energía
2. las **energías**: I don't have the energy to go out no tengo energías para salir; **we should try and save energy** deberíamos intentar ahorrar energía; **alternative energy** energía alternativa.

engaged [ɪn'geɪdʒd] *adjective*
1. **comprometido**: they are engaged están comprometidos
2. *UK* **ocupado**: the line is engaged la línea está ocupada
▷ **to get engaged** comprometerse: they have just got engaged acaban de comprometerse.

engagement [ɪn'geɪdʒmənt] *noun* ■ el **compromiso**
▷ **engagement ring** anillo de compromiso.

engine ['endʒɪn] *noun*
1. el **motor**: their car has a powerful engine su coche tiene un motor potente
2. la **locomotora**: a steam engine una locomotora a vapor.

engineer [ˌendʒɪ'nɪəʳ] *noun* ■ el **ingeniero**, la **ingeniera**: the engineer that designed the bridge el ingeniero que diseñó el puente.

England ['ɪŋglənd] *noun* ■ **Inglaterra**.

English ['ɪŋglɪʃ] *(adjective & noun)*
■ *adjective*

Remember not to use a capital letter for the adjective or the language in Spanish:

inglés: the English countryside la campiña inglesa
■ *noun*

In Spanish, a capital letter is not used for the inhabitants of a country or region:

el **inglés**: do you speak English? ¿hablas inglés?
▷ **the English** los ingleses.

Englishman ['ɪŋglɪʃmən] *(plural* Englishmen ['ɪŋglɪʃmən]*) noun* ■ el **inglés** *(plural* los **ingleses***)*.

Englishwoman ['ɪŋglɪʃˌwʊmən] *(plural* Englishwomen ['ɪŋglɪʃˌwɪmɪn]*) noun* ■ la **inglesa**.

enjoy [ɪn'dʒɔɪ] *verb*
1. **disfrutar**: I enjoy listening to music disfruto escuchando música
2. **gustar**: she enjoyed the book le gustó el libro
▷ **to enjoy oneself** divertirse: I really enjoyed myself at the party realmente me divertí en la fiesta.

enormous [ɪ'nɔːməs] *adjective* ■ **enorme**.

enough [ɪ'nʌf] *(adjective, adverb & pronoun)*
■ *adjective*
suficiente: do you have enough money? ¿tienes suficiente dinero?; **there isn't enough room** no hay suficiente espacio
■ *adverb & pronoun*
suficiente: would you like some more or have you got enough? ¿quieres más o tienes suficiente?
▷ **that's enough!** ¡basta ya!

enquire *UK* [ɪn'kwaɪəʳ] *verb*
▷ **to enquire about something** informarse sobre algo: he enquired about the departure time se informó sobre la hora de salida.

enquiry [ɪn'kwaɪərɪ] *(plural* enquiries*) noun* ■ la **investigación**, la **pregunta**
▷ **to make enquiries** hacer averiguaciones.

enter ['entəʳ] *verb*
1. **entrar**: he knocked on the door and entered llamó a la puerta y entró
2. **entrar en**: everyone looked at her when she entered the room todos la miraron cuando entró en la habitación
3. **presentarse a**: I entered a competition me presenté a un concurso
4. **introducir**: enter your password and click on OK introduzca su contraseña y haga clic en "OK"
▷ **the enter key** la tecla "enter".

entertainment [ˌentə'teɪnmənt] *noun* ■ el **entretenimiento**: this film is good family entertainment la película es un buen entretenimiento para toda la familia
▷ **the entertainment business** la industria del espectáculo.

enthusiasm [ɪn'θjuːzɪæzm] *noun* ■ el entusiasmo.

enthusiastic [ɪnˌθjuːzɪ'æstɪk] *adjective* ■ entusiasta.

entire [ɪn'taɪəʳ] *adjective* ■ entero: he ate an entire chicken se comió un pollo entero.

entirely [ɪn'taɪəlɪ] *adverb* ■ completamente: it's entirely my fault el error es completamente mío.

entrance ['entrəns] *noun* ■ la entrada: wait for me at the school entrance espérame en la entrada del colegio

an entrance exam un examen de ingreso.

entry ['entrɪ] *noun* ■ la entrada

no entry prohibida la entrada.

entryphone ['entrɪfəʊn] *noun* ■ el portero automático.

envelope ['envələʊp] *noun* ■ el sobre: he put the letter in the envelope puso la carta en el sobre.

environment [ɪn'vaɪərənmənt] *noun*

the environment el medio ambiente: we must protect the environment debemos proteger el medio ambiente.

episode ['epɪsəʊd] *noun* ■ el episodio: the first episode is on TV tonight esta noche dan el primer episodio por la tele.

equal ['iːkwəl] *(adjective & verb)*

■ *adjective*
igual: I divided the cake into two equal parts corté el pastel en dos partes iguales
equal opportunities igualdad de oportunidades

■ *verb*
ser igual a: 4 plus 5 equals 9 4 más 5 es igual a 9.

equator [ɪ'kweɪtəʳ] *noun* ■ el ecuador.

equipment [ɪ'kwɪpmənt] *uncountable noun* ■ el equipo: camping equipment equipo de acampada.

equivalent [ɪ'kwɪvələnt] *(adjective & noun)*
■ *adjective*
equivalente

to be equivalent to something equivaler a algo: this is equivalent to 5 pounds esto equivale a 5 libras
■ *noun*
el equivalente: it costs the equivalent of 50 dollars cuesta el equivalente a 50 dólares.

eraser [ɪ'reɪzəʳ] *noun* ■ la goma: have you seen my eraser? ¿has visto mi goma?

error ['erəʳ] *noun* ■ el error

a printing error un error de imprenta.

erupt [ɪ'rʌpt] *verb* ■ entrar en erupción: the volcano erupted el volcán entró en erupción.

escalator ['eskəleɪtəʳ] *noun* ■ la escalera mecánica.

escape [ɪ'skeɪp] *(noun & verb)*
■ *noun*
la fuga: the escape of the prisoners la fuga de los prisioneros
I had a narrow escape me salvé por un pelo
■ *verb*
1. escaparse: a monkey escaped from the zoo un mono se escapó del zoológico
2. fugarse: he escaped from prison se fugó de la cárcel.

especially [ɪ'speʃəlɪ] *adverb* ■ especialmente: I like all animals, especially horses me gustan todos los animales, especialmente los caballos.

essay ['eseɪ] *noun* ■ la redacción *(plural* las redacciones*)*: an essay on the environment una redacción sobre el medio ambiente.

estimate ['estɪmeɪt] *verb* ■ calcular: he estimated the price at 500 euros calculó el precio en 500 euros.

EU ['iːjuː] *(abbreviation of* European Union*)* *noun* ■ la Unión Europea.

euro ['jʊərəʊ] *(plural* euro OR euros*)* *noun* ■ el euro: it costs 50 euros cuesta 50 euros.

Europe ['jʊərəp] *noun* ■ Europa.

European [ˌjʊərə'piːən] *(adjective & noun)*
■ *adjective*
Remember not to use a capital letter for the adjective in Spanish:

europeo: the European continent el continente europeo
> the European Union la Unión Europea
◼ *noun*

In Spanish, a capital letter is not used for the inhabitants of a country or region:

el **europeo,** la **europea:** many Europeans travel frequently muchos europeos viajan con frecuencia.

eve [iːv] *noun* ◼ la **víspera**
> Christmas Eve Nochebuena
> New Year's Eve Nochevieja.

even [ˈiːvn] *(adjective & adverb)*
◼ *adjective*
1. **liso:** the surface is even la superficie es lisa
2. **par:** four is an even number el cuatro es un número par
> their chances are about even tienen casi las mismas posibilidades
> to get even with somebody vengarse de alguien
◼ *adverb*
1. **incluso:** it has everything, even a tennis court tiene de todo, incluso una pista de tenis
2. **aún:** it's even better now ahora está aún mejor; it's even more difficult es aún más difícil
> not even ni siquiera: he can't even sing ni siquiera sabe cantar

Aunque is followed by a verb in the subjunctive in Spanish when it means "even if".

> even if aunque: even if he comes it won't make any difference aunque venga, no habrá ninguna diferencia
> even though a pesar de que: he went to school even though he wasn't well fue al colegio a pesar de que no se encontraba bien.

evening [ˈiːvnɪŋ] *noun*
1. *before dark* la **tarde:** at 6 in the evening a las 6 de la tarde; I'm staying at home this evening esta tarde me quedo en casa; yesterday evening ayer por la tarde
2. *after dark* la **noche:** at 10 o'clock in the evening a las 10 de la noche
> good evening! ¡buenas noches!
> evening classes clases nocturnas.

event [ɪˈvent] *noun*
1. el **acontecimiento:** it's an important event es un acontecimiento importante
2. la **prueba:** he participated in three events at the athletics meeting participó en tres pruebas en el encuentro de atletismo.

eventual [ɪˈventʃʊəl] *adjective* ◼ **final:** the eventual conclusions will be published las conclusiones finales serán publicadas.

eventually [ɪˈventʃʊəlɪ] *adverb* ◼ **finalmente:** he left eventually finalmente se fue.

ever [ˈevəʳ] *adverb*
1. **nunca:** nothing ever happens nunca pasa nada; I hardly ever watch television casi nunca veo televisión
2. **jamás:** it's the best film I've ever seen es la mejor película que he visto jamás
3. **alguna vez:** have you ever been to China? ¿has estado alguna vez en China?
> as ever como siempre: she's as cheerful as ever está tan alegre como siempre
> for ever para siempre: he left for ever se fue para siempre
> ever since desde que: it's been raining ever since I arrived ha estado lloviendo desde que llegué.

every [ˈevrɪ] *adjective* ◼ **todos**

"Every" + a singular noun is usually translated by **todos los** or **todas las** + a plural noun in Spanish. You can also use **cada** + singular noun, if you want to emphasize that you mean "every single one":

every student in the class passed the exam todos los estudiantes de la clase aprobaron el examen; every house in the street has a garden todas las casas de esta calle tienen un jardín; every student recited a different poem cada estudiante recitó un poema diferente
> every day todos los días
> every other day un día sí y otro no
> every time cada vez: he wins every time cada vez gana
> every time that cada vez que: every time that I go to London I visit my uncle cada vez que voy a Londres visito a mi tío.

everybody ['evrɪ,bɒdɪ], **everyone** ['evrɪwʌn] *pronoun* ■ **todos:** everybody knows him todos lo conocen; everyone was enjoying themselves todos se estaban divirtiendo.

everyplace *US adverb* ➤ everywhere.

everything ['evrɪθɪŋ] *pronoun* ■ **todo:** do you have everything? ¿lo tienes todo?; I've told you everything I know te he dicho todo lo que sé.

everywhere ['evrɪweəʳ], **everyplace** *US* ['evrɪ,pleɪs] *adverb*
1. **en todas partes:** I've looked for it everywhere lo he buscado en todas partes
2. **dondequiera que:** she follows me everywhere I go ella me sigue dondequiera que vaya

Dondequiera que is followed by a verb in the subjunctive.

evidence ['evɪdəns] *uncountable noun*
1. **las pruebas:** there's no evidence that he robbed the bank no hay pruebas de que él haya atracado el banco
2. **el testimonio:** his evidence was very important in the case su testimonio era muy importante para el caso.

evil ['iːvl] *(adjective & noun)*
■ *adjective*
malvado: he's an evil man es un hombre malvado
■ *noun*
el **mal: to tell good from evil** distinguir el bien del mal.

exact [ɪg'zækt] *adjective* ■ **exacto: what is the exact time?** ¿cuál es la hora exacta?

exactly [ɪg'zæktlɪ] *adverb* ■ **exactamente:** that's exactly what I mean eso es exactamente lo que quiero decir
it's exactly 6 o'clock son las 6 en punto.

exaggerate [ɪg'zædʒəreɪt] *verb* ■ **exagerar:** don't exaggerate! ¡no exageres!

exam [ɪg'zæm], **examination** [ɪg,zæmɪ'neɪʃn] *noun* ■ el **examen** *(plural* los **exámenes)*. I passed my English exam aprobé el examen de inglés.

examine [ɪg'zæmɪn] *verb* ■ **examinar:** he examined the fly through the microscope examinó la mosca por el microscopio.

example [*UK* ɪg'zɑːmpl, *US* ɪg'zæmpl] *noun* ■ el **ejemplo**
for example por ejemplo.

excellent ['eksələnt] *adjective* ■ **excelente:** she's an excellent teacher es una profesora excelente.

except [ɪk'sept] *preposition & conjunction* ■ **excepto:** everyone can swim except me todos saben nadar excepto yo
except that salvo que: I don't remember anything except that I was scared no recuerdo nada salvo que tenía miedo.

exception [ɪk'sepʃn] *noun* ■ la **excepción** *(plural* las **excepciones)*: it's an exception to the rule es una excepción a la regla
to make an exception hacer una excepción: I'll make an exception for you haré una excepción contigo.

exchange [ɪks'tʃeɪndʒ] *(verb & noun)*
■ *verb*
cambiar: she exchanged the CD for a book cambió el CD por un libro
■ *noun*
I gave him a camera in exchange for a watch le di una cámara a cambio de un reloj
the exchange rate la tasa de cambio.

excited [ɪk'saɪtɪd] *adjective* ■ **entusiasmado.**

exciting [ɪk'saɪtɪŋ] *adjective* ■ **emocionante.**

exclamation mark *UK* [,eksklə'meɪʃnmɑːk], **exclamation point** *US* [,eksklə'meɪʃnpɔɪnt] *noun* ■ el **signo de exclamación.**

excuse *(noun & verb)*
■ *noun* [ɪk'skjuːs]
la **excusa: that's just an excuse!** ¡eso no es más que una excusa!
■ *verb* [ɪk'skjuːz]
disculpar: excuse me! ¡discúlpeme!

exercise ['eksəsaɪz] *noun* ■ el **ejercicio:** he doesn't get enough exercise no hace suficiente ejercicio.

exhausted [ɪg'zɔːstɪd] *adjective* ■ **agotado:** I'm exhausted estoy agotado.

exhausting [ɪg'zɔːstɪŋ] *adjective* ■ **agotador:** the work is exhausting el trabajo es agotador.

exhaust pipe [ɪg'zɔːspaɪp] *noun* ■ el tubo de escape.

exhibit *US* [ɪg'zɪbɪt] *noun* ■ la **exposición** *(plural* las **exposiciones)***:* there's a big exhibit in New York hay una gran exposición en Nueva York.

exist [ɪg'zɪst] *verb* ■ **existir:** that company doesn't exist anymore esa compañía ya no existe.

exit ['eksɪt] *noun* ■ la **salida**

 Exit es un falso amigo, no significa "éxito".

exotic [ɪg'zɒtɪk] *adjective* ■ **exótico.**

expect [ɪk'spekt] *verb*
1. **esperar:** I wasn't expecting his visit no esperaba su visita; she's expecting a baby está esperando un bebé

The verb **esperar** is followed by a verb in the subjunctive in Spanish:

I was expecting him to be here esperaba que él estuviera aquí

2. **suponer que:** I expect he has left the country supongo que ha salido del país; I expect so supongo que sí.

expel [ɪk'spel] *(past tense & past participle* expelled, *present participle* expelling*) verb* ■ **expulsar:** they expelled Fred from school expulsaron a Fred del colegio.

expenses [ɪk'spensəz] *plural noun* ■ los gastos: we pay your travel expenses te pagamos los gastos de viaje.

expensive [ɪk'spensɪv] *adjective* ■ **caro:** this dress is too expensive este vestido es demasiado caro.

experience [ɪk'spɪərɪəns] *noun* ■ la **experiencia:** he has a lot of experience tiene mucha experiencia.

experiment [ɪk'sperɪmənt] *(noun & verb)*
■ *noun*
el **experimento:** they did an experiment in the laboratory hicieron un experimento en el laboratorio
■ *verb*
experimentar: she experimented with drugs experimentó con las drogas.

expert ['ekspɜːt] *noun* ■ el **experto:** he's a computer expert es experto en ordenadores.

explain [ɪk'spleɪn] *verb* ■ **explicar:** can you explain what happened? ¿puedes explicar lo que ocurrió?

explanation [ˌeksplə'neɪʃn] *noun* ■ la **explicación** *(plural* las **explicaciones)***:* I demand an explanation exijo una explicación.

explode [ɪk'spləʊd] *verb*
1. **estallar:** the bomb exploded la bomba estalló
2. **hacer estallar:** the police exploded the bomb la policía hizo estallar la bomba.

exploit *(noun&verb)*
■ *noun* ['eksplɔɪt]
la **hazaña**
■ *verb* [ɪk'splɔɪt]
explotar: they exploit their workers explotan a sus trabajadores.

explore [ɪk'splɔːʳ] *verb* ■ **explorar:** they explored the ruins exploraron las ruinas.

explorer [ɪk'splɔːrəʳ] *noun* ■ el **explorador,** la **exploradora.**

explosion [ɪk'spləʊʒn] *noun* ■ la **explosión** *(plural* las **explosiones)** .

export [ɪk'spɔːt] *verb* ■ **exportar:** Brazil exports coffee Brasil exporta café.

express [ɪk'spres] *(adjective & verb)*
■ *adjective*
expreso: an express train un tren expreso
■ *verb*

expresar: she expressed her feelings expresó sus sentimientos

> **to express oneself** expresarse: he expresses himself well in Spanish se expresa bien en español.

expression [ɪkˈspreʃn] noun ■ la **expresión** (plural las **expresiones**): it's a common expression es una expresión común; her expression changed le cambió la expresión; she had a funny expression on her face tenía una expresión curiosa en la cara.

expressway US [ɪkˈspresweɪ] noun ■ la **autopista.**

extend [ɪkˈstend] verb

1. **prolongar:** I'm going to extend my stay voy a prolongar mi estancia
2. **tender:** he extended his hand tendió la mano
3. **extenderse:** the plain extends to the mountain la llanura se extiende hasta la montaña.

extension [ɪkˈstenʃn] noun

1. la **ampliación** (plural las **ampliaciones**): we've built an extension hicimos una ampliación
2. la **extensión:** you can call me on extension 429 me puedes llamar a la extensión 429.

extent [ɪkˈstent] noun

> **to a certain extent** hasta cierto punto: to a certain extent you're right hasta cierto punto tienes razón.

exterior [ɪkˈstɪərɪər] adjective ■ **exterior:** an exterior wall un muro exterior.

extinct [ɪkˈstɪŋkt] adjective ■ **extinguido:** this species is extinct esta especie está extinguida

> **to become extinct** extinguirse: that type of whale is becoming extinct ese tipo de ballenas se está extinguiendo.

extra [ˈekstrə] (adjective, adverb & noun)
■ adjective

1. **extra:** he's taking extra lessons está asistiendo a clases extra
2. **de más:** I have an extra pencil tengo un lápiz de más

■ adverb
más: it's worth paying extra for quality vale la pena pagar más para obtener mayor calidad
■ noun

1. el **suplemento:** the price is fixed and there are no extras el precio es fijo y no hay suplementos
2. el/la **extra:** he's an extra in the film es un extra en la película.

extraordinary [ɪkˈstrɔːdnrɪ] adjective ■ **extraordinario.**

extravagant [ɪkˈstrævəgənt] adjective

1. **derrochador:** he's very extravagant with his money es muy derrochador con su dinero
2. **extravagante:** he wears very extravagant outfits usa ropas muy extravagantes.

extreme [ɪkˈstriːm] (adjective & noun)
■ adjective
extremo: extreme sports deportes extremos
■ noun
el **extremo:** she goes from one extreme to another va de un extremo a otro.

extremely [ɪkˈstriːmlɪ] adverb ■ **sumamente:** it's an extremely interesting book es un libro sumamente interesante.

eye [aɪ] noun ■ el **ojo:** she has green eyes tiene ojos verdes

> **to keep an eye on something** vigilar algo: can you keep an eye on my luggage? ¿puedes vigilar mi equipaje?

eyebrow [ˈaɪbraʊ] noun ■ la **ceja.**

eyedrops [ˈaɪdrɒps] plural noun ■ el **colirio.**

eyelash [ˈaɪlæʃ] (plural eyelashes) noun ■ la **pestaña:** she has long eyelashes tiene las pestañas largas.

eyelid [ˈaɪlɪd] noun ■ el **párpado.**

eyesight [ˈaɪsaɪt] noun ■ la **vista:** he has good eyesight tiene buena vista.

eyewitness [ˌaɪˈwɪtnɪs] noun ■ el/la **testigo ocular.**

fabric ['fæbrɪk] *noun* ■ la **tela**, el **tejido**: cotton fabric tela de algodón

 Fabric es un falso amigo, no significa "fábrica".

fabulous ['fæbjʊləs] *adjective* ■ **fabuloso**: we had a fabulous evening pasamos una tarde fabulosa.

face [feɪs] *(noun & verb)*

■ *noun*

1. la **cara**: she has a beautiful face tiene una cara hermosa
2. la **mueca**: he made a face hizo una mueca
3. la **esfera**: the clock face is broken la esfera del reloj está rota

■ *verb*

1. **enfrentarse**: we must face these problems tenemos que enfrentarnos a estos problemas
2. **dar a**: our house faces the sea nuestra casa da al mar

   face to face cara a cara

   to face somebody OR something volverse hacia alguien OR algo

face up to *phrasal verb* ■ **afrontar**: he faced up to the problem afrontó el problema.

facilities [fə'sɪlətɪz] *plural noun* ■ las **instalaciones**: the school has good sports facilities el colegio tiene buenas instalaciones deportivas.

fact [fækt] *noun*

1. el **hecho**: that's a fact es un hecho
2. *(uncountable noun)* la **realidad**: fact and fiction realidad y ficción
▸ in fact de hecho.

factory ['fæktərɪ] *(plural* factories*) noun* ■ la **fábrica**: a car factory una fábrica de coches.

fade [feɪd] *verb*

1. **desteñirse**: your jeans have faded se te han desteñido los vaqueros
2. **apagarse**: the light is fading la luz se está apagando
3. **perder intensidad**: the colour has faded with time el color ha perdido intensidad con el tiempo.

fail [feɪl] *verb*

1. **suspender**: he failed the exam suspendió el examen
2. **fracasar**: I tried to persuade him but I failed traté de convencerlo, pero fracasé
3. **fallar**: the brakes failed los frenos fallaron
▸ to fail to do something no lograr hacer algo: I failed to convince him no logré convencerlo
▸ the letter failed to arrive la carta no llegó.

failure ['feɪljər] *noun* ■ el **fracaso**: it ended in failure terminó en fracaso; he's a failure es un fracasado
▸ a power failure un apagón.

faint [feɪnt] *(adjective & verb)*

■ *adjective*

1. **leve**: there's a faint smell of smoke hay un leve olor a humo
2. **borroso**: the text is too faint to read el texto está demasiado borroso para poder leerlo
3. **débil**: your voice is a bit faint tu voz es un poco débil
4. **tenue**: a faint light una luz tenue
▸ to feel faint sentirse mareado: he suddenly felt faint de pronto, se sintió mareado

■ *verb*

   desmayarse: she fainted se desmayó.

fair [feər] *(adjective & noun)*

■ *adjective*

1. **justo**: it's not fair! ¡no es justo!
2. **bastante**: she has a fair chance of winning tiene bastantes posibilidades de ganar
3. **rubio**: Donald has fair hair Donald tiene el pelo rubio
4. **blanco**: Carol has fair skin Carol tiene la piel blanca
5. **buen**: the weather is fair hace buen tiempo

◾ *noun*

la **feria**: we went to the book **fair** fuimos a la feria del libro.

fairly [ˈfeəlɪ] *adverb*

1. **bastante**: it's fairly late es bastante tarde
2. **justamente**: he was fairly treated fue justamente tratado
3. **equitativamente**: they divided the money fairly repartieron el dinero equitativamente.

fairy [ˈfeərɪ] *(plural* fairies*) noun* ◾ el **hada** *(feminine)*

➤ a **fairy tale** un cuento de hadas.

faith [feɪθ] *noun*

1. la **confianza**: I've lost faith in him perdí la confianza en él
2. la **fe**: the Christian faith la fe cristiana.

faithful [ˈfeɪθfʊl] *adjective* ◾ **fiel.**

fake [feɪk] *(adjective & noun)*

◾ *adjective*

falso: these pearls are fake estas perlas son falsas

◾ *noun*

la **falsificación** *(plural* las **falsificaciones***)*: this painting is a fake esta pintura es una falsificación.

fall [fɔːl] *(noun & verb)*

◾ *noun*

1. la **caída**: a hard fall una fuerte caída; he had a fall sufrió una caída
2. *US* el **otoño**: in the fall en otoño

◾ *verb (past tense* fell*, past participle* fallen*)*

1. **caerse**: I slipped and fell me resbalé y me caí
2. **bajar**: the temperature has fallen ha bajado la temperatura

➤ to **fall asleep** dormirse: she fell asleep se durmió

➤ to **fall in love** enamorarse: he fell in love with Britney se enamoró de Britney

fall down *phrasal verb* ◾ **caerse**: the little girl fell down la niña se cayó

fall off *phrasal verb* ◾ **caerse**: he fell off his bicycle se cayó de la bicicleta

fall out *phrasal verb*

1. **caerse**: the keys fell out of my pocket se me cayeron las llaves del bolsillo

2. **pelearse**: he's fallen out with his best friend se peleó con su mejor amigo

fall over *phrasal verb*

1. **caerse**: the vase fell over se cayó el jarrón
2. **tropezarse**: he fell over a log se tropezó con un tronco.

fallen [ˈfɔːln] *past participle* ➤ fall.

false [fɔːls] *adjective*

1. **falso**: what he said is false lo que dijo es falso
2. **postizo**: he has false teeth tiene la dentadura postiza.

fame [feɪm] *noun* ◾ la **fama.**

familiar [fəˈmɪljəʳ] *adjective* ◾ **familiar**: your face is familiar to me tu cara me es familiar.

family [ˈfæmlɪ] *(plural* families*) noun* ◾ la **familia**: the Smith family la familia Smith.

famous [ˈfeɪməs] *adjective* ◾ **famoso**: she's a famous artist es una artista famosa.

fan [fæn] *(noun*

1. el **abanico**: she was holding a fan llevaba un abanico
2. el **ventilador**: an electric fan un ventilador eléctrico
3. el/la **fan**, el **admirador**, la **admiradora**: she's a fan of the Beatles es una fan de los Beatles
4. el/la **hincha**: soccer fans hinchas de fútbol.

fancy [ˈfænsɪ] *(adjective & verb)*

◾ *adjective*

1. **extravagante**: she's wearing a fancy hat lleva un sombrero extravagante
2. **elegante**: they went to a fancy restaurant fueron a un restaurante elegante

➤ **fancy dress** *UK* el disfraz: she was in fancy dress iba disfrazada

➤ a **fancy dress party** una fiesta de disfraces

◾ *verb UK informal*

1. **apetecer**: do you fancy going to see a film? ¿te apetece ir a ver una película?
2. **gustar**: he fancies the girl next door le gusta la vecina de al lado.

fantastic [fænˈtæstɪk] *adjective* ◾ **fantástico**: we had a fantastic evening pasamos una velada fantástica.

far [fɑːʳ] *(comparative* farther, further, *superlative* farthest, furthest*) (adverb & adjective)*

■ *adverb*

1. **lejos:** is the bank far? ¿está lejos el banco?; it's not far OR it's not far away no queda lejos; Oxford isn't far from London Oxford no queda lejos de Londres

2. **mucho:** I feel far better me siento mucho mejor

➤ **how far is it?** ¿a qué distancia está?: **how far is it to Miami?** ¿a qué distancia está de Miami?

➤ **as far as I know** que yo sepa: she's not coming, as far as I know no va a venir, que yo sepa

➤ **so far** hasta ahora: so far so good hasta ahora, todo bien

➤ **that's far too much** es demasiado

■ *adjective*

extremo: the far right la extrema derecha

➤ **at the far end of the road** al otro extremo de la calle

➤ **the Far East** el Extremo Oriente

➤ **in the far north** en el extremo norte.

fare [feəʳ] *noun* ■ la **tarifa:** the fares have gone up las tarifas han subido; the train fare to London la tarifa de tren a Londres.

farm [fɑːm] *noun* ■ la **granja.**

farmer ['fɑːməʳ] *noun* ■ el **agricultor,** la **agricultora.**

farmhouse ['fɑːmhaʊs] *noun* ■ la **granja.**

farming ['fɑːmɪŋ] *(noun* ■ la **agricultura.**

farther ['fɑːðəʳ] *(comparative of* far) *(adverb & adjective)*

■ *adverb*

más lejos: we have to walk a bit farther tenemos que andar un poco más lejos

■ *adjective*

más alejado: on the farther side of the room en la parte más alejada de la habitación.

farthest ['fɑːðəst] *(superlative of* far) *(adverb & adjective)*

■ *adverb*

lo más lejos: he went the farthest he could fue lo más lejos que pudo

■ *adjective*

el más alejado: the farthest tree from the house el árbol más alejado de la casa.

fascinating ['fæsɪneɪtɪŋ] *adjective* ■ **fascinante.**

fashion ['fæʃn] *noun* ■ la **moda:** it's the latest fashion es la última moda

➤ **in fashion** de moda: this coat is in fashion este abrigo está de moda

➤ **it has gone out of fashion** ha pasado de moda: that hairstyle has gone out of fashion este corte de pelo ha pasado de moda

➤ **a fashion show** un desfile de moda.

fashionable ['fæʃnəbl] *adjective* ■ **de moda:** she likes to buy fashionable clothes le gusta comprar ropa de moda.

fast [*UK* fɑːst, *US* fæst] *(adjective & adverb)*

■ *adjective*

rápido: this train is very fast este tren es muy rápido

➤ **my watch is fast** mi reloj va adelantado; the clock is ten minutes fast el reloj va adelantado diez minutos

➤ **fast food** comida rápida

➤ **a fast-food restaurant** un restaurante de comida rápida

■ *adverb*

rápido: he works fast trabaja rápido

➤ **to be fast asleep** estar profundamente dormido: the baby is fast asleep el bebé está profundamente dormido.

fasten [*UK* 'fɑːsn, *US* 'fæsn] *verb*

1. **abrocharse:** fasten your seat belts abróchense los cinturones

2. **cerrar:** she fastened her bag cerró su bolso.

fat [fæt] *(comparative* fatter, *superlative* fattest*) (adjective & noun)*

■ *adjective*

gordo: he's very fat es muy gordo

➤ **to get fat** engordar: she doesn't want to get fat no quiere engordar

■ *noun*

la grasa: there's too much fat on this ham este jamón tiene mucha grasa; gelatine contains no fat la gelatina no contiene grasas

➤ **a low-fat yoghurt** un yogur desnatado.

fatal ['feɪtl] *adjective*
1. **mortal**: he had a fatal accident tuvo un accidente mortal
2. **fatídico**: it was a fatal mistake fue un error fatídico.

father ['fɑːðəʳ] *noun* ■ el **padre**
➤ Father's Day el Día del Padre.

father-in-law ['fɑːðəʳɪnlɔː] *(plural fathers-in-law) noun* ■ el **suegro**.

fattening ['fætnɪŋ] *adjective*
➤ to be fattening engordar: cakes are fattening los pasteles engordan.

fault ['fɔːlt] *noun*
1. la **culpa**: whose fault is it? ¿de quién es la culpa?; it's my fault yo tengo la culpa
2. el **defecto**: he has many faults tiene muchos defectos.

favour *UK*, **favor** *US* ['feɪvəʳ] *noun* ■ el **favor**
➤ to do somebody a favour hacerle un favor a alguien: can you do me a favour? ¿puedes hacerme un favor?
➤ to be in favour of something estar a favor de algo: we're all in favour of world peace todos estamos a favor de la paz mundial.

favourite *UK*, **favorite** *US* ['feɪvrɪt] *(adjective & noun)*
■ *adjective*
favorito: purple is my favourite colour el violeta es mi color favorito
■ *noun*
el **favorito**, la **favorita**: let's listen to this CD, it's my favourite escuchemos este CD, es mi favorito.

fax [fæks] *(noun & verb)*
■ *noun*
el **fax**: he sent me a fax me envió un fax
➤ a fax machine un fax
■ *verb*
enviar por fax: I faxed the letter to Eric le envié la carta a Eric por fax.

fear [fɪəʳ] *(noun & verb)*
■ *noun*
el **miedo**: have no fear! ¡no tengas miedo!
■ *verb*
temer: she fears nothing no le teme a nada.

feast [fiːst] *noun*
1. el **banquete**
2. la **festividad**: the feast of San Juan la festividad de San Juan.

feather ['feðəʳ] *noun* ■ la **pluma**.

feature ['fiːtʃəʳ] *noun*
1. la **característica**: an interesting feature of the landscape una característica interesante del paisaje
2. el **rasgo**: she has fine features tiene rasgos delicados.

February ['februərɪ] *noun*

In Spanish the months of the year do not start with a capital letter:

febrero *(masculine)*: in February en febrero; next February el próximo febrero; last February el pasado febrero.

fed [fed] *past tense & past participle* ➤ **feed**

fed up ['fedʌp] *adjective* ■ *informal*
➤ to be fed up estar harto: I'm fed up! ¡estoy harta!
➤ to be fed up with something estar harto de algo: I'm fed up with waiting estoy harto de esperar.

feed [fiːd] *(past tense & past participle fed) verb*
■ **alimentar**: she's feeding the dogs está alimentando a los perros.

feel [fiːl] *(past tense & past participle felt) verb*
1. **sentirse**: how do you feel? ¿cómo te sientes?; I don't feel very well no me siento muy bien

When "feel" is used with certain adjectives (cold, hot, hungry or thirsty), you should translate it with the Spanish verb **tener**:

I feel cold tengo frío; my hands feel cold tengo las manos frías; do you feel hungry? ¿tienes hambre?

2.

When you are describing how something feels to the touch, you should use the verb **ser** or **estar**:

this bed feels very hard esta cama es muy dura; the water feels cold el agua está fría
3. **sentir**: I felt the ground shake sentí la sacudida del suelo

4. tocar: he felt his pockets se tocó los bolsillos
➤ to feel as if OR to feel as though tener la sensación de que: I feel as if I'm going to faint tengo la sensación de que me voy a desmayar
➤ to feel like doing something tener ganas de hacer algo: I feel like going to bed tengo ganas de irme a la cama.

feeling ['fiːlɪŋ] *noun*
1. el **sentimiento**: a feeling of sadness un sentimiento de tristeza
2. la **sensación** *(plural* las **sensaciones)*: I have a funny feeling in my leg tengo una sensación extraña en la pierna.

feet *plural* ➤ foot.

fell [fel] *past tense* ➤ fall.

fellow ['feləʊ] *(adjective & noun)*
■ *adjective*
➤ a fellow countryman un compatriota
➤ a fellow student un compañero de estudios
➤ a fellow worker un compañero de trabajo
■ *noun*
tipo: he's a fine fellow es un buen tipo.

felt [felt] *(noun & verb)*
■ *noun*
el **fieltro**
■ *past tense & past participle*
➤ feel.

felt-tip pen ['felttɪppen] *noun* ■ el **rotulador**.

female ['fiːmeɪl] *(noun & adjective)*
■ *noun*
la hembra
■ *adjective*
1. hembra: a female kangaroo un canguro hembra
2. femenino: I heard a female voice oí una voz femenina
➤ a female student una estudiante.

feminine ['femɪnɪn] *adjective* ■ **femenino.**

fence [fens] *noun* ■ la **valla.**

Ferris wheel ['ferɪswiːl] *noun* ■ la **noria.**

ferry ['ferɪ] *(plural* ferries) *noun* ■ el **ferry** *(plural* los **ferrys)*: we took the ferry to Santander cogimos el ferry a Santander.

festival ['festəvl] *noun* ■ el **festival:** there's a film festival in Leeds next week hay un festival de cine en Leeds la próxima semana.

fever ['fiːvər] *noun* ■ la **fiebre: Chris has a fever** Chris tiene fiebre.

few [fjuː] *(comparative* fewer, *superlative* fewest) *(adjective & pronoun)*
■ *adjective*
pocos: few people come here aquí vienen pocas personas
➤ a few unos cuantos: a few people came vinieron unas cuantas personas
➤ I need a few books necesito unos cuantos libros
■ *pronoun*
pocos: few of them agree pocos están de acuerdo
➤ a few unos pocos: a few stayed till the end unos pocos se quedaron hasta el final.

fewer ['fjuːər] *(adjective & pronoun)*
■ *adjective*
menos: we have fewer problems than last year tenemos menos problemas que el año pasado
■ *pronoun*
menos: I have a lot fewer than you tengo mucho menos que tú.

fewest ['fjuːəst] *(adjective & pronoun)*
■ *adjective*
➤ the fewest mistakes possible el menor número de faltas posibles
■ *pronoun*
menos: I have the fewest soy la que menos tengo.

fiancé [fɪ'ɒnseɪ] *noun* ■ el **prometido.**

fiancée [fɪ'ɒnseɪ] *noun* ■ la **prometida.**

fiction ['fɪkʃn] *uncountable noun* ■ la **ficción:** he can't distinguish between fact and fiction no puede distinguir la realidad de la ficción; he reads a lot of fiction lee mucha ficción.

fidget ['fɪdʒɪt] *verb* ■ **moverse ruidosamente**
➤ stop fidgeting! ¡estate quieto!

field [fiːld] *noun* ■ el **campo:** they grow corn in that field cultivan maíz en ese campo; she's an expert in that field es experta en ese campo; they're playing on the football field están jugando en el campo de fútbol.

fierce [fɪəs] *adjective*
1. **feroz:** a fierce animal un animal feroz
2. **violento:** it was a fierce battle fue una batalla violenta.

fifteen [fɪf'tiːn] *number* ■ **quince:** fifteen people came to the party quince personas vinieron a la fiesta
she's fifteen tiene quince años.

fifteenth [fɪf'tiːnθ] *number* ■ **decimo-quinto:** he was the fifteenth person to arrive fue la decimoquinta persona en llegar
it's the fifteenth of May *UK* OR it's May fifteenth *US* es el quince de mayo .

fifth [fɪfθ] *number* ■ **quinto:** he came fifth llegó quinto
it's the fifth of November *UK* OR it's November fifth es el 5 de noviembre.

fifty ['fɪftɪ] *number* ■ **cincuenta:** there were fifty people in the classroom había cincuenta personas en la clase
she's fifty tiene cincuenta años
fifty-one cincuenta y uno
fifty-two cincuenta y dos.

fight [faɪt] *(noun & verb)*
■ *noun*
1. **la lucha:** the fight against disease la lucha contra la enfermedad
2. **la pelea:** there was a fight in the street hubo una pelea en la calle
to have a fight pelearse: he had a fight with his brother se peleó con su hermano
■ *verb (past tense & past participle* fought*)*
1. **pelear:** they were fighting in the street estaban peleando en la calle
2. **luchar contra:** we must fight against apathy debemos luchar contra la apatía.

figure [*UK* 'fɪgər, *US* 'fɪgjər] *(noun & verb)*
■ *noun*
1. **la cifra:** I added up the figures you gave me sumé las cifras que me diste
2. **la figura:** he's a well-known figure in politics es una figura muy conocida en política; she's got a great figure tiene una estupenda figura

■ *verb US*
figurarse: I figure he'll be late me figuro que llegará tarde

figure out *phrasal verb*
1. **entender:** I can't figure out why no entiendo por qué
2. **calcular:** I tried to figure out the total intenté calcular el total.

file [faɪl] *(noun & verb)*
■ *noun*
1. **el fichero:** there are 20 files on the disk hay 20 ficheros en el disco
2. **el expediente:** the police have a file on him la policía tiene un expediente de él
3. **la carpeta:** I put my notes in a red file puse mis notas en una carpeta roja
a nail file una lima de uñas
in single file en fila india: we walked in single file caminamos en fila india
■ *verb*
1. **archivar:** she's filing her papers está archivando sus papeles
2. **limarse:** she's filing her nails se está limando las uñas.

fill [fɪl] *verb* ■ **llenar:** I filled the bottle with water llené la botella con agua

fill in *phrasal verb* ■ **rellenar:** he filled in the hole rellenó el agujero; I filled in the form rellené el formulario

fill out *phrasal verb* ■ **rellenar:** she filled out the form rellenó el formulario

fill up *phrasal verb* ■ **llenar:** I'm going to fill up the tank voy a llenar el depósito.

fillet ['fɪlɪt] *noun* ■ **el filete:**
a fillet steak un solomillo.

filling ['fɪlɪŋ] *(adjective & noun)*
■ *adjective*
the meal was very filling la comida llenaba mucho
■ *noun*
1. **el empaste:** the dentist gave me a filling el dentista me puso un empaste
2. **el relleno:** this filling is very tasty este relleno es muy sabroso.

film [fɪlm] *noun*

1. la **película**: there's a good film on television están dando una buena película en la televisión
2. el **carrete**: I need some more film for my camera necesito otro carrete para mi cámara
> a film star una estrella del cine.

filthy [ˈfɪlθɪ] *adjective* ■ **mugriento**.

fin [fɪn] *noun* ■ la **aleta**: fish have fins los peces tienen aletas.

final [ˈfaɪnl] *(adjective & noun)*

■ *adjective*

1. **último**: this is my final lesson esta es mi última clase
2. **final**: that's my final decision es mi decisión final

■ *noun*

la **final**: England are in the finals Inglaterra está en la final.

finally [ˈfaɪnəlɪ] *adverb*

1. **finalmente**: he has finally arrived finalmente llegó
2. **por último**: finally you add the vanilla por último agregas la vainilla.

financial [fɪˈnænʃl] *adjective* ■ **económico, financiero**: they have financial problems tienen problemas económicos.

find [faɪnd] *(past tense & past participle* found*)* *verb* ■ **encontrar**: I can't find my address book no puedo encontrar mi libreta de direcciones; have you found the address? ¿has encontrado la dirección?

find out *phrasal verb*

1. **averiguar**: I'm going to find out what's going on out there voy a averiguar qué está pasando allí fuera
2. **descubrir**: he found out the truth descubrió la verdad.

fine [faɪn] *(adjective, adverb, noun & verb)*

■ *adjective*

1. **excelente**: he did a fine job hizo un trabajo excelente
2. **bien**: how are you? – I'm fine! ¿cómo estás? –¡bien!
3. **delicado**: she has fine features tiene rasgos delicados

4. **buen tiempo**: the weather is fine today hoy hace buen tiempo
> the fine arts las bellas artes

■ *adverb*

bien: he feels fine se siente bien

■ *noun*

la **multa**: he got a 20-pounds fine le pusieron una multa de 20 libras

■ *verb*

poner una multa a: they fined Peter 20 dollars a Peter le pusieron una multa de 20 dólares.

finger [ˈfɪŋgəʳ] *noun* ■ el **dedo**.

fingernail [ˈfɪŋgəneɪl] *noun* ■ la **uña**.

fingerprint [ˈfɪŋgəprɪnt] *noun* ■ la **huella dactilar**: the police took his fingerprints la policía le tomó las huellas dactilares.

finish [ˈfɪnɪʃ] *(verb & noun)*

■ *verb*

terminar: she has finished her homework ha terminado sus deberes; the film finishes at 11 o'clock la película termina a las 11 en punto
> to finish doing something terminar de hacer algo: I've finished eating he terminado de comer

■ *noun*

1. el **fin**: from start to finish de principio a fin
2. el **final**: we watched the finish of the race vimos el final de la carrera.

fire [ˈfaɪəʳ] *(noun & verb)*

■ *noun*

1. el **fuego**: he lit a fire encendió un fuego
2. el **incendio**: they are trying to put out the fire están tratando de apagar el incendio
3. *UK* la **estufa**: can you put the fire on? ¿puedes encender la estufa?
> on fire en llamas, ardiendo: the house is on fire la casa está en llamas
> to catch fire prenderse
> to set fire to something prenderle fuego a algo, incendiar algo: they set fire to the house le prendieron fuego a la casa
> a fire alarm una alarma contra incendios
> the fire brigade *UK* OR the fire department *US* el cuerpo de bomberos

a **fire engine** un coche de bomberos

a **fire escape** una escalera de incendios

the **fire exit** la salida de incendios

a **fire extinguisher** un extintor

the **fire station** el parque de bomberos

■ *verb*

1. **disparar: they fired at him** le dispararon; **she fired the gun** disparó la pistola

2. **despedir: he fired the secretary** despidió a la secretaria.

firefighter *US* ['faɪə'faɪtər] *noun* ■ el **bombero,** la **bombera.**

fireman *UK* ['faɪəmən] *(plural* firemen ['faɪəmən]*) noun* ■ el **bombero.**

fireplace ['faɪəpleɪs] *noun* ■ la **chimenea: they sat by the fireplace** se sentaron junto a la chimenea.

fireworks ['faɪəwɜːks] *plural noun* ■ los **fuegos artificiales.**

firm [fɜːm] *(adjective & noun)*

■ *adjective*

1. **duro: the cushion is firm** el cojín es duro

2. **estricto: he was firm with me** fue estricto conmigo

■ *noun*

la **empresa: she works for a firm in Scotland** trabaja para una empresa en Escocia.

first [fɜːst] *(adjective, adverb & noun)*

■ *adjective*

primero: it's the first time I've seen him es la primera vez que lo veo

Primer is used before a masculine singular noun:

he was the first man to arrive fue el primer hombre en llegar

■ *adverb*

primero: I saw it first yo lo vi primero; **he came first in the race** quedó primero en la carrera; **I want to have something to eat first** me gustaría comer algo primero

■ *noun*

el **primero,** la **primera: she was the first to leave** fue la primera en irse; **May the first** el primero de mayo

first of all antes que nada: **first of all tell me your name** antes que nada, dime tu nombre

at first al principio: **at first I thought he was mad** al principio pensé que estaba loco

first aid los primeros auxilios: **a first-aid kit** un botiquín de primeros auxilios

the **first floor**

1. *UK* la **primera planta,** el **primer piso**

2. *US* la **planta baja**

first name nombre de pila.

first-class ['fɜːst,klɑːs] *adjective*

1. **de primera clase: I bought a first-class ticket** compré un billete de primera clase

2. **de primera: the food in this restaurant is first class** la comida en este restaurante es de primera.

fish [fɪʃ] *(noun & verb)*

■ *noun (plural* fish)

1. el **pez** *(plural* los **peces): there are lots of fish in the lake** hay muchos peces en el lago

2. el **pescado: he doesn't like fish** no le gusta el pescado

fish and chips *UK* pescado rebozado con patatas fritas

■ *verb*

pescar: he was fishing in the river estaba pescando en el río.

fishing ['fɪʃɪŋ] *uncountable noun* ■ la **pesca: to go fishing** irse de pesca

a **fishing boat** un bote de pesca

a **fishing rod** una caña de pescar.

fishmonger *UK* ['fɪʃ,mʌŋgər] *noun* ■ el **pescadero,** la **pescadera**

the **fishmonger's** la pescadería.

fist [fɪst] *noun* ■ el **puño: he clenched his fist** cerró el puño.

fit [fɪt] *(adjective, noun & verb)*

■ *adjective*

en forma: he tries to keep fit trata de mantenerse en forma

■ *noun*

1. el **ataque: an epileptic fit** un ataque de epilepsia

2. el **arrebato: a fit of anger** un arrebato de ira

my mother had a fit when she saw the mess a mi madre le dio un infarto cuando vio el desorden

■ verb (past tense & past participle fitted OR US fit, present participle fitting)

1. **quedar bien:** these trousers don't fit estos pantalones no me quedan bien
2. **caber:** the pillow doesn't fit in the case la almohada no cabe en la funda
3. **entrar:** the key didn't fit the lock la llave no entraba en la cerradura
4. **instalar:** he fitted an alarm in his car instaló una alarma en el coche
5. **encajar:** the plug doesn't fit el enchufe no encaja.

fitting room ['fɪtɪŋruːm] noun ■ el probador.

five [faɪv] number ■ **cinco:** there are five pieces of cake hay cinco pedazos de pastel; she's five tiene cinco años; I went out at five salí a las cinco.

fix [fɪks] verb

1. **fijar:** I fixed the mirror to the wall fijé el espejo en la pared; can we fix a date? ¿podemos fijar una fecha?
2. **arreglar:** he's trying to fix the TV está tratando de arreglar el televisor
3. **preparar:** she's fixing us something to eat nos está preparando algo de comer.

fizzy ['fɪzɪ] adjective ■ **con gas, gaseoso:** she likes fizzy drinks le gustan las bebidas con gas.

flag [flæg] noun ■ la **bandera.**

flame [fleɪm] noun ■ la **llama:** careful with the flame! ¡cuidado con la llama!; the house was in flames la casa estaba en llamas.

flan [flæn] noun ■ la **tarta.**

flap [flæp] (past tense & past participle flapped, present participle flapping) verb

1. **batir:** the eagle flapped its wings el águila batió sus alas
2. **agitarse:** the flag flapped in the wind la bandera se agitaba con el viento.

flash [flæʃ] (noun & verb)

■ noun

1. el **destello:** the flash blinded me for a few seconds el destello me deslumbró por unos segundos

2. el **flash:** this camera has a flash esta cámara fotográfica tiene flash
> a flash of lightning un relámpago
■ verb

encenderse y apagarse: all the lights are flashing todas las luces se están encendiendo y apagando
> to flash one's headlights hacer una señal con los faros.

flashlight US ['flæʃlaɪt] noun ■ la **linterna.**

flat [flæt] (adjective & noun)

■ adjective

1. **plano:** a flat surface una superficie plana
2. **llano:** the countryside is flat around our town el paisaje es llano alrededor del pueblo
> a flat tyre un neumático desinflado.

flavour UK, **flavor** US ['fleɪvəʳ] noun ■ el **sabor:** this soup doesn't have much flavour este sopa no tiene mucho sabor; which flavour ice cream do you want? ¿de qué sabor quieres el helado?

flea [fliː] noun ■ la **pulga**
> the flea market el mercadillo.

fleece [fliːs] noun ■ la **lana:** the sheep's fleece keeps it warm la lana de la oveja la mantiene caliente
> a fleece jacket chaleco de forro polar.

flew [fluː] past tense ➤ fly.

flick [flɪk] verb ■ **encender (con movimiento rápido):** I flicked the TV switch encendí la tele

flick through phrasal verb ■ hojear: she flicked through the magazine hojeó la revista.

flies UK [flaɪz] plural noun ■ la **bragueta:** your flies are undone llevas la bragueta abierta.

flight [flaɪt] noun ■ el **vuelo:** the flight to Rome is at 2 o'clock el vuelo a Roma es a las 2 en punto
> a flight of stairs un tramo de escaleras.

fling [flɪŋ] (past tense & past participle flung) verb ■ **arrojar:** he flung his things on the floor arrojó sus cosas al suelo.

flip-flop UK ['flɪpflɒp] noun ■ la chancleta.

flipper ['flɪpəʳ] noun ■ la aleta: seals have flippers las focas tienen aletas; the diver's wearing flippers el buceador lleva aletas.

float [fləʊt] verb ■ flotar: a bottle is floating in the water una botella está flotando en el agua.

flock [flɒk] noun

1. la **bandada**: a flock of birds una bandada de pájaros
2. el **rebaño**: a flock of sheep un rebaño de ovejas.

flood [flʌd] (noun & verb)

■ noun

1. la **inundación** (plural las inundaciones): there have been floods in this area ha habido inundaciones en esta zona
2. la **avalancha**: we got a flood of letters recibimos una avalancha de cartas

■ verb

inundarse: the fields flooded se inundaron los campos.

floor [flɔːʳ] noun

1. el **suelo**: the floor's wet el suelo está mojado
2. el **piso**, la **planta**: which floor do you live on? ¿en qué piso vives?
   - on the first floor
1. UK en el primer piso OR planta
2. US en la planta baja
   - on the ground floor en la planta baja
   - on the floor en el suelo

⚠️ Floor es un falso amigo, no significa "flor".

floppy disk ['flɒpɪdɪsk] noun ■ el disquete: put the floppy disk into the drive pon el disquete en la disquetera.

florist ['flɒrɪst] noun ■ el/la florista the florist's la floristería.

flour ['flaʊəʳ] noun ■ la harina.

flow [fləʊ] verb ■ correr: the water flows through the pipe el agua corre por la cañería.

flower ['flaʊəʳ] (noun & verb)

■ noun

la **flor**: a bunch of flowers un ramo de flores; she picked some flowers cogió algunas flores

■ verb

florecer: these roses are about to flower estas rosas están a punto de florecer.

flowerpot ['flaʊəpɒt] noun ■ la maceta.

flown [fləʊn] past participle ➤ fly.

flu [fluː] uncountable noun ■ la gripe: she has flu UK OR she has the flu US tiene gripe.

fluent ['fluːənt] adjective

she's fluent in Spanish OR she speaks fluent Spanish habla español con fluidez.

flung [flʌŋ] past tense & past participle ➤ fling.

flush [flʌʃ] verb ■ tirar de la cadena: you didn't flush the toilet! ¡no has tirado de la cadena!

flute [fluːt] noun ■ la flauta: he plays the flute toca la flauta.

fly [flaɪ] (noun & verb)

■ noun (plural flies)

1. la **mosca**: there's a fly in my soup hay una mosca en mi sopa
2. US la **bragueta**: your fly is undone llevas la bragueta abierta

■ verb (past tense flew, past participle flown)

1. **volar**: thousands of birds flew over us miles de pájaros volaron por encima nuestro
2. **hacer volar**: he's flying a kite está haciendo volar una cometa
3. **viajar en avión**: he flies often viaja en avión a menudo; I'm afraid of flying me da miedo viajar en avión
4. **pilotar**: can you fly a plane? ¿sabes pilotar un avión?

fly away phrasal verb ■ salir volando: the bird flew away el pájaro salió volando.

focus ['fəʊkəs] (noun & verb)

■ noun

el **foco**: you have to adjust the focus tienes que ajustar el foco in focus enfocado: the picture is in focus la foto está enfocada

out of focus desenfocado: the picture is out of focus la foto está desenfocada

■ verb

enfocar: she focused the camera enfocó la cámara fotográfica

to focus on something centrarse en algo: he focused on the importance of education se centró en la importancia de la educación.

fog [fɒg] noun ■ la **niebla.**

foggy ['fɒgɪ] adjective

it's foggy hay niebla; it was a foggy day era un día de niebla.

fold [fəʊld] verb ■ **doblar:** I folded the paper in half doblé el papel por la mitad

to fold one's arms cruzarse de brazos: she folded her arms se cruzó de brazos.

folder ['fəʊldər] noun ■ la **carpeta:** I put my papers in the folder puse mis papeles en la carpeta.

folding ['fəʊldɪŋ] adjective ■ **plegable:** a folding chair una silla plegable.

follow ['fɒləʊ] verb ■ **seguir:** she was following me me estaba siguiendo; follow me! ¡síganme!

following ['fɒləʊɪŋ] adjective ■ **siguiente:** it happened the following month sucedió al mes siguiente

the following day al día siguiente.

fond [fɒnd] adjective

to be fond of somebody OR something gustarle alguien OR algo: he's very fond of chocolate le gusta mucho el chocolate.

food [fuːd] uncountable noun ■ la **comida:** there's enough food for everyone hay comida suficiente para todos.

fool [fuːl] noun ■ el/la **idiota:** what a fool! ¡qué idiota!

foolish ['fuːlɪʃ] adjective ■ **estúpido:** it was a foolish decision fue una decisión estúpida.

foot [fʊt] (plural feet [fiːt]) noun ■ el **pie:** I hurt my foot me hice daño en el pie; let's go on foot vayamos a pie; he's 6 feet tall mide 6 pies.

football ['fʊtbɔːl] noun

1. UK el **fútbol:** they are playing football están jugando a fútbol

2. US el **fútbol americano:** we went to a football game fuimos a un partido de fútbol americano

a football match UK un partido de fútbol

3. la **pelota de fútbol, el balón de fútbol:** he kicked the football chutó la pelota de fútbol

a football team un equipo de fútbol americano.

footballer ['fʊtbɔːlər] noun ■ el/la **futbolista:** he's a footballer él es futbolista.

footpath [UK 'fʊtpɑːθ, US 'fʊtpæθ] noun ■ el **sendero.**

footprint ['fʊtprɪnt] noun ■ la **huella:** we saw footprints in the snow vimos huellas en la nieve.

footstep ['fʊtstep] noun ■ el **paso:** I heard footsteps on the stairs oí pasos en la escalera.

for [fɔːr] preposition

1. para: this is for you esto es para ti; a knife for cutting bread un cuchillo para cortar pan

2. por: he paid 200 dollars for the car pagó 200 dólares por el coche; thanks for helping me gracias por ayudarme; we are going away for the weekend vamos a estar fuera por el fin de semana

3. durante

When you are talking about completed actions in the past, you should use a verb in the past tense + **durante**:

she lived in Spain for two years vivió en España durante dos años

4. hace: he has lived in France for five years vive en Francia desde hace cinco años; I've been waiting for two hours hace dos horas que estoy esperando

for sale en venta

T for Tony la T de Tony

we walked for miles caminamos varias millas

what for? ¿para qué?: I need some money — what for? necesito un poco de dinero —¿para qué?

forbid [fə'bɪd] *(past tense* forbade, *past participle* forbidden) verb ■ **prohibir: I forbid you to go to that party** te prohíbo que vayas a esa fiesta.

forbidden [fə'bɪdn] *adjective* ■ **prohibido: smoking is forbidden** prohibido fumar.

force [fɔːs] *(noun & verb)*
■ *noun*
la **fuerza: the ball hit me with great force** la pelota me dio con mucha fuerza
▶ **by force** a la fuerza: **they took him away by force** se lo llevaron a la fuerza
■ *verb*
obligar: he forced me to tell the truth me obligó a decir la verdad
▶ **to force one's way into something** entrar a la fuerza: **he forced his way into the office** entró en la oficina a la fuerza.

forecast [*UK* 'fɔːkɑːst, *US* 'fɔːkæst] *noun* ■ **el pronóstico**
▶ **the weather forecast** el pronóstico del tiempo: **what's the weather forecast for tomorrow?** ¿cuál es el pronóstico del tiempo para mañana?

forehead ['fɔːhed] *noun* ■ **la frente.**

foreign ['fɒrən] *adjective* ■ **extranjero: foreign languages** lenguas extranjeras; **she lives in a foreign country** vive en un país extranjero.

foreigner ['fɒrənə'] *noun* ■ **el extranjero, la extranjera: he's a foreigner** es un extranjero.

forest ['fɒrɪst] *noun* ■ **el bosque: she got lost in the forest** se perdió en el bosque.

forever [fə'revə'] *adverb* ■ **para siempre: he's gone forever** se ha ido para siempre; **it won't last forever** no va a durar para siempre.

forgave [fə'geɪv] *past tense* ➤ forgive.

forge [fɔːdʒ] *verb* ■ **falsificar: she forged her mother's signature** falsificó la firma de su madre.

forgery ['fɔːdʒərɪ] *(plural* forgeries) *noun* ■ **la falsificación** *(plural* las **falsificaciones): she was arrested for forgery** fue arrestada por falsificación

> **this passport is a forgery** este pasaporte es falso.

forget [fə'get] *(past tense* forgot, *past participle* forgotten) *verb* ■ **olvidarse: I've forgotten your address** se me ha olvidado tu dirección; **don't forget to call!** ¡no te olvides de llamar!; **she forgot her purse** se le olvidó el monedero.

forgive [fə'gɪv] *(past tense* forgave, *past participle* forgiven) *verb* ■ **perdonar: I forgive you** te perdono; **I forgave him for not telling the truth** lo perdoné por no haber dicho la verdad.

forgot [fə'gɒt] *past tense* ➤ forget.

forgotten [fə'gɒtn] *past participle* ➤ forget.

fork [fɔːk] *noun*
1. **el tenedor: a knife and fork** un cuchillo y un tenedor
2. **la bifurcación** *(plural* las **bifurcaciones): we came to a fork in the road** llegamos a una bifurcación en la carretera.

form [fɔːm] *(noun & verb)*
■ *noun*
1. la **forma: there are different forms of life on the planet** hay diferentes formas de vida en el planeta
2. el **formulario: I filled in the form** rellené el formulario
3. *UK* el **curso: what form are you in?** ¿en qué curso estás?
■ *verb*
formar: the children formed a circle los niños formaron un corro.

formal ['fɔːml] *adjective* ■ **formal: they made a formal announcement** hicieron un anuncio formal.

former ['fɔːmə'] *adjective*
1. **antiguo: he's a former student of mine** es un antiguo alumno mío
2. **primero: do you mean the former or the latter?** te refieres al primero o al último?

Primer is used before a masculine singular noun.

I'm referring to the former case me refiero al primer caso.

formula ['fɔːmʊlə] *noun* ■ la **fórmula:** they stole the secret formula robaron la fórmula secreta.

fort [fɔːt] *noun* ■ el **fuerte.**

fortnight UK ['fɔːtnaɪt] *noun* ■ la **quincena:** the first fortnight in June la primera quincena de junio; I'll be away for a fortnight estaré ausente quince días; I see him every fortnight lo veo cada quince días.

fortunately ['fɔːtʃnətlɪ] *adverb* ■ afortunadamente: fortunately, everyone is safe afortunadamente, todos están a salvo.

fortune ['fɔːtʃuːn] *noun* ■ la **fortuna:** he made his fortune before he was 30 hizo su fortuna antes de cumplir los 30; he had the good fortune to get an excellent education tuvo la buena fortuna de recibir una excelente educación

➤ to tell somebody's fortune leerle la suerte a alguien.

forty ['fɔːtɪ] *number* ■ **cuarenta:** he's forty tiene cuarenta años; forty-one cuarenta y uno; forty-two cuarenta y dos.

forward ['fɔːwəd], **forwards** ['fɔːwədz] *adverb* ■ **hacia adelante:** he leaned forward se inclinó hacia adelante

➤ to move forward avanzar: the army is moving forward el ejército está avanzando

➤ to put the clocks forward adelantar los relojes.

fought [fɔːt] *past tense & past participle* ➤ fight.

foul [faʊl] *(adjective & noun)*

■ *adjective*
asqueroso: what a foul smell! ¡qué asqueroso olor!

■ *noun*
la **falta:** Beckham committed a foul Beckham cometió una falta.

found [faʊnd] *past tense & past participle* ➤ find.

fountain ['faʊntɪn] *noun* ■ la **fuente:** I'll see you at the fountain at 8 nos vemos en la fuente a las 8

➤ a fountain pen una estilográfica.

four [fɔːʳ] *number* ■ **cuatro:** they have four children tienen cuatro hijos; she's four tiene cuatro años; we went out at four salimos a las cuatro.

fourteen [ˌfɔːˈtiːn] *number* ■ **catorce:** he's fourteen tiene catorce años.

fourth [fɔːθ] *number* ■ **cuarto:** he came fourth llegó cuarto

➤ it's the fourth of March UK OR it's March fourth US estamos a cuatro de marzo

➤ the Fourth of July US el 4 de julio

THE FOURTH OF JULY

El 4 de julio o **Fourth of July,** también llamado **Independence Day,** es una de las fiestas de mayor importancia en los Estados Unidos; conmemora el momento en que el país declaró su independencia de Inglaterra en el año 1776. Como parte de los festejos se organizan desfiles por las calles y, por la noche, se encienden castillos de fuegos artificiales en los que predominan los colores rojo, blanco y azul. Los edificios se decoran con adornos de estos mismos colores o con banderas estadounidenses.

fox [fɒks] *(plural* foxes [fɒksɪz]*) noun* ■ el **zorro.**

fraction ['frækʃn] *noun* ■ la **fracción** *(plural* las **fracciones***).*

fragile ['frædʒaɪl] *adjective* ■ **frágil.**

frame [freɪm] *noun* ■ el **marco:** I put the photo in a frame puse la foto en un marco.

France [UK frɑːns, US fræns] *noun* ■ **Francia.**

fraternity [US frəˈtɜːrnəti] *(plural* fraternities*) noun* ■ asociación estudiantil universitaria

FRATERNITY

Los clubes de estudiantes masculinos **(fraternities)** son un elemento sobresaliente de la vida social universitaria estadounidense. Cada club posee su propio nombre, constituido por letras del alfabeto griego y tiene su sede en el edificio donde reside la mayoría de sus miembros. Estos clubes realizan trabajos para instituciones de asistencia social, pero también son famosas sus juergas con alcohol y sus reuniones secretas. Algunas universidades han decidido prohibirlos porque sus ceremonias de iniciación incluían novatadas crueles y peligrosas.

freckle ['frekl] *noun* ■ la **peca: Rachel has freckles** Raquel tiene pecas.

free [fri:] *(adjective & verb)*
■ *adjective*
1. **libre: are you free tonight?** ¿estás libre esta noche?; **is this seat free?** ¿está libre este asiento?
2. **gratis: it's free of charge** es gratis; **you can download the program for free** puedes descargar gratis el programa
3. **gratuito: a free magazine** una revista gratuita
> **a free kick** un tiro libre
> **you're free to go** puedes irte
■ *verb*
liberar: they freed the prisoners liberaron a los prisioneros.

freedom ['fri:dəm] *noun* ■ la **libertad: freedom of speech** libertad de expresión.

freeway *US* ['fri:weɪ] *noun* ■ la **autopista.**

freeze [fri:z] *(past tense* **froze,** *past participle* **frozen)** *verb*
1. **congelarse: the lake had frozen overnight** el lago se congeló durante la noche
2. **congelar: I froze the chicken** congelé el pollo.

freezer ['fri:zə'] *noun* ■ el **congelador: she put the ice cream in the freezer** puso el helado en el congelador.

freezing ['fri:zɪŋ] *adjective* ■ **helado: your hands are freezing** tienes las manos heladas
> **I'm freezing** estoy helado
> **it's freezing today** hoy hace un frío espantoso.

French [frentʃ] *(adjective & noun)*
■ *adjective*
Remember not to use a capital letter for the adjective in Spanish:

francés *(feminine* **francesa)**: **I like French cooking** me gusta la cocina francesa
> **French fries** *US* patatas fritas
■ *noun*

In Spanish, a capital letter is not used for the language or the inhabitants of a country or region:

el francés: he speaks French habla francés
> **the French** los franceses.

frequent ['fri:kwənt] *adjective* ■ **frecuente: accidents are frequent here** los accidentes son frecuentes aquí.

frequently ['fri:kwəntlɪ] *adverb* ■ **frecuentemente, con frecuencia.**

fresh [freʃ] *adjective*
1. **fresco: fresh bread** pan fresco
2. **nuevo: start a fresh page** comienza una página nueva
> **he wants to make a fresh start** quiere empezar de nuevo
> **fresh air** aire fresco: **let's go and get some fresh air** vamos a salir a tomar un poco de aire fresco.

freshen up ['freʃnʌp] *phrasal verb* ■ **refrescarse: I'm just going to freshen up** sólo voy a refrescarme.

Friday ['fraɪdɪ] *noun* ■ el **viernes** *(plural* los **viernes)**: **it's Friday today** hoy es viernes; **next Friday** el próximo viernes; **last Friday** el viernes pasado
> **on Friday** el viernes: **I'll see you on Friday** te veo el viernes
> **on Fridays** los viernes: **Sam goes swimming on Fridays** Sam va a nadar los viernes

In Spanish the days of the week do not start with a capital letter.

fridge *UK* [frɪdʒ] *noun* ■ la **nevera.**

fried [fraɪd] *(adjective & verb form)*
■ *adjective*
frito: fried chicken pollo frito
> **a fried egg** un huevo frito
■ *past tense & past participle*
> **fry.**

friend [frend] *noun* ■ el **amigo,** la **amiga: we're friends** somos amigos; **Sally is my best friend** Sally es mi mejor amiga

> to make friends hacer amigos: **she has trouble making friends** tiene problemas para hacer amigos.

friendly ['frendlɪ] *adjective* ■ **simpático**: **he's very friendly** es muy simpático

> they gave her a friendly welcome le dieron una cordial bienvenida.

friendship ['frendʃɪp] *noun* ■ **la amistad**.

fries *US* [fraɪz] *plural noun* ■ **las patatas fritas**: **she ordered a burger with fries** pidió una hamburguesa con patatas fritas.

fright [fraɪt] *noun* ■ **el miedo**: **she was pale with fright** estaba pálida de miedo

> to give someone a fright darle un susto a alguien: **she gave me a fright** me dio un susto.

frighten ['fraɪtn] *verb* ■ **asustar**: **you frightened me** me has asustado.

frightened ['fraɪtnd] *adjective*

> to be frightened estar asustado: **we were cold, frightened and tired** teníamos frío y estábamos asustados y cansados.

frightening ['fraɪtnɪŋ] *adjective* ■ **aterrador** *(feminine* **aterradora***)*: **she told us a frightening story** nos contó un cuento aterrador.

fringe *UK* [frɪndʒ] *noun* ■ **el flequillo**.

frog [frɒg] *noun* ■ **la rana**

> to have a frog in one's throat tener carraspera.

from [frəm, frɒm] *preposition*

1. **de**: **I got a letter from my brother** recibí una carta de mi hermano; **I come from Chicago** soy de Chicago; **oranges from Valencia** naranjas de Valencia; **the house is 5 miles from the sea** la casa queda a 5 millas del mar

> Remember that **de + el = del**.

2.

> When you say what country a person is from, you should use an adjective to give the person's nationality in Spanish:

Andy is from Wales Andy es galés

3. **desde**: **from the bridge you can see the quay** desde el puente puedes ver el muelle

> from now on a partir de ahora: **from now on I'll be working at the other shop** a partir de ahora trabajaré en la otra tienda

> from... to...

1. **desde...hasta...**: **the bank is open from 9a.m. to 4p.m.** el banco está abierto desde las 9 de la mañana hasta las 4 de la tarde

2. **de... a...**: **we took the train from London to Cardiff** cogimos el tren de Londres a Cardiff.

front [frʌnt] *(adjective & noun)*

■ *adjective*

1. **de delante**: **they are playing in the front garden** están jugando en el jardín de delante

2. **delantero**: **the front seat** el asiento delantero

3. **primero**: **we sat in the front row** nos sentamos en la primera fila

> the front page of a newspaper la primera plana de un periódico

■ *noun*

1. la **parte de delante**: **the front of your shirt is dirty** la parte de delante de la camisa está sucia

2. la **parte delantera**: **the front of the car** la parte delantera del coche

> in front of delante de: **George is standing in front of the house** George está de pie delante de la casa

> in front delante: **Bob was walking in front** Bob iba caminando delante

> the front door la puerta principal.

frontier ['frʌnˌtɪəʳ] *noun* ■ **la frontera**.

frost [frɒst] *noun* ■ **la escarcha**: **there was frost on the windows** había escarcha en las ventanas.

frosty ['frɒstɪ] *adjective*

> it's frosty today hoy ha helado.

frown [fraʊn] *verb* ■ **fruncir el ceño**

> to frown at someone mirar a alguien con el ceño fruncido: **she frowned at me** me miró con el ceño fruncido.

froze [frəʊz] *past tense* ➤ **freeze**.

frozen ['frəʊzn] *(adjective & verb form)*

■ *adjective*

congelado: **she bought some frozen vegetables** compró verduras congeladas; **my hands are frozen** tengo las manos congeladas

■ *past participle*
➤ freeze.

fruit [fruːt] *uncountable noun* ■ la **fruta**: a piece of fruit una fruta
fruit juice zumo de fruta
fruit salad ensalada de frutas.

fry [fraɪ] *(past tense & past participle* fried*) verb*
■ **freír**: he's frying some fish está friendo pescado.

frying pan ['fraɪŋˌpæn] *noun* ■ la **sartén**.

ft. *(abbreviation of* foot OR feet*)*
he's 6 ft. tall mide 6 pies de alto.

fuel [fjʊəl] *noun* ■ el **combustible**: our fuel supplies are running low nos queda poco combustible.

full [fʊl] *adjective*
1. **lleno**: the glass is full of water el vaso está lleno de agua
2. **completo**: please state your full name escriba su nombre completo, por favor; the hotel is full el hotel está completo
3. **apretado**: I've had a full day he tenido un día apretado
➤ a full moon luna llena: there's a full moon tonight esta noche hay luna llena
➤ at full speed a toda velocidad
➤ a full stop *UK* un punto: put a full stop at the end of the sentence pon un punto al final de la frase.

full-time ['fʊltaɪm] *(adjective & adverb)*
■ *adjective*
de tiempo completo: he has a full-time job tiene un trabajo de tiempo completo
■ *adverb*
a tiempo completo: he works full-time trabaja a tiempo completo.

fully ['fʊlɪ] *adverb* ■ **totalmente**: she never fully recovered nunca se recuperó totalmente.

fun [fʌn] *(adjective & noun)*
■ *adjective*
divertido: Steve is such a fun guy Steve es un tipo muy divertido
■ *noun*
➤ to have fun divertirse: we had so much fun today hoy nos hemos divertido mucho

➤ have fun! ¡que te diviertas!
➤ to be fun ser divertido: this game is a lot of fun este juego es muy divertido
➤ to make fun of somebody reírse de alguien: don't make fun of your brother no te rías de tu hermano.

funeral ['fjuːnərəl] *noun* ■ el **funeral**.

funny ['fʌnɪ] *adjective*
1. **divertido**: the film is very funny la película es muy divertida
2. **raro**: what a funny smell! ¡qué olor tan raro!

fur [fɜːʳ] *noun* ■ el **pelo**: he was stroking the cat's fur estaba acariciando el pelo del gato
➤ a fur coat un abrigo de piel.

furious ['fjʊərɪəs] *adjective* ■ **furioso**: he's furious with me está furioso conmigo.

furniture ['fɜːnɪtʃəʳ] *uncountable noun* ■ los **muebles**: the furniture is very modern los muebles son muy modernos
➤ a piece of furniture un mueble.

further ['fɜːðəʳ] *(comparative of* far*) (adverb & adjective)*
■ *adverb*
más lejos: they went a little further fueron un poco más lejos
➤ is it much further? ¿cuánto falta?
■ *adjective*
➤ do you have any further questions? ¿tienen más preguntas?
➤ until further notice hasta nuevo aviso: the concert is postponed until further notice el concierto se aplaza hasta nuevo aviso.

furthest ['fɜːðɪst] *(superlative of* far*) (adverb & adjective)*
■ *adverb*
más lejos: he walked furthest fue el que más lejos caminó
■ *adjective*
más alejado: the furthest house la casa más alejada.

fuse [fjuːz] *noun* ■ el **fusible**: one of the fuses blew se fundió uno de los fusibles.

fuss [fʌs] *noun* ■ el **alboroto**: what's all the fuss about? ¿a qué viene tanto alboroto?

to make a fuss armar un escándalo: **please don't make a fuss** por favor, no arméis un escándalo.

fussy ['fʌsɪ] *adjective* ■ **quisquilloso: he's such a fussy eater** es tan quisquilloso con la comida.

future ['fjuːtʃə'] *noun* ■ **el futuro: we can't predict the future** no podemos predecir el futuro
- **the future tense** el futuro
- **in future** de ahora en adelante: **I won't help you in future** de ahora en adelante no te ayudaré.

gadget ['gædʒɪt] *noun* ■ **el aparato.**

gain [geɪn] *verb* ■ **conseguir: what do you hope to gain by behaving like this?** ¿qué esperas conseguir comportándote así?
- **to gain weight** engordar: **he gained a lot of weight** engordó mucho
- **he managed to gain my respect** consiguió ganarse mi respeto
- **what did you gain from your experience?** ¿qué provecho sacaste de tu experiencia?

gale [geɪl] *noun* ■ **el vendaval: there was a gale blowing** soplaba un fuerte vendaval.

gallery ['gælərɪ] *(plural galleries) noun* ■ **la galería: we visited an art gallery** fuimos a una galería de arte; **I bought a painting**

from a gallery compré un cuadro en una galería.

gallon ['gælən] *noun* ■ **el galón** *(plural los* **galones***) (UK = 4,546 litros; US = 3,785 litros).*

gallop ['gæləp] *(noun & verb)*
- *noun*
  el galope
- *verb* **galopar: the horses galloped along the beach** los caballos galopaban por la playa.

gamble ['gæmbl] *verb* ■ **jugarse algo: she gambled 100 dollars** se jugó 100 dólares.

gambler ['gæmblə'] *noun* ■ **el jugador, la jugadora: he's a keen gambler** es muy aficionado al juego.

gambling ['gæmblɪŋ] *noun* ■ **el juego: gambling is banned in this state** el juego está prohibido en este estado.

game [geɪm] *noun*
1. **el juego: a computer game** un juego de ordenador
2. **el partido: what time is the football game?** ¿a qué hora es el partido de fútbol?
3. **la partida: a game of chess** una partida de ajedrez.

gang [gæŋ] *noun* ■ **la pandilla.**

gap [gæp] *noun*
1. **la abertura: they went through a gap in the fence** pasaron por una abertura en la valla
2. **la laguna: there are big gaps in his knowledge** tiene grandes lagunas en sus conocimientos
3. **la separación, la distancia: the gap between rich and poor** la separación entre ricos y pobres; **there's a large age gap between us** hay una gran distancia generacional entre nosotros
- **she has a gap in her teeth** tiene los dientes separados.

garage [*UK* 'gærɑːʒ, *US* 'gærɪdʒ] *noun* ■ **el garaje: the house has a two-car garage** la casa tiene un garaje de dos plazas.

garbage US ['gɑːbɪdʒ] noun ■ la **basura**
a garbage can un cubo de la basura.
a garbage truck el camión de la basura.

garden ['gɑːdn] noun ■ el **jardín** (plural
los **jardines**).

gardener ['gɑːdnəʳ] noun ■ el **jardinero**,
la **jardinera**.

gardening ['gɑːdnɪŋ] noun ■ la **jardinería**: she loves gardening le encanta la
jardinería.

garlic ['gɑːlɪk] noun ■ el **ajo**
garlic bread pan de ajo.

gas [gæs] noun

1. el gas: a gas cooker una cocina de gas
2. US la **gasolina**: my car is almost out of gas
casi no le queda gasolina al coche
a gas station una estación de servicio.

gasoline US ['gæsəliːn] noun ■ la **gasolina**.

gate [geɪt] noun

1. el **portón** (plural los **portones**): I opened the
gate and walked up the path abrí el portón
y caminé por el sendero
2. la **puerta**: we'll be boarding at gate 4 vamos a embarcar por la puerta 4.

gather ['gæðəʳ] verb

1. reunirse: people are gathering in front of
the embassy la gente se está reuniendo delante de la embajada
2. recoger: she's gathering blackberries está
recogiendo moras
3. reunir: you need to gather all the necessary information debes reunir toda la información necesaria
to gather speed adquirir velocidad: the train
was gathering speed el tren iba adquiriendo
velocidad.

gave [geɪv] past tense ➤ give.

gaze [geɪz] verb ■ mirar: she's gazing out
of the window está mirando por la ventana.

gear [gɪəʳ] noun

1. la marcha: he changed gear cambió la marcha del coche
2. velocidad: my bike has ten gears mi bici
tiene diez velocidades

3. el **equipo**: he had all his fishing gear tenía
todo su equipo de pesca.

geese [giːs] plural ➤ goose.

gel [dʒel] noun ■ el **gel**
hair gel gel para el pelo.

gem [dʒem] noun ■ la **gema**.

gene [dʒiːn] noun ■ el **gen**.

general ['dʒenərəl] (adjective & noun)

■ adjective
general: it's a general question es una pregunta general
a general election UK unas elecciones generales
general knowledge cultura general
the general public el público en general
in general en general

■ noun
el/la general: he's a general in the army es
general del ejército.

generally ['dʒenərəlɪ] adverb ■ generalmente: they generally go to bed at 10
o'clock generalmente se acuestan a las 10.

generation [ˌdʒenə'reɪʃn] noun ■ la **generación** (plural las **generaciones**): the
younger generation la generación más joven.

generous ['dʒenərəs] adjective ■ generoso: he's very generous es muy generoso.

genetic [dʒɪ'netɪk] adjective ■ genético:
genetic engineering ingeniería genética.

genius ['dʒiːnjəs] noun ■ el **genio**: she's
a genius es un genio.

gentle ['dʒentl] adjective

1. dulce: he's very gentle with the baby es
muy dulce con el bebé
2. suave: there's a gentle breeze hay una
brisa suave.

gentleman ['dʒentlmən] (plural gentlemen ['dʒentlmən]) noun ■ el **caballero**:
come in, gentlemen! ¡entren, caballeros!

genuine ['dʒenjʊɪn] adjective

1. auténtico: it's genuine gold es oro auténtico
2. sincero: she's very genuine es muy sincera.

geography [dʒɪˈɒgrəfɪ] *noun* ■ la geografía.

germ [dʒɜːm] *noun* ■ el **germen** (*plural* los gérmenes).

German [ˈdʒɜːmən] (*adjective & noun*)
■ *adjective*

Remember not to use a capital letter for the adjective in Spanish:

alemán (*feminine* **alemana**): Dieter is a German name Dieter es un nombre alemán
■ *noun*

In Spanish, a capital letter is not used for the language or the inhabitants of a country or region:

1. el **alemán**, la **alemana**: the Germans los alemanes
2. el **alemán**: she speaks German habla alemán.

Germany [ˈdʒɜːmənɪ] *noun* ■ **Alemania**.

gesture [ˈdʒestʃər] *noun* ■ el **gesto**.

get [get] (*past tense* got, *past participle UK* get OR *US* gotten) *verb*

1. *when get means "receive"* **recibir**: I got a letter from my brother recibí una carta de mi hermano; how many presents did you get? ¿cuántos regalos has recibido?
2. *when get means "achieve"* **sacar**: she gets good grades saca buenas notas
3. *when get means "find"* **conseguir**: where did you get that book? ¿dónde conseguiste ese libro?
4. *when get means "buy"* **comprar**: I'm going to the shop to get some milk voy a la tienda a comprar leche; I don't know what to get Harry for his birthday no sé qué comprarle a Harry para su cumpleaños
5. *when get means "fetch"* **ir a buscar**, **traer**: go and get the doctor ve a buscar al doctor; can you get my slippers? ¿me puedes traer las zapatillas?
6. *when get means "catch"* **coger**: he got a cold cogió un resfriado; did they get the thief? ¿cogieron al ladrón?
7. *when get means "take"* **tomar**: let's get a cab to the station tomemos un taxi hasta la estación

8. *when get means "become"*

When **get** means "become" and is followed by an adjective, it can sometimes be translated by **hacerse** + adjective. You will often find there is a single verb in Spanish that can replace **hacerse** + adjective (to get angry = enfadarse):

she's getting old se está haciendo vieja; he got angry se enfadó; he got married last June se casó el junio pasado; it's getting dark está oscureciendo
9. *when get means "arrive" or "go"* **llegar**: when did you get here? ¿cuándo llegasteis aquí?; how do you get to the station? ¿cómo se llega a la estación?
10. *when get means "understand"* **entender**: he didn't get the joke no entendió el chiste ➤ have

➤ to get something ready preparar algo: he's getting dinner ready está preparando la cena
➤ to get something done mandar hacer algo: I must get the yard cleaned tengo que mandar limpiar el patio; he's going to get his hair cut va a cortarse el pelo
➤ to get somebody to do something mandar a alguien hacer algo: I got him to clean the car le he mandado limpiar el coche

get along *phrasal verb* ■ **llevarse bien**: my brother and I don't get along mi hermano y yo no nos llevamos bien

get away *phrasal verb* ■ **escaparse**: the thief got away el ladrón se escapó

get back *phrasal verb*
1. **volver**: I got back late volví tarde
2. **devolver**: did you get your money back? ¿te devolvieron el dinero?

get down *phrasal verb* ■ **bajar**: he got down from the tree bajó del árbol

get in *phrasal verb*
1. **entrar**: they got in through the window entraron por la ventana
2. **subirse a**: get in the car! ¡súbete al coche!

get off *phrasal verb*
1. **bajarse de**: he got off the bus se bajó del autobús

2. bajarse: where do we get off? ¿dónde tenemos que bajarnos?

get on *phrasal verb*

1. subirse a: they got on the train se subieron al tren

2. llevarse bien: I don't get on with Sam no me llevo bien con Sam

get out *phrasal verb* ■ salir por: I got out of the window salí por la ventana
➤ she got out of the taxi se bajó del taxi
➤ get out! ¡fuera!

get up *phrasal verb* ■ levantarse: what time did you get up? ¿a qué hora te levantaste?; Sam gets up at dawn Sam se levanta al amanecer.

ghost [gəʊst] *noun* ■ el fantasma: do you believe in ghosts? ¿crees en fantasmas?

giant ['dʒaɪənt] *noun* ■ el gigante, la giganta.

giddy ['gɪdɪ] *adjective* ■ mareado: I feel giddy me siento mareado.

gift [gɪft] *noun*

1. el regalo: I gave her a gift le di un regalo; a gift shop una tienda de regalos

2. el don: she has a gift for languages tiene un don para los idiomas.

gifted ['gɪftɪd] *adjective* ■ superdotado: his son is gifted su hijo es superdotado.

gigantic [dʒaɪ'gæntɪk] *adjective* ■ gigantesco: they live in a gigantic house viven en una casa gigantesca.

giggle ['gɪgl] *verb* ■ reírse tontamente: the girls were giggling las niñas se estaban riendo tontamente.

ginger ['dʒɪndʒəʳ] *(noun & adjective)*
■ *noun*
el jengibre: there's a bit of ginger in the sauce la salsa tiene un poco de jengibre
■ *adjective UK*
pelirrojo: she has ginger hair tiene el pelo pelirrojo.

gipsy ['dʒɪpsɪ] ➤ gypsy.

giraffe [UK dʒɪ'rɑːf, US dʒɪ'ræf] *noun* ■ la jirafa.

girl [gɜːl] *noun* ■ la niña: a little girl una niña pequeña
➤ a girl guide *UK* OR a girl scout *US* una scout.

girlfriend ['gɜːlfrend] *noun*

1. la novia: Bob has a new girlfriend Bob tiene una novia nueva

2. la amiga: she went out with her girlfriends salió con sus amigas.

give [gɪv] *(past tense* gave, *past participle* given) verb

1. dar: to give something to somebody darle algo a alguien; give me the book dame el libro; give it to me! ¡dámelo!; he gave them some money les dio algo de dinero

2. regalar: she gave him a CD for his birthday le regaló un CD para su cumpleaños
➤ to give somebody a present hacerle un regalo a alguien
➤ to give something back to somebody devolverle algo a alguien: he gave the book back to me me devolvió el libro

give in *phrasal verb* ■ ceder: his mother gave in and let him go out su madre cedió y le dejó salir

give out *phrasal verb* ■ repartir: the teacher gave out the exam papers el profesor repartió las hojas de examen

give up *phrasal verb*

1. rendirse: it's too hard, I give up es muy difícil, me rindo

2. dejar de: he gave up smoking dejó de fumar.

given ['gɪvn] *past participle* ➤ give.

glad [glæd] *adjective*

Alegrarse de que is followed by a verb in the subjunctive:
➤ to be glad alegrarse: I'm glad you came me alegro de que hayas venido.

glamor *US* ➤ glamour *UK*.

glamorous ['glæmərəs] *adjective*

1. glamouroso: she's very glamorous es muy glamourosa

2. atractivo: she has a glamorous job tiene un trabajo atractivo.

glamour *UK,* **glamor** *US* ['glæmər] *noun*
■ el **glamour**: the glamour of Hollywood el glamour de Hollywood.

glance [*UK* glɑːns, *US* glæns] *(noun & verb)*
■ *noun*
la **mirada**: have a quick glance at this échale una mirada rápida a esto
> at first glance a primera vista
■ *verb*
> to glance at something echarle una mirada a algo: he glanced at his watch le echó una mirada a su reloj.

glass [*UK* glɑːs, *UK* glæs] *noun*
1. el **vaso**: can I have a glass of water? ¿me podrías dar un vaso de agua?
2. el **vidrio**: it's made of glass es de vidrio.

glasses [*UK* 'glɑːsɪz, *UK* 'glæsɪz] *plural noun* ■ las **gafas**: I can't see without my glasses no veo sin mis gafas.

glide [glaɪd] *verb* ■ **deslizarse**: they glided around the dance floor se deslizaban por la pista de baile.

glider [glaɪdər] *noun* ■ el **planeador**.

glitter ['glɪtər] *(verb & noun)*
■ *noun*
la **purpurina**
■ *verb*
brillar: the diamond glittered in the light el diamante brillaba con la luz.

global ['gləʊbl] *adjective* ■ **global**
> global warming calentamiento global.

globe [gləʊb] *noun* ■ el **globo terráqueo**.

gloomy ['gluːmɪ] *adjective*
1. **lúgubre**: this is such a gloomy house ésta es una casa tan lúgubre
2. **triste**: you look gloomy today pareces triste hoy.

glorious ['glɔːrɪəs] *adjective* ■ **espléndido**: what a glorious day! ¡qué día tan espléndido!

glove [glʌv] *noun* ■ el **guante**: he was wearing black gloves llevaba guantes negros.

glow [gləʊ] *(noun & verb)*
■ *uncountable noun*
la **luz**: the fire gave off a warm glow el fuego daba una luz cálida
■ *verb*
1. **brillar**: the fire was glowing el fuego brillaba
2. **rebosar**: she was glowing with health rebosaba de salud.

glue [gluː] *(noun & verb)*
■ *noun*
el **pegamento**: use some glue to stick the pieces back together usa un poco de pegamento para pegar los pedazos
■ *verb*
pegar: he glued the two pieces together pegó los dos pedazos
> to be glued to something estar pegado a algo: we were glued to the TV all day estuvimos pegados a la tele todo el día.

go [gəʊ] *(verb & noun)*
■ *verb*
1. **ir**: I'm going to Australia voy a Australia; we went for a walk fuimos a dar un paseo; how's it going? ¿cómo va todo?; the party went well la fiesta fue bien
2. **salir**: the train has already gone el tren ya ha salido
3. **irse**: she left home se fue de casa; I must be going now ya tengo que irme; let's go! ¡vámonos!; we're going on holiday nos vamos de vacaciones
4. **pasar**: time goes quickly el tiempo pasa rápido
5. **funcionar**: the car won't go el coche no funciona
6. **volverse**: he went crazy se volvió loco
> to be going to do something ir a hacer algo: I'm going to call my parents voy a llamar a mis padres; it's going to rain va a llover; what are you going to do? ¿qué vas a hacer?
> her hair has gone white se la ha puesto el pelo blanco
> ready, steady, go! ¡preparados, listos, ya!

go around, **go round** *UK phrasal verb*
■ **andar (por ahí)**: they went around the museum anduvieron por el museo

go away *phrasal verb* ■ **irse:** she's gone away se ha ido

➤ **go away!** ¡vete!

go back *phrasal verb* ■ **volver:** I went back to the shop volví a la tienda

➤ **to go back to sleep** volverse a dormir: I couldn't go back to sleep no pude volverme a dormir

go down *phrasal verb* ■ **bajar:** she has gone down to the cellar ha bajado al sótano; we went down the hill bajamos la colina; prices have gone down han bajado los precios

go in *phrasal verb* ■ **entrar:** Sam knocked on the door and went in Sam golpeó en la puerta y entró

go off *phrasal verb*

1. **explotar:** the bomb went off la bomba explotó

2. **sonar:** the alarm clock went off at 6 a.m. el despertador sonó a las 6 de la mañana

3. **irse:** she went off without me se fue sin mí

4. **apagarse:** the heating went off se apagó la calefacción

5. **echarse a perder:** the milk has gone off la leche se ha echado a perder

go on *phrasal verb*

1. **seguir:** they went on talking siguieron hablando

2. **pasar:** what's going on? ¿qué pasa?

go out *phrasal verb* ■ **salir:** I'm going out tonight voy a salir esta noche; he's going out with Tina está saliendo con Tina

go round *UK verb* ➤ go around

go up *phrasal verb* ■ **subir:** they went up the hill subieron a la colina; prices have gone up han subido los precios

go without *phrasal verb* ■ **pasar sin:** we'll have to go without bread tendremos que pasar sin pan.

go [gəʊ] *noun* ■ **el turno:** it's your go te toca a ti

➤ **to have a go** intentar: have another go! ¡inténtalo otra vez!

goal [gəʊl] *noun*

1. **el objetivo:** our goal is to succeed nuestro objetivo es triunfar

2. **el gol:** he scored the winning goal marcó el gol de la victoria.

goalkeeper [ˈgəʊlˌkiːpəʳ] *noun* ■ **el portero, la portera.**

goat [gəʊt] *noun* ■ **la cabra.**

god [gɒd] *noun* ■ **el dios:** she believes in God cree en Dios

➤ **oh my God!** ¡Dios mío!

goddaughter [ˈgɒdˌdɔːtəʳ] *noun* ■ **la ahijada.**

goddess [ˈgɒdɪs] *noun* ■ **la diosa.**

godfather [ˈgɒdˌfɑːðəʳ] *noun* ■ **el padrino.**

godmother [ˈgɒdˌmʌðəʳ] *noun* ■ **la madrina.**

godson [ˈgɒdsʌn] *noun* ■ **el ahijado.**

goes [gəʊz] ➤ go.

goggles [ˈgɒglz] *plural noun* ■ **las gafas**

➤ **safety goggles** gafas protectoras

➤ **ski goggles** gafas de esquí

➤ **swimming goggles** gafas de natación.

gold [gəʊld] *uncountable noun* ■ **el oro:** it's made of gold es de oro

➤ **a gold medal** una medalla de oro.

golden [ˈgəʊldən] *adjective* ■ **dorado.**

goldfish [ˈgəʊldfɪʃ] *(plural goldfish) noun* ■ **el pez de colores** *(plural* los peces de colores*).*

goldmine [ˈgəʊldmaɪn] *noun* ■ **la mina de oro.**

golf [gɒlf] *noun* ■ **el golf:** he plays golf juega al golf

➤ **a golf ball** una pelota de golf

➤ **a golf club**

1. **un club de golf**

2. **un palo de golf**

➤ **a golf course** un campo de golf.

gone [gɒn] *past participle* ➤ go.

good [gʊd] *(adjective & noun)*

■ *adjective*
bueno

Bueno becomes **buen** before a masculine noun:

it's a really good book es un libro realmente bueno; did you have a good holiday? ¿tuviste unas buenas vacaciones?; have a good day! ¡que tengas un buen día!; that cake looks good el pastel tiene buen aspecto; exercise is good for you el ejercicio es muy bueno
> be good! ¡pórtate bien!
> they were very good to me se portaron muy bien conmigo
> to have a good time pasarlo bien: did you have a good time? ¿lo pasaste bien?
> good morning! ¡buenos días!
> good afternoon! ¡buenas tardes!
> good evening! ¡buenas tardes!; ¡buenas noches!
> good night! ¡buenas noches!
■ *noun*
> el **bien**: good and evil el bien y el mal
> it'll do you good te va a hacer bien
> it's no good crying de nada sirve llorar
> for good para siempre: she left for good se fue para siempre.

goodbye [ˌgʊdˈbaɪ] *exclamation* ■ ¡adiós!

gooseberry [UK 'gʊzbərɪ, US 'guːsbərɪ] *(plural* gooseberries*) noun* ■ la **grosella silvestre.**

good-looking [gʊdˈlʊkɪŋ] *adjective* ■ **guapo, atractivo:** he's very good-looking es muy guapo.

goods [gʊdz] *plural noun* ■ los **bienes,** los **productos.**

goose [guːs] *(plural* geese [giːs]*) noun* ■ el **ganso.**

gorgeous ['gɔːdʒəs] *adjective*
1. **precioso:** what a gorgeous hat! ¡qué sombrero tan precioso!
2. **guapísimo:** she's gorgeous es guapísima.

gorilla [gəˈrɪlə] *noun* ■ el/la **gorila.**

gossip ['gɒsɪp] *(noun & verb)*
■ *noun*
1. el **cotilleo,** los **chismes:** that's just gossip son sólo chismes

2. la **cotilla:** she's a real gossip es muy cotilla
> a piece of gossip un chisme
■ *verb*
cotillear
> to gossip about somebody cotillear sobre alguien.

got [gɒt] *past tense & past participle* ➤ get.

gotten US ['gɒtn] *past participle* ➤ get.

government ['gʌvnmənt] *noun* ■ el **gobierno.**

grab [græb] *(past tense & past participle* grabbed, *present participle* grabbing*) verb* ■ **agarrar:** he grabbed the rope agarró la cuerda.

graceful ['greɪsfʊl] *adjective* ■ **elegante:** the dancer's movements are graceful los movimientos de la bailarina son elegantes.

grade [greɪd] *noun*
1. la **nota:** she always gets good grades siempre saca buenas notas
2. US el **curso:** what grade are you in? ¿en qué curso estás?
> grade school US escuela primaria.

gradually ['grædʒʊəlɪ] *adverb* ■ **poco a poco:** things gradually got better las cosas mejoraron poco a poco.

graduate *(noun & verb)*
■ *noun* ['grædʒʊət]
el **licenciado,** la **licenciada:** she's a university graduate es licenciada universitaria
> graduate school US escuela de posgrado
■ *verb* ['grædʒʊeɪt]
licenciarse: I graduated in 2003 me licencié en 2003.

graffiti [grəˈfiːtɪ] *noun* ■ las **pintadas:** there's some graffiti on the wall hay unas pintadas en la pared.

grain [greɪn] *noun* ■ el **grano:** a grain of sand un grano de arena; a grain of rice un grano de arroz.

gram , **gramme** UK [græm] *noun* ■ el **gramo:** there are 1000 grams in a kilo un kilo tiene 1000 gramos.

grammar ['græmə^r] *noun* ■ la **gramática**.

grammar school ['græmə^rsku:l] *noun*
1. *UK* el **instituto de enseñanza**
2. *US* la **escuela primaria**.

grandchild ['græntʃaɪld] *(plural* grand-children ['græntʃɪldɪ ən]) *noun* ■ **el nieto,** la **nieta:** Mrs. Evans has four grandchildren la señora Evans tiene cuatro nietos.

granddad ['grændæd] *noun* ■ *informal* el **abuelito**.

granddaughter ['græn,dɔːtə^r] *noun* ■ la **nieta**.

grandfather ['grænd,fɑːðə^r] *noun* ■ el **abuelo**.

grandma ['grænmɑː] *noun* ■ *informal* la **abuelita**.

grandmother ['græn,mʌðə^r] *noun* ■ la **abuela**.

grandpa ['grænpɑː] *noun* ■ *informal* el **abuelito**.

grandparents ['græn,peərənts] *plural noun* ■ los **abuelos**.

grandson ['grænsʌn] *noun* ■ el **nieto**.

granny ['grænɪ] *(plural* grannies [græniːz]) *noun* ■ *informal* la **abuelita**.

grant [*UK* grɑːnt, *US* grænt] *(noun & verb)*
■ *noun*
la **beca:** they have a research grant tienen una beca de investigación
■ *verb*
conceder: he granted us permission to enter nos concedió permiso para entrar.

grape [greɪp] *noun* ■ la **uva**
a bunch of grapes un racimo de uvas.

grapefruit ['greɪpfruːt] *noun* ■ el **pomelo**.

graph [*UK* grɑːf, *US* græf] *noun* ■ el **gráfico:** the graph shows the company's profits el gráfico muestra las ganancias de la empresa.

grasp [*UK* grɑːsp, *US* græsp] *verb* ■ **agarrar:** he grasped my hand me agarró la mano.

grass [*UK* grɑːs, *US* græs] *noun*
1. la **hierba:** we lay on the grass nos estiramos en la hierba
2. el **césped:** don't walk on the grass prohibido pisar el césped; I'm going to cut the grass voy a cortar el césped.

grasshopper [*UK* 'grɑːs,hɒpə^r, *US* 'græs,hɒpə^r] *noun* ■ el **saltamontes** *(plural* los **saltamontes***)*.

grate [greɪt] *verb* ■ **rallar:** can you grate some cheese? ¿podrías rallar un poco de queso?

grateful ['greɪtfʊl] *adjective* ■ **agradecido:** I'm very grateful to you te estoy muy agradecido.

grave [greɪv] *noun* ■ la **tumba:** I placed some flowers on the grave puse unas flores en la tumba.

graveyard ['greɪvjɑːd] *noun* ■ el **cementerio**.

gravity ['grævəɪ] *noun* ■ la **gravedad:** the force of gravity la fuerza de la gravedad.

gravy ['greɪvɪ] *uncountable noun* ■ la **salsa (de la carne asada)**.

gray *US* [greɪ] *adjective* ➤ grey *UK*.

grease [griːs] *noun* ■ la **grasa:** the mechanic's hands are covered in grease las manos del mecánico están llenas de grasa.

greasy ['griːzɪ] *adjective*
1. **graso:** her hair was greasy tenía el pelo graso
2. **grasiento:** a greasy rag un trapo grasiento.

great [greɪt] *adjective*
1. **grande**

Grande becomes **gran** before a masculine singular noun:

it's a great success es un gran éxito
2. *informal* **sensacional:** he's a great guy es un tipo sensacional; what a great view! ¡qué vista tan sensacional!
➤ I feel great me siento estupendamente
➤ a great deal of mucho: he has a great deal of money tiene mucho dinero.

Great Britain ['greɪt'brɪtn] *noun* ■ **Gran Bretaña.**

great-grandfather [greɪt'grænd,fɑː-ðəʳ] *noun* ■ el **bisabuelo.**

great-grandmother [greɪt'grænd,mʌ-ðəʳ] *noun* ■ la **bisabuela.**

greedy ['griːdɪ] *adjective*

1. **glotón** *(plural* **glotones),** **glotona:** I want some more cake — don't be greedy! quiero un poco más de pastel –¡no seas glotón!
2. **codicioso:** a greedy businessman un hombre de negocios codicioso.

green [griːnₗ] *adjective* ■ **verde:** she has green eyes tiene los ojos verdes
> a green salad una ensalada verde
> green beans judías verdes
> the Green Party el Partido Verde.

greengrocer *UK* ['griːnₗgrəʊsəʳ] *noun* ■ el **verdulero,** la **verdulera:** the greengrocer's shop la verdulería.

greenhouse ['griːnhaʊs] *noun* ■ el **invernadero**
> the greenhouse effect el efecto invernadero.

greet [griːt] *verb* ■ **saludar:** I greeted him with a wave lo saludé con la mano.

greetings card *UK* ['griːtɪŋzkɑːd], **greeting card** ['griːtɪŋkɑːd] *noun* ■ la **tarjeta de felicitación.**

grew [gruː] *past tense* ➤ **grow.**

grey *UK,* **gray** *US* [greɪ] *adjective* ■ **gris:** the sky is grey el cielo está gris
> she has grey hair tiene el pelo canoso.

grief [griːf] *noun* ■ el **dolor.**

grill [grɪl] *(noun & verb)*
■ *noun*
la **parrilla:** he cooked the fish under the grill hizo el pescado en la parrilla
■ *verb*
asar a la parrilla: I grilled the chicken asé el pollo a la parrilla.

grin [grɪn] *(noun & verb)*
■ *noun*
la **sonrisa:** he had a big grin on his face tenía una gran sonrisa en la cara

■ *verb (past tense & past participle* grinned, *present participle* grinning)
sonreír: she was grinning at me me estaba sonriendo.

grind [graɪnd] *(past tense & past participle* ground) *verb* ■ **moler:** it's for grinding spices sirve para moler especias.

grip [grɪp] *(past tense & past participle* gripped, *present participle* gripping) *verb* ■ **agarrar:** I gripped his arm le agarré el brazo; she was gripping my hand tightly me agarraba la mano con fuerza.

groan [grəʊn] *(noun & verb)*
■ *noun*
el **gemido:** I could hear the patient's groans oía los gemidos del paciente
■ *verb*
gemir: he groaned with pain gemía de dolor.

groceries ['grəʊsərɪz] *noun* ■ los **comestibles:** she's gone to get the groceries fue a comprar comestibles.

grocery store *US* ['grəʊsərɪ,stɔːʳ] *noun* ■ la **tienda de comestibles.**

groom [gruːm] *noun* ■ el **novio**
> the bride and groom la novia y el novio.

gross [grəʊs] *adjective*
1. **grosero:** his behaviour is really gross su comportamiento es realmente grosero
2. **bruto:** his gross income sus ingresos brutos.

ground [graʊnd] *(noun & adjective)*
■ *noun*
1. el **suelo:** I dug a hole in the ground hice un hoyo en el suelo
2. la **zona:** a recreation ground una zona de recreo
3. **campo:** a football ground un campo de fútbol
4. **motivo:** grounds for divorce motivo de divorcio
> on the ground en el suelo: I was sitting on the ground estaba sentada en el suelo
> the ground floor la planta baja: I took the lift to the ground floor tomé el ascensor hasta la planta baja
■ *adjective*
molido: ground coffee café molido
> ground beef *US* carne picada.

group [gruːp] *noun* ■ el **grupo: a large group** of tourists un grupo grande de turistas.

grow [grəʊ] *(past tense* **grew,** *past participle* **grown)** *verb*

1. **crecer: these plants grow quickly** estas plantas crecen rápido

2. **aumentar: the number of net users has grown** ha aumentado el número de usuarios de la red

3. **cultivar: we grow a lot of vegetables** cultivamos muchas verduras

4. **dejarse crecer: she's growing her hair** se está dejando crecer el pelo
- **to grow bigger** crecer
- **to grow old** envejecer: **he's growing old** está envejeciendo

grow up *phrasal verb* ■ **criarse: I grew up in Oxford** me crié en Oxford
- **I want to be a pilot when I grow up** cuando sea mayor, quiero ser piloto.

growl [graʊl] *verb* ■ **gruñir: the dog growled** el perro gruñó.

grown [grəʊn] *past participle* ➤ **grow.**

grown-up ['grəʊnʌp] *(adjective & noun)*

■ *adjective*
adulto: children must be accompanied by a grown-up los niños deben ir acompañados de un adulto

■ *noun*
la persona mayor: you're a grown-up now ya eres una persona mayor.

growth [grəʊθ] *noun* ■ el **crecimiento: economic growth** crecimiento económico.

grumble ['grʌmbl] *verb* ■ **quejarse: she's always grumbling about something** siempre está quejándose de algo.

grumpy ['grʌmpɪ] *adjective* ■ **gruñón** *(plural* gruñones), **gruñona: a grumpy old man** un viejo gruñón.

grunt [grʌnt] *verb* ■ **gruñir: the pigs were grunting** los cerdos estaban gruñendo.

guarantee [ˌgærən'tiː] *(noun & verb)*

■ *noun*
la garantía: it has a five-year guarantee tiene cinco años de garantía

■ *verb*
garantizar: I can't guarantee I'll come no puedo garantizar que vaya a venir
- **my watch is guaranteed** mi reloj tiene garantía.

guard [gɑːd] *(noun & verb)*

■ *noun*
el/la guardia: he's a prison guard es guardia de prisión
- **to be on guard** estar de guardia
- **a guard dog** un perro guardián

■ *verb*
vigilar: the soldiers are guarding the building los soldados están vigilando el edificio.

guava ['gwɑːvə] *noun* ■ la **guayaba.**

guess [ges] *(noun & verb)*

■ *noun*
la suposición *(plural* las **suposiciones): it's just a guess** es sólo una suposición
- **to take a guess** adivinar

■ *verb*

1. **adivinar: I couldn't guess the answer** no pude adivinar la respuesta; **guess what I did!** ¡adivina qué hice!

2. **suponer: I guess so** supongo que sí.

guest [gest] *noun*

1. el **invitado,** la **invitada: we're having guests for dinner** tenemos invitados a cenar

2. el/la **huésped: the hotel has over 100 guests** el hotel tiene más de 100 huéspedes.

guesthouse ['gesthaʊs, *plural* 'gesthaʊzɪz] *noun* ■ la **casa de huéspedes.**

guide [gaɪd] *(noun & verb)*

■ *noun*
el/la **guía: he's a tour guide** es guía turístico
- **a guide book** una guía
- **a guide dog** un perro lazarillo

■ *verb*
guiar: he guided us to the castle nos guió hasta el castillo.

guilty ['gɪltɪ] *adjective* ■ **culpable: he's not guilty of theft** no es culpable de robo; **I feel guilty about lying to her** me siento culpable por haberle mentido.

guinea pig ['gɪnɪpɪg] *noun* ■ el **conejillo de Indias.**

guitar [gɪˈtɑːʳ] *noun* ■ la **guitarra: I'm learning to play guitar** estoy aprendiendo a tocar la guitarra.

gum [gʌm] *noun* ■ el **chicle: a stick of gum** un chicle.

gums [gʌmz] *plural noun* ■ la **encía.**

gun [gʌn] *noun*

1. el **revólver,** la **pistola: he has a gun in his hand** lleva un revólver en la mano; **the thief threw his gun to the ground** el ladrón tiró la pistola al suelo

2. el **fusil: he bought a gun for hunting** compró un fusil de caza

3. el **arma: he fired a gun** disparó un arma.

gunfire [ˈgʌnfaɪəʳ] *uncountable noun* ■ los **disparos: we could hear gunfire** escuchábamos disparos.

gutter [ˈgʌtəʳ] *noun* ■ la **cuneta.**

guy [gaɪ] *noun* ■ *informal* el **tipo: he's a nice guy** es un tipo simpático.

Guy Fawkes' Night [gaɪˈfɔksnaɪt] *noun* ■ *fiesta celebrada en Gran Bretaña el 5 de noviembre*

GUY FAWKES' NIGHT

El 5 de noviembre, los británicos celebran la **Guy Fawkes' Night** o **Bonfire Night** en recuerdo de la Conspiración de la pólvora de 1605, durante la que un grupo de católicos comandados por Guy Fawkes intentó hacer volar el Parlamento. El complot fue descubierto el 4 de noviembre y los conspiradores fueron ajusticiados. Hoy, la gente lanza fuegos artificiales y se encienden grandes hogueras sobre las que se quema la efigie de Guy Fawkes.

gym [dʒɪm] *noun*

1. el **gimnasio: I go to the gym on Mondays** voy al gimnasio los lunes

2. la **gimnasia: we have gym class after lunch** tenemos clase de gimnasia después del almuerzo.

gypsy , gipsy [ˈdʒɪpsɪ] *(plural* gypsies OR gipsies [ˈdʒɪpsiːz]*) noun* ■ el **gitano,** la **gitana.**

habit [ˈhæbɪt] *noun* ■ la **costumbre: she has some bad habits** tiene algunas malas costumbres

➤ **I've got into the habit of exercising** me he acostumbrado a hacer ejercicio.

hacker [ˈhækəʳ] *noun* ■ el **pirata informático,** la **pirata informática.**

had [hæd] *past tense & past participle* ➤ have.

hadn't [ˈhædnt] = had not: **I hadn't finished** no había terminado.

hail [heɪl] *(noun & verb)*

■ *noun*

el **granizo**

■ *verb*

1. **granizar: it's hailing** está granizando

2. **hacerle señas a: he hailed a cab** le hizo señas a un taxi.

hair [heəʳ] *noun* ■ el **pelo: she has black hair** tiene el pelo negro; **his hair is very long** tiene el pelo muy largo; **there's dog hair everywhere** hay pelos del perro por todas partes; **there's a hair in my soup** hay un pelo en la sopa

➤ **to do one's hair** peinarse: **she's doing her hair** se está peinando

➤ **a hair clip** una horquilla para el pelo.

hairbrush [ˈheəbrʌʃ] *noun* ■ el **cepillo.**

haircut [ˈheəkʌt] *noun* ■ el **corte de pelo: she has a great haircut** lleva un corte de pelo sensacional; **I'm going to have a haircut** voy a cortarme el pelo.

hairdresser [ˈheəˌdresəʳ] *noun* ■ **el peluquero, la peluquera**: she's a hairdresser es peluquera
the hairdresser's la peluquería.

hairdryer [ˈheəˌdraɪəʳ] *noun* ■ **el secador de pelo.**

hairspray [ˈheəspreɪ] *noun* ■ **la laca.**

hairstyle [ˈheəstaɪl] *noun* ■ **el peinado**: she hasn't changed her hairstyle in years hace años que no cambia de peinado.

hairy [ˈheərɪ] *adjective* ■ **peludo**: he has hairy arms tiene los brazos peludos.

half [*UK* hɑːf, *US* hæf] *(noun & adverb)*
■ *noun*
1. **la mitad**: he ate half the cake se comió la mitad del pastel
2. *in time expressions* an hour and a half una hora y media; half an hour media hora; it's half past three son las tres y media; two and a half years dos años y medio
3. **el tiempo**: the first half of the game el primer tiempo del partido
to cut something in half partir algo por la mitad
■ *adverb*
medio: she's half asleep está medio dormida
he's half Spanish, half English es mitad español, mitad inglés
half term *UK* vacaciones de una semana a mediados de cada trimestre escolar.

half-time [*UK* ˈhɑːfˌtaɪm, *US* ˈhæfˌtaɪm] *noun* ■ **el descanso**: he came back after half-time volvió después del descanso.

halfway [*UK* hɑːfˈweɪ, *US* hæfˈweɪ] *adverb* ■ **a medio camino**: halfway between Manchester and London a medio camino entre Manchester y Londres
halfway through the film en la mitad de la película.

hall [hɔːl] *noun*
1. **el vestíbulo**: he hung his coat up in the hall colgó el abrigo en el vestíbulo
2. **la sala**: there's a large hall where meetings take place hay una amplia sala donde tienen lugar las reuniones.

Halloween [ˌhæləʊˈiːn] *noun* ■ **Halloween** *(masculine)*

> **HALLOWEEN**
>
> Se pensaba que el 31 de octubre, víspera del Día de Todos los Santos, los espíritus de los muertos venían a visitar a los vivos. Hoy en día, los niños se disfrazan de brujas y fantasmas y van de puerta en puerta, diciendo "trick or treat!" (susto o caramelo) para pedir golosinas.

hallway [ˈhɔːlweɪ] *noun* ■ **el vestíbulo.**

halt [hɔːlt] *noun*
to come to a halt detenerse: the car came to a halt el coche se detuvo.

ham [hæm] *noun* ■ **el jamón** *(plural* los jamones*)*: a ham sandwich un bocadillo de jamón.

hamburger [ˈhæmbɜːgəʳ] *noun* ■ **la hamburguesa**: Mum's making hamburgers for dinner mamá está preparando hamburguesas para la cena.

hammer [ˈhæməʳ] *noun* ■ **el martillo.**

hamster [ˈhæmstəʳ] *noun* ■ **el hámster** *(plural* los hámsters)

hand [hænd] *(noun & verb)*
■ *noun*
1. **la mano**: he writes with his left hand escribe con la mano izquierda
2. **la manecilla**: the hands of a clock las manecillas de un reloj
to hold hands ir de la mano: they were holding hands iban de la mano
to give somebody a hand echarle una mano a alguien: he gave me a hand with my suitcases me echó una mano con las maletas
■ *verb*
pasar: can you hand me a pencil? ¿puedes pasarme un lápiz?

hand in *phrasal verb* ■ **entregar**: they handed in their homework entregaron los deberes

hand out *phrasal verb* ■ **repartir**: the teacher handed out the papers la profesora repartió los papeles

hand over *phrasal verb* ■ **entregar:** I handed the money over to her le entregué el dinero.

handbag [ˈhændbæg] *noun* ■ el **bolso.**

handcuffs [ˈhændkʌfs] *plural noun* ■ las **esposas.**

handkerchief [ˈhæŋkətʃɪf] *(plural hand-kerchiefs OR handkerchieves* [ˈhæŋkətʃɪvz]*) noun* ■ el **pañuelo.**

handle [ˈhændl] *(noun & verb)*
■ *noun*
1. la **manilla:** he turned the door handle giró la manilla de la puerta
2. el **asa** *(feminine)*

> Although **asa** is a feminine noun, it takes **un** or **el** in the singular.

hold the cup by the handle coge la taza por el asa
3. el **mango:** the frying pan handle is broken el mango de la sartén está roto
■ *verb*
1. **manejar:** he handled the situation well manejó bien la situación
2. **tratar:** he knows how to handle people sabe tratar a las personas.

handlebars [ˈhændlbɑːz] *plural noun* ■ el **manillar.**

handmade [ˌhændˈmeɪd] *adjective* ■ hecho a mano.

handrail [ˈhændreɪl] *noun* ■ la **barandi-lla:** hold on to the handrail cógete a la barandilla.

handset [ˈhændset] *noun* ■ el **auricular.**

handsome [ˈhænsəm] *adjective* ■ **guapo, apuesto:** he's very handsome es muy guapo.

handy [ˈhændɪ] *adjective*
1. **práctico:** it's a handy little tool es una pe-queña herramienta muy útil
2. **a mano:** I always have extra batteries handy siempre tengo pilas de más a mano
3. **muy cerca:** the shops are handy las tiendas están muy cerca.

hang [hæŋ] *(past tense & past participle* hung*) verb*
1. **colgar:** he hung the picture on the wall colgó el cuadro en la pared; the picture is hanging on the wall el cuadro está colgado en la pared
2. *(past tense & past participle* hanged*)* **ahorcar:** they hanged the murderer ahorcaron al asesino

hang on *phrasal verb* ■ *informal* **esperar:** can you hang on a minute? ¿puedes espe-rar un minuto?

hang up *phrasal verb* ■ **colgar:** hang up your coat cuelga tu abrigo; they hung the decorations up colgaron los adornos; after the phone call he hung up después de la llamada telefónica, colgó.

hanger [ˈhæŋəʳ] *noun* ■ la **percha:** put your jacket on the hanger cuelga tu cha-queta en la percha.

happen [ˈhæpən] *verb* ■ **pasar:** what happened? ¿qué pasó?; it happened last week pasó la semana pasada; guess what happened to me! ¡adivina lo que me pasó!; what's happening? ¿qué pasa?

happier [ˈhæpɪəʳ] *comparative* ➤ happy.

happiest [ˈhæpɪəst] *superlative* ➤ happy.

happiness [ˈhæpɪnɪs] *uncountable noun* ■ la **felicidad.**

happy [ˈhæpɪ] *(comparative* happier, *su-perlative* happiest*) adjective* ■ **contento:** I'm very happy to see you estoy muy contento de verte; Karen looks happier today Karen parece más contenta hoy
➤ Happy birthday! ¡Feliz cumpleaños!
➤ Happy Christmas! ¡Feliz Navidad!
➤ Happy New Year! ¡Feliz Año Nuevo!

harbour *UK*, **harbor** *US* [ˈhɑːbəʳ] *noun* ■ el **puerto:** the ships are in the harbour los barcos están en el puerto.

hard [hɑːd] *(adjective & adverb)*
■ *adjective*
1. **duro:** the bed is very hard la cama es muy dura

2. difícil: that's a hard question ésa es una pregunta difícil

she's very hard on him es muy dura con él

the hard disk el disco duro

adverb

duro: she works hard trabaja duro

to try hard esforzarse: I tried very hard to succeed me esforcé mucho para lograrlo.

hard-boiled [hɑːd'bɔɪld] adjective

a hard-boiled egg un huevo duro.

hardly ['hɑːdlɪ] adverb ■ apenas: I hardly know him apenas lo conozco

hardly ever casi nunca: he hardly ever phones casi nunca llama por teléfono.

hardware ['hɑːdweəʳ] noun ■ el hardware: I'm installing the new hardware on the computer estoy instalando el nuevo hardware en el ordenador

a hardware store una ferretería.

hare [heəʳ] noun ■ la liebre.

harm [hɑːm] (noun & verb)

noun

el daño: it won't do him any harm no le hará ningún daño

verb

1. hacerle daño a: he wouldn't harm a fly no le haría daño ni a una mosca

2. dañar: the gases could harm the environment los gases podrían dañar el medio ambiente.

harmful ['hɑːmfʊl] adjective ■ perjudicial: the harmful effects of smoking los efectos perjudiciales del tabaco.

harmless ['hɑːmlɪs] adjective ■ inofensivo: these animals are harmless estos animales son inofensivos.

harmonica ['hɑːmɒnɪ] noun ■ la armónica: he plays the harmonica toca la armónica.

harsh [hɑːʃ] adjective ■ severo: it's a harsh punishment es un castigo severo.

harvest ['hɑːvɪst] noun ■ la cosecha: there's a lot of work at harvest time hay mucho trabajo en época de cosecha.

has [həz, hæz] ➤ have.

hasn't ['hæznt] = has not: he hasn't finished no ha terminado.

hat [hæt] noun ■ el sombrero: she's wearing a big hat lleva puesto un sombrero grande.

hate [heɪt] verb ■ odiar: I hate liver odio el hígado

to hate doing something odiar hacer algo: he hates getting up early odia levantarse temprano.

hatred ['heɪtrɪd] noun ■ el odio.

haunted ['hɔːntɪd] adjective ■ embrujado: this house is haunted esta casa está embrujada.

have [hæv] (past tense & past participle had) verb

1. tener: I have a dog called Sammy OR I've got a dog called Sammy tengo un perro que se llama Sammy; do you have any brothers? OR have you got any brothers? ¿tienes hermanos?; Rosie has blue eyes OR Rosie has got blue eyes Rosie tiene los ojos azules; they didn't have time no tenían tiempo

2.

When "have" is used with certain nouns, you can use a single verb in Spanish to translate "have" + noun:

I'm going to have a shower voy a ducharme; I'll have some coffee tomaré café; what time do you have breakfast? ¿a qué hora desayunas?; we had a sandwich for lunch almorzamos un bocadillo; let's have dinner vamos a cenar

3. pasar: we had a nice evening pasamos una tarde agradable; I hope you have a good time espero que te lo pases bien

4. in the perfect tenses haber: have you seen my glasses? ¿has visto mis gafas?; she had forgotten to phone se había olvidado de llamar; he has become very rich se ha hecho muy rico

5.

"Have to" and "have got to" are translated by tener que + infinitive:

I have to leave OR I've got to leave tengo que irme; he had to go to the dentist tuvo que ir al dentista

To say you "don't have to", use the construction **no tener que** + infinitive:

you don't have to come no tienes que venir
▸ **to have something done** mandar hacer algo: **I'm going to have the rugs cleaned** voy a mandar limpiar las alfombras
▸ **to have a party** tener una fiesta: **I'm having a party on Friday** tengo una fiesta el viernes.

haven't ['hævnt] = have not: **I haven't been to Spain** no he estado en España.

hay [heɪ] *uncountable noun* ■ el **heno: the cows are eating hay** las vacas están comiendo heno
▸ **hay fever** fiebre del heno: **she has hay fever** tiene fiebre del heno.

hazardous ['hæzədəs] *adjective* ■ **peligroso.**

hazelnut ['heɪzl,nʌt] *noun* ■ la **avellana.**

he [hiː] *personal pronoun* ■ **él**

In Spanish, **he** is not usually translated:

he's called John se llama John; **he came to see me** vino a verme; **he's a clever man** es un hombre listo

Use **él** for emphasis or to avoid ambiguity:

he did it él lo hizo; **he doesn't know it but she does** él no lo sabe pero ella sí
▸ **there he is!** ¡ahí está!

head [hed] *noun*
1. la **cabeza: my head hurts** me duele la cabeza
2. el **jefe**, la **jefa: he's the head of state** es el jefe de Estado
3. *UK* el **director**, la **directora: the head of the school** la directora de la escuela
▸ **heads or tails?** ¿cara o cruz?

head for *phrasal verb* ■ **dirigirse hacia: they're heading for the exit** se dirigen hacia la salida.

headache ['hedeɪk] *noun* ■ el **dolor de cabeza: she has a headache** tiene dolor de cabeza.

headlight ['hedlaɪt] *noun* ■ el **faro: the driver put the headlights on** el conductor encendió los faros.

headline ['hedlaɪn] *noun* ■ el **titular: to read the headlines** leer los titulares.

headmaster *UK* [,hed'mɑːstəʳ] *noun* ■ **director: he's headmaster of the school** es el director del colegio.

headmistress *UK* [,hed'mɪstrɪs] *noun* ■ la **directora: she's headmistress of the school** es la directora del colegio.

headphones ['hedfəʊnz] *plural noun* ■ los **auriculares: she put on her headphones to listen to the music** se puso los auriculares para escuchar música.

heal [hiːl] *verb*
1. **cicatrizar: the wound is healing** la herida está cicatrizando
2. **curar: this will heal your wounds** esto curará tus heridas.

health [helθ] *uncountable noun* ■ la **salud: he's in good health** tiene buena salud.

healthy ['helθɪ] *adjective*
1. **sano: she's very healthy** es muy sana; **he leads a healthy life** lleva una vida sana; **a healthy diet** una dieta sana
2. **saludable: a healthy climate** un clima saludable.

heap [hiːp] *noun* ■ el **montón** *(plural los* **montones***): a heap of leaves** un montón de hojas; **his clothes are lying in a heap** su ropa está tirada en un montón.

hear [hɪəʳ] *(past tense & past participle* heard [hɜːd]*) verb*
1. **oír: I can't hear you** no te oigo; **she heard a noise** oyó un ruido; **I heard him laughing** lo oí reírse; **have you heard the news?** ¿has oído las noticias?
2. **enterarse: I've heard he was ill** me he enterado de que estaba enfermo; **I've heard you've got a new car** me he enterado de que tienes un coche nuevo

hear from *phrasal verb* ■ **tener noticias de: I haven't heard from her for ages** hace años que no tengo noticias de ella

hear of *phrasal verb* ■ **oír hablar de:** I've never heard of him nunca he oído hablar de él.

heart [hɑːt] *noun* ■ **el corazón** *(plural los corazones)*: my heart missed a beat me dio un vuelco el corazón
by heart de memoria: I know the poem by heart me sé el poema de memoria
a heart attack un ataque al corazón
the ace of hearts el as de corazones.

heat [hiːt] *(noun & verb)*
■ *noun*
el calor: I don't like the heat no me gusta el calor
■ *verb*
calentar: heat the water for ten minutes caliente el agua durante diez minutos

heat up *phrasal verb*
1. **calentar:** I heated the pizza up in the oven calenté la pizza en el horno; I heated up the milk calenté la leche
2. **calentarse:** the water is heating up el agua se está calentando.

heater ['hiːtə'] *noun* ■ **el calentador:** he turned the heater on encendió el calentador.

heating ['hiːtɪŋ] *noun* ■ **la calefacción:** he put the heating on puso la calefacción.

heaven ['hevn] *noun* ■ **el cielo:** will he go to heaven? ¿irá al cielo?

heavy ['hevɪ] *(comparative* heavier, *superlative* heaviest) *adjective*
1. **pesado:** my luggage is very heavy mi equipaje es muy pesado
2. **grueso:** a heavy coat un abrigo grueso
3. **apretado:** I had a heavy week tuve una semana muy apretada
the traffic is heavy at weekends los fines de semana hay mucho tráfico
how heavy is it? ¿cuánto pesa?; is your bag heavy? ¿pesa mucho tu bolsa?

he'd [hiːd]
1. = he had: he'd already finished ya había terminado
2. = he would: he'd like to come le gustaría venir.

hedge [hedʒ] *noun* ■ **el seto:** there's a hedge around the garden hay un seto alrededor del jardín.

hedgehog ['hedʒhɒg] *noun* ■ **el erizo.**

heel [hiːl] *noun*
1. **el talón** *(plural los talones)*: these socks have a hole in the heel estos calcetines tienen un agujero en el talón
2. **el tacón** *(plural los tacones)*: her shoes have very high heels sus zapatos tienen los tacones muy altos.

height [haɪt] *noun*
1. **la altura:** what is the height of the wall? ¿qué altura tiene la pared?
2. **la estatura:** she's of average height es de estatura mediana.

heir [eə'] *noun* ■ **el heredero, la heredera.**

held [held] *past tense & past participle* ➤ **hold.**

helicopter ['helɪkɒptə'] *noun* ■ **el helicóptero.**

hell [hel] *noun* ■ **el infierno:** heaven and hell el cielo y el infierno.

he'll [hiːl] = he will: he'll be here soon pronto llegará.

hello [hə'ləʊ] *exclamation*
1. **hola:** hello, how are you? hola, ¿cómo estás?
2. **¡dígame!, ¿sí?:** hello — is Paul there? ¡dígame! —¿está Paul?

helmet ['helmɪt] *noun* ■ **el casco:** you should wear a helmet when you ride your bike deberías usar casco cuando vayas en bicicleta.

help [help] *(noun, exclamation & verb)*
■ *noun*
la ayuda: do you need any help? ¿necesitas ayuda?; he asked for help pidió ayuda
■ *exclamation*
socorro: help, I'm drowning! ¡socorro! ¡que me ahogo!
■ *verb*
ayudar: can I help you? ¿te ayudo?; can you help me with my homework? ¿puedes ayudarme con los deberes?; I helped her wash the car la ayudé a lavar el coche

➤ **I can't help it** no puedo evitarlo
➤ **help yourself!** ¡sírvete!: **can I have some water? — help yourself!** ¿puedo beber agua? –sí, ¡sírvete!
➤ **I helped myself to some cheese** me serví un poco de queso.

helpful ['helpfʊl] adjective

1. **servicial: he's always very helpful** siempre es muy servicial
2. **útil: your advice was helpful** tu consejo fue útil.

helping ['helpɪŋ] noun ■ la **ración,** la **porción** (plural las **porciones**): **I had a big helping of rice** me serví una buena ración de arroz
➤ **to have a second helping** repetir: **would you like to have a second helping of cake?** ¿quieres repetir pastel?

hen [hen] noun ■ la **gallina.**

her [hɜːʳ] (pronoun & adjective)

■ personal pronoun

1. direct object **la: can you see her?** ¿la ves?; **call her!** ¡llámala!; **I didn't see her** no la vi; **he has always loved her** siempre la ha amado
2. indirect object **le: I gave her the flowers** le dí las flores

> Use **se** instead of **le** when **her** is used with a direct object pronoun:
>
> **give them to her!** ¡dáselas!

3. after a preposition **ella: these chocolates are for her** estos chocolates son para ella; **I'm taller than her** soy más alto que ella

■ possessive adjective
su

> In Spanish the possessive adjective agrees in number (singular or plural) with the noun that follows:
>
> **her father is a doctor** su padre es médico; **her car won't start** su coche no arranca; **she lent me her books** me prestó sus libros

> Use the definite article (**el, la, los** or **las**), not the possessive adjective, with parts of the body:

she raised her hand levantó la mano; **I'm brushing my teeth** me estoy cepillando los dientes.

herb [UK hɜːrb, US ɜːrb] noun ■ la **hierba: basil is an aromatic herb** la albahaca es una hierba aromática.

herd [hɜːd] noun ■ el **rebaño: a herd of sheep** un rebaño de ovejas.

here [hɪəʳ] adverb ■ **aquí: come here!** ¡ven aquí!
➤ **here is** OR **here's** aquí está: **here's Jenny** aquí está Jenny
➤ **here are** aquí están: **here are your keys** aquí están tus llaves.

hero ['hɪərəʊ] (plural heroes) noun ■ el **héroe: he's my hero** es mi héroe.

heroin ['herəʊɪn] noun ■ la **heroína: heroin is a very addictive dangerous drug** la heroína es una droga muy adictiva y peligrosa.

heroine ['herəʊɪn] noun

1. la **heroína: she's my heroine** es mi heroína
2. la **protagonista: who is the heroine of the book?** ¿quién es la protagonista del libro?

herring ['herɪŋ] noun ■ el **arenque.**

hers [hɜːz] possessive pronoun

1. **el suyo**

> In Spanish the possessive pronoun agrees in gender (masculine or feminine) and number (singular or plural) with the noun it replaces:
>
> **my blouse is blue, hers is red** mi blusa es azul, la suya es roja

2. **suyo: that book's not hers** ese libro no es suyo; **she's a friend of hers** es una amiga suya.

herself [hɜːˈself] pronoun

1. **se: she's washing herself** se está lavando; **she enjoyed herself** se divirtió
2. **ella misma: she made it herself** lo hizo ella misma
➤ **she's pleased with herself** está satisfecha consigo misma
➤ **by herself** sola: **Amy is all by herself** Amy está completamente sola; **she did it by herself** lo hizo ella sola.

he's [hiːz]

1. = he is: **he's a teacher** es profesor
2. = he has: (got) **he's got a dog** tiene un perro.

hesitate ['hezɪteɪt] *verb* ■ dudar: I hesitated for a moment dudé por un momento; don't hesitate to call me! ¡no dudes en llamarme!

hi [haɪ] *exclamation* ■ *informal* hola: hi, how are you? hola, ¿qué tal?

hiccup ['hɪkʌp] *noun* ■ el hipo: I've got the hiccups tengo hipo.

hid [hɪd] *past tense* ➤ hide.

hidden ['hɪdn] *past participle* ➤ hide.

hide [haɪd] *(past tense* hid, *past participle* hidden) *verb*

1. esconder: hide the presents! ¡esconde los regalos!
2. esconderse: she hid behind the sofa se escondió detrás del sofá.

hide-and-seek [haɪdɔndsiːk] *noun* ■ el escondite: they're playing hide-and-seek están jugando al escondite.

hi-fi ['haɪfaɪ] *noun* ■ el equipo de alta fidelidad.

high [haɪ] *adjective*

1. alto: this fence is very high esta valla es muy alta; prices are high in New York los precios son altos en Nueva York; how high is the tower? ¿qué altura tiene la torre?, it's 6 metres high tiene 6 metros de altura
2. agudo: she has a high voice tiene una voz aguda
➤ the high jump el salto de altura
➤ at high speed a alta velocidad: the train travels at high speed el tren va a gran velocidad.

higher ['haɪəʳ] *(comparative of* high *)*
➤ higher education educación superior.

highlight ['haɪlaɪt] *(noun & verb)*
■ *noun*
1. lo más destacado: the speech was the highlight of the evening el discurso fue lo más destacado de la noche
■ *verb*
1. marcar con rotulador fluorescente: I've highlighted the important words in yellow marqué con rotulador fluorescente amarillo las palabras importantes

2. resaltar: double-click on a word to highlight it haz doble clic sobre una palabra para resaltarla.

highlighter ['haɪlaɪtəʳ] *noun* ■ el rotulador fluorescente.

high school [haɪskuːl] *noun*

1. *US* el instituto de enseñanza secundaria: he's still in high school todavía está en instituto
2. *UK* la escuela secundaria *(normalmente femenina)*.

high-tech , hi-tech [haɪ'tek] *adjective* ■ de alta tecnología: it's a high-tech computer es un ordenador de alta tecnología
➤ a high-tech industry una industria de alta tecnología.

highway *US* ['haɪweɪ] *noun* ■ la autopista
➤ the highway code el código de circulación.

hijack ['haɪdʒæk] *verb* ■ secuestrar: a plane has been hijacked secuestraron un avión.

hijacker ['haɪdʒækəʳ] *noun* ■ el secuestrador, la secuestradora.

hike [haɪk] *noun* ■ la excursión a pie, la caminata: we went on a hike in the morning fuimos de excursión por la mañana.

hiking ['haɪkɪŋ] *noun* ■ el excursionismo, el senderismo: do you want to go hiking? ¿quieres hacer excursionismo?

hilarious [hɪ'leərɪəs] *adjective* ■ divertidísimo: the show was hilarious el programa fue divertidísimo.

hill [hɪl] *noun* ■ la colina: there's a house on the top of the hill hay una casa en la cima de la colina; they walked up the hill subieron la colina andando.

him [hɪm] *personal pronoun*

1. *direct object* lo, le: I can't see him no lo veo; find him! ¡encuéntralo!; I saw him lo vi
2. *indirect object* le: she gave him a kiss le dio un beso; tell him to come dile que venga

Use se instead of le when him is used with a direct object pronoun:

give them to him! dáselos

3. *after preposition* **él: these CDs are for him** estos CDs son para él; **I'm taller than him** soy más alta que él.

himself [hɪm'self] *pronoun*

1. se: he's washing himself se está lavando; **he cut himself** se cortó

2. él mismo: he made it himself lo hizo él mismo **Jack's very pleased with himself** Jack está muy satisfecho consigo mismo

➤ **by himself** solo: **he's all by himself** está completamente solo; **he did it by himself** lo hizo él solo.

hip [hɪp] *noun* ■ la **cadera**.

hippopotamus [ˌhɪpə'pɒtəməs], **hippo** ['hɪpəʊ] *noun* ■ el **hipopótamo**.

hire ['haɪəʳ] *(verb & noun)*

■ *verb*

1. *UK* **alquilar: we hired a car** alquilamos un coche

2. contratar: the factory hired 20 new workers la fábrica contrató 20 nuevos trabajadores

■ *noun*

➤ **for hire** se alquila: **this car is for hire** se alquila este coche.

his [hɪz] *(adjective & pronoun)*

■ *possessive adjective*

su

In Spanish the possessive adjective agrees in number (singular or plural) with the noun that follows:

his brother is called Dan su hermano se llama Dan; **his car won't start** su coche no arranca; **his parents are away** sus padres han salido

Use the definite article (**el, la, los** or **las**), not the possessive adjective, with parts of the body:

he raised his hand levantó la mano; **he's washing his face** se está lavando la cara

■ *possessive pronoun*

1. el suyo

In Spanish the possessive pronoun agrees in gender (masculine or feminine) and number (singular or plural) with the noun it replaces:

my shirt is green, his is blue mi camisa es verde, la suya es azul

2. suyo: it's his es suyo; **he's a friend of his** es un amigo suyo.

hiss [hɪs] *verb* ■ **silbar: the snake hissed** la serpiente silbó.

history ['hɪstərɪ] *noun* ■ la **historia: they're studying American history** están estudiando la historia de Estados Unidos.

hit [hɪt] *(verb & noun)*

■ *verb (past tense & past participle* hit*)*

1. golpear: she hit him lo golpeó

2. chocar: the car hit a tree el coche chocó contra un árbol

3. atropellar: she was hit by a car la atropelló un coche

4. golpearse: I hit my knee on the table me golpeé la rodilla con la mesa

5. dar en: the bullet hit the target la bala dio en el blanco

■ *noun*

el éxito: her book was a big hit su libro fue un gran éxito.

hitchhike ['hɪtʃhaɪk] *verb* ■ **hacer autostop: she hitchhiked to Madrid** hizo autostop hasta Madrid.

hi-tech *adjective* ➤ high-tech.

hoarse [hɔːs] *adjective* ■ **ronco: my voice is hoarse** tengo la voz ronca.

hobby ['hɒbɪ] *(plural* hobbies ['hɒbɪz]*)* *noun* ■ el **hobby** *(plural* los **hobbies***)*: **do you have any hobbies?** ¿tienes algún hobby?

hockey ['hɒkɪ] *noun*

1. *UK* el **hockey sobre hierba: they're playing hockey** están jugando a hockey

2. *US* el **hockey sobre hielo**.

Hogmanay ['hɒgmənei] *noun* ■ la *Nochevieja en Escocia*.

hold [həʊld] *(past tense & past participle* held*)* *verb*

1. sostener, tener en la mano: I was holding the key in my hand tenía la llave en la mano

2. tener una capacidad de: the bottle holds two litres of water la botella tiene una capacidad de dos litros de agua

3. celebrar: we're holding a meeting tomorrow vamos a celebrar una reunión mañana

⟩ to hold one's breath contener la respiración: how long can you hold your breath? ¿cuánto tiempo puedes contener la respiración?

⟩ please hold the line! no cuelgue, por favor

⟩ hold it! ¡espera!

⟩ to get hold of something conseguir algo: I couldn't get hold of his address no pude conseguir su dirección

hold on phrasal verb

1. esperar: hold on a minute! ¡espera un minuto!

2. agarrarse: hold on tight! ¡agárrate fuerte!

⟩ to hold onto something cogerse a algo: hold onto the railing cógete a la barandilla

hold out phrasal verb ■ tender: he held out his hand le tendió la mano

hold up phrasal verb

1. levantar: she held up her hand levantó la mano

2. retrasarse: we were held up in a traffic jam nos retrasamos debido a un embotellamiento

3. atracar: three men held up the bank tres hombres atracaron el banco.

hold-up ['həʊldʌp] noun

1. el atraco: there was a hold-up at the bank hubo un atraco en el banco

2. el retraso: what's the hold-up? ¿de cuánto es el retraso?

hole [həʊl] noun ■ el agujero: the puppy was digging a hole el cachorro estaba haciendo un agujero.

holiday ['hɒlɪdeɪ] noun

1. UK las vacaciones: they're on holiday están de vacaciones; I'm going on holiday next week me voy de vacaciones la próxima semana; did you have a nice holiday? ¿has tenido unas buenas vacaciones?; the school holidays las vacaciones escolares

2. el día festivo: 26th December is a holiday in the UK el 26 de diciembre es un día festivo en Gran Bretaña

⟩ the holidays las vacaciones: what are you doing for the holidays ¿qué vas a hacer en vacaciones?

hollow ['hɒləʊ] adjective ■ hueco: the tree trunk is hollow el tronco del árbol está hueco.

holly ['hɒlɪ] noun ■ el acebo.

Hollywood ['hɒlɪwʊd] noun ■ Hollywood (masculine)

HOLLYWOOD

Hollywood es una zona de Los Angeles, California, donde se producen la mayor parte de las películas estadounidenses desde hace casi un siglo y donde viven muchas estrellas. Las primeras productoras cinematográficas se establecieron allí en 1908 porque el clima privilegiado permitía rodar en exteriores todo el año. Las décadas de 1930 y 1940 fueron la época dorada de Hollywood.

holy ['həʊlɪ] adjective ■ santo.

home [həʊm] (noun & adverb)

■ noun

la casa: you have a lovely home tienes una casa preciosa

⟩ a home page una página de inicio

■ adverb

casa: she took me home me llevó a mi casa

⟩ at home en casa: I stayed at home today hoy me he quedado en casa

⟩ make yourself at home! ¡estás en tu casa!

⟩ to go home irse a casa: I want to go home quiero irme a casa

⟩ James got home late James llegó a casa tarde.

homeless ['həʊmlɪs] noun

⟩ to be homeless estar sin hogar

⟩ the homeless los sin techo.

homemade [ˌhəʊm'meɪd] adjective ■ casero: they served homemade bread sirvieron pan casero.

homesick ['həʊmsɪk] adjective

⟩ she was homesick for most of the trip echó de menos a su familia durante la mayor parte del viaje

⟩ to feel homesick tener morriña.

homework ['həʊmwɜːk] uncountable noun ■ los deberes: do you have any homework? ¿tienes deberes?; have you done your homework ¿has hecho los deberes?

honest [ˈɒnɪst] *adjective*
1. **honrado**: she's a very honest person es una persona muy honrada
2. **sincero**: be honest with me sé sincero conmigo.

honesty [ˈɒnɪstɪ] *noun* ■ la **honradez**.

honey [ˈhʌnɪ] *noun* ■ la **miel**: she put some honey in her tea le puso un poco de miel a su té.

honeymoon [ˈhʌnɪmuːn] *noun* ■ la **luna de miel**: they spent their honeymoon in India pasaron su luna de miel en la India.

honour *UK*, **honor** *US* [ˈɒnəʳ] *noun* ■ el **honor**.

hood [hʊd] *noun*
1. la **capucha**: put the hood of your coat up súbete la capucha del abrigo
2. *US* el **capó**: the hood of the car el capó del coche.

hoof [huːf, hʊf] *(plural* hoofs OR hooves [huːvz]*) noun*
1. el **casco**: horses have hooves los caballos tienen cascos
2. la **pezuña**: cows and sheep have hooves las vacas y las ovejas tienen pezuñas.

hook [hʊk] *noun*
1. el **gancho**: the picture is hanging on a hook el cuadro está colgado de un gancho
2. el **anzuelo**: he caught the fish on a hook pescó el pez con un anzuelo
  ▸ the phone is off the hook el teléfono está descolgado.

hooray ➤ **hurray**.

hop [hɒp] *(past tense & past participle* hopped, *present participle* hopping*) verb*
1. **cruzar de un salto**: he hopped over the ditch cruzó de un salto la zanja
2. **saltar a la pata coja**
  ▸ to hop in **subirse a**: she hopped in the car and drove off se subió al coche y se fue.

hope [həʊp] *(noun & verb)*
■ *noun*
la **esperanza**: the news gave me hope la noticia me dio esperanzas

■ *verb*
esperar: I hope she succeeds espero que lo logre; he was hoping for an answer tonight esperaba tener una respuesta esta noche; I hope to see you soon espero verte pronto
  ▸ I hope so espero que sí
  ▸ I hope not espero que no.

hopeful [ˈhəʊpfʊl] *adjective*
1. **esperanzado**: everybody is hopeful todos están esperanzados
2. **esperanzador**: the news is hopeful la noticia es esperanzadora.

hopefully [ˈhəʊpfəlɪ] *adverb*
hopefully, it will be sunny tomorrow esperemos que mañana haga sol

  Esperar que is followed by a verb in the subjunctive.

hopeless [ˈhəʊplɪs] *adjective*
1. **desesperado**: the situation is hopeless la situación es desesperada
2. **negado**: he's hopeless at sports es un negado para los deportes.

horizon [həˈraɪzn] *noun* ■ el **horizonte**: I can see a ship on the horizon veo un barco en el horizonte.

horn [hɔːn] *noun*
1. el **cuerno**: bulls have horns los toros tienen cuernos
2. el **claxon**: he sounded the horn tocó el claxon.

horoscope [ˈhɒrəskəʊp] *noun* ■ el **horóscopo**.

horrible [ˈhɒrəbl] *adjective* ■ **horrible**: what a horrible place! ¡qué lugar tan horrible!

horror [ˈhɒrəʳ] *noun* ■ el **horror**
  a horror film una película de terror.

horse [hɔːs] *noun* ■ el **caballo**: can you ride a horse? ¿sabes montar a caballo?
  ▸ horse racing carreras de caballos
  ▸ horse riding la equitación: she goes horse riding monta a caballo.

horseback [ˈhɔːsbæ] *noun*
  ▸ on horseback a caballo
  ▸ horseback riding *US* la equitación.

horseshoe ['hɔːsʃuː] *noun* ■ la **herradura**: horseshoes bring good luck las herraduras traen buena suerte.

hose [həʊz], **hosepipe** ['həʊzpaɪp] *noun* ■ la **manguera**: a garden hose una manguera de jardín.

hospital ['hɒspɪtl] *noun* ■ el **hospital**: they took him to the hospital lo llevaron al hospital

in hospital *UK* OR in the hospital *US* en el hospital: she's in hospital está en el hospital.

host [həʊst] *noun* ■ el **anfitrión** *(plural* los anfitriones*)*: Gary is a very gracious host Gary es un anfitrión muy amable.

hostage ['hɒstɪdʒ] *noun* ■ el **rehén** *(plural* los rehenes*)*: they have 12 hostages in there tienen 12 rehenes allí dentro; she was taken hostage fue tomada como rehén.

hostess ['həʊstes] *noun* ■ la **anfitriona**.

hot [hɒt] *adjective*

1. **caliente**: the water's hot el agua está caliente
2. **picante**: he likes hot food le gusta la comida picante
   › a hot sauce una salsa picante
   › to be hot
   1. **tener calor**: I'm hot tengo calor
   2. **hacer calor**: it's hot today hace calor hoy
   › a hot dog un perrito caliente.

hotel [həʊ'tel] *noun* ■ el **hotel**: we stayed in a hotel nos alojamos en un hotel.

hour ['aʊəʳ] *noun* ■ la **hora**: I waited for two hours esperé dos horas

› an hour and a half una hora y media
› half an hour media hora
› a quarter of an hour un cuarto de hora.

house [haʊs, *plural* 'haʊzɪz] *noun* ■ la **casa**: he lives in a small house vive en una casa pequeña; you can stay at my house puedes quedarte en mi casa; I went to her house fui a su casa

› the House of Commons la Cámara de los Comunes
› the House of Lords la Cámara de los Lores

› the Houses of Parliament el Parlamento británico ➤ Political Parties
› the House of Representatives la Cámara de Representantes.

housewife ['haʊswaɪf] *(plural* housewives ['haʊswaɪvz]*) noun* ■ el **ama de casa** *(plural* las **amas de casa***)*

Feminine noun that takes un or el in the singular.

housework ['haʊswɜːk] *uncountable noun* ■ las **tareas domésticas**: he hates doing the housework odia las tareas domésticas.

housing estate *UK* ['haʊzɪŋ'esteɪt], **housing project** *US* ['haʊzɪŋ'prɒdʒekt] *noun* ■ la **urbanización**.

hovercraft [*UK* 'hɒvəkrɑːft, *US* 'hɒvəkræft] *noun* ■ el **aerodeslizador**.

how [haʊ] *adverb*

1. **cómo**: how are you? ¿cómo estás?; how was the test? ¿cómo fue la prueba?; tell me how you did it cuéntame cómo lo hiciste
2. *with "much" and "many"* **cuánto**: how much is it? ¿cuánto es?; how much money do you have? ¿cuánto dinero tienes?; how many continents are there? ¿cuántos continentes hay?
3. *in exclamations* **qué**: how pretty you look! ¡qué guapa estás!; how kind! ¡qué amable!
   › to know how to do something saber hacer algo: I don't know how to drive no sé conducir; do you know how to ski? ¿sabes esquiar?
   › how long will it take? ¿cuánto tiempo va a tardar?
   › how long is the rope? ¿qué longitud tiene la cuerda?
   › how old are you? ¿cuántos años tienes?

however [haʊ'evəʳ] *adverb* ■ **sin embargo**: she worked hard; however, she failed the final exam trabajó duro, sin embargo, no aprobó el examen final.

howl [haʊl] *verb* ■ **aullar**.

hug [hʌg] *(noun & verb)*

■ *noun*

el **abrazo**: she gave me a big hug me dio un gran abrazo

■ *verb (past tense & past participle* hugged, *present participle* hugging)
abrazar: I hugged him lo abracé.

huge [hju:dʒ] *adjective* ■ **enorme:** elephants are huge animals los elefantes son animales enormes; a huge building un edificio enorme.

hum [hʌm] *verb*
1. **tararear:** he was humming a tune estaba tarareando una melodía
2. **zumbar:** we could hear the bees humming oíamos zumbar las abejas.

human [ˈhju:mən] *adjective* ■ **humano:** we're all human todos somos humanos
➤ a human being un ser humano.

humid [ˈhju:mɪd] *adjective* ■ **húmedo:** it's very humid está muy húmedo.

humour UK, **humor** US [ˈhju:məʳ] *noun* ■ el **humor:** Suzanne has a good sense of humour Suzanne tiene un buen sentido del humor.

hump [hʌmp] *noun* ■ la **joroba:** a camel with two humps un camello con dos jorobas.

hunchback [ˈhʌntʃbæk] *noun* ■ el **jorobado,** la **jorobada.**

hundred [ˈhʌndrəd] *number*

Use **cien** before a noun:

a hundred dollars cien dólares; a hundred people cien personas; she's a hundred years old tiene cien años

When **hundred** is preceded by another number, use the compound form **doscientos, trescientos etc,** which must agree with the noun:

three hundred trescientos; two hundred people doscientas personas; three hundred and one trescientos uno

But use **cien** when **hundred** is followed by **thousand** or **million:**

one hundred thousand dollars cien mil dólares; one hundred million euros cien millones de euros
➤ there were hundreds of people at the party había cientos de personas en la fiesta.

hung [hʌŋ] *past tense & past participle* ➤ hang.

hunger [ˈhʌŋgəʳ] *noun* ■ el **hambre**

Feminine noun that takes **un** or **el** in the singular.

hungry [ˈhʌŋgrɪ] *adjective*
➤ to be hungry tener hambre: I'm hungry tengo hambre; are you very hungry? ¿tienes mucha hambre?

hunt [hʌnt] *verb*
1. **cazar:** they hunt deer cazan ciervos
2. **buscar:** the police are hunting the murderer la policía está buscando al asesino
➤ to hunt for something buscar algo: he's hunting for his keys está buscando sus llaves.

hunter [ˈhʌntəʳ] *noun* ■ el **cazador,** la **cazadora:** he's a hunter es cazador.

hunting [ˈhʌntɪŋ] *noun* ■ la **caza.**

hurl [hɜ:l] *verb* ■ **lanzar:** she hurled the ball through the window lanzó la pelota por la ventana.

hurray , hooray [hʊˈreɪ] *exclamation* ■ **hurra.**

hurricane [ˈhʌrɪkən] *noun* ■ el **huracán** *(plural* los **huracanes***).*

hurry [ˈhʌrɪ] *(noun & verb)*
■ *noun*
➤ to be in a hurry tener prisa: she's always in a hurry siempre tiene prisa; take your time, I'm not in a hurry tómate tu tiempo, no tengo prisa
➤ to do something in a hurry hacer algo a toda prisa: she did her homework in a hurry hizo los deberes a toda prisa
■ *verb (past tense & past participle* hurried*)*
darse prisa: she hurried to catch the bus se dio prisa para coger el autobús

hurry up *phrasal verb* ■ **darse prisa:** hurry up! ¡date prisa!

hurt [hɜ:t] *(adjective & verb)*
■ *adjective*
1. **herido:** he's badly hurt está gravemente herido

2. dolido: she's hurt that you didn't invite her está dolida porque no la invitaste

▪ verb (past tense & past participle hurt)

1. doler: ouch, that hurts! ¡ay! eso duele; my head hurts me duele la cabeza

2. hacer daño: stop it, you're hurting me basta ya, me estás haciendo daño

3. herir: what he said hurt me me hirió lo que dijo

▸ to hurt someone's feelings herir los sentimientos de alguien: I didn't mean to hurt your feelings no quise herir tus sentimientos

▸ I hurt my leg me hice daño en la pierna

▸ to hurt oneself hacerse daño: did you hurt yourself? ¿te has hecho daño?

husband ['hʌzbənd] noun ▪ el **marido:** she met her husband at university conoció a su marido en la universidad.

hut [hʌt] noun ▪ la **choza,** la **cabaña:** the shepherd built a hut in the forest el pastor construyó una cabaña en el bosque.

hymn [hɪm] noun ▪ el **himno.**

hyphen ['haɪfn] noun ▪ el **guion** (plural los guiones): "e-mail" is written with a hyphen "e-mail" se escribe con un guion.

I [aɪ] pronoun ▪ **yo:** she and I went dancing ella y yo fuimos a bailar

I is usually not translated:

I live in Spain vivo en España; I went to see him fui a verlo

Use **yo** for emphasis or to avoid ambiguity:

I did it yo lo hice; he doesn't know it but I do él no lo sabe pero yo sí

▸ here I am! ¡aquí estoy!

ice [aɪs] noun ▪ el **hielo:** the children are skating on the ice los niños están patinando sobre hielo; there's ice on the road hay hielo en la calle; do you want ice in your drink? ¿quieres hielo en la bebida?

▸ an ice cube un cubito de hielo

▸ ice hockey hockey sobre hielo

▸ an ice lolly UK un polo

▸ an ice rink una pista de hielo.

iceberg ['aɪsbɜːg] noun ▪ el **iceberg** (plural los **icebergs**).

ice cream [,aɪs'kriːm] noun ▪ el **helado:** do you want some ice cream? ¿quieres helado?; a chocolate ice cream un helado de chocolate

▸ an ice cream van una furgoneta de helados

ICE CREAM VAN

Con el buen tiempo, las calles de Gran Bretaña saludan la llegada del vendedor ambulante de helados. Con una furgoneta de vivos colores y un inconfundible campanilleo, hace su entrada en los barrios donde grandes y pequeños salen a la calle para hacer cola frente al mostrador.

ice skate ['aɪsskeɪt] noun ▪ el **patín para el hielo** (plural los **patines para el hielo**).

ice skating [aɪs'skeɪtɪŋ] noun ▪ el **patinaje sobre hielo**

▸ we're going ice skating in the park vamos a patinar sobre hielo en el parque.

icicle ['aɪsɪkl] noun ▪ el **carámbano:** there are icicles hanging from the trees hay carámbanos colgando de los árboles.

icing ['aɪsɪŋ] noun ▪ el **glaseado:** a cake with pink icing un pastel con glaseado rosa

▸ icing sugar UK azúcar glas.

icon ['aɪkɒn] noun ▪ el **icono:** click on the icon to open the program haga clic sobre el icono para abrir el programa.

icy ['aɪsɪ] *adjective*
1. helado: an icy wind un viento helado
2. cubierto de hielo: be careful, the road is icy ten cuidado, la calle está cubierta de hielo.

I'd [aɪd]
1. = I had
2. = I would.

ID [aɪ'diː] *(abbreviation of* identification*)* *noun* ■ la documentación, el carné de identidad: do you have any ID? ¿tienes algún documento de identidad?

idea [aɪ'dɪə] *noun* ■ la idea: that's a good idea es una buena idea; where is he? — I have no idea ¿dónde está? —no tengo ni idea.

ideal [aɪ'dɪəl] *adjective* ■ ideal: it's an ideal place for a party es un lugar ideal para hacer una fiesta.

identical [aɪ'dentɪkl] *adjective* ■ idéntico identical twins gemelos idénticos.

identification [aɪ,dentɪfɪ'keɪʃn] *noun* ■ la identificación *(plural* las identificaciones*)*: do you have any identification? ¿tienes alguna identificación?
identification papers documentos de identidad.

identify [aɪ'dentɪfaɪ] *(past tense & past participle* identified*)* *verb* ■ identificar: they've identified the body han identificado el cuerpo.

identity [aɪ'dentətɪ] *(plural* identities*)* *noun* ■ la identidad: he revealed the murderer's identity reveló la identidad del asesino
an identity card un carné de identidad.

idiom ['ɪdɪəm] *noun* ■ el modismo

⚠️ La palabra inglesa idiom es un falso amigo, no significa "idioma".

idiot ['ɪdɪət] *noun* ■ el/la idiota: what an idiot! ¡qué idiota!

if [ɪf] *conjunction* ■ si: you can come if you want puedes venir si quieres; if I knew the answer I'd tell you si supiera la respuesta, te la diría; I don't know if she's back no sé si ha vuelto
if not si no: I must go, if not, I'll be late tengo que irme, si no, llegaré tarde

if only ojalá: if only I could go! ¡ojalá pudiera ir!

Ojalá is followed by a verb in the subjunctive.

ignore [ɪg'nɔːʳ] *verb* ■ ignorar: he ignored my advice ignoró mi consejo; I saw her in the street but she ignored me la vi en la calle, pero me ignoró.

ill [ɪl] *adjective* ■ enfermo: he's very ill está muy enfermo
to feel ill sentirse mal: Alan feels ill Alan se siente mal
to be taken ill ponerse enfermo.

I'll [aɪl] = I will OR I shall: I'll phone you tomorrow te llamaré mañana.

illegal [ɪ'liːgl] *adjective* ■ ilegal: it's illegal to drive through a red light es ilegal pasarse un semáforo en rojo.

illness ['ɪlnɪs] *noun* ■ la enfermedad: leukaemia is a serious illness la leucemia es una enfermedad grave.

illustration [,ɪlə'streɪʃn] *noun* ■ la ilustración *(plural* las ilustraciones*)*: there are lots of illustrations in the book hay muchas ilustraciones en el libro.

I'm [aɪm] = I am.

image ['ɪmɪdʒ] *noun* ■ la imagen *(plural* las imágenes*)*: the company has changed its image la compañía ha cambiado de imagen.

imaginary [ɪ'mædʒɪnrɪ] *adjective* ■ imaginario: she has an imaginary playmate tiene un compañero de juegos imaginario.

imagination [ɪ,mædʒɪ'neɪʃn] *noun* ■ la imaginación *(plural* las imaginaciones*)*: the boy had a great imagination el niño tenía mucha imaginación.

imagine [ɪ'mædʒɪn] *verb* ■ imaginar: imagine a princess beside a lake imagina a una princesa junto a un lago; I imagine he's happy me imagino que es feliz.

imitation [,ɪmɪ'teɪʃn] *noun* ■ la imitación *(plural* las imitaciones*)*.

immediate [ɪ'miːdjət] *adjective* ■ inmediato: I need an immediate answer necesito una respuesta inmediata.

immediately [ɪ'miːdjətlɪ] *adverb* ■ **inmediatamente**: tell him to see me immediately dígale que me venga a ver inmediatamente.

immigrant ['ɪmɪgrənt] *noun* ■ **el/la inmigrante**.

impatient [ɪm'peɪʃnt] *adjective* ■ **impaciente**: he's impatient to leave está impaciente por irse

to get impatient **impacientarse**: she's beginning to get impatient está empezando a impacientarse.

import [ɪm'pɔːt] *verb* ■ **importar**: they import goods from China importan mercancías de China.

importance [ɪm'pɔːtns] *noun* ■ la **importancia**: it's a matter of great importance es un asunto de gran importancia.

important [ɪm'pɔːtnt] *adjective* ■ **importante**: she's an important person es una persona importante; it's not important no es importante.

impossible [ɪm'pɒsəbl] *adjective* ■ **imposible**: this word is impossible to pronounce esta palabra es imposible de pronunciar; it's impossible to get tickets for the concert es imposible conseguir entradas para el concierto.

impression [ɪm'preʃn] *noun* ■ la **impresión** *(plural* las **impresiones)**: she made a good impression on them les causó una buena impresión.

improve [ɪm'pruːv] *verb* ■ **mejorar**: she wants to improve her Spanish quiere mejorar su español; the weather's improving el tiempo está mejorando.

improvement [ɪm'pruːvmənt] *noun* ■ la **mejora**: this model is an improvement on the previous one este modelo es mejor que el anterior

> there's been an improvement in his work su trabajo ha mejorado.

in [ɪn] *(preposition & adverb)*

■ *preposition*

1. **en**: there's a desk in my room hay un escritorio en mi cuarto; put this photo in an envelope mete esta foto en un sobre; Lisa lives in Ireland Lisa vive en Irlanda; it's written in Spanish está escrito en español

2. **a**: they arrived in Mexico this morning llegaron a México esta mañana; they sat in the sun se sentaron al sol

3. **dentro de**: in two weeks dentro de dos semanas; she'll be back in an hour volverá dentro de una hora

4. *in time expressions, seasons* **en**: my birthday's in May mi cumpleaños es en mayo; he was born in 1932 nació en 1932; I woke up in the night me levanté por la noche; the film starts in ten minutes la película empieza en diez minutos; in the nineties en los noventa; in winter en invierno

5. *with morning, afternoon, evening* I went for a walk in the afternoon salí a pasear por la tarde; I'll call you in the morning te llamaré por la mañana; it's 3 o'clock in the morning son las 3 de la madrugada

6. *with superlatives* **de**: Everest is the tallest mountain in the world el Everest es la montaña más alta del mundo; she's the best student in the class es la mejor alumna de la clase

> we were caught in the rain nos pilló la lluvia

> she's dressed in black va vestida de negro

> he spent all day in his pyjamas pasó todo el día en pijama

■ *adverb*

1. **en casa**: we had a night in por la noche nos quedamos en casa

2. *informal* **de moda**: are hats in? ¿están de moda los sombreros?

> is Dan in? ¿está Dan en casa?

> he's not in today hoy no está

> nobody was in no había nadie

> the tide's in la marea está alta

> in writing por escrito.

inch [ɪntʃ] *noun* ■ la **pulgada** *(2,5 centímetros)*.

include [ɪn'kluːd] *verb* ■ **incluir**: I wasn't included in the team no me incluyeron en el equipo

> service is included el servicio está incluido.

including [ɪn'kluːdɪŋ] *preposition*

> everyone's coming, including Thomas vienen todos, incluyendo a Thomas

> that's 20 pounds including service son 20 libras con el servicio incluido.

income ['ɪŋkʌm] *uncountable noun* ■ los **ingresos**: a source of income una fuente de ingresos

> income tax impuesto sobre la renta.

increase *(noun & verb)*

■ *noun* ['ɪnkriːs]
el **aumento**: there's been an increase in the price ha habido un aumento del precio

■ *verb* [ɪn'kriːs]
aumentar: the number of users is increasing está aumentando el número de usuarios; they've increased the price han aumentado el precio.

incredible [ɪn'kredəbl] *adjective* ■ **increíble**.

indecisive [ˌɪndɪ'saɪsɪv] *adjective* ■ **indeciso**.

indeed [ɪn'diːd] *adverb*

1. **realmente**: I'm very tired indeed estoy realmente cansado
2. **efectivamente**: indeed there is a problem efectivamente, hay un problema

> thank you very much indeed muchísimas gracias.

independence [ˌɪndɪ'pendəns] *noun* ■ la **independencia**

> Independence Day *US* el Día de la Independencia ➤ Fourth of July.

independent [ˌɪndɪ'pendənt] *adjective* ■ **independiente**.

index ['ɪndeks] *noun* ■ el **índice**: look it up in the index búscalo en el índice

> the index finger el dedo índice.

indicate ['ɪndɪkeɪt] *verb*

1. **indicar**: he indicated the quickest route nos indicó el camino más rápido
2. *UK* **poner el intermitente**: you must indicate before you turn tienes que poner el intermitente antes de girar.

indicator *UK* ['ɪndɪkeɪtəʳ] *noun* ■ el **intermitente**.

indigestion [ˌɪndɪ'dʒestʃn] *uncountable noun* ■ la **indigestión**: he has indigestion tiene indigestión.

individual [ˌɪndɪ'vɪdʒʊəl] *(adjective & noun)*

■ *adjective*
individual: an individual room una habitación individual

■ *noun*
el **individuo**.

indoor ['ɪndɔːʳ] *adjective*

1. **de interior**: indoor plants plantas de interior
2. **bajo techo**: indoor sports deportes en pista cubierta

> an indoor pool una piscina cubierta.

indoors [ˌɪn'dɔːz] *adverb* ■ **dentro**: they're indoors están dentro

> to go indoors OR to come indoors entrar: come indoors, it's raining entra, está lloviendo.

industrial [ɪn'dʌstrɪəl] *adjective* ■ **industrial**: an industrial zone una zona industrial.

industry ['ɪndəstrɪ] *(plural* industries*)* *noun* ■ la **industria**: he works in the film industry trabaja en la industria cinematográfica.

infant school *UK* ['ɪnfənt,skuːl] *noun* ■ el **parvulario**.

infection [ɪn'fekʃn] *noun* ■ la **infección** *(plural* las **infecciones***)*

> a throat infection una infección de garganta.

infinitive [ɪn'fɪnɪtɪv] *noun* ■ el **infinitivo**.

infirmary [ɪn'fɜːmərɪ] *(plural* infirmaries*)* *noun* ■ el **hospital**.

inflatable [ɪn'fleɪtəbl] *adjective* ■ **inflable**: an inflatable toy un juguete inflable.

influence ['ɪnflʊəns] *(noun & verb)*

■ *noun*
la **influencia**: she has a lot of influence on her brother tiene mucha influencia sobre su hermano

■ *verb*
influir: don't let him influence you no dejes que te influya.

inform [ɪn'fɔːm] *verb* ■ **informar**: I informed him I was leaving le informé de que me iba.

informal [ɪnˈfɔːml] *adjective*
1. **informal:** an informal atmosphere un ambiente informal; **wear informal clothes** llevad ropa informal
2. **familiar:** an informal expression una expresión familiar.

information [ˌɪnfəˈmeɪʃn] *uncountable noun* ■ la **información** *(plural* las **informaciones)*: **I'd like some information about train times** quisiera información sobre el horario de los trenes
> **the information desk** el mostrador de información
> **the information superhighway** la autopista de la información
> **information technology** la informática.

infrared [ˌɪnfrəˈred] *adjective* ■ **infrarrojo:** an infrared beam un rayo infrarrojo.

ingredient [ɪnˈgriːdjənt] *noun* ■ el **ingrediente:** mix the ingredients together in a bowl mezcle los ingredientes en un bol.

inhabitant [ɪnˈhæbɪtənt] *noun* ■ el/la **habitante:** our town has 100,000 inhabitants nuestra ciudad tiene 100.000 habitantes.

inherit [ɪnˈherɪt] *verb* ■ **heredar:** he inherited some money from his great-aunt heredó dinero de su tía abuela.

initials [ɪˈnɪʃlz] *plural noun* ■ la **inicial:** his initials are GWS sus iniciales son GWS.

injection [ɪnˈdʒekʃn] *noun* ■ la **inyección** *(plural* las **inyecciones)*: the doctor gave him an injection el médico le puso una inyección.

injure [ˈɪndʒər] *verb* ■ **lesionar:** he has injured his leg se lesionó la pierna.

injured [ˈɪndʒəd] *adjective* ■ **lesionado.**

injury [ˈɪndʒərɪ] *(plural* injuries) *noun* ■ la **lesión** *(plural* las **lesiones)*: he has serious injuries tiene lesiones graves
> **injury time** tiempo de descuento.

ink [ɪŋk] *noun* ■ la **tinta:** an ink stain una mancha de tinta.

innocent [ˈɪnəsənt] *adjective* ■ **inocente:** he was found innocent fue declarado inocente.

inquire [ɪnˈkwaɪər] *verb* ■ **pedir información**
> **to inquire about something** pedir información sobre algo: he inquired about the departure times pidió información sobre los horarios de salida.

inquiry [ɪnˈkwaɪərɪ] *(plural* inquiries) *noun* ■ la **investigación** *(plural* las **investigaciones)*.

insane [ɪnˈseɪn] *adjective* ■ **loco:** she is insane está loca
> **to go insane** volverse loco: he has gone insane se ha vuelto loco.

insect [ˈɪnsekt] *noun* ■ el **insecto.**

inside [ɪnˈsaɪd] *(preposition, adverb, adjective & noun)*
■ *preposition*
dentro de: the keys are inside the car las llaves están dentro del coche
■ *adverb*
dentro: I've put them inside las puse dentro
> **to come inside** OR **to go inside** entrar: come inside! ¡entra!; let's go inside entremos
■ *adjective*
interior: the inside pages of the book las páginas interiores del libro
■ *noun*
el **interior:** the inside of the box el interior de la caja
> **inside out** del revés: your shirt is inside out llevas la camisa del revés.

insist [ɪnˈsɪst] *verb* ■ **insistir:** Ann insisted on coming Ann insistió en venir.

inspect [ɪnˈspekt] *verb* ■ **examinar, inspeccionar:** they want to inspect our passports quieren examinar nuestros pasaportes.

inspector [ɪnˈspektər] *noun* ■ el **inspector,** la **inspectora:** he's a police inspector es inspector de policía.

inspire [ɪnˈspaɪər] *verb* ■ **inspirar:** the music inspired me la música me inspiró.

install , **instal** US [ɪnˈstɔːl] *verb* ■ **instalar:** click on the icon to install the program haga clic en el icono para instalar el programa.

instance ['ɪnstəns] *noun*
> for instance por ejemplo.

instant ['ɪnstənt] *adjective*

1. inmediato: the album was an instant success el disco fue un éxito inmediato
2. instantáneo: I don't like instant coffee no me gusta el café instantáneo.

instead [ɪn'sted] *adverb* ■ así que: I don't eat meat, I'll have vegetables instead no como carne, así que voy a comer verduras
> instead of en lugar de: instead of helping us, he got in the way en lugar de ayudarnos, se nos puso en medio
> instead of somebody en lugar de alguien: Jenny's going to the meeting instead of me Jenny va a ir a la fiesta en mi lugar.

instructions [ɪn'strʌkʃnz] *plural noun* ■ las instrucciones: follow my instructions seguid mis instrucciones; read the instructions before you use the camera lea las instrucciones antes de usar la cámara.

instructor [ɪn'strʌktər] *noun* ■ el instructor, la instructora: he's a driving instructor es instructor de autoescuela.

instrument ['ɪnstrʊmənt] *noun* ■ el instrumento: musical instruments instrumentos musicales; she plays an instrument toca un instrumento.

insult *(verb & noun)*
■ *verb* [ɪn'sʌlt]
insultar: he insulted his teacher insultó a su profesor
■ *noun* ['ɪnsʌlt]
el insulto: the crowd was shouting insults la multitud estaba gritando insultos.

insurance [ɪn'ʃʊərəns] *noun* ■ el seguro: I took out some fire insurance contraté un seguro contra incendios
> an insurance policy una póliza de seguros.

insure [ɪn'ʃʊər] *verb* ■ asegurar: she insured her car against theft aseguró el coche contra robos.

intelligent [ɪn'telɪdʒənt] *adjective* ■ inteligente.

intend [ɪn'tend] *verb* ■ tener la intención de: I intend to go to Australia tengo la intención de ir a Australia.

intensive [ɪn'tensɪv] *adjective* ■ intensivo
> in intensive care en cuidados intensivos.

intercom ['ɪntəkɒm] *noun* ■ el interfono.

interest ['ɪntrəst] *(noun & verb)*
■ *noun*

1. el interés *(plural los intereses)*: they charge 10% interest cobran un 10% de interés
2. la afición *(plural las aficiones)*: what are your interests? ¿cuáles son tus aficiones?
> to take an interest in something interesarse por algo: she takes an interest in other people se interesa por las personas
> to lose interest in something perder interés en algo
> to be in one's best interest convenir: it's in your best interest to finish your degree te conviene terminar tus estudios universitarios
■ *verb*
interesar: archaeology interests me la arqueología me interesa.

interested ['ɪntrəstɪd] *adjective* ■ interesado: he seems interested parece estar interesado; Toby is interested in motorbikes Toby está interesado en las motos; I'm not interested in that eso no me interesa.

interesting ['ɪntrəstɪŋ] *adjective* ■ interesante: he led an interesting life llevó una vida interesante.

interfere [,ɪntə'fɪər] *verb* ■ entrometerse: to interfere in somebody's business entrometerse en los asuntos de alguien
> don't interfere! ¡no te metas!

intermediate [,ɪntə'miːdjət] *adjective* ■ de nivel intermedio: he's in the intermediate class está en la clase de nivel intermedio.

internal [ɪn'tɜːnl] *adjective* ■ interno: an internal modem un módem interno.

international [,ɪntə'næʃənl] *adjective* ■ internacional.

Internet , internet ['ɪntənet] *noun* ■ el/la Internet: you'll find the information

on the Internet encontrarás la información en Internet

an Internet café un cibercafé

an Internet Service Provider un proveedor de servicios de Internet.

interpreter [ɪn'tɜːprɪtəʳ] *noun* ■ el/la intérprete: **she's an interpreter** es intérprete.

interrupt [ˌɪntəˈrʌpt] *verb* ■ interrumpir: **she interrupted the teacher** interrumpió a la profesora.

interruption [ˌɪntəˈrʌpʃn] *noun* ■ la interrupción *(plural* las **interrupciones***)*.

intersection [ˌɪntəˈsekʃn] *noun* ■ el cruce: **turn left at the intersection** dobla a la izquierda en el cruce.

interval ['ɪntəvl] *noun*

1. el **intervalo**: **at regular intervals** a intervalos regulares

2. *UK* el **intermedio.**

interview ['ɪntəvjuː] *(noun & verb)*

■ *noun*

la **entrevista**: **he has a job interview** tiene una entrevista de trabajo

■ *verb*

entrevistar: **he interviewed the President** entrevistó al presidente.

into ['ɪntʊ] *preposition*

1. **en**: **he put the book into his bag** puso el libro en su bolso; **he cut the cake into three pieces** cortó el pastel en tres pedazos; **he got into bed** se metió en la cama

2. **a**: **she translated the letter into Spanish** tradujo la carta al español.

introduce [*UK* ˌɪntrəˈdjuːs, *US* ˌɪntrəˈduːs] *verb*

1. **presentar**: **she introduced me to her mother** me presentó a su madre; **let me introduce you to Brian** déjame presentarte a Brian

2. **introducir**: **he introduced a new fashion** introdujo una nueva moda.

introduction [ˌɪntrəˈdʌkʃn] *noun* ■ la **introducción** *(plural* las **introducciones***)*: **the book has a good introduction** el libro tiene una buena introducción.

invade [ɪnˈveɪd] *verb* ■ **invadir**: **tourists invaded the town** los turistas invadieron la ciudad.

invasion [ɪnˈveɪʒn] *noun* ■ la **invasión** *(plural* las **invasiones***)*.

invent [ɪnˈvent] *verb* ■ **inventar**: **who invented the telephone?** ¿quién inventó el teléfono?

invention [ɪnˈvenʃn] *noun* ■ el **invento.**

inventor [ɪnˈventəʳ] *noun* ■ el **inventor**, la **inventora.**

inverted commas *UK* [ɪnˌvɜːtɪdˈkɒməz] *plural noun* ■ las **comillas**: **in inverted commas** entre comillas.

investigate [ɪnˈvestɪgeɪt] *verb* ■ **investigar**. **they're investigating the accident** están investigando el accidente.

investigation [ɪnˌvestɪˈgeɪʃn] *noun* ■ la **investigación** *(plural* las **investigaciones***)*: **a police investigation** una investigación policial.

invisible [ɪnˈvɪzɪbl] *adjective* ■ **invisible.**

invitation [ˌɪnvɪˈteɪʃn] *noun* ■ la **invitación** *(plural* las **invitaciones***)*: **an invitation to a party** una invitación a una fiesta.

invite [ɪnˈvaɪt] *verb* ■ **invitar**: **I invited Tara to my party** invité a Tara a mi fiesta.

involve [ɪnˈvɒlv] *verb*

1. **suponer**: **it involves a lot of work** supone mucho trabajo

2. **afectar**: **it involves us all** nos afecta a todos

3. **involucrar**: **I'm not involved in the project** no estoy involucrado en el proyecto

> **to be involved** estar metido: **he's involved in some nasty business** está metido en asuntos desagradables.

Ireland ['aɪələnd] *noun* ■ **Irlanda.**

Irish ['aɪrɪʃ] *(adjective & noun)*

■ *adjective*

Remember not to use a capital letter for the adjective or the language in Spanish:

irlandés: **Sinéad is an Irish name** Sinéad es un nombre irlandés

■ noun

el **irlandés: he speaks Irish** habla irlandés

In Spanish, a capital letter is not used for the inhabitants of a country or region:

> the Irish los irlandeses.

iron ['aɪən] (noun & verb)

■ noun

1. (uncountable) el **hierro: it's made of iron** es de hierro
2. la **plancha: the iron is too hot** la plancha está demasiado caliente

■ verb

planchar: he's ironing his shirt está planchando su camisa.

ironing ['aɪənɪŋ] noun ■ **she's doing the ironing** está planchando

> **an ironing board** una tabla de planchar.

irregular [ɪ'regjʊlə'] adjective ■ **irregular: irregular verbs** verbos irregulares.

irritating ['ɪrɪteɪtɪŋ] adjective ■ **irritante.**

is [ɪz] ➤ be.

island ['aɪlənd] noun ■ la **isla.**

Islamic [ɪz'læmɪk] adjective ■ **islámico.**

isle [aɪl] noun ■ la **isla: the Isle of Wight** la isla de Wight.

isn't ['ɪznt] = is not: **she isn't ready** no está lista.

issue ['ɪʃuː] noun

1. el **número: it's the first issue of the magazine** es el primer número de la revista
2. el **asunto: it's an important issue** es un asunto importante.

it [ɪt] pronoun

1. subject pronoun

In Spanish, it is not usually translated:

where's my book? — it's over there ¿dónde está mi libro? —está ahí; **do you like my dress? — yes, it's lovely** ¿te gusta mi vestido? —sí, es precioso

2. direct object pronoun

Use lo when "it" stands for a masculine noun and la for a feminine noun:

I've got an extra ticket, do you want it? tengo una entrada de más, ¿la quieres?; **I've lost my dog, have you seen it?** he perdido mi perro, ¿lo has visto?

3. indirect object pronoun

Use le when "it" represents an indirect object:

give it a push dale un empujón

4. impersonal usages

It is not translated.

it's raining está lloviendo; **it's cold** hace frío; **it's hot today** hoy hace calor; **what time is it?** ¿qué hora es?; **it's ten o'clock** son las diez; **it's me!** ¡soy yo!

IT (abbreviation of information technology) noun ■ la **informática: she works in IT** trabaja en informática.

Italian [ɪ'tæljən] (adjective & noun)

■ adjective

Remember not to use a capital letter for the adjective or the language in Spanish:

italiano: I like Italian ice cream me gusta el helado italiano

■ noun

1. el **italiano,** la **italiana: Italians are known for their good food** los italianos son famosos por su buena comida

In Spanish, a capital letter is not used for the inhabitants of a country or region:

2. el **italiano: she speaks Italian** habla italiano.

italic [ɪ'tælɪk] noun ■ la **cursiva: in italics** en cursiva.

Italy ['ɪtəlɪ] noun ■ **Italia.**

itch [ɪtʃ] verb ■ **picar: my arm itches** me pica el brazo; **I itch all over** me pica todo.

itchy ['ɪtʃɪ] adjective

> **my nose is itchy** me pica la nariz
> **this pullover is itchy** este jersey pica.

it'd ['ɪtəd]

1. = it had: **it'd stopped raining** había dejado de llover

. = it would: **it'd be nice if you could come** sería perfecto si pudieras venir.

it'll [ɪtl] = it will: **it'll take you a long time to do it** tardarás mucho tiempo en hacerlo.

its [ɪts] *possessive adjective* ■ **su**

In Spanish the possessive adjective agrees in number (singular or plural) with the noun that follows:

put the camera back in its case guarda la cámara en su estuche; **the woman handed me her shoes** la mujer me alcanzó sus zapatos.

it's [ɪts]

. = it is: **it's my turn to play** me toca jugar a mí

2. = it has: **it's stopped raining** dejó de llover.

itself [ɪt'self] *pronoun*

1. se, a sí mismo: **the cat is washing itself** el gato se está lavando

2. en sí: **the town itself is not very big** la ciudad en sí no es muy grande

by itself solo: **the door closed by itself** la puerta se cerró sola.

I've [aɪv]

1. = I have: **I've decided to leave** he decidido irme

2. = I have (got). **I've got two sisters** tengo dos hermanas.

ivory ['aɪvərɪ] *noun* ■ el **marfil.**

ivy ['aɪvɪ] *noun* ■ la **hiedra**

IVY LEAGUE

El término **Ivy League** se utiliza en Estados Unidos para referirse al colegio universitario de Dartmouth y a las universidades de Brown, Columbia, Cornell, Harvard, Pensilvania, Princeton y Yale, que son algunos de los centros académicos más antiguos del país. El nombre de la liga alude a la hiedra, **ivy**, que suele trepar por las paredes de los antiguos edificios que albergan estas universidades. Un título de la **Ivy League** es un aval para el éxito profesional.

jacket ['dʒækɪt] *noun* ■ la **chaqueta**
a **jacket potato** una patata asada con piel.

jackpot ['dʒækpɒt] *noun* ■ el **(premio) gordo: John won the jackpot** John ganó el gordo.

jail [dʒeɪl] *(noun & verb)*
■ *noun*
la **cárcel: they sent him to jail** lo mandaron a la cárcel
■ *verb*
encarcelar: **they jailed the suspect immediately** encarcelaron al sospechoso inmediatamente.

jam [dʒæm] *noun*
1. la **mermelada: raspberry jam** mermelada de frambuesa
2. el **embotellamiento: a traffic jam** un embotellamiento
to be in a jam estar en apuros.

jammed [dʒæm] *adjective* ■ **atascado: the drawer's jammed** el cajón está atascado.

janitor *US* ['dʒænɪtər] *noun* ■ el/la **conserje: Mr Freeman is a janitor** el señor Freeman es conserje.

January ['dʒænjʊərɪ] *noun*

In Spanish the months of the year do not start with a capital letter:

enero *(masculine)*: **in January** en enero; **next January** el enero próximo; **last January** el enero pasado.

Japan [dʒə'pæn] *noun* ■ **Japón.**

Japanese [ˌdʒæpə'niːz] *(adjective & noun)*
■ *adjective*

Remember not to use a capital letter for the adjective or the language in Spanish:

japonés *(feminine* **japonesa***)*: I like Japanese cooking me gusta la comida japonesa
■ *noun*

el **japonés**: they speak Japanese hablan japonés

In Spanish, a capital letter is not used for the inhabitants of a country or region:

the Japanese los japoneses.

jar [dʒɑːʳ] *noun* ■ el **tarro**: a jar of jam un tarro de mermelada.

jaw [dʒɔː] *noun* ■ la **mandíbula**: Dan has a square jaw Dan tiene la mandíbula cuadrada.

jazz [dʒæz] *noun* ■ el **jazz.**

jealous ['dʒeləs] *adjective* ■ **celoso.**

jeans [dʒiːnz] *plural noun* ■ los **vaqueros**: a pair of jeans un par de vaqueros; he's wearing jeans lleva puestos unos vaqueros.

jelly *UK* ['dʒelɪ], **Jell-O®** *US* ['dʒeləʊ] *noun* ■ la **gelatina**: the children had jelly for dessert los niños comieron gelatina de postre.

jellyfish ['dʒelɪfɪʃ] *(plural* jellyfish*) noun* ■ la **medusa.**

jersey ['dʒɜːzɪ] *noun* ■ el **jersey** *(plural* los jerséis*).*

jet [dʒet] *noun*
1. **chorro**: a water jet un chorro de agua
2. el **avión** *(plural* los **aviones***)*: she took a jet to the United States cogió un avión a los Estados Unidos
➤ jet lag jet lag: he's suffering from jet lag tiene jet lag.

Jew [dʒuː] *noun* ■ el **judío, la judía.**

jewel ['dʒuːəl] *noun* ■ la **joya.**

jeweller *UK*, **jeweler** *US* ['dʒuːələʳ] *noun* ■ el **joyero, la joyera**
➤ the jeweller's *UK* OR the jeweler's *US* la joyería.

jewellery *UK*, **jewelry** *US* ['dʒuːəlrɪ] *noun* ■ las **joyas**: that actress has a lot of jewellery esa actriz tiene muchas joyas; gold jewellery joyas de oro.

Jewish ['dʒuːɪʃ] *adjective*

The Spanish adjective does not start with a capital letter:

judío: a Jewish tradition una tradición judía
➤ a Jewish man un judío.

jigsaw ['dʒɪgsɔː], **jigsaw puzzle** ['dʒɪgsɔː'pʌzl] *noun* ■ el **rompecabezas** *(plural* los **rompecabezas***)*: he's doing a jigsaw puzzle está haciendo un rompecabezas.

job [dʒɒb] *noun* ■ el **trabajo**: he has a job in a bookshop tiene un trabajo en una librería; you've done a good job has hecho un buen trabajo.

jobless ['dʒɒblɪs] *adjective* ■ **parado, desempleado**: he's jobless está parado.

jog [dʒɒg] *(past tense & past participle* jogged, *present participle* jogging*) verb* ■ **hacer footing**: I jog once a week hago footing una vez por semana.

jogging ['dʒɒgɪŋ] *noun* ■ **hacer footing**: I go jogging every day hago footing todos los días.

join [dʒɔɪn] *verb*
1. **unir**: you have to join the two ends together tienes que unir las dos puntas
2. **sentarse con**: can I join you? ¿puedo sentarme contigo?
3. **hacerse socio de**: Sally joined the judo club Sally se hizo socia del club de judo
➤ to join the army alistarse en el ejército
➤ to join the queue *UK* hacer cola

join in *phrasal verb*
1. **participar**: Charlie wanted to join in Charlie quería participar; everyone joined in the conversation todos participaron en la conversación.

joint [dʒɔɪnt] *(noun & adjective)*
■ *noun*

la **articulación** *(plural* las **articulaciones***)*: my joints ache in the winter en invierno, me duelen las articulaciones

adjective
conjunto: they have a joint account tienen una cuenta conjunta.

joke [dʒəʊk] *(noun & verb)*
noun
• el **chiste: he told us a joke** nos contó un chiste
• la **broma: they played a joke on Simon** le hicieron una broma a Simon
verb
bromear: are you joking? ¿estás bromeando?

journalist [ˈdʒɜːnəlɪst] *noun* ■ el/la **periodista: she's a journalist** es periodista.

journey [ˈdʒɜːnɪ] *noun*
• el **viaje: they went on a long journey** hicieron un largo viaje
2. el **trayecto: the journey to school** el trayecto al colegio; **it's an hour's journey on the bus** es un trayecto de una hora en autobús.

joy [dʒɔɪ] *noun* ■ la **alegría: the children are jumping for joy** los niños están saltando de alegría.

joystick [ˈdʒɔɪstɪk] *noun* ■ la **palanca de mandos** *(en videojuegos).*

judge [dʒʌdʒ] *(noun & verb)*
noun
el/la **juez** *(plural* los/las **jueces): he's a judge** es juez
verb
juzgar: they will judge the defendant tomorrow van a juzgar al acusado mañana.

judo [ˈdʒuːdəʊ] *noun* ■ el **judo: he does judo** hace judo.

jug *UK* [dʒʌg] *noun* ■ la **jarra.**

juggle [ˈdʒʌgl] *verb* ■ **hacer malabarismos: do you know how to juggle?** ¿sabes hacer malabarismos?

juice [dʒuːs] *noun* ■ el **zumo: orange juice** zumo de naranja.

juicy [ˈdʒuːsɪ] *adjective* ■ **jugoso.**

July [dʒuːˈlaɪ] *noun*

In Spanish the months of the year do not start with a capital letter:

julio *(masculine)*: **in July** en julio; **next July** el julio próximo; **last July** el julio pasado.

jumble sale *UK* [ˈdʒʌmblseɪl] *noun* ■ el **rastrillo,** el **mercadillo.**

jump [dʒʌmp] *(noun & verb)*
■ *noun*
el **salto: the high jump** el salto de altura
■ *verb*
saltar: she jumped out of the window saltó por la ventana
➤ **you made me jump** me asustaste.

jumper *UK* [ˈdʒʌmpəʳ] *noun* ■ el **jersey** *(plural* los **jerséis).**

June [dʒuːn] *noun*

In Spanish the months of the year do not start with a capital letter:

junio: in June en junio; **next June** el junio próximo; **last June** el junio pasado.

jungle [ˈdʒʌngl] *noun* ■ la **selva.**

junior [ˈdʒuːnjəʳ] *(adjective & noun)*
■ *adjective*
1. **subalterno: he's a junior employee** es un empleado subalterno
2. **júnior: the junior tennis championship** el campeonato de tenis júnior
■ *noun*
UK el **alumno (de primaria)**
➤ **junior school** *UK* escuela de primaria
➤ **junior high school** *US* escuela de secundaria.

junk [dʒʌŋk] *uncountable noun*
1. los **trastos: the house is full of junk** la casa está llena de trastos
2. *informal* la **basura: it's a piece of junk!** ¡es una basura!
➤ **junk food** la comida basura
➤ **junk shop** tienda de objetos usados.

jury [ˈdʒʊərɪ] *(plural* juries) *noun* ■ el **jurado: Mrs Davies is on the jury** la señora Davies está en el jurado.

just [dʒʌst] *adverb*
1. **justo: it happened just after midnight** ocurrió justo después de la medianoche; **we have just enough time** tenemos el tiempo

justo; **you're just in time!** ¡has llegado justo
a tiempo!; **that's just what I need** eso es justo lo que necesito
2. **sólo: she's just seven** sólo tiene siete años;
just add water añada sólo agua
➤ **he's just arrived** acaba de llegar
➤ **I was just about to leave** estaba a punto de
irme
➤ **it's just about ready** está casi listo
➤ **just a minute!** ¡espera un minuto!

justice ['dʒʌstɪs] *noun* ■ la **justicia.**

kangaroo [ˌkæŋgə'ruː] *noun* ■ el **canguro.**

karate [kə'rɑːtɪ] *noun* ■ el **kárate: he
does karate** hace kárate.

keen [kiːn] *adjective* ■ **entusiasta: he's a
keen supporter of Manchester City** es un
hincha entusiasta del Manchester City
➤ **to be keen on something** ser aficionado a
algo: **Alex is keen on rugby** Alex es aficionado al rugby
➤ **to be keen to do something** tener muchas
ganas de hacer algo: **I'm keen to see the
new film** tengo muchas ganas de ver la nueva película.

keep [kiːp] *(past tense & past participle* **kept)**
verb
1. **quedarse con: keep the change** quédese
con el cambio

2. **guardar: can you keep a secret?** ¿puedes
guardar un secreto?
3. **mantener: we must keep calm** debemos
mantener la calma; **he kept his promise**
mantuvo su promesa
4. **criar: they keep chickens** crían pollos
➤ **to keep doing** OR **to keep on doing** seguir
haciendo: **I kept on working** seguí trabajando; **she keeps calling me** me sigue llamando
➤ **to keep somebody from doing something**
impedir que alguien haga algo: **nothing will
keep me from going** nada impedirá que me
vaya
➤ **to keep somebody waiting** hacer esperar a
alguien: **I'm sorry to keep you waiting**
lamento hacerte esperar
➤ **to keep fit** estar en forma
➤ **to keep quiet** mantener la boca cerrada:
they kept quiet mantuvieron la boca cerrada
➤ **keep quiet!** ¡cállate!

keep off *phrasal verb*
➤ **keep off the grass** prohibido pisar el césped

keep out *phrasal verb*
➤ **keep out!** ¡prohibida la entrada!

keep up *phrasal verb* ■ **seguir el ritmo:
don't go so fast, I can't keep up** no vayas
tan rápido, no puedo seguir tu ritmo.

kept [kept] *past tense & past participle* ➤
keep.

ketchup ['ketʃəp] *uncountable noun* ■ el
ketchup: do you want some ketchup?
¿quieres ketchup?

kettle ['ketl] *noun* ■ la **tetera eléctrica.**

key [kiː] *noun*
1. la **llave: I've lost my keys** perdí mis llaves
2. la **tecla: the computer keys are dirty** las
teclas del ordenador están sucias.

keyboard ['kiːbɔːd] *noun* ■ el **teclado:
we need a new keyboard for the computer**
necesitamos un teclado nuevo para el ordenador.

keyhole ['kiːhəʊl] *noun* ■ la **cerradura.**

keypad ['ki:pæd] *noun* ■ el **teclado numérico.**

key ring ['ki:rɪŋ] *noun* ■ el **llavero.**

khaki ['kɑ:kɪ] *adjective* ■ el **caqui.**

kick [kɪk] *(noun & verb)*
■ *noun*
la **patada**: he gave me a kick me dio una patada
■ *verb*
1. dar una **patada**: he kicked me me dio una patada; she kicked the ball chutó la pelota
2. **patalear**: stop kicking! ¡deja de patalear!

kid [kɪd] *informal (noun & verb)*
■ *noun*
1. el **niño**: there are 20 kids in the class hay 20 niños en la clase
2. el **hijo**: they have four kids tienen cuatro hijos
he's my kid brother es mi hermano pequeño
■ *verb*
bromear: I'm only kidding! ¡sólo estoy bromeando!

kidnap ['kɪdnæp] *(past tense & past participle* kidnapped, *present participle* kidnapping*) verb* ■ **secuestrar**: they kidnapped the rich man for his money secuestraron al hombre rico por su dinero.

kidney ['kɪdnɪ] *noun* ■ el **riñón** *(plural los riñones)*
kidney beans alubias rojas

kill [kɪl] *verb* ■ **matar**: he killed a bear mató un oso.

kilo ['ki:ləʊ] *(abbreviation of* kilogram*) noun* ■ el **kilo.**

kilogram , **kilogramme** UK ['kɪləgræm] *noun* ■ el **kilogramo.**

kilometre UK [kɪ'ləmɪtər], **kilometer** US [kɪ'lɒmɪtər] *noun* ■ el **kilómetro**: they're driving at 50 kilometres an hour van a 50 kilómetros por hora.

kind [kaɪnd] *(adjective & noun)*
■ *adjective*
amable: that's very kind of you es muy amable de tu parte

■ *noun*
el **tipo**: it's a kind of bird es un tipo de pájaro; I like all kinds of music me gusta todo tipo de música
what kind of plant is it? ¿qué especie de planta es?

kindergarten ['kɪndə,gɑ:tn] *noun* ■ el **jardín de infancia**: she goes to kindergarten va al jardín de infancia.

kindness ['kaɪndnɪs] *noun* ■ la **amabilidad.**

king [kɪŋ] *noun* ■ el **rey**: King Harold el rey Harold.

kingdom ['kɪŋdəm] *noun* ■ el **reino**: the United Kingdom el Reino Unido; the animal kingdom el reino animal.

kiosk ['ki:ɒsk] *noun* ■ el **quiosco**: she bought a newspaper from the kiosk compró un periódico en el quiosco.

kiss [kɪs] *(noun & verb)*
■ *noun*
el **beso**: she gave her father a kiss le dio un beso a su padre
love and kisses besos y abrazos
■ *verb*
1. **besar**: she kissed me on the cheek me besó en la mejilla
2. **besarse**: they kissed and said goodbye se besaron y se despidieron.

kit [kɪt] *noun*
a first-aid kit un botiquín de primeros auxilios
a tool kit una caja de herramientas.

kitchen ['kɪtʃɪn] *noun* ■ la **cocina**: he's in the kitchen making dinner está en la cocina preparando la cena.

kite [kaɪt] *noun* ■ la **cometa.**

kitten ['kɪtn] *noun* ■ el **gatito.**

knee [ni:] *noun* ■ la **rodilla**: he was on his knees estaba de rodillas.

kneel [ni:l] *(past tense & past participle* knelt [nelt] OR kneeled [ni:ld]*) verb* ■ **arrodillarse**: he knelt down se arrodilló; he was kneeling estaba arrodillado.

knelt *past tense & past participle* ➤ kneel.

knew [nju:] *past tense* ➤ know.

knife [naɪf] *(plural* knives [naɪvz]*) noun*
■ el **cuchillo**: a bread knife un cuchillo para cortar pan.

knight [naɪt] *noun*
1. el **caballero**: the Knights of the Round Table los caballeros de la mesa redonda
2. el **caballo**: the knight is a piece used in a game of chess el caballo es una pieza del ajedrez.

knit ['nɪt] *(past tense & past participle* knitted, *present participle* knitting*) verb* ■ **tejer, hacer punto**: I knitted a scarf tejí una bufanda.

knitting ['nɪtɪŋ] *noun* ■ la **labor de punto**: she likes knitting le gusta hacer punto
> a knitting needle la aguja de punto.

knives [naɪvz] *plural* ➤ knife.

knob [nɒb] *noun*
1. el **dial**: turn the knob to the right gira el dial hacia la derecha
2. el **pomo**: a door knob el pomo de una puerta.

knock [nɒk] *(noun & verb)*
■ *noun*
el **golpe**: I heard a knock at the door oí un golpe en la puerta
■ *verb*
1. **llamar**: somebody's knocking at the door alguien está llamando a la puerta
2. **golpearse**: I knocked my head on the shelf me golpeé la cabeza con el estante
3. **clavar**: he knocked the nail into the wall clavó el clavo en la pared

knock down *phrasal verb*
1. **derribar**: they knocked that building down derribaron ese edificio
2. **atropellar**: he was knocked down by a car lo atropelló un coche

knock out *phrasal verb*
1. **dejar sin sentido**: the thief knocked the guard out el ladrón dejó sin sentido al guardia

2. **eliminar**: England knocked Spain out o▮ the tournament Inglaterra eliminó a Españ▮ del torneo

knock over *phrasal verb* ■ **tirar**: I knocke▮ the glass over tiré el vaso.

knot [nɒt] *noun* ■ el **nudo**: he tied ▮ knot in the string hizo un nudo en la cuer▮ da.

know [nəʊ] *(past tense* knew, *past particip▮* known*) verb*

Use the verb **saber** for knowing facts. Use the verb **conocer** for knowing people or places.

1. **saber**: I know you're right sé que tienes▮ razón; he's Italian — yes, I know es italiano▮ —sí, lo sé; I don't know where he is no s▮ dónde está; she doesn't know any English▮ no sabe nada de inglés
2. **conocer**: do you know Vanessa? ¿conoces▮ a Vanessa?; I'm slowly getting to know▮ him lo voy conociendo poco a poco; I don't▮ know London very well no conozco muy▮ bien Londres
> how should I know? ¿cómo quieres que lo▮ sepa?
> to know how to do something saber hacer▮ algo: do you know how to swim? ¿sabes▮ nadar?

know about *phrasal verb*
1. **enterarse**: do you know about the accident? ¿te has enterado del accidente?
2. **saber de**: he knows all about computers sabe mucho de ordenadores.

know-how ['nəʊhaʊ] *noun* ■ los **conocimientos prácticos**: he doesn't have the know-how no tiene los conocimientos prácticos.

knowledge ['nɒlɪdʒ] *uncountable noun* ■ el **conocimiento**: she has a good knowledge of English tiene buenos conocimientos de inglés.

known [nəʊn] *past participle* ➤ know.

lab [læb] *(abbreviation of* laboratory*)* noun
■ *informal* el **laboratorio: a chemistry lab**
un laboratorio de química.

label ['leɪbl] *noun* ■ la **etiqueta.**

labor US ['leɪbə'] *noun* ➤ labour UK
Labor Day el Día del Trabajo *(primer lunes de septiembre)*
a labor union un sindicato de trabajadores.

laboratory [UK 'ləbrə,tɔːrɪ, US 'læbrə,tɔː-
rɪ] *(plural* laboratories*)* noun ■ el **laboratorio.**

labour UK, **labor** US ['leɪbə'] *noun* ■ la
mano de obra: skilled labour mano de obra
especializada
➤ **the Labour Party** UK el partido laborista
➤ Political Parties.

lace [leɪs] *noun*
1. el cordón *(plural* los cordones*)*: **he tied his
laces** se ató los cordones
2. el **encaje: a lace tablecloth** un mantel de
encaje.

lack [læk] *(noun & verb)*
■ *noun*
la **falta: through lack of experience** por falta de experiencia
■ *verb*
carecer de: she lacks confidence carece
de confianza en sí misma.

ladder ['lædə'] *noun* ■ la **escalera (de
mano): he climbed up the ladder** se subió
a la escalera.

lady ['leɪdɪ] *(plural* ladies*)* noun ■ la **señora: there's a lady waiting to see you** hay
una señora esperando para verte

ladies' clothes ropa de mujer
➤ **Ladies and Gentlemen!** ¡señoras y señores!
➤ **the ladies** UK OR **the ladies' room** US el
lavabo de señoras: **where is the ladies?**
¿dónde está el lavabo de señoras?

lager ['lɑːɡə'] *noun* ■ la **cerveza rubia.**

laid [leɪd] *past tense & past participle* ➤ lay.

laid-back ['leɪdbæk] *adjective* ■ *informal*
**tranquilo: people are very laid-back in Cali-
fornia** la gente de California es muy tranquila.

lain [leɪn] *past participle* ➤ lie.

lake [leɪk] *noun* ■ el **lago.**

lamb [læm] *noun* ■ el **cordero.**

lame [leɪm] *adjective* ■ **cojo: his horse is
lame** su caballo está cojo.

lamp [læmp] *noun* ■ la **lámpara.**

lamppost ['læmpəʊst] *noun* ■ la **farola.**

lampshade ['læmpʃeɪd] *noun* ■ la **pantalla (de lámpara).**

land [lænd] *(noun & verb)*
■ *noun*
la **tierra: this land is very fertile** esta tierra
es muy fértil
➤ **a piece of land** un terreno
■ *verb*
aterrizar: the plane lands at 6 o'clock el
avión aterriza a las 6.

landing ['lændɪŋ] *noun*
1. el **aterrizaje: the pilot made an emergency
landing** el piloto hizo un aterrizaje forzoso
2. el **rellano: the bathroom is on the landing** el
baño está en el rellano.

landlady ['lænd,leɪdɪ] *(plural* landladies*)*
noun ■ la **casera.**

landlord ['lændlɔːrd] *noun* ■ el **casero.**

landscape ['lændskeɪp] *noun* ■ el
**paisaje: the fields and woods of the English
landscape** los prados y bosques del paisaje inglés.

lane [leɪn] *noun*
1. el **camino: a country lane** un camino rural
2. el **carril: this motorway has four lanes** esta
autopista tiene cuatro carriles.

language ['læŋgwɪdʒ] *noun*
1. la **lengua: can you speak a foreign language?** ¿sabes alguna lengua extranjera?
2. el **lenguaje: legal language** el lenguaje legal
> **a language laboratory** un laboratorio de lenguas.

lap [læp] *noun*
1. el **regazo: the baby is sitting on her lap** el bebé está sentado en su regazo
2. la **vuelta: the runners did two laps** los corredores dieron dos vueltas.

laptop ['læptɒp] *noun* ■ el **ordenador portátil: he wants a laptop** quiere un ordenador portátil.

large [lɑːdʒ] *adjective*
1. **grande: London is a very large city** Londres es una ciudad muy grande
2. **importante: a large sum** una cantidad importante de dinero.

laser ['leɪzər] *noun* ■ el **láser: a laser beam** un rayo láser.

last [*UK* lɑːst, *US* læst] *(adjective, adverb, noun & verb)*
■ *adjective*
1. **último: that's the last time I listen to you!** ¡es la última vez que te hago caso!
2. **pasado: it happened last week** ocurrió la semana pasada; **Greg arrived last Tuesday** Greg llegó el martes pasado
> **last name** apellido: **what is your last name?** ¿cuál es tu apellido?
■ *adverb*
1. **último: she came last** fue la última en llegar
2. la **última vez: I last saw her in Boston** la última vez que la vi fue en Boston
■ *noun*
> el **último,** la **última: he's the last in the class** es el último de la clase
■ *verb*
> **durar: the film lasted two hours** la película duró dos horas
> **last night** anoche: **I saw him last night** lo vi anoche
> **the year before last** hace dos años
> **the next to last** penúltimo
> **at last** por fin: **we're home at last** ¡por fin estamos en casa!

late [leɪt] *adjective & adverb* ■ **tarde: I'm sorry I'm late** perdón por llegar tarde; **he arrived late** llegó tarde; **it's too late** es demasiado tarde; **I went to bed late** me acosté tarde; **he arrived two hours late** llegó dos horas tarde; **he arrived two hours late** llegó dos horas tarde; **he**
> **in late June** a finales de junio.

lately ['leɪtlɪ] *adverb* ■ **últimamente: have you seen him lately?** ¿lo has visto últimamente?

later ['leɪtər] *(comparative of late) adverb* ■ **después: I'll do it later** lo haré después
> **see you later!** ¡hasta luego!

latest ['leɪtɪst] *(superlative of late)*
■ *adjective*
> **último: here is the latest news** estas son las últimas noticias
> **at the latest** como muy tarde: **it will be ready by tomorrow at the latest** estará listo mañana, como muy tarde.

Latin ['lætɪn] *(adjective & noun)*
■ *adjective*

Remember not to use a capital letter for the adjective or the language in Spanish:

latino
> **Latin America** América Latina: **Peru is in Latin America** Perú está en América Latina
> **Latin American** latinoamericano
■ *noun*
> el **latín: he's studying Latin** está estudiando latín.

laugh [*UK* lɑːf, *US* læf] *(noun & verb)*
■ *noun*
> la **risa**
> **for a laugh** para divertirse: **we did it for a laugh** lo hicimos para divertirnos
> **to have a good laugh** divertirse mucho
■ *verb*
> **reírse: the audience was laughing** el público se estaba riendo; **she burst out laughing** se echó a reír
> **laugh at** *phrasal verb* ■ **reírse de: he was laughing at me** se estaba riendo de mí.

laughter ['lɑːftər] *uncountable noun* ■ la **risa: I can hear laughter** oigo risas.

launderette UK [lɔːnˈdret], **Laundromat®** US [ˈlɔːndrəmæt] *noun* ■ la **lavandería.**

laundry [ˈlɔːndrɪ] *(uncountable noun & noun)*
■ *uncountable noun*
la **ropa sucia: put the laundry in the basket** coloca la ropa sucia en el cesto
to do the laundry hacer la colada
■ *noun (plural* **laundries)**
la **lavandería.**

lavender [ˈlævəndəʳ] *noun* ■ la **lavanda.**

lavatory [ˈlævətrɪ] *(plural* **lavatories)** *noun*
■ el **baño: where is the lavatory?** ¿dónde está el baño?

law [lɔː] *noun*
1. la **ley: we must obey the law** debemos obedecer la ley; **to break the law** violar la ley
2. el **derecho: he's studying law** estudia derecho
it's against the law va contra la ley
law and order la ley y el orden.

lawn [lɔːn] *noun* ■ el **césped: she's mowing the lawn** está cortando el césped.

lawnmower [ˈlɔːn.məʊəʳ] *noun* ■ el **cortacésped** *(plural* los **cortacésped).**

lawyer [ˈlɔːjəʳ] *noun* ■ el **abogado,** la **abogada: Cheryl's a lawyer** Cheryl es abogada.

lay [leɪ] *(verb & verb form)*
■ *verb (past tense & past participle* **laid)**
poner: he laid his hand on my shoulder me puso la mano sobre el hombro
to lay an egg poner un huevo: **the hen laid an egg** la gallina puso un huevo
■ *past tense*
➤ **lie.**

layer [ˈleɪəʳ] *noun* ■ la **capa: there's a thick layer of snow on the roof** hay una gruesa capa de nieve sobre el tejado.

lazy [ˈleɪzɪ] *adjective* ■ **perezoso.**

lead [liːd] *(verb & adjective)*
■ *verb (past tense & past participle* **led)**
1. **llevar: this path leads to the village** este sendero lleva al pueblo; **he leads a busy life** lleva una vida muy ajetreada

2. **ir ganando por: Spain is leading 3 goals to 2** España va ganando por 3 goles a 2
➤ **to lead the way** mostrar el camino
■ *noun*
UK la **correa: you must keep your dog on a lead** debes llevar el perro sujeto con una correa
➤ **to be in the lead** llevar la delantera: **Shadowfax is in the lead** Shadowfax lleva la delantera
■ *adjective* [liːd]
solista: he's the lead trumpet of the orchestra es el trompetista solista de la orquesta.

lead [led] *noun*
1. el **plomo: the pipes are made of lead** las cañerías son de plomo
2. la **mina: the lead in a pencil** la mina de un lápiz.

leader [ˈliːdəʳ] *noun*
1. el/la **líder: the leader of our party** el líder de nuestro partido; **the leader of the gang** el líder de la pandilla
2. el **presidente: the leader of the country** el presidente del país.

leaf [liːf] *(plural* **leaves** [liːvz]*) noun* ■ la **hoja: the trees are losing their leaves** los árboles están perdiendo las hojas.

leaflet [ˈliːflɪt] *noun* ■ el **folleto.**

league [liːg] *noun* ■ la **liga: our team is at the top of the league** nuestro equipo encabeza la liga.

leak [liːk] *(noun & verb)*
■ *noun*
el **escape: there has been a gas leak** ha habido un escape de gas
■ *verb*
1. **gotear: the bucket is leaking** el cubo está goteando
2. **hacer agua: the boat's leaking** el barco está haciendo agua.

lean [liːn] *verb*
1. **apoyar: I leaned the ladder against the wall** apoyé la escalera contra la pared; **my bike is leaning against the wall** mi bicicleta está apoyada contra la pared

2. **apoyarse:** she leaned on the door se apoyó en la puerta

3. **inclinarse:** he leaned forward se inclinó hacia delante

lean out *phrasal verb* ■ **asomarse:** she leaned out of the window se asomó por la ventana

lean over *phrasal verb* ■ **inclinarse:** he leaned over to speak to me se inclinó para hablarme.

leap [liːp] *(past tense & past participle* leapt OR leaped) *verb* ■ **saltar:** the cat leaped on the mouse el gato saltó sobre el ratón; she leapt out of bed saltó de la cama

▶ to leap to one's feet ponerse de pie de un salto.

leapt [lept] *past tense & past participle* ➤ leap.

leap year [ˈliːpjɪər] *noun* ■ el **año bisiesto:** there's a leap year every four years hay un año bisiesto cada cuatro años.

learn [lɜːn] *verb* ■ **aprender: we're** learning English estamos aprendiendo inglés; she's learning to swim OR she's learning how to swim está aprendiendo a nadar.

learner [ˈlɜːnər] *noun* ■ el/la **principiante.**

least [liːst] *(superlative of* little) *(adjective, adverb & pronoun)*

■ *adjective*

▶ the least: he has the least money es el que menos dinero tiene; I don't have the least idea no tengo la menor idea

■ *adverb*

▶ the least

1. *with verbs* el que menos: I like those ones the least esos son los que menos me gustan

2. *with adjectives and nouns* menos: the least expensive restaurant el restaurante menos caro; the least funny joke la broma menos graciosa

■ *pronoun*

▶ the least menos: Sarah ate the least Sarah es la que menos comió

▶ at least

1. **al menos:** it'll cost at least 100 dollars costará al menos 100 dólares

2. **por lo menos:** she's never met him, at least that's what she says no lo conoce, por lo menos eso es lo que dice

▶ it's the least I can do es lo menos que puedo hacer.

leather [ˈleðər] *noun* ■ el **cuero,** la **piel.**

leave [liːv] *(noun & verb)*

■ *noun*

el **permiso:** the secretary has two days' leave la secretaria tiene dos días de permiso

■ *verb (past tense & past participle* left)

1. **irse:** I'm leaving tomorrow me voy mañana; she has already left ya se ha ido

2. **salir:** she left the country this morning ha salido del país esta mañana

3. **dejar:** I left the door open dejé la puerta abierta; leave me alone! ¡déjame en paz!; leave the book at home deja el libro en casa

leave out *phrasal verb* ■ **omitir:** you've left a word out has omitido una palabra.

leaves *plural* ➤ leaf.

lecture [ˈlektʃər] *noun*

1. la **charla:** he gave a lecture on archaeology dio una charla sobre arqueología

2. la **clase:** he missed his history lecture se perdió la clase de historia

⚠ Lecture es un falso amigo, no significa "lectura".

led [led] *past tense & past participle* ➤ lead.

left [left] *(adjective, adverb, noun & verb form)*

■ *adjective*

izquierdo: he took it with his left hand lo cogió con la mano izquierda

■ *adverb*

izquierdo: turn left at the end of the road dobla a la izquierda al final de la calle

■ *noun*

la **izquierda:** look to the left mira hacia la izquierda; you drive on the left in Britain en Gran Bretaña, se conduce por la izquierda

■ *past tense & past participle*

➤ leave

▶ to be left quedar: do you have any money left? ¿te queda algo de dinero?; there's none left no queda nada.

left-hand ['lefthænd] *adjective* ■ **de la izquierda**: the left-hand drawer el cajón de la izquierda
on the left-hand side del lado izquierdo.

left-handed [,left'hændɪd] *adjective* ■ **zurdo**: he's left-handed es zurdo.

left-luggage office [left'lʌgɪdʒ'ɒfɪs] *noun* ■ **la consigna.**

leftovers ['leftəʊvə'z] *plural noun* ■ **las sobras**: I threw away the leftovers tiré las sobras.

leg [leg] *noun* ■ **la pierna**: Colin has broken his leg Colin se ha roto una pierna
to pull somebody's leg tomarle el pelo a alguien: he's pulling your leg te está tomando el pelo
a leg of lamb una pierna de cordero
a chicken leg un muslo de pollo.

legal ['li:gl] *adjective* ■ **legal.**

legend ['ledʒənd] *noun* ■ **la leyenda**: he became a legend se convirtió en una leyenda.

leggings ['legɪŋz] *plural noun* ■ **las mallas.**

leisure [*UK* 'leʒə', *US* 'li:ʒər] *uncountable noun* ■ **el ocio**
a leisure centre *UK* un centro recreativo
leisure time tiempo libre: what do you do in your leisure time? ¿qué haces en tu tiempo libre?

lemon ['lemən] *noun* ■ **el limón** *(plural* los limones)*: a slice of lemon una rodaja de limón
lemon juice zumo de limón.

lemonade [,lemə'neɪd] *noun*
1. la limonada
2. *UK* la gaseosa.

lend [lend] *(past tense & past participle* lent) *verb* ■ **prestar**
to lend something to somebody prestarle algo a alguien: can you lend me your pencil? ¿puedes prestarme el lápiz?

length [leŋθ] *noun*
1. el largo: what length is it? ¿cuánto mide de largo?; it's five metres in length mide cinco metros de largo

2. la duración: the length of a prison sentence la duración de una condena de prisión.

lens [lenz] *(plural* lenses [lenzɪz]*) noun*
1. el objetivo: the lens of a camera el objetivo de la cámara
2. el cristal: my glasses have thick lenses mis gafas tienen cristales gruesos
3. la lente de contacto: she wears contact lenses usa lentes de contacto.

lent [lent] *past tense & past participle* ➤ lend.

Lent [lent] *noun* ■ **la Cuaresma.**

lentil ['lentɪl] *noun* ■ **la lenteja.**

leopard ['lepəd] *noun* ■ **el leopardo.**

less [les] *(comparative of* little) *(adjective, adverb & pronoun)*
■ *adjective*
menos: I have less money than you tengo menos dinero que tú
■ *adverb*
menos: you should eat less deberías comer menos; it's less serious than I thought es menos grave de lo que pensaba; the more I see him, the less I like him cuanto más lo veo, menos me gusta
■ *pronoun*
1. menos de: he'll be here in less than two hours estará aquí en menos de dos horas
2. menos que: he has less than me tiene menos que yo.

lesson ['lesn] *noun*
1. la lección *(plural* las lecciones)*: we will study that lesson in the book tomorrow estudiaremos esa lección del libro mañana
2. la clase: she's taking English lessons está yendo a clases de inglés
that'll teach him a lesson! ¡eso le servirá de lección!

let [let] *(past tense & past participle* let) *verb*
1. *in suggestions* let's go! ¡vamos!; let's go to the cinema tonight ¿vamos al cine esta noche?
2. dejar: to let somebody do something dejar a alguien hacer algo; my parents won't let me go out mis padres no me van a dejar salir; let me explain déjame que te explique

> to let go of somebody OR something soltar a alguien o algo: **let me go!** ¡suéltame!
> to let somebody know something informar de algo a alguien: **I'll let you know what time I arrive** te informaré de a qué hora llego
> **let us know** avísanos

let down *phrasal verb* ■ **fallar: she let me down at the last minute** me falló en el último momento

let in *phrasal verb* ■ **dejar entrar: he went to the door and let them in** fue hasta la puerta y los dejó entrar; **they wouldn't let us in the club** no nos dejaron entrar en el club

let off *phrasal verb* ■ **perdonar: I'll let you off this time, but don't do it again** te perdono esta vez, pero no lo vuelvas a hacer.

let's [lets] = let us.

letter ['letər] *noun*
1. la **carta: I sent him a letter** le mandé una carta
2. la **letra: the letters of the alphabet** las letras del abecedario.

letterbox *UK* ['letəbɒks] *noun* ■ el **buzón de correos** *(plural* los **buzones de correos***)*.

lettuce ['letɪs] *noun* ■ la **lechuga.**

level ['levl] *(noun & adjective)*
■ *noun*
el **nivel: they're on the same level** están al mismo nivel
■ *adjective*
1. **llano: the ground is level** el terreno es llano
2. **derecho: the pictures aren't level** los cuadros no están derechos
3. **empatado: the teams were level after the first half** los equipos iban empatados después de la primera parte.

lever [*UK* 'liːvəʳ, *US* 'levər] *noun* ■ la **palanca: the gear lever** la palanca de cambios.

liar ['laɪəʳ] *noun* ■ el **mentiroso,** la **mentirosa: he's a liar** es un mentiroso.

liberal ['lɪbərəl] *adjective* ■ **liberal**
the Liberal Democrats *UK* el Partido Liberal Demócrata ➤ Political Parties.

liberty ['lɪbətɪ] *noun* ■ la **libertad.**

librarian [laɪ'breərɪən] *noun* ■ el **bibliotecario,** la **bibliotecaria.**

library ['laɪbrərɪ] *(plural* libraries*) noun* ■ la **biblioteca**
> a **library book** un libro de la biblioteca

 La palabra inglesa **library** es un falso amigo, no significa "librería".

licence *UK*, **license** *US* ['laɪsəns] *noun* ■ la **licencia**
> a **license plate** *US* una placa de la matrícula
> a **driving licence** *UK* un carné de conducir.

lick [lɪk] *verb* ■ **lamer**
> the cat's licking its paws el gato se está lamiendo las patas.

licorice *US noun* ➤ liquorice *UK*.

lid [lɪd] *noun* ■ la **tapa: put the lid back on the saucepan** ponerle la tapa a la olla.

lie [laɪ] *(noun & verb)*
■ *noun*
la **mentira: it's all lies!** ¡son todo mentiras! to **tell lies** decir mentiras: **he's telling lies** está diciendo mentiras
■ *verb*
1. *(past tense & past participle* lied, *present participle* lying)* **mentir: you're lying** estás mintiendo; **she lied to me** me mintió
2. *(past tense* lay, *past participle* lain, *present participle* lying)* **echarse, tumbarse: he lay on the grass** se echó en el césped; **she's lying on the sofa** está tumbada en el sofá

lie down *phrasal verb* ■ **echarse, acostarse: I want to lie down on the bed** quiero echarme en la cama; **go and lie down for a while** ve y échate un rato
> to be lying down OR to be lying estar echado: **Marcus was lying down** Marcus estaba echado.

life [laɪf] *(plural* lives [laɪvz]*) noun* ■ la **vida: you saved my life!** ¡me salvaste la vida!; **that's life!** ¡así es la vida!
> a **life belt** *UK* un salvavidas
> a **life jacket** *UK* OR a **life preserver** *US* un chaleco salvavidas.

lifeboat ['laɪfbəʊt] *noun* ■ el **bote sal-vavidas.**

lifeguard ['laɪfgɑːd] *noun* ■ el/la **soco-rrista.**

lift [lɪft] *(noun & verb)*

noun

UK el **ascensor: I took the lift to the second floor** cogí el ascensor hasta el segundo piso
to give somebody a lift llevar a alguien en coche: **she gave me a lift to school** me llevó a la escuela en coche; **can I give you a lift?** ¿quieres que te lleve a algún lado?

verb

levantar: this suitcase is too heavy, I can't lift it la maleta es muy pesada, no la puedo levantar; **he lifted his arm** levantó el brazo.

light [laɪt] *(adjective, noun & verb)*

adjective

1. **ligero: it's as light as a feather** es tan ligero como una pluma; **we had a light meal** tomamos una comida ligera
2. **claro: he's wearing a light green shirt** lleva puesta una camisa verde claro
3. **luminoso: my bedroom is very light** mi habitación es muy luminosa

noun

1. la **luz** *(plural* las **luces): there's not enough light to read by** no hay suficiente luz para leer; **can you switch the light on?** ¿puedes encender la luz?; **the driver put his lights on** el conductor encendió las luces
2. el **fuego: have you got a light?** ¿tienes fuego?
   a traffic light un semáforo: **the traffic light is red** el semáforo está en rojo
   a light bulb una bombilla

verb (past tense & past participle **lit)**

encender: she lit the candle encendió la vela.

lighter ['laɪtəʳ] *noun* ■ el **encendedor: a cigarette lighter** un mechero.

lighthouse ['laɪthaʊs] *noun* ■ el **faro.**

lightning ['laɪtnɪŋ] *uncountable noun* ■ los **relámpagos, los rayos: there was thunder and lightning** había truenos y relámpagos
a flash of lightning un relámpago: **I saw a flash of lightning** vi un relámpago
as quick as lightning rápido como un rayo

the barn was struck by lightning cayó un rayo en el granero.

like [laɪk] *(preposition & verb)*

■ *preposition*

como: their house is like ours su casa es como la nuestra
what's he like? ¿cómo es él?
what's the weather like? ¿qué tiempo hace?
to look like somebody parecerse a alguien: **she looks like her sister** se parece a su hermana
do it like this hazlo así

■ *verb*

In Spanish, the verb **gustar** is used for express-ing likes and dislikes. When you use this verb, don't forget that the object liked or disliked be-comes the subject of the sentence, since **gustar** literally means "to be pleasing to":

I like music me gusta la música; **she doesn't like sardines** no le gustan las sardinas; **do you like dancing?** ¿te gusta bailar?

To ask someone if he or she would like to do something, or if he or she would like something, you often use the verb **gustar** in the condition-al. You can also use the verb **querer** in the in-dicative or in the past subjunctive. This also ap-plies to you stating your own desires:

if you like si quieres
I would like OR **I'd like** quisiera
I'd like a cup of tea quisiera una taza de té
would you like some more cake? ¿te gus-taría un poco más de pastel?
I'd like to me gustaría: **I'd like to go to Egypt** me gustaría ir a Egipto.

likely ['laɪklɪ] *adjective* ■ **probable: that's not very likely** eso no es muy probable; **it's likely to rain** es probable que llueva.

lilac ['laɪlək] *noun* ■ el **lila.**

lily ['lɪlɪ] *(plural* lilies) *noun* ■ el **lirio.**

lime [laɪm] *noun* ■ la **lima: lime juice** zu-mo de lima.

limit ['lɪmɪt] *(noun & verb)*

■ *noun*

el **límite: he knows his limits** conoce sus límites

■ *verb*
limitar: we have to try and limit our expenses tenemos que tratar de limitar nuestros gastos.

limp [lɪmp] *(verb & noun)*

■ *verb*
cojear: she's limping está cojeando

■ *noun*
> to have a limp cojear.

line [laɪn] *(noun & verb)*

■ *noun*
1. la **línea**: draw a straight line traza una línea recta; the line is engaged está comunicando
2. la **fila**: there was a long line of cars había una larga fila de coches
> to stand in line *US* hacer cola
> to drop somebody a line escribirle unas líneas a alguien: I dropped her a line le escribí unas líneas
> hold the line! ¡no cuelgue!

■ *verb*
1. **bordear**: trees lined the avenue los árboles bordeaban la avenida
2. **forrar**: a coat lined with silk un abrigo forrado de seda

line up *phrasal verb* ■ **ponerse en fila**: the children have lined up los niños se han puesto en fila.

linen [ˈlɪnɪn] *uncountable noun* ■ el **lino**.

link [lɪŋk] *(noun & verb)*

■ *noun*
la **conexión** *(plural* las **conexiones)**: there's a link between the two events hay una conexión entre los dos hechos

■ *verb*
1. **conectar**: the two towns are linked by rail los dos pueblos están conectados por ferrocarril
2. **relacionar**: the two events are linked los dos acontecimientos están relacionados.

lion [ˈlaɪən] *noun* ■ el **león** *(plural* los **leones)**: the lion roared el león rugió.

lioness [ˈlaɪənes] *noun* ■ la **leona**.

lip [lɪp] *noun* ■ el **labio**: I bit my lip me mordí el labio.

lip-read [ˈlɪpriːd] *verb* ■ **leer los labios**.

lipstick [ˈlɪpstɪk] *noun* ■ el **lápiz de labios**.

liquid [ˈlɪkwɪd] *noun* ■ el **líquido**.

liquor *US* [ˈlɪkər] *noun* ■ el **alcohol**
> a liquor store una tienda de vinos y licores.

liquorice *UK*, **licorice** *US* [ˈlɪkərɪs] *noun* ■ el **regaliz**.

list [lɪst] *(noun & verb)*

■ *noun*
la **lista**: her name is on the list su nombre está en la lista; make a list haz una lista

■ *verb*
hacer una lista: I've listed the presents to buy he hecho una lista de regalos que hay que comprar.

listen [ˈlɪsn] *verb* ■ **escuchar**: she's listening to the music está escuchando música.

lit [lɪt] *past tense & past participle* ➤ light.

liter *US* ➤ litre *UK*.

literature [ˈlɪtrətʃər] *noun* ■ la **literatura**.

litre *UK*, **liter** *US* [ˈliːtər] *noun* ■ el **litro**.

litter [ˈlɪtər] *uncountable noun* ■ la **basura**.

little [ˈlɪtl] *(adjective & adverb)*

■ *adjective*
1. **pequeño**: a little boy un niño pequeño
2. **poco**: there's very little hope hay muy poca esperanza
> her little sister su hermanita

■ *adverb*
poco: he eats very little come muy poco
> a little un poco de: I'm a little hungry tengo un poco de hambre; I have a little money tengo un poco de dinero
> a little bit un poquito
> little by little poco a poco.

live *(verb & adjective)*

■ *verb* [lɪv]
vivir: he lives with his father vive con su padre; Martha lives in Chicago Martha vive en Chicago

■ *adjective* [laɪv]
1. **en directo**: the programme is live el programa es en directo

2. vivo: experiments on live animals experimentos con animales vivos.

lively [ˈlaɪvlɪ] *adjective*

1. vivo: she's very lively es muy viva
2. animado: a lively place un lugar animado.

liver [ˈlɪvəʳ] *noun* ■ el **hígado**.

lives *plural* ➤ life.

living [ˈlɪvɪŋ] *noun*

to earn a living ganarse la vida

what do you do for a living? ¿a qué te dedicas?

living room [ˈlɪvɪŋruːm] *noun* ■ la **sala de estar**.

lizard [ˈlɪzəd] *noun* ■ el **lagarto**.

llama [ˈlɑːmə] *noun* ■ la **llama**.

load [ləʊd] *(noun & verb)*

■ *noun*

la **carga**: a heavy load una carga pesada

loads of *informal* un montón de: he's got loads of money tiene un montón de dinero

■ *verb*

cargar: they loaded the luggage into the car cargaron el equipaje en el coche; he loaded the gun cargó el arma

to load a camera ponerle carrete a la cámara.

loaf [ləʊf] *(plural loaves [ləʊvz]) noun* ■ el pan: a loaf of bread una barra de pan.

loan [ləʊn] *(noun & verb)*

■ *noun*

el **préstamo**: the bank gave him a loan el banco le dio un préstamo

■ *verb*

prestar: he loaned me his camera me prestó su cámara.

loaves *plural* ➤ loaf.

lobby [ˈlɒbɪ] *(plural lobbies) noun* ■ el **vestíbulo**: he's waiting for me in the lobby of the hotel me está esperando en el vestíbulo del hotel.

lobster [ˈlɒbstəʳ] *noun* ■ la **langosta**.

local [ˈləʊkl] *adjective*

1. local: a local newspaper un periódico local

2. de la zona: the local inhabitants los habitantes de la zona.

locally [ˈləʊkəlɪ] *adverb* ■ en la zona: she lives locally vive en la zona.

location [ləʊˈkeɪʃn] *noun* ■ la **ubicación** *(plural las ubicaciones)*: the house is in a beautiful location la casa tiene una ubicación preciosa.

lock [lɒk] *(noun & verb)*

■ *noun*

la **cerradura**: she put the key in the lock metió la llave en la cerradura

■ *verb*

cerrar con llave: she locked the door cerró la puerta con llave

lock in *phrasal verb* ■ encerrar: they locked her in her room la encerraron en su cuarto

lock out *phrasal verb* ■ quedarse fuera sin llaves: I locked myself out me quedé fuera sin llaves.

locker [ˈlɒkəʳ] *noun* ■ la **taquilla**: he keeps his books in his locker guarda sus libros en la taquilla

the locker room el vestuario.

lodger [ˈlɒdʒəʳ] *noun* ■ el **inquilino**, la **inquilina**.

log [lɒg] *(noun & phrasal verb)*

■ *noun*

el **tronco**: put a log on the fire pon un tronco en el fuego

a log cabin una cabaña de madera

log in , **log on** *phrasal verb* ■ entrar en el sistema

log off , **log out** *phrasal verb* ■ salir del sistema.

logical [ˈlɒdʒɪkl] *adjective* ■ **lógico**.

lollipop [ˈlɒlɪpɒp] *noun* ■ el **pirulí**.

lolly *UK* [ˈlɒlɪ] *(plural lollies) noun* ■ *informal* la **piruleta**

an ice lolly un polo.

London [ˈlʌndən] *noun* ■ **Londres**: I live in London vivo en Londres; we're going to London vamos a Londres

lonely ['ləʊnlɪ] *adjective*

1. **solo**: she feels lonely OR she's lonely se siente sola
2. **solitario**: a lonely beach una playa solitaria.

long [lɒŋ] *(adjective & adverb)*

■ *adjective*

largo: her skirt is too long su falda es demasiado larga
▶ the fence is ten metres long la valla tiene diez metros de largo
▶ the concert is three hours long el concierto dura tres horas
▶ a long time mucho tiempo: I've been waiting a long time hace mucho tiempo que espero; it takes a long time lleva mucho tiempo
▶ it's a long way queda lejos

■ *adverb*

tiempo: I didn't wait long no esperé mucho tiempo
▶ I won't be long no voy a tardar
▶ how long will it take? ¿cuánto tiempo te llevará?; how long will you be? ¿cuánto tiempo estarás?; how long have you been here? ¿cuánto hace que estás aquí?

When "as long as" means "provided that" the verb that follows must be in the subjunctive:

▶ as long as el tiempo que, mientras
▶ I'll wait as long as you like esperaré el tiempo que quieras: as long as you are there, you're safe mientras estés aquí, estás a salvo
▶ so long! adiós.

loo UK [luː] *noun* ■ *informal* el **cuarto de baño**.

look [lʊk] *(noun & verb)*

■ *noun*

la **mirada**: he gave me a funny look me miró de un modo gracioso

▶ to have a look at something echar un vistazo a algo: can I have a look? ¿puedo echar un vistazo?

■ *verb*

1. **mirar**: don't look! ¡no mires!
2. **parecer**: you look tired pareces cansado
▶ it looks as if it's going to snow parece que va a nevar
▶ to look like somebody parecerse a alguien: Felicia looks like her mother Felicia se parece a su madre

look after *phrasal verb* ■ **cuidar**: he's looking after his little brother está cuidando a su hermano menor

look around ➤ look round UK

look at *phrasal verb* ■ **mirar**: look at the photos mira las fotos; he looked at her él la miró

look for *phrasal verb* ■ **buscar**: I'm looking for my keys estoy buscando mis llaves

look forward to *phrasal verb*

1. **desear**: I'm really looking forward to Christmas estoy deseando que llegue Navidad
2. **esperar**: I look forward to hearing from you espero tener noticias tuyas

look out *phrasal verb* ■ **tener cuidado**: look out! ¡cuidado!

look round UK, **look around** *phrasal verb*

1. **mirar alrededor**: he looked round when I called him miró alrededor cuando lo llamé
2. **mirar**: I'm just looking round sólo estoy mirando
3. **recorrer**: let's look round the museum vamos a recorrer el museo

look up *phrasal verb*

1. **alzar la vista**: I looked up when he came in alcé la vista cuando entró
2. **buscar**: look the word up in the dictionary busca la palabra en el diccionario.

loose [luːs] *adjective*

1. **flojo**: this screw is loose este tornillo está flojo
2. **holgado**: loose clothes ropa holgada

to come loose aflojarse: the knot has come loose el nudo se aflojó

loose change dinero suelto.

lord [lɔːd] *noun*

1. el señor: he lives like a lord vive como un rey

2. *UK* el **lord**

the Lords *UK* la Cámara de los Lores.

lose [luːz] *(past tense & past participle* lost*) verb*

■ **perder:** I've lost my ticket he perdido mi entrada; the team lost by three goals to one el equipo perdió por tres a uno

to lose one's way perderse: he lost his way se perdió.

loser ['luːzəʳ] *noun*

1. el **perdedor,** la **perdedora:** he's a bad loser es un mal perdedor

2. *informal* el **fracasado,** la **fracasada:** he's a real loser es un verdadero fracasado.

loss [lɒs] *noun* ■ la **pérdida.**

lost [lɒst] *(adjective & verb form)*

■ *adjective*

perdido

to get lost perderse: I got lost in the woods me perdí en el bosque

the lost property office *UK* OR the lost-and-found *US* la oficina de objetos perdidos

■ *past tense & past participle*

➤ lose.

lot [lɒt] *noun*

a lot mucho: he eats a lot come mucho

thanks a lot! ¡muchas gracias!

he has a lot of friends tiene muchos amigos

lots *informal* un montón de: she has lots of money tiene un montón de dinero

the lot *informal* todo: she ate the lot se lo comió todo.

lotion ['ləʊʃn] *noun* ■ la **loción** *(plural* las **lociones)**

suntan lotion el bronceador.

lottery ['lɒtərɪ] *(plural* lotteries) *noun* ■ la **lotería.**

loud [laʊd] *adjective & adverb* ■ **fuerte:** the music's too loud la música está muy fuerte; can you speak a bit louder? ¿puedes hablar un poco más fuerte?

out loud en voz alta: he spoke out loud habló en voz alta; to read out loud leer en voz alta.

loudspeaker [ˌlaʊd'spiːkəʳ] *noun* ■ el **altavoz.**

lounge *UK* [laʊndʒ] *noun* ■ el **salón:** they're watching TV in the lounge están viendo la tele en el salón

the departure lounge la sala de embarque.

louse *UK* [laʊs] *noun* ■ el **piojo.**

lousy ['laʊzɪ] *adjective* ■ *informal* **horrible, malísimo:** the weather's lousy el tiempo es malísimo.

love [lʌv] *(noun & verb)*

■ *noun*

el **amor**

a love song una canción de amor

to be in love estar enamorado: he's in love with her él está enamorado de ella

to fall in love enamorarse: she fell in love with him se enamoró de él

give her my love dale recuerdos de mi parte

■ *verb*

1. **querer, amar:** I love you te quiero

2. **encantar:** I'd love to come to your party me encantaría ir a tu fiesta; he loves chocolate le encanta el chocolate; I love dancing me encanta bailar.

lovely ['lʌvlɪ] *adjective*

1. **precioso:** that's a lovely dress es un vestido precioso; you look lovely, Claire! Claire, ¡estás preciosa!

2. **encantador:** he's a lovely man es un hombre encantador

3. **delicioso:** this tastes lovely esto está delicioso

we had a lovely time lo pasamos muy bien

what lovely weather! hace un tiempo estupendo.

low [ləʊ] *(adjective & adverb)*

■ *adjective*

bajo: the ceiling is very low el techo es muy bajo

■ *adverb*
bajo: the plane is flying low el avión está volando bajo.

lower [ˈləʊəʳ] *(adjective, adverb & verb)*
■ *adjective (comparative of* low *)*
inferior: the lower level of the bus el piso inferior del autobús
■ *adverb (comparative of* low *)*
más abajo: put the painting a bit lower pon el cuadro un poco más abajo
■ *verb*
bajar: they've lowered the prices han bajado los precios.

low-fat [ləʊfæt] *adjective*
1. **bajo en grasas**: a low-fat meal una comida baja en grasas
2. **desnatado**: low-fat yoghurt yogur desnatado.

luck [lʌk] *uncountable noun* ■ la **suerte**: you're in luck estás de suerte
➤ **good luck!** ¡buena suerte!
➤ **bad luck!** ¡mala suerte!

lucky [ˈlʌkɪ] *adjective*
➤ to be lucky
1. **tener suerte**: she's very lucky tiene mucha suerte
2. **dar suerte**: horseshoes are lucky las herraduras dan suerte
➤ a lucky charm un amuleto.

luggage [ˈlʌgɪdʒ] *uncountable noun* ■ el **equipaje**: my luggage is very heavy mi equipaje pesa mucho
➤ a luggage rack una baca, un portaequipajes.

lullaby [ˈlʌləbaɪ] *(plural* lullabies*) noun* ■ la **nana**.

lump [lʌmp] *noun*
1. **el terrón** *(plural* los **terrones***)*: a lump of sugar un terrón de azúcar
2. **el chichón** *(plural* los **chichones***)*: she has a lump on her forehead tiene un chichón en la frente.

lunch [lʌntʃ] *noun* ■ el **almuerzo**, la **comida**: what did you have for lunch? ¿qué has almorzado?
➤ to have lunch almorzar, comer

➤ we have lunch at one o'clock comemos a la una
➤ the lunch hour la hora del almuerzo, la hora de la comida.

lunchtime [ˈlʌntʃtaɪm] *noun* ■ la **hora del almuerzo**, la **hora de la comida**: it's nearly lunchtime es casi la hora del almuerzo.

lung [lʌŋ] *noun* ■ el **pulmón** *(plural* los **pulmones***)*.

luxury [ˈlʌkʃərɪ] *(plural* luxuries*) noun* ■ el **lujo**: she lives in luxury vive con lujo
➤ a luxury hotel un hotel de lujo.

lying [ˈlaɪɪŋ] ➤ lie.

lyrics [ˈlɪrɪks] *plural noun* ■ la **letra**: who wrote the lyrics for this song? ¿quién escribió la letra de esta canción?

macaroni [ˌmækəˈrəʊnɪ] *uncountable noun* ■ los **macarrones**.

machine [məˈʃiːn] *noun* ■ la **máquina**: a sewing machine una máquina de coser
➤ a machine gun una ametralladora.

mackerel [ˈmækrəl] *noun* ■ la **caballa**.

mad [mæd] *adjective*
1. **loco**: he's mad está loco; you must be going mad debes estar volviéndote loco
2. **furioso**: I'm mad at him estoy furioso con él
➤ to be mad about something estar loco por algo: he's mad about football está loco por el fútbol

to be mad about somebody estar loco por alguien: he's mad about her está loco por ella.

madam ['mædəm] *noun* ■ la **señora: can I help you, madam?** ¿qué desea, señora?

made [meɪd] *past tense & past participle* ➤ make.

magazine [ˌmægə'ziːn] *noun* ■ la **revista: a fashion magazine** una revista de moda.

magic ['mædʒɪk] *(noun & adjective)*
■ *noun*
la **magia: he likes to do magic** le gusta hacer magia
■ *adjective*
mágico: a magic wand una varita mágica
a magic trick un truco de magia.

magician [mə'dʒɪʃn] *noun* ■ el **mago,** la **maga.**

magnet ['mægnɪt] *noun* ■ el **imán** *(plural* los **imanes)**.

magnetic [mæg'netɪk] *adjective* ■ **magnético.**

magnificent [mæg'nɪfɪsənt] *adjective* ■ **magnífico.**

magnifying glass ['mægnɪfaɪɪŋglɑːs] *noun* ■ la **lupa.**

magpie ['mægpaɪ] *noun* ■ la **urraca.**

maid [meɪd] *noun* ■ la **sirvienta.**

maiden name ['meɪdnneɪm] *noun* ■ el **apellido de soltera.**

mail [meɪl] *(noun & verb)*
■ *noun*
1. la **correspondencia: you have mail** tienes correspondencia
2. el **correo: I'll send it to you by mail** te lo mandaré por correo
■ *verb*
US **mandar (por correo): to mail a letter to somebody** mandarle una carta a alguien.

mailbox *US* ['meɪlbɒks] *(plural* mailboxes) *noun* ■ el **buzón** *(plural* los **buzones)**.

mailman *US* ['meɪlmən] *(plural* mailmen ['meɪlmən]) *noun* ■ el **cartero.**

main [meɪn] *adjective* ■ **principal**
➤ the main course el plato principal
➤ a main road una carretera principal.

mainly ['meɪnlɪ] *adverb* ■ **principalmente.**

maize [meɪz] *uncountable noun* ■ el **maíz.**

Majesty ['mædʒəstɪ] *(plural* Majesties) *noun* ■ la **Majestad: Her Majesty the Queen** su Majestad la Reina

major ['meɪdʒəʳ] *(adjective & noun)*
■ *adjective*
muy importante: it's a major event es un acontecimiento muy importante
➤ a major road una carretera principal
➤ It's of major importance esto es de enorme importancia
■ *noun*
1. el/la **comandante**
2. *US* la **especialidad: my major is physics** mi especialidad es la física.

majority [mə'dʒɒrətɪ] *(plural* majorities) *noun* ■ la **mayoría: he won by a big majority** ganó por una amplia mayoría
➤ the majority of people la mayoría de las personas.

make [meɪk] *(verb & noun)*
■ *verb (past tense & past participle* made)
1. **hacer: I made this vase myself** yo mismo hice este jarrón; **have you made the bed?** ¿has hecho la cama?
2. **fabricar: these cars are made in Germany** estos coches están fabricados en Alemania
3. **preparar: to make a meal** preparar una comida
4. **ganar: he makes a lot of money** gana mucho dinero
➤ to be made of ser de: this ring is made of gold este anillo es de oro
➤ to make somebody do something hacer a alguien hacer algo: she made me laugh me hizo reír
➤ the film made me sad la película me puso triste
➤ to make do arreglárselas; we'll have to make do vamos a tener que arreglárnoslas; to make do with something conformarse con algo; they made do with the leftovers se conformaron con las sobras

▷ **to make sure** asegurarse (de algo): **make sure the oven is turned off** asegúrate de que el horno esté apagado

▷ **make yourself at home** siéntete como en tu casa

▷ **3 and 4 make 7** 3 y 4 son 7

make out *phrasal verb*

1. **descifrar**: **I can't make out what the inscription says** no puedo descifrar lo que dice la inscripción

2. **entender**: **I can't make out what they are saying** no puedo entender lo que dicen

3. **dar a entender**: **she's not as rich as she makes out** no es tan rica como da a entender

make up *phrasal verb*

1. **inventar**: **he made up an excuse** inventó una excusa

2. **hacer las paces**: **they had an argument, but they've made up now** discutieron, pero ahora han hecho las paces

▷ **to make up one's mind** decidirse

make up for *phrasal verb*

1. **compensar**: **to make up for a loss** compensar una pérdida

2. **recuperar**: **we must make up for lost time** debemos recuperar el tiempo perdido.

make [meɪk] *noun* ■ **marca**: **what make of car is that?** ¿qué marca de coche es esa?

make-up [meɪkʌp] *uncountable noun* ■ **el maquillaje**

▷ **a make-up bag** un neceser de maquillaje

▷ **to wear make-up** maquillarse: **Susan doesn't wear make-up** Susan no se maquilla.

male [meɪl] *(noun & adjective)*

■ *noun*

el varón *(plural* **los varones**)*, el **macho**

■ *adjective*

1. **macho**: **a male hamster** un hámster macho

2. **masculino**: **I heard a male voice** escuché una voz masculina

▷ **a male nurse** un enfermero

▷ **a male student** un estudiante.

mall [mɔːl] *noun* ■ **el centro comercial**: **a shopping mall** un centro comercial.

mammal [ˈmæml] *noun* ■ **el mamífero**.

man [mæn] *(plural* **men** [men]*) noun* ■ **el hombre**: **men's clothes** ropa de hombre

▷ **he's an old man** es un anciano

▷ **a young man** un joven

▷ **the men's room** el lavabo de hombres: **where is the men's room?** ¿dónde está el baño de hombres?

manage [ˈmænɪdʒ] *verb*

1. **arreglárselas**: **I can manage by myself** me las puedo arreglar solo

2. **dirigir**: **he manages a big company** dirige una gran empresa

▷ **to manage to do something** arreglárselas para hacer algo: **how did you manage to carry your suitcase?** ¿cómo te las arreglaste para llevar tu maleta?

management [ˈmænɪdʒmənt] *noun* ■ **la dirección**: **the management does not accept responsibility** la dirección no asume responsabilidad alguna

▷ **management studies** administración de empresas.

manager [ˈmænɪdʒəʳ] *noun*

1. **el/la gerente, el director, la directora**: **the bank manager** el gerente del banco

2. **el encargado, la encargada**: **a shop manager** un encargado de tienda

3. **el entrenador, la entrenadora**: **he's the team manager** es el entrenador del equipo.

mango [ˈmæŋgəʊ] *noun* ■ **el mango**.

Manhattan [ˈmænˌhætən] *noun* ■ **Manhattan** *(masculine)*: **Edward lives in Manhattan** Edward vive en Manhattan

MANHATTAN

Manhattan es el distrito central de Nueva York. Se divide en tres barrios: **Downtown, Midtown** y **Uptown** y acoge lugares tan conocidos como **Central Park**, la **Quinta Avenida, Broadway**, la **Estatua de la Libertad** y **Greenwich Village**, así como rascacielos tan famosos como el **Empire State Building** y el **Chrysler Building**. La **Manhattan Skyline** es la famosa vista de Nueva York dominada por los rascacielos que incluían las torres gemelas del World Trade Center, hasta su destrucción en los ataques terroristas del 11 de septiembre de 2001.

mankind [mæn'kaɪnd] *noun* ■ la humanidad.

man-made ['mænmeɪd] *adjective*
1. artificial: a man-made lake un lago artificial
2. sintético: a man-made fabric una tela sintética.

manner ['mænəʳ] *noun* ■ la **manera**: she treated me in a decent manner me trató de manera amable.

manners ['mænəʳz] *plural noun* ■ los **modales**: he has very good manners tiene muy buenos modales.

mantelpiece ['mæntlpiːs] *noun* ■ la **repisa de la chimenea**.

mansion ['mænʃn] *noun* ■ la **mansión** *(plural* las **mansiones***)*.

manual ['mænjʊəl] *noun* ■ el **manual**: an instruction manual un manual de instrucciones.

many ['menɪ] *(adjective & pronoun)*
■ *adjective*
muchos: she has many friends tiene muchos amigos
> were there many people at the match? ¿había mucha gente en el partido?
■ *pronoun*
muchos: don't eat all the sweets, there aren't many left no te comas todos los caramelos, no quedan muchos
> how many? ¿cuántos?: how many are there? ¿cuántos hay?; how many presents did you get? ¿cuántos regalos recibiste?
> too many demasiados: I ate too many sweets comí demasiados caramelos
> there are too many people here hay demasiada gente aquí
> as many tantos como: I don't have as many CDs as my brother no tengo tantos cedés como mi hermano
> take as many as you like coge todos los que quieras.

map [mæp] *noun*
1. el **mapa**: a map of Spain un mapa de España
2. el **plano**: a map of Madrid un plano de Madrid.

maple ['meɪpl] *noun* ■ el **arce**
> maple syrup jarabe de arce.

marathon ['mærəθn] *noun* ■ el/la **maratón** *(plural* los/las **maratones***)*.

marble ['mɑːbl] *noun*
1. el **mármol**: a marble statue una estatua de mármol
2. la **canica**: they're playing marbles están jugando a las canicas.

march [mɑːtʃ] *verb* ■ **desfilar**: the soldiers were marching los soldados estaban desfilando; **forward march!** ¡adelante, marchen!

March [mɑːtʃ] *noun*

In Spanish the months of the year do not start with a capital letter:

marzo: in March en marzo; next March el próximo marzo; last March el pasado marzo.

margarine [ˌmɑːgə'riːn] *uncountable* ■ la **margarina**.

margin ['mɑːdʒɪn] *noun* ■ el **margen** *(plural* los **márgenes***)*: he wrote something in the margin escribió algo en el margen.

mark [mɑːk] *(noun & verb)*
■ *noun*
1. la **mancha**: there's a mark on your T-shirt tienes una mancha en la camiseta; there are marks all over his body tiene manchas en todo el cuerpo
2. *UK* la **nota**: I got good marks in English saqué buenas notas en inglés
■ *verb*
1. **marcar**: X marks the spot el lugar está marcado con una X
2. **corregir**: the teacher has marked our homework el profesor ha corregido los deberes.

market ['mɑːkɪt] *noun* ■ el **mercado**: I'm going to the market voy al mercado.

marriage ['mærɪdʒ] *noun* ■ el **matrimonio**: this is her second marriage éste es su segundo matrimonio.

married ['mærɪd] *adjective* ■ **casado**: are you married? ¿estás casado?
> to get married casarse: they're getting married se van a casar.

marry ['mærɪ] *(past tense & past participle married) verb* ■ **casarse con: she married Ian Jones** se casó con Ian Jones; **will you marry me?** ¿te quieres casar conmigo?

marvellous *UK,* **marvelous** *US* ['mɑːvələs] *adjective* ■ **maravilloso.**

marzipan ['mɑːzɪpæn] *uncountable noun* ■ **el mazapán.**

masculine ['mæskjʊlɪn] *adjective* ■ **masculino.**

mashed potatoes [mæʃtpə'teɪtəʊz] *plural noun* ■ **el puré de patatas.**

mask [*UK* mɑːsk, *US* mæsk] *noun* ■ **la máscara: he's wearing a mask** lleva puesta una máscara.

mass [mæs] *noun*
1. **el montón** *(plural* los **montones***):* **a mass of papers** un montón de papeles
2. **la misa: Catholics go to mass on Sunday** los católicos van a misa los domingos
> **masses of** un montón de: **Bill has masses of computer games** Bill tiene un montón de videojuegos.

massage [*UK* 'mæsɑːʒ, *US* mə'sɑːʒ] *noun* ■ **el masaje.**

massive ['mæsɪv] *adjective* ■ **masivo.**

mast [*UK* mɑːst, *US* mæst] *noun* ■ **el mástil.**

master ['mɑːstəʳ] *noun* ■ **el dueño: the master of the house** el dueño de casa.

masterpiece [*UK* 'mɑːstəpiːs, *US* 'mæstərpiːs] *noun* ■ **la obra maestra.**

mat [mæt] *noun*
1. **la colchoneta: an exercise mat** una colchoneta para hacer gimnasia
2. **el felpudo: wipe your feet on the mat before you come in** límpiate los pies en el felpudo antes de entrar
> **a place mat** un mantel individual.

match [mætʃ] *(noun & verb)*
■ *noun*
1. **la cerilla: a box of matches** una caja de cerillas

2. **el partido: a tennis match** un partido de tenis; **a football match** un partido de fútbol
> **a boxing match** un combate de boxeo
■ *verb*
1. **hacer juego con: that tie doesn't match your shirt** esa corbata no hace juego con tu camisa
2. *in negative sentences* **estar desparejado: those socks don't match** esos calcetines están desparejados.

matchbox ['mætʃbɒks] *noun* ■ **la caja de cerillas.**

matching ['mætʃɪŋ] *adjective* ■ **a juego: matching dress and shoes** vestido y zapatos a juego.

material [mə'tɪərɪəl] *noun*
1. **el material: building materials** materiales de construcción
2. **la tela: she bought some curtain material** compró tela para hacer cortinas
> **raw materials** materia prima.

math *US* ➤ maths *UK* .

mathematics [ˌmæθə'mætɪks] *uncountable noun* ■ **las matemáticas.**

maths *UK* [mæθs], **math** *US* [mæθ] *(abbreviation of* mathematics*) uncountable noun* ■ *informal* **mates: I like maths** me gustan las mates; **maths is fun** las mates son divertidas.

matter ['mætəʳ] *(noun & verb)*
■ *noun*
el asunto: it's a delicate matter es un asunto delicado
it's a matter of time es cuestión de tiempo
> **as a matter of fact** de hecho
> **what's the matter?** ¿qué pasa?
> **what's the matter with her?** ¿qué le pasa?
> **there's nothing the matter** no pasa nada
■ *verb*
importar: it doesn't matter no importa.

mattress ['mætrɪs] *noun* ■ **el colchón** *(plural* los **colchones***)* .

mature [mə'tjʊəʳ] *adjective* ■ **maduro: he's very mature for his age** es muy maduro para su edad.

mauve [məʊv] *adjective* ■ **malva.**

maximum ['mæksɪməm] *(adjective & noun)*
adjective
máximo: what's the maximum speed?
¿cuál es la velocidad máxima?
noun
el **máximo:** there'll be a maximum of 20
habrá un máximo de 20.

may [meɪ] *modal verb*
possibility

In Spanish, when "may" is used with another verb to say something is possible, you can translate it using the expression **puede que** followed by a verb in the subjunctive:

we may come puede que vengamos; it may rain puede que llueva; she may have called puede que haya llamado

2. *asking and giving permission* **poder:** may I open the window? ¿puedo abrir la ventana?; you may sit down pueden sentarse.

May [meɪ] *noun*

In Spanish the months of the year do not start with a capital letter:

mayo: in May en mayo; next May el próximo mayo; last May el pasado mayo
May Day el primero de mayo.

maybe ['meɪbiː] *adverb* ■ **quizás**

Quizás must be followed by a verb in the subjunctive:

maybe I'll come quizás venga; maybe you're right quizás tengas razón
maybe not quizás no.

mayonnaise [ˌmeɪə'neɪz] *noun* ■ la **mayonesa.**

mayor [meəʳ] *noun* ■ el **alcalde,** la **alcaldesa:** he's the mayor of New York es el alcalde de Nueva York.

maze [meɪz] *noun* ■ el **laberinto:** this building is a real maze este edificio es un verdadero laberinto.

me [miː] *personal pronoun*
1. *direct and indirect object* **me:** she doesn't know me no me conoce; can you hear me? ¿puedes oírme?; **give it to me!** ¡dámelo!

2. *after prepositions* **mí:** is that for me? ¿eso es para mí?; she left without me se fue sin mí

In Spanish, "with me" has a special form:

come with me ven conmigo
3. *in comparisons* **yo:** he's taller than me es más alto que yo.

meal [miːl] *noun* ■ la **comida:** she made a big meal preparó una gran comida
➤ enjoy your meal! ¡buen provecho!

mean [miːn] *(adjective & verb)*
■ *adjective*
1. **tacaño:** he's mean, he never buys me anything es un tacaño, nunca me compra nada
2. **malo:** he's always mean to his sister siempre es malo con su hermana
■ *verb (past tense & past participle* meant*)*
1. **significar:** what does this expression mean? ¿qué significa esta expresión?; it doesn't mean anything esto no significa nada
2. **querer decir:** what do you mean? ¿qué quieres decir?; that's not what he meant eso no es lo que quería decir
3. **querer:** I mean to leave at 6 o'clock quiero irme a las 6 en punto; I didn't mean to hurt you no quise herirte
➤ I meant it lo dije en serio
➤ to be meant for ser para: this present is meant for your sister este regalo es para tu hermana.

meaning ['miːnɪŋ] *noun* ■ el **significado:** what's the meaning of this word? ¿cuál es el significado de esta palabra?

means [miːnz] *noun* ■ el **medio:** it's a means to get what he wants es un medio para obtener lo que quiere
➤ by means of por medio de: they communicate by means of a variety of sounds se comunican por medio de una variedad de sonidos
➤ the thief got in by means of a ladder el ladrón entró usando una escalera
➤ a means of transport un medio de transporte.

meant [ment] *past tense & past participle* ➤ mean.

meantime ['miːnˌtaɪm] *noun*
➤ in the meantime mientras tanto.

meanwhile ['miːnˌwaɪl] *adverb* ■ **mientras tanto:** meanwhile, I was out with my friends mientras tanto, yo estaba fuera con mis amigos.

measles ['miːzlz] *noun* ■ el **sarampión:** she has measles tiene sarampión.

measure ['meʒəʳ] *verb* ■ **medir:** she measured the chair with a tape measure midió la silla con una cinta métrica; the room measures 20 square metres la habitación mide 20 metros cuadrados.

measurement ['meʒəmənt] *noun* ■ la **medida:** he took my measurements me tomó las medidas

MEASUREMENTS

En Gran Bretaña (aunque oficialmente se haya adoptado el sistema métrico) y Estados Unidos no se usa normalmente el sistema métrico, sino que se emplean las medidas del antiguo sistema inglés, conocido como **imperial system**. Las unidades más comunes son: **inches** (pulgadas); **feet** (pies); **yards** (yardas); **miles** (millas); **ounces** (onzas); **pounds** (libras); **degrees Fahrenheit** (grados Fahrenheit). 1 inch = 2,54 cm, 1 foot = 30,48 cm, 1 yard = 91,44 cm, 1 mile = 1,6 km, 1 ounce = 28,35 g, 1 pound = 0,453 kg, 1 degree Fahrenheit = −17,22 grados centígrados.

meat [miːt] *uncountable noun* ■ la **carne:** she doesn't like meat no le gusta la carne.

mechanic [mɪ'kænɪk] *noun* ■ el **mecánico,** la **mecánica.**

mechanical [mɪ'kænɪkl] *adjective* ■ **mecánico.**

medal ['medl] *noun* ■ la **medalla:** she won a gold medal ganó una medalla de oro.

media ['miːdjə] *noun*

the media los medios de comunicación: the event was reported in the media el acontecimiento fue divulgado por los medios de comunicación.

medical ['medɪkl] *adjective* ■ **médico:** medical treatment tratamiento médico

a medical student un estudiante de medicina.

medicine ['medsɪn] *noun*

1. la **medicina:** Andrew's studying medicine Andrew está estudiando medicina

2. el **medicamento:** I must take my medicine debo tomar mi medicamento.

medium ['miːdjəm] *adjective* ■ **mediano:** he's of medium height es de estatura mediana.

medium-sized ['miːdjəmsaɪzd] *adjective* ■ **tamaño mediano:** a medium-sized town una ciudad de tamaño mediano.

meet [miːt] *(past tense & past participle* met*) verb*

1. **conocer:** have you met Lisa's brother? ¿conoces al hermano de Lisa?

2. **encontrarse:** we met by chance in the street nos encontramos por casualidad en la calle; let's meet in front of the cinema por qué no quedamos delante del cine

3. **reunirse:** the board met today hoy se ha reunido el consejo

4. **buscar:** I'm going to meet them at the airport at 3 o'clock voy a buscarlos al aeropuerto a las 3 en punto

▶ I met Sue outside the shop me encontré con Sue fuera de la tienda

▶ pleased to meet you encantado de conocerlo.

meeting ['miːtɪŋ] *noun*

1. la **reunión** *(plural* las **reuniones***):* I have a meeting today hoy tengo una reunión

2. el **encuentro:** this was our first meeting éste era nuestro primer encuentro.

megabyte ['megəbaɪt] *noun* ■ el **megabyte.**

melody ['melədɪ] *(plural* melodies*) noun* ■ la **melodía.**

melon ['melən] *noun* ■ el **melón** *(plural* los **melones***)*.

melt [melt] *verb* ■ **derretirse:** the ice is melting el hielo se está derritiendo.

member ['membəʳ] *noun* ■ el **socio,** la **socia:** Rita's a member of the chess club Rita es socia del club de ajedrez

▶ a Member of Congress *US* un miembro del Congreso

a Member of Parliament *UK* un diputado, una diputada ➤ The Houses of Parliament.

memorial [mɪ'mɔːrɪəl] *noun* ■ el **monumento**: a war memorial un monumento a los caídos.

memorize , memorise *UK* ['meməraɪz] *verb* ■ **memorizar**: you must memorize your password debes memorizar tu contraseña.

memory ['memərɪ] *(plural* memories*) noun*
1. la **memoria**: she has a good memory tiene buena memoria; the new computer has a lot of memory el nuevo ordenador tiene mucha memoria
2. el **recuerdo**: I have good memories of that evening tengo buenos recuerdos de esa noche.

men *plural* ➤ man.

mend [mend] *verb*
1. *UK* **arreglar**: can you mend the radio? ¿puedes arreglar la radio?
2. **remendar**: I'm going to mend this shirt voy a remendar esta camisa.

mental ['mentl] *adjective* ■ **mental**.

mention ['menʃn] *verb* ■ **mencionar**: he mentioned your name mencionó tu nombre
➤ thank you! — don't mention it! ¡gracias! —¡no hay de qué!

menu ['menjuː] *noun*
1. la **carta**: can I see the menu, please? ¿me trae la carta, por favor?
2. el **menú** *(plural* los **menús***)*: choose Print from the File menu elija Imprimir en el menú Archivo
➤ the set menu el menú del día.

meow *US* ➤ miaow *UK*.

mercy ['mɜːsɪ] *noun* ■ la **piedad**: he showed no mercy no tuvo piedad.

mermaid ['mɜːmeɪd] *noun* ■ la **sirena**.

merry ['merɪ] *adjective*
Merry Christmas! ¡Feliz Navidad!

merry-go-round ['merɪɡəʊraʊnd] *noun* ■ el **tiovivo**.

mess [mes] *uncountable noun* ■ el **desorden**: what a mess! ¡qué desorden!

➤ to make a mess dejar patas arriba: the workmen made a mess los obreros lo dejaron todo patas arriba

mess around *phrasal verb* ■ *informal*
1. **perder el tiempo**: stop messing around! ¡deja de perder el tiempo!
2. **entretenerse**: the children are messing around in the garden los niños se están entreteniendo en el jardín
➤ don't mess around with my guitar ¡deja mi guitarra tranquila!

mess up *phrasal verb* ■ *informal*
1. **desordenar**: he's messed up the kitchen desordenó la cocina
2. **estropear**: that's messed up my plans eso estropeó mis planes
3. **meter la pata**: I really messed up my exam realmente metí la pata en el examen.

message ['mesɪdʒ] *noun* ■ el **mensaje**.

messenger ['mesɪndʒər] *noun* ■ el **mensajero**, la **mensajera**.

messy ['mesɪ] *adjective* ■ **desordenado**: my room is very messy mi habitación está muy desordenada; you're very messy eres muy desordenado
➤ it's a messy job es un trabajo sucio.

met [met] *past tense & past participle* ➤ meet.

metal ['metl] *noun* ■ el **metal**.

meter ['miːtər] *noun*
1. el **contador**: a water meter un contador de agua
2. *US* el **metro**: it's two meters long tiene dos metros de largo
➤ a parking meter un parquímetro.

method ['meθəd] *noun* ■ el **método**: we must change our methods debemos cambiar nuestros métodos.

metre *UK*, **meter** *US* ['miːtər] *noun* ■ el **metro**: it's 4 metres long tiene 4 metros de largo.

metric ['metrɪk] *adjective* ■ **métrico**: the metric system el sistema métrico.

Mexican ['meksɪkn] *(adjective & noun)*
■ *adjective*

Remember not to use a capital letter for the adjective in Spanish:

mexicano: I like Mexican food me gusta la comida mexicana
■ *noun*

In Spanish, a capital letter is not used for the inhabitants of a country or region:

el mexicano, la mexicana: the Mexicans are famous for their cuisine los mexicanos son famosos por su cocina.

Mexico ['meksɪkəʊ] *noun* ■ **México.**

miaow *UK* [miːˈaʊ], **meow** *US* [mɪˈaʊ] *(noun & verb)*
■ *noun*
el **maullido**
■ *verb*
maullar.

mice ➤ mouse.

microphone ['maɪkrəfəʊn] *noun* ■ el **micrófono.**

microscope ['maɪkrəskəʊp] *noun* ■ el **microscopio.**

microwave ['maɪkrəweɪv] *noun* ■ el **microondas** *(plural* los **microondas)** .

midday [mɪdˈdeɪ] *noun* ■ el **mediodía: she went out at midday** salió al mediodía.

middle ['mɪdl] *(adjective & noun)*
■ *adjective*
del medio: he sat in the middle chair se sentó en la silla del medio
➤ **the Middle Ages** la Edad Media
➤ **the Middle East** el Oriente Medio: **she lives in the Middle East** vive en el Oriente Medio
➤ **middle name** segundo nombre: **what is your middle name?** ¿cuál es tu segundo nombre?
■ *noun* el **centro,** el **medio: the table's in the middle of the room** la mesa está en el centro de la habitación
➤ **it happened in the middle of the night** ocurrió en medio de la noche.

middle-aged ['mɪdleɪdʒd] *adjective* ■ **de mediana edad: she's middle-aged** ella es de mediana edad.

middle-class ['mɪdlklɑːs] *adjective* ■ **de clase media: he's very middle-class** es muy de clase media.

midnight ['mɪdnaɪt] *noun* ■ la **medianoche: he came back at midnight** volvió a medianoche.

might [maɪt] *modal verb*

In Spanish, you can use the expression **puede que** followed by a verb in the subjunctive to translate "might":

they might be away puede que se hayan ido; **it might snow** puede que nieve; **she might have got lost** puede que se haya perdido.

mighty ['maɪtɪ] *adjective* ■ **poderoso: he was a mighty king** fue un rey poderoso.

mike [maɪk] *(abbreviation of* microphone*)* *noun* ■ *informal* el **micrófono: he was talking into the mike** estaba hablando por el micrófono.

mild [maɪld] *adjective* ■ **templado: the climate is very mild** el clima es muy templado.

mile [maɪl] *noun* ■ la **milla: she was driving at 50 miles an hour** iba conduciendo a 80 kilómetros por hora; **I walked for miles** caminé kilómetros y kilómetros.

military ['mɪlɪtrɪ] *adjective* ■ **militar: a military band** una banda militar.

milk [mɪlk] *noun* ■ la **leche: a glass of milk** un vaso de leche
➤ **milk chocolate** chocolate con leche
➤ **a milk shake** un batido.

milkman ['mɪlkmən] *(plural* milkmen ['mɪlkmən])* *noun* ■ el **lechero.**

mill [mɪl] *noun* ■ el **molino.**

millennium [mɪˈlenɪəm] *(plural* millenniums OR millennia [mɪˈlenɪə])* *noun* ■ el **milenio: it's the new millennium** es el nuevo milenio.

millimetre *UK,* **millimeter** *US* ['mɪlɪˌmiːtəʳ] *noun* ■ el **milímetro.**

million ['mɪljən] *noun* ■ el **millón** *(plural* los **millones***)*: three million tres millones; a million dollars un millón de dólares.

millionaire [ˌmɪljə'neəʳ] *noun* ■ el **millonario**, la **millonaria**.

mince *UK* [mɪns] *(noun & verb)*
■ *noun*
la **carne picada**
■ *verb*
picar: you have to mince the meat tienes que picar la carne.

mind [maɪnd] *(noun & verb)*
■ *noun*
la **mente**: he has a very agile mind tiene una mente muy ágil
it never crossed my mind ni se me pasó por la cabeza
to have something on one's mind tener algo en mente: she has something on her mind tiene algo en mente
to make one's mind up decidirse: I haven't made up my mind yet no me he decidido todavía
to change one's mind cambiar de opinión: she's changed her mind cambió de opinión
■ *verb*
1. tener cuidado con: mind the step! ¡cuidado con el escalón!
2. cuidar: could you mind the children this evening? ¿puedes cuidar a los niños esta noche?
I don't mind no me importa: I don't mind waiting no me importa esperar
I'm sorry about the noise — oh, I don't mind perdón por el ruido –ah, no me molesta
do you mind if I open the window? ¿te importa si abro la ventana?
never mind! ¡no importa!
I wouldn't mind a coffee me tomaría un café
mind your own business! ¡no te metas en lo que no te importa!

mine [maɪn] *(pronoun & noun)*
■ *possessive pronoun*
mío

In Spanish the possessive pronoun agrees in gender (masculine or feminine) and number (singular or plural) with the noun it replaces:

his computer's a PC, mine is a Mac su ordenador es un PC, el mío es un Mac; her skirt is blue, mine is red su falda es azul, la mía es roja; his books are on the table, mine are on the shelf sus libros están sobre la mesa, los míos están en el estante; is this glass mine? ¿es mío este vaso?; he's a friend of mine es amigo mío
■ *noun*
la **mina**: a coal mine una mina de carbón; the tank hit a mine el tanque chocó contra una mina.

miner ['maɪnəʳ] *noun* ■ el **minero**, la **minera**: he's a miner es minero.

mineral water ['mɪnərəl'wɔːtəʳ] *noun* ■ el **agua mineral**

Feminine noun that takes un or el in the singular.

miniature [*UK* 'mɪnətʃəʳ, *US* 'mɪnətʃʊəʳ] *adjective* ■ **en miniatura.**

minidisc ['mɪnɪdɪsk] *noun* ■ el **minidisco.**

minimum ['mɪnɪməm] *(noun & adjective)*
■ *noun*
el **mínimo**: you have to pay a minimum of 50 dollars tienes que pagar un mínimo de 50 dólares
■ *adjective*
mínimo: what's the minimum wage? ¿cuál es el salario mínimo?

miniskirt ['mɪnɪskɜːt] *noun* ■ la **minifalda.**

minister ['mɪnɪstəʳ] *noun*
1. el **ministro**, la **ministra**: the Environment Minister el ministro de Medio Ambiente
2. el **pastor**, la **pastora**: he's a minister in the church es pastor de la iglesia.

ministry ['mɪnɪstrɪ] *(plural* ministries*)* *noun* ■ el **ministerio**: the Ministry of Education el Ministerio de Educación y Ciencia.

mink [mɪŋk] *(plural* mink*)* *noun* ■ el **visón** *(plural* los **visones***)* .

minivan ['mɪnɪvæn] *noun* ■ la **furgoneta.**

minor ['maɪnəʳ] *adjective* ■ **menor**: it's a minor problem es un problema menor.

minority [maɪˈnɒrətɪ] *(plural* minorities*)* *noun* ■ la **minoría: we're in the minority** estamos en minoría.

mint [mɪnt] *noun*
1. la **menta: he likes mint ice cream** le gusta el helado de menta
2. la **pastilla de menta: would you like a mint?** ¿quieres una pastilla de menta?

minus [ˈmaɪnəs] *preposition* ■ **menos: 20 minus 7 equals 13** 20 menos 7 es igual a 13
▷ **it's minus three degrees** hay tres grados bajo cero
▷ **the minus sign** el signo menos OR signo negativo.

minute [ˈmɪnɪt] *noun* ■ el **minuto: he left five minutes ago** se fue hace cinco minutos; **wait a minute!** ¡espera un minuto!
▷ **stop this minute!** ¡para ahora mismo!

mirror [ˈmɪrəʳ] *noun*
1. el **espejo: he was looking at himself in the mirror** se estaba mirando en el espejo
2. el **espejo retrovisor: look in your mirror before you pass that car** mira por el espejo retrovisor antes de adelantar a ese coche.

misbehave [ˌmɪsbɪˈheɪv] *verb* ■ **portarse mal: they always misbehave in class** siempre se portan mal en clase.

mischief [ˈmɪstʃɪf] *uncountable noun* ■ la **travesura: he's always up to mischief** siempre está haciendo travesuras.

miser [ˈmaɪzəʳ] *noun* ■ el **avaro,** la **avara.**

miserable [ˈmɪzrəbl] *adjective*
1. **deprimido: he looks miserable** parece deprimido
2. **deprimente: the weather's miserable** el tiempo es deprimente.

misery [ˈmɪzərɪ] *noun* ■ la **desdicha: it'll bring nothing but misery** no traerá más que desdichas.

miss [mɪs] *verb*
1. **perder: I missed the train** perdí el tren
2. **perderse: the film was terrible, you didn't miss anything** la película fue espantosa, no te perdiste nada

▷ **I miss you** te echo de menos
▷ **it's a big house, you can't miss it** es una casa grande, la vas a ver enseguida

miss out *UK phrasal verb* ■ **saltar, omitir: I missed out a word in this sentence** me he saltado una palabra en esta frase.

Miss [mɪs] *noun* ■ **señorita: can I help you, Miss?** ¿qué desea, señorita?; **Miss Janet Brown** la señorita Janet Brown.

missing [ˈmɪsɪŋ] *adjective* ■ **desaparecido: a missing person** una persona desaparecida
▷ **to be missing** faltar: **how many pieces are missing?** ¿cuántas piezas faltan?; **there's something missing** falta algo
▷ **fill in the missing words** completa las palabras que faltan.

mission [ˈmɪʃn] *noun* ■ la **misión,** las **misiones: our mission is to find him** nuestra misión es encontrarlo.

mist [mɪst] *noun* ■ la **neblina.**

mistake [mɪˈsteɪk] *(noun & verb)*
■ *noun*
1. la **equivocación** *(plural* las **equivocaciones**): **it was a big mistake** fue una gran equivocación
2. el **error: it was a big mistake** ése fue su gran error
3. la **falta: a spelling mistake** una falta de ortografía
▷ **to make a mistake** cometer un error: **I made a mistake by telling him** cometí un error al decírselo; **I made a lot of mistakes in my essay** cometí muchos errores en mi redacción
▷ **to make a mistake** equivocarse: **I'm sorry, I must have made a mistake** perdón, debo haberme equivocado; **anyone can make a mistake** cualquiera puede equivocarse
▷ **by mistake** por equivocación: **he took my pencil by mistake** tomó mi lápiz por equivocación
■ *verb (past tense* mistook [mɪˈstʊk], *past participle* mistaken [mɪˈsteɪkn]*)*
▷ **to mistake someone for somebody else** confundir: **I mistook you for your brother** te confundí con tu hermano.

mistaken *past participle* ➤ mistake.

mistletoe ['mɪsltəʊ] *noun* ■ el **muérdago**: to kiss under the mistletoe besarse bajo el muérdago.

mistook *past tense* ➤ mistake.

misunderstand [ˌmɪsʌndə'stænd] *(past tense & past participle* misunderstood [ˌmɪsʌndə'stʊd]*) verb* ■ **entender mal**: I misunderstood you te entendí mal.

misunderstanding [ˌmɪsʌndə'stændɪŋ] *noun* ■ **malentendido**: there's been a misunderstanding hubo un malentendido.

misunderstood *past tense & past participle* ➤ misunderstand.

mix [mɪks] *(noun & verb)*

noun

la **mezcla**: it's a mix of two cultures es una mezcla de dos culturas

a cake mix un preparado para hacer pasteles

verb

mezclar: mix all the ingredients together mezcle todos los ingredientes juntos

mix up *phrasal verb*

1. **confundir**: he mixed me up with my brother me confundió con mi hermano; you're mixing me up me estás confundiendo

2. **desordenar**: he's mixed up all the photos ha desordenado todas las fotos

I'm getting mixed up me estoy confundiendo.

mixed [mɪkst] *adjective*

1. **surtido**: a bag of mixed sweets una bolsa de caramelos surtidos

2. **mixto**: it's a mixed school es una escuela mixta; a mixed salad una ensalada mixta.

mixture ['mɪkstʃəʳ] *noun* ■ la **mezcla**: it's a mixture of rap and jazz es una mezcla de rap y jazz.

mix-up [mɪksʌp] *noun* ■ la **confusión**: there's been a mix-up ha habido una confusión.

moan [məʊn] *verb*

1. **gemir**: the patient moaned with pain el paciente gimió de dolor

2. *informal* **quejarse**: stop moaning! ¡deja de quejarte!

mobile ['məʊbaɪl] *noun & adjective* ■ **móvil** a mobile phone un teléfono móvil.

mock exam [mɒkɪg'zæm] *noun* ■ un examen de prueba.

model ['mɒdl] *noun*

1. el **modelo**: it's the latest model es el último modelo

2. el/la **modelo**: she's a model es modelo

3. la **maqueta**: a model plane una maqueta de avión.

modem ['məʊdem] *noun* ■ el **módem** *(plural* los **módems***)*.

modern ['mɒdən] *adjective* ■ **moderno** modern languages lenguas modernas.

modest ['mɒdɪst] *adjective* ■ **modesto**: Fred's very modest Fred es muy modesto.

moldy *US* ➤ mouldy *UK.*

mole [məʊl] *noun*

1. el **lunar**: she has a mole on her arm tiene un lunar en el brazo

2. el **topo**: moles live under the ground los topos viven debajo de la tierra.

mom *US* [mɒm] *noun* ■ *informal* la **mamá**: his mom's a nurse su mamá es enfermera.

moment ['məʊmənt] *noun* ■ el **momento**: he's not here at the moment no está aquí en este momento

wait a moment! ¡espera un momento!

mommy *UK* ['mɒmɪ] *noun* ■ *informal* la **mami**.

monastery ['mɒnəstrɪ] *(plural* monasteries*) noun* ■ el **monasterio**.

Monday ['mʌndɪ] *noun*

In Spanish the days of the week do not start with a capital letter:

el **lunes** *(plural* los **lunes***)*: it's Monday today hoy es lunes; next Monday el lunes que viene; last Monday el lunes pasado

on Monday el lunes: I'll see you on Monday nos vemos el lunes

on Mondays los lunes: he does judo on Mondays hace judo los lunes.

money ['mʌnɪ] *uncountable noun* ■ el **dinero**: I don't have any money no tengo dinero.

mongrel ['mʌngrəl] *noun* ■ el **perro mestizo**.

monk [mʌŋk] *noun* ■ el **monje**: he's a monk es monje.

monkey ['mʌŋkɪ] *noun* ■ el **mono**, la **mona**.

monster ['mɒnstə'] *noun* ■ el **monstruo**.

month [mʌnθ] *noun* ■ el **mes**: this month este mes; next month el mes que viene; last month el mes pasado; we see each other twice a month nos vemos dos veces al mes.

monument ['mɒnjʊmənt] *noun* ■ el **monumento**: it's a historic monument es un monumento histórico.

moo [muː] *(past tense & past participle* mooed [muːd]*) verb* ■ **mugir**: I can hear the cows mooing oigo las vacas mugiendo.

mood [muːd] *noun* ■ el **humor**: she's in a good mood está de buen humor; I'm in a bad mood estoy de mal humor.

moody ['muːdɪ] *adjective*
1. **malhumorado**: you're very moody today hoy estás muy malhumorado
2. **temperamental**: she's a moody person es muy temperamental.

moon [muːn] *noun* ■ la **luna**: there's a full moon tonight esta noche hay luna llena.

moonlight ['muːnlaɪt] *noun* ■ la **luz de la luna**: I went for a walk in the moonlight salí a pasear a la luz de la luna.

moped ['məʊped] *noun* ■ el **ciclomotor**: she rides a moped to work va a trabajar en ciclomotor.

moral ['mɒrəl] *(adjective & noun)*
■ *adjective*
moral: we're here to give moral support estamos aquí para dar apoyo moral
■ *noun*
la **moraleja**: what's the moral of the story? ¿cuál es la moraleja de la historia?

morale [məˈrɑːl] *noun* ■ la **moral**: we have to boost their morale tenemos que levantarles la moral.

more [mɔː'] *(adjective, adverb & pronoun)*
■ *adjective (comparative of* many, much *and a lot of)*
más: there are more trains in the morning hay más trenes por la mañana; he has more money than me tiene más dinero que yo; there isn't any more bread no hay más pan; I need three more tickets necesito tres billetes más; would you like some more cake? ¿quieres un poco más de pastel?; do you have any more questions? ¿tienes más preguntas?
■ *adverb*
más: it's more expensive es más caro; she's more intelligent than him ella es más inteligente que él; Tom reads more than me Tom lee más que yo; you have to work more debes trabajar más
▸ once more otra vez
▸ she doesn't live here any more ya no vive aquí
■ *pronoun (comparative of* many, much *and a lot)*
más: it costs more than 100 dollars cuesta más de 100 dólares; he eats more than I do come más que yo; there aren't any more no hay más; I need more of them necesito más; I like this cake, can I have some more? me gusta este pastel, ¿puedo comer más?
▸ more and more cada vez más: she travels more and more viaja cada vez más; more and more people are taking up yoga cada vez más gente empieza a hacer yoga
▸ more or less más o menos: the new program does more or less the same as the old one el nuevo programa hace más o menos lo mismo que el viejo.

morning ['mɔːnɪŋ] *noun* ■ la **mañana**: he's not going to school this morning no va a ir a la escuela esta mañana; she works in the morning trabaja por la mañana; at 6 o'clock in the morning a las 6 de la mañana; I'll do it in the morning lo haré por la mañana; she stayed in bed all morning se quedó en la cama toda la mañana
▸ every morning todas las mañanas
▸ yesterday morning ayer por la mañana
▸ tomorrow morning mañana por la mañana.

Moslem ➤ Muslim.

mosque [mɒsk] *noun* ■ la **mezquita:** they go to the mosque on Fridays van a la mezquita los viernes.

mosquito [mə'skiːtəʊ] *noun* ■ el **mosquito:** I'm covered in mosquito bites estoy lleno de picaduras de mosquito.

most [məʊst] *(adjective, adverb & pronoun)*

■ *adjective*

• la **mayoría de:** most tourists visit the Tower of London la mayoría de los turistas visitan el edificio de la Torre de Londres

2. **más:** she has the most money es la que tiene más dinero

■ *adverb*

más: he's the most experienced player on the team es el jugador con más experiencia del equipo; it's the most beautiful city in the world es la ciudad más bonita del mundo; the most expensive present el regalo más caro

■ *pronoun*

la **mayor parte:** most of the tourists are American la mayor parte de los turistas son estadounidenses; I spent most of the day in bed me pasé la mayor parte del día en la cama; most of them left early la mayoría se fueron temprano

Paul ate the most Paul fue el que más comió.

mostly ['məʊstlɪ] *adverb* ■ **en su mayoría, principalmente:** there were lots of customers, mostly young people había muchos clientes, en su mayoría gente joven.

motel [məʊ'tel] *noun* ■ el **motel:** we stopped at a motel for the night paramos en un motel para pasar la noche.

moth [mɒθ] *noun* ■ la **polilla.**

mother ['mʌðəʳ] *noun* ■ la **madre**
Mother's Day el Día de la Madre.

mother-in-law ['mʌðəʳɪnlɔː] *(plural* mothers-in law) *noun* ■ la **suegra.**

mother-of-pearl [ˌmʌðəʳɒv'pɜːl] *noun* ■ el **nácar.**

motion picture [ˌməʊʃn'pɪktʃəʳ] *noun* ■ la **película de cine.**

motivated ['məʊtɪveɪtɪd] *adjective* ■ **motivado:** my students are very motivated mis estudiantes están muy motivados.

motivation [ˌməʊtɪ'veɪʃn] *noun* ■ la **motivación** *(plural* las **motivaciones**)**:** he seems to lack motivation parece que le falta motivación.

motive ['məʊtɪv] *noun* ■ el **motivo:** what was the motive for the crime? ¿cuál fue el motivo del crimen?

motor ['məʊtəʳ] *noun* ■ el **motor:** an electric motor un motor eléctrico
motor racing las carreras de coches.

motorbike UK ['məʊtəbaɪk] *noun* ■ la **moto.**

motorboat ['məʊtəbəʊt] *noun* ■ la **lancha a motor.**

motorcycle ['məʊtəˌsaɪkl] *noun* ■ la **motocicleta:** let's go for a ride on your motorcycle vamos a dar una vuelta en tu motocicleta.

motorcyclist ['məʊtəˌsaɪklɪst] *noun* ■ el/la **motociclista.**

motorist UK ['məʊtərɪst] *noun* ■ el **conductor,** la **conductora.**

motorway UK ['məʊtəweɪ] *noun* ■ la **autopista.**

motto ['mɒtəʊ] *noun* ■ el **lema:** our motto is "quality above all" nuestro lema es "calidad por encima de todo".

mouldy UK, **moldy** US ['məʊldɪ] *adjective* ■ **mohoso**
to go mouldy enmohecerse.

mount [maʊnt] *(verb & noun)*

■ *verb*

1. **subirse a:** Dan mounted his horse Dan se subió a su caballo

2. **aumentar:** the construction costs are mounting los costes de la construcción están aumentando

3. **montar:** they have mounted a campaign against terrorism han montado una campaña contra el terrorismo

■ noun
el **monte**
> Mount Rushmore el Monte Rushmore

> MOUNT RUSHMORE
>
> Se trata de un gigantesco relieve de los bustos de los presidentes estadounidenses Washington, Jefferson, Lincoln y Theodore Roosevelt, excavado en un lado del monte Rushmore (Dakota del Sur). Es un monumento nacional y una popular atracción turística. Los bustos se esculpieron utilizando taladros neumáticos y miden 28 metros de altura.

mountain ['mauntɪn] noun ■ la **montaña**: they set out to climb the mountain salieron para escalar la montaña
> a mountain bike una bicicleta de montaña.

mountaineer [,mauntɪ'nɪər] noun ■ el/la **alpinista**.

mountaineering [,mauntɪ'nɪərɪŋ] noun ■ el **alpinismo**
> to go mountaineering hacer alpinismo.

mouse [maus] (plural mice [maɪs]) noun ■ el **ratón** (plural los **ratones**): a mouse ran across the room un ratón atravesó la habitación
> use the mouse to move around the screen usa el ratón para moverte por la pantalla
> a mouse pad una almohadilla para el ratón.

mousse [mu:s] noun ■ el/la **mousse**: chocolate mousse mousse de chocolate.

moustache UK [mə'stɑ:ʃ], **mustache** US ['mʌstæʃ] noun ■ el **bigote**: he has a moustache lleva bigote.

mouth [mauθ] noun ■ la **boca**: don't talk with your mouth full! ¡no hables con la boca llena!; he didn't open his mouth no abrió la boca.

move [mu:v] (noun & verb)
■ noun
1. el **paso**: selling that stock was a wise move vender esas acciones fue un paso acertado
2. la **mudanza**: the vase broke during the move el florero se rompió durante la mudanza
3. *in games* la **jugada**: that was a very good move ésa fue una excelente jugada
> it's your move te toca jugar

■ verb
1. **mover**: I can't move my arm no puedo mover el brazo
2. **moverse**: don't move no te muevas; come on, get moving! ¡vamos, muévete!
3. **correr**: we have to move the furniture to paint the room tenemos que correr los muebles para pintar la habitación
4. **avanzar**: the expedition moved slowly la expedición avanzó lentamente
5. **mudarse**: they're moving next week se mudan la semana que viene; we're moving to Brighton nos mudamos a Brighton
6. **conmover**: his speech really moved me su discurso verdaderamente me conmovió; she was very moved estaba muy conmovida

move forward phrasal verb ■ **avanzar**: the soldiers are moving forward los soldados están avanzando

move in phrasal verb ■ **mudarse**: the new tenant just moved in el nuevo inquilino acaba de mudarse

move off phrasal verb ■ **ponerse en marcha**: the convoy moved off la caravana se puso en marcha

move out phrasal verb ■ **mudarse**: he moved out last month se mudó el mes pasado

move over phrasal verb ■ **corrar**: move over, I don't have enough room córrete, no tengo suficiente espacio.

movement ['mu:vmənt] noun ■ el **movimiento**: she made a sudden movement hizo un movimiento repentino.

movie US ['mu:vɪ] noun ■ la **película**: let's go to a movie vayamos a ver una película
> the movies el cine: I went to the movies with a friend fui al cine con un amigo
> a movie theater un cine.

mow [məu] (past tense mowed [məud], past participle mowed OR mown [məun]) verb ■ **cortar**: she's mowing the lawn está cortando el césped.

mower ['məuər] noun ■ el **cortacésped** (plural los **cortacésped**).

mown past participle ➤ mow.

MP UK [ˌem'piː] (abbreviation of Member of Parliament) noun ■ el **diputado**, la **diputada**: she's an MP es diputada.

MP3 [empiː'θriː] noun ■ el **archivo MP3**: to download an MP3 descargar un archivo MP3 an MP3 player un reproductor de MP3.

Mr ['mɪstər] noun

. el **señor**: Mr Smith is here el señor Smith está aquí

:. in correspondence **Sr.** (masculine).

Mrs ['mɪsɪz] noun

. la **señora**: Mrs Smith is here la señora Smith está aquí

:. in correspondence **Sra.** (feminine).

Ms [mɪz] noun

. la **señora**: Ms Brown is here to see you la señora Brown está aquí para verlo

:. in correspondence **Sra.** (feminine).

much [mʌtʃ] (comparative **more**, superlative **most**) (adjective, pronoun & adverb)

■ adjective

mucho: I don't have much time no tengo mucho tiempo

■ pronoun

mucho: I don't want much no quiero mucho

■ adverb

mucho: she doesn't go out much no sale mucho; thank you very much muchas gracias

➤ how much cuánto: how much does it cost? ¿cuánto cuesta?; how much money do you have? ¿cuánto dinero tienes?

➤ too much demasiado: she talks too much habla demasiado; there's too much sugar in my coffee hay demasiado azúcar en mi café

➤ so much tanto: I missed you so much te eché tanto de menos; he got into so much trouble at school se metió en tantos problemas en la escuela

➤ have as much as you like coge todo lo que quieras

➤ he doesn't have as much time as I do no tiene tanto tiempo como yo.

mud [mʌd] noun ■ el **barro**: the car is covered in mud el coche está cubierto de barro.

muddle ['mʌdl] (noun & verb)

■ noun

➤ to be in a muddle estar revuelto: all my notes are in a muddle tengo todos los apuntes revueltos

muddle up phrasal verb

1. **desordenar, armar un lío**: you've muddled up my papers has desordenando mis papeles

2. **confundirse, hacerse un lío**: he got muddled up se hizo un lío.

muddy ['mʌdɪ] adjective ■ **embarrado**: the ground is very muddy el suelo está muy embarrado.

mug [mʌg] (noun & verb)

■ noun

la **taza alta**: a mug of coffee un taza alta de café

■ verb (past tense & past participle **mugged**, present participle **mugging**)

atracar: she was mugged in the street la atracaron en la calle.

mugger [ˌmʌgər] noun ■ el/la **asaltante**: the police caught the mugger la policía atrapó al asaltante.

multimedia [ˌmʌltɪ'miːdjə] noun ■ el/la **multimedia**: a multimedia display una presentación multimedia.

multiple-choice test [ˌmʌltɪpl'tʃɔɪstest] noun ■ la **prueba de opción múltiple**.

multiplication [ˌmʌltɪplɪ'keɪʃn] noun ■ la **multiplicación** (plural las **multiplicaciones**): to do a multiplication hacer una multiplicación

➤ multiplication sign signo de multiplicar

➤ multiplication table tabla de multiplicar.

multiply ['mʌltɪplaɪ] (past tense & past participle **multiplied**) verb ■ **multiplicar**: what's 3 multiplied by 7? ¿cuánto es 3 multiplicado por 7?

mum UK [mʌm] noun ■ informal la **mamá**: my mum's a teacher mi mamá es profesora.

mummy ['mʌmɪ] (plural **mummies**) noun

1. UK informal la **mami**

2. la **momia**.

murder ['mɜːdəʳ] *(noun & verb)*

■ *noun*

el **asesinato**: he was accused of murder lo acusaron de asesinato

■ *verb*

asesinar: somebody was murdered near the station asesinaron a alguien cerca de la estación.

murderer ['mɜːdərəʳ] *noun* ■ el **asesino**, la **asesina**.

muscle ['mʌsl] *noun* ■ el **músculo**.

museum [mjuːˈziːəm] *noun* ■ el **museo**.

mushroom ['mʌʃrʊm] *noun* ■ el **champiñón** *(plural* los **champiñones***).*

music ['mjuːzɪk] *noun* ■ la **música**: he's listening to music está escuchando música.

musical ['mjuːzɪkl] *(adjective & noun)*

■ *adjective*

a musical instrument un instrumento musical: she plays a musical instrument toca un instrumento musical

■ *noun*

el **musical**: we're going to see a musical vamos a ver un musical.

musician [mjuːˈzɪʃn] *noun* ■ el **músico**, la **música**: she's a musician es música.

Muslim ['mʊzlɪm], **Moslem** ['mɒzləm] *(adjective & noun)*

■ *adjective*

Remember not to use a capital letter for the adjective or the noun in Spanish:

musulmán

■ *noun*

el **musulmán** *(plural* los **musulmanes***),* la **musulmana**.

mussel ['mʌsl] *noun* ■ el **mejillón** *(plural* los **mejillones***).*

must [mʌst] *modal verb* ■ **deber**

You can use the verb **deber** + infinitive to translate "must," or you can use the impersonal construction **hay que** + infinitive. You can also use **tener que** + infinitive:

you mustn't tell anyone no debes contárselo a nadie; you must always read the in-

structions siempre hay que leer las instrucciones; I must go tengo que irme; you must come and see us tienes que venir a vernos

To make deductions, you use the verb **deber** in Spanish:

he must be English debe ser inglés; she must have got lost debe haberse perdido.

mustache *US* ➤ moustache *UK*.

mustard ['mʌstəd] *noun* ■ la **mostaza**.

mustn't [mʌsnt] = must not: you mustn't go no debes ir.

must've ['mʌstəv] = must have: he must've left already debe haberse ido ya.

mutton ['mʌtn] *noun* ■ la **carne de oveja**: we never eat mutton nunca comemos carne de oveja.

my [maɪ] *possessive adjective* ■ **mi**

In Spanish the possessive adjective agrees in number (singular or plural) with the noun that follows:

my dog is called Spike mi perro se llama Spike; my car won't start mi coche no arranca; my parents are on holiday mis padres están de vacaciones

Use the definite article (**el, la, los** or **las**), not the possessive adjective, with parts of the body:

I broke my leg me rompí la pierna; I'm going to wash my hair voy a lavarme el pelo.

myself [maɪˈself] *pronoun*

1. **me**: I'm washing myself me estoy lavando; I'm enjoying myself me estoy divirtiendo
2. **yo mismo**: I asked him myself yo mismo le pregunté
3. **mí mismo**: I often talk about myself a menudo hablo de mí mismo
   ▶ I'm enjoying myself me estoy divirtiendo
   ▶ by myself solo: I did it by myself lo hice solo.

mysterious [mɪˈstɪərɪəs] *adjective* ■ **misterioso**.

mystery ['mɪstərɪ] *(plural* mysteries*) noun* ■ el **misterio**: it's a real mystery es un verdadero misterio

➤ a murder mystery una novela policíaca.

myth [mɪθ] *noun* ■ el **mito**: the Greek myths los mitos griegos.

mythology [mɪˈθɒlədʒɪ] *noun* ■ la **mitología**: Greek mythology la mitología griega.

nag [næg] *(past tense & past participle* nagged, *present participle* nagging*) verb* ■ **fastidiar, dar la lata** *informal*: stop nagging me deja de fastidiarme, deja de darme la lata.

nail [neɪl] *(noun & verb)*
■ *noun*
1. el **clavo**: he hammered a nail into the wall clavó un clavo en la pared
2. la **uña**: he bites his nails se come las uñas
> a nail file una lima de uñas
> nail polish el esmalte de uñas
■ *verb*
clavar: she nailed the sign to the door clavó el cartel en la puerta.

naked [ˈneɪkɪd] *adjective* ■ **desnudo**: he was completely naked estaba completamente desnudo.

name [neɪm] *noun* ■ el **nombre**: he has a foreign name tiene un nombre extranjero
> what's your name? ¿cómo te llamas?
> my name is Paul me llamo Paul.

nanny [ˈnænɪ] *(plural* nannies*) noun* ■ la **niñera**.

nap [næp] *noun* ■ la **siesta**: I took a nap me eché una siesta.

nappy *UK* [næpɪ] *(plural* nappies*) noun* ■ el **pañal**.

napkin [ˈnæpkɪn] *noun* ■ la **servilleta**: a paper napkin una servilleta de papel.

narrow [ˈnærəʊ] *adjective* ■ **estrecho**: this street is very narrow esta calle es muy estrecha.

nasty [*UK* ˈnɑːstɪ, *US* ˈnæstɪ] *adjective*
1. **muy desagradable**: this cheese has a nasty taste este queso tiene un sabor muy desagradable
2. **malo**: she was nasty to him fue muy mala con él.

nation [ˈneɪʃn] *noun* ■ la **nación** *(plural* las naciones*)*.

national [ˈnæʃənl] *adjective* ■ **nacional**
> the national anthem el himno nacional
> the National Health Service *UK* la Seguridad Social
> a national park un parque nacional

NATIONAL PARK

Los parques nacionales en Estados Unidos y Gran Bretaña son grandes extensiones naturales abiertas al público. Están protegidas tanto para preservar el equilibrio ecológico como el interés paisajístico. Yellowstone y Yosemite son famosos parques nacionales estadounidenses; los más conocidos de Gran Bretaña son el Snowdonia, el Lake District y el Peak District. En todos ellos hay lugares donde se puede acampar.

nationality [ˌnæʃəˈnælətɪ] *(plural* nationalities*) noun* ■ la **nacionalidad**: what nationality are you? ¿de qué nacionalidad eres?

native [ˈneɪtɪv] *(adjective & noun)*
■ *adjective*
1. **natal**: Spain is his native country España es su país natal
2. **materno**: English is my native language el inglés es mi lengua materna
> a native English speaker un hablante nativo de inglés
■ *noun*
> she is a native of Mexico es originaria de México

NATIVE AMERICAN

Las tribus de aborígenes americanas que poblaban Estados Unidos antes de la llegada de los europeos reciben el nombre de **Native American**. Cada una poseía su propia lengua y modo de vida. Muchos indios murieron combatiendo a los colonos europeos o tras contraer alguna de las enfermedades que estos llevaron a América. Otros muchos fueron obligados a vivir en reservas, territorios acotados especialmente para ellos. A lo largo del siglo XX, el gobierno estadounidense procuró conceder más derechos a los grupos étnicos nativos de Estados Unidos. Al mismo tiempo, en las últimas décadas, en el país se ha generado cada vez un mayor interés por su historia y su cultura tradicional.

natural ['nætʃrəl] *adjective* ■ **natural: I like to wear natural fibres** me gusta vestirme con fibras naturales; **it's natural to feel that way** es natural que te sientas así.

naturally ['nætʃrəlı] *adverb*
1. **naturalmente: naturally, I was angry** naturalmente, estaba enfadado
2. **por naturaleza: she's naturally generous** es generosa por naturaleza.

nature ['neɪtʃər] *noun* ■ **la naturaleza: I'm a real nature lover** soy un verdadero amante de la naturaleza; **he has a very kind nature** es amable por naturaleza
> **a nature reserve** una reserva natural.

naughty ['nɔːtɪ] *adjective* ■ **travieso: he's a naughty boy!** ¡es un niño travieso!
> **they've been very naughty** se han portado muy mal.

nauseous [*UK* 'nɔːsjəs, *US* 'nɔːʃəs] *adjective* ■ **mareado**
> **to feel nauseous** sentirse mareado.

navel ['neɪvl] *noun* ■ **el ombligo**.

navy ['neɪvɪ] *(noun & adjective)*
■ *noun*
  la **marina: he's in the navy** está en la marina
■ *adjective*
  azul marino *(plural* azul marino*)*: **she's wearing a navy skirt** lleva una falda azul marino
> **navy blue** azul marino.

near [nɪəʳ] *(adjective, adverb & preposition)*
■ *adjective*
  cercano: where is the nearest hospital? ¿dónde está el hospital más cercano?
> **the nearest thing** lo más cercano: **she's the nearest thing to a mother I ever had** es lo más cercano a una madre que yo he tenido
> **in the near future** en el futuro próximo: **we're going to buy a house in the near future** vamos a comprar una casa en un futuro próximo
> **his story is nearer to the truth** su historia se acerca más a la verdad
■ *adverb*
  cerca: the station is very near la estación está muy cerca
■ *preposition*
  cerca de: there's a supermarket near the school hay un supermercado cerca de la escuela; **is there a restaurant near here?** ¿hay un restaurante cerca de aquí?
> **near to** cerca de.

nearby [nɪə'baɪ] *(adjective & adverb)*
■ *adjective*
  cercano: there was a fire in a nearby town hubo un incendio en un pueblo cercano
■ *adverb*
  cerca: there's a school nearby hay una escuela cerca.

nearly ['nɪəlɪ] *adverb* ■ **casi: it's nearly 8 o'clock** son casi las 8; **I nearly started laughing when she said that** casi me pongo a reír cuando dijo eso.

nearsighted *US* [,nɪə'saɪtɪd] *adjective* ■ **miope: she's nearsighted** es miope.

neat [niːt] *adjective*
1. **ordenado: the house is very neat** la casa está muy ordenada
2. **pulcro: she always looks neat** siempre tiene un aspecto pulcro
3. *US informal* **fantástico: that was a neat movie!** ¡ésa fue una película fantástica!

neatly ['niːtlɪ] *adverb* ■ **cuidadosamente: she writes very neatly** escribe cuidadosamente.

necessary [*UK* 'nesəsrɪ, *US* 'nesəserɪ] *adjective* ■ **necesario: I'll make the necessary arrangements** haré los arreglos necesarios.

neck [nek] *noun* ■ el **cuello**: she has a scarf round her neck lleva una bufanda alrededor del cuello.

necklace ['neklɪs] *noun* ■ el **collar**: she's wearing a gold necklace lleva puesto un collar de oro.

nectarine ['nektərɪn] *noun* ■ la **nectarina**.

need [niːd] *(noun & verb)*
■ *noun*
la **necesidad**: there is no need to go no hay necesidad de ir
to be in need of something necesitar algo: the children are in need of medical attention los niños necesitan atención médica
■ *verb*
■. **necesitar**: he needs a new bike necesita una bicicleta nueva; I need to get some sleep necesito dormir un poco
c. *when need means "have to"*

You can use the constructions **tener que** or **hay que** + infinitive to translate 'need':

I need to leave right away tengo que irme ahora mismo; do we need to show our passports? ¿hay que enseñar los pasaportes?

To translate 'don't need to' or 'needn't', you can use the Spanish construction **no tener que hacer algo** or the impersonal constructions **no es necesario que** or **no hace falta que**:

you don't need to wait OR you needn't wait no tienes que esperar; we don't need to pick him up no es necesario que lo pasemos a recoger.

needle ['niːdl] *noun* ■ la **aguja**: I can't find a needle to sew on the button no puedo encontrar una aguja para coser el botón.

needn't ['niːdnt] = need not: you needn't come no hace falta que vengas.

negative ['negətɪv] *(adjective & noun)*
■ *adjective*
negativo: we got a negative answer nos dieron una respuesta negativa
■ *noun*
el **negativo**: he printed a photo from the negative sacó una copia de una foto usando el negativo.

negotiate [nɪ'gəʊʃɪeɪt] *verb* ■ **negociar**.

negotiation [nɪ'gəʊʃɪeɪʃən] *noun* ■ la **negociación**.

neigh [neɪ] *verb* ■ **relinchar**: the horse neighed el caballo relinchó.

neighbour UK, **neighbor** US ['neɪbəʳ] *noun* ■ el **vecino**, la **vecina**: he doesn't like his neighbours no le gustan sus vecinos.

neighbourhood UK, **neighborhood** US ['neɪbəhʊd] *noun* ■ el **barrio**: there are a lot of restaurants in the neighbourhood hay muchos restaurantes en este barrio.

neither ['naɪðəʳ, 'niːðəʳ] *(conjunction, adjective & pronoun)*
■ *conjunction*
ı. **ni**: it's neither good nor bad no es ni bueno ni malo; he's neither English nor American no es inglés ni americano
2. **tampoco**: he doesn't know and neither does she él no lo sabe y ella tampoco; she can't swim — neither can I ella no sabe nadar —yo tampoco
■ *adjective & pronoun*
ninguno: neither book is any good ninguno de los libros es bueno; neither of them came ninguno de ellos vino; which dress do you want? — neither ¿qué vestido quieres? —ninguno.

neon ['niːɒn] *noun* ■ el **neón**
neon lights luces de neón.

nephew ['nefjuː] *noun* ■ el **sobrino**.

nerve [nɜːv] *noun*
ı. el **nervio**: it's a disease that attacks the nerves es una enfermedad que ataca los nervios; she had an attack of nerves before the show tuvo un ataque de nervios antes del espectáculo
2. el **valor**: he didn't have the nerve to tell her the truth no tuvo el valor de decirle la verdad
3. el **descaro**: she had the nerve to come without being invited tuvo el descaro de venir sin ser invitada
to get on somebody's nerves sacar de quicio a alguien: that guy really gets on my nerves ese tipo realmente me saca de quicio.

nervous ['nɜːvəs] *adjective* ■ **nervioso:** going to the dentist makes me nervous me pone nervioso ir al dentista; he's a nervous driver es un conductor nervioso

‣ to be nervous estar nervioso: actors are often nervous before they go on stage los actores generalmente están nerviosos antes de salir al escenario

‣ I'm nervous about speaking in public me pone nervioso hablar en público

‣ a nervous breakdown una crisis nerviosa.

nest [nest] *noun* ■ **el nido:** a bird's nest un nido de pájaros.

net [net] *noun* ■ **la red**

‣ a fishing net una red de pescar

‣ the Net la Red: she spends hours surfing the Net pasa horas navegando por la Red.

netball *UK* ['netbɔːl] *noun* ■ deporte parecido al baloncesto, que se practica en los colegios femeninos del Reino Unido.

nettle ['netl] *noun* ■ la **ortiga.**

network ['netwɜːk] *noun* ■ la **red:** a computer network una red de ordenadores.

never ['nevər] *adverb*

1. nunca: he never drinks no bebe nunca; I've never been to Rome no he estado nunca en Roma

   If **nunca** is used before the verb it is not necessary to use "no":

   I've never spoken to her nunca he hablado con ella

2. jamás: will you tell me your secret? — never! ¿me dirás tu secreto? –¡jamás!

‣ never again! ¡nunca más!

‣ never mind! ¡no importa!

new [*UK* njuː, *US* nuː] *adjective* ■ **nuevo:** this is my new address ésta es mi nueva dirección; Harriet has a new boyfriend Harriet tiene un novio nuevo; there's a new moon tonight hay luna nueva esta noche

‣ brand new completamente nuevo: I've got a brand new bike tengo una bicicleta completamente nueva

‣ what's new? ¿qué hay de nuevo?

newborn [*UK* 'njuːbɔːn, *US* 'nuːbɔːn] *adjective* ■ **recién nacido:** a newborn baby un bebé recién nacido.

newcomer [*UK* 'njuːˌkʌmər, *US* 'nuːˌkʌmər] *noun* ■ **el recién llegado, la recién llegada:** I'd like to welcome any newcomers quisiera darles la bienvenida a los recién llegados.

news [*UK* 'njuːz, *US* 'nuːz] *uncountable noun*

1. la **noticia:** do you have any news from him? ¿tienes alguna noticia de él?; I have some good news tengo buenas noticias; what bad news! ¡qué mala noticia!

2. las **noticias:** he's listening to the news on the radio está escuchando las noticias en la radio

‣ a piece of news una noticia.

newsagent *UK* ['njuːzeɪdʒənt], **newsdealer** *US* ['nuːzdiːlər] *noun* ■ **el vendedor de periódicos, la vendedora de periódicos.**

newspaper [*UK* 'njuːzˌpeɪpər, *US* 'nuːzˌpeɪpər] *noun* ■ **el periódico:** I read the newspaper over breakfast leí el periódico durante el desayuno.

newsstand [*UK* 'njuːzstænd, *US* 'nuːzstænd] *noun* ■ **el kiosco de periódicos.**

New Year [*UK* njuːˈjɪər, *US* nuːˈjɪər] *noun* ■ they celebrated New Year in the Caribbean celebraron el Año Nuevo en el Caribe

‣ Happy New Year! ¡Feliz Año Nuevo!

‣ New Year's Day el día de Año Nuevo

‣ New Year's Eve la noche de Fin de Año

NEW YEAR

En Estados Unidos y Gran Bretaña la gente celebra fiestas para recibir o **to see in** (ver entrar) el nuevo año. Cuando los relojes dan las doce campanadas, todo el mundo se desea un **Happy New Year** (feliz año nuevo), se abraza y se besa. Se suele entonar el **Auld Lang Syne**, una canción tradicional. Al día siguiente, Año Nuevo, es fiesta nacional.

New Zealand [*UK* njuːˈziːlənd, *US* nuːˈziːlənd] *noun* ■ **Nueva Zelanda:** they're going to New Zealand se van a Nueva Zelanda.

New Zealander [UK njuː'ziːləndər, US nuː'ziːləndər] noun

In Spanish, a capital letter is not used for the inhabitants of a country or region:

el **neozelandés,** la **neozelandesa.**

next [nɛkst] (adjective & adverb)

adjective

. **próximo: the big game is next week** el gran partido es la próxima semana; **I'll see you next Tuesday** te veré el próximo martes; **we're going to Jamaica next year** vamos a Jamaica el próximo año

2. **siguiente: it's on the next page** está en la página siguiente; **next, please!** ¡el siguiente, por favor!; **the next day was a holiday** el día siguiente era festivo; **the next day she came to see me** al día siguiente vino a verme

3. **de al lado: who's in the next room?** ¿quién está en el cuarto de al lado?

adverb

después: what happened next? ¿qué pasó después?

▸ **when I see him next I'll tell him** la próxima vez que lo vea se lo voy a decir

▸ **next door** al lado: **they live next door** viven al lado

▸ **our next-door neighbours** nuestros vecinos de al lado

▸ **next to** al lado: **the bank is next to the bookshop** el banco está al lado de la librería

▸ **next to nothing** casi nada: **it cost next to nothing** no costó casi nada

NHS UK (abbreviation of National Health Service) [ˌeneɪtʃ'es] noun ➤ la Seguridad Social británica.

nice [naɪs] adjective

1. **simpático: Mrs. Thompson is very nice** la Sra. Thompson es muy simpática

2. **bonito: that's a nice dress** qué vestido más bonito

3. **bueno: it's a nice day** hace un buen día; **this cake is very nice** este pastel es muy bueno

4. **agradable: we had a very nice day** pasamos un día muy agradable

▸ **have a nice time!** ¡que lo pases bien!

nicely ['naɪslɪ] adverb

1. **bien: she was nicely dressed** iba bien vestida

2. **amablemente, con buenos modales: ask nicely!** ¡pídelo con buenos modales!

nickel ['nɪkl] noun

1. el **níquel**

2. US la **moneda de cinco céntimos.**

nickname ['nɪkneɪm] noun ■ el **apodo: his nickname is "Killer"** su apodo es "Killer".

niece [niːs] noun ■ la **sobrina.**

night [naɪt] noun ■ la **noche: did you have a good night?** ¿pasaste una buena noche?; **we danced all night** bailamos toda la noche

▸ **last night** anoche: **it happened last night at 8 o'clock** pasó anoche a las 8; **what did you do last night?** ¿qué hiciste anoche?

▸ **at night** de noche: **badgers come out at night** los tejones salen de noche

▸ **to have an early night** acostarse temprano; **to have a late night** acostarse tarde

▸ **good night!** ¡buenas noches!

nightclub ['naɪtklʌb] noun ■ el **club nocturno: the band is playing at a nightclub** la banda toca en un club nocturno.

nightie ['naɪtɪ] noun ■ informal el **camisón** (plural los **camisones).**

nightmare ['naɪtmeər] noun ■ la **pesadilla: I had a terrible nightmare** tuve una pesadilla espantosa.

nighttime ['naɪttaɪm] noun ■ la **noche: it's very noisy at nighttime** hay mucho ruido de noche.

nil UK [nɪl] noun ■ **cero: they won three nil** ganaron tres a cero.

nine [naɪn] number ■ **nueve: there are nine girls in the group** hay nueve niñas en el grupo; **Bill is nine** Bill tiene nueve años; **she went out at nine** salió a las nueve.

nineteen [ˌnaɪn'tiːn] number ■ **diecinueve: Lisa is nineteen** Lisa tiene diecinueve años.

nineteenth [ˌnaɪn'tiːn] number ■ **decimonoveno: it's her nineteenth birthday** es su decimonoveno cumpleaños it's the nineteenth of May UK OR it's May nineteenth today US estamos a 19 de mayo.

ninety ['naɪntɪ] *number* ■ **noventa:** she's ninety tiene noventa años

ninety-two noventa y dos.

ninth [naɪnθ] *number* ■ **noveno:** on the ninth floor en el noveno piso

it's the ninth of October UK OR it's October ninth today US estamos a 9 de octubre.

no [nəʊ] *(adverb & adjective)*

■ *adverb*

no: do you like seafood? — no, I don't ¿te gusta el marisco? —no; no, thank you no, gracias

■ *adjective*

In Spanish **no** is not used before the noun but before the verb:

she has no money no tiene dinero; there are no buses on Sundays no hay autobuses los domingos; there's no hope no hay esperanza.

nobody ['nəʊbədɪ], **no one** ['nəʊwʌn] *pronoun* ■ **nadie:** nobody came no vino nadie

If **nadie** is used before the verb it is not necessary to use "no":

nobody saw me nadie me vio; who did you see? — nobody! ¿a quién viste? —a nadie; there's no one in here no hay nadie aquí dentro.

nod [nɒd] *(past tense & past participle* nodded, *present participle* nodding) *verb*

1. asentir con la cabeza: I asked him if he was coming and he nodded le pregunté si vendría y asintió con la cabeza

2. saludar con la cabeza: he didn't say hello, but he nodded to me no dijo "hola", pero me saludó con la cabeza.

noise [nɔɪz] *uncountable noun* ■ **el ruido:** you're making too much noise estás haciendo demasiado ruido.

noisy ['nɔɪzɪ] *adjective* ■ **ruidoso:** your computer is very noisy tu ordenador es muy ruidoso.

none [nʌn] *pronoun*

1. ninguno: how many cards do you have left? — none ¿cuántas cartas te quedan? —ninguna; none of the pictures is for sale ninguno de los cuadros está a la venta; none of us won ninguno de nosotros ganó

2. *with uncountable nouns* nada: do you have any money? — no, none at all ¿tienes dinero? —no, no tengo nada; there's none left no queda nada.

nonsense ['nɒnsəns] *uncountable* ■ **las tonterías:** you're talking nonsense estás diciendo tonterías

nonsense! ¡tonterías!

non-smoker [,nɒn'sməʊkər] *noun* ■ **el no fumador,** la **no fumadora.**

nonstop [,nɒn'stɒp] *(adjective & adverb)*

■ *adjective*

sin escalas: we took a nonstop flight cogimos un vuelo sin escalas

■ *adverb*

sin parar: I'm working nonstop estoy trabajando sin parar.

noodles ['nuːdlz] *plural noun* ■ **los fideos**

egg noodles fideos de huevo.

noon [nuːn] *noun* ■ **el mediodía:** we're meeting at noon nos vamos a encontrar al mediodía.

no one *pronoun* ➤ nobody.

nor ['nɔːr] *conjunction* ■ **ni:** neither Fred nor Lucy is coming ni Fred ni Lucy vienen.

normal ['nɔːml] *adjective* ■ **normal:** that's quite normal eso es bastante normal

we'll meet at the normal time nos encontraremos a la hora de siempre.

normally ['nɔːməlɪ] *adverb* ■ **normalmente:** I normally get up at 7 o'clock normalmente me levanto a las 7.

north [nɔːθ] *(noun, adjective & adverb)*

■ *noun*

el **norte:** Manchester is in the north of England Manchester está en el norte de Inglaterra

■ *adjective*

norte *(plural* norte): she lives on the north coast vive en la costa norte

North America América del Norte: **Texas is in North America** Texas está en América del Norte
the North Pole el Polo Norte
the North Sea el Mar del Norte
adverb
norte: we are going north vamos hacia el norte
north of al norte de: **Boston is north of New York** Boston está al norte de Nueva York.

northeast [ˌnɔːθˈiːst] *(noun, adjective & verb)*
■ *noun*
el **noreste: Hannah lives in the northeast of England** Hannah vive en el noreste de Inglaterra
■ *adjective*
noreste: the northeast coast la costa noreste
■ *adverb*
noreste: we headed northeast nos dirigimos hacia el noreste.

northern [ˈnɔːðən] *adjective* ■ **del norte:**
Northern Europe Europa del Norte
Northern Ireland Irlanda del Norte.

northwest [ˌnɔːθˈwest] *(noun, adjective & adverb)*
■ *noun*
el **noroeste: we live in the northwest of the country** vivimos en el noroeste del país
■ *adjective*
noroeste: the northwest coast la costa noroeste
■ *adverb*
noroeste: we headed northwest nos dirigimos hacia el noreste.

nose [nəʊz] *noun* ■ la **nariz** *(plural* las **narices)*: **he has a big nose** tiene la nariz grande
to blow one's nose sonarse la nariz: **blow your nose!** ¡suénate la nariz!

nosebleed [ˈnəʊzbliːd] *noun*
she had a nosebleed after falling down le sangró la nariz después de caerse.

nosey ➤ **nosy.**

nostril [ˈnɒstrəl] *noun* ■ la **fosa nasal.**

nosy , nosey [ˈnəʊzɪ] *adjective* ■ **fisgón: our neighbours are so nosy** nuestros vecinos son tan fisgones
don't be so nosy! ¡no seas tan fisgón!

not [nɒt] *adverb* ■ **no: he's not coming** no viene

> Por lo general **not** se usa en la forma contraída "-n't", en cuyo caso va unida al verbo que la precede:

I don't think so no lo creo; **Hank didn't come** Hank no vino; **are you coming or not?** ¿vienes o no?; **do you go out on Saturday nights? — not always** ¿sales los sábados por la noche? —no siempre
I'm afraid not me temo que no
not at all en absoluto: **do you mind? — not at all** ¿te importa? —¡en absoluto!
not really en realidad no: **do you want to come? — not really** ¿quieres venir? —en realidad no
not yet todavía no: **are you ready? — not yet** ¿estás listo? —todavia no.

note [nəʊt] *(noun & verb)*
■ *noun*
1. la **nota: she's taking notes** está tomando notas; **I sent him a note** le mandé una nota
2. *UK* el **billete: she gave me a ten-pound note** me dio un billete de diez libras
■ *verb*
notar, tener en cuenta: please note that some products are out of stock sírvase notar que algunos productos están agotados

note down *phrasal verb* ■ **anotar: she noted down the phone number** anotó el número de teléfono.

notebook [ˈnəʊtbʊk] *noun* ■ el **cuaderno.**

notepad [ˈnəʊtpæd] *noun* ■ el **bloc de notas** *(plural* los **blocs de notas)*.

nothing [ˈnʌθɪŋ] *pronoun* ■ **nada: I've got nothing to do** no tengo nada que hacer; **she has nothing left** no le queda nada; **did you see anything? — no, nothing!** ¿viste algo? —¡no, nada!
I didn't pay for it, I got it for nothing no lo pagué, lo conseguí gratis.

notice [ˈnəʊtɪs] *(noun & verb)*
■ *noun*
1. el **letrero: they put up a notice on the door** pusieron un letrero en la puerta

2. el **aviso**: until further notice hasta nuevo aviso

> to take no notice of someone no hacerle caso a alguien: he took no notice of her no le hizo caso

 La palabra inglesa **notice** es un falso amigo, no significa "noticia".

■ *verb*
darse cuenta: I didn't notice you standing there no me di cuenta de que estabas ahí de pie.

noticeboard *UK* ['nəʊtɪsbɔːd] *noun* ■ el **tablón de anuncios**.

nought *UK* [nɔːt] *number* ■ **cero**: nought point five cero coma cinco.

noun [naʊn] *noun* ■ el **sustantivo**: "dog", "London", and "happiness" are all nouns "perro", "Londres" y "felicidad" son todos sustantivos.

novel ['nɒvl] *noun* ■ la **novela**: Katie is reading a novel Katie está leyendo una novela.

novelist ['nɒvəlɪst] *noun* ■ el/la **novelista**: Agatha Christie is a famous novelist Agatha Christie es una famosa novelista.

November [nə'vembəʳ] *noun*

In Spanish the months of the year do not start with a capital letter:

noviembre *(masculine)*: in November en noviembre; next November el próximo noviembre; last November el pasado noviembre.

now [naʊ] *adverb* ■ **ahora**: what shall we do now? ¿qué haremos ahora?

> from now on de ahora en adelante: I'll be more careful from now on tendré más cuidado de ahora en adelante

> any time now en cualquier momento: I'm expecting her any time now la espero en cualquier momento

> right now ahora mismo: get over here right now! ¡ven aquí ahora mismo!

> he should be here by now ya tendría que estar aquí

> now and then OR now and again de vez en cuando: I still see him now and then todavía lo veo de vez en cuando.

nowadays ['naʊədeɪz] *adverb* ■ **hoy en día**: a lot of people work on computers nowadays hoy en día mucha gente trabaja con ordenador.

nowhere ['nəʊweəʳ] *adverb* ■ **where are you going? — nowhere** ¿adónde vas? —a ninguna parte; there's nowhere to sit down no hay ningún lugar para sentarse

> nowhere near lejísimos: Newcastle is nowhere near London Newcastle queda lejísimos de Londres.

nuclear [*UK* 'njuːklɪəʳ, *US* 'nuːklɪəʳ] *adjective* ■ **nuclear**

> a nuclear bomb una bomba nuclear
> nuclear power energía nuclear
> a nuclear power station una central nuclear.

nude [*UK* njuːd, *US* nuːd] *(adjective & noun)*
■ *adjective*
desnudo: they were completely nude estaban completamente desnudos
■ *noun*
> in the nude desnudo: she poses in the nude posa desnuda.

nudge [nʌdʒ] *verb* ■ **dar un codazo**: she nudged me me dio un codazo.

nuisance [*UK* 'njuːsns, *US* 'nuːsns] *noun* ■ el **pesado**, la **pesada**: my little brother is such a nuisance mi hermano pequeño es un pesado.

numb [nʌm] *adjective* ■ **dormido, entumecido**: my hand has gone numb se me ha dormido la mano.

number ['nʌmbəʳ] *noun* ■ el **número**: what's your telephone number? ¿cuál es tu número de teléfono?; we live at number 210 vivimos en el número 210; odd numbers and even numbers números pares y números impares; a large number of people un gran número de personas; your password should contain letters and numbers tu contraseña debe tener letras y números; the numbers on the keyboard los números en el teclado

> number plate *UK* la matrícula
> Number Ten *la residencia oficial del Primer Ministro británico* ➤ Downing Street.

numeral ['njuːmərəl] *noun* ■ el **número**: Roman numerals números romanos.

nun [nʌn] *noun* ■ la **monja**: she's a nun es monja.

nurse [nɜːs] *noun* ■ el **enfermero**, la enfermera: Sue is a nurse Sue es enfermera.

nursery ['nɜːsərɪ] *(plural* nurseries) *noun*

. la **guardería**: there's a nursery for employees' children hay una guardería para los hijos de los empleados

. el **cuarto de los niños**: the baby sleeps in the nursery el bebé duerme en el cuarto de los niños

. el **vivero**: I bought the plants at a nursery compré las plantas en el vivero

a nursery rhyme una canción infantil

nursery school el parvulario, el jardín de infancia: Amy goes to nursery school Amy va al parvulario.

nut [nʌt] *noun*

. el **fruto seco (de cáscara dura)**: the cake was topped with nuts el pastel tenía frutos secos encima

. la **tuerca**: the table is assembled with nuts and bolts la mesa está montada con tuercas y tornillos.

nylon ['naɪlɒn] *noun* ■ el **nailon**: a nylon shirt una camisa de nailon.

oak [əʊk] *noun* ■ el **roble**: an oak tree un roble; an oak table una mesa de roble.

oar [ɔːʳ] *noun* ■ el **remo**.

oasis [əʊ'eɪsɪs] *(plural* oases [əʊ'eɪsiːz]) *noun* ■ el **oasis** *(plural* los **oasis**).

oatmeal ['əʊtmiːl] *noun* ■ el **copo de avena**: I had oatmeal for breakfast desayuné copos de avena.

oats [əʊts] *plural noun* ■ la **avena**: porridge oats copos de avena.

obedient [ə'biːdjənt] *adjective* ■ obediente: Fido's a very obedient dog Fido es un perro muy obediente.

obey [ə'beɪ] *verb*

. **obedecer**: she has always obeyed her parents siempre ha obedecido a sus padres

. **cumplir**: you must obey the rules debes cumplir las reglas.

object ['ɒbdʒɪkt] *noun*

. el **objeto**: what is that strange object? ¿qué es ese objeto raro?

. el **objetivo**: the object of the game is to get rid of all your cards el objetivo del juego es deshacerse de todas las cartas.

oblong ['ɒblɒŋ] *adjective* ■ rectangular: an oblong table una mesa rectangular.

oboe ['əʊbəʊ] *noun* ■ el **oboe**: she plays the oboe toca el oboe.

observation [ɒbzə'veɪʃən] *noun* ■ la **observación** *(plural* las observaciones). the doctors are keeping her in for observation los médicos la mantienen en observación; he made some intelligent observations hizo algunas observaciones inteligentes.

observe [əb'zɜːv] *verb* ■ observar: he carefully observed the procedure observó el procedimiento cuidadosamente.

obsessed [əb'sest] *adjective* ■ obsesionado: she's obsessed with dinosaurs está obsesionada con los dinosaurios.

obstacle ['ɒbstəkl] *noun* ■ el **obstáculo** an obstacle race una carrera de obstáculos.

obtain [əb'teɪn] *verb* ■ obtener: he obtained permission to leave obtuvo permiso para irse.

obvious ['ɒbvɪəs] *adjective* ■ **obvio**: it was obvious that he was nervous era obvio que estaba nervioso.

obviously ['ɒbvɪəslɪ] *adverb*
she's obviously right es obvio que tiene razón
obviously he's not coming está claro que no va a venir.

occasion [ə'keɪʒn] *noun* ■ **la ocasión** *(plural las ocasiones)*: he's been here on several occasions ha estado aquí en varias ocasiones; it's an important occasion es una ocasión importante.

occasionally [ə'keɪʒnəlɪ] *adverb* ■ **de vez en cuando**: I see her occasionally la veo de vez en cuando.

occupation [ˌɒkjʊ'peɪʃn] *noun* ■ **la profesión** *(plural las profesiones)*: what is his occupation? ¿cuál es su profesión?

occur [ə'kɜːʳ] *(past tense & past participle occurred, present participle occurring) verb*
1. **ocurrir**: the incident occurred yesterday el incidente ocurrió ayer
2. **ocurrirse**: it never occurred to me to call nunca se me ocurrió llamar.

ocean ['əʊʃn] *noun* ■ **el océano**: the Atlantic Ocean el Océano Atlántico.

o'clock [ə'klɒk] *adverb* ■ **it's three o'clock** son las tres; at two o'clock a las dos.

October [ɒk'təʊbəʳ] *noun*

In Spanish the months of the year do not start with a capital letter:

octubre *(masculine)*: in October en octubre; next October el próximo octubre; last October el pasado octubre.

octopus ['ɒktəpəs] *noun* ■ **el pulpo**.

odd [ɒd] *adjective*
1. **raro**: that's very odd eso es muy raro
2. **impar**: five is an odd number el cinco es un número impar.

of [əv, ɒv] *preposition*
1. **de**: in the middle of London en el centro de Londres; he ate half of the cake se comió la mitad del pastel; there are thousands of

people hay miles de personas; a kilo of apples un kilo de manzanas; a cup of coffee una taza de café; the ring is made of silver el anillo es de plata; three of them left early tres de ellos se fueron temprano
2. *giving the date* the 4th of July el 4 de julio
how many cups are there? — there are seven of them ¿cuántas tazas hay? –hay siete
there are four of us somos cuatro.

off [UK ɒf, US ɔːf] *(adjective, adverb & preposition)*
■ *adjective*
1. **apagado**: the lights are off las luces están apagadas; is the TV off? ¿está apagada la tele?
2. **suspendido**: the game is off el partido está suspendido
3. **estropeado**: the meat is off la carne se ha estropeado
4. **cortado**: the milk is off la leche se ha cortado
he's off this week tiene esta semana libre
■ *adverb*
he took a week off se tomó una semana libre; it's my day off es mi día libre; he turned the light off apagó la luz; turn the tap off cierra el grifo; the jeans are 10% off los vaqueros tienen un descuento del 10%
■ *preposition*
he got off the train se bajó del tren; she took the book off the shelf cogió el libro del estante; the island is just off the coast la isla está a poca distancia de la costa; he's off work no está en el trabajo; she's off school UK no ha ido al colegio.

offence UK, **offense** US [ə'fens] *noun* ■ **la infracción** *(plural las infracciones)*: he committed an offence cometió una infracción
to take offence ofenderse: I think he took offence at what I said creo que se ofendió por lo que dije.

offend [ə'fend] *verb* ■ **ofender**: I didn't mean to offend you no quise ofenderte.

offense US ➤ offence UK.

offer [UK 'ɒfəʳ, US 'ɔːfəʳ] *(noun & verb)*
■ *noun*
1. **el ofrecimiento**: I appreciate the offer aprecio el ofrecimiento

la **oferta**: they made me a good **offer** me hicieron una buena oferta

it's on special **offer** está de oferta

■ *verb*

ofrecer: I **offered** her something to drink le ofrecí algo de beber

she **offered** to come with me se ofreció a acompañarme.

office [*UK* 'ɒfɪs, *US* 'ɔːfɪs] *noun*

. la **oficina**: Bill works in an **office** Bill trabaja en una oficina

2. el **despacho**: go to the director's **office** ve al despacho del director

an **office block** *UK* OR an **office building** *US* un edificio de oficinas.

officer ['ɒfɪsə^r] *noun* ■ el/la **oficial**: he's an officer in the army es un oficial del ejército

a police **officer** un agente de policía.

official [ə'fɪʃl] *adjective* ■ **oficial**: an official announcement un anuncio oficial.

off-licence *UK* ['ɒf,laɪsns] *noun* ■ **tienda de bebidas alcohólicas**.

offline , off-line [*UK* ,ɒf'laɪn, *US* ,ɔːf'laɪn] *adjective* ■ **fuera de línea**: I'm working offline estoy trabajando fuera de línea

to go **offline** desconectarse.

offside [*UK* ,ɒf'saɪd, *US* ,ɔːf'saɪd] *adjective* ■ **fuera de juego**: Giggs was offside Giggs estaba fuera de juego.

often [*UK* 'ɒfn, *UK* 'ɒftn, *UK* 'ɔːftn] *adverb* ■ **a menudo**: she often plays tennis juega al tenis a menudo

how **often**? ¿cada cuánto, ¿con qué frecuencia?: ¿how often do you see her? ¿cada cuánto la ves?

oil [ɔɪl] *noun*

1. el **aceite**: tuna in oil atún en aceite; I'm having the car's oil changed le estoy haciendo un cambio de aceite a mi coche

2. el **petróleo**: they've found oil in the area encontraron petróleo en la zona

an **oil slick** una mancha de petróleo

an **oil well** un pozo petrolífero.

ointment ['ɔɪntmənt] *noun* ■ la **pomada**: put this ointment on your skin ponte esta pomada en la piel.

OK , okay [,əʊ'keɪ] *adjective*

1. **vale, de acuerdo**: do you want to come? — OK! ¿quieres venir? –¡vale!; I'll see you tomorrow, OK? nos vemos mañana, ¿de acuerdo?

2. **bien**: how are you? — I'm OK! ¿cómo estás? –¡estoy bien!

is that OK with you? ¿te parece bien?

how was the film? — It was OK ¿qué tal la película? –no estuvo mal.

old [əʊld] *adjective*

1. **viejo**: it's an old house es una casa vieja; he's an old man es un hombre viejo

2. **antiguo**: that's my old school ése es mi antiguo colegio

how old are you? ¿cuántos años tienes?

I'm 13 years old tengo trece años

old age la vejez

an old age pensioner un/una pensionista.

older [əʊldə^r] *(comparative of* old*) adjective* ■ **mayor**: she's my older sister es mi hermana mayor; she's older than me es mayor que yo; he's three years older than me es tres años mayor que yo.

oldest ['əʊldəst] *(superlative of* old*) adjective*

1. **mayor**: she's the oldest daughter in the family es la hija mayor de la familia

2. **más antiguo**: it's the oldest church in the town es la iglesia más antigua del pueblo.

old-fashioned [,əʊld'fæʃnd] *adjective*

1. **pasado de moda**: she wore an old-fashioned coat usó un abrigo pasado de moda

2. **chapado a la antigua**: his parents are very old-fashioned sus padres son muy chapados a la antigua.

olive ['ɒlɪv] *noun* ■ la **aceituna**

olive oil aceite de oliva

an olive tree un olivo.

Olympic [ə'lɪmpɪk] *adjective* ■ **olímpico**: an Olympic champion un campeón olímpico

the Olympics las Olimpíadas.

omelette , omelet US ['ɒmlɪt] *noun* ■
la **tortilla francesa**
➤ a potato omelette una tortilla de patatas.

on [ɒn] *(adjective, adverb & preposition)*
■ *adjective*
encendido: the lights are on las luces están
encendidas; **the dryer is on** la secadora está encendida
■ *adverb*
put the lid on ponle la tapa; **I'm going
to put a sweater on** me voy a poner un jersey; **what's on at the Rex?** ¿qué hay dan en
el Rex?; **put the radio on** enciende la radio
■ *preposition*
1. **en: he sat on a chair** se sentó en una silla; **the
map is on the table** el mapa está en la mesa;
the information is on the hard disk la información está en el disco duro; **there's a picture
on the wall** hay un cuadro en la pared; **she has
a ring on her finger** lleva un anillo en el dedo;
what's on TV? ¿qué hay en la tele?
2. **a: we went on foot** fuimos a pie; **my house
is on the left** mi casa está a la izquierda
3. *in time expressions*

When talking about days and dates, instead of a
preposition use **el** or **los:**

I'm coming on Thursday vengo el jueves;
she goes swimming on Tuesdays hace natación los martes; **he left on May 17th** se fue
el 17 de mayo
4. **sobre: it's a book on Australia** es un libro
sobre Australia
➤ **I don't have money on me** no llevo dinero
encima
➤ **she's on the phone** está hablando por teléfono
➤ **I'm having a party on my birthday** voy a
dar una fiesta para mi cumpleaños.

once [wʌns] *adverb*
1. **una vez: once a day** una vez al día
2. **antes: this part of the city was once a village** esta parte de la ciudad era antes una
aldea
➤ **once more** una vez más: **I'd like to go once
more** me gustaría ir una vez más
➤ **once and for all** de una vez por todas: **we'll
have to solve this problem once and for**

all tenemos que resolver este problema de
una vez por todas
➤ **once in a while** de vez en cuando: **he comes
to see me once in a while** viene a verme de
vez en cuando
➤ **once upon a time** érase una vez: **once upon
a time there was a beautiful princess** había
una vez una hermosa princesa
➤ **at once**
1. **enseguida: I must leave at once** tengo que
irme enseguida
2. **a la vez: don't all speak at once** no habléis
todos a la vez.

one [wʌn] *(number & pronoun)*
■ *number*
uno

Uno becomes **un** before masculine nouns:

one day un día; **chapter one** el capítulo uno;
one, two, three, go! ¡uno, dos y tres!; **we
have one dog and two cats** tenemos un perro y dos gatos; **there's only one plate** hay
sólo un plato
➤ **one hundred** cien
■ *pronoun*
1. **uno, una: one of those books is mine** uno
de esos libros es mío; **one of the girls is
Mexican** una de las chicas es mexicana; **do
you need a stamp? — no, I've got one**
¿necesitas un sello? —no, ya tengo uno; **I have
two caps, you can have one** tengo dos go-
rras, puedes quedarte con una
2. *referring to a particular person or thing*
which one? ¿cuál?; **this one, not that one**
éste, no aquél; **this bike is better than the
old one** esta bici es mejor que la vieja
3. *impersonal pronoun* **uno: one must be
sure** uno debe estar seguro
➤ **they love one another** se aman el uno al otro
➤ **one never knows** nunca se sabe.

oneself [wʌn'self] *pronoun*
1. **se: to wash oneself** lavarse; **to enjoy oneself** divertirse
2. **uno mismo: to do something oneself** hacer
algo uno mismo
3. **sí mismo: to talk about oneself** hablar de sí
mismo
➤ **by oneself** solo.

one-way [ˌwʌn'weɪ] *adjective*

a one-way street una calle de único sentido

a one-way ticket un billete de ida.

onion ['ʌnjən] *noun* ■ la **cebolla.**

online , **on-line** ['ɒnlaɪn] *(adjective & adverb)*

adjective

en línea, conectado: online help ayuda en línea; she's online está conectada

adverb

en línea: I love to shop online me encanta comprar en línea

to go online conectarse.

only ['əʊnlɪ] *(adjective & adverb)*

adjective

único: he's the only friend I have es el único amigo que tengo

an only child hijo único: Susan is an only child Susan es hija única

adverb

sólo: she only reads science-fiction sólo lee ciencia ficción; there are only three seats left sólo quedan tres localidades; how much do you have left? — only twenty euros ¿cuánto dinero te queda? —sólo veinte euros

not only no sólo: he's not only tall but he's good-looking too no sólo es alto sino que también es guapo.

onto , **on to** [UK 'ɒntuː, US 'ɑːntuː] *preposition* ■ he threw his books onto the table tiró los libros sobre la mesa; he jumped onto the horse se subió al caballo de un salto; the house looks onto the park la casa da al parque.

onwards ['ɒnwədz], **onward** US ['ɒnwəd] *adverb* ■ en adelante: read from page 50 onwards leed de la página 50 en adelante.

open ['əʊpn] *(adjective, noun & verb)*

adjective

abierto: the door's open la puerta está abierta

wide open abierto de par en par: he left the window wide open dejó la ventana abierta de par en par

■ *noun*

out in the open al aire libre: we slept out in the open dormimos al aire libre

■ *verb*

1. **abrir:** I opened the door abrí la puerta; open the window! ¡abrid la ventana!; the shops open at 9 o'clock las tiendas abren a las 9

2. **abrirse:** the door opened and I walked in la puerta se abrió y entré.

opera ['ɒpərə] *noun* ■ la **ópera.**

operate ['ɒpəreɪt] *verb*

1. **hacer funcionar:** he can't operate the video no puede hacer funcionar el vídeo

2. **operar:** the doctors operated on him but couldn't save him los médicos lo operaron pero no pudieron salvarlo.

operation [ˌɒpə'reɪʃn] *noun* ■ la **operación** *(plural* las **operaciones)**

to have an operation operarse: I'm going to have an operation on my knee me voy a operar de la rodilla.

operator ['ɒpəreɪtər] *noun*

1. el **operador,** la **operadora:** I dialled the operator for assistance llamé al operador para que me ayudara

2. el **operario,** la **operaria:** he's a fork-lift operator es operario de carretilla elevadora

a switchboard operator una telefonista.

opinion [ə'pɪnjən] *noun* ■ la **opinión** *(plural* las **opiniones):** it's a matter of opinion es cuestión de opiniones

what's your opinion on this matter? ¿tú qué opinas sobre este tema?

in my opinion en mi opinión: in my opinion, you should ask her to leave en mi opinión, deberías pedirle que se vaya

an opinion poll un sondeo de opinión.

opponent [ə'pəʊnənt] *noun* ■ el **adversario,** la **adversaria:** he's facing a tough opponent se enfrenta a un duro adversario.

opportunity [UK ˌɒpə'tjuːnətɪ, US ɒpər-'tuːnətɪ] *(plural* opportunities) *noun* ■ la **oportunidad:** it will give you the opportunity to travel te dará la oportunidad de viajar.

opposed [ə'pəʊzd] *adjective*
> to be opposed to something estar en contra de algo: **she's opposed to nuclear weapons** está en contra de las armas nucleares.

opposite ['ɒpəzɪt] *(adjective, noun, preposition & adverb)*
■ *adjective*
1. contrario: **he went in the opposite direction** se fue en dirección contraria
2. opuesto: **the opposite sex** el sexo opuesto
> **the bank is on the opposite side of the street** el banco está al otro lado de la calle
■ *noun*
lo contrario: **the opposite of "sad" is "happy"** lo contrario de "triste" es "contento"; **he always does the opposite of what he is told** siempre hace lo contrario de lo que le dicen
■ *preposition*
frente a: **the school is opposite the station** la escuela está frente a la estación
■ *adverb*
enfrente: **she lives opposite** ella vive enfrente.

optician [ɒp'tɪʃn] *noun* ■ el **óptico**, la **óptica: she's an optician** es óptica.
> **the optician's** la óptica.

optimistic [,ɒptɪ'mɪstɪk] *adjective* ■ **optimista: I'm not very optimistic** no soy muy optimista.

option ['ɒpʃn] *noun* ■ la **opción** *(plural* las **opciones): I have no other option** no tengo otra opción.

optional ['ɒpʃənl] *adjective* ■ **optativo: the German class is optional** la clase de alemán es optativa.

or [ɔːʳ] *conjunction*
1. o: **do you want tea or coffee?** ¿quieres té o café?; **are you coming or not?** ¿vienes o no?; **hurry up or we'll miss the train** date prisa o vamos a perder el tren
2. ni: **I can't come today or tomorrow** no puedo venir hoy ni mañana; **he couldn't eat or sleep** no podía comer ni dormir.

oral ['ɔːrəl] *adjective* ■ **oral**
> **an oral exam** un examen oral.

orange ['ɒrɪndʒ] *(noun & adjective)*
■ *noun*
la **naranja**
> **orange juice** zumo de naranja
> **an orange tree** un naranjo
■ *adjective*
naranja: Bob's wearing an orange shirt Bob lleva puesta una camisa naranja.

orchard ['ɔːtʃəd] *noun* ■ el **huerto de árboles frutales.**

orchestra ['ɔːkɪstrə] *noun* ■ la **orquesta: she plays in an orchestra** toca en una orquesta.

order ['ɔːdəʳ] *(noun & verb)*
■ *noun*
1. el **orden: the names are in alphabetical order** los nombres están en orden alfabético; **I hope everything is in order** espero que todo esté en orden
2. la **orden** *(plural* las **órdenes): he gave me an order** me dio una orden
3. el **pedido: we placed the order yesterday** hicimos el pedido ayer; **the waiter took our order** el camarero tomó nota de lo que habíamos pedido
> **out of order** fuera de servicio: **the lift is out of order** el ascensor está fuera de servicio
> **in order to** para: **he came back home in order to see his parents** volvió a su casa para ver a sus padres
■ *verb*
1. ordenar: **she ordered me to leave** me ordenó que me fuera
2. pedir: **Oliver ordered fish** Oliver pidió pescado.

ordinary [*UK* 'ɔːdənrɪ, *US* 'ɔːdənerɪ] *adjective* ■ **normal: it was an ordinary day** fue un día normal
> **Austin's just an ordinary guy** Austin es un tipo del montón
> **out of the ordinary** fuera de lo común: **I didn't notice anything out of the ordinary** no noté nada fuera de lo común.

organ ['ɔːgən] *noun* ■ el **órgano.**

organic [ɔː'gænɪk] *adjective* ■ **orgánico: organic compound** compuesto orgánico.

organization , organisation UK
[ˌɔːgənaɪˈzeɪʃn] noun ■ la **organización** (plural las **organizaciones**): the Red Cross is an international organization la Cruz Roja es una organización internacional.

organize , organise UK [ˈɔːgənaɪz] verb ■ organizar: we're organizing a trip to Canada estamos organizando un viaje a Canadá.

original [ɒˈrɪdʒənl] adjective
. original: it's an original idea es una idea original
2. primero: who were the original inhabitants of the country? ¿quiénes fueron los primeros habitantes del país?

originally [əˈrɪdʒənəlɪ] adverb ■ en un principio: the house was originally painted white en un principio, la casa estaba pintada de blanco.

ornament [ˈɔːnəmənt] noun ■ el adorno: there were a lot of ornaments on the Christmas tree había muchos adornos en el árbol de Navidad.

orphan [ˈɔːfn] noun ■ el **huérfano**, la **huérfana**: she's an orphan es huérfana.

orphanage [ˈɔːfənɪdʒ] noun ■ el orfanato.

ostrich [ˈɒstrɪtʃ] el **avestruz** (plural los avestruces).

other [ˈʌðər] adjective & pronoun ■ otro: the other shirt is dirty la otra camisa está sucia; I saw Darren the other day vi a Darren el otro día; they had other problems tenían otros problemas
the other one el otro: I'll take the other one me llevo el otro
the others los otros: the others are not coming los otros no vienen.

otherwise [ˈʌðəwaɪz] (conjunction & adverb)
■ conjunction
si no: go now, otherwise you'll miss your train iros ahora, si no vais a perder el tren
■ adverb
aparte de eso: we couldn't do otherwise aparte de eso, no pudimos hacer otra cosa.

ouch [aʊtʃ] exclamation ■ ¡ay!: ouch, that hurts! ¡ay, eso duele!

ought [ɔːt] modal verb

"Ought" is translated by the verb **deber** in the conditional tense:

you ought to go to the dentist deberías ir al dentista; they ought to be here soon deberían llegar pronto.

ounce [aʊns] la **onza** (28,35 gramos): add four ounces of chocolate añada 120 gramos de chocolate.

our [ˈaʊər] possessive adjective ■ nuestro

In Spanish the possessive adjective agrees in number (singular or plural) with the noun that follows:

our dog is called Sammy nuestro perro se llama Sammy; our cousins live in Canada nuestros primos viven en Canadá

Use the definite article (el, la, los or las), not the possessive adjective, with parts of the body:

we brushed our teeth nos lavamos los dientes.

ours [ˈaʊəz] possessive pronoun
1. nuestro

In Spanish the possessive pronoun agrees in gender (masculine and feminine) and number (singular or plural) with the noun it replaces:

their house is big, ours is small la casa de ellos es grande, la nuestra es pequeña; their books are new, ours are old sus libros son nuevos, los nuestros, viejos
2. nuestro: this book isn't ours este libro no es nuestro; he's a friend of ours es nuestro amigo.

ourselves [aʊəˈselvz] pronoun
1. nos: we're enjoying ourselves nos estamos divirtiendo
2. nosotros mismos: we asked him ourselves le preguntamos nosotros mismos
by ourselves solos.

out [aʊt] adverb & preposition
1. fuera: it's hot out hace calor fuera; they're out in the garden están fuera en el jardín; come out here ven aquí fuera

2. pasado de moda: long skirts are out las faldas largas están pasadas de moda
➤ the lights are out se apagaron las luces
➤ she's out ha salido
➤ I'm going out voy a salir
➤ he ran out salió corriendo

out of *preposition*
1. *with verbs of motion* he took a book out of his bag sacó un libro de su bolsa; he came out of the room salió del cuarto; get out of here! ¡salid de aquí!; she jumped out of bed se levantó de la cama de un salto
2. por: she did it out of love lo hizo por amor
3. de: ten out of every twenty diez de cada veinte
➤ we drank out of china cups bebimos en tazas de porcelana.

outdoor ['aʊtdɔːʳ] *adjective*
1. al aire libre: outdoor sports deportes al aire libre
2. descubierto: an outdoor swimming pool una piscina descubierta.

outdoors [aʊt'dɔːz] *adverb* ■ al aire libre: we had lunch outdoors almorzamos al aire libre.

outer ['aʊtəʳ] *adjective* ■ externo: the outer layer is made of metal la capa externa es de metal
➤ outer space el espacio exterior.

outfit ['aʊtfɪt] *noun* ■ el conjunto: that's a nice outfit ése es un conjunto bonito.

outgrew ['aʊtgruː] *past tense* ➤ outgrow.

outgrow ['aʊtgrəʊ] *(past participle* outgrown, *past tense* outgrew) *verb* ■ babies outgrow their clothes so quickly a los bebés la ropa les queda pequeña muy rápidamente.

outgrown ['aʊtgrəʊn] *past participle* ➤ outgrow.

outing ['aʊtɪŋ] *noun* ■ la excursión *(plural* las excursiones)*: we're going on an outing to the museum vamos a ir de excursión al museo.

outlaw ['aʊtlɔː] *noun* ■ el forajido, la forajida.

outlet ['aʊtlet] *noun*
1. el desagüe
2. *US* la toma de corriente: plug the computer into the nearest outlet enchufa el ordenador en la toma de corriente más cercana.

outline ['aʊtlaɪn] *noun* ■ el contorno: you can see the outline of the tower puedes ver el contorno de la torre.

out of date [,aʊtəv'deɪt] *adjective* ■ caducado: your ticket is out of date tu billete está caducado.

outrageous [aʊt'reɪdʒəs] *adjective*
1. escandaloso: his behaviour has been outrageous su comportamiento ha sido escandaloso
2. exorbitante: they charge outrageous prices cobran unos precios exorbitantes
3. extravagante: an outrageous hat un sombrero extravagante.

outside ['aʊtsaɪd, ,aʊt'saɪd] *(adjective, adverb, noun & preposition)*
■ *adjective*
exterior: the outside walls las paredes exteriores
■ *adverb* [,aʊt'saɪd]
fuera: wait for me outside espérame fuera
■ *noun*
el exterior: the outside of the box is red el exterior de la caja es rojo
■ *preposition*
en las afueras: she lives outside the city vive en las afueras de la ciudad.

outskirts ['aʊtskɜːts] *noun* ■ las afueras: they live on the outskirts of Liverpool viven en las afueras de Liverpool.

oval ['əʊvl] *(adjective & noun)*
■ *adjective*
ovalado: an oval window una ventana ovalada
■ *noun*
el óvalo.

oven ['ʌvn] *noun* ■ el horno: put the chicken in the oven mete el pollo en el horno.

over ['əʊvəʳ] *(adjective, adverb & preposition)*
■ *adjective*
➤ to be over terminar: finals are over on Friday los exámenes finales terminan el viernes

adverb

más: you have to be 1.65 metres or over to go on the ride tienes que medir 1,65 metros o más para subirte a las atracciones
I invited him over lo invité a casa

preposition

encima de: there's a light over the table hay una lámpara encima de la mesa

por encima de: he jumped over the fence saltó por encima de la valla

más de: she's over 40 tiene más de 40

durante: it happened over the Christmas holidays esto sucedió durante las vacaciones de Navidad
over here aquí: the shop is over here la tienda queda por aquí
over there ahí: look over there mirad ahí
all over por todo: there were papers all over the floor había papeles por todo el suelo
it's all over now ya pasó todo.

overalls ['əʊvərɔːlz] *plural noun* ■ el mono (de trabajo): he wears overalls at work usa un mono para trabajar.

overcame *past tense* ➤ overcome.

overcharge [,əʊvə'tʃɑːdʒ] *verb* ■ cobrar de más: I was overcharged at the restaurant me cobraron de más en el restaurante.

overcome [,əʊvə'kʌm] *(past tense* overcame [,əʊvə'keɪm], *past participle* overcome*) verb* ■ superar: she tried to overcome the problem trató de superar el problema.

overlook [,əʊvə'lʊk] *verb*

1. **dar a:** our room overlooks the sea nuestro cuarto da al mar

2. **pasar por alto:** she overlooked an important detail pasó por alto un detalle importante.

overnight [,əʊvə'naɪt] *adverb*

1. **durante la noche:** we travelled overnight viajamos durante la noche

2. **de la noche a la mañana:** she changed overnight cambió de la noche a la mañana
he stayed overnight se quedó a pasar la noche.

overseas ['əʊvəsiːz] *(adjective & adverb)*

■ *adjective*

extranjero: they are overseas students son estudiantes extranjeros

■ *adverb*

en el extranjero: she lives overseas vive en el extranjero.

oversleep [,əʊvə'sliːp] *(past tense & past participle* overslept*) verb* ■ **quedarse dormido:** I overslept this morning esta mañana me he quedado dormido.

overslept *past tense & past participle* ➤ oversleep.

overtake *UK* [,əʊvə'teɪk] *(past tense* overtook, *past participle* overtaken*) verb* ■ **adelantar:** he overtook the bus adelantó al autobús.

overtaken *UK* [,əʊvə'teɪkən] *past participle* ➤ overtake.

overtime ['əʊvətaɪm] *uncountable* ■ **las horas extra:** she's doing overtime está haciendo horas extra.

overtook *UK* [,əʊvə'tʊk] *past tense* ➤ overtake.

overweight [,əʊvə'weɪt] *adjective* ■ **con sobrepeso:** being overweight is bad for your health tener sobrepeso es perjudicial para la salud.

owe [əʊ] *verb* ■ **deber:** I owe him fifty euros le debo cincuenta euros.

owl [aʊl] *noun* ■ el búho.

own [əʊn] *(adjective & verb)*

■ *adjective*

propio: do you have your own bike? ¿tienes tu propia bicicleta?

➤ on one's own solo: I'll do it on my own lo haré solo

■ *verb*

ser dueño de: she owns a car es dueña de un coche

own up *phrasal verb* ■ **admitir tener la culpa**

➤ own up to something admitir algo: he owned up to taking the money admitió que había robado el dinero.

owner ['əʊnəʳ] *noun* ■ el dueño, la dueña.

ox [ɒks] *(plural* oxen ['ɒksn]*) noun* ■ el buey.

oxygen ['ɒksɪdʒən] *noun* ■ el oxígeno
➤ an oxygen mask una máscara de oxígeno.

oyster [ˈɔɪstəʳ] *noun* ■ la **ostra**.

oz. *(abbreviation of* ounce & ounces*)* ➤ ounce.

ozone [ˈəʊzəʊn] *noun* ■ el **ozono** the ozone layer la capa de ozono.

p UK *(abbreviation of* penny & pence*)* ➤ penny: it costs 20p vale 20 peniques.

pace [peɪs] *(noun & verb)*
■ *noun*
1. el **paso**: she walked at a brisk pace andaba con paso enérgico
2. el **ritmo**: he couldn't take the pace no pudo mantener el ritmo
■ *verb*
to pace up and down pasearse de un lado a otro.

Pacific [pəˈsɪfɪk] *noun*
3. the Pacific el Pacífico; the Pacific Ocean el océano Pacífico.

pacifier US [ˈpæsɪfaɪəʳ] *noun* ■ el **chupete**: the baby dropped his pacifier al bebé se le cayó el chupete.

pack [pæk] *(noun & verb)*
■ *noun*
1. el **paquete**: a pack of cigarettes un paquete de cigarrillos
2. la **manada**: a pack of wolves una manada de lobos
a pack of cards una baraja de cartas

■ *verb*
1. hacer la maleta: he packed his bags hizo las maletas
2. abarrotar: the crowd packed into the stadium la multitud abarrotaba el estadio.

package [ˈpækɪdʒ] *noun* ■ el **paquete**: the postman has left a package for you el cartero ha dejado un paquete para ti.

packed [pækt] *adjective* ■ **abarrotado**: the train was packed today hoy el tren iba abarrotado.

packet [ˈpækɪt] *noun* ■ el **paquete**: she bought a packet of biscuits compró un paquete de galletas.

pad [ˈpæd] *(noun & verb)*
■ *noun*
el **bloc**: a desk pad un bloc de notas
■ *verb (past tense & past participle* padded, *present participle* padding*)*
acolchar: I padded the bottom to make it more comfortable acolché la parte de abajo para hacerla más cómoda.

paddle [ˈpædl] *(noun & verb)*
■ *noun*
el **remo**: he dropped his paddle into the water se le cayó el remo al agua
to go for a paddle ir a mojarse los pies
■ *verb*
1. mojarse los pies (en la orilla)
2. remar
to paddle a canoe dirigir remando una canoa.

paddling pool UK [ˈpædlɪŋpuːl] *noun* ■ la **piscina**.

padlock [ˈpædlɒk] *noun* ■ el **candado**: he put a padlock on his bike le puso un candado a la bici.

page [peɪdʒ] *noun* ■ la **página**: turn the page pasa la página.

paid [peɪd] *past tense & past participle* ➤ pay.

pain [peɪn] *noun*
1. el **dolor**: I felt a sharp pain in my side sentí un dolor agudo en el costado
2. la **lata** *informal*: what a pain to have to do it again ¡qué lata tener que hacerlo otra vez!

to be in pain tener dolor: **she's in a lot of pain** tiene muchos dolores
a pain in the neck un pesado: **my little sister is a pain in the neck** mi hermana pequeña es una pesada.

painful ['peɪnfʊl] *adjective* ■ **doloroso**: **sunburn is very painful** la quemadura solar es muy dolorosa.

paint [peɪnt] *(noun & verb)*
■ *noun*
la **pintura**: **"wet paint"** "recién pintado"
■ *verb*
pintar: **he paints landscapes** pinta paisajes.

paintbrush ['peɪntbrʌʃ] *noun* ■ el **pincel**.

painter ['peɪntər] *noun* ■ el **pintor**, la **pintora**: **Vincent's a painter** Vincent es pintor.

painting ['peɪntɪŋ] *noun*
1. la **pintura**: **she likes painting** le gusta la pintura
2. el **cuadro**: **it's a painting by Monet** es un cuadro de Monet.

pair [peər] *noun* ■ el **par**: **a pair of shoes** un par de zapatos
a pair of trousers UK OR **a pair of pants** US unos pantalones.

pajamas US *plural noun* ➤ **pyjamas** UK.

pal [pæl] *noun* ■ *informal* el/la **colega**.

palace ['pælɪs] *noun* ■ el **palacio**.

pale [peɪl] *adjective*
1. **pálido**: **I was so pale at the end of the winter** estaba tan pálido al final del invierno
2. **claro**: **her dress was pale blue** su vestido era azul claro.

palm [pɑːm] *noun*
1. la **palma**: **she was holding an egg in the palm of her hand** tenía un huevo en la palma de la mano
2. la **palmera**: **a palm tree** una palmera.

pamphlet ['pæmflɪt] *noun* ■ el **folleto**.

pan [pæn] *noun* ■ la **sartén** *(plural* las sartenes): **put the bacon in the pan** pon el beicon en la sartén.

Panama [pænəmɑː] *noun* ■ **Panamá**.

pancake ['pænkeɪk] *noun* ■ la **crepe**: **I made pancakes for breakfast** preparé crepes para desayunar.

panda ['pændə] *noun* ■ el **panda**.

pane [peɪn] *noun* ■ el **vidrio**, el **cristal**: **a pane of glass** un vidrio.

panic ['pænɪk] *(noun & verb)*
■ *noun*
el **pánico**
■ *verb (past tense & past participle* panicked, *present participle* panicking)*
he panicked when the car broke down le entró el pánico cuando el coche se averió; **don't panic!** ¡que no cunda el pánico!

pant [pænt] *verb* ■ **jadear**: **the dog was panting in the heat** el perro jadeaba por el calor.

panties ['pæntɪz] *plural noun* ■ las **bragas**: **a pair of panties** unas bragas.

pantomime UK ['pæntəmaɪm] *noun* ■ la **comedia musical navideña**.

pants [pænts] *plural noun*
1. UK los **calzoncillos**: **a pair of pants** un par de calzoncillos
2. US los **pantalones**: **a pair of pants** unos pantalones.

pantyhose US ['pæntɪhəʊz] *plural noun* ■ las **medias**, los **pantys**.

paper ['peɪpər] *noun*
1. el **papel**: **he wrote the number on a piece of paper** escribió el número en un pedazo de papel; **a paper bag** una bolsa de papel
2. el **periódico**: **David was reading the paper** David estaba leyendo el periódico
▸ **a paper clip** un clip
▸ **the paper shop** UK el quiosco.

paperback ['peɪpəbæk] *noun* ■ el **libro en rústica**.

parachute ['pærəʃuːt] *noun* ■ el **paracaídas** *(plural* los **paracaídas**): **he came down in a parachute** saltó en paracaídas.

parade [pə'reɪd] *noun* ■ el **desfile**: **a fashion parade** un desfile de moda.

187

paradise ['pærədaɪs] *noun* ■ el **paraíso.**

paragraph ['pærəgrɑːf] *noun* ■ el párrafo

full stop, new paragraph punto y aparte.

Paraguay ['pærəgwaɪ] *noun* ■ **Paraguay.**

parallel ['pærəlel] *adjective* ■ **paralelo:** parallel lines líneas paralelas.

paralysed *UK*, **paralyzed** *US* ['pærəlaɪzd] *adjective* ■ **paralítico:** she was paralysed in a riding accident quedó paralítica en un accidente de equitación.

pardon ['pɑːdn] *noun*

> pardon? ¿cómo?: pardon? — I said it's that way ¿cómo? —dije que era en esa dirección.

parenthesis [pə'renθəsɪz] *(plural* parentheses [pə'renθəsiːz]*)* plural *noun* ■ el **paréntesis** *(plural* los **paréntesis***)*: in parentheses entre paréntesis.

parents ['peərənts] plural *noun* ■ los **padres.**

park [pɑːk] *(noun & verb)*

■ *noun*

el **parque:** let's go to the park vamos al parque

■ *verb*

aparcar: where can we park? ¿dónde podemos aparcar?; I parked the car aparqué el coche.

parking ['pɑːkɪŋ] *noun* ■ el **estacionamiento**

> "no parking" "prohibido aparcar"

> a parking lot *US* el aparcamiento

> a parking meter el parquímetro

> a parking ticket una multa por aparcamiento indebido.

parliament ['pɑːləmənt] *noun* ■ el **parlamento.**

parrot ['pærət] *noun* ■ el **loro.**

parsley ['pɑːslɪ] *noun* ■ el **perejil.**

part [pɑːt] *(noun & verb)*

■ *noun*

1. la **parte:** I liked parts of the book me gustaron algunas partes del libro

2. el **papel:** he plays a big part in the play tiene un papel importante en la obra

3. la **pieza:** I bought some spare parts for the car compré unas piezas de repuesto para el coche

4. *US* la **raya:** she has a center part lleva la raya en medio

> to take part in something participar en algo: he took part in the race participó en la carrera

■ *verb*

separarse: they parted at the door se separaron en la puerta

> to part one's hair peinarse con raya: she parts her hair in the middle se peina con la raya en medio

part with *phrasal verb* ■ **desprenderse de:** I had to part with my favourite sweater tuve que desprenderme de mi jersey favorito.

participle ['pɑːtɪsɪpl] *noun* ■ el **participio:** the past participle el participio pasado.

particular [pə'tɪkjʊləʳ] *adjective*

1. en **particular:** why do you need that particular book? ¿por qué necesitas ese libro en particular?

2. exigente: she's very particular about her clothes es muy exigente con la ropa

> in particular en particular: are you looking for something in particular? ¿estás buscando algo en particular?

particularly [pə'tɪkjʊləlɪ] *adverb* ■ **particularmente:** I'm not particularly interested in going no estoy particularmente interesada en ir.

parting *UK* ['pɑːtɪŋ] *noun* ■ la **raya:** he has a middle parting lleva la raya en medio.

partner ['pɑːtnəʳ] *noun* ■ el **socio,** la **socia**

> a business partner un socio comercial.

part-time [pɑːttaɪm] *adjective & adverb* ■ a tiempo parcial: he has a part-time job tiene un trabajo a tiempo parcial; she works part-time trabaja a tiempo parcial.

party ['pɑːtɪ] *(plural* parties*)* noun

1. la **fiesta:** we're having a party vamos a dar una fiesta; a birthday party una fiesta de cumpleaños

2. el **partido**: the Labour Party el partido Laborista; the Democratic party el partido Demócrata

3. el **grupo**: a party of tourists un grupo de turistas.

pass [UK pɑːs, US pæs] (noun & verb)

▪ noun

. el **pase**: you need a pass to get in necesitas un pase para poder entrar; he made a pass to Owen le hizo un pase a Owen

2. el **abono**: a bus pass un abono de autobús

3. el **paso**: a mountain pass el paso de montaña

4. UK el **aprobado**: I got a pass in history he aprobado historia

➢ a boarding pass una tarjeta de embarque

▪ verb

1. **pasar**: can you pass me the salt? ¿podrías pasarme la sal?; they played cards to pass the time jugaron a las cartas solo para pasar el tiempo; the evening passed quickly la tarde pasó rápido; what's the capital of Poland? — pass! ¿cuál es la capital de Polonia? —¡paso!

2. **pasar por delante de**: I pass the museum on my way to school paso por delante del museo de camino al colegio

3. **adelantar a**: he passed the car in front adelantó al coche de delante

4. **aprobar**: he passed his driving test aprobó el examen de conducir; the law was passed last year la ley fue aprobada el año pasado

pass on phrasal verb ▪ **pasar**: can you pass the message on? ¿puedes pasar el mensaje?

pass out phrasal verb ▪ **desmayarse**: she passed out se desmayó.

passage ['pæsɪdʒ] noun

1. el **pasillo**: the toilet is at the end of the passage el baño está al final del pasillo

2. el **pasaje**: it's an interesting passage from the book es un pasaje interesante del libro.

passenger ['pæsɪndʒəʳ] noun ▪ el **pasajero**, la **pasajera**.

passerby [UK ˌpɑːsəˈbaɪ, US ˈpæsəʳˌbaɪ] (plural passersby [UK ˌpɑːsəzˈbaɪ, US ˈpæsəʳzˈbaɪ]) noun ▪ el/la **transeúnte**.

passion ['pæʃn] noun ▪ la **pasión**: she has a passion for music siente pasión por la música

➢ passion fruit el maracuyá.

passive ['pæsɪv] (adjective & noun)

▪ adjective

pasivo

▪ noun

la **voz pasiva**: in the passive en voz pasiva.

Passover [UK 'pɑːsˌəʊvəʳ, US 'pæsˌəʊvəʳ] noun ▪ la **Pascua judía**.

passport [UK 'pɑːspɔːt, US 'pæspɔːt] noun ▪ el **pasaporte**.

password [UK 'pɑːswɜːd, UK 'pæswɜːd] noun ▪ la **contraseña**: what's the password? ¿cuál es la contraseña?

past [UK pɑːst, US pæst] (adjective, noun & preposition)

▪ adjective

1. **último**: during the past few days durante los últimos días

2. **pasado**: the past tense el tiempo pasado

▪ noun

el **pasado**: she often thinks about the past piensa a menudo en el pasado

➢ in the past en el pasado: there are more students now than in the past hay más estudiantes ahora que en el pasado

▪ preposition

por delante de: we drove past the school pasamos en coche por delante de la escuela

➢ it's just past the church queda justo después de la iglesia

➢ half past y media: it's half past eight son las ocho y media; it's ten past six son las seis y diez.

pasta ['pæstə] uncountable noun ▪ la **pasta**: pasta with tomato sauce pasta con salsa de tomate.

pastime [UK 'pɑːstaɪm, US 'pæstaɪm] noun ▪ el **pasatiempo**: my favourite pastime is swimming mi pasatiempo preferido es la natación.

pastry ['peɪstrɪ] (plural pastries) noun

1. el **pastel**: we offer a selection of pastries ofrecemos una variedad de pasteles

2. (uncountable) la **masa**: she's making pastry for an apple pie está haciendo la masa para una tarta de manzana.

pat [pæt] (noun & verb)

■ noun

la **palmadita**: he gave the boy a friendly pat on the shoulder le dio al niño una palmadita amistosa en el hombro

■ verb (past tense & past participle patted, present participle patting)

acariciar (dando palmaditas): can I pat your dog? ¿puedo acariciar al perro?

patch [pætʃ] (plural patches [pætʃɪz]) (noun & verb)

■ noun

1. el **parche**: his jeans had patches on the knees sus vaqueros tenían parches en las rodillas

2. la **zona**: there were icy patches on the road había zonas con hielo en la carretera

to be going through a bad patch pasar por una mala racha

■ verb

ponerle un parche a: she patched the holes in her sweater le puso un parche a los agujeros del suéter

path [UK pɑ:θ, US pæθ] noun ■ el **sendero**, el **camino**: this path leads to the river este sendero lleva al río.

pathetic [pə'θetɪk] adjective ■ **penoso**: that's a pathetic excuse es una excusa penosa.

patience ['peɪʃns] noun ■ la **paciencia**: she has a lot of patience tiene mucha paciencia.

patient ['peɪʃnt] (adjective & noun)

■ adjective

paciente: he's very patient with the children es muy paciente con los niños

■ noun

el/la **paciente**.

patiently ['peɪʃntlɪ] adverb ■ **pacientemente**: he waited patiently for her la esperó pacientemente.

patriotic [UK ,pætrɪ'ɒtɪk, US ,peɪtrɪ'ɒtɪk] adjective ■ **patriótico**.

patrol [pə'trəʊl] noun ■ la **patrulla**: the soldiers are on patrol los soldados están de patrulla

a patrol car un coche patrulla.

pattern ['pætən] noun ■ el **estampado**: I like the pattern on your dress me gusta el estampado de tu vestido.

pause [pɔ:z] (noun & verb)

■ noun

la **pausa**: there was a slight pause between songs hubo una breve pausa entre las canciones

■ verb

detenerse: I paused before entering the room me detuve antes de entrar la habitación.

pavement ['peɪvmənt] noun ■ la **acera**: walk on the pavement anda por la acera.

paw [pɔ:] noun ■ la **pata**: the dog scratched himself with his paw el perro se rascaba con la pata.

pay [peɪ] (past tense & past participle paid) verb ■ **pagar**: I'll pay the bill pagaré la cuenta; he's paid by the week le pagan por semana

to pay attention prestar atención: I wasn't paying attention no estaba prestando atención; to pay somebody a visit ir a ver a alguien

pay back phrasal verb ■ **devolver el dinero**: I'll pay you back later te devolveré el dinero después

pay for phrasal verb ■ **pagar**: I've already paid for the meal ya he pagado la cena; he paid 30 euros for that shirt pagó treinta euros por esa camisa.

payment ['peɪmənt] noun ■ el **pago** payment in cash pago al contado.

payphone ['peɪfəʊn] noun ■ el **teléfono público**.

PC [,pi:'si:] (abbreviation of personal computer) noun ■ el **PC**.

PE [,pi:'i:] (abbreviation of physical education) noun ■ la **educación física**.

pea [piː] *noun* ■ el **guisante**.

peace [piːs] *noun* ■ la **paz** *(plural* las paces*)*: they made peace hicieron las paces ▸ to leave somebody in peace dejar a alguien en paz ▸ peace and quiet paz y tranquilidad: I came here looking for peace and quiet vine aquí buscando paz y tranquilidad.

peaceful ['piːsfʊl] *adjective*
1. tranquilo: it's a very peaceful town es un pueblo muy tranquilo
2. pacífico: we took part in a peaceful demonstration participamos en una manifestación pacífica ▸ it's very peaceful in the country hay mucha tranquilidad en el campo.

peach [piːtʃ] *(plural* peaches [piːtʃɪz]*) noun* ■ el **melocotón** *(plural* los **melocotones**).

peacock ['piːkɒk] *noun* ■ el **pavo real**.

peak [piːk] *noun*
1. la **cumbre**: he reached the peak of the mountain llegó a la cumbre de la montaña
2. el **apogeo**: she died at the peak of her film career murió en el apogeo de su carrera cinematográfica ▸ the peak season la temporada alta.

peanut ['piːnʌt] *noun* ■ el **cacahuete** ▸ peanut butter mantequilla de cacahuete.

pear [peəʳ] *noun* ■ la **pera**.

pearl [pɜːl] *noun* ■ la **perla**: she wore a pearl necklace llevaba puesto un collar de perlas.

pebble ['pebl] *noun* ■ el **guijarro**.

peculiar [pɪ'kjuːljəʳ] *adjective* ■ **raro**: it has a peculiar smell huele raro.

pedal ['pedl] *(noun & verb)*
■ *noun*
el **pedal**: put your foot on the pedal pon el pie en el pedal
■ *verb*
pedalear: you have to pedal harder when you go up a hill tienes que pedalear más fuerte cuando subes una pendiente.

pedestrian [pɪ'destrɪən] *noun* ■ el **peatón** *(plural* los **peatones***)*: this street is for pedestrians only esta calle es sólo para peatones ▸ a pedestrian precinct *UK* OR a pedestrian zone *US* una zona peatonal ▸ a pedestrian crossing *UK* un paso de peatones.

pee [piː] *noun* ■ *informal* **pis** ▸ to have a pee hacer pis.

peek ➤ peep.

peel [piːl] *(noun & verb)*
■ *noun*
la **piel**: take the peel off before you eat the fruit quita la piel antes de comerte la fruta
■ *verb*
1. pelar: he's peeling the potatoes está pelando las patatas
2. pelarse: my skin is peeling me estoy pelando

peel off *phrasal verb* ■ **despegar**: peel the label off despega la etiqueta.

peep [piːp], **peek** [piːk] *(noun & verb)*
■ *noun*
el **vistazo**
▸ to have a peep echar un vistazo: I had a peep into the kitchen to see how dinner was coming along eché un vistazo en la cocina para ver cómo iba la cena
■ *verb*
espiar
▸ no peeping! ¡no miren!

peg [peg] *noun*
1. *UK* la **pinza**: hang up the clothes with these pegs tiende la ropa con estas pinzas
2. el **colgador**: put your coat on the peg pon tu abrigo en el colgador.

pelican ['pelɪkən] *noun* ■ el **pelícano**.

pen [pen] *noun* ■ el **bolígrafo**: can I borrow a pen? ¿me prestas un bolígrafo?

penalty ['penltɪ] *(plural* penalties*) noun*
1. la **pena**: the death penalty la pena de muerte
2. *in sports* el **penalti**.

pence [pens] *UK* ➤ penny: a 50-pence piece una moneda de 50 peniques.

pencil ['pensl] *noun* ■ el **lápiz** *(plural* los lápices*)*: write your name in pencil escribe tu nombre con lápiz

➤ a pencil case un estuche de lápices
➤ a pencil sharpener un sacapuntas.

pendant ['pendənt] *noun* ■ el **colgante**: she's wearing a pendant lleva un colgante.

penfriend ['penfrend] *UK noun* ■ el **amigo por correspondencia, la amiga por correspondencia.**

penguin ['peŋgwɪn] *noun* ■ el **pingüino.**

penknife ['pennaɪf] *(plural* penknives [pennaɪvz]*) noun* ■ la **navaja.**

penny ['penɪ] *noun*

1. *(plural* pence*) UK* el **penique**: he dropped a penny on the floor se le cayó un penique al suelo; it costs 20 pence vale 20 peniques
2. *(plural* pennies*) US* el **centavo**: do you have a couple of pennies? ¿tienes algunos centavos?

pension ['penʃn] *noun* ■ la **pensión** *(plural* las pensiones*)*

➤ to live on a pension vivir de una pensión: mi grandfather lives on a pension mi abuelo vive de una pensión.

pensioner *UK* ['penʃənər] el/la **pensionista.**

Pentagon ['pentəgən] *noun* ■ the Pentagon el Pentágono

THE PENTAGON

El edificio del Pentágono, llamado así por su forma, y que se encuentra en las afueras de la ciudad de Washington, es la sede de la secretaría de la defensa estadounidense. Muchas veces se habla del Pentágono para referirse al poder militar de los Estados Unidos en general. Un parte del Pentágono fue destruida en los ataques terroristas del 11 de septiembre de 2001.

penthouse ['penthaʊs] *noun* ■ el **ático de lujo.**

people ['piːpl] *plural noun*

1. la **gente**

Gente is a singular noun and is used with a verb in the singular:

they're nice people es gente agradable; there are a lot of people here hay mucha gente aquí
2. las **personas**: there's enough room for ten people hay espacio suficiente para diez personas

➤ people say that... dicen que...: people say that he's mean dicen que es tacaño
➤ English people los ingleses
➤ a people carrier un monovolumen.

pepper ['pepər] *noun*

1. la **pimienta**: salt and pepper sal y pimienta
2. el **pimiento**: I'd like green peppers and mushrooms on the pizza quisiera una pizza con pimientos verdes y champiñones.

peppermint ['pepəmɪnt] *noun* ■ la **menta.**

per [pɜːr] *preposition* ■ **por**: it costs 10 pounds per person cuesta 10 libras por persona.

per cent , percent *US* [pɜːrˈsent] *adverb* ■ **por ciento**: 20 percent of the students are absent today hoy falta el 20 por ciento de los alumnos.

perfect ['pɜːfɪkt] *adjective* ■ **perfecto**: the weather is perfect el tiempo es perfecto.

perfectly ['pɜːfɪktlɪ] *adverb* ■ **perfectamente**: she speaks Spanish perfectly habla español perfectamente

➤ I'm perfectly happy estoy muy contento.

perform [pəˈfɔːm] *verb*

1. **actuar**: he's performing in a play está actuando en una obra de teatro
2. **realizar**: a computer can perform several tasks at once un ordenador puede realizar varias tareas a la vez.

performance [pəˈfɔːməns] *noun*

1. la **función** *(plural* las funciones*)*: the performance lasts two hours la función dura dos horas
2. la **actuación**: the team's performance was excellent la actuación del equipo fue excelente

el rendimiento: the students' perform-ance has been good el rendimiento de los alumnos ha sido bueno.

perfume ['pɜːfjuːm] noun ■ **el perfume:** she's wearing perfume lleva perfume.

perhaps [pə'hæps] adverb ■ **quizás:** per-haps you're right quizás tengas razón perhaps not quizás no.

period ['pɪərɪəd] noun

. **el periodo:** a long period of drought un largo periodo de sequía

2. **la clase:** I have history next period la próxi-ma clase es de historia

3. **la regla:** she has her period está con la regla

4. US **el punto:** don't forget the period at the end of the sentence no olvides poner el pun-to al final de la frase.

perm [pɜːm] noun ■ **la permanente:** she's going to get a perm se va a hacer la permanente.

permanent ['pɜːmənənt] adjective ■ **permanente:** it's part of the museum's permanent collection es parte de la colec-ción permanente del museo.

permission [pə'mɪʃn] noun ■ **el per-miso:** she gave me permission to leave me dio permiso para irme.

permit (noun & verb)
noun ['pɜːmɪt]
el permiso: his work permit has expired su permiso de trabajo ha caducado
verb [pə'mɪt] (past tense & past participle permit-ted, present participle permitting)
permitir: her parents won't permit her to travel alone sus padres no le van a permitir que viaje sola
smoking is not permitted no está permitido fumar.

person ['pɜːsn] (plural people) noun ■ **la persona:** there's room for one more person hay sitio para una persona más
in person en persona: she came to see me in person vino a verme en persona.

personal ['pɜːsənl] adjective ■ **personal:** it's a personal letter es una carta personal
a personal stereo un walkman®.

personality [ˌpɜːsə'nælətɪ] (plural per-sonalities) noun ■ **la personalidad:** he has a strong personality tiene una personalidad fuerte.

persuade [pə'sweɪd] verb ■ **convencer:** he persuaded me to go me convenció de que fuera; I persuaded him not to go out lo convencí de que no saliera.

pessimistic [ˌpesɪ'mɪstɪk] adjective ■ **pesimista.**

pet [pet] noun

1. **el animal doméstico:** do you have any pets? ¿tienes algún animal doméstico?

2. **el preferido, la preferida:** he's the teacher's pet es el preferido del profesor
a pet shop una tienda de animales.

petal ['petl] noun ■ **el pétalo.**

petrol UK ['petrəl] noun ■ **la gasolina.**

pharmacy ['fɑːməsɪ] (plural pharmacies) noun ■ **la farmacia:** the pharmacy is open until 8 la farmacia está abierta hasta las 8.

pheasant ['feznt] noun ■ **el faisán** (plural los faisanes).

philosopher [fɪ'lɒsəfəʳ] noun ■ **el filó-sofo, la filósofa:** Plato was a Greek philoso-pher Platón fue un filósofo griego.

philosophy [fɪ'lɒsəfɪ] noun ■ **la filo-sofía:** she's studying philosophy estudia filosofía.

phobia ['fəʊbjə] noun ■ **la fobia:** she has a phobia about spiders tiene fobia a las arañas.

phone [fəʊn] (noun & verb)
■ noun
el teléfono: where's the phone? ¿dónde está el teléfono?
to be on the phone estar hablando por telé-fono: Fred's on the phone Fred está hablan-do por teléfono
the phone book la guía telefónica: look up the number in the phone book busca el número en la guía telefónica
a phone booth OR a phone box UK una cabi-na telefónica
a phone call una llamada telefónica

a phone number un número de teléfono: what's your phone number? ¿cuál es tu número de teléfono?

■ *verb*

llamar por teléfono: I have to phone my parents tengo que llamar por teléfono a mis padres

phone back *phrasal verb* ■ volver a llamar: I'll phone you back tonight te vuelvo a llamar esta noche.

phonecard ['fəʊnkɑːd] *noun* ■ la tarjeta telefónica.

phony , phoney *UK* ['fəʊnɪ] *adjective* ■ falso: she gave a phoney name dio un nombre falso.

photo ['fəʊtəʊ] *noun* ■ la foto: he took a photo sacó una foto

> to take a photo sacarle una foto: he took a photo of me sacó una foto.

photocopy ['fəʊtəʊˌkɒpɪ] *(plural* photocopies) *(noun & verb)*

■ *noun*

la fotocopia: I'll make a photocopy of the article voy a hacer una fotocopia del artículo

■ *verb (past tense & past participle* photocopied*)*

fotocopiar: I photocopied the letter fotocopié la carta.

photograph [*UK* 'fəʊtəgrɑːf, *US* 'fəʊtəgræf] *noun* ■ la fotografía: she was taking photographs estaba sacando fotografías

> to take a photograph sacarle una fotografía: he took a photograph of the bridge le sacó una fotografía al puente.

photographer [fə'tɒgrəfə^r] *noun* ■ el fotógrafo, la fotógrafa: she's a photographer es fotógrafa.

photography [fə'tɒgrəfɪ] *noun* ■ la fotografía: he's studying photography at college está estudiando fotografía en el instituto.

phrase [freɪz] *noun* ■ la frase, la locución

> a phrase book una guía de conversación para viajeros.

physical ['fɪzɪkl] *adjective* ■ físico: he does a lot of physical exercise hace mucho ejercicio físico

> physical education educación física.

physician *US* [fɪ'zɪʃn] *noun* ■ el médico, la médica: he's a physician es médico.

physics ['fɪzɪks] *uncountable noun* ■ la física: physics is my favourite subject mi materia favorita es física.

pianist ['pɪənɪst] *noun* ■ el/la pianista: Mary's a pianist María es pianista.

piano [pɪ'ænəʊ] *noun* ■ el piano: Pete plays the piano Pete toca el piano.

pick [pɪk] *(noun & verb)*

■ *noun*

> go ahead, take your pick! ¡vamos, adelante, elige la que quieras!

> an ice pick un punzón para el hielo

■ *verb*

1. elegir: I picked the green shirt elegí la camisa verde

2. recoger: we went to pick apples fuimos a recoger manzanas

3. coger: she's picking flowers está cogiendo flores

> to pick a fight buscar pelea

> to pick one's nose hurgarse la nariz

pick on *phrasal verb* ■ meterse con: they're always picking on him at school siempre se están metiendo con él en el colegio

pick up *phrasal verb*

1. coger: he bent down and picked up the coin se agachó y cogió la moneda

2. recoger: I'll pick you up at the station te recogeré en la estación; pick up those toys right now recoge esos juguetes ahora mismo

3. aprender: she picked up a bit of Italian aprendió un poco de italiano.

pickpocket ['pɪkˌpɒkɪt] *noun* ■ el/la carterista: beware of pickpockets ten cuidado con los carteristas.

picnic ['pɪknɪk] *noun* ■ el picnic *(plural* los picnics)*: we're going on a picnic nos vamos de picnic

> to have a picnic irse de picnic.

picture ['pɪktʃə^r] *noun*

1. el dibujo: she's drawing a picture está haciendo un dibujo

. la **ilustración** (plural las **ilustraciones**): are there any pictures in this book? ¿hay ilustraciones en este libro?

. la **foto**: I took a picture of him le saqué una foto.

pie [paɪ] noun ■ la **tarta**: I baked an apple pie hice una tarta de manzana.

piece [piːs] noun

. el **trozo**: a piece of bread un trozo de pan

2. el **pedazo**: it fell to pieces se hizo pedazos

3. la **pieza**: I lost a piece of the jigsaw puzzle perdí una pieza del rompecabezas

to take something to pieces desmontar algo

a piece of furniture un mueble

a piece of advice un consejo.

pierced [pɪəst] adjective ■ I have pierced ears tengo hechos los agujeros de las orejas.

pig [pɪg] noun

1. el **cerdo**: they keep pigs on the farm crían cerdos en la granja

2. el **glotón** (plural los **glotones**), la **glotona**: you greedy pig! ¡mira que eres glotón!

pigeon ['pɪdʒɪn] noun ■ la **paloma**.

piggyback ['pɪgɪbæk] adjective

to give someone a piggyback llevar a alguien a caballo: he gave me a piggyback me llevó a caballo.

piggybank ['pɪgɪbæŋk] noun ■ la **hucha en forma de cerdito**.

pigtail ['pɪgteɪl] noun ■ la **coleta**: she wears her hair in pigtails lleva coletas.

pile [paɪl] (noun & verb)

■ noun

el **montón** (plural los **montones**): she left her clothes in a pile on the floor dejó su ropa en un montón en el suelo; there was a pile of books on his desk había un montón de libros en su escritorio

■ verb

amontonar, apilar: he neatly piled his clothes on the bed amontonó cuidadosamente la ropa sobre la cama

pile into phrasal verb ■ **meterse**: we all piled into the van nos metimos todos en la furgoneta

pile up phrasal verb ■ **amontonarse**: the dirty plates are piling up in the sink los platos sucios se están amontonando en el fregadero.

pill [pɪl] noun ■ la **píldora**: he swallowed the pill se tragó la píldora.

pillar ['pɪlər] noun ■ el **pilar**: tall marble pillars held up the roof grandes pilares de mármol sostenían el techo.

pillow ['pɪləʊ] noun ■ la **almohada**.

pillowcase ['pɪləʊkeɪs] noun ■ la **funda de almohada**.

pilot ['paɪlət] noun ■ el/la **piloto**: Ted's father is a pilot el padre de Ted es piloto.

pimple ['pɪmpəl] noun ■ el **grano**: there's a pimple on my nose! ¡tengo un grano en la nariz!

pin [pɪn] (noun & verb)

■ noun

el **alfiler**: she pricked her finger with a pin se pinchó el dedo con un alfiler

■ verb

prender: he had a rose pinned in his buttonhole tenía una rosa prendida en el ojal

she pinned a sign on the noticeboard puso un letrero en el tablón de anuncios.

PIN [pɪn] (abbreviation of personal identification number) noun ■ el **número de identificación personal**.

pinch [pɪntʃ] verb

1. **pellizcar**: she pinched me on the arm me pellizcó el brazo

2. UK informal **birlar**: somebody has pinched my bike alguien me ha birlado la bici.

pine [paɪn] noun ■ el **pino**

a pine tree un pino.

pineapple ['paɪnæpl] noun ■ la **piña**.

pink [pɪŋk] adjective ■ **rosa**: she's wearing a pink skirt lleva una falda rosa

bright pink rosa brillante.

pint [paɪnt] noun

1. la **pinta**: it costs 90 pence a pint va a 90 peniques la pinta

2. *UK* la **cerveza:** I'm going to have a pint me voy a tomar una cerveza.

pipe [paɪp] *noun*

1. la **cañería:** the pipes are frozen las cañerías están congeladas

2. la **pipa:** he smokes a pipe fuma en pipa.

pirate ['paɪrət] *noun* ■ el/la **pirata.**

pistol ['pɪstl] *noun* ■ la **pistola.**

pitch *UK* [pɪtʃ] *(plural* pitches*) noun* ■ el **campo:** a football pitch un campo de fútbol.

pitcher *US* ['pɪtʃəʳ] *noun* ■ la **jarra.**

pity ['pɪtɪ] *(noun & verb)*

■ *noun*

1. la **compasión:** she did it out of pity lo hizo por compasión

2. la **lástima:** what a pity! ¡qué lástima!; it's a pity you didn't see it es una lástima que no lo hayas visto

Use a verb in the subjunctive after **lástima que.**

> she took pity on them se compadeció de ellos

■ *verb*

compadecer: I pity him lo compadezco.

pizza ['piːtsə] *noun* ■ la **pizza**

> a pizza parlour una pizzería.

place [pleɪs] *(noun & verb)*

■ *noun*

1. el **lugar:** what is your place of birth? ¿cuál es su lugar de nacimiento?

2. el **sitio:** can you save me a place? ¿podrías guardarme un sitio?; a parking place un sitio para aparcar

3. el **puesto:** they took first place in the tournament obtuvieron el primer puesto en el torneo

> my place mi casa

> to change places cambiar el sitio: can I change places with you? ¿me cambias el sitio?

> to take place tener lugar: when did the game take place? ¿cuándo tuvo lugar el partido?

> all over the place por todas partes: he spilled milk all over the place derramó leche por todas partes

■ *verb*

poner: place your hands on the table pon las manos sobre la mesa.

plain [pleɪn] *(adjective & noun)*

■ *adjective*

1. **sencillo:** he's wearing a plain blue tie lleva una sencilla corbata azul; he likes his food plain le gusta la comida sencilla

2. **liso:** a plain blue blouse una blusa azul lisa

3. **claro:** it's plain that he's lying está claro que está mintiendo

4. **poco agraciado:** she's rather plain es bastante poco agraciada

> plain yogurt yogur natural

■ *noun*

la **llanura:** the battle took place on the plain la batalla tuvo lugar en la llanura.

plait [plæt] *noun* ■ la **trenza:** Jane wears plaits Jane lleva trenzas.

plan [plæn] *(noun & verb)*

■ *noun*

1. el **plan:** what are your plans for the future? ¿qué planes tienes para el futuro?

2. el **plano:** she drew a plan of the house dibujó un plano de la casa

> to go according to plan salir según lo previsto: everything went according to plan todo salió según lo previsto

■ *verb*

planear: they're planning a surprise party están planeando una fiesta sorpresa

> to plan to do something tener planeado hacer algo: I'm planning to go to Europe tengo planeado ir a Europa.

plane [pleɪn] *noun* ■ el **avión** *(plural* los **aviones***):* John has his own plane John tiene su propio avión.

planet ['plænɪt] *noun* ■ el **planeta.**

plant [*UK* plɑːnt , *US* plænt] *(noun & verb)*

■ *noun*

la **planta:** I forgot to water the plants olvidé regar las plantas

■ *verb*

plantar: we are going to plant an apple tree vamos a plantar un manzano.

plaster [UK ˈplɑːstəʳ, US ˈplæstəʳ] noun
la **escayola**: his arm is in plaster lleva el brazo escayolado
▸ la **tirita**: he had a plaster on his finger llevaba una tirita en el dedo.

plastic [ˈplæstɪk] (adjective & noun)
■ adjective
de **plástico**: a plastic bag una bolsa de plástico
■ noun
el **plástico**: it's made out of plastic es de plástico.

plate [pleɪt] noun ■ el **plato**: the plates are in the cupboard los platos están en el armario; a plate of spaghetti un plato de espaguetis.

platform [ˈplætfɔːm] noun
▸ el **andén** (plural los **andenes**): the passengers are waiting on platform 2 los pasajeros esperan en el andén 2
2. la **tarima**: there was a platform for the band había una tarima para la banda.

play [pleɪ] (noun & verb)
■ noun
la **obra de teatro**: she's acting in the school play actúa en la obra de teatro del colegio; Macbeth is a play by Shakespeare Macbeth es una obra de Shakespeare
■ verb
1. **jugar**: they're playing in the park están jugando en el parque; do you want to play chess? ¿quieres jugar al ajedrez?
2. **tocar**: can you play the guitar? ¿tocas la guitarra?
3. **poner**: let's play a CD pongamos un CD
4. **interpretar**: the part of the Queen was played by her daughter su hija interpretó el papel de reina
▸ to play a part in something desempeñar un papel en algo: she played an important part in the negotiations desempeñó un papel importante en las negociaciones.

player [ˈpleɪəʳ] noun ■ el **jugador,** la **jugadora**: he's a football player es jugador de fútbol
▸ a piano player un pianista.

playful [ˈpleɪfʊl] adjective ■ **juguetón** (feminine **juguetona**): the kitten is very playful el gatito es muy juguetón.

playground [ˈpleɪgraʊnd] noun
1. UK el **patio**: the teacher supervised the students in the playground el profesor vigilaba a los estudiantes en el patio
2. los **columpios**: we went to the playground in the park fuimos a los columpios del parque.

play-off [ˈpleɪɒf] noun ■ el **desempate**.

plead [pliːd] (past tense pleaded OR US pled) verb ■ **suplicar**: I pleaded with him not to go le supliqué que no fuera
▸ to plead guilty/not guilty declararse culpable/inocente: the prisoner pleaded guilty to murder el preso se declaró culpable del asesinato

pleasant [ˈpleznt] adjective ■ **agradable**: we spent a pleasant day at the beach pasamos un día agradable en la playa.

please [pliːz] (adverb & verb)
■ adverb
por favor: can you tell me the time, please? ¿puede decirme la hora, por favor?; please, tell me! ¡por favor, dímelo!
■ verb
complacer: you can't please all the people all the time no puedes complacer siempre a todo el mundo
▸ please yourself! ¡como quieras!, ¡tú mismo!

pleased [pliːzd] adjective ■ **contento**: she's not very pleased no está muy contenta
▸ pleased to meet you! ¡encantado de conocerte!

pleasure [ˈpleʒəʳ] noun ■ el **placer**: she reads for pleasure lee por placer; it's a pleasure to meet you es un placer conocerte
▸ my pleasure! ¡no hay de qué!: thank you for your help — my pleasure! gracias por la ayuda –¡no hay de qué!
▸ with pleasure con mucho gusto.

plenty [ˈplentɪ] pronoun ■ **de sobra**: we have plenty of time hay tiempo de sobra
▸ there's plenty to eat hay mucha comida
▸ that's plenty es suficiente.

pliers ['plaɪərz] *noun* ■ los **alicates**: use the pliers to bend the end of the wire usa los alicates para doblar la punta del alambre.

plot [plɒt] *(noun & verb)*
■ *noun*
1. la **conspiración** *(plural* las **conspiraciones)*: the plot to kill the president failed fracasó la conspiración para matar al presidente
2. el **argumento**: the film has a complicated plot la película tiene un argumento complejo
■ *verb (past tense & past participle* plotted, *present participle* plotting)*
   conspirar: they're plotting against the king están conspirando contra el rey.

plough *UK,* **plow** *US* [plaʊ] *(noun & verb)*
■ *noun*
   el **arado**
■ *verb*
   arar.

plug [plʌg] *noun*
1. el **enchufe**: put the plug back in the socket vuelve a conectar el enchufe
2. el **tapón** *(plural* los **tapones)**: I pulled the plug out of the sink saqué el tapón del fregadero

plug in *phrasal verb (past tense & past participle* plugged in, *present participle* plugging in)* ■ **enchufar**: she plugged the television in enchufó la televisión.

plum [plʌm] *noun* ■ la **ciruela.**

plumber ['plʌmə^r] *noun* ■ el **fontanero**: he's a plumber es fontanero.

plural ['plʊərəl] *noun* ■ el **plural**: in the plural en plural.

plus [plʌs] *preposition* ■ **más**: 10 plus 5 equals 15 10 más 5 es igual a 15
   a plus sign el signo de más, el signo positivo.

p.m. [ˌpiː'em] *adverb*
1. de la tarde: at 3 p.m. a las 3 de la tarde
2. de la noche: at 8 p.m. a las 8 de la noche.

pocket ['pɒkɪt] *noun* ■ el **bolsillo**
   pocket money la paga.

pocketbook ['pɒkɪtbʊk] *noun*
1. el **cuaderno de notas**
2. *US* la **cartera.**

poem ['pəʊɪm] *noun* ■ el **poema.**

poet ['pəʊɪt] *noun* ■ el **poeta,** la **poetisa.**

poetry ['pəʊɪtrɪ] *noun* ■ la **poesía**: do you like poetry? ¿te gusta la poesía?

point [pɔɪnt] *(noun & verb)*
■ *noun*
1. la **punta**: she found a stick with a sharp point encontró un palo con una punta afilada
2. el **punto**: the point where the river divides el punto donde el río se divide; a meeting point un punto de encuentro; you get two points for each correct answer obtienes dos puntos por cada respuesta correcta
3. el **momento**: at that point, the police arrived en ese momento, llegó la policía
4. el **sentido**: what's the point of the game? ¿qué sentido tiene este juego?; I don't see the point of going no veo qué sentido tiene ir
> what's the point? ¿para qué?
> two point seven dos coma siete
> point of view punto de vista: what's your point of view? ¿cuál es tu punto de vista?
> to have a point tener un poco de razón: you have a good point there tienes un poco de razón en lo que dices
> to make a point of doing something asegurarse de hacer algo: I made a point of saying hello to her me aseguré de saludarla
> to get to the point ir al grano
> to miss the point no entender
■ *verb*
   señalar con el dedo: she pointed at the tower señaló la torre con el dedo
> he pointed the gun at the guard apuntó al guardia con el arma

point out *phrasal verb*
1. señalar: he pointed out the opera house to me me señaló el edificio de la ópera
2. indicar: he pointed out that no one had paid indicó que nadie había pagado.

pointed ['pɔɪntɪd] *adjective* ■ **puntiagudo**: he's wearing pointed shoes lleva puestos unos zapatos puntiagudos.

pointless ['pɔɪntlɪs] *adjective* ■ **inútil**: it's pointless to try again es inútil intentarlo de nuevo.

poison [ˈpɔɪzn] *(noun & verb)*
noun
el **veneno**: arsenic is a poison el arsénico es un veneno
verb
envenenar: she poisoned her husband envenenó a su marido.

poisonous [ˈpɔɪznəs] *adjective* ■ **venenoso**: these mushrooms are poisonous estas setas son venenosas.

poke [pəʊk] *verb*
she poked me in the ribs me dio un codazo en las costillas
she poked me in the eye me metió un dedo en el ojo.

polar bear [ˈpəʊləˈbeəʳ] *noun* ■ el **oso polar**.

pole [pəʊl] *noun*
1. el **poste**, el **palo**: he stuck a pole in the ground clavó un palo en el suelo; a telegraph pole un poste telegráfico
2. la **pértiga**: the pole vault el salto con pértiga
3. el **polo**: the North Pole el Polo norte; the South Pole el Polo Sur.

police [pəˈliːs] *plural noun* ■ la **policía**:
the police are on their way la policía está en camino
a police car un coche patrulla
a police officer un agente de policía
the police station la comisaría.

policeman [pəˈliːsmən] *(plural* policemen [pəˈliːsmən]*) noun* ■ el **policía**: he's a policeman es policía.

policewoman [pəˈliːsˌwʊmən] *(plural* policewomen [pəˈliːsˌwɪmɪn]*) noun* ■ la **policía**: she's a policewoman es policía.

polish [ˈpɒlɪʃ] *(noun & verb)*
■ *noun*
1. la **cera**: furniture polish cera para muebles
2. el **abrillantador**: floor polish abrillantador de suelos
nail polish esmalte de uñas
shoe polish betún
■ *verb*
limpiar: he's polishing his shoes se está limpiando los zapatos.

polite [pəˈlaɪt] *adjective* ■ **educado**: he's very polite es muy educado.

political [pəˈlɪtɪkl] *adjective* ■ **político**

POLITICAL PARTIES

En Gran Bretaña y en Estados Unidos hay menos partidos políticos que en España. En Gran Bretaña, los dos partidos mayoritarios son el **Conservative Party** (partido de los conservadores) y el **Labour Party** (partido de corte socialdemócrata). En Estados Unidos, los dos grandes partidos son el **Republican Party** (de tendencia conservadora y cuyo símbolo es un elefante) y el **Democratic Party** (de ideas más progresistas y con un asno como símbolo).

politician [ˌpɒlɪˈtɪʃn] *noun* ■ el **político**, la **política**: he's a politician es político.

politics [ˈpɒlətɪks] *noun* ■ la **política**: she's interested in politics le interesa la política.

poll [pəʊl] *noun* ■ la **encuesta**
an opinion poll una encuesta de opinión.

pollen [ˈpɒlən] *noun* ■ el **polen**.

pollute [pəˈluːt] *verb* ■ **contaminar**: they fine any factories that pollute the river multan a las industrias que contaminan el río.

pollution [pəˈluːʃn] *uncountable noun* ■ la **contaminación**: pollution is a serious problem in the city la contaminación es un problema serio en la ciudad
air pollution contaminación del aire.

polo neck UK [ˈpəʊləʊnek] *noun* ■ el **cuello alto**.

pomegranate [ˈpɒmɪˌɡrænɪt] *noun* ■ la **granada**.

pond [pɒnd] *noun* ■ el **estanque**.

pony [ˈpəʊnɪ] *(plural* ponies*) noun* ■ el **poni**.

ponytail [ˈpəʊnɪteɪl] *noun* ■ la **cola de caballo**: she put her hair in a ponytail se hizo una cola de caballo.

poodle [ˈpuːdl] *noun* ■ el **caniche**.

pool [puːl] *noun*
1. la **piscina**: he's swimming in the pool está nadando en la piscina

2. el **charco**: a pool of water formed under the pipes se formó un charco debajo de la cañería
3. el **billar americano**: they're playing pool están jugando al billar americano
   > the pools *UK* las quinielas.

poor [pɔːʳ] *adjective*
1. **pobre**: they are very poor son muy pobres; poor thing! I hope she'll be all right ¡pobre! espero que esté bien
2. **malo**: that's a poor excuse ésa es una mala excusa

   Malo becomes **mal** before a masculine singular noun:

   the weather has been poor ha hecho mal tiempo.

pop [pɒp] *(adjective, noun & verb)*
■ *adjective*
   pop: she used to play in a pop group solía tocar en un grupo pop
■ *noun*
1. la **música pop**: she likes listening to pop le gusta escuchar música pop
2. la **gaseosa**
3. *US informal* el **papá**
   > the balloon made a loud pop el globo hizo ¡pum!
■ *verb (past tense & past participle* popped, *present participle* popping)*
   reventar: he popped the balloon reventó el globo

pop by *phrasal verb* ■ Annie popped by last night Annie pasó por casa anoche

pop in *phrasal verb* ■ **pasar un momento**: I'll pop in and see you voy a pasar un momento a verte.

popcorn [ˈpɒpkɔːn] *uncountable noun* ■ las **palomitas de maíz**.

pope [pəʊp] *noun*
   > the Pope el Papa.

poppy [ˈpɒpɪ] *(plural* poppies) *noun* ■ la **amapola**.

popular [ˈpɒpjʊləʳ] *adjective* ■ **popular**: he's a very popular singer es un cantante muy popular

> Janet's very popular Janet le cae bien a todo el mundo.

population [ˌpɒpjʊˈleɪʃn] *noun* ■ la **población** *(plural* las **poblaciones**): what is the population of Scotland? ¿cuál es la población de Escocia?

porch [pɔːtʃ] *noun*
1. *US* el **porche**: let's sit outside on the porch sentémonos afuera en el porche
2. *UK* la **entrada**: leave your boots in the porch deja las botas en la entrada.

pork [pɔːk] *noun* ■ la **carne de cerdo**: we're having pork chops tonight hoy vamos a cenar chuletas de cerdo.

porridge [ˈpɒrɪdʒ] *uncountable noun* ■ las **gachas de avena**.

port [pɔːt] *noun*
1. el **puerto**: New York is a port Nueva York es un puerto
2. el **oporto**: a glass of port una copa de oporto.

portable [ˈpɔːtəbl] *adjective* ■ **portátil**: a portable TV un televisor portátil.

porter [ˈpɔːtəʳ] *noun*
1. *hotel* el **portero**, la **portera**: the porter carried our luggage el portero nos llevó el equipaje
2. *station* el **mozo de equipajes**, la **moza de equipajes**.

portion [ˈpɔːʃn] *noun* ■ la **porción** *(plural* las **porciones**), la **ración** *(plural* las **raciones**): they serve large portions at this restaurant sirven raciones abundantes en este restaurante.

portrait [ˈpɔːtreɪt] *noun* ■ el **retrato**: he painted a portrait of his father pintó un retrato de su padre.

posh [pɒʃ] *adjective*
1. **de lujo**: it's a posh hotel es un hotel de lujo
2. **pijo**: she has a posh accent tiene acento pijo.

position [pəˈzɪʃn] *noun*
1. la **posición** *(plural* las **posiciones**): he changed position cambió de posición; what position does Beckham play in? ¿en qué posición juega Beckham?

. la **situación** *(plural* las **situaciones***)*: I'm in a difficult position estoy en una situación difícil
to be in position estar en posición
to get into position ponerse en posición.

positive ['pɒzətɪv] *adjective*
. **positivo**: he has a positive attitude tiene una actitud positiva
.. **seguro**: I'm positive about it estoy seguro de eso.

possessions [pə'zeʃnz] *noun*
she took all her possessions with her se llevó todas sus pertenencias.

possibility [,pɒsə'bɪlətɪ] *(plural* possibilities*)* *noun* ■ la **posibilidad**: that's a possibility ésa es una posibilidad.

possible ['pɒsəbl] *adjective* ■ **posible**: is it possible to change the tickets? ¿es posible cambiar las entradas?
as soon as possible lo antes posible: come and see me as soon as possible ven a verme lo antes posible.

possibly ['pɒsəblɪ] *adverb* ■ **posiblemente, tal vez**: will you finish today? — possibly ¿vas a terminar hoy? —posiblemente
I can't possibly accept your money me es imposible aceptar tu dinero.

post [pəʊst] *(noun & verb)*
■ *noun*
1. el **poste**: the net is fixed between two posts la red está atada a dos postes
2. *UK* el **correo**: he sent it by post lo envió por correo; there's some post for you hay correo para ti
the post office la oficina de correos: where's the post office? ¿dónde está la oficina de correos?
■ *verb*
1. *UK* **echar al correo**: she posted the letter echó la carta al correo
2. **fijar**: he posted a sign on the door fijó un letrero en la puerta
3. **colgar**: he posted a message on the web site colgó un mensaje en el sitio web.

postbox *UK* ['pəʊstbɒks] *(plural* postboxes*)* *noun* ■ el **buzón**.

postcard ['pəʊstkɑːd] *noun* ■ la **postal**: I got a postcard from my friend recibí una postal de mi amigo.

postcode *UK* ['pəʊstkəʊd] *noun* ■ el **código postal**.

poster ['pəʊstər] *noun* ■ el **póster** *(plural* los pósters*)*: they put up posters advertising the concert pusieron pósters anunciando el concierto.

postman *UK* ['pəʊstmən] *(plural* postmen ['pəʊstmən]*)* *noun* ■ el **cartero**.

postpone [,pəʊst'pəʊn] *verb* ■ **aplazar**: the meeting has been postponed aplazaron la reunión.

potato [pə'teɪtəʊ] *(plural* potatoes*)* *noun* ■ la **patata**
potato crisps *UK* OR potato chips *US* las patatas fritas (de bolsa).

pottery ['pɒtərɪ] *noun* ■ la **cerámica**: I'm taking a pottery class this term estoy tomando clases de cerámica este trimestre; she has a collection of pottery tiene una colección de cerámica.

poultry ['pəʊltrɪ] *noun* ■ las **aves de corral**.

pound [paʊnd] *noun*
1. *(abbreviation* lb.*)* la **libra** *(453,6 gramos)*: it weighs about two pounds pesa alrededor de dos libras
2. *(abbreviation* £*)* la **libra (esterlina)**: a five-pound note un billete de cinco libras.

pour [pɔːr] *verb*
1. **echar**: she poured the water into the glass echó el agua en el vaso
2. **servir**: can you pour me a juice? ¿me puedes servir un zumo?
it's pouring with rain llueve a cántaros.

poverty ['pɒvətɪ] *noun* ■ la **pobreza**.

powder ['paʊdər] *noun* ■ el **polvo**
baby powder polvos de talco.

power ['pauə^r] *noun*

1. el **poder**: a new party is in power un nuevo partido ocupa el poder; they took power by force tomaron el poder por la fuerza
2. la **fuerza**: the power of the explosion knocked him off his feet la fuerza de la explosión lo tiró al suelo
3. la **electricidad**: there was a power cut hubo un apagón
4. la **energía**
> nuclear power la energía nuclear
> solar power la energía solar
> a power station una central eléctrica.

powerful ['pauəful] *adjective*

1. **poderoso**: a powerful nation una nación poderosa
2. **potente**: it's a very powerful computer es un ordenador muy potente.

practical ['præktɪkl] *adjective* ■ **práctico**: she's very practical es muy práctica.
> a practical joke una broma: he played a practical joke on his teacher le hizo una broma a la profesora.

practice ['præktɪs] *(noun & verb)*

■ *noun*

1. la **práctica**: she needs practice le falta práctica
2. el **entrenamiento**: I've got football practice tonight tengo entrenamiento de fútbol esta noche
3. el **bufete**: she joined our practice after law school pasó a ser parte de nuestro bufete después de licenciarse en derecho
> out of practice desentrenado: she's out of practice está desentrenada

■ *verb US*
➤ practise UK.

practise UK, **practice** US ['præktɪs] *verb*

1. **practicar**: she needs to practise more necesita practicar más
2. **entrenar**: the team practises every Saturday el equipo entrena todos los sábados.

praise [preɪz] *(uncountable noun & verb)*

■ *uncountable noun*
el **elogio**: you deserve all this praise te mereces todos estos elogios

■ *verb*
elogiar: they praised us for our work nos elogiaron por nuestro trabajo.

pram [præm] *noun* ■ el **cochecito de niño**.

prawn [prɔːn] *noun* ■ la **gamba**.

pray [preɪ] *verb* ■ **rezar**: they prayed to God le rezaron a Dios.

prayer [preə^r] *noun* ■ la **oración** *(plural* las **oraciones***)*: she was saying her prayers estaba rezando sus oraciones.

precaution [prɪ'kɔːʃn] *noun* ■ la **precaución** *(plural* las **precauciones***)*: we must take precautions tenemos que tomar precauciones.

precinct UK ['priːsɪŋkt] *noun*
> a pedestrian precinct una zona peatonal
> a shopping precinct una zona comercial.

precious ['preʃəs] *adjective*

1. **valioso**: water is a precious resource el agua es un recurso valioso
2. **precioso**: a precious stone una piedra preciosa
3. **querido**: my children are very precious to me mis hijos son lo más querido para mí.

precise [prɪ'saɪs] *adjective* ■ **preciso**: can you be more precise in describing the mugger? ¿puedes ser más preciso al describir al atracador?

precisely [prɪ'saɪslɪ] *adverb* ■ **exactamente**: tell us precisely what happened cuéntanos exactamente lo que sucedió.

predict [prɪ'dɪkt] *verb* ■ **predecir**: we can't predict the future no podemos predecir el futuro.

prefer [prɪ'fɜː^r] *(past tense & past participle* preferred, *present participle* preferring*) verb* ■ **preferir**: which one do you prefer? ¿cuál prefieres?; she prefers chicken to fish prefiere el pollo al pescado.

pregnant ['pregnənt] *adjective* ■ **embarazada**: she's seven months pregnant está embarazada de siete meses.

prehistoric [ˌpriːhɪ'stɒrɪk] *adjective* ■ **prehistórico**: prehistoric animals animales prehistóricos.

prejudice ['predʒʊdɪs] *noun* ■ el pre-juicio: he has a prejudice against women tiene prejuicios contra las mujeres; racial prejudice prejuicios raciales.

prejudiced ['predʒʊdɪst] *adjective* to be prejudiced against somebody tener prejuicios contra alguien: he was prejudiced against foreigners tenía prejuicios contra los extranjeros.

preparation [ˌprepəˈreɪʃn] *noun* ■ la preparación *(plural* las **preparaciones***)*: it takes a lot of preparation to get to that level necesitas mucha preparación para llegar a ese nivel

to make preparations for something hacer preparativos para algo: they're making preparations for their trip están haciendo preparativos para el viaje.

prepare [prɪˈpeəʳ] *verb*
1. preparar: she's preparing dinner está preparando la cena
2. prepararse: she's preparing for her exam se está preparando para el examen.

prepared [prɪˈpeəd] *adjective* ■ dis-puesto: are you prepared to do it? ¿estás dispuesto a hacerlo?; Harry was prepared for anything Harry estaba dispuesto a todo.

preposition [ˌprepəˈzɪʃn] *noun* ■ la preposición *(plural* las **preposiciones***)*.

prescription [prɪˈskrɪpʃn] *noun* ■ la re-ceta: the doctor gave me a prescription for the pills el médico me dio una receta para las pastillas

by prescription con receta médica: this medicine is only available by prescription este medicamento sólo se vende con receta médica.

present *(adjective, noun & verb)*
■ *adjective* ['preznt]
1. actual: in the present circumstances en las circunstancias actuales
2. presente: I was present at the meeting es-taba presente en la reunión

the present tense el tiempo presente: put the verb in the present tense pon el verbo en el tiempo presente

■ *noun* ['preznt]
1. el regalo: he gave me a birthday present me dio un regalo de cumpleaños
2. el presente: I try to enjoy the present trato de disfrutar el presente

at present en este momento: that colour is not available at present este color no está disponible en este momento
■ *verb* [prɪˈzent]
1. presentar: she presents a quiz show pre-senta un concurso televisivo
2. entregar: they presented her with a medal le entregaron una medalla.

presenter UK [prɪˈzentəʳ] *noun* ■ el pre-sentador, la **presentadora**: he's a tele-vision presenter es presentador de televisión.

president ['prezɪdənt] *noun* ■ el **presi-dente**, la **presidenta**: he's the president of the United States es el presidente de los Es-tados Unidos.

press [pres] *(noun & verb)*
■ *noun*
la prensa: the press followed her every move la prensa seguía todos sus movimientos
■ *verb*
apretar: you have to press the button tienes que apretar el botón; the potter pressed down on the clay el ceramista apretaba la arcilla.

press-up UK ['presʌp] *noun* ■ la flexión: he does ten press-ups every day hace diez flexiones cada día.

pressure ['preʃəʳ] *noun* ■ la presión *(plu-ral* las **presiones***)*: she's under pressure está bajo presión

to put pressure on somebody presionar a alguien.

presume [UK prɪˈzjuːm, US prɪˈzuːm] *verb* ■ suponer: I presume you're right supongo que tienes razón.

pretend [prɪˈtend] *verb* ■ fingir: I was just pretending sólo estaba fingiendo; he pretended to be surprised fingió estar sor-prendido

⚠ La palabra inglesa **pretend** es un fal-so amigo, no significa "pretender".

pretty ['prɪtɪ] *(adjective & adverb)*

■ *adjective*

bonito: what a pretty dress! ¡qué vestido más bonito!

■ *adverb*

bastante: the book was pretty good el libro era bastante bueno.

prevent [prɪ'vent] *verb* ■ **impedir**

> to prevent someone from doing something impedir que alguien haga algo: she tried to prevent me from coming in trató de impedir que entrara

The verb following **impedir que** must be in the subjunctive.

previous ['priːvjəs] *adjective*

1. **anterior:** they refer to the subject in the previous paragraph se hace referencia al tema en el párrafo anterior

2. **previo:** they have no previous experience no tienen experiencia previa.

prey [preɪ] *noun* ■ **la presa**

> a bird of prey un ave rapaz.

price [praɪs] *noun* ■ **el precio:** what price did you pay? ¿qué precio pagaste?

> a price tag una etiqueta de precio

> the price list la lista de precios.

prick [prɪk] *verb* ■ **pincharse:** she pricked her finger se pinchó el dedo.

prickly ['prɪklɪ] *adjective* ■ **espinoso:** this is a prickly cactus éste es un cactus espinoso.

pride [praɪd] *uncountable noun* ■ **el orgullo:** she looked at her daughter with pride miró a su hija con orgullo; it hurt his pride hirió su orgullo

> to take pride in somebody OR something estar orgulloso de alguien o de algo: she takes pride in her daughter está orgullosa de su hija.

priest [priːst] *noun* ■ **el sacerdote:** he's a priest es sacerdote.

primary ['praɪmərɪ] *adjective* ■ **primario:** a primary school una escuela primaria.

prime minister [praɪm'mɪnɪstər] *noun* ■ **el primer ministro, la primera ministra.**

prince [prɪns] *noun* ■ **el príncipe:** the Prince of Wales el príncipe de Gales; Prince Charming el príncipe azul.

princess [prɪn'ses] *noun* ■ **la princesa.**

principal ['prɪnsəpl] *(adjective & noun)*

■ *adjective*

principal: that's the principal reason ésa es la razón principal

■ *noun*

el director: the teacher sent him to the principal's office la profesora lo mandó a la oficina del director.

principle ['prɪnsəpl] *noun* ■ **el principio:** lying goes against my principles mentir va en contra de mis principios.

print [prɪnt] *(noun & verb)*

■ *noun*

1. **la letra:** the sign was written in large print el letrero estaba escrito en letras grandes

2. **la copia:** I want to make a print from the negative quiero sacar una copia del negativo

3. **la huella:** the police took his prints la policía le tomó las huellas

■ *verb*

1. **imprimir:** I printed the letter imprimí la carta

2. **escribir con letra de imprenta, escribir con mayúsculas:** print your name escriba su nombre con letra de imprenta.

printer ['prɪntər] *noun* ■ **la impresora:** turn the printer on enciende la impresora.

prison ['prɪzn] *noun* ■ **la cárcel:** he's in prison está en la cárcel

> they sent him to prison lo encarcelaron.

prisoner ['prɪznər] *noun* ■ **el prisionero:** he was taken prisoner lo hicieron prisionero

> a prisoner of war un prisionero de guerra.

private ['praɪvɪt] *(adjective & noun)*

■ *adjective*

privado: he doesn't talk much about his private life no habla mucho sobre su vida privada; he flew in on his private jet voló en su avión privado; can we discuss this somewhere more private? ¿podemos discutir esto en algún lugar más privado?

> a private detective un detective privado

private property propiedad privada
a private school un colegio privado

■ *noun*

el **soldado**: Private Jones el soldado Jones
in private en privado: **I need to talk to you
in private** tengo que hablarte en privado.

privately ['praɪvɪtlɪ] *adverb* ■ **en privado:**
she told me privately me lo contó en privado.

privilege ['prɪvɪlɪdʒ] *noun* ■ el **privilegio:**
it's a real privilege to be here tonight es un
verdadero privilegio estar aquí esta noche.

prize [praɪz] *noun* ■ el **premio: she won
first prize** ganó el primer premio.

prizewinner ['praɪzˌwɪnər] *noun*
1. el **ganador, la ganadora: a lottery prizewinner** el ganador de la lotería
2. el **premio: he was the Nobel prizewinner
in 2004** obtuvo el premio Nobel en 2004.

probably ['prɒbəblɪ] *adverb* ■ **probablemente: he'll probably come tonight** probablemente venga esta noche; **are you going?
– probably not** ¿vas a ir? –probablemente no.

problem ['prɒbləm] *noun* ■ el **problema: what's the problem?** ¿algún problema?; **the roadworks are likely to cause
problems** es probable que las obras en la
carretera causen problemas
no problem! ¡no hay ningún problema!

process ['prəʊses] *(noun & verb)*

■ *noun*

el **proceso: the peace process** el proceso de
paz
to be in the process of doing something
estar haciendo algo
she's in the process of painting the house
está pintando la casa

■ *verb*

**procesar: the computer can process a lot
of data** el ordenador puede procesar muchos
datos.

produce [UK prə'djuːs, US prə'duːs] *verb*
■ **producir: these toys are produced in
China** en China producen estos juguetes.

producer [UK prə'djuːsər, US prə'duːsər]
noun ■ el **productor, la productora: he's a**

television producer es productor de televisión.

product ['prɒdʌkt] *noun* ■ el **producto:
they're bringing out a new product** van a
sacar un nuevo producto.

production [prə'dʌkʃn] *noun* ■ la **producción** *(plural* las **producciones)**: **the new
machines will increase production** las
nuevas máquinas aumentarán la producción;
the film is a multinational production la
película es una producción multinacional.

profession [prə'feʃn] *noun* ■ la **profesión** *(plural* las **profesiones)**: **what is your
profession?** ¿cuál es tu profesión?

professional [prə'feʃənl] *(adjective & noun)*

■ *adjective*

**profesional: he's a professional photo-
grapher** es fotógrafo profesional

■ *noun*

el/la **profesional: we hired a professional
to install the lighting** contratamos a un profesional para instalar la iluminación.

professor [prə'fesər] *noun* ■ el **cate-
drático, la catedrática: she's a professor
at Cambridge** es catedrática en Cambridge.

profit ['prɒfɪt] *noun* ■ la **ganancia,** el
beneficio: they made large profits obtuvieron grandes ganancias.

program ['prəʊgræm] *(noun & verb)*

■ *noun*

1. el **programa: a computer program** un programa informático
2. US ➤ programme UK

■ *verb (past tense & past participle* programmed,
present participle programming)
**programar: do you know how to program a
computer?** ¿sabes programar un ordenador?

programme UK, **program** US
['prəʊgræm] *noun* ■ el **programa: a TV programme** un programa de televisión; **I picked
up a programme before the performance**
cogí un programa antes de la función.

progress ['prəʊgres] *uncountable noun* ■
el **progreso: we made good progress on
our project** hicimos bastantes progresos en
nuestro proyecto.

project [ˈprɒdʒekt] *noun* ■ el **proyecto**:
we're doing a project on rainforests estamos
haciendo un proyecto sobre la selva tropical

> a housing project *US* un complejo de vi-
viendas sociales.

prom [prɑː] *US noun* ■ *baile de fin de curso
de las escuelas secundarias*

PROM

 Prom es el baile formal que se celebra cada primavera en las escuelas
secundarias de Estados Unidos. Es sin duda el
evento social más importante del año escolar.
Muchos jóvenes se ponen sus mejores galas y
alquilan limusinas para esa noche.

promise [ˈprɒmɪs] *(noun & verb)*

■ *noun*
la **promesa**: Jane kept her promise Jane
cumplió su promesa

■ *verb*
prometer: I promised to help her prometí
ayudarla.

promote [prəˈməʊt] *verb*

1. **promocionar**: he's promoting his new film
está promocionando su nueva película

2. **ascender**

> to be promoted ser ascendido: I've been
promoted to vice-president me han ascendido a vicepresidente.

promotion [prəˈməʊʃn] *noun* ■ el **ascenso**: she got promotion at work obtuvo
un ascenso en el trabajo.

pronoun [ˈprəʊnaʊn] *noun* ■ el
pronombre: "he" is a personal pronoun
"él" es un pronombre personal.

pronunciation [prəˌnʌnsɪˈeɪʃn] *noun* ■
la **pronunciación** *(plural* las **pronuncia-
ciones)*: her pronunciation is very good su
pronunciación es muy buena.

proof [pruːf] *uncountable noun* ■ la **prueba**: do you have any proof? ¿tienes alguna
prueba?

proper [ˈprɒpəʳ] *adjective* ■ **correcto**: I'll
show you the proper way to do it te en-
señaré la manera correcta de hacerlo.

properly [ˈprɒpəlɪ] *adverb* ■ **correctamente**: you're not doing it properly no lo
estás haciendo correctamente.

property [ˈprɒpətɪ] *(plural* **properties)**
noun ■ la **propiedad**: the sign says "private
property" el cartel dice "propiedad privada"

> personal property bienes personales
> public property propiedad pública.

proposal [prəˈpəʊzl] *noun* ■ la **propuesta**: she made a proposal to the committee
hizo una nueva propuesta al comité; she accepted his marriage proposal aceptó su
propuesta de matrimonio.

propose [prəˈpəʊz] *verb* ■ **proponer**:
he's proposing a new way of doing things
propone una nueva manera de hacer las cosas

> to propose to someone proponerle matri-
monio a alguien: he proposed to her at the
restaurant le propuso matrimonio en el
restaurante.

prospects [ˈprɒspekts] *plural noun* ■ **perspectivas**: the job has good future prospects
el empleo ofrece buenas perspectivas de futuro.

protect [prəˈtekt] *verb* ■ **proteger**: a
helmet will protect you if you fall un casco
te protegerá si te caes.

protection [prəˈtekʃn] *noun* ■ la **protección**: a society for the protection of birds
una asociación para la protección de las aves.

protein [ˈprəʊtiːn] *noun* ■ la **proteína**.

protest *(noun & verb)*

■ *noun* [ˈprəʊtest]
la **protesta**: she did it as a sign of protest
lo hizo en señal de protesta

■ *verb* [prəˈtest]
protestar: many people are protesting
against the new law mucha gente está
protestando contra la nueva ley.

Protestant [ˈprɒtɪstənt] *(noun & adjective)*

■ *noun*
el/la **protestante**

■ *adjective*
protestante.

proud [praʊd] *adjective* ■ **orgulloso**: he's
proud of his son está orgulloso de su hijo.

prove [pruːv] *(past tense* proved OR proven*) verb* ■ **probar:** I can't prove he's lying no puedo probar que miente.

proverb [ˈprɒvɜːb] *noun* ■ **el refrán.**

provide [prəˈvaɪd] *verb* to provide something for someone proporcionarle algo a alguien: they provided a home for the refugees proporcionaron un hogar a los refugiados.

provided [prəˈvaɪdɪd] *conjunction* ■ **siempre que:** she'll do the work provided they pay her hará el trabajo siempre que le paguen

The verb following **siempre que** must be in the subjunctive.

prune [pruːn] *noun* ■ **la ciruela pasa.**

pseudonym [ˈsjuːdənɪm] *noun* ■ **el seudónimo.**

psychiatrist [saɪˈkaɪətrɪst] *noun* ■ **el/la psiquiatra:** she's a psychiatrist es psiquiatra.

psychologist [saɪˈkɒlədʒɪst] *noun* ■ **el psicólogo, la psicóloga:** he's a psychologist es psicólogo.

pub UK [pʌb] *noun* ■ **el bar.**

public [ˈpʌblɪk] *(adjective & noun)* ■ *adjective*
público: this is a public place éste es un lugar público
a public holiday UK un día festivo
public opinion la opinión pública
a public school
1. UK una escuela privada
2. US una escuela pública
public transport el transporte público
■ *noun*
the public el público: the museum isn't open to the public today el museo no está abierto al público hoy
in public en público: I don't like singing in public no me gusta cantar en público.

publicity [pʌbˈlɪsɪtɪ] *uncountable noun* ■ **la publicidad:** her new video got a lot of publicity su nuevo video tuvo mucha publicidad.

publish [ˈpʌblɪʃ] *verb* ■ **publicar.**

pudding [ˈpʊdɪŋ] *noun*
1. UK el **postre:** what's for pudding? ¿qué hay de postre?
2. el **budín** *(plural* los **budines***),* el **pudín** *(plural* los **pudines***):* chocolate pudding budín de chocolate
rice pudding el arroz con leche.

puddle [ˈpʌdl] *noun* ■ **el charco.**

puff [pʌf] *verb* ■ **resoplar:** he was puffing and panting resoplaba y jadeaba.

pull [pʊl] *verb*
1. **tirar:** don't pull so hard no tires tan fuerte
2. **tirar de:** he pulled her hair le tiró del pelo; she was pulling on the rope tiraba de la cuerda

pull down *phrasal verb*
1. **bajar:** pull the blind down baja la persiana
2. **derribar:** they pulled down the old building derribaron el viejo edificio

pull into *phrasal verb* ■ **llegar:** the train pulled into the station el tren llegó a la estación

pull out *phrasal verb* ■ **sacar:** he pulled something out of his pocket sacó algo del bolsillo; the dentist pulled his tooth out el dentista le sacó el diente

pull through *phrasal verb* ■ **recuperarse:** don't worry, she'll pull through no te preocupes, se recuperará

pull up *phrasal verb*
1. **subirse:** he pulled his socks up se subió los calcetines
2. **parar:** a car pulled up in front of the house un coche paró frente a la casa.

pullover [ˈpʊl,əʊvəʳ] *noun* ■ **el jersey.**

pulse [pʌls] *noun* ■ **el pulso:** the doctor took my pulse el doctor me tomó el pulso.

pump [pʌmp] *(noun & verb)*
■ *noun*
la **bomba:** a bicycle pump una bomba de bicicleta
a petrol pump UK OR a gas pump US un surtidor de gasolina
■ *verb*

bombear: he pumped the water out of the pond sacó bombeando el agua del estanque

pump up *phrasal verb* ■ **inflar:** he's pumping up the tyres está inflando las ruedas.

pumpkin ['pʌmpkɪn] *noun* ■ la **calabaza:** a pumpkin pie una tarta de calabaza.

punch [pʌntʃ] *(noun & verb)*
■ *noun*
1. el **puñetazo:** he knocked me out with a single punch me dejó inconsciente de un solo puñetazo
2. el **ponche:** a glass of punch un vaso de ponche
■ *verb*
1. **darle un puñetazo a:** she punched him le dio un puñetazo
2. **picar:** the inspector punched my ticket el inspector me picó el billete.

punctuation [ˌpʌŋktʃʊ'eɪʃn] *noun* ■ la **puntuación** *(plural* las **puntuaciones***)*: punctuation marks signos de puntuación.

puncture *UK* ['pʌŋktʃə^r] *noun* ■ el **pinchazo**
to have a puncture tener un pinchazo.

punish ['pʌnɪʃ] *verb* ■ **castigar:** they punished him for staying out all night lo castigaron por pasar toda la noche fuera.

punishment ['pʌnɪʃmənt] *noun* ■ el **castigo:** your punishment will be to wash up for a week tu castigo será lavar los platos durante una semana.

pupil ['pjuːpl] *noun*
1. el **alumno,** la **alumna:** there are 600 pupils in the school hay 600 alumnos en el colegio
2. la **pupila:** the doctor looked at his pupils el médico le miró las pupilas.

puppet ['pʌpɪt] *noun* ■ el **títere:** a puppet show un espectáculo de títeres.

puppy ['pʌpɪ] *(plural* puppies*)* noun* ■ el **cachorro:** our dog had puppies nuestra perra tuvo cachorros.

purchase ['pɜːtʃəs] *(noun & verb)*
■ *noun*
la **compra:** she showed me her newest purchase me enseñó su última compra

■ *verb*
comprar: they purchased a new car compraron un coche nuevo.

pure [pjʊə^r] *adjective* ■ **puro:** she studies pure maths estudia matemáticas puras; it was pure coincidence fue pura coincidencia
pure silk seda natural.

purple ['pɜːpl] *adjective* ■ **morado.**

purpose ['pɜːpəs] *noun* ■ el **propósito:** what is the purpose of your visit? ¿cuál es el propósito de su visita?
on purpose a propósito: I didn't do it on purpose no lo hice a propósito.

purr [pɜː^r] *verb* ■ **ronronear:** the cat purred happily el gato ronroneó alegremente.

purse [pɜːs] *noun*
1. *UK* el **monedero**
2. *US* el **bolso.**

push [pʊʃ] *verb*
1. **empujar:** she pushed the door open empujó la puerta para abrirla; we had to push the car tuvimos que empujar el coche
2. **pulsar:** I pushed the button pulse el botón

push in *phrasal verb* ■ **colarse:** there was a long queue so they pushed in había mucha cola y se colaron.

pushchair *UK* ['pʊʃtʃeə^r] *noun* ■ la **silla de paseo (de niño).**

push-up [pʊʃʌp] *noun* ■ la **flexión de brazos** *(plural* las **flexiones de brazos***)*: he does 100 push-ups a day hace 100 flexiones de brazos al día.

put [pʊt] *(past tense & past participle* put*) verb*
1. **poner:** put the plates on the table pon los platos en la mesa; put it over there ponlo allí
2. **decir:** I don't know how to put it no sé cómo decirlo
3. **invertir:** Bob put a lot of money into the project Bob invirtió mucho dinero en el proyecto
he put his arm around her la rodeó con un brazo

put away *phrasal verb* ■ **guardar:** she put all her things away guardó todas sus cosas

put back *phrasal verb* ■ **volver a poner en su lugar**: put the scissors back when you've finished with them vuelve a poner las tijeras en su lugar cuando hayas terminado

put down *phrasal verb* ■ **soltar**: he put the gun down soltó el arma
to put the phone down **colgar**: he put the phone down on me me colgó el teléfono

put off *phrasal verb*

. **aplazar**: the party has been put off la fiesta ha sido aplazada; she's putting off the decision está aplazando la decisión

. **disuadir**: she tried to put him off taking the job trató de disuadirle de su intención de aceptar el trabajo

. **apagar**: she put the TV off apagó el televisor
it put me off mussels for life hizo que me dejaran de gustar los mejillones para siempre

put on *phrasal verb*

. **ponerse**: she put her hat on se puso el sombrero

. **encender**: I'll put the light on voy a encender la luz

. **representar**: we're putting on a Christmas show estamos representando un espectáculo navideño

. *informal* **tomar el pelo**: you're putting me on me estás tomando el pelo
I've put on weight he engordado
to put the brakes on frenar

put out *phrasal verb*

. **apagar**: put the lights out apaga las luces

. **tender**: he put his hand out tendió la mano

. **sacar**: I'll put out the rubbish voy a sacar la basura

. **molestar**: will it put you out if we change the meeting to Monday? ¿te molesta si cambiamos la reunión para el lunes?
to be put out estar molesto

put up *phrasal verb*

. **montar**: where shall we put the tent up? ¿dónde montamos la tienda?

. **colgar**: Perry put some posters up on his bedroom wall Perry colgó algunos pósters en la pared de su dormitorio

3. *UK* **subir**: they've put the prices up han subido los precios

4. **alojar**: can you put me up for the night? ¿podéis alojarme esta noche?
to put one's hand up **levantar la mano**: put your hand up if you know the answer levantad la mano si sabéis la respuesta

put up with *phrasal verb* ■ **aguantar**: I won't put up with this kind of behaviour no voy a aguantar este tipo de comportamiento.

puzzle ['pʌzl] *noun*

. el **misterio**: her disappearance remains a puzzle su desaparición sigue siendo un misterio

. el **rompecabezas** *(plural* los **rompecabezas)**: he played with a puzzle on the floor jugaba con un rompecabezas en el suelo
a crossword puzzle un crucigrama
a jigsaw puzzle un rompecabezas.

puzzled ['pʌzld] *adjective* ■ **perplejo**: I was puzzled by her comments me quedé perplejo con sus comentarios.

pyjamas *UK,* **pajamas** *US* [pə'dʒɑːməz] *plural noun* ■ el **pijama**: he was still in his pyjamas todavía estaba en pijama
a pair of pyjamas un pijama.

pyramid ['pɪrəmɪd] *noun* ■ la **pirámide**.

quack [kwæk] *verb* ■ **graznar**.

qualification [ˌkwɒlɪfɪ'keɪʃn] *noun* ■ el **título**: list your academic qualifications enumere sus títulos académicos.

qualified ['kwɒlɪfaɪd] *adjective* ■ **titulado:** he's a qualified teacher es un profesor titulado.

qualify ['kwɒlɪfaɪ] *(past tense & past participle* qualified*) verb*
1. **sacarse el título:** she qualified as a nurse in May se sacó el título de enfermera en mayo
2. **clasificarse:** our team qualified for the championship nuestro equipo se clasificó para el campeonato.

quality ['kwɒlətɪ] *(plural* qualities*) noun*
1. **la cualidad:** she has many good qualities tiene muchas buenas cualidades
2. **la calidad:** our products are of the finest quality nuestros productos son de la mejor calidad.

quantity ['kwɒntətɪ] *(plural* quantities*) noun* ■ **la cantidad:** he has a large quantity of books tiene una gran cantidad de libros.

quarrel ['kwɒrəl] *(noun & verb)*
■ *noun*
la **pelea:** they had a quarrel tuvieron una pelea
■ *verb (past tense & past participle UK* quarrelled OR *US* quarreled, *present participle UK* quarrelling OR *US* quarreling)
pelear: we quarrelled all morning peleamos toda la mañana.

quart ['kwɔːt] *noun* ■ **el cuarto de galón** *(UK = 1,14 litros; US = 0,95 litros)*.

quarter ['kwɔːtəʳ] *noun*
1. **el cuarto:** he ate a quarter of the cake se comió un cuarto del pastel; a quarter of an hour un cuarto de hora; three quarters of an hour tres cuartos de hora; it's a quarter past two *UK* OR it's a quarter after two *US* son las dos y cuarto; it's a quarter to six son las seis menos cuarto
2. *US* **la moneda de 25 centavos:** this candy costs a quarter este caramelo cuesta 25 centavos.

quarter final ['kwɔːtəʳˌfaɪnl] *noun* ■ **los cuartos de final.**

quay [kiː] *noun* ■ **el muelle.**

queasy ['kwiːzɪ] *adjective* ■ **mareado** to feel queasy tener náuseas.

queen [kwiːn] *noun* ■ **la reina:** the Queen of England la reina de Inglaterra; the Queen Mother la reina madre.

query ['kwɪərɪ] *(plural* queries*) noun* ■ **la pregunta:** do you have any queries? ¿tienes alguna pregunta?

question ['kwestʃn] *(noun & verb)*
■ *noun*
la **pregunta:** I asked the teacher a question le hice una pregunta al profesor; he answered all my questions contestó todas mis preguntas
▸ that's out of the question es imposible
▸ a question mark un signo de interrogación
■ *verb*
interrogar: the police want to question him la policía quiere interrogarlo.

queue *UK* [kjuː] *(noun & verb)*
■ *noun*
la **cola:** there was a queue in front of the cinema había cola en la puerta del cine
■ *verb*
hacer cola: we had to queue for tickets tuvimos que hacer cola para las entradas.

quick [kwɪk] *(adjective & adverb)*
■ *adjective*
rápido: what's the quickest way back? ¿cuál es el camino de vuelta más rápido?; I have to make a quick phone call tengo que hacer una llamada rápida
▸ be quick! ¡date prisa!
■ *adverb*
rápido: quick, here he comes! ¡rápido, aquí viene!

quickly ['kwɪklɪ] *adverb* ■ **rápidamente:** he finished quickly terminó rápidamente.

quiet ['kwaɪət] *adjective*
1. **tranquilo:** a quiet street una calle tranquila; we had a quiet evening tuvimos una tarde tranquila
2. **silencioso:** the car has a quiet engine el coche tiene un motor silencioso

bajo: she spoke in a quiet voice habló en voz baja

be quiet! ¡silencio!

to keep quiet no decir nada: keep quiet about the party no digas nada sobre la fiesta.

quietly [ˈkwaɪətlɪ] adverb

sin hacer ruido: she left the room quietly dejó la habitación sin hacer ruido

en voz baja: he speaks very quietly habla en voz muy baja.

quilt [kwɪlt] noun ■ el **edredón** (plural los edredones).

quince [kwɪns] noun ■ el **membrillo.**

quit [kwɪt] (past tense & past participle quit OR quitted, present participle quitting) verb ■ dejar: she quit her job dejó su trabajo

to quit smoking US dejar de fumar: I'm trying to quit smoking estoy tratando de dejar de fumar.

quite [kwaɪt] adverb ■ **bastante:** she's quite pretty es bastante guapa

not quite no del todo: are you finished? – not quite ¿has terminado? –no del todo

to be quite right tener toda la razón.

quiz [kwɪz] (plural quizzes [ˈkwɪzɪz]) noun

1. el **concurso:** he won the money on a TV quiz show ganó el dinero en un concurso televisivo

2. US el **examen:** we had a geography quiz today hoy hemos tenido un examen de geografía.

quotation [kwəʊˈteɪʃn] noun ■ la **cita:** it's a quotation from Shakespeare es una cita de Shakespeare

quotation marks comillas

in quotation marks entre comillas.

quote [kwəʊt] (noun & verb)

■ noun

la cita: it's a quote from Oscar Wilde es una cita de Oscar Wilde

quotes comillas: his words were in quotes sus palabras estaban entre comillas

■ verb

citar: she quoted Homer citó a Homero.

rabbi [ˈræbaɪ] noun ■ el **rabino:** he's a rabbi es rabino.

rabbit [ˈræbɪt] noun ■ el **conejo.**

race [reɪs] (noun & verb)

■ noun

1. la carrera: she won the race ganó la carrera

2. la raza: the human race la raza humana

a race car US un coche de carreras

a race car driver US un piloto de carreras

■ verb

1. correr: she raced to the door corrió a la puerta

2. echar una carrera: I'll race you te echo una carrera.

racecourse UK [ˈreɪskɔːs] noun ■ el **hipódromo.**

racehorse [ˈreɪshɔːs] noun ■ el **caballo de carreras.**

racetrack [ˈreɪstræk] noun ■ el **circuito:** the cars sped around the racetrack los coches aceleraban por el circuito.

racing car UK [ˈreɪsɪŋkɑːʳ] noun ■ el **coche de carreras.**

racing driver UK [ˈreɪsɪŋˌdraɪvəʳ] noun ■ el **piloto de carreras.**

racism [ˈreɪsɪzm] noun ■ el **racismo.**

racist [ˈreɪsɪst] adjective ■ **racista.**

rack [ræk] noun ■ el **portaequipajes** (plural los **portaequipajes)**

a towel rack un toallero.

racket ['rækɪt] *noun*
1. la **raqueta: a tennis racket** una raqueta de tenis
2. *informal* el **alboroto: what's all the racket for?** ¿a qué viene todo este alboroto?

racquet ['rækɪt] *noun* ■ la **raqueta: a tennis racquet** una raqueta de tenis.

radiator ['reɪdɪeɪtəʳ] *noun* ■ el **radiador: put the radiator on** enciende el radiador.

radio ['reɪdɪəʊ] *noun* ■ la **radio: I heard it on the radio** lo escuché en la radio
▷ **a radio station** una emisora de radio.

radish ['rædɪʃ] *noun* ■ el **rábano.**

raft [ræft] *noun* ■ la **balsa: they built a raft out of logs** construyeron una balsa con troncos.

rag [ræg] *noun* ■ el **trapo: he wiped his hands on an oily rag** se limpió las manos con un trapo aceitoso

rags *plural noun* ■ el **harapo: he was dressed in rags** iba vestido con harapos.

rage [reɪdʒ] *noun* ■ la **rabia: he was speechless with rage** estaba mudo de rabia
▷ **she flew into a rage when she heard the news** se puso furiosa cuando escuchó la noticia.

raid [reɪd] *(noun & verb)*
■ *noun*
1. la **redada: a police raid** una redada policial
2. *UK* el **atraco: a bank raid** un atraco de banco
▷ **a bombing raid** un bombardeo aéreo
■ *verb*
1. **hacer una redada: the police raided their offices** la policía hizo una redada en sus oficinas
2. **saquear: he raided the fridge in the middle of the night** saqueó la nevera en mitad de la noche
3. *UK* **atracar: three men raided the bank** tres hombres atracaron el banco.

rail [reɪl] *noun*
1. la **barandilla: hold onto the rail when you come down the stairs** cógete de la barandilla al bajar la escalera
2 el **raíl,** el **riel: electrified rails** raíles electrificados

▷ **by rail** en tren: **she prefers to travel by rail** ella prefiere viajar en tren
▷ **the train went off the rails** el tren descarriló.

railings ['reɪlɪŋz] *plural noun*
1. la **barandilla: he leaned over the railings on the balcony** se inclinó sobre la barandilla del balcón
2. la **verja: they jumped over the railings** saltaron la verja.

railway *UK* ['reɪlweɪ], **railroad** *US* ['reɪlrəʊd] *noun* ■ el **ferrocarril**
▷ **a railway line** una línea ferroviaria
▷ **a railway station** una estación de ferrocarril
▷ **a railway track** una vía férrea.

rain [reɪn] *(noun & verb)*
■ *noun*
la **lluvia: we're expecting rain today** hoy esperamos lluvia
■ *verb*
llover: it's going to rain this afternoon esta tarde lloverá.

rainbow ['reɪnbəʊ] *noun* ■ el **arco iris** *(plural* los **arco iris): how many colours are there in a rainbow?** ¿cuántos colores tiene el arco iris?

raincoat ['reɪnkəʊt] *noun* ■ el **impermeable.**

rainforest ['reɪn'fɒrɪst] *noun* ■ la **selva tropical: the rainforests of Brazil** las selvas tropicales de Brasil.

raise [reɪz] *(verb & noun)*
■ *verb*
1. **levantar: she raised her hand** levantó la mano; **they raised the barrier** levantaron la barrera
2. **aumentar: they've raised their prices** han aumentado los precios
3. **mejorar: we must raise university standards** debemos mejorar el nivel universitario
4. **criarse: the children were raised in Canada** los niños se criaron en Canadá
▷ **to raise one's voice** levantar la voz: **she raised her voice to make herself heard** levantó la voz para hacerse oír
▷ **to raise money** recaudar fondos: **the school is trying to raise money for a new library**

la escuela está tratando de recaudar fondos para una nueva biblioteca
noun
US el **aumento**: all the staff got a raise todo el personal tuvo un aumento.

raisin ['reɪzn] noun ■ la **pasa.**

rake [reɪk] noun ■ el **rastrillo**: he used a rake to gather all the leaves usó un rastrillo para amontonar todas las hojas.

RAM [ræm] (abbreviation of Random Access Memory) noun ■ la **memoria de acceso aleatorio**, la **memoria RAM.**

rambling ['ræmblɪŋ] uncountable noun ■ la **excursión**: to go rambling ir de excursión.

ramp [ræmp] noun ■ la **rampa**: he pushed the cart up the ramp empujó el carrito por la rampa; the exit ramp was full of cars la rampa de salida estaba llena de automóviles.

ran [ræn] past tense ➤ run.

ranch [UK rɑːntʃ, US ræntʃ] (plural ranches) noun ■ el **rancho.**

random ['rændəm] adjective
at random al azar: choose a number at random elige un número al azar.

rang [ræŋ] past tense ➤ ring.

range [reɪndʒ] (noun & verb)
noun
1. la **gama**: there is a wide range of colours hay una amplia gama de colores
2. el **alcance**: the target is out of range el objetivo está fuera del alcance
3. US la **cocina**: they bought a new range compraron una cocina nueva
   it's out of my price range está fuera de mis posibilidades
   a mountain range una cadena montañosa
verb
to range from... to... oscilar entre... y...: prices range from 50 to 500 dollars los precios oscilan entre los 50 y los 500 dólares.

rank [ræŋk] (noun & verb)
noun
1. el **rango**: the rank of colonel is above captain el rango de coronel está por encima del de capitán

2. la **fila**: the soldiers broke ranks los soldados rompieron filas
verb
clasificar: he's ranked second in the world está clasificado segundo en el mundo.

rap [ræp] noun ■ el **rap**: a rap singer un cantante de rap.

rare [reəʳ] adjective
1. raro: this is a rare animal éste es un animal raro
2. poco hecho: I'd like my steak rare quiero el filete poco hecho.

rarely ['reəlɪ] adverb ■ pocas veces: they rarely go out salen pocas veces.

rash [ræʃ] noun ■ el **sarpullido**: he broke out in a rash le salió un sarpullido.

raspberry ['rɑːzbərɪ] (plural raspberries) noun ■ la **frambuesa.**

rat [ræt] noun ■ la **rata.**

rate [reɪt] noun
1. la **tasa**: the birth rate la tasa de natalidad
2. el **tipo**: interest rates are low los tipos de interés son bajos
3. la **tarifa**: are there special rates for students? ¿hay tarifas especiales para estudiantes?

rather [UK 'rɑːðəʳ, US 'ræðəʳ] adverb ■ mejor
rather than en lugar de: he did it alone rather than ask for help lo hizo solo en lugar de pedir ayuda
I'd rather go now preferiría irme ahora
she'd rather not talk to him preferiría no hablar con él.

rattle ['rætl] noun ■ el **sonajero**: the baby dropped its rattle al bebé se le cayó el sonajero.

rattlesnake ['rætlsneɪk] noun ■ la **serpiente de cascabel**: rattlesnakes are poisonous las serpientes de cascabel son venenosas.

raw [rɔː] adjective ■ crudo: a raw carrot una zanahoria cruda
raw materials materias primas.

ray [reɪ] *noun* ■ el **rayo**: the sun's rays warmed the ground los rayos de sol calentaron el suelo.

razor ['reɪzəʳ] *noun* ■ la **navaja**
➤ a razor blade una hoja de afeitar.

Rd. *(abbreviation of* road*)* ➤ road.

reach [riːtʃ] *(verb & noun)*
■ *verb*
1. **llegar a**: we reached Madrid before dark llegamos a Madrid antes del anochecer; the snow reached the window la nieve llegó hasta la ventana; they've reached a decision llegaron a una decisión
2. **alcanzar**: I can't reach the book on the top shelf no alcanzo el libro del estante de arriba
3. **ponerse en contacto**: you can reach me on this number puedes ponerte en contacto conmigo en este número
■ *noun*
➤ within arm's reach al alcance de la mano: the telephone is within reach el teléfono está al alcance de la mano
➤ within easy reach a poca distancia: the school is within easy reach of my house la escuela está a poca distancia de mi casa
➤ out of reach fuera del alcance

reach out *phrasal verb* ■ **extender la mano**: he reached out and touched her arm extendió la mano y le tocó el brazo.

react [rɪ'ækt] *verb* ■ **reaccionar**: he didn't react to her speech no reaccionó ante su discurso.

reaction [rɪ'ækʃn] *noun* ■ la **reacción** *(plural* las **reacciones***)*: what was her reaction when you told her the news? ¿cuál fue su reacción cuando le contaste la noticia?

read [riːd] *(past tense & past participle* read [red]*) verb* ■ **leer**: she's reading the newspaper está leyendo el periódico; have you read this book? ¿has leído este libro?
➤ to read out loud leer en voz alta: she read the story out loud to the class leyó el cuento en voz alta para toda la clase.

reading ['riːdɪŋ] *noun* ■ la **lectura**: reading is my favourite hobby la lectura es mi pasatiempo favorito.

ready ['redɪ] *adjective*
1. **listo**: are you ready to go? ¿estás listo para salir?
2. **dispuesto**: she's always ready to help siempre está dispuesta a ayudar
➤ to get ready prepararse: she's getting ready to leave se está preparando para irse
➤ to get something ready preparar algo: he's getting lunch ready está preparando el almuerzo.

real ['rɪəl] *adjective*
1. **verdadero**: that's not the real reason ése no es el verdadero motivo; he's a real crook es un verdadero sinvergüenza
2. **auténtico**: it's made of real leather es de piel auténtica
3. **real**: the real world el mundo real
➤ real estate *US* la propiedad inmobiliaria: her father's in real estate su padre trabaja en la propiedad inmobiliaria.

realistic [ˌrɪə'lɪstɪk] *adjective* ■ **realista**: the film shows a realistic vision of war la película muestra una visión realista de la guerra.

reality [rɪ'ælətɪ] *noun* ■ la **realidad**.

realize , realise *UK* ['rɪəlaɪz] *verb* ■ **darse cuenta de**: he realized his mistake se dio cuenta de su error; I didn't realize what the time was no me di cuenta de la hora que era.

really ['rɪəlɪ] *adverb*
1. **realmente**: she's really pretty es realmente muy guapa
2. **muy**: it's really late es muy tarde
3. **de verdad**: are you really going to Australia? ¿vas de verdad a Australia?
➤ really? ¿en serio?, ¿de verdad?: Ann won the lottery! — really? a Ann le tocó la lotería —¿en serio?
➤ do you want to go to the party? — not really ¿quieres ir a la fiesta? —en realidad, no.

rear [rɪəʳ] *(adjective & noun)*
■ *adjective*
trasero: please use the rear entrance por favor, utilice la entrada trasera
■ *noun*
la **parte trasera**: I was sitting at the rear of the bus estaba sentado en la parte trasera del autobús.

reason ['riːzn] *noun* ■ la **razón** *(plural* las razones*)*: that's the reason she left ésa es la razón por la que se fue.

reasonable ['riːznəbl] *adjective* ■ **razonable**: Alex is usually such a reasonable person Alex suele ser una persona tan razonable; the prices are reasonable in that shop en esa tienda los precios son razonables.

reasonably ['riːznəblɪ] *adverb* ■ **bastante**: she's reasonably happy es bastante feliz
the food is reasonably good la comida es bastante buena.

reassure [ˌriːə'ʃʊəʳ] *verb* ■ **tranquilizar**: I tried to reassure her traté de tranquilizarla.

receipt [rɪ'siːt] *noun* ■ el **recibo**: I'd like a receipt, please quisiera un recibo, por favor.

receive [rɪ'siːv] *verb* ■ **recibir**: I received a letter this morning recibí una carta esta mañana.

receiver [rɪ'siːvəʳ] *noun* ■ el **auricular**: he picked up the receiver levantó el auricular.

recent ['riːsnt] *adjective* ■ **reciente**: recent research into AIDS las investigaciones más recientes sobre el sida.

recently ['riːsntlɪ] *adverb* ■ **recientemente**: we hired Kim recently recientemente contratamos a Kim
until recently hasta hace poco: until recently he lived in London hasta hace poco vivía en Londres.

reception [rɪ'sepʃn] *noun* ■ la **recepción** *(plural* las recepciones*)*: the reception will be held at the Waldorf la recepción se celebrará en el Waldorf
the reception desk la recepción
a wedding reception un banquete de bodas.

receptionist [rɪ'sepʃənɪst] *noun* ■ el/la **recepcionista**: she's a receptionist es recepcionista.

recess *US* ['riːses] *noun* ■ el **recreo**: it's recess time es la hora del recreo.

recipe ['resɪpɪ] *noun* ■ la **receta**: can I have your biscuit recipe? ¿me das tu receta de galletas?

reckon ['rekən] *verb*
1. **creer**: I reckon you're right creo que tienes razón
2. **calcular**: the age of the Earth is reckoned at 4,600 years se calcula que la edad de la Tierra es de 4.600 años.

recognize , recognise *UK* ['rekəgnaɪz] *verb* ■ **reconocer**: I didn't recognize you no te reconocí.

recommend [ˌrekə'mend] *verb* ■ **recomendar**: he recommended this book to me me recomendó este libro.

record *(noun & verb)*
■ *noun* ['rekɔːd]
1. el **récord** *(plural* los récords*)*: she has broken the world record ha batido el récord mundial
2. el **disco**: I like listening to old records me gusta escuchar discos antiguos
3. el **historial**: he has a good academic record tiene un buen historial académico
a record player un tocadiscos
a criminal record antecedentes penales
to keep a record of something llevar un registro de algo: you should keep a record of your expenses deberías llevar un registro de tus gastos
■ *verb* [rɪ'kɔːd]
grabar; I've recorded the film grabé la película.

recorded delivery ['rekɔːdɪddɪ'lɪvərɪ] *noun*
to send something recorded delivery enviar algo por correo certificado.

recorder ['rekɔːdəʳ] *noun* ■ la **flauta dulce**.

recording [rɪ'kɔːdɪŋ] *noun* ■ la **grabación** *(plural* las grabaciones*)*: this is a bad recording ésta es una mala grabación.

recover [rɪ'kʌvəʳ] *verb* ■ **recuperarse**: she's recovering from a cold se está recuperando de un resfriado.

recovery [rɪ'kʌvərɪ] *noun* ■ la **recuperación**
best wishes for a quick recovery! ¡que te mejores pronto!

rectangle ['rek,tæŋgl] *noun* ■ el **rectángulo**.

recycle [,riː'saɪkl] *verb* ■ **reciclar**: we recycle bottles and newspapers reciclamos botellas y periódicos
▷ recycled paper papel reciclado.

recycling [,riː'saɪklɪŋ] *uncountable noun* ■ el **reciclaje**: a recycling facility un centro de reciclaje.

red [red] *adjective* ■ **rojo**: a red apple una manzana roja; a bright red hat un sombrero rojo vivo
▶ she has red hair es pelirroja
▶ the Red Cross la Cruz Roja
▶ a red light un semáforo en rojo: he went through a red light se pasó un semáforo en rojo
▶ to go red ruborizarse.

redhead ['redhed] *noun* ■ el **pelirrojo**, la **pelirroja**: Julie is a natural redhead Julie es pelirroja natural.

redo [,riː'duː] *(past tense* redid, *past participle* redone) *verb* ■ **rehacer**: she had to redo her homework tuvo que rehacer sus deberes.

reduce [*UK* rɪ'djuːs, *US* rɪ'duːs] *verb* ■ **reducir**: they've reduced the price han reducido el precio.

reduction [rɪ'dʌkʃn] *noun* ■ la **reducción** *(plural* las **reducciones***)*: we've seen a reduction in traffic in this area hemos visto una reducción del tráfico en esta zona.

redundant *UK* [rɪ'dʌndənt] *adjective*
▶ to be made redundant ser despedido.

reef [riːf] *noun* ■ el **arrecife**: a coral reef un arrecife de coral.

refer [rɪ'fɜːʳ] *(past tense & past participle* referred, *present participle* referring) *verb* ■ **referirse**: I don't know what you're referring to no se a qué te refieres
▶ to refer to referirse a: she's referring to your son se refiere a tu hijo.

referee [,refə'riː] *noun* ■ el **árbitro**, la **árbitra**: the referee blew his whistle el árbitro hizo sonar el silbato.

reference ['refrəns] *noun*
1. la **referencia**: she made a reference to her family hizo referencia a su familia
2. las **referencias**: could you give me a reference for the job? ¿podría darme referencias para el trabajo?
▷ a reference book un libro de consulta
▷ a reference number un número de referencia.

reflection [rɪ'flekʃn] *noun* ■ el **reflejo**: I can see my reflection in the mirror veo mi reflejo en el espejo
▷ on reflection, I don't think it's a good idea pensándolo bien, no creo que sea una buena idea.

reflex ['riːfleks] *noun* ■ el **reflejo**: he has good reflexes tiene buenos reflejos.

reflexive [rɪ'fleksɪv] *adjective* ■ **reflexivo**: 'to wash oneself' is a reflexive verb 'lavarse' es un verbo reflexivo.

refreshing [rɪ'freʃɪŋ] *adjective* ■ **refrescante**: I took a refreshing shower me di una ducha refrescante.

refrigerator [rɪ'frɪdʒəreɪtəʳ] *noun* ■ el **frigorífico**.

refugee [,refjʊ'dʒiː] *noun* ■ el **refugiado**, la **refugiada**.

refund *(noun & verb)*
■ *noun* ['riːfʌnd]
el **reembolso**: we'll give you a refund if you are not satisfied le devolvemos el dinero si usted no queda satisfecho
■ *verb* [rɪ'fʌnd]
reembolsar: they refunded my money me reembolsaron el dinero.

refuse *(verb & noun)*
■ *verb* [rɪ'fjuːz]
negarse: I refuse to do it me niego a hacerlo
■ *noun* ['refjuːs]
la **basura**
▷ refuse collector el basurero, la basurera.

regard [rɪ'gɑːd] *verb* ■ **considerar**: I regard her as my sister la considero mi hermana; he's regarded as the best player in the world está considerado el mejor jugador del mundo.

regards [rɪ'gɑːdz] *plural noun* ■ **los recuerdos**: **give her my regards** dale recuerdos de mi parte; **he sends his regards** te manda recuerdos.

region ['riːdʒən] *noun* ■ **la región** (*plural* **las regiones**): **Tibet is a mountainous region** el Tíbet es una región montañosa.

register ['redʒɪstəʳ] (*noun & verb*)
noun
. el **registro**: **she signed the register** firmó el registro
. *UK* la **lista**
to take the register pasar lista: **the teacher took the register** el profesor pasó lista
verb
. **inscribirse**: **she wants to register for a Spanish course** quiere inscribirse en un curso de español
. *UK* **facturar**: **we have to register our luggage** tenemos que facturar el equipaje.

registered letter [,redʒɪstəd'letəʳ] *noun* ■ la **carta certificada**.

registered trademark [,redʒɪstəd-'treɪdmɑːk] *noun* ■ la **marca registrada**.

registration number *UK* [,redʒɪs'treə-ʃn'nʌmbəʳ] *noun* ■ el **número de matrícula**.

regret [rɪ'gret] (*noun & verb*)
noun
do you have any regrets? ¿te arrepientes de algo?; **I have no regrets** no me arrepiento de nada
verb
arrepentirse: **he regrets breaking up with her** se arrepiente de haber terminado con ella.

regular ['regjʊləʳ] *adjective*
1. **regular**: **the vibrations occur at regular intervals** las vibraciones se presentan a intervalos regulares
2. **habitual**: **I'll see you at the regular time** te veo a la hora habitual; **he's a regular customer** es un cliente habitual
3. **normal**: **a regular portion of chips** una porción normal de patatas fritas.

regularly ['regjʊləlɪ] *adverb* ■ **regularmente**: **I go to the dentist regularly** voy al dentista regularmente.

regulations [,regjʊ'leɪʃnz] *plural noun* ■ el **reglamento**: **it's against regulations** va en contra del reglamento.

rehearsal [rɪ'hɜːsl] *noun* ■ el **ensayo**: **there's a rehearsal for the play tonight** hay un ensayo de la obra esta noche.

rehearse [rɪ'hɜːs] *verb* ■ **ensayar**: **the band is rehearsing this afternoon** la banda ensaya esta tarde.

reign [reɪn] (*noun & verb*)
noun
el **reinado**: **during the reign of Henry VIII** durante el reinado de Enrique VIII
verb
reinar: **the king reigned for 50 years** el rey reinó durante 50 años.

reindeer ['reɪn,dɪəʳ] (*plural* **reindeer**) *noun* ■ el **reno**.

reins [reɪnz] *plural noun* ■ las **riendas**: **she was holding the horse's reins** llevaba las riendas del caballo.

reject [rɪ'dʒekt] *verb* ■ **rechazar**: **they rejected my book** rechazaron mi libro.

related [rɪ'leɪtɪd] *adjective* ■ **relacionado**: **the two problems aren't related** los dos problemas no están relacionados
how is Sam related to Ted? ¿qué parentesco tiene Sam con Ted?
they are related son parientes.

relation [rɪ'leɪʃn] *noun*
1. el/la **pariente**: **Vicky has relations in Miami** Vicky tiene parientes en Miami
2. la **relación** (*plural* las **relaciones**): **there's no relation between the two crimes** no hay relación entre los dos crímenes; **the two countries have good relations** ambos países tienen buenas relaciones.

relationship [rɪ'leɪʃnʃɪp] *noun* ■ la **relación** (*plural* las **relaciones**): **they have a good relationship** tienen una buena relación.

relative ['relətɪv] *noun* ■ el/la **pariente**: **he has relatives in Dublin** tiene parientes en Dublín.

relax [rɪ'læks] *verb* ■ **relajarse: a massage will help you relax** un masaje te ayudará a relajarte

> **relax, everything is fine** tranquilo, no pasa nada.

relaxation [ˌriːlæk'seɪʃn] *noun*

1. **el descanso: a good place to find relaxation** un buen lugar para el descanso
2. **la relajación: what do you do for relaxation?** ¿qué haces para relajarte?

relaxed [rɪ'lækst] *adjective* ■ **relajado: he's been very relaxed since he came back from his holidays** está muy relajado desde que volvió de las vacaciones.

relaxing [rɪ'læksɪŋ] *adjective* ■ **relajante: she had a relaxing bath** se dio un baño relajante

> **it was a relaxing weekend** fue un fin de semana de descanso.

relay ['riːleɪ], **relay race** ['riːleɪreɪs] *noun* ■ **la carrera de relevos.**

release [rɪ'liːs] *(noun & verb)*

■ *noun*

la **liberación** *(plural* las **liberaciones)*: **we've arranged for the release of the hostages** hemos organizado la liberación de los rehenes

> **a new release** un nuevo disco: **his new release is called "No Good Blues"** su nuevo disco se llama "No Good Blues"
> **a press release** un comunicado de prensa

■ *verb*

1. **liberar: they released the prisoners** liberaron a los prisioneros
2. **sacar a la venta: they've just released a new album** acaban de sacar a la venta un nuevo álbum.

reliable [rɪ'laɪəbl] *adjective*

1. **de fiar: he's a reliable person** es una persona de fiar
2. **fiable: this engine isn't very reliable** este motor no es muy fiable.

relief [rɪ'liːf] *noun* ■ **el alivio: what a relief!** ¡qué alivio!

relieve [rɪ'liːv] *verb* ■ **aliviar: this aspirin will relieve the pain** esta aspirina le aliviará el dolor.

religion [rɪ'lɪdʒn] *noun* ■ **la religión** *(plural* las **religiones)*.

religious [rɪ'lɪdʒəs] *adjective* ■ **religioso: what are your religious beliefs?** ¿cuáles son tus creencias religiosas?; **she's very religious** es muy religiosa.

reluctant [rɪ'lʌktənt] *adjective* ■ **reacio**

> **to be reluctant to do something** mostrarse reacio a hacer algo: **I was reluctant to leave** me mostraba reacio a irme.

reluctantly [rɪ'lʌktəntlɪ] *adverb* ■ **de mala gana: he reluctantly went to bed** se fue a la cama de mala gana.

rely [rɪ'laɪ] *(past tense & past participle* relied*)* *verb*

> **to rely on someone** OR **something** depender de alguien o algo: **I've always relied on my parents** siempre he dependido de mis padres
> **it's a car you can rely on** es un coche en el que se puede confiar.

remain [rɪ'meɪn] *verb*

1. **quedarse: he remained at home** se quedó en casa
2. **permanecer: the house remained abandoned for years** la casa permaneció abandonada durante años.

remaining [rɪ'meɪnɪŋ] *adjective* ■ **restante: the remaining passengers arrived late** el resto de los pasajeros llegó tarde.

remains [rɪ'meɪnz] *plural noun* ■ **los restos: they found human remains** encontraron restos humanos; **the remains of an ancient city** los restos de una antigua ciudad.

remark [rɪ'mɑːk] *noun* ■ **el comentario: she made a critical remark** hizo un comentario crítico.

remarkable [rɪ'mɑːkəbl] *adjective* ■ **excepcional: she's a remarkable woman** es una mujer excepcional.

remember [rɪ'membər] *verb*

1. **acordarse: I don't remember** no me acuerdo
2. **acordarse de: I remember what happened** me acuerdo de lo que sucedió; **she doesn't remember me** no se acuerda de mí

. recordar: I remember visiting that museum when I was a child recuerdo haber estado en ese museo cuando era pequeño
to remember to do something acordarse de hacer algo: remember to take your umbrella acuérdate de llevar el paraguas
as far as I remember que yo recuerde.

remind [rɪ'maɪnd] *verb* ■ recordar: you remind me of my brother me recuerdas a mi hermano; remind me to call David recuérdame que llame a David

The verb following **recordarle a alguien que** must be in the subjunctive.

remote [rɪ'məʊt] *adjective* ■ remoto: a remote mountain village un pueblo remoto de la montaña
the remote control el mando a distancia.

remove [rɪ'muːv] *verb*
. retirar: he removed the plates from the table retiró los platos de la mesa
2. quitar: it's the best thing for removing stains es lo mejor para quitar las manchas.

renew [*UK* rɪ'njuː, *US* rɪ'nuː] *verb* ■ renovar: I have to renew my passport tengo que renovar mi pasaporte.

rent [rent] *(noun & verb)*
■ *noun*
el alquiler: how much rent do you pay? ¿cuánto pagas de alquiler?
■ *verb*
alquilar: they rented a house for the summer alquilaron una casa para el verano
"for rent" "se alquila".

rental ['rentl] *(noun & adjective)*
■ *noun*
el alquiler
■ *adjective*
de alquiler: a rental car un coche de alquiler.

repair [rɪ'peər] *(noun & verb)*
■ *noun*
la reparación: the repair cost 50 dollars la reparación costó 50 dólares
■ *verb*
arreglar: he repaired the television arregló la televisión.

repeat [rɪ'piːt] *(verb & noun)*
■ *verb*
repetir: can you repeat what you just said? ¿puedes repetir lo que acabas de decir?
■ *noun*
la reposición: this programme is a repeat este programa es una reposición.

replace [rɪ'pleɪs] *verb*
1. cambiar: I replaced the broken window cambié la ventana rota
2. volver a colocar: replace the book on the shelf vuelve a colocar el libro en el estante.

reply [rɪ'plaɪ] *(noun & verb)*
■ *noun*
la respuesta: we're waiting for a reply estamos esperando una respuesta
■ *verb (past tense & past participle* replied*)*
responder: I have to reply to this e-mail tengo que responder a este mensaje de correo electrónico.

report [rɪ'pɔːt] *(noun & verb)*
■ *noun*
1. el informe: I read the police report leí el informe de la policía
2. el reportaje: we read the report in the paper leímos el reportaje en el periódico
3. *UK* las notas: he got a good report ha sacado buenas notas
a report card *US* el boletín de calificaciones: we're getting our report cards today hoy nos entregan el informe escolar
■ *verb*
1. dar parte de: we reported the accident to the police dimos parte del accidente a la policía
2. divulgar: the news was reported in the paper divulgaron la noticia en el periódico
3. presentarse: please report to my office por favor, preséntese en mi oficina.

reporter [rɪ'pɔːtər] *noun* ■ el/la periodista: she's a reporter es periodista.

represent [,reprɪ'zent] *verb* ■ representar: the dotted line represents the border la línea punteada representa la frontera; Ms. Smith will represent the company at the convention la señora Smith representará a la compañía en la convención.

representative [ˌreprɪˈzentətɪv] *noun* ■ el/la **representante**: Scott is our representative in Texas Scott es nuestro representante en Texas.

reptile [ˈreptaɪl] *noun* ■ el **reptil**.

republic [rɪˈpʌblɪk] *noun* ■ la **república**.

Republican [rɪˈpʌblɪkən] *(adjective & noun)*

■ *adjective*
republicano: the Republican Party el Partido Republicano

■ *noun*
el **republicano**, la **republicana**: my parents are both Republicans mis padres son republicanos.

request [rɪˈkwest] *(noun & verb)*

■ *noun*
la **petición** *(plural* las **peticiones**): they made a request for help presentaron una petición de ayuda

■ *verb*
pedir: I'll have to request more supplies tendré que pedir más provisiones
to request that pedir que: we requested that they provide more information pedimos que nos proporcionaran más información

The verb following **pedir que** must be in the subjunctive.

require [rɪˈkwaɪər] *verb* ■ **requerir**: this work requires a lot of concentration este trabajo requiere mucha concentración.

resat UK [riːsæt] *past tense & past participle*
➤ **resit**.

rescue [ˈreskjuː] *(noun & verb)*

■ *noun*
el **rescate**: a rescue operation una operación de rescate; a rescue team un equipo de rescate
➤ he came to my rescue acudió en mi ayuda

■ *verb*
rescatar: they rescued her from the fire la rescataron del incendio.

research [ˌrɪˈsɜːtʃ, ˈrɪsɜːtʃ] *(noun & verb)*

■ *noun*
la **investigación** *(plural* las **investigaciones**): he's doing research on genetics está haciendo una investigación sobre genética

■ *verb*
investigar: they're researching alternative energy sources están investigando fuentes de energía alternativa.

researcher [rɪˈsɜːtʃər, ˈrɪsɜːtʃər] *noun* ■ el **investigador**, la **investigadora**: he's a researcher at the university trabaja como investigador en la universidad.

resemblance [rɪˈzembləns] *noun* ■ el **parecido**: I don't see the resemblance between you and your sister no veo el parecido entre tú y tu hermana.

resemble [rɪˈzembl] *verb* ■ **parecerse**: the baby resembles his father el bebé se parece a su padre.

reservation [ˌrezəˈveɪʃn] *noun* ■ la **reserva**: I made a reservation for dinner hice una reserva para la cena.

reserve [rɪˈzɜːv] *(noun & verb)*

■ *noun*
la **reserva**: our water reserves are getting low nuestras reservas de agua están disminuyendo
➤ a nature reserve una reserva natural

■ *verb*
reservar: she reserved a table for six reservó una mesa para seis.

residence [ˈrezɪdəns] *noun* ■ la **residencia**: it's the president's official residence es la residencia oficial del presidente.

resident [ˈrezɪdənt] *noun*

1. el/la **residente**: he's a UK resident es residente británico
2. el **vecino**, la **vecina**: the residents are opposed to the proposal los vecinos se oponen a la propuesta
3. el/la **huésped**: hotel residents los huéspedes de hotel.

resign [rɪˈzaɪn] *verb* ■ **dimitir**: he resigned from his job dimitió de su puesto de trabajo.

resist [rɪˈzɪst] *verb*

1. **resistir**: I couldn't resist his blue eyes no pude resistir sus ojos azules
2. **resistirse a**: she resisted their efforts to change her mind se resistió a sus esfuerzos de hacerla cambiar de idea.

resit UK [ˌriːˈsɪt] (past tense & past participle re-sat, present participle resitting) verb ■ **volver a presentarse:** he had to resit the exam tuvo que volver a presentarse al examen.

resort [rɪˈzɔːt] noun

. el **centro de vacaciones: a very popular seaside resort** un centro de vacaciones costero muy popular

:. el **recurso: we can call Dad as a last resort** podemos llamar a papá como último recurso **a ski resort** una estación de esquí.

resource [rɪˈsɔːs] noun ■ el **recurso natural resources** recursos naturales.

respect [rɪˈspekt] (noun & verb)

■ noun
el **respeto: he has no respect for his parents** no les tiene ningún respeto a sus padres
■ verb
respetar: everybody respects her todo el mundo la respeta.

responsibility [rɪˌspɒnsəˈbɪlətɪ] noun ■ la **responsabilidad: he has more responsibilities in his new job** tiene más responsabilidades en su nuevo trabajo.

responsible [rɪˈspɒnsəbl] adjective ■ **responsable: she's responsible for the accident** es responsable del accidente.

rest [rest] (noun & verb)

■ noun
el **descanso: you need a good rest** necesitas un buen descanso
> **the rest** el resto: **the rest of the book was more interesting** el resto del libro era más interesante
> **to have a rest** descansar: **let's have a rest for a while** descansemos un rato
> **the rest rooms** US los servicios
■ verb
ı. **descansar: sit down and rest your legs** siéntate y descansa las piernas; **I want to rest for a few minutes** quiero descansar unos minutos
2. **apoyar: she rested her bike against the wall** apoyó la bicicleta contra la pared.

restaurant [ˈrestərɒnt] noun ■ el **restaurante.**

result [rɪˈzʌlt] noun ■ el **resultado: the doctor has your test results** el doctor tiene el resultado de sus análisis.

résumé US [UK ˈrezjuːmeɪ, US ˈrezuːmeɪ] noun ■ el **currículo.**

retire [rɪˈtaɪəʳ] verb ■ **jubilarse: she retired at 60** se jubiló a los 60 años.

return [rɪˈtɜːn] (noun & verb)

■ noun
ı. la **vuelta: I will call on my return from Madrid** llamaré a mi vuelta de Madrid
2. UK el **billete de ida y vuelta: I'd like a return to London** quisiera un billete de ida y vuelta a Londres
> **a return match** un partido de vuelta
> **a return ticket** UK un billete de ida y vuelta
> **in return** a cambio: **he didn't want anything in return** no quiso nada a cambio
■ verb
ı. **volver: she returned to the office at 3** volvió a la oficina a las 3
2. **devolver: he returned the book I lent him** devolvió el libro que le presté.

reunion [ˌriːˈjuːnjən] noun ■ la **reunión** (plural las **reuniones): a family reunion** una reunión familiar.

reveal [rɪˈviːl] verb ■ **revelar: she revealed my secret** reveló mi secreto.

revenge [rɪˈvendʒ] noun ■ la **venganza to get one's revenge** OR **to take revenge** vengarse: **I swore I'd get my revenge** juré que me vengaría; **he took revenge on us** se vengó de nosotros.

reverse [rɪˈvɜːs] (adjective, noun & verb)

■ adjective
inverso: the letters are in reverse order las letras están en orden inverso
■ noun
la **marcha atrás: put the car in reverse** da marcha atrás
■ verb
dar marcha atrás: watch out — he's reversing! ¡cuidado! —¡está dando marcha atrás! **to reverse the charges** UK llamar a cobro revertido.

review [rɪ'vjuː] *noun* ■ la **crítica**: his new film got great reviews su nueva película tuvo críticas excelentes.

revise UK [rɪ'vaɪz] *verb* ■ **repasar**: he's revising for his exams está repasando para los exámenes.

revolting [rɪ'vəʊltɪŋ] *adjective* ■ **asqueroso**: the soup was revolting la sopa estaba asquerosa.

revolution [ˌrevə'luːʃn] *noun* ■ la **revolución** *(plural* las **revoluciones***)*.

reward [rɪ'wɔːd] *(noun & verb)*
■ *noun*
la **recompensa**: they're offering a reward están ofreciendo una recompensa
■ *verb*
recompensar: he was rewarded for his efforts lo recompensaron por sus esfuerzos.

rewind [ˌriː'waɪnd] *(past tense & past participle* rewound [ˌriː'waʊnd]*) verb* ■ **rebobinar**: I'll rewind the tape voy a rebobinar la cinta.

rewound *past tense & past participle* ➤ rewind.

rhinoceros [raɪ'nɒsərəs] *noun* ■ el **rinoceronte**.

rhyme [raɪm] *(noun & verb)*
■ *noun*
1. la **rima**: I need a rhyme for "rain" necesito una palabra que rime con "lluvia"
2. el **poema**: a book of rhymes for children un libro de poemas infantiles
3. la **canción** *(plural* las **canciones***)*: a nursery rhyme una canción infantil
■ *verb*
rimar: "bad" rhymes with "mad" "bad" rima con "mad".

rhythm ['rɪðm] *noun* ■ el **ritmo**.

rib [rɪb] *noun* ■ la **costilla**.

ribbon ['rɪbən] *noun* ■ la **cinta**: the girl had a ribbon in her hair la niña llevaba una cinta en el pelo.

rice [raɪs] *uncountable noun* ■ el **arroz**
➤ fried rice arroz frito
➤ rice pudding arroz con leche
➤ brown rice arroz integral.

rich [rɪtʃ] *adjective* ■ **rico**: he's one of the richest men in the world es uno de los hombres más ricos del mundo.

rid [rɪd] *(past tense & past participle* rid*) verb*
➤ to get rid of something deshacerse de algo: he got rid of his old toys se deshizo de sus viejos juguetes.

ridden ['rɪdn] *past participle* ➤ ride.

riddle ['rɪdl] *noun* ■ la **adivinanza**: he asked me a riddle me preguntó una adivinanza.

ride [raɪd] *(noun & verb)*
■ *noun*
el **paseo**: she went for a ride on her bike fue a dar un paseo en bicicleta
➤ to give somebody a ride **llevar a alguien**: can you give me a ride to school? ¿me llevas al colegio?
■ *verb (past tense* rode, *past participle* ridden*)*
1. **ir**: he can't ride a bicycle no sabe ir en bicicleta; she rides her bike to school va en bicicleta al colegio
2. **montar a caballo**: he rides his horse every day monta a caballo cada día.

ridiculous [rɪ'dɪkjʊləs] *adjective* ■ **ridículo**: you look ridiculous in that hat ese sombrero te queda ridículo.

riding ['raɪdɪŋ] *noun* ■ la **equitación**: she likes riding le gusta montar a caballo
➤ a riding school una escuela de equitación.

rifle ['raɪfl] *noun* ■ el **rifle**: a hunting rifle un rifle de caza.

right [raɪt] *(adjective, adverb & noun)*
■ *adjective*
1. **derecho**: give me your right hand dame la mano derecha
2. **correcto**: that's the right answer ésa es la respuesta correcta; is that the right size? ¿es ésa la talla correcta?
3. **bien**: it's not right to steal robar no está bien
➤ to be right **tener razón**: she was right to protest tenía razón en protestar
➤ that's right así es: are you going to Turkey? — yes, that's right ¿te vas a Turquía? —sí, así es

right? ¿verdad?: you're Kathy, right? tú eres Kathy, ¿verdad?

a right angle un ángulo recto

adverb

. **a la derecha:** turn right at the corner dobla a la derecha en la esquina

. **bien:** she got the question right entendió bien la pregunta

. **recto:** go right to the end of the corridor siga recto hasta el final del pasillo

. **justo:** it happened right after Christmas ocurrió justo después de Navidad

right now OR **right away** ahora mismo: you have to go right now tienes que ir ahora mismo

noun

. la **derecha:** look to the right mira hacia la derecha

. el **derecho:** you have the right to remain silent tiene derecho a permanecer en silencio

human rights derechos humanos

he can't tell right from wrong no distingue lo que está bien de lo que está mal

right of way prioridad de paso: you have the right of way tienes prioridad de paso.

right-hand [raɪthænd] *adjective* ■ it's in the right-hand drawer está en el cajón de la derecha

it's on the right-hand side está a mano derecha.

right-handed [raɪthændɪd] *adjective* ■ **diestro:** she's right-handed es diestra.

ring [rɪŋ] *(noun & verb)*

■ *noun*

. el **anillo:** she has a diamond ring on her finger lleva un anillo de diamantes en el dedo

. el **círculo:** they formed a ring around him formaron un círculo a su alrededor

. el **ring** *(plural* los **rings):** the boxers climbed into the ring los boxeadores subieron al ring

an engagement ring un anillo de compromiso

a wedding ring un anillo de boda

a ring binder una carpeta de anillas

to give somebody a ring UK llamar a alguien (por teléfono): I'll give you a ring tomorrow te llamaré mañana

there was a ring at the door sonó el timbre de la puerta

■ *verb (past tense* rang, *past participle* rung)

. UK **llamar:** I forgot to ring you me olvidé de llamarte; I'll ring you tonight te llamaré esta noche

. **sonar:** the phone is ringing esta sonando el teléfono

to ring the doorbell tocar el timbre: somebody rang the doorbell alguien tocó el timbre

ring back UK *phrasal verb* ■ volver a llamar: I'll ring you back tomorrow te volveré a llamar mañana

ring up UK *phrasal verb* ■ he rang me up last night me llamó (por teléfono) anoche.

rink [rɪŋk] *noun*

an ice rink una pista de hielo

a roller-skating rink una pista de patinaje sobre ruedas.

rinse [rɪns] *verb*

. **enjuagar:** rinse the glass before using it enjuaga el vaso antes de utilizarlo

. **aclarar:** she rinsed her hair with warm water se aclaró el pelo con agua tibia; you have to rinse the baby's clothes properly tienes que aclarar bien la ropa del bebé

to rinse out one's mouth enjuagarse la boca.

riot ['raɪət] *noun* ■ los **disturbios:** a riot broke out in the street empezaron disturbios en la calle.

rip [rɪp] *(past tense & past participle* ripped, *present participle* ripping) *verb*

. **rasgarse:** he ripped his shirt se rasgó la camisa; my coat has ripped se me rasgó el abrigo

. **arrancar:** he ripped the poster off the wall arrancó el póster de la pared.

ripe [raɪp] *adjective* ■ **maduro:** these bananas are very ripe estos plátanos están muy maduros.

rip-off [rɪpɒf] *noun* ■ *informal* el **timo:** what a rip-off ¡qué timo!

rise [raɪz] *(noun & verb)*

■ *noun*

1. la **subida**: a major rise in temperature in the South una gran subida de las temperaturas en el sur
2. *UK* el **aumento**
  a pay rise un aumento de sueldo: Colin has just had a pay rise Colin acaba de recibir un aumento de sueldo

■ *verb (past tense* rose, *past participle* risen)

1. **subir**: prices are rising los precios están subiendo
2. **salir**: the sun rises in the east el sol sale por el este; smoke rose from the chimney el humo salió por la chimenea.

risen ['rɪzn] *past participle* ➤ rise.

risk [rɪsk] *noun* ■ **riesgo**: he doesn't like taking risks no le gusta correr riesgos.

risky ['rɪskɪ] *adjective* ■ **arriesgado**: it's too risky es demasiado arriesgado.

rival ['raɪvl] *noun* ■ el **rival**: Chelsea defeated their rivals el Chelsea venció a sus rivales.

river ['rɪvəʳ] *noun* ■ el **río**: they were swimming in the river estaban nadando en el río; the Tagus is the longest river on the Iberian Peninsula el Tajo es el río más largo de la Península Ibérica
  the Mississippi River el río Mississippi
  the river Thames el río Támesis.

road [rəʊd] *noun*

1. la **carretera**: we took the road from London to Bristol cogimos la carretera de Londres a Bristol
2. la **calle**: she lives on the other side of the road vive al otro lado de la calle
  on the road de viaje: I was on the road all day estaba siempre de viaje
  a road map un mapa de carreteras
  a road sign una señal de tránsito
  road works las obras.

roar [rɔːʳ] *verb* ■ **rugir**: the lion roared el león rugió.

roast [rəʊst] *adjective* ■ **asado**: a roast chicken un pollo asado
  roast beef el rosbif.

rob [rɒb] *(past tense & past participle* robbed, *present participle* robbing) *verb*

1. **robar**: I've been robbed me han robado
2. **asaltar**: somebody robbed the bank alguien asaltó el banco.

robber ['rɒbəʳ] *noun* ■ el **ladrón** *(plural* los **ladrones***)*
  a bank robber un asaltante de bancos.

robbery ['rɒbərɪ] *(plural* robberies*) noun* ■ el **robo**: there have been several robberies in the area ha habido varios robos en la zona
  a bank robbery un asalto a un banco.

robot ['rəʊbɒt] *noun* ■ el **robot** *(plural* los **robots***)*.

rock [rɒk] *noun*

1. la **roca**: they drilled through the rock perforaron la roca
2. la **piedra**: he threw a rock at me me tiró una piedra
3. el **rock**: Susie loves rock music a Susie le encanta la música rock
  rock and roll el rock and roll
  a rock band una banda de rock
  a rock star una estrella de rock.

rocket ['rɒkɪt] *noun* ■ el **cohete**: they sent a rocket into space enviaron un cohete al espacio.

rocking chair ['rɒkɪntʃeəʳ] *noun* ■ la **mecedora**.

rocking horse ['rɒkɪŋhɔːs] *noun* ■ el **caballito de balancín**.

rocky ['rɒkɪ] *adjective* ■ **pedregoso**: a rocky path un camino pedregoso
  the Rocky Mountains OR the Rockies las Montañas Rocosas

ROCKY MOUNTAINS

Las Rocky Mountains, o Montañas Rocosas, es la cordillera que va desde Canadá hasta México y atraviesa los Estados Unidos de norte a sur en la zona oeste del país. Son famosas por su gran belleza natural y son la sede de populares centros de esquí como Vail y Aspen.

rod [rɒd] *noun*
a fishing rod una caña de pescar.

rode [rəʊd] *past tense* ➤ ride.

role [rəʊl] *noun* ■ el **papel** *(plural* los **pape-les)*: he has an important role hace un papel importante.

roll [rəʊl] *(noun & verb)*
noun
■ el **rollo**: a roll of toilet paper un rollo de papel higiénico
■ el **panecillo**: a bread roll un panecillo
verb
■ **rodar**: the ball rolled under the chair la pelota rodó debajo de la silla
■ **hacer rodar**: they rolled the barrel all the way hicieron rodar el barril todo el camino
■ **tirar**: roll the dice tira los dados

roll up *phrasal verb*
■ **enrollar**: she rolled up the map enrolló el mapa
2. **remangarse**: Danny rolled up his sleeves Danny se remangó.

roller ['rəʊlə'] *noun* ■ el **rulo**: her hair is in rollers lleva rulos en el pelo.

Rollerblades® ['rəʊləbleɪdz] *plural noun*
■ los **patines en línea**: a pair of Roller-blades® un par de patines en línea.

rollerblading ['rəʊləbleɪdɪŋ] *uncount-able noun* ■ el **patinaje en línea**: she loves rollerblading le encanta el patinaje en línea.

roller coaster ['rəʊlə'kəʊstə'] *noun* ■ la **montaña rusa** *(plural* las **montañas rusas)*: let's go on the roller coaster vamos a la montaña rusa.

roller skates ['rəʊlə'skeɪts] *plural noun* ■ los **patines**: a pair of roller skates un par de patines.

roller-skating ['rəʊlə'skeɪtɪŋ] *uncount-able noun* ■ el **patinaje sobre ruedas**: do you like roller-skating? ¿te gusta el patinaje sobre ruedas?

ROM [*UK* rɒm, *US* rɑːm] *(abbreviation of* Read-Only Memory) *noun* ■ la **memoria Rom**.

Roman ['rəʊmən] *(adjective & noun)*
■ *adjective*

Remember not to use a capital letter for the adjective in Spanish:

romano: Roman numerals números romanos
➤ the Roman empire el Imperio romano
■ *noun*
■ el **romano**: the Romans arrived in Britain in 55 B.C. los romanos llegaron a Gran Bretaña en el año 55 a.C.

Roman Catholic ['rəʊmən'kæθlɪk] *ad-jective & noun* ■ **católico**: he's Roman Catholic es católico
➤ the Roman Catholic Church la Iglesia Católica.

romance [rəʊ'mæns] *noun*
1. el **romance**: a fairytale romance un romance de cuento de hadas
2. el **encanto**: the romance of travel el encanto de viajar.

romantic [rəʊ'mæntɪk] *adjective* ■ **romántico**: he's very romantic es muy romántico.

roof [ruːf] *noun* ■ el **tejado**: the cat climbed onto the roof el gato subió al tejado.

room [ruːm, rʊm] *noun*
1. la **habitación**: there are only two rooms free sólo quedan dos habitaciones libres; she was playing in the back room estaba jugando en la habitación de atrás
2. el **cuarto**, el **dormitorio**: go to your room! ¡vete a tu cuarto!
3. la **sala**: the school has a large room for concerts la escuela tiene una gran sala para conciertos
4. el **espacio**: there isn't enough room no hay suficiente espacio; the boxes take up a lot of room las cajas ocupan mucho espacio
➤ a single room una habitación individual
➤ a double room una habitación doble
➤ a meeting room una sala de reuniones.

roommate *US* ['ruːmmeɪt] *noun* ■ el **compañero de cuarto** *(plural* los **compañe-ros de cuarto)*: we were roommates in college fuimos compañeros de cuarto en la universidad.

root [ruːt] *noun* ■ la **raíz** *(plural* las **raíces***):* the roots of the tree are very strong las raíces del árbol son muy fuertes.

rope [rəʊp] *noun* ■ la **cuerda,** la **soga:** tie the rope to the tree ata la cuerda al árbol.

rose [rəʊz] *(noun & verb form)*
■ *noun*
la **rosa:** he gave her a bouquet of red roses le dio un ramo de rosas rojas
■ *past tense*
➤ **rise.**

rot [rɒt] *(past tense & past participle* rotted, *present participle* rotting) *verb* ■ **pudrirse:** this melon will rot if you don't eat it este melón se va a pudrir si no te lo comes.

rotten ['rɒtn] *adjective*
1. **podrido:** rotten bananas plátanos podridos
2. *informal* **malísimo:** it was a rotten party fue una fiesta malísima
3. *informal* **fatal:** I feel rotten this morning me siento fatal esta mañana
➤ that was a rotten thing to do fue horrible lo que hiciste.

rough [rʌf] *adjective*
1. **áspero:** the table has a rough surface la mesa tiene una superficie áspera
2. **agitado:** the sea is rough today hoy el mar está agitado
3. **accidentado:** rough terrain terreno accidentado
4. **brusco:** he's very rough with his sister es muy brusco con su hermana
5. **duro:** he led a rough life tuvo una vida dura
6. **peligroso:** it's a rough neighbourhood es un barrio peligroso
7. **vago:** I have a rough idea of what to do tengo una vaga idea de qué hacer
➤ a rough copy un borrador
➤ a rough road una carretera en mal estado.

roughly ['rʌflɪ] *adverb*
1. **aproximadamente:** it costs roughly 200 euros cuesta aproximadamente 200 euros
2. **bruscamente, violentamente**
➤ to treat something OR somebody roughly maltratar algo O a alguien: he treats his dog roughly maltrata a su perro.

round [raʊnd] *(adjective, preposition, adverb & noun)*
■ *adjective*
redondo: a round window una ventana redonda
➤ a round trip *US* un viaje de ida y vuelta
➤ a round trip ticket *US* un billete de ida y vuelta: I bought a round trip ticket to Boston compré un billete de ida y vuelta a Boston
■ *preposition UK*
alrededor de: they're sitting round the table están sentados alrededor de la mesa
➤ it's just round the corner está a la vuelta de la esquina
➤ round here por aquí cerca
■ *adverb UK*
por todos lados: there are mountains all round hay montañas por todos lados
➤ round about alrededor de: I'll be there round about 8 llegaré allí alrededor de las 8
➤ to turn round volverse: he turned round to see what was happening se volvió para ver qué pasaba
➤ come round and see us ven a vernos a casa
■ *noun*
1. la **vuelta:** they lost in the first round of the tournament perdieron en la primera vuelta del torneo
2. *in boxing* el **asalto:** he was knocked out in the first round fue noqueado en el primer asalto
3. la **ronda:** the doctor is doing his rounds el médico está haciendo una ronda de visitas; a second round of negotiations una segunda ronda de negociaciones
➤ a round of ammunition un disparo
➤ a round of applause un aplauso: he got a huge round of applause recibió un gran aplauso.

roundabout *UK* ['raʊndəbaʊt] *noun*
1. la **rotonda,** la **glorieta:** he went round the roundabout dio la vuelta a la rotonda
2. el **tiovivo:** the children had a ride on the roundabout los niños se subieron al tiovivo.

route [ruːt] *noun*

. el **camino**: what is the quickest route? ¿cuál es el camino más rápido?

. la **carretera**: Route 66 la carretera 66.

routine [ruːˈtiːn] *noun* ■ la **rutina**: exercise is part of my daily routine el ejercicio es parte de mi rutina diaria.

row *(noun & verb)*

noun [rəʊ]

. la **hilera**: a row of houses una hilera de casas

. la **fila**: they are sitting in the second row están sentados en la segunda fila

. [raʊ] la **pelea**: they had a row tuvieron una pelea

in a row seguido: he phoned her three times in a row la llamó tres veces seguidas

verb [rəʊ]

. **remar**: he rowed for three hours remó durante tres horas

to row across the river cruzar el río a remo.

rowboat *US* [ˈrəʊbəʊt] *noun* ■ el **bote a remos**.

rowdy [ˈraʊdɪ] *adjective* ■ **bullicioso**: a rowdy class una clase bulliciosa.

rowing [ˈrəʊɪŋ] *uncountable noun* ■ el **remo**: he likes rowing le gusta el remo

a rowing boat *UK* un bote de remos.

royal [ˈrɔɪəl] *adjective* ■ **real**: the royal family la familia real.

rub [rʌb] *(past tense & past participle* rubbed, *present participle* rubbing) *verb*

1. **frotar**: don't rub so hard no frotes tan fuerte

2. **frotarse**: he rubbed his eyes se frotó los ojos

rub out *phrasal verb* ■ **borrar**: she rubbed the word out on the blackboard borró la palabra de la pizarra.

rubber [ˈrʌbəʳ] *noun*

1. la **goma**: the ball is made of rubber la pelota es de goma

2. *UK* la **goma de borrar**: can I borrow your rubber? ¿me prestas tu goma de borrar?

> a rubber ball una pelota de goma

> a rubber band una goma elástica.

rubbish *UK* [ˈrʌbɪʃ] *(noun & adjective)*

■ *uncountable noun*

1. la **basura**: they collect the rubbish on Wednesdays recogen la basura los miércoles; this shop only sells rubbish esta tienda sólo vende basura

2. las **tonterías**: you're talking rubbish estás diciendo tonterías

> rubbish bin el cubo de la basura

> the rubbish dump el vertedero

■ *adjective*

malísimo: the film was rubbish la película era malísima.

ruby [ˈruːbɪ] *noun* ■ el **rubí** *(plural* los rubíes)*: a ruby necklace un collar de rubíes.

rucksack [ˈrʌksæk] *noun* ■ la **mochila**.

rude [ruːd] *adjective*

1. **maleducado, grosero**: she was rude to her mother fue grosera con su madre

2. **de mala educación**: it's rude to talk with your mouth full es de mala educación hablar con la boca llena.

rug [rʌg] *noun* ■ la **alfombra**: there's a rug in front of the fireplace hay una alfombra frente a la chimenea.

rugby [ˈrʌgbɪ] *noun* ■ el **rugby**: they're playing rugby están jugando al rugby.

ruin [ˈruːɪn] *(noun & verb)*

■ *noun*

la **ruina**: they found the ruins of an old castle encontraron las ruinas de un viejo castillo

in ruins en ruinas: the city is in ruins la ciudad está en ruinas

■ *verb*

arruinar: he ruined my party arruinó mi fiesta; the stock market crash ruined him la caída de la bolsa lo arruinó.

rule [ruːl] *(noun & verb)*

■ *noun*

1. la **regla**: what are the rules of the game? ¿cuáles son las reglas del juego?; he broke the rules rompió las reglas

2. la **norma**

to be against the rules ir en contra de las normas: smoking is against the rules fumar va en contra de las normas

■ *verb*

gobernar: who is going to rule the country? ¿quién va a gobernar el país?

rule out *phrasal verb* ■ **descartar:** we can't rule out the possibility of rain no podemos descartar la posibilidad de que llueva.

ruler ['ruːləʳ] *noun*

1. la **regla:** use a ruler to measure the line usa una regla para medir la línea

2. el **gobernante:** the ruler of the country el gobernante del país.

rum [rʌm] *noun* ■ el **ron.**

rumour *UK,* **rumor** *US* ['ruːməʳ] *noun* ■ el **rumor** *(plural los **rumores**):* it's just a rumour sólo es un rumor.

run [rʌn] *(noun & verb)*

■ *noun*

1. la **carrera:** a five-mile run una carrera de cinco millas; he scored 4 runs anotó 4 carreras

2. la **vuelta:** they went for a run in the car fueron a dar una vuelta en coche

▸ **in the long run** a la larga: in the long run it won't really matter a la larga, no importará realmente

▸ **to go for a run** ir a correr.

■ *verb (past tense* ran, *past participle* run*)*

1. **correr:** she ran 5 miles corrió 5 millas; you left the water running dejaste el agua corriendo; she ran across the road cruzó la carretera corriendo

2. **organizar:** they run courses in computing organizan cursos de informática

3. **dirigir:** she runs a big company dirige una gran empresa

4. **gotear:** my nose is running me gotea la nariz

5. **funcionar:** the bus runs on gas el autobús funciona con gas; the engine is running el motor está en marcha

6. **circular:** the trains don't run on Sundays los trenes no circulan los domingos

7. **pasar:** she ran her hand through her hair se pasó la mano por el cabello

8. **ser candidato a:** Bush is running for president Bush es candidato a presidente

9. **desteñirse:** my T-shirt has run in the washing machine se me ha desteñido la camiseta en la lavadora

10. **llevar (en coche):** can I run you to the station? ¿quieres que te lleve a la estación?

run away *phrasal verb* ■ **huir:** the thieves ran away los ladrones huyeron

run out *phrasal verb* ■ **agotarse:** their supplies ran out se les agotaron las provisiones

▸ **time is running out** se está acabando el tiempo

▸ **to run out of something** quedarse sin algo: they ran out of milk se quedaron sin leche

run over *phrasal verb* ■ **atropellar:** he was run over by a car lo atropelló un coche

▸ **to get run over** ser atropellado.

rung [rʌŋ] *past participle* ➤ **ring.**

runner ['rʌnəʳ] *noun* ■ el **corredor,** la **corredora:** there are ten runners in this race hay diez corredores en esta carrera.

runner bean [ˌrʌnəʳˈbiːn] *noun* ■ la **judía verde.**

runner-up ['rʌnəʳʌp] *noun* ■ el **subcampeón** *(plural los **subcampeones**),* la **subcampeona:** she was runner-up in her category fue subcampeona en su categoría.

running ['rʌnɪŋ] *noun* ■ he took up running at 40 empezó a correr a los 40 años.

runny ['rʌnɪ] *adjective*

▸ **to have a runny nose** gotear la nariz: I have a runny nose me gotea la nariz.

runway ['rʌnweɪ] *noun* ■ la **pista de aterrizaje:** the plane is on the runway el avión está en la pista de aterrizaje.

rush [rʌʃ] *(noun & verb)*

■ *noun*

la **prisa:** what's the rush? ¿qué prisa hay?

▸ **in a rush** deprisa: I did my homework in a rush hice los deberes deprisa

▸ **to be in a rush** tener prisa: I'm in a rush! ¡tengo prisa!

▸ **rush hour** hora punta: traffic is awful at rush hour el tráfico es terrible a la hora punta

verb

- **darse prisa, apresurarse:** you'll have to rush if you want to catch the train tendrás que darte prisa si quieres coger el tren
- **precipitarse, salir corriendo:** they rushed towards the exit se precipitó hacia la salida ▪ **to rush somebody to hospital** llevar a alguien urgentemente al hospital: **she was rushed to hospital** la llevaron urgentemente al hospital.

rust ['rʌst] *noun* ■ el **óxido:** your bike is covered in rust tu bicicleta está cubierta de óxido.

rusty ['rʌsti] *adjective* ■ **oxidado:** a rusty old nail un viejo clavo oxidado ▪ **my Italian is rusty** tengo muy olvidado el italiano.

rye [raɪ] *noun* ■ el **centeno:** rye bread pan de centeno.

sack [sæk] *(noun & verb)*
■ *noun*
el **saco:** a sack of potatoes un saco de patatas ▪ **to get the sack** US ser despedido (del trabajo)
■ *verb* UK
despedir (del trabajo): he's been sacked le han despedido.

sad [sæd] *adjective* ■ **triste:** she looks sad parece triste.

saddle ['sædl] *noun* ■ la **montura:** the jockey climbed into the saddle el jinete subió a su montura.

sadly ['sædlɪ] *adverb*
1. **con tristeza:** he looked at me sadly me miró con tristeza
2. **lamentablemente:** sadly she died lamentablemente murió.

sadness ['sædnɪs] *noun* ■ la **tristeza.**

safe [seɪf] *(adjective & noun)*
■ *adjective*
1. **sin peligro:** it's safe to swim here aquí se puede nadar sin peligro
2. **a salvo:** he's safe now ahora está a salvo
3. **seguro:** this ladder isn't very safe esta escalera no es muy segura
4. **prudente:** he's a safe driver es un conductor prudente
▸ **to feel safe** sentirse seguro
▸ **to be in a safe place** estar en un lugar seguro: **the jewels are in a safe place** las joyas están en un lugar seguro
▸ **it's not safe** no es seguro
■ *noun*
la **caja fuerte:** there's a lot of money in the safe hay mucho dinero en la caja fuerte.

safety ['seɪftɪ] *noun* ■ la **seguridad:** they say they do it for our safety dicen que lo hacen por nuestra seguridad
▸ **a safety belt** un cinturón de seguridad
▸ **a safety pin** un imperdible.

said [sed] *past tense & past participle* ➤ say.

sail [seɪl] *(noun & verb)*
■ *noun*
la **vela:** a ship in full sail un barco con las velas desplegadas
▸ **to set sail** zarpar: they set sail at dawn zarparon al amanecer
■ *verb*
1. **navegar:** the boat is sailing to Mallorca el barco está navegando hacia Mallorca
2. **zarpar:** we sail tomorrow mañana zarpamos.

sailboard ['seɪlbɔːrd] *noun* ■ la **tabla de windsurf.**

sailboat US [ˈseɪlbəʊt] noun ■ el **velero**.

sailing [ˈseɪlɪŋ] uncountable noun ■ **navegar: he goes sailing at the weekend** sale a navegar los fines de semana
➤ a **sailing boat** UK un barco de vela.

sailor [ˈseɪləʳ] noun ■ el **marinero: he's a sailor** es marinero.

saint [seɪnt] noun ■ el **santo**, la **santa: he's a saint** es un santo

Before a man's name, **Santo** is shortened to **San**, except before Tomás and Domingo:

Saint Paul San Pablo; **Saint Thomas** Santo Tomás; **Saint Catherine** Santa Catalina
➤ **Saint Patrick's Day** el día de San Patricio

SAINT PATRICK'S DAY

El 17 de marzo, día de san Patricio, es la fiesta nacional de Irlanda. Los irlandeses y sus descendientes en todos los rincones del planeta lo celebran por todo lo alto. Unos espectaculares desfiles recorren las calles de Dublín y Nueva York. Es tradición llevar una hoja de trébol, símbolo de Irlanda, o alguna prenda verde, el color nacional. En Estados Unidos, algunos bares llegan al extremo de servir cerveza verde.

sake [seɪk] noun
➤ **for somebody's sake** por alguien: **do it for my sake** hazlo por mí.

salad [ˈsæləd] noun ■ la **ensalada: do you want some salad?** ¿quieres ensalada?; **a mixed salad** una ensalada variada
➤ **salad dressing** el aderezo de ensalada.

salary [ˈsælərɪ] (plural salaries) noun ■ el **sueldo**.

sale [seɪl] noun
1. la **venta: the sales department** el departamento de ventas
2. la **rebaja: Bloomingdale's is having a sale** hay rebajas en Bloomingdale's
➤ **in the sales** UK OR **on sale** US en las rebajas: **I bought this coat in the sales** compré este abrigo en las rebajas
➤ **on sale** UK a la venta
➤ **for sale** se vende: **their house is not for sale** su casa no se vende

➤ **on sale** UK a la venta: **it's on sale in all the bookshops** está a la venta en todas las librerías.

sales assistant UK [ˈseɪlzəˈsɪstənt] noun ■ el **dependiente**, la **dependienta**.

sales clerk US [ˈseɪlzklɜːk] noun ■ el **dependiente**, la **dependienta**.

salesman [ˈseɪlzmən] (plural salesmen [ˈseɪlzmən]) noun ■ el **vendedor: he's an insurance salesman** es vendedor de seguros.

saleswoman [ˈseɪlzwʊmən] (plural saleswomen [ˈseɪlzwɪmɪn]) noun ■ la **vendedora: she's an insurance saleswoman** es vendedora de seguros.

salmon [ˈsæmən] noun ■ el **salmón** (plural los **salmones**)**: smoked salmon** salmón ahumado.

salon [ˈsælɒn] noun ■ el **salón** (plural los **salones**)**: a beauty salon** un salón de belleza.

salt [sɒlt] noun ■ la **sal: can you pass me the salt?** ¿me pasas la sal?

salty [ˈsɔːltɪ] adjective ■ **salado: this soup is too salty** esta sopa está demasiado salada.

salute [səˈluːt] verb ■ **saludar: the general saluted the troops** el general saludó a las tropas.

same [seɪm] (adjective & pronoun)
■ adjective
mismo: she's wearing the same sweater as I am lleva el mismo suéter que yo; **we left at the same time** nos fuimos al mismo tiempo
■ pronoun
lo **mismo: I'm going to order the same as you** voy a pedir lo mismo que tú
➤ **to look the same** parecerse: **they all look the same** todos se parecen
➤ **thanks all the same** gracias de todos modos.

sand [sænd] uncountable noun ■ la **arena**
➤ a **sand castle** un castillo de arena
➤ a **sand dune** una duna de arena.

sandal [ˈsændl] noun ■ la **sandalia: she's wearing sandals** lleva sandalias.

sandwich [UK 'sænwɪdʒ, US 'sænwɪtʃ] noun

1. with sliced bread el **sándwich** (plural los **sándwiches**): a cheese sandwich un sándwich de queso

2. with French bread el **bocadillo**: a tuna sandwich un bocadillo de atún.

sang [sæŋ] past tense ➤ sing.

sanitary towel UK ['sænɪtrɪ'taʊəl], **sanitary napkin** US ['sænɪtrɪ'næpkɪn] noun ■ la **compresa.**

sank [sæŋk] past tense ➤ sink.

Santa Claus ['sæntə,klɔːz] noun ■ **Papá Noel.**

sarcastic [sær'kæstɪk] adjective ■ **sarcástico.**

sardine [sɑː'diːn] noun ■ la **sardina.**

sat [sæt] past tense & past participle ➤ sit.

satchel ['sætʃəl] noun ■ la **cartera (escolar).**

satellite ['sætəlaɪt] noun ■ el **satélite:** satellite TV televisión por satélite
a satellite dish una antena parabólica.

satisfied ['sætɪsfaɪd] adjective ■ **satisfecho:** I'm not satisfied with your work no estoy satisfecha con tu trabajo.

Saturday ['sætədɪ] noun

In Spanish the days of the week do not start with a capital letter:

el **sábado:** it's Saturday today hoy es sábado; next Saturday el sábado que viene; last Saturday el sábado pasado
on Saturday el sábado: I'll see you on Saturday te veo el sábado
on Saturdays los sábados: he comes to see me on Saturdays viene a verme los sábados.

sauce [sɔːs] noun ■ la **salsa:** tomato sauce salsa de tomate.

saucepan ['sɔːspən] noun ■ la **cacerola.**

sauna ['sɔːnə] noun ■ la **sauna.**

sausage ['sɒsɪdʒ] noun ■ la **salchicha.**

save [seɪv] verb

1. **salvar:** she saved my life me salvó la vida

2. **ahorrar:** we must try and save water debemos intentar ahorrar agua

3. **ahorrarse:** I saved a hundred dollars me ahorré cien dólares

4. **guardar:** he saved the cake for later guardó el pastel para más tarde; I saved my file onto a floppy disk guardé el archivo en un disquete
to save time ahorrar tiempo: that will save you a lot of time eso te ahorrará mucho tiempo

save up phrasal verb ■ **ahorrar:** he's saving up to buy a guitar está ahorrando para comprar una guitarra.

savings ['seɪvɪŋz] plural noun ■ los **ahorros:** she has spent all her savings se ha gastado todos sus ahorros.

savoury UK, **savory** US ['seɪvərɪ] adjective ■ **salado:** I prefer savoury foods to sweet foods prefiero lo salado a lo dulce.

saw [sɔː] (noun, verb & verb form)
■ noun
la **sierra:** a power saw una sierra eléctrica
■ verb (past tense sawed, past participle UK sawn, US sawed)
serrar: he sawed the board in half serró la tabla a la mitad
■ past tense
➤ see.

sawn UK [sɔːn] past participle ➤ saw.

saxophone ['sæksəfəʊn] noun ■ el **saxofón** (plural los **saxofones**): she plays the saxophone toca el saxofón.

say [seɪ] (past tense & past participle said) verb ■ **decir:** what did you say? ¿qué dijiste tú?; I said I was tired dije que estaba cansado
could you say that again? ¿podrías repetir eso?

saying ['seɪɪŋ] noun ■ el **dicho:** it's a well-known saying es un dicho muy conocido.

scale [skeɪl] noun

1. la **escala:** this map has a scale of 1/100 este mapa tiene una escala de 1/100; she's practising her scales está practicando las escalas musicales

2. la **magnitud:** the scale of the problem la magnitud del problema

scales *plural noun*

la **balanza:** put your luggage on the scales coloque su equipaje sobre la balanza
➤ **bathroom scales** una báscula.

scampi ['skæmpɪ] *uncountable noun* ■ las **gambas rebozadas.**

scan [skæn] *(noun & verb)*
■ *noun*
la **ecografía,** el **escáner**
■ *verb (past tense & past participle* scanned, *present participle* scanning)
escanear: I scanned the photo escaneé la foto.

scandal ['skændl] *noun* ■ el **escándalo:** it caused a scandal causó escándalo.

scanner ['skænər] *noun* ■ el **escáner** *(plural* los **escáneres**)**:** put the photo in the scanner pon la foto en el escáner.

scar [skɑːr] *noun* ■ la **cicatriz** *(plural* las **cicatrices**)*.*

scare [skeər] *(noun & verb)*
■ *noun*
el **susto:** you gave me a scare me diste un susto
➤ **a bomb scare** una amenaza de bomba
■ *verb*
asustar: Juan scares me Juan me asusta.

scarecrow ['skeəkrəʊ] *noun* ■ el **espantapájaros** *(plural* los **espantapájaros**)*.*

scared ['skeəd] *adjective*
➤ **to be scared** tener miedo: I was scared of him le tenía miedo; I'm not scared of flying no tengo miedo a volar; don't be scared no tengas miedo.

scarf [skɑːf] *(plural* scarfs [skɑːfs] OR scarves [skɑːvz]) *noun*
1. la **bufanda:** a woollen scarf una bufanda de lana
2. el **pañuelo:** a silk scarf un pañuelo de seda.

scary ['skeərɪ] *adjective*
➤ **to be scary** ser aterrador: it's a scary film es una película de miedo.

scarves *plural* ➤ scarf.

scene [siːn] *noun*
1. la **escena:** there is a very funny scene in the film hay una escena muy divertida en la película
2. el **lugar:** the scene of the crime el lugar del crimen
➤ **behind the scenes** entre bastidores.

scenery ['siːnərɪ] *uncountable noun* ■ el **paisaje:** I love the scenery in this part of the country me encanta el paisaje en esta zona del país.

schedule [*UK* 'ʃedjuːl, *US* 'skedʒʊl] *noun*
1. el **programa:** according to the schedule, the building will be finished next year según el programa, el edificio se acabará el año que viene
2. *US* el **horario:** the train schedule el horario de los trenes
➤ **we're on schedule** estamos al día
➤ **we're ahead of schedule** vamos adelantados
➤ **we're behind schedule** vamos con retraso.

scheme [skiːm] *noun* ■ el **plan:** it's a scheme to make money es un plan para ganar dinero.

scholarship ['skɒləʃɪp] *noun* ■ la **beca:** he got a scholarship obtuvo una beca.

school [skuːl] *noun*
1. el **colegio**
2. la **escuela:** a language school una escuela de idiomas
3. la **facultad:** law school la facultad de derecho
➤ **a school bus** un autobús escolar
➤ **the school year** el año escolar

SCHOOL

En Gran Bretaña, los niños van primero a la **primary school** (de 5 a 11 años) o a la **infant school** (de 5 a 7 años). Luego, asisten a la **junior school** (de 7 a 11 años). A partir de los 11 y hasta los 16 o 18 estudian en la **secondary school**.

El sistema educativo de Estados Unidos se divide en dos niveles básicos: primaria y secundaria. La escuela primaria (**elementary school, grade school** o **grammar school**) abarca de los 6 a los 12 años. Luego se pasa a la **junior high school** (de los 12 a los 14 años,) para acabar en una **high school** (a partir de los 14 años).

schoolbook ['sku:lbʊk] *noun* ■ el **libro de texto**: don't forget your schoolbooks no te olvides de tus libros de texto.

schoolchildren ['sku:ltʃɪldrən] *plural noun* ■ los **escolares.**

science ['saɪəns] *noun* ■ la **ciencia**: science and technology ciencia y tecnología; Chris wants to study science Chris quiere estudiar ciencias
science fiction ciencia ficción: it's a science fiction book es un libro de ciencia ficción.

scientific [,saɪən'tɪfɪk] *adjective* ■ **científico**: a scientific method un método científico.

scientist ['saɪəntɪst] *noun* ■ el **científico**, la **científica**: she's a scientist es científica.

scissors ['sɪzəz] *plural noun* ■ las **tijeras** a pair of scissors unas tijeras.

scoop [sku:p] *noun* ■ la **bola**: three scoops of ice cream tres bolas de helado.

scooter ['sku:tə'] *noun*
1. el **escúter**: a lot of people use scooters to get around mucha gente usa un escúter para desplazarse
2. el **patinete**: the child was playing on his scooter el niño jugaba con su patinete.

score [skɔ:'] *(noun & verb)*
■ *noun*
el **resultado**: the final score was one-nil el resultado final fue uno a cero
what's the score? ¿cómo van?
■ *verb*
marcar: he scored a goal marcó un gol; they haven't scored yet no han marcado todavía.

scorpion ['skɔ:pjən] *noun* ■ el **escorpión** *(plural* los **escorpiones***)*.

Scotland ['skɒtlənd] *noun* ■ **Escocia.**

Scottish ['skɒtɪʃ] *adjective*

Remember not to use a capital letter for the adjective in Spanish:

escocés: the Scottish countryside is beautiful la campiña escocesa es hermosa.

scout [skaʊt] *noun* ■ el/la **boyscout.**

scrambled eggs ['skræmbldegz] *plural noun* ■ los **huevos revueltos.**

scrap paper *UK* [skræp'peɪpə'] *noun* ■ el **papel de borrador.**

scratch [skrætʃ] *(noun & verb)*
■ *noun*
el **rasguño**, el **arañazo**: my legs are covered with scratches tengo las piernas llenas de rasguños; there's a scratch on this CD este CD tiene un arañazo
to start from scratch empezar desde cero: we'll just have to start from scratch vamos a tener que empezar desde cero
■ *verb*
1. **rascar**: can you scratch my back? ¿me rascas la espalda?
2. **rascarse**: don't scratch no te rasques; he was scratching his leg se estaba rascando la pierna
3. **arañar**: the cat scratched my hand el gato me arañó la mano.

scratch paper *US* [skrætʃ'peɪpə'] *noun* ■ el **papel de borrador.**

scream [skri:m] *(noun & verb)*
■ *noun*
el **grito**: I could hear screams oía gritos
■ *verb*
gritar: she screamed when the vampire appeared gritó cuando apareció el vampiro.

screen [skri:n] *noun* ■ la **pantalla**: it's a good film to see on the big screen es una buena película para ver en pantalla grande; the computer screen is very bright la pantalla del ordenador brilla mucho
a screen saver un protector de pantalla.

screw [skru:] *(noun & verb)*
■ *noun*
el **tornillo**: he went to buy some screws fue a comprar tornillos
■ *verb*
1. **atornillar**: you have to screw the mirror to the wall tienes que atornillar el espejo a la pared
2. **enroscar**: I screwed the top on the bottle enrosqué la tapa de la botella.

screwdriver ['skruː,draɪvəʳ] *noun* ■ el destornillador.

scroll [skrəʊl] *verb* ■ desplazarse: scroll down to the end of the document desplázate hacia abajo, hasta el final del documento.

scruffy ['skrʌfɪ] *adjective* ■ desaliñado: he looked scruffy tenía un aspecto desaliñado.

sculptor ['skʌlptəʳ] *noun* ■ el escultor, la escultora: Rodin was a sculptor Rodin era escultor.

sculpture ['skʌlptʃəʳ] *noun* ■ la escultura: an exhibition of modern sculptures una exposición de esculturas modernas.

sea [siː] *noun* ■ el mar: I like swimming in the sea me gusta nadar en el mar
- by sea en barco
- by the sea a orillas del mar.

seafood ['siːfuːd] *uncountable noun* ■ el marisco.

seagull ['siːgʌl] *noun* ■ la gaviota.

seal [siːl] *(noun & verb)*

■ *noun*
la **foca**: seals are mammals that live in cold waters las focas son mamíferos que viven en aguas frías

■ *verb*
cerrar: have you sealed the envelope yet? ¿ya has cerrado el sobre?

search [sɜːtʃ] *(noun & verb)*

■ *noun*
1. la **búsqueda**: there was a search for the missing boy se llevó a cabo una búsqueda del chico desaparecido
2. el **registro**: the police carried out a search of the house la policía efectuó un registro domiciliario
- a search engine un buscador
- a search party un grupo de rescate

■ *verb*
1. **buscar**: we searched the whole town buscamos por toda la ciudad; I searched my pockets busqué en mis bolsillos
2. **registrar**: the police searched the apartment la policía registró el apartamento

search for *phrasal verb* ■ **buscar**: I'm searching for my keys estoy buscando mis llaves.

seashell ['siːʃel] *noun* ■ la concha marina.

seasick ['siːsɪk] *adjective*
- to be seasick estar mareado: she was seasick estaba mareada
- to get seasick marearse.

seaside ['siːsaɪd] *noun* ■ la playa: we're going to the seaside for our holidays vamos a ir a la playa por vacaciones.

season ['siːzn] *noun*
1. la **estación** *(plural* las **estaciones***)*: my favourite season is spring mi estación favorita es la primavera
2. la **temporada**: the football season la temporada de fútbol
- a season ticket un abono: I'm going to get a season ticket voy a comprar un abono.

seat [siːt] *noun*
1. el **asiento**: your book's on the back seat of the car tu libro está en el asiento trasero del coche
2. el **escaño**: he has a seat in parliament tiene un escaño en el parlamento
3. la **localidad**: I reserved two seats for the play reservé dos localidades para ver la obra
4. **plaza**: there are no free seats on the flight no quedan plazas libres en el vuelo
- a seat belt un cinturón de seguridad: fasten your seat belts abróchense los cinturones de seguridad.

seaweed ['siːwiːd] *uncountable noun* ■ el alga marina

Feminine noun that takes un or el in the singular.

second ['sekənd] *(adjective & noun)*

■ *adjective*
segundo: that's the second time he has rung ésa es la segunda vez que toca el timbre
- it's the second of June *UK* OR it's June second *US* estamos a dos de junio
- on the second floor
1. *UK* en el segundo piso
2. *US* en el primer piso
- to come second llegar segundo

noun
el **segundo**: wait a second! ¡espera un segundo!
to have **seconds** repetir: may I have seconds? ¿puedo repetir?

secondary school [UK 'sekəndrıskuːl, US 'sekəndərıskuːl] *noun* ■ una **escuela secundaria**.

second-class [ˌsekənd'klɑːs] *adjective* ■ de **segunda clase**: a second-class ticket un billete de segunda clase
second-class post correo de franqueo normal.

second-hand [ˌsekənd'hænd] *(adjective & adverb)*
■ *adjective*
de **segunda mano**: it's a second-hand bike es una bicicleta de segunda mano
■ *adverb*
de **segunda mano**: I bought it second-hand la compré de segunda mano.

secret ['siːkrıt] *(adjective & noun)*
■ *adjective*
secreto: it's a secret meeting place es un lugar de encuentro secreto
■ el **secreto**: he can't keep a secret no sabe guardar un secreto
we met in **secret** nos encontramos en secreto.

secretary [UK 'sekrətrı, US 'sekrətərı] *(plural secretaries) noun* ■ el **secretario**, la **secretaria**.

section ['sekʃn] *noun* ■ la **sección** *(plural las secciones)*: there are three sections to the newspaper hay tres secciones en el periódico.

security [sı'kjʊərətı] *noun* ■ la **seguridad**: security at the airport has been tightened han reforzado la seguridad en el aeropuerto
a security guard un guardia de seguridad.

see [siː] *(past tense* saw, *past participle* seen) *verb* ■ **ver**: I saw Jack yesterday ayer vi a Jack; have you seen any good films recently? ¿has visto alguna buena película últimamente?; I can't see no veo; I'll see what I can do veré lo que puedo hacer

➤ we'll see veremos
➤ see you soon! ¡hasta pronto!
➤ see you! ¡nos vemos!

see off *phrasal verb* ■ **despedir**: he saw me off at the airport me despidió en el aeropuerto

see to *phrasal verb* ■ **encargarse de**: I can't close the door — I'll see to it no puedo cerrar la puerta —yo me encargo de eso.

seed [siːd] *noun*
1. la **semilla**: she planted some sunflower seeds plantó unas semillas de girasol
2. el **favorito**, la **favorita**: he's number two seed in the tournament es el segundo de los favoritos del torneo.

seek [siːk] *(past tense & past participle* sought) *verb* ■ **buscar**: we're seeking a solution estamos buscando una solución.

seem [siːm] *verb* ■ **parecer**: she seems sad parece triste; you seem to be having problems parece que tienes problemas; there seems to be a delay parece que hay un retraso
➤ so it seems eso parece.

seen [siːn] *past participle* ➤ see.

seesaw ['siːsɔː] *noun* ■ el **balancín** *(plural los balancines)*.

seize [siːz] *verb* ■ **coger**: she seized my arm me cogió del brazo.

select [sı'lekt] *verb* ■ **seleccionar**: she selected the CDs she wanted seleccionó los CD que quería.

selection [sı'lekʃn] *noun*
1. la **selección** *(plural las selecciones)*: you've made a good selection has hecho una buena selección
2. el **surtido**: there's a good selection of food in the market hay un gran surtido de comida en el mercado.

self-confident [ˌself'kɒnfıdənt] *adjective* ■ **seguro de sí mismo**: Kim's very self-confident Kim está muy segura de sí misma.

self-conscious [ˌself'kɒnʃəs] *adjective* ■ **cohibido**: I feel very self-conscious in my red hat me siento muy cohibida con este sombrero rojo.

self-control [ˌselfkən'trəʊl] *noun* ■ el **dominio de sí mismo**: he lost his self-control perdió el dominio de sí mismo.

self-defence *UK,* **self-defense** *US* [ˌselfdɪ'fens] *noun* ■ la **defensa personal**: a self-defence course un curso de defensa personal

➤ in self-defence en defensa propia: she shot him in self-defence le disparó en defensa propia.

selfish ['selfɪʃ] *adjective* ■ **egoísta**: he's very selfish es muy egoísta.

self-service [ˌself's3ːvɪs] *adjective*
➤ a self-service restaurant un (restaurante) autoservicio.

sell [sel] *(past tense & past participle* sold*) verb* ■ **vender**: I'm trying to sell my computer estoy tratando de vender mi ordenador; she sold it for 100 euros lo vendió por 100 euros; I sold him my bike le vendí mi bici

sell out *phrasal verb* ■ all the tickets are sold out todas las entradas están agotadas; we've sold out of coffee se nos ha terminado el café.

Sellotape® *UK* ['seləteɪp] *noun* ■ el **celo®**.

semester [sɪ'mestər] *noun* ■ el **semestre**.

semicircle ['semɪs3ːkl] *noun* ■ el **semicírculo**.

semicolon [ˌsemɪ'kəʊlən] *noun* ■ el **punto y coma**.

semi-detached house *UK* ['semɪdɪ-'tætʃhaʊs] *noun* ■ la **casa pareada**.

Senate *US* ['senɪt] *noun* ■ the Senate el **Senado**.

senator *US* ['senətər] *noun* ■ el **senador,** la **senadora**: he's a New York senator es senador por Nueva York.

send [send] *(past tense & past participle* sent*) verb* ■ **mandar, enviar**: he sent me a letter me mandó una carta

➤ send them my love salúdales de mi parte
➤ to send somebody home mandar a alguien a casa

send back *phrasal verb* ■ **devolver**: if you don't want it, you can send it back si no lo quieres, puedes devolverlo

send for *phrasal verb* ■ **mandar a buscar**: I sent for the doctor mandé a buscar al médico

send off *phrasal verb*
1. **enviar (por correo)**: Ray sent off the package yesterday Ray envió el paquete ayer
2. **expulsar**: the player was sent off el jugador fue expulsado.

senior ['siːnjər] *(adjective & noun)*

■ *adjective*
1. **mayor**: she is two years senior to me es dos años mayor que yo
2. **alto**: these are senior people in the government estos son altos cargos del gobierno
➤ a senior citizen una persona de la tercera edad
➤ senior pupils *UK* los alumnos de escuela secundaria (de 16 a 18 años)
➤ senior year *US* el último año de la universidad: Raul's in his senior year Raúl está en el último año de la universidad

■ *noun*
1. *UK* el **alumno de escuela secundaria,** la **alumna de escuela secundaria** *(de 16 a 18 años)*
2. *US* el/la **estudiante del último año**: the school's seniors are taking their final exams los estudiantes del último año están haciendo sus exámenes finales.

sense [sens] *noun*
1. el **sentido**: what you say doesn't make sense lo que dices no tiene sentido; the five senses los cinco sentidos
2. el **sentido común**: you have no sense no tienes sentido común
➤ that makes sense eso tiene sentido
➤ a sense of humour el sentido del humor: she doesn't have a sense of humour no tiene sentido del humor
➤ the sense of smell el sentido del olfato
➤ the sense of touch el sentido del tacto.

sensible ['sensəbl] *adjective* ■ **sensato**: she's a sensible girl es una chica sensata

 La palabra inglesa **sensible** es un falso amigo, no significa "sensible".

sensitive ['sensɪtɪv] *adjective* ■ **sensible:** he's a sensitive boy es un muchacho sensible she's sensitive about her weight no le gusta que hagan comentarios sobre su peso.

sent [sent] *past tense & past participle* ➤ send.

sentence ['sentəns] *(noun & verb)*
■ *noun*
1. la **oración** *(plural* las **oraciones***):* a sentence should begin with a capital letter and end with a full stop una oración debe empezar con mayúscula y terminar con un punto
2. la **condena:** a five-year sentence una condena de cinco años
■ *verb*
condenar: he was sentenced to five years in prison lo condenaron a cinco años de prisión.

separate *(adjective & verb)*
■ *adjective* ['seprət]
1. **aparte:** put it in a separate envelope ponlo en un sobre aparte
2. **diferente:** these are two separate issues estos son dos temas diferentes
3. **separado:** can we have separate receipts? ¿podría darnos recibos separados?
➤ she has a separate room tiene su propia habitación
■ *verb* ['sepəreɪt]
1. **separar:** they separated the boys from the girls separaron a los niños de las niñas
2. **separarse:** they separated after ten years of marriage se separaron después de diez años de matrimonio.

September [sep'tembər] *noun*

In Spanish the months of the year do not start with a capital letter:

septiembre *(masculine):* school starts in September las clases empiezan en septiembre; next September el próximo septiembre; last September el pasado septiembre.

sequel ['siːkwəl] *noun* ■ la **continuación** *(plural* las **continuaciones***):* have you seen the sequel to the film? ¿has visto la continuación de la película?

sergeant ['sɑːdʒənt] *noun* ■ el/la **sargento:** he's a sergeant in the army es sargento del ejército; he's a police sergeant es sargento de policía.

serial ['sɪərɪəl] *noun* ■ la **serie:** a television serial una serie de televisión.

series ['sɪəriːz] *(plural* series*) noun* ■ la **serie:** we've had a series of problems hemos tenido una serie de problemas
➤ The World Series la Serie Mundial (de béisbol).

serious ['sɪərɪəs] *adjective*
1. **serio:** he always looks serious siempre está serio
2. **grave:** she has a serious illness padece una enfermedad grave.

seriously ['sɪərɪəslɪ] *adverb*
1. **en serio: seriously, what do you think?** en serio, ¿qué crees tú?
2. **gravemente:** he was seriously injured estaba gravemente herido.

serve [sɜːv] *verb* ■ **servir:** dinner is served at 7 o'clock la cena se sirve a las 7 en punto
➤ that serves you right lo tienes bien merecido.

service ['sɜːvɪs] *noun*
1. el **servicio:** the service is good in this restaurant el servicio en este restaurante es bueno; service is not included el servicio no está incluido
2. la **revisión** *(plural* las **revisiones***):* I'm going to take the car for a service voy a llevar el coche para que le hagan la revisión
➤ a service provider un proveedor de servicios
➤ a service station una estación de servicio.

session ['seʃn] *noun* ■ la **sesión** *(plural* las **sesiones***):* a recording session una sesión de grabación.

set [set] *(noun, adjective & verb)*
■ *noun*
1. el **juego:** a set of keys un juego de llaves; a chess set un juego de ajedrez
2. la **colección** *(plural* las **colecciones***):* a set of encyclopaedias una colección de enciclopedias
3. el **set:** Sampras won the first set Sampras ganó el primer set

a dinner set una vajilla

a television set un televisor

■ *adjective*

listo: they were set to leave estaban listos para salir

a set menu un menú del día

■ *verb (past tense & past participle* set, *present participle* setting)*

1. **poner**: she set the vase on the table puso el jarrón sobre la mesa; he set his bike against the wall puso su bici contra la pared; I'll set the alarm for 6 a.m. voy a poner el despertador a las 6 de a mañana.

2. **fijar**: let's set a time and a place fijemos una hora y lugar

3. **establecer**: he set a new world record estableció un nuevo récord mundial

4. **ponerse**: the sun's setting el sol se está poniendo

5. **programar**: have you set the video? ¿has programado el video?

▷ to set somebody free poner en libertad a alguien

▷ to set something on fire prenderle fuego a algo

▷ to set the table poner la mesa

▷ the film's set in Casablanca la película está ambientada en Casablanca

set off *phrasal verb*

1. **salir**: they set off at dawn salieron al amanecer

2. **tirar**: they set some fireworks off tiraron fuegos artificiales

3. **hacer explotar**: they set the bomb off hicieron explotar la bomba

4. **hacer sonar**: the burglar set the alarm off el ladrón hizo sonar la alarma

set out *phrasal verb*

1. **proponerse**: he set out to find the buried treasure se propuso encontrar el tesoro enterrado

2. **salir**: they set out early in the morning salieron pronto por la mañana

set up *phrasal verb*

1. **montar**: he set up a new business montó un nuevo negocio

2. **instalar**: he set the computer up in his room instaló el ordenador en su habitación

3. **montar**: they set the tent up in the garden montaron la tienda en el jardín.

set square ['setskweə^r] *noun* ■ la **escuadra.**

settee [se'tiː] *noun* ■ el **sofá.**

settle ['setl] *verb*

1. **zanjar**: we settled the argument zanjamos la discusión

2. **pagar**: may I settle the bill now? ¿podría pagar la cuenta ahora?

3. **establecerse**: they settled in Canada se establecieron en Canadá

▷ that's settled queda decidido

settle down *phrasal verb*

1. **calmarse**: settle down! ¡cálmate!

2. **acomodarse**: she settled down in the armchair se acomodó en el sillón.

seven ['sevn] *number* ■ **siete**: the seven wonders of the world las siete maravillas del mundo; she's seven tiene siete años; he went out at seven salió a las siete.

seventeen [,sevn'tiːn] *number* ■ **diecisiete**: there are seventeen girls in the class hay diecisiete niñas en la clase; she's seventeen tiene diecisiete años.

seventeenth [,sevn'tiːnθ] *number* ■ **decimoséptimo**

▷ it's her seventeenth birthday cumple diecisiete años

▷ it's the seventeenth of May UK OR it's May seventeenth US estamos a 17 de mayo.

seventh ['sevnθ] *number* ■ **séptimo**: on the seventh floor en el séptimo piso

▷ it's the seventh of November UK OR it's November seventh US estamos a 7 de noviembre.

seventy ['sevntɪ] *number* ■ **setenta**: she's seventy tiene setenta años

▷ seventy-one setenta y uno

▷ seventy-two setenta y dos.

several ['sevrəl] *(adjective & pronoun)*

■ *adjective*

varios: she called me several times me llamó varias veces

pronoun
varios: he ate several of them se comió varios.

sew [səʊ] *(past tense* sewed, *past participle* sewn OR sewed) *verb* ■ **coser: do you know how to sew?** ¿sabes coser?; **she sewed the button on** cosió el botón.

sewing ['səʊɪŋ] *uncountable noun* ■ **la costura**
a sewing machine una máquina de coser.

sewn [səʊn] *past participle* ➤ sew.

sex [seks] *noun* ■ el **sexo: there were young people of both sexes** había jóvenes de ambos sexos
to have sex with somebody tener relaciones sexuales con alguien.

sexist ['seksɪst] *adjective* ■ **sexista: don't be sexist** no seas sexista.

sexy ['seksɪ] *adjective* ■ **sexy** *(plural* sexys): **she was wearing a sexy dress** llevaba un vestido sexy.

shade [ʃeɪd] *noun*
1. la **sombra: I was sitting in the shade** estaba sentado a la sombra; **it was 30 degrees in the shade** hacía 30 grados a la sombra
2. el **tono: choose another shade of green** elige otro tono de verde.

shadow ['ʃædəʊ] *noun* ■ la **sombra: I saw a shadow on the wall** vi una sombra en la pared.

shake [ʃeɪk] *(past tense* shook, *past participle* shaken) *verb*
1. **sacudir: shake the tree to make the apples fall** sacude el árbol para que caigan las manzanas
2. **agitar: you have to shake the bottle first** tienes que agitar la botella primero
3. **temblar: my legs are shaking** me tiemblan las piernas; **she's shaking with cold** está temblando de frío
   to shake hands with somebody darle la mano a alguien: **we shook hands** nos dimos la mano
   to shake one's head negar con la cabeza: **I asked if she was coming and she shook her head** le pregunté si venía y negó con la cabeza.

shaken ['ʃeɪkn] *past participle* ➤ shake.

shall [ʃəl, ʃæl] *verb*
1. *the future tense* **I shall see him tomorrow** lo veré mañana
2. *making suggestions* **shall I open the window?** ¿abro la ventana?; **let's go, shall we?** ¿qué les parece si vamos?

shallow ['ʃæləʊ] *adjective* ■ **poco profundo: the river is shallow here** el río es poco profundo aquí.

shame [ʃeɪm] *noun* ■ la **vergüenza: he put me to shame** me hizo pasar vergüenza
it's a shame es una lástima: **it's a shame that you lost** es una lástima que hayas perdido
what a shame! ¡qué lástima!

shampoo [ʃæm'puː] *noun* ■ el **champú** *(plural* los champús).

shan't UK [ʃɑːnt] = shall not: **I shan't be long** no tardaré; **we shan't be able to come** no podremos venir.

shape [ʃeɪp] *noun* ■ la **forma: a cake in the shape of a heart** un pastel en forma de corazón
to be in good shape estar en buena forma: **he's in good shape** está en buena forma.

share [ʃeər] *(noun & verb)*
■ *noun*
la **parte: I didn't get my share** no obtuve mi parte
■ *verb*
compartir: I share a room with him comparto habitación con él
share out *phrasal verb* ■ **repartir: they shared out the sweets** repartieron los caramelos.

shares ['ʃeərz] *plural noun* ■ las **acciones: we have shares in the company** tenemos acciones en la compañía.

shark [ʃɑːk] *noun* ■ el **tiburón** *(plural* los tiburones): **these waters are full of sharks** estas aguas están llenas de tiburones.

sharp [ʃɑːp] *(adjective & adverb)*
■ *adjective*
1. **afilado: a sharp knife** un cuchillo afilado

2. **puntiagudo**: a sharp needle una aguja puntiaguda
3. **brusco**: a sharp rise in prices una subida brusca de los precios
4. **agudo**: he's very sharp es muy agudo
■ adverb
at 8 o'clock sharp a las 8 en punto.

shave [ʃeɪv] (noun & verb)
■ noun
un **afeitado**
➤ you need a shave necesitas un afeitado
➤ to have a shave afeitarse
■ verb
afeitarse: he shaves every day se afeita todos los días; he shaved off his beard se afeitó la barba
➤ to shave one's legs afeitarse las piernas.

shaver ['ʃeɪvəʳ] noun ■ la **máquina de afeitar**.

shaving cream ['ʃeɪvɪŋkriːm] noun ■ la **crema de afeitar**.

shaving foam ['ʃeɪvɪŋfəʊm] noun ■ la **espuma de afeitar**.

shawl [ʃɔːl] noun ■ el **chal**.

she [ʃiː] pronoun ■ **ella**

The pronoun "she" is often not translated unless it is needed for emphasis or clarification:

she's called Eileen se llama Eileen; she came to see me vino a verme; she did it ella lo hizo; she doesn't know it but he does ella no lo sabe pero él sí
➤ there she is! ¡ahí está!

shed [ʃed] noun ■ el **cobertizo**: there's a shed in the garden hay un cobertizo en el jardín.

she'd [ʃɪd, ʃiːd]
1. = she had: she'd forgotten to bring her camera se había olvidado de llevar la cámara
2. = she would: she'd like to come with us le gustaría venir con nosotros.

sheep [ʃiːp] (plural sheep) noun ■ la **oveja**.

sheet [ʃiːt] noun
1. la **sábana**: the sheets are clean las sábanas están limpias

2. la **hoja**: give me a sheet of paper dame una hoja de papel.

shelf [ʃelf] (plural shelves [ʃelvz]) noun ■ la **estante**: I put the book on the shelf puse el libro en el estante.

shell [ʃel] noun
1. la **concha**: there are lots of shells on the beach hay muchas conchas en la playa
2. el **caparazón** (plural los **caparazones**): the turtle has a very big shell la tortuga tiene un caparazón muy grande
3. la **cáscara**: the shell of the egg la cáscara del huevo
4. el **obús** (plural los **obuses**): the shell exploded in the field el obús explotó en el campo.

she'll [ʃiːl] = she will OR she shall: she'll be here soon llegará pronto.

shelter ['ʃeltəʳ] (noun & verb)
■ noun
el **refugio**: we were looking for shelter estábamos buscando refugio
➤ to take shelter refugiarse: he took shelter from the storm se refugió de la tormenta
■ verb
1. **refugiarse**: we sheltered from the rain in the tube station nos refugiamos de la lluvia en la estación de metro
2. **proteger**: he sheltered the girl with his body protegió a la niña con su cuerpo.

shelves plural ➤ shelf.

shepherd ['ʃepəd] noun ■ el **pastor**.

sheriff US ['ʃerif] noun ■ el/la **sheriff**: he's the sheriff of Great Rock es el sheriff de Great Rock.

she's [ʃiːz]
1. = she is: she's happy to be here está contenta de estar aquí
2. = she has: she's taken my pen me ha cogido el bolígrafo.

shield [ʃiːld] noun ■ el **escudo**: the soldiers used shields to protect themselves los soldados usaban escudos para protegerse.

shin [ʃɪn] noun ■ la **espinilla**.

shine [ʃaɪn] *(past tense & past participle* shone) *verb* ■ **brillar**: the sun was shining el sol brillaba.

shiny ['ʃaɪnɪ] *adjective* ■ **brillante**.

ship [ʃɪp] *noun* ■ **el barco**: the ship sank el barco se hundió
we went by ship fuimos en barco.

shipwreck ['ʃɪprek] *noun* ■ **el naufragio**.

shipwrecked ['ʃɪprekt] *adjective*
to be shipwrecked naufragar.

shirt [ʃɜːt] *noun* ■ **la camisa**: he was wearing a shirt and tie llevaba camisa y corbata.

shiver ['ʃɪvəʳ] *verb*

1. **tiritar**: it's so cold she's shivering hace tanto frío que está tiritando
2. **temblar**: she heard the scream and shivered oyó los gritos y tembló.

shock [ʃɒk] *(noun & verb)*
■ *noun*

1. **la conmoción**: the news of his death left his fans in shock la noticia de su muerte causó conmoción entre sus fans
2. **la descarga**: he got an electric shock recibió una descarga eléctrica
■ *verb*
escandalizar: his behaviour shocked me OR I was shocked by his behaviour su comportamiento me escandalizó

shocking ['ʃɒkɪŋ] *adjective* ■ **escandaloso**: his attitude is shocking su actitud es escandalosa.

shoe [ʃuː] *noun* ■ **el zapato**: put your shoes on! ¡ponte los zapatos!; I took my shoes off me quité los zapatos
> a pair of shoes un par de zapatos
> a shoe shop una zapatería.

shoelace ['ʃuːleɪs] *noun* ■ **el cordón de los zapatos** *(plural* los **cordones de los zapatos***)*: your shoelaces are undone llevas los cordones desatados.

shone [ʃɒn] *past tense & past participle* ➤ shine.

shook [ʃʊk] *past tense* ➤ shake.

shoot [ʃuːt] *(past tense & past participle* shot) *verb*

1. **disparar**: where did you learn to shoot? ¿dónde aprendiste a disparar?
2. **pegarle un tiro a**: he was shot in the leg le pegaron un tiro en la pierna
3. **fusilar**: they shot him at dawn lo fusilaron al amanecer
4. **rodar**: they shot the film in New Zealand rodaron la película en Nueva Zelanda
5. **chutar, tirar**: the forward shoot a goal el delantero chutó a la portería
> he was shot dead in the robbery lo mataron a tiros en el atraco.

shop [ʃɒp] *(noun & verb)*
■ *noun*
la tienda: that shop sells used books esa tienda vende libros usados
> a shop assistant *UK* un dependiente, una dependienta
> a shop window un escaparate
■ *verb (past tense & past participle* shopped, *present participle* shopping)
hacer compras: we often shop at that supermarket a menudo hacemos compras en este supermercado.

shopkeeper ['ʃɒpˌkiːpəʳ] *noun* ■ **el/la comerciante**.

shopping ['ʃɒpɪŋ] *uncountable noun* ■ **las compras**
> to go shopping ir de compras: he goes shopping every Friday va de compras todos los viernes
> a shopping bag una bolsa de la compra
> a shopping centre *UK* OR a shopping center *US* OR a shopping mall *US* un centro comercial.

shore [ʃɔːʳ] *noun* ■ **la orilla**: we were walking on the shore paseábamos por la orilla.

short [ʃɔːt] *adjective*

1. **corto**: Sam has short hair Sam lleva el pelo corto; it's a short film es una película corta
2. **bajo**: he's very short es muy bajo
> Dan is short for Daniel Dan es el diminutivo de Daniel
> they call him Bob for short lo llaman Bob para abreviar.

shortcut [ˈʃɔːtkʌt] *noun* ■ el **atajo**: she took the shortcut tomó el atajo.

shortly [ˈʃɔːtlɪ] *adverb* ■ **dentro de poco**: I'll see you again shortly te veré de nuevo dentro de poco.

shorts [ʃɔːts] *plural noun* ■ los **pantalones cortos**: he was wearing shorts llevaba pantalones cortos.

shortsighted UK [ˌʃɔːtˈsaɪtɪd] *adjective* ■ **miope**.

shot [ʃɒt] *(noun & verb form)*
■ *noun*
1. el **disparo**: we heard shots oímos disparos
2. la **vacuna**, la **inyección**: the baby has had all his shots al bebé le han puesto todas las vacunas
3. la **toma**: this is a nice shot ésta es una buena toma
➤ good shot! ¡buen tiro!
■ *past tense & past participle*
➤ shoot.

shotgun [ˈʃɒtɡʌn] *adjective* ■ la **escopeta**.

should [ʃʊd] *verb*

"Should" is translated by the verb **deber** in the conditional tense:

you should go deberías irte; they should have won the match deberían haber ganado el partido.

shoulder [ˈʃəʊldər] *noun* ■ el **hombro**: he put his hand on her shoulder le puso la mano en el hombro.

shouldn't [ˈʃʊdnt] = should not.

should've [ˈʃʊdəv] = should haver.

shout [ʃaʊt] *(noun & verb)*
■ *noun*
el **grito**: I heard a shout oí un grito
■ *verb*
gritar: he was shouting at me estaba gritándome.

show [ʃəʊ] *(noun & verb)*
■ *noun*
1. el **espectáculo**: we're going to see a show on Broadway vamos a ver un espectáculo en Broadway

2. el **programa**: it's a live television show es un programa de televisión en directo
3. la **exposición**: he's got a show at the Guggenheim tiene una exposición en el Guggenheim
■ *verb (past tense* showed, *past participle* shown OR showed*)*
1. **enseñar**: I showed them the photos les enseñé las fotos
2. **indicar**: can you show me the way? ¿puedes indicarme el camino?
3. **dar**: they are going to show the film tomorrow van a dar la película mañana

show off *phrasal verb* ■ **presumir**: he's always showing off siempre está presumiendo

show up *phrasal verb* ■ **presentarse**: she hasn't shown up yet todavía no se ha presentado.

shower [ˈʃaʊər] *noun*
1. la **ducha**: he's in the shower está en la ducha
2. el **chubasco**: it's not raining much, it's only a shower no está lloviendo mucho, es sólo un chubasco
➤ to have a shower **ducharse**: I'm going to have a shower voy a ducharme.

shown [ʃəʊn] *past participle* ➤ show.

show-off [ˈʃəʊɒf] *noun* ■ el **fanfarrón** *(plural* los **fanfarrones***), la* **fanfarrona**: he's a show-off es un fanfarrón.

shrank [ʃræŋk] *past tense* ➤ shrink.

shrimp [ʃrɪmp] *noun* ■ el **camarón** *(plural* los **camarones***)*.

shrink [ʃrɪŋk] *(past tense* shrank, *past participle* shrunk*) verb* ■ **encoger**: this material shrinks esta tela encoge.

Shrove Tuesday [*UK* ˌʃrəʊvˈtjuːzdɪ, *US* ˌʃrəʊvˈtuːzdɪ] *noun* ■ el **Martes de Carnaval**.

shrug [ʃrʌɡ] *(past tense & past participle* shrugged, *present participle* shrugging*) verb*
➤ to shrug one's shoulders **encogerse de hombros**: he shrugged his shoulders se encogió de hombros.

shrunk [ʃrʌŋk] *past participle* ➤ shrink.

shuffle [ˈʃʌfl] *verb*
to shuffle the cards barajar las cartas.

shut [ʃʌt] *(adjective & verb)*
adjective
cerrado: the window is shut la ventana está cerrada
verb (past tense & past participle shut, *present participle* shutting*)*
cerrar: she shut the door cerró la puerta

shut up *phrasal verb* ■ **callarse:** will you shut up! ¿quieres callarte?

shutter [ˈʃʌtəʳ] *noun* ■ la **contraventana:** close the shutters cierra las contraventanas.

shuttle [ˈʃʌtl] *adjective*
1. el **transbordador:** a space shuttle el transbordador espacial
2. el **puente aéreo:** the shuttle from Barcelona to Madrid el puente aéreo de Barcelona a Madrid.

shy [ʃaɪ] *adjective* ■ **tímido.**

sick [sɪk] *adjective* ■ **enfermo:** he's not at school because he's sick no ha venido a la escuela porque está enfermo
▸ to be sick *UK* devolver
▸ to feel sick *UK* tener ganas de devolver
▸ to be sick of something estar harto de algo: I'm sick of your lies estoy harto de tus mentiras.

side [saɪd] *noun*
1. el **lado:** the school is on the other side of the road la escuela está al otro lado de la calle; his dog stood by his side su perro estaba a su lado
2. la **orilla:** there's a house by the side of the river hay una casa a la orilla del río
3. el **equipo:** our side won the match nuestro equipo ganó el partido
▸ side by side uno al lado del otro: they were walking side by side caminaban uno al lado del otro
▸ to be on somebody's side estar de parte de alguien: are you on my side? ¿estás de mi parte?
▸ to take sides tomar partido.

sideboard [ˈsaɪdbɔːd] *noun* ■ el **aparador.**

sideboards *UK* [ˈsaɪdbɔːdz], **sideburns** [ˈsaɪdbɜːnz] *plural noun* ■ las **patillas:** he has sideboards lleva patillas.

sidewalk *US* [ˈsaɪdwɔːk] *noun* ■ la **acera.**

sideways [ˈsaɪdweɪz] *adverb* ■ **de lado:** crabs walk sideways los cangrejos andan de lado.

sigh [saɪ] *(noun & verb)*
noun
el **suspiro:** he gave a sigh of relief dio un suspiro de alivio
verb
suspirar: she sighed with frustration suspiró de frustración.

sight [saɪt] *noun* ■ la **vista:** I have good sight tengo buena vista; I've lost sight of her la he perdido de vista; at first sight a primera vista
▸ he faints at the sight of blood se desmaya con sólo ver la sangre
▸ to catch sight of something divisar algo: we caught sight of the pyramids divisamos las pirámides
▸ I know him by sight lo conozco de vista
▸ what a funny sight! ¡vaya pinta!
▸ she's a sight está horrorosa.

sights [saɪts] *plural noun* ■ los **lugares de interés turístico:** we went to see the sights of New York visitamos los lugares de interés turístico de Nueva York.

sightseeing [ˈsaɪtˌsiːɪŋ] *noun* ■ let's go sightseeing vamos a visitar los lugares de interés turístico.

sign [saɪn] *(noun & verb)*
noun
1. la **señal:** Harry made a sign to me Harry me hizo una señal; the victory sign la señal de la victoria
2. el **letrero:** follow the signs to the station sigue los letreros hacia la estación
verb
firmar: can you sign here, please? ¿puede firmar aquí, por favor?

signal [ˈsɪgnl] *noun* ■ la **señal:** the teacher gave them the signal to start la maestra les hizo una señal para que comenzaran.

signature ['sɪgnətʃəʳ] *noun* ▪ la **firma**: I can't read the signature no puedo leer la firma.

significant [sɪg'nɪfɪkənt] *adjective* ▪ **significativo**: it's a significant discovery es un descubrimiento significativo.

signpost ['saɪnpəʊst] *noun* ▪ la **señal**.

Sikh [siːk] *(adjective & noun)*
▪ *adjective*
sij: the Sikh religion la religión sij
▪ *noun*
el/la **sij**: he's a Sikh es sij.

silence ['saɪləns] *noun* ▪ el **silencio**: a sudden noise broke the silence un ruido repentino rompió el silencio.

silent ['saɪlənt] *adjective*
1. **silencioso**: a silent place un lugar silencioso
2. **callado**: they kept silent se mantuvieron callados.

silicon chip [ˌsɪlɪkən'tʃɪp] *noun* ▪ el chip de silicio *(plural* los **chips de silicio***)*.

silk [sɪlk] *noun* ▪ la **seda**: it's made of silk es de seda
➤ a silk blouse una blusa de seda.

silly ['sɪlɪ] *adjective* ▪ **tonto**: don't be silly! ¡no seas tonto!

silver ['sɪlvəʳ] *adjective* ▪ la **plata**: it's made of silver es de plata
➤ a silver bracelet una pulsera de plata.

similar ['sɪmɪləʳ] *adjective* ▪ **parecido**: these two colours are similar estos dos colores son parecidos
➤ to be similar to something ser parecido a algo: her coat's similar to mine su abrigo es parecido al mío.

simple ['sɪmpl] *adjective* ▪ **sencillo**: it's a simple question es una pregunta sencilla.

sin [sɪn] *noun* ▪ el **pecado**: it's a sin to lie es pecado mentir.

since [sɪns] *(preposition, conjunction & adverb)*
▪ *preposition*
desde: it's been raining since Sunday está lloviendo desde el domingo; I've lived in England since 1990 vivo en Inglaterra desde 1990; she'd been waiting since 7 p.m. esperaba desde las 7 de la tarde
➤ since then desde entonces
▪ *conjunction*
1. **conocer**: I've known him since I was 10 lo conozco desde que tenía 10 años
2. **como**: since it's raining, we might as well stay at home como está lloviendo, más vale que nos quedemos en casa
▪ *adverb*
desde entonces: I haven't seen her since no la he visto desde entonces.

sincere [sɪn'sɪəʳ] *adjective* ▪ **sincero**.

sincerely [sɪn'sɪəlɪ] *adverb*
➤ Yours sincerely *UK* OR Sincerely yours *US* Atentamente.

sing [sɪŋ] *(past tense* sang, *past participle* sung*) verb* ▪ **cantar**: he sang a song cantó una canción; she sings very well canta muy bien.

singer ['sɪŋəʳ] *noun* ▪ el/la **cantante**.

singing ['sɪŋɪŋ] *uncountable noun* ▪ el **canto**: singing lessons clases de canto.

single ['sɪŋgl] *(adjective & noun)*
▪ *adjective*
1. **solo**: there isn't a single book in their house no hay ni un solo libro en su casa
2. **soltero**: she's single es soltera
▪ *noun*
1. el **single** *(plural* los **singles***)*: their latest single is on the album su último single viene en el álbum
2. *UK* el **billete de ida**: can I have a single to Birmingham, please? ¿me da un billete de ida a Birmingham, por favor?
➤ a single bed una cama individual
➤ the single currency la moneda única
➤ in single file en fila india: they were walking in single file andaban en fila india
➤ a single parent un padre soltero, una madre soltera: she's a single parent es madre soltera
➤ the men's singles los individuales masculinos.

singular ['sɪŋgjʊləʳ] *noun* ▪ **singular**: put this noun in the singular pon este sustantivo en singular.

sink [sɪŋk] *(noun & verb)*
noun
el **fregadero**: the dishes are in the sink los platos están en el fregadero
verb (past tense sank, *past participle* sunk*)*
hundirse: the Titanic sank in 1912 el Titanic se hundió en 1912; our feet sank into the mud se nos hundieron los pies en el barro.

sip [sɪp] *(past tense & past participle* sipped, *present participle* sipping*) verb* ■ **beber a sorbos**: he was sipping his tea estaba bebiendo el té a sorbos.

sir [sɜːʳ] *noun* ■ **señor**: excuse me, sir disculpe, señor; yes, sir! sí, señor
Dear Sir,… Estimado señor:…

sister ['sɪstəʳ] *noun* ■ la **hermana**: he has two sisters tiene dos hermanas.

sister-in-law ['sɪstəʳɪnlɔː] *(plural* sisters-in-law*) noun* ■ la **cuñada**.

sit [sɪt] *(past tense & past participle* sat, *present participle* sitting*) verb* ■ **sentarse**: come and sit here ven a sentarte aquí
to be sitting estar sentado: Vicky was sitting on the floor Vicky estaba sentada en el suelo
to sit an exam *UK* presentarse a un examen

sit down *phrasal verb* ■ **sentarse**: sit down! ¡siéntate!; he sat down in the armchair se sentó en el sillón.

site [saɪt] *noun*
1. el **lugar**: the museum stands on the site of an old factory el museo ocupa el lugar de una antigua fábrica
2. el **sitio web**: have you visited the BBC site? ¿has visitado el sitio web de la BBC?
3. el **emplazamiento**: here is the site of the new offices aquí está el emplazamiento de las nuevas oficinas
a building site una obra: Bill works on a building site Bill trabaja en una obra
an archaeological site un yacimiento arqueológico.

sitting room ['sɪtɪŋruːm] *noun* ■ la **sala de estar**: there's a TV in the sitting room hay un televisor en la sala de estar.

situation [ˌsɪtjʊ'eɪʃn] *noun* ■ la **situación** *(plural* las **situaciones**): we're in a difficult situation estamos en una situación difícil.

six [sɪks] *number* ■ **seis**: there are six states in Australia Australia tiene seis estados; he's six tiene seis años; we went out at six salimos a las seis.

sixteen [sɪks'tiːn] *number* ■ **dieciséis**: there are sixteen boys in the class hay dieciséis chicos en la clase; he's sixteen tiene dieciséis años.

sixteenth [sɪks'tiːnθ] *number* ■ **decimosexto**
it's his sixteenth birthday cumple dieciséis años
it's the sixteenth of June *UK* OR it's June sixteenth *US* estamos a dieciséis de junio

sixth [sɪksθ] *number* ■ **sexto**: on the sixth floor en el sexto piso
it's the sixth of January *UK* OR it's January sixth *US* estamos a seis de enero.

sixty ['sɪkstɪ] *number* ■ **sesenta**: she's sixty tiene sesenta años
sixty-one sesenta y uno
sixty-two sesenta y dos.

size [saɪz] *noun*
1. el **tamaño**: the two rooms are the same size las dos habitaciones tienen el mismo tamaño
2. la **talla**: what size are you? ¿qué talla usas?; I'm a size 40 uso la talla 40
3. el **número**: what shoe size do you take? ¿qué número de zapatos calzas?; I take a size 7 shoe calzo el número 7.

skate [skeɪt] *noun* ■ el **patín** *(plural* los **patines**): I'm getting some new skates me voy a comprar patines nuevos.

skateboard ['skeɪtbɔːd] *noun* ■ el **monopatín** *(plural* los **monopatines**).

skating ['skeɪtɪŋ] *noun*
to go skating ir a patinar: we go skating on the lake in winter en invierno vamos a patinar al lago
a skating rink una pista de patinaje.

skeleton [ˈskelɪtn] *noun* ■ el **esqueleto**: there's a skeleton in the grave hay un esqueleto en la tumba.

sketch [sketʃ] *(noun & verb)*
■ *noun*
el **bosquejo**: I drew a sketch dibujé un bosquejo
■ *verb*
hacer un bosquejo: he sketched the White House hizo un bosquejo de la Casa Blanca.

sketchpad [ˈsketʃpæd] *noun* ■ el **bloc de dibujo.**

ski [skiː] *(noun & verb)*
■ *noun*
el **esquí** *(plural* **esquís** OR **esquíes***)*: he's wearing skis lleva puestos los esquís
▸ ski boots botas de esquí
▸ a ski lift un telesilla
▸ a ski pole un bastón de esquí
▸ a ski slope una pista de esquí
▸ a ski tow un telesquí
■ *verb (past tense & past participle* skied, *present participle* skiing)
esquiar: she's learning how to ski está aprendiendo a esquiar.

skier [ˈskiːəʳ] *noun* ■ el **esquiador,** la **esquiadora**: she's a good skier es buena esquiadora.

skid [skɪd] *(past tense & past participle* skidded, *present participle* skidding) verb* ■ **derrapar**: the car skidded on the ice el coche derrapó sobre el hielo.

skies *plural* ➤ sky.

skiing [ˈskiːɪŋ] *uncountable noun* ■ el **esquí**: he's having skiing lessons está recibiendo clases de esquí
▸ to go skiing ir a esquiar: they go skiing every weekend van a esquiar cada fin de semana.

skilful UK, **skillful** US [ˈskɪlfʊl] *adjective* ■ **hábil**: he's a skilful player es un jugador hábil.

skill [skɪl] *noun* ■ la **habilidad**: this job requires great skill este trabajo requiere una gran habilidad.

skillful US ➤ skilful UK.

skimmed milk [ˈskɪmdmɪlk] *noun* ■ la **leche desnatada.**

skin [skɪn] *noun* ■ la **piel**: she has fair skin tiene la piel blanca
▸ a banana skin una piel de plátano.

skinny [ˈskɪnɪ] *adjective* ■ **flaco.**

skin-tight [skɪntaɪt] *adjective* ■ **muy ceñido**: she was wearing skin-tight jeans tenía puestos unos vaqueros muy ceñidos.

skip [skɪp] *(past tense & past participle* skipped, *present participle* skipping) verb*
1. **saltarse**: she skipped breakfast se saltó el desayuno
2. **faltar**: he skipped his class faltó a clase
3. UK **saltar a la comba**: can you skip? ¿sabes saltar a la comba?

skipping rope UK [ˈskɪpɪŋrəʊp] *noun* ■ la **cuerda,** la **comba.**

skirt [skɜːt] *noun* ■ la **falda.**

skull [skʌl] *noun* ■ el **cráneo.**

sky [skaɪ] *(plural* skies [skaɪz]*) noun* ■ el **cielo**: the sky's blue el cielo es azul
▸ sky blue azul celeste: the walls are sky blue las paredes son azul celeste.

skylight [ˈskaɪlaɪt] *noun* ■ la **claraboya.**

skyscraper [ˈskaɪˌskreɪpəʳ] *noun* ■ el **rascacielos** *(plural* los **rascacielos***)*.

slam [slæm] *(past tense & past participle* slammed, *present participle* slamming) verb*
■ **cerrar de golpe**: I slammed the door cerré la puerta de golpe
▸ the door slammed la puerta se cerró de un portazo.

slang [slæŋ] *noun* ■ el **argot**: it's a young people's slang word es una palabra del argot juvenil.

slap [slæp] *(noun & verb)*
■ *noun*
1. la **bofetada**: he gave me a slap in the face me dio una bofetada
2. la **palmada**: he gave me a slap on the back me dio una palmada en la espalda

verb (past tense & past participle slapped, *present participle* slapping)
- darle una bofetada a: I slapped him in the face le di una bofetada
- darle una palmada a: he slapped me on the back me dio una palmada en la espalda.

slave [sleɪv] *noun* ■ el **esclavo**, la **esclava**: there were slaves at that time había esclavos en esa época.

slavery ['sleɪvərɪ] *noun* ■ la **esclavitud**: slavery was abolished in 1833 in Britain and in 1865 in the US la esclavitud fue abolida en Inglaterra en 1833 y en EE.UU. en 1865.

sledge *UK* [sledʒ], **sled** *US* [sled] *noun* ■ el **trineo**: they came down the hill in a sledge bajaron la colina en un trineo.

sleep [sliːp] *(noun & verb)*
noun
el **sueño**: it's the lack of sleep es la falta de sueño
I need some sleep necesito dormir
verb (past tense & past participle slept)
dormir: she's sleeping está durmiendo; we slept at the Imperial dormimos en el Imperial
to go to sleep dormirse: he went to sleep straightaway se durmió enseguida

sleep in *phrasal verb* ■ **dormir hasta tarde**: I sleep in when I don't have to go to school duermo hasta tarde cuando no tengo que ir al colegio

sleep over *phrasal verb* ■ **quedarse a dormir**: I slept over at Patty's house me quedé a dormir en casa de Patty.

sleeping bag ['sliːpɪŋbæg] *noun* ■ el **saco de dormir**.

sleepy ['sliːpɪ] *adjective*
to be sleepy OR to feel sleepy tener sueño: I feel sleepy tengo sueño.

sleeve [sliːv] *noun* ■ la **manga**
he rolled up his sleeves se arremangó.

slender ['slendər] *adjective* ■ **delgado**.

slept [slept] *past tense & past participle* ➤ sleep.

slice [slaɪs] *(noun & verb)*
noun
1. la **rebanada**: he cut a slice of bread cortó una rebanada de pan
2. la **loncha**: a slice of cheese una loncha de queso
3. la **rodaja**: a slice of lemon una rodaja de limón
verb
cortar: can you slice the bread? ¿puedes cortar el pan?

slid [slɪd] *past tense & past participle* ➤ slide.

slide [slaɪd] *(noun & verb)*
noun
1. el **tobogán** *(plural* los **toboganes***)*: the children are playing on the slide los niños están jugando en el tobogán
2. la **diapositiva**: they showed us their slides nos enseñaron sus diapositivas
3. *UK* el **pasador (para el pelo)**
verb (past tense & past participle slid*)*
deslizarse: he was sliding on the ice se deslizaba en el hielo.

slight [slaɪt] *adjective* ■ **leve**: there has been a slight improvement ha habido una leve mejoría.

slightly ['slaɪtlɪ] *adverb* ■ **un poco**: I feel slightly better me siento un poco mejor.

slim [slɪm] *adjective* ■ **delgado**: Nicole's very slim Nicole es muy delgada.

sling [slɪŋ] *noun* ■ el **cabestrillo**: his arm is in a sling lleva el brazo en cabestrillo.

slip [slɪp] *(noun & verb)*
noun
la **combinación** *(plural* las **combinaciones***)*: she needs to wear a slip with that dress necesita ponerse una combinación con ese vestido
a slip of paper un papelito: I wrote it on a slip of paper lo escribí en un papelito
verb (past tense & past participle slipped, *present participle* slipping*)*
1. **resbalarse**: I slipped me resbalé
2. **meter disimuladamente**: he slipped some money into my pocket me metió disimuladamente dinero en el bolsillo.

slipper ['slɪpə^r] *noun* ■ la **zapatilla**: he put on his slippers se puso las zapatillas.

slope [sləʊp] *noun* ■ la **pendiente**: it's a very steep slope es una pendiente muy empinada.

slot [slɒt] *noun* ■ la **ranura**: put your money in the slot introduzca su dinero en la ranura
> a slot machine una máquina tragaperras.

slow [sləʊ] (*adjective, adverb & verb*)
■ *adjective*
lento: this bus is very slow este autobús es muy lento
> my watch is slow mi reloj se atrasa: my watch is five minutes slow mi reloj se atrasa cinco minutos
> in slow motion a cámara lenta
■ *adverb*
despacio: we're going slow vamos despacio
■ *verb*
reducir la velocidad: she slowed to a stop fue reduciendo la velocidad hasta detenerse

slow down *phrasal verb* ■ **reducir la velocidad**: you're driving too fast, slow down estás conduciendo muy rápido, reduce la velocidad.

slowly ['sləʊlɪ] *adverb*
1. **lentamente**: I was walking slowly caminaba lentamente
2. **despacio**: speak slowly! ¡habla despacio!

smack [smæk] (*noun & verb*)
■ *noun*
la **palmada**: she gave him a smack le dio una palmada
> a smack in the face una bofetada
■ *verb*
dar una palmada: she smacked him on the bottom le dio una palmada en el trasero.

small [smɔːl] *adjective* ■ **pequeño**: they live in a small village viven en un pueblo pequeño
> small change el dinero suelto, la calderilla: do you have any small change? ¿tienes suelto?

smart [smɑːt] *adjective*
1. UK **elegante**: you look smart in that dress estás muy elegante con ese vestido; we went to a smart restaurant fuimos a un restaurante elegante
2. **listo**: his child is very smart su hijo es muy listo.

smash [smæʃ] *verb*
1. **romper**: he smashed a window rompió una ventana
2. **romperse**: the glass smashed on the floor el vaso se rompió en el suelo.

smell [smel] (*noun & verb*)
■ *noun*
el **olor**: I love the smell of cut grass me encanta el olor del césped cortado
> the sense of smell el sentido del olfato
■ *verb* (*past tense & past participle* smelt OR smelled)
1. **oler**: I can smell gas huelo a gas; that cake smells good ese pastel huele bien
2. **oler mal**: your socks smell! ¡tus calcetines huelen mal!

smelly ['smelɪ] *adjective* ■ **maloliente**: a smelly, narrow street una calle estrecha y maloliente
> you've got smelly feet te huelen los pies.

smelt [smelt] *past tense & past participle*
➤ smell.

smile [smaɪl] (*noun & verb*)
■ *noun*
la **sonrisa**: he gave me a big smile me sonrió de oreja a oreja
■ *verb*
sonreír: she smiled at me me sonrió.

smiley ['smaɪlɪ] *noun* ■ el **emoticón** (*plural* los **emoticones**).

smoke [sməʊk] (*noun & verb*)
■ *noun*
el **humo**: the room is full of smoke la habitación está llena de humo
■ *verb*
fumar: he was smoking a cigarette estaba fumando un cigarrillo.

smoker ['sməʊkə^r] *noun* ■ el **fumador**, la **fumadora**
> he's a heavy smoker fuma mucho.

smoking ['sməʊkɪŋ] *noun* ■ el **tabaquismo**

there is no cure for smoking el tabaquismo no tiene cura
to give up smoking dejar de fumar
"no smoking" "prohibido fumar".

smooth [smuːð] *adjective* ■ **suave**: he has smooth skin tiene la piel suave.

SMS [esemes] *(abbreviation of* Short Message Service*) noun* ■ el **SMS** *(abbreviation of* Servicio de Mensajes Cortos*)*.

snack [snæk] *noun* ■ el **tentempié**
to have a snack picar algo de comer
a snack bar una cafetería.

snail [sneɪl] *noun* ■ el **caracol**.

snake [sneɪk] *noun* ■ la **serpiente**.

snap [snæp] *(past tense & past participle* snapped*, present participle* snapping*) verb*
romperse: the rope snapped la cuerda se rompió
partir: I snapped the branch in two partí la rama en dos.

snatch [snætʃ] *verb* ■ **arrebatar**: he snatched my bag from my hands me arrebató la bolsa de las manos.

sneakers ['sniːkəz] *plural noun* ■ las **zapatillas de deportes**: Ben's wearing sneakers Ben lleva puestas unas zapatillas de deporte.

sneeze [sniːz] *verb* ■ **estornudar**: I sneezed estornudé.

sniff [snɪf] *verb* ■ **olfatear**: the dog sniffed the bone el perro olfateó el hueso.

snob [snɒb] *noun* ■ el/la **esnob** *(plural* los/las **esnobs***)*: you're a snob eres un esnob.

snore [snɔːʳ] *verb* ■ **roncar**: he snores at night ronca de noche.

snorkel ['snɔːkl] *noun* ■ el **tubo de bucear**.

snorkelling *UK*, **snorkeling** *US* ['snɔːklɪŋ] *noun* ■ el **buceo con tubo**
to go snorkelling ir a bucear con tubo.

snow [snəʊ] *(noun & verb)*
■ *noun*
la **nieve**: there's snow on the top of the mountains hay nieve en la cima de las montañas

■ *verb*
nevar: it's snowing está nevando.

snowball ['snəʊbɔːl] *noun* ■ la **bola de nieve**.

snowboard ['snəʊˌbɔːd] *noun* ■ la **tabla de snowboard**.

snowboarding ['snəʊˌbɔːdɪŋ] *noun* ■ el **snowboard**: to go snowboarding practicar snowboard.

snowman ['snəʊmæn] *(plural* snowmen ['snəʊmen]*) noun* ■ el **muñeco de nieve**: they made a snowman hicieron un muñeco de nieve.

so [səʊ] *(adverb & conjunction)*
■ *adverb*
1. **tan**: she's so beautiful! ¡es tan guapa!; don't be so stupid! ¡no seas tan estúpido!
2. **también**: he's American and so is she él es americano y ella también; she has a dog and so do I ella tiene un perro y yo también
3. *with 'think', 'hope', 'say', 'suppose'* I don't think so no creo; I think so creo que sí; I hope so espero que sí; I suppose so supongo que sí
> **so far** hasta ahora: so far I haven't made any mistakes hasta ahora no he cometido ningún error
> **so many** tantos: she has so many friends! ¡tiene tantos amigos!
> I'd never seen so many people nunca había visto tanta gente
> **so much** tanto: I have so much work! ¡tengo tanto trabajo!; I'd never seen so much money nunca había visto tanto dinero; I love you so much te quiero tanto
> **or so** más o menos: thirty or so treinta más o menos

■ *conjunction*
así: I'll be on holiday, so I won't be able to come estaré de vacaciones, así que no voy a poder venir; my bike was broken so I repaired it mi bici estaba rota, así que la arreglé
> **so what's the point then?** ¿para qué entonces?
> **so what?** ¿y qué?
> **so long!** adiós

> so that para que: he worked hard so that everything would be ready in time trabajó mucho para que todo estuviera listo a tiempo

The conjunction **para que** is followed by a verb in the subjunctive in Spanish.

soak ['səʊk] *verb* ■ **poner en remojo:** she soaked the shirt in soapy water puso la camisa en remojo con agua y jabón.

soaking ['səʊkɪŋ] *adjective* ■ **empapado:** I'm soaking OR I'm soaking wet estoy empapado

> first soak the lentils primero pon las lentejas en remojo.

soap [səʊp] *noun* ■ el **jabón** *(plural* los **jabones***):* a bar of soap una pastilla de jabón

> a soap opera una telenovela.

soccer ['sɒkəʳ] *noun* ■ el **fútbol:** I play soccer every Saturday juego al fútbol todos los sábados

> a soccer player un jugador de fútbol

SOCCER

Soccer es la palabra que se utiliza en Estados Unidos para referirse al deporte mundialmente conocido como fútbol. Ha ganado mucha popularidad en años recientes y hoy en día muchos niños y niñas estadounidenses practican este deporte.

social ['səʊʃəl] *adjective* ■ **social:** social sciences ciencias sociales; the social services los servicios sociales

> social security la seguridad social.

socialist ['səʊʃəlɪst] *(adjective & noun)*

■ *adjective*
socialista

■ *noun*
el/la **socialista.**

society [sə'saɪətɪ] *(plural* societies*) noun*

1. la **sociedad:** we live in a multicultural society vivimos en una sociedad multicultural

2. la **asociación** *(plural* las **asociaciones***):* Jenny is in a drama society Jenny está en una asociación teatral.

sock [sɒk] *noun* ■ el **calcetín** *(plural* los **calcetines***):* he's wearing black socks lleva puestos unos calcetines negros.

soda US ['səʊdə] *noun*

1. el **refresco:** Cheryl's drinking a soda Cheryl está tomando un refresco

2. la **gaseosa.**

sofa ['səʊfə] *noun* ■ el **sofá:** he's sitting on the sofa está sentado en el sofá.

soft [sɒft] *adjective*

1. **suave:** the baby has soft skin el bebé tiene la piel suave

2. **blando:** the butter is soft la mantequilla está blanda; a soft mattress un colchón blando; a soft leather bag un bolso de cuero blando

> a soft drink un refresco.

softly ['sɒftlɪ] *adverb* ■ **en voz baja:** she was singing softly estaba cantando en voz baja.

software ['sɒftweəʳ] *uncountable noun* ■ el **software:** the computer comes with a lot of software el ordenador viene con mucho software.

soggy ['sɒgɪ] *adjective* ■ **empapado:** the ground was soggy el suelo estaba empapado.

soil [sɔɪl] *noun* ■ la **tierra:** the soil is red in Australia la tierra es roja en Australia.

solar ['səʊləʳ] *adjective* ■ **solar:** solar energy la energía solar.

sold [səʊld] *past tense & past participle* ➤ sell.

soldier ['səʊldʒəʳ] *noun* ■ el/la **soldado.**

sole [səʊl] *noun* ■ la **suela:** there's a hole in the sole of my shoe hay un agujero en la suela de mi zapato.

solicitor UK [sə'lɪsɪtəʳ] *noun* ■ el **notario, la notaria:** he's a solicitor es notario.

solid ['sɒlɪd] *adjective*

1. **sólido:** the bridge is very solid el puente es muy sólido

2. **macizo:** he wears a solid gold chain lleva una cadena de oro macizo.

solution [sə'luːʃn] *noun* ■ la **solución** *(plural* las **soluciones***):* we're trying to find a

solution estamos tratando de encontrar una solución.

solve [sɒlv] *verb* ■ **resolver: he has solved the problem** ha resuelto el problema.

some [sʌm] *(adjective, pronoun & adverb)*
adjective

When "some" refers to something that is un-countable, it is often not translated in Spanish:

do you want some coffee? ¿quieres café?; **I bought some meat** compré carne; **he gave me some money** me dio dinero; **let's go and buy some sweets** vamos a comprar caramelos

2. **alguno: some swans are black** algunos cisnes son negros; **some people like his music** a algunos les gusta su música

Alguno becomes *algún* before masculine nouns.

some day algún día
pronoun

alguno: some are red, some are blue algunos son rojos, algunos son azules; **I bought a kilo of oranges, some of them were bad** compré un kilo de naranjas, algunas estaban en mal estado

that cake looks nice, can I have some? este pastel tiene buen aspecto, ¿puedo comer un poco?
adverb

unos: there were some 7,000 people at the concert había unas 7.000 personas en el concierto.

somebody ['sʌmbədɪ], **someone** ['sʌmwʌn] *pronoun* ■ **alguien: somebody came to see you** alguien vino a verte; **he's somebody famous** es alguien famoso; **somebody else** otra persona.

someday ['sʌmdeɪ] *adverb* ■ **algún día: someday I'll be rich and famous** algún día seré rico y famoso.

somehow ['sʌmhaʊ] *adverb* ■ **de alguna manera: I'll do it somehow** de alguna manera lo haré

somehow, I don't think he'll come back no sé por qué, pero no creo que él vuelva.

someone *pronoun* ➤ somebody.

someplace *US adverb* ➤ somewhere.

something ['sʌmθɪŋ] *pronoun* ■ **algo: I have something in my eye** tengo algo en el ojo; **don't just stand there, do something!** ¡no te quedes ahí parado, haz algo!; **something odd happened** pasó algo extraño; **would you like something to drink?** ¿quieres algo de beber?

I'll have something else voy a tomar otra cosa
that was something else! ¡eso fue genial!
he's something else! ¡es fuera de serie!

sometime ['sʌmtaɪm] *adverb* ■ **algún día, alguna vez: come and see me sometime** ven a verme algún día; **I'll see you sometime next week** te veré algún día de la semana que viene.

sometimes ['sʌmtaɪmz] *adverb* ■ **a veces: she sometimes writes to me** a veces me escribe; **sometimes I make mistakes** a veces cometo errores.

somewhere ['sʌmweər], **someplace** *UK* ['sʌmpleɪs] *adverb* ■ **en algún lugar, algún sitio: they live somewhere in Scotland** viven en algún lugar de Escocia; **I'm looking for somewhere to live** estoy buscando algún sitio donde vivir

somewhere else otro lugar: **let's go somewhere else** vamos a otro lugar.

son [sʌn] *noun* ■ **el hijo: they have three sons** tienen tres hijos

song [sɒŋ] *noun* ■ **la canción** *(plural* las canciones)**: he was singing a love song** estaba cantando una canción de amor.

son-in-law [sʌnɪnlɔː] *(plural* sons-in-law) *noun* ■ **el yerno.**

soon [suːn] *adverb* ■ **pronto: he'll soon be here** estará aquí pronto; **I'll see you soon!** ¡te veré pronto!

soon after poco después: **she left soon after** se fue poco después
as soon as en cuanto, tan pronto como

En cuanto and **tan pronto como**, when used to express "as soon as" with an event that has not yet occurred, must be followed by a verb in the subjunctive:

I'll tell you as soon as he leaves te lo diré en cuanto él se vaya

➤ as soon as possible lo antes posible, cuanto antes: leave as soon as possible vete lo antes posible

➤ I'll be back soon! ¡volveré pronto!

sooner ['su:nə^r] (comparative of soon) adverb

■ antes: you should have come sooner deberías haber venido antes

➤ sooner or later tarde o temprano: sooner or later you'll have to tell me tarde o temprano me lo tendrás que decir

➤ the sooner the better cuanto antes, mejor.

sorcerer ['sɔ:sərə^r] noun ■ el brujo.

sore [sɔ:^r] adjective

1. dolorido

2. US informal enfadado: he's sore at me está enfadado conmigo

➤ this burn on my hand is really sore esta quemadura en la mano me duele mucho

➤ she has a sore throat le duele la garganta.

sorrow ['sɒrəʊ] noun ■ la pena: his death caused me great sorrow su muerte me causó una gran pena.

sorry ['sɒrɪ] adjective

➤ I'm really sorry, I have to go lo siento mucho, pero tengo que irme

➤ I'm sorry I'm late siento llegar tarde

➤ sorry? ¿cómo?: sorry? what did you say? ¿cómo?, ¿qué has dicho?

➤ sorry! ¡perdón!

➤ you'll be sorry! te arrepentirás

➤ say sorry to your sister pídele perdón a tu hermana

➤ he said he was sorry pidió perdón

➤ to feel sorry for somebody compadecer a alguien: I feel sorry for him lo compadezco.

sort [sɔ:t] (noun & verb)

■ noun

el tipo: what sort of computer have you got? ¿qué tipo de ordenador tienes?; there were all sorts of people había todo tipo de gente

■ verb

clasificar: the computer sorts the words in alphabetical order el ordenador clasifica las palabras por orden alfabético

sort out phrasal verb

1. ordenar: I'm going to sort out all my papers voy a ordenar todos mis papeles

2. solucionar: he managed to sort the problem out consiguió solucionar el problema

3. encargarse: I'll sort the tickets out me voy a encargar de las entradas.

sought [sɔ:t] past tense & past participle ➤ seek.

soul [səʊl] noun ■ el alma

Feminine noun that takes un or el in the singular.

sound [saʊnd] (noun & verb)

■ noun

1. el sonido: I recognized the sound of her voice reconocí el sonido de su voz

2. el volumen: turn the sound up sube el volumen

3. el ruido: I heard a sound oí un ruido

➤ sound effects efectos sonoros

■ verb

1. hacer sonar: they sounded the alarm hicieron sonar la alarma

2. sonar: this wall sounds hollow esta pared suena hueca; your idea sounds good tu idea suena bien

3. parecer: he sounds happy parece contento; it sounds as if they have a problem parece que tienen un problema

➤ to sound one's horn tocar el claxon: he sounded his horn tocó el claxon.

soundtrack ['saʊndtræk] noun ■ la banda sonora: I bought the soundtrack to the film compré la banda sonora de la película.

soup [su:p] noun ■ la sopa: a bowl of onion soup un tazón de sopa de cebolla.

sour ['saʊə^r] adjective ■ agrio: this yogurt tastes sour este yogur sabe agrio

➤ the milk has gone sour la leche se ha cortado.

source [sɔ:s] noun ■ la fuente: the Internet is a good source of information Internet es una buena fuente de información.

south [saʊθ] (noun, adjective & adverb)

■ noun

el sur: London is in the south of England Londres está en el sur de Inglaterra adjective

sur *(plural* sur*)*: **the prettiest beaches are on the south coast** las playas más hermosas están en la costa sur

adverb

hacia el sur: a lot of birds fly south in the winter muchos pájaros vuelan hacia el sur en invierno

south of al sur de: **Sitges is south of Barcelona** Sitges está al sur de Barcelona.

South America [ˌsaʊθəˈmərɪkə] *noun* ■ **América del Sur.**

South American [ˌsaʊθəˈmərɪkn] *(adjective & noun)*

adjective

Remember not to use a capital letter for the adjective in Spanish:

sudamericano: I like South American music me gusta la música sudamericana

noun

In Spanish, a capital letter is not used for the inhabitants of a country or region:

el sudamericano, la sudamericana: many South Americans speak Spanish or Portuguese muchos sudamericanos hablan español o portugués.

southeast [ˌsaʊθˈiːst] *noun* ■ **el sureste: Kent is in the southeast of England** Kent está en el sureste de Inglaterra.

southwest [ˌsaʊθˈwest] *noun* ■ **el suroeste: Cornwall is in the southwest of England** Cornwall está en el suroeste de Inglaterra.

souvenir [ˌsuːvəˈnɪəʳ] *noun* ■ **el recuerdo: he bought a lot of souvenirs in Madrid** compró muchos recuerdos en Madrid.

soya [ˈsɔɪə] *noun* ■ **la soja: soya beans** las semillas de soja.

soy sauce [ˌsɔɪˈsɔːs] *noun* ■ **la salsa de soja.**

space [speɪs] *noun*

1. **el espacio: who was the first man to travel in space?** ¿quién fue el primer hombre en viajar al espacio?; **leave a space for corrections** deja un espacio para las correcciones;

there's not enough space for a bed no hay suficiente espacio para una cama

2. **el sitio: can you make a space for me?** ¿puedes hacerme sitio?
   > **a parking space** un sitio para aparcar
   > **to stare into space** mirar al vacío
   > **a space shuttle** un transbordador espacial.

spaceship [ˈspeɪsʃɪp] *noun* ■ **la nave espacial.**

spacesuit [ˈspeɪssuːt] *noun* ■ **el traje espacial.**

spade [speɪd] *noun*

1. **la pala: the children were playing with their buckets and spades on the beach** los niños estaban jugando con los cubos y las palas en la playa

2. **la carta de picas**
   > **the queen of spades** la reina de picas

   ⚠ Spade es un falso amigo, no significa "espada".

spaghetti [spəˈgetɪ] *uncountable noun* ■ **los espaguetis.**

Spain [speɪn] *noun* ■ **España.**

Spanish [ˈspænɪʃ] *(adjective & noun)*

■ adjective

Remember not to use a capital letter for the adjective in Spanish:

español: sangria is a Spanish drink la sangría es una bebida española

■ noun

el español, el castellano: she speaks Spanish habla español

In Spanish, a capital letter is not used for the inhabitants of a country or region:

> **the Spanish** los españoles.

spanner *UK* [ˈspænəʳ] *noun* ■ **la llave inglesa.**

spare [speəʳ] *(adjective & verb)*

■ adjective

1. **de más: I've got a spare ticket** tengo una entrada de más

2. **libre: there's a spare seat at the back** hay un asiento libre en el fondo

> a spare part un repuesto
> a spare room un cuarto de huéspedes: **we have a spare room** tenemos un cuarto de huéspedes
> spare time tiempo libre: **I don't have any spare time** no tengo tiempo libre
> a spare tyre una rueda de repuesto
■ *verb*
> can you spare a few minutes? ¿tienes unos minutos?
> I can't spare the time no tengo tiempo
> I arrived with half an hour to spare llegué con media hora de antelación.

sparkling ['spɑːklɪŋ] *adjective* ■ **con gas**: a bottle of sparkling water una botella de agua con gas
> sparkling wine el vino espumoso.

sparrow ['spærəʊ] *noun* ■ el **gorrión** (*plural* los **gorriones**).

spat [spæt] *past tense & past participle* ➤ spit.

speak [spiːk] (*past tense* spoke, *past participle* spoken) *verb* ■ **hablar**: do you speak English? ¿hablas inglés?; speak more slowly habla más despacio; I spoke to my parents about the party hablé con mis padres sobre la fiesta; can I speak to Henry, please? ¿podría hablar con Henry, por favor?
> who's speaking? ¿de parte de quién?
> this is Kate speaking soy Kate.

speaker ['spiːkə'] *noun* ■ el **altavoz** (*plural* los **altavoces**): don't put the speakers too close together no pongas los altavoces muy cerca el uno del otro
> he's an English speaker es anglófono.

special ['speʃl] *adjective* ■ **especial**: you need special shoes to run in necesitas zapatos especiales para correr; this is a special case es un caso especial; this ring is very special to me este anillo es muy especial para mí.

specialist ['speʃəlɪst] *noun* ■ el/la **especialista**.

speciality UK [ˌspeʃɪ'ælətɪ] (*plural* specialities), **specialty** US ['speʃltɪ] (*plural* specialties) *noun* ■ la **especialidad**: steak is that restaurant's speciality el filete es la especialidad de este restaurante.

specially ['speʃəlɪ] *adverb* ■ **especialmente**: I wrote it specially for you lo escribí especialmente para ti.

specialty US *noun* ➤ speciality UK.

species ['spiːʃiːz] (*plural* species) *noun* ■ la **especie**: this species is extinct esta especie está extinguida.

spectacles UK ['spektəklz] *plural noun* ■ las **gafas**: Harry wears spectacles Harry lleva gafas.

spectacular [spek'tækjʊlə'] *adjective* ■ **espectacular**: the monument was spectacular el monumento era espectacular.

spectator [spek'teɪtə'] *noun* ■ el **espectador**, la **espectadora**: there were 5,000 spectators at the match asistieron 5.000 espectadores al partido.

sped [sped] *past tense & past participle* ➤ speed.

speech [spiːtʃ] *noun* ■ el **discurso**: he gave a speech pronunció un discurso.

speed [spiːd] (*noun & verb*)
■ *noun*
la **velocidad**: at the speed of light a la velocidad de la luz
> at top speed a toda velocidad: they were driving at top speed conducían a toda velocidad
> the speed limit el límite de velocidad: the speed limit is 50 miles an hour el límite de velocidad es de 50 millas por hora
■ *verb* (*past tense & past participle* sped OR speeded)
ir a toda velocidad: the driver was speeding el conductor iba a toda velocidad

speed up *phrasal verb* ■ **acelerar**: can you speed up a bit? ¿puedes acelerar un poco?

speedboat ['spiːdbəʊt] *noun* ■ la **lancha motora**.

speeding ['spiːdɪŋ] *uncountable noun* ■ el **exceso de velocidad**: he was fined for speeding lo multaron por exceso de velocidad.

speedometer [spɪ'dɒmɪtə'] *noun* ■ el **velocímetro**: his speedometer is broken se le rompió el velocímetro.

spell [spel] *(noun & verb)*

noun

el **hechizo**

to cast a spell on somebody hechizar a alguien: the sorcerer cast a spell on him el brujo lo hechizó

verb (past tense & past participle spelled OR spelt *UK)*

in writing escribir: how do you spell that? ¿cómo se escribe eso?

aloud deletrear: could you spell your name for me? ¿podrías deletrearme tu nombre?

spell-checker ['spelt∫ekə'] *noun* ■ el corrector ortográfico.

spelling ['spelɪŋ] *noun* ■ la **ortografía**: a spelling mistake una falta de ortografía.

spelt *UK* ['spelt] *past tense & past participle* ➤ spell.

spend [spend] *(past tense & past participle* spent) *verb*

gastar: how much did you spend? ¿cuánto gastaste?

pasar: I'd like to spend a few days in New York me gustaría pasar unos pocos días en Nueva York.

spent [spent] *past tense & past participle* ➤ spend.

spice [spaɪs] *noun* ■ la **especia**: pepper is a spice la pimienta es una especia.

spicy ['spaɪsɪ] *adjective* ■ **picante**: he doesn't like spicy food no le gusta la comida picante.

spider ['spaɪdə'] *noun* ■ la **araña**: he's afraid of spiders le dan miedo las arañas.

spill [spɪl] *(past tense & past participle* spilled OR spilt *UK) verb*

1. derramar: I spilled the water derramé el agua
2. derramarse: the milk spilled on the floor la leche se derramó por el suelo.

spilt *UK* [spɪlt] *past tense & past participle* ➤ spill.

spin [spɪn] *(past tense & past participle* spun, *present participle* spinning) *verb*

1. girar: the planet spins on its axis el planeta gira sobre su eje

2. hacer girar: he spun the wheel hizo girar la rueda

my head is spinning la cabeza me da vueltas

spin around , spin round *UK phrasal verb*

1. dar vueltas: the moon spins around the earth la luna da vueltas alrededor de la Tierra
2. darse la vuelta: she suddenly spun around de repente se dio la vuelta.

spinach [*UK* 'spɪnɪdʒ, *US* 'spɪnɪt∫] *uncountable noun* ■ las **espinacas**.

spine [spaɪn] *noun* ■ la **columna vertebral**: the spine forms the central part of the skeleton la columna vertebral es la parte central del esqueleto.

spiral staircase ['spaɪərəl'steəkeɪs] *noun* ■ la **escalera de caracol**.

spit [spɪt] *(past tense & past participle* spat OR spit, *present participle* spitting) *verb* ■ **escupir**: she spat the mushroom out escupió la seta.

spite [spaɪt] *noun* ■ el **rencor**

in spite of a pesar de: in spite of the rain, they went for a walk a pesar de la lluvia, salieron a dar un paseo

out of spite por despecho: she did it out of spite lo hizo por despecho.

splash [splæ∫] *(noun & verb)*

■ *noun*

el **chapoteo**: I heard a loud splash oí un fuerte chapoteo; the car splashed me with mud el coche me salpicó de barro

■ *verb*

salpicar: you've splashed me me has salpicado.

splendid ['splendɪd] *adjective* ■ **espléndido**: the weather was splendid el tiempo era espléndido.

splinter ['splɪntə'] *noun* ■ la **astilla**.

split [splɪt] *(past tense & past participle* split, *present participle* splitting) *verb*

1. partir: he split some wood for the fire partió leña para el fuego
2. romperse: the frame has split se rompió el marco
3. romperse: I've split my trousers se me han roto los pantalones

4. dividir: let's split the work dividamos el trabajo; he split the class into two groups dividió la clase en dos grupos

split up *phrasal verb* ■ **separarse:** the band split up last year la banda se separó el año pasado.

spoil [spɔɪl] *(past tense & past participle* spoiled OR spoilt*) verb*

1. echar a perder: you spoiled my party me echaste a perder la fiesta

2. mimar demasiado: they've spoiled their daughter han mimado demasiado a su hija.

spoiled [spɔɪld], **spoilt** [spɔɪlt] *adjective* ■ **mimado:** he's a spoiled child es un niño mimado.

spoke [spəʊk] *(noun & verb form)*
■ *noun*
el **radio:** the spokes of the wheel los radios de la rueda
■ *past tense*
➤ speak.

spoken ['spəʊkn] *past participle* ➤ speak.

sponge [spʌndʒ] *noun* ■ la **esponja:** she wiped the table with a sponge limpió la mesa con una esponja
➤ a sponge cake un bizcocho.

spooky ['spuːkɪ] *adjective* ■ **fantasmal, aterrador:** a spooky old house una vieja casa fantasmal.

spoon [spuːn] *noun* ■ la **cuchara:** a soup spoon una cuchara sopera.

spoonful ['spuːnfʊl] *noun* ■ la **cucharada:** add a spoonful of lemon juice agregue una cucharada de zumo de limón.

sport [spɔːt] *noun* ■ el **deporte:** they play a lot of sport hacen mucho deporte
➤ he's a bad sport es un mal perdedor
➤ a sports car un coche deportivo
➤ a sports ground un campo de deportes.

sportsman ['spɔːtsmən] *(plural* sportsmen ['spɔːtsmən]*) noun* ■ el **deportista.**

sportswoman ['spɔːtswʊmən] *(plural* sportswomen ['spɔːtswɪmən]*) noun* ■ la **deportista.**

sporty ['spɔːtɪ] *adjective* ■ **deportista:** he's very sporty es muy deportista.

spot [spɒt] *(noun & verb)*
■ *noun*
1. la **mancha:** a grease spot una mancha de grasa
2. el **lunar:** a shirt with red spots una camisa con lunares rojos
3. *UK* el **grano:** he's got a few spots on his face tiene algunos granos en la cara
4. el **sitio:** I know a nice spot where we can eat conozco un bonito sitio donde comer
■ *verb*
ver: I spotted her in the distance la vi a lo lejos
➤ he spotted the mistake descubrió el error.

spotlight ['spɒtlaɪt] *noun* ■ el **foco**
➤ he's in the spotlight es el foco de atención.

sprain [spreɪn] *verb*
to sprain one's ankle torcerse el tobillo: I've sprained my ankle me torcí el tobillo.

spray [spreɪ] *(noun & verb)*
■ *noun*
el **aerosol** *(plural* los **aerosoles***),* el **spray:** a deodorant spray un desodorante en aerosol; an insect spray un insecticida en aerosol
■ *verb*
1. rociar: she sprayed the leaves with water roció las hojas con agua
2. fumigar: they're spraying the crops están fumigando los cultivos
➤ she sprayed perfume in her hair se puso perfume en el pelo con un atomizador
➤ somebody has sprayed graffiti on the wall alguien ha hecho unas pintadas en la pared con un aerosol.

spread [spred] *(past tense & past participle* spread*) verb*
1. untar: he spread butter on the bread untó mantequilla en el pan
2. extender: they spread a blanket on the lawn extendieron una manta en el césped
3. desplegar: the bird spread its wings el pájaro desplegó las alas
4. divulgar: we must spread the news debemos divulgar la noticia

extenderse: the fire is beginning to spread el fuego está comenzando a extenderse

spread out *phrasal verb* ■ **dispersarse:** the search party spread out el equipo de rescate se dispersó.

spring [sprɪŋ] *noun*

la **primavera:** plants begin to grow again in the spring las plantas comienzan a crecer nuevamente en primavera

el **muelle:** this bed has a spring mattress esta cama tiene un colchón de muelles

el **manantial:** the water comes from a mountain spring el agua viene de un manantial en la montaña.

spring onion *UK* [sprɪŋ'ʌnjən] *noun* ■ la **cebolleta.**

springtime ['sprɪŋtaɪm] *uncountable noun* ■ la **primavera:** the swallows start to come back in springtime las golondrinas comienzan a volver en primavera.

sprouts [spraʊts] *plural noun* Brussels sprouts las coles de Bruselas.

spun [spʌn] *past tense & past participle* ➤ spin.

spy [spaɪ] *(noun & verb)*

noun

el/la **espía** a spy film una película de espionaje

verb

espiar to spy on somebody espiar a alguien.

square [skweəʳ] *(adjective & noun)*

adjective

cuadrado: the box is square la caja es cuadrada; two square metres dos metros cuadrados

noun

1. el **cuadrado:** it's a square not a circle es un cuadrado, no un círculo

2. la **plaza:** the hotel is near the market square el hotel está cerca de la plaza del mercado the town square la plaza del pueblo.

squash [skwɒʃ] *(noun & verb)*

noun

1. el **squash:** they're playing squash están jugando a squash

2. *US* la **calabaza:** he doesn't like eating squash no le gusta comer calabaza

3. *UK* el **refresco (de frutas edulcorado):** an orange squash un refresco de naranja

verb

aplastar: he squashed my hat aplastó mi sombrero; you're squashing me! ¡me estás aplastando!

squeeze [skwiːz] *verb*

1. **exprimir:** she squeezed the sponge exprimió la esponja; a glass of freshly squeezed orange juice un vaso de zumo de naranja recién exprimido

2. **apretar:** I squeezed her hand le apreté la mano

3. **meter a presión:** I squeezed my things into the suitcase metí a presión mis cosas en la maleta.

squirrel ['skwɜːrəl] *noun* ■ la **ardilla.**

St

1. *(abbreviation of* street*)* **calle:** 13 Barrow St el número 13 de la calle Barrow

2. *(abbreviation of* saint*)* **Sto., Sta.:** St Thomas Sto. Tomás.

stab [stæb] *(past tense & past participle* stabbed, *present participle* stabbing*) verb* ■ **apuñalar:** the robbers stabbed him los ladrones lo apuñalaron.

stable ['steɪbl] *noun* ■ el **establo:** the horses are in the stable los caballos están en el establo.

stack [stæk] *noun* ■ la **pila:** there's a stack of newspapers on the floor hay una pila de periódicos en el suelo.

stadium ['steɪdjəm] *(plural* stadiums OR stadia ['steɪdjə]*) noun* ■ el **estadio.**

staff [*UK* stɑːf, *US* stæf] *noun*

1. el **personal:** the staff of our firm el personal de nuestra empresa

2. *UK* el **profesorado:** the staff of our school el profesorado de nuestro colegio.

stage [steɪdʒ] *noun*

1. el **escenario:** the actors are on the stage los actores están en el escenario

2. la **etapa**: we are doing this in stages lo estamos haciendo por etapas
➤ **at this stage** a estas alturas.

stagger ['stægər] *verb* ■ **tambalearse**: he was so drunk he was staggering estaba tan borracho que se tambaleaba.

stain [steɪn] *(noun & verb)*
■ *noun*
la **mancha**: there's a stain on your jacket tienes una mancha en la chaqueta
■ *verb*
manchar: the wine stained my dress el vino me manchó el vestido.

stair [steər] *noun* ■ el **peldaño**: he's sitting on the bottom stair está sentado en el último peldaño.

staircase ['steəkeɪs] *noun* ■ la **escalera**: the staircase leads to the attic la escalera lleva al desván.

stairs [steərz] *plural noun* ■ las **escaleras**: she went down the stairs bajó las escaleras.

stale [steɪl] *adjective* ■ **duro**: the bread is stale el pan está duro.

stammer ['stæmər] *verb* ■ **tartamudear**: she stammers tartamudea.

stamp [stæmp] *(noun & verb)*
■ *noun*
el **sello**: he stuck on the stamp pegó el sello
■ *verb*
sellar: they stamped my passport sellaron mi pasaporte
➤ **to stamp one's foot** dar una patada en el suelo: she stamped her foot in rage dio una patada en el suelo de rabia.

stand [stænd] *(noun & verb)*
■ *noun*
1. el **pabellón**, la **caseta**: we have a stand at the exhibition tenemos un pabellón en la exposición
2. la **tribuna**: the stands in a stadium las tribunas de un estadio
➤ **a newspaper stand** un puesto de periódicos
➤ **a taxi stand** una parada de taxis
➤ **an umbrella stand** un paragüero

■ *verb (past tense & past participle* **stood***)*
1. **estar de pie**: she's standing by the door está de pie al lado de la puerta
2. **ponerse de pie**: everyone stood when the judge came in todo el mundo se puso de pie cuando entró el juez
3. **estar**: the house stands in the valley la casa está en el valle
4. **soportar**: I can't stand racism no soporto el racismo
➤ **stand still!** ¡estáte quieto!

stand for *phrasal verb*
1. **significar**: what does FAQ stand for? ¿qué significa FAQ?
2. **tolerar**: I won't stand for this behaviour! ¡no voy a tolerar esta conducta!

stand out *phrasal verb* ■ **destacarse**: the colours stand out against the background los colores destacan sobre el fondo
➤ she stands out in a crowd sobresale entre la multitud

stand up *phrasal verb* ■ **ponerse de pie**: she stood up when I came in se puso de pie cuando entré

stand up for *phrasal verb* ■ **defender**: he stands up for his little brother defiende a su hermano menor.

standard ['stændəd] *(noun & adjective)*
■ *noun*
1. el **nivel**: the standard is very high el nivel es muy alto
2. el **criterio**, el **valor**: what standards are you judging it by? ¿con qué criterios lo estás juzgando?
➤ his parents have very strict standards sus padres tienen unos principios muy estrictos
➤ the standard of living el nivel de vida: they have a high standard of living tienen un alto nivel de vida
➤ he has high standards es muy exigente
■ *adjective*
estándar: it's a standard hotel room es una habitación estándar; this is the standard size éste es el tamaño estándar.

stank [stæŋk] *past tense* ➤ stink.

staple ['steɪpl] (noun & verb)

noun

la **grapa**: the staple has come out se ha salido la grapa

verb

grapar: I stapled the papers together grapé los papeles.

stapler ['steɪplə'] noun ■ la **grapadora**.

star [stɑː'] (noun & verb)

noun

la **estrella**: there are lots of stars tonight hay muchas estrellas esta noche; he's an international star es una estrella internacional to read one's stars leer el horóscopo: she reads her stars in the newspaper every day lee su horóscopo cada día en el periódico

verb

1. **tener como protagonista**: the film stars Mel Gibson la película tiene como protagonista a Mel Gibson

2. **protagonizar**: Julia Roberts stars in the film Julia Roberts protagoniza la película.

stare [steə'] verb ■ **mirar fijamente**: he stared at me me miró fijamente.

Stars and Stripes ['stɑː'zəndstraɪps] noun ■ the Stars and Stripes la bandera de Estados Unidos, las barras y estrellas

THE STARS AND STRIPES

The Stars and Stripes es el nombre que se le da a la bandera estadounidense ya que su diseño incluye 13 bandas blancas y rojas, representando las 13 colonias originales de la época en que se fundó el país, y un campo azul con 50 estrellas blancas que representan los 50 estados actuales.

start [stɑːt] (noun & verb)

noun

el **comienzo**, el **principio**: it's a start es un comienzo; at the start of the film al principio de la película

verb

1. **empezar**: the film starts at 4 o'clock la película empieza a las 4; he wants to start a business quiere empezar un negocio

2. **arrancar**: the car won't start el coche no arranca

3. **poner en marcha**: can you start the washing machine? ¿podrías poner en marcha la lavadora?

> to start again empezar de nuevo

> to start to do something OR to start doing something ponerse a hacer algo: he started learning English a year ago empezó a estudiar inglés hace un año

> she started crying OR she started to cry se puso a llorar

> it started snowing se puso a nevar

start off , **start out** phrasal verb ■ **salir**: we started off at dawn salimos al amanecer.

starter UK ['stɑːtə'] noun ■ el primer plato: we had salad as a starter de primer plato tomamos ensalada.

startle ['stɑːtl] verb ■ **asustar**: you startled me me has asustado.

starve [stɑːv] verb ■ **morirse de hambre**: millions of people are starving all over the world millones de personas se mueren de hambre en el mundo

> I'm starving me muero de hambre.

state [steɪt] noun

1. la **condición** (plural las **condiciones**): she's not in any state to drive no está en condiciones de conducir

2. el **estado**: the head of state el jefe del estado; what are the member states of the European Union ¿cuáles son los estados miembros de la Unión Europea?; Alaska is the biggest state in the United States Alaska es el estado más grande de Estados Unidos

> the States Estados Unidos: Vic lives in the States Vic vive en Estados Unidos.

statement ['steɪtmənt] noun ■ la **declaración**: the president made a statement to the press el presidente hizo unas declaraciones a la prensa.

station ['steɪʃn] noun ■ la **estación** (plural las **estaciones**): I'll meet you at the station te voy a buscar a la estación

> a radio station una emisora de radio

> a bus station una terminal de autobuses

> a railway station UK OR a train station US una estación de ferrocarril

> a tube station *UK* OR a subway station *US* una estación de metro
> the police station la comisaría
> a station wagon un monovolumen.

stationery ['steɪʃnərɪ] *uncountable noun* ■ el **material de papelería**: I bought some stationery compré material de papelería
> a stationery shop *UK* OR a stationery store *US* una papelería.

statue ['stætʃuː] *noun* ■ la **estatua**: there's a statue of Nelson in Trafalgar Square hay una estatua de Nelson en Trafalgar Square
> the Statue of Liberty la estatua de la Libertad

THE STATUE OF LIBERTY

Se trata de un monumento regalado por el gobierno de Francia a los Estados Unidos en 1886 en reconocimiento de la alianza forjada entre estas dos naciones durante la revolución americana. La estatua mide 93 metros de altura y se encuentra en una isla (**Liberty Island**), en el puerto de Nueva York. Con el tiempo se convirtió en un símbolo de bienvenida a los inmigrantes que llegaban al país procedentes de todo el mundo. Actualmente es una popular atracción turística.

stay [steɪ] *(noun & verb)*

■ *noun*
la **estancia**: I enjoyed my stay in Madrid disfruté de mi estancia en Madrid

■ *verb*
1. **quedarse**: stay here! ¡quédate aquí!; I'll stay at home me voy a quedar en casa; he stayed for a week se quedó una semana; I stayed in a hotel me quedé en un hotel; she stayed awake all night se quedó despierta toda la noche
> to stay the night quedarse a dormir: do you want to stay the night? ¿quieres quedarte a dormir?

stay away *phrasal verb* ■ **mantenerse alejado**: stay away from the door mantente alejado de la puerta

stay out *phrasal verb*
he stayed out all night pasó toda la noche fuera

stay up *phrasal verb* ■ **quedarse levantado**: she stayed up all night se quedó levantada toda la noche.

steady ['stedɪ] *adjective*
1. **firme**: the chair isn't very steady la silla no es muy firme; he has steady hands tiene el pulso firme
2. **fijo**: she has a steady job tiene un trabajo fijo
> we're making steady progress seguimos mejorando.

steak [steɪk] *noun* ■ el **filete**: I like my steak well-done me gusta el filete muy hecho.

steal [stiːl] *(past tense* stole, *past participle* stolen) verb* ■ **robar**: someone stole my wallet alguien me robó la cartera.

steam [stiːm] *noun*
1. el **vapor**: a steam engine una máquina de vapor
2. el **vaho**: the bathroom filled with steam el baño se llenó de vaho.

steel [stiːl] *uncountable noun* ■ el **acero.**

steep [stiːp] *adjective*
1. **empinado**: the stairs are steep las escaleras son empinadas
2. **escarpada**: it's a steep hill es una colina escarpada.

steering wheel ['stɪərɪŋwiːl] *noun* ■ el **volante.**

step [step] *(noun & verb)*

■ *noun*
1. el **paso**: she took one step backwards dio un paso atrás
2. el **escalón** *(plural* los **escalones**): he was sitting on the step estaba sentado en el escalón

■ *verb (past tense & past participle* stepped, *present participle* stepping)
pisar: he stepped on an ant pisó una hormiga; he stepped on my foot me pisó

step forward *phrasal verb* ■ **dar un paso adelante**: can you step forward? ¿podrías dar un paso adelante?

stepbrother ['step‚brʌðər] *noun* ■ el **hermanastro.**

stepdaughter ['step,dɔːtəʳ] *noun* ■ la hijastra.

stepfather ['step,fɑːðəʳ] *noun* ■ el padrastro.

stepmother ['step,mʌðəʳ] *noun* ■ la madrastra.

stepsister ['step,sɪstəʳ] *noun* ■ la hermanastra.

stepson ['stepsʌn] *noun* ■ el hijastro.

stereo ['sterɪəʊ] *noun* ■ el **equipo de música**: he bought a new stereo compró un equipo de música nuevo
a personal stereo un walkman®.

stew [*UK* stjuː, *US* stuː] *noun* ■ el **estofado**: a beef stew un estofado de ternera.

stick [stɪk] *(noun & verb)*

■ *noun*

. el **palo**: he hit the tree with a stick golpeó el árbol con un palo

2. el **bastón** *(plural* los **bastones***)*: she was walking with a stick caminaba con un bastón

■ *verb (past tense & past participle* stuck*)*

. **pegar**: I stuck the stamps on the envelope pegué los sellos en el sobre

2. **pegarse**: the label won't stick la etiqueta no se pega

3. **clavar**: he stuck the penknife into the wood clavó la navaja en la madera

4. *informal* **poner**: stick your bag over there pon tu bolso allí

stick out *phrasal verb* ■ **verse**: your shirt is sticking out se te ve la camisa

> to stick one's tongue out sacar la lengua: he stuck his tongue out sacó la lengua.

sticker ['stɪkəʳ] *noun* ■ la **pegatina**: her case is covered in stickers su maleta está cubierta de pegatinas.

sticky ['stɪkɪ] *adjective*

. **pegajoso**: my hands are sticky tengo las manos pegajosas

2. **adhesivo**: a sticky label una etiqueta adhesiva.

stiff [stɪf] *adjective*

. **rígido**: stiff cardboard cartón rígido

2. **duro**: it was a stiff exam fue un examen duro

> to be stiff tener agujetas: I'm stiff all over tengo agujetas por todo el cuerpo

> to have a stiff neck tener tortícolis

> he's bored stiff *informal* se aburre como una ostra

> she's scared stiff *informal* está muerta de miedo.

still [stɪl] *(adverb & adjective)*

■ *adverb*

. **todavía**: are you still at this address? ¿todavía vives en esta dirección?; that's better still eso es todavía mejor

2. **aún así**: he's very lazy but she still likes him es muy vago pero aún así ella lo quiere

■ *adjective*
quieto: the lizard was very still la lagartija estaba muy quieta

> to keep still quedarse quieto: she won't keep still no se queda quieta

> sit still! ¡quédate quieto!, ¡no te muevas!

sting [stɪŋ] *(noun & verb)*

■ *noun*
la **picadura**: a bee sting una picadura de abeja

■ *verb (past tense & past participle* stung*)*
picar: a bee has me me picó una abeja.

stink [stɪŋk] *(past tense* stank, *past participle* stunk*) verb* ■ **apestar**: it stinks in here! ¡aquí dentro apesta!

stir [stɜːʳ] *(past tense & past participle* stirred, *present participle* stirring*) verb* ■ **remover**: stir the sauce until it boils remueve la salsa hasta que hierva.

stitch [stɪtʃ] *(noun & verb)*

■ *noun*

. la **puntada**: you can see the stitches on the hem se ven las puntadas en el dobladillo

2. el **punto**: they gave him three stitches in his arm le pusieron tres puntos en el brazo

3. el **flato**: I've got a stitch tengo flato

■ *verb*
coser: she stitched the button back on volvió a coser el botón.

stock [stɒk] *noun*

. la **reserva**: we have a stock of canned food at home tenemos una reserva de comida enlatada en casa

2. el **caldo:** chicken stock caldo de pollo
➤ in stock en existencias
➤ they are out of stock están agotados
➤ the stock exchange OR the stock market el mercado de valores, la bolsa.

stocking ['stɒkɪŋ] *noun* ■ la **media:** she's wearing silk stockings lleva unas medias de seda.

stole [stəʊl] *past tense* ➤ steal.

stolen ['stəʊln] *past participle* ➤ steal.

stomach ['stʌmək] *noun* ■ el **estómago.**

stomachache ['stʌməkeɪk] *noun* ■ el dolor de estómago
➤ I've got stomachache me duele el estómago.

stone [stəʊn] *noun*
1. la **piedra:** she threw a stone at the window tiró una piedra a la ventana; **opal is a precious stone** el ópalo es una piedra preciosa
2. UK el **hueso:** an olive stone un hueso de aceituna
3. *(plural* stone*)* UK **6,348 kg:** she weighs ten stone pesa sesenta y tres kilos.

stood [stʊd] *past tense & past participle* ➤ stand.

stool [stuːl] *noun* ■ el **taburete:** she's sitting on a stool está sentada en un taburete.

stop [stɒp] *(noun & verb)*
■ *noun*
a **parada:** what's the next stop? ¿cuál es la próxima parada?; **a bus stop** una parada de autobús
➤ to come to a stop detenerse: the train came to a stop el tren se detuvo
■ *verb (past tense & past participle* stopped, *present participle* stopping*)*
1. **parar:** the bus stopped in front of the school el autobús paró enfrente de la escuela; she stopped the car paró el coche
2. **pararse:** my watch has stopped se me ha parado el reloj
➤ to stop doing something dejar de hacer algo: it has stopped raining at last finalmente ha dejado de llover

Impedir que must be followed by a verb in the subjunctive:

➤ to stop somebody from doing something impedir que alguien haga algo: I tried to stop him from leaving traté de impedir que se fuera.

stopwatch ['stɒpwɒtʃ] *noun* ■ el cronómetro.

store [stɔːʳ] *(noun & verb)*
■ *noun*
US la **tienda:** he went into the store on the corner entró en la tienda de la esquina
➤ a department store unos grandes almacenes
■ *verb*
1. **guardar:** we store wine in the cellar guardamos vino en la bodega
2. **almacenar:** the latest computers can store even more information los últimos ordenadores pueden almacenar aún más información.

storey UK, **story** US ['stɔːrɪ] *noun* ■ el **piso:** the building has ten storeys el edificio tiene diez pisos.

stork [stɔːk] *noun* ■ la **cigüeña.**

storm [stɔːm] *noun* ■ la **tormenta.**

stormy ['stɔːmɪ] *adjective* ■ **tormentoso:** it's stormy today hoy es un día tormentoso.

story ['stɔːrɪ] *(plural* stories*)* *noun*
1. la **historia:** she told us a story nos contó una historia
2. US ➤ storey UK
➤ a fairy story un cuento de hadas.

straight [streɪt] *(adjective & adverb)*
■ *adjective*
1. **recto:** draw a straight line dibuja una línea recta
2. **lacio:** he has straight hair tiene el pelo lacio
3. **franco:** he's always very straight with me siempre es muy franco conmigo
■ *adverb*
1. **directamente:** he went straight to the police fue directamente a la policía
2. **recto:** walk straight ahead camina recto
3. **inmediatamente:** it happened straight after that sucedió inmediatamente después de eso.

strain [streɪn] *verb*
➤ to strain a muscle hacerse un esguince: he strained a muscle se hizo un esguince

to **strain one's eyes** forzar la vista: **don't strain your eyes** no fuerces la vista.

strange [streɪndʒ] *adjective*
raro: **it's strange that she's late** es raro que no haya llegado todavía; **she's a strange woman** es una mujer rara
. desconocido: **there are a lot of strange faces** hay un montón de caras desconocidas; **in a strange town** en un pueblo desconocido.

stranger ['streɪndʒər] *noun* ■ el **desconocido**, la **desconocida**: **he's a complete stranger** es un perfecto desconocido.

strangle ['stræŋgl] *verb* ■ **estrangular**: **the murderer strangled her** el asesino la estranguló.

strap [stræp] *noun*
. el **tirante**: **my bra strap has broken** se me ha roto el tirante del sostén
:. la **correa**: **I need a new strap for my watch** necesito una correa nueva para mi reloj
:. el **asa**: **the strap on my bag is too long** el asa de mi bolso es demasiado larga.

straw [strɔː] *noun*
. la **paja**: **there's straw all over the floor** hay paja tirada por todo el suelo
2. la **pajita**: **he was drinking through a straw** estaba bebiendo con una pajita.

strawberry ['strɔːbərɪ] *(plural* strawberries) *noun* ■ la **fresa**
strawberry jam mermelada de fresa.

stream [striːm] *noun* ■ el **arroyo**: **we crossed the stream** cruzamos el arroyo.

street [striːt] *noun* ■ la **calle**: **cross the street at the lights** cruza la calle por los semáforos; **he parks his car in the street** aparca el coche en la calle
a street lamp OR **a street light** un farol.

streetcar US [striːtkɑːr] *noun* ■ el **tranvía**.

streetwise ['striːtwaɪz] *adjective* ■ **pillo**: **these kids are very streetwise** estos chicos son muy pillos.

strength [streŋθ] *noun* ■ la **fuerza**: **I don't have the strength to get up** no tengo fuerzas para levantarme.

stress [stres] *noun*
1. el **estrés**: **this job involves a lot of stress** este trabajo implica mucho estrés
2. el **acento**: **the stress is on the first syllable** el acento recae sobre la primera sílaba
> **he's under a lot of stress** está muy estresado.

stressed ['stresd] *adjective* ■ **estresado**: **she's stressed** está estresada.

stretch [stretʃ] *verb*
1. **estirarse**: **she woke up and stretched** se despertó y se estiró
2. **estirar**: **they stretched the net between the two poles** estiraron la red entre los dos palos; **stretch your arms towards the ceiling** estira los brazos hacia el techo
> **to stretch one's legs** estirar las piernas: **I went outside to stretch my legs** salí fuera a estirar las piernas

stretch out *phrasal verb*
1. **estirar**: **she stretched her hand out to take it** estiró la mano para cogerlo; **he stretched his legs out** estiró las piernas
2. **tumbarse**: **they stretched out on the grass** se tumbaron en el césped.

stretcher ['stretʃər] *noun* ■ la **camilla**: **they carried her on a stretcher** la llevaban en una camilla.

strict [strɪkt] *adjective* ■ **estricto**: **his parents are very strict** sus padres son muy estrictos.

strike [straɪk] *(noun & verb)*
■ *noun*
la **huelga**
> **to be on strike** estar en huelga
> **to go on strike** declararse en huelga
■ *verb (past tense & past participle* struck*)*
1. **pegar**: **someone struck me** alguien me pegó
2. **dar**: **the clock struck six** el reloj dio las seis
3. **llamar la atención**: **I was struck by her beauty** me llamó la atención su belleza
4. **chocar contra**: **the car struck a tree** el coche chocó contra un árbol
> **to strike a match** encender una cerilla: **she struck a match** encendió una cerilla.

string [strɪŋ] *noun* ■ la **cuerda**: I tied the package with string até el paquete con cuerda; the guitar has a broken string la guitarra tiene una cuerda rota
> a piece of string una cuerda.

strip [strɪp] *(noun & verb)*
■ *noun*
la **tira**: a strip of paper una tira de papel
■ *verb (past tense & past participle* stripped, *present participle* stripping)
desnudarse: he stripped and had a shower se desnudó y se duchó.

stripe [straɪp] *noun* ■ la **raya**: there are red and green stripes on her dress su vestido tiene rayas verdes y rojas.

striped [straɪpt] *adjective* ■ **a rayas**: Don's wearing a striped shirt Don lleva puesta una camisa a rayas.

stroke [strəʊk] *(noun & verb)*
■ *noun*
1. el **trazo**: he made several strokes on the canvas with his brush dibujó diferentes trazos en el lienzo con el pincel
2. el **derrame cerebral**: he had a stroke tuvo un derrame cerebral
> a stroke of luck un golpe de suerte
■ *verb*
acariciar: she was stroking the cat estaba acariciando al gato.

stroll [strəʊl] *(noun & verb)*
■ *noun*
el **paseo**: we're going for a stroll vamos a dar un paseo
■ *verb*
pasear: they were strolling through the park estaban paseando por el parque.

stroller *US* ['strəʊləʳ] *noun* ■ la **silla de paseo**: she was pushing the baby in the stroller llevaba al bebé en la silla de paseo.

strong [strɒŋ] *adjective* ■ **fuerte**: Hercules was very strong Hércules era muy fuerte; she likes her coffee strong le gusta el café fuerte; as strong as an ox fuerte como un toro.

struck [strʌk] *past tense & past participle* ➤ strike.

structure ['strʌktʃəʳ] *noun* ■ la **estructura**.

struggle ['strʌgl] *(noun & verb)*
■ *noun*
la **lucha**: a struggle to survive una lucha para sobrevivir
■ *verb*
1. **luchar**: he struggled to survive in the jungle luchó para sobrevivir en la selva
2. **forcejear**: she struggled to get free forcejeó para escaparse
3. **tener dificultades**: he's struggling to finish his homework tiene dificultades para terminar los deberes.

stubborn ['stʌbən] *adjective* ■ **terco**
> as stubborn as a mule terco como una mula.

stuck [stʌk] *(adjective & verb form)*
■ *adjective*
1. **atascado**: the window is stuck la ventana está atascada
2. **atrapado**: we're stuck in a snowstorm estamos atrapados en una tormenta de nieve
> to get stuck
1. **atascarse**: my drawer got stuck se me atascó el cajón
2. **quedar atrapado**: his head got stuck in the window se le quedó la cabeza atrapada en la ventana
■ *past tense & past participle*
> stick.

stuck-up [stʌkʌp] *adjective* ■ *informal* **creído**: she's really stuck-up es muy creída.

student [*UK* 'stjuːdnt, *US* 'stuːdnt] *noun* ■ el/la **estudiante**.

studio [*UK* 'stjuːdɪəʊ, *US* 'stuːdɪəʊ] *(plural* studios) *noun*
1. el **estudio**: a television studio un estudio de televisión
2. el **taller**: a painter's studio el taller de un pintor
> a studio apartment un estudio.

study ['stʌdɪ] *(noun & verb)*
■ *noun (plural* studies)
los **estudios**: he wants to continue his studies quiere continuar sus estudios

verb
estudiar: Flora's studying Spanish Flora está estudiando español
to study for an exam estudiar para un examen: **I'm studying for my exam** estoy estudiando para el examen.

stuff [stʌf] *informal (noun & verb)*
noun
1. la **cosa:** what's that stuff you're eating? ¿qué es esa cosa que estás comiendo?; what's all this stuff on the table? ¿qué hacen todas estas cosas en la mesa?
2. las **cosas:** don't forget to take your stuff with you acuérdate de llevarte tus cosas
verb
meterse: he stuffed the keys into his pocket se metió las llaves en el bolsillo.

stumble ['stʌmbl] *verb* ■ **tropezarse:** she stumbled down the stairs se tropezó bajando las escaleras.

stung [stʌŋ] *past tense & past participle* ➤ sting.

stunk [stʌŋk] *past tense* ➤ stink.

stunned ['stʌnd] *adjective* ■ **atónito, pasmado:** he was stunned by the news las noticias lo dejaron atónito.

stunning ['stʌnɪŋ] *adjective*
1. **asombroso:** it's stunning news es una noticia asombrosa
2. **impresionante:** the scenery is stunning el paisaje es impresionante.

stunt [stʌnt] *noun* ■ el **truco**
a stunt man un doble (para escenas peligrosas).

stupid [UK 'stjuːpɪd, US 'stuːpɪd] *adjective* ■ **estúpido.**

stutter ['stʌtər] *verb* ■ **tartamudear:** she stutters tartamudea.

style [staɪl] *noun*
1. la **moda:** a new style of sportswear una nueva moda en ropa deportiva
2. el **estilo:** James Bond has a lot of style James Bond tiene mucho estilo.

subject ['sʌbdʒekt] *noun*

1. el **tema:** what's the subject of the book? ¿cuál es el tema del libro?
2. la **asignatura:** history is my favourite subject historia es mi asignatura preferida.

submarine [ˌsʌbməˈriːn] *noun* ■ el **submarino.**

subscription [səbˈskrɪpʃn] *noun* ■ la **suscripción** *(plural* las **suscripciones)**
➤ **to have a subscription to a magazine** estar suscrito a una revista.

substance ['sʌbstəns] *noun* ■ la **sustancia:** a sticky substance una sustancia pegajosa.

substitute [UK 'sʌbstɪtjuːt, US 'sʌbstɪtuːt] *noun* ■ el **sustituto,** la **sustituta:** the teams can have three substitutes los equipos pueden tener tres sustitutos.

subtitle ['sʌbˌtaɪtl] *noun* ■ el **subtítulo:** I can't read the subtitles no puedo leer los subtítulos.

subtle ['sʌtl] *adjective* ■ **sutil.**

subtract [səbˈtrækt] *verb* ■ **restar:** subtract 78 from 100 resta 78 de 100.

suburb ['sʌbɜːb] *noun* ■ el **barrio residencial:** Wanstead is a suburb of London Wanstead es un barrio residencial de Londres
➤ **the suburbs** las afueras.

subway ['sʌbweɪ] *noun*
1. *UK* el **paso subterráneo**
2. *US* el **metro.** it's best to take the subway into Manhattan para ir a Manhattan es mejor coger el metro.

succeed [səkˈsiːd] *verb*
1. **tener éxito:** you have to work hard to succeed tienes que trabajar duro para tener éxito
2. **conseguir:** he succeeded in getting into Oxford consiguió entrar a Oxford.

success [səkˈses] *noun* ■ el **éxito:** it's a great success es un gran éxito; a successful writer un escritor de éxito

⚠ Success es un falso amigo, no significa "suceso".

successful [səkˈsesful] *adjective* ■ **de éxito:** it was a successful evening fue una tarde de éxito to be successful tener éxito: **she's success-ful in whatever she does** tiene éxito en todo lo que hace.

successfully [sək'sesfʊlɪ] *adverb* ■ **con éxito.**

such [sʌtʃ] *adjective & adverb*

1. **tal: such situations are common** tales situaciones son frecuentes; **in such cases** en tales casos
2. **tanto: he has such a lot of books** tiene tantos libros; **I waited such a long time** esperé tanto tiempo
3. **tan: it's such a beautiful view!** ¡es una vista tan bonita!; **he's such a clever man** es un hombre tan inteligente; **I'd never seen such a big dog** nunca había visto un perro tan grande
   > **it's such a pity** es una lástima
   > **there's no such thing** no existe tal cosa
   > **such as** como: **animals such as lions and tigers** animales como los leones y los tigres.

suck [sʌk] *verb* ■ **chuparse: he's sucking his thumb** se está chupando el pulgar.

sudden ['sʌdn] *adjective* ■ **repentino: there was a sudden shower** hubo un chubasco repentino
> **all of a sudden** de repente: **all of a sudden she got angry** de repente se enfadó.

suddenly ['sʌdnlɪ] *adverb* ■ **de repente: suddenly he left** de repente se fue.

suede [sweɪd] *uncountable noun* ■ **el ante.**

suffer ['sʌfəʳ] *verb* ■ **sufrir: he's really suffering** está sufriendo de verdad
> **to be suffering from a cold** estar resfriado.

sugar ['ʃʊgəʳ] *noun* ■ **el azúcar: I don't take sugar** no tomo azúcar
> **a sugar lump** un terrón de azúcar.

suggest [*UK* sə'dʒest, *US* sə'gʒest] *verb*

1. **sugerir: what do you suggest?** ¿qué sugieres?
2. **aconsejar: I suggest you leave now** te aconsejo que te vayas ahora

> Aconsejar que must be followed by a verb in the subjunctive.

suggestion [*UK* sə'dʒestʃn, *US* sə'gʒestʃn] *noun* ■ **la sugerencia: can I make a suggestion?** ¿puedo hacer una sugerencia?

suicide ['sʊɪsaɪd] *noun* ■ **el suicidio**
> **to commit suicide** suicidarse: **she committed suicide** se suicidó.

suit [suːt] *(noun & verb)*

■ *noun*

1. **el traje: he's wearing a suit** lleva un traje
2. **el palo: the four suits are hearts, diamonds, clubs and spades** los cuatro palos de la baraja son corazones, diamantes, tréboles y picas

■ *verb*

1. **quedar bien: that skirt suits you** esa falda te queda bien
2. **venir bien: does Monday suit you?** ¿te viene bien el lunes?
   > **suit yourself!** ¡haz lo que quieras!

suitable ['suːtəbl] *adjective*

1. **apropiado: that dress isn't suitable for the occasion** este vestido no es apropiado para la ocasión
2. **adecuado: it's a suitable present for a small child** es un regalo adecuado para un niño
3. **conveniente: I'll call you at the most suitable time for you** le llamaré a la hora más conveniente para usted.

suitcase ['suːtkeɪs] *noun* ■ **la maleta: I'm going to pack my suitcase** voy a hacer la maleta.

suite [swiːt] *noun* ■ **la suite: they have a suite at the Ritz** tienen una suite en el Ritz.

sulk [sʌlk] *verb*
> **she's sulking** está enfurruñada.

sum [sʌm] *(noun & verb)*

■ *noun*

1. **la suma: that's a large sum of money** ésa es una gran suma de dinero
2. **el cálculo: he's good at sums** es bueno en cálculo

sum up *phrasal verb* ■ **resumir: let's sum up what we've done so far** resumamos lo que hemos hecho hasta el momento.

summary ['sʌmərɪ] *(plural* summaries*)* *noun* ■ **el resumen** *(plural* los resúmenes*).*

summer ['sʌməʳ] *noun* ■ **el verano: in the summer** en el verano; **they go to Corsica**

every summer se van a Córcega todos los veranos
a summer camp un campamento de verano
summer clothes ropa de verano
the summer holidays *UK* OR the summer vacation *US* las vacaciones de verano.

summertime ['sʌmətaɪm] *uncountable noun* ■ el **verano**: it happened in the summertime sucedió en verano.

summit ['sʌmɪt] *noun* ■ la **cumbre**: Edmund Hillary and Tenzing Norgay reached the summit of Everest in 1953 Edmund Hillary y Tenzing Norgay llegaron a la cumbre del Everest en 1953.

sun [sʌn] *noun* ■ el **sol**: the sun's shining el sol brilla
in the sun al sol: I don't want to go out in the sun no quiero salir al sol.

sunbathe ['sʌnbeɪð] *verb* ■ **tomar el sol**: she was sunbathing on the beach estaba tomando el sol en la playa.

sunburn ['sʌnbɜːn] *uncountable noun* ■ las **quemaduras de sol**: I have sunburn on my arms tengo quemaduras de sol en los brazos.

Sunday ['sʌndɪ] *noun*

In Spanish the days of the week do not start with a capital letter:

el **domingo**: it's Sunday today hoy es domingo; next Sunday el domingo que viene; last Sunday el domingo pasado
on Sunday el domingo: I'll see you on Sunday te veo el domingo
on Sundays los domingos: he comes to see me on Sundays viene a verme los domingos
to be in one's Sunday best ir vestido de domingo.

sundown *US* ['sʌndaʊn] *uncountable noun* ■ el **atardecer**: they stopped work at sundown dejaron de trabajar al atardecer.

sunflower ['sʌnflaʊər] *noun* ■ el **girasol**
sunflower oil el aceite de girasol
a sunflower seed una pipa de girasol.

sung [sʌŋ] *past participle* ➤ sing.

sunglasses ['sʌnˌglɑːsɪz] *plural noun* ■ las **gafas de sol**.

sunk [sʌŋk] *past participle* ➤ sink.

sunlight ['sʌnlaɪt] *uncountable noun* ■ la **luz del sol**: in the sunlight a la luz del sol.

sunny ['sʌnɪ] *adjective* ■ **soleado**: it was a sunny day era un día soleado
it's sunny hace sol.

sunrise ['sʌnraɪz] *noun* ■ la **salida del sol**: I woke up before sunrise me desperté antes de la salida del sol.

sunset ['sʌnset] *noun* ■ la **puesta de sol**: I came home after sunset llegué a casa después de la puesta de sol.

sunshine ['sʌnʃaɪn] *uncountable noun* ■ el **sol**: there isn't much sunshine today hoy no hay mucho sol.

suntan ['sʌntæn] *noun* ■ el **bronceado**: she has a nice suntan tiene un bonito bronceado
suntan lotion bronceador.

super ['suːpər] *adjective* ■ *informal* **genial**: it's a super film es una película genial
the Super Bowl *US* la Super Bowl

THE SUPER BOWL

La Super Bowl es un partido de fútbol americano en el que se enfrentan los campeones de las dos ligas o conferences más importantes del fútbol profesional en Estados Unidos. Se celebra al final de la temporada –a finales de enero de cada año– y una gran cantidad de gente en Estados Unidos y otros países presencian el encuentro por televisión.

superhighway *US* ['suːpəˌhaɪweɪ] *noun* ■ la **autopista**
the information superhighway la autopista de la información.

superior [suːˈpɪərɪər] *adjective* ■ **superior** goods of superior quality productos de calidad superior.

supermarket ['suːpəˌmɑːkɪt] *noun* ■ el **supermercado**.

supernatural [ˌsuːpəˈnætʃrəl] *adjective* ■ **sobrenatural**.

superstitious [ˌsuːpəˈstɪʃəs] *adjective* ∎ **supersticioso.**

supper [ˈsʌpər] *noun* ∎ la **cena: supper time** la hora de la cena
> **to have supper** cenar: **we had fish for supper** cenamos pescado.

supply [səˈplaɪ] *(noun & verb)*
∎ *noun (plural* **supplies***)*
el **suministro: the supplies are running out** se están acabando los suministros
> **supply and demand** la oferta y la demanda
∎ *verb (past tense & past participle* **supplied***)*
suministrar: the school supplies pencils la escuela suministra los lápices
> **to supply someone with something** facilitarle algo a alguien: **I supplied him with the details** le facilité los detalles.

support [səˈpɔːt] *(noun & verb)*
∎ *noun*
el **apoyo: thanks to their support, he was elected mayor** gracias a su apoyo, fue elegido alcalde
∎ *verb*
1. **apoyar: I will always support you** siempre te apoyaré
2. **ser hincha de: she supports Manchester United** es hincha del Manchester United.

supporter [səˈpɔːtər] *noun*
1. el **partidario,** la **partidaria: he's a supporter of feminism** es partidario del feminismo
2. el/la **hincha: he's a Leeds supporter** es hincha del Leeds.

suppose [səˈpəʊz] *verb*
1. **suponer: I suppose he'll come tomorrow** supongo que vendrá mañana
2. **creer: do you suppose he'll pass his exam?** ¿crees que aprobará el examen?
> **suppose you were rich...** imagínate que eres rico...
> **I suppose so** supongo que sí
> **we are supposed to wait here** se supone que tenemos que esperar aquí.

sure [ʃʊər] *adjective* ∎ **seguro: are you sure she'll come?** ¿estás seguro de que vendrá?; **I'm not sure** no estoy seguro

> **they are sure to be late** con toda seguridad van a llegar tarde
> **to make sure** asegurarse: **make sure you don't forget!** ¡asegúrate de no olvidarte!

surf [sɜːf] *verb*
1. **hacer surf: he likes surfing** le gusta hacer surf
2. **navegar: he surfs the Net for hours at a time** navega por Internet durante horas.

surface [ˈsɜːfɪs] *noun* ∎ la **superficie: I can see something on the surface of the water** veo algo en la superficie del agua.

surfboard [ˈsɜːfbɔːd] *noun* ∎ la **tabla de surf.**

surfing [ˈsɜːfɪŋ] *uncountable noun* ∎ el **surf: to go surfing** hacer surf; **he goes surfing every weekend** hace surf todos los fines de semana.

surgeon [ˈsɜːdʒən] *noun* ∎ el **cirujano,** la **cirujana.**

surname [ˈsɜːneɪm] *noun* ∎ el **apellido: what's your surname?** ¿cuál es tu apellido?

surprise [səˈpraɪz] *(noun & verb)*
∎ *noun*
la **sorpresa: what a surprise!** ¡qué sorpresa!
∎ *verb*
sorprender: that surprises me eso me sorprende.

surrender [səˈrendər] *verb* ∎ **rendirse: the soldiers surrendered** los soldados se rindieron.

surround [səˈraʊnd] *verb* ∎ **rodear: the house is surrounded by a wall** la casa está rodeada por un muro; **the police surrounded the building** la policía rodeó el edificio.

survey [ˈsɜːveɪ] *noun* ∎ la **encuesta.**

survive [səˈvaɪv] *verb* ∎ **sobrevivir: two people survived** sobrevivieron dos personas.

survivor [səˈvaɪvər] *noun* ∎ el/la **superviviente.**

suspect *(noun & verb)*
∎ *noun* [ˈsʌspekt]
el **sospechoso,** la **sospechosa: he's a suspect** es sospechoso

verb [sə'spekt]
sospechar: they suspect her of stealing the diamond sospechan que robó el diamante.

suspense [sə'spens] *uncountable noun* ■ el **suspense**: the film was full of suspense la película tenía mucho suspense.

suspicion [sə'spɪʃn] *noun* ■ la **sospecha**: do you have any suspicions? ¿tienes alguna sospecha?

suspicious [sə'spɪʃəs] *adjective*
. **desconfiado**: he became suspicious se volvió desconfiado
²**. sospechoso**: she looks very suspicious tiene un aspecto sospechoso
to be suspicious of somebody desconfiar de alguien.

swallow ['swɒləʊ] *(noun & verb)*
■ *noun*
la **golondrina**: swallows migrate to Africa in the winter las golondrinas emigran a África en invierno
■ *verb*
tragarse: she swallowed the pill se tragó la píldora.

swam [swæm] *past tense* ➤ swim.

swamp [swɒmp] *noun* ■ el **pantano**: there are alligators in this swamp hay caimanes en este pantano.

swan [swɒn] *noun* ■ el **cisne**.

swap , swop US [swɒp] *(past tense & past participle* swapped OR swopped, *present participle* swapping OR swopping) *verb*
¹. **cambiarse**: let's swap jackets cambiémonos las chaquetas
². **cambiar**: I swapped my bike for a moped cambié mi bici por una moto.

swear [sweə^r] *(past tense* swore, *past participle* sworn) *verb*
¹. **decir palabrotas**: don't swear no digas palabrotas
². **jurar**: I swear I'm telling the truth juro que estoy diciendo la verdad
to swear at somebody insultar a alguien.

swearword ['sweəwɜːd] *noun* ■ la **palabrota**: don't say that, it's a swearword no digas eso, es una palabrota.

sweat [swet] *(noun & verb)*
■ *uncountable noun*
el **sudor**: I'm covered in sweat estoy cubierta de sudor
■ *verb*
sudar: I'm sweating estoy sudando.

sweater ['swetə^r] *noun* ■ el **suéter**: he's wearing a red sweater lleva puesto un suéter rojo.

sweep [swiːp] *(past tense & past participle* swept) *verb* ■ **barrer**: he's sweeping the floor está barriendo el suelo.

sweet [swiːt] *(adjective & noun)*
■ *adjective*
¹. **dulce**: the cake is too sweet el pastel es demasiado dulce; she's very sweet es muy dulce
². **mono**: what a sweet baby! ¡qué bebé más mono!
sweet dreams! ¡dulces sueños!
a sweet potato un boniato
■ *noun UK*
¹. el **caramelo**: she loves sweets le encantan los caramelos
². el **postre**: what's for sweet? ¿qué hay de postre?

swell [swel] *(past tense* swelled, *past participle* swollen) *verb* ■ **hincharse**: my lip started to swell se me empezó a hinchar el labio

swell up *phrasal verb* ■ **hincharse**: her face has swollen up se le ha hinchado la cara.

swept [swept] *past tense & past participle* ➤ sweep.

swim [swɪm] *(noun & verb)*
■ *noun*
to go for a swim OR to have a swim ir a nadar, bañarse: they went for a swim in the lake fueron a bañarse al lago
■ *verb (past tense* swam, *past participle* swum)
nadar: can you swim? ¿sabes nadar?

swimmer ['swɪmə^r] *noun* ■ el **nadador**, la **nadadora**: he's a good swimmer es buen nadador.

swimming ['swɪmɪŋ] *uncountable noun* ■ la **natación**: I love swimming me encanta la natación

> a swimming costume *UK* un bañador, un traje de baño (de mujer): **she's wearing a swimming costume** lleva bañador
> **to go swimming** ir a nadar
> **a swimming pool** una piscina
> **swimming trunks** el traje de baño (de caballero).

swimsuit ['swimsu:t] *noun* ■ el **traje de baño (de mujer)**.

swing [swɪŋ] *(noun & verb)*
■ *noun*
el **columpio: there are swings in the park** hay columpios en el parque
■ *verb (past tense & past participle* swung*)*
1. **balancearse: the monkeys were swinging in the trees** los monos se balanceaban en los árboles
2. **balancear: he was swinging his arms** balanceaba los brazos.

switch [swɪtʃ] *(noun & verb)*
■ *noun (plural* switches*)*
el **interruptor: where's the light switch?** ¿dónde está el interruptor de la luz?
■ *verb*
cambiar de: let's switch places cambiemos de sitio

switch off *phrasal verb* ■ **apagar: I switched off the light** apagué la luz; **he switched off the engine** apagó el motor

switch on *phrasal verb* ■ **encender: she switched the light on** encendió la luz; **I switched the engine on** encendí el motor.

swollen ['swəʊln] *past participle* ➤ swell.

sword [sɔ:d] *noun* ■ la **espada**.

swordfish ['sɔ:dfɪʃ] *noun* ■ el **pez espada**.

swore [swɔːʳ] *past tense* ➤ swear.

sworn [swɔːn] *past participle* ➤ swear.

swum [swʌm] *past participle* ➤ swim.

swung [swʌŋ] *past tense & past participle* ➤ swing.

syllable ['sɪləbl] *noun* ■ la **sílaba: "happiness" has three syllables** "happiness" tiene tres sílabas.

syllabus ['sɪləbəs] *(plural* syllabuses OR syllabi*) noun* ■ el **plan de estudios: Spanish isn't on the syllabus any more** el español ya no está en el plan de estudios.

symbol ['sɪmbl] *noun* ■ el **símbolo: the white dove is a symbol of peace** la paloma blanca es un símbolo de paz.

sympathetic [ˌsɪmpə'θetɪk] *adjective* ■ **comprensivo: they were very sympathetic after hearing about our problem** fueron muy comprensivos después de enterarse de nuestro problema

 Sympathetic es un falso amigo, no significa "simpático".

sympathy ['sɪmpəθɪ] *uncountable noun* ■ la **compasión: he has no sympathy for them** no siente ninguna compasión por ellos.

syrup ['sɪrəp] *uncountable noun* ■ el **jarabe: a cough syrup** un jarabe para la tos
> **maple syrup** jarabe de arce
> **peaches in syrup** melocotones en almíbar.

system ['sɪstəm] *noun* ■ el **sistema: it's a very good system** es un sistema muy bueno
> **operating system** sistema operativo.

table ['teɪbl] *noun* ■ la **mesa: the plates are on the table** los platos están en la mesa; **the guests are sitting at the table** los invitados están sentados a la mesa to lay the table OR to set the table poner la mesa: **shall I lay the table?** ¿pongo la mesa? **table tennis** ping-pong: **they're playing table tennis** están jugando al ping-pong.

tablecloth ['teɪblklɒθ] *noun* ■ el **mantel**: **put the tablecloth on the table** pon el mantel en la mesa.

tablespoon ['teɪblspuːn] *noun* ■ la **cuchara de servir** a **tablespoon of sugar** una cucharada de azúcar.

tablet ['tæblɪt] *noun* ■ la **pastilla**: **take one tablet every four hours** tome una pastilla cada cuatro horas.

tadpole ['tædpəʊl] *noun* ■ el **renacuajo**.

tag [tæg] *noun* ■ la **etiqueta**: **what's the price on the tag?** ¿cuál es el precio de la etiqueta?

tail [teɪl] *noun* ■ la **cola**: **the dog's wagging its tail** el perro está moviendo la cola **heads or tails?** ¿cara o cruz?

tailor ['teɪlər] *noun* ■ el **sastre**.

take ['teɪk] *(past tense* took, *past participle* taken) *verb*

1. **coger**: **let's take the bus** cojamos el autobús
2. **tomar**: **I haven't taken my medicine** no he tomado mi medicina
3. **llevarse**: **he took my bike while I wasn't looking** se llevó mi bici cuando yo no estaba mirando
4. **sacar**: **take the book off the shelf** saca el libro del estante; **I took a lot of photos** saqué muchas fotos
5. **llevar**: **take the chairs into the garden** lleva las sillas al jardín; **they took her some flowers** le llevaron flores; **he took me to the cinema** me llevó al cine
6. **hacer**: **to take an exam** hacer un examen
7. **aceptar**: **they don't take credit cards** no aceptan tarjetas de crédito
8. **soportar**: **he can't take criticism** no soporta la crítica
9. *when "take" means "require"* **it takes patience** hace falta paciencia; **it takes two hours to get there** se tarda dos horas en lle-

gar allí; **how long will it take?** ¿cuánto tiempo va a tardar?; **it took us two days to finish** tardamos dos días en terminar
▸ **what size do you take?** ¿qué talla usas?
▸ **what shoe size do you take?** ¿qué número de zapatos calzas?

take after *phrasal verb* ■ **parecerse a**: **she takes after her grandmother** se parece a su abuela

take apart *phrasal verb* ■ **desmontar**: **Jack took the car apart** Jack desmontó el coche

take away *phrasal verb*
1. **llevarse**: **she took the plates away** se llevó los platos; **the police took him away** la policía se lo llevó
2. **quitar**: **he was afraid they would take his car away from him** tenía miedo de que le quitaran el coche

take back *phrasal verb* ■ **devolver**: **I took the jeans back to the shop** devolví los vaqueros a la tienda

take down *phrasal verb*
1. **desmontar**: **they took the tent down** desmontaron la tienda
2. **quitar**: **she took the poster down** quitó el póster
3. **anotar**: **he took down her name and address** anotó su nombre y dirección

take off *phrasal verb*
1. **despegar**: **the plane takes off at 5 a.m.** el avión despega a las 5 de la mañana
2. **quitarse**: **she took her shoes off** se quitó los zapatos
▸ **to take one's clothes off** quitarse la ropa: **he took his clothes off** se quitó la ropa

take out *phrasal verb* ■ **sacar**: **I'm going to take some money out of the bank** voy a sacar dinero del banco
▸ **to take somebody out to dinner** invitar a alguien a cenar fuera

take up *phrasal verb* ■ **ocupar**: **that box takes up too much room** esa caja ocupa demasiado espacio
▸ **he's taken up golf** ha empezado a jugar al golf.

takeaway *UK* ['teɪkə,weɪ], **takeout** *US* ['teɪkaʊt] *noun*
1. la **comida para llevar**
2. el **restaurante de comida para llevar**.

take-off ['teɪkɒf] *noun* ■ el **despegue**: passengers must wear their seat belts during take-off los pasajeros deben usar los cinturones de seguridad durante el despegue.

tale [teɪl] *noun* ■ el **cuento**: she likes fairy tales le gustan los cuentos de hadas.

talent ['teɪlənt] *noun* ■ el **talento**.

talk [tɔːk] *(noun & verb)*
■ *noun*
1. la **conversación** *(plural* las **conversaciones***)*: I had a talk with my father tuve una conversación con mi padre
2. la **charla**: he gave a talk on the environment dio una charla sobre el medio ambiente
■ *verb*
hablar: he's talking to his girlfriend está hablando con su novia; we talked about the future hablamos sobre el futuro.

tall [tɔːl] *adjective* ■ **alto**: Thomas is very tall Thomas es muy alto; the building is tall el edificio es alto
➤ how tall are you? ¿cuánto mides?; how tall is the Eiffel Tower? ¿cuánto mide la Torre Eiffel?

tambourine [tæmbə'riːn] *noun* ■ la **pandereta**: she plays the tambourine toca la pandereta.

tame [teɪm] *adjective* ■ **domesticado**.

tan [tæn] *noun* ■ el **bronceado**: what a great tan! ¡qué bronceado tan sensacional!
➤ to have a tan estar bronceado.

tangerine [,tændʒə'riːn] *noun* ■ la **mandarina**.

tangle ['tæŋgl] *noun* ■ el **enredo**
➤ to be in a tangle estar enredado: my hair's in a tangle mi pelo está enredado
➤ to get in a tangle enredarse: the wires have got in a tangle los cables se han enredado.

tank [tæŋk] *noun*
1. el **depósito**: the fuel tank is empty el depósito de combustible está vacío

2. el **tanque**: there are a lot of tanks on the border hay muchos tanques en la frontera
➤ a fish tank una pecera.

tanned [tænd] *adjective* ■ **bronceado**: you're very tanned estás muy bronceada.

tap [tæp] *(noun & verb)*
■ *noun*
1. el **grifo**: turn the tap on abre el grifo; turn the tap off cierra el grifo
2. el **golpecito**: I felt a tap on my arm sentí un golpecito en el brazo
■ *verb (past tense & past participle* tapped, *present participle* tapping)*
darle un golpecito a: someone tapped me on the shoulder alguien me dio un golpecito en el hombro
➤ he was tapping his fingers on the table tamborileaba con los dedos en la mesa

 Tap es un falso amigo, no significa "tapa".

tape [teɪp] *(noun & verb)*
■ *noun*
1. la **cinta (de vídeo)**: do you have a blank tape to record this film? ¿tienes una cinta virgen para grabar esta película?
2. **cinta (de radiocasete)**: we listened to a Beatles tape escuchamos una cinta de los Beatles
3. la **cinta adhesiva**: stick this down with tape pega esto con una cinta adhesiva
➤ a tape measure una cinta métrica
➤ on tape grabado: I've got some good music on tape tengo grabada buena música; I've got "Star Wars" on tape tengo "La guerra de las galaxias" grabada en vídeo
➤ a tape recorder una grabadora
■ *verb*
grabar: I taped the film grabé la película.

tart *UK* [tɑːt] *noun* ■ la **tarta**: an apple tart una tarta de manzana.

target ['tɑːgɪt] *noun* ■ el **blanco**: you've hit the target has dado en el blanco.

task [*UK* tɑːsk, *US* tæsk] *noun* ■ la **tarea**: it's a difficult task es una tarea difícil.

taste [teɪst] (noun & verb)

noun

• el **sabor**: this fish has a funny taste el pescado tiene un sabor raro

• el **gusto**
to have good taste tener buen gusto; Jane has very good taste Jane tiene muy buen gusto
have a taste! ¡pruébalo!

verb

• **probar**: taste this delicious soup prueba esta sopa deliciosa

• **saber**: it tastes delicious sabe delicioso
to taste like something OR to taste of something saber a algo: it tastes like honey sabe a miel.

tasty ['teɪstɪ] adjective ▪ **sabroso.**

tattoo [tə'tuː] noun ▪ el **tatuaje.**

taught [tɔːt] past tense & past participle
➤ teach.

tax [tæks] noun ▪ el **impuesto**: we all have to pay taxes todos tenemos que pagar impuestos.

taxi ['tæksɪ] noun ▪ el **taxi**: let's take a taxi tomemos un taxi
a taxi driver un taxista
a taxi stand una parada de taxis.

tea [tiː] uncountable noun

• el **té**: I'd like a cup of tea me gustaría una taza de té

• la **merienda**: what time is tea? ¿a qué hora es la merienda?
a tea towel un trapo de cocina.

teabag ['tiːbæg] noun ▪ la **bolsita de té.**

teach [tiːtʃ] (past tense & past participle taught) verb

1. **enseñar**: my brother is teaching me Spanish mi hermano me está enseñando español

2. **dar clases**: she teaches at a secondary school da clases en un instituto.

teacher ['tiːtʃər] noun

1. el **profesor**, la **profesora**: he's a maths teacher es profesor de matemáticas

2. el **maestro**, la **maestra**: she's a teacher in a primary school es maestra de una escuela primaria.

teacup ['tiːkʌp] noun ▪ la **taza para el té.**

team [tiːm] noun ▪ el **equipo.**

teapot ['tiːpɒt] noun ▪ la **tetera.**

tear [tɪər] noun ▪ la **lágrima**
he was in tears estaba llorando.

tear [teər] (noun & verb)

▪ noun
el **desgarro**: can you mend this tear? ¿puedes arreglar este desgarro?

▪ verb (past tense tore, past participle torn)

1. **romper**: I tore the page rompí la página

2. **romperse**: this cloth tears very easily esta tela se rompe muy fácilmente

tear down phrasal verb ▪ **derribar**: they're going to tear the old factory down van a derribar la vieja fábrica

tear out phrasal verb ▪ **arrancar**: I tore the page out arranqué la página

tear up phrasal verb ▪ **hacer pedazos**: he tore up the letter hizo pedazos la carta.

tease [tiːz] verb ▪ **tomarle el pelo a**: he's always teasing his little brother siempre le está tomando el pelo a su hermano pequeño.

teaspoon ['tiːspuːn] noun ▪ la **cucharilla**: I need a teaspoon for my coffee necesito una cucharilla para el café
add one teaspoon of sugar agregue una cucharadita de azúcar.

technical ['teknɪkl] adjective ▪ **técnico.**

technique [tek'niːk] noun ▪ la **técnica**: a new technique for making memory chips una nueva técnica para fabricar chips de memoria.

techno ['teknəʊ] noun ▪ el **tecno**: Yvonne likes techno a Yvonne le gusta el tecno.

technological [ˌteknə'lɒdʒɪkl] adjective ▪ **tecnológico**
a technological breakthrough un avance tecnológico.

technology [tek'nɒlədʒɪ] noun ▪ la **tecnología.**

teddy bear ['tedɪbeər] noun ▪ el **oso de peluche.**

teen [tiːn] *noun* ■ el/la **adolescente**
a teen magazine una revista para adolescentes.

teenage ['tiːneɪdʒ] *adjective* ■ **adolescente**: he has a teenage son tiene un hijo adolescente.

teenager ['tiːnˌeɪdʒəʳ] *noun* ■ el/la **adolescente**: he's a teenager es un adolescente.

teens [tiːnz] *plural noun*
to be in one's teens ser adolescente: he's in his teens es adolescente.

teeth *plural* ➤ tooth.

telephone ['telɪfəʊn] *noun* ■ el **teléfono**: the telephone's ringing está sonando el teléfono; he answered the telephone contestó al teléfono
to be on the telephone estar hablando por teléfono: she's on the telephone at the moment está hablando por teléfono en este momento
the telephone book OR the telephone directory la guía telefónica
a telephone booth OR a telephone box UK una cabina telefónica
a telephone call una llamada telefónica: there's a telephone call for you tienes una llamada telefónica
a telephone number un número de teléfono: what's your telephone number? ¿cuál es tu número de teléfono?

telescope ['telɪskəʊp] *noun* ■ el **telescopio**.

television ['telɪˌvɪʒn] *noun* ■ la **televisión**: I watched it on television lo vi en la televisión; put the television on pon la televisión
a television programme un programa de televisión
a television set un televisor.

tell [tel] *(past tense & past participle* told*) verb* ■ **decir**: I told him I would be late le dije que llegaría tarde
I can tell he's really angry me doy cuenta de que está realmente enfadado
to tell a story contar una historia
to tell the time decir la hora
to tell somebody about something contar a alguien algo: I told her about my trip le conté mi viaje

tell off *phrasal verb* ■ **reñir**: my teacher told me off mi profesor me riñó.

temper ['tempəʳ] *noun* ■ el **genio**: she has an awful temper tiene muy mal genio
to lose one's temper perder los estribos: I lost my temper perdí los estribos.

temperature ['temprətʃəʳ] *noun*
1. la **temperatura**: what is the temperature outside? ¿qué temperatura hay fuera?; I took her temperature le tomé la temperatura
2. la **fiebre**: he has a temperature tiene fiebre.

temple ['templ] *noun* ■ el **templo**: a Greek temple un templo griego.

temporary ['tempərəri] *adjective* ■ **temporal**.

tempt [tempt] *verb* ■ **tentar**
I'm tempted to say no estoy tentado de decir que no.

ten [ten] *number* ■ **diez**: the Ten Commandments los Diez Mandamientos; she's ten tiene diez años; he went out at ten salió a las diez.

tenant ['tenənt] *noun* ■ el **inquilino**, la **inquilina**.

tend [tend] *verb*
to tend to do something tener tendencia a hacer algo: she tends to exaggerate tiene tendencia a exagerar.

tender ['tendəʳ] *adjective* ■ **tierno**: the meat is very tender la carne es muy tierna.

tennis ['tenɪs] *noun* ■ el **tenis**: she's playing tennis está jugando al tenis; a game of tennis un partido de tenis
a tennis ball una pelota de tenis
a tennis court una pista de tenis
a tennis player un tenista
a tennis racket una raqueta de tenis
tennis shoes zapatillas de tenis.

tense [tens] *adjective* ■ **tenso**: the atmosphere was very tense el ambiente era muy tenso.

tension ['tenʃn] *noun* ■ la **tensión** (*plural* las **tensiones**)*:* there's a lot of tension between them hay mucha tensión entre ellos.

tent [tent] *noun* ■ la **tienda de campaña**.

tenth [tenθ] *number* ■ **décimo: on the tenth floor** en el décimo piso
it's the tenth of November UK OR **it's November tenth** US estamos a 10 de noviembre.

term [tɜːm] *noun*
UK el **trimestre: there are three terms in the school year** hay tres trimestres en el año escolar
el **término: it's a technical term** es un término técnico
to be on good terms with somebody tener buenas relaciones con alguien
to come to terms with something aceptar algo.

terminal [ˈtɜːmɪnl] *noun* ■ la **terminal: there are three terminals at the airport** hay tres terminales en el aeropuerto
the bus terminal la terminal de autobuses.

terrace [ˈterəs] *noun* ■ la **terraza**.

terraced house UK [ˈterəsthaʊs] *noun* ■ la **casa adosada**.

terrible [ˈterəbl] *adjective* ■ **terrible**.

terrific [təˈrɪfɪk] *adjective* ■ **estupendo: it's a terrific book** es un libro estupendo.

territory [UK ˈterətrɪ, US ˈterɪtɔːrɪ] *(plural* territories) *noun* ■ el **territorio**.

terrorism [ˈterərɪzm] *noun* ■ el **terrorismo**.

terrorist [ˈterərɪst] *noun* ■ el/la **terrorista: a terrorist attack** un ataque terrorista.

test [test] *(noun & verb)*
■ *noun*
la **prueba: we had a test this morning** tuvimos una prueba esta mañana
I'm taking my driving test voy a hacer el examen de conducir
a blood test un análisis de sangre
nuclear tests pruebas nucleares
a test tube un tubo de ensayo
an eye test una revisión de la vista
■ *verb*
1. **probar: I'd like to test the computer before I buy it** me gustaría probar el ordenador antes de comprarlo

2. **hacerle una prueba a: the teacher tested us on irregular verbs** la profesora nos hizo una prueba sobre los verbos irregulares.

text [tekst] *(noun & verb)*
■ *noun*
el **texto: a text file** un archivo de texto
■ *verb*
to text somebody enviar un mensaje de texto a alguien: **you can text me on my mobile** puedes enviarme un mensaje de texto al móvil.

textbook [ˈtekstbʊk] *noun* ■ el **libro de texto: a biology textbook** un libro de texto de biología.

text-message [tekstˈmesɪdʒ] *noun* ■ el **mensaje de texto: he sent me a text-message** me envió un mensaje de texto.

than [ðən, ðæn] *conjunction*
1. **que: Tina's taller than Ted** Tina es más alta que Ted; **I've got less than you** OR **I've got less than you have** tengo menos que tú
2. *with quantities* **de: it costs less than 50 euros** cuesta menos de 50 euros; **he stayed more than three months** se quedó más de tres meses.

thank [θæŋk] *verb* ■ **agradecer: I'd like to thank you for your help** quiero agradecerle su ayuda
thank you! ¡gracias!: **thank you very much!** ¡muchas gracias!
thank God! ¡gracias a Dios!

thanks [θæŋks] *exclamation & noun*
thanks! ¡gracias!: **thanks a lot!** ¡muchas gracias!
thanks to gracias a.

Thanksgiving [ˈθæŋksˌgɪvɪŋ] *noun* ■ la **Acción de Gracias**

THANKSGIVING

La fiesta de **Thanksgiving**, el cuarto jueves de noviembre, conmemora el establecimiento de los primeros colonos en lo que hoy son los Estados Unidos. La cena, que ese día generalmente se celebra en familia, consiste en un pavo con salsa de arándanos, acompañado de boniatos al horno y el tradicional pastel de calabaza como postre.

that [ðæt] *(adjective, pronoun, conjunction & adverb)*

■ *adjective (plural* **those***)*

A demonstrative adjective must agree in gender (masculine or feminine) and number (singular or plural) with the noun it precedes.

1. **ese, esa:** *give me that book* dame ese libro; *that soup is cold* esa sopa está fría
2. **aquel, aquella**

Use **aquel** and **aquella** to express more distance between the speaker and the object:

I don't want that dress on the table, I want that dress over there no quiero ese vestido que está en la mesa, quiero aquel vestido de allí

■ *pronoun*

A demonstrative pronoun must agree in gender (masculine or feminine) and number (singular or plural) with the noun to which it refers. If it does not refer to something that can be assigned gender, the neuter form **eso** is used.

1. **ése, ésa, eso:** *who's that?* ¿quién es ése?; *is that Janet?* ¿es ésa Janet?; *that's my brother* ése es mi hermano; *that's not true* eso no es cierto; *what's that?* ¿qué es eso?
2. **aquél, aquélla, aquello**

Use **aquél, aquélla** or **aquello** to express more distance between the speaker and the object:

I don't want this one, I want that one no quiero éste, quiero aquél; *this hat won't do, we must have that one in the window* este sombrero no es adecuado, debemos coger aquél que está en el escaparate

> *is that you?* ¿eres tú?

■ *pronoun*

1. *subject or object of the verb* **que:** *where's the path that leads to the wood?* ¿dónde está el camino que conduce al bosque?; *the man that he saw* el hombre que él vio
2. *after a preposition* **el que**

The relative pronoun becomes **el que, la que, los que** or **las que** after a preposition, according to the gender (masculine or feminine) and number (singular or plural) of the noun to which it refers:

the chair that he was sitting on collapsed la silla en la que estaba sentado se vino abajo; *the boys that he's talking to are his cousins* los chicos con los que está hablando son sus primos

■ *conjunction*

que: *she said that she was coming* dijo que venía

■ *adverb*

tan: *it's not that bad* no es tan malo.

that's [ðæts]

1. = that is: *that's not my dog* ese no es mi perro
2. = that has: *that's got nothing to do with it* eso no tiene nada que ver.

the [ðə, ði:] *definite article* ■ **el**

The definite article must agree in gender (masculine or feminine – **el, la**) and number (singular or plural – **los, las**) with the noun it precedes:

give me the book dame el libro; *look at the flower* mira la flor; *where are the children?* ¿dónde están los niños?; *put the flowers in a vase* pon las flores en un florero

When you say "of the" or "to the" in Spanish, the prepositions **de** and **a** combine with **el** to make one word: **de + el = del**, and **a + el = al**:

I can't remember the name of the village no puedo recordar el nombre del pueblo; *she gave the ball to the dog* le dio la pelota al perro.

theatre *UK,* **theater** *US* [ˈθɪətəʳ] *noun* ■ el **teatro:** *we're going to the theatre* vamos a ir al teatro.

theft [θeft] *noun* ■ el **robo.**

their [ðeəʳ] *possessive adjective*

In Spanish the possessive adjective agrees in number (singular or plural) with the noun that follows:

su: *their house is in the countryside* su casa está en el campo; *their parents are doctors* sus padres son médicos

Use the definite article (**el, la, los** or **las**), not the possessive adjective, with parts of the body and clothing when it's clear who the possessor is:

they're brushing their teeth se están lavando los dientes; *she put on her coat* se puso el abrigo.

theirs [ðeəz] *possessive pronoun*

In Spanish the possessive pronoun agrees in gender (masculine or feminine) and number (singular or plural) with the noun it replaces:

• el **suyo**, la **suya**: our dog is big, **theirs is small** nuestro perro es grande, el suyo es pequeño; **your books are here, theirs are on the table** tus libros están aquí, los suyos están en la mesa

• **suyo, suya**: those books aren't theirs esos libros no son suyos; **she's a friend of theirs** es amiga suya.

them [ðəm, ðem] *pronoun*

• *direct object* **los, las**: I can't see them no los puedo ver; **find them!** ¡encuéntralos!; I saw them los vi

• *indirect object* **les**: she gave them a kiss les dio un beso; **tell them to come** diles que vengan

Instead of "les", use **se** as an indirect object when there is also a direct object pronoun:

I gave it to them se lo di a ellos

• *after a preposition* **ellos, ellas**: I'm going with them voy con ellos.

themselves [ðem'selvz] *pronoun*

1. **se**: the boys are washing themselves los muchachos se están lavando; **they're enjoying themselves** se están divirtiendo

2. **ellos mismos**: they made it themselves lo hicieron ellos mismos

3. **sí mismos**: they often talk about themselves a menudo hablan de sí mismos

• **by themselves** solos; **they did it by themselves** lo hicieron solos.

then [ðen] *adverb*

1. **entonces**: we lived in London then entonces vivíamos en Londres; **it's too sweet — don't drink it then** es muy dulce —entonces no lo bebas

2. **luego**: I had dinner then I went to bed cené y luego me fui a acostar.

there [ðeər] *(pronoun & adverb)*

▪ *pronoun*

▸ **there is** OR **there are** hay

▸ **there's a message for you** hay un mensaje para ti; **there are a lot of people here** hay mucha gente aquí; **there isn't any bread** no hay pan; **there was a storm** hubo una tormenta

▪ *adverb*

ahí, allí, allá: put it there ponlo ahí; **there he is!** ¡ahí está!; **up/down there** allí arriba/abajo; **put it over there** ponlo allí; **I'm going there next week** voy para allá la próxima semana

▸ **is Lance there?** ¿está Lance?

therefore ['ðeəfɔːr] *adverb* ▪ **por lo tanto**: he's only 15 and therefore can't drive tiene sólo 15 años, por lo tanto no puede conducir.

there's [ðeəz]

1. = there is

2. = there has.

thermometer [θə'mɒmɪtər] *(noun* ▪ el termómetro.

these [ðiːz] *(plural of this) (adjective & pronoun)*

▪ *adjective*

A demonstrative adjective must agree in gender (masculine or feminine) and number (singular or plural) with the noun it precedes:

estos *(plural* estas): these shoes are mine estos zapatos son míos; **I prefer these flowers** prefiero estas flores

▪ *pronoun*

A demonstrative pronoun must agree in gender (masculine or feminine) and number (singular or plural) with the noun to which it refers.

éstos, éstas: these are my keys éstas son mis llaves; **can I try these on?** ¿puedo probarme éstos?; **which books do you want, these or those?** ¿qué libros quieres, éstos o aquéllos?

they [ðeɪ] *pronoun* ▪ **ellos, ellas**

"They" is not usually translated unless necessary for emphasis or clarification. Spanish nouns are either masculine or feminine. Remember to use **ellos** for masculine subjects and **ellas** for feminine subjects. When "they" includes male and female, use **ellos**:

they're American son norteamericanos; **where are my glasses? — they're on the**

table ¿dónde están mis gafas? —están en la mesa; **they did** it ellos lo hicieron
▸ **here they are!** ¡aquí están!

they'd [ðeɪd]
1. = they had
2. = they would.

they'll [ðeɪl]
1. = they shall
2. = they will.

they're [ðeəʳ] = they are.

they've [ðeɪv] = they have.

thick [θɪk] adjective ■ **grueso: it's a thick book** es un libro grueso
▸ **the walls are ten centimetres thick** las paredes tienen diez centímetros de espesor.

thief [θiːf] (plural thieves [θiːvz]) noun ■ **el ladrón** (plural los **ladrones**).

thigh [θaɪ] noun ■ **el muslo: this exercise works the thigh muscles** este ejercicio trabaja los músculos del muslo.

thin [θɪn] adjective
1. **delgado: he's too thin** es muy delgado
2. **fino: a thin slice of lemon** una rodaja fina de limón.

thing [θɪŋ] noun ■ **la cosa: he has a lot of things to do** tiene muchas cosas que hacer
▸ **my things** mis cosas
▸ **I can't see a thing** no veo nada
▸ **the poor thing!** ¡pobrecito!

think [θɪŋk] (past tense & past participle thought) verb
1. **pensar: what do you think?** ¿qué piensas?; **think carefully before you make a decision** piensa con cuidado antes de tomar una decisión;
2. **imaginar: think how life will be in ten years** imagina cómo será la vida dentro de diez años
3. **creer opinar: I think you're mad** creo que estás loco
▸ **I think so** creo que sí
▸ **I don't think so** creo que no

think about phrasal verb
1. **pensar en: what are you thinking about?** ¿en qué estás pensando?; **I'm thinking about the party** estoy pensando en la fiesta

2. **parecer: what did you think about the film?** ¿qué te pareció la película?
▸ **I'll think about it** lo pensaré

think of phrasal verb ■ **pensar de: what do you think of her?** ¿qué piensas de ella?

third [θɜːd] (adjective & noun)
■ adjective
tercero

Tercero becomes "tercer" before masculine singular nouns:

the third Tuesday of each month el tercer martes de cada mes
▸ **third time lucky** a la tercera va la vencida
▸ **the Third World** el Tercer Mundo
■ noun
el tercio: he ate a third of the cake se comió un tercio del pastel
▸ **it's the third of November** UK OR **it's November third** US estamos a tres de noviembre.

thirst [θɜːst] noun ■ **la sed: I'm dying of thirst** estoy muerto de sed.

thirsty ['θɜːstɪ] adjective
▸ **to be thirsty** tener sed: **I'm thirsty** tengo sed.

thirteen [ˌθɜː'tiːn] number ■ **trece: thirteen is my lucky number** el trece es mi número de la suerte; **she's thirteen** tiene trece años.

thirteenth [ˌθɜː'tiːnθ] number ■ **décimo tercero**
▸ **it's the thirteenth of April** UK OR **it's April thirteenth** US estamos a trece de abril.

thirtieth [ˌθɜːtɪəθ] number ■ **trigésimo**
▸ **it's the thirtieth of December** UK OR **it's December thirtieth** US estamos a treinta de diciembre.

thirty ['θɜːtɪ] numeral ■ **treinta: she's thirty** tiene treinta años
▸ **thirty-one** treinta y uno
▸ **thirty-two** treinta y dos.

this [ðɪs] (plural these) (adjective, pronoun & adverb)
■ adjective

A demonstrative adjective must agree in gender (masculine or feminine) and number (singular or plural) with the noun it precedes.

este, esta (plural estos, estas): he left this morning se fue esta mañana; **I prefer this CD** prefiero este CD

pronoun

A demonstrative pronoun must agree in gender (masculine or feminine) and number (singular or plural) with the noun to which it refers. If it does not refer to something that can be assigned gender, the neuter form **esto** is used.

éste, ésta, esto: I don't want that dress, I want this one no quiero ese vestido, quiero éste; **do you like that shirt? — no I like this one** ¿te gusta esa falda? –no, me gusta ésta; **this is for you** esto es para ti; **what's this?** ¿qué es esto?
who's this? ¿quién es?
this is Jackie Brown
. *introducing somebody* le presento a Jackie Brown
2. *on the phone* soy Jackie Brown
adverb
it was this big era así de grande
I didn't know it was this far no sabía que estaba tan lejos.

thorn [θɔːn] *noun* ■ la **espina.**

thorough ['θʌrə] *adjective*

1. **riguroso: they did a thorough test on the aeroplane** hicieron una prueba rigurosa del avión
2. **meticuloso: he's thorough in his work** es meticuloso en su trabajo.

thoroughly ['θʌrəlɪ] *adverb*

1. **totalmente: I thoroughly agree** estoy totalmente de acuerdo
2. **minuciosamente: he studied his case thoroughly** estudió su caso minuciosamente.

those [ðəʊz] (plural of that) (adjective & pronoun)
■ *adjective*

A demonstrative adjective must agree in gender (masculine or feminine) and number (singular or plural) with the noun it precedes.

1. **esos, esas: those books are mine** esos libros son míos; **I prefer those flowers** prefiero esas flores
2. **aquellos, aquellas**

Use **aquellos** and **aquellas** to express more distance between the speaker and the object:

she'd like those shoes over there a ella le gustarían aquellos zapatos de allí
■ *pronoun*

A demonstrative pronoun must agree in gender (masculine or feminine) and number (singular or plural) with the noun to which it refers. If it does not refer to something that can be assigned gender, the neuter form **esos** is used.

1. **ésos, ésas: those are my books** ésos son mis libros; **can I try those on?** ¿puedo probarme ésos?; **I don't want these books, I want those** no quiero estos libros, quiero ésos
2. **aquéllos, aquéllas**

Use **aquéllos** and **aquéllas** to express more distance between the speaker and the object:

those flowers are nice, but those over there are nicer esas flores son bonitas, pero aquéllas de allí son más bonitas
those who want to come should put their hand up los que quieran venir que levanten la mano.

though [ðəʊ] (conjunction & adverb)
■ *conjunction*
aunque: though the car's old, it's still in good condition aunque el coche es viejo, todavía está en buenas condiciones
■ *adverb*
pero: we lost! — it was a good game though ¡perdimos! –pero fue un buen partido.

thought [θɔːt] (noun & verb form)
■ *noun*
la **idea: he had an interesting thought** tuvo una idea interesante
she was lost in her thoughts estaba abstraída en sus pensamientos
■ *past tense & past participle*
➤ think.

thousand ['θaʊznd] *number* ■ **mil: it costs a thousand euros** cuesta mil euros
a thousand and one mil uno
thousands of miles de: **there were thousands of people** había miles de personas.

thread [θred] *noun* ■ el **hilo.**

threat [θret] *noun* ■ la **amenaza.**

threaten ['θretn] *verb* ■ **amenazar:** she threatened to leave the team amenazó con retirarse del equipo.

three [θriː] *numeral* ■ **tres:** you get three chances tienes tres oportunidades; she's three tiene tres años; he went out at three salió a las tres.

three-D [,θriː'diː], **three-dimensional** [,θriːdɪ'menʃənl] *adjective* ■ **tridimensional:** a three-dimensional object un objeto tridimensional

➤ a film in three-D una película en tres dimensiones.

threw [θruː] *past tense* ➤ throw.

thrill [θrɪl] *(noun & verb)*

■ *noun*

la **emoción** *(plural* las **emociones***)*: what a thrill! ¡qué emoción!

➤ seeing Everest was a real thrill ver el Everest fue verdaderamente emocionante

■ *verb*

emocionar: I was thrilled to see her again estaba emocionado de verla otra vez.

thriller ['θrɪləʳ] *noun* ■ la **novela (o película) de suspense.**

throat [θrəʊt] *noun* ■ la **garganta:** I have a sore throat me duele la garganta.

throne [θrəʊn] *noun* ■ el **trono:** Queen Elizabeth came to the throne in 1952 la reina Isabel subió al trono en 1952.

through *US* [θruː] *(preposition & adverb)*

■ *preposition*

1. **por:** she was looking through the window estaba mirando por la ventana

2. **durante:** she talked all through the film habló durante toda la película

➤ I got the job through a friend conseguí el trabajo gracias a un amigo

➤ to go through a red light saltarse un semáforo en rojo

➤ Monday through Friday *US* de lunes a viernes

➤ to go through atravesar: the bullet went through the wall la bala atravesó la pared; we went through the park atravesamos el parque

■ *adverb*

➤ the arrow went right through la flecha lo atravesó completamente

➤ to get through pasar: can you get through? ¿puedes pasar al otro lado?

➤ to get through to somebody comunicarse con alguien: I can't get through to him on the phone no puedo comunicarme con él por teléfono

➤ to let somebody through dejar pasar a alguien.

throughout [θruː'aʊt] *preposition*

1. **durante:** he slept throughout the meeting durmió durante toda la reunión

2. **por todo:** throughout the house por toda la casa

➤ throughout Spain en toda España.

throw [θrəʊ] *(past tense* **threw,** *past participle* thrown*) verb* ■ **tirar, lanzar:** throw me the ball! ¡tírame la pelota!; they were throwing stones at the police le estaban tirando piedras a la policía

➤ to throw a party dar una fiesta

throw away *phrasal verb* ■ **tirar a la basura:** I threw my ticket away tiré mi billete a la basura

throw out *phrasal verb*

1. **tirar a la basura:** I'm going to throw this stale bread out voy a tirar este pan duro a la basura

2. **expulsar:** they threw him out lo expulsaron

throw up *phrasal verb* ■ **vomitar:** he threw up vomitó.

thrown [θrəʊn] *past participle* ➤ throw.

thumb [θʌm] *noun* ■ el **pulgar.**

thunder ['θʌndəʳ] *uncountable noun* ■ el **trueno.**

thunderstorm ['θʌndəstɔːm] *noun* ■ la **tormenta eléctrica.**

Thursday ['θɜːzdɪ] *noun*

In Spanish the days of the week do not start with a capital letter:

el **jueves:** it's Thursday today hoy es jueves; next Thursday el jueves que viene; last Thursday el jueves pasado on Thursday el jueves: **I'll see you on Thursday** te veré el jueves

on Thursdays los jueves: **he comes to see me on Thursdays** viene a verme los jueves.

ticket ['tɪkɪt] *noun*

. el **billete**: **a plane ticket** un billete de avión; **a train ticket** un billete de tren

2. la **entrada**: **I bought two tickets for the concert** compré dos entradas para el concierto

3. el **recibo**, el **resguardo**: **I've lost the cloak-room ticket** he perdido el resguardo del guardarropa

a parking ticket una multa por estacionamiento indebido

a ticket machine una máquina expendedora de billetes

the ticket office la taquilla.

tickle ['tɪkl] *verb* ■ **hacer cosquillas**: **that tickles!** ¡eso hace cosquillas!

tide [taɪd] *noun* ■ la **marea**: **it's high tide** OR **the tide is in** la marea está alta; **it's low tide** OR **the tide is out** la marea está baja.

tie [taɪ] *(noun & verb)*

■ *noun*

1. la **corbata**: **he's wearing a tie** lleva corbata

2. el **empate**: **who won the game? — It was a tie** ¿quién ganó el partido? —hubo empate

■ *verb (present participle* tying*)*

1. **atar**: **they tied his hands to the chair** le ataron las manos a la silla; **tie the rope around the tree** ata la cuerda alrededor del árbol

2. **atarse**: **tie your shoelaces** átate los cordones de los zapatos

3. **empatar**: **they tied two all** empataron a dos **he tied his scarf around his neck** se envolvió el cuello con la bufanda

to tie a knot hacer un nudo: **she tied a knot in her handkerchief** le hizo un nudo al pañuelo

tie up *phrasal verb* ■ **atar**: **she tied the package up with ribbon** ató el paquete con una cinta; **they tied up the prisoner** ataron al prisionero.

tiger ['taɪgər] *noun* ■ el **tigre**: **tigers come from Asia** los tigres proceden de Asia.

tight [taɪt] *adjective*

1. **ajustado**: **this dress is too tight** este vestido es muy ajustado; **she was wearing tight jeans** llevaba unos vaqueros muy ajustados

2. **apretado**: **this knot is too tight** este nudo está muy apretado.

tighten ['taɪtn] *verb* ■ **apretar**: **he tightened the screw** apretó el tornillo.

tightly ['taɪtlɪ] *adverb* ■ **she was holding his hand tightly** le agarraba la mano con fuerza.

tights ['taɪts] *plural noun* ■ las **medias**.

tile [taɪl] *noun*

1. la **teja**: **a tile fell off the roof** cayó una teja del tejado

2. el **azulejo**: **the floor and the walls in the bathroom are covered in blue tiles** el suelo y las paredes del baño están revestidos de azulejos azules.

till [tɪl] *(noun, preposition & conjunction)*

■ *noun*

la **caja**: **pay at the till** pague en caja

■ *preposition*

hasta: **we'll play till six** vamos a jugar hasta las seis

■ *conjunction*

hasta que

> The conjunction **hasta que** is followed by a verb in the subjunctive when referring to an event that has not yet happened:

I'll stay here till he comes me quedaré aquí hasta que llegue

till now hasta ahora.

time [taɪm] *noun*

1. el **tiempo**: **I don't have time** no tengo tiempo; **take your time** tómate tu tiempo; **you're just in time for lunch** llegas justo a tiempo para almorzar; **all the time** todo el tiempo; **most of the time** la mayor parte del tiempo

2. la **hora**: **what time is it?** ¿qué hora es?; **the train's on time** el tren viene a la hora

3. la **época**: **in Roman times** en la época romana

4. el **momento**: he arrived at the right time llegó en un buen momento

5. la **vez**: how many times have you seen the **film?** ¿cuántas veces has visto la película?; **the first time I saw you** la primera vez que te vi; **four times a year** cuatro veces al año

➤ **four at a time** de cuatro en cuatro

➤ **6 times 7 is 42** 6 por 7 es 42

➤ **from time to time** de vez en cuando

➤ **for the time being** por el momento

➤ **a long time** mucho tiempo: **we waited for a long time** esperamos mucho tiempo; **I've been here for a long time** he estado aquí mucho tiempo

➤ **it's time for bed** es hora de acostarse

➤ **it's time to go** es hora de irse

➤ **it's about time he left** ya es hora de que se vaya

➤ **to have a good time** pasarlo bien: **I had a really good time at the party** lo pasé muy bien en la fiesta

➤ **in a week's time** dentro de una semana.

timetable ['taɪm,teɪbl] *noun* ■ el **horario**: check the timetable to see when the next train is revisa el horario para ver cuándo pasa el próximo tren.

tin [tɪn] *noun*

1. *UK* la **lata**: **a tin of sardines** una lata de sardinas

2. el **estaño**: **it's made of tin** es de estaño

➤ **a tin can** una lata

➤ **a tin opener** *UK* un abrelatas.

tinfoil ['tɪnfɔɪl] *uncountable noun* ■ el **papel de aluminio**.

tiny ['taɪnɪ] *adjective* ■ **diminuto**.

tip [tɪp] *(noun & verb)*

■ *noun*

1. la **punta**: **the tips of your fingers** la punta de tus dedos; **it's on the tip of my tongue** lo tengo en la punta de la lengua

2. la **propina**: **I gave the waiter a tip** le di propina al camarero

3. el **consejo**: **safety tips** consejos de seguridad

4. *UK* el **vertedero (de basura)**: **you must take your rubbish to the tip** tienes que llevar la basura al vertedero

■ *verb (past tense & past participle* tipped, *present participle* tipping)*

dar propina: she tipped the waiter le dio propina al camarero

tip over *phrasal verb*

1. **volcar**: she tipped the bottle over volcó la botella

2. **volcarse**: the glass tipped over se volcó el vaso.

tiptoe ['tɪptəʊ] *noun*

on tiptoe de puntillas: he was walking on tiptoe andaba de puntillas.

tire *US* ['taɪəʳ] *noun* ➤ tyre *UK*.

tired ['taɪəd] *adjective* ■ **cansado**: he's very tired está muy cansado

➤ **to be tired of something** estar cansado de algo: **I'm tired of all these arguments** estoy cansado de todas estas discusiones; **he's tired of waiting** está cansado de esperar.

tiring ['taɪərɪŋ] *adjective* ■ **cansado**: this work is tiring este trabajo es cansado.

tissue ['tɪʃuː] *noun* ■ el **pañuelo de papel**: can you give me a tissue? ¿me puedes dar un pañuelo de papel?

title ['taɪtl] *noun* ■ el **título**: what's the title of the film? ¿cuál es el título de la película?

to [tə, tuː] *preposition*

1. **a**: do you want to go to the beach? ¿quieres ir a la playa?; **let's go to London** vamos a Londres; she wrote to her brother le escribió a su hermano; **from 9 to 5** de 9 a 5

> When a combines with el it becomes al: **give these bones to the dog** dale estos huesos al perro

2. **hasta**: count to 10 cuenta hasta 10

3. *telling the time* **menos**: it's quarter to four son las cuatro menos cuarto; it's ten to seven son las siete menos diez

4. *with infinitives*

> When "to" is used as part of an infinitive after certain verbs (begin to do, try to do), it is usually translated by a or de depending on the verb used in Spanish:

she began to sing empezó a cantar; he tried to help me intenté ayudarme

When "to" is used after an adjective (easy to do, hard to do), it is usually translated by **de** when the infinitive has no object:

it's easy to understand es fácil de entender; **it's hard to believe** es difícil de creer

When the infinitive has an object, "to" is not translated:

it's hard to understand him es difícil entenderlo; **it's not easy to help him** no es fácil ayudarlo

When "to" means "in order to", it is translated by **para**:

he worked hard to pass his exam trabajó mucho para aprobar el examen; **she went to town to buy a coat** fue al centro para comprar un abrigo.

toad [təʊd] *noun* ■ el **sapo**.

toadstool ['təʊdstuːl] *noun* ■ la **seta venenosa**.

toast [təʊst] *noun* ■ la **tostada**: I had toast for breakfast comí tostadas para desayunar
a piece of toast una tostada
to drink a toast to somebody brindar por alguien: let's drink a toast to Gary brindemos por Gary.

toaster ['təʊstər] *noun* ■ el **tostador (eléctrico)**.

tobacco [tə'bækəʊ] *noun* ■ el **tabaco**.

tobacconist UK [tə'bækənɪst] *noun* ■ el **estanquero**, la **estanquera**
tobacconist's el estanco.

today [tə'deɪ] *adverb* ■ **hoy**: what did you do today? ¿qué has hecho hoy?; what day is it today? ¿qué día es hoy?

toe [təʊ] *noun* ■ el **dedo del pie**: I hurt my toe me he hecho daño en el dedo del pie.

together [tə'geðər] *adverb* ■ **juntos**: they arrived together llegaron juntos
together with junto con: together with the CD, you get a booklet junto con el CD, viene un folleto.

toilet ['tɔɪlɪt] *noun*
1. *in a public place* los **aseos**: where are the toilets? ¿dónde están los aseos?
2. *in a house* el **lavabo**, el **baño**: he's gone to the toilet ha ido al lavabo
a toilet bag un neceser
toilet paper el papel higiénico
a toilet roll un rollo de papel higiénico.

toiletries ['tɔɪlɪtrɪz] *plural noun* ■ los **artículos de tocador**.

token ['təʊkn] *noun* ■ la **muestra**: they gave her a gift as a token of their appreciation le dieron un regalo como muestra de su agradecimiento
a gift token un cheque-regalo.

told [təʊld] *past tense & past participle* ➤ tell.

toll [təʊl] *noun* ■ el **peaje**: you have to pay a toll at the bridge tienes que pagar peaje en el puente.

toll-free US [təʊlfriː] *adverb*
to call toll-free llamar gratis: I called toll-free llamé gratis.

tomato [UK tə'mɑːtəʊ, US tə'meɪtəʊ] *(plural tomatoes) noun* ■ el **tomate**
tomato sauce la salsa de tomate.

tomb [tuːm] *noun* ■ la **tumba**.

tomorrow [tə'mɒrəʊ] *adverb* ■ **mañana**: I'll do it tomorrow lo haré mañana
tomorrow morning mañana por la mañana
tomorrow evening mañana por la tarde
the day after tomorrow pasado mañana: I'll come over the day after tomorrow pasaré por ahí pasado mañana.

ton [tʌn] *noun* ■ la **tonelada**: it weighs a ton pesa una tonelada
tons of *informal* montones de: she has tons of friends tiene montones de amigos.

tone [təʊn] *noun* ■ el **tono**: don't speak to me in that tone no me hables en ese tono; the phone isn't working, there's no tone el teléfono no funciona, no hay tono de llamada
speak after the tone hable después de la señal
mobile ring tones melodías de móvil.

tongue [tʌŋ] *noun* ■ la **lengua**: she stuck her tongue out at me me sacó la lengua.

tonight [tə'naɪt] *adverb* ■ **esta noche**: I'm going out tonight salgo esta noche.

tonsils ['tɒnslz] *plural noun* ■ las **amígdalas**: he had his tonsils out lo operaron de las amígdalas.

too [tu:] *adverb*

1. **también**: are you coming too? ¿tú también vienes?; I'm hungry — me too tengo hambre —yo también

2. **demasiado**: it's too late es demasiado tarde
➤ too many demasiados: there are too many cars hay demasiados coches
➤ there are too many people hay demasiada gente
➤ too much demasiado: you drink too much coffee bebes demasiado café.

took [tʊk] *past tense* ➤ take.

tool [tu:l] *noun* ■ la **herramienta**
➤ a tool box una caja de herramientas.

tooth [tu:θ] *(plural* teeth [ti:θ]*) noun* ■ el **diente**: she's brushing her teeth se está lavando los dientes.

toothache ['tu:θeɪk] *noun* ■ el **dolor de muelas**
➤ she has toothache UK OR she has a toothache US le duelen las muelas.

toothbrush ['tu:θbrʌʃ] *noun* ■ el **cepillo de dientes**.

toothpaste ['tu:θpeɪst] *noun* ■ la **pasta de dientes**, el **dentífrico**: a tube of toothpaste un tubo de pasta de dientes.

top [tɒp] *(noun & adjective)*
■ *noun*
1. la **cima**: at the top of the mountain en la cima de la montaña
2. la **parte superior**: at the top of the page en la parte superior de la hoja
3. la **parte de arriba**: at the top of the stairs en la parte de arriba de la escalera
4. *garment* la **parte de arriba**: the bikini top la parte de arriba del biquini
5. la **superficie**: she polished the top of the table limpió la superficie de la mesa

6. el **tapón** *(plural* los **tapones***)*: put the top back on the bottle ponle el tapón a la botella
7. el **capuchón**: the top of a pen el capuchón de un bolígrafo
➤ on top of encima de: he was sitting on top of the table estaba sentado encima de la mesa
➤ on top of that, he's stupid además, es estúpido
➤ he's at the top of the class es el mejor de la clase
➤ on top encima: a cake with a cherry on top un pastel con una cereza encima
■ *adjective*
1. de **arriba**: the top drawer el cajón de arriba; the top stair la escalera de arriba
2. **destacado**: he's a top tennis player es un destacado tenista
➤ the top floor el último piso: they live on the top floor viven en el último piso.

topic ['tɒpɪk] *noun* ■ el **tema**: the main topic of conversation el tema principal de conversación.

topping ['tɒpɪŋ] *noun*
➤ what toppings do you want on your pizza? ¿con qué ingredientes quiere la pizza?

top-secret [,tɒp'si:krɪt] *adjective* ■ **secreto**: top-secret information información secreta.

tore [tɔ:ʳ] *past tense* ➤ tear.

torn [tɔ:n] *past participle* ➤ tear.

tortoise ['tɔ:təs] *noun* ■ la **tortuga**.

toss [tɒs] *verb* ■ **tirar**: he tossed me the ball me tiró la pelota
➤ to toss a coin echarlo a cara o cruz: let's toss a coin echémoslo a cara o cruz

total ['təʊtl] *(noun & adjective)*
■ *noun*
el **total**: it costs a total of 200 euros cuesta un total de 200 euros
➤ in total en total
■ *adjective*
total: the total price el precio total.

touch [tʌtʃ] *(noun & verb)*
■ *noun*
el **tacto**: the sense of touch el sentido del tacto; it's soft to the touch es suave al tacto

to keep in touch with somebody mantenerse en contacto con alguien

to get in touch with somebody ponerse en contacto con alguien: **I got in touch with him** me puse en contacto con él

to lose touch with somebody perder el contacto con alguien: **I lost touch with them** perdí el contacto con ellos

verb

tocar: the meat is tough le toqué la mano.

touchdown ['tʌtʃdaʊn] *noun*

. *plane* el **aterrizaje**

2.*spacecraft* el **alunizaje**

3.*in American football* el **ensayo**.

tough [tʌf] *adjective*

. **duro**: the meat is tough la carne está dura; **it's a tough life** es una vida dura

2. **difícil**: it's a tough problem es un problema difícil

3. **peligroso**: this is a tough neighbourhood éste es un barrio peligroso

tough luck! ¡mala suerte!

tour [tʊər] *noun*

1. el **viaje turístico**, el **recorrido turístico**: we went on a tour of Spain hicimos un recorrido turístico por España

2. la **visita**: we went on a tour of the museum hicimos una visita al museo

3. la **gira**: Jennifer López is on tour Jennifer López está de gira.

tourism ['tʊərɪzm] *noun* ■ el **turismo**.

tourist ['tʊərɪst] *noun* ■ el/la **turista**

a tourist office OR a tourist information office una oficina de turismo OR una oficina de información turística.

tournament ['tɔːnəmənt] *noun* ■ el **torneo**: a chess tournament un torneo de ajedrez.

towards [təˈwɔːdz], **toward** US [təˈwɔːd] *preposition*

1. **hacia**: he was walking towards me venía hacia mí

2. **con**: she was very kind towards us fue muy amable con nosotros.

towel ['taʊəl] *noun* ■ la **toalla**: a bath towel una toalla de baño.

tower ['taʊər] *noun* ■ la **torre**.

a tower block UK un bloque de pisos.

town [taʊn] *noun*

1. el **pueblo**: he lives in a small town vive en un pequeño pueblo

2. la **ciudad**: we went into town fuimos a la ciudad

the town centre UK el centro de la ciudad

the town hall el ayuntamiento.

toy [tɔɪ] *noun* ■ el **juguete**

a toy shop UK OR a toy store US una juguetería.

track [træk] *noun*

1. el **camino**: a mountain track un camino de montaña

2. la **pista**: he did three laps around the track dio tres vueltas a la pista

3. la **canción**: can I listen to the next track? ¿puedo escuchar la siguiente canción?

4. la **huella**: the tyre tracks led to the river las huellas de los neumáticos conducían al río

a railway track UK OR a railroad track US una vía férrea.

tracksuit ['træksuːt] *noun* ■ el **chándal** (*plural* los chandals OR los chándales).

tractor ['træktər] *noun* ■ el **tractor**.

trade [treɪd] *noun*

1. el **oficio**: he's a chef by trade es chef de oficio

2. el **comercio**: international trade comercio internacional.

trademark ['treɪdmɑːk] *noun* ■ la **marca**: a registered trademark una marca registrada.

tradition [trəˈdɪʃn] *noun* ■ la **tradición** (*plural* las tradiciones): it's a Christmas tradition to kiss under the mistletoe es una tradición navideña besarse debajo del muérdago.

traditional [trəˈdɪʃənl] *adjective* ■ tradicional.

traffic ['træfɪk] *uncountable noun* ■ el tráfico: there's a lot of traffic hay mucho tráfico

a traffic circle US una rotonda

a traffic jam un atasco: we got caught in a traffic jam quedamos atrapados en un atasco

> the **traffic lights** el semáforo: **stop at the traffic lights** pare en el semáforo
> a **traffic warden** UK un guardia de tráfico.

tragedy ['trædʒədɪ] (plural tragedies) noun ▪ la **tragedia**.

trail [treɪl] noun ▪ el **rastro**: **we are on their trail** les estamos siguiendo el rastro.

trailer ['treɪlər] noun
1. el **avance**: **I liked the trailer for the film** me gustó el avance de la película
2. el **remolque**: **the car was pulling a trailer** el coche llevaba un remolque
3. US la **caravana**: **they live in a trailer** viven en una caravana.

train [treɪn] (noun & verb)
▪ noun
el **tren**: **I went to Bristol by train** fui a Bristol en tren
▪ verb
1. **formar**: **he is training the new assistant** está formando al nuevo empleado
2. **estudiar**: **she's training as a doctor** está estudiando medicina
3. **entrenar**: **he's training for the race** está entrenando para la carrera.

trainer ['treɪnər] noun ▪ el **entrenador**, la **entrenadora**: **the team has a new trainer** el equipo tiene un nuevo entrenador.

trainers UK ['treɪnərz] plural noun ▪ las **zapatillas de deporte**.

training ['treɪnɪŋ] uncountable noun ▪ la **formación**: **he did his training in Spain** hizo su formación en España
> **to be in training** estar entrenándose: **he's in training for the tournament** se está entrenando para el torneo
> **to be out of training** estar desentrenado.

tram UK [træm] noun ▪ el **tranvía**: **there are trams in Amsterdam** hay tranvías en Amsterdam.

tramp [træmp] noun ▪ el **vagabundo**, la **vagabunda**.

trampoline ['træmpəliːn] noun ▪ la **cama elástica**.

translate [trænsˈleɪt] verb ▪ **traducir**: **can you translate this letter into English?** ¿puedes traducir esta carta al inglés?

translation [trænsˈleɪʃn] noun ▪ la **traducción** (plural las **traducciones**).

translator [trænsˈleɪtər] noun ▪ el **traductor**, la **traductora**.

transparent [trænsˈpærənt] adjective ▪ **transparente**.

transport noun & verb
▪ noun ['trænspɔːt]
el **transporte**: **we went by public transport** fuimos en transporte público
▪ verb [trænsˈpɔːt]
transportar.

trap [træp] (noun & verb)
▪ noun
la **trampa**: **it's a trap** es una trampa
▪ verb (past tense & past participle **trapped**, present participle **trapping**)
1. **atrapado**: **I'm trapped, I can't get out** estoy atrapado, no puedo salir
2. **cazar con una trampa**: **the hunters trapped the lion** los cazadores cazaron al león con una trampa.

trash US [træʃ] uncountable noun ▪ la **basura**: **there's a pile of trash in the corner** hay una pila de basura en el rincón
> **put it in the trash** tíralo a la basura
> **put the trash out** saca la basura.

trashcan US ['træʃkæn] noun ▪ el **cubo de la basura**.

travel ['trævl] (noun & verb)
▪ uncountable noun
el **viajar**, los **viajes**: **travel broadens the mind** viajar abre la mente
> **a travel agency** una agencia de viajes
▪ verb (past tense & past participle **travelled** UK OR **traveled** US, present participle **travelling** UK OR **traveling** US)
1. **viajar**: **he travels a lot** viaja mucho
2. **recorrer**: **I've travelled 30 kilometres** he recorrido 30 kilómetros.

traveller UK, **traveler** US ['trævlər] noun ▪ el **viajero**, la **viajera**

a **traveller's cheque** UK OR a **traveler's check** US un cheque de viaje.

tray [treɪ] noun ■ la **bandeja: put the plates on a tray** pon los platos en una bandeja.

treasure ['treʒəʳ] uncountable noun ■ el **tesoro: they found treasure on the shipwreck** encontraron un tesoro en los restos del naufragio.

treat [triːt] (verb & noun)

■ verb

tratar: she treats him well lo trata bien

to treat somebody to something invitar a alguien a algo: **he treated me to an ice cream** me invitó a tomar un helado

■ noun

el **capricho: today I'm going to give myself a treat** hoy me voy a dar un capricho

el **placer: it was a treat to see you again** fue un placer verte otra vez

it's my treat invito yo.

treatment ['triːtmənt] noun ■ el **tratamiento: he's having treatment at the hospital** está recibiendo tratamiento en el hospital.

treaty ['triːtɪ] (plural treaties) noun ■ el **tratado: a peace treaty** un tratado de paz.

tree [triː] noun ■ el **árbol: we sat under a tree** nos sentamos bajo un árbol

a family tree un árbol genealógico

a tree trunk un tronco.

tremble ['trembl] verb ■ **temblar: I was trembling all over** estaba temblando.

trend [trend] noun

1. la **moda: the latest trend** la última moda

2. la **tendencia: a new trend in music** una nueva tendencia musical.

trendy [trendɪ] adjective ■ informal **muy de moda, moderno: we went to a trendy club** fuimos a un club muy de moda.

trial ['traɪəl] noun ■ el **juicio: he pleaded guilty at the trial** se declaró culpable en el juicio

to go on trial ir a juicio.

triangle ['traɪæŋgl] noun ■ el **triángulo**.

tribe [traɪb] noun ■ la **tribu: an Amazonian tribe** una tribu amazónica.

trick [trɪk] (noun & verb)

■ noun

1. la **broma: he played a trick on his brother** le gastó una broma a su hermano

2. el **truco: there's a trick to opening the door** abrir la puerta tiene truco

■ verb

engañar: you tricked me me engañaste.

tried [traɪd] past tense & past participle ➤ **try**.

trigger ['trɪgəʳ] noun ■ el **gatillo: she pulled the trigger** apretó el gatillo.

trim [trɪm] (noun & verb)

■ noun

➤ **to have a trim** cortarse las puntas (del pelo)

■ verb (past tense & past participle **trimmed**, present participle **trimming**)

recortar

➤ **I need to have my hair trimmed** necesito cortarme las puntas.

trip [trɪp] (noun & verb)

■ noun

1. el **viaje: they went on a trip to Italy** se fueron de viaje a Italia

2. la **excursión: we're going on a trip to the beach today** hoy nos vamos de excursión a la playa

■ verb (past tense & past participle **tripped**, present participle **tripping**)

tropezar: I tripped and fell tropecé y me caí.

trolley UK ['trɒlɪ] noun ■ el **carrito: a shopping trolley** el carrito de la compra.

trophy ['trəʊfɪ] (plural trophies) noun ■ el **trofeo**.

tropical ['trɒpɪkl] adjective ■ **tropical: a tropical rainforest** una selva tropical.

trot [trɒt] (past tense & past participle **trotted**, present participle **trotting**) verb ■ **trotar: the horses were trotting round the field** los caballos trotaban por el campo.

trouble ['trʌbl] *(noun & verb)*
■ *uncountable noun*
1. el **problema**: he made a lot of trouble for me me causó muchos problemas; that's the trouble ése es el problema
2. la **molestia**: he has gone to a lot of trouble to help me se tomó muchas molestias para ayudarme
▸ to be in trouble estar metido en problemas: he's in a lot of trouble está metido en muchos problemas
▸ to get into trouble meterse en problemas: I don't want to get into trouble no quiero meterme en problemas
▸ what's the trouble? ¿qué pasa?
■ *verb*
molestar: I'm sorry to trouble you siento molestarlo.

trousers *UK* ['traʊzəz] *plural noun* ■ los **pantalones**: Paul's wearing red trousers Paul lleva pantalones rojos
▸ a pair of trousers unos pantalones

trout [traʊt] *noun* ■ la **trucha**.

truant *UK* ['truːənt] *noun*
▸ to play truant hacer novillos: he often plays truant hace novillos a menudo.

truck [trʌk] *noun* ■ el **camión** *(plural* los **camiones***)*: the rubbish truck el camión de la basura
▸ a truck driver el camionero.

trucker *UK* ['trʌkə'] *noun* ■ el **camionero**, la **camionera**.

true [truː] *adjective* ■ **verdadero**: a true love un amor verdadero
▸ it's true es verdad
▸ to come true hacerse realidad: her dream came true su sueño se hizo realidad.

trumpet ['trʌmpɪt] *noun* ■ la **trompeta**: Louis plays the trumpet Louis toca la trompeta.

trunk [trʌŋk] *noun*
1. el **tronco**: a tree trunk un tronco
2. la **trompa**: elephants suck up water with their trunks los elefantes succionan agua con la trompa
3. el **baúl**: they put the trunk away in the attic guardaron el baúl en el desván

4. el **maletero**: put your bags into the trunk of the car pon tus maletas en el maletero del coche.

trust [trʌst] *(noun & verb)*
■ *uncountable noun*
la **confianza**: she has a lot of trust in you tiene mucha confianza en ti
■ *verb*
confiar: I trust you confío en ti.

truth [truːθ] *noun* ■ la **verdad**: he's telling the truth está diciendo la verdad.

try [traɪ] *(noun & verb)*
■ *noun*
el **intento**: I'll give it a try haré el intento
■ *verb (past tense & past participle* tried*)*
1. **intentar**: I tried to open the door intenté abrir la puerta
2. **probar**: try a bit of this cake prueba un poquito de este pastel
▸ to try one's best OR to try one's hardest hacer todo lo posible

try on *phrasal verb* ■ **probarse**: try this hat on pruébate este sombrero.

T-shirt [tiːʃɜːt] *noun* ■ la **camiseta**.

tube [*UK* tjuːb, *US* tuːb] *noun* ■ el **tubo**: a tube of toothpaste un tubo de pasta de dientes
▸ the tube *UK* el metro.

Tuesday [*UK* 'tjuːzdɪ, *US* 'tuːzdɪ] *noun*

In Spanish the days of the week do not start with a capital letter:

el **martes** *(plural* los **martes***)*: it's Tuesday today hoy es martes; next Tuesday el martes que viene; last Tuesday el martes pasado
▸ on Tuesday el martes: I'll see you on Tuesday te veo el martes
▸ on Tuesdays los martes: he comes to see me on Tuesdays viene a verme los martes.

tulip [*UK* 'tjuːlɪp, *US* 'tuːlɪp] *noun* ■ el **tulipán** *(plural* los **tulipanes***)*.

tummy ['tʌmɪ] *noun* ■ *informal* la **barriga**: I have a tummy ache me duele la barriga.

tuna [*UK* 'tjuːnə, *US* 'tuːnə] *(plural* tuna OR tunas) *noun* ■ el **atún** *(plural* los **atunes***)*.

tune [UK tjuːn, US tuːn] noun ■ la melodía: I don't know the words, but I'll sing you the tune no sé la letra, pero te cantaré la melodía

out of tune desafinado: he's singing out of tune está desafinando.

tunnel ['tʌnl] noun ■ el túnel: we went through a tunnel pasamos por un túnel.

turkey ['tɜːkɪ] noun ■ el pavo: we eat turkey at Christmas en Navidad comemos pavo.

turn ['tɜːn] (noun & verb)

noun
. el turno
2. la curva: there's a turn in the road hay una curva en la carretera
it's my turn me toca a mí
it's your turn to wash the dishes te toca a ti lavar los platos
to take turns at doing something turnarse para hacer algo

verb
. torcer: turn left at the light tuerza a la izquierda en el semáforo
2. girar: turn the knob to the right gira el pomo hacia la derecha
3. volverse: he turned towards me se volvió hacia mí
4. ponerse: she turned pale se puso pálida; her face turned red se le puso la cara colorada

turn around , turn round UK phrasal verb
. darse la vuelta: he turned around when I came in se dio la vuelta cuando entré
2. dar la vuelta: the car turned around el coche dio la vuelta

turn back phrasal verb ■ regresar: we walked for an hour and then turned back caminamos durante una hora y después regresamos

turn down phrasal verb ■ rechazar: they turned my offer down rechazaron mi oferta

turn into phrasal verb
. convertir: the witch turned the prince into a frog la bruja convirtió al príncipe en una rana

2. convertirse: the caterpillar turned into a butterfly el gusano se convirtió en una mariposa

turn off phrasal verb ■ apagar: turn the TV off apaga la tele

turn on phrasal verb ■ encender: turn the radio on enciende la radio; he turned the light on encendió la luz

turn over phrasal verb
. dar la vuelta: he turned his cards over dio la vuelta a sus cartas
2. darse la vuelta: she turned over and went back to sleep se dio la vuelta y se volvió a dormir
3. cambiar de canal: this film is boring, let's turn over esta película es aburrida, cambiemos de canal

turn round UK phrasal verb ➤ turn around

turn up phrasal verb
. subir: turn the music up sube la música
2. aparecer: he didn't turn up no apareció; don't worry, it'll turn up no te preocupes, ya aparecerá.

turnip ['tɜːnɪp] noun ■ el nabo.

turnpike US ['tɜːnpaɪk] noun ■ la autopista de peaje.

turquoise ['tɜːkwɔɪz] adjective ■ turquesa.

turtle ['tɜːtl] noun ■ la tortuga (marina).

tusk [tʌsk] noun ■ el colmillo: elephants have long tusks los elefantes tienen colmillos largos.

TV [ˌtiːˈviː] (abbreviation of television) noun ■ la tele: they're watching TV están viendo tele; what's on TV? ¿qué dan en la tele?

twelfth [twelfθ] numeral ■ duodécimo
on the twelfth floor en el piso doce
it's the twelfth of November UK OR it's November twelfth US estamos a doce de noviembre.

twelve [twelv] numeral ■ doce: the twelve apostles los doce apóstoles; she's twelve tiene doce años; I'll meet you at twelve nos encontramos a las doce.

twentieth ['twentɪəθ] *numeral* ■ **vigési-mo**: in the twentieth century en el siglo veinte
it's the twentieth of May *UK* OR it's May twentieth *US* estamos a veinte de mayo.

twenty ['twentɪ] *numeral* ■ **veinte**: it's twenty to four son las cuatro menos veinte; she's twenty tiene veinte años
twenty-one veintiuno
the twenty-first century el siglo veintiuno.

twice [twaɪs] *adverb* ■ **dos veces**: I go swimming twice a week voy a nadar dos veces por semana; she earns twice as much as him ella gana el doble que él.

twin [twɪn] *noun* ■ **el gemelo, la gemela, el mellizo, la melliza**: they are twins son mellizos; his twin brother su hermano gemelo.

twist [twɪst] *verb*
1. **retorcer**: he twisted my arm me retorció el brazo
2. **girar**: I twisted the knob to the left giré el pomo hacia la izquierda
3. **enrollar**: twist the thread around the bobbin enrolla el hilo en la bobina
to get twisted enroscarse: the cable has got twisted el cable se enroscó
to twist one's ankle torcerse el tobillo: I twisted my ankle me torcí el tobillo.

two [tuː] *numeral* ■ **dos**: I cut the paper in two corté el papel en dos; she's two tiene dos años; he left at two se fue a las dos.

type [taɪp] *(noun & verb)*
■ *noun*
el **tipo**: there are different types of houses hay diferentes tipos de casas
■ *verb*
escribir a máquina: he typed the letter escribió la carta a máquina
I have to type up the notes on the computer tengo que pasar los apuntes al ordenador.

typewriter ['taɪp,raɪtər] *noun* ■ **la máquina de escribir**.

typical ['tɪpɪkl] *adjective* ■ **típico**.

tyre *UK*, **tire** *US* ['taɪər] *noun* ■ **el neumático**: he pumped up the tyres infló los neumáticos.

UFO ['uːfəʊ] *(abbreviation of* unidentified flying object) *noun* ■ **el OVNI**.

ugly ['ʌglɪ] *adjective* ■ **feo**: the house is very ugly la casa es muy fea.

UK [,juː'keɪ] *(abbreviation of* United Kingdom) *noun*
the UK el Reino Unido.

umbrella [ʌm'brelə] *noun* ■ **el paraguas** *(plural* los **paraguas**)*: he put up his umbrella abrió el paraguas.

umpire ['ʌmpaɪər] *noun* ■ **el árbitro, la árbitra**.

UN [,juː'en] *(abbreviation of* United Nations) *noun*
the UN la ONU.

unable [ʌn'eɪbl] *adjective*
to be unable to do something no poder hacer algo: he was unable to help me no pudo ayudarme
she's unable to read no sabe leer.

unbearable [ʌn'beərəbl] *adjective* ■ **insoportable**.

unbelievable [,ʌnbɪ'liːvəbl] *adjective* ■ **increíble**.

uncle ['ʌŋkl] *noun* ■ **el tío**.

uncomfortable [,ʌn'kʌmftəbl] *adjective* ■ **incómodo**
to be uncomfortable ser incómodo: this chair is really uncomfortable esta silla es realmente incómoda
to feel uncomfortable sentirse incómodo: I felt very uncomfortable at the party me sentí muy incómodo en la fiesta.

under ['ʌndəʳ] *(preposition & adverb)*
preposition
- **debajo de:** the dog's under the sofa el perro está debajo del sofá
- **menos de:** it weighs under 5 kilos pesa menos de 5 kilos
- **menor de:** a game for children under five un juego para niños menores de cinco años
  it's under there está ahí debajo
  the road goes under the bridge la carretera pasa por debajo del puente
adverb
- **debajo:** he saw the bed and crawled under vio la cama y se metió debajo
2. **menos:** children of ten and under niños de diez años o menos.

underground ['ʌndəɡraʊnd] *(adjective, adverb & noun)*
adjective
subterráneo: an underground passage un pasaje subterráneo
adverb
bajo tierra: the animal went underground el animal se metió bajo tierra
noun
UK **el metro:** we took the underground cogimos el metro.

underline [ˌʌndə'laɪn] *verb* ■ **subrayar:** he underlined the heading subrayó el título.

underneath [ˌʌndə'niːθ] *(preposition & adverb)*
preposition
debajo de: I looked underneath the chair miré debajo de la silla
adverb
debajo: I bent down and looked underneath me incliné y miré debajo.

underpants ['ʌndəpænts] *plural noun* ■ los **calzoncillos:** a pair of blue underpants unos calzoncillos azules.

underpass [*UK* 'ʌndəpɑːs, *US* 'ʌndəpæs] *noun* ■ el **paso subterráneo.**

undershirt *US* ['ʌndəʃɜːt] *noun* ■ la **camiseta (interior).**

understand [ˌʌndə'stænd] *(past tense & past participle* understood) *verb* ■ **entender:**

do you understand? ¿entiendes?; I don't understand Spanish no entiendo español.

understood [ˌʌndə'stʊd] *past tense & past participle* ➤ understand.

underwater [ˌʌndə'wɔːtəʳ] *adjective* ■ **submarino:** an underwater camera una cámara submarina.

underwear ['ʌndəweəʳ] *uncountable noun* ■ la **ropa interior.**

undid [ˌʌn'dɪd] *past tense* ➤ undo.

undo [ˌʌn'duː] *(past tense* undid, *past participle* undone) *verb*
1. **desabrochar:** he undid his jacket se desabrochó la chaqueta
2. **deshacer:** I can't undo this knot no puedo deshacer este nudo
3. **desatar:** she undid her shoelaces se desató los cordones de los zapatos.

undone [ˌʌn'dʌn] *adjective & past participle* ➤ undo.

undress [ˌʌn'dres] *verb* ■ **desvestir**
➤ to get undressed desvestirse: he got undressed se desvistió.

unemployed [ˌʌnɪm'plɔɪd] *adjective* ■ **parado, en el paro:** he's unemployed está en el paro
➤ the unemployed los parados.

unemployment [ˌʌnɪm'plɔɪmənt] *noun* ■ el **desempleo,** el **paro**
➤ unemployment benefit *UK* OR unemployment compensation *US* subsidio de desempleo.

unexpected [ˌʌnɪk'spektɪd] *adjective* ■ **inesperado.**

unfair [ˌʌn'feəʳ] *adjective* ■ **injusto.**

unfortunately [ʌn'fɔːtʃnətlɪ] *adverb* ■ **lamentablemente, por desgracia:** unfortunately, there isn't any cake left lamentablemente, no queda más pastel.

unfriendly [ˌʌn'frendlɪ] *adjective* ■ **antipático.**

unhappy [ʌn'hæpɪ] *adjective* ■ **infeliz** *(plural* infelices).

unhealthy [ʌnˈhelθɪ] *adjective*

I. **enfermizo:** he looks really unhealthy tiene un aspecto realmente enfermizo

2. **poco saludable:** it's an unhealthy climate es un clima poco saludable.

uniform [ˈjuːnɪfɔːm] *noun* ■ el **uniforme.**

union [ˈjuːnjən] *noun* ■ el **sindicato:** they belong to a union pertenecen a un sindicato

▸ the Union Jack la bandera del Reino Unido

THE UNION JACK

La bandera oficial del Reino Unido se llama the Union Jack o the Union Flag. Las cruces de san Jorge, san Andrés y san Patricio representan respectivamente a Inglaterra, Escocia e Irlanda del Norte. El País de Gales, aunque forma parte del Reino Unido, tiene su propia bandera, un dragón rojo sobre un fondo verde y blanco.

unit [ˈjuːnɪt] *noun* ■ la **unidad.**

United Kingdom [juːˌnaɪtɪdˈkɪŋdəm] *noun* ■ the United Kingdom el Reino Unido.

United Nations [juːˌnaɪtɪdˈneɪʃnz] *plural noun*

▸ the United Nations las Naciones Unidas.

United States [juːˌnaɪtɪdˈsteɪts] *noun*

▸ the United States los Estados Unidos.

universe [ˈjuːnɪvɜːs] *noun* ■ el **universo.**

university [ˌjuːnɪˈvɜːsətɪ] *(plural* universities*) noun* ■ la **universidad:** he goes to university *UK* OR he goes to the university *US* va a la universidad; she's a university student es una estudiante universitaria.

unleaded [ˌʌnˈledɪd] *adjective* ■ **sin plomo:** *UK* unleaded petrol OR *US* unleaded gas la gasolina sin plomo.

unless [ənˈles] *conjunction* ■ **a menos que, a no ser que, si no**

The conjunctions a menos que and a no ser que are followed by a verb in the subjunctive:

I'll stay here unless he comes to pick me up me quedaré aquí a menos que él venga a buscarme.

unlike [ˌʌnˈlaɪk] *preposition* ■ **a diferencia de:** unlike other systems, this one is easy to install a diferencia de otros sistemas, este es fácil de instalar.

unlikely [ʌnˈlaɪklɪ] *adjective* ■ **poco probable, improbable:** he's unlikely to win es poco probable que él gane.

unlock [ˌʌnˈlɒk] *verb* ■ **abrir (con llave):** I will unlock the door voy a abrir la puerta.

unlucky [ʌnˈlʌkɪ] *adjective*

▸ to be unlucky tener mala suerte: he's so unlucky tiene tan mala suerte

▸ it's unlucky to walk underneath a ladder pasar por debajo de una escalera trae mala suerte.

unpack [ˌʌnˈpæk] *verb* ■ **deshacer:** we unpacked our suitcases deshicimos las maletas

▸ I unpacked my clothes saqué la ropa de la maleta.

untidy [ʌnˈtaɪdɪ] *adjective*

I. **desordenado:** your room is untidy tu habitación está desordenada; Nick is very untidy Nick es muy desordenado

2. **descuidado, desaliñado:** he looks untidy tiene un aspecto descuidado.

untie [ˌʌnˈtaɪ] *(present participle* untying*) verb*

I. **deshacer:** I untied the knot deshice el nudo

2. **desatar:** they untied the prisoner desataron al prisionero.

until [ənˈtɪl] *(preposition & conjunction)*

■ *preposition*
hasta: we'll play until 6 o'clock vamos a jugar hasta las 6; until now hasta ahora

■ *conjunction*
hasta que

The conjunction hasta que is followed by a verb in the subjunctive when referring to an event that hasn't yet occurred:

I'll stay here until he comes me quedaré aquí hasta que venga.

unusual [ʌnˈjuːʒl] *adjective*

I. **poco común:** an unusual colour un color poco común

raro: it's unusual for her to arrive late es raro que llegue tarde

The expression **es raro que** is followed by a verb in the subjunctive.

original: she wears unusual clothes lleva ropa original.

unwrap [ˌʌnˈræp] *(past tense & past participle* unwrapped, *present participle* unwrapping) verb* ■ **desenvolver**: she unwrapped her presents desenvolvió sus regalos.

up [ʌp] *(adverb, preposition & adjective)*

adverb

arriba: it's up here es aquí arriba
don't look up no mires hacia arriba

preposition

en lo alto, arriba de: the house is up the hill la casa está en lo alto de la colina; the cat's up the tree el gato está arriba del árbol

2.

When "up" is used with a verb of movement in English (to come up or to go up), you often use a verb alone in Spanish to translate it:

she went up the stairs subió las escaleras; they ran up the road corrieron por la calle
their house is just up the road su casa queda un poco más adelante por esta calle
up to hasta: the water came up to my knees el agua me llegaba hasta las rodillas
up to 30 people hasta 30 personas
it's up to you depende de ti
I don't feel up to going out no me siento con ánimos para salir
what's he up to? ¿qué está haciendo?
he's up to something está tramando algo

adjective

levantado: I was up at dawn estaba levantado al amanecer; is she up? ¿está levantada?
time's up! ¡ya es la hora!
what's up? *informal* ¿qué pasa?

update [ˌʌpˈdeɪt] *verb* ■ **actualizar**: I updated the file actualicé el fichero.

uphill [ˌʌpˈhɪl] *adverb*
to go uphill ir cuesta arriba: the path goes uphill el camino va cuesta arriba.

upon [əˈpɒn] *preposition* ■ *formal* **en, sobre**: she put the book upon the table puso el libro sobre la mesa

upper [ˈʌpər] *adjective* ■ **superior**: the upper lip el labio superior
the upper classes las clases altas.

upright [ˌʌpˈraɪt] *adjective & adverb* ■ **derecho**: stand upright! ¡ponte derecho!

upset [ʌpˈset] *(adjective & verb)*

■ *adjective*
afectado: she was very upset at the news estaba muy afectada por las noticias
to be upset **enfadarse**: don't get upset at what I said no te enfades por lo que dije
to have an upset stomach **estar mal del estómago**

■ *verb (past tense & past participle* upset, *present participle* upsetting)*

1. **afectar**: it upsets me to think about it me afecta pensar en eso
2. **disgustar**: this decision will upset a lot of people esta decisión va a disgustar a mucha gente
3. **desbaratar**: this has upset my plans esto ha desbaratado mis planes
4. **derramar**: I upset some coffee derramé un poco de café.

upside down [ˌʌpsaɪdˈdaʊn] *adverb* ■ **al revés**: the picture is upside down el cuadro está al revés.

upstairs [ˌʌpˈsteəz] *(adverb & adjective)*

■ *adverb*
arriba: wait for me upstairs esperadme arriba
to come upstairs OR to go upstairs **subir**: can you come upstairs? ¿puedes subir?

■ *adjective*
del piso de arriba: the upstairs rooms las habitaciones del piso de arriba.

up-to-date [ˌʌptəˈdeɪt] *adjective*
1. **al día**: the information is up-to-date la información está al día
2. **actualizado**: an up-to-date computer un ordenador actualizado.

upwards [ˈʌpwədz], **upward** *US* [ˈʌpwəd] *adverb* ■ **hacia arriba**: we looked upwards miramos hacia arriba.

urgent ['ɜːdʒənt] *adjective* ■ **urgente: I must speak to you, it's urgent** tengo que hablar contigo, es urgente.

us [ʌs] *pronoun*

1. *as a direct or indirect object pronoun* **nos: she calls us every week** nos llama todas las semanas; **he gave the papers to us** nos dio los papeles
2. *after a preposition and the verb "to be"* **nosotros: is that for us?** ¿eso es para nosotros?; **it's us** somos nosotros.

US [ˌjuːˈes] *(abbreviation of* United States*) noun*
▷ **the US** los EE.UU.

USA [ˌjuːesˈeɪ] *(abbreviation of* United States of America*) noun*
▷ **the USA** los EE.UU.

use *(noun & verb)*
■ *noun* [juːs]
el uso: there's a ban on the use of certain products está prohibido el uso de ciertos productos; **for my own use** para mi uso personal
▷ **directions for use** instrucciones de uso
▷ **to be of use** servir
▷ **the lift is out of use** el ascensor está fuera de servicio
▷ **it's no use** es inútil
▷ **what's the use?** ¿para qué sirve?
■ *verb* [juːz]

1. **usar: I used a new method** usé un método nuevo; **she uses vinegar to clean the windows** usa vinagre para limpiar los cristales; **can I use your phone?** ¿puedo usar el teléfono?
2. **utilizar: they use water as energy** utilizan el agua como energía; **he showed me how to use the Internet** me enseñó cómo utilizar Internet.

used [juːzd] *adjective* ■ **usado: a used car** un coche usado
▷ **to be used to doing something** estar acostumbrado a hacer algo: **I'm used to going to bed late** estoy acostumbrada a acostarme tarde
▷ **to get used to doing something** acostumbrarse a hacer algo: **you'll get used to getting up early** te acostumbrarás a levantarte temprano.

used to ['juːzdˈtə, 'juːzdˈtʊ, 'juːzdˈtuː] *modal verb* ■ **I used to go swimming twice a week** solía nadar dos veces por semana; **he used to study English** antes estudiaba inglés.

useful ['juːsfʊl] *adjective* ■ **útil: take the guidebook, it could be useful** llévate la guía, puede serte útil.

useless ['juːslɪs] *adjective*

1. **inservible: a useless piece of diving equipment** un equipo de buceo inservible
2. **inútil: he's completely useless** es totalmente inútil
▷ **it's useless** es inútil: **it's useless asking her** es inútil preguntarle.

user ['juːztər] *noun* ■ **el usuario,** la **usuaria**
▷ **the user name** el nombre de usuario.

usual ['juːʒəl] *adjective* ■ **de costumbre: we'll meet at the usual time** nos veremos a la hora de costumbre
▷ **as usual** como de costumbre: **she arrived early, as usual** llegó temprano, como de costumbre
▷ **later than usual** más tarde que de costumbre.

usually ['juːʒəlɪ] *adverb* ■ **normalmente: she usually leaves the house at nine** normalmente sale de la casa a las nueve.

vacant ['veɪkənt] *adjective* ■ **libre: is this seat vacant?** ¿está libre este asiento?

vacation *US* [vəˈkeɪʃn] *uncountable noun* ■ **las vacaciones: they spent their vacation in Greece** pasaron las vacaciones en Grecia
▷ **on vacation** de vacaciones: **she's on vacation** está de vacaciones

where are you going on vacation?
¿adónde vas a ir de vacaciones?

vacuum ['vækjʊəm] *(noun & verb)*

noun

el **vacío**

la **aspiradora**

a vacuum cleaner una aspiradora

verb

pasar la **aspiradora**: he's vacuuming the hall está pasando la aspiradora en el vestíbulo.

vacuum-packed ['vækjʊəm'pækt] *adjective* ■ **envasado al vacío.**

vain [veɪn] *adjective* ■ **vanidoso**: he's very vain es muy vanidoso

in vain en vano: I tried in vain to help him intenté en vano ayudarlo.

valid ['vælɪd] *adjective* ■ **válido**: your ticket isn't valid su billete no es válido.

valley ['vælɪ] *noun* ■ **el valle.**

valuable ['væljʊəbl] *adjective*

de **valor**: a valuable necklace un collar de valor

valioso: your advice has been very valuable tu consejo ha sido muy valioso.

valuables ['væljʊəblz] *plural noun* ■ **los objetos de valor**: she keeps her valuables in a safe guarda los objetos de valor en una caja fuerte.

value ['vælju:] *noun* ■ **el valor**: the value of their house has doubled se ha duplicado el valor de su casa.

van [væn] *noun* ■ **la furgoneta.**

vanilla [və'nɪlə] *noun* ■ **la vainilla.**

vanish ['vænɪʃ] *verb* ■ **desaparecer**: he vanished desapareció.

variety [və'raɪətɪ] *(plural varieties) noun* ■ **la variedad**: there are many different varieties of flowers hay muchas variedades diferentes de flores.

various ['veərɪəs] *adjective* ■ **varios**: for various reasons por varias razones.

varnish ['vɑːnɪʃ] *noun* ■ **el barniz**: give it a coat of varnish dale una mano de barniz nail varnish esmalte de uñas.

vary ['veərɪ] *(past tense & past participle varied) verb* ■ **variar**: the weather varies from day to day el tiempo varía de día en día.

vase [*UK* vɑːz, *US* veɪz] *noun* ■ **el florero**: I put the flowers in the vase puse las flores en el florero

⚠ Vase es un falso amigo, no significa "vaso".

veal [viːl] *uncountable noun* ■ **la carne de ternera.**

vegetable ['vedʒtəbl] *noun* ■ **la verdura.**

vegetarian [,vedʒɪ'teərɪən] *noun* ■ **el vegetariano, la vegetariana.**

vehicle ['viːɪkl] *noun* ■ **el vehículo.**

veil [veɪl] *noun* ■ **el velo**: she's wearing a veil lleva un velo.

vein [veɪn] *noun* ■ **la vena**: veins carry blood to the heart las venas transportan la sangre al corazón.

velvet ['velvɪt] *noun* ■ **el terciopelo.**

vending machine ['vendɪŋmə'ʃiːn] *noun* ■ **la máquina expendedora.**

verb [vɜːb] *noun* ■ **el verbo.**

verse [vɜːs] *noun*

1. el **verso**: the poem has three verses el poema tiene tres versos

2. el **versículo**: a verse from the Bible un versículo de la Biblia.

version ['vɜːʃn] *noun* ■ **la versión** *(plural las versiones)*: there are two versions of the story hay dos versiones de la historia.

versus ['vɜːsəs] *preposition* ■ **contra**: Liverpool versus Barcelona Liverpool contra Barcelona.

vertical ['vɜːtɪkl] *adjective* ■ **vertical**: a vertical line una línea vertical.

very ['verɪ] *adverb* ■ **muy**: he's very happy está muy contento

very much mucho: I like him very much él me gusta mucho

the very same day el mismo día.

vest [vest] *noun*
1. *UK* la **camiseta (interior):** he's wearing a vest under his shirt lleva una camiseta debajo de la camisa
2. *US* el **chaleco:** he's wearing a suit and a vest lleva un traje con chaleco.

vet [vet], **veterinarian** *US* [ˌvetərɪ'neərɪən] *noun* ■ el **veterinario,** la **veterinaria.**

vicar ['vɪkəʳ] *noun* ■ el **párroco.**

vicious ['vɪʃəs] *adjective*
1. **brutal:** a vicious attack una agresión brutal
2. **feroz** *(plural* feroces)*:* a vicious dog un perro feroz
➤ a vicious circle un círculo vicioso.

victim ['vɪktɪm] *noun* ■ el/la **víctima.**

victory ['vɪktərɪ] *(plural* victories) *noun* ■ la **victoria.**

video ['vɪdɪəʊ] *noun* ■ el **vídeo:** they're watching a video están viendo un vídeo
➤ on video en vídeo: the film's out on video la película está en vídeo
➤ a video camera una videocámara
➤ a video cassette un videocasete
➤ a video club un videoclub
➤ a video game un videojuego
➤ a video recorder un aparato de vídeo.

view [vju:] *noun*
1. la **vista:** there's a great view from the top of the Eiffel Tower hay una vista espectacular desde lo alto de la Torre Eiffel
2. el **punto de vista:** what is your view on the subject? ¿cuál es tu punto de vista sobre el tema?

viewer ['vju:əʳ] *noun* ■ el **espectador,** la **espectadora:** the programme attracts millions of viewers el programa atrae a millones de espectadores.

village ['vɪlɪdʒ] *noun* ■ el **pueblo:** they live in a village in the mountains viven en un pueblo de montaña.

vine [vaɪn] *noun* ■ la **vid:** grapes grow on vines la uva crece en las vides.

vinegar ['vɪnɪgəʳ] *noun* ■ el **vinagre.**

vineyard ['vɪnjəd] *noun* ■ la **viña.**

violence ['vaɪələns] *noun* ■ la **violencia.**

violent ['vaɪələnt] *adjective* ■ **violento:** he's a violent man es un hombre violento.

violin [ˌvaɪə'lɪn] *noun* ■ el **violín** *(plural* los violines)*:* she plays the violin toca el violín.

virus ['vaɪrəs] *noun* ■ el **virus** *(plural* los virus).

visa ['vi:zə] *noun* ■ el **visado.**

visit ['vɪzɪt] *(noun & verb)*
■ *noun*
la **visita:** I paid a visit to my uncle le hice una visita a mi tío
■ *verb*
visitar: I visited my uncle visité a mi tío.

visitor ['vɪzɪtəʳ] *noun*
1. la **visita:** we have visitors tomorrow mañana tenemos visitas
2. el/la **visitante:** the park attracts a lot of visitors el parque atrae a muchos visitantes.

vitamin [*UK* 'vɪtəmɪn, *US* 'vaɪtəmɪn] *noun* ■ la **vitamina.**

vocabulary [və'kæbjʊlərɪ] *(plural* vocabularies) *noun* ■ el **vocabulario.**

voice [vɔɪs] *noun* ■ la **voz** *(plural* las voces)*:* he has a deep voice tiene una voz grave
➤ she has a loud voice habla muy alto
➤ voice mail buzón de voz.

volcano [vɒl'keɪnəʊ] *(plural* volcanoes OR volcanos) *noun* ■ el **volcán** *(plural* los volcanes)*:* the volcano erupted el volcán entró en erupción.

volleyball ['vɒlɪbɔ:l] *noun* ■ el **voleibol:** they're playing volleyball están jugando al voleibol.

volume ['vɒlju:m] *noun* ■ el **volumen** *(plural* los **volúmenes***):* can you turn the volume up? ¿puedes subir el volumen?

voluntary ['vɒləntrɪ] *adjective* ■ **voluntario:** she does voluntary work hace trabajo voluntario.

volunteer [ˌvɒlən'tɪəʳ] *(noun & verb)*
noun
el **voluntario**, la **voluntaria**: they don't get paid, they're volunteers no les pagan, son voluntarios
verb
to volunteer to do something ofrecerse a hacer algo: he volunteered to help us se ofreció a ayudarnos.

vomit ['vɒmɪt] *verb* ■ **vomitar**: he vomited vomitó.

vote [vəʊt] *(noun & verb)*
noun
la **votación** *(plural* las **votaciones***)*: they organized a vote organizaron una votación
el **voto**: they won by 20 votes to 4 ganaron por 20 votos a 4
verb
votar: he voted for the Green Party votó al Partido Verde.

voucher ['vaʊtʃəʳ] *noun* ■ el **vale**: a voucher for a free drink un vale de bebida gratis; a gift voucher un vale de regalo.

vowel ['vaʊəl] *noun* ■ la **vocal**.

vulture ['vʌltʃəʳ] *noun* ■ el **buitre**.

wade [weɪd] *verb* ■ **vadear**: they're wading in the stream están vadeando el arroyo.

wag [wæg] *(past tense & past participle* wagged, *present participle* wagging*) verb* ■ **menear**: the dog's wagging its tail el perro está meneando la cola.

wage [weɪdʒ] *noun* ■ el **sueldo**: the wages are good los sueldos son buenos.

waist [weɪst] *noun* ■ la **cintura**: she has a small waist tiene una cintura pequeña.

waistcoat UK ['weɪstkəʊt] *noun* ■ el **chaleco**: he's wearing a suit and a waistcoat lleva un traje con chaleco.

wait [weɪt] *(noun & verb)*
■ *noun*
la **espera**: it was a long wait fue una larga espera
■ *verb*
esperar: we waited a long time esperamos un rato largo; wait a minute! ¡espera un momento!; I waited until he had left OR I waited for him to leave esperé hasta que se fuera

> The verb that follows esperar hasta que must be in the subjunctive.

I can't wait to see you tengo muchas ganas de verte
to keep somebody waiting hacer esperar a alguien: I'm sorry to keep you waiting perdón por hacerte esperar

wait for *phrasal verb* ■ **esperar**: wait for me! ¡esperadme!; he's waiting for the bus está esperando el autobús.

waiter ['weɪtəʳ] *noun* ■ el **camarero**.

waiting room ['weɪtɪŋruːm] *noun* ■ la sala de espera.

waitress ['weɪtrɪs] *noun* ■ la **camarera**.

wake [weɪk] *(past tense* woke, *past participle* woken) *verb* ■ **despertar**: wake me at six despiértame a las seis

wake up *phrasal verb*
1. **despertar**: can you wake me up in the morning? ¿puedes despertarme por la mañana?
2. **despertarse**: I woke up at seven me desperté a las siete.

walk [wɔːk] *(noun & verb)*
■ *noun*
el **paseo**: let's go for a walk vamos a dar un paseo

> it's a long walk es una larga caminata
> it's a five-minute walk queda a cinco minutos a pie
■ verb
1. ir a pie: I always walk to school siempre voy a pie al colegio
2. andar: we walked along the beach hemos andado por la playa
3. pasear: we walked three kilometres paseamos tres kilómetros
> to walk the dog sacar a pasear al perro

walk out phrasal verb ■ irse: he just got up and walked out se levantó y se fue.

walking ['wɔːkɪŋ] uncountable noun ■ walking is a good form of exercise andar es una buena forma de hacer ejercicio
> a walking stick un bastón.

Walkman® ['wɔːkmən] noun ■ el walkman® (plural los walkman).

wall [wɔːl] noun
1. la pared: he put a poster on his bedroom wall puso un póster en la pared de su habitación
2. el muro: he jumped over the wall saltó el muro.

wallet ['wɒlɪt] noun ■ la cartera: he took a 20-euro note out of his wallet sacó un billete de 20 euros de la cartera.

wallpaper ['wɔːlˌpeɪpər] noun ■ el papel pintado.

walnut ['wɔːlnʌt] noun ■ la nuez (plural las nueces).

wand [wɒnd] noun ■ la varita: a magic wand una varita mágica.

wander ['wɒndər] verb ■ dar vueltas: we wandered around the town dimos vueltas por el pueblo.

want [wɒnt] verb ■ querer: do you want some tea? ¿quieres té?; I want to go to the cinema quiero ir al cine
> to want somebody to do something querer que alguien haga algo: she wants me to stay quiere que me quede

The verb that follows querer que must be in the subjunctive.

wanted ['wɒntɪd] adjective
> he's wanted by the police lo busca la policía
> you're wanted in the kitchen te necesitan en la cocina.

war [wɔːr] noun ■ la guerra: the Second World War la Segunda Guerra Mundial
> to be at war estar en guerra: the two countries are at war los dos países están en guerra.

wardrobe ['wɔːdrəub] noun ■ el armario: put your coat in the wardrobe pon el abrigo en el armario.

warehouse ['weəhaus] noun ■ el almacén (plural los almacenes).

warm [wɔːm] (adjective & phrasal verb)
■ adjective
1. caliente, templado: the water is warm el agua está templada; the oven is warm el horno está caliente
2. caluroso: he got a warm welcome tuvo un recibimiento caluroso
> to be warm tener calor
> it's warm today hoy hace calor

warm up phrasal verb
1. calentar, entrar en calor: I'll warm up some apple pie voy a calentar un poco de tarta de manzana; the athletes are warming up los atletas están calentando
2. calentarse: come and warm up in front of the fire ven a calentarte frente al fuego

warmth [wɔːmθ] noun ■ el calor.

warn [wɔːn] verb ■ advertir: I warned you te lo advertí
> to warn somebody not to do something aconsejarle a alguien que no haga algo: I warned you not to go te aconsejé que no fueras

The verb that follows aconsejar que must be in the subjunctive.

warning ['wɔːnɪŋ] noun ■ la advertencia: this is my final warning ésta es mi última advertencia.

warranty ['wɒrəntɪ] (plural warranties) noun ■ la garantía: the computer is still under warranty el ordenador todavía está en garantía.

wart [wɔːt] *noun* ■ la **verruga**.

was [wəz] *past tense* ➤ be.

wash [wɒʃ] *(noun & verb)*
■ *noun*
to have a wash *UK* lavarse
his shirt is in the wash su camisa está para
lavar
■ *verb*
. **lavar**: he's washing his clothes está lavando la ropa
2. **lavarse**: I'm washing me estoy lavando; she
washed her hands se lavó las manos; he's
washing his hair se está lavando el pelo

wash up *phrasal verb* ■
1. *UK* **lavar los platos**: who's going to wash
up? ¿quién va a lavar los platos?
2. *US* **lavarse**: go and wash up before dinner
ve a lavarte antes de comer.

washing machine ['wɒʃɪŋməˌʃiːn] *noun*
■ la **lavadora**.

washing-up *UK* ['wɒʃɪŋʌp] *noun* ■ to
do the washing-up lavar los platos

wasn't [wɒznt] = was not.

wasp [wɒsp] *noun* ■ la **avispa**.

waste [weɪst] *noun & verb)*
1. el **desperdicio**: what a waste! ¡qué desperdicio!
2. los **desechos, los residuos**: industrial waste
desechos industriales
➤ It's a waste of time es una pérdida de tiempo
■ *verb*
1. **derrochar**: he wastes money derrocha el
dinero
2. **perder**: he wastes a lot of time pierde mucho tiempo.

wastepaper basket *UK* [ˌweɪstˈpeɪpəˈ-
ˌbɑːskɪt], **wastebasket** *US* ['weɪstˌbɑːskɪt]
noun ■ la **papelera**.

watch [wɒtʃ] *(noun & verb)*
■ *noun*
el **reloj**: my watch has stopped se me paró el
reloj
■ *verb*
1. **ver**: they're watching television están viendo la televisión

2. **cuidar**: I'm watching their luggage for
them les estoy cuidando las maletas

watch out *phrasal verb* ■ **tener cuidado**:
watch out, there's a car coming! ¡ten
cuidado que viene un coche!

water ['wɔːtəʳ] *(noun & verb)*
■ *uncountable noun*
el **agua**

Feminine noun that takes **un** or **el** in the singular.

■ *verb*
regar: remember to water the plants no te
olvides de regar las plantas
➤ my eyes are watering me lloran los ojos
➤ my mouth's watering se me hace la boca
agua.

waterfall ['wɔːtəfɔːl] *noun* ■ la **catarata**.

watermelon ['wɔːtəˌmelən] *noun* ■ la
sandía.

waterproof ['wɔːtəpruːf] *adjective*
1. **impermeable**: a waterproof jacket una
chaqueta impermeable
2. **sumergible**: a waterproof watch un reloj
sumergible.

water-skiing ['wɔːtəˈskiːɪŋ] *uncountable
noun* ■ el **esquí acuático**: they go water-skiing often practican esquí acuático a menudo.

wave [weɪv] *(noun & verb)*
■ *noun*
la **ola**: the waves are big today hoy las olas
son grandes
➤ he gave me a wave me saludó con la mano
■ *verb*
1. **hacerle una señal con la mano**: he waved
to me when he saw me me hizo una señal
con la mano cuando me vio
2. **agitar**: the children are waving flags los
niños están agitando banderas
➤ to wave goodbye hacer adiós con la mano: I
waved goodbye to them les hice adiós con
la mano.

wax [wæks] *uncountable noun* ■ la **cera**.

waxworks [wækswɜːks] *noun* ■ el
museo de cera.

way [weɪ] *noun*
1. la **forma**: I like the way she dresses me gusta su forma vestir
2. el **camino**: the quickest way to the town centre el camino más rápido para llegar al centro; it's on my way me queda de camino; we stopped on the way paramos en el camino
3. la **manera**: I did it my way lo hice a mi manera
> in the same way de la misma manera
> in a way en cierto modo
> can you tell me the way to the museum? ¿podría decirme cómo llegar al museo?
> he got his own way se salió con la suya
> the way in la entrada
> the way out la salida
> to be in the way estar bloqueando el camino: you're in the way estás bloqueando el camino
> to get out of the way quitarse del medio: get out of the way! ¡quítate del medio!
> he's on his way está en camino
> it's a long way está lejos
> which way is it? ¿por dónde es?
> this way
1. **así**: do it this way hazlo así
2. **por aquí**: the hotel's this way el hotel está por aquí
> that way
1. **por allí**: he went that way se fue por allí
2. **así**: don't do it that way no lo hagas así
> is this the right way? ¿vamos por aquí?
> he went the wrong way se equivocó de camino
> no way! ¡ni hablar!

WC [ˌdʌblju:ˈsi:] *noun* ■ el **retrete**.

we [wi:] *pronoun* ■ **nosotros, nosotras**

"We" is not usually translated unless necessary for emphasis or clarification:

we live in Leeds vivimos en Leeds; we're going to the cinema vamos al cine

Spanish nouns are either masculine or feminine. Remember to use **nosotros** for masculine subjects and **nosotras** for feminine subjects. When "we" includes male and female, use **nosotros**:

we did it lo hicimos nosotros; we know it but they don't nosotros lo sabemos pero ellos no.

weak [wi:k] *adjective* ■ **débil**.

wealthy [ˈwelθɪ] *adjective* ■ **rico**
> the wealthy los ricos.

weapon [ˈwepən] *noun* ■ el **arma**.

Feminine noun that takes **un** or **el** in the singular.

wear [weəʳ] (*past tense* **wore**, *past participle* **worn**) *verb*
1. **llevar puesto**: Carol's wearing a dress Carol lleva puesto un vestido
2. **ponerse**: what are you going to wear? ¿qué te vas a poner?

wear out *phrasal verb*
1. **desgastar**: I've worn out my shoes he desgastado los zapatos
2. **desgastarse**: my shoes wear out quickly los zapatos se me desgastan rápido
3. **agotar**: that journey has worn me out ese viaje me agotó.

weather [ˈweðəʳ] *uncountable noun* ■ el **tiempo**: what's the weather like? ¿qué tiempo hace?; the weather is awful hace un tiempo horrible; the weather is fine hace buen tiempo
> the weather forecast el pronóstico del tiempo: what's the weather forecast? ¿cuál es el pronóstico del tiempo?

web [web] *noun*
> the Web la Web: I found his address on the Web encontré su dirección en la Web
> a web page OR a Web page una página web.

website [websaɪt] *noun* ■ el **sitio web**: have you visited the Larousse website? ¿has entrado en el sitio web de Larousse?

we'd [wi:d]
1. = we had
2. = we would.

wedding [ˈwedɪŋ] *noun* ■ la **boda**
> a wedding anniversary un aniversario de bodas
> a wedding cake una pastel de boda
> a wedding dress un vestido de novia
> a wedding ring un anillo de boda.

Wednesday [ˈwenzdɪ] *noun*

In Spanish the days of the week do not start with a capital letter:

el **miércoles** (plural los **miércoles**): it's Wednesday today hoy es miércoles; next Wednesday el miércoles que viene; last Wednesday el miércoles pasado

on Wednesday el miércoles: **I'll see you on Wednesday** te veo el miércoles

on Wednesdays los miércoles: **she has a Spanish class on Wednesdays** los miércoles tiene una clase de español.

weed [wiːd] noun ■ la **mala hierba**: **I'm going to dig up the weeds** voy a arrancar las malas hierbas.

week [wiːk] noun ■ la **semana**: **in a week's time** dentro de una semana; **this week** esta semana; **next week** la semana que viene; **last week** la semana pasada

a week on Saturday UK OR a week from Saturday US una semana a partir del sábado.

weekend [ˌwiːkˈɒnd] noun ■ el **fin de semana**: **what are you doing this weekend?** ¿qué vas a hacer este fin de semana?; **next weekend** el próximo fin de semana; **last weekend** el fin de semana pasado

at the weekend UK OR on the weekend US el fin de semana: **I'll see you at the weekend** te veo el fin de semana.

weep [wiːp] (past tense & past participle **wept**) verb ■ **llorar**: **she started weeping** se echó a llorar.

weigh [weɪ] verb ■ **pesar**: **she weighs 40 kilos** pesa 40 kilos; **can you weigh these apples?** ¿podría pesar estas manzanas?

weight [weɪt] noun ■ el **peso**

to put on weight engordar: **I've put on weight** he engordado

to lose weight adelgazar: **she lost weight** adelgazó.

weird [wɪəd] adjective ■ **raro**.

welcome ['welkəm] (noun, verb & adjective)
■ noun
la **bienvenida**: **they gave me a warm welcome** me dieron una calurosa bienvenida
■ verb
recibir a alguien: **they welcomed me with open arms** me recibieron con los brazos abiertos

■ adjective
bienvenido: **you're always welcome** siempre eres bienvenida

welcome! ¡bienvenido!: **welcome to England!** ¡bienvenido a Inglaterra!

thank you! — you're welcome! ¡gracias! —¡de nada!

we'll [wiːl]
1. = we shall
2. = we will.

well [wel] (adjective, adverb, noun & exclamation)
■ adjective (comparative **better**)
bien: **I'm very well, thank you** estoy muy bien, gracias; **all is well** todo está bien
■ adverb (superlative **best**)
bien: **the party went well** la fiesta fue bien; **she sings really well** canta realmente bien
well done! ¡muy bien!
as well también: **he came as well** él también vino
as well as además de: **they sell records as well as CDs** venden discos además de CDs
■ noun
el **pozo**: **an oil well** un pozo de petróleo
■ exclamation
1. **bueno**: **oh well, never mind!** ¡bueno, no importa!; **well, who was it then?** bueno ¿quién fue entonces?
2. **vaya**: **well, look who it is!** ¡vaya, mirad quién es!

well-behaved [ˌwelbɪˈheɪvd] adjective ■ **que se porta bien, educado**
the children were well-behaved los niños se portaron bien.

well-known [ˌwelˈnəʊn] adjective ■ **conocido**: **it's a well-known restaurant** es un restaurante conocido.

Welsh [welʃ] (adjective & noun)
■ adjective
galés: **a Welsh choir** un coro galés

Remember not to use a capital letter for the adjective or the language in Spanish.

■ noun
galés: **he speaks Welsh** habla galés

In Spanish, a capital letter is not used for the inhabitants of a country or region:

the Welsh los galeses.

went [went] *past tense* = go.

wept [wept] *past tense & past participle* = weep.

were [wɜːʳ] *past tense* = be.

we're [wɪəʳ] = we are.

weren't [wɜːnt] = were not.

west [west] *(noun, adjective & adverb)*
- *noun*
el **oeste**: the sun sets in the west el sol se pone por el oeste
- *adjective*
oeste *(plural* oeste*)*: San Francisco is on the west coast San Francisco está en la costa oeste
- *adverb*
hacia el **oeste**: go west vayan hacia el oeste
- west **of** al oeste de: Chicago is west of Detroit Chicago está al oeste de Detroit.

western ['westən] *(adjective & noun)*
- *adjective*
occidental: Western Europe Europa Occidental
- *noun*
la **película del oeste**: he prefers westerns to thrillers prefiere las películas del oeste a las películas de suspense.

wet [wet] *adjective*
1. **mojado**: my hair's wet tengo el pelo mojado
2. **lluvioso**: the weather is wet el tiempo está lluvioso
- to get wet mojarse: I got wet me mojé; I got my shirt wet me mojé la camisa.

we've [wiːv] = we have .

whale [weɪl] *noun* ■ la **ballena**.

what [wɒt] *(adjective, pronoun & exclamation)*
- *adjective*
qué: what colour is it? ¿de qué color es?; what time is it? ¿qué hora es?; what books do you want? ¿qué libros quieres?; what a pity! ¡qué lástima!; what lovely flowers! ¡qué flores tan bonitas!
- *pronoun*
1. *in questions*

You generally translate "what" as **qué**:

what's that? ¿qué es eso?; what's happening? ¿qué está pasando?; what's wrong?

¿qué pasa?; what are you doing? ¿qué estás haciendo?; what are they talking about? ¿de qué están hablando?; what are you thinking about? ¿en qué estás pensando?

Translate "what is" by **cuál es**:

what's your address? ¿cuál es tu dirección?; what is your phone number? ¿cuál es tu número de teléfono?

2. *in relative clauses*

Translate "what" as **lo que**:

I saw what happened vi lo que pasó; you can't always get what you want no siempre puedes tener lo que quieres; tell me what she said dime lo que dijo
- what about going out for a meal? ¿qué tal si salimos a comer?
- what about me? ¿y yo qué?
- what is it about? ¿de qué se trata?
- *exclamation*
what! ¡qué!; what? ¿qué?

whatever [wɒt'evəʳ] *(pronoun & adjective)*
- *pronoun*
1.

When "whatever" means "no matter what", it's often translated by a repetition of the verb in its subjunctive form:

whatever happens, don't tell Joe pase lo que pase, no le digas a Joe; whatever he says, don't go with him diga lo que diga, no vayas con él

2.

When "whatever" means "everything", it's usually translated with **(todo) lo que** followed by a verb in the subjunctive:

I'll do whatever I can haré todo lo que pueda
- *adjective*
cualquiera que

Cualquiera que should be followed by a verb in the subjunctive:

whatever decision you make, I'll support you cualquiera que sea la decisión que tomes, te apoyaré.

wheat [wiːt] *noun* ■ el **trigo**.

wheel [wiːl] *noun*

- la **rueda: bicycles have two wheels** las bicicletas tienen dos ruedas
- el **volante: who was behind the wheel?** ¿quién estaba al volante?

wheelbarrow [ˈwiːlˌbærəʊ] *noun* ■ la carretilla.

wheelchair [ˈwiːlˌtʃeəʳ] *noun* ■ la silla de ruedas.

when [wen] *(adverb & conjunction)*

■ *adverb*

cuándo: when are you going? ¿cuándo vas?; **tell me when you're coming** dime cuándo vienes

■ *conjunction*

cuando: he visited me when I lived in Paris me visitó cuando yo vivía en París; **he always gets annoyed when I sing** siempre se molesta cuando canto

Cuando is followed by a verb in the subjunctive when it refers to the future:

I'll tell her when she gets here se lo diré cuando llegue; **I'll buy you a car when you are 18** te compraré un coche cuando tengas 18.

whenever [wenˈevəʳ] *conjunction*

1. **cuando**

Cuando is followed by a verb in the subjunctive when it refers to an event that has not yet happened:

come whenever you like ven cuando quieras

2. **siempre que: whenever I see them we argue** discutimos siempre que nos vemos.

where [weəʳ] *(adverb & conjunction)*

■ *adverb*

dónde: where is the station? ¿dónde queda la estación?; **tell me where you hid it** dime dónde lo escondiste

- **where are you going?** ¿adónde vas?

■ *conjunction*

donde: this is the town where I grew up este es el pueblo donde crecí.

wherever [weərˈevəʳ] *conjunction* ■ **dondequiera que: he followed her wherever she went** la seguía dondequiera que ella iba

Dondequiera que is followed by a verb in the subjunctive when it refers to an event that has not yet happened:

he'll follow you wherever you go te va a seguir dondequiera que vayas

- **sit wherever you like** siéntate donde quieras.

whether [ˈweðəʳ] *conjunction* ■ **si: I don't know whether she's coming** no sé si va a venir.

which [wɪtʃ] *(adjective & pronoun)*

■ *adjective*

qué

In questions, qué is often used before nouns to translate "which":

which bike is yours? ¿qué bici es la tuya?; **which flowers do you like?** ¿qué flores te gustan?

- **which one?** ¿cuál?: **there are two bags, which one is yours?** hay dos bolsas, ¿cuál es la tuya?

■ *pronoun*

1. *in questions* **cuál, cuáles: out of the two dresses, which do you prefer?** de los dos vestidos, ¿cuál prefieres?; **which of the shoes are yours?** ¿cuál de los zapatos son tuyos?

2. *in relative clauses* **que: houses which are on the beach cost more** las casas que están en la playa cuestan más; **the book which you lent me was good** el libro que me prestaste era bueno

When "which" is used with a preposition it is translated by el que, la que, los que or las que depending on the gender (masculine or feminine) and the number (singular or plural) of the noun it refers to:

the chair on which he was sitting la silla en la que estaba sentado

3. **lo cual: the computers don't work, which is a serious problem** los ordenadores no funcionan, lo cual es un problema grave.

while [waɪl] *(conjunction & noun)*

■ *conjunction*

1. **mientras: I was reading while you were sleeping** yo estaba leyendo mientras tú dormías

2. mientras que: he likes to go out while his brother prefers to watch TV le gusta salir mientras que a su hermano le gusta ver la tele
■ *noun*
el **rato: let's stay here for a while** quedémonos aquí un rato
➤ **after a while** después de un rato: **after a while he got tired** después de un rato, se cansó
➤ **for a while** un rato: **he went to the party for a while, but then returned home** fue un rato a la fiesta, pero después volvió a la casa.

whisper ['wɪspə'] *verb* ■ **susurrar: she whispered something to me** me susurró algo.

whistle ['wɪsl] *(noun & verb)*
■ *noun*
el **silbato: the referee blew his whistle** el árbitro hizo sonar el silbato
■ *verb*
silbar: can you whistle? ¿sabes silbar?

white [waɪt] *adjective* ■ **blanco: a white shirt** una camisa blanca
➤ **white coffee** café con leche
➤ **a white lie** una mentira piadosa
➤ **the White House** la Casa Blanca

WHITE HOUSE

La Casa Blanca **(the White House)** es la residencia oficial y el lugar de trabajo del presidente de los Estados Unidos. Se encuentra en Washington D.C., que además de ser la capital del país es la sede del gobierno federal. La Casa Blanca es un símbolo tanto de la presidencia como del ramo ejecutivo del gobierno estadounidense.

who [hu:] *pronoun*
1. *in direct and indirect questions* **quién: who are you?** ¿quién eres?; **who are you talking about?** ¿de quién estás hablando?; **I don't know who she is** no sé quién es ella
2. *in relative clauses* **que: she's the woman who lives in that big house** es la mujer que vive en esa casa grande

After a preposition, **que** becomes **el que, la que, los que** or **las que** depending on the gender (masculine or feminine) and the number (singular or plural) of the noun it refers to:

the men who we were talking to disappeared los hombres con los que estábamos hablando desaparecieron.

who'd [hu:d]
1. = who had
2. = who would

whoever [hu:'evə'] *pronoun*
1. **quien**

When "whoever" means "anyone who", the verb that follows **quien** is in the subjunctive:

you can invite whoever you like puedes invitar a quien quieras
2. **quienquiera que**

When "whoever" means "the one who", the verb that follows **quienquiera que** is in the subjunctive:

whoever wins will get this cup quienquiera que gane obtendrá esta copa.

whole [həʊl] *(adjective & noun)*
■ *adjective*
entero: she ate the whole cake se comió el pastel entero
■ *noun*
➤ **the whole of** todo: **the whole of the summer** todo el verano; **the whole of London is talking about it** todo Londres está hablando de eso
➤ **on the whole** en general.

who'll [hu:l] = who will OR who shall.

whom [hu:m] *pronoun formal*
1. *in questions* **quién: with whom did she leave?** ¿con quién se fue?
2. *in relative clauses* **quien: the man whom she married** el hombre con quien se casó; **to whom it may concern** a quien corresponda.

who's [hu:z] *noun*
1. = who is
2. = who has.

whose [hu:z] *(adjective & pronoun)*
■ *adjective*
1. **de quién: whose car is this?** ¿de quién es ese coche?
2. **cuyo**

In Spanish the adjective agrees in gender (masculine or feminine) and number (singular or plural) with the noun to which it refers:

that's the boy whose father is an astronaut ése es el niño cuyo padre es astronauta; **the lady whose bags are in my car** la mujer cuyas bolsas están en mi coche

■ *pronoun*
de quién: whose is it? ¿de quién es esto?

who've [huːv] = who have.

why [waɪ] *adverb* ■ **por qué: why did you lie?** ¿por qué mentiste?; **why don't you come too?** ¿por qué no vienes tú también?; **I don't know why he said that** no sé por qué dijo eso; **do you want to go out? — OK, why not?** ¿quieres salir? –bueno, ¿por qué no?

wicked [ˈwɪkɪd] *adjective*
1. **malvado: he's a wicked man** es un hombre malvado
2. *informal* **genial: this song is wicked** esta canción es genial.

wide [waɪd] *(adjective & adverb)*
■ *adjective*
1. **ancho: a wide road** una calle ancha; **how wide is the river?** ¿cómo es de ancho el río?; **it's nine metres wide** tiene nueve metros de ancho
2. **gran: a wide variety** una gran variedad
■ *adverb*
▶ **open wide!** ¡abre bien la boca!
▶ **wide awake** completamente despierto: **she's wide awake** está completamente despierta
▶ **wide open** abierto de par en par: **the window's wide open** la ventana está abierta de par en par.

widow [ˈwɪdəʊ] *noun* ■ **la viuda.**

widower [ˈwɪdəʊəʳ] *noun* ■ **el viudo.**

width [wɪdθ] *noun* ■ **el ancho.**

wife [waɪf] *(plural wives [waɪvz]) noun* ■ **la esposa: Jane is my wife** Jane es mi esposa.

wig [wɪg] *noun* ■ **la peluca: he wears a wig** lleva peluca.

wild [waɪld] *adjective*
1. **salvaje: wild animals** animales salvajes
2. **silvestre: wild flowers** flores silvestres.

will [wɪl] *(verb & noun)*
■ *verb (negative* won't OR will not)
1. *the future tense* **I'll leave for Spain in the autumn** me iré a España en otoño; **when will you call?** ¿cuándo llamarás?; **will we arrive on time?** ¿llegaremos a tiempo?

In Spanish you can use the present tense of the verb **ir** + infinitive to talk about the future:

I'll do it now lo voy a hacer ahora; **it will change everything** va a cambiarlo todo

You can also use the present tense to talk about the near future:

will you help me? ¿me ayudas?; **I'll go with you** yo voy contigo

2. *in invitations and requests* **querer: will you have some more cake?** ¿quieres más pastel?; **will you close the window?** ¿quieres cerrar la ventana?
▶ **he won't help me** no quiere ayudarme
▶ **the car won't start** el coche no arranca
▶ **that'll be your father** ése debe ser tu padre
■ *noun*
1. **la voluntad: I did it against my will** lo hice contra mi voluntad
2. **el testamento: to make a will** hacer un testamento
▶ **she has a strong will** tiene una gran fuerza de voluntad.

willing [ˈwɪlɪŋ] *adjective*
▶ **to be willing to do something** estar dispuesto a hacer algo: **I'm willing to help you** estoy dispuesto a ayudarte.

win [wɪn] *(past tense & past participle* won, *present participle* winning*) verb* ■ **ganar: she won the race** ganó la carrera; **we won the competition** ganamos el concurso.

wind *(noun & verb)*
■ *noun* [wɪnd]
el viento: there's a strong wind hace un viento fuerte
▶ **a wind instrument** un instrumento de viento
■ *verb* [waɪnd] *(past tense & past participle* wound*)*
1. **enrollar: wind the rope around the pole** enrolla la cuerda alrededor del poste
2. **darle cuerda a: I forgot to wind the clock** me olvidé de darle cuerda al reloj

wind up *phrasal verb* ■ **terminar:** he wound up in jail terminó en la cárcel.

windmill ['wɪndmɪl] *noun* ■ el **molino de viento.**

window ['wɪndəʊ] *noun*
1. la **ventana:** open the window abre la ventana
2. la **ventanilla:** he's cleaning the car windows está limpiando las ventanillas del coche
3. el **escaparate:** she's looking in the shop window está mirando el escaparate.

windscreen *UK* ['wɪndskriːn], **windshield** *US* ['wɪndʃiːld] *noun* ■ el **parabrisas** (plural los **parabrisas**)
➤ windscreen wipers *UK* OR windshield wipers *US* los limpiaparabrisas.

windsurfing ['wɪnd,sɜːfɪŋ] *noun* ■ el **windsurf:** he goes windsurfing at weekends hace windsurf los fines de semana.

windy ['wɪndɪ] *adjective*
➤ it's windy hace viento
➤ it was a very windy day era un día de mucho viento.

wine [waɪn] *noun* ■ el **vino:** a glass of red wine una copa de vino tinto.

wineglass ['waɪnɡlɑːs] *noun* ■ la **copa para vino.**

wing [wɪŋ] *noun* ■ el **ala**

Feminine noun that takes **un** or **el** in the singular.

pelicans have large wings los pelícanos tienen las alas grandes.

wink [wɪŋk] *verb* ■ **guiñar el ojo:** he winked at me me guiñó el ojo.

winner ['wɪnər] *noun* ■ el **ganador,** la **ganadora.**

winter ['wɪntər] *noun* ■ el **invierno:** it's cold in winter en invierno hace frío
➤ winter sports deportes de invierno.

wintertime ['wɪntətaɪm] *uncountable noun* ■ el **invierno:** in the wintertime en invierno.

wipe [waɪp] *verb* ■ **limpiar:** he's wiping the table está limpiando la mesa

wipe up *phrasal verb* ■ **limpiar:** she wiped up the coffee from the floor limpió el café del suelo.

wire ['waɪər] *noun*
1. el **alambre:** a barbed wire fence una valla de alambre de espino
2. el **cable:** somebody cut the telephone wires alguien cortó los cables del teléfono.

wisdom ['wɪzdəm] *noun* ■ la **sabiduría**
➤ a wisdom tooth una muela del juicio.

wise [waɪz] *adjective* ■ **sabio:** he's a very wise man es un hombre muy sabio.

wish [wɪʃ] (noun & verb)

■ *noun*
➤ el **deseo:** his wish came true su deseo se hizo realidad
➤ best wishes on your birthday muchas felicidades por tu cumpleaños
➤ best wishes, Andrew un abrazo, Andrew
■ *verb*
➤ **desear:** you can stay here if you wish puedes quedarte aquí si lo deseas; he wished me a happy birthday me deseó un feliz cumpleaños
➤ I wish I had a yacht! ¡ojalá tuviera un yate!
➤ I wish you were here ¡ojalá estuvieras aquí!

The verb that follows **ojalá** must be in the subjunctive:

witch [wɪtʃ] (plural witches) *noun* ■ la **bruja.**

with [wɪð] *preposition*
1. **con:** I danced with Mary bailé con Mary; Tom came with us Tom vino con nosotros; with pleasure con mucho gusto; I cut it with a knife lo corté con un cuchillo
2. **de:** the man with the hat el hombre del sombrero; she was trembling with fear estaba temblando de miedo.

within [wɪ'ðɪn] *preposition*
1. **en menos de:** the doctor came within ten minutes el médico vino en menos de diez minutos
2. **dentro de:** the house is situated within a large property la casa está situada dentro de una gran propiedad

a menos de: **we're within 50 kilometres of Madrid** estamos a menos de 50 kilómetros de Madrid.

without [wɪð'aʊt] *preposition* ■ **sin: I won't go without you** no voy a ir sin ti; **he left without saying goodbye** se fue sin despedirse

to go without something OR **to do without something** arreglárselas sin algo: **we can't go without water** no podemos arreglárnoslas sin agua.

witness ['wɪtnɪs] *(plural* witnesses*) noun* ■ el/la **testigo.**

witty ['wɪtɪ] *adjective* ■ **ocurrente: he's very witty** es muy ocurrente.

wives *plural* ➤ **wife.**

wizard ['wɪzəd] *noun* ■ el **mago.**

woke [wəʊk] *past tense* ➤ **wake.**

woken ['wəʊkn] *past participle* ➤ **wake.**

wolf [wʊlf] *(plural* wolves ['wʊlvz]*) noun* ■ el **lobo.**

woman ['wʊmən] *(plural* women*) noun* ■ la **mujer**

a woman architect una arquitecta.

won [wʌn] *past tense & past participle* ➤ **win.**

wonder ['wʌndər] *(noun & verb)*

■ *noun*

la **maravilla: the seven wonders of the world** las siete maravillas del mundo

no wonder! ¡con razón!: **no wonder you're tired!** ¡con razón estás cansado!

■ *verb*

preguntarse: I wonder what he's doing me pregunto qué estará haciendo.

wonderful ['wʌndəfʊl] *adjective* ■ **maravilloso: it was a wonderful party** fue una fiesta maravillosa.

won't [wəʊnt] = will not.

wood [wʊd] *noun* ■ la **madera: the table is made of wood** la mesa es de madera.

wooden ['wʊdn] *adjective* ■ **de madera: a wooden table** una mesa de madera.

wool [wʊl] *noun* ■ la **lana: it's made of wool** es de lana.

word [wɜːd] *noun*

1. la **palabra: she didn't say a word** no dijo ni una palabra; **what does this word mean?** ¿qué significa esta palabra?

2. la **letra: do you know the words to this song?** ¿sabes la letra de esta canción?

➤ **to give somebody one's word** darle la palabra a alguien: **I gave you my word** te di mi palabra

➤ **to have a word with somebody** hablar con alguien: **I'm going to have a word with your teacher** voy a hablar con tu profesora

➤ **word processing** tratamiento de textos.

wore [wɔːr] *past tense* ➤ **wear.**

work [wɜːk] *(noun & verb)*

■ *noun*

1. el **trabajo: I have a lot of work to do** tengo mucho trabajo que hacer; **she's not here, she's at work** no está aquí, está en el trabajo

2. la **obra: the complete works of Shakespeare** las obras completas de Shakespeare

➤ **a work of art** una obra de arte

➤ **to be out of work** estar sin trabajo

■ *verb*

1. **trabajar: where do you work?** ¿dónde trabajas?

2. **funcionar: the TV isn't working** la tele no funciona

3. **hacer funcionar algo: I can't work this machine** no puedo hacer funcionar esta máquina

work out *phrasal verb*

1. **encontrar: I've worked out the answer** encontré la respuesta

2. **resolver: have you worked out the problem?** ¿has resuelto el problema?

3. **calcular: I'll work out the total** voy a calcular el total

4. **entender: I can't work it out** no logro entenderlo

5. **resultar: everything worked out well** todo resultó bien

6. **hacer ejercicios: he works out every morning** hace ejercicios todas las mañanas.

worker [ˈwɜːkə^r] *noun* ■ el **trabajador,** la **trabajadora**
> an office worker un oficinista
> a factory worker un obrero.

workshop [ˈwɜːkʃɒp] *noun* ■ el **taller:** a drama workshop un taller de teatro.

world [wɜːld] *noun* ■ el **mundo**
> the Second World War la Segunda Guerra Mundial
> the First World War la Primera Guerra Mundial
> the world champion el campeón del mundo
> the World Cup el Mundial
> the World Series la Serie Mundial

WORLD SERIES

La **World Series** o Serie Mundial es un conjunto de hasta siete partidos de béisbol en los que se enfrentan, al final de la temporada, los campeones de las dos ligas principales: la **National League** y la **American League**. Se proclama campeón el primero en obtener cuatro victorias. Éste es uno de los acontecimientos deportivos anuales de mayor importancia en los Estados Unidos; la tradición marca que sea el presidente de la nación quien lance la primera bola del encuentro.

worm [wɜːm] *noun* ■ el **gusano.**

worn [wɔːn] *(adjective & verb form)*
■ *adjective*
gastado: the carpet is worn la alfombra está gastada
> worn out gastado: my shoes are worn out mis zapatos están gastados
■ *past participle*
➤ wear.

worried [ˈwʌrɪd] *adjective* ■ **preocupado:** you look worried te ves preocupado
> to be worried about somebody OR something estar preocupado por alguien OR algo: I'm very worried about him estoy muy preocupado por él
> I'm worried sick estoy preocupadísimo.

worry [ˈwʌrɪ] *(noun & verb)*
■ *noun (plural worries)*
la **preocupación** *(plural* las **preocupaciones***)*: he has a lot of worries tiene muchas preocupaciones

■ *verb (past tense & past participle worried)*
1. **preocuparse:** he's worrying about the exams se preocupa por los exámenes; don't worry! ¡no te preocupes!
2. **preocupar:** the situation worries me me preocupa la situación.

worse [wɜːs] *(adjective & adverb)*
■ *adjective (comparative of bad)*
peor: it could have been worse podría haber sido peor
> to get worse empeorar: things are getting worse las cosas están empeorando
■ *adverb (comparative of badly)*
peor: he sings worse than I thought canta peor de lo que yo pensaba.

worst [wɜːst] *(adjective, adverb & noun)*
■ *adjective (superlative of bad)*
peor: it's the worst film I've ever seen es la peor película que he visto en mi vida
■ *adverb (superlative of badly)*
peor: he plays worst es el que juega peor
■ *noun*
> the worst el peor, la peor: of all the players I know, you're the worst de todos los jugadores que conozco, tú eres el peor
> at worst en el peor de los casos: at worst you'll be an hour late en el peor de los casos llegarás una hora tarde.

worth [wɜːθ] *(noun & adjective)*
■ *noun*
el **valor:** a jewel of great worth una joya de gran valor
> I have ten dollars' worth of change tengo diez dólares en monedas
■ *adjective*
> to be worth doing something valer la pena hacer algo: it's worth reading the book vale la pena leer el libro
> it's worth it vale la pena.

would [wʊd] *verb (negative* **wouldn't** OR **would not***)*

"Would" is usually translated by a verb in the conditional tense in Spanish:

if I won the lottery, I would buy a sports car si ganara la lotería, me compraría un coche deportivo; if I were you, I wouldn't do

it yo que tú, no lo haría; **we would have missed the train if we'd waited** habríamos perdido el tren, si hubiéramos esperado; **she said she would come** dijo que vendría
would you like another biscuit? ¿quieres otra galleta?

I'd like a cup of coffee quisiera una taza de café.

wouldn't ['wʊdnt] = would not.

would've ['wʊdəv] = would have.

wound [wuːnd] (noun, verb & verb form)
■ noun
la **herida: he has a wound on his leg** tiene una herida en la pierna
■ verb
herir: she wounded him in the arm lo hirió en el brazo
■ past tense & past participle [waund]
➤ wind.

wrap [ræp] (past tense & past participle wrapped, present participle wrapping) verb
1. **envolver: he's wrapping the presents** está envolviendo los regalos
2. **envolverse: she wrapped herself in a blanket** se envolvió en una manta.

wreck [rek] (noun & verb)
■ noun
los **restos** (de un naufragio, un accidente): **there was a wreck on the motorway** había restos de un vehículo accidentado en la autopista
■ verb
1. **destrozar: the tsunami wrecked the village** el tsunami destrozó el pueblo
2. **arruinar: the weather has wrecked all our plans** el tiempo arruinó todos nuestros planes.

wrestler ['reslər] noun ■ el **luchador,** la **luchadora.**

wrestling ['reslɪŋ] uncountable noun ■ la **lucha libre.**

wrinkle ['rɪŋkl] noun ■ la **arruga: he has a wrinkled forehead** tiene la frente arrugada; **he has a lot of wrinkles** tiene muchas arrugas.

wrist [rɪst] noun ■ la **muñeca: she broke her wrist** se rompió la muñeca.

write [raɪt] (past tense wrote, past participle written) verb ■ **escribir: she's writing a letter to her sister** está escribiendo una carta a su hermana.

write back phrasal verb ■ **contestar: I sent her a letter but she didn't write back** le envié una carta pero no me contestó

write down phrasal verb ■ **anotar: he wrote down everything I said** anotó todo lo que dije.

writer ['raɪtər] noun ■ el **escritor,** la **escritora.**

writing ['raɪtɪŋ] uncountable noun ■ la **letra: she has nice writing** tiene una letra bonita

writing paper papel de escribir.

written ['rɪtn] past participle ➤ write.

wrong [rɒŋ] (adjective & adverb)
■ adjective
1. **incorrecto: your calculations are wrong** tus cálculos son incorrectos; **that's the wrong answer** ésa es la respuesta incorrecta
2. **mal: it's wrong to lie** está mal mentir
   they went in the wrong direction se equivocaron de camino
   to be wrong estar equivocado: **you're wrong** estás equivocado
   you have the wrong number se ha equivocado de número
   what's wrong? ¿qué pasa?
   there's something wrong with my bike algo le pasa a mi bici
■ adverb
mal: she wrote my name wrong escribió mal mi nombre
to get something wrong equivocarse en algo: **you've got the date wrong** te equivocaste en la fecha
to go wrong
1. **equivocarse: I've gone wrong again** me he equivocado otra vez
2. **salir mal: my plans have gone wrong** mis planes salieron mal
3. **estropearse: the radio has gone wrong** la radio se ha estropeado.

wrote [rəʊt] past tense ➤ write.

Xmas ['eksməs, 'krɪsməs] *(abbreviation of Christmas) noun* ■ la **Navidad.**

X-ray ['eksreɪ] *noun* ■ la **radiografía: he needs to have an X-ray** necesita hacerse una radiografía.

xylophone ['zaɪləfəʊn] *noun* ■ el **xilófono.**

yacht [jɒt] *noun* ■ el **yate.**

yard [jɑːd] *noun*
1. el **patio: the children are playing in the yard** los niños están jugando en el patio
2. *US* el **jardín** *(plural* los **jardines***): **the house has a small yard** la casa tiene un pequeño jardín
3. la **yarda** *(91,44 cm.).*

yawn [jɔːn] *verb* ■ **bostezar: he's yawning** está bostezando.

year [jɪəʳ] *noun* ■ el **año: we waited a whole year** esperamos un año entero; **she's 21 years old** tiene 21 años
> **next year** el año que viene
> **last year** el año pasado
> **the New Year** el Año Nuevo.

yellow ['jeləʊ] *adjective* ■ **amarillo: she was wearing a yellow dress** llevaba un vestido amarillo.

yes [jes] *adverb* ■ **sí: would you like some cake? — yes, please** ¿quieres un poco de pastel? –sí, por favor.

yesterday ['jestədɪ] *adverb* ■ **ayer: I saw her yesterday** la vi ayer
> **yesterday morning** ayer por la mañana
> **yesterday evening** ayer por la tarde
> **the day before yesterday** anteayer: **he came home the day before yesterday** vino a casa anteayer.

yet [jet] *adverb*
1. **todavía: I haven't seen them yet** no los he visto todavía
2. **ya: have they finished yet?** ¿ya han terminado?
> **not yet** todavía no: **has she arrived? — no, not yet** ¿ha llegado? –no, todavía no.

yoga ['jəʊgə] *noun* ■ el **yoga: she practices yoga** hace yoga.

yoghurt , yogurt [*UK* 'jɒgət, *US* 'jəʊgərt] *noun* ■ el **yogur** *(plural* los **yogures***).*

yolk [jəʊk] *noun* ■ la **yema.**

you [juː] *pronoun*

"You" as the subject of the verb is not usually translated unless necessary for emphasis or clarification.

subject of a verb
1. *informal* **tú: are you coming with us?** ¿vienes con nosotros?; **you don't know it** no lo sabes; **you said it** tú lo dijiste; **you are ready but she is not** tú estás preparado pero ella no
2. *formal* **usted, ustedes: how are you?** ¿cómo está usted?; **this is for you** esto es para usted; **would you like some tea?** ¿quieren un poco de té?

3. *plural informal* **vosotros, vosotras: you don't know what happened** no sabéis lo que ocurrió; **I'm coming with you** vengo con vosotras
direct object of a verb

1. *informal* **te: hello Jane, I called you yesterday** hola Jane, te llamé ayer; **I saw you at the concert** te vi en el concierto

2. *formal* **le, lo, la: I haven't seen you** no le he visto; **do I know him?** ¿lo conozco?; **I can take you in my car** la puedo llevar en mi coche

3. *informal* **os: she'll tell you later** os lo dirá luego; **I saw you at the restaurant** os vi en el restaurante

4. *plural formal* **los, las: I remember you all** los recuerdo a todos; **I'm watching you** las estoy vigilando
direct object of a verb

1. *informal* **te: I told you yesterday** te lo dije ayer

2. *formal* **le: I gave you my address** le di mi dirección

Use **se** instead of **le** when **you** is used with a direct-object pronoun:

I gave it to you all se la di a todos ustedes

3. *plural informal* **os: I'll give it to you tomorrow** os lo daré mañana

4. *plural formal* **les: I have given them the news** les he dado la noticia

Use **se** instead of **les** when **you** is used with a direct-object pronoun:

I told you on Monday se lo dije el lunes
after preposition

1. *informal* **ti: thanks to you** gracias a ti

2. *formal* **usted, ustedes: this is for you** esto es para usted; **I'll come with you** voy con usted; **I've been thinking about you all** he estado pensando en todos ustedes

3. *plural informal* **vosotros, vosotras: does he work with you?** ¿trabaja con vosotros?; **we're going without you** nos vamos sin vosotras.

you'd [juːd]
1. = you had
2. = you would.

you'll [juːl] = you will.

young [jʌŋ] *adjective* ■ **joven** *(plural jóvenes)*

young people la gente joven.

younger [ˈjʌŋgəʳ] *(comparative of younger)* *adjective* ■ **he's ten years younger than me** tiene diez años menos que yo; **my younger brother** mi hermano menor.

youngest [ˈjʌŋgɪst] *(superlative of young)* *adjective* ■ **menor: he's the youngest child** es el hijo menor.

your [jɔːʳ] *possessive adjective*

The possessive adjective must agree in number (singular or plural) with the noun that follows. Use **tu** (or **tus**) or **vuestro** (**vuestra, vuestros, vuestras**) to translate "your" when you are talking to someone you know well, your family or friends and use **su** (or **sus**) when you are talking to someone you don't know:

1. **tu: she likes your brother** le gusta tu hermano; **can I listen to your CDs?** ¿puedo escuchar tus CDs?

Use the definite article (**el, la, los** or **las**), not the possessive adjective, with parts of the body and personal possessions:

have you washed your hands? ¿te has lavado las manos?

2. **su: your dog bit me** su perro me mordió; **leave your coats here** dejen aquí sus abrigos

Use the definite article (**el, la, los** or **las**), not the possessive adjective, with parts of the body and personal possessions:

close your eyes cierra los ojos

3. **vuestro: I like your car** me gusta vuestro coche; **can you give me your address?** ¿me podéis dar vuestra dirección?; **do they know your parents?** ¿conocen a vuestros padres?; **I know your sisters** conozco a vuestras hermanas

Use the definite article (**el, la, los** or **las**), not the possessive adjective, with parts of the body and personal possessions:

don't forget to brush your teeth no olvidéis cepillaros los dientes.

you're [jɔːʳ] = you are.

yours [jɔːz] *possessive pronoun*

The possessive pronoun must agree in gender (masculine or feminine) and number (singular or plural) with the noun it replaces. Use **tuyo** (or **tuya, tuyos** or **tuyas**) or **vuestro** (**vuestra, vuestros, vuestras**) to translate "yours" when you are talking to someone you know well, your family or friends, and use **su** (or **sus**), when you are talking to someone you don't know:

1. **tuyo**: that bracelet is yours esa pulsera es tuya; my bike has ten gears, yours has twelve mi bici tiene diez cambios y la tuya doce
2. **suyo**: my surname is English, yours is Spanish mi apellido es inglés, el suyo es español
3. **vuestro**: this is your car éste es vuestro coche; is this suitcase yours? ¿es vuestra esta maleta?; are these magazines yours? ¿son vuestras estas revistas?
> sincerely yours *UK*, sincerely yours *UK* atentamente.

yourself [jɔːˈself] *pronoun*
1.

In Spanish there are two ways to translate "yourself". When you are talking to somebody you don't know, you use **se** or **usted mismo**. This is known as the polite form. When you are talking to somebody you know well, your friends or your family, you can use the informal form **te** or **tú mismo** or **ti mismo**:

te: can you describe yourself in three words? ¿te puedes describir con tres palabras?
2. **tú mismo**: did you do it yourself? ¿lo hiciste tú mismo?
3. **ti mismo**: you were talking about yourself estabas hablando de ti mismo
4. **se**: don't cut yourself no se corte
5. **usted mismo**: did you make that yourself? ¿hizo eso usted mismo?
> keep it for yourself quédate con él
> by yourself solo: were you by yourself? ¿estabas solo?

yourselves [jɔːˈselvz] *pronoun*
1.

Use **os, vosotros mismos, se** or **ustedes mismos** when talking to more than one person:

os: did you enjoy yourselves? ¿os divertisteis?
2. **vosotros mismos**: do it yourselves! ¡hacedlo vosotros mismos!
3. **se**: did you hurt yourselves? ¿se han hecho daño?
4. **ustedes mismos**: do it yourselves háganlo ustedes mismos
> help yourselves! ¡serviros!
> by yourselves solos: were you by yourselves? ¿estabais solos?

you've [juːv] = you have.

zebra [*UK* ˈzebrə, *US* ˈziːbrə] *noun* ■ la **cebra**.

zero [ˈzɪərəʊ] *noun* ■ el **cero**: the temperature is below zero la temperatura está bajo cero; the Yankees won 16 to zero los Yankees ganaron 16 a cero.

zip code *US* [ˈzɪpkəʊd] *noun* ■ el **código postal**.

zip *UK* [zɪp], **zipper** *US* [ˈzɪpəʳ] *noun* ■ la **cremallera**.

zone [zəʊn] *noun* ■ la **zona**.

zoo [zuː] *noun* ■ el **zoológico**.

zucchini *US* [zuːˈkiːnɪ] *(plural* zucchini) *noun* ■ el **calabacín** *(plural* los **calabacines**).

zodiac [ˈzəʊdɪæk] *noun* ■ el **zodíaco**: there are 12 signs of the zodiac hay 12 signos del zodíaco.

Verbos irregulares ingleses

Infinitive	Past tense	Past participle	Infinitive	Past tense	Past participle
arise	arose	arisen	feel	felt	felt
awake	awoke	awoken	fight	fought	fought
be	was/	been	find	found	found
	were		flee	fled	fled
bear	bore	born(e)	fling	flung	flung
beat	beat	beaten	fly	flew	flown
become	became	become	forbid	forbade	forbidden
begin	began	begun	forget	forgot	forgotten
bend	bent	bent	forgive	forgave	forgiven
bet	bet/	bet/	freeze	froze	frozen
	betted	betted	get	got	got,
bid	bid	bid			US gotten
bide	bode/	bided	give	gave	given
	bided		go	went	gone
bind	bound	bound	grind	ground	ground
bite	bit	bitten	grow	grew	grown
bleed	bled	bled	hang	hung/	hung/
blow	blew	blown		hanged	hanged
break	broke	broken	have	had	had
breed	bred	bred	hear	heard	heard
bring	brought	brought	hide	hid	hidden/
broadcast	broadcast	broadcast			hid
build	built	built	hit	hit	hit
burn	burnt/	burnt/	hold	held	held
	burned	burned	hurt	hurt	hurt
burst	burst	burst	keep	kept	kept
buy	bought	bought	kneel	knelt,	knelt,
can	could	–		US kneeled	US kneeled
cast	cast	cast	know	knew	known
catch	caught	caught	lay	laid	laid
choose	chose	chosen	lead	led	led
cling	clung	clung	lean	leant/	leant/
come	came	come		leaned	leaned
cost	cost	cost	leap	leapt/	leapt/
creep	crept	crept		leaped	leaped
cut	cut	cut	learn	learnt/	learnt/
deal	dealt	dealt		learned	learned
dig	dug	dug	leave	left	left
dive	dived,	dived	lend	lent	lent
	US dove	dived	let	let	let
do	did	done	light	lighted/	lighted/
draw	drew	drawn		lit	lit
dream	dreamed/	dreamed/	lose	lost	lost
	dreamt	dreamt	make	made	made
drink	drank	drunk	may	might	–
drive	drove	driven	mean	meant	meant
eat	ate	eaten	meet	met	met
fall	fell	fallen	mistake	mistook	mistaken
feed	fed	fed	misunderstand	misunderstood	misunderstood

I

Verbos irregulares ingleses

Infinitive	Past tense	Past participle	Infinitive	Past tense	Past participle
mow	mowed	mowed/ mown	sow	sowed	sowed/ sown
outgrow	outgrew	outgrown	speak	spoke	spoken
overcome	overcame	overcome	speed	speeded/ sped	speeded/ sped
oversleep	overslept	overslept			
overtake	overtook	overtaken	spell	spelled/ spelt	spelled/ spelt
pay	paid	paid			
prove	proved	proved/ proven	spend	spent	spent
			spill	spilled/ spilt	spilled/ spilt
put	put	put			
quit	quit/ quitted	quit/ quitted	spin	spun/ span	spun
read	read	read	spit	spat	spat
rerun	reran	rerun	split	split	split
rewind	rewound	rewound	spoil	spoiled/ spoilt	spoiled/ spoilt
rid	rid/ ridded	rid/ ridded	spread	spread	spread
ride	rode	ridden	spring	sprang	sprung
ring	rang	rung	stand	stood	stood
rise	rose	risen	steal	stole	stolen
run	ran	run	stick	stuck	stuck
saw	sawed	sawed/ sawn	sting	stung	stung
			stink	stank/ stunk	stunk
say	said	said			
see	saw	seen	strike	struck	struck
seek	sought	sought	swear	swore	sworn
sell	sold	sold	sweep	swept	swept
send	sent	sent	swell	swelled	swollen
set	set	set	swim	swam	swum
sew	sewed	sewed/ sewn	swing	swung	swung
			take	took	taken
shake	shook	shaken	teach	taught	taught
shall	should	—	tear	tore	torn
shed	shed	shed	tell	told	told
shine	shone	shone	think	thought	thought
shoot	shot	shot	throw	threw	thrown
show	showed	shown/ showed	tread	trod	trodden/ trod
shrink	shrank	shrunk	understand	understood	understood
shut	shut	shut	upset	upset	upset
sing	sang	sung	wake	woke	woken
sink	sank	sunk	wear	wore	worn
sit	sat	sat	weave	wove	woven
sleep	slept	slept	weep	wept	wept
slide	slid	slid	win	won	won
sling	slung	slung	wind	wound	wound
smell	smelled/ smelt	smelled/ smelt	wring	wrung	wrung
			write	wrote	written

Ilustraciones temáticas en color

Themed colour plates

Índice

Index

La casa

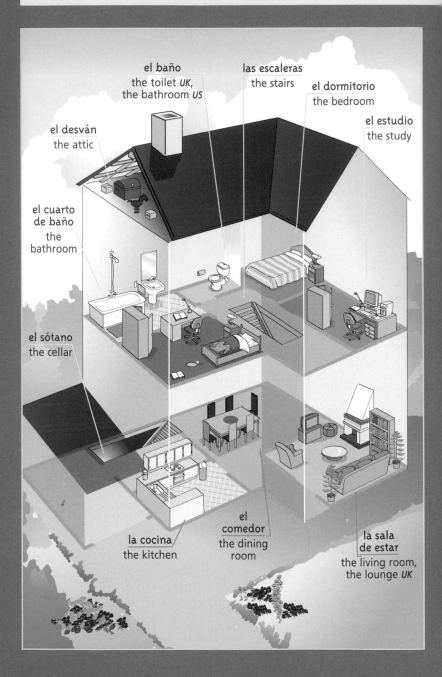

el baño
the toilet *UK*,
the bathroom *US*

las escaleras
the stairs

el dormitorio
the bedroom

el estudio
the study

el desván
the attic

el cuarto
de baño
the
bathroom

el sótano
the cellar

el comedor
the dining
room

la cocina
the kitchen

la sala
de estar
the living room,
the lounge *UK*

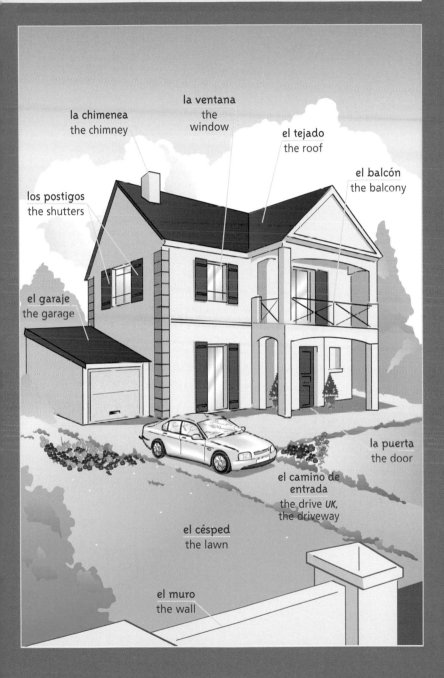

la chimenea
the chimney

la ventana
the window

el tejado
the roof

el balcón
the balcony

los postigos
the shutters

el garaje
the garage

la puerta
the door

el camino de entrada
the drive *UK*, the driveway

el césped
the lawn

el muro
the wall

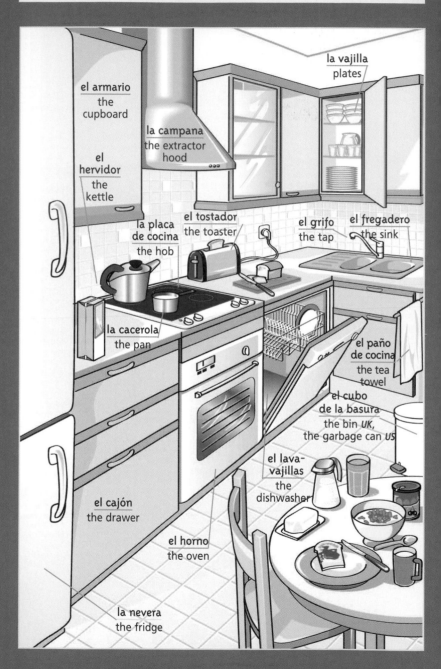

la vajilla
plates

el armario
the cupboard

la campana
the extractor hood

el hervidor
the kettle

la placa de cocina
the hob

el tostador
the toaster

el grifo
the tap

el fregadero
the sink

la cacerola
the pan

el paño de cocina
the tea towel

el cubo de la basura
the bin *UK*,
the garbage can *US*

el lava-vajillas
the dishwasher

el cajón
the drawer

el horno
the oven

la nevera
the fridge

el cuadro
the painting

las cortinas
the curtains

la televisión
the television

el sofá
the sofa

la maceta
the flowerpot

la mesita baja
the coffee table

el aparador
the side-board

la mesa del comedor
the table

el tenedor
the fork

el cuchillo
the knife

la servilleta
the napkin

el banco
the bench

la silla
the chair

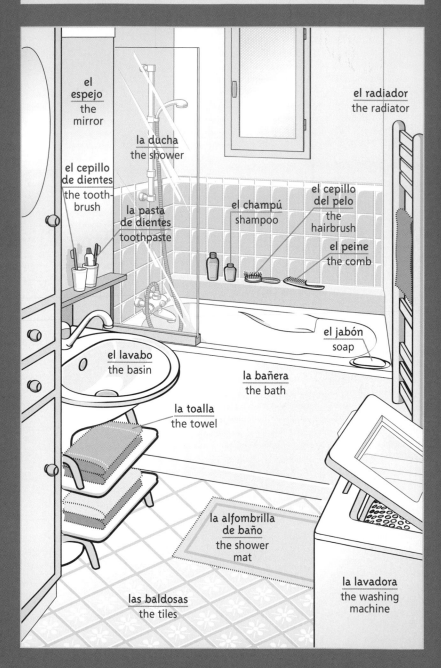

el espejo
the mirror

el radiador
the radiador

la ducha
the shower

el cepillo de dientes
the toothbrush

el cepillo del pelo
the hairbrush

la pasta de dientes
toothpaste

el champú
shampoo

el peine
the comb

el lavabo
the basin

el jabón
soap

la bañera
the bath

la toalla
the towel

la alfombrilla de baño
the shower mat

la lavadora
the washing machine

las baldosas
the tiles

el póster
the poster

las estanterías
the shelves

el armario
the wardrobe

el pez de colores
the goldfish

la lámpara
the lamp

la cama
the bed

la almohada
the pillow

el edredón
the duvet *UK*,
the comforter *US*

la cómoda
the chest
of drawers

el despertador
the alarm clock

la mesilla
de noche
the bedside
table

la alfombra
the rug

el escritorio
the desk

el walkman
the walkman

la silla
the chair

una batería
drums

un platillo
a cymbal

un xilófono
a xylophone

una pandereta
a tambourine

unas maracas
maracas

una trompeta
a trumpet

una flauta
a flute

un trombón
a trombone

un saxofón
a saxophone

un clarinete
a clarinet

una armónica
a harmonica

un piano
a piano

un contrabajo
a double
bass

una
guitarra
a guitar

un violín
a violin

bisabuela
great-grandmother

bisabuelo
great-grandfather

abuela
grandmother

abuelo
grandfather

madre
mother

padre
father

tía
aunt

tío
uncle

hija, hermana
daughter, sister

hijo, hermano
son, brother

prima
cousin

primo
cousin

María está contenta,
está sonriendo

María is happy,
she's smiling

Gemma está
enfadada, está gritando

Gemma is angry,
she's shouting

Pedro está triste,
está llorando

Pedro is sad,
he's crying

Óscar tiene miedo,
está temblando

Óscar is afraid,
he's trembling

Roberto está cansado, está
bostezando

Roberto is tired,
he's yawning

Isabel es tímida, se
está sonrojando

Isabel is shy,
she's blushing

Hugo está soprendido,
se ha sobresaltado

Hugo is surprised,
he jumped

Elena está enamorada,
está soñando despierta

Elena is in love,
she's daydreaming

*Miguel está enfadado,
frunce el ceño*
Miguel is annoyed,
he's frowning

*a Pablo le da igual, se
encoge de hombros*
Pablo doesn't care, he's
shrugging his shoulders

*Ana está ofendida,
está enfurruñada*
Ana is hurt,
she's sulking

*Benjamín no está de acuerdo,
niega con la cabeza*
Benjamín disagrees,
he's shaking his head

*Eva está de acuerdo,
asiente con la cabeza*
Eva agrees,
she's nodding

*Lucía se está
divirtiendo, se ríe*
Lucía is enjoying herself,
she's laughing

*Tomás se aburre,
suspira*
Tomás is bored,
he's sighing

*a Alicia no le gustan las
espinacas, pone mala cara*
Alicia doesn't like spinach,
she's pulling a face

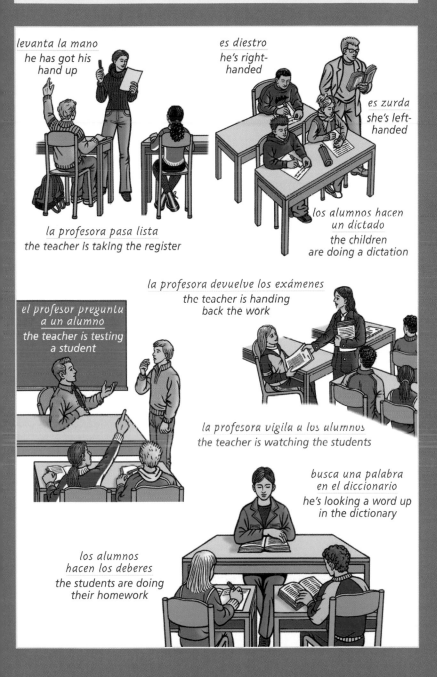

levanta la mano
he has got his hand up

la profesora pasa lista
the teacher is taking the register

es diestro
he's right-handed

es zurda
she's left-handed

los alumnos hacen un dictado
the children are doing a dictation

la profesora devuelve los exámenes
the teacher is handing back the work

el profesor pregunta a un alumno
the teacher is testing a student

la profesora vigila a los alumnos
the teacher is watching the students

busca una palabra en el diccionario
he's looking a word up in the dictionary

los alumnos hacen los deberes
the students are doing their homework

la entrada
the starter

el postre
dessert

el plato principal
the main course

la verdura
vegetables

la carne
meat

la bandeja
the tray

la jarra de agua
the water jug

un plato
a plate

el yogur
yoghurt

un pastel
a cake

el vaso
the glass

el queso
cheese

los cubiertos
the cutlery

el pan
bread

la ensalada
salad

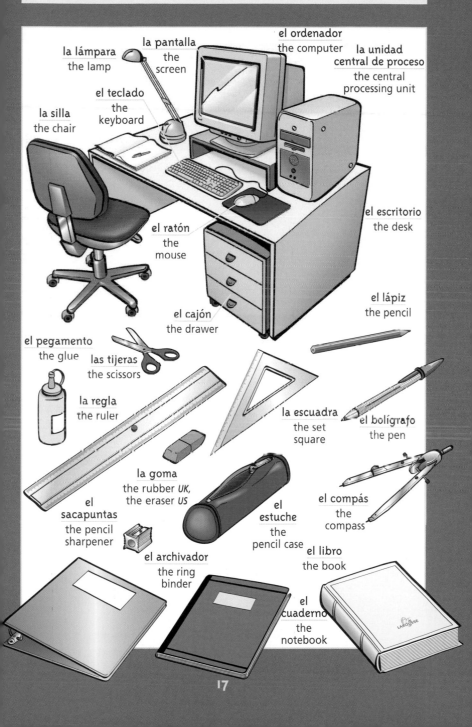

la pantalla
the screen

la lámpara
the lamp

el ordenador
the computer

la unidad central de proceso
the central processing unit

el teclado
the keyboard

la silla
the chair

el escritorio
the desk

el ratón
the mouse

el lápiz
the pencil

el cajón
the drawer

el pegamento
the glue

las tijeras
the scissors

la regla
the ruler

la escuadra
the set square

el bolígrafo
the pen

la goma
the rubber *UK*,
the eraser *US*

el sacapuntas
the pencil sharpener

el estuche
the pencil case

el compás
the compass

el archivador
the ring binder

el libro
the book

el cuaderno
the notebook

17

Los oficios

es bombero
he's a fireman,
he's a
firefighter US

es médica
she's a doctor

es química
she's a chemist

es profesor
he's a teacher

es periodista
she's a journalist

es piloto
he's a pilot

es mecánico
he's a mechanic

es cartero
he's
a postman,
he's
a mailman US

es policía
she's a policewoman

es abogada
she's a lawyer

es banquero
he's a banker

es arquitecta
she's an architect

es ingeniero
he's an engineer

es informático
he's a computer scientist

es pintora
she's a painter

es actriz
she's an actress

es fotógrafa
she's a photographer

es peluquera
she's a hairdresser

es vendedora
she's a sales assistant UK,
she's a sales clerk US

es estilista
he's a
designer

El cuerpo humano

la ceja
eyebrow

la frente
forehead

las pestañas
eyelashes

el ojo
eye

la mejilla
cheek

los dientes
teeth

la boca
mouth

la lengua
tongue

la oreja
ear

la nariz
nose

la barbilla
chin

la espalda
back

el brazo
arm

la cintura
waist

la cadera
hip

las nalgas
buttocks

la pierna
leg

el pie
foot

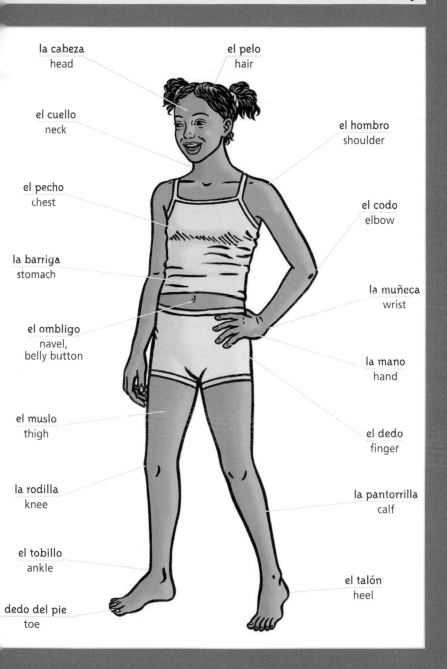

la cabeza
head

el pelo
hair

el cuello
neck

el hombro
shoulder

el pecho
chest

el codo
elbow

la barriga
stomach

la muñeca
wrist

el ombligo
navel,
belly button

el muslo
thigh

la mano
hand

el dedo
finger

la rodilla
knee

la pantorrilla
calf

el tobillo
ankle

el talón
heel

dedo del pie
toe

el hockey sobre hielo
ice hockey *UK*,
hockey *US*

el baloncesto
basketball

el rugby
rugby

el voleibol
volleyball

el fútbol
football *UK*,
soccer *US*

el béisbol
baseball

el fútbol
americano
American
football

la natación
swimming

el tenis
tennis

el esquí
skiing

la equitación
riding

el golf
golf

el judo
judo

la vela
sailing

el patinaje
skating

la esgrima
fencing

el windsurf
windsurfing

el piragüismo
canoeing

el atletismo
running

El movimiento — La posición

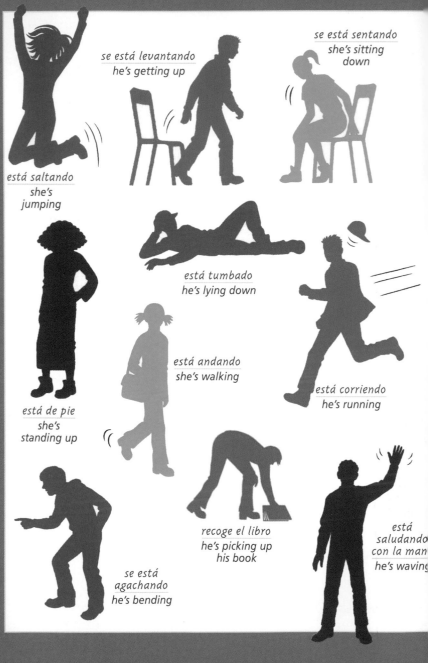

se está levantando
he's getting up

se está sentando
she's sitting down

está saltando
she's jumping

está tumbado
he's lying down

está de pie
she's standing up

está andando
she's walking

está corriendo
he's running

se está agachando
he's bending

recoge el libro
he's picking up his book

está saludando con la man
he's waving

se cae
he's falling

está en cuclillas
he's squatting
down

está sentada con las
piernas cruzadas
she's sitting
cross-legged

está sentado con lus
piernas cruzadas
he is sitting
with his legs
crossed

camina de
puntillas
she's walking
on tiptoes

baila
she's dancing

está con los
codos apoyados
en la mesa
he's resting his
elbows on
the table

está acurrucada
en un sillón
she's curled up
in an armchair

está apoyada
contra la pared
she's leaning
against the wall

está de
rodillas
she's kneeling

Lucía es pelirroja, tiene el pelo corto y pecas

Lucía is a redhead, she has short hair and freckles

Alicia tiene el pelo recogido y lleva pendientes

Alicia is wearing her hair up and has earrings on

Óscar tiene el pelo corto y una cicatriz en la barbilla

Óscar has short hair and a scar on his chin

Miguel lleva el pelo cortado a lo cepillo y tiene granos en las mejillas

Miguel has a crew cut and spots on his cheeks

Tomás tiene un remolino en el pelo y las cejas pobladas

Tomás' hair sticks up and he has thick eyebrows

Elena tiene el pelo largo y lleva una cinta

Elena has long hair and is wearing a headband

Pedro es castaño, de ojos azules

Pedro has brown hair and blue eyes

María es rubia, de ojos verdes

María is blonde with green eyes

Gemma es morena, media melena y lleva la raya al medio

Gemma has brown hair cut in a bob with a middle parting UK / part US

Pablo tiene el pelo rizado y un lunar en la mejilla

Pablo has curly hair and a mole on his cheek

Roberto tiene los ojos marrones y lleva una gorra roja

Roberto has brown eyes and is wearing a red cap

Eva tiene la nariz respingona y lleva una coleta

Eva has a turned-up nose and a ponytail

Isabel tiene el pelo rizado y lleva un collar

Isabel has curly hair and is wearing a necklace

Benjamín lleva gafas y la raya de lado

Benjamín is wearing glasses and has a side parting UK or part US

Hugo tiene el brazo roto

Hugo has a broken arm

Ana tiene flequillo y una trenza

Ana has a fringe and a plait / braid US

La ropa

un sujetador
a bra

unas bragas
panties

un camisón
a nightie

un albornoz
de felpa
a towelling robe

unas medias
tights *UK*,
pantyhose *US*

un vestido
floreado
a flowery
dress

un vestido
de lunares
a dress with
dots on

unas gafas
de sol
sunglasses

un bañador
a swimming
costume *UK*,
a bathing suit

unas sandalias
sandals

una minifalda
a mini skirt

un vestido
a dress

un gorro de lana
a woolly hat *UK*,
a wooly hat *US*

unos guantes
gloves

una chaqueta de lana
a wool jacket

una bufanda
a scarf

un abrigo
a coat

un suéter de cuello de pico
a V-neck sweater,
a V-neck jumper *UK*

un suéter de cuello vuelto
a polo neck *UK*,
a turtle neck
sweater *US*

una chaqueta
a cardigan

una blusa
a blouse

una falda acampanada
a flared skirt

una falda
a skirt

unas botas
boots

La ropa

unos calzoncillos
underpants

un pijama
pyjamas

unos
calcetines
socks

una bata
a dressing gown

unas
zapatillas
slippers

una camiseta
de manga corta
a short-sleeved
T-shirt

una camiseta
de manga larga
a long-sleeved T-shirt

una camiseta
a rayas
a striped T-shirt

un chándal
a tracksuit *UK*,
a sweatsuit *US*

un bañador
a swimming
costume

unas zapatillas
de deporte
trainers *UK*,
sneakers *US*

una chaqueta
a jacket

una cazadora de cuero
a leather jacket

un
impermeable
a raincoat

una camisa
a shirt

una camisa
a cuadros
a checked shirt

un suéter
a sweater,
a jumper UK

unos
pantalones de pinzas
pleated trousers UK /
pleated pants US

unos
pantalones de pana
corduroy trousers UK /
corduroy pants US

unos pantalones
de cintura baja
trousers UK / pants US
with a low waist

unos vaqueros
jeans

unos zapatos
shoes

un oso
a bear

un murciélago
a bat

un pájaro
a bird

una ardilla
a squirrel

una rana
a frog

un pez
a fish

una tortuga
a tortoise,
a turtle *US*

un lobo
a wolf

una serpiente
a snake

un pato
a duck

un ratón
a mouse

una oveja
a sheep

un gato
a cat

un perro
a dog

un conejo
a rabbit

una vaca
a cow

una gallina
a hen

un caballo
a horse

un cerdo
a pig

un loro
a parrot

un león
a lion

un mono
a monkey

un elefante
an elephant

un jirafa
a giraffe

una cebra
a zebra

un rinoceronte
a rhinoceros

un hipopótamo
a hippopotamus

un delfín
a dolphin

un pingüino
a penguin

una ballena
a whale

un tiburón
a shark

una
tuga marina
a turtle

una llama
a llama

un canguro
a kangaroo

un cocodrilo
a crocodile

La fruta

uvas
grapes

grosellas
redcurrants

arándanos
blueberries

arándanos rojos
cranberries

grosellas negras
blackcurrants

una frambuesa
a raspberry

una mora
a blackberry

cerezas
cherries

ciruelas
plums

una fresa
a strawberry

un albaricoque
an apricot

una pera
a pear

una manzana
an apple

un melocotón
a peach

un melón
a melon

una sandía
a watermelon

36

un higo
a fig

un maracuyá
a passion fruit

un limón
a lemon

un plátano
a banana

una lima
a lime

un kiwi
a kiwi

una naranja
an orange

una granada
a pomegranate

una piña
a pineapple

un aguacate
an avocado

una guayaba
a guava

un coco
a coconut

un mango
a mango

La verdura

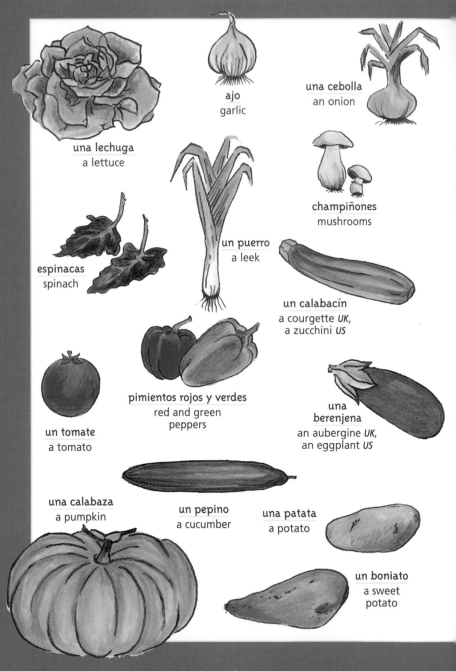

una lechuga
a lettuce

ajo
garlic

una cebolla
an onion

champiñones
mushrooms

espinacas
spinach

un puerro
a leek

un calabacín
a courgette *UK*,
a zucchini *US*

pimientos rojos y verdes
red and green
peppers

una
berenjena
an aubergine *UK*,
an eggplant *US*

un tomate
a tomato

una calabaza
a pumpkin

un pepino
a cucumber

una patata
a potato

un boniato
a sweet
potato

una
anahoria
a carrot

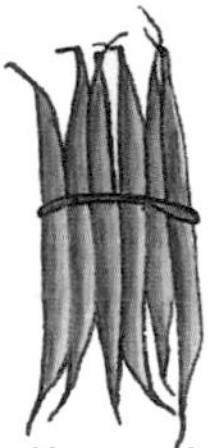

judías verdes
green beans,
string beans US

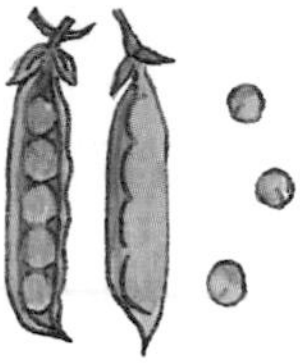

guisantes
peas

el apio
celery

alubias
kidney beans

un nabo
a turnip

remolacha
beetroot UK,
a beet US

brotes
de soja
beansprouts

rábanos
radishes

espárragos
asparagus

una
alcachofa
an artichoke

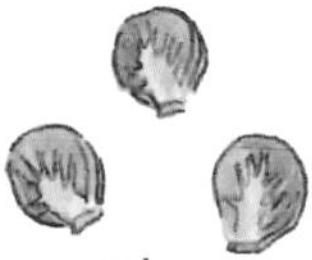

coles
de Bruselas
brussels sprouts

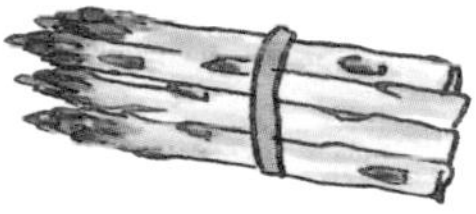

una coliflor
a cauliflower

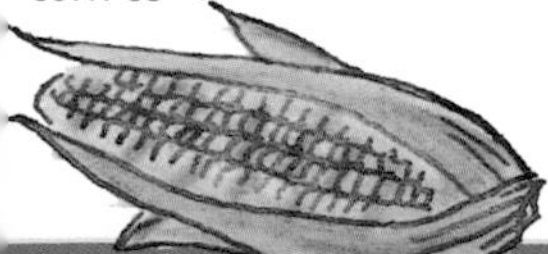

maíz
eetcorn UK,
corn US

el brócoli
broccoli

39

un roble
an oak tree

un abeto
a fir tree

un pino
a pine

un olivo
an olive tree

un arce
a maple

un plátano
a plane
tree

una palmera
a palm tree

un haya
a beech tree

un clavel
a carnation

muguete
lily of the valley

una rosa
a rose

una margarita
a daisy

violetas
violets

geranios
geraniums

un cardo
a thistle

una orquídea
an orchid

una amapola
a poppy

un tulipán
a tulip

una lila
lilac

un lirio
an iris

un girasol
a sunflower

El tiempo – Las estaciones   The weather – The seasons

el sol
the sun

las nubes
the clouds

la tormenta
the storm

los relámpagos
lightning

el granizo
hail

la primavera
spring

el verano
summer

el viento
wind

la nieve
snow

la lluvia
rain

la niebla
fog

el otoño
autumn / fall US

el invierno
winter

Las catástrofes naturales

una erupción volcánica
a volcanic eruption

un volcán
a volcano

un cráter
a crater

un río de lava
a lava flow

un maremoto
a tidal wave

una ola
a wave

la orilla
the shore

una inundación
a flood

los equipos de socorro
the rescuers

un deslizamiento de tierras
a landslide

la crecida del río
the flooding of a river

un ciclón
a cyclone

un torbellino
a whirlwind

un terremoto
an earthquake

la falla
the fault line

los daños materiales
material damage

una casa inundada
a flooded house

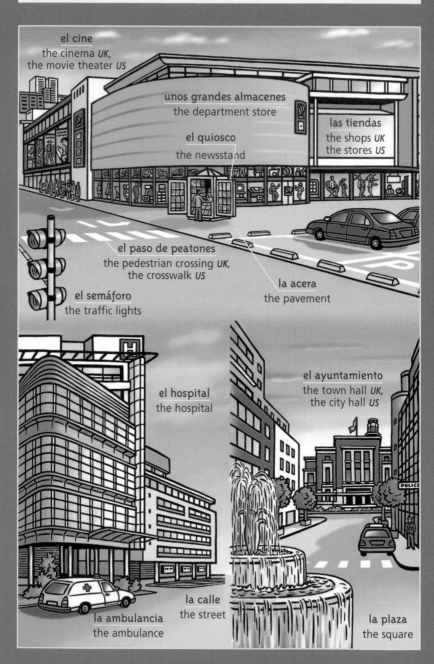

el cine
the cinema *UK*,
the movie theater *US*

unos grandes almacenes
the department store

las tiendas
the shops *UK*
the stores *US*

el quiosco
the newsstand

el paso de peatones
the pedestrian crossing *UK*,
the crosswalk *US*

la acera
the pavement

el semáforo
the traffic lights

el hospital
the hospital

el ayuntamiento
the town hall *UK*,
the city hall *US*

la calle the street

la ambulancia
the ambulance

la plaza
the square

se prueba una chaqueta
he's trying on a jacket

el probador
the fitting room

la escalera mecánica
the escalator

el perchero
the rack

la vendedora
the sales assistant *UK*,
the sales clerk *US*

el maniquí
the dummy

la cajera devuelve el cambio al cliente
the cashier is giving the customer her change

los billetes
banknotes

una percha
a clothes hanger

las monedas
coins

el expositor
the display shelf

la caja
the cash desk

un monedero
a purse *UK*,
a wallet *US*

una clienta
a customer

unas llaves
keys

un teléfono móvil
a mobile phone

una mochila
a rucksack

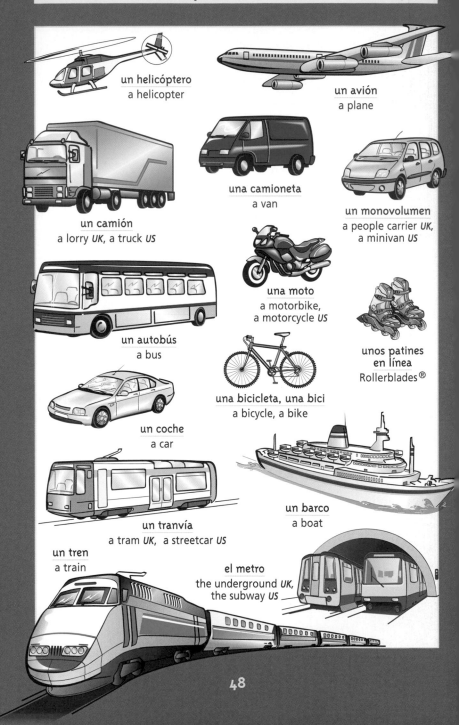

un helicóptero
a helicopter

un avión
a plane

una camioneta
a van

un camión
a lorry *UK*, a truck *US*

un monovolumen
a people carrier *UK*,
a minivan *US*

una moto
a motorbike,
a motorcycle *US*

un autobús
a bus

unos patines
en línea
Rollerblades®

una bicicleta, una bici
a bicycle, a bike

un coche
a car

un tranvía
a tram *UK*, a streetcar *US*

un barco
a boat

un tren
a train

el metro
the underground *UK*,
the subway *US*

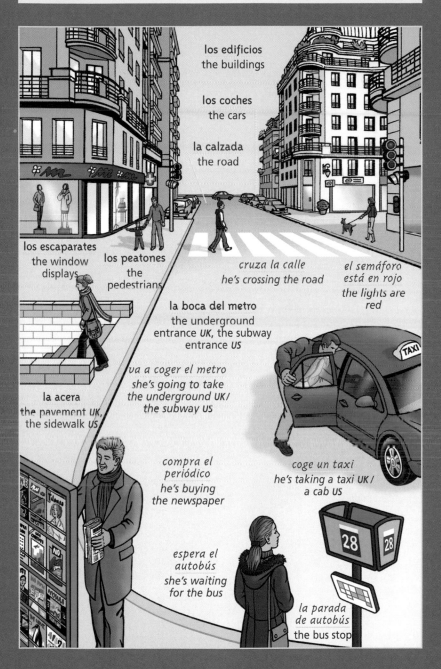

los edificios
the buildings

los coches
the cars

la calzada
the road

los escaparates
the window
displays

los peatones
the
pedestrians

cruza la calle
he's crossing the road

*el semáforo
está en rojo*
*the lights are
red*

la boca del metro
the underground
entrance *UK*, the subway
entrance *US*

va a coger el metro
*she's going to take
the underground UK/
the subway US*

la acera
the pavement *UK*,
the sidewalk *US*

*compra el
periódico*
*he's buying
the newspaper*

coge un taxi
*he's taking a taxi UK/
a cab US*

TAXI

*espera el
autobús*
*she's waiting
for the bus*

28 28

*la parada
de autobús*
the bus stop

*va **a casa de** su amiga*
she's going **to** her
friend's house

*el sombrero
está colgado
en el perchero*
the hat
is hanging **on**
the peg

*va **a** la playa*
he's going **to**
the beach

*está **en** la biblioteca*
she's **in** the library

*está **en** su casa*
he's **at** home

*Carlos camina **sobre** el césped, Emma
está sentada **debajo de** la sombrilla*
Carlos is walking **on** the grass, Emma is
sitting **under** a parasol

*el coche pasa **por encima del** puente,
el barco pasa **por debajo del** puente*
the car is going **over** the bridge,
the boat is going **under** the bridge

cuelga el cuadro
encima de la chimenea
he's hanging the picture
above the fireplace

el helicóptero
sobrevuela la ciudad
the helicopter is flying
over the town

el perro pasa **por
encima de** la valla
the dog is jumping
over the fence

lleva una chaqueta con un
suéter de cuello vuelto **por debajo**
she's wearing a jacket with
a polo neck UK /
turtleneck US **underneath**

el gato pasa **por
debajo de** la valla
the cat is going
under the fence

apoya la escalera
contra el muro
he's leaning
the ladder **against**
the wall

la cama está
contra la pared
the bed is **against**
the wall

Situar en el espacio

Pablo está **a la derecha de** María, y **a la izquierda de** Javier

Pablo is **on** María's **right**, but he is **on** Javier's **left**

Miguel está sentado **delante de** María, María está sentada **detrás de** Miguel

Miguel is sitting **in front of** María, María is sitting **behind** Miguel

Jaime está sentado **al lado de** Pedro

Jaime is sitting **next to** Pedro

Tomás está **en el medio**, **entre** Gabriel **y** Julia

Tomás is **in the middle**, he is **between** Gabriel **and** Julia

Pedro está **arriba de** las escaleras, Zoe está **abajo de** las escaleras

Pedro's **at the top of** the stairs, Zoe's **at the bottom of** the stairs

Tomás está sentado **enfrente de** Luisa

Tomás is sitting **opposite** Luisa

la llave está
en la cerradura
the key is
in the lock

pone el azúcar
en el armario
she's putting
the sugar
in the cupboard

un pedazo de tarta
con una cereza
encima
a slice of cake with
a cherry **on top**

de la ventana **a** la
cama hay un metro
it is one metre UK
or meter US **from** the
window **to** the bed

tiene que correr
hasta la línea de meta
he must run
to the finishing line

el perro corre **hacia** Tomás
the dog is running
towards Tomás

se cayó **al** suelo
he **fell down**

53

Los opuestos

la carretera es ancha,
el camino es estrecho

the road is wide,
the path is narrow

el coche es rápido,
el patinete es lento

the car is fast,
the scooter is slow

la bicicleta roja es grande,
la azul es pequeña

the red bike is big,
the blue one is small

el edificio es alto,
la casa es baja

the building is tall,
the house is small

el espejo está derecho,
el cuadro está torcido

the mirror is straight,
the painting is crooked

el paisaje es bonito,
el cuadro es feo

the scenery is beautiful,
the painting is ugly

la puerta está abierta,
la ventana está cerrada

the door is open, the
window is closed

el jarrón es transparente,
la ventana es opaca

the vase is transparent,
the window pane
is opaque

la camiseta está sucia, los pantalones cortos están limpios

the T-shirt is dirty, the shorts are clean

el pantalón verde es largo, el marrón es corto

the green trousers UK / pants US are long, the brown ones are short

Pablo es gordo, Pedro es delgado

Pablo is fat, Pedro is thin

el libro es grueso, la libreta es fina

the book is thick, the exercise book is thin

la goma es flexible, la regla es rígida

the rubber is flexible, the ruler is rigid

la pesa es pesada, la pluma es ligera

the weight is heavy, the feather is light

el helado está frío, la sopa está caliente

the ice cream is cold, the soup is hot

la botella está llena, el vaso está vacío

the bottle is full, the glass is empty

la punta de las tijeras es redondeada, la hoja del cuchillo es afilada

the ends of the scissors are rounded, the blade of the knife is sharp

el terrón de azúcar es duro, la mantequilla es blanda

the sugar lump is hard, the butter is soft

Las figuras geométricas | Geometric shapes

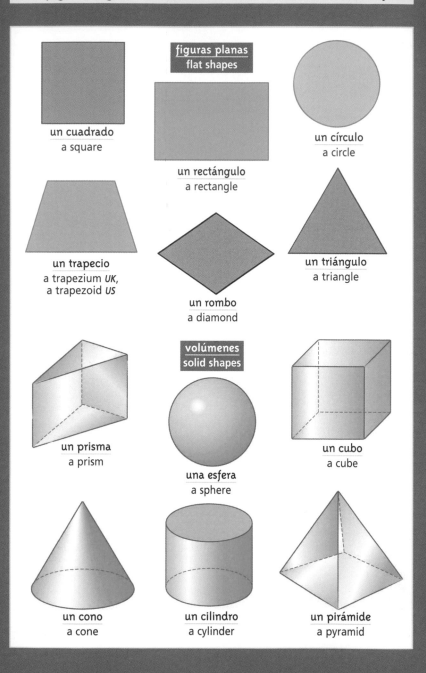

figuras planas
flat shapes

un cuadrado
a square

un rectángulo
a rectangle

un círculo
a circle

un trapecio
a trapezium *UK*,
a trapezoid *US*

un rombo
a diamond

un triángulo
a triangle

volúmenes
solid shapes

un prisma
a prism

una esfera
a sphere

un cubo
a cube

un cono
a cone

un cilindro
a cylinder

un pirámide
a pyramid

56

Los colores

Colours *UK*, Colors *US*

naranja
orange

azul
blue

marrón
brown

verde
green

rojo
red

amarillo
yellow

blanco
white

negro
black

verde claro
light
green

verde oscuro
dark
green

morado
purple

burdeos
burgundy

rosa
pink

azul
marino
navy blue

rosa fuerte
bright pink

gris
grey *UK*, gray *US*

azul celeste
sky blue

57

*son las
cuatro y diez*
it's ten past four
it's ten after four US

*son las
cuatro y cuarto*
it's (a) quarter past
four / it's a quarter
after four US

*son las
cuatro y media*
it's half past four

*son las cinco
menos cuarto*
it's (a) quarter to five
it's a quarter of five US

*son las cinco
menos diez*
it's ten to five
it's ten of five US

*son las cinco
(en punto)*
it's five o'clock

*son las doce del
mediodía*
it's midday

*son las doce
de la noche*
it's midnight

enero

1	sábado	Saturday
2	domingo	Sunday
3	lunes	Monday
4	martes	Tuesday ☾
5	miércoles	Wednesday
6	jueves	Thursday
7	viernes	Friday
8	sábado	Saturday
9	domingo	Sunday
10	lunes	Monday
11	martes	Tuesday ●
12	miércoles	Wednesday
13	jueves	Thursday
14	viernes	Friday
15	sábado	Saturday
16	domingo	Sunday
17	lunes	Monday
18	martes	Tuesday ☽
19	miércoles	Wednesday
20	jueves	Thursday
21	viernes	Friday
22	sábado	Saturday
23	domingo	Sunday
24	lunes	Monday
25	martes	Tuesday ○
26	miércoles	Wednesday
27	jueves	Thursday
28	viernes	Friday
29	sábado	Saturday
30	domingo	Sunday
31	lunes	Monday

enero January

febrero February

marzo March

abril April

mayo May

junio June

julio July

agosto August

septiembre September

octubre October

noviembre November

diciembre December

Ana nació el 6 de junio
Ana was born
on 6th June

las vacaciones de Semana
Santa comienzan el 23 de abril
the Easter holidays start on
23rd April UK ,
the Easter vacation starts
on 23rd April US

el examen de matemáticas
es dentro de una semana
the maths test is
in one week's time

hoy estamos a
16 de enero
it is 16th January
today

este año el 1 de
noviembre cae en martes
this year 1st November
is on a Tuesday

el cumpleaños
de Tomás es el
7 de febrero
Tomás' birthday
is on 7th February

El mundo hispanoparlante   The Spanish-speaking world

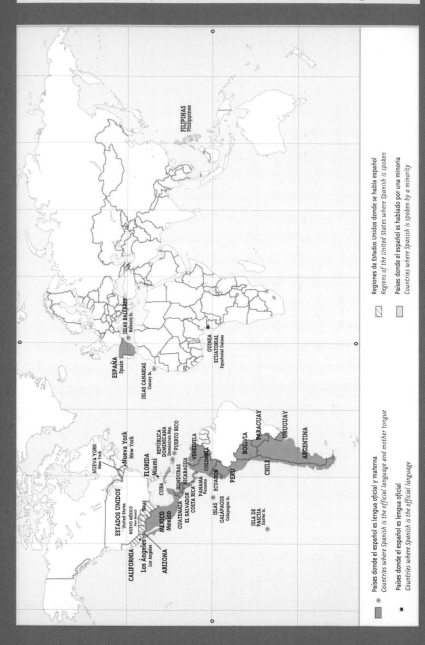

FILIPINAS
Philippines

ESPAÑA
Spain

ISLAS BALEARES
Balearic Is.

ISLAS CANARIAS
Canary Is.

GUINEA
ECUATORIAL
Equatorial Guinea

NUEVA YORK
New York

Nueva York
New York

REPÚBLICA
DOMINICANA
Dominican Rep.

PUERTO RICO

VENEZUELA

FLORIDA
Miami

CUBA

HONDURAS

NICARAGUA

COLOMBIA

PARAGUAY

BOLIVIA

URUGUAY

ARGENTINA

ESTADOS UNIDOS
United States

NUEVO MÉXICO

TEXAS

GUATEMALA

EL SALVADOR

COSTA RICA

PANAMÁ
Panama

ECUADOR

PERÚ

CHILE

CALIFORNIA

Los Ángeles
Los Angeles

ARIZONA

MÉXICO
Mexico

ISLAS
GALÁPAGOS
Galápagos Is.

ISLA DE
PASCUA
Easter Is.

Regiones de Estados Unidos donde se habla español
Regions of the United States where Spanish is spoken

Países donde el español es hablado por una minoría
Countries where Spanish is spoken by a minority

Países donde el español es lengua oficial y materna
Countries where Spanish is the official language and mother tongue

Países donde el español es lengua oficial
Countries where Spanish is the official language

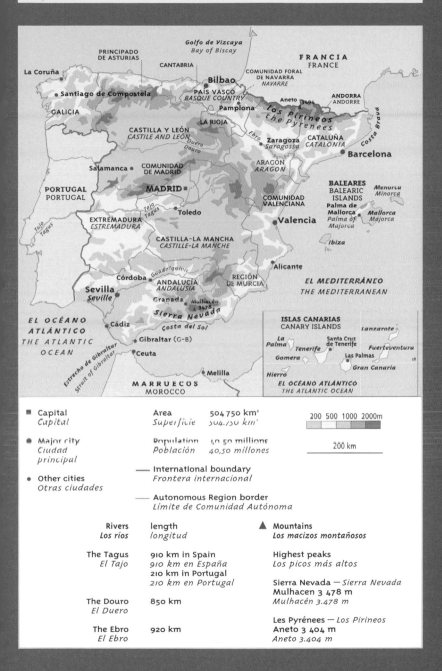

Capital / *Capital*

Major city / *Ciudad principal*

Other cities / *Otras ciudades*

Area / *Superficie*   504 750 km² / *504.750 km²*

Population / *Población*   40-50 millions / *40,50 millones*

200 500 1000 2000m

200 km

—— **International boundary** / *Frontera internacional*

—— **Autonomous Region border** / *Límite de Comunidad Autónoma*

Rivers / *Los ríos*   **length** / *longitud*

▲ **Mountains** / *Los macizos montañosos*

The Tagus / *El Tajo*   910 km in Spain / *910 km en España*   210 km in Portugal / *210 km en Portugal*

Highest peaks / *Los picos más altos*

Sierra Nevada — *Sierra Nevada*
Mulhacen 3 478 m / *Mulhacén 3.478 m*

The Douro / *El Duero*   850 km

Les Pyrénées — *Los Pirineos*
Aneto 3 404 m / *Aneto 3.404 m*

The Ebro / *El Ebro*   920 km

ORKNEY ISLANDS
Islas Orcadas

SHETLAND ISLANDS
Islas Shetland

WESTERN ISLES
Islas Hébridas

Scotland
Escocia

NORTH SEA
MAR DEL NORTE

Ben Nevis
4406 ft
1.344 m

ATLANTIC OCEAN
OCÉANO ATLÁNTICO

Edinburgh
Edimburgo

Glasgow

UNITED KINGDOM
REINO UNIDO

Northern
Ireland
Irlanda del Norte

Ulster

IRELAND
IRLANDA

Belfast

Isle of Man
Isla de Man

England
Inglaterra

Leeds

Irish Sea
Mar de Irlanda

Manchester

Liverpool

Sheffield

Shannon

DUBLIN
Dublín

Wales
País
de Gales

Birmingham

Limerick

Cambridge

Cork

Oxford

St. George's Channel
Canal de San Jorge

Cardiff

Bristol

Thames
Támesis

LONDON
Londres

CORNWALL
Cornualles

ISLE OF WIGHT
Isla de Wight

ENGLISH CHANNEL
CANAL DE LA MANCHA

ISLES OF SCILLY
Islas Scilly

■ Capital de estado
   State capital

100 km

200 500 m

● Ciudad principal
   Major city

Superficie 253 500 km²
Area

● Otras ciudades
   Other cities

Población 58 400 000
Population

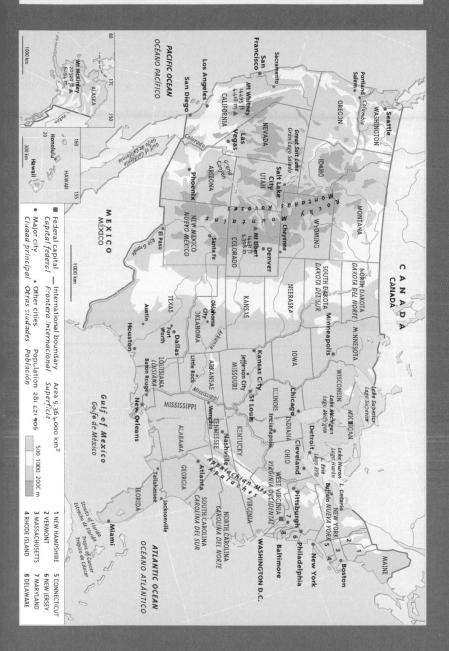

OCÉANO PACÍFICO
PACIFIC OCEAN

ALASKA
Mt McKinley
20320 ft
6194 m
Yukon

1000 km
60
170
150

Honolulu
HAWAII
Hawaii
160
155
20
300 km
Golfo de California
Gulf of California

Seattle
WASHINGTON
Portland
Salem
Columbia
OREGON
Colorado
San Francisco
Sacramento
CALIFORNIA
Los Angeles
San Diego
Mt Whitney
14495 ft
4418 m
NEVADA
Las Vegas
Great Salt Lake
Gran Lago Salado
Salt Lake City
UTAH
IDAHO
MONTANA
Montañas
WYOMING
Cheyenne
Gand Canyon
ARIZONA
Phoenix
El Paso
NEW MEXICO
NUEVO MÉXICO
Santa Fe
Rio Grande
Mt Elbert
14431 ft
4398 m
Rocosas
Rocky
Mountains
COLORADO
Denver

MÉXICO
MEXICO

CANADA
CANADÁ

NORTH DAKOTA
DAKOTA DEL NORTE
SOUTH DAKOTA
DAKOTA DEL SUR
MINNESOTA
Minneapolis
NEBRASKA
KANSAS
Kansas City
Oklahoma City
OKLAHOMA
TEXAS
Austin
Fort Worth
Dallas
Houston
Arkansas
LOUISIANA
LUISIANA
Baton Rouge
New Orleans
MISSISSIPPI
Little Rock
ARKANSAS
MISSOURI
St Louis
Jefferson City
IOWA
WISCONSIN
Lago Superior
Lake Superior
Lago Michigan
Lake Michigan
Lago Huron
Lake Huron
MICHIGAN
ILLINOIS
Chicago
INDIANA
Indianapolis
Memphis
TENNESSEE
Nashville
KENTUCKY
OHIO
Cleveland
Detroit
L. Erie
Lago Erie
Pittsburgh
WEST VIRGINIA
VIRGINIA OCCIDENTAL
VIRGINIA
WASHINGTON D.C.
Baltimore
L. Ontario
Lago Ontario
Buffalo
NEW YORK
NUEVA YORK
Philadelphia
New York
Boston
MAINE
Appalaches
Appalachian Mountains
ALABAMA
GEORGIA
Atlanta
NORTH CAROLINA
CAROLINA DEL NORTE
SOUTH CAROLINA
CAROLINA DEL SUR
Tallahassee
Jacksonville
FLORIDA
Miami
Straits of Florida
Estrecho de Florida
Trópico de Cáncer
Tropic of Cancer

Gulf of Mexico
Golfo de México

ATLANTIC OCEAN
OCÉANO ATLÁNTICO

Mississippi

■ Federal capital — International boundary
   Capital federal   Frontera internacional
● Major city   Area 9,364,000 km²
   Ciudad principal   Superficie
● Other cities   Population 281,421,906
   Otras ciudades   Población

500 1000 2000 m

1 NEW HAMPSHIRE   5 CONNECTICUT
2 VERMONT   6 NEW JERSEY
3 MASSACHUSETTS   7 MARYLAND
4 RHODE ISLAND   8 DELAWARE

a *preposición*

1. **to:** vamos a una fiesta we're going to a party; dáselo a tu hermano give it to your brother
2. **on:** a la derecha on the right
3. **in:** llegó a España he arrived in Spain
4. **at:** nos vamos a encontrar en el cine a las 4 de la tarde we're meeting at the cinema theater at 4 p.m.; a 100 kilómetros por hora at 100 kilometres per hour.

abajo *adverbio*

1. **below:** he visto al vecino del piso de abajo I've seen the neighbour from the flat below
2. **downstairs:** mamá está abajo Mom is downstairs
> **boca abajo** face down: se echó boca abajo she lay face down.

abandonar [1] *verbo*

1. **to abandon:** no podemos abandonar a los cachorros, tenemos que alimentarlos we can't abandon the puppies, we have to feed them
2. **to leave:** abandonó su ciudad she left her town
3. **to give up:** no puedo abandonar el trabajo ahora I can't give up my job now
> **¡no abandones!** don't give up!

el **abanico** ■ fan.

abarcar [8] *verbo* ■ **to cover:** el curso de historia abarca desde el siglo XVI hasta el presente the history course covers from the 16th century to the present.

abarrotado, da *adjetivo* ■ **packed:** el mercado estaba abarrotado de gente the market was packed with people.

el **abdomen** *(plural* los abdómenes*)* ■ abdomen.

abdominal *adjetivo* ■ **abdominal:** tiene dolor abdominal he's suffering from abdominal pain.

los **abdominales** ■ **sit-ups:** hice 50 abdominales I did 50 sit-ups.

el **abecedario** ■ alphabet.

la **abeja** ■ bee.

el **abeto** ■ fir tree.

la **abertura** ■ **crack:** por la abertura de la puerta se colaba el frío the crack in the door let in a cold draught.

abierto, ta *adjetivo* ■ **open:** la puerta está abierta the door is open.

el **abismo** ■ abyss.

ablandar [1] *verbo* ■ **to soften:** el agua ablandó la pasta the water softened the pasta

ablandarse *verbo pronominal* ■ **to soften:** la mantequilla se ablandó con el calor the butter softened in the heat.

el **abogado** , la **abogada** ■ **lawyer:** mi madre es abogada my mother is a lawyer.

abolir [57] *verbo* ■ **to abolish:** abolieron la pena de muerte they abolished the death penalty.

abonar [1] *verbo*

1. **to fertilize:** abonamos la tierra para que la planta crezca fuerte y sana we fertilized the soil so the plant would grow strong and healthy ·
2. **to pay:** debe abonar la cantidad en metálico you must pay the amount in cash.

abonarse *verbo pronominal*

1. to buy a season ticket: nos hemos abonado para toda la temporada we've bought a season ticket for the whole season
2. to subscribe: se ha abonado a un canal de cine he's subscribed to a cinema channel.

el **abono**

1. fertilizer: el abono natural no daña el medio ambiente natural fertilizer doesn't harm the environment
2. season ticket: tengo un abono para el torneo de baloncesto I have a season ticket for the basketball championship.

el **aborto** ■ abortion.

aborrecer [22] *verbo* ■ to hate: mi primo aborrece las espinacas my cousin hates spinach.

abotonarse [1] *verbo pronominal* ■ to button up: abotónate el abrigo, que te vas a enfriar button up your coat or you'll catch a cold.

abrasar [1] *verbo* ■ to burn: el sol ha abrasado las plantas th sun has burnt the plants

abrasarse *verbo pronominal* ■ to get burned: Marta se ha abrasado de estar demasiado tiempo al sol Marta has got burnt by staying in the sun too long.

abrazar [10] *verbo* ■ to hug: antes de subir al avión, abrazamos a la familia we hugged our relatives before getting on the plane

abrazarse *verbo pronominal*

1. to hug each other: los amigos se abrazaron afectuosamente the friends hugged each other affectionately.

el **abrazo** ■ hug: dale un abrazo a tu abuelo give your grandfather a hug.

el **abrebotellas** *(plural* los abrebotellas) ■ bottle opener.

el **abrelatas** *(plural* los abrelatas) ■ tin opener UK, can opener US.

abreviar [1] *verbo*

1. to abbreviate: ¿cómo se abrevia "señora"? how do you abbreviate "señora"?
2. to keep something short: no hay mucho espacio, intenta abreviar al máximo there's not a lot of space, try to keep it as short as possible.

la **abreviatura** ■ abbreviation: "Sr." es la abreviatura de "señor" "Sr." is the abbreviation of "señor".

abrigar [12] *verbo*

1. to wrap up: abriga bien al niño wrap the baby up warm
2. to be warm: esta cazadora abriga demasiado this jacket is too warm

abrigarse *verbo pronominal* ■ to wrap up: nos abrigamos con mantas de lana we wrapped ourselves up in wool blankets.

el **abrigo** ■ coat: ese abrigo rojo es muy bonito that red coat is very nice.

abril *sustantivo masculino* ■ April: en abril in April; el próximo abril next April; el pasado abril last April

En inglés los nombres de los meses se escriben con mayúscula.

abrir [3] *verbo*

1. to open: no puedo abrir esta caja I can't open this box
2. to turn on: abre el grifo del agua fría turn on the cold water tap.

abrocharse [1] *verbo pronominal* ■ to fasten: abróchense los cinturones de seguridad fasten your seat belts.

absoluto, ta *adjetivo* ■ absolute: un silencio absoluto absolute silence

en absoluto not at all: ¿te importa? — en absoluto do you mind? —not at all; no me molestas en absoluto you're not bothering me at all.

absorber [2] *verbo* ■ to absorb: la tierra seca absorbe rápidamente el agua de la lluvia dry earth quickly absorbs rainwater.

la **absorción** *(plural* las absorciones) ■ absorption: el algodón es una fibra con alto poder de absorción cotton is a very absorbent fibre.

abstenerse [52] *verbo pronominal* ■ **to abstain**: en la votación, 20 diputados se abstuvieron 20 MPs abstained from voting.

abstracto, ta *adjetivo* ■ **abstract**: no entiendo esa idea tan abstracta, dame un ejemplo concreto I don't understand such an abstract idea, give me a concrete example.

absurdo, da *adjetivo* ■ **absurd**: el relato del testigo es absurdo the witness' testimony is absurd.

la **abuela** ■ **grandmother**.

el **abuelo** ■ **grandfather**
mis abuelos my grandparents.

la **abundancia** ■ **abundance**: había comida en abundancia there was an abundance of food
vivir en la abundancia to be well-off.

abundante *adjetivo* ■ **plentiful**: la cosecha ha sido abundante este año the crop was plentiful this year.

abundar [1] *verbo* ■ **to abound**: en los pueblos de mar abundan las gaviotas seagulls abound in coastal towns.

aburrido, da *adjetivo* ■ **boring**: la película que vi ayer era muy aburrida the film I saw yesterday was very boring.

aburrirse [3] *verbo pronominal* ■ **to get bored**: nos aburrimos mucho en la fiesta we got really bored at the party.

abusar [1] *verbo*
1. **to abuse**: abusó de su posición he abused his position; muchos adultos abusan del alcohol many adults abuse alcohol
2. **to take advantage of**: no quiero abusar de su hospitalidad I don't want to take advantage of your hospitality.

el **abuso**
1. **abuse**: es muy difícil combatir el abuso de drogas it's very hard to combat drug abuse
2. **outrage**: ¡esto es un abuso! this is an outrage!

3. **imposition**: su acción es un abuso de nuestra generosidad what he did is an imposition on our generosity
el abuso del alcohol alcohol abuse
los precios de este restaurante son un abuso the prices in this restaurant are outrageous.

acabar [1] *verbo* ■ **to finish**: cuando acabe este capítulo llamaré a mi amiga I'll call my friend when I finish this chapter

acabarse *verbo pronominal* ■ **to run out**: se ha acabado el pan, iré a comprar más we've ran out of bread, I'll go and buy some more.

la **academia**
1. **academy**: la Real Academia Española se creó en 1713 the Royal Academy of the Spanish Language was founded in 1713
2. **school**: María va tres veces por semana a la academia de danza María goes to dance school three times a week

LA REAL ACADEMIA ESPAÑOLA

This official institution, based in Spain but with counterparts in other Spanish-speaking countries, attempts to set lexical and syntactical standards for Spanish-speakers both in Spain and in Latin America. It publishes periodicals, grammars and a dictionary, the **Diccionario de la Real Academia (DRAE)**.

la **acampada** ■ **camp**
ir de acampada to go camping: iremos de acampada a la montaña we'll go camping in the mountains.

acampar [1] *verbo* ■ **to camp**: acamparemos en un prado we'll camp in a field.

acariciar [1] *verbo* ■ **to stroke**: al niño le encanta acariciar al gato the boy loves stroking the cat.

acaso *adverbio*

After **acaso** in the sense of "maybe", the verb in Spanish has to be in the subjunctive:

maybe: acaso tenga frío maybe she's cold
por si acaso just in case: tráete el abrigo, por si acaso bring your coat, just in case.

acatarrarse [1] *verbo pronominal* ■ **to catch a cold.**

acceder [2] *verbo*

1. **to agree:** al final el profesor accedió a la petición de los alumnos in the end the teacher agreed to the students' request
2. **to obtain:** el estudio permite acceder a mejores puestos de trabajo education can allow you to obtain better jobs
3. **to gain access:** para acceder a las habitaciones hay que atravesar el patio to gain access to the rooms you have to cross a courtyard.

accesible *adjetivo*

1. **approachable:** la nueva profesora es muy accesible the new teacher is very approachable
2. **comprehensible:** la lección de matemáticas fue accesible gracias a la explicación del profesor the maths lesson was made comprehensible thanks to the teacher's explanation.

el **acceso**

1. **access:** esta entrada te da acceso a todas las exposiciones this ticket gives you access to all the exhibitions
2. **means of access:** éste es el acceso principal al edificio this is the main means of access to the building.

el **accidente** ■ **accident:** un conductor distraído provocó el accidente a careless driver caused the accident
> **sufrir un accidente** to have an accident.

la **acción** *(plural* las acciones)

1. **action:** estamos listos para entrar en acción, capitán we're ready to go into action, captain
2. **deed:** hizo una buena acción she performed a good deed
3. **share:** tenemos acciones en esta empresa we have shares in this company
> **ponerse en acción** to go into action.

acechar [1] *verbo* ■ **to lie in wait for:** el gato está siempre acechando al ratón the cat is always lying in wait for the mouse.

el **aceite** ■ **oil**
> **aceite de oliva** olive oil.

la **aceituna** ■ **olive**
> **aceituna negra** black olive
> **aceituna verde** green olive.

la **aceleración** *(plural* las aceleraciones) ■ **acceleration:** la aceleración se calcula con una fórmula acceleration is calculated by using a formula.

el **acelerador** *(plural* los aceleradores) ■ **accelerator:** vas muy rápido, no pises más el acelerador you're going too fast, stop pressing the accelerator.

acelerar [1] *verbo* ■ **to accelerate:** tendrás que acelerar si lo quieres adelantar you'll have to accelerate if you want to overtake him.

la **acelga** ■ **Swiss chard.**

el **acento**

1. **accent:** "café" lleva acento en la "e" "café" has an accent on the "e"; el acento andaluz es diferente al acento gallego the Andalusian accent is different from the Galician accent
2. **stress:** ¿cuál es la sílaba con acento en la palabra "silla"? what syllable does the stress fall on in the word "silla"?

acentuar [6] *verbo*

1. **to accentuate:** el vestido acentuaba su cintura the dress accentuated her waist
2. **to stress:** ¿cómo se acentúan las palabras en español? how do you stress words in Spanish?

acentuarse *verbo pronominal* ■ **to be stressed:** "café" se acentúa en la última sílaba "café" is stressed on the last syllable.

aceptar [1] *verbo* ■ **to accept:** Juan aceptó el trabajo que le ofrecieron Juan accepted the job they offered him.

la **acera** ■ **pavement** *UK,* **sidewalk** *US.*

acerca de *adverbio* ■ **about:** la historia es acerca de una familia de extraterrestres the story is about a family of aliens.

acercar [8] *verbo* ■ **to move closer:** acerca la silla a la mesa para estar más cómodo move your chair closer to the table, you'll be more comfortable

acercarse *verbo pronominal* ■ **to get closer:** me acerqué al fuego para entrar en calor I got closer to the fire to warm up.

el **acero** ■ steel
> acero inoxidable stainless steel.

acertar [14] *verbo*
1. **to get right:** acerté sólo cinco preguntas I only got five of the questions right
2. **to guess:** ¿a que no aciertas cuántas páginas tiene este libro? I bet you can't guess how many pages this book has.

ácido, da *adjetivo* ■ **acidic:** los limones son muy ácidos lemons are very acidic.

el **ácido** ■ acid.

el **acierto**
1. **right answer:** Álex tuvo 80 aciertos en el test Álex got 80 right answers in the test
2. **good idea:** ha sido un acierto coger el paraguas it was a good idea to take the umbrella.

aclarar [1] *verbo*
1. **to rinse:** aclara la ropa en el fregadero rinse the clothes in the sink
2. **to clarify:** tienes que aclarar tus ideas you have to clarify your ideas
> ¡no me aclaro! I can't work it out.

acoger [11] *verbo*
1. **to welcome:** me acogieron con los brazos abiertos they welcomed me with open arms
2. **to take in:** esta ONG acoge a los inmigrantes this NGO takes in inmigrants.

acomodarse [1] *verbo pronominal* ■ **to make yourself comfortable:** la abuela se acomodó en el sofá y se quedó dormida grandma made herself comfortable on the sofa and fell asleep.

acompañar [1] *verbo*
1. **to go with:** ¿queréis acompañarme al supermercado? do you want to go to the supermarket with me?
2. **to come with:** ¿puedo acompañarte? can I come with you?
3. **to accompany:** un pianista lo acompañó en su recital de flauta a pianist accompanied him during his flute recital.

aconsejar [1] *verbo* ■ **to advise:** me aconsejó que aprendiera inglés she advised me to learn English.

el **acontecimiento** ■ **event:** su llegada fue un gran acontecimiento her arrival was a great event.

acordar [16] *verbo* ■ **to agree:** los enemigos acordaron firmar el tratado de paz the enemies agreed to sign the peace treaty

acordarse *verbo pronominal* ■ **to remember:** siempre me acuerdo de vosotros cuando voy ahí I always remember you when I go there
> acordarse de algo to remember something: no me acuerdo del nombre de la calle I can't remember the name of the street
> acordarse de hacer algo to remember to do something: acuérdate de sacar la basura remember to take out the rubbish.

el **acordeón** *(plural* los acordeones*)* ■ accordion.

acorralar [1] *verbo* ■ **to corner:** acorralaron al conejo para meterlo en la jaula they cornered the rabbit to put it in the cage.

acostar [16] *verbo* ■ **to put to bed:** ya es hora de acostar a los niños it's time to put the children to bed

acostarse *verbo pronominal* ■ **to go to bed:** se acostaron tarde, por eso están tan cansados they went to bed late, that's why they're so tired
> acostarse con alguien to sleep with somebody.

acostumbrar [1] *verbo*
> acostumbrar a alguien a algo to get someone used to something: hay que acostumbrar al niño a que se duerma temprano you have to get the baby used to going to sleep early

acostumbrarse *verbo pronominal* ■ **to get used to:** al cabo de los años se acostumbraron al frío they got used to the cold after a few years.

el/la **acróbata** ■ acrobat.

la **actitud** ■ attitude.

la **actividad** ■ activity (plural **activities**)
➤ **actividades extraescolares** extracurricular activities.

activo, va adjetivo ■ **active**.

el **acto**
1. **action**: los adultos son responsables de sus actos adults are responsible for their actions
2. **ceremony**: fuimos al acto de inauguración del museo we went to the museum's opening ceremony
➤ **en el acto** immediately: acudió a mi llamada en el acto he answered my call immediately; se hacen reparaciones en el acto repairs done while you wait.

el **actor** ■ **actor**.

la **actriz** (plural las actrices) ■ **actress**.

actual adjetivo
1. **present**: la situación actual nos obliga a ahorrar the present situation forces us to save
2. **modern**: no les gusta mucho la música actual they don't like modern music

 The Spanish word **actual** is a false friend, it does not mean "actual".

la **actualidad** ■ **current affairs**: Manuel sigue la actualidad con mucho interés Manuel follows current affairs with a lot of interest
➤ **en la actualidad** currently: en la actualidad, mucha gente usa el ordenador currently, a lot of people use computers.

actualmente adverbio ■ **nowadays**: actualmente, mucha gente tiene un móvil nowadays a lot of people have mobile phones

 The Spanish word **actualmente** is a false friend, it does not mean "actually".

actuar [6] verbo ■ **to act**: actuaron rápidamente y evitaron un accidente they acted quickly and avoided an accident; actuó muy mal en las dos últimas películas en que trabajó he acted badly in the last two films he was in.

la **acuarela** ■ **watercolour** UK, **watercolor** US.

el **acuario**
1. **aquarium**: me regalaron un acuario para mi cumpleaños I was given an aquarium for my birthday; el domingo fuimos a visitar el acuario we went to the aquarium on Sunday.

acuático, ca adjetivo ■ **aquatic**: en este lago hay muchas plantas acuáticas there are many aquatic plants in the lake.

el **acuerdo** ■ **agreement**: los presidentes firmaron un acuerdo the presidents signed an agreement
➤ **estar de acuerdo** to agree: estoy de acuerdo contigo I agree with you.

acumular [1] verbo ■ **to accumulate**: las ardillas acumulan frutos secos para el invierno squirrels accumulate nuts for the winter

acumularse verbo pronominal ■ **to pile up**: se me acumula el trabajo my work's piling up.

el **acusado**, la **acusada** ■ **defendant**: la acusada se declaró culpable the defendant pleaded guilty.

acusar [1] verbo ■ **to accuse**: lo acusaron sin razón they accused him for no reason.

adaptar [1] verbo ■ **to adapt**: adaptaron la novela a la película they adapted the novel into a film

adaptarse verbo pronominal ■ **to adapt**: después de varios años, se adaptaron al frío they adapted to the cold after a few years.

adecuado, da adjetivo
1. **appropriate**: ese vestido no es adecuado para el funeral that dress isn't appropriate for the funeral
2. **right**: el momento adecuado the right moment.

adelantar [1] verbo
1. **to move forward**: adelantaron la boda un mes they moved the wedding forward a month
2. **to make progress**: hace dos horas que estás leyendo, ¿cuánto has adelantado? you've been reading for two hours, how much progress have you made?

3. to gain time: este reloj adelanta this clock is gaining time

4. to overtake: "prohibido adelantar" decía ese cartel that sign said "do not overtake"

adelantarse *verbo pronominal*

1. to go ahead: me adelanté para coger sitio I went ahead to get a place

2. to arrive early: este año el invierno se ha adelantado winter arrived early this year.

adelante *adverbio* ■ **forward:** veremos mejor si pasamos adelante we'll see better if we move forward

➤ **más adelante**

1. *en el tiempo* **later**

2. *en el espacio* **further on**

➤ **de ahora en adelante** from now on: de ahora en adelante no quiero más discusiones from now on I don't want any more arguments

➤ **¡adelante!**

1. *al animar* go ahead!

2. *al llamar* come in!

adelgazar [10] *verbo* ■ **to lose weight:** adelgazó 5 kilos en un mes she lost 5 kilos in a month.

además *adverbio*

1. as well as: además de traductora, es intérprete as well as being a translator, she's an interpreter

2. in addition: la casa es grande y además tiene un jardín precioso in addition to being big, the house has a beautiful garden

3. besides: además, llegaste tarde besides, you were late.

adentro *adverbio* ■ **inside:** pasad adentro, no os quedéis en la puerta come inside, don't stand in the doorway.

adherir [20] *verbo* ■ **to stick:** asegúrate de adherir bien las etiquetas make sure to stick the labels on well.

adhesivo, va *adjetivo* ■ **adhesive.**

la **adición** *(plural* las adiciones*)* ■ **addition.**

¡adiós! *interjección* ■ **goodbye:** dijo "adiós" al despedirse he said goodbye as he was leaving.

la **adivinanza** ■ **riddle**

➤ **jugar a las adivinanzas** to play at guessing riddles.

adivinar [1] *verbo* ■ **to guess:** ¡adivina lo que tengo para ti! guess what I have for you!

el **adjetivo** ■ **adjective.**

la **administración** *(plural* las administraciones*)* ■ **administration.**

el **administrador** , la **administradora** ■ **administrator**

➤ **administrador de Web** Webmaster.

administrativo, va *adjetivo* ■ **administrative:** se ocupa de las tareas administrativas he's in charge of the administrative work.

la **admiración** *(plural* las admiraciones*)* ■ **admiration:** se debatía entre la envidia y la admiración he was caught between envy and admiration; tiene gran admiración por su hermano mayor he has a great deal of admiration for his older brother

➤ **signo de admiración** exclamation mark.

admirar [1] *verbo* ■ **to admire:** es la mejor de la clase, todos la admiran everyone admires her, she's the best in the class.

admitir [3] *verbo*

1. to accept: nos acaban de admitir al club we've just been accepted into the club

2. to admit: al final admitió que le gustaba Pedro she finally admitted that she liked Pedro

3. to allow: mi madre no admite que le grite my mother doesn't allow me to shout at her.

la **adolescencia** ■ **adolescence.**

adolescente *adjetivo* ■ **adolescent**

el/la **adolescente** ■ **teenager.**

adonde *adverbio* ■ **where:** el pueblo adonde vamos es muy bonito the village where we go is very pretty

➤ **adonde fueres, haz lo que vieres** when in Rome, do as the Romans do.

adónde *adverbio* ■ **where:** ¿adónde vas? where are you going?

Adónde takes an accent in direct and indirect questions.

adoptar [1] *verbo* ■ **to adopt:** los padres de Juan han decidido adoptar un bebé Juan's parents have decided to adopt a baby.

adorar [1] *verbo*

1. **to worship:** los antiguos egipcios adoraban al dios Sol the ancient Egyptians worshiped the Sun god
2. **to adore:** Carlos y María adoran a sus padres Carlos and María adore their parents.

adornar [1] *verbo* ■ **to decorate:** hemos adornado la casa para la fiesta we have decorated the house for the party.

el **adorno** ■ **decoration:** las calles están llenas de adornos de Navidad the streets are full of Christmas decorations.

adquirir [59] *verbo*

1. **to acquire:** la escuela adquirió más ordenadores the school acquired more computers
2. **to gain:** adquirió mucha experiencia trabajando en esa oficina she gained a lot of experience working in that office.

la **adquisición** *(plural* las adquisiciones*)* ■ **acquisition:** es mi más reciente adquisición it's my most recent acquisition.

adrede *adverbio* ■ **on purpose:** no creo que lo haya hecho adrede I don't think she did it on purpose.

la **aduana** ■ **customs** *(plural)*: pasar por la aduana to go through customs.

adulto, ta *adjetivo* ■ **adult**

el **adulto** la **adulta** ■ **adult:** los adultos deben responsabilizarse de sus actos adults have to take responsibility for their actions.

el **adverbio** ■ **adverb**

Los adverbios en inglés terminan en general en "-ly", lo que facilita su reconocimiento.

el **adversario**, la **adversaria** ■ **opponent:** mi adversario trató de conseguir el primer puesto, pero no lo consiguió my opponent tried to take first place, but failed.

la **advertencia** ■ **warning:** advertencia: no entre en la obra sin casco protector warning: hard hats must be worn on the building site.

advertir [20] *verbo*

1. **to warn:** el profesor advirtió que no toleraría tramposos the teacher warned that he would not put up with cheats
2. **to be aware:** no advertí la presencia del ladrón I was not aware of the thief's presence.

aéreo, a *adjetivo* ■ **air**

El adjetivo inglés **air** siempre se usa antes del sustantivo:

te lo enviaré por correo aéreo I'll send it by air mail.

aerobic ■ **aerobics:** los martes va a su clase de aerobic she goes to aerobics class on Tuesdays.

el **aeroplano** ■ **aeroplane** *UK,* **airplane** *US.*

el **aeropuerto** ■ **airport.**

el **aerosol** ■ **aerosol.**

afectar [1] *verbo* ■ **to affect:** la violencia afecta a millones de personas violence affects millions of people.

el **afecto** ■ **affection:** el afecto es muy importante en la amistad affection is very important in friendship.

afeitarse [1] *verbo pronominal* ■ **to shave:** mi hermano se afeita todas las mañanas my brother shaves every morning.

la **afición** *(plural* las aficiones*)*

1. **hobby:** Pablo tiene afición por el deporte Pablo's hobby is sports
2. **fans:** la afición apoyó al equipo the fans supported the team

> por afición as a hobby.

el **aficionado**, la **aficionada**

1. **enthusiast:** es un aficionado al bricolage he's a DIY enthusiast
2. **amateur:** un cineasta aficionado an amateur film-maker.

afilar [1] *verbo* ■ **to sharpen:** hay que afilar el cuchillo antes de usarlo you should sharpen the knife before using it.

afinar [1] *verbo* ■ **to tune:** los músicos afinaron los instrumentos the musicians tuned their instruments.

la **afirmación** *(plural* las afirmaciones)
■ **statement.**

afirmar [1] *verbo* ■ **to state:** Carmen afirmó que le gusta aprender idiomas Carmen stated that she likes to learn foreign languages.

afirmativo, va *adjetivo* ■ **affirmative.**

aflojar [1] *verbo* ■ **to loosen:** no puedo aflojar este nudo I can't loosen this knot.

afortunado, da *adjetivo* ■ **lucky:** Ana es muy afortunada Ana is very lucky.

África ■ **Africa.**

africano, na *adjetivo*

En inglés, los adjetivos que se refieren a un país o una región se escriben con mayúscula:

African: el elefante africano es más grande que el elefante indio the African elephant is bigger than the Indian elephant

el **africano** , la **africana**

En inglés, los gentilicios se escriben con mayúscula:

African: los africanos the Africans.

afuera *adverbio* ■ **outside:** vamos afuera let's go outside

las **afueras** ■ **outskirts:** las fábricas están en las afueras de la ciudad the factories are on the outskirts of town.

agacharse [1] *verbo pronominal*
1. **to bend down:** agáchate y coge el libro bend down and pick up the book
2. **to crouch down:** me agaché para estar a la misma altura que los niños I crouched down to be on the same level as the children.

agarrar [1] *verbo*
1. **to catch:** en pocas horas la policía agarró al ladrón the police caught the thief in just a few hours
2. **to grab:** agarra al niño de la mano para cruzar la calle grab the child's by the hand when you cross the street

agarrarse *verbo pronominal* ■ **to hold on:** ¡agárrate bien! hold on tight!

la **agencia** ■ **agency** *(plural* agencies): he comprado mi billete en la agencia de viajes I bought my ticket at the travel agency.

el/la **agente** ■ **agent:** el agente secreto se lleva a la chica the secret agent took the girl away
➤ agente de policía *hombre* policeman, *mujer* policewoman
➤ agente de bolsa stockbroker
➤ agente de seguros insurance broker.

ágil *adjetivo* ■ **agile:** las gimnastas son ágiles y flexibles gymnasts are agile and flexible.

agitar [1] *verbo* ■ **to shake:** agita el envase antes de servir el zumo shake the carton before pouring the juice.

la **aglomeración** *(plural* las aglomeraciones) ■ **crowd:** se produjo una aglomeración a crowd formed.

agosto *sustantivo masculino*

En inglés, los meses del año se escriben con mayúscula:

August: en agosto in August; hoy es 28 de agosto today is 28th August.

agotar [1] *verbo* ■ **to use up:** hemos agotado las reservas de agua we've used up our water supplies

agotarse *verbo pronominal*
1. **to become exhausted:** mamá se ha agotado después de tanto esfuerzo Mum was exhausted after all that effort
2. **to sell out:** se han agotado todas las entradas all the tickets are sold out.

agradable *adjetivo* ■ **pleasant:** en primavera, la temperatura es más agradable que en invierno the temperature is more pleasant in the spring than in the winter.

agradecer [22] *verbo* ■ **to thank:** los novios nos agradecieron los regalos the newlyweds thanked us for the presents.

agrario, ria *adjetivo* ■ **agricultural:** la principal producción agraria de Valencia son los cítricos citrus fruit is Valencia's main agricultural product.

agredir [57] *verbo* ■ **to attack:** agredió al árbitro he attacked the referee.

agregar [12] *verbo* ■ **to add:** agrega la leche después de la harina add the milk after the flour.

la **agresividad** ■ aggression.

agresivo, va *adjetivo* ■ **aggressive:** es muy agresiva she's very aggressive.

el **agricultor** , la **agricultora** ■ **farmer:** el agricultor trabaja en el campo the farmer works in the fields.

la **agricultura** ■ agriculture
> agricultura ecológica organic farming.

agrio, a *adjetivo* ■ **sour:** la leche está agria the milk is sour.

el **agua** *sustantivo femenino*

Feminine noun that takes **un** or **el** in the singular.

water
> agua con gas sparkling water
> agua corriente running water
> agua dulce fresh water
> agua mineral mineral water
> agua potable drinking water
> agua salada salt water
> agua sin gas still water.

el **aguacate** ■ avocado.

el **aguacero** ■ downpour.

aguantar [1] *verbo*

1. **to stand:** no aguanto más el ruido de esa sirena I can't stand the noise of that siren any more

2. **to hold:** yo no puedo aguantar la respiración más de 30 segundos I can only hold my breath for 30 seconds

3. **to take:** la bolsa no ha aguantado el peso de las naranjas the bag couldn't take the weight of the oranges

4. **to last:** no creo que mis zapatos aguanten mucho más I don't think my shoes will last much longer.

agudo, da *adjetivo*

1. **high:** "si" es una nota mucho más aguda que "fa" "si" is a higher note than "fa"

2. **sharp:** sentí un dolor agudo en una muela I felt a sharp pain in my tooth

el **aguijón** *(plural* los aguijones*)* ■ sting.

el **águila** *sustantivo femenino*

Feminine noun that takes **un** or **el** in the singular.

eagle.

el **aguinaldo** ■ Christmas bonus

EL AGUINALDO

In Spanish-speaking countries, workers often receive a year-end bonus known as an **aguinaldo**. It is usually paid in December and is generally designated for holiday preparations and for buying presents for Christmas and the Feast of the Epiphany in January.

la **aguja** ■ **needle:** necesitas una aguja e hilo you need a needle and thread
> las agujas del reloj the hands of the clock.

las **agujetas** ■ tengo agujetas I'm all stiff.

el **agujero** ■ hole.

ahí *adverbio*

1. *cuando quiere decir 'en o a ese lugar'* **there:** ¿quién está ahí? who's there?; yo ahí no voy I'm not going there

2. *cuando quiere decir 'en ese momento'* **then:** ahí fue cuando me acordé that was when I remembered; de ahí en adelante from then on

3. *cuando quiere decir 'en eso'* **that:** ahí está el problema that's the problem
> ahí mismo right there
> por ahí

1. *en algún lugar* there somewhere: debe estar por ahí it has to be there somewhere

2. *en ese lugar* over there: busquemos por ahí let's look over there

3. *aproximadamente* or so: unas 100 personas o por ahí a hundred or so people.

la **ahijada** ■ goddaughter.

el **ahijado** ■ godson: sus ahijados her godchildren.

ahogarse [12] *verbo pronominal*
1. to drown: se ahogó en el mar he drowned in the sea
2. to suffocate: me ahogo con tanto humo I'm suffocating with all this smoke.

ahora *adverbio* ■ now: ahora no está lloviendo it's not raining now
➤ de ahora en adelante from now on: de ahora en adelante él es el jefe from now on he is the boss
➤ ahora mismo right now: ahora mismo no está she's not here right now
➤ hasta ahora so far: hasta ahora todo va bien so far, so good
➤ ¡hasta ahora! see you soon!
➤ por ahora for now.

ahorcar [8] *verbo* ■ to hang

ahorcarse *verbo pronominal* ■ to hang oneself: se ahorcó con un cinturón he hanged himself with his belt.

ahorrar [1] *verbo* ■ to save: ahorra tiempo y dinero it saves you time and money.

el **aire**
1. air: el aire que respiramos the air we breathe
2. wind: soplaba un aire frío a cold wind was blowing
➤ tomar el aire to get some fresh air
➤ aire acondicionado air conditioning
➤ al aire libre outdoors.

aislar [58] *verbo*
1. to isolate: tuvieron que aislar al enfermo they had to isolate the patient
2. to insulate: hay que aislar el techo we need to insulate the roof.

el **ajedrez**
1. chess: jugar al ajedrez to play chess
2. chess set: el ajedrez está guardado en el cajón the chess set is in the drawer.

ajeno, na *adjetivo* ■ las cosas ajenas other people's things; por razones ajenas a su voluntad for reasons beyond his control.

el **ajo** ■ garlic.

ajustado, da *adjetivo* ■ tight: estos pantalones me quedan muy ajustados these trousers are too tight on me.

ajustar [1] *verbo*
1. to adjust: ajustaron los frenos they adjusted the brakes
2. to tighten: hay que ajustar estos tornillos I have to tighten these screws
3. to fit: la tapa no ajusta bien the lid doesn't fit very well
4. to take in: la modista ajustó esta falda the seamstress took this skirt in

ajustarse *verbo pronominal* ■ to fasten: se ajustó el cinturón he fastened his belt.

al

Contraction of a and el.

➤ a; ➤ el.

el **ala** *sustantivo femenino*

Feminine noun that takes un or el in the singular.

1. wing: las alas del cóndor the wings of the condor; el ala izquierda del avión the plane's left wing
2. brim: un sombrero de ala ancha a wide-brimmed hat
➤ ala delta hang gliding: hacer ala delta to hang glide
➤ me gusta el ala delta I like hang gliding.

la **alambrada** ■ wire fence.

el **alambre** ■ wire
➤ alambre de espino barbed wire.

el **álamo** ■ poplar.

alargar [12] *verbo*
1. to lengthen: quiero alargar estos pantalones I want to lengthen these trousers
2. to extend: van a alargar las vacaciones they're going to extend their holidays

alargarse *verbo pronominal* ■ to get longer: en esta época los días se van alargando the days get longer at this time of year.

la **alarma** ■ alarm: empezó a sonar la alarma the alarm went off; **dieron la alarma** they sounded the alarm
➤ alarma antirrobo antitheft alarm
➤ alarma contra incendios fire alarm.

alarmar [1] *verbo* ■ to alarm: no queremos alarmar a nadie we don't want to alarm anyone

alarmarse *verbo pronominal* ■ to be alarmed: no hay por qué alarmarse there's no need to be alarmed.

el **alba** *sustantivo femenino*

Feminine noun that takes **un** or **el** in the singular.

dawn
➤ al alba at dawn.

el/la **albañil**
1. *que construye* **construction worker**
2. *que coloca ladrillos* **bricklayer.**

el **albaricoque** ■ apricot.

el **albergue** ■ hostel
➤ un albergue juvenil a youth hostel.

la **albóndiga** ■ meatball.

el **albornoz** *(plural* los albornoces*)* ■ bathrobe.

el **alboroto** ■ racket: los niños armaron un alboroto tremendo the kids made an enormous racket.

el **álbum** *(plural* los álbumes*)* ■ album.

la **alcachofa** ■ artichoke.

el **alcalde** , la **alcaldesa** ■ mayor.

el **alcance**
1. **reach**: no lo dejes al alcance de los niños don't leave it within the children's reach
2. **range**: un telescopio de largo alcance a long-range telescope.

la **alcantarilla**
1. *para la lluvia* **drain**
2. *cloaca* **sewer.**

alcanzar [10] *verbo*
1. **to reach**: queríamos alcanzar la cima we wanted to reach the top

2. **to catch up with**: si te das prisa, lo alcanzas if you hurry you can catch up with him
3. **to hand**: me alcanzó la sal he handed me the salt
4. **to be enough**: los vasos no alcanzan para todos there aren't enough glasses for everyone.

el **alcohol** ■ alcohol
➤ una bebida sin alcohol a non-alcoholic drink.

alcohólico, ca *adjetivo* ■ alcoholic
el **alcohólico** , la **alcohólica** ■ alcoholic.

la **aldea** ■ village.

el **aldeano** , la **aldeana** ■ villager.

alegrar [1] *verbo* ■ to cheer up: sus nietos siempre le alegran his grandchildren always cheer him up; me alegró mucho recibir tu carta your letter really cheered me up
➤ me alegra que hayas podido venir I'm so glad you could come

alegrarse *verbo pronominal*
1. **to cheer up**: anda, ¡alégrate! come on, cheer up!
2. **to be glad**: he sacado muy buenas notas —¡cuánto me alegro! I got very good grades – I'm so glad!
➤ alegrarse de algo to be happy about something: nos alegramos de que vengas we're so happy you're coming
➤ alegrarse por alguien to be happy for someone.

alegre *adjetivo*
1. **cheerful**: es una chica muy alegre she's a very cheerful girl; ¡qué alegre estás hoy! you're very cheerful today
2. **bright**: usa ropa de colores alegres he wears bright clothes.

la **alegría** ■ joy: los niños saltaban de alegría the children jumped for joy
➤ ¡qué alegría! how wonderful!
➤ sentí mucha alegría al verlo I was so happy to see him.

alejarse [1] *verbo pronominal* ■ to move away
➤ alejarse de algo to move away from something: alejaos de la orilla move away from the shore
➤ no te alejes demasiado don't go too far.

alemán, alemana *adjetivo*

En inglés, los adjetivos que se refieren a un país o una región se escriben con mayúscula:

German: tiene un apellido alemán he has a German surname

el **alemán** , la **alemana**

En inglés, los gentilicios se escriben con mayúscula:

German: los alemanes the Germans

el **alemán**

En inglés, los idiomas se escriben con mayúscula.

German.

Alemania ■ Germany.

la **alergia** ■ allergy *(plural* **allergies)**

➤ **tener alergia a algo** to be allergic to something: **tengo alergia al polen** I'm allergic to pollen.

alérgico, ca *adjetivo* ■ **allergic: soy alérgico a los gatos** I'm allergic to cats.

la **alerta** ■ alert

➤ **dar la alerta** to raise the alarm: **alguien dio la alerta** someone raised the alarm

➤ **estar alerta** to be alert

➤ **una alerta de bomba** a bomb scare.

la **aleta**
1. *de pez* **fin**
2. *de bucear* **flipper.**

el **alfabeto** ■ alphabet.

la **alfarería** ■ pottery.

el **alfarero** , la **alfarera** ■ potter.

el **alfiler** ■ pin.

la **alfombra**
1. *grande* **carpet: una alfombra de pared a pared** wall-to-wall carpeting
2. *más pequeña* **rug: una alfombra persa** a Persian rug.

el **alga** *sustantivo femenino*

Feminine noun that takes **un** or **el** in the singular.

seaweed: algunos peces se alimentan de algas some fish eat seaweed.

el **álgebra** *sustantivo femenino*

Feminine noun that takes **un** or **el** in the singular.

algebra.

algo *(pronombre & adverbio)*

■ *pronombre*

En oraciones afirmativas y en preguntas cuando se espera una respuesta afirmativa **algo** se suele traducir por **something**. En oraciones condicionales y en el resto de las oraciones interrogativas, por lo general se traduce por **anything**:

1. **something: he comprado algo para ti** I've bought something for you; **¿quieres tomar algo?** do you want something to drink?
2. **anything: ¿le dijiste algo a la profesora?** did you say anything to the teacher?; **si algo sale mal, es por su culpa** if anything goes wrong it's her fault

➤ **o algo así** or something like that: **su apellido es Laren o algo así** her last name is Laren or something like that

■ *adverbio*

1. **rather: es algo difícil de explicar** it's rather difficult to explain
2. **a little: hablo algo de inglés** I speak a little English.

el **algodón** *(plural* los algodones)
1. **cotton: unos calcetines de algodón** cotton socks
2. **cotton wool: se limpió la herida con un poco de algodón** she cleaned her wound with a cotton wool.

alguien *pronombre* ■

En oraciones afirmativas y en preguntas cuando se espera una respuesta afirmativa **alguien** se suele traducir por **somebody**. En oraciones condicionales y en el resto de las oraciones interrogativas se traduce por **anybody**:

1. **somebody: alguien preguntó por ti** somebody was asking for you; **¿puede alguien cerrar la puerta?** can somebody close the door?
2. **anybody: si alguien pregunta, dile que no lo sabes** if anybody asks tell them you don't know; **¿ha llamado alguien?** did anybody call?

algún *adjetivo*

Shortened form of **alguno** used before masculine singular nouns.

alguno, na *(adjetivo & pronombre)*

■ *adjetivo*

En oraciones afirmativas el adjetivo **alguno** se suele traducir por **some**. En preguntas y en oraciones condicionales, por lo general se traduce por **any**:

1. **some**: vinieron algunas amigas some friends came over
2. **any**: ¿practicas algún deporte? do you play any sports?; si tenéis alguna pregunta, hacedla al final de la clase if you have any questions please ask them at the end of class
➤ ¿has estado alguna vez en España? have you ever been to Spain?
➤ ¿alguna cosa más? anything else?
➤ en alguna parte somewhere

■ *pronombre*

1. *en singular* **one**: compra alguno barato buy a cheap one; alguna de ellas lo sabe one of them should know
2. *en plural* **some**: algunas tienen techo de madera some of them have wooden roofs.

la **alianza**

1. **alliance**: la alianza entre ambos partidos the alliance between both parties
2. **wedding ring**: llevaba una alianza en el dedo she wore a wedding ring on her finger.

aliarse [7] *verbo* ■ **to form an alliance**: se aliaron con los ingleses they formed an alliance with the English.

los **alicates** ■ **pliers.**

el **aliento** ■ **breath**: tiene mal aliento he has bad breath
➤ llegué arriba sin aliento I was out of breath when I got upstairs
➤ dar aliento a alguien to encourage somebody: lo que dijo nos dio aliento para seguir what he said encouraged us to keep going.

la **alimentación** *(plural las alimentaciones)*

1. **diet**: es importante una alimentación equilibrada a balanced diet is important

2. **feeding**: yo me hago cargo de la alimentación de mi perro I'm in charge of feeding my dog.

alimentar [1] *verbo*

1. **to feed**: tienen problemas para alimentar a su familia they are having problems feeding their family
2. **to be nutritious**: come cosas que no alimentan he eats things that aren't nutritious

alimentarse *verbo pronominal* ■ **to eat**: debes alimentarte bien you should try to eat well
➤ se alimentan de hierba they live on grass.

el **alimento** ■ **food**: alimentos ricos en proteínas foods high in protein.

aliñar [1] *verbo* ■ **to dress**: aliñó la ensalada con aceite y vinagre he dressed the salad with oil and vinegar.

el **aliño** ■ **dressing.**

aliviar [1] *verbo*
➤ esto te aliviará this will make you feel better
➤ la pastilla me alivió el dolor de cabeza the pill got rid of my headache.

el **alivio** ■ **relief**
➤ ¡qué alivio! what a relief!: ¡qué alivio sentí cuando lo encontré! what a relief when I found it!

allá *adverbio* ■ **over there**: los demás están allá the others are over there
➤ ya van para allá they're on their way over
➤ allá arriba up there
➤ allá fuera out there
➤ más allá further over: échate más allá, por favor move a little further over, please
➤ más allá de beyond
➤ allá tú it's your problem: allá tú si no quieres estudiar it's your problem if you don't want to study
➤ el más allá the beyond.

allí *adverbio* ■ **there**: estuvieron allí toda la mañana they were there all morning
➤ allí abajo down there

14

➤ **allí mismo** right there: **allí mismo encontrarás la biblioteca** they found the library right there.

el **alma** *sustantivo femenino*

Feminine noun that takes **un** or **el** in the singular.

soul: el cuerpo y el alma body and soul
➤ **te lo agradezco en el alma** I'm very grateful
➤ **siento en el alma no poder ir** I'm so sorry I can't go.

el **almacén** *(plural* los almacenes*)* ■ **warehouse**
➤ **grandes almacenes** department store.

almacenar [1] *verbo* ■ **to store.**

la **almeja** ■ **clam.**

la **almendra** ■ **almond.**

el **almíbar** ■ **syrup: melocotones en almíbar** peaches in syrup.

la **almohada** ■ **pillow.**

almorzar [26] *verbo*

1. *al mediodía* **to have lunch: almorzamos en el colegio** we had lunch at school; **hoy he almorzado un bistec con patatas** today I had steak and chips for lunch
2. *a media mañana* **to have as a mid morning snack: he almorzado fruta y pan** I had fruit and roll as a mid-morning snack.

el **almuerzo**

1. *al mediodía* **lunch**
2. *a media mañana* **mid-morning snack.**

el **alojamiento** ■ **accommodation** *UK,* **accommodations** *US:* **encontraron alojamiento en un albergue juvenil** they found accommodation at a youth hostel.

alojarse [1] *verbo pronominal* ■ **to stay: nos alojamos en un hotel de lujo** we stayed at a luxury hotel.

el **alpinismo** ■ **mountain climbing: hacer alpinismo** to go mountain climbing.

▮/la **alpinista** ■ **mountain climber.**

alquilar [1] *verbo* ■ **to rent: le alquila la habitación a un estudiante** she rents the room to a student; **alquilé una bicicleta** I rented a bicycle
➤ **se alquila** for rent.

el **alquiler** ■ **rent: ¿cuánto pagas de alquiler?** how much rent do you pay?
➤ **coche de alquiler** rental car
➤ **piso de alquiler** rented flat.

alrededor *adverbio* ■ **around: los niños se sentaron a su alrededor** the children sat around him
➤ **alrededor de** around: **corrimos alrededor de la piscina** we ran around the pool; **estudió inglés alrededor de tres años** she studied English for around three years.

los **alrededores** ■ **outskirts: vive en los alrededores de la ciudad** she lives on the outskirts of the city
➤ **hay muchas casas en los alrededores del aeropuerto** there are a lot of houses in the area around the airport.

el **alta** *sustantivo femenino*
➤ **dar de alta a alguien** to discharge somebody: **lo dieron de alta en el hospital** they discharged him from the hospital.

el **altar** ■ **altar.**

el **altavoz** *(plural* los altavoces*)* ■ **loudspeaker.**

alterar [1] *verbo*

1. **to change: tuvimos que alterar los planes** we had to change our plans
2. **to disturb: no debes alterar a la abuela** you shouldn't disturb your grandmother

alterarse *verbo pronominal* ■ **to upset: evita que tu padre se altere** try not to upset your father.

la **alternativa** ■ **alternative: no tiene más alternativa que aceptar la propuesta** he has no alternative but to accept the offer.

la **altitud** ■ **altitude.**

alto, ta *adjetivo*

1. **high: una de las montañas más altas del continente** one of the highest mountains on the continent

2. **tall:** es muy alto para su edad he's very tall for his age
- alta fidelidad high fidelity
- en alta mar on the high seas

alto *adverbio*

1. **high:** es un avión que vuela muy alto it's a plane that flies very high; ponen el volumen muy alto they turn the volume up too high
2. **loud:** no habléis tan alto don't talk so loud
- pasar por alto algo to overlook something

el **alto**

- tiene dos metros de alto it's two metres high
- hicieron un alto para descansar they made a rest stop
- el alto al fuego the ceasefire.

la **altura** ■ **height:** esos aviones pueden volar a mucha altura those planes can fly at great heights
- el Teide tiene cerca de 4.000 metros de altura the Teide is nearly 4,000 metres high
- a estas alturas at this point: a estas alturas no hay nada que podamos hacer at this point there's nothing we can do.

alucinar [1] *verbo* ■ **to be amazed:** alucino con tu dominio del japonés I'm amazed at your good command of Japanese.

el **alud** ■ **avalanche.**

alumbrar [1] *verbo* ■ **to light:** llévate una linterna para alumbrar el camino take a torch to light the way.

el **aluminio** ■ **aluminium** *UK,* **aluminum** *US.*

el **alumno** , la **alumna**

1. *de colegio* **pupil**
2. *de universidad* **student.**

el **alza** *sustantivo femenino*

Feminine noun that takes **un** or **el** in the singular.

increase: habrá un alza en el precio de las entradas there will be an increase in ticket prices

- en alza on the rise: el índice de criminalidad está en alza the crime rate is on the rise.

alzar [10] *verbo* ■ **to raise:** si queréis que os oiga, alzad la voz if you want me to hear you, raise your voices

- ¡no me alces la voz! don't raise your voice to me!

amable *adjetivo* ■ **kind:** la secretaria es muy amable the secretary is very kind

- ¿sería tan amable de abrir la ventana? would you be so kind as to open the window?

amamantar [1] *verbo*

1. *a un bebé* **to nurse**
2. *a un animal* **to suckle.**

el **amanecer** ■ **dawn**

- al amanecer at dawn.

amanecer [22] *verbo*

1. **to get light:** en esta época amanece más temprano it gets light early at this time of year
2. **to wake up:** amaneció enfermo he woke up ill
- hoy amaneció lloviendo it was raining when we got up.

el/la **amante**

1. **lover:** Romeo y Julieta eran amantes Romeo and Juliet were lovers
- los amantes de la música pop pop music lovers.

la **amapola** ■ **poppy** *(plural* **poppies).**

amar [1] *verbo* ■ **to love.**

amargado, da *adjetivo* ■ **bitter:** es una persona amargada she's a bitter person.

amargar [12] *verbo* ■ **to spoil:** eso nos amargó el paseo it spoiled our outing

- le amarga la vida a sus padres he makes his parents' life miserable

amargarse *verbo pronominal* ■ **to get upset:** no te amargues por lo que ha pasado don't get upset over what happened.

amargo, ga *adjetivo* ■ **bitter.**

amarillo, lla *adjetivo* ■ **yellow**

el **amarillo** ■ **yellow.**

la ambición *(plural* las ambiciones*)* ■ ambition: tiene la ambición de ser astronauta her ambition is to be an astronaut.

el ambientador ■ air freshener.

el ambiente

1. atmosphere: es un ambiente ideal para los niños it's an ideal atmosphere for children

2. spirit: aquí hay un ambiente de camaradería there's a real spirit of camaraderie here

➢ una fiesta con mucho ambiente a really happening party

➢ abrid las ventanas, el ambiente está muy cargado open the windows, it's very stuffy in here

➢ un cambio de ambiente le haría bien a change of scenery would do him good.

ambos, bas *adjetivo & pronombre* ■ both: los alumnos de ambos colegios the students from both schools; ambos pasaron de curso they both passed; los castigaron a ambos they were both punished.

la ambulancia ■ ambulance.

la amenaza ■ threat.

amenazar [10] *verbo* ■ to threaten: me amenazó con dejarme castigado she threatened to ground me.

ameno, na *adjetivo* ■ enjoyable: sus clases son muy amenas her classes are very enjoyable.

americano, na *adjetivo*

En inglés, los adjetivos que se refieren a un país o una región se escriben con mayúscula:

1. de América Latina **Latin American**
2. de América, de Estados Unidos **American**

el americano , la **americana**

En inglés, los gentilicios se escriben con mayúscula:

1. de América Latina **Latin American**
2. de América, de Estados Unidos **American**.

la amígdala ■ tonsil: lo operaron de las amígdalas he had his tonsils removed.

el amigo , la **amiga** ■ friend: es mi mejor amigo he's my best friend; son muy amigos they're good friends

➢ hacer amigos to make friends

➢ hacerse amigo de alguien to become friends with somebody

EL AMIGO INVISIBLE

The **amigo invisible** (invisible friend) is a widespread tradition throughout Spain. A group of friends or workmates draws lots to decide who will give a present and who will be the recipient. The presents are usually inexpensive and are given on a specific date such as Christmas. The interest of the game lies in the fact that nobody knows the identity of the person giving the presents and they have to guess who it is when they are being given out.

la amistad ■ friendship: valoro mucho tu amistad I really value your friendship

➢ las amistades friends: vinieron todas sus amistades all her friends came.

amistoso, sa *adjetivo* ■ friendly.

el amo , el **ama** ■ owner: lo abandonó su amo it was abandoned by its owner

➢ un ama de casa housewife.

amontonar [1] *verbo* ■ to pile up: amontonaron los libros en el suelo they piled the books up on the floor.

el amor ■ love

➢ hacer el amor to make love.

ampliar [7] *verbo*

1. to expand: van a ampliar su negocio they're going to expand their business

2. to extend: están ampliando la terminal 1 they're extending terminal 1; ampliaron el plazo para la matrícula they extended the registration period

3. to enlarge: quiero ampliar esta foto I want to enlarge this photo.

el amplificador ■ amplifier.

amplio, plia *adjetivo*

1. **spacious:** su casa es bastante amplia their house is pretty spacious
2. **wide:** una amplia avenida a wide avenue
3. **loose:** prefiere la ropa amplia she prefers loose clothing.

la **ampolla** ■ blister.

amueblar [1] *verbo* ■ **to furnish:** amueblaron el cuarto they furnished the room
➤ un piso sin amueblar an unfurnished flat.

el **analfabetismo** ■ illiteracy.

analfabeto, ta *adjetivo* ■ illiterate.

el **analgésico** ■ painkiller.

el **análisis** (*plural* los análisis)

1. **analysis** (*plural* analyses): hicimos un análisis gramatical we did a grammatical analysis
2. **test:** un análisis de sangre a blood test.

analizar [10] *verbo* ■ **to analyse** *UK*, **to analyze** *US*.

la **anatomía** ■ anatomy.

ancho, cha *adjetivo*

1. **wide:** una avenida muy ancha a very wide avenue
2. **loose:** prefiero las camisetas anchas I like loose t-shirts
➤ esta falda me queda demasiado ancha this skirt is too big for me
➤ ser ancho de espaldas to have broad shoulders
➤ a lo ancho crosswise

el **ancho** ■ **width:** mide el ancho de la ventana measure the width of the window
➤ ¿cuánto mide de ancho? how wide is it?
➤ tiene dos metros de ancho it's two metres wide.

la **anchura** ■ width.

la **anciana** ■ elderly woman.

anciano, na *adjetivo* ■ elderly

el **anciano** ■ elderly man
➤ los ancianos the elderly.

el **ancla** ■ anchor

Feminine noun that takes **un** or **el** in the singular.

anda *interjección*

1. **come on!:** ¡anda! que vamos a llegar tarde come on! we're going to be late
2. **hey!:** ¡anda! mira lo que encontré hey! look what I found!
➤ ¡anda ya! come off it!

Andalucía ■ Andalusia.

andaluz, za *adjetivo*

En inglés, los adjetivos que se refieren a un país o una región se escriben con mayúscula:

Andalusian: el flamenco es un baile andaluz flamenco is an Andalusian dance

el **andaluz**, la **andaluza**

En inglés, los gentilicios se escriben con mayúscula:

Andalusian: los andaluces the Andalusians.

andar [37] *verbo*

1. **to walk:** vine andando I walked here
2. **to work:** mi reloj no anda my watch isn't working
3. **to be:** ando muy ocupado I am very busy; ¿qué tal andas? how's it going?; ando buscando a la profesora I'm looking for the teacher
➤ andar mal de dinero to be short of money
➤ andar con alguien to go out with someone
➤ anda por los treinta she's about thirty
➤ hay que andarse con cuidado you should be careful.

el **andén** (*plural* los andenes) ■ platform.

Andorra ■ Andorra.

andorrano, na *adjetivo*

En inglés, los adjetivos que se refieren a un país o una región se escriben con mayúscula:

Andorran: tiene un apellido andorrano he has an Andorran surname el **andorrano** , la **andorrana**

En inglés, los gentilicios se escriben con mayúscula:

Andorran: los andorranos the Andorrans.

la **anestesia**

1. *proceso* anaesthesia UK, anesthesia US: **anestesia local** local anaesthesia
2. *sustancia* anaesthetic UK, anesthetic US: **aún está bajo los efectos de la anestesia** he's still under the anaesthetic.

la **anécdota** ■ anecdote.

el **ángel** ■ angel.

as **anginas**

▷ **tener anginas** to have a sore thoat.

angosto, ta *adjetivo* ■ narrow: **un pasillo angosto** a narrow corridor.

el **ángulo** ■ angle
▷ **un ángulo recto** a right angle.

el **anillo** ■ ring
▷ **un anillo de boda** a wedding ring
▷ **un anillo de compromiso** an engagement ring.

animado, da *adjetivo*

1. cheerful: **¡qué animado estás hoy!** you're very cheerful today!
2. lively: **las playas tienen un ambiente muy animado** the beaches have a very lively atmosphere
▷ **dibujos animados** cartoons.

animal *adjetivo* ■ animal: **el reino animal** the animal kingdom

el **animal** ■ animal: **le encantan los animales** she loves animals
▷ **un animal doméstico** a pet
▷ **un animal salvaje** a wild animal.

animar [1] *verbo*

1. to cheer up: **fuimos para animarlo un poco** we went to try to cheer him up a little
2. to cheer on: **animaron al equipo** they cheered on the team

3. to encourage: **hay que animarlo para que siga estudiando** we have to encourage him to carry on studying
4. to liven up: **animó la fiesta** he livened up the party

animarse *verbo pronominal* ■ to cheer up: **¡anda, anímate!** come on, cheer up!
▷ **animarse a hacer algo** to be up for something: **vamos a nadar ¿quién más se anima?** we're going swimming – who else is up for it?

ánimo *interjección*

▷ **¡ánimo! todo se va a arreglar** cheer up! it'll all work out
▷ **¡ánimo! que ya casi terminamos** come on! we're nearly finished

el **ánimo**

▷ **está de muy buen ánimo** he's in very good spirits
▷ **no tengo ánimos para salir** I'm not in the mood to go out
▷ **lo que me dijo me dio ánimos** what she told me really lifted my spirits
▷ **me dieron ánimos para que siguiera estudiando** they encouraged me to stay at school.

el **aniversario** ■ anniversary (plural anniversaries): **es el aniversario de boda de mis padres** it's my parents' wedding anniversary.

anoche *adverbio* ■ last night: **anoche fuimos al cine** we went to the cinema last night.

el **anochecer** ■ nightfall
▷ **volvieron al anochecer** they came back at nightfall.

anochecer [22] *verbo* ■ to get dark: **en esta época anochece más temprano** it gets dark early at this time of year

anónimo, ma *adjetivo* ■ anonymous.

el **anorak** ■ anorak.

anotar [1] *verbo*

1. to write down: **anotó su número de teléfono en la tarjeta** she wrote down her phone number on the card
2. to score: **anotó nueve puntos en el primer tiempo** she scored nine goals in the first half.

ante *preposición*

1. **before:** tiene que presentarse ante el director she has to appear before the manager
2. **facing:** estamos ante un grave problema we are facing a serious problem

el **ante** ■ **suede:** unos guantes de ante suede gloves.

anteanoche *adverbio* ■ **the night before last.**

anteayer *adverbio* ■ **the day before yesterday.**

el **antebrazo** ■ **forearm.**

los **antecedentes** ■ **record**
> antecedentes penales police record.

antemano *adverbio*
> de antemano beforehand: preparé las preguntas de antemano I prepared the questions beforehand.

la **antena** ■ **antenna:** la antena de la tele está rota the tv aerial is broken
> una antena parabólica a satellite dish.

el **antepasado**, la **antepasada** ■ **ancestor:** estoy orgulloso de mis antepasados I'm proud of my ancestors.

anterior *adjetivo*

1. **previous:** mi colegio anterior era mucho mejor my previous school was much better
2. **front:** las patas anteriores the front legs.

anteriormente *adverbio* ■ **previously.**

antes *adverbio*

1. **before:** esto lo deberías haber hecho antes you should have done this before
2. **first:** ella llegó antes she got here first
> antes de before: antes de salir, limpiemos la cocina let's clean the kitchen before we go out
> antes que nada first of all
> cuanto antes mejor the sooner, the better
> lo antes posible as soon as possible.

el **antibiótico** ■ **antibiotic.**

anticipado, da *adjetivo*
> por anticipado in advance.

anticipar [1] *verbo*

1. **to advance:** ¿me podría anticipar un 20% de mi sueldo? could you advance me 20% of my salary?
2. **to move forward:** estamos considerando anticipar nuestro viaje we're thinking of moving forward our trip

anticiparse *verbo pronominal* ■ **to come early:** se anticipó el invierno winter has come early
> anticiparse a su tiempo to be ahead of one's time: el artista se anticipó a su tiempo the artist was ahead of his time
> anticiparse a alguien to get in before somebody: se me anticipó y contestó la pregunta de la profesora she got in before me and answered the teacher's question.

anticonceptivo, va *adjetivo* ■ **contraceptive**

el **anticonceptivo** ■ **contraceptive.**

anticuado, da *adjetivo* ■ **old-fashioned.**

el **anticuerpo** ■ **antibody** (*plural* **antibodies**).

el **antídoto** ■ **antidote.**

antiguamente *adverbio* ■ **in the old days:** antiguamente, todo esto era campo in the old days, this was all countryside.

la **antigüedad**
> de gran antigüedad ancient: restos arqueológicos de gran antigüedad ancient archaelogical remains

las **antigüedades** ■ **antiques**
> tienda de antigüedades antique shop.

antiguo, gua *adjetivo*

1. **antique:** un jarrón antiguo an antique vase
2. **ancient:** las civilizaciones antiguas ancient civilizations
3. **old:** un antiguo amigo an old friend.

la **antipatía** ■ **dislike:** no pude disimular mi antipatía hacia ella I couldn't hide my dislike for her.

antipático, ca *adjetivo* ■ **unpleasant:** ¡que persona más antipática! what an unpleasant person!

el **ántrax** ■ anthrax.

anual *adjetivo* ■ **yearly:** el promedio anual the yearly average.

anular [1] *verbo*

1. **to cancel:** no será fácil anular el contrato it won't be easy to cancel the contract
2. **to disallow:** el árbitro anuló el gol the referee disallowed the goal
3. **to overturn:** el juez anuló el fallo the judge overturned the verdict.

anunciar [1] *verbo*

1. **to announce:** el gobierno anunció una bajada de impuestos the government announced a tax cut
2. **to advertise:** anuncian el producto en televisión the product is advertised on TV.

el **anuncio**

1. **advertisement:** puedes poner un anuncio en el diario you can put an advertisement in the paper
2. **commercial:** cada día hay más anuncios en la tele there are more commercials on TV every day
3. **announcement:** el anuncio de su partida nos sorprendió the announcement of his departure surprised us.

el **anzuelo** ■ hook.

añadir [3] *verbo* ■ **to add:** le añadió un poco de pimienta a la salsa he added a little pepper to the sauce.

los **añicos**

> el perro hizo añicos tu sombrero the dog tore your hat to shreds.

el **año**

1. *tiempo* **year:** el año que viene next year
2. *edad* ¿cuántos años tienes? —tengo 14 años how old are you? – I'm 14; en marzo cumpliré 15 años I'll be 15 this March
> año escolar school year
> el año pasado last year
> año bisiesto leap year
> Año Nuevo New Year: ¡Feliz Año Nuevo! Happy New Year!

apagar [12] *verbo*

1. **to turn off:** apaga la televisión antes de subir turn the TV off before going upstairs
2. **to put out:** se olvidó de apagar el cigarrillo he forgot to put out his cigarette.

el **aparato**

1. **appliance:** aparatos electrodomésticos household appliances
2. **system:** el aparato circulatorio the circulatory system
> aparato dental brace *UK*, braces *US*.

el **aparcamiento** ■ car park *UK*, parking lot *US*.

aparcar [8] *verbo* ■ **to park:** "prohibido aparcar" "no parking".

aparecer [22] *verbo* ■ **to appear.**

aparentar [1] *verbo* ■ **to look:** aparenta más de 16 años she looks older than 16.

la **apariencia** ■ **appearance:** deberías preocuparte más de tu apariencia you should take more care of your appearance
> las apariencias engañan appearances can be deceptive.

apartado, da *adjetivo* ■ **isolated:** vive en un lugar muy apartado he lives in a very isolated place
> estar apartado de to be away from: se mantiene apartado de su familia he stays away from his family

el **apartado** ■ **section:** contesta las preguntas en el apartado A answer the questions in section A
> apartado de correos P.O. Box.

el **apartamento** ■ apartment.

apartar [1] *verbo*

1. **to move out of the way:** aparta esa basura de ahí move that rubbish out of the way
2. **to set aside:** te apartaré un pedazo de pastel I'll set aside a piece of cake for you

apartarse *verbo pronominal* ■ **to stand aside:** ¡apártate! stand aside!

aparte *(adverbio & adjetivo)*

■ *adverbio*

1. **to the side:** voy a dejar tus cosas aparte I'll put your things to one side
2. **apart from:** aparte de la coliflor, come de todo he eats everything, apart from cauliflower

■ *adjetivo*

separate: eso es un caso aparte that's a separate issue.

apasionar [1] *verbo* ■ **to be fascinated by:** me apasiona el arte I'm fascinated by art.

la **apatía** ■ apathy.

el **apellido** ■ surname

> **LOS APELLIDOS**
>
> In Spain and Latin American, people commonly use the last names of both their father and their mother (in that order). Thus, if Alejandro Gómez Ortega and Isabel Ruiz Costa have a daughter named María, she will be known as María Gómez Ruiz. When a woman gets married, she keeps her full maiden name, but she can choose to adopt her husband's first surname as her second, or she can be known by her husband's name. So if María Gómez Ruiz marries Gustavo Núñez Lago, she could either keep her own name, change it to María Gómez de Núñez, or be known as Señora de Núñez.

apenas *adverbio*

1. **hardly:** apenas podía respirar por el calor I could hardly breathe because of the heat
2. **barely:** hace apenas dos semanas que nos conocemos we met barely two weeks ago
3. **as soon as:** apenas había llegado cuando empezaron con las preguntas they started asking questions as soon as I walked in.

el **aperitivo** ■ aperitif.

apetecer [22] *verbo*

1. **to feel like:** ¿te apetece ir al cine? dou you feel like going to de cinema?
2. **to fancy:** ¿te apetece un poco de tarta? do you fancy a bit of pie?

apestar [1] *verbo* ■ **to stink:** ¡tu ropa apesta a puros! your clothes stink of cigars!

el **apetito** ■ appetite.

aplastar [1] *verbo* ■ **to squash:** ¡me estás aplastando! you're squashing me!

aplaudir [3] *verbo* ■ **to applaud:** el público aplaudió su discurso the public applauded his speech.

el **aplauso** ■ applause.

aplicar [8] *verbo*

1. **to apply:** primero, aplicamos la pintura first, we apply the paint
2. **to put into practice:** ahora vamos a aplicar lo que hemos aprendido now we'll put what we've learned into practice

aplicarse *verbo pronominal* ■ **to apply oneself:** ¡no te has aplicado mucho en este trabajo! you haven't applied yourself much in this job!

apostar [16] *verbo* ■ **to bet:** apuesto a que no viene I bet he won't come.

apoyar [1] *verbo*

1. **to support:** sus amigos lo apoyaron en los momentos difíciles his friends supported him during difficult times
2. **to rest:** apoya tus piernas en la mesa de centro rest your legs on the coffee table

apoyarse *verbo pronominal* ■ **to lean:** se apoyó en la pared he leaned against the wall.

el **apoyo** ■ support.

apreciar [1] *verbo* ■ **to value:** te aprecio mucho como amigo I really value your friendship.

aprender [2] *verbo* ■ **to learn:** hoy he aprendido a nadar I learned to swim today

aprenderse *verbo pronominal* ■ **to learn:** me he aprendido la lección I've learned the lesson.

apretar [14] *verbo*

1. **to press:** apriete el botón rojo press the red button
2. **to squeeze:** ¡me estás apretando la mano muy fuerte! you're squeezing my hand too tightly!

aprobar [16] *verbo*

1. **to pass:** me han aprobado las matemáticas I passed maths; han aprobado la ley they have passed the law
2. **to approve of:** su padre no lo aprueba his father didn't approve of it.

apropiado, da *adjetivo* ■ **suitable.**

aprovechar [1] *verbo* ■ **to make the most of:** aprovéchalo mientras puedas make the most of it while you can

> aprovechar la ocasión para hacer algo to take the opportunity to do something: aprovechó la ocasión para hablar con ella he took the opportunity to talk to her

aprovecharse *verbo pronominal*

> aprovecharse de alguien to take advantage of somebody: se aprovechó de sus amigos he took the opportunity to talk to her.

apto, ta *adjetivo* ■ **suitable**

> ser apto para algo to be suitable for something: no es apto para niños it's not suitable for children.

la **apuesta** ■ **bet:** hicimos una apuesta we made a bet.

apuntar [1] *verbo*

1. **to write down:** déjame apuntar tu teléfono let me write down your number
2. **to point:** la aguja de la brújula apunta al norte the needle of the compass points north.

los **apuntes** ■ **notes**

> tomar apuntes to take notes.

el **apuro** ■ **jam:** nos vimos en apuros we found ourselves in a jam

> dar apuro to feel embarrassed: me da apuro pedirle un favor I feel embarrassed to ask him a favour.

aquel, aquella *adjetivo* ■ **that:** está en aquel cajón it's in that drawer; en aquellos días vivía en Madrid in those days he lived in Madrid.

aquél, aquélla *pronombre* ■ **that one:** pásame aquél, por favor pass me that one, please.

aquello *pronombre*

1. **that:** aquello fue demasiado that was too much
2. **what:** aquello que me dijiste me decepcionó I was disappointed by what you said me.

aquí *adverbio*

1. **here:** no eres de por aquí, ¿verdad? you're not from around here, are you?
> aquí abajo down here
> aquí arriba up here
> aquí mismo right here
2. **now**
> de aquí en adelante from now on.

Aragón ■ **Aragon.**

aragonés, aragonesa *adjetivo*

En inglés, los adjetivos que se refieren a un país o una región se escriben con mayúscula:

Aragonese: tiene un apellido aragonés he has an Aragonese surname

el **aragonés** , la **aragonesa**

En inglés, los gentilicios se escriben con mayúscula:

Aragonese: los aragoneses the Aragonese.

la **araña** ■ **spider.**

arañar [1] *verbo* ■ **to scratch:** el gato arañó la mejilla de la niña the cat scratched the little girl's cheek.

el **árbitro** , la **árbitra** ■ **referee:** el árbitro le mostró una tarjeta amarilla the referee showed him a yellow card.

el **árbol** ■ **tree**

> árbol genealógico family tree
> árbol de Navidad Christmas tree.

el **arbusto** ■ **bush.**

archivar [1] *verbo* ■ **to file:** archivaré los documentos alfabéticamente I'll file the documents alphabetically.

el **archivo**

1. **archive:** los archivos históricos the historical archives
2. **file:** este archivo sólo ocupa 30Kb this file takes up only 30Kb.

el arco
1. arch: un arco de triunfo a triumphal arch
2. bow: puso una flecha en el arco he placed an arrow in the bow
> el arco iris rainbow.

arder [2] *verbo*
1. to burn: ¡mira, está ardiendo el bosque! look, the forest's burning
2. to be boiling hot: ¡la sopa está ardiendo! the soup's boiling hot.

la ardilla ■ squirrel.

el área *sustantivo femenino*

Feminine noun that takes **un** or **el** in the singular.

area: área metropolitana metropolitan area.

la arena ■ sand: hicimos un castillo de arena we built a sand castle
> arenas movedizas quicksand.

Argentina ■ Argentina.

argentino, na *adjetivo*

En inglés, los adjetivos que se refieren a un país o una región se escriben con mayúscula:

Argentinian: tiene un primo argentino he has an Argentinian cousin

el argentino , la argentina

En inglés, los gentilicios se escriben con mayúscula:

Argentinian: los argentinos the Argentinians.

el argumento
1. argument: presentó sus argumentos en contra de la nueva ley he presented his arguments against the new law
2. plot: el argumento de la película the plot of the film.

la aristocracia ■ aristocracy.

el/la aristócrata ■ aristocrat.

la aritmética ■ arithmetic.

el arma *sustantivo femenino*

Feminine noun that takes **un** or **el** in the singular.

weapon: había un arma en su coche there was a weapon in his car

> arma blanca knife
> arma de fuego firearm
> armas químicas chemical weapons.

armar [1] *verbo* ■ to arm: armaron a la población they armed the population
> armar jaleo to make a racket

armarse *verbo pronominal* ■ to arm oneself: se armaron para la guerra they armed themselves for war
> armarse de paciencia to be patient/to arm oneself with patience: lo mejor es armarse de paciencia y esperar the best thing is to be patient and wait
> armarse de valor to pluck up courage/to arm oneself with courage: tuvo que armarse de valor y decírselo he had to pluck up courage and tell her.

el armario ■ cupboard *UK,* closet *US*
> armario empotrado built-in closet
> armario ropero wardrobe.

la armonía ■ harmony *(plural* **harmonies***)*: estar en armonía to be in harmony.

la armónica ■ harmonica.

el aro
1. ring
2. hoop: el león pasó por el aro the lion jumped through the hoop
> los aros olímpicos the Olympic hoops.

el aroma
1. aroma: el intenso aroma del café the intense aroma of coffee
2. scent: el aroma dulce de las flores the sweet scent of the flowers.

la arqueología ■ archaeology.

el arquitecto , la arquitecta ■ architect: mi padre es arquitecto my father is an architect.

la arquitectura ■ architecture.

arrancar [8] *verbo*
1. to pull up: trata de no arrancar las flores try not to pull up the flowers
2. to tear out: arranqué todas las páginas del libro I tore out all the pages of the book

3. **to start:** el coche no arranca the car won't start.

arrastrar [1] *verbo* ■ **to drag:** Pedro arrastró su mochila por el suelo Pedro dragged his rucksack on the floor.

arreglar [1] *verbo*

1. **to fix:** Javier arregló mi reloj Javier fixed my watch
2. **to sort out:** no te preocupes, todo está arreglado don't worry, everything's sorted
3. **to clean up:** arreglemos la casa antes de que lleguen let's clean up the house before they arrive

arreglarse *verbo pronominal*

1. **to manage:** yo me las arreglo solo I'll manage on my own
2. **to get ready:** lleva dos horas en el baño arreglándose she's been in the bathroom getting ready for two hours
3. **to get sorted out:** las cosas no se arreglan solas things don't just get sorted out by themselves.

el **arreglo**

1. **repair:** el coche necesita bastantes arreglos the car needs a lot of repairs
> tener arreglo to have a solution: esto no tiene arreglo there's no solution to this problem
> arreglo floral flower arrangement
> arreglo musical musical arrangement.

arrepentirse [20] *verbo pronominal* ■ **to regret:** me arrepiento de no haberlo hecho antes I regret not having done it sooner.

arrestar [1] *verbo* ■ **to arrest:** han arrestado a los ladrones they've arrested the thieves.

arriba *adverbio*

1. **top:** mira en el cajón de arriba look in the top drawer
2. **upstairs:** tu hermano está arriba your brother is upstairs
> hacia arriba upwards
> más arriba further up
> mirar alguien de arriba abajo to look somebody up and down.

arriesgar [12] *verbo* ■ **to risk:** arriesgó su vida para salvarme she risked her life to save me

arriesgarse *verbo pronominal* ■ **to take risks:** no se arriesgó a provocarla he didn't risk provoking her.

arrimar [1] *verbo* ■ **to bring closer:** arrima tu silla para que te pueda ver mejor bring your chair closer so I can see you better.

arrodillarse [1] *verbo pronominal* ■ **to kneel down:** nos arrodillamos frente al altar we kneeled down in front of the altar.

arrogante *adjetivo* ■ **arrogant:** ¡no seas tan arrogante! don't be so arrogant!

arrojar [1] *verbo* ■ **to throw:** arrojaron la basura por la ventana they threw the rubbish out of the window.

el **arroyo** ■ **stream:** bebimos agua de un pequeño arroyo we drank water from a small stream.

el **arroz** ■ **rice**
> arroz blanco boiled rice
> arroz integral brown rice
> arroz con leche rice pudding.

la **arruga**

1. **wrinkle:** tiene muchas arrugas en la frente he has a lot of wrinkles on his forehead
2. **creases:** su camisa estaba llena de arrugas his shirt was full of creases.

arrugado, da *adjetivo* ■ **wrinkled:** el vestido está muy arrugado this dress is very wrinkled.

arruinar [1] *verbo* ■ **to ruin:** la lluvia arruinó la fiesta the rain ruined the party

arruinarse *verbo pronominal* ■ **to lose everything:** su padre se arruinó jugando his father lost everything gambling.

el **arte** *(plural* las artes) ■ **art:** el arte moderno modern art
> las bellas artes the fine arts
> las artes marciales martial arts.

el **artículo** ■ article: tienes que leer este artículo you have to read this article; "el" es un artículo "el" is an article.

artificial *adjetivo* ■ artificial.

el/la **artista** ■ artist: cada cuadro va firmado por el artista each painting is signed by the artist
> artista de cine film star.

artístico, ca *adjetivo* ■ artistic.

la **artritis** ■ arthritis.

el **as** ■ ace
> el as de picas the ace of spades
> ser un as to be brilliant

⚠ The Spanish word as is a false friend, it does not mean "ass".

el **asa** *sustantivo femenino* ■

Feminine noun that takes un or el in the singular.

handle: cógelo por las asas take it by the handles.

asado, da *adjetivo*
1. roast: castañas asadas roast chestnuts
2. baked: patatas asadas baked potatoes

el **asado** ■ roast: asado de cordero roast lamb.

asaltar [1] *verbo*
1. to hold up: asaltaron el banco they held up the bank
2. to mug: me asaltaron a dos manzanas de mi casa I was mugged two blocks from my house.

el **asalto** ■ raid: hubo un asalto al banco there was a bank raid.

la **asamblea**
1. assembly: la asamblea legislativa está reunida the legislative assembly is in session
2. meeting: resolvieron el problema en asamblea they solved the problem in a meeting.

asar [1] *verbo* ■ to roast: voy a asar la carne I'll roast the meat too
> ¡me estoy asando! I'm roasting!

ascender [15] *verbo*
1. to climb: ascendimos la montaña lentamente we climbed the mountain slowly
2. to be promoted: ascendió a gerente he was promoted to manager.

el **ascensor** ■ lift *UK*, elevator *US*.

el **asco** ■ me dan asco las babosas I find slugs disgusting
> ¡qué asco! how disgusting!

asear [1] *verbo* ■ to clean: deberías asear tu habitación de vez en cuando you should clean your bedroom from time to time.

asegurar [1] *verbo*
1. to assure: le aseguro que no fue así I can assure you that it didn't happen like that
2. to insure: he asegurado mi casa contra incendios I've insured my house against fire
3. to secure: mejor asegurarlo con un candado it's better to secure it with a padlock

asegurarse *verbo pronominal* ■ to make sure: asegúrate de que has cerrado la puerta make sure you've locked the door.

el **aseo** ■ cleanliness: el aseo es muy importante cleanliness is very important
> aseo personal personal hygiene
> los aseos toilets *UK*, restrooms *US*.

asesinar [1] *verbo*
1. to murder: asesinaron a los secuestrados they murdered the kidnap victims
2. *a presidente, rey* to assassinate: asesinaron al presidente the president was assassinated.

el **asesinato**
1. murder
2. *de presidente, rey* assassination.

el **asesino** , la **asesina**
1. murderer
2. *de presidente, rey* assassin.

asfixiar [1] *verbo* ■ to suffocate: casi me asfixio I nearly suffocated.

así *adverbio*
1. like that: ¡no seas así! don't be like that!

2. **like this: me dijo que lo hiciera así** she told me to do it like this

➤ **¡así de fácil!** it's that easy!

➤ **así como así** just like that

➤ **así es** that's right

➤ **¡así me gusta!** that's the way I like it!

➤ **así así** so, so

➤ **así que** so: **así que te habló mal de mí** so, he said bad things about me.

Asia ■ Asia.

asiático, ca *adjetivo*

En inglés, los adjetivos que se refieren a un país o una región se escriben con mayúscula:

Asian: **la cocina asiática** Asian cooking

el **asiático** , la **asiática**

En inglés, los gentilicios se escriben con mayúscula:

Asian: **los asiáticos** the Asians.

el **asiento** ■ seat: **tome asiento** take a seat.

el **asilo**

1. home: **un asilo de ancianos** an old people's home

2. asylum: **el asilo político** political asylum.

asimilar [1] *verbo* ■ to assimilate: **es difícil asimilar tanta información** it's hard to assimilate so much information.

la **asistente** ■ assistant: **mandó a su asistente por café** she sent her assistant out for coffee

➤ **asistente social** social worker.

asistir [3] *verbo*

1. to attend: **¿cuántas personas asistieron a la boda?** how many people attended the wedding?

2. to assist: **salió del coche y asistió a los heridos** he came out of the car and assisted the injured.

el **asma** *sustantivo femenino*

Feminine noun that takes **un** or **el** in the singular.

asthma.

el **asno** ■ ass.

la **asociación** *(plural* las asociaciones*)* ■ association: **es miembro de la asociación de vecinos** he's member of the residents association.

asociar [1] *verbo* ■ to associate: **asocio ese olor con mi niñez** I associate that smell with my childhood

asociarse *verbo pronominal*

1. to join: **se ha asociado a una ONG** she's joined an ONG

2. to go into partnership: **estoy pensando asociarme con Juan** I'm thinking about going into partnership with Juan.

asomar [1] *verbo*

1. to stick out: **asomó la cabeza por la ventana** he stuck his head out of the window

2. to lean out: **asómate a la ventana para que lo puedas ver** lean out of the window so you can see it.

asombrar [1] *verbo* ■ to astonish: **me asombró lo que me dijo** I was astonished by what she told me.

el **asombro** ■ astonishment.

el **aspecto**

1. appearance: **tiene un aspecto muy refinado** he has a very refined appearance

2. aspect: **me interesa más el aspecto creativo** I'm more interested in the creative aspect.

áspero, ra *adjetivo*

1. rough: **tengo la piel áspera** my skin feels rough

2. harsh: **¡que voz más áspera!** what a harsh voice!

la **aspiración** *(plural* las aspiraciones*)* ■ aspiration: **tengo aspiraciones de ser músico** my aspiration is to become a musician.

la **aspiradora** ■ vacuum cleaner

➤ **pasar la aspiradora** to vacuum.

la **aspirina**® ■ aspirin.

asqueroso, sa *adjetivo* ■ disgusting: **limpia tu habitación, está asquerosa** clean your bedroom, it's disgusting.

el **asterisco** ■ asterisk.

la **astilla** ■ splinter: tengo una astilla en el dedo I have a splinter in my finger.

la **astrología** ■ astrology.

el/la **astronauta** ■ astronaut: cuando sea mayor quiero ser astronauta when I grow up I want to be an astronaut.

la **astronomía** ■ astronomy.

astronómico, ca *adjetivo* ■ astronomical: las facturas de este mes son astronómicas this month's bills are astronomical.

asturiano, na *adjetivo*

En inglés, los adjetivos que se refieren a un país o una región se escriben con mayúscula:

Asturian: la fabada es un plato asturiano fabada is an Asturian dish

el **asturiano** , la **asturiana**

En inglés, los gentilicios se escriben con mayúscula:

Asturian: los asturianos the Asturians.

Asturias ■ Asturias.

astuto, ta *adjetivo* ■ shrewd: eres muy astuto para los negocios you're a very shrewd businessman.

asumir [3] *verbo*

1. to take on: no quiero asumir esa responsabilidad I don't want to take on that responsibility

2. to deal with: me cuesta asumir que se fue I'm having trouble dealing with her leaving

3. to accept: hay que asumir las propias limitaciones we must accept our limitations.

el **asunto** ■ matter: esto es un asunto muy complicado this is a very complicated matter
➤ no es asunto suyo it's none of his business.

asustar [1] *verbo* ■ to frighten: lo asustaron esos ruidos those noises frightened him

asustarse *verbo pronominal* ■ to get scared: se asustó cuando vio al monstruo he got scared when he saw the monster; no te asustes, no pasa nada don't be scared, everything's all right.

atacar [8] *verbo* ■ to attack: nos atacaron con palos they attacked us with sticks.

el **atajo** ■ short cut: tomamos un atajo we took a short cut.

el **ataque** ■ attack: el ataque nos pilló por sorpresa the attack took us by surprise; le dio un ataque de alergia he had an allergy attack
➤ ataque cardíaco heart attack
➤ tener un ataque de nervios to panic.

atar [1] *verbo* ■ to tie: ató el perro a una farola he tied the dog to a lamppost

atarse *verbo pronominal* ■ to tie: átate los zapatos tie your shoelaces.

el **atardecer** ■ dusk: los mosquitos salen al atardecer mosquitoes come out at dusk.

atardecer [22] *verbo* ■ to get dark: está atardeciendo it's getting dark.

el **atasco** ■ traffic jam.

el **ataúd** ■ coffin.

la **atención** *(plural las atenciones)*

1. attention: hay que prestar atención al profesor you have to pay attention to your teacher

2. service: recibimos excelente atención en el hotel the service at the hotel was excellent
➤ a la atención de for the attention of
➤ llamar la atención to attract attention
➤ llamarle la atención a alguien to reprimand someone.

atención *interjección* ■ attention!
➤ ¡atención, por favor! your attention, please!

atender [15] *verbo*

1. to pay attention: no me estás atendiendo you're not paying attention to me

2. to take care of: atiende muy bien a sus pacientes he takes good care of his patients

3. to attend to: ahora tengo que atender a un cliente I have to attend to a client now; ¿le atienden? are you being served?

el **atentado**
➤ un atentado contra el presidente an assassination attempt on the president
➤ un atentado terrorista a terrorist attack.

atento, ta *adjetivo*

1. attentive: loa alumnos estaban muy atentos the pupils were very attentive
2. thoughtful: ¡qué atento! that's very thoughtful of you!

el **ateo** , la **atea** ■ atheist.

el **aterrizaje** ■ landing: el aterrizaje fue muy suave the landing was very smooth
> aterrizaje forzoso emergency landing.

aterrizar [10] *verbo* ■ to land: aterrizaremos en 20 minutos we will be landing in 20 minutes.

aterrorizar [10] *verbo* ■ to terrorize: esos dos matones aterrorizan a todos los otros niños those two bullies terrorize all the other children.

atlántico, ca *adjetivo*

En inglés, los adjetivos que se refieren a un océano se escriben con mayúscula:

Atlantic: la costa atlántica the Atlantic coast

el **Atlántico** ■ the Atlantic Ocean o the Atlantic.

el **atlas** ■ atlas.

/la **atleta** ■ athlete.

el **atletismo** ■ athletics UK, track and field US: soy un fanático del atletismo I'm a huge fan of athletics.

la **atmósfera** ■ atmosphere.

atmosférico, ca *adjetivo* ■ atmospheric.

atómico,ca *adjetivo* ■ atomic.

el **átomo** ■ atom.

atormentar [1] *verbo* ■ to torment: ¿por qué me estás atormentando con tantas preguntas? why are you tormenting me with all these questions?

atracar [8] *verbo*

1. to hold up: dos hombres atracaron la joyería two men held up a jeweller's shop
2. to mug: le atracaron en el metro he was mugged on the underground.

la **atracción** *(plural* las atracciones) ■ attraction: la atracción entre ellos era obvia the attraction between them was palpable
> atracciones turísticas tourist attractions.

atractivo, va *adjetivo* ■ attractive: el candidato es joven y atractivo the candidate is young and attractive.

atraer [53] *verbo*

1. to attract: ese bar atrae gente bohemia that bar attracts an arty crowd
2. to appeal: el esquí no me atrae nada skiing doesn't appeal to me at all.

atrapar [1] *verbo* ■ to catch: atraparon al delincuente they caught the criminal.

atrás *adverbio* ■ back: échate para atrás move back
> ¡atrás! get back!
> la puerta de atrás the back door
> años atrás years ago.

atrasado, da *adjetivo*

1. slow: mi reloj está atrasado diez minutos my watch is ten minutes slow
2. behind: va atrasada en la escuela she's behind in school
3. behind schedule: el proyecto está atrasado the project is behind schedule.

atravesar [14] *verbo* ■ to cross: el río atraviesa el país entero the river crosses the entire country; atravesamos la frontera al amanecer we cross the border at dawn.

atreverse [2] *verbo pronominal* ■ to dare: no me atrevo a decírselo I daren't tell him.

atropellar [1] *verbo* ■ to run over: ¡casi me atropellas! you nearly ran me over.

el **atún** ■ tuna
> un bocadillo de atún a tuna fish sandwich.

audaz *(plural* audaces) *adjetivo* ■ daring: un piloto audaz a daring pilot.

el **audífono** ■ hearing aid: mi abuelo usa audífono my grandfather wears a hearing aid.

el **auditorio** ■ auditorium.

el **aula** *sustantivo femenino*

Feminine noun that takes **un** or **el** in the singular.

classroom.

el **aullido** ■ **howl:** los aullidos de los perros no me dejaron dormir the dogs' howls kept me awake.

aumentar [1] *verbo*

1. **to go up, to increase:** ha aumentado el número de alumnos the number of pupils has gone up
2. **to increase, to put up:** me han aumentado el sueldo they've put up my salary
➤ aumentar de peso to put on weight.

el **aumento**

1. **increase:** un aumento en el número de alumnos an increase in the number of pupils; los precios han sufrido un aumento del 5% prices have increased by 5%
2. **rise:** un aumento de sueldo a pay rise.

aun *adverbio* ■ **even:** aun así, no lo creo even so, I don't believe it.

aún *adverbio*

1. **still:** aún no me ha dicho qué va a hacer she still hasn't told me what she's going to do
2. **yet:** aún no he terminado I haven't finished yet
3. **even:** ¡eres aún más guapa de lo que me imaginaba! you're even more beautiful than I imagined!

aunque *conjunción*

1. **although:** me apetece un filete, aunque normalmente no como carne I fancy a steak, although I don't usually eat meat
2. **even though:** te ayudaré, aunque estoy agotado I'll help you even though I'm exhausted
3. **even if:** tenemos que ir aunque no quieras we have to go even if you don't want to.

el **auricular** ■

1. *del teléfono* **receiver**
2. *de aparato de música* **headphones.**

la **ausencia** ■ **absence:** no había cambiado nada en mi ausencia nothing had changed during my absence.

ausente *adjetivo*

1. **absent:** has estado ausente demasiadas veces you've been absent too many times
2. **distracted:** hoy pareces estar ausente you look distracted today

el/la **ausente** ■ **absentee:** hoy hay tres ausentes en esta clase there are three absentees in this class today.

Australia ■ **Australia.**

australiano, na *adjetivo*

En inglés, los adjetivos que se refieren a un país o una región se escriben con mayúscula:

Australian: el equipo australiano the Australian team

el **australiano**, la **australiana**

En inglés, los gentilicios se escriben con mayúscula:

Australian: había dos australianos en el grupo there were two Australians in the group.

auténtico, ca *adjetivo* ■ **genuine:** un diamante auténtico an genuine diamond.

el **autobús** *(plural* los autobuses) ■ **bus.**

el **autocar** *(plural* los autocares) ■ **bus.**

la **autoescuela** ■ **driving school.**

el **autoestop** ■ **hitchhiking:** hacer autoestop to hitchhike.

automático, ca *adjetivo* ■ **automatic.**

la **autopista** ■ **motorway** *UK,* **freeway** *US*
➤ autopista de peaje toll motorway *UK,* turnpike *US.*

el **autor**, la **autora** ■ **author:** es la autora del poema she's the author of the poem
➤ el autor de la música the composer
➤ el autor del cuadro the painter
➤ los autores del crimen the perpetrators.

la **autoridad** ■ **authority:** no tiene ninguna autoridad sobre los alumnos she doesn't have any authority over the students
➤ las autoridades the authorities.

la **autorización** *(plural* las autorizaciones*)*
■ authorization: necesito la autorización del director I need authorization from the manager.

autorizar [10] *verbo* ■ to authorize

➤ autorizar a alguien para que haga algo to authorize someone to do something: nos autorizaron a salir más temprano we were authorized to leave early.

el **auxilio** ■ help: tuvimos que pedir auxilio we had to call for help

➤ ¡auxilio! help!

➤ los primeros auxilios first aid.

avanzar [10] *verbo*

1. to make progress: ha avanzado mucho en sus estudios he has made a lot of progress in school

2. to move forward: la cola avanzaba muy lentamente the queue moved forward slowly.

avaro, ra *adjetivo* ■ miserly

el **avaro** , la **avara** ■ miser.

el **ave** *sustantivo femenino*

Feminine noun that takes **un** or **el** in the singular.

bird

➤ aves de corral poultry

➤ un ave de rapiña a bird of prey.

la **avellana** ■ hazelnut.

la **avena** ■ oatmeal.

la **avenida** ■ avenue.

la **aventura** ■ adventure: el viaje fue toda una aventura the journey was quite an adventure

➤ ir a la aventura to go on an adventure.

avergonzar [10] *verbo*

1. to embarrass: me avergonzó delante de la clase he embarrassed me in front of the class

2. to be ashamed: ¿no te avergüenza ir con esa ropa? aren't you ashamed to go around dressed like that?

avergonzarse *verbo pronominal* ■ to be ashamed: no tienes por qué avergonzarte you have nothing to be ashamed of

➤ avergonzarse de algo to be ashamed of something: me avergüenzo de haberlo acusado I'm ashamed of accusing him.

la **avería** ■ breakdown: su coche tuvo una avería their car had a breakdown.

averiguar [33] *verbo* ■ to find out: tengo que averiguar la fecha exacta I have to find out the exact date.

la **aviación** *(plural* las aviaciones*)*

1. aviation: quiere estudiar aviación civil he wants to study civil aviation

2. air force: es teniente de aviación he's a lieutenant in the air force

➤ un accidente de aviación a plane crash.

el **avión** *(plural* los aviones*)* ■ aeroplane UK, airplane US: le encantan los aviones she loves aeroplanes

➤ vamos a ir en avión we're going by plane

➤ mandé el paquete por avión I sent the package by airmail.

avisar [1] *verbo*

1. to warn: te aviso que vas a tener problemas I'm warning you – you'll have problems

2. to let know: ¿le avisaste que no ibas a ir? did you let her know you weren't going?; avísame con tiempo let me know in advance

➤ siempre llega sin avisar he always comes without letting us know.

el **aviso**

1. notice: el aviso daba información acerca del cambio de dirección the notice informed us of the change of address

2. warning: el profesor me dijo que no habría un nuevo aviso the teacher told me there wouldn't be a second warning

➤ hasta nuevo aviso until further notice

➤ sin previo aviso without warning.

la **avispa** ■ wasp.

la **axila** ■ armpit.

¡ay! *interjección*

1. *para expresar dolor* ouch!: ¡ay! me haces daño ouch! that hurts!

2. *para expresar sorpresa* **oops!:** ¡ay! casi me caigo oops! I nearly fell down

3. *para expresar susto* **oh!:** ¡ay! me has asustado oh! you startled me.

ayer *adverbio* ■ **yesterday:** ayer la vi I saw her yesterday

➤ antes de ayer the day before yesterday

➤ ayer por la mañana yesterday morning

➤ ayer por la noche last night

➤ ayer por la tarde yesterday afternoon, yesterday evening.

la **ayuda** ■ **help:** ¿necesitas ayuda? do you need help?; me pidió ayuda she asked me for help.

ayudar [1] *verbo* ■ **to help:** me ha ayudado mucho it's helped me a lot

➤ ayudar a alguien a hacer algo to help someone do something: mi padre me ayudó a hacer los deberes my dad helped me do my homework.

el **ayuntamiento** ■ **town hall** UK, **city hall** US: un curso organizado por el ayuntamiento a course organized by town hall; vivo cerca del ayuntamiento I live near town hall.

la **azafata** ■ **flight attendant, air hostess** UK.

el **azar** ■ **chance:** me enteré por azar I only found out by chance

➤ al azar at random: escoge una carta al azar pick a card at random.

el/la **azúcar** ■ **sugar:** no le echo azúcar al café I don't put sugar in my coffee

➤ azúcar moreno brown sugar.

azul *adjetivo* ■ **blue:** un vestido azul a blue dress; es de color azul it's blue

el **azul** ■ **blue:** no me gusta el azul I don't like blue; iba vestida de azul she was dressed in blue

➤ azul celeste sky blue

➤ azul marino navy blue.

el **azulejo** ■ **tile.**

el **babero** ■ **bib.**

la **babosa** ■ **slug.**

el **bacalao** ■ **cod** *(plural* cod*).*

el **bache** ■ **pothole:** hay muchos baches en el camino there are a lot of potholes on this road

➤ están pasando por un mal bache they're going through a bad patch.

el **bachillerato** ■ **high school course.**

la **bacteria** ■ **bacteria.**

la **bahía** ■ **bay.**

bailar [1] *verbo* ■ **to dance:** anoche fuimos a bailar we went out dancing last night

➤ estoy aprendiendo a bailar salsa I'm learning to dance salsa.

el **bailarín** , la **bailarina** ■ **dancer:** quiere ser bailarina she wants to be a dancer.

el **baile** ■ **dance:** las sevillanas es un baile andaluz the Sevillanas is an Andalusian dance; da clases de baile she takes dance lessons; lo van a celebrar con un baile they're going to celebrate with a dance

➤ un baile de etiqueta a ball

➤ un baile de disfraces a fancy dress ball

➤ el baile de salón ballroom dancing.

la **baja**

➤ estar de baja to be off sick: estuve dos meses de baja I was off sick for two months

darse de baja to cancel one's membership: **me di de baja en el club** I cancelled my club membership.

la **bajada** ■ way down: **la bajada es siempre más fácil** the way down is always easier

una bajada muy pronunciada a steep descent.

bajar [1] *verbo*

1. **to go down:** **voy a bajar por las escaleras** I'll go down the stairs

2. **to come down:** **baja que quiero decirte algo** come down, I need to tell you something; **ya bajo** I'm coming down

3. **to take down:** **voy a bajar el teléfono a la cocina** I'm going to take the phone down to the kitchen

4. **to bring down:** **por favor, bájame un suéter que aquí hace frío** please bring me down a sweater – it's cold here

5. **to get down:** **baja el diccionario del estante** get the dictionary down from the shelf

6. **to lower:** **han bajado el precio de la entrada** they've lowered the ticket prices

7. **to download:** **acabo de bajar esta canción** I just downloaded this song

8. **to turn down:** **baja la música, por favor** please turn down the music

¡bajad la voz que no puedo estudiar! keep your voices down, I'm trying to study!

bajarse de algo

1. *de un autobús, avión, bicicleta* **to get off:** **nos bajamos juntos del tren** we got off the train together

2. *de un coche* **to get out of:** **se bajó de un taxi** she got out of a taxi

3. *de un árbol, mesa* **to come down from:** **¡bájate de ahí que te vas a caer!** get down from there before you fall!

bajo, ja *adjetivo*

1. **short:** **José es muy bajo** José is very short

2. **low:** **la silla es muy baja** the chair is very low; **saqué notas muy bajas** I got very low marks; **las temperaturas no son muy bajas** temperatures aren't too low

la planta baja the ground floor

hablaban en voz baja they were talking quietly

pon la música más baja turn the music down

alimentos bajos en calorías low-calorie foods.

bajo *(adverbio & preposición)*

■ *adverbio*

low: **iba volando muy bajo** it was flying very low

hablad más bajo please lower your voices

■ *preposición*

under: **escribe bajo un seudónimo** she writes under a pseudonym

bajo cero below zero: **tres grados bajo cero** three degrees below zero

bajo tierra underground.

la **bala** ■ bullet.

la **balanza** ■ scales: **me pesé en la balanza del baño** I weighed myself on the bathroom scales.

el **balazo** ■ shot: **oímos unos balazos** we heard some shots

lo mataron de un balazo he was shot to death.

el **balcón** *(plural* los balcones*)* ■ balcony *(plural* balconies*)*.

el **balde** ■ bucket: **un balde de agua** a bucket of water

en balde in vain: **hicimos el viaje en balde porque no estaba** he was out, so our trip was in vain.

la **baldosa** ■ tile.

Baleares ■ the Balearic Islands

las islas Baleares the Balearic Islands.

la **ballena** ■ whale.

el **balón** *(plural* los balones*)* ■ ball

 Balón is a false friend, it does not mean "balloon".

la **balsa** ■ raft.

el **banco**

1. **bank:** **depositó el cheque en el banco** he deposited the cheque at the bank

2. **bench:** **me senté en un banco de la plaza** I sat on a bench in the square

los bancos de la iglesia the pews
un banco de sangre a blood bank.

la **banda**
1. band: toca en la banda del colegio she plays in the school band
2. gang: detuvieron a una banda de ladrones they caught a gang of thieves
3. sash: llevaba una banda con el nombre de su país she wore a sash with her country's name on it
la banda sonora de la película the film soundtrack.

la **bandeja** ■ tray.

la **bandera** ■ flag.

el **banquero** , la **banquera** ■ banker: su padre es banquero his father is a banker.

el **banquete** ■ banquet: los invitaron a un banquete they were invited to a banquet
el banquete de bodas the wedding reception.

el **bañador** ■
1. de hombre swimming trunks
2. de mujer swimsuit.

bañarse [1] verbo pronominal
1. to have a bath: puedes bañarte o ducharte you can have a bath or a shower
2. to swim: nos bañamos en el mar we swam in the sea.

la **bañera** ■ bath, bathtub.

el **baño** ■ bathroom: ¿dónde está el baño, por favor? can you tell me where the bathroom is, please?; una casa con tres baños a house with three bathrooms
darse un baño
1. en el mar, la piscina to go for a swim
2. en la bañera to have a bath.

el **bar** ■ bar.

la **baraja** ■ pack of cards

BARAJA ESPAÑOLA

Card games using the French pack are very common in Spain but there are also a wide variety of games played with the Spanish pack, such as **mus**, **tute** or **brisca**. The Spanish pack consists of 48 cards, with numerals ranging from one to seven (the eight and nine are hardly ever used), followed by the **sota** (jack), the **caballo** (horse) and the **rey** (king), which are the figures in the pack. The colours are called **oros** (represented by gold coins), **copas** (cups), **bastos** (batons) and **espadas** (swords).

barato, ta adjetivo ■ cheap: ¿cuál es más barato? which one is the cheapest?

barato adverbio ■ cheaply: aquí podemos comer barato we can eat cheaply here
el viaje nos salió bastante barato our trip was pretty cheap.

la **barba** ■ beard
dejarse barba to grow a beard: se está dejando barba he's growing a beard.

la **barbacoa** ■ barbecue: hacer una barbacoa to have a barbecue.

la **barbaridad** ■ atrocity (plural atrocities): las barbaridades cometidas en la guerra the atrocities committed during the war
no digas tantas barbaridades don't talk such nonsense
tengo una barbaridad de tareas para mañana I've got a load of jobs for tomorrow
¡qué barbaridad! mira qué tarde es oh my God! look how late it is!

la **barbilla** ■ chin.

la **barca** ■ boat: una barca de remos a rowing boat UK, a row boat US.

Barcelona ■ Barcelona.

el **barco**
1. grande ship
2. de menor tamaño boat
un barco de guerra a warship
un barco de vela a sailing boat.

el **barniz** (plural los barnices) ■ varnish.

la **barra** ■ bar: tomamos unas bebidas en la barra we had drinks at the bar; una barra de metal a metal bar

una barra de labios a lipstick

una barra de pan a loaf of bread.

el **barranco** ■ ravine.

barrer [2] *verbo* ■ to sweep: tengo que barrer la cocina I have to sweep the kitchen.

la **barrera** ■ barrier

la barrera del sonido the sound barrier.

la **barriga** ■ belly *(plural* **bellies***)*: tiene una barriga tremenda he has a huge belly

me duele la barriga my tummy hurts.

el **barril** ■ barrel: un barril de petróleo an oil barrel.

el **barrio** ■ neighbourhood *UK*, **neighborhood** *US*: un barrio residencial a residential neighbourhood; va a un colegio del barrio she goes to a neighbourhood school.

el **barro**

1. clay: una olla de barro a clay pot
2. mud: llegó con los zapatos llenos de barro he arrived with his shoes covered in mud.

el **barullo**

1. racket: había mucho barullo en la clase there was a lot of racket in the classroom
2. mess

se armó un barullo con las cuentas he got into a mess with the accounts.

basarse [1] *verbo pronominal* ■ to be based on: el libro se basa en una historia real the book is based on a true story.

la **báscula** ■ scales.

la **base**

1. base: la base de la pirámide the base of the pyramid; corrió a la tercera base she ran to third base
2. basis: la base de su éxito fue el estudio studying was the basis for his success

lo consiguió a base de esfuerzo he did it through hard work

las bases del concurso the rules of the competition

una base aérea an air base

una base de datos a database.

básico, ca *adjetivo* ■ basic.

bastante *(adjetivo & adverbio)*

■ *adjetivo*

> Cuando tiene el sentido de suficiente, el adjetivo **bastante** se traduce por **enough**. Si se refiere a una cantidad o número considerable se traduce por a **lot of**:

1. enough: hay bastante comida para todos there's enough food for everyone
2. a lot of: había bastante gente there were a lot of people; mañana tengo bastantes cosas que hacer I have a lot of things to do tomorrow

■ *adverbio*

pretty: son bastante caras they're pretty expensive; habla bastante bien inglés she speaks English pretty well

tengo bastante hambre I'm quite hungry

tardamos bastante en llegar we got there pretty late.

bastar [1] *verbo* ■ to be enough: basta con un pellizco de sal a pinch of a salt is enough

¡basta! that's enough!

el **bastón** ■ cane.

la **basura** ■ garbage: pasan a recoger la basura los lunes they pick up the garbage on Monday

tirar algo a la basura to throw something in the garbage.

el **basurero** , la **basurera** ■ refuse collector, dustman *UK*, garbage collector *US*: es basurero he's a dustman

el **basurero** ■ rubbish dump *UK*, garbage dump *US*: lo encontró en el basurero she found it in the rubbish dump.

la **bata**

1. dressing gown *UK*, robe *US*: seguía en bata a las 3 de la tarde she was still in her dressing gown at 3 o'clock in the afternoon
2. coat: los médicos usan batas blancas doctors wear white coats.

la **batalla** ■ battle.

el **bateador** , la **bateadora** ■ batter.

la **batería**

1. battery (plural **batteries**): necesito una nueva batería para mi coche I need a new battery for my car
2. drums: estoy aprendiendo a tocar la batería I'm learning to play the drums
> tengo que recargar la batería del móvil I have to recharge my mobile phone battery.

la **batidora** ■ blender.

batir [3] verbo

1. to beat: bate los huevos ligeramente beat the eggs lightly
2. to whip: primero hay que batir la nata you have to whip the cream first
3. to break: ha batido todos los récords he has beaten all the records.

el **baúl** ■ trunk.

bautizar [10] verbo ■ to christen: la bautizan el sábado she's being christened on Saturday.

el **bautizo** ■ christening.

beber [2] verbo ■ to drink: no bebas esa agua don't drink that water
> se bebieron todo el vino they drank all the wine
> tienes que bebértelo todo you have to drink all of it.

la **bebida** ■ drink.

la **beca**

1. del gobierno grant: recibimos una beca del gobierno we got a government grant
2. de universidad, institución privada scholarship: le han dado una beca para ir a Harvard they've given her a scholarship to go to Harvard.

el **béisbol** ■ baseball.

belga adjetivo

En inglés, los gentilicios se escriben con mayúscula:

Belgian: chocolatinas belgas Belgian chocolates

el/la **belga**

En inglés, los gentilicios se escriben con mayúscula:

Belgian: los belgas the Belgians.

Bélgica ■ Belgium.

la **belleza** ■ beauty.

bendecir [48] verbo ■ to bless.

la **bendición** (plural las bendiciones) ■ blessing.

beneficiar [1] verbo ■ to benefit: la nueva ley beneficia a todos the new law benefits everybody

beneficiarse verbo pronominal ■ to benefit: con este cambio nadie se beneficia nobody benefits from this change.

el **beneficio** ■ profit: la empresa tuvo un beneficio de 2000 dólares the company made a profit of 2000 dollars.

benéfico, ca adjetivo ■ benefit: una cena benéfica a benefit dinner.

benigno, na adjetivo

1. benign: un tumor benigno a benign tumour
2. mild: un clima benigno a mild climate.

la **berenjena** ■ aubergine UK, eggplant US.

el **berrinche** ■ tantrum: cogió un berrinche tremendo he threw a terrible tantrum.

besar [1] verbo ■ to kiss: le besó en la frente she kissed him on the forehead

besarse verbo pronominal ■ to kiss, to kiss each other: se estaban besando they were kissing; Juan y María se besaron Juan and María kissed each other.

el **beso** ■ kiss: le dio un beso he gave her a kiss.

el **biberón** (plural los biberones) ■ bottle: voy a darle el biberón al niño I'm going to give the baby his bottle.

la **Biblia** ■ Bible.

la **biblioteca** ■ library (plural **libraries**): la biblioteca de la escuela the school library.

el **bibliotecario** , la **bibliotecaria** ■ librarian.

el **bicho** ■ insect
> *familiar* ser un bicho to be a nasty piece of work.

la **bici** ■ bike.

la **bicicleta** ■ bicycle
> montar en bicicleta to ride a bicycle: no sabe montar en bicicleta he doesn't know how to ride a bicycle
> bicicleta de montaña mountain bike.

bien *adverbio*
1. good: me siento bien I feel good
2. very: repítelo bien fuerte repeat it very loudly
3. great: ¡bien, vamos al cine! great, let's go to the cinema!
4. all right: está bien: te dejo el coche it's all right: I'm leaving you the car
5. well: ¡cierra bien la puerta! close the door well!
> lo pasamos muy bien we had a good time
> ¡bien hecho! well done!
> ¿te parece bien? is that OK with you?
> ¡qué bien! how wonderful!

el **bien**
1. good: el bien y el mal good and evil
2. well-being: lo hizo por tu bien she did it for your well-being
> los bienes goods.

la **bienvenida**
> dar la bienvenida a alguien to welcome somebody: me dieron la bienvenida they welcomed me.

bienvenido, da *adjetivo* ■ welcome: bienvenido a nuestra casa welcome to our home.

el **bigote** ■ moustache *UK*, mustache *US*.

Bilbao ■ Bilbao.

el **billete**
1. note *UK*, bill *US:* un billete de 100 euros a 100 euro note
2. ticket: un billete de tren a train ticket.

la **billetera** ■ wallet: una billetera de cuero a leather wallet.

la **biografía** ■ biography *(plural* biografías*)*.

ia **biología** ■ biology.

biológico, ca *adjetivo* ■ biological.

el **bis** ■ encore: pidieron un bis en el concierto they asked for an encore at the concert.

la **bisabuela** ■ great-grandmother.

el **bisabuelo** ■ great-grandfather
> mis bisabuelos my great-grandparents.

la **bisnieta** ■ great-granddaughter.

el **bisnieto** ■ great-grandson
> mis bisnietos my great-grandchildren.

el **bistec** ■ steak.

bizco, ca *adjetivo* ■ cross-eyed.

el **bizcocho** ■ sponge cake.

blanco, ca *adjetivo* ■ white: una pared blanca a white wall

el **blanco**
1. white: el blanco es mi color preferido white is my favourite colour
2. target: fue el blanco de todas las críticas he was the target of all the criticism; el ciervo fue el blanco de los cazadores the deer was the hunter's target
> dejar algo en blanco to leave something blank: deje esa parte del documento en blanco leave that part of the document blank
> quedarse en blanco to go blank: en el examen oral me quedé en blanco my mind went blank during the oral exam.

blando, da *adjetivo*
1. soft: una superficie blanda a soft surface
2. indulgent: es muy blando con sus hijos he's very indulgent with his children.

el **bloque** ■ block: un bloque de cemento a cement block
> un bloque de pisos a block of facts.

bloquear [1] *verbo* ■ to block: el camión bloqueaba la entrada the lorry was blocking the entrance

bloquearse *verbo pronominal*

1. **to jam:** se ha bloqueado la cerradura the lock has jammed
2. **to go blank:** cuando tiene miedo, se bloquea when he's afraid, his mind goes blank.

el **bloqueo** ■ blockade.

la **blusa** ■ blouse.

bobo, ba *adjetivo* ■ **silly:** no seas bobo don't be silly

el **bobo**, la **boba** ■ **fool:** Guillermo es un bobo Guillermo is a fool.

la **boca**

1. **mouth:** una boca pequeña a small mouth
2. **entrance:** quedamos en la boca del metro let's meet at the entrance of the underground
 ➣ quedarse con la boca abierta to be dumbfounded
 ➣ se me hace agua la boca my mouth is watering
 ➣ boca abajo face down
 ➣ boca arriba face up.

el **bocado** ■ **bite:** probé un bocado de esa comida I tried a bite of that food.

la **bocina** ■ **horn:** el conductor tocó la bocina the driver honked the horn.

la **boda** ■ wedding.

la **bodega**

1. **cellar:** una bodega de vino a wine cellar
2. **hold:** el equipaje está en la bodega del barco the luggage is in the ship's hold.

la **bofetada** ■ **slap:** le dio una fuerte bofetada she gave him a hard slap.

el **bol** ■ bowl.

la **bola**

1. **ball:** me tiró una bola de papel he threw a ball of paper at me
2. **fib:** ¡deja de contar bolas! stop telling fibs!

el **bolígrafo** ■ **pen:** marca las correcciones con un bolígrafo rojo mark the corrections with a red pen.

Bolivia ■ Bolivia.

boliviano, na *adjetivo*

En inglés, los adjetivos que se refieren a un país o una región se escriben con mayúscula:

Bolivian: los tejidos bolivianos son de alta calidad Bolivian textiles are high quality

el **boliviano**, la **boliviano**

En inglés, los gentilicios se escriben con mayúscula:

Bolivian: los bolivianos the Bolivians.

el **bollo** ■ **bun:** me gustan los bollos de chocolate I like chocolate buns.

la **bolsa**

1. **bag:** traje las compras en una bolsa de papel I carried the shopping in a paper bag
2. **stock market:** la Bolsa ha subido the stock market has gone up
 ➣ una bolsa de agua caliente a hot-water bottle
 ➣ una bolsa de aire an air pocket
 ➣ una bolsa de deportes a sports bag
 ➣ una bolsa de viaje a travel bag.

el **bolsillo** ■ **pocket:** este pantalón tiene dos bolsillos these trousers have two pockets
 ➣ un libro de bolsillo a paperback.

el **bolso** ■ **bag:** un bolso de cuero a leather bag
 ➣ un bolso de mano handbag *UK*, purse *US*.

la **bomba**

1. **bomb:** estalló una bomba en una tienda a bomb exploded in a store
2. **pump:** usamos una bomba para sacar el agua we used a pump to get the water out
 ➣ pasarlo bomba to have a great time: en la fiesta lo pasamos bomba we had a great time at the party
 ➣ la noticia fue una bomba the news was a bombshell.

bombear [1] *verbo* ■ **to pump out:** los voluntarios bombearon el agua del pozo the volunteers pumped out the water from the well.

el **bombero**, la **bombera** ■ *hombre* fireman, *mujer* firewoman, firefighter: los bomberos apagaron el fuego the firefighters put out the fire.

la **bombilla** ■ light bulb: necesitamos una bombilla para la lámpara we need a light bulb for the lamp.

el **bombón** (plural los bombones) ■ chocolate.

el **boniato** ■ sweet potato (plural sweet potatoes).

bonito, ta adjetivo ■ pretty: esta blusa es muy bonita this blouse is very pretty.

el **bonito** ■ tuna.

el **bono**
1. voucher: me han dado un bono por el 10% de mi compra they've given me a voucher for 10% of my purchase
2. pass: Beatriz compró un bono mensual Beatriz bought a monthly pass.

el **bordado** ■ embroidery.

el **borde** ■ edge: es peligroso asomarse al borde del barranco it's dangerous to get close to the edge of the ravine
▷ estar al borde de algo to be on the verge of something: está al borde de una crisis nerviosa he's on the verge of a nervous breakdown.

bordo sustantivo masculino
▷ a bordo on board: subimos a bordo de la lancha we got on board the boat.

la **borrachera**
▷ coger una borrachera to get drunk: Juan cogió una borrachera tremenda Juan got really drunk.

borracho, cha adjetivo ■ drunk: estaba borracho he was drunk.

el **borrador**
1. rough draft: es un borrador de la redacción it's a rough draft of the essay
2. board rubber UK, eraser US: la profesora pidió un borrador nuevo the teacher asked for a new board rubber.

borrar [1] verbo
1. to rub out, to erase: el estudiante borró la pizarra the student rubbed out the black board
2. to delete: he borrado un fichero sin querer I've deleted a file accidentally.

el **borrego**, la **borrega** ■ lamb.

el **borrón** (plural los borrones) ■ smudge: este papel está lleno de borrones this paper is covered with smudges.

borroso, sa adjetivo
1. blurred: una fotografía borrosa a blurred photograph
2. vague: un recuerdo borroso a vague memory.

el **bosque**
1. grande forest
2. pequeño wood.

bostezar [10] verbo ■ to yawn: Pedro bostezó durante toda la conferencia Pedro yawned during the whole conference.

la **bota** ■ boot: me he comprado unas botas de cuero I've bought leather boots.

la **botánica** ■ botany.

botar [1] verbo ■ to bounce: el balón ya no bota the ball doesn't bounce anymore.

el **bote**
1. can: hemos comprado un bote de pintura we've bought a tin of paint
2. boat: hoy hay muchos botes en el lago there are lots of boats on the lake today
▷ pasear en bote to go sailing
▷ tener a alguien en el bote to have someone eating out of one's hand.

la **botella** ■ bottle: una botella de vidrio a glass bottle; una botella de agua a bottle of water.

el **botón** (plural los botones) ■ button: perdió dos botones de la blusa she lost two buttons off her blouse; debes apretar el botón you have to press the button.

la **bóveda** ■ vault.

el **boxeo** ■ boxing: un campeonato de boxeo a boxing championship.

las **bragas** ■ knickers: me he comprado unas bragas de algodón I've bought a pair of cotton knickers.

la **brasa** ■ hot coal: hay que avivar las brasas we have to stoke the hot coals.

Brasil ■ Brazil.

brasileño, ña *adjetivo*

En inglés, los adjetivos que se refieren a un país o una región se escriben con mayúscula:

Brazilian: el equipo brasileño salió campeón the Brazilian team were the champions

el **brasileño** , la **brasileña**

En inglés, los gentilicios se escriben con mayúscula:

Brazilian: los brasileños the Brazilians.

bravo *interjección* ■ **well done!**

el **brazo** ■ arm: Ricardo se ha roto el brazo Ricardo has broken his arm; los brazos del sillón están gastados the arms of the chair are worn

➤ una brazo de gitano a swiss roll
➤ cruzarse de brazos to fold one's arms.

breve *adjetivo*

1. brief: una breve pausa a brief pause
2. short: un discurso breve a short speech
➤ en breve shortly.

brillante *adjetivo*

1. shiny: una superficie brillante a shiny surface
2. brilliant: es una estudiante brillante she's a brilliant student

el **brillante** ■ diamond: un anillo de brillantes a diamond ring.

brillar [1] *verbo*

1. to shine: las estrellas brillan the stars are shining
2. to sparkle: sus ojos brillaban his eyes sparkled.

el **brillo**

1. shine: el brillo del vidrio me ciega the shine from the glass is blinding me
2. sparkle: adoro el brillo de tus ojos I adore the sparkle of your eyes.

brincar [8] *verbo* ■ **to jump up and down**: el niño brincaba de emoción the boy was jumping up and down with excitement.

el **brinco**
➤ pegar un brinco to jump: pegó un brinco en el aire she jumped in the air.

brindar [1] *verbo*

1. to offer: te brindo mi amor I offer you my love
➤ brindar por to drink a toast to: en la fiesta brindamos por los novios at the party we drank a toast to the bride and groom

brindarse *verbo pronominal*
➤ brindarse a hacer algo to offer to do something: me brindé a lavar los platos I offered to do the dishes.

el **brindis** (plural los brindis) ■ toast: hagamos un brindis por los novios let's drink a toast to the bride and groom.

la **brisa** ■ breeze: hay una brisa muy agradable there's a very pleasant breeze.

británico, ca *adjetivo*

En inglés, los adjetivos que se refieren a un país o una región se escriben con mayúscula:

British: tiene acento británico he has a British accent

el **británico** , la **británica**

En inglés, los gentilicios se escriben con mayúscula:

British person: los británicos the British.

la **brocha** ■ paintbrush.

el **broche**

1. fastener: se rompió el broche del collar the fastener of the necklace broke
2. brooch: me gusta usar un broche en la solapa I like to wear a brooch on my lapel.

la **broma** ■ joke: le gusta hacer bromas he likes to make jokes
➤ gastar una broma a alguien to play a joke on somebody: gastamos una broma a Cristina we played a joke on Cristina
➤ lo decía en broma I was just joking.

bromear [1] *verbo* ■ **to joke**: sólo estábamos bromeando we were only joking.

bromista ■ joker: mi hermano es muy bromista my brother is a real joker.

a bronca ■ row: se armó una bronca terrible en el partido there was a terrible row during the game

echar la bronca a alguien to tell somebody off: nos echaron la bronca por llegar tarde they told us off for being late.

bronceado, da *adjetivo* ■ tanned: su piel estaba bronceada his skin was tanned

ponerse bronceado to get a tan: me pongo bronceado después de sólo una hora al sol I get a tan after only one hour in the sun

el bronceado ■ suntan.

el bronceador ■ suntan lotion: siempre utilizo bronceador I always use suntan lotion.

el brote ■ shoot: esta planta tiene brotes sanos this plant has healthy shoots.

la bruja ■ witch.

el brujo ■ wizard.

la brújula ■ compass.

la bruma ■ mist: hay una espesa bruma sobre el mar there's a heavy mist over the sea.

brusco, ca *adjetivo* ■ sudden: hizo un movimiento brusco he made a sudden movement.

brutal *adjetivo* ■ brutal: fue una guerra brutal it was a brutal war.

bruto, ta *adjetivo*

1. uncouth: es un niño muy bruto he's a very uncouth boy
2. gross: los beneficios brutos gross profits.

bucal *adjetivo* ■ oral: tienes una infección bucal you have an oral infection.

bucear [1] *verbo* ■ to dive: nos vamos a bucear we're going diving.

el buceo ■ diving: me gustaría practicar el buceo I would like to go diving.

buen *adjetivo*

Buen is a shortened form of bueno used in front of a masculine singular noun. Example: es un buen año, es un año bueno.

good: es un buen principio it's a good beginning.

bueno, na *adjetivo* ■ good: sacó muy buenas notas en el examen he got very good marks in the exam; su hermana es muy buena her sister's very good.

bueno *(adverbio & interjección)*

■ *adverbio*

OK: bueno, comamos pizza OK, let's eat pizza; ¿vienes? —bueno, vale are you coming? – ok

■ *interjección*

right!: ¡bueno, esto es demasiado! right, this is too much.

el buey ■ ox *(plural* oxen*)*.

la bufanda ■ scarf *(plural* scarves*)*.

el búho ■ owl.

el buitre ■ vulture.

el bulbo ■ bulb.

la bulla ■ ruckus: los niños armaron una gran bulla the children raised a terrible ruckus.

el bullicio ■ racket: el bullicio de la calle era insoportable the racket of the street was unbearable.

el bulto

1. bulge: la cartera te hace un bulto en el bolsillo your wallet makes a bulge in your pocket
2. piece of luggage: viajan con cuatro bultos they're travelling with four pieces of luggage
3. shape: sólo puedo distinguir dos bultos grandes en este cuarto oscuro I can only distinguish two large shapes in this dark room.

el buque ■ ship.

la burbuja ■ bubble.

la burguesía ■ middle class.

la burla ■ taunt: las burlas de sus compañeros fueron crueles the taunts of his colleagues were cruel.

burlarse [1] *verbo pronominal*

burlarse de alguien to make fun of somebody: se burlaron cruelmente del niño they cruelly made fun of the boy.

la **burocracia** ■ bureaucracy.

el/la **burócrata** ■ bureaucrat.

burocrático, ca *adjetivo* ■ bureaucratic: debemos completar estos trámites burocráticos we have to complete these bureaucratic formalities.

burro, rra *adjetivo* ■ *informal* stupid: era tan burro que pensaba que el número dos era impar he was so stupid that he thought that two was an odd number

el **burro** ■ donkey.

el **bus** ■ bus: cogimos el bus para ir al museo we took the bus to the museum.

buscar [8] *verbo*

1. to look for: estoy buscando trabajo I'm looking for work
2. to pick up: va a buscar a los niños al colegio todos los días she goes to pick up the children from school every day
➤ se busca caniche blanco white poodle wanted
➤ se la está buscando he's looking for trouble.

la **búsqueda** ■ search: la búsqueda de la niña duró dos días the search for the girl lasted two days; he hecho una búsqueda en internet I've done a search on the Internet.

el **busto** ■ bust: inauguraron un busto del famoso poeta they unveiled a bust of the famous poet.

la **butaca** ■ armchair.

el **buzo** ■ diver: los buzos están buscando el barco en el fondo del mar the divers are looking for the ship at the bottom of the sea.

el **buzón** *(plural* los buzones)*

1. letter box *UK*, mailbox *US:* encontré dos cartas en el buzón I found two letters in the letter box
2. post box *UK*, mailbox *US:* en esta calle no hay ningún buzón there are no post boxes in this street
➤ el buzón de voz voicemail
➤ eché una carta al buzón I posted a letter.

caballería ■ cavalry.

caballero *adjetivo* ■ gentlemanly: es muy caballero he's very gentlemanly

el **caballero** ■ gentleman *(plural* gentlemen): estas cosas no deberían pasar entre caballeros these things shouldn't happen among gentlemen

➤ damas y caballeros ladies and gentlemen.

el **caballo**

1. horse: el caballo es mi animal favorito the horse is my favourite animal
2. knight: no te conviene mover el caballo o te haré jaque al rey it's not a good idea for you to move your knight because I'll check your king
➤ montar a caballo to ride.

la **cabaña** ■ cabin: fuimos a pasar el fin de semana a la cabaña we went to spend the weekend at the cabin.

cabecear [1] *verbo*

1. to nod off: el viejo cabeceaba frente a la tele the old man was nodding off in front of the TV
2. to head: el jugador cabeceó y marcó un gol the player headed the ball and scored a goal

la **cabecera**

1. headboard: la cabecera de la cama era de madera the headboard of the bed was made of wood
2. head: el invitado se sentó a la cabecera de la mesa the guest sat down at the head of the table.

el **cabello** ■ hair: tiene un cabello suave y brillante she has smooth, glossy hair.

caber [38] *verbo* ■ **to fit:** en esta habitación caben diez personas ten people fit in this room; estos pantalones ya no me caben these trousers don't fit me anymore.

la **cabeza**

1. **head:** me duele la cabeza I've got a headache
2. **person:** sale a 100 euros por cabeza it's 100 euros per person
> **a la cabeza** at the head: el sacerdote iba a la cabeza de la procesión the priest was at the head of the procession
> **perder la cabeza** to lose one's head: perdió la cabeza por esa chica he lost his head over that girl
> **romperse la cabeza** to rack one's brains: me he roto la cabeza tratando de entender este ejercicio I've racked my brains trying to understand this exercise
> **cabeza de ajo** clove of garlic
> **cabeza de familia** head of the household
> **a ver si sientas la cabeza** let's see if you can settle down.

la **cabina**

1. **booth:** hay una cabina telefónica a dos manzanas there's a telephone box two blocks away
2. *del piloto* **cockpit,** *de los pasajeros* **cabin:** se prendió fuego en la cabina del avión the airplane's cockpit caught on fire.

el **cable**

1. **cable:** se tropezó con un cable he tripped on a cable
2. **message:** recibí un cable del exterior I received a message from abroad
3. **cable television:** tengo cable en casa I have cable television at home.

el **cabo**

1. **end:** pásame el cabo de la cuerda pass me the end of the rope
2. **corporal:** el sargento ordenó al cabo que saliera the sergeant ordered the corporal to leave
3. **cape:** esta costa tiene muchos cabos this coast has many capes
> **llevar a cabo** to carry out: la empresa llevó a cabo un proyecto original the company carried out an original project

> **atar cabos** to put two and two together: el inspector ató cabos hasta dar con el asesino the inspector put two and two together and found the murderer.

la **cabra** ■ **goat**
> **estar como una cabra** to be crazy: Rubén está como una cabra Rubén is crazy.

la **caca** *Informal* ■ **poo** *UK*, **poop** *US:* la calle está llena de cacas de perro the street is full of dog poo.

el **cacahuete** ■ **peanut**
> **mantequilla de cacahuete** peanut butter.

el **cacao** ■ **cocoa.**

el **cacareo** ■ **crowing:** el cacareo de los gallos era insoportable the crowing of the roosters was unbearable.

la **cacería** ■ **hunt:** la cacería del zorro the fox hunt.

la **cacerola** ■ **pan:** puse las verduras crudas en la cacerola I put the raw vegetables in the pan.

el **cacharro**

1. **piece of junk:** el sótano está lleno de cacharros viejos the basement is full of old pieces of junk
2. **piece of pot:** todavía tengo que lavar los cacharros de la comida I still have to wash the pots from dinner.

el **cachete** ■ **slap:** el padre le pegó un cachete the father gave the boy a slap.

el **cachorro** , la **cachorra**

1. *de perro* **puppy** (*plural* **puppies**)
2. *de gato* **kitten**
3. *de león, oso* **cub.**

el **cacique**

1. **chief:** el cacique de la tribu era un hombre de gran sabiduría the chief of the tribe was a man of great wisdom
2. **political leader:** la región está dominada por caciques corruptos the region is dominated by corrupt political leaders.

el **cactus** (*plural* los cactus) ■ **cactus** (*plural* cacti).

cada *adjetivo*

1. **each:** cada alumno trajo su propio cuaderno each student brought his own notebook
2. **every:** viene a casa cada quince días he comes home every two weeks
   - dices cada cosa you say the funniest things
   - cada vez más more and more
   - cada vez menos less and less.

el **cadáver** ■ corpse.

la **cadena**

1. **chain:** me regalaron una cadena de plata they gave me a silver chain; el magnate compró una cadena de hoteles the magnate bought a chain of hotels
2. **channel:** una sola cadena de televisión transmitirá el partido only one television channel will show the game
   - cadena perpetua life imprisonment: lo condenaron a cadena perpetua they sentenced him to life imprisonment; una cadena de música a music system
   - una cadena montañosa a mountain range
   - tirar de la cadena to flush the toilet.

la **cadera** ■ hip.

el **cadete** ■ cadet: los cadetes tienen libre el fin de semana the cadets have the weekend free.

caducado, da *adjetivo* ■ expired: mi pasaporte está caducado my passport has expired.

la **caducidad**

3. *de medicamentos* expiry UK, expiration US: es importante leer la fecha de caducidad it's important to read the expiry date
   - estar caducado to be past its sell-by date: los yogures están caducados the yoghurts are past their sell-by date.

caer [39] *verbo*

1. **to fall:** cayó un meteorito a meteorite fell; cayó la dictadura the dictatorship fell; este año el carnaval cae en marzo this year the carnival falls in March
2. **to understand:** ahora caigo now I understand
3. **to like:** Antonio me cae muy bien I like Antonio very much

- dejar caer to drop: dejé caer el vaso I dropped the glass
- caer en la cuenta to realize: caí en la cuenta de que mentía I realized that he was lying
- me cae mal el pescado frito fried fish disagrees with me
- al caer la noche at nightfall
- estar al caer to be about to arrive: Ana está al caer Ana's about to arrive
- los exámenes están al caer the exams are just around the corner

caerse *verbo pronominal* ■ to fall: se cayó por la escalera she fell down the stairs.

el **café**

1. **coffee:** todas las mañanas tomo café I drink coffee every morning
2. **café:** me encontré con Juan en el café de la esquina I met Juan at the café on the corner
   - café con leche UK white coffee, regular coffee US
   - café cortado espresso with a dash of milk
   - café descafeinado decaffeinated coffee
   - café solo black coffee.

la **cafetera**

1. *para preparar café* coffee machine
2. *para servir café* coffee pot.

la **cafetería** ■ café.

la **caída** ■ fall: como consecuencia de una caída, se rompió una pierna because of a fall, he broke his leg; los precios sufrieron una fuerte caída prices suffered a sharp fall.

el **caimán** *(plural los caimanes)* ■ alligator.

la **caja**

1. **box:** me han regalado una caja de madera they gave me a wooden box
2. **checkout:** tenemos que pagar en la caja we have to pay at the checkout
   - caja de ahorros savings bank
   - caja de cambios gearbox
   - caja fuerte safe
   - caja negra black box.

el **cajero** , la **cajera** ■ cashier: el cajero me cobró de menos the cashier undercharged me un cajero automático an automated teller machine, cashpoint machine UK.

el cajón (plural los cajones) ■ drawer: guardo las medias en el cajón izquierdo I keep my stockings in the left drawer.

la cal ■ lime

cerrar a cal y canto to close tight.

la cala ■ cove.

el calabacín (plural los calabacines) ■ courgette UK, zucchini US.

la calabaza ■ pumpkin

dar calabazas to give somebody the cold shoulder.

el calamar ■ squid.

el calambre
1. cramp: me dio un fuerte calambre en la pierna I got a strong cramp in my leg
2. shock: si lo tocas te puede dar un calambre if you touch it you could get a shock.

la calamidad ■ disaster: el accidente fue una gran calamidad the accident was a terrible disaster.

calar [1] verbo ■ to soak: la tormenta nos caló hasta los huesos the storm soaked us to the skin

calarse verbo pronominal
1. to get soaked
2. to stall: se me caló el coche my car stalled.

la calavera ■ skull.

el calcetín (plural los calcetines) ■ sock.

el calcio ■ calcium.

la calculadora ■ calculator.

calcular [1] verbo
1. to calculate: calcula la cantidad total y multiplícala por dos calculate the total amount and multiply it by two
2. to reckon: calculo que llegaremos antes del mediodía I reckon we'll arrive before noon.

el cálculo
1. estimate: hice un cálculo de los costes I made an estimate of the costs
2. calculus: el cálculo es realmente difícil calculus is really difficult

3. calculation: según mis cálculos, estaremos en casa para la cena according to my calculations, we will be at home for dinner
4. stone: me operé de unos cálculos en el riñón I was operated on for some kidney stones.

la caldera ■ boiler: las calderas de la fábrica funcionan todo el día the factory's boilers operate all day

la calefacción central central heating.

el caldo ■ broth: haz el arroz en un caldo de gallina cook the rice in chicken stock.

la calefacción (plural las calefacciones) ■ heating: esta casa tiene muy buena calefacción this house has very good heating.

el calendario
1. calendar: en el calendario solar el año tiene aproximadamente 365 días by the solar calendar the year has approximately 365 days; marca los días festivos en el calendario mark the holidays on the calendar
2. schedule: el calendario para el proyecto es el siguiente the schedule for the project is the following.

el calentador ■ heater: el calentador se ha roto the heater has broken.

calentar [14] verbo
1. to heat up: calienta la comida heat up the food
2. to warm up: necesito calentar antes del partido I need to warm up before the match.

la calidad ■ quality: este mueble es de muy buena calidad this piece of furniture is very good quality

la calidad de vida quality of life.

caliente adjetivo
1. hot: la plancha está muy caliente the iron is very hot
2. heated: es una discusión caliente it's a heated discussion.

la calificación (plural las calificaciones) ■ mark: saqué muy buenas calificaciones en el examen I got very good marks in the exam.

calificar [8] *verbo*
1. **to describe:** lo calificó de atrevido she described him as daring
2. **to grade:** los profesores calificaron generosamente the teachers graded generously.

callar [1] *verbo* ■ **to keep quiet:** en estas circunstancias prefiero callar under these circumstances I prefer to keep quiet

callarse *verbo pronominal* ■ **to stop talking:** todos se callaron cuando el viejo empezó a hablar everybody stopped talking when the old man began to speak
> callarse la boca to shut up: ¡cállate la boca! shut up!

la **calle** ■ street
> en la calle out: el delincuente ya está en la calle the delinquent is out already
> calle peatonal pedestrian street.

el **callejón** (*plural* los callejones) ■ alley: un callejón sin salida dead end.

el **callo**
1. **callus:** tengo un callo en la mano izquierda I have a callus on my left hand
2. **corn:** tengo un callo en el pie derecho I have a corn on my right foot.

la **calma** ■ calm: disfruto mucho la calma del campo I really enjoy the calm of the countryside
> mantengan la calma keep calm
> no pierdas la calma don't lose your cool.

el **calmante**
1. **painkiller:** tomé un calmante para el dolor de cabeza I took a painkiller for my headache
2. **tranquillizer** *UK,* **tranquilizer** *US:* le dio un calmante para los nervios she gave him a tranquillizer for his nerves.

calmar [1] *verbo*
1. **to calm:** la niña calmó a su hermano con palabras suaves the girl calmed her brother with gentle words
2. **to relieve:** la aspirina calma el dolor de cabeza aspirin relieves headaches

calmarse *verbo pronominal* ■ **to calm down:** cálmate, que ya llegamos calm down, we'll arrive soon.

el **calor** ■ **heat:** no aguanto este calor I can't stand this heat
> ha hecho mucho calor estos días it's been really hot recently
> tengo calor I'm hot.

la **caloría** ■ calorie.

calvo, va *adjetivo* ■ bald.

la **calzada** ■ road.

el **calzado** ■ footwear: aquí el calzado es de muy buena calidad the footwear is very good quality here.

calzar [10] *verbo* ■ **to put shoes on:** los niños están descalzos, cálzalos the children are barefoot, put their shoes on
> ¿qué número calzas? what size shoe do you take?

calzarse *verbo pronominal* ■ **to put one's shoes on:** cálzate, que vamos a salir put your shoes on, we're going out.

los **calzoncillos** ■ underpants, underwear
> se te ven los calzoncillos your underpants are showing.

la **cama** ■ **bed:** hacer la cama to make one's bed
> una cama individual a single bed
> una cama de matrimonio a double bed.

la **cámara** ■ **camera:** me voy a comprar una cámara de fotos digital I'm going to buy myself a digital camera
> una cámara de aire an air chamber
> una cámara frigorífica a cold store
> la Cámara de los Lores The House of Lords.

la **camarera** ■ waitress.

el **camarero** ■ waiter.

el **camarón** (*plural* los camarones) ■ **prawn** *UK,* **shrimp** *US.*

el **camarote** ■ cabin: este barco tiene 400 camarotes this ship has 400 cabins.

cambiar [1] *verbo*
1. **to change:** Pedro ha cambiado mucho últimamente Pedro has changed a lot recently; ayúdame a cambiar las sábanas help me change the sheets

2. to exchange: ¿dónde puedo cambiar dinero? where can I exchange money?

3. to trade: te cambio mis medias rojas por las tuyas verdes I'll trade my red stockings for your green ones

> cambiar de idea to change one's mind

> cambiar de ropa to change clothes

cambiarse *verbo pronominal* ■ to change: este vestido está sucio, me voy a cambiar this dress is dirty, I'm going to change

> cambiarse de casa to move: se han cambiado de casa, ya no somos vecinos they've moved, we are no longer neighbours.

el **cambio**

1. change: en las sociedades modernas, los cambios suceden muy rápido in modern societies, changes happen very rapidly; el cajero me dio mal el cambio the cashier gave me the wrong change

2. exchange: no se admiten cambios ni devoluciones exchanges and refunds are not allowed

3. small change: no tengo cambio para el autobús I don't have small change for the bus

4. gearshift: este coche es automático, no tiene cambio this car is automatic, it doesn't have a manual gearbox

> en cambio on the other hand: a mí me gusta el rojo, en cambio él prefiere el azul I like the red one; on the other hand, he prefers the blue one.

el **camello** ■ camel.

la **camilla**

1. *en una ambulancia* stretcher

2. *en la consulta* couch.

caminar [1] *verbo* ■ to walk.

el **camino**

1. *de un pueblo a otro* route: tomemos el camino más corto let's take the shortest route

2. *de una casa a otra* path: el camino no es muy ancho the path is not very wide

3. way: fuimos a mi casa y por el camino compramos una pizza we went to my house and on the way we bought a pizza; ya están de camino they're on their way

CAMINO DE SANTIAGO

From the Middle Ages onwards, many devotees began to travel the **camino de Santiago** (the Way of Saint James) on a pilgrimage to the tomb of the apostle. The tradition of the pilgrimage, which had almost died out by the 17th century, has attracted new followers since the 1960s due to the efforts of the Catholic church. Nowadays, the **camino de Santiago** is always busy, especially during jubilee years, the holy years when Saint James's Day (25th July) falls on a Sunday. The pilgrims, who come from every corner of Europe, enter Spain by two Pyrenean mountain passes — Somport and Roncesvalles — and stop off at the monasteries, churches and refuges built for this purpose.

el **camión** *(plural* los camiones*)* ■ **lorry** UK *(plural* **lorries***)*, **truck** US.

la **camioneta** ■ van.

la **camisa** ■ shirt.

la **camiseta**

1. *exterior* T-shirt

2. *interior* vest UK, undershirt US.

el **camisón** *(plural* los camisones*)* ■ nightdress.

el **campamento**

1. camp: levantaron el campamento junto al río they set up camp next to the river

2. camping: estuvimos de campamento una semana we went camping for a week.

la **campana** ■ bell.

la **campanada** ■ peal: son las 2, acaban de sonar 2 campanadas it's two o'clock, two peals just rang out

> las 12 campanadas the 12 chimes of midnight.

la **campaña** ■ campaign: la campaña contra el tabaco durará todo un mes the campaign against tobacco use will last a whole month

> una campaña electoral electoral campaign

> una campaña publicitaria advertising campaign.

el **campeón** , la **campeona** (*plural* los campeones) ■ champion.

el **campeonato** ■ championship.

el **campesino** , la **campesina** ■ peasant.

el **camping**
1. camping: ir de camping to go camping
2. campsite: estábamos en un camping we were on a campsite.

el **campo**
1. country: mis abuelos viven en el campo my grandparents live in the country
2. countryside: el campo está muy bonito en esta época the countryside looks very pretty right now
3. field: un campo de trigo a field of wheat
4. pitch *UK*, field *US:* un campo de fútbol a football pitch
5. camp: un campo de refugiados a refugee camp.

la **cana** ■ white hair.

Canadá ■ Canada.

canadiense *adjetivo*

En inglés, los adjetivos que se refieren a un país o una región se escriben con mayúscula:

Canadian: tiene acento canadiense he has a Canadian accent

el/la **canadiense**

En inglés, los gentilicios se escriben con mayúscula:

Canadian: los canadienses the Canadians.

el **canal**
1. channel: este canal es muy malo this channel is very poor; un canal de riego an irrigation channel
2. canal
  ➤ el Canal de Panamá the Panama Canal
  ➤ el Canal de la Mancha The English Channel.

Canarias ■ the Canaries
➤ las islas Canarias the Canary Islands.

canario, ria *adjetivo*

En inglés, los adjetivos que se refieren a un país o una región se escriben con mayúscula:

of the Canary Isles: los plátanos canarios son deliciosos the bananas of the Canary Isles are delicious

el **canario** , la **canaria**

En inglés, los gentilicios se escriben con mayúscula:

Canary Islander: los canarios the Canary Islanders

el **canario** ■ canary (*plural* canaries).

la **canasta** ■ basket.

cancelar [1] *verbo* ■ to cancel.

el **cáncer** ■ cancer: la lucha contra el cáncer the fight against cancer.

la **cancha**
1. *de fútbol* pitch *UK* field *US*
2. *de baloncesto, tenis* court.

la **canción** (*plural* las canciones) ■ song: una canción de amor a love song.

el **candado** ■ padlock.

el **candelabro** ■ candelabra.

el **candidato** , la **candidata** ■ candidate: ser candidato a la presidencia to be a candidate for the presidency.

la **canela** ■ cinnamon.

el **cangrejo** ■ crab.

el **canguro**
1. *animal* kangaroo
2. *persona* babysitter.

la **canica** ■ marble
➤ jugar a las canicas to play marbles: le gusta jugar a las canicas he likes playing marbles.

la **canilla**
➤ canilla de la pierna shinbone
➤ canilla del brazo armbone.

el **canino** ■ canine tooth (*plural* canine teeth).

la **canoa** ■ canoe.

canoso, sa *adjetivo* ■ white-haired.

cansado, da *adjetivo* ■ tired: estoy cansado I'm tired.

el cansancio ■ exhaustion

> ¡qué cansancio! I'm exhausted!

cansar [1] *verbo* ■ to tire: estudiar muchas horas seguidas me cansa studying for hours in a row tires me

> cansarse de algo to get tired of something: me cansé de sus mentiras I got tired of his lies.

Cantabria ■ Cantabria.

cantábrico, ca *adjetivo*

En inglés, los adjetivos que se refieren a un océano se escriben con mayúscula:

Cantabrian: la costa cantábrica the Cantabrian coast

el Cantábrico ■ the Cantabrian Sea.

cántabro, bra *adjetivo*

En inglés, los adjetivos que se refieren a un país o una región se escriben con mayúscula:

Cantabrian

el cántabro , la cántabra

En inglés, los gentilicios se escriben con mayúscula:

Cantabrian: los cántabros the Cantabrians.

la cantante ■ singer.

cantar [1] *verbo* ■ to sing: canta muy bien she sings very well.

la cantidad *(plural* las cantidades)

1. a lot: Luisa tiene cantidad de fotos Luisa has a lot of photos
2. quantity *(plural* quantities): hay que considerar la calidad más que la cantidad one must consider quality above quantity; ¿qué cantidad de harina pongo? what quantity of flour do you need?

el canto

1. singing: María estudia canto, quiere ser soprano María studies singing; she wants to be a soprano
2. song: es bonito el canto de ese canario that canary's song is beautiful.

la caña ■ cane

> caña de azúcar sugar cane

> caña de pescar fishing rod

> caña de cerveza small glass of beer.

la cañería ■ pipes: pusimos cañerías nuevas en la casa we put new pipes in the house.

el cañón *(plural* los cañones)

1. cannon: en ese fuerte hay varios cañones antiguos in that fort there are several old cannons
2. canyon: hay muchos cañones en esa cordillera there are a lot of canyons in that mountain range

> el Gran Cañón the Grand Canyon.

el caos ■ chaos.

la capa

1. cloak: Caperucita llevaba una capa roja Little Red Riding Hood wore a red cloak
2. layer: sacude la capa de polvo que hay sobre los muebles brush off the layer of dust that is on the furniture

> la capa de ozono the ozone layer.

la capacidad

1. capacity: la capacidad de esta jarra es un litro the capacity of this jar is one litre
2. talent: tiene mucha capacidad para las ciencias she has a lot of talent for sciences
3. ability: la capacidad de adaptación al clima the ability to adapt to the climate.

el caparazón *(plural* los caparazones) ■ shell: la tortuga escondió patas y cabeza en su caparazón the turtle hid his feet and head inside his shell.

capaz *adjetivo* ■ capable: es un alumno muy capaz he's a very capable student

> ser capaz de algo to be capable of something: Pedro no sería capaz de algo así Pedro wouldn't be capable of something like that.

la capilla ■ chapel.

la capital ■ capital: Madrid es la capital de España Madrid is the capital of Spain.

el capital ■ capital: el capital necesario para abrir ese negocio es muy grande the capital necessary to open this business is a lot.

el capitalismo ■ capitalism.

el **capitán** , la **capitana** (plural los capitanes) ■ captain.

el **capítulo** ■ chapter.

el **capó** ■ bonnet UK, hood US: el capó del coche está sucio the car bonnet is dirty.

el **capricho** ■ whim: su tía le consiente todos los caprichos her aunt caters to all her whims.

la **cápsula** ■ capsule: estas cápsulas son antibióticos these capsules are antibiotics; fueron a la luna en una cápsula espacial they went to the moon in a space capsule.

captar [1] verbo

1. to grasp: no capté lo que me dijiste I didn't grasp what you told me
2. to receive: el televisor está estropeado, no capta las imágenes the television is broken; it doesn't receive the pictures.

capturar [1] verbo ■ to capture: la policía enseguida capturó a los asesinos the police immediately captured the murderers.

la **capucha** ■ hood.

la **cara**

1. face: ve a lavarte la cara go and wash your face
2. cheek: ¡qué cara! what a cheek!
3. side: la otra cara de un problema the other side of a problem
> cara o cruz heads or tails
> dar la cara to face the consequences of one's actions
> cara a cara face to face
> tener buena cara to look well
> tener mala cara to look ill.

el **caracol** ■ snail.

el **carácter** (plural los caracteres) ■ character: una mujer de carácter a woman of character
> tener buen carácter to be good-natured
> tener mal carácter to be bad-tempered.

la **característica** ■ characteristic: una característica de su escritura es que siempre es muy sencilla a characteristic of his writing is that it's always very simple.

característico, ca adjetivo ■ characteristic: la alegría es un rasgo característico de los optimistas happiness is characteristic of optimists.

el **caramelo** ■ sweet UK, candy US (plural candies): no comas caramelos antes del almuerzo don't eat sweets before lunch.

el **carbón** (plural los carbones) ■ coal
> carbón de leña charcoal.

la **carcajada** ■ guffaw: oímos una carcajada we heard a guffaw
> reírse a carcajadas to roar with laughter: nos reímos a carcajadas con las historias de Pablo we roared with laughter at Pablo's stories.

la **cárcel** ■ prison: aún no ha salido de la cárcel he still hasn't got out of prison.

el **cardenal**

1. cardinal: los cardenales eligen al Papa the cardinals elect the Pope
2. bruise: tuvo un accidente y está lleno de cardenales he had an accident and is covered with bruises.

cardíaco, ca adjetivo ■ cardiac
> un paro cardiaco a cardiac arrest.

cardinal adjetivo ■ cardinal: los puntos cardinales the cardinal points.

la **cardiología** ■ cardiology.

el **cardo** ■ thistle.

la **carencia** ■ lack: la carencia de alimentos ocasiona debilidad lack of food causes weakness.

la **carga**

1. load: la carga máxima es de 30 kilos the maximum load is 30 kilos
2. burden: puedes quedarte en casa, no eres ninguna carga you can stay in my home, you're not a burden
> carga y descarga loading and unloading.

el **cargamento** ■ load: el camión traía un cargamento de manzanas the lorry was carrying a load of apples.

cargar [12] verbo

1. to load: cargamos las maletas en el coche y salimos hacia la estación we loaded the suit-

cases into the car and left for the station; **cargó el rifle y empezó a disparar** he loaded the rifle and began to shoot

2. **to charge: necesito cargar la batería del móvil** I need to charge the mobile phone battery.

el cargo ■ position: **la presidencia es el principal cargo de gobierno** the presidency is the foremost governmental position.

la caricia ■ caress: **una tierna caricia** a gentle caress

▷ **hacerle una caricia a alguien** to caress somebody: **le hizo una caricia a su hijo** she caressed her son.

la caridad ■ charity (plural **charities**).

la caries (plural **las caries**)

1. **tooth decay: este dentífrico previene las caries** this toothpaste prevents tooth decay

2. **cavity** (plural **cavities**): **voy al dentista a que me arregle tres caries** I'm going to the dentist so he can fill three cavities.

el cariño

1. **affection: había mucho cariño en ese hogar** there was a lot of affection in that home

2. **liking: al cabo de una semana, el perro y el gato se tomaron cariño** by the end of one week, the dog and the cat took a liking to each other

3. **darling: cariño, espera un momento** wait a moment, darling

4. **caress**

▷ **hacerle cariños a alguien** to caress somebody: **siempre está haciéndole cariños al bebé** she's always caressing the baby.

el carnaval ■ carnival

CARNAVAL

Carnival is celebrated in many parts of Spain and South American countries, lasting between three days and a week before Ash Wednesday, the beginning of Lent. The festivities include costume parades, entertainment, and water displays. In some regions of South America, indigenous rituals are incorporated into the celebrations. Among the more famous Spanish carnivals are the ones in Cádiz and Santa Cruz de Tenerife.

la carne ■ meat

▷ **carne de cerdo** pork

▷ **carne de cordero** lamb

▷ **carne picada** minced meat UK, ground meat US

▷ **carne picada** ground beef

▷ **carne de cerdo** pork

▷ **carne de vaca** beef.

el carné , **el carnet** ■ card

▷ **carné de conducir** driver's license

▷ **carné de identidad** identity card

▷ **carné de estudiante** student card.

la carnicería ■ butcher's shop.

el carnicero , **la carnicera** ■ butcher.

caro, ra adjetivo ■ expensive: **siempre compra ropa cara** she always buys expensive clothes.

caro adverbio ■ expensive: **el viaje salió demasiado caro** the trip came out too expensive.

la carpeta ■ folder.

el carpintero , **la carpintera** ■ carpenter.

la carrera

1. **race: con mucho esfuerzo gané la carrera** with a lot of effort I won the race

2. **degree: mi hermano está estudiando la carrera de medicina** my brother is studying for a degree in medicine

3. **career: mi carrera es muy importante para mí** my career is very important to me

4. **ladder: tengo una carrera en las medias** I've got a ladder in my stockings.

la carreta ■ cart.

la carretera ■ road.

el carril ■ lane

▷ **un carril bici** a bicycle lane

▷ **un carril bus** a bus lane.

el carro

1. **cart: un carro tirado por dos caballos** a horse-drawn cart

2. trolley *UK*, cart *US*: **voy a buscar un carro para las maletas** I'm going to look for a trolley for the suitcases
> **un carro de supermercado** grocery cart.

la **carroza**
1. *arrastrada por caballos* **carriage**
2. *en cabalgata* **float.**

el **carrusel** *(plural* los carruseles)* ■ **roundabouts** *UK*, **merry-go-round** *US*.

la **carta**
1. **letter: recibí una carta de mi prima** I received a letter from my cousin
2. **card: jugamos a las cartas toda la tarde** we played cards all afternoon
3. **menu: este restaurante tiene una carta muy variada** this restaurant has a very varied menu.

el **cartel** *(plural* los carteles)*
1. **sign: ahí hay un cartel de "stop"** there's a stop sign there
2. **poster: un cartel publicitario** an advertising poster.

la **cartelera** ■ **what's on section** *UK*, **theater section** *US*: **no veo la película en la cartelera de este diario** I don't see the film in the what's on section of this newspaper
> **la obra estuvo más de un año en cartelera** the play ran for more than a year.

la **cartera**
1. *para dinero* **wallet, billfold** *US*
2. *para documentos* **briefcase**
3. *de colegio* **satchel.**

el **cartero** , la **cartera**
hombre **postman** *UK*, **mailman** *US* ; *mujer* **postwoman** *UK*, **mailwoman** *US*.

el **cartón** *(plural* los cartones)*
1. **cardboard: necesito una caja de cartón para los zapatos** I need a cardboard box for the shoes
2. **carton: hemos comprado dos cartones de leche** we've bought two cartons of milk.

el **cartucho** ■ **cartridge: necesito cartuchos para la impresora** I need cartridges for the printer; **no quedan cartuchos en la escopeta** there are no cartridges left in the shotgun.

la **cartulina** ■ **card.**

la **casa**
1. **house: vive en una casa pequeña** she lives in a small house
2. **home: estoy en casa** I'm at home
> **bienvenido a casa** welcome home.

casar [1] *verbo* ■ **to marry: el sacerdote los casó en una ceremonia rápida** the priest married them in a quick ceremony

casarse *verbo pronominal* ■ **to get married: se casaron hace tres años** they got married three years ago
> **casarse con** to get married to: **Ana se casó con Pedro** Ana got married to Pedro.

la **cascada** ■ **waterfall.**

la **cáscara**
1. *de huevo, nuez* **shell**
2. *de limón, naranja* **rind.**

el **casco** ■ **helmet: siempre lleva casco** he always wears a helmet.

los **cascos** ■ **headphones: he perdido los cascos del discman** I've lost my discman headphones.

casero, ra *adjetivo* ■ **homemade: la comida casera es la más rica** homemade food is the most delicious

el **casero** , la **casera**
hombre **landlord,** *mujer* **landlady: mi casero vino a cobrar el alquiler** my landlord came to collect the rent.

el/la **casete** ■ **cassette.**

casi *adverbio*
1. **almost: son casi las once, vamos a dormir** it's almost eleven o'clock, let's go to sleep
2. **hardly: casi no he dormido en toda la noche** I hardly slept all night.

la **casilla**
1. **box: complete todas las casillas** complete all the boxes
2. **space: te saltaste una casilla, vuelve para atrás** you skipped a space, go back.

el casillero

1. compartment: en este casillero tengo las cuentas y en aquél las cartas I have the bills in this compartment, and the letters in that one
2. locker: dejó la ropa en un casillero he left his clothes in a locker.

el caso ■ case: el caso del asesino en serie fue muy comentado the case of the serial killer was discussed a lot

> hacer caso to pay attention: hazle caso a tu madre pay attention to your mother; no le hagas caso a tu hermano cuando se burla de ti don't pay attention to your brother when he makes fun of you.

la caspa ■ dandruff.

la castaña ■ chestnut

castaño, ña adjetivo ■ chestnut

el castaño ■ chestnut tree.

castellano, na adjetivo

En inglés, los adjetivos que se refieren a un país o una región se escriben con mayúscula:

Castilian: hemos visitado varios pueblos castellanos we have visited some Castilian towns

el castellano , la castellana

En inglés, los gentilicios se escriben con mayúscula:

Castilian: los castellanos the Castilians

el castellano

En inglés, los idiomas se escriben con mayúscula.

Spanish: estamos aprendiendo castellano we're learning Spanish.

castigar [12] verbo ■ to punish: los niños se portaron mal y su padre los castigó the children behaved badly and their father punished them.

el castigo ■ punishment: como castigo, lavarás los platos hasta fin de mes as a punishment, you will wash the dishes until the end of the month.

Castilla-La Mancha ■ Castile and La Mancha.

Castilla y León ■ Castile and León.

el castillo ■ castle.

la casualidad ■ coincidence: fue una casualidad que nos encontráramos en el parque it was a coincidence that we met in the park

> de casualidad by coincidence: nos encontramos en el parque de casualidad we met in the park by coincidence
> por casualidad by chance: ¿por casualidad viste a mi perro? by chance did you see my dog?

catalán, catalana adjetivo

En inglés, los adjetivos que se refieren a un país o una región se escriben con mayúscula:

Catalan: las cuatro provincias catalanas son Gerona, Lérida, Barcelona y Tarragona the four Catalan provinces are Gerona, Lérida, Barcelona and Tarragona

el catalán , la catalana

En inglés, los gentilicios se escriben con mayúscula:

Catalan: los catalanes the Catalans

el catalán

En inglés, los idiomas se escriben con mayúscula.

Catalan.

Cataluña ■ Catalonia.

el catálogo ■ catalogue UK, catalog US.

la catarata

1. waterfall: visitamos las cataratas del Iguazú we visited the Iguazú waterfalls
2. cataract: a la abuela la operaron de cataratas they operated on my grandmother's cataracts.

el catarro ■ cold: he pillado un catarro I've caught a cold.

la catástrofe ■ catastrophe.

la catedral ■ cathedral.

la categoría

1. category (plural categories): había tres categorías: principiantes, intermedios y avanzados there were three categories: beginners, intermediate, and advanced

2. **quality:** es un hotel de categoría it's a quality hotel.

católico, ca *adjetivo*

En inglés las religiones y los miembros de una religión se escriben con mayúscula:

Catholic

el **católico** , la **católica** ■ Catholic.

catorce *numeral* ■ **fourteen**

➤ hoy es catorce de octubre today is the fourteenth of October.

el **cauce** ■ bed: el cauce del río se secó the river bed dried up.

el **caucho** ■ rubber.

el **caudillo** ■ leader.

la **causa** ■ cause: descubrieron la causa del incendio they discovered the cause of the fire

➤ a causa de because of: hubo inundaciones a causa de las fuertes lluvias there were floods because of the heavy rain.

causar [1] *verbo* ■ to cause: un cortocircuito causó el incendio a short circuit caused the fire.

cautivo, va *adjetivo* ■ captive

el **cautivo** , la **cautiva** ■ captive.

cavar [1] *verbo* ■ to dig: cavó varios hoyos para plantar flores he dug several holes to plant flowers.

la **caverna** ■ cavern.

la **caza** ■ hunting: mi tío es aficionado a la caza my uncle is fond of hunting.

el **cazador** , la **cazadora** ■ hunter.

la **cazadora** ■ jacket: me he comprado una cazadora I've bought myself a leather jacket.

cazar [10] *verbo* ■ to hunt.

el **cazo**

1. **saucepan:** calienta el agua en un cazo heat the water in a saucepan

2. **ladle:** sirve la sopa con un cazo serve the soup with a ladle.

la **cazuela**

1. **pan:** pon esa cazuela en el horno put that pan in the oven

2. **stew:** comimos una cazuela de marisco deliciosa we ate a delicious seafood stew.

el **CD** *(plural* los CDs*)* ■ **CD.**

el **CD-ROM** *(plural* los CD-ROMs*)* ■ **CD-ROM.**

la **cebolla** ■ onion.

la **cebra** ■ zebra.

ceder [2] *verbo*

1. **to give in:** al final, mi madre cedió y me prestó el coche in the end, my mother gave in and loaned me the car

2. **to give way:** el televisor era demasiado pesado y la mesa cedió the television was too heavy and the table gave way.

la **ceguera** ■ blindness.

la **ceja** ■ eyebrow.

la **celda** ■ cell.

la **celebración** *(plural* las celebraciones*)* ■ celebration.

celebrar [1] *verbo*

1. **to celebrate:** celebró su cumpleaños con una fiesta he celebrated his birthday with a party

2. **to hold:** celebraron la reunión en el salón de actos they held the meeting in the assembly hall.

el **celo®** ■ Sellotape®, *UK.* Scotch tape® *US:* he pegado el póster con celo I've stuck up the poster with sellotape.

los **celos** ■ jealousy: lo hizo por celos she did it out of jealousy

➤ Pepe tiene celos de su hermana Pepe is jealous of his sister

➤ coquetea con otras chicas para darle celos he flirts with other girls to make her jealous.

celoso, sa *adjetivo* ■ **jealous:** es muy celosa she's a jealous person; está celoso de Begoña he's jealous of Begoña.

la **célula** ■ cell.

el **cementerio** ■ cemetery (plural **cemeteries**): el funeral se celebró en el cementerio the funeral was held at the cemetery

> un cementerio de automóviles a scrapyard UK, a salvage yard US.

el **cemento** ■ cement

cemento armado reinforced cement.

la **cena** ■ dinner.

cenar [1] verbo ■ to have dinner: cenamos a las 9 we have dinner at 9 o'clock

> sólo cené pescado I only ate fish for dinner.

el **cenicero** ■ ashtray.

la **ceniza** ■ ash.

el **céntimo** ■ cent: cuesta tres euros y cuarenta céntimos it costs three euros and forty cents

> no tengo ni un céntimo I'm broke.

central adjetivo ■ central.

la **central**

1. oficina central **head office**
2. de energía **power station**

> una central eléctrica a power plant
> una central nuclear a nuclear power plant.

el **centro** ■ center: vivo en el centro de Salamanca I live in the center of Salamanca

> tengo que ir al centro I have to go into town
> las tiendas del centro the downtown stores
> un centro comercial a shopping centre UK, a shopping mall US.

el **ceño** ■ frown

> frunció el ceño he frowned
> lo miró con el ceño fruncido she frowned at him.

cepillar [1] verbo ■ to brush: cepilla el abrigo para sacarle el polvo brush the coat to remove the dust

cepillarse verbo pronominal ■ to brush: se cepilló los dientes he brushed his teeth; se cepilló el pelo he brushed his hair.

el **cepillo** ■ brush

> el cepillo de pelo the hairbrush
> el cepillo de dientes the toothbrush.

la **cera** ■ wax.

la **cerámica** ■ pottery: mi madre estudia cerámica my mother studies pottery

> una cerámica a piece of pottery.

cerca adverbio ■ close: mi casa está muy cerca my house is very close

> ¿hay una farmacia cerca? is there a chemist's nearby?
> queda cerca de la escuela it's near the school
> cerca de 100 personas around 100 people
> me acerqué para verlo de cerca I drew near in order to see it close up
> los exámenes ya están cerca the exams are already coming up soon

la **cerca**

1. de madera, alambre **fence**
2. de piedra **wall**.

cercano, na adjetivo

1. **nearby:** los pueblos cercanos the nearby towns
2. **close:** un pariente cercano a close relative; la zona cercana a la estación the area close to the station

> una cifra cercana al millón a figure approaching a million.

el **cerdo** , la **cerda**

1. animal **pig:** crían cerdos they raise pigs
2. carne **pork:** ayer comimos cerdo yesterday we ate pork

> comí como un cerdo informal I ate like a pig.

el **cereal** ■ cereal: siempre desayuno cereales I always eat cereal for breakfast.

el **cerebro** ■ brain.

la **ceremonia** ■ ceremony (plural **ceremonies**).

la **cereza** ■ cherry (plural **cherries**).

la **cerilla** ■ match: no juegues con cerillas don't play with matches.

el **cero**

1. **zero** (plural **zeroes** o **zeros**), **nought** UK

> el primer número es cero the first number is zero; cero coma dos zero point two, nought point two

2. O *UK* [oʊ], **zero** *US:* mi número de teléfono es dos cuatro cero seis ocho nueve seis my phone number is two four 0 six eight nine six *UK,* my phone number is two four zero six eight nine six *US*

3. *en fútbol* **nil** *UK,* **zero** *US:* tres a cero three-nil

4. *en tenis* **love:** cuarenta a cero forty-love

➤ estamos a dos grados bajo cero it's two degrees below zero

➤ fue un empate a cero it was a no-score draw

➤ tuvimos que empezar desde cero we had to start from scratch.

cerrado, da *adjetivo* ■ **closed:** la tienda estaba cerrada the shop was closed

➤ está cerrado con llave it's locked

➤ deja el grifo cerrado leave the tap off

➤ el sobre venía cerrado the envelope came sealed.

la **cerradura** ■ **lock.**

cerrar [14] *verbo*

1. to close: cerró la ventana he closed the window; la biblioteca cierra a las 5 the library closes at 5

2. to turn off: cierra bien el grifo turn the tap off completely

➤ ¿has cerrado la puerta con llave? have you locked the door?

cerrarse *verbo pronominal* ■ **to close:** la ventana se cerró con el viento the window closed with the wind

➤ se me cerraban los ojos I couldn't keep my eyes open.

el **cerro** ■ **hill.**

el **cerrojo** ■ **bolt.**

certificado, da *adjetivo* ■ **registered:** mandé la carta certificada I sent the letter registered.

el **certificado** ■ **certificate.**

la **cerveza** ■ **beer:** fueron a tomar unas cervezas they went to have a few beers

➤ cerveza de barril draught beer.

el **césped** ■ **lawn**

➤ "prohibido pisar el césped" "keep off the lawn".

la **cesta** ■ **basket**

➤ la cesta de la compra the shopping basket.

el **cesto** ■ **basket**

➤ el cesto de la ropa sucia the laundry basket.

Ceuta ■ **Ceuta.**

ceutí *(plural* ceutíes) *adjetivo* ■ **of** OR **relating to Ceuta.**

el/la **ceutí** ■ **inhabitant** OR **native of Ceuta.**

el **chaleco** ■ **waistcoat** *UK,* **vest** *US*

➤ un chaleco salvavidas a life jacket.

el **champán** *(plural* los champanes) ■ **champagne.**

el **champiñón** *(plural* los champiñones) ■ **mushroom.**

el **champú** *(plural* los champús) ■ **shampoo.**

la **chancleta** ■ **flip-flop.**

el **chándal** *(plural* los chandals O los chándales) ■ **tracksuit.**

el **chantaje** ■ **blackmail:** un caso de chantaje a case of blackmail

➤ le hicieron un chantaje they blackmailed him.

chantajear [1] *verbo* ■ **to blackmail:** lo chantajearon por mucho dinero they blackmailed him for a lot of money.

la **chapa**

1. *de metal, madera* **sheet**

2. *cerradura* **lock**

3. *insignia* **badge**

4. *de botella* **cap.**

el **chaparrón** *(plural* los chaparrones) ■ **downpour.**

chapotear [1] *verbo* ■ **to splash around:** los niños chapotearon en la piscina the children splashed around in the swimming pool.

el **chapuzón** *(plural* los chapuzones) ■ **dip**

➤ nos dimos un chapuzón we went for a dip.

la **chaqueta**

1. *americana* **jacket**

2. *de punto* **cardigan**

➤ una chaqueta de fuerza a straitjacket.

el charco ■ puddle.

la charla

1. chat: estaban de charla they were having a chat

2. talk: dio una charla sobre el medioambiente she gave a talk about the environment.

charlar [1] *verbo* ■ to chat: charlaron de sus novios they chatted about their boyfriends.

charlatán, charlatana *adjetivo* ■ talkative

el charlatán, la **charlatana** ■ chatterbox.

el chasco ■ disappointment: ¡qué chasco! what a disappointment!

> nos llevamos un chasco we were disappointed.

la chatarra ■ junk.

el chaval *(plural* los chavales*)* ■ kid: los chavales del pueblo están en la plaza the kids of the village are in the square

> estar hecho un chaval to look young: a sus 60 años está hecho un chaval he looks young for 60.

el cheque ■ cheque *UK*, check *US*

> un cheque de viaje a traveller's cheque *UK*, a traveler's check *US*.

el chichón *(plural* los chichones*)* ■ bump: tiene un chichón en la cabeza he has a bump on his head.

el chicle ■ chewing gum: le gusta mascar chicle she likes to chew chewing gum

> ¿me das un chicle? may I have a piece of chewing gum?

la chica ■ girl: es una chica muy simpática she's a very nice girl.

chico, ca *adjetivo*

1. *de tamaño* small: el baño es muy chico the bathroom is very small; estos pantalones me quedan chicos these trousers are too small for me

2. *de edad* young: cuando era chica jugaba con él when she was young she played with him

el chico ■ boy: hay diez chicos en mi clase there are ten boys in my class

> los chicos del vecino the neighbour's kids.

el chile ■ chilli pepper *UK*, chili pepper *US*.

Chile ■ Chile.

chileno, na *adjetivo*

En inglés, los adjetivos que se refieren a un país o una región se escriben con mayúscula:

Chilean: el paisaje chileno es muy bonito the Chilean landscape is very beautiful

el chileno, la **chilena**

En inglés, los gentilicios se escriben con mayúscula:

Chilean: los chilenos the Chileans.

chillar [1] *verbo*

1. *una persona* to scream

2. *un cerdo* to squeal

3. *un ratón* to squeak

4. *una gaviota* to squawk.

la chimenea

1. fireplace: nos sentamos frente a la chimenea we sat down in front of the fireplace

2. chimney: las chimeneas de la fábrica the factory chimneys.

el chimpancé *(plural* los chimpancés*)* ■ chimpanzee.

China ■ China.

chino, na *adjetivo*

En inglés, los adjetivos que se refieren a un país o una región se escriben con mayúscula:

Chinese: la cocina china Chinese cooking

el chino, la **china**

En inglés, los gentilicios se escriben con mayúscula:

Chinese: los chinos the Chinese

el chino

En inglés, los idiomas se escriben con mayúscula:

Chinese.

la **chincheta** ■ drawing pin *UK*, thumb-tack *US*.

el **chiquillo** , la **chiquilla** ■ child.

chirriar [7] *verbo*

1. *una puerta, bisagra* to squeak
2. *los frenos, neumáticos* to squeal.

el **chisme**

1. piece of gossip (*plural* gossip): ella nos explicó un chisme muy interesante she told us an interesting piece of gossip
> se pasó dos horas contando chismes he spent two hours gossiping
2. thing: ¿para qué sirve este chisme? what is this thing for?

la **chispa** ■ spark: saltaron chispas del fuego sparks popped out of the fire
> tiene mucha chispa he's lively.

el **chiste** ■ joke: estaban contando chistes they were telling jokes
> un chiste picante a dirty joke
> un chiste verde a dirty joke.

chocar [8] *verbo* ■ to crash: chocó contra un árbol he crashed into a tree
> choqué con él a la salida I bumped into him on the way out
> chocaron de frente they collided head on
> me choca el vocabulario que usan the vocabulary that they use shocks me
> ¡chócala! give me five!

el **chocolate** ■ chocolate: me encanta el chocolate I love chocolate
> me dio un chocolate she gave me a piece of chocolate
> me tomé un chocolate caliente I drank a hot chocolate.

el/la **chófer**

1. *de un coche, camión* driver
2. *empleado* chauffeur
> una limusina con chófer a chauffeur-driven limousine.

el **choque** ■ crash: hubo un choque frente al colegio there was a crash in front of the school.

el **chorizo** ■ spicy pork sausage.

el **chorro** ■ stream: un chorro de agua a stream of water
> el agua salía a chorros the water was gushing out.

la **choza** ■ hut.

el **chubasquero** ■ raincoat.

la **chuchería** ■ sweet *UK*, candy *US* (*plural* candies).

la **chuleta**

1. chop: una chuleta de cordero a lamb chop
2. crib sheet *UK*, cheat sheet *US:* lo sorprendieron con una chuleta they caught him copying from a crib sheet.

chulo, la *adjetivo*

1. sweet *UK*, cute *US:* mira, ¡qué vestido tan chulo! look, what a sweet dress!
2. cocky: eres un poco chulo you're a bit cocky

chupar [1] *verbo* ■ to suck: no te chupes el dedo don't suck your thumb.

el **chupete** ■ dummy *UK*, pacifier *US*.

el **churro** ■ *twisted strip of deep-fried batter sprinkled with sugar*

LOS CHURROS

Churros are a kind of elongated doughnut which are deep-fried and sprinkled with sugar. They are eaten hot, dipped in a cup of thick hot chocolate. Traditionally, they are served for breakfast, but nowadays they are eaten in the early morning of holidays, such as New Year's Eve, or after a wedding. **Churros** are also served in some cafés with hot chocolate and sold at special bakeries known as **churrerías**.

---

el **cibercafé** ■ Internet café.

la **cicatriz** (*plural* las cicatrices) ■ sacar: le va a quedar una cicatriz en la frente she's going to have a scar on her forehead.

el **ciclismo** ■ cycling: el ciclismo es un deporte bastante popular cycling is a pretty popular sport.

e/la **ciclista** ■ cyclist.

el **ciclo** ■ cycle: el ciclo de las estaciones the cycle of the seasons

mi hermana menor está en el primer ciclo my little sister is in the first year.

el **ciclón** *(plural* los ciclones*)* ■ cyclone.

ciego, ga *adjetivo* ■ blind: es ciega she's blind

se quedó ciego he went blind
es ciego de nacimiento he's blind from birth.

el **cielo**

1. sky *(plural* skies*)*: el cielo estaba despejado the sky was clear
2. heaven: dice que su perro está en el cielo she says that her dog is in heaven.

cien *numeral* ■ a hundred: vinieron cerca de cien personas around a hundred people came; más de cien mil dólares more than a hundred thousand dollars

cien por cien one hundred percent: es cien por cien biodegradable it's one hundred percent biodegradable.

la **ciencia** ■ science: la ciencia moderna modern science; mañana tengo ciencias tomorrow I have science

ciencia ficción science fiction: una película de ciencia ficción a science fiction film
ciencias naturales natural sciences.

científico, ca *adjetivo* ■ scientific

el **científico** , **la** **científica** ■ scientist.

ciento *numeral* ■ a hundred: ciento cincuenta euros a hundred and fifty euros

había cientos de personas there were hundreds of people

por ciento percent: el treinta por ciento de los alumnos thirty percent of the students.

el **cierre**

1. *de collar, pulsera* clasp
2. *de una fábrica, discoteca* closing-down.

cierto, ta *adjetivo*

1. true: ¡eso no es cierto! that's not true!
2. certain: ciertas personas piensan que es culpable certain people think that he's guilty
por cierto by the way: por cierto, ¿no teníamos que ir a la farmacia? by the way, didn't we have to go to the chemist's?

el **ciervo** , **la** **cierva** ■ deer *(plural* deer*)*.

la **cifra** ■ figure: un número de dos cifras a two-figure number.

el **cigarrillo** ■ cigarette.

el **cigarro** ■ cigar.

la **cigüeña** ■ stork.

la **cima** ■ top: subieron hasta la cima they went up to the top

en la cima at the peak: el cantante está en la cima de su carrera the singer is at the peak of his career.

los **cimientos** ■ foundations.

cinco *numeral* ■ five: tiene cinco hijos she has five children; mi hermana tiene cinco años my sister is five years old

son las cinco it's five o'clock
el cinco de abril the fifth of April.

cincuenta *numeral* ■ fifty: unas cincuenta personas some fifty people; tiene cincuenta años he's fifty years old.

el **cine**

1. cinema *UK*, movie theater *US*: fuimos al cine we went to the cinema
un cine de barrio a local cinema
2. cinema: el cine español Spanish cinema
un actor de cine a film actor *UK*, a movie actor *US*.

cínico, ca *adjetivo* ■ cynical: es muy cínico he's very cynical

el **cínico** , **la** **cínica** ■ cynic.

la **cinta**

1. ribbon: se ató el pelo con una cinta she tied her hair back with a ribbon
2. tape: una cinta virgen a blank tape
cinta adhesiva adhesive tape
una cinta de vídeo a videotape
una cinta métrica a tape-measure.

la **cintura** ■ waist: me aprieta en la cintura it's too tight in the waist.

el **cinturón** *(plural* los cinturones*)* ■ belt
cinturón de seguridad safety belt.

el **circo** ■ circus.

el **circuito**

1. *deportes* **track:** una vuelta al circuito a lap around the track
2. *electricidad* **circuit:** circuito cerrado de televisión closed-circuit television.

la **circulación** *(plural* las circulaciones*)*

1. **traffic:** una calle de mucha circulación a street with a lot of traffic
2. **circulation:** tengo muy buena circulación I have very good circulation.

circular [1] *verbo*

1. *en coche* **to drive:** en ese país circulan por la izquierda in that country they drive on the left side of the road
2. *las personas* **to move about:** podemos circular libremente por el colegio we can move about freely through the school
3. *la sangre, el aire* **to circulate:** abrid la puerta para que circule el aire open the door so that the air will circulate
4. *un rumor, una noticia* **to go around:** son rumores que circulan en el colegio they're rumours that are going around the school
   ➤ ¡circulen, por favor! move along, please!

el **círculo** ■ **circle:** dibujamos un círculo we drew a circle; nos sentamos en círculo we sat down in a circle.

la **circunferencia** ■ **circumference.**

la **circunstancia** ■ **circumstance:** no se conocen las circunstancias del accidente the circumstances of the accident are unknown
➤ bajo ninguna circunstancia under no circumstance
➤ dadas las circunstancias given the circumstances.

la **ciruela** ■ **plum.**

la **cirugía** ■ **surgery:** se hizo la cirugía estética she had plastic surgery.

el **cirujano** , la **cirujana** ■ **surgeon.**

el **cisne** ■ **swan.**

la **cita**

1. **appointment:** mi madre tiene una cita con el director my mother has an appointment with the director

2. *romántica* **date:** tiene una cita con su novio she has a date with her boyfriend
3. **quotation:** una cita de Machado a quotation from Machado.

citar [1] *verbo* ■ **to quote:** citó un pasaje de la Biblia he quoted a passage from the Bible
➤ la citaron a las 9 they gave her an appointment for 9 o'clock
➤ se citaban a escondidas they were meeting secretly.

la **ciudad**

> City hace referencia a ciudades grandes y **town** a un pueblo grande o ciudad pequeña.

1. **city** *(plural* **cities***):* en ciudades como Valencia in cities like Valencia
2. **town:** vive en una ciudad de muy pocos habitantes he lives in a town with very few inhabitants
➤ una ciudad balneario a coastal resort
➤ la ciudad universitaria the university campus.

el **ciudadano** , la **ciudadana** ■ **citizen:** es ciudadano español he's a Spanish citizen.

civil *adjetivo* ■ **civil**
➤ derechos civiles civil rights.

la **civilización** *(plural* las civilizaciones*)* ■ **civilization:** las grandes civilizaciones antiguas the great ancient civilizations.

la **clara** ■ **egg white:** hay que batir las claras you have to beat the egg whites.

claro, ra *adjetivo*

1. **clear:** su explicación fue muy clara his explanation was very clear; está claro que miente it's clear that he's lying
2. **light:** prefiere los colores claros she prefers light colours; tiene los ojos verde claro he has light green eyes
➤ no saqué nada en claro de su explicación I couldn't make any sense of his explanation
➤ dejó en claro que no iba a ir he made it clear that he wasn't going to go

claro *adverbio* ■ **clearly:** no lo veo muy claro I don't see it very clearly
➤ tienes que hablarle claro you have to be frank with him

> ¡claro! of course!
> ¡claro que sí! yes, of course!
> ¡claro que no! of course not!

la clase

1. classroom: los alumnos estaban en la clase cuando llegó el maestro the students were in the classroom when the teacher arrived
2. class: esa chica está en mi clase that girl is in my class; hoy tuvimos clase de historia today we had history class
3. type: en esta región crecen varias clases de manzana in this region they grow various types of apple
   clase baja lower class
   clase media middle class
   clase alta upper class.

clásico, ca adjetivo ■ classical: le gusta la música clásica she likes classical music

el **clásico** ■ classic: Cervantes es un clásico de la literatura Cervantes is a literary classic.

clasificar [8] verbo ■ to classify: en la clase de biología clasificamos varias plantas in biology class we classified a number of plants

clasificarse verbo pronominal ■ to quantify: se han clasificado para las semifinales they've qualified for the semi-finals.

clavar [1] verbo ■ to nail: no permiten clavar nada en estas paredes they don't allow anything to be nailed into these walls

clavarse verbo pronominal ■ to prick oneself: cuidado no vayas a clavarte una espina careful not to prick yourself on a thorn; se clavó una aguja she stuck a needle into herself.

la clave

1. key: descubrimos la clave del problema we discovered the key to the problem
2. code: este mensaje está en clave, por eso no lo entendemos this message is in code; that's why we don't understand it.

el **clavel** ■ carnation.

la **clavícula** ■ collar bone.

el **clavo** ■ nail.

la **clemencia** ■ clemency.

el **clero** ■ clergy.

el **cliente**, la **clienta**

1. de empresa client
2. de tienda, restaurante customer
3. de hotel guest.

el **clima** ■ climate.

la **clínica** ■ clinic.

el **clip** (plural los clips)

1. para papel paper clip
2. para pelo hairgrip UK, bobby pin US.

el **cloro** ■ chlorine.

el **club** (plural los clubes) ■ club
un club de tenis a tennis club.

el **cm** (abreviatura de centímetro) ■ cm.

coagularse [1] verbo pronominal ■ to clot: la sangre se coagula rápidamente blood clots quickly.

cobarde adjetivo ■ cowardly
> ¡no seas cobarde! don't be a coward!

la **cobaya** ■ guinea pig.

el **cobrador**, la **cobradora**

1. de recibos, deudas collector
2. de autobús conductor
3. de tren inspector.

cobrar [1] verbo

1. to charge: me cobraron 100 euros por el almuerzo they charged me 100 euros for lunch
2. to earn: cobra 1.000 euros al mes she earns 1,000 euros a month
3. to collect: viene todos los meses a cobrar el alquiler he comes every month to collect the rent
   cóbrese, por favor the bill, please.

el **cobre** ■ copper.

la **cocción** (plural las cocciones) ■ cooking time: este arroz necesita sólo diez minutos de cocción this rice only needs ten minutes cooking time.

cocer [30] *verbo*
1. to cook: cuece el pescado 20 minutos en la cacerola cook the fish for 20 minutes in the pan
2. to boil: cuece las zanahorias 15 minutos you boil the carrots for 15 minutes
   este arroz tarda sólo diez minutos en cocerse this rice only takes ten minutes to cook.

el **coche**
1. *automóvil* car
2. *para bebés* pram UK, baby carriage US
3. *de tren* carriage UK, car US
   un coche de bomberos a fire engine.

la **cochera** ■ garage.

cochino, na *adjetivo* ■ filthy: ¡qué pantalones más cochinos! what filthy trousers!

el **cochino** ■ pig.

el **cocido** ■ stew.

la **cocina**
1. kitchen: esta casa tiene una cocina muy amplia this house has a very spacious kitchen
2. cooker UK, stove US: ayer compramos una cocina nueva yesterday we bought a new cooker
   un curso de cocina a cooking course
   un libro de cocina a cookery book UK, a cookbook US.

cocinar [1] *verbo* ■ to cook: voy a cocinar un pollo I'm going to cook a chicken.

el **cocinero**, la **cocinera** ■ cook: es cocinero he's a cook.

el **coco** ■ coconut.

el **cocodrilo** ■ crocodile.

la **codicia** ■ greed.

el **código** ■ code
   un código de barras a bar code
   un código postal a postcode UK, a zip code US
   un código secreto a password.

el **codo** ■ elbow: se hizo daño en el codo he hurt his elbow.

la **codorniz** *(plural* las codornices) ■ quail.

coger [11] *verbo*
1. to take: coge todas las manzanas que quieras take all the apples you want

2. to catch: la policía lo cogió robando the police caught him stealing
3. to get: voy a coger las entradas I'm going to get the tickets
4. to take, to catch: cogí el autobús para ir al cine I took the bus to go to the cinema
5. to pick up: cogió sus llaves y salió he picked up his keys and left
6. to borrow: ¿puedo coger tu abrigo? may I borrow your coat?

el **cohete** ■ rocket.

coincidir [3] *verbo* ■ to coincide: su cumpleaños coincide con Navidad his birthday coincides with Christmas.

cojear [1] *verbo*
1. to limp: la anciana cojea mucho the old woman limps a lot
2. to wobble: esa mesa cojea that table wobbles.

el **cojín** *(plural* los cojines) ■ cushion.

la **col** ■ cabbage.

la **cola**
1. tail: el pavo real tiene una cola preciosa the peacock has a beautiful tail
2. line: si llegas temprano, no tendrás que hacer cola if you arrive early, you won't have to queue
3. glue: tengo que pegar estos dos papeles con cola I have to paste these two papers with glue.

colaborar [1] *verbo*
1. to work, to collaborate: colaboró con nuestra empresa en la promoción del producto he worked with us in the promotion of the product
2. to help, to collaborate: colabora con la limpieza, no tires papeles al suelo help with the cleaning, don't throw paper on the floor.

el **colador** ■ strainer.

colar [16] *verbo* ■ to strain: cuela la pasta, mientras yo rallo el queso strain the pasta while I grate the cheese

colarse *verbo pronominal* ■ to slip into: siempre hay alguien que se cuela en la fila there is always somebody who pushes in the queue.

la colcha ■ bedspread.

el colchón (plural los colchones) ■ mattress.

la colección (plural las colecciones) ■ collection: tiene una colección de sellos de todo el mundo he has a collection of stamps from all over the world.

coleccionar [1] verbo ■ to collect: hace muchos años que colecciona sellos he has been collecting stamps for many years.

la colega
1. de profesión colleague
2. familiar amigo mate UK, buddy US: es un colega del barrio he's a mate from the neighbourhood.

el colegio ■ school: no le gusta ir al colegio he doesn't like to go to school
▸ un colegio privado a private school, a public school UK
▸ un colegio público a state school.

la cólera ■ anger.

el cólera ■ cholera.

colgar [28] verbo
1. to hang: cuelga tu chaqueta en esa percha hang your jacket on that hanger
2. to hang up: colgó sin despedirse he hung up without saying goodbye
▸ ¡no cuelgue, por favor! hold the line, please!

el cólico ■ colic.

la coliflor ■ cauliflower.

la colina ■ hill.

el collar
1. joya necklace
2. de animal collar.

la colmena ■ beehive.

el colmillo
1. de persona eye-tooth (plural eye-teeth)
2. de elefante tusk
3. de perro fang.

el colmo ■ height: el colmo de arrogancia the height of arrogance
▸ ¡esto es el colmo! this is the limit!

colocar [8] verbo
1. to place: coloca este florero encima de la mesa place this vase on the table
2. to arrange: he colocado los CDs por grupos musicales I've arranged the CDs by musical groups

colocarse verbo pronominal ■ to place oneself: colocaos cerca de los árboles place yourselves close to the trees
▸ colócate en la fila get in line.

Colombia ■ Colombia.

colombiano, na adjetivo

En inglés, los adjetivos que se refieren a un país o una región se escriben con mayúscula:

Colombian

el colombiano , la colombiana

En inglés, los gentilicios se escriben con mayúscula:

Colombian: los colombianos the Colombians.

la colonia
1. perfume: prefiero las colonias florales I prefer floral perfumes
2. colony (plural colonies): España tenía colonias en América y África Spain had colonies in America and Africa
▸ una colonia de verano a summer camp.

colonizar [10] verbo ■ to colonize: los españoles colonizaron una gran parte de América the Spanish colonized a large part of America.

el color ■ colour UK, color US.

colorado, da adjetivo ■ red
▸ ponerse colorado to blush.

colorear [1] verbo ■ to colour UK, to color US: después de dibujar el paisaje, coloréalo after you've drawn the landscape, colour it in.

la columna
1. column: la fachada está adornada con columnas the façade is adorned with columns

2. **spine:** el ortopeda trata los problemas de la columna the orthopaedist treats problems of the spine
> columna vertebral spinal column.

columpiar [1] *verbo* ■ **to push:** ¿puedes columpiarme? can you push me?

columpiarse *verbo pronominal* ■ **to swing.**

el **columpio** ■ **swing.**

la **coma**
1. **comma:** en esa oración no hay que poner coma that sentence doesn't require a comma
2. **point:** tres coma cinco three point five.

el **coma** ■ **coma**
> estar en coma to be in a coma.

el **combate**
1. **battle:** el combate fue largo y dejó varios heridos the battle was long and left a number of wounded people
2. **fight:** hay que implicarse en la lucha contra las drogas we have to get involved in the fight against drugs.

combatir [3] *verbo*
1. **to fight:** estos soldados combatieron en la última guerra these soldiers fought in the last war
2. **to combat:** es importante combatir la desnutrición it's important to combat malnutrition.

la **combinación** *(plural* las combinaciones*)* ■ **combination:** azul y rojo es una buena combinación de colores blue and red is a good colour combination.

el **combustible** ■ **fuel:** este coche necesita combustible urgentemente this car needs fuel urgently.

la **combustión** *(plural* las combustiones*)* ■ **combustion:** la combustión se estudia en clase de química combustion is studied in chemistry class.

la **comedia** ■ **comedy** *(plural* **comedies***)*: Molière es autor de excelentes comedias Molière is the author of excellent comedies
> una comedia musical a musical.

el **comedor**
1. *en casa* **dining room**
2. *en colegio* **cafeteria**
3. *en lugar de trabajo* **canteen.**

comentar [1] *verbo*
1. **to discuss:** en clase comentamos los textos que leemos en casa in class we discuss the texts that we read at home
2. **to comment:** comentó que hacía mucho frío fuera he commented that it was very cold outside.

comenzar [10] *verbo* ■ **to begin:** las clases comienzan a las 8 classes begin at 8 o'clock.

comer [2] *verbo*
1. **to eat:** ¿has comido suficiente? have you eaten enough?
2. *a mediodía* **to lunch:** normalmente comemos a las dos we usually have lunch at two; he comido pollo con patatas I had chicken and chips for lunch.

comercial
1. *zona, relación* **business**
2. *guerra* **trade**
3. *película* **commercial**
> un centro comercial a shopping centre *UK*, a shopping mall *US*.

el **comercio** ■ **commerce**
> comercio electrónico e-commerce.

comestible *adjetivo* ■ **edible**

el **comestible** ■ **food:** hay que llevar comestibles para los tres días de campamento we have to take food for the three days of camp
> tienda de comestibles grocer's shop *UK*, grocery store *US*.

la **cometa** ■ **kite.**

el **cometa** ■ **comet.**

cometer [2] *verbo*
1. **to commit:** cometió muchos crímenes antes de morir he committed many crimes before he died
2. **to make:** cometí un error muy grave I made a very serious mistake.

el **cómic** ■ comic: me encanta leer cómics I love reading comics.

cómico, ca *adjetivo*

1. funny: hizo un comentario muy cómico he made a very funny comment
2. comic: un actor cómico a comic actor

el **cómico** ■ comedian: Cantinflas fue un cómico muy famoso Cantinflas was a very famous comedian.

la **comida**

1. food: me gusta preparar la comida con productos frescos I like to prepare the food with fresh products
2. meal: tomar un comprimido antes de cada comida take one pill before each meal
3. *al mediodía* lunch
4. *por la noche* dinner
> comida basura junk food

COMIDA

In some Spanish-speaking countries (Bolivia, Uruguay, and Venezuela) comida can refer to lunch or dinner, while in other places (Chile, Colombia, and Peru) it only refers to dinner, and in Spain, it only refers to lunch. This can lead to confusion, so it's best to make sure you know which meal the speaker is referring to if you are invited to a comida.

---

el **comienzo** ■ beginning.

las **comillas** ■ quotation marks.

la **comisaría** ■ police station.

como *(adverbio & conjunción)*

■ *adverbio*

1. like: tu bicicleta es como la mía your bicycle is like mine
2. as: eres tan inteligente como ella you're as intelligent as her; como te decía la semana pasada... as I was telling you last week...
3. around: llegaron como a las 10 they arrived around 10 o'clock

■ *conjunción*

1. since: como llegué tarde, no me dejaron entrar since I arrived late, they didn't allow me to enter

2. if: como me desobedezcas, no volverás a salir if you disobey me, you won't go out again.

cómo *adverbio* ■

Cómo takes an accent in direct and indirect questions.

how: ¿cómo te ha ido el examen? how did the exam go?; no sé cómo resolver este problema I don't know how to solve this problem
> ¡cómo me gusta! I really like it!; ¡cómo está de alto! how tall you are!
> ¿cómo dices? sorry?
> ¡cómo no! of course!: ¿me ayudarás? —¡cómo no! will you help me? – of course!

cómodo, da *adjetivo*

1. comfortable: una silla muy cómoda a comfortable chair; ponte cómodo make yourself confortable
2. convenient: tener el metro cerca es muy cómodo having the underground nearby is very convenient.

compacto, ta *adjetivo* ■ compact.

compadecer [22] *verbo* ■ to sympathize with: qué examen tan difícil, te compadezco what a difficult exam, I sympathize with you.

el **compañero** , la **compañera**

1. *en la escuela* classmate
2. *en el trabajo* colleague
3. *pareja* partner.

la **compañía** ■ company *(plural* companies): trabaja en una compañía inglesa she works for an English company; esta noche se presenta una compañía de teatro extranjera a foreign theatre company is performing tonight; mis amigos me hicieron compañía toda la tarde my friends kept me company all afternoon.

comparar [1] *verbo* ■ to compare: no le gusta que la comparen con su hermana she doesn't like to be compared with her sister.

compartir [3] *verbo* ■ to share: compartió con sus amigos los dulces que le regalaron he shared the sweets they gave him with his friends.

el **compás** *(plural* los compases*)*

1. *de música* **rhythm**: bailaron al compás de un tango they danced to the rhythm of a tango
2. **(a pair of) compasses**: dibuja el círculo con un compás draw the circle with a pair of compasses.

la **compasión** *(plural* las compasiones*)* ■ compassion.

la **competencia**

1. **rivalry**: hay mucha competencia entre los dos equipos there is a lot of rivalry between the two teams
2. **competition**: quiso desacreditar a la competencia he wanted to discredit the competition.

competente *adjetivo* ■ **competent.**

la **competición** *(plural* las competiciones*)* ■ **competition**: ha ganado la competición de atletismo she's won the athletics competition.

competir [19] *verbo* ■ **to compete**: esos dos supermercados compiten entre sí those two supermarkets compete against each other; compite mañana por la medalla de oro she competes tomorrow for the gold medal.

complacer [22] *verbo* ■ **to please**: es difícil complacer a todo el mundo it's difficult to please everybody; me complace presentarles a este cantante it's pleasure for me to introduce this singer to you.

el **complejo** ■ **complex**: por aquí se va al complejo deportivo de la universidad this is the way to the university's sports complex; tiene complejo porque es muy alto he has a complex because he's very tall.

el **complemento** ■ **complement**: ese verbo no tiene complemento that verb doesn't have a complement
- **complemento directo** direct object
- **complemento indirecto** indirect object
- **ropa de mujer y complementos** ladies' clothes and accessories.

completar [1] *verbo*

1. **to finish, to complete**: ya ha completado sus estudios he's already finished his studies

2. **to complete**: complete las frases con la palabra adecuada complete the sentences with the right word.

completo, ta *adjetivo*

1. **complete**: acabo de comprar las obras completas de Cervantes I've just bought the complete works of Cervantes
2. **comprehensive**: ese diccionario es muy completo that dictionary is very comprehensive
3. **full**: el avión venía completo the aeroplane was full
4. **complete**: Alberto es un completo desastre Alberto is a complete disaster; se olvidó por completo he completely forgot.

complicado, da *adjetivo* ■ **complicated.**

el/la **cómplice** ■ **accomplice.**

componer [47] *verbo*

1. **to make up**: estos diez jugadores componen el equipo these ten players make up the team
2. **to compose**: Beethoven compuso nueve sinfonías Beethoven composed nine symphonies
- **el equipo se compone de estos diez jugadores** the team consists of these ten players.

la **composición** *(plural* las composiciones*)* ■ **composition**: las composiciones de Chopin son muy bellas Chopin's compositions are very beautiful.

el **comportamiento** ■ **behaviour** *UK*, **behavior** *US*.

el **compositor**, la **compositora** ■ **composer.**

la **compra**

1. **shopping**: deja la compra en la cocina leave the shopping in the kitchen; tengo que ir de compras, nos falta comida I have to go shopping, we need food
2. **purchase**: la última compra que hice fue este libro the last purchase that I made was this book.

comprar [1] *verbo* ■ **to buy**: me he comprado una moto I've bought myself a moped; antes de comprar conviene comparar precios before buying, it's good to compare prices; le he comprado el coche a una amiga I've bought the car from a friend tienes que comprarte zapatos nuevos you have to buy yourself new shoes.

comprender [2] *verbo*

1. to understand: no comprendo por qué no vienes I don't understand why you're not coming

2. to include: el precio comprende dos excursiones a las islas the price includes two trips to the islands.

la compresa ■ sanitary towel *UK,* sanitary napkin *US.*

comprensivo, va *adjetivo* ■ understanding: María es una persona muy comprensiva María is a very understanding person.

comprimir [3] *verbo* ■ to compress.

comprobar [16] *verbo* ■ to check: comprueba que la puerta esté bien cerrada check that the door is closed properly.

comprometerse [2] *verbo pronominal*

1. to promise: se ha comprometido a entregar el trabajo mañana he has promised to hand in the paper tomorrow

2. to commit oneself: no quiso comprometerse, porque no sabía cuándo podría entregar el trabajo he refused to commit himself, because he didn't know when he would be able to hand in the paper.

el compromiso

1. engagement: no podré verte mañana porque tengo varios compromisos I can't see you tomorrow because I have several engagements

poner a alguien en un compromiso to put somebody in an awkward position.

compuesto, ta *adjetivo* ■ compound: "sacacorchos" es una palabra compuesta "sacacorchos" is a compound word.

común *(plural* comunes) *adjetivo* ■ common: "Pérez" es un apellido muy común "Pérez" is a very common surname; los alumnos cuentan con una sala de lectura común there is a common reading room for students

en común in common: tenemos varios intereses en común we have several things in common.

la comunicación *(plural* las comunicaciones) ■ communication: el lenguaje es el principal medio de comunicación language is the main means of communication

se ha cortado la comunicación we've been cut off.

comunicar [8] *verbo*

1. to inform: nos comunicó su proyecto de casarse he informed us of his plan to get married

2. to be engaged *UK,* to be busy *US:* te he llamado pero comunicabas I called you but you were engaged

comunicarse *verbo pronominal*

1. to communicate: le cuesta comunicarse con sus amigos he finds it difficult to communicate with his friends

2. to be connected: la habitación se comunica con el baño the bedroom is connected to the bathroom.

la comunidad ■ community: la comunidad latina es numerosa en esta región there is a large Latin community in this area

la Comunidad Europea the European Community

una comunidad autónoma a self-governing region.

la comunión *(plural* las comuniones) ■ communion: primera comunión first communion.

con *preposición* ■ with: viajé con mis padres I travelled with my parents; rellené los calamares con carne I filled the squid with meat

conduzca con prudencia drive carefully

con tal de as long as: con tal de verte, voy adonde sea as long as I can see you I'll go anywhere

con tal de que in order to: con tal de que lo aplaudan es capaz de hacer cualquier cosa he'll do anything in order to get the applause.

conceder [2] *verbo* ■ to grant: el hada madrina le concedió tres deseos her fairy godmother granted her three wishes.

la **concentración** *(plural* las concentraciones*)* ■ concentration: estudiar requiere mucha concentración studying requires a lot of concentration.

concentrarse [1] *verbo pronominal*

1. to concentrate: no logro concentrarme porque estáis haciendo demasiado ruido I can't concentrate because you're making too much noise

2. to gather: varias personas se concentraron en la puerta del teatro several people gathered at the theatre doors.

la **conciencia** ■ conscience: la voz de la conciencia the voice of conscience

➤ no tiene conciencia del daño que le ha hecho he's not aware of the damage he's done to her

➤ tener la conciencia tranquila to have a clear conscience.

el **concierto** ■ concert: fuimos a un concierto de rock we went to a rock concert.

concluir [36] *verbo*

1. to finish: concluimos el trabajo a tiempo we finished the work on time

2. to conclude: concluyo que no te interesa participar en el proyecto I can only conclude that you're not interested in participating in the project.

la **conclusión** *(plural* las conclusiones*)* ■ conclusion: he llegado a la conclusión de que no se lo merece I've reached the conclusion that he doesn't deserve it.

concreto, ta *adjetivo*

1. concrete: quiero un ejemplo concreto I want a concrete example

2. specific: necesito una fecha concreta I need a specific date.

el/la **concursante** ■ contestant.

concursar [1] *verbo* ■ to be a contestant: concursó en un programa de preguntas y respuestas he was a contestant on a quiz show.

el **concurso** ■ competition: ha participado en un concurso fotográfico he's taken part in a photography competition

➤ un concurso de belleza a beauty contest

➤ un concurso televisivo a game show.

la **condena** ■ sentence.

condenar [1] *verbo* ■ to sentence: lo condenaron a diez años de prisión he was sentenced to ten years in prison.

la **condición** *(plural* las condiciones*)* ■ condition: te lo presto, con la condición de que me lo devuelvas mañana I'll lend it to you on condition that you give it back to me tomorrow

las **condiciones**

1. shape: mi coche está en muy malas condiciones my car is in very bad shape

2. condition: la abuela no está en condiciones de hacer un viaje tan largo grandmother is in no condition to make such a long trip.

conducir [23] *verbo*

1. *un coche* to drive: no sabe conducir he can't drive

2. *una moto* to ride

3. *actitud* to lead: tu actitud no conduce a nada your attitude is leading nowhere.

la **conducta** ■ behaviour *UK,* behavior *US.*

el **conductor** , la **conductora** ■ driver

⚠ The Spanish word **conductor** is a false friend, it does not mean "conductor".

conectar [1] *verbo* ■ to connect: esa carretera conecta mi pueblo con la capital this road connects my town to the capital; sólo falta conectar el teléfono we just have to connect the phone

conectarse *verbo pronominal* ■ to connect: me voy a conectar a Internet para mirar mi correo I'm going to connect to the Internet to look at my e-mails.

el **conejo** , la **coneja** ■ rabbit.

la **conferencia**

1. lecture: voy a dar una conferencia en la facultad de derecho I'm giving a lecture at the law faculty

2. conference: fue a una conferencia médica he went to a medical conference

➤ una conferencia telefónica a long-distance phone call.

confesar [14] *verbo*

1. **to confess:** el ladrón confesó el crimen the thief confessed to the crime
2. **to admit:** Pablo me confesó que está enamorado de Ana Pablo admitted he's in love with Ana
> confesarse to go to confession.

el **confesor** ■ confessor.

la **confianza**

1. **trust:** nunca me ha mentido, le tengo total confianza he's never lied to me, I trust him completely
2. **familiarity:** nos trata con confianza porque nos conocemos hace mucho he treats us with familiarity because we've known each other a long time
> tener confianza en sí mismo to be self-confident.

confiar [7] *verbo*

1. **to trust:** confía en su amiga y por eso le presta el coche she trusts her friend so she lets her borrow the car
2. **to entrust:** su padre le confió el cuidado de la tienda his father entrusted him with the running of the shop
3. **to be trusting:** no debes confiarte demasiado you mustn't be too trusting.

la **configuración** *(plural* las configuraciones) ■ configuration.

configurar [8] *verbo* ■ to configure.

la **confirmación** *(plural* las confirmaciones) ■ confirmation: la confirmación de la reserva the booking confirmation
> ya tengo la confirmación de mi vuelo my flight is confirmed.

confirmar [1] *verbo* ■ to confirm: antes de viajar, es importante confirmar el vuelo it's important to confirm your flights before you travel.

el **conflicto** ■ conflict.

conforme *adjetivo* ■ satisfied: conforme vayan pasando las horas as the hours go by.

conforme *adverbio* ■ as: conforme vayan terminando la prueba, pueden salir you may leave as you finish the test.

confortable *adjetivo* ■ comfortable.

confundir [3] *verbo*

1. **to mix up:** siempre confundo a las dos gemelas I always mix up the twins
2. **to confuse:** con esa jugada lograste confundir a tu rival you managed to confuse your opponent with that move
> ¡me he confundido! I've made a mistake!

confundirse *verbo pronominal* ■ to get confused: me confundí en el camino porque no había señales I got confused on the way because there were no signs
> no te confundas de chaqueta don't take the wrong jacket.

la **confusión** *(plural* las confusiones) ■ confusion: en la confusión de la mañana se me olvidaron las llaves I forgot my keys in all the confusion this morning.

congelado, da *adjetivo* ■ frozen

los **congelados** ■ frozen food.

congelar [1] *verbo* ■ to freeze: voy a congelar el pollo que acabo de comprar I'm going to freeze the chicken I've just bought; el agua se ha congelado the water's frozen; me estoy congelando I'm freezing.

el **congreso**

1. **conference:** fue a un congreso de cirugía en Mallorca he went to a surgical conference in Mallorca
2. **Congress:** lo eligieron para el congreso he was elected to Congress.

la **conjugación** *(plural* las conjugaciones) ■ conjugation.

conjugar [12] *verbo* ■ conjugate: estamos aprendiendo a conjugar los verbos irregulares we're learning to conjugate irregular verbs.

la **conjunción** *(plural* las conjunciones) ■ conjunction: "y" es una conjunción "y" is a conjunction.

el **conjunto**

1. **band:** un conjunto de rock a rock band
2. **outfit:** me he comprado un conjunto de pantalón y chaqueta I've bought myself an outfit with a jacket and matching trousers.

conmemorar [1] *verbo* ■ to commemorate.

conmigo *pronombre*

1. with me: ayer vino conmigo al cine she came to the cinema with me yesterday
2. to me: siempre fue muy buena conmigo she was always very good to me.

conmover [17] *verbo* ■ to move: sus lágrimas lo conmovieron her tears moved him.

el **cono** ■ cone
➢ el Cono Sur the Southern Cone.

conocer [22] *verbo*

1. to meet: quiero que conozcas a mi hermana I'd like you to meet my sister
2. to know: a Juan lo conozco hace más de diez años I've known Juan for over ten years
3. to go to: me gustaría conocer Irlanda I'd like to go to Ireland
➢ no conozco Egipto I have never been to Egypt

conocerse *verbo pronominal* ■ to meet: nos conocimos en Madrid we met in Madrid; ¿os conocéis? have you met?

el **conocido**, la **conocida** ■ acquaintance: tiene algunos amigos y muchos conocidos he has some friends and a lot of acquaintances.

el **conocimiento**

1. knowledge: el conocimiento del sistema solar knowledge of the solar system
2. consciousness: perder el conocimiento to lose consciousness
➢ conocimientos knowledge: tiene buenos conocimientos de historia he has a good knowledge of history.

el **conquistador**, la **conquistadora** ■ conqueror.

conquistar [1] *verbo*

1. to conquer: conquistamos la cima we conquered the summit
2. to win over: la conquisté con flores I won her over with flowers.

consciente *adjetivo*

1. aware: no es consciente de lo que hace he's not aware of what he's doing

2. responsible: deberías ser más consciente you should be more responsible
3. conscious: el herido está consciente the victim is conscious.

la **consecuencia** ■ consequence: tendrá que pagar las consecuencias she'll have to pay the consequences
➢ a consecuencia de as a result of: a consecuencia de las heridas perdió el conocimiento he lost consciousness as a result of his injuries.

consecutivo, va *adjetivo* ■ consecutive: lo vi durante tres días consecutivos I saw him on three consecutive days.

conseguir [32] *verbo*

1. to get: consiguió lo que quería he got what he wanted
2. to achieve: si te dedicas, puedes conseguir cualquier cosa you can achieve anything if you make the effort
➢ finalmente conseguí que me enseñara inglés I finally got her to teach me English
➢ ¡lo conseguiste! you did it!

el **consejo** ■ advice, piece of advice: déjame darte un consejo let me give you some advice; me dio un consejo he gave me a piece of advice.

e/la **conserje**

1. *de edificio, colegio* caretaker *UK*, janitor *US*
2. *de hotel* receptionist.

consentir [20] *verbo*

1. to allow: les consienten todo they are allowed to do whatever they want
2. to spoil: su padre siempre la ha consentido her father has always spoiled her.

la **conserva** ■ canned food, tinned food *UK*
➢ espárragos en conserva tinned asparagus.

conservado, ra *adjetivo* ■ conservative: sus padres son muy conservadores her parents are very conservative.

conservar [1] *verbo*

1. to keep: has conservado tu figura you've kept your figure

2. **to preserve: quieren conservar sus tradiciones** they want to preserve their traditions

▷ **conservar en un sitio fresco y seco** keep in a cool dry place: **los huevos se conservan en la nevera** the eggs are kept in the fridge
▷ **conserva las amistades** he keeps his friends.

considerado, da *adjetivo*

1. **considerate: debería ser más considerado con nosotros** he should be more considerate towards us

2. **regarded: está muy bien considerado entre otros músicos** he is highly regarded by other musicians.

considerar [1] *verbo* ■ to consider: **la profesora consideró que valía la pena** the teacher considered it worthwhile

▷ **considerar los pros y los contras** to weigh up the pros and cons
▷ **considerar que** to take into account that: **tenemos que considerar que ha faltado** we have to take into account that he's been absent.

consigo *pronombre*

1. *con él* **with him: Luis llevó su tienda consigo** Luis brought his tent with him

2. *con ella* **with her: María trajo su traje de baño consigo** María brought her swimsuit with her

3. *con usted, ustedes* **with you: traiga consigo lo que necesite** bring whatever you need with you

▷ **consigo mismo/a** himself/herself: **Carlos habala consigo mismo** Carlos talks to himself; **Inés está muy contenta consigo misma** Inés is very pleased with herself.

consistir [3] *verbo* ■ involve: **¿en qué consiste este juego?** what does this game involve?

▷ **consistir en** to consist of: **la obra consiste en dos actos** the play consists of two acts
▷ **en eso consiste el juego** this is what the game consists of.

consolar [16] *verbo* ■ to comfort: **lo abrazó para consolarlo** she comforted him with a hug.

la **consonante** ■ consonant.

constante *adjetivo* ■ constant: **tengo un dolor de cabeza constante** I have a constant headache

▷ **ser constante** to persevere: **para tener éxito hay que ser constante** you have to persevere to be successful.

constipado, da *adjetivo*

▷ **estar constipado** to have a cold: **Elena está muy constipada** Elena has a bad cold

⚠️ The Spanish word **constipado** is a false friend, it does not mean "constipated".

la **constitución** *(plural* las constituciones) ■ constitution

▷ **la Constitución española** the Spanish Constitution.

constituir [36] *verbo*

1. **to constitute: los dos grupos constituyen una verdadera amenaza** the two groups constitute a real threat

2. **to make up: España está constituida por 52 provincias** Spain is made up of 52 provinces.

la **construcción** *(plural* las construcciones) ■ construction: **hace siete años que ese edificio está en construcción** that building has been under construction for seven years; **una empresa de construcción** a construction company; **este sitio está en construcción** this website is under construction.

construir [36] *verbo* ■ **to build: construyó su propia casa** he built his own house.

el **consuelo** ■ consolation: **su único consuelo es que no suspendió** his only consolation is that he didn't fail the exam.

el/la **cónsul** ■ consul.

el **consulado** ■ consulate.

la **consulta** ■ office: **el médico está en su consulta de 9 a 3** the doctor is in his surgery from 9 to 3

▷ **hacer una consulta a alguien** to ask somebody for advice
▷ **consulta a domicilio** house call

> **hacer una consulta** to see a patient
> **horas de consulta** office hours.

consultar [1] *verbo* ■ **to consult:** mejor consulta con el médico you should consult your doctor
> **consultar un libro** to look something up in a book.

el **consumidor** , la **consumidora** ■ consumer: derechos del consumidor consumer rights.

consumir [3] *verbo*
1. **to consume:** en este país se consume mucho azúcar in this country we consume a lot of sugar
2. **to use:** su coche consume mucha gasolina his car uses a lot of petrol
> **consumir preferentemente antes de...** best before...

el **consumo** ■ consumption: cómprate un coche de bajo consumo buy a car with low petrol consumption
> **el consumo de drogas** drug use.

la **contabilidad** ■ accounting: estudiar contabilidad to study accounting.

el **contacto**
1. **contact:** echo de menos el contacto humano I miss human contact
2. **touch:** he perdido el contacto con ella I've lost touch with her
> **ponerse en contacto con alguien** to get in touch with someone.

el **contado** ■ cash: pagar al contado to pay in cash.

contagiar [1] *verbo* ■ **to give:** mi hermano me ha contagiado la gripe my brother has given me his flu.

contagioso, sa *adjetivo*
1. **contagious:** esa enfermedad es muy contagiosa it's a very contagious disease
2. **infectious:** tu risa es contagiosa you have an infectious laugh.

la **contaminación** *(plural* las contaminaciones) ■ **pollution:** la contaminación del medio ambiente environmental pollution.

contaminar [1] *verbo* ■ **to pollute:** las fábricas han contaminado el río the factories have polluted the river.

contar [16] *verbo*
1. **to count:** cuenta hasta diez count to ten
2. **to tell:** ¿te cuento un cuento? do you want me to tell you a story?
> **contar con alguien** to count on someone
> **ese gol no cuenta** that goal doesn't count.

contener [52] *verbo* ■ **to contain:** el paquete contiene libros the package contains books

contenerse *verbo pronominal* ■ **to contain oneself:** no pudo contenerse de alegría she could hardly contain herself she was so happy.

el **contenido** ■ contents: el contenido de la caja the contents of the box; el contenido del sitio web the contents of the website.

contento, ta *adjetivo* ■ **happy:** está muy contento con sus notas he's very happy with his grades.

contestar [1] *verbo*
1. **to answer:** contesta el teléfono, por favor can you answer the phone, please?
2. **to reply to:** tengo que contestar su mensaje electrónico I have to reply to his e-mail

 The Spanish word **contestar** is a false friend, it does not mean "contest".

contigo *pronombre* ■ **with you:** ¿puedo ir contigo? can I come with you?
> **contigo mismo** with yourself: ¿estás contento contigo mismo? are you happy with yourself?

el **continente** ■ continent.

continuar [6] *verbo* ■ **to continue:** podemos continuar la conversación después de la comida we can continue this conversation after lunch
> **no puedes continuar así** you can't go on like this.

contra *preposición* ■ **against:** me he chocado contra el cristal I hit himself against the glass

> **estar en contra de algo** to be against something: **estoy en contra de esta ley** I'm against this law; **estoy en contra de la discriminación** I'm against discrimination.

el **contrabajo** ■ double bass.

contradecir [48] *verbo* ■ to contradict: **siempre me contradices** you're always contradicting me.

la **contradicción** (*plural* las contradicciones) ■ contradiction.

contrario, ria *adjetivo*

1. opposing: **el equipo contrario no es muy bueno** the opposing team isn't very good
2. opposite: **vamos en sentido contrario** we're going in the opposite direction
3. conflicting: **tienen opiniones contrarias** they have conflicting opinions
> **al contrario** on the contrary
> **de lo contrario** otherwise: **de lo contrario, tendrás en problemas** otherwise, you'll be in trouble.

el **contraste** ■ contrast: **la tele tiene demasiado contraste** there's too much contrast on the TV.

el **contrato** ■ contract: **ayer firmó el contrato** she signed the contract yesterday.

la **contribución** (*plural* las contribuciones)
1. contribution: **hice una contribución voluntaria** I made a voluntary contribution
2. tax: **la contribución municipal** council tax *UK*, local property tax *US*.

/la **contribuyente** ■ taxpayer.

/la **contrincante** ■ opponent: **su contrincante es muy hábil** his opponent is very skilful.

el **control** ■ control: **todo está bajo control** everything's under control; **perdió el control del coche** he lost control of his car
> **control de calidad** quality control
> **control de natalidad** birth control
> **control remoto** remote control
> **control de carretera** checkpoint
> **control de matemáticas** maths test.

controlar [1] *verbo*
1. to control: **deberías aprender a controlarte** you should learn to control yourself
2. to monitor: **estaremos controlando la situación** we'll be monitoring the situation
> **todo está controlado** everything's under control.

convencer [9] *verbo*
1. to convince: **su argumento no me convenció** his argument didn't convince me
2. to persuade: **no la pude convencer para que viniera** I couldn't persuade her to come.

convencional *adjetivo* ■ conventional: **su pensamiento es muy convencional** her way of thinking is very conventional.

conveniente *adjetivo* ■ convenient: **no me resulta conveniente** it's not convenient for me.

convenir [55] *verbo* ■ to be convenient: **me conviene más a las 11** 11 o'clock is more convenient for me
> **no sabes lo que te conviene** you don't know what's good for you.

el **convento** ■ convent.

la **conversación** (*plural* las conversaciones) ■ conversation: **mantuvimos una conversación** we had a conversation for two hours
> **conversaciones** talks: **las conversaciones de paz** the peace talks.

convertir [20] *verbo* ■ to turn into: **convirtieron la bodega en un cuarto de juegos** they turned the warehouse into a games room

convertirse *verbo pronominal*
1. to convert: **se convirtió al budismo** she converted to Buddhism
2. to turn into: **se convirtió en un pesado** he turned into a bore
3. to be turned into: **el edificio se ha convertido en un hotel** the building has been turned into a hotel.

la **cooperación** (*plural* las cooperaciones) ■ cooperation: **la cooperación entre países** cooperation between countries.

cooperar [1] *verbo* ■ **to cooperate:** es–peramos que cooperes con nosotros we hope you'll cooperate with us.

la **cooperativa** ■ cooperative.

la **coordenada** ■ **coordinate:** la coorde-nada "y" the "y" coordinate.

coordinar [1] *verbo* ■ **to coordinate:** le cuesta coordinar sus movimientos he has trouble coordinating his movements; no sé coordinar la ropa I don't know how to coor-dinate my clothes.

la **copa**

1. **glass:** ¿quieres una copa de vino? would you like a glass of wine?
2. **drink:** te invito a una copa I'll buy you a drink
3. **cup:** ganaron la Copa Mundial they won the World Cup
> la copa de un árbol the top of a tree.

la **copia** ■ **copy** *(plural* **copies***):* hizo tres copias del artículo she made three copies of the article.

copiar [1] *verbo* ■ **to copy.**

el **copión**, la **copiona** *informal* ■ copy-cat: ¡José es un copión! José is a copycat!

el **copo** ■ **flake:** un copo de nieve a snowflake
> copos de maíz cornflakes.

coqueto, ta *adjetivo* ■ **flirtations:** Mer-cedes es muy coqueta Mercedes is very flir-tations.

coquetear [1] *verbo* ■ **to flirt:** le encanta coquetear she loves to flirt.

el **coraje**

1. **courage:** hay que tener mucho coraje para hacer eso it takes a lot of courage to do that
2. **anger:** me da mucho coraje that makes me very angry.

el **corazón** *(plural* los corazones*)* ■ **heart:** el ejercicio es bueno para el corazón exercise is good for the heart
> corazones *en cartas* hearts: la reina de co-razones the queen of hearts
> Pepe es un hombre de buen corazón Pepe is a kind-hearted man.

la **corbata** ■ **tie:** lleva corbata he wears a tie.

el **corcho** ■ cork.

el **cordel** ■ **string:** átalo con este cordel tie it with this string.

el **cordero** ■ **lamb:** me gustan mucho las chuletas de cordero I like lamb chops very much.

la **cordillera** ■ **mountain range:** tuvieron que atravesar la cordillera they had to cross the mountain range
> la cordillera de los Pirineos the Pyrenean mountain range.

Córdoba ■ Cordova.

el **cordón** *(plural* los cordones*)*

1. **shoelace:** átate los cordones tie your shoelaces
2. **cord:** necesitamos un cordón más fuerte we need a stronger cord
> el cordón umbilical the umbilical cord.

la **córnea** ■ cornea.

la **corneta**

1. **bugle:** tocaba la corneta en el ejército he played the bugle in the army
2. **cornet:** prefiero la trompeta a la corneta I prefer the trumpet to the cornet.

el **coro** ■ **choir:** Lucía canta en el coro Lucía sings in the choir.

la **corona** ■ crown.

el/la **coronel** ■ colonel.

la **corporación** *(plural* las corporaciones*)* ■ **corporation:** las corporaciones multi-nacionales multinational corporations.

corporal *adjetivo* ■ **physical:** el trabajo corporal physical labour
> el castigo corporal corporal punishment
> la temperatura corporal body temperature.

el **corral** ■ **pen:** hay muchas gallinas en el corral there are a lot of chickens in the pen.

la **correa**

1. **strap:** se me rompió la correa del reloj my watch strap broke

2. lead *UK*, **leash** *US*: ponle la correa al perro put the dog's lead on.

correcto, ta *adjetivo*

1. correct: la mayoría de sus respuestas fueron correctas most of her answers were correct

2. polite: es un niño muy correcto he's a very polite boy

> ¡correcto! that's right!

el **corredor** , la **corredora** ■ runner.

corregir [31] *verbo*

1. to correct: me corrigió las faltas de ortografía she corrected my spelling mistakes

2. to grade *UK*, to grade *US*: estuvo horas corrigiendo los exámenes she spent hours marking tests.

el **correo** ■ mail, post *UK*: mándamelo por correo send it to me by post

> correo aéreo air mail
> correo certificado registered mail
> correo electrónico e-mail
> Correos post office.

correr [2] *verbo*

1. to run: corre muy rápido he runs very fast

2. to go fast: no corras tanto que vas a chocar don't go so fast or you'll crash

3. to hurry up: le dije que corriera para no llegar tarde I told him to hurry up so he wouldn't be late

4. to move over: diles que se corran para que nos podamos sentar tell them to move over so we can sit down

> el río corre de norte a sur the river runs from north to south.

la **correspondencia**

1. correspondence: no hay correspondencia entre sonidos y letras there is no correspondence between sounds and letters; a curso por correspondencia a correspondence course

2. mail: le llega mucha correspondencia he gets a lot of mail.

corresponder [2] *verbo* ■ to belong: ponlo donde corresponde put it where it belongs

> hacer algo como corresponde to do something properly
> le corresponde a él hacerlo it's his job to do it.

la **corrida** ■ bullfight.

corriente *(adjetivo & sustantivo)*

■ *adjetivo*

common: un nombre muy corriente a very common name

> al corriente up to date
> mantenme al corriente de tu situación keep me informed of your situation

■ *sustantivo femenino*

1. draught *UK*, draft *US*: cierra la ventana que entra una corriente close the window – there's a draught

2. current: corriente eléctrica electric current

> no parece haber corriente there doesn't seem to be any power
> se cortó la corriente there was a power cut.

corromper [2] *verbo* ■ to corrupt: el poder corrompe power corrupts.

la **corrupción** *(plural las corrupciones)* ■ corruption.

corrupto, ta *adjetivo* ■ corrupt: un político corrupto a corrupt politician.

cortado, da *adjetivo*

1. chapped: tengo los labios cortados my lips are chapped

2. closed: la calle está cortada por obras the street is closed due to roadworks

3. curdled: la nata está cortada the cream is curdled

el **cortado** ■ espresso coffee with a dash of milk.

cortar [1] *verbo*

1. to cut: Ana sabe cortar el pelo Ana knows how to cut hair; cortaron la escena porque era demasiado violenta they cut the scene because it was too violent

2. to cut off: me cortaron el teléfono the phone was cut off

3. to turn off: corta la luz turn the light off

cortarse *verbo pronominal*

1. to cut oneself: me corté con un cuchillo I cut myself with a knife

2. to have cut: voy a cortarme el pelo I'm going to have my hair cut

3. to be cut off: se ha cortado la comunicación we've been cut off.

el **cortaúñas** (plural los cortaúñas) ■ nail clippers.

el **corte** ■ cut: tengo un corte en la mano I've got a cut on my hand

▸ un corte de pelo a haircut

▸ dar corte to be embarrassed: me da corte hablar en público I'm embarrassed to speak in public.

la **corte** ■ court: la corte del rey the royal court

▸ Corte Suprema Supreme Court.

cortés adjetivo ■ polite: un caballero muy cortés a very polite gentleman

▸ lo cortés no quita lo valiente politeness isn't a sign of weakness.

la **cortesía** ■ courtesy, politeness

▸ de cortesía complimentary

▸ por cortesía out of politeness.

la **corteza**

1. bark: la corteza del árbol the tree bark

2. crust: quita la corteza del pan remove the crust from the bread

3. peel: la corteza del limón lemon peel

4. rind: la corteza del queso the cheese rind

▸ la corteza terrestre the earth's crust.

la **cortina** ■ curtain.

corto, ta adjetivo ■ short: te queda bien el pelo corto you look good with short hair

▸ ser corto de vista to be shortsighted.

la **cosa** ■ thing: pásame esa cosa verde pass me that green thing

▸ cualquier cosa anything

▸ no es cosa tuya it's none of your business

▸ ¡son cosas de la vida! that's life!

la **cosecha**

1. harvest: es época de cosecha it's harvest time

2. crop: el granizo arruinó la cosecha hail ruined the crop.

cosechar [1] verbo ■ to harvest.

coser [2] verbo ■ to sew: si supiera coser, te arreglaría la camisa if I knew how to sew I'd mend your shirt

▸ ser coser y cantar to be a piece of cake: preparar este plato es coser y cantar making this dish is a piece of cake.

el **cosmético** ■ cosmetic.

cósmico, ca adjetivo ■ cosmic.

las **cosquillas**

▸ ¡no me hagas cosquillas! stop tickling me!

▸ tener cosquillas to be ticklish.

la **costa** ■ coast: tiene una casa en la costa he has a house on the coast

▸ a toda costa at all costs

▸ vivir a costa de los demás to live at other people' expense.

el **costado** ■ side: túmbate de lado lie on your side.

costar [16] verbo

1. to cost: ¿cuánto cuesta? how much does it cost?

2. to take: me costó tres días acabarlo it took me three days to finish it

▸ me está costando aprender alemán I'm finding it hard to learn German.

Costa Rica ■ Costa Rica.

costarricense adjetivo

En inglés, los adjetivos que se refieren a un país o una región se escriben con mayúscula:

Costa Rican

el/la **costarricense**

En inglés, los gentilicios se escriben con mayúscula:

Costa Rican: los costarricenses the Costa Ricans.

costarriqueño, ña adjetivo

En inglés, los adjetivos que se refieren a un país o una región se escriben con mayúscula:

Costa Rican

el costarriqueño , la costarriqueña

> En inglés, los gentilicios se escriben con mayúscula:
>
> **Costa Rican: los costarriqueños** the Costa Ricans.

la costilla ■ rib.

el costo ■ cost.

la costra ■ scab: **no te rasques la costra** don't scratch the scab.

la costumbre
1. habit: **una mala costumbre** a bad habit
2. custom: **una costumbre local** a local custom
> **como de costumbre** as usual
> **no tengo la costumbre** I'm not used to it.

la costura
1. sewing: **a Paula le gusta la costura** Paula likes sewing
2. seam: **una costura mal hecha** a badly-sewn seam
> **alta costura** haute couture.

cotidiano, na *adjetivo* ■ everyday: **la vida cotidiana** everyday life.

el coyote ■ coyote.

el cráneo ■ skull.

la creación *(plural* **las creaciones***)* ■ creation.

crear [1] *verbo* ■ to create: **crearon una base de datos** they created a database
> **crear falsas expectativas** to raise false hopes
> **crear problemas** to cause problems.

crecer [22] *verbo*
1. to grow: **has crecido mucho** you've grown a lot
2. to grow up: **creció en Toledo** she grew up in Toledo
3. to rise: **ha crecido la inflación y el desempleo** inflation and unemployment have risen.

el crecimiento ■ growth: **la leche es beneficiosa para el crecimiento del niño** milk is beneficial for a child's growth; **los niños deben comer bien durante el crecimiento** children must eat well while they are growing.

el crédito
1. credit: **comprar algo a crédito** to buy something on credit
2. loan: **¿crees que te darán un crédito?** do you think they'll give you a loan?

la creencia ■ belief: **no estoy atacando tus creencias** I'm not attacking your beliefs.

creer [35] *verbo*
1. to believe: **no lo puedo creer** I can't believe it
2. to think: **creo que tienes razón** I think you're right
> **se creen muy listos** they think they're very clever; **creo que sí** I think so; **creo que no** I don't think so.

creído, da *adjetivo* ■ conceited: **José es muy creído** José is really conceited.

la crema
1. *pastelera* confectioner's custard
2. *de leche* cream
> **crema de espárragos** cream of asparagus soup
> **crema de champiñones** mushroom soup
> **crema para las manos** hand cream
> **crema de afeitar** shaving cream.

la cremallera ■ zip: **súbete la cremallera** do up your zip.

el creyente , la creyente ■ believer.

la cría ■ young: **una hembra con sus crías** a female with her young
> **una cría de elefante** a baby elephant
> **una cría de león** a lion cub.

el criado , la criada ■ servant.

criar [7] *verbo*
1. to bring up: **sus padres la criaron bien** her parents brought her up well
2. to breed: **crían perros** they breed dogs
3. to grow up: **nos criamos juntos** we grew up together.

el crimen *(plural* **los crímenes***)* ■ murder: **cometer un crimen** to commit murder
> **crimen de guerra** war crime
> **crimen organizado** organized crime.

el/la **criminal** ■ criminal.

el **crío** , la **cría** ■ kid: se ha llevado los
  críos al parque she's taken the kids to the
  park; Sara no es más que una cría Sara's
  just a kid.

la **crisis** *(plural las crisis)* ■ crisis: una crisis
  económica an economic crisis
  ▸ crisis cardíaca heart failure
  ▸ una crisis nerviosa a nervous breakdown.

el **cristal**
  1. glass: una botella de cristal a glass bottle
  2. crystal: una copa de cristal de Bohemia a
    Bohemian crystal glass.

el **cristiano** , la **cristiana** ■ Christian.

  Cristo *sustantivo masculino* ■ Christ.

la **crítica**
  1. criticism: no aguantó tanta crítica y se fue
    he couldn't stand so much criticism so he left
  2. review: voy a escribir una crítica del libro
    I'm going to write a review of the book.

  criticar [4] *verbo*
  1. to criticize: la critica constantemente he's
    constantly criticizing her
  2. to review: criticar una película to review a
    film.

el **crítico** , la **crítica** ■ critic
  ▸ un crítico de cine a film critic.

el **cromo** ■ picture card.

el **cronómetro** ■ stopwatch.

  cronometrar [1] *verbo* ■ to time.

la **croqueta** ■ croquette.

el **cruce** ■ crossing: un cruce fronterizo a
  border crossing
  ▸ un cruce de carreteras a crossroads
  ▸ un cruce de peatones a pedestrian crossing.

el **crucigrama** ■ crossword.

  crudo, da *adjetivo*
  1. raw: carne cruda raw meat
  2. undercooked: el pollo está crudo the
    chicken's undercooked; tenerlo crudo to
    have a hard time.

  cruel *adjetivo* ■ cruel.

  crujiente *adjetivo*
  1. crunchy: una manzana crujiente a crunchy
    apple
  2. crispy: lonchas de beicon crujiente crispy
    rashers of bacon.

  crujir [3] *verbo*
  1. to creak: la cama crujía cada vez que me
    movía the bed creaked every time I moved
  2. to rustle: las hojas secas crujían con el
    viento the dry leaves rustled in the wind
  3. to grind: le crujen los dientes he grinds his
    teeth
  4. to crunch: la nieve crujía bajos nuestros
    pies the snow crunched under our feet.

la **cruz** *(plural las cruces)* ■ cross.

  cruzar [10] *verbo* ■ to cross: ten cuidado
  al cruzar la calle be careful when you cross
  the street
  ▸ cruzar los brazos to fold your arms
  ▸ cruzarse con alguien to run into someone.

el **cuaderno** ■ notebook: un cuaderno
  de espiral a spiral notebook.

la **cuadra** ■ stable: los caballos están en
  la cuadra the horses are in the stable.

  cuadrado, da *adjetivo* ■ square: una
  caja cuadrada a square box
  ▸ diez metros cuadrados ten square metres
  ▸ tu hermano está muy cuadrado our brother
  is really square.

el **cuadrado** ■ square.

  cuadriculado, da *adjetivo* ■ papel
  cuadriculado graph paper.

el **cuadro**
  1. painting: colecciona cuadros she collects
    paintings
  2. pictures: tiene la casa llena de cuadros her
    house is full of pictures; un pantalón a
    cuadros checked trousers.

  cual *pronombre* ■ who, whom *formal:* las
  personas con las cuales pasé la tarde the
  people who I spent the afternoon; la chica de
  la cual te hablé the girl whom I told you about
  ▸ cada cual everyone: cada cual en su lugar
  everyone in their place

➤ **sea cual sea** whatever
➤ **sea cual sea el resultado, lo aceptamos** whatever the result is, we'll accept it.

cuál *pronombre*

1. **what:** ¿cuál es tu nombre? what's your name?
2. **which:** ¿cuáles son tus libros? which books are yours?
3. **which one:** ¿cuál prefieres? which one do you prefer?; ¿cuáles son las tuyas? which ones are yours

cualidad ■ **quality:** tiene buenas cualidades she has good qualities.

cualquier *adjetivo* ➤ cualquiera.

cualquiera (*plural* cualesquiera) (*adjetivo & pronombre*)

■ *adjetivo*

any: a cualquier hora any time; este examen lo puede aprobar cualquier alumno any student can pass this exam; puedes comprar una mesa cualquiera you can buy any kind of table; no es un amigo cualquiera he's no ordinary friend; cualquier día de estos te llamaré I'll call you any of these days.

■ *adjetivo*

1. **anyone:** cualquiera puede aprobar el examen si estudia anyone can pass the test if they study
2. **either:** ¿cuál de los dos prefieres? —cualquiera which of the two do you prefer? – either
3. **any of them:** llévate cualquiera take any of them.

cuando *conjunción*

1. **when:** ven cuando puedas come when you can
2. **if:** cuando Miguel lo dice, debe ser por algo if Miguel says so it must be for a reason
➤ **cuando quieras** whenever you like
➤ **de cuando en cuando** every so often.

cuándo *adverbio* ■ **when:** ¿cuándo llegaste? when did you arrive?; no sé cuándo fue I don't know when it was.

cuanto *adverbio* ■ **as much as:** come cuanto quieras eat as much as you like
➤ **cuanto antes** as soon as possible

➤ **en cuanto** as soon as: nos vamos en cuanto termine de llover we'll go as soon as it stops raining
➤ **en cuanto a** as for: en cuanto a tu sueldo, lo discutiremos mañana as for your salary, we'll discuss it tomorrow
➤ **cuanto más la conozco, más me gusta** the more I get to know her, the more I like her.

cuánto *adjetivo & pronombre*

1. *en singular* **how much:** ¿cuánto pan compro? how much bread do I buy?
2. *en plural* **how many:** ¿cuántos libros tienes? how many books do you have?; ¿a cuánto estamos? what's the date?; ¡cuánta gente hay! what a lot of people!; ¿cuánto tiempo llevas ahí? how long have you been there?

cuarenta *adjetivo* ■ **forty:** me dio cuarenta euros he gave me forty euros; tiene cuarenta años she's forty.

el **cuartel** ■ **barracks.**

cuarto, ta *adjetivo* ■ **fourth:** eres la cuarta persona en llegar you're the fourth person to arrive
➤ **la cuarta parte** a quarter.

el **cuarto**

1. **room:** la casa tiene cinco cuartos the house has five rooms
2. **quarter:** ha hecho tres cuartos de los deberes he's done three quarters of his homework
➤ **las diez y cuarto** a quarter past ten *UK*, a quarter after ten *US*
➤ **las diez menos cuarto** a quarter to ten.

cuatro *numeral* ■ **four:** tiene cuatro hijos she has four children
➤ **mi hermana tiene cuatro años** my sister is four years old
➤ **son las cuatro** it's four o'clock
➤ **el cuatro de abril** the fourth of April *UK*, April fourth *US*.

Cuba ■ Cuba.

cubano, na *adjetivo*

En inglés, los adjetivos que se refieren a un país o una región se escriben con mayúscula:

Cuban

el **cubano** , la **cubana**

En inglés, los gentilicios se escriben con mayúscula:

Cubans: los cubanos the Cubans.

cúbico, ca *adjetivo* ■ **cubic: diez metros cúbicos** ten cubic metres.

la **cubierta**
1. **cover: un libro con cubiertas de cuero** a book with leather covers
2. **deck: voy a subir a la cubierta para ver el mar** I'm going up on deck to look at the sea.

el **cubito** ■ ice cube.

el **cubierto** ■ **cover charge: cobran bastante por cada cubierto** the cover charge is pretty high
➤ **cubiertos** cutlery: **cubiertos de plata** silver cutlery.

el **cubo**
1. **bucket: un cubo de agua** a bucket of water
2. **cube: los cubos tienen seis caras** cubes have six sides
➤ **el cubo de la basura** the rubbish bin *UK*, the trash can *US*.

cubrir [3] *verbo* ■ **to cover: se cubrió la cara con las manos** she covered her face with her hands.

la **cucaracha** ■ cockroach.

la **cuchara** ■ spoon.

la **cucharada** ■ **spoonful: una cucharada de azúcar** a spoonful of sugar.

la **cucharadita** ■ **teaspoon: una cucharadita de azúcar** a teaspoon of sugar.

la **cucharilla** ■ **teaspoon: ¿me traes una cucharilla?** can you bring me a teaspoon?

el **cucharón** *(plural* los cucharones*)* ■ ladle.

cuchichear [1] *verbo* ■ **to whisper: cuchicheó algo al oído de Sonia** she whispered something into Sonia's ear.

el **cuchillo** ■ knife *(plural* knives*)*.

cuclillas *adverbio* ■ **tienes que ponerte en cuclillas** you have to crouch down.

el **cuello**
1. **neck: me duele el cuello** my neck hurts
2. **collar: el cuello de la camisa me aprieta** the shirt collar is too tight for me.

la **cuenta**
1. **count: perder la cuenta** to lose count
2. **account: una cuenta corriente** a current account *UK*, a checking account *US*
3. **bill: la cuenta del teléfono** the phone bill
4. **bill** *UK*, **check** *US*: **la cuenta, por favor** can I have the bill, please
➤ **darse cuenta** to realize: **no me di cuenta de que te habías ido** I didn't realize you'd left
➤ **las cuentas** the accounts
➤ **tener en cuenta** to take into account.

el **cuento** ■ **story: cuéntame un cuento** tell me a story
➤ **no me vengas con cuentos** I don't want to hear your excuses
➤ **un cuento de hadas** a fairy tale.

la **cuerda**
1. **rope: afloja la cuerda** loosen the rope
2. **string: ata el paquete con una cuerda** tie the package with some string; **se me ha roto una cuerda de la guitarra** I've broken a guitar string
➤ **dar cuerda a un reloj** to wind (up) a watch
➤ **saltar a la cuerda** to skip
➤ **la cuerda floja** the tightrope.

el **cuerno** ■ horn.

el **cuero** ■ **leather: guantes de cuero** leather gloves.

el **cuerpo** ■ **body: el cuerpo humano** the human body.

la **cuesta** ■ **slope: esta cuesta es muy empinada** this is a very steep slope
➤ **ir cuesta abajo** to go downhill
➤ **ir cuesta arriba** to go uphill
➤ **me llevó a cuestas** he carried me on his shoulders.

el **cuestionario** ■ questionnaire.

la **cueva** ■ cave.

el **cuidado** ■ **care: el cuidado de la piel** skin care

ten cuidado al cruzar la calle be careful crossing the street

con cuidado carefully

¡cuidado! watch out!

cuidados intensivos intensive care.

cuidar [1] *verbo* ■ to take care: deberías cuidar más tu salud you should take better care of your health

cuidar de to look after: cuida de sus hermanos she looks after her brothers

¡cuídate! take care!

la **culebra** ■ snake.

el **culo** ■ *familiar* bottom, bum *UK*.

la **culpa**

1. fault: ha sido culpa mía it was my fault
2. blame: me echó la culpa she put the blame on me.

culpable *adjetivo* ■ guilty: me siento culpable por haberlo dicho I feel guilty for saying it

la **culpable** ■ culprit: no han encontrado al culpable they haven't found the culprit

¿quién es el culpable de este desorden? who's the responsible for this mess?

cultivar [1] *verbo*

1. to grow: cultiva lechugas en su jardín she grows lettuce in her garden
2. to farm: cultivar la tierra to farm the land
3. to cultivate: ha estado cultivando amistades he's been cultivating friendships.

el **cultivo** ■ farming: el cultivo intensivo intensive farming.

culto, ta *adjetivo*

1. educated: una persona muy culta a well-educated person
2. formal: usa lenguaje muy culto she uses very formal language

el **culto** ■ worship: el culto al sol sun worship.

la **cultura** ■ culture: la cultura popular popular culture.

la **cumbre** ■ summit.

el **cumpleaños** (*plural* los cumpleaños) ■ birthday: ¡feliz cumpleaños! happy birthday!

el **cumplido** ■ compliment: le hice un cumplido I gave her a compliment.

cumplir [3] *verbo*

1. to carry out: cumplió con el encargo que le hice he carried out the commission I gave him
2. to keep: no cumple sus promesas she doesn't keep her promises
3. to serve: le faltan dos años para cumplir su condena he has two years left to serve his sentence
4. to meet: tiene que cumplir los requisitos mínimos he has to meet the minimum requirements

cumplir quince años to turn fifteen years old.

la **cuna** ■ cradle.

la **cuñada** ■ sister-in-law.

el **cuñado** ■ brother-in-law.

la **cuota**

1. fee: la cuota de socio anual the yearly membership fee
2. quota: la cuota de exportación the export quota.

el **cupón** (*plural* los cupones) ■ coupon.

el **cura** ■ priest.

la **cura** ■ cure: esa enfermedad no tiene cura that illness doesn't have a cure.

curar [1] *verbo*

1. to cure: saben curar varias formas de cáncer they know how to cure several types of cancer
2. to treat: la enfermera me curó la herida the nurse treated my wound

curarse *verbo pronominal*

1. to heal: se me curó la herida rápidamente my wound healed quickly
2. to recover: Belén tardó dos meses en curarse Belén took two months to recover.

la **curiosidad** ■ curiosity

por curiosidad out of curiosity: lo ha preguntado por curiosidad he asked out of curiosity

tener curiosidad to be curious: tenía curiosidad por saberlo he was curious to know.

curioso, sa *adjetivo*
1. **strange:** ¡qué curioso! how strange
2. **inquisitive:** los alumnos son bastante curiosos the students are pretty inquisitive.

el **currículo** ■ CV *UK*, résumé *US*.

el **curso**
1. **class:** estamos en el mismo curso we're in the same class
2. **course:** quiero apuntarme a un curso de inglés I want to enrol in an English course
   en el curso de las discusiones in the course of the discussions
   el curso escolar the school year.

la **curva** ■ **curve:** esa carretera tiene muchas curvas that road has a lot of curves.

cuyo, ya *pronombre* ■ **whose:** el señor cuyo nombre no voy a mencionar the man whose name I won't mention; conozco a un chico cuya madre es novelista I know a boy whose mother is a novelist.

d

el **dado** ■ **dice** *(plural* **dice)**
> **jugar a los dados** to play dice
> ¡tira el dado! throw the dice!

la **dama** ■ **lady** *(plural* **ladies):** damas y caballeros ladies and gentlemen
> **damas** draughts *UK,* **checkers** *US:* no sé jugar a las damas I don't know how to play checkers.

la **danza** ■ **dance:** una danza tradicional a traditional dance.

dañar [1] *verbo*
1. **to harm:** ¡no dañes al gato! don't harm the cat!
2. **to damage:** eso dañará la mercancía that will damage the merchandise; el tabaco daña la salud tobacco damages your health.

el **daño** ■ **damage:** el daño que el barco sufrió es leve the damage that the boat suffered is slight
> **hacer daño a alguien** to hurt somebody
> **hacerse daño** to hurt oneself.

dar [40] *verbo* ■ **to give:** le di mi dirección I gave her my address; ¿me da un kilo de patatas? could I have a kilogram of potatoes?; me dio permiso para salir he gave me permission to go out
> **dar a** to overlook: el jardín da a la playa the garden overlooks the beach
> **dar las gracias** to thank: ¿le has dado las gracias? have you thanked him?
> **da lo mismo** it doesn't matter
> **dar una fiesta** to have a party
> **el reloj dio las tres** the clock struck three
> **si se entera le va a dar un ataque** if he finds out, he'll have a fit
> **dar clases** to teach
> **da clases de historia** she teaches history
> **me voy a dar un baño** I'm going to have a bath
> **dar los buenos días** to say hello
> **¿qué dan hoy en la tele?** what's on TV today?
> **darse una ducha** to have a shower
> **darse un golpe** to hit oneself: se dio un golpe contra el estante he hit himself on the self.

el **dátil** ■ **date.**

el **dato** ■ **piece of information:** un dato interesante an interesting piece of information
> **datos personales** personal details.

de *preposición*
1. **of:** una taza de té a cup of tea; uno de sus hermanos one of his brothers
2. **from:** Juan es de Guadalajara Juan is from Guadalajara
3. **in:** la montaña más alta del mundo the highest mountain in the world

4. by: una película de Spielberg a film by Spielberg; estaba rodeado de admiradores he was surrounded by fans

5. than: he tardado más de lo que esperaba I took longer than I expected; había más de mil personas there were more than a thousand people

▸ esto es de Pepe this is Pepe's

▸ la clase de matemáticas the maths class

▸ salgo de mi casa muy temprano I leave home very early

▸ son las tres de la tarde it's three o'clock in the afternoon

▸ una pulsera de plata a silver bracelet

▸ de lunes a sábado from Monday to Saturday.

debajo *adverbio* ■ **under:** ponte algo debajo de la chaqueta put something on under your jacket

▸ pasar por debajo to go under.

el **deber** ■ **duty** *(plural* **duties***):* es tu deber hacerlo it's your duty to do it

▸ los deberes homework.

deber [2] *verbo*

1. to owe: me debes cinco euros you owe me five euros

2. must: debes pedir perdón you must ask for forgiveness

▸ deberías hacerlo you should do it

▸ se debe a que no estudias it's because you don't study.

débil *adjetivo* ■ **weak.**

la **debilidad** ■ **weakness:** la debilidad del puente lo hace peligroso the weakness of the bridge makes it dangerous

▸ tengo debilidad por los dulces I have a weakness for sweets; tengo debilidad por mi sobrina I have a soft spot for my niece.

debilitar [1] *verbo* ■ **to weaken.**

la **década** ■ **decade.**

decente *adjetivo* ■ **decent:** es un hombre decente he's a decent man; su casa es bastante decente his house is pretty decent; un sueldo decente a decent salary.

la **decepción** *(plural* las decepciones*)* ■ **disappointment:** el libro fue una decepción the book was a disappointment

 The Spanish word **decepción** is a false friend, it does not mean "deception".

decidido, da *adjetivo* ■ **determined:** está decidido a pasar el examen he's determined to pass the exam; un hombre muy decidido a very determined man.

decidir [3] *verbo* ■ **to decide:** decidió hacerlo después de todo he decided to do it after all

▸ ¿por cuál te has decidido? which one did you have chosen?

▸ ¡decídete! make your mind up!

decir [41] *verbo*

1. to say: di algo say something; dijo que no he said no

2. to tell: dime como te va tell me how you're doing; dime que no es cierto tell me it's not true; nadie me dijo que la película había empezado nobody told me the film had begun; dile que me llame tell him to call me

▸ es decir that is to say: son buenos, es decir, mejor que los otros they're good, that is to say, better than the others

▸ ¡no me digas! no way!

▸ por decirlo así so to speak

▸ ¿qué quiere decir esto? what does this mean?

▸ ¿y ellos, qué dicen? what do they think?

▸ es un decir it's just a figure of speech

▸ ¿diga? hello?

▸ decir la verdad to tell the truth

▸ decir mentiras to tell lies.

la **decisión** *(plural* las decepciones*)* ■ **decision:** tomó la decisión de irse he made the decision to leave.

la **declaración** *(plural* las decepciones*)*

1. declaration: una declaración de amor a declaration of love

2. statement: esperamos oír la declaración del presidente we are waiting to hear the president's statement

3. testimony: el testigo prestó declaración the witness gave testimony.

declarar [1] *verbo*

1. **to announce:** declaró que era inocente he announced he was innocent
2. **to declare:** acaban de declarar la guerra they've just declared war
   > lo declararon inocente they found him not guilty
   > se declaró a María he declared his love to María.

la **decoración** *(plural* las decoraciones*)* ■ **decoration.**

decorar [1] *verbo* ■ **to decorate:** decoraron el árbol de Navidad they decorated the Christmas tree.

la **dedicación** ■ **dedication:** si quieres ganar necesitas dedicación if you want to win, you need dedication.

dedicar [8] *verbo*

1. **to dedicate:** le dedicó el poema a su hija she dedicated the poem to her daughter
2. **to devote:** deberías dedicar más tiempo al estudio you should devote more time to studying.

la **dedicatoria** ■ **dedication:** le pedí que me escribiera una dedicatoria en su libro I asked him to write a dedication to me in his book.

el **dedo**

1. *de la mano* **finger:** se ha hecho un corte en el dedo he cut his finger
2. *del pie* **toe:** el dedo gordo del pie the big toe
   > el dedo gordo de la mano the thumb
   > hacer dedo to hitch a ride
   > no mover un dedo not to lift a finger.

el **defecto**

1. **defect:** tu abrigo tiene un defecto en la manga your coat has a defect on the sleeve
2. **flaw:** es un defecto de su personalidad it's a personality flaw of his.

defender [15] *verbo* ■ **to defend:** ¡siempre lo defiendes a él! you always defend him!

la **defensa** ■ **defence** *UK*, **defense** *US:* salió en mi defensa he came to my defence
> defensa personal self-defence.

deficiente *adjetivo* ■ **inadequate:** la atención a los pacientes es deficiente the attention to the patients is inadequate
> una dieta deficiente en calcio a diet deficient in calcium.

la **definición** *(plural* las definiciones*)* ■ **definition.**

definir [3] *verbo* ■ **to define:** ¿cómo defines el amor? how do you define love?

deformar [1] *verbo*

1. **to distort:** el espejo deforma la imagen the mirror distorts the image
2. **to deform:** quedó deformado después del accidente he was left deformed after the accident.

dejar [1] *verbo*

1. **to leave:** déjalo ahí leave it over there; su novia le ha dejado his girlfriend has left him
2. **to let:** le dejamos entrar we let him in
3. **to lend:** le he dejado mi bufanda I've lent him my scarf
4. **to give up** *UK,* **to quit** *US:* dejó la gimnasia por culpa de una lesión he gave up gymnastics because of an injury
   > dejar de hacer algo to stop doing something: ¡deja de molestarme! stop bothering me!; dejar de fumar to give up smoking
   > ¡déjame en paz! leave me alone!

del *preposición*

> **del** is a contraction of **de** and **el.**

➤ de.

delante *adverbio* ■ **in front:** ve delante go in front
> delante de in front of: se paró delante de mí he stopped in front of me; ha pasado delante de mi casa he passed in front of my house; inclínate hacia delante lean forward.

delantero, ra *adjetivo* ■ **front:** la rueda delantera the front wheel.

el **delfín** *(plural* los delfines*)* ■ **dolphin.**

delgado, da *adjetivo* ■ **thin:** estás mucho más delgada que antes you're much thinner than before.

delicado, da *adjetivo*

1. **delicate:** ¡que manos tan delicadas! what delicate hands!
2. **fragile:** estas copas son muy delicadas these glasses are very fragile
3. **sensitive:** tengo la piel muy delicada my skin is very sensitive
4. **tactful:** tienes que aprender a ser más delicado you should learn to be more tactful.

delicioso, sa *adjetivo* ■ **delicious.**

la **delincuencia** ■ **crime:** la delincuencia es un problema en este barrio crime is a problem in this area.

la **delincuente** ■ **criminal**
un delincuente juvenil a juvenile delinquent.

el **delito** ■ **crime:** lo que estoy haciendo no es un delito what I'm doing isn't a crime.

la **demanda** ■ **demand:** ese juguete tiene mucha demanda that toy is in great demand
▸ presentar una demanda contra alguien **to sue somebody:** presentamos una demanda contra la empresa we sued the company.

demandar [1] *verbo* ■ **to sue:** demandar a alguien to sue somebody.

demás *(adjetivo & pronombre)*
■ *adjetivo*
other: los demás alumnos entraron por otra puerta the other students came in by another door
■ *pronombre*
▸ lo demás the rest: lo demás es para mañana the rest is for tomorrow
▸ todo lo demás everything else: estudia esto e ignora todo lo demás study this and ignore everything else
▸ los demás the others: los demás no habían estudiado the others hadn't studied.

demasiado, da *adjetivo*

1. **too much:** le has puesto demasiada sal you've put too much salt on it

2. **too many:** tiene demasiados libros he's got too many books; siempre hay demasiada gente there are always too many people.

demasiado *adverbio*

1. **too:** hablas inglés demasiado rápido para mí you speak English too quickly for me
2. **too much:** comes demasiado you eat too much.

la **democracia** ■ **democracy** *(plural* **democracies***)*.

democrático, ca *adjetivo* ■ **democratic.**

el **demonio** ■ **devil:** estos alumnos son unos pequeños demonios these students are little devils.

la **demostración** *(plural* las demostraciones*)* ■ **demonstration:** tenían varios aparatos de demostración they had several pieces of equipment for demonstration.

demostrar [16] *verbo*

1. **to demonstrate:** ahora vamos a demostrar cómo funciona now we shall demonstrate how it works
2. **to show:** demostró interés she showed interest
3. **to prove:** ha demostrado su habilidad she's proven her ability.

la **densidad** ■ **density.**

denso, sa *adjetivo*

1. **dense:** un líquido denso a dense liquid; una niebla densa a dense fog
2. **heavy:** un libro denso a heavy book.

la **dentadura** ■ **teeth:** tiene una buena dentadura she has good teeth.

el **dentífrico** ■ **toothpaste.**

el/la **dentista** ■ **dentist.**

dentro *adverbio* ■ **inside:** no sé que hay dentro I don't know what's inside; límpialo por dentro clean it on the inside
▸ ponlo dentro de la caja put it in the box
▸ dentro de poco in a while.

la **denuncia** ■ **report:** voy a presentar una denuncia por robo I'm going to have to file a report about the robbery.

denunciar [1] *verbo*
1. **to report:** denunció el crimen a la policía he reported the crime to the police
2. **to condemn:** denunciaron el abuso de poder they condemned the abuse of power.

el **departamento**
1. **department:** el departamento de muebles the furniture department
> el Departamento de Física the Physics Department.

depender [2] *verbo* ■ **to depend:** ¿puedes venir el martes? —depende can you come on Tuesday? – it depends
> depender de to depend on: depende de la ayuda de los demás he depends on the help of others
> no depende mí it's not up to me.

el **dependiente**, la **dependienta** ■ shop assistant *UK*, sales clerk *US*.

el **deporte** ■ **sport:** mi deporte preferido es el fútbol my favourite sport is football.

el/la **deportista** ■ *hombre* **sportsman** (*plural* **sportsmen**), *mujer* **sportwoman** (*plural* **sportwomen**).

deportivo, va *adjetivo*
1. **sporting:** el espíritu deportivo del equipo the sporting spirit of the team
2. **casual:** siempre lleva ropa deportiva he always wear casual clothes.

depositar [1] *verbo*
1. **to leave:** deposite su basura aquí leave your rubbish here
2. **to deposit:** tienes que depositar el dinero antes de las 3 you have to deposit the money before 3 o'clock.

el **depósito**
1. *de gasolina, agua* **tank**
2. *de dinero* **deposit**.

la **depresión** (*plural* las depresiones) ■ **depression**.

deprimir [3] *verbo* ■ **to depress:** la película nos deprimió the film depressed us.

deprisa *adverbio* ■ **quickly:** hazlo deprisa do it quickly.

la **derecha** ■ **right hand**
> a la derecha on the right: el primer edificio a la derecha the first building on the right; gira a la derecha turn on the right; coge la primera calle a la derecha take the first street on the right; María está sentada a la derecha de Juan María is seated to the right of Juan
> la derecha *política* the right
> conducir por la derecha to drive on the right.

derecho, cha *adjetivo* ■ **right:** la pierna derecha the right leg

el **derecho**
1. **right:** el derecho a voto the right to vote; los derechos humanos human rights
2. **law:** quiere estudiar derecho she wants to study law
> ¡no hay derecho! it's not fair!

derecho *adverbio* ■ **straight:** siéntate derecho sit up straight
> todo derecho straight ahead.

derramar [1] *verbo* ■ **to spill:** Ana derramó leche sobre su blusa Ana spilled milk on her blouse.

derrapar [1] *verbo* ■ **to skid.**

derretir [19] *verbo* ■ **to melt:** debes derretir la mantequilla you have to melt the butter
> se derritió el helado the ice-cream melted.

derribar [1] *verbo*
1. **to demolish:** derribaron un edificio viejo they demolished an old building
2. **to shoot down:** derribaron el avión enemigo they shot down the enemy aeroplane
3. **to overthrow:** quieren derribar al gobierno they want to overthrow the government.

derrotar [1] *verbo* ■ **to defeat:** logré derrotar a los otros corredores I managed to defeat the other runners.

derrumbar [1] *verbo* ■ **to demolish:** los albañiles derrumbaron la casa vieja the builders demolished the old house.

desabrochar [1] *verbo* ■ **to undo:** llevas los pantalones desabrochados your trousers are undone; desabróchate la chaqueta undo your jacket; se te ha desabrochado la chaqueta your blouse is undone.

desafiar [7] *verbo*
1. to challenge: el héroe desafió a su enemigo the hero challenged his enemy
2. to defy: los bomberos desafían a la muerte todos los días firefighters defy death every day.

el **desafío** ■ challenge.

desafortunado, da *adjetivo* ■ unfortunate: fue un comentario desafortunado that was an unfortunate comment.

desagradable *adjetivo* ■ unpleasant: el olor a comida podrida es muy desagradable the smell of rotting food is very unpleasant
➤ ¡no seas tan desagradable! don't be so unpleasant!

desagradecido, da *adjetivo* ■ ungrateful.

el **desagüe** ■ drain: el desagüe está tapado con hojas the drain is blocked with leaves.

desahogar [12] *verbo* ■ to vent: Esther desahogó todos sus problemas con su madre Esther vented all her problems on her mother
➤ a veces grita para desahogarse sometimes she screams to let off steam.

desanimado, da *adjetivo* ■ dejected.

desanimar [1] *verbo* ■ to discourage: la falta de dinero nos desanimó the lack of money discouraged us; no te desanimes don't be discouraged.

desaparecer [22] *verbo* ■ to disappear: mis llaves han desaparecido my keys have disappeared.

la **desaparición** ■ disappearance.

desarmar [1] *verbo*
1. to disarm: el policía desarmó con facilidad al atracador the police officer easily disarmed the robber.

el **desarme** ■ disarmament.

desarrollar [1] *verbo*
1. to develop: eso es importante para el desarrollo del niño that's important for a child's development

2. to carry out: desarrolla un trabajo indispensable she carries out indispensable work.

el **desarrollo** ■ development: el desarrollo de las niñas comienza antes que el de los niños girls' development begins before that of boys
➤ países en vías de desarrollo developing countries.

el **desastre** ■ disaster: la fiesta ha sido un desastre the party was a disaster
➤ ¡eres un desastre! you're hopeless!
➤ vas hecho un desastre you look a mess.

desatar [1] *verbo*
1. to untie: desatamos al perro we untied the dog
2. to undo: ayúdame a desatar este nudo help me undo this knot

desatarse *verbo pronominal*
1. to come undone: se ha desatado el nudo the knot has come undone; se te han desatado los cordones your shoelaces have come undone
2. to break: se desató una tormenta muy violenta a very violent storm broke.

desayunar [1] *verbo* ■ to have breakfast: ya es hora de desayunar it's time to have breakfast
➤ desayunar algo to have some breakfast: ¿quieres desayunar algo? would you like to have some breakfast?
➤ desayunaré cereales I'll have cereal for breakfast.

el **desayuno** ■ breakfast.

descalzarse [10] *verbo pronominal* ■ to take one's shoes off: por favor, descalzaos antes de entrar please take your shoes off before entering.

descalzo, za *adjetivo* ■ barefoot: me gusta correr descalzo por la playa I like to run barefoot on the beach.

descansar [1] *verbo* ■ to rest: descansamos durante las vacaciones we rested during the holidays
➤ ¡que descanses! get some rest!

el **descanso**
1. **rest:** necesito un buen descanso I need a good rest
2. **break:** vamos a hacer un descanso de diez minutos we're going to take a ten minute break
3. **intermission:** esta obra de teatro tiene un descanso de cinco minutos this play has a five minute intermission.

el **descapotable** ■ convertible.

descargar [12] *verbo*
1. **to unload:** descargaron la mercancía they unloaded the merchandise
2. **to fire:** descargó su arma sobre víctimas inocentes he fired his weapon at innocent victims
3. **to download:** descarga muchos programas de Internet she downloads a lot of programs from the Internet

descargarse *verbo pronominal* ■ **to go flat:** se ha descargado la batería del coche the car battery has gone flat.

descender [15] *verbo*
1. **to go down:** descendió la temperatura the temperature went down
2. **to be relegated:** nuestro equipo descendió de categoría our soccer team was relegated
3. **to be descended:** desciendo de una familia de origen alemán I am descended from a family of German origin.

el **descenso**
1. **descent:** el descenso de esta montaña es muy peligroso the descent from this mountain is very dangerous
2. **fall:** un fuerte descenso de los precios a sharp fall in prices.

descifrar [1] *verbo* ■ **to decipher:** descifró el jeroglífico he deciphered the hieroglyph.

descolgar [28] *verbo*
1. **to take down:** descolgamos todos los cuadros we took down all the pictures
2. **to pick up:** descuelga el teléfono pick up the telephone

descolgarse *verbo pronominal* ■ **to lower oneself:** las fuerzas especiales se descolgaron por la ventana the special forces lowered themselves through the window.

desconectar [1] *verbo*
1. **to disconnect:** desconectemos este cable let's disconnect this cable
2. **to unplug:** hay que desconectar el aparato you have to unplug the appliance.

desconfiar [7] *verbo* ■ desconfío de sus palabras I distrust his words.

desconfiado, da *adjetivo* ■ **distrustful.**

descongelar [1] *verbo* ■ **to defrost.**

desconocer [22] *verbo* ■ **to be unfamiliar with:** desconocen el tema they are unfamiliar with the subject.

desconocido, da *adjetivo*
1. **unknown:** una actriz desconocida ganó el premio an unknown actress won the prize
2. **unrecognizable:** estás desconocido con ese corte de pelo you're unrecognizable with that haircut

el **desconocido** , **la** **desconocida** unknown person *(plural* **unknown people***)*: dos desconocidos secuestraron al embajador two unknown people kidnapped the ambassador.

el **desconsuelo** ■ grief.

descontar [16] *verbo* ■ **to deduct:** he descontado 10 euros del total I deducted 10 euros from the total.

descontrolarse [1] *verbo pronominal* ■ **to lose control:** se descontroló y empezó a gritarme she lost control and began to shout at me.

descortés *adjetivo* ■ **rude:** su comportamiento fue muy descortés his behaviour was very rude.

describir [3] *verbo* ■ **to describe:** describí el problema I described the problem.

la **descripción** *(plural* las descripciones*)* ■ **description:** hizo una detallada descripción de la situación he gave a detailed description of the situation.

descubierto, ta *adjetivo* ■ **exposed:** era un lugar descubierto it was an exposed place.

el **descubrimiento** ■ **discovery** *(plural discoveries)*: el descubrimiento de la rueda the discovery of the wheel.

descubrir [3] *verbo*

1. **to discover:** descubrieron una isla desierta they discovered a desert island
2. **to uncover:** descubrí el desfalco I uncovered the embezzlement
3. **to unveil:** la novia descubrió su rostro the bride unveiled her face
4. **to find out:** ¡me han descubierto! they have found me out!

el **descuento**

1. **discount:** me hicieron un 15% de descuento they gave me a 15% discount
2. **extra time** *UK,* **overtime** *US:* el árbitro agregó cuatro minutos de descuento en la final the referee added four minutes of extra time in the final.

descuidar [1] *verbo* ■ **to neglect:** no deberías descuidar tu aspecto you shouldn't neglect your appearance

descuidarse *verbo pronominal* ■ **to be careless**

se descuidó un momento y se saltó un semáforo en rojo he lost concentration for a moment and he went through a red light.

el **descuido** ■ **oversight:** provocó un accidente por un descuido he caused an accident through an oversight.

desde *preposición*

1. **since:** vivo en Toledo desde 1998 I have lived in Toledo since 1998; has cambiado desde que te conozco you've changed since I met you
2. **from:** viajamos desde Vigo a Madrid we traveled from Vigo to Madrid; vi el volcán desde el tren I saw the volcano from the train; vivo aquí desde hace cuatro meses I've lived here for four months

desde entonces since then
desde luego of course.

la **desdicha** ■ **unhappiness:** su muerte nos causó una gran desdicha his death caused us great unhappiness.

desear [1] *verbo* ■ **to wish:** te deseo toda la suerte del mundo I wish you all the luck in the world; deseo hablar con el encargado I wish to speak with the person in charge.

desechar [1] *verbo*

1. **to throw out:** desechamos la ropa vieja we threw out the old clothes
2. **to reject:** deseché la idea de viajar I rejected the idea of travelling.

el **desecho** ■ **waste:** los desechos tóxicos son un problema mundial toxic waste is a worldwide problem.

desembarcar [8] *verbo*

1. **to disembark:** los viajeros desembarcaron al llegar al puerto the travellers disembarked upon arriving at the port
2. **to unload:** desembarcaron el equipaje de los pasajeros they unloaded the passengers' luggage.

la **desembocadura** ■ **mouth:** la desembocadura del río queda a dos kilómetros the mouth of the river is two kilometres away.

desembocar [8] *verbo*

1. **to lead into:** esta calle desemboca en la avenida principal this street leads into the main avenue
2. **to flow into:** el Tajo desemboca en el Océano Atlántico the Tagus flows into the Atlantic Ocean.

desempeñar [1] *verbo* ■ **to occupy:** desempeña un cargo ejecutivo she occupies an executive position.

el **desempleo** ■ **unemployment:** el desempleo ha aumentado mucho unemployment has increased a lot.

desencadenar [1] *verbo* ■ **to set off:** la intervención de las tropas desencadenó represalias the intervention of the troops set off reprisals.

desenchufar [1] *verbo* ■ **to unplug**: desenchufa la lámpara unplug the lamp.

desenfocado, da *adjetivo* ■ **out of focus**: las fotos están un poco desenfocadas the photos are a bit out of focus.

el **desengaño** ■ **disappointment**.

el **desenlace** ■ **outcome**: el desenlace de los acontecimientos fue inesperado the outcome of the events was unexpected.

desenredar [1] *verbo*
1. **to untangle**: se desenredó el pelo con el cepillo he untangle his hair with a brush
2. **to unravel**: desenredé el misterio I unraveled the mystery.

desenvolver [17] *verbo* ■ **to unwrap**: desenvolvimos los regalos después de la fiesta we unwrapped the gifts after the party

desenvolverse *verbo pronominal* ■ **to manage**: se desenvolvió bien durante la entrevista she managed well during the interview.

el **deseo**
1. **desire**: mi mayor deseo es hacerte feliz my greatest desire is to make you happy
2. **wish**: pide tres deseos antes de apagar las velas make three wishes before blowing out the candles.

desértico, ca *adjetivo* ■ **desert-like**: atravesamos una zona desértica we crossed a desert-like area.

la **desesperación** *(plural* las desesperaciones) ■ **despair**: la desesperación lo llevó a la locura despair drove him insane.

desesperado, da *adjetivo* ■ **desperate**: estoy desesperado por encontrarla I'm desperate to find her.

desesperar [1] *verbo* ■ **to drive crazy**: me desespera la falta de puntualidad unpunctuality drives me crazy

desesperarse *verbo pronominal* ■ **to lose hope**: no te desesperes que aún puedes ganar don't lose hope, you can still win.

desfilar [1] *verbo* ■ **to parade**: el ejército desfiló ante el Presidente the army paraded

before the President; los escolares desfilaron para carnaval the schoolchildren paraded for carnival.

el **desfile**
1. **parade**: el desfile militar duró tres horas the military parade lasted three hours
2. **procession**: nos encantó el desfile de carnaval we loved the Carnival procession
   ➤ un desfile de moda a fashion show.

desgarrar [1] *verbo* ■ **to tear**: desgarró la tela con un cuchillo he tore the material with a knife.

desgastar [1] *verbo*
1. **to wear out**: has desgastado los zapatos muy rápido you're worn out your shoes quickly
2. **to tear away**: la erosión ha desgastado las rocas erosion has worn away the rocks
3. **to wear down**: este conflicto me ha desgastado terriblemente this conflict has worn me down terribly

desgastarse *verbo pronominal* ■ **to get worn out**: las suelas de las botas se han desgastado the soles of the boots have got worn out.

la **desgracia** ■ **tragedy** *(plural* **tragedies)**: este accidente fue una verdadera desgracia this accident was a real tragedy

➤ por desgracia unfortunately: por desgracia perdimos el campeonato unfortunately we lost the championship.

deshabitado, da *adjetivo* ■ **uninhabited**: es una zona deshabitada it's an uninhabited zone.

deshacer [43] *verbo*
1. **to take apart**: deshice el puzzle I took the puzzle apart
2. **to melt**: tienes que deshacer la mantequilla you have to melt the butter
3. **to undo**: el nudo se deshizo al amarrar el barco the knot came undone as the boat moored
4. **to unpack**: ya he deshecho las maletas I've already unpacked the suitcases

deshacerse *verbo pronominal*

1. to melt: el buen chocolate se deshace en la boca good chocolate melts in your mouth
2. to come undone: el nudo se deshizo solo the knot came undone

> deshacerse de algo to get rid of something: el capitán se deshizo de la carga más pesada the captain got rid of the heaviest cargo
> deshacerse en elogios to shower with praise.

deshidratarse [1] *verbo pronominal* ■ to get dehydrated: se deshidrató a causa del sol he got dehydrated because of the sun.

desierto, ta ■ deserted: la calle está desierta the street is deserted

el **desierto** ■ desert.

la **desilusión** *(plural* las desilusiones*)* ■ disappointment: me llevé una gran desilusión con su comportamiento I suffered a terrible disappointment because of his behaviour; ¡qué desilusión! what a disappointment!

desilusionar [1] *verbo* ■ to disappoint: me has desilusionado con tus malas notas you've disappointed me with your bad grades

desilusionarse *verbo pronominal* ■ to be disappointed: se desilusionó al ver la reacción de su novio she was disappointed to see her boyfriend's reaction.

el **desinfectante** ■ disinfectant.

desinfectar [1] *verbo* ■ to disinfect: el médico desinfectó la herida the doctor disinfected the wound.

desinflar [1] *verbo* ■ to deflate: ayúdame a desinflar la colchoneta help me deflate the mattress.

desintegrarse [1] *verbo pronominal*

1. to disintegrate: las partículas se desintegraron the particles disintegrated
2. to break up: la familia se desintegró the family broke up
3. to split up: el grupo musical se desintegró en 1980 the group split up in 1980.

el **desinterés**

1. lack of interest: hay un gran desinterés de los jóvenes por la política there's a

huge lack of interest in politics among young people
2. unselfishness: me ayudó con total desinterés he helped me with total unselfishness.

desinteresado, da *adjetivo* ■ impartial: te voy a dar un consejo desinteresado I'm going to give you an impartial piece of advice.

deslizar [10] *verbo* ■ to slip: deslizó la carta por debajo de la puerta he slipped the letter under the door

deslizarse *verbo pronominal* ■ to slide: el esquiador se deslizó por la pendiente the skier slid down the slope.

deslumbrante *adjetivo* ■ dazzling: tuvo una actuación deslumbrante he gave a dazzling performance.

deslumbrar [1] *verbo* ■ to dazzle: me deslumbró con su belleza she dazzled me with her beauty.

desmayarse [1] *verbo pronominal* ■ to faint: se desmayó en medio de la clase she fainted in the middle of the class; se desmayó de dolor he fainted from the pain.

el **desmayo** ■ faint
> sufrir un desmayo to faint.

desmontar [1] *verbo*

1. *un mueble* to take apart
2. *un motor* to strip
3. *jinete* to dismount.

desnatado, da *adjetivo*

1. *leche* skimmed
2. *yogur* low-fat.

desnudar [1] *verbo* ■ to undress

desnudarse *verbo pronominal* ■ to get undressed: le da vergüenza desnudarse he's embarrassed about getting undressed.

desnudo, da *adjetivo* ■ naked: estaba completamente desnudo he was totally naked.

la **desnutrición** *(plural* las desnutriciones*)* ■ malnutrition.

desobedecer [22] *verbo* ■ to disobey.

la **desobediencia** ■ disobedience.

desobediente *adjetivo* ■ **disobedient.**

desocupar [1] *verbo* ■ **to vacate:** desocuparon la casa de al lado they vacated the house next door.

el **desodorante** ■ **deodorant.**

el **desorden** *(plural* los desórdenes*)* ■ **mess:** tienes que arreglar el desorden de tu cuarto you have to tidy up the mess in your room

2. **disturbance:** causaron desórdenes públicos they caused public disturbances.

desorientar [1] *verbo*

1. **to disorientate:** la niebla los desorientó the strong fog disorientated them

2. **to confuse:** me desorientó su actitud his attitude confused me.

despachar [1] *verbo*

1. **to attend to:** nos despachó una empleada muy amable a very nice shop assistant attended to us

2. **to deal with:** despachó el tema rápidamente she dealt with the issue quickly

3. **to sell:** esta tienda despacha productos extranjeros this shop sells foreign products.

el **despacho**

1. **office:** me recibió en su despacho he received me in his office

2. **study:** el despacho de mi padre está al lado de la cocina my father's study is next to the kitchen.

despacio *adverbio* ■ **slowly:** caminamos muy despacio we walked very slowly.

despedir [19] *verbo*

1. **to fire:** despidieron a cuatro obreros they fired four workers

2. **to see off:** la despedimos en la estación we saw her off at the station

despedirse *verbo pronominal* ■ **to say goodbye:** se despidieron en la estación they said goodbye at the station

▸ **despedirse de alguien** to say goodbye to somebody: nos despedimos de nuestros padres en el aeropuerto we said goodbye to our parents at the airport.

despegar [12] *verbo*

1. **to take off:** el avión ya ha despegado the aeroplane has already taken off

2. **to peel off:** no despegues la etiqueta don't peel off the label.

despeinado, da *adjetivo* ■ **dishevelled:** estás muy despeinado you look very dishevelled.

despeinarse [1] *verbo pronominal* ■ **to get messed up:** me he despeinado con el viento my hair's got messed up in the wind.

despejado, da *adjetivo* ■ **clear:** el cielo está despejado the sky is clear.

la **despensa** ■ **pantry** *(plural* pantries*)*: guardo los dulces en la despensa I keep the sweets in the pantry.

desperdiciar [1] *verbo* ■ **to throw away:** desperdició muy buenas oportunidades he threw away very good opportunities.

el **desperdicio** ■ **waste:** es un desperdicio no comer esa carne it's a waste not to eat that meat

▸ **no tires los desperdicios** don't throw out the scraps.

el **desperfecto** ■ **flaw:** este coche tiene algunos desperfectos this car has some flaws.

el **despertador** ■ **alarm clock:** mi despertador suena a las 6 de la mañana my alarm clock goes off at 6 in the morning.

despertar [14] *verbo*

1. **to wake:** desperté a mi hijo temprano I woke my son early

2. **to arouse:** su actitud despertó sospechas his attitude aroused suspicion

despertarse to wake up: me desperté con el ruido de la calle I woke up with the noise of the street.

despierto, ta *adjetivo*

1. **awake:** aún non está despierto he's not awake yet

2. **bright:** es una niña muy despierta she's a very bright child.

el **despiste** ■ **slip:** fue un despiste it was just a slip.

despistado, da *adjetivo* ■ **absent-minded.**

desplazar [10] *verbo* ■ **to take the place of:** el avión ha desplazado al barco the airplane has taken the place of the ship

desplazarse **to travel:** me desplazo por la ciudad en coche I travel around the city by car.

desplegar [25] *verbo*

1. **to unfold:** desplegó la tela she unfolded the cloth

2. **to spread:** el pájaro desplegó las alas the bird spread its wings.

despoblado, da *adjetivo* ■ **uninhabited:** atravesamos una zona despoblada we crossed an uninhabited area.

despoblarse [16] *verbo pronominal* ■ **to become depopulated:** el campo se ha despoblado the countryside has become depopulated.

despojarse [1] *verbo* ■ **to remove:** se despojó de la ropa he removed his clothes.

despreciar [1] *verbo*

1. **to look down on:** desprecia a sus empleados he looks down on his employees

2. **to reject:** despreció la invitación de Ana he rejected Ana's invitation.

el **desprecio** ■ **disdain:** una mirada de desprecio a look of disdain.

desprender [2] *verbo* ■ **to give off:** desprende un agradable olor it gives off a nice smell

desprenderse *verbo pronominal*

desprenderse de algo to part with something: no quiere desprenderse del sofá viejo she doesn't want to part with her old sofa.

despreocuparse [1] *verbo pronominal* ■ **to stop worrying:** despreocúpate y descansa un rato stop worrying and rest for a while.

desprevenido, da *adjetivo* ■ **unaware:** su reacción me cogió desprevenido his reaction caught me unaware

la noticia me cogió desprevenida the news took me by surprise.

después *adverbio*

1. **afterwards:** después, iremos a bailar afterwards, we'll go dancing

2. **later:** vino después she came later; un año después volví a mi trabajo a year later I went back to work

3. **then:** primero le pones sal y después le pones pimienta first you put in the salt and then you put in the pepper

después de after: después de cenar te llamaré after dinner I'll call you; después de todo after all

después de Cristo Anno Domini.

destacar [8] *verbo*

1. **to emphasize:** destacó sus valores morales he emphasized his moral values

2. **to stand up:** destaca por su altura he stands out because of his height.

destapar [1] *verbo* ■ **to open:** destapé la limonada I opened the lemonade.

el **destello** ■ **glimmer:** vi un destello de luz en la distancia I saw a glimmer of light in the distance.

destinar [1] *verbo*

1. **to set aside:** han destinado el dinero a obras benéficas they've set aside the money for charity

2. **to assign:** lo han destinado al departamento de contabilidad they have assigned him to the accounting department

3. **to post:** me han destinado a Bilbao they've posted me to Bilbao.

el **destinatario** , **la** **destinataria** ■ **addressee:** Raúl es el destinatario de esta carta Raúl is the addressee of this letter.

el **destino**

1. **destiny** *(plural* **destinies***)*: mi destino es ayudar a los demás my destiny is to help others

2. **destination:** no sabe el destino del vuelo he doesn't know the destiny of the flight; los pasajeros con destino Roma deben embarcar ahora the passengers for Rome must board now.

la **destreza** ■ **skill:** tiene una destreza increíble con las manos he has incredible skill with his hands.

el **destornillador** ■ screwdriver.

destrozar [10] *verbo*

1. to destroy: la explosión destrozó el barrio the explosion destroyed the neighbourhood
2. to ruin: el perro ha destrozado el sofá the dog has ruined the sofa
3. to break: me ha destrozado el corazón she's broken my heart.

destructor, ra *adjetivo* ■ destructive: tuvo efectos destructores it had destructive effects.

destruir [36] *verbo* ■ to destroy: la tormenta destruyó las casas del pueblo the storm destroyed the houses in the town.

el **desván** ■ attic.

desvelar [1] *verbo*

1. to keep awake: el café me desvela coffee keeps me awake
2. to reveal: me desveló la verdad he revealed the truth to me

desvelarse por algo to be concerned about something: se desvela por nuestra felicidad he's concerned about our happiness.

la **desventaja** ■ disadvantage.

la **desviación** *(plural* las desviaciones*)* ■ detour: tuvimos que tomar una desviación en el camino we had to make a detour on the way

desviación de fondos diversion of funds.

desviar [7] *verbo* ■ to divert: desviaron el tránsito they diverted the traffic

desviarse *verbo pronominal* ■ to turn off: nos desviamos de la ruta principal we turned off from the main route.

el **detalle** ■ detail: me contó los detalles de la historia he told me the details of the story

¡qué detalle! how thoughtful!

detectar [1] *verbo* ■ to detect: el radar detectó el peligro the radar detected the danger.

el/la **detective** ■ detective

un detective privado a private detective.

detener [52] *verbo*

1. to stop: el conductor detuvo el coche the driver stopped the car
2. to arrest: la policía detuvo a los sospechosos the police arrested the suspects

detenerse *verbo pronominal* ■ to stop: no te detengas, sigue andando don't stop, keep walking.

el **detenido** , la **detenida** ■ prisoner.

el **detergente** ■ detergent.

deteriorar [1] *verbo* ■ to damage: el mar deteriora las casas de la costa the sea damages the coastal houses

deteriorarse to deteriorate: su salud se ha deteriorado rápidamente her health has deteriorated quickly.

determinado, da *adjetivo* ■ certain: esta práctica era común en determinada época this practice was common at a certain time period.

determinar [1] *verbo*

1. to determine: el juez determinó la sentencia de los acusados the judge determined the sentence of the accused
2. to decide: determinamos una fecha para la reunión we decided a date for the meeting
3. to state: la ley determina que tenemos ciertos derechos y obligaciones the law states that we have certain rights and obligations
4. to bring about: el excelente trabajo de los empleados determinó el éxito del negocio the excellent work of the employees brought about the success of the business.

detrás *adverbio* ■ at the back: siéntate detrás sit at the back

uno detrás de otro one after another

detrás de behind

el gato se escondió detrás de la puerta the cat hid behind the door.

la **deuda** ■ debt: tengo una deuda con el banco I have a debt with the bank.

el **deudor** , la **deudora** ■ debtor: los deudores tienen problemas para pagar the debtors are having problems paying.

la **devaluación** *(plural* las devaluaciones*)*
■ devaluation: la devaluación de la moneda provocó una baja en el consumo interno the devaluation of the currency caused a decrease in internal consumption
> la devaluación de la moneda the devaluation of the currency.

la **devoción** ■ devotion.

la **devolución**
1. *de libro, carta* return
2. *de dinero* refund.

devolver [17] *verbo*
1. to return: ya he devuelto los libros a la biblioteca I've already returned the books to the library
2. to repay: le devolveremos el importe we'll repay the amount to him
3. to throw up: el bebé devolvió la comida the baby threw up the food.

devorar [1] *verbo*
1. to devour: el jabalí devoró al cordero the wild boar devoured the lamb; los niños devoraron la merienda the children devoured the snack
2. to consume: las llamas devoraron el almacén the flames consumed the warehouse.

el **día** ■ day: los días son más largos en verano the days are longer in the summer; marzo tiene 31 días March has 31 days; los murciélagos duermen de día bats sleep during the day
> ¡buenos días! good morning!
> es de día it's daylight
> un día festivo a holiday
> un día laborable a working day
> hacer buen día to be a fine day
> hoy en día nowadays
> todos los días every day
> poner al día to catch up: se puso al día con el trabajo he caught up with his work.

el **diablo** ■ devil: el diablo representa el mal the devil represents evil.

el **diagnóstico** ■ diagnosis: el médico dio un diagnóstico favorable the doctor gave a favourable diagnosis.

el **diálogo**
1. dialogue: el diálogo condujo a una solución pacífica the dialogue led to a peaceful solution
2. conversation: mantuvimos un diálogo muy interesante we had a very interesting conversation.

el **diamante** ■ diamond: me regaló un anillo con un diamante he gave me a diamond ring.

el **diámetro** ■ diameter: calcula el diámetro de este círculo calculate the diameter of this circle.

la **diana** ■ target: dar en la diana to hit the target.

la **diapositiva** ■ slide.

diario, ria *adjetivo* ■ daily: hago tres comidas diarias I have three meals daily
> a diario every day: va en bici a diario he rides his bike every day

el **diario**
1. newspaper: pásame el diario de la mañana pass me the morning newspaper
2. diary *(plural* diaries*)*: escribo en mi diario todos los días I write in my diary every day.

el/la **dibujante**
1. cartoonist: el dibujante hizo un oso animado the cartoonist drew an animated bear
2. *hombre* draughtsman UK, draftsman US *(plural* draughtsmen UK, draftsmen US*), mujer* draughtswoman UK, draftswoman UK *(plural* draughtswomen UK, draftswomen US*)*: los dibujantes terminaron el plano the draughtsmen finished the plan.

dibujar [1] *verbo* ■ to draw: dibujó un paisaje he drew a landscape; no sabe dibujar he can't draw.

el **dibujo** ■ drawing: hizo un dibujo de su madre he did a drawing of his mother
> los dibujos animados cartoons.

el **diccionario** ■ dictionary *(plural* dictionaries*)*: compró un diccionario de inglés he bought an English dictionary.

la **dicha** ■ happiness: su familia es su mayor dicha his family is his greatest happiness.

el **dicho** ■ saying: **abusa de los dichos y proverbios** she abuses sayings and proverbs; **es un dicho popular** it's a popular saying
> **dicho y hecho** no sooner said than done.

dichoso, sa *adjetivo* ■ happy: **se siente dichosa con su embarazo** she feels happy about her pregnancy
> **¡dichosa música!** that damn music!

diciembre *sustantivo masculino*

En inglés los nombres de los meses se escriben con mayúscula.

December: **en diciembre** in December; **el próximo diciembre** next December; **el pasado diciembre** last December; **jueves seis de diciembre** Thursday the sixth of December *UK*, Thursday, December sixth *US*.

el **dictado** ■ dictation: **la maestra pone un dictado todas las semanas** the teacher assigns a dictation every week.

el **dictador** , la **dictadora** ■ dictator: **el dictador gobernó durante diez años** the dictator governed for ten years.

la **dictadura** ■ dictatorship.

dictar [1] *verbo*
1. to dictate: **el jefe le dictó una carta a la secretaria** the boss dictated a letter to his secretary
2. to pronounce: **el juez dictó sentencia** the judge pronounced the sentence.

diecinueve *numeral* ■ nineteen: **la abuela tiene diecinueve nietos** grandma has nineteen grandchildren; **mi hermano tiene diecinueve años** my brother is nineteen; **el diecinueve de febrero** the nineteenth of February *UK*, February nineteenth *US*.

dieciocho *numeral* ■ eighteen: **por fin cumpliré dieciocho años** I'll be eighteen at last; **el dieciocho de julio** the eighteenth of July *UK*, July eighteenth *US*.

dieciséis *numeral* ■ sixteen: **mañana cumplo dieciséis años** I'll be sixteen tomorrow; **el dieciséis de octubre** the sixteenth of October *UK*, October sixteenth *US*.

diecisiete *numeral* ■ seventeen: **un grupo de diecisiete personas** a group of seventeen people; **el diecisiete de abril** the seventeenth of April *UK*, April seventeenth *US*.

el **diente** ■ tooth *(plural* teeth*)*: **al bebe le están saliendo los dientes** the baby's teeth are coming through; **la sierra tiene los dientes gastados** the teeth of the saw are worn out
> **un diente de ajo** a clove of garlic
> **un diente de leche** a milk tooth.

diestro, tra *adjetivo*
1. skilful *UK*, skillful *US*: **es muy diestro manejando los caballos** he's very skilful at handling the horses
2. right-handed: **un chico diestro y uno zurdo** a right-handed boy and a left-handed one.

la **dieta** ■ diet: **la dieta mediterránea es muy saludable** the Mediterranean diet is very healthy; **el lunes me pongo a dieta** on Monday I start the diet.

el/la **dietista** ■ dietician: **el dietista me recomendó que no comiera grasas** the dietician recommended that I don't eat fats.

diez *numeral* ■ ten: **tiene diez hijos** she has ten children
> **mi hermana tiene diez años** my sister is ten years old
> **son las diez** it's ten o'clock
> **el diez de abril** the tenth of April *UK*, April tenth *US*.

la **diferencia** ■ difference: **hay una gran diferencia de edad entre los dos hermanos** there's a big age difference between the two brothers; **los socios tuvieron graves diferencias** the partners had serious differences.

diferente *(adjetivo & adverbio)*
■ *adjetivo*
different: **sus hijos son muy diferentes** his children are very different
■ *adverbio*
differently: **Ana come diferente porque está a dieta** Ana is eating differently because she's on a diet.

difícil *adjetivo* ■ difficult: **no encuentro salida para esta difícil situación** I can't find a way out of this difficult situation; **este problema de matemáticas es muy difícil**

this maths problem is very difficult; **una persona difícil** a difficult person.

la **dificultad** ■ difficulty *(plural* **difficulties)**: **este viaje está lleno de dificultades** this trip is full of difficulties.

dificultar [1] *verbo* ■ to hinder: **la niebla dificulta la visión** the fog hinders vision.

difundir [3] *verbo*

1. to spread: **la luz eléctrica se difundió por todo el mundo** electric light spread throughout the whole world

2. to broadcast: **la televisión difunde las noticias** television broadcasts the news.

digerir [20] *verbo* ■ to digest: **digiere la comida con dificultad** he digests food with difficulty.

la **digestión** *(plural* **las digestiones)** ■ digestion.

digital *adjetivo* ■ digital

> **una cámara digital** a digital camera; **las huellas digitales** fingerprints.

la **dignidad**

1. dignity: **habla con dignidad** he speaks with dignity

2. honour *UK*, honor *US*: **su dignidad le impidió aceptar la oferta** his honour prevented him from accepting the offer.

digno, na *adjetivo* ■ worthy: **su trabajo es digno de mención** his work is worthy of mention.

dilatar [1] *verbo*

1. to expand: **el calor dilata los cuerpos** heat expands substances

2. to put off: **dilataron la respuesta intencionalmente** they put off the answer intentionally.

diluir [36] *verbo* ■ to dilute: **diluye la pintura con agua** dilute the paint with water.

la **dimensión** *(plural* **las dimensiones)**

1. dimension: **¿cuáles son las dimensiones del coche?** what are de dimensions of the car?

2. measurement: **necesito las dimensiones exactas de la habitación** I need the exact measurements of the room

3. scope: **las dimensiones de la catástrofe son incalculables** the scope of the catastrophe is incalculable

> **en grandes dimensiones** very large: **es una casa de grandes dimensiones** it's a very large house.

el **diminutivo** ■ the diminutive.

diminuto, ta *adjetivo* ■ tiny: **tiene una cicatriz diminuta** she has a tiny scar.

la **dimisión** ■ resignation: **el director ha presentado su dimisión** the director handed in his resignation.

dimitir [3] *verbo* ■ to resign: **ha dimitido a causa del escándalo** he's resigned because of the scandal.

dinámico, ca *adjetivo* ■ dynamic: **es una persona tan dinámica que trabaja 15 horas al día** she's such a dynamic person that she works 15 hours a day.

la **dinamita** ■ dynamite.

el **dinero** ■ money: **heredé una fuerte suma de dinero** I inherited a large sum of money; **ando muy mal de dinero** I'm very short of money.

el **dios** ■ god: **en su religión adoran a más de un dios** in their religion they worship more than one god; **según la Biblia Dios creó al hombre** according to the Bible, God created man

> **Dios mediante** God willing

> **¡Dios mío!** my God!

la **diosa** ■ goddess: **la diosa del mar protege a los pescadores** the goddess of the sea protects fishermen.

el **diploma** ■ diploma.

la **diplomacia** ■ diplomacy.

el **diplomático**, la **diplomática** ■ diplomat.

el **diputado**, la **diputada**

1. *en el congreso* deputy *(plural* **deputies)**

2. member of parliament, MP *UK*

3. representative *US*.

la **dirección** *(plural* **las direcciones)**

1. direction: **estamos yendo en dirección norte** we are going in a northerly direction

2. **management:** la dirección incorporará más trabajadores the management are going to take on more workers

3. **address:** tengo la dirección de la fiesta I have the address of the party

4. **steering:** está fallando la dirección del coche the car's steering is failing.

directo, ta *adjetivo*

1. **direct, non-stop** *US:* este es un vuelo directo a Barcelona this is a direct flight to Barcelone

2. **direct:** tengo órdenes directas del jefe I have direct orders from the boss

3. **straight:** fui directo a casa I went straight home

➢ **en directo** live: están transmitiendo el partido en directo they are broadcasting the match live.

el **director** , **la** **directora**

1. **director:** la directora de la empresa prometió llamarnos the director of the company promised to call us; ¿quién es el director de la película? who is the director of the film?

2. **headteacher** *UK,* **principal** *US* la directora de esa escuela es muy joven the headteacher of that school is very young

3. **conductor:** el director de la orquesta tiene mucha experiencia the conductor of the orchestra has a lot of experience

4. **editor:** mi tío es el director de ese periódico my uncle is the editor of that newspaper.

el **directorio**

1. **board of directors:** el directorio de la empresa es muy exigente the company's board of directors is very demanding

2. **directory** *(plural* **directories***)*: tengo muchos directorios en mi ordenador I have a lot of directories in my computer.

dirigir [11] *verbo*

1. **to address:** esta carta está dirigida a mi jefe this letter is addressed to my boss

2. **to manage:** el Sr. López dirige esta empresa Mr. López manages this company

3. **to direct:** Spielberg ha dirigido muchas películas Spielberg has directed a lot of films

4. **to conduct:** el hombre que dirige esta orquesta es muy famoso en Europa the man who conducts this orchestra is very famous in Europe

dirigirse *verbo pronominal*

1. **to head towards:** nos dirigimos hacia el oeste we headed towards the west

2. **to address:** se dirigió a los estudiantes he addressed the students.

la **disciplina** ■ **discipline:** la disciplina es muy importante en esta institución discipline is very important in this institution.

el **discípulo** , **la** **discípula**

1. **follower:** Carlos es discípulo de un artista famoso Carlos is a follower of a famous artist

2. **disciple:** Jesús escogió a 12 discípulos Jesus chose 12 disciples.

el **disco**

1. **disc** *UK,* **disk** *US:* cortamos esta masa en forma de disco we cut this dough into the shape of a disc

2. **record:** tiene una colección de discos de jazz she has a collection of jazz records

3. **disk:** tiene problemas con el disco duro he's got problems with the hard disk

➢ **un disco compacto** a compact disc.

la **discordia** ■ **discord.**

la **discoteca** ■ **discotheque.**

la **discreción** *(plural* las discreciones*)* ■ **discretion:** me pidió discreción cuando me reveló su problema he asked me for discretion when he disclosed his problem to me.

discreto, ta *adjetivo* ■ **discreet:** se viste de manera muy discreta she dresses in a very discreet manner.

la **discriminación** *(plural* las descripciones*)* ■ **discrimination:** discriminación racial racial discrimination.

discriminar [1] *verbo*

1. **to discriminate:** hay leyes que discriminan según el sexo there are laws that discriminate according to sex

2. **to tell the difference:** tienes que discriminar entre lo que está bien y lo que está mal you have to tell the difference between what's good and what's bad.

la **disculpa** ■ **apology** *(plural* **apologies***)*: su disculpa no fue suficiente his apology was not enough pedirle disculpas a alguien por algo to apologize to somebody for something: te pido disculpas por lo que dije I apologize to you for what I said.

disculpar [1] *verbo* ■ to excuse: te disculpo esta vez I'll excuse you this time

disculpe, ¿me deja pasar? excuse me, can I get by?

disculparse to apologize: el profesor se disculpó por haber llegado tarde the teacher apologized for having arrived late.

el **discurso** ■ speech: pronunció un discurso muy emotivo he gave a very moving speech.

la **discusión** *(plural* las discusiones)*

1. discussion: la discusión sobre el tema se hizo interminable the discussion of the subject became endless

2. argument: tuvimos una discusión con el encargado del restaurante we had an argument with the manager of the restaurant.

discutir [3] *verbo*

1. to discuss: discutimos el tema de la crisis financiera we discussed the subject of the financial crisis

2. to argue: discutieron con el encargado del restaurante they argued with the manager of the restaurant.

diseñar [1] *verbo* ■ to design: el arquitecto diseñó una casa con cuatro dormitorios the architect designed a house with four bedrooms; Ana diseña moda femenina Ana designs ladies' fashion.

el **diseño** ■ design: se encargó del diseño de la próxima colección de vestidos she took charge of the design of the next collection of dresses.

el **disfraz** *(plural* los disfraces)* ■ disguise: el niño se puso un disfraz de pirata the boy put on a pirate disguise.

disfrazar [10] *verbo* ■ to dress up: disfrazó a su hijo para el carnaval she dressed her son up for the carnival

disfrazarse *verbo pronominal*

disfrazarse de to dress up as: se disfrazó de vaquero he dressed up as a cowboy.

disfrutar [1] *verbo* ■ to enjoy oneself: disfruté en la fiesta I enjoyed myself at the party

disfrutar de algo to enjoy something: disfruta de tus vacaciones en la playa enjoy your holidays at the seaside.

disgustar [1] *verbo* ■ to upset: a los clientes les disgustan estas respuestas these answers upset the clients

disgustarse *verbo pronominal* ■ to get upset: el jefe se disgustó con uno de los empleados the boss got upset with one of the employees

 The Spanish word **disgustar** is a false friend, it does not mean "to disgust".

el **disgusto**

darle un disgusto a alguien to upset somebody: su respuesta me dio un gran disgusto his answer upset me a lot

llevarse un disgusto to get upset: se llevó un disgusto cuando suspendió he got upset when he failed.

disimular [1] *verbo* ■ to hide: disimularon su enfado they hid their anger

no disimules, que te he visto stop pretending, I know what you're up to.

disminuir [36] *verbo* ■ to decrease: disminuye la velocidad en la curva decrease your speed on the curve; la inflación ha disminuido un 1% inflation has decreased by 1%.

disolver [17] *verbo*

1. to dissolve: tuvimos que disolver la pastilla en el agua we had to dissolve the tablet in the water

2. to break up: la policía disolvió la manifestación the police broke up the demonstration

disolverse *verbo pronominal* ■ to dissolve: el medicamento se disuelve en el agua the medicine dissolves in water.

disparar [1] *verbo* ■ to shoot: la policía disparó sa los ladrones the police fired at the thieves

dispara la fotografía take the picture.

el **disparate** ■ nonsense: lo que dices es un disparate what you're saying is nonsense.

el **disparo** ■ shot: el disparo retumbó en la habitación the shot echoed in the room.

disponer [47] *verbo*

1. to arrange: dispusimos las sillas junto a las mesas we arranged the chairs close to the tables

2. to order: el jefe dispuso que trabajáramos toda la noche the boss ordered us to work all night

disponerse *verbo pronominal*

disponerse a to get ready to: nos disponíamos a salir cuando llegó mi madre we were getting ready to leave when my mother arrived.

disponible *adjetivo* ■ available.

la **disposición** (*plural* las disposiciones)

1. arrangement: no me gusta la disposición de las sillas en esta sala I don't like the arrangement of the chairs in this room

2. aptitude: no tiene disposición para las matemáticas he has no aptitude for mathematics

3. provision: la disposición del gobierno regula el comercio interno the provision of the government regulates internal commerce.

el **disquete** ■ diskette: copia el archivo en un disquete copy the file onto a diskette.

la **distancia** ■ distance: hay una distancia de 100 km entre las dos ciudades there's a distance of 100 km between the two cities

¿a qué distancia está la tienda? how far away is the shop?

a dos millas de distancia two miles away.

distante *adjetivo*

1. far away: vive en una zona distante de la capital he lives in an area far away from the capital

2. distant: tiene una actitud distante con respecto al problema she has a distant attitude regarding the problem.

distinguir [13] *verbo*

1. to distinguish: no puedo distinguir a un mellizo del otro I can't distinguish one twin from the other

2. to set apart: la calidad de nuestros productos nos distingue de los demás the quality of our products sets us apart from the rest

3. to make out: no puedo distinguirlo entre la multitud I can't make him out among the crowd

4. to honour: lo distinguieron con el primer premio they honored him with first prize.

distinto, ta *adjetivo* ■ different: cada hijo es distinto each child is different; es muy distinto verlo en directo it's very different to see it live.

la **distracción** (*plural* las distracciones)

1. lapse of concentration: una distracción del conductor provocó el accidente a lapse of concentration from the driver caused the accident

2. pastime: el cine es una buena distracción the cinema is a good pastime.

distraer [53] *verbo*

1. to distract: el ruido me distrae cuando estudio noise distracts me when I'm studying

2. to entertain: las películas me distraen films entertain me

distraerse *verbo pronominal*

1. to get distracted: el niño se distrae fácilmente en clase the boy gets distracted easily in class

2. to entertain oneself: me distraigo viendo televisión I entertain myself watching television.

distribuir [36] *verbo*

1. to distribute: distribuiremos las tareas entre todos we'll distribute the work between everybody

2. to hand out: el profesor distribuyó los exámenes the teacher handed out the exams.

el **distrito** ■ district: es el encargado de la seguridad del distrito he's the one in charge of the district's safety

distrito federal federal district: México es un Distrito Federal Mexico City is a Federal District.

diurno, na *adjetivo* ■ day: me tocó el turno diurno en el trabajo I got the day shift at work.

la **diversidad** ■ variety: hay una gran diversidad de artículos en esta tienda there's a wide variety of goods in this shop.

la **diversión** *(plural* las diversiones*)*

1. amusement: le dedica más tiempo a la diversión que al trabajo he dedicates more time to amusement than to work

2. pastime: el cine es mi diversión preferida the cinema is my favourite pastime

⚠ The Spanish word **diversión** is a false friend, it does not mean "diversion".

diverso, sa *adjetivo*

1. diverse: tiene gustos muy diversos he has very diverse tastes

2. various: tuvimos varios problemas we had various problems.

divertido, da *adjetivo* ■ enjoyable: pasamos un rato muy divertido en la fiesta we had a very enjoyable time at the party

➤ ¡qué divertido! what fun!

divertir [20] *verbo* ■ to amuse: los payasos no me divierten en absoluto clowns don't amuse me at all

➤ nos divertimos en la fiesta we had fun at the party.

dividir [3] *verbo*

1. to divide: un tabique dividía la habitación en dos a partition divided the room in two; divide 464 entre cuatro divide 464 by four

2. to divide up: dividimos los caramelos entre todos los niños we divided up the sweets among all the children.

la **división** *(plural* las divisiones*)* ■ division: la división de los bienes fue problemática the division of the goods was problematic; su hijo ya hace divisiones en la escuela her son is already doing divisions at school; su equipo juega en segunda división his team plays in the second division.

divorciarse *verbo pronominal* ■ to get divorced: se divorciaron después de diez años de casados they got divorced after being married for ten years.

el **divorcio** ■ divorce: los trámites del divorcio fueron muy costosos the divorce proceedings were very costly.

divulgar [12] *verbo* ■ to spread: los medios divulgaron la noticia the media spread the news.

DNI *(plural* los DNI*) (abreviatura de* Documento Nacional de Identidad*)* ■ identity card: tengo que renovar el DNI I have to renew my ID card.

doblar [1] *verbo*

1. to fold: doblé la ropa antes de guardarla en el armario I folded the clothes before putting them in the wardrobe

2. to double: le doblaron el sueldo they doubled his salary

3. to turn: tenemos que doblar en la primera esquina we turned at the first corner

4. to dub: doblaron la película al español they dubbed the film into Spanish.

doble *(adjetivo & adverbio)*

■ *adjetivo*

double: he reservado una habitación doble I've booked a double room

■ *adverbio*

double: como había perdido la entrada, tuvo que pagar doble since he had lost the ticket, he had to pay double

el **doble**

1. double: contrataron un doble para las escenas peligrosas they hired a double for the dangerous scenes

2. el doble twice as much; gana el doble que yo he earns twice as much as I do.

doce *numeral* ■ twelve: tiene doce sobrinos she has twelve nephews

➤ mi hermana tiene doce años my sister is twelve years old

➤ son las doce it's twelve o'clock

➤ el doce de abril the twelfth of April UK, April twelfth US.

la **docena** ■ dozen.

el **doctor** , la **doctora** ■ doctor: la doctora me dio de alta the doctor pronounced me fit.

el **documento** ■ document: me piden un documento que pruebe mi fecha de nacimiento they are asking me for a document that proves my date of birth

un documento de identidad an identity card: para comprar bebidas alcohólicas necesitas mostrar el documento de identidad in order to buy alcoholic beverages you need to show your identity card.

el **dólar** ■ dollar.

doler [17] *verbo*

1. to ache: me duele la espalda my back aches
2. to hurt: le dolió mucho que su novia lo dejara it hurt him a lot that his girlfriend left him.

el **dolor** ■ pain: la noticia de su muerte le causó mucho dolor the news of his death caused her a lot of pain

tener dolor de cabeza to have a headache
tener dolor de muelas to have toothache.

domesticar [8] *verbo* ■ to tame: consiguieron domesticar un jabalí they managed to tame a wild boar.

doméstico, ca *adjetivo* ■ domestic: las tareas domésticas domestic chores

compramos un lavaplatos de uso doméstico we bought a dishwasher for home use
un animal doméstico a pet.

el **domicilio** ■ residence

domicilio familiar family residence
escriba su nombre y domicilio en este formulario write your name and address on this form.

dominar [1] *verbo*

1. to rule over: el ejército enemigo dominaba toda la zona the enemy army ruled over all the area
2. to control: domina la pelota de manera increíble he controls the ball in an incredible way.

el **domingo**

En inglés, los días de la semana se escriben con mayúscula:

Sunday: hoy es domingo today is Sunday; el próximo domingo next Sunday; el domingo pasado last Sunday; el domingo on Sunday; te veré el domingo I'll see you on Sunday; los domingos on Sundays; los domingos vamos al parque on Sundays we go to the park.

dominicano, na *adjetivo*

En inglés, los adjetivos que se refieren a un país o una región se escriben con mayúscula:

Dominican

el **domicano**, la **domicana**

En inglés, los gentilicios se escriben con mayúscula:

Dominicans: los dominicanos the Dominicans.

el **dominio**

1. control: tiene un dominio total de la situación he has total control over the situation
2. command: tiene un dominio excelente del español he has an excellent command of Spanish.

el **dominó** ■ dominoes: los sábados jugamos al dominó on Saturdays we play dominoes.

el **don**

1. gift: tiene un don para los idiomas he has a gift for languages
2. Mr.: don Mario López Mr. Mario López.

donar [1] *verbo* ■ to donate: donó la casa a los más necesitados he donated the house to the most needy.

donde *adverbio* ■ where: ahí fue donde encontramos la mochila there's where we found the rucksack; iré hasta donde quieras I'll go wherever you want me to.

dónde *adverbio* ■ where: ¿dónde estabas ayer a esta misma hora? where were you yesterday at this time?; ¿dónde vas a ir de viaje? where are you going for your trip?; ¿de dónde eres? where are you from?; no sé dónde he puesto el libro I don't know where I've put the book

por dónde which way: ¿por dónde se va a tu casa? which is the way to your home?

la **doña** ■ Mrs.: doña Beatriz García Mrs. Beatriz García.

dorado, da *adjetivo* ■ gold.

dormir [18] *verbo*

1. to sleep: durmió profundamente toda la noche he slept deeply all night
2. to stay: dormimos en un hotel de cinco estrellas we stayed in a five-star hotel
3. to anaesthetize *UK*, to anesthetize *US*: te duermen únicamente la zona que te van a operar they anesthetize only the area they're going to operate on

> se me durmió el pie my foot fell asleep

dormirse *verbo pronominal* ■ **to fall asleep**: me dormí enseguida I fell asleep straight away.

el **dormitorio** ■ bedroom: la casa tiene cuatro dormitorios the house has four bedrooms.

el **dorso** ■ back: firme al dorso del documento sign on the back of the document.

dos *numeral* ■ two: tiene dos hijos she has two children

> mi hermana tiene dos años my sister is two years old
> son las dos it's two o'clock
> el dos de abril the second of April.

la **dosis** *(plural las dosis)* ■ dose: aumentaron la dosis del medicamento they increased his dose of medicine.

el **drama** ■ drama: el drama es el género que más me gusta drama is the genre that I like most; la enfermedad de su hijo es un verdadero drama her son's illness is a real drama.

dramático, ca *adjetivo*

1. dramatic: el accidente tuvo consecuencias dramáticas the accident had dramatic consequences
2. drama: este autor destacó en el género dramático this author stood out in the drama genre.

el **drenaje** ■ drainage.

drenar [1] *verbo* ■ to drain: drenaron la zona después de las inundaciones they drained the area after the floods.

la **droga** ■ drug: es una droga muy peligrosa it's a very dangerous drug
> drogas duras hard drugs
> drogas blandas soft drugs.

drogarse [12] *verbo pronominal* ■ to take drugs.

la **drogadicción** *(plural las drogadicciones)* ■ drug addiction.

la **ducha** ■ shower: me di una ducha antes de acostarme I had a shower before going to bed; la ducha de este baño es pequeña the shower in this bathroom is small
> darse una ducha to take a shower: me di una ducha después de hacer deporte I took a shower after playing sports.

ducharse [1] *verbo pronominal* ■ to take a shower: me ducho siempre por la mañana I always take a shower in the morning.

la **duda**

1. doubt: tengo dudas sobre la honestidad de su respuesta I have doubts about the honesty of his reply
2. question: la profesora preguntó si alguien tenía alguna duda sobre el tema the teacher asked if anybody had any questions about the topic
> tengo la duda de si llamar a Diego o no I don't know whether to call Diego or not.

dudar [1] *verbo*

1. to doubt: dudo que venga I doubt that he'll come
2. to hesitate: dudo entre ir al cine o ir al teatro I am hesitating between going to the cinema and going to the theatre
3. to question: dudo de sus buenas intenciones I question his good intentions.

el **dueño** , la **dueña**

1. owner: es el dueño de un edificio entero he's the owner of a whole building
2. *dueño de la casa* landlord, *dueña de la casa* landlady *(plural* landladies): tenemos que pagar el alquiler al dueño de la casa we have to pay the rent to the landlord of the flat.

dulce *adjetivo*

1. sweet: este postre es muy dulce this dessert is very sweet

2. gentle: su hija es la niña más dulce que conozco her daughter is the most gentle girl I know

el **dulce** ■ sweet: sus hijos adoran los dulces his children adore sweets.

la **duración** *(plural* las duraciones*)* ■ length.

durante *preposición*

1. during: ha trabajado durante todo el verano he's worked all summer; durmió durante toda la película he slept through the film

2. for: estudió química durante ocho años she studied chemistry for eight years.

durar [1] *verbo*

1. to last: estos zapatos nuevos me duraron sólo dos meses these new shoes lasted me only two months

2. to go on: este partido de tenis está durando demasiado this tennis match is going on too long.

la **dureza**

1. *de material* toughness, hardness.

2. *de carácter* harshness, hardness.

duro, ra *adjetivo*

1. hard: este tipo de madera es más duro que el otro this type of wood is harder than the other

2. tough: la carne estaba tan dura que era incomible the meat was so tough that it was inedible

3. hard: ha tenido una vida muy dura she's had a very hard life

4. harsh: el Gobierno dio una dura respuesta a la oposición the government gave a harsh reply to the opposition

➤ a duras penas with great difficulty: a duras penas gana para vivir he makes living with great difficulty

➤ el duro five-peseta coin: no tengo ni un duro I'm broke

duro *adverbio* ■ hard: estudió duro para el examen I am studying hard for the exam.

el **DVD** *(abreviatura de* Disco Versátil Digital*)* ■ DVD.

e *conjunción* ■ and: María e Inés son compañeras de clase María and Inés are classmates

e replaces y before words that begin with "i" or "hi"

ebrio, a *adjetivo* ■ drunk: una persona ebria no debe conducir a drunk person shouldn't drive.

echar [1] *verbo*

1. to throw: echaron las piedras al río they threw stones into the river

2. to throw out: lo echaron de casa they threw him out of the house

3. to expel: los han echado del colegio they've expelled them from the school

4. to sack: lo han echado del trabajo they've sacked him from work

5. to grow: esta planta ya ha echado raíces this plant has already grown roots

6. to put: le eché sal a la sopa I put salt in the soup

➤ echar de menos to miss: te vamos a echar de menos cuando estés de viaje we're going to miss you when you're on your trip

➤ echar a perder to spoil: vas a echar a perder a la niña con tantos regalos you're going to spoil the girl with so many gifts

➤ ¿qué echan esta noche en la tele? what's on TV tonight?

echarse *verbo pronominal* ■ to lie down: se echó en la cama he lay down on the bed.

el **eclipse** ■ eclipse

➤ un eclipse de sol a solar eclipse

➤ un eclipse de luna a lunar eclipse.

el eco ■ echo *(plural* **echoes***)*: **en esta cueva hay eco** there's an echo in this cave.

la economía

1. **economy**: **la economía no anda muy bien** the economy is not doing very well

2. **economics**: **es profesor de economía** he's a professor of economics.

económico, ca *adjetivo*

1. **economic**: **tienen serios problemas económicos** they have serious economic problems

2. **inexpensive**: **este restaurante es el más económico** this restaurant is the most inexpensive

3. **economical**: **este coche es más económico que el otro** this car is more economical than the other.

el ecuador ■ equator.

Ecuador ■ Ecuador.

ecuatoriano, na *adjetivo*

En inglés, los adjetivos que se refieren a un país o una región se escriben con mayúscula:

Ecuadorian: **los tapices ecuatorianos son muy bonitos** Ecuadorian carpets are very pretty

el ecuatoriano , la ecuatoriana

En inglés, los gentilicios se escriben con mayúscula:

Ecuadorian: **los ecuatorianos** the Ecuadorians.

la edad ■ age: **a la edad de tres años** at the age of three

> **tiene cinco años de edad** he's five years old

> **¿qué edad tienes?** how old are you?; **no tienes edad para eso** you're not old enough for that

> **la tercera edad** senior citizens.

el edificio ■ building.

la educación *(plural* las educaciones*)*

1. **education**: **el tema de la educación preocupa al Gobierno** the subject of education concerns the government

2. **upbringing**: **este niño ha tenido una muy buena educación** this boy has had a very good upbringing

> **educación a distancia** distance education

> **educación física** physical education

> **educación secundaria** secondary education.

educar [8] *verbo*

1. **to educate**: **educaron a sus hijos en los mejores colegios** they educated their children in the best secondary schools

2. **to bring up**: **no han educado a su hija de una manera muy tradicional** they haven't brought up their daughter in a very traditional manner.

EE. UU. *(abreviatura de* Estados Unidos*)* ■ USA.

el efectivo ■ cash: **tengo que pagar en efectivo** I have to pay in cash.

el efecto

1. **effect**: **el medicamento me hizo efecto en pocos minutos** the medicine took effect on me in just a few minutes

2. **spin**: **devolvió la pelota con efecto** he put some spin on the ball

> **en efecto** in fact: **en efecto, tienes toda la razón** in fact, you're absolutely right

> **efectos especiales** special effects.

la eficacia ■ effectiveness: **este medicamento destaca por su eficacia** this medicine stands out for its effectiveness.

eficaz *adjetivo*

1. **effective**: **este medicamento es muy eficaz para curar los dolores de cabeza** this medicine is very effective in curing headaches

2. **efficient**: **es un empleado muy eficaz** he's a very efficient employee.

la eficiencia ■ efficiency: **la eficiencia es la mejor de sus virtudes** efficiency is the best of his virtues.

el egoísmo ■ selfishness: **su egoísmo lo ha llevado al aislamiento** his selfishness has led to his loneliness.

egoísta *adjetivo* ■ selfish: **es una de las personas más egoístas que conozco** he's one of the most selfish people I know.

el eje

1. **axle**: **se rompió uno de los ejes de la rueda** one of the axles of the wheel broke

2. **axis** *(plural* **axes***)*: el eje de la Tierra es una línea imaginaria the earth's axis is an imaginary line
3. **focal point**: el eje de sus conversaciones siempre es el dinero the focal point of their conversations is always money.

ejecutar [1] *verbo*
1. **to carry out**: ejecutaron sus órdenes sin protestar they carried out his orders without protesting
2. **to execute**: ejecutaron a los prisioneros they executed the prisoners.

ejemplar *adjetivo* ■ **exemplary**: comportamiento ejemplar exemplary behaviour.

el **ejemplar** ■ **copy** *(plural* **copies***)*: le mandó un ejemplar de su libro he sent her a copy of his book.

el **ejemplo** ■ **example**: siguieron el buen ejemplo de su madre they followed the good example of their mother
> **por ejemplo** for example
> **ponme un ejemplo** give me an example
> **debes dar ejemplo a tus hijos** you must set an example to your children.

el **ejercicio**
1. **exercise**: la profesora puso varios ejercicios de geometría the teacher set several geometry exercises
2. **financial year**: el balance del ejercicio fue muy positivo the result of the financial year was very positive
> **hacer ejercicio** to exercise: el médico me recomendó que hiciera ejercicio the doctor recommended that I exercise.

ejercitar [1] *verbo* ■ **to exercise**: la cantante ejercita su voz todas las mañanas the singer exercises her voice every morning.

el **ejército** ■ **army** *(plural* **armies***)*: el ejército ocupó la ciudad the army occupied the city.

el **artículo** ■ **the**: el avión sale a las 11 the aeroplane leaves at 11

Las partes del cuerpo llevan en español artículo pero deben traducirse al inglés con un pronombre posesivo:

me duele el brazo my arm hurts

> **el Sr. Díaz compró el sombrero** Mr. Díaz bought the hat
> **este reloj y el de Roberto son iguales** this watch and Robert's are the same
> **me encanta el chocolate** I love chocolate

Los nombres abstractos llevan artículo en español pero no en inglés:

> **la vida es difícil** life is difficult

Para describir el aspecto físico de una persona se usa el artículo en español pero no en inglés:

> **tiene el pelo rubio** he has blond hair.

él *pronombre*
1. **he**: él no vino he didn't come
2. **him**: este regalo es para él this gift is for him
3. **it**: se le rompió el bastón y no puede estar sin él his walking stick broke and he can't be without it
> **él mismo** himself: lo hizo él mismo he did it himself
> **de él** his: el coche es de él it's his car

In Spanish **él** as a subject is normally omitted unless it's used for emphasis or to contrast with another person.

elaborar [1] *verbo*
1. **to produce**: elaboran quesos they produce cheeses
2. **to work out**: elaboré un plan nuevo I worked out a new plan.

la **elasticidad** ■ **elasticity.**

elástico, ca *adjetivo* ■ **elastic.**

la **elección** *(plural* **las elecciones***)*
1. **choice**: no tengo elección I have no choice; has hecho una buena elección you've made a good choice
2. **election**: no se presentará a las próximas elecciones he won't stand in the next elections.

la **electricidad** ■ **electricity.**

el/la **electricista** ■ **electrician**: he llamado al electricista I've called the electrician.

eléctrico, ca *adjetivo*
1. **electric**: he comprado un cepillo eléctrico I've bought an electric toothbrush; tengo una guitarra eléctrica I've got an electric guitar

2. electrical: ha habido un fallo eléctrico there's been an electrical failure.

la **electrónica** ■ electronics.

electrónico, ca adjetivo ■ electronic: es un aparato electrónico it's an electronic device.

el **elefante** , la **elefanta** ■ elephant.

elegante adjetivo ■ elegant: se compró un vestido elegante she bought herself an elegant dress.

elegir [31] verbo

1. to choose: elegimos esta casa por el precio we chose this house because of the price

2. to elect: lo han elegido para el cargo de gerente they have elected him to the position of director.

elemental adjetivo ■ elementary: este ejercicio es de nivel elemental this exercise is elementary level.

el **elemento** ■ element: describe los elementos de un sistema informático describe the elements of the computer system; su opinión es un elemento esencial en este debate your opinion is an essential element in this debate.

eliminar [1] verbo

1. to eliminate: el equipo rival nos eliminó en la final the rival team eliminated us in the finals

2. to get rid of: el agua ayuda a eliminar las sustancias tóxicas del cuerpo water helps to get rid of the body's toxic substances.

ella pronombre

1. she: ella no está she's not here

2. her: me enamoré de ella I fell in love with her

3. it: se me ha estropeado la impresora y sin ella no puedo imprimir my printer's broken and I can't print without it

➤ ella misma herself: lo hizo ella misma she did it herself

➤ de ella her: el apartamento es de ella it's her apartment

In Spanish ella as a subject is normally omitted unless it's used for emphasis or to contrast with another person.

ello pronombre

➤ por ello that's why: no estudiamos y por ello suspendimos el examen we didn't study and that's why we failed the exam.

ellos, ellas pronombre

1. they: ellos fueron al concierto they went to the concert

2. them: salí de noche con ellas I went out at night with them

➤ ellos mismos themselves: lo hicieron ellos mismos they did it themselves

➤ de ellos their

➤ la casa es de ellas it's their house

In Spanish ellos and ellas as a subject is normally omitted unless it's used for emphasis or to contrast with another person.

El Salvador ■ El Salvador.

la **embajada** ■ embassy (plural embassies): la embajada está en el centro de la ciudad the embassy is in the centre.

el **embajador** , la **embajadora** ■ ambassador.

embarazada adjetivo ■ pregnant: está embarazada de tres meses she's three months pregnant; se ha quedado embarazada she's got pregnant

⚠ The Spanish word embarazada is a false friend, it does not mean "embarrassed".

el **embarazo** ■ pregnancy (plural pregnancies): el embarazo ha sido difícil the pregnancy has been difficult.

la **embarcación** (plural las embarcaciones) ■ boat.

embarcar [8] verbo ■ to board: los pasajeros ya están embarcando the passengers are already boarding.

emborracharse [1] verbo pronominal ■ to get drunk: su novio se emborrachó durante la fiesta her boyfriend got drunk during the party.

el **embrague** ■ clutch: suelta el embrague despacio release the clutch slowly.

embrujar [1] *verbo* ■ **to put a spell on:** cree que la han embrujado she believes that they've put a spell on her.

el **embutido** ■ **sausage:** hacen el embutido con carne de cerdo they make the sausage with pork.

la **emergencia** ■ **emergency** *(plural* emergencies*):* llámame si surge alguna emergencia call me if an emergency arises.

emigrar [1] *verbo*

1. **to emigrate:** mi abuelo emigró de Europa a principios del siglo XX my grandfather emigrated from Europe at the beginning of the 20th century

2. **to migrate:** muchos pájaros emigran al sur antes del invierno many birds migrate to the south before winter.

emitir [3] *verbo*

1. **to emit:** la televisión emitía un sonido raro the television was emitting a strange sound

2. **to issue:** el Gobierno emitirá nuevos billetes the government will issue new notes

3. **to broadcast:** emiten el partido en el canal 2 they've broadcasting the match on channel 2.

la **emoción** *(plural* las emociones*)* ■ **emotion:** no puedo expresar la emoción que sentía I can't express the emotion I felt.

emocionante *adjetivo* ■ **exciting:** es una noticia realmente emocionante it's really exciting news.

emotivo, va *adjetivo* ■ **moving:** su discurso fue muy emotivo his speech was very moving.

la **empanada** ■ **pasty** *(plural* **pasties***):* comimos unas ricas empanadas de carne we ate some tasty meat pasties.

empañar [1] *verbo* ■ **to steam up:** se empañaron los cristales del coche the car windows steamed up.

empaparse [1] *verbo pronominal* ■ **to get soaked:** se me empapó el abrigo con el chaparrón my coat got soaked in the downpour.

empatar [1] *verbo* ■ **to tie:** empataron a cero they tied nil-nil.

el **empate** ■ **tie:** hubo un empate en la final de fútbol there was a tie at the football finals.

empeñar [1] *verbo* ■ **to pawn:** empeñó las joyas de la abuela he pawned his grandmother's jewels

empeñarse *verbo pronominal* ■ **to insist** se empeña en seguir haciendo deporte he insists on continuing to play sports.

el **empeño** ■ **determination:** pone mucho empeño en todo lo que hace he puts a lot of determination into everything he does.

empeorar [1] *verbo*

1. **to get worse:** el tiempo ha empeorado the weather has got worse

2. **to make worse:** eso empeorará las cosas that will make things worse.

empezar [24] *verbo* ■ **to begin:** ya ha empezado la clase class has already began

empezar a **to begin to:** empiezan a pintar la casa el próximo sábado they'll begin to paint the house next Saturday.

el **empleado** , la **empleada** ■ **employee:** los empleados de esta oficina trabajan ocho horas the employees in this office work eight hours.

emplear [1] *verbo*

1. **to use:** emplean materiales reciclados they use recycled materials

2. **to hire:** la empresa emplea a 100 trabajadores the company employs 100 workers

le está bien empleado it serves him right.

el **empleo**

1. **job:** me ofrecieron empleo en una escuela they offered me a job at a school

2. **employment:** ha bajado el índice de empleo the employment rate has gone down

3. **use:** está prohibido el uso de esas sustancias the use of these substance is prohibited.

empollar [1] *verbo* ■ **to bone up, to swot (up)** *UK:* tendré que empollar para ese examen I'll have to swot up for the exam.

el **empollón** , la **empollona** ■ swot UK, grind US: Eva es la empollona de la clase Eva is the class swot.

emprender [2] verbo ■ to take on: emprendieron un nuevo negocio they took on a new business.

la **empresa**

1. company (plural companies): contratamos a una empresa de seguridad we hired a security company

2. management: la empresa no se hace responsable de este accidente the management is not responsible for this accident.

la **empresaria** ■ businesswoman (plural businesswomen).

el **empresario** ■ businessman (plural businessmen): es una reunión de empresarios it's a meeting for businessmen.

empujar [1] verbo ■ to push: empujamos el coche unos metros we pushed the car a few metres; no me empujes don't push me.

el **empujón** (plural los empujones) ■ push: le dieron un empujón tan grande que se cayó por la escalera they gave him such a hard push that he fell down the stairs

> se abrió paso a empujones he shoved his way through.

en preposición

1. in: vive en el campo he lives in the country; en el año 2006 in the year 2006; en primavera in spring; pagar en euros to pay in euros; puedes hacerlo en una hora you can do it in an hour

2. by: viajo a menudo en avión I often travel by plane

3. on: el sobre está en la mesa the envelope is on the table; el cuadro está en la pared the painting is on the wall; vivo en el sexto piso I live on the sixth floor

4. into: entró en la sala he went into the room

5. at: pasé tres horas en la playa I spent three hours at the beach; en casa at home; en el trabajo at work; vive en el número 20 he lives at number 20.

enamorarse [1] verbo pronominal ■ to fall in love: se enamora fácilmente she falls in love easily

enamorarse de to fall in love with: se enamoró de Carolina he fell in love with Carolina.

enano, na adjetivo ■ dwarf: es una planta enana it's a dwarf plant

el **enano** , la **enana** ■ dwarf (plural dwarves): soy una enana si me comparo con tu altura I'm a dwarf if I compare myself with your height.

encabezar [10] verbo

1. to head: encabezo la lista de candidatos I head the list of candidates

2. to lead: fueron arrestados quienes encabezaron los disturbios those who led the riots were arrested.

encadenar [1] verbo ■ to chain: encadené la bicicleta a un árbol I chained the bicycle to a tree.

encantado, da adjetivo

1. delighted: está encantado con su bicicleta nueva he's delighted with this new bicycle

2. haunted: un castillo encantado a haunted castle

> encantado de conocerle pleased to meet you.

encantador, ra adjetivo ■ charming: tiene tres niñas encantadoras she has three charming girls.

encantar [1] verbo

1. to love: les encanta jugar al fútbol they love to play football

2. to enchant: el hada encantó al príncipe the fairy enchanted the prince.

encarcelar [1] verbo ■ to jail: encarcelaron a los delincuentes they jailed the criminals.

el **encargado** , la **encargada** ■ manager: voy a hablar con la encargada de la tienda I'm going to speak to the manager of the shop.

encargar [12] verbo

1. to ask: le encargué que me introdujera estos datos en el ordenador I asked him to enter this data into the computer

2. to order: encargamos dos libros por Internet we ordered two books on the Internet

encargarse *verbo pronominal*

encargarse de to take care of: **el jefe se encarga de estos problemas** the boss takes care of these problems.

encender [15] *verbo*

1. to light: **encendimos la vela** we lit the candle
2. to turn on: **encendió la luz** he turned on the light; **enciende la tele** turn on the TV
3. to start up: **encendió el motor** she started up the engine.

encerar [1] *verbo* ■ to wax: **enceró el suelo de la oficina** he waxed the office floor.

encerrar [14] *verbo* ■ to shut in: **encerró al perro en el baño** she shut the dog in the bathroom

encerrarse *verbo pronominal* ■ to shut oneself away: **Gloria se ha encerrado en su habitación** she shut herself away in her room.

enchufar [1] *verbo* ■ to plug in: **enchufa el ordenador** plug in the computer.

enchufado, da *adjetivo*

1. plugged in: **la impresora no está enchufada** the printer isn't plugged in
2. well connected: **lo han ascendido porque está enchufado** they have promoted him because he's well connected.

el **enchufe** ■ plug: **compré un enchufe nuevo para el televisor** I bought a new plug for the television

consiguió trabajo gracias a un enchufe she got the job through contacts.

la **enciclopedia** ■ encyclopedia, encyclopaedia *UK*.

encima *adverbio*

1. on: **siempre llevo encima los documentos** I always carry the documents on me; **déjalo allí encima** leave it on there
2. on top of that: **es feo y encima caro** it's ugly and on top of that expensive

ya tenemos encima el período de exámenes the exam period is upon us

por encima superficially: **me lo ha explicado por encima** he explained it to me superficially

por encima de over: **salta por encima de la cuerda** jump over the rope

encima de on top of: **puse la caja más pequeña encima de la más grande** I put the smallest box on top of the largest; **encima de pagarle la cena, le dio dinero para un taxi** on top of paying for his dinner, she gave him money for a taxi.

encoger [11] *verbo* ■ to shrink: **este pantalón encogió con el lavado** these trousers shrank when washed

encogerse *verbo pronominal* ■ to shrink: **se me ha encogido el jersey** my sweater has shrunk

encogerse de hombros to shrug one's shoulders: **se encogió de hombros cuando le di la noticia** he shrugged his shoulders when I gave him the news.

encontrar [16] *verbo* ■ to find: **encontramos un reloj en la calle** we found a watch in the street; **lo encuentro un poco tímido** I find him a little shy

encontrarse *verbo pronominal*

1. to meet: **se encontraron en el parque** they met in the park
2. to be located: **la farmacia se encuentra en esta calle** the chemist's is located on this street
3. to feel: **Luis se encuentra mejor** Luis feels better

encontrarse con alguien to run into somebody: **me encontré con Francisco en el restaurante** I ran into Francisco in the restaurant.

el **encuentro**

1. meeting: **el encuentro de antiguos alumnos es el sábado** the alumni meeting is on Saturday
2. match: **ayer se realizó el encuentro deportivo más popular del año** yesterday the most popular sports match of the year took place.

la **encuesta** ■ survey.

endurecer [22] *verbo*

1. to harden: **la vida lo ha endurecido** life has hardened him

2. **to tone:** estos ejercicios endurecen los músculos these exercises tone the muscles

endurecerse *verbo pronominal* ■ **to harden:** la masa se endureció demasiado the dough hardened too much.

enemigo, ga *adjetivo* ■ **enemy:** el ejército enemigo invadió la ciudad the enemy army invaded the city

el **enemigo** , la **enemiga** ■ **enemy** *(plural enemies)*.

la **energía** ■ **energy:** el sol es una fuente importante de energía the sun is an important source of energy

➤ no tengo energías para salir I don't have the energy to go out

➤ energía eólica wind power

➤ energía nuclear nuclear energy

➤ energía solar solar energy.

enérgico, ca *adjetivo*

1. **energetic:** tiene una forma de actuar muy enérgica he has a very energetic way of acting

2. **bold:** el gobierno tomó medidas enérgicas frente a la crisis the government took bold measures in facing the crisis.

enero *sustantivo masculino*

En inglés los nombres de los meses se escriben con mayúscula:

January: en enero in January; el próximo enero next January; el pasado enero last January.

enfadado, da *adjetivo* ■ **angry:** está enfadado conmigo he's angry with me.

enfadarse [1] *verbo pronominal* ■ **to get angry:** se enfadó con los niños por sus travesuras she got angry with the children because of their pranks.

el **énfasis** ■ **stress, emphasis**

➤ poner énfasis en to stress: hay que poner énfasis en la primera sílaba you have to stress the first syllable; puso énfasis en la importancia de la solidaridad he stressed the importance of solidarity.

la **enfermedad**

1. **illness:** se recupera de una enfermedad muy grave she's recovering from a very serious illness

2. **disease:** tiene una enfermedad hereditaria he has a hereditary disease.

el **enfermero** , la **enfermera** ■ **nurse:** los enfermeros de este hospital son excelentes the nurses in this hospital are excellent.

enfermo, ma *adjetivo* ■ **ill:** mi profesor de lengua está enfermo my language teacher is ill; está gravemente enferma she's seriously ill

el **enfermo** , la **enferma**

1. **sick person:** de noche cuida enfermos at night she cares for sick people

2. **patient:** mi médico atiende solo diez enfermos por día my doctor sees only ten patients a day; un enfermo de asma está esperando al doctor an asthma patient is waiting for the doctor.

enfrentar [1] *verbo*

1. **to face:** tenemos que enfrentar el problema we have to face the problem; enfrenta cargos por difamación he faces charges for slander

2. **to bring face to face:** las elecciones enfrentaron a los dos candidatos the elections brought the two candidates face to face

enfrentarse *verbo pronominal*

1. **to face:** se enfrentó con optimismo a la nueva situación he faced the new situation with optimism

2. **to play against:** el equipo de fútbol local se enfrenta hoy con su tradicional rival the local football team is playing against its traditional rival today.

enfrente *adverbio* ■ **opposite:** mis amigos estaban sentados enfrente my friends were sitting opposite

➤ de enfrente across the way: la oficina de enfrente está cerrada the office across the way is closed.

enfriar [7] *verbo* ■ **to cool:** esta nevera no enfría bien this refrigerator doesn't cool well dejar enfriar to let cool: dejó enfriar la salsa he let the sauce cool

enfriarse *verbo pronominal*

1. **to go cold:** se enfriará la comida the food will go cold

2. **to get cold:** te vas a enfriar si no te pones la chaqueta you'll get cold if you don't put on your jacket

3. **to cool down:** deja que se enfríe antes de enchufarlo let it cool down before you plug it in.

enganchar [1] *verbo* ■ **to hook:** engancha la caravana al coche hook the caravan onto the car.

engañar [1] *verbo*

1. **to mislead:** me engañaron diciéndome que este producto era de buena calidad they misled me, telling me that this was a high quality product

2. **to be unfaithful to:** Sofía engaña a su esposo Sofía is being unfaithful to her husband

3. **to deceive:** me estás engañando you're deceiving me.

el **engaño**

1. **sham:** el contrato fue un engaño the contract was a sham

2. **deception:** soy víctima de un engaño I'm the victim of a deception.

engañoso, sa *adjetivo* ■ **deceitful:** es una persona engañosa he's a deceitful person; siempre tuvo una conducta engañosa he always had a deceitful manner.

engordar [1] *verbo*

1. **to put on weight:** he engordado mucho durante las vacaciones I put on a lot of weight during the holidays

2. **to be fattening:** la mayonesa engorda mayonnaise is fattening.

el **engranaje** ■ **gear.**

la **enhorabuena**

dar la enhorabuena a alguien to congratulate somebody: dimos la enhorabuena a los padres we congratulated the parents
¡enhorabuena! congratulations!

enjabonar [1] *verbo* ■ **to soap:** enjabona el cuello y los puños soap the collar and cuffs

enjabonarse *verbo pronominal* ■ **to soap:** me enjaboné primero la espalda I soaped my back first.

enjuagar [12] *verbo* ■ **to rinse:** enjuagó todos los platos she rinsed all the plates.

el **enlace** ■ **link:** hay un enlace entre los dos crímenes there's a link between the two crimes; sigue el enlace para encontrar la otra página web follow the link to find the other web page.

enorgullecerse [22] *verbo pronominal* ■ **to be proud:** nos enorgullecemos de nuestros hijos we are proud of our children.

enorme *adjetivo* ■ **enormous:** comió un pedazo de tarta enorme he ate an enormous piece of cake.

enredar [1] *verbo* ■ **to complicate:** su mala actitud enredó más las cosas his bad attitude complicated things more

enredarse *verbo pronominal* ■ **to get tangled:** se me enreda mucho el pelo my hair gets very tangled.

enriquecer [22] *verbo* ■ **to make rich:** el turismo enriqueció a toda la zona tourism made the whole area rich

enriquecerse *verbo pronominal* ■ **to get rich:** se enriqueció con su trabajo he got rich with his work.

la **ensalada** ■ **salad.**

ensanchar [1] *verbo* ■ **to widen:** han ensanchado la avenida principal they've widened the main avenue.

ensayar [1] *verbo* ■ **to rehearse:** ensayó esta obra durante seis meses he rehearsed this piece for six months.

el **ensayo**

1. **rehearsal:** ayer fui al ensayo de un concierto yesterday I went to a concert rehearsal

2. **test:** los ensayos nucleares son altamente peligrosos nuclear tests are extremely dangerous
un ensayo general a dress rehearsal.

enseguida *adverbio* ■ **right away:** enseguida comienza la función the performance will begin right away
enseguida vuelvo I'll be right back.

la **enseñanza** ■ **teaching:** la enseñanza no me atrae como profesión teaching doesn't appeal to me by profession
enseñanza primaria primary education *UK*, elementary education *US*
enseñanza secundaria secondary education
enseñanza universitaria university education.

enseñar [1] *verbo*
1. **to teach:** en este colegio nos enseñan a razonar at this school they teach us to reason
2. **to show:** me enseñó su ordenador nuevo he showed me his new computer.

ensuciar [1] *verbo* ■ **to make dirty:** el perro ensució el piso the dog made the flat dirty

ensuciarse *verbo pronominal* ■ **to get dirty:** me ensucié en el jardín I got dirty in the garden; ¡te vas a ensuciar! you'll get dirty!

entender [15] *verbo* ■ **to understand:** no entiendo lo que dices I don't understand what you're saying
hacerse entender to make oneself understood: no se hace entender con claridad he doesn't make himself clearly understood
entender de to know about: no entiendo de ordenadores I don't understand about computers

entenderse *verbo pronominal* ■ **to get on, to get along:** mi novia y yo nos entendemos muy bien my girlfriend and I get on very well.

el **entendimiento** ■ **understanding:** falta entendimiento entre las partes there's a lack of understanding between the parties.

enterarse [1] *verbo pronominal*
1. **to find out:** me he enterado de que vas a estudiar química I found out that you're going to take chemistry
2. **to hear:** no quiero que se enteren de lo nuestro I don't want them to hear about us

3. **to understand:** me lo ha explicado pero no me he enterado he explained it to me but I didn't understand.

entero, ra *adjetivo* ■ **whole:** tiene una colección entera de figuritas she has a whole collection of figurines; me pasé la tarde entera andando I spent the whole afternoon walking.

enterrar [14] *verbo* ■ **to bury:** lo enterraron en un cementerio privado they buried him in a private cemetery; he enterrado las monedas debajo del árbol I've buried the coins under the tree.

el **entierro** ■ **burial:** el entierro es hoy a las tres the burial is today at three o'clock

ENTIERRO DE LA SARDINA

The **entierro de la sardina** (the burial of the sardine) is a lively celebration held on Ash Wednesday throughout most of Spain to mark the end of Carnival and the beginning of Lent. The festival involves the imaginary burial of a sardine, accompanied by a colourful funeral procession. In former times, people buried a pig – *cerdina* – and this word has now been transformed into sardina.

entonar [1] *verbo*
1. **to sing:** entonó una canción he sang a song
2. **to sing in tune:** esta chica entona muy bien this girl sings really in tune.

entonces *adverbio*
1. **then:** hablé con la maestra y entonces me dijo que había suspendido el examen I spoke with the teacher and then she told me that I had failed the exam; para entonces ya estará fuera del país by then he will already be out of the country; entonces no existía el teléfono the telephone didn't exist then
2. **so:** entonces lo mejor que puedes hacer es pedir perdón so the best that you can do is to say sorry
desde entonces since then: desde entonces no nos hemos vuelto a ver we haven't seen each other again since then.

la **entrada**

1. **entrance:** se rompió la puerta de entrada the entrance door broke
2. **admission:** la entrada al concierto fue muy desorganizada admission to the concert was very disorganized
3. **ticket:** compramos cinco entradas para el teatro we bought five tickets for the theatre
4. **entry** (plural **entries**): este diccionario tiene miles de entradas this dictionary has thousands of entries
- **de entrada** from the outset: **de entrada no me gustó nada** I didn't like it at all from the outset.

el **entrante** ■ starter: de entrante comimos melón con jamón we had melon with ham for a starter.

entrar [1] verbo

1. **to go in:** entraron en la tienda de enfrente they went in the store across the way
2. **to come in:** ¿puedo entrar? can I come in?
3. **to fit:** estos pantalones ya no me entran these trousers don't fit me anymore
4. **to begin:** entró en la universidad el año pasado he began university last year
- **entrar en calor** to get warm: **con este vino entramos en calor rápidamente** we got warm quickly with this wine
- **entrar en coma** to go into a coma
- **entrar en razón** to see reason
- **entrar en el precio** to be included in the price
- **me entró una pereza terrible** I felt terribly lazy.

entre preposición

1. **between:** llegará entre las cuatro y las cinco he'll arrive between four and five o'clock; **siempre viaja entre diciembre y febrero** she always travels between December and February; **la escuela queda entre tu casa y la mía** the school is between your house and mine
2. **among:** acampamos entre los árboles we camped among the trees; **siempre están discutiendo entre ellos** they're always arguing among themselves
3. **divided by:** ocho entre cuatro es igual a dos eight divided by four equals two

- **entre sí** among themselves: **discutieron entre sí acaloradamente** they argued heatedly among themselves
- **entre todos** together: **lo pueden hacer entre todos** together they can do it.

la **entrega**

1. **presentation:** la entrega de premios fue muy emotiva the award presentation was very moving
2. **dedication:** su entrega hacia los demás es totalmente desinteresada her dedication to others is totally unselfish.

entregar [12] verbo

1. **to deliver:** entregué el paquete al supervisor I delivered the parcel to the supervisor
2. **to hand in:** entregamos los trabajos al profesor we handed in the papers to the teacher

entregarse verbo pronominal ■ **to surrender:** los delincuentes se entregaron a la policía the criminals surrendered to the police.

el **entrenador**, la **entrenadora** ■ trainer.

el **entrenamiento** ■ training: esta tarde tengo entrenamiento I've got training this afternoon.

entrenar [1] verbo ■ **to train:** entreno todas las mañanas para la competencia I train every morning for the competition.

entretenerse [52] verbo pronominal

1. **to hang around:** me entretuve charlando con unos amigos I hung around talking with some friends
2. **to entertain oneself:** me entretengo mucho con los dibujos animados I entertain myself a lot with cartoons.

el **entretenimiento**

1. **entertainment:** este programa nos ofrece lo último en entretenimiento this programme offers us the latest in entertainment
2. **pastime:** su entretenimiento favorito es coleccionar sellos his favourite pastime is collecting stamps.

la **entrevista** ■ interview: hoy he tenido una entrevista de trabajo today I had a job interview.

entrevistar [1] *verbo* ■ **to interview:** entrevistamos a cientos de personas para la encuesta we interviewed hundreds of people for the survey.

entrometerse [2] *verbo pronominal* ■ **to interfere:** no te entrometas en mi vida privada don't interfere in my private life.

el **entrometido**, la **entrometida** ■ busybody *(plural* busybodies): es un entrometido insoportable que siempre opina donde no debe he's an intolerable busybody who always gives his opinion when he shouldn't.

entusiasmar [1] *verbo*
1. to fill with enthusiasm: el fútbol le entusiasma football fill him with enthusiasm
2. to love: la obra de teatro me ha entusiasmado I loved the play.

el **entusiasmo** ■ enthusiasm: el entusiasmo del público era increíble the enthusiasm of the public was incredible
▸ con entusiasmo enthusiastically.

envasar [1] *verbo*
1. *en cajas, paquetes* to pack
2. *en bolsas* to bag
3. *en latas* to can.

el **envase** ■ container: el envase de este producto ha cambiado the container of this product has changed.

envejecer [22] *verbo* ■ **to age:** todos envejecemos tarde o temprano we all age sooner or later.

el **envejecimiento** ■ ageing, aging: el envejecimiento es un proceso natural ageing is a natural process.

envenenar [1] *verbo* ■ **to poison:** el gas tóxico envenenó a la población the toxic gas poisoned the population.

enviar [7] *verbo* ■ **to send:** enviamos el cheque por correo we sent the cheque by post.

la **envidia** ■ envy: la envidia puede destruir una relación envy can destroy a relationship

▸ tener envidia a to envy: le tiene envidia a su hermano she envies her brother.

envidioso, sa *adjetivo* ■ envious.

el **envío** ■ shipment: aquella oficina se encarga de los envíos de la fábrica that office is in charge of the factory's shipments
▸ envíos a domicilio home delivery
▸ envíos contra reembolso cash on delivery.

la **envoltura** ■ wrapping: se rompió la envoltura del paquete the package's wrapping was torn.

envolver [17] *verbo* ■ **to wrap:** envolvimos el regalo we wrapped the gift; ¿se lo envuelvo para regalo? do you want it gift-wrapped?

la **epidemia** ■ epidemic.

el **epílogo** ■ epilogue.

el **episodio** ■ episode: sólo he visto dos episodios de esta serie I've only seen two episodes of this series.

la **época** ■ time: es la época más calurosa del año it's the hottest time of the year; estas cosas no pasaban en mi época these things didn't happen in my time.

equilibrar [1] *verbo* ■ **to balance:** equilibró el peso de la estantería he balanced the weight of the shelving.

el **equilibrio** ■ balance: perdió el equilibrio y cayó al suelo he lost his balance and fell to the floor; intenta mantener el equilibrio try and keep your balance.

el **equipaje** ■ luggage: llevo mucho equipaje I'm carrying a lot of luggage
▸ equipaje de mano hand luggage.

equipar [1] *verbo* ■ **to equip:** equiparon la escuela con tecnología moderna they equipped the school with modern technology.

el **equipo**
1. equipment: trajimos el equipo de camping completo we brought the complete set of camping equipment
2. team: hoy compiten los mejores equipos de baloncesto compiten hoy the best basketball teams compete today
▸ equipo de música stereo.

equitativo, va *adjetivo* ■ **fair:** repartieron el dinero de manera equitativa they shared out the money in a fair manner.

la **equivalencia** ■ equivalence.

equivalente *adjetivo* ■ **equivalent:** los significados de estas dos palabras son equivalentes the two words have equivalent meanings

el **equivalente** ■ **equivalent:** me pagaron el equivalente a dos meses de trabajo they paid me the equivalent of two months of work.

la **equivocación** *(plural* las equivocaciones) ■ **mistake:** he cometido varias equivocaciones en mi vida I've made several mistakes in my life.

equivocarse [8] *verbo pronominal* ■ **to make a mistake:** debes admitirlo cuando te equivocas you must admit it when you make a mistake
> me equivoqué de salida en la autopista I took the wrong exit on the motorway.

la **erosión** *(plural* las erosiones) ■ erosion.

erradicar [8] *verbo* ■ **to eradicate:** el gobierno intenta erradicar la pobreza the government is trying to eradicate poverty.

erróneo, a *adjetivo* ■ **mistaken:** su lógica es errónea his logic is mistaken.

el **error** ■ **error:** cometió un grave error en el examen he committed a serious error in the exam
> por error by mistake: me llevé tu lápiz por error I took your pencil by mistake
> un error de imprenta a misprint.

la **erupción** *(plural* las erupciones)
1. **eruption:** la erupción del volcán mató a tres personas the eruption of the volcano killed three people
2. **rash:** le salió una erupción en la cara a rash broke out on his face
> estar en erupción to erupt: el volcán está en erupción the volcano is erupting.

la **escala**
1. **stopover:** el avión hizo escala en Londres the aeroplane had a stopover in London

2. **scale:** sacó ocho en una escala del uno al diez he got an eight on a scale of one to ten; ¿cuál es la escala del mapa? what is the scale of the map?
> a escala to scale.

escalar [1] *verbo* ■ **to scale:** escalamos una montaña nevada we scaled a snowy mountain.

la **escalera**
1. **stairs:** ¿subo por las escaleras? shall I go up the stairs?
2. **staircase:** la casa tiene una escalera de madera the house has a wooden staircase
> una escalera de caracol a spiral staircase
> una escalera de incendios a fire escape
> una escalera de mano a ladder
> una escalera mecánica an escalator.

el **escalofrío**
1. **shiver:** sólo de pensarlo me da escalofríos just thinking about it gives me the shivers
2. **chill:** esta gripe me produce escalofríos this flu is making me have chills.

el **escalón** *(plural* los escalones) ■ **step:** cuidado con el escalón mind the step.

la **escama** ■ **scale:** le sacamos las escamas al pescado we took the scales off of fish.

el **escándalo**
1. **scandal:** un escándalo de corrupción a corruption scandal
2. **outrage:** la película provocó un escándalo the film caused an outrage
3. **racket:** ¡dejad de armar tanto escándalo! stop making such a racket!

escapar [1] *verbo* ■ **to escape:** escaparon de la policía they escaped from the police; no dejes escapar esta oportunidad don't pass up this opportunity

escaparse *verbo pronominal* ■ **to escape:** se escapó de la cárcel he escaped from prison
> se me escapó un grito I let out a scream.

el **escaparate** ■ **shop window** UK, **store window** US.

escarbar [1] *verbo* ■ **to dig:** el perro escarbaba en el jardín the dog was digging in the garden.

la **escarcha** ■ frost.

escaso, sa _adjetivo_

1. scarce: el platino es un metal muy escaso platinum is a very scarce metal
2. meagre _UK_, meager _US_: es gente de escasos recursos they're people of meagre resources
> escaso de algo short of something: siempre ando escaso de tiempo he's always short of time
> duró una hora escasa it lasted just under an hour.

la **escayola**

1. plaster: mezcla la escayola con agua mix the plaster with water
2. plaster cast: Marga lleva una escayola en el brazo Marga has a plaster cast on her arm.

la **escena** ■ scene.

el **escenario** ■ stage: los actores salieron al escenario the actors went out on stage.

la **esclavitud** ■ slavery.

el **esclavo** , la **esclava** ■ slave
> no quiero ser esclavo de la moda I don't want to be a slave to fashion.

la **escoba** ■ broom: tenemos que comprar una escoba para la cocina we need to buy a broom for the kitchen
> pasar la escoba to sweep: pasó la escoba por la entrada he swept the entrance
> un palo de escoba a broom handle.

escocer [30] _verbo_ ■ to sting: me escuece la herida my wound stings.

escoger [11] _verbo_ ■ to choose: es difícil escoger entre los dos it's difficult to choose between the two; hay que escoger uno de este montón we have to choose one from this pile.

escolar _adjetivo_ ■ school: el autobús escolar the school bus

■/la **escolar** ■ schoolboy, schoolgirl
> la parada estaba llena de escolares the bus stop was full of schoolchildren.

los **escombros** ■ rubble.

esconder [2] _verbo_ ■ to hide: tenemos que esconder los regalos we have to hide the gifts

esconderse _verbo pronominal_ ■ to hide: se escondió detrás de la puerta he hid behind the door.

las **escondidas**
> a escondidas secretly: fuman a escondidas they smoke secretly.

el **escondite** ■ hiding place: el escondite de los ladrones the thieves' hiding place
> jugar al escondite to play hide-and-seek.

la **escopeta** ■ shotgun.

el **escorpión** _(plural_ los escorpiones) ■ scorpion.

escribir [3] _verbo_ ■ to write: ha escrito varios libros she's written several books; nos escribe muy a menudo he writes to us often
> no sabe leer ni escribir he doesn't know how to read or write
> ¿cómo se escribe su nombre? how do you spell her name?
> han dejado de escribirse they have stopped writing to each other.

escrito, ta _adjetivo_ ■ written: un examen escrito a written exam
> una nota escrita a mano a hand-written note
> por escrito in writing
> tienes que pedirlo por escrito you have to request it in writing.

el **escritor** , la **escritora** ■ writer.

el **escritorio** ■ desk: déjalo encima del escritorio leave it on the desk.

la **escritura** ■ writing: la escritura árabe Arabic writing.

escuchar [1] _verbo_

1. to listen: ¡escucha! alguien viene listen! somebody's coming; escuchaban con mucha atención they were listening very attentively
2. to listen to: me encanta escuchar música I love to listen to music; tienes que escuchar a la profesora you have to listen to the teacher; no escucha a nadie he doesn't listen to anybody.

el escudo

1. **shield:** llevaban escudos para protegerse they carried shields to protect themselves
2. **badge:** una camiseta con el escudo del equipo a shirt with the team badge.

la escuela ■ **school:** no pudo ir a la escuela he couldn't go to school
▸ está en la escuela primaria she's in primary school.

la escultura ■ **sculpture.**

escupir [3] *verbo* ■ **to spit:** escupió en el suelo he spat on the floor.

ese, esa *adjetivo* ■ **that:** María vive en esa casa María lives in that house; ¿quién es ese chico que pregunta por ti? who is that guy who's asking for you?

ése, ésa *pronombre* ■ **that one:** me gusta ése I like that one
▸ ése es el que compramos that's the one we bought
▸ ése es el problema that's the problem.

esencial *adjetivo* ■ **essential:** la lectura es algo esencial reading is something that's essential
▸ lo esencial the main thing: lo esencial es comprenderlo the main thing is to understand it.

la esfera ■ **sphere.**

esforzarse [26] *verbo pronominal* ■ **to make an effort:** tienes que esforzarte más en los estudios you have to make more effort with your studies.

el esfuerzo ■ **effort:** vas a tener que hacer un esfuerzo you're going to have to make an effort
▸ saltó sin ningún esfuerzo he jumped effortlessly
▸ no lo hacen porque es mucho esfuerzo they don't do it because it takes a lot of effort.

la esgrima ■ **fencing.**

el esguince ■ **sprain**
▸ tengo un esguince en el tobillo I've sprained my ankle.

la esmeralda ■ **emerald.**

el esmero ■ **care:** todo lo hace con mucho esmero she does everything with great care.

el esmog ■ **smog.**

eso *pronombre* ■ **that:** ¿para qué sirve eso? what is that for?; eso no es cierto that's not true
▸ por eso that's why
▸ por eso llegó tarde that's why she arrived late
▸ pasé de curso y eso que no estudié mucho I passed the course in spite of the fact that I didn't study much
▸ ¡eso es! así es como hay que hacerlo that's it! that's how you have to do it.

esos, esas *adjetivo* ■ **those:** esas fotos son mías those photos are mine; ¿de quién son esos cuadernos? whose are those notebooks?

ésos, ésas *pronombre* ■ **those:** ésos son más bonitos those are the prettiest.

espacial *adjetivo* ■ **space:** construyeron una estación espacial they built a space station
▸ una nave espacial a spaceship.

el espacio

1. **room:** no hay suficiente espacio para una cama there's not enough room for a bed; esto ocupa demasiado espacio this takes up too much room
2. **space:** hay que dejar espacio para las correcciones you have to leave space for the corrections; deja un espacio entre las dos palabras leave a space between the two words
▸ llena los espacios en blanco fill in the blanks
▸ el espacio space: el primer hombre en el espacio the first man in space.

la espada ■ **sword**

 The Spanish word **espada** is a false friend, it doesn't mean "spade".

los espaguetis ■ **spaghetti.**

la espalda ■ **back:** me duele la espalda my back hurts
▸ dar la espalda a alguien
1. **to turn one's back to somebody:** le estás dando la espalda, date la vuelta you're turning your back to him, turn round

2. **dar la espalda a alguien** to turn one's back on somebody: **los amigos nunca te dan la espalda** friends never turn their backs on you.

el **espantapájaros** *(plural* los espantapájaros*)* ■ **scarecrow.**

espantoso, sa *adjetivo*

1. **terrifying: hubo un choque espantoso** there was a terrifying crash; **mostraron unas escenas espantosas** they showed some terrifying scenes

2. *informal* **dreadful: ¡qué color más espantoso!** what a dreadful colour!; **está espantosa con ese peinado** she looks dreadful with that hairstyle
   - **tenía un miedo espantoso** she was terribly frightened
   - **el calor era espantoso** the heat was terrible.

España ■ **Spain.**

español, la *adjetivo*

En inglés, los adjetivos que se refieren a un país o una región se escriben con mayúscula:

Spanish: es una costumbre española it's a Spanish custom

el **español** , la **española**

En inglés, los gentilicios se escriben con mayúscula:

Spaniard: los españoles Spaniards

el **español**

En inglés, los idiomas se escriben con mayúscula:

Spanish.

especial *adjetivo* ■ **special: es un precio especial para estudiantes** it's a special price for students; **lo uso sólo en ocasiones especiales** I use it only on special occasions
   - **la película no tiene nada de especial** the film is nothing special
   - **en especial** especially: **son todos inteligentes, en especial Carlos** they're all intelligent, especially Carlos.

la **especialidad** ■ **speciality** UK, **specialty** US *(plural* **specialities***)*.

especialmente *adverbio* ■ **especially.**

la **especie** ■ **species: una especie en vías de extinción** a species in the process of extinction
   - **una especie de** a type of: **llevaba una especie de turbante en la cabeza** he was wearing a type of turban on his head.

específico, ca *adjetivo* ■ **specific.**

espectacular *adjetivo* ■ **spectacular.**

el **espectáculo**

1. **show: un espectáculo para gente joven** a show for young people

2. **spectacle: un espectáculo muy lamentable** a very pitiful spectacle
   - **dar un espectáculo** to make a scene: **deja de gritar que estás dando un espectáculo** stop shouting, you're making a scene.

el **espectador** , la **espectadora**

1. **spectator: un espectador saltó al campo** a spectator jumped onto the field

2. **audience member: hicieron salir del cine a un espectador** they made an audience member leave the cinema
   - **los espectadores**

1. *en cine, concierto* the audience

2. *en estadio* the spectators.

el **espejo** ■ **mirror: se miró al espejo** he looked at himself in the mirror
   - **el espejo retrovisor** the rear-view mirror.

la **esperanza** ■ **hope: eso me ha dado esperanzas** that's given me hope
   - **no tiene ninguna esperanza de salir de vacaciones** he doesn't have any hope that he'll go on holiday
   - **no pierdo las esperanzas** I don't lose hope.

esperar [1] *verbo*

1. **to wait: voy a esperar hasta mañana** I'm going to wait until tomorrow; **espere en la sala, por favor** wait in the room, please

2. **to wait for: ¿qué estás esperando?** what are you waiting for?; **estoy esperando el tren** I'm waiting for the train; **te espero a la salida** I'll wait for you at the exit

3. **to expect: espera aprobar el examen** she expects to pass the exam; **no esperaba verte aquí** I didn't expect to see you here

4. to hope: espero volverlo a ver I hope to see him again; ¿crees que dejará de llover? —espero que sí do you think it will stop raining? – I hope so

▸ no estudió nada —bueno, eso era de esperar he didn't study at all – well, that was to be expected

▸ está esperando un bebé she's expecting a baby

▸ ¡espera un poco, no seas impaciente! wait a little bit, don't be impatient!

espeso, sa *adjetivo* ■ **thick.**

el/la **espía** ■ spy *(plural* **spies**)*.*

espiar [7] *verbo* ■ **to spy on:** espiaron a los políticos they spied on the politicians.

la **espina**

1. thorn: las espinas de los rosales the thorns of the rosebushes

2. bone: un pescado con muchas espinas a fish with a lot of bones.

las **espinacas** ■ spinach: las espinacas son parecidas a las acelgas spinach is similar to chard.

la **espiral** ■ spiral.

el **espíritu**

1. spirit: hay que tener espíritu de equipo you have to have team spirit

2. ghost: dicen que aquí hay muchos espíritus they say that there are a lot of ghosts here.

espléndido, da *adjetivo* ■ **splendid:** hace un tiempo espléndido the weather's splendid.

la **esponja** ■ sponge.

esponjoso, sa *adjetivo* ■ **spongy.**

la **esposa** ■ wife.

las **esposas** ■ handcuffs

▸ la policía le puso las esposas the police handcuffed him.

el **esposo** ■ husband.

la **espuma**

1. *del jabón, champú* foam

2. *de la cerveza* froth

▸ la espuma de las olas the surf.

el **esqueleto** ■ skeleton.

el **esquema**

1. diagram: les hice un esquema de mi casa I drew them a diagram of my house

2. outline: hice un esquema de lo que iba a escribir I made an outline of what I was going to write.

el **esquí**

1. ski: un par de esquís a pair of skis

2. skiing: el esquí es su deporte favorito skiing is his favourite sport

▸ esquí acuático water skiing

▸ esquí de fondo cross-country skiing.

esquiar [7] *verbo* ■ **to ski:** ¿sabe esquiar? does he know how to ski?

esquimal *adjetivo*

En inglés, los adjetivos que se refieren a un país o una región se escriben con mayúscula:

Inuit

el/la **esquimal**

En inglés, los gentilicios se escriben con mayúscula:

Inuit.

la **esquina** ■ corner

▸ está a la vuelta de la esquina it's right around the corner

▸ doblar la esquina to turn the corner.

esquivar [1] *verbo* ■ **to avoid:** me agaché para esquivar el golpe I ducked to avoid the blow.

estable *adjetivo* ■ **stable.**

establecer [22] *verbo* ■ **to establish:** han establecido relaciones diplomáticas they've established diplomatic relations; estableció el récord mundial en jabalina he established the world record in the javelin

establecerse *verbo pronominal* ■ **to settle:** se establecieron en Granada they settled in Granada.

el **establo** ■ barn.

la **estación** (plural las estaciones)

1. season: la estación de las lluvias the rainy season
2. station: se baja en la siguiente estación he gets off at the next station
> una estación de esquí a ski resort
> una estación de servicio a service station.

el **estacionamiento** ■ parking: es una zona de estacionamiento prohibido it's a no parking zone.

estacionar [1] verbo ■ to park.

el **estadio** ■ stadium (plural stadia o stadiums).

el **estado** ■ state: ¿en qué estado quedó la moto? what state was the motorcycle in?; su estado de salud ha mejorado mucho her state of health has improved a lot
> en buen estado in good condition
> en mal estado in bad condition
> trabaja en una oficina del Estado he works in a government office
> estado civil marital status
> tiene una beca del Estado she has a scholarship from the state
> en uno de los estados del norte in one of the northern states.

Estados Unidos ■ United States.

estadounidense adjetivo

En inglés, los adjetivos que se refieren a un país o una región se escriben con mayúscula:

American

la **estadounidense**

En inglés, los gentilicios se escriben con mayúscula:

American: los estadounidenses the Americans.

la **estafa** ■ fraud.

estafar [1] verbo ■ to swindle: han estafado al banco they swindled the bank
> en esa tienda me estafaron they ripped me off in that shop.

estallar [1] verbo

1. to go off: un bomba estalló en ese lugar a bomb went off in that place
2. to break out: ha estallado una guerra a war has broken out.

la **estancia**

1. stay: durante nuestra estancia en el extranjero during our stay abroad
2. room: las estancias de palacio the palace rooms.

el **estanque** ■ pond.

el **estante** ■ shelf (plural shelves): el libro está en el estante the book is on the shelf.

estar [42] verbo

En términos generales estar se traduce por **to be**:

to be: está muy cerca it's very close; no ha estado nunca en Cancún she has never been to Cancún; ¿está Pedro? is Pedro there?; hola, ¿cómo estás? hello, how are you?; está enfermo he is ill; estoy estudiando I am studying
2. indicando fechas, precio ¿a cuánto estamos? what's the date?; estamos a dos de marzo it's the second of March UK, it's March second US; ¿a cuánto están los melones? how much are the melons?; estaban a dos euros el kilo they were two euros per kilo
> está lloviendo it's raining
> está muy delgada she looks very thin
> Pepe está con paperas Pepe has the mumps
> ¡estáte quieto! be still!

la **estatua** ■ statue.

la **estatura** ■ height: es de estatura normal he's of normal height
> mide casi dos metros de estatura he's almost two metres tall.

este ■ east: Barcelona está en la costa este de España Barcelona is on the east coast of Spain

el **este** ■ the east: el sol sale por el este the sun rises in the east; fuimos hacia el este we went east
> al este de east of: Cuenca está al este de Madrid Cuenca is east of Madrid.

este, esta adjetivo ■ this: tengo que leer este libro I have to read this book.

éste, ésta *pronombre* ■ **this one:** éste es mejor this one is better

> ésta es mi casa this is my house

> éste no es el que yo quería this is not the one that I wanted.

esterilizar [10] *verbo* ■ **to sterilize.**

el **estiércol**

1. *excremento* **dung**

2. *abono* **manure.**

estilarse [1] *verbo pronominal*

> **to be in fashion:** esa clase de peinado ya no se estila that type of hairstyle is no longer in fashion.

el **estilo** ■ **style:** es su estilo it's his style

> salen a caminar, andar en bicicleta y cosas por el estilo they go out for walks, bike rides and that sort of thing

> estilo de vida lifestyle

> estilo gótico gothic style.

estimular [1] *verbo*

1. **to encourage:** nos estimulan para que leamos más they encourage us to read more

2. **to stimulate:** un tónico para estimular el apetito a tonic to stimulate the appetite.

estirar [1] *verbo* ■ **to stretch:** los niños estiraban de la cuerda the children stretched the rope; salí a estirar las piernas un poco I went out to stretch my legs a little.

esto *pronombre* ■ **this:** ¿para qué sirve esto? what is this for?; esto es a lo que me refiero this is what I'm referring to

> todo esto es mío all this is mine.

el **estómago** ■ **stomach**

> me duele el estómago my stomach hurts.

estorbar [1] *verbo* ■ **to be in the way:** estas cajas estorban these boxes are in the way.

el **estorbo** ■ **hindrance:** estas cosas aquí son un estorbo these things here are a hindrance.

estornudar [1] *verbo* ■ **to sneeze.**

el **estornudo** ■ **sneeze.**

estos, estas *adjetivo* ■ **these:** tengo que devolver estos libros I have to return these books; ¿de quién son estas llaves? whose keys are these?

éstos, éstas *pronombre* ■ **these:** me quedo con éstos I'm keeping these; éstas son mis compañeras de curso these are my classmates

> éstas son las que hay que estudiar these are the ones we have to study

> un día de éstos one of these days.

el **estornudo** ■ **sneeze.**

estrecho, cha *adjetivo*

1. **narrow:** es una calle muy estrecha it's a very narrow street

2. **tight:** le gustan los jerséis estrechos she likes tight sweaters.

el **estrecho** ■ **strait**

> el Estrecho de Gibraltar the Strait of Gibraltar.

la **estrella** ■ **star**

> una estrella del cine a film star *UK,* a movie star *US*

> una estrella fugaz a shooting star; una estrella de mar a starfish

> un hotel de tres estrellas a three-star hotel.

estrellarse [1] *verbo pronominal* ■ **to crash:** el autobús se estrelló contra un camión the bus crashed into a lorry.

estrenar [1] *verbo* ■ van a estrenar la película en mayo they're going to release the movie in May; todavía no hemos estrenado la piscina we still haven't used the swimming pool.

el **estreno** ■ **premiere:** fui al estreno de la película I went to the première of the film.

el **estreñimiento** ■ **constipation**

> tener estreñimiento to be constipated.

el **estrés** ■ **stress.**

estricto, ta *adjetivo* ■ **strict.**

estropear [1] *verbo*

1. **to break:** si sigues jugando con eso lo vas a estropear if you keep on playing with that you're going to break it

2. **to ruin:** la lluvia nos estropeó el picnic the rain ruined our picnic

estropearse *verbo pronominal*

1. **to break:** se nos ha estropeado el televisor our television broke
2. **to break down:** se le ha estropeado el coche his car has broken down
3. **to spoil:** se estropeó la comida con el calor the food spoiled with the heat.

la **estructura** ■ structure.

el **estuche** ■ case: un estuche para lápices a pencil case.

la **estudiante** ■ student.

estudiar [1] *verbo* ■ to study: me voy porque tengo que estudiar I'm going because I've got to study; le gustaría estudiar arquitectura she'd like to study architecture.

el **estudio**

1. **study:** ha dedicado su vida al estudio de la fauna he's dedicated his life to the study of animals
2. **studio apartment:** vive en un estudio she lives in a studio apartment

tengo dos horas de estudio entre las clases I have a two-hour study break between classes

dedica muy poco tiempo al estudio she devotes very little time to her studies

un estudio de televisión a television studio

estudios ■ studies: terminó sus estudios a los 20 años he completed his studies when he was 20

no pudieron darle estudios a su hijo they couldn't give their son a college education.

estudioso, sa *adjetivo* ■ studious: mi hermano es muy estudioso my brother is very studious.

la **estufa** ■ heater: nos acercamos a la estufa para calentarnos we moved closer to the heater to warm up.

estupendo, da *adjetivo* ■ wonderful: he pasado una tarde estupenda I've had a wonderful evening.

estúpido, da *adjetivo* ■ stupid: ¡qué pregunta más estúpida! what a stupid question!

el **estúpido** , la **estúpida** idiot: es un estúpido he's an idiot.

la **etapa**

1. **stage:** lo vamos a hacer por etapas we're going to do it in stages
2. **time:** la etapa más feliz de mi vida the happiest time of my life.

eterno, na *adjetivo* ■ eternal.

la **etiqueta** ■ label: una etiqueta adhesiva an adhesive label; quítale la etiqueta al pantalón remove the label from the trousers.

étnico, ca *adjetivo* ■ ethnic.

el **euro** ■ euro: el euro es la moneda de la Unión Europea the Euro is the monetary unit of the European Union

una moneda de dos euros a two-euro coin.

Europa ■ Europe.

europeo, a *adjetivo*

En inglés, los adjetivos que se refieren a un país o una región se escriben con mayúscula:

European

el **europeo** , la **europea**

En inglés, los gentilicios se escriben con mayúscula:

European: los europeos the Europeans.

evacuar [1] *verbo* ■ to evacuate.

la **evaluación** *(plural* las evaluaciones*)* ■ assessment.

evaluar [6] *verbo* ■ to assess.

evaporarse [1] *verbo pronominal* ■ to evaporate: el agua se evaporó con el calor del sol the water evaporated with the heat of the sun.

evidente *adjetivo* ■ obvious: es evidente que no ha estudiado it's obvious he hasn't studied.

evitar [1] *verbo*

1. **to avoid:** a esa hora evitamos el tráfico we can avoid traffic at that time
2. **to prevent:** lo hacen para evitar accidentes they do it to prevent accidents

3. to save: **eso nos habría evitado muchas molestias** that would have saved us a lot of trouble
- **no pude evitarlo** I couldn't help it.

la **evolución** *(plural* las evoluciones) ■ development: **gracias a la evolución de la medicina** thanks to medical developments
- **la teoría de la evolución** the theory of evolution.

la **exactitud** ■ precision: **la exactitud de un test** the precision of a test
- **no lo recuerdo con exactitud** I can't remember precisely.

exacto, ta *adjetivo* ■ exact: **¿me puedes decir la hora exacta?** can you tell me the exact time?
- **el avión salió a la hora exacta** the plane left right on time
- **¡exacto!** that's right!

exagerado, da *adjetivo* ■ exaggerated: **la polémica sobre la película fue exagerada** the controversy about the film was exaggerated
- **no seas tan exagerado** don't exaggerate.

exagerar [1] *verbo* ■ to exaggerate: **no exageres** don't exaggerate.

el **examen** *(plural* los exámenes) ■ exam: **tengo que estudiar para el examen de inglés** I have to study for my English exam
- **un examen de conducir** a driving test.

examinar [1] *verbo* ■ to examine: **este es el médico que me examinó** this is the doctor who examined me.

examinarse *verbo pronominal* ■ to take an exam: **se examina mañana** she's taking an exam tomorrow.

excavar [1] *verbo* ■ to dig: **hay varios arqueólogos excavando el lugar** there are several archaeologists digging on the site.

excelente *adjetivo* ■ excellent.

excéntrico, ca *adjetivo* ■ eccentric.

la **excepción** *(plural* las excepciones) ■ exception: **es una excepción a la regla** it's the exception to the rule

hacer una excepción to make an exception: **hicieron una excepción con él** they made an exception for him
- **a excepción de** except: **me lo he estudiado todo a excepción de esto** I've studied everything except this.

excepto *preposición* ■ except: **todos llevaron algo excepto yo** everybody except me brought something.

el **exceso** ■ excess: **todos los excesos son malos** all excesses are bad
- **en exceso** to excess: **hay gente que bebe en exceso** some people drink to excess
- **exceso de equipaje** excess baggage
- **exceso de velocidad** speeding.

excitarse [1] *verbo pronominal* ■ to get worked up: **se excita mucho cuando discute** he gets very worked up when he argues.

la **exclamación** *(plural* las exclamaciones) ■ exclamation
- **signo de exclamación** exclamation mark.

excluir [36] *verbo* ■ to exclude: **lo excluyeron del equipo** he was excluded from the team
- **fueron todos, excluyendo Pepe** they all went except for Pepe.

exclusivo, va *adjetivo* ■ exclusive.

la **excursión** *(plural* las excursiones) ■ trip: **hicimos una excursión a un pueblo cercano** we made a trip to a nearby town; **el martes vamos de excursión con el colegio** we're going on a school field trip on Tuesday.

el/la **excursionista** ■ hiker.

la **excusa** ■ excuse.

la **exhibición** *(plural* las exhibiciones) ■ exhibition: **una exhibición de arte africano** an exhibition of African art.

exhibir [3] *verbo* ■ to show: **van a exhibir uno de sus cuadros** they're going to show one of his paintings
- **le encanta exhibirse** she loves to show off.

exigente *adjetivo* ■ demanding: **es una profesora muy exigente** she's a very demanding teacher.

exigir [11] *verbo*

1. **to demand:** la profesora nos exige mucho the teacher demands a great deal from us
2. **to require:** eso exige mucha fuerza de voluntad that requires a lot of will power.

el **exiliado** , la **exiliada** ■ exile: un exiliado político a political exile.

existir [3] *verbo* ■ **to exist:** está convencido de que los ovnis existen he's convinced that UFOs exist.

el **éxito** ■ success: la película fue todo un éxito the film was a real success
> tener éxito to be successful: su libro ha tenido mucho éxito her book has been very successful

> ⚠ The Spanish word éxito is a false friend, it doesn't mean "exit".

exitoso, sa *adjetivo* ■ **successful.**

exótico, ca *adjetivo* ■ **exotic.**

la **expedición** *(plural* las expediciones*)* ■ **expedition.**

la **experiencia** ■ experience: tiene mucha experiencia she has a lot of experience; no es necesario tener experiencia previa no previous experience is necessary
> necesitan a una persona con experiencia they need an experienced person.

experimentar [1] *verbo*

1. **to experiment:** experimentan con conejos they experiment on rabbits
2. **to experience:** nunca había experimentado algo así I'd never experienced anything like it.

el **experimento** ■ experiment.

el **experto** , la **experta** ■ expert: es una experta en informática she's an expert in computers.

la **explicación** *(plural* las explicaciones*)* ■ explanation: debe haber una explicación para todo esto there has to be an explanation for all of this
> pedir explicaciones to demand an explanation
> dar explicaciones to give an explanation.

explicar [8] *verbo* ■ **to explain:** no lo pudo explicar she couldn't explain it; nos explicó cómo lo descubrieron she explained how they discovered it
> explicarle algo a alguien to explain something to someone
> no sé si me explico bien I don't know if I'm making myself clear
> no me lo puedo explicar I can't understand it.

el **explorador** , la **exploradora** ■ explorer.

explorar [1] *verbo* ■ **to explore.**

la **explosión** *(plural* las explosiones*)* ■ explosion: se produjo una gran explosión there was a big explosion
> hacer explosión to explode.

el **explosivo,va** ■ **explosive.**

la **explotación** *(plural* las explotaciones*)* ■ **exploitation.**

explotar [1] *verbo*

1. **to explode:** la bomba va explotar en 10 minutos the bomb will explode in 10 minutes
2. **to exploit:** han explotado los recursos al máximo they've exploited their resources to the full; dice que la explotan en su trabajo she says they exploit her at work.

exponer [47] *verbo*

1. **to exhibit:** van a exponer sus cuadros en una galería they're going to exhibit her paintings in a gallery
2. **to set out:** expuso sus ideas muy claramente she set out her ideas very clearly
> exponen su vida para salvar a otros they risk their lives to save others
> no deberías exponerte demasiado al sol you shouldn't expose yourself to the sun too much.

exportar [1] *verbo* ■ **to export.**

la **exportación** *(plural* las exportaciones*)* ■ export
> artículos de exportación export goods.

la **exposición** *(plural* las exposiciones*)* ■ exhibition: una exposición de pinturas a painting exhibition
> montar una exposición to set up an exhibition.

expresar [1] *verbo* ■ to express: **le cuesta expresar lo que siente** he has trouble expressing his feelings; **no sabe expresarse muy bien** she's not very good at expressing herself.

la **expresión** *(plural* las expresiones*)* ■ expression: **tenía una expresión de tristeza en la cara** she had a sad expression on her face; **es una expresión típica española** it's a typical Spanish expression.

exprimir [3] *verbo* ■ to squeeze.

expulsar [1] *verbo*
1. to expel: **lo expulsaron del colegio** he was expelled from school
2. to send off: **lo expulsaron en el primer tiempo** he was sent off in the first half.

exquisito, ta *adjetivo* ■ delicious: **nos sirvieron una comida exquisita** they served us a delicious meal.

extender [15] *verbo*
1. to spread: **extendió la sábana sobre la cama** she spread the sheet on the bed; **hay que extender bien el bronceador por todo el cuerpo** you have to spread the tanning lotion all over your body; **el fuego se extendió por toda la costa** the fire spread along the coast
2. to extend: **extendió su mano** he extended his hand; **la llanura se extiende hasta la montaña** the plain extends to the mountain.

la **extensión** *(plural* las extensiones*)*
1. area, expanse: **es dueño de una gran extensión de terreno** he owns a vast expanse of land
2. extension: **¿sabes el número de su extensión?** do you know her extension?; **no consiguió la extensión de su visado** she didn't get the visa extension.

extenso, sa *adjetivo* ■ extensive.

exterior *adjetivo*
1. outside: **hay que subir por la escalera exterior** you have to climb up the outside ladder; **la parte exterior es más antigua** the outside is older
2. foreign: **el comercio exterior** foreign trade

el **exterior** ■ outside
➤ el exterior
1. the outside: **pintaron de blanco el exterior de la casa** they painted the outside of the house white
2. abroad: **informaron sobre las noticias del exterior** they reported the news from abroad.

externo, na *adjetivo*
1. external: **la pomada es de uso externo** the ointment is for external use
2. outside: **la parte externa de una flor** the outside of the flower.

la **extinción** *(plural* las extinciones*)* ■ extinction: **¿qué provocó la extinción de los dinosaurios?** what caused the extinction of the dinosaurs?
➤ **el viento hizo difícil la extinción del incendio** the wind made it difficult to put out the fire
➤ **especies en vías de extinción** endangered species.

extra *adjetivo* ■ extra: **pueden poner una cama extra** they can set up an extra bed
➤ **tiempo extra** extra time *UK*, overtime *US*
➤ **trabajar horas extras** to work overtime.

extraer [53] *verbo* ■ to extract: **me han extraído dos muelas** they've extracted two teeth.

extraescolar *adjetivo*
➤ **actividades extraescolares** out-of-school activities.

extranjero, ra *adjetivo* ■ foreign: **un visitante extranjero** a foreign visitor

el **extranjero** , la **extranjera** ■ foreigner: **muchos extranjeros viven en esta zona** a lot of foreigners live in this area

el **extranjero** ■ **le gustaría viajar al extranjero** she'd like to travel abroad
➤ **ir al extranjero** to go abroad.

extrañar [1] *verbo* ■ **me extraña que...** I'm surprised that...: **me extrañó no verte en clase** I was surprised that you weren't in class.

extraño, ña *adjetivo* ■ strange: **una costumbre muy extraña** a strange custom
➤ **¡qué extraño!** how strange!

extraordinario, ria *adjetivo* ■ **extraordinary**: **hace falta una paciencia extraordinaria** it takes extraordinary patience
> **no tiene nada de extraordinario** there's nothing unusual about that.

la **extraterrestre** ■ **extraterrestrial**.

extremo, ma *adjetivo* ■ **extreme**: **en el desierto tienen temperaturas extremas** they have extreme temperatures in the desert

el **extremo** ■ **end**: **ató los dos extremos de la cuerda** he tied the two ends of the rope
> **Extremo Oriente** Far East
> **vive al otro extremo de la ciudad** he lives on the other side of the city
> **recorrió el país de extremo a extremo** he travelled from one end of the country to the other
> **en caso extremo** as a last resort: **en caso extremo puedes llamarme** as a last resort, you can call me.

la **fábrica** ■ **factory**: **trabaja en una fábrica de automóviles** she works in a car factory

⚠️ The Spanish word **fábrica** is a false friend, it doesn't mean "fabric".

fabricar [8] *verbo* ■ **to manufacture**: **fabrican zapatos para niños** they manufacture children's shoes
> **fabricado en Corea** made in Korea
> **fabricar en serie** to mass-produce.

fabuloso, sa *adjetivo* ■ **fabulous**.

la **facha** *informal* ■ **look**: **no quiero que nadie me vea con esta facha** I don't want anyone to see me looking like this.

la **fachada** ■ **façade**: **están pintando la fachada del colegio** they're painting the school's façade.

fácil *adjetivo* ■ **easy**: **unos deberes fáciles** an easy homework assignment; **es muy fácil equivocarse** it's very easy to make a mistake
> **es fácil de convencer** he's easy to convince
> **lleva paraguas porque es fácil que llueva** bring an umbrella because it could easily rain.

la **facilidad** ■ **ease**: **aprobó los exámenes con facilidad** she passed her exams with ease
> **tiene mucha facilidad para las matemáticas** he's good at math
> **con facilidad** easily: **ganaron con facilidad** they won easily.

el **factor** ■ **factor**: **el clima es un factor importante** the climate is an important factor.

la **factura**
1. **invoice**: **envíe su factura al finalizar el trabajo** send your invoice when the job is finished
2. **bill**: **la factura del teléfono** the telephone bill.

la **facultad** ■ **faculty** *(plural* **faculties***)*: **tiene todas sus facultades mentales** he's in full possession of his mental faculties
> **la Facultad de Medicina** the Faculty of Medicine
> **fueron a la misma facultad** they went to the same faculty.

la **falda**
1. **skirt**: **una falda larga** a long skirt
2. **side**: **un pueblo en la falda de la montaña** a town on the side of the mountain.

fallar [1] *verbo* ■ **to fail**: **le está fallando la memoria** her memory is failing her; **le fallaron los frenos** his brakes failed
> **fallar un tiro** to miss a shot
> **cuento contigo, no me vayas a fallar** I'm counting on you, don't let me down.

las **Fallas** ■ *festivities held in Valencia every year on 19th March*

LAS FALLAS DE VALENCIA

Every year, on 19th March, the city of Valencia celebrates the **día de San José** (Saint Joseph's Day). Saint Joseph is the patron saint of carpenters, and in the months leading up to the festival, the residents of every neighbourhood build huge papier-mâché sculptures, known as **fallas**, caricaturing famous figures and current events. The **fallas** are real works of art and are put on display in the city's streets. On the night of 19th March, the **fallas** are set alight around the city and the festivities continue until the early hours of the morning, amid the noise of crackers and fireworks.

el **fallo**

1. failure: todo se debió a un fallo en el sistema it was all due to a failure in the system
2. mistake: ¡qué fallo! what a mistake!
3. flaw: devolví el juguete porque tenía un fallo I returned the toy because it had a flaw
   - un fallo mecánico a mechanical failure
   - un fallo humano a human error

falsificar [8] *verbo* ■ to forge: falsificó su firma he forged her signature.

falso, sa *adjetivo*

1. false: usaba un nombre falso she was using a false name
2. fake: el pasaporte era falso the passport was fake
   - un billete falso a counterfeit note *UK* o a counterfeit bill *US*
   - lo que dijo es falso what he said is false
   - una falsa alarma a false alarm
   - falso amigo false friend: "librería" y "library" son falsos amigos "librería" and "library" are false friends.

la **falta**

1. lack: por falta de experiencia due to lack of experience
2. foul: el árbitro no marcó la falta the referee didn't call the foul
   - faltas de ortografía spelling mistakes
   - tiene dos faltas de asistencia he's been absent twice

- es por falta de costumbre it's because I'm not used to it
- es una falta de educación it's bad manners
- hace falta más disciplina we need more discipline
- me hace falta un buen diccionario I need a good dictionary
- sin falta without fail: mañana sin falta lo llamo I'll call him tomorrow without fail.

faltar [1] *verbo* ■ to be missing: a este libro le falta una página this book is missing a page; ¿quién falta? who's missing?

- no falta nunca a clase she never misses class
- ha faltado dos semanas a clase he's been absent from class for two weeks
- le falta experiencia he lacks experience
- va a faltar comida we won't have enough food
- a esto le falta sabor it's lacking in taste
- falta una semana para mi cumpleaños it's a week until my birthday
- falta poco para terminar we're almost finished
- ¿te falta mucho? do you have a lot more to do?
- sólo me falta poner la fecha I just need to add the date
- ¡era lo último que nos faltaba! that's the last thing we need!

la **fama**

1. fame: alcanzó la fama con su primer disco she shot to fame with her first record
2. reputation: tiene fama de vago he has a reputation for being lazy; tiene muy mala fama he has a bad reputation.

la **familia** ■ family (*plural* families): fue a visitar a su familia she went to visit her family; tiene familia en Galicia he's got family in Galicia

- es de buena familia he comes from a good family
- celebramos la Navidad en familia we celebrated Christmas with the family
- a large family una familia numerosa.

familiar *adjetivo*

1. family: hay un ambiente familiar en este restaurante this restaurant has a family atmosphere

2. familiar: su cara le era familiar her face was familiar to him

viene en envase familiar it comes in a family-size pack

la **familiar** ■ relative: vive con un familiar she lives with a relative.

famoso, sa *adjetivo* ■ famous.

la **fan** *(plural* los/las fans) ■ fan: mi hermana es fan de Enrique Iglesias my sister is a fan of Enrique Iglesias

un club de fans a fan club.

fanático, ca *adjetivo* ■ fanatical

el **fanático** , la **fanática** ■ fanatic: es una fanática de la música pop she's a pop music fanatic.

la **fantasía** ■ fantasy *(plural* fantasies)

un mundo de fantasía a fantasy world

joyas de fantasía costume jewellery.

el **fantasma** ■ ghost.

fantástico, ca *adjetivo*

1. imaginary: en ese cuento hay muchos personajes fantásticos in this story there are a lot of imaginary characters

2. fantastic: nuestro viaje a Egipto fue fantástico our trip to Egypt was fantastic.

la **farmacia** ■ chemist's *UK*, pharmacy *(plural* pharmacies) *US*, drugstore *US*.

el **faro**

1. lighthouse: podíamos ver el faro en la distancia we could see the lighthouse in the distance

2. headlight: encendí los faros del coche I switched on the car's headlights.

la **farola**

1. street light, lamp-post: las farolas se encienden a las 8 the street lights go on at 8 o'clock; ha chocado contra la farola he crashed into a lamp-post.

el **farsante** ■ fraud: me ha engañado varias veces, es un farsante he's conned me several times, he's a fraud.

fascinar [1] *verbo* ■ to fascinate: me fascinan sus cuadros his pictures fascinate me.

la **fase** ■ phase: las fases de la luna son cuatro the moon has four phases.

fastidiar [1] *verbo*

1. to annoy: me fastidia que los vecinos hagan tanto ruido it really annoys me that the neighbours make so much noise

2. to bother: no fastidies a tu hermana, que está haciendo los deberes don't bother your sister, she's doing her homework

3. to spoil: el tiempo nos fastidió el fin de semana the weather spoilt our weekend.

el **fastidio** ■ nuisance: ¡qué fastidio tener que salir con esta lluvia! what a nuisance to have to go out in this rain!

¡es un fastidio! it's a pain!: es un fastidio tener que madrugar tanto it's a pain having to get up so early.

fatal *adjetivo*

1. fatal: fue un error fatal it was a fatal error

2. awful: me encuentro fatal I feel awful; fue un día fatal, todo lo que hice me salió mal it was an awful day – everything I did went wrong.

la **fatiga** ■ fatigue.

el **favor** ■ favour *UK*, favor *US*: me han hecho varios favores y por eso les estoy agradecida they've done me a few favours so I'm grateful to them

a favor de in favour of: están a favor de la educación bilingüe they're in favour of bilingual education

por favor please: cierra la puerta, por favor close the door please.

favorecer [22] *verbo*

1. to favour *UK*, to favor *US*: esa ley favorece a los ricos that law favours the rich

2. to be flattering: ese color te favorece, deberías usarlo más a menudo that colour is very flattering, you should wear it more often.

favorito, ta *adjetivo* ■ favourite *UK*, favorite *US*.

el **fax** *(plural* los faxes)

1. fax machine: acabo de instalar el nuevo fax I just set up the new fax machine

2. **fax:** ha llegado un fax con la información que faltaba a fax has arrived with the missing information
- mandar algo por fax to fax something.

la **fe** ■ **faith:** tengo fe en que todo va a salir bien I have faith that everything will turn out all right
- de buena fe in good faith
- de mala fe dishonestly
- fe en Dios faith in God.

la **fealdad** ■ **ugliness.**

febrero *sustantivo masculino*

En inglés los nombres de los meses se escriben con mayúscula:

February: en febrero in February; el próximo febrero next February; el pasado febrero last February.

la **fecha** ■ **date:** ¿cuál es la fecha del examen? what's the date of the exam?
- fecha de nacimiento date of birth.

fecundar [1] *verbo* ■ **to fertilize.**

la **federación** *(plural* las federaciones*)* ■ **federation.**

la **felicidad** ■ **happiness:** el dinero no compra la felicidad money can't buy you happiness
- es mi cumpleaños —¡muchas felicidades! it's my birthday today – happy birthday!
- ¡muchas felicidades por el nuevo trabajo! congratulations on your new job!

las **felicitaciones** ■ **congratulations:** los ganadores recibieron las felicitaciones del público the winners received the spectators' congratulations.

felicitar [1] *verbo* ■ **to congratulate:** vamos a felicitarlo por sus buenos resultados let's congratulate him on his good results
- llamamos a nuestros amigos para felicitarlos por Navidad we called our friends to wish them a merry Christmas; tengo que felicitarla por su cumpleaños I have to wish her a happy birthday.

feliz *(plural* felices*) adjetivo* ■ **happy:** Sofía es muy feliz en Sevilla Sofía is very happy in Seville
- ¡feliz cumpleaños! happy birthday!
- ¡Feliz Navidad! Happy Christmas!
- ¡Feliz Año Nuevo! Happy New Year!

el **felpudo** ■ **doormat.**

femenino, na *adjetivo*
1. **feminine:** Rebeca es muy femenina Rebeca is very feminine
2. **female:** el sexo femenino the female sex
3. **women's, ladies':** el fútbol femenino women's football; la moda femenina ladies' fashion.

fenomenal *adjetivo* ■ **fantastic:** lo hemos pasado fenomenal we had a fantastic time.

el **fenómeno** ■ **phenomenon** *(plural* phenomena*).*

feo, a *adjetivo*
1. **ugly:** ese cuadro no me gusta nada, es muy feo I don't like that picture at all, it's so ugly
2. **nasty:** una herida fea a nasty wound
3. **not nice:** es muy feo mentir, no lo vuelvas a hacer it's not nice to lie, don't do it again.

el **féretro** ■ **coffin.**

la **feria** ■ **fair:** he ganado el muñeco en la feria I won the doll at the fair; mañana se inaugura la feria del juguete the toy fair opens tomorrow
- feria de Abril *festivities held in Seville every year*

LA FERIA DE ABRIL

The **Feria de Abril** (April Fair) is held every year in Seville, about a fortnight after Easter. The Festivities, which last for a week, take place in a big park, where green-and white-striped marquees and pavilions, known as **casetas**, are set up and decorated with flowers and lanterns. Groups of friends and entire families get together in the **casetas** to have a drink, eat some **tapas** and dance **sevillanas** until the early hours of the morning. The organisers host concerts and other entertainments, and processions in traditional costumes are also held. The **Feria** also marks the beginning of the bullfighting season.

fermentar [1] *verbo* ■ to ferment.

feroz *adjetivo* ■ fierce.

la ferretería ■ hardware store.

el ferrocarril ■ railway *UK*, railroad *US*.

fértil *adjetivo* ■ fertile.

el fertilizante ■ fertilizer.

fertilizar [10] *verbo* ■ to fertilize.

el festival ■ festival
festival de cine film festival.

la festividad ■ festivity (*plural* **festivities**):
las festividades duraron todo el fin de semana the festivities went on all weekend; la festividad de San Juan es el 24 de junio the festivity of Saint John is on 24th June.

festivo, a *adjetivo* ■ festive: el primero de mayo es un día festivo the first of May is a holiday.

el feto ■ foetus *UK*, fetus *US*.

el fiambre ■ cold cut: de todos los fiambres, el jamón es mi preferido ham is my favorite cold cut.

fiar [7] *verbo*

1. to be trustworthy: Ramón es una persona de fiar Ramón is a trustworthy person
2. to be reliable: esa marca de electrodomésticos no es de fiar this brand of appliances isn't very reliable
3. to give credit: en esta tienda me fían in this shop they give me credit

fiarse *verbo pronominal*

1. to believe: no te fíes de todo lo que oyes don't believe everything you hear
2. to trust: no te fíes de todos los que vengan a ofrecerte ayuda don't trust everyone that offers to help you.

la fibra ■ fibre *UK*, fiber *US*: el pan integral contiene mucha fibra wholemeal bread contains a lot of fibre; el algodón es una excelente fibra natural cotton is an excellent natural fibre.

la ficción (*plural* las ficciones)■ fiction: sólo escribe ficción she only writes fiction.

la ficha

1. card: en esta ficha anotaré tus datos I'll write your details on this card
2. piece: faltan algunas fichas rojas some of the red pieces are missing
> una ficha médica medical records
> una ficha policial a police record.

el fichero

1. file: un fichero informático a computer file
2. filing cabinet: guardo los informes en el fichero I keep the reports in the filing cabinet.

el fideo ■ noodle: el primer plato es sopa de fideos the starter is noodle soup
> estar como un fideo to be as thin as a rake: tu prima está como un fideo your cousin is as thin as a rake.

la fiebre ■ fever: le di una aspirina para bajarle la fiebre I gave her an aspirin to lower the fever.

fiel *adjetivo*

1. loyal: Juan siempre ha sido fiel a sus amigos Juan has always been loyal to his friends
2. faithful: le es fiel a su esposa he's faithful to his wife.

la fiera ■ wild animal: en este bosque viven varias fieras several wild animals live in this forest
> ponerse como una fiera to fly into a rage
> ser una fiera en algo to be whizz at something.

la fiesta

1. party (*plural* **parties**): hicimos una fiesta para su cumpleaños we threw a party for his birthday
2. holiday: el viernes es fiesta Friday is a holiday
> ir de fiesta to go out partying: el sábado iremos de fiesta we're going out partying on Saturday
> estar de fiesta to be celebrating: la familia está de fiesta por el nacimiento del niño the family is celebrating the birth of the baby
fiesta mayor local celebrations

FIESTA MAYOR

La **fiesta mayor** consists of a round of cultural and recreational events organized in a town to celebrate the festival of its patron saint.

la **figura** ■ **figure:** dibujamos figuras de diferentes tamaños we drew different size figures; tras el parto he recuperado la figura I got my figure back after the birth; Tony es una gran figura del baloncesto Tony is a major figure in basketball; una figura de porcelana a porcelain figure.

figurar [1] *verbo* ■ **to appear:** tu nombre no figura en esta lista your name doesn't appear on this list.

fijar [1] *verbo* ■ **to set:** hay que fijar la fecha de la boda we have to set the date for the wedding

fijarse *verbo pronominal*

1. **to look carefully:** fíjate si tienes las llaves en el bolso look carefully in your bag for the keys
2. **to notice:** no me fijé en la ropa que llevaba I didn't notice the clothes she was wearing
   ▸ ¡fíjate en eso! look at that!

fijo, ja *adjetivo*

1. **fixed:** la estantería está fija, ya puedes poner tus libros the shelves are fixed to the wall so you can put your books on them
2. **set:** pagamos una cuota fija todos los meses we pay a set fee every month; no hay una fecha fija para las vacaciones there's no set date for the holidays
3. **permanent:** todavía no tengo trabajo fijo I don't have a permanent job yet.

la **fila**

1. **file, line:** nos pusieron en fila we were lined up
2. **row:** conseguimos asientos en tercera fila we got seats in the third row
   ▸ estacionar en doble fila to double park
   ▸ ponerse en fila to get in line.

las **Filipinas** ■ **the Philippines.**

filmar [1] *verbo* ■ **to film:** Pedro filmó el nacimiento de su hijo Pedro filmed the birth of his son.

el **filo** ■ **blade:** el filo del cuchillo estaba oxidado the knife had a rusty blade
▸ sacarle filo a algo to sharpen something: tengo que sacarle filo a este cuchillo I need to sharpen this knife

este cuchillo tiene poco filo this knife isn't very sharp
▸ de doble filo double-edged.

la **filosofía** ■ **philosophy.**

filtrar [1] *verbo* ■ **to filter:** tienes que filtrar el agua you have to filter the water

filtrarse *verbo pronominal* ■ **to leak:** se está filtrando agua por el techo the roof is leaking.

el **filtro** ■ **filter.**

el **fin**

1. **end:** se acerca el fin del año escolar we're approaching the end of the school year
2. **purpose:** ¿cuál es el fin de tu viaje? what is the purpose of your trip?
   "fin" "the end"
   ▸ ¡al fin! finally!: ¡al fin llegaste! you're finally here!
   ▸ al fin y al cabo after all
   ▸ en fin well: en fin, ¿qué piensas hacer ahora? well, what are you going to do now?
   ▸ ¡por fin! finally: ¡por fin has terminado! you've finally finished!
   ▸ el fin de año New Year's Eve
   ▸ el fin de semana the weekend.

el **final** ■ **end:** no me gustó el final del cuento I didn't like the end of the story
▸ a finales de at the end of: viajaremos a finales de diciembre we're going on holiday at the end of December
▸ un final feliz a happy ending: me encantan las películas con final feliz I love films with a happy ending

la **final** ■ **final:** España ganó la final Spain won the final.

finalizar [10] *verbo* ■ **to finish.**

financiar [1] *verbo* ■ **to finance:** el gobierno financió la construcción del puente the government financed the construction of the bridge.

las **finanzas** ■ **finances:** las finanzas de una empresa a company's finances.

la **finca** ■ **country estate.**

fingir [11] *verbo* ■ **to pretend:** no finjas que duermes, sé que estás despierta stop pretending you're asleep, I know you're awake.

fino, na *adjetivo*

1. **fine:** tengo el pelo muy fino I have very fine hair

2. **slender:** la pianista tenía manos largas y dedos finos the pianist had long hands with slender fingers

3. **thin:** corta el jamón en lonchas finas cut the jam in thin slices.

la **firma** ■ **signature:** aquí está la firma de mi padre here's my father's signature.

firmar [1] *verbo* ■ **to sign:** firme aquí, por favor sign here please.

firme *adjetivo*

1. **steady:** necesito una mesa firme para dibujar I need a steady table to draw at

2. **firm:** adoptaron una decisión firme they made a firm decision

> **ponerse firme** to stand one's ground: el soldado se puso firme the soldier stood his ground.

la **fiscal** ■ **public prosecutor** UK, **district attorney** US.

la **física** ■ **physics.**

físico, ca *adjetivo* ■ **physical:** el niño no tiene ningún problema físico the child has no physical problems

> **educación física** physical education

> **ejercicio físico** physical exercise

el **físico**, la **física** ■ **physicist.**

flaco, ca *adjetivo* ■ **skinny.**

flamante *adjetivo* ■ **brand-new:** un coche flamante a brand-new car.

el **flamenco**

1. **flamenco:** fuimos a ver un espectáculo de flamenco we went to see a flamenco show

2. **flamingo:** el flamenco es un ave de color rosado the flamingo is a pink bird

EL FLAMENCO

Flamenco has its origins in an Andalusian style of song known as **cante jondo**, created by the gypsies who moved to Andalusia in the 15th century. **Cante jondo** is a cry from the heart, expressing the suffering of a people that have been persecuted and denigrated. The songs of the **cante jondo** are sung to the simple accompaniment of a guitar. Initially, they were performed in taverns in Andalusia but spread to the rest of Spain in about 1850 when these watering holes became fashionable. This is how **flamenco** was born. The poet of the Andalusian people, García Lorca, studied **cante jondo** with his teacher, the composer Manuel de Falla, and helped popularise this musical genre in the 1920s. Enrique Morente and the late Camarón de la Isla rank among some of the great flamenco performers.

el **flan** ■ **crème caramel.**

la **flauta** ■ **flute:** toca muy bien la flauta he plays the flute very well

> **flauta dulce** recorder.

la **flecha** ■ **arrow.**

el **fleco** ■ **fringe:** llevaba una chaqueta con flecos she wore a jacket with a fringe on it.

el **flequillo** ■ **fringe** UK, **bangs** US.

flexible *adjetivo* ■ **flexible.**

la **flexión** *(plural* las flexiones) ■ **push-up:** ayer hice 100 flexiones I did 100 push-ups yesterday.

flojo, ja *adjetivo*

1. **loose:** este nudo está muy flojo this knot is very loose

2. **weak:** estás flojo en historia you're history grades are weak; el café me gusta flojo I like my coffee weak

3. **poor:** hice un examen un poco flojo I did a rather poor exam.

la **flor** ■ **flower:** un ramo de flores a bunch of flowers.

florecer [22] *verbo* ■ **to blossom:** los árboles florecieron temprano este año the trees blossomed early this year.

el **florero** ■ vase: me regalaron un precioso florero de cristal they gave me a beautiful crystal vase.

la **floristería** ■ florist's.

la **flota** ■ fleet: la flota pesquera partió antes del amanecer the fishing fleet left before dawn.

el **flotador** ■ rubber ring.

flotar [1] verbo ■ to float: había muchas hojas flotando en la piscina there were a lot of leaves floating in the pool.

fluorescente adjetivo ■ fluorescent.

la **foca** ■ seal.

el **foco**
1. spotlight: los focos iluminaron el escenario the spotlights lit up the stage
2. floodlight: los focos del estadio se encendieron the floodlights in the stadium came on
➤ fuera de foco out of focus: esa imagen está fuera de foco this picture is out of focus.

el **folio**
1. sheet of paper: escríbelo en este folio write it on this sheet of paper
2. page: un informe de diez folios a ten-page report.

el **folleto**
1. de una hoja leaflet
2. como un librito brochure.

el **fondo**
1. bottom: están explorando el fondo del mar they are exploring the bottom of the sea
2. background: el retrato tenía un fondo azul the portrait had a blue background
3. end: el baño está al fondo del pasillo the bathroom is at the end of the corridor
➤ a fondo in-depth: estudiaron el problema a fondo they did an in-depth study of the problem
➤ en el fondo deep down: pelean mucho, pero en el fondo se quieren they fight a lot, but deep down they love each other.

los **fondos** ■ funds: están recaudando fondos para el hospital they're raising funds for the hospital.

el **fontanero** , la **fontanera** ■ plumber.

forestal adjetivo ■ forest: el guardia forestal detectó el incendio the forest ranger spotted the fire.

el **footing** ■ jogging: hago footing todas las mañanas I go jogging every morning.

la **forma**
1. shape: encuentra todas las formas circulares find all the circular shapes
2. way: no me gusta su forma de ser, siempre está de mal humor I don't like the way she acts, she's always in a bad mood; este ejercicio puede resolverse de diferentes formas this problem can be solved in different ways
➤ de cualquier forma anyway
➤ de todas formas anyway: de todas formas tendrás que ordenar tu cuarto you'll have to tidy your room anyway
➤ mantenerse en forma to stay in shape: Ana camina tres kilómetros cada día para mantenerse en forma Ana walks three kilometres a day to stay in shape.

la **formación** ■ education: es importante tener una buena formación para conseguir un buen trabajo it's important to have a good education to get a good job.

formal adjetivo
1. reliable: necesitamos trabajadores más formales we need more reliable workers
2. responsible: es un chico muy formal he's a very responsible boy
3. formal: una invitación formal al banquete a formal invitation to the banquet.

formar [1] verbo
1. to make: si unes los puntos formarás la figura de un elefante if you connect the dots you'll make an elephant
2. to form: Juan y sus amigos formaron un grupo de rap Juan and his friends formed a rap group
3. to train: la universidad se ocupa de formar a los jóvenes it's the university's job to train young people
4. to make up: Pablo y yo formamos un buen equipo Pablo and I make up a good team.

a **fórmula**

1. formula: es difícil recordar todas las fórmulas matemáticas it's hard to remember all the mathematical formulas

2. set expression: tienes que empezar la carta con una fórmula de cortesía you should start the letter with a polite set expression
una **fórmula mágica** a magic formula.

el **formulario** ■ form: tienes que rellenar este formulario you have to till this form.

forrar [1] verbo

1. to cover: voy a forrar los cuadernos para protegerlos I'm going to cover my notebooks to protect them

2. to line: me van a forrar el abrigo they're going to line my coat

forrarse verbo pronominal ■ to make a fortune: se ha forrado con un sitio en Internet he's made a fortune from an Internet site.

fortalecer [22] verbo ■ to strengthen: el ejercicio físico fortalece los músculos physical exercise strengthens the muscles.

la **fortaleza**

1. strength: su fortaleza lo ayudó a recuperarse pronto his strength helped him recover quickly

2. fortress: a lo largo de la costa hay varias fortalezas antiguas there are several old fortresses along the coast.

la **fortuna** ■ fortune: su fortuna personal es de cerca de diez millones de dólares her personal fortune comes to nearly ten million dollars; tuvo la fortuna de conocer personalmente a su actor favorito he had the good fortune to meet his favourite actor.

forzar [10] verbo ■ to force: forzaron la cerradura para poder entrar they forced the lock to enter; el mal tiempo nos forzó a quedarnos en casa todo el fin de semana the bad weather forced us to stay at home all weekend.

la **foto** ■ picture: hemos hecho unas fotos muy bonitas we took some lovely photos.

la **fotocopia** ■ photocopy (plural photocopies).

la **fotocopiadora** ■ photocopier.

fotocopiar [1] verbo ■ to photocopy.

la **fotografía**

1. photograph

2. photography: estudia fotografía en el instituto he studies photography at college
hacer una fotografía de alguien to take a picture of someone.

el **fotógrafo** , la **fotógrafa** ■ photographer.

fracasar [1] verbo ■ to fail: nuestros planes de viaje fracasaron por falta de dinero our travel plans failed due to lack of money.

el **fracaso** ■ failure: el espectáculo fue un fracaso, no vino nadie the show was a failure, nobody came.

la **fracción** (plural las fracciones) ■ fraction: en clase hoy hemos estudiado las fracciones we studied fractions in class today.

la **fractura** ■ fracture: la caída le produjo varias fracturas she sustained several fractures from the fall.

frágil adjetivo ■ fragile.

fragmentar [1] verbo ■ to fragment.

la **frambuesa** ■ raspberry (plural raspberries).

francés, francesa

En inglés, los adjetivos que se refieren a un país o una región se escriben con mayúscula:

French: tiene acento francés he has a French accent

el **francés** , la **francesa** (plural los franceses)

En inglés, los gentilicios se escriben con mayúscula:

Frenchman (plural Frenchmen), Frenchwoman (plural Frenchwomen)
los franceses the French

el **francés**

En inglés, los idiomas se escriben con mayúscula:

French.

Francia ■ France.

franco, ca *adjetivo* ■ **frank**: te voy a ser franco, no confío en él I'll be frank, I don't trust him

➤ para serte franco to be honest.

la **franja** ■ **stripe**: la bandera española tiene tres franjas horizontales: roja, amarilla y roja the Spanish flag has three horizontal stripes: red, yellow and red.

el **frasco**

1. **bottle**: el perfume viene en un frasco muy bonito the perfume comes in a pretty bottle

2. **jar**: no puedo abrir el frasco de la mayonesa I can't open the mayonnaise jar.

la **frase**

1. **sentence**: esta frase no tiene verbo this sentence doesn't have a verb

2. **phrase**: una frase hecha a set phrase.

el **fraude** ■ **fraud**

➤ un fraude fiscal a tax fraud.

la **frecuencia** ■ **frequency** *(plural* **frequencies***)*: las ondas de una frecuencia tan alta no se oyen you can't hear waves of such a high frequency

➤ con frecuencia frequently: somos buenas amigas y nos vemos con frecuencia we're good friends and see each other frequently; con qué frecuencia visitas a tus abuelos? how often do you visit your grandparents?.

frecuente *adjetivo* ■ **frequent.**

fregar [12] *verbo* ■ **to wash**: tengo que fregar la sartén I have to wash the frying pan

➤ fregar los platos to wash the dishes

➤ fregar el suelo to mop the floor.

freír [21] *verbo* ■ **to fry.**

frenar [1] *verbo* ■ **to brake**: no pudo frenar a tiempo y provocó un accidente he couldn't brake in time and caused an accident.

el **freno** ■ **brake**

➤ el freno de mano the handbrake.

el **frente** ■ **front**: un frente de aire cálido a warm air front; vivió experiencias terribles en el frente de batalla he experienced terrible things at the battle front

➤ al frente at the helm: está al frente de la empresa she's at the helm of the company

➤ de frente head-on: chocaron de frente they had a head-on collision

➤ frente a opposite: la farmacia está frente a la panadería the chemist's is opposite the baker's

➤ hacer frente to face: tuvo que hacer frente a muchos problemas he had to face a lot of problems.

la **frente** ■ **forehead**: era guapa, tenía los pómulos altos y la frente ancha she was pretty, with high cheekbones and a wide forehead.

la **fresa** ■ **strawberry** *(plural* **strawberries***).*

fresco, ca *adjetivo*

1. **cool**: soplaba un viento fresco a cool wind was blowing; una habitación fresca a cool room; en verano siempre llevo ropa fresca in summer I always wear cool clothing

2. **fresh**: es importante comer verduras y fruta fresca it's important to eat fresh fruit and vegetables; nos ha traído noticias frescas he brought us fresh news

3. **chilly**: esta mañana hace fresco it's chilly this morning.

el **frigorífico** ■ **fridge** UK, **refrigerator**: guarda la mayonesa en el frigorífico keep the mayonnaise in the fridge.

frío, a *adjetivo* ■ **cold**: la sopa está fría the soup is cold; Jaime es una persona muy fría Jaime is a very cold person; el azul es un color frío blue is a cold colour

el **frío** ■ **cold**: hace frío it's cold; tengo frío I'm cold.

frito, ta *adjetivo* ■ **fried**: voy a hacer un pescado frito I'm going to do fried fish.

frontal *adjetivo* ■ **head-on**: fue un choque frontal it was a head-on crash.

la **frontera** ■ **border**: en la frontera tuve que mostrar el pasaporte I had to show the passport at the border.

frotar [1] *verbo* ■ **to rub**: tienes que frotarte las piernas con esta loción you have to rub your legs with this lotion; frota bien para quitar la mancha rub it well to remove the stain.

la **frustración** (*plural* las frustraciones) ■ frustration.

frustrar [1] *verbo* ■ to spoil: el mal tiempo frustró nuestros planes de viaje the bad weather spoiled our plans

frustrarse *verbo pronominal* ■ to be frustrated: me frustré un poco al quedar segundo en la carrera I was a bit frustrated at coming second in the race.

la **fruta** ■ fruit: me encanta la fruta I love fruit

fruta del tiempo seasonal fruit.

la **frutería** ■ fruit shop.

el **fruto** ■ fruit: el árbol está cargado de frutos the tree is full of fruit

los frutos secos nuts and dried fruit.

el **fuego** ■ fire: no consiguieron controlar el fuego they couldn't control the fire

fuegos artificiales fireworks.

la **fuente**

1. **fountain:** construyeron una hermosa fuente en medio del parque they built a beautiful fountain in the middle of the park

2. **bowl:** ¿tienes una fuente para poner la fruta? do you have a bowl to put the fruit in?

3. **source:** el turismo es la principal fuente de ingresos en esa región tourism is the main source of income in that area.

fuera *adverbio*

1. **outside:** el perro duerme fuera de la casa the dog sleeps outside the house; te está esperando fuera he's waiting for you outside; por fuera es rojo it's red on the outside

2. **away:** he estado fuera una semana I've been away for a week

esta noche vamos a cenar fuera tonight we're going out for dinner

fuera de lugar out of place: ese comentario está fuera de lugar that comment is out of place

estar fuera de sí to be beside oneself: Daniel estaba fuera de sí Daniel was beside himself.

fuerte *adjetivo*

1. **strong:** ese pescado tiene un olor muy fuerte that fish has a very strong smell

2. **loud:** la música está muy fuerte the music is too loud

3. **bad:** fui al dentista con un fuerte dolor de muelas I went to the dentist with a bad toothache

4. **bold:** para la ropa, prefiero los colores fuertes I prefer clothes with bold colours

5. **hard:** se dio un golpe tan fuerte que empezó a llorar he hit himself so hard he started to cry

el **fuerte** ■ fort.

la **fuerza**

1. **strength:** vamos a descansar para recuperar fuerzas let's have a break to recover our strength

2. **force:** la fuerza del viento obligó al velero a girar the force of the wind made the sailing boat turn around

la fuerza de gravedad the force of gravity

tiene tanta fuerza que partió un ladrillo de un golpe he's so strong he broke a brick with one blow

a fuerza de by: se hizo rico a fuerza de trabajar he got rich by working

a la fuerza by force: los alborotadores fueron sacados a la fuerza the rioters were taken away by force

me han hecho venir a la fuerza they forced me to come.

la **fuga**

1. **escape:** los prisioneros planearon su fuga the prisoners planned their escape

2. **leak:** encontramos una fuga de gas en la cocina we found a gas leak in the kitchen.

fugarse [12] *verbo pronominal* ■ to escape.

fugaz *adjetivo* ■ fleeting.

fugitivo, va *adjetivo* ■ fugitive

el **fugitivo** , la **fugitiva** ■ fugitive.

fumar [1] *verbo* ■ to smoke: fumar en pipa to smoke a pipe

prohibido fumar no smoking

dejar de fumar to give up smoking.

la **función** *(plural* las funciones*)*
1. role: ¿cuál es tu función en la empresa? what is your role in the company?
2. performance: la próxima función empieza a las cinco the next performance starts at five
3. function: aún no conoce todas las funciones del ordenador he still doesn't know all the functions of the computer.

funcionar [1] *verbo* ■ to work: la licuadora ya no funciona the blender doesn't work any more; ¿cómo funciona este aparato? how does this appliance work?; no funciona it doesn't work.

el **funcionario** , la **funcionaria** ■ government employee, civil servant *UK*.

la **funda**
1. *de cojín, CD, sofá* cover
2. *de gafas* case
una funda de almohada a pillowcase.

fundamental *adjetivo* ■ fundamental.

fundar [1] *verbo* ■ to found: según la leyenda, Rómulo y Remo fundaron Roma according to the legend, Romulus and Remus founded Rome.

fundir [3] *verbo*
1. to melt: el sol fundió la nieve the sun melted the snow
2. to smelt: los altos hornos sirven para fundir metales blast furnaces are used to smelt metal

fundirse *verbo pronominal*
1. to melt: la mantequilla se funde si la dejas al calor butter melts if you leave it out in the heat
2. to blow: la bombilla se ha fundido the light bulb has blown.

fúnebre *adjetivo* ■ funereal.

el **funeral** ■ funeral.

la **funeraria** ■ undertaker's *UK*, funeral parlor *US*.

la **furia** ■ rage.

furioso, sa *adjetivo* ■ furious: una mirada furiosa a furious look

ponerse furioso to get angry: me pongo furioso cuando el ordenador no funciona I get angry when the computer doesn't work.

el **fusil** ■ rifle.

fusionar [1] *verbo* ■ to merge: varias pequeñas empresas se fusionaron para lograr mantenerse en el mercado several small companies merged so they could stay in business.

el **fútbol** ■ football *UK*, soccer *US*: un jugador de fútbol a football player *UK*, a football soccer *US*; los domingos juega al fútbol he plays football on Sundays
> fútbol americano American football.

el **futbolín** ■ table football.

el/la **futbolista** ■ football player *UK*, soccer player *US*.

futuro, ra *adjetivo* ■ future: las generaciones futuras future generations; el futuro marido the future husband
> la futura madre the mother-to-be

el **futuro** ■ future: el futuro del verbo "ser" the future of the verb "ser"; el futuro de los jóvenes the future of young people.

la **gabardina** ■ raincoat.

las **gafas** ■ glasses: mi hermano lleva gafas my brother wears glasses
> gafas de sol sunglasses
> gafas graduadas prescription glasses
> gafas protectoras protective goggles.

a **gafe** ■ accident-prone: María es una gafe María is accident-prone.

a **galaxia** ■ galaxy (plural **galaxies**).

a **galería** ■ gallery (plural **galleries**): una galería de arte an art gallery
una galería comercial a shopping arcade UK, a shopping mall US.

Galicia ■ Galicia.

gallego, ga adjetivo

En inglés, los adjetivos que se refieren a un país o una región se escriben con mayúscula:

Galician: el marisco gallego es muy bueno Galician seafood is very good

el **gallego** , la **gallega**

En inglés, los gentilicios se escriben con mayúscula:

el **gallego**

En inglés, los idiomas se escriben con mayúscula.

Galician: estamos aprendiendo gallego we're learning Galician.

la **galleta** ■ biscuit UK, cookie US: compré un paquete de galletas I bought a pack of biscuits
una galleta salada a cracker.

la **gallina** ■ chicken.

el **gallo** ■ cockerel UK, rooster.

la **gamba** ■ prawn UK, shrimp US.

la **gamberrada** ■ yobbish behavior US, loutish behaviour: siempre están haciendo gamberradas they always act like a yob.

el **gamberro** , la **gamberra** ■ yob UK, hooligan: unos gamberros me han pinchado las ruedas del coche some yobs punctured my car tyres.

la **gana**
¡no me da la gana! I don't feel like it
me muero de ganas de ir al cine I'm dying to go to the cinema
chutó la pelota con ganas he kicked the ball hard

tener ganas de hacer algo to feel like doing something: tengo ganas de tomarme un helado I feel like having an ice cream cone
de buena gana willingly: de buena gana se ofreció a acompañarla he willingly offered to go with her
de mala gana reluctantly: me contestó de mala gana he answered reluctantly
llegamos tarde y nos quedamos con las ganas de ver la película we didn't get to see the film because we were late.

la **ganadería**
1. actividad cattle breeding
2. conjunto de ganado cattle.

el **ganado** ■ livestock.

el **ganador** , la **ganadora** ■ winner: el presidente entregó el trofeo al ganador the president presented the trophy to the winner.

las **ganancias** ■ profits: las pérdidas y las ganancias losses and profits.

ganar [1] verbo
1. to win: nuestra escuela ganó el campeonato de fútbol our school won the football championship
2. to earn: gana mil euros al mes she earns a thousand euros a month
ganarle a alguien to beat someone: la tenista rusa le ganó a la francesa the Russian tennis player beat the French one

ganarse verbo pronominal ■ to earn: se gana la vida como camarero he earns a living as a waiter; se ganó la confianza de todos she earned everybody's trust.

el **gancho**
1. hook: lo colgó de un gancho he hung it on a hook
2. hanger: colgamos la ropa en ganchos de plástico we hung up the clothes on plastic hangers
tener gancho
1. to be catchy: esta canción tiene gancho that song is catchy
2. to have charm: Eduardo tiene gancho Eduardo has charm.

la **ganga** ■ bargain: ese televisor es una ganga that television is a bargain.

el **ganso** , la **gansa** ■ goose.

el **garaje** ■ garage.

la **garantía** ■ guarantee: este equipo de música tiene un año de garantía this stereo system has a one-year guarantee.

garantizar [10] *verbo* ■ to guarantee: garantizan la calidad del producto they guarantee the quality of the product; te garantizo que llegaremos a tiempo I guarantee you we'll get there on time.

el **garbanzo** ■ chickpea, garbanzo bean *US*.

la **garganta** ■ throat: me duele la garganta I have a sore throat.

la **garra**
1. claw: el lobo lo hirió con sus garras the wolf wounded him with its claws; las garras del gato the cat's claws
2. talon: las garras del águila son muy peligrosas the eagle's talons are very dangerous
3. clutches: cayó en las garras de la mafia she fell into the clutches of the mob.

el **gas** ■ gas: la explosión se produjo por un escape de gas the explosion was caused by a gas leak.

la **gaseosa** ■ lemonade *UK*, soda *US*.

la **gasolina** ■ petrol *UK*, gas *US*: tenemos que poner gasolina we need to get petrol.

la **gasolinera** ■ petrol station *UK*, gas station *US*: la gasolinera más cercana está a dos manzanas the nearest petrol station is two blocks away.

gastar [1] *verbo*
1. to spend: gastamos mucho dinero en la reforma de la cocina we spent a lot of money redoing the kitchen
2. to use: este coche gasta demasiada gasolina this car uses too much petrol
3. to wear out: este niño gasta mucho los zapatos this child really wears out his shoes
➤ gastar una broma to play a joke: le hemos gastado una broma we played a joke on him.

el **gasto**
1. expense: el gasto más importante en nuestra casa es la comida our biggest household expense is on food; tengo muchos gastos I've got a lot of expenses
2. waste: el gasto de energía es exagerado en este país the waste of energy in this country is ridiculous
➤ gastos de envío shipping and handling
➤ gastos de mantenimiento maintenance costs
➤ el gasto público public expenditure.

gatas
➤ a gatas on all fours: caminábamos a gatas en la oscuridad we were going around on all fours in the dark.

gatear [1] *verbo* ■ to crawl: mi hija gatea por toda la casa my daughter crawls all over the house.

el **gato** , la **gata** ■ cat: le encantan los gatos she loves cats

el **gato** ■ jack: no tenemos un gato para cambiar el neumático we don't have a jack for changing the wheel.

la **gaviota** ■ seagull.

el **gazpacho** ■ *cold soup made with tomatoes and other vegetables.*

la **gema** ■ gem.

gemelo, la *adjetivo* ■ twin: tiene un hermano gemelo she has a twin brother

el **gemelo** , la **gemela** ■ twin: la profesora siempre confunde a los gemelos de su clase the teacher always confuses the twins in her class

los **gemelos**
1. cuff links: compré unos gemelos para la camisa I bought some cuff links for the shirt
2. binoculars: observaban los pájaros con unos gemelos they watched the birds through binoculars.

gemir [19] *verbo* ■ to whine: el perro del vecino gimió toda la noche the neighbour's dog whined all night long
➤ gemir de dolor to moan with pain: el niño gimió de dolor cuando se hizo daño the boy moaned with pain when he hurt himself.

el **gen** ■ gene.

la **generación** (plural las generaciones) ■ generation: somos la segunda generación de inmigrantes en mi familia we're the second generation of immigrants in my family; este cantante pertenece a la generación de mis padres this singer is from my parent's generation.

general adjetivo ■ general: hubo una reunión general en la escuela there was a general meeting at the school; un resumen general a general summary

➤ en general in general

➤ por lo general generally: por lo general comemos fuera los domingos we generally eat out on Sundays

el **general** ■ general.

la **generalidad** ■ generality (plural generalities).

el **género**

1. genus: estudia el género humano she's studying the human genus

2. gender: género masculino masculine gender; muchos sustantivos de género masculino terminan con la letra "o" a lot of masculine nouns end in "o"

3. type: también tengo problemas de ese género I also have that type of problem

4. genre: el género policíaco me gusta mucho I really enjoy the detective genre.

generoso, sa adjetivo ■ generous: es una persona muy generosa con los demás she's very generous to other people; en este restaurante sirven platos muy generosos the portions are very generous in this restaurant.

genial adjetivo ■ brilliant: tuvo una idea genial she had a brilliant idea; pocos escritores son tan geniales como él few writers are as brilliant as he is.

la **genética** ■ genetics.

el **genio**

1. temper: su hermano tiene mal genio her brother has a bad temper

2. genius: fue un verdadero genio de la literatura he was a true literary genius

3. genie: Aladino y el genio de la lámpara Aladdin and the genie of the lamp.

la **gente** ■ people: la gente se paraba para mirar people stopped to look; había mucha gente en la fiesta there were a lot of people at the party

➤ ser buena gente to be nice: Teresa es muy buena gente Teresa is very nice

➤ gente bien well-to-do people

➤ gente de bien good people.

la **geografía** ■ geography.

la **geometría** ■ geometry.

el/la **gerente** ■ manager.

el **gesto** ■ expression: tenía un gesto de tristeza en la cara she had an expression of sadness on her face

➤ hacer un gesto to gesture: me hizo un gesto para que me acercara he gestured for me to come closer

➤ un gesto simbólico a symbolic gesture.

gigante adjetivo

1. giant: una pantalla gigante a giant screen

2. huge, gigantic: este apartamento es gigante this apartment is huge

el **gigante** ■ giant: el gigante vivía en un castillo the giant lived in a castle.

la **gimnasia** ■ gymnastics: hacer gimnasia to do gymnastics.

el **gimnasio** ■ gym.

el/la **gimnasta** ■ gymnast.

girar [1] verbo

1. to revolve: la tierra gira alrededor del sol the earth revolves around the sun

2. to turn: giró hacia la derecha he turned to the right

➤ girar en torno a to revolve around: su vida gira en torno al dinero her life revolves around money.

el **girasol** ■ sunflower.

el **giro**

1. turn: un giro a la izquierda a turn to the left; la situación tuvo un giro inesperado the situation took an unexpected turn

2. wire: mandé un giro de 2000 euros I sent a wire for 2000 euros.

gitano, na *adjetivo* ■ **gypsy** (plural **gypsies**): tiene alma gitana he has a gypsy soul

el **gitano**, la **gitana** ■ **gypsy:** una gitana me adivinó el futuro a gypsy told my fortune.

el **globo**

1. balloon: trajimos globos de colores para los niños we brought coloured balloons for the kids

2. hot-air balloon: mi sueño es viajar en globo my dream is to travel in a hot-air balloon

▷ un globo terráqueo a globe.

glotón, glotona *adjetivo* ■ **glutton:** es tan glotón que en un minuto se comió todo el postre he's such a glutton that he ate all of his dessert in just a minute.

el **gobernador**, la **gobernadora** ■ governor.

gobernar [1] *verbo* ■ **to govern:** este partido ha gobernado en el país durante los últimos 10 años the party has governed the country for the last 10 years.

el **gobierno**

1. government: el gobierno tomó drásticas medidas económicas the government took drastic economic measures

2. management: la dirección declina toda responsabilidad the management does not accept responsibility

el **gol** ■ goal

▷ marcar un gol to score a goal.

el **golfo** ■ gulf.

la **golondrina** ■ swallow.

la **golosina** ■ **sweet** UK, **candy** US (plural **candies**): compré golosinas para los niños I bought some sweets for the children.

el **golpe** ■ **blow:** la noticia fue un duro golpe para Pedro the news was a harsh blow to Pedro

▷ se dio un golpe en la cabeza she bumped her head

▷ de golpe suddenly: empezó a llover de golpe it suddenly began to rain

▷ no dar golpe not to do a stroke of work

▷ un golpe de Estado a coup d'état

▷ un golpe de suerte a stroke of luck

▷ un golpe de vista a glance.

golpear [1] *verbo*

1. to bang: golpeó la mesa con la mano he banged on the table with his hand

2. to hit: le golpeó en la cara she hit him in the face; se golpeó el codo contra la mesa he hit his elbow on the table.

la **goma**

1. rubber: la goma es un material impermeable rubber is a waterproof material; unos guantes de goma rubber gloves

2. rubber UK, **eraser** US: necesito una goma para borrar los errores I need a rubber to rub out my mistakes

3. elastic band: ¿tienes una goma para sujetar estos papeles? have you got an elastic band to secure these papers?

▷ una goma de borrar an eraser

▷ la goma de mascar chewing gum

gordo, da *adjetivo*

1. fat: José está más gordo que nunca José is fatter than ever

2. thick: estoy leyendo un libro muy gordo I'm reading a very thick book

3. big: tenemos un problema muy gordo we've got a very big problem

▷ Antonio me cae gordo I can't stand Antonio.

el **gordo** ■ jackpot

EL GORDO DE LA LOTERÍA

The **gordo** is the general term used to describe a lottery jackpot in Spanish. The biggest jackpot of all is paid out at the special Christmas lottery draw, held every year on 22nd December. The winning number and the lucky winners appear on the front page of all the Spanish newspapers the following day.

la **gorra** ■ **cap:** en la playa me pongo siempre una gorra I always wear a cap on the beach

▷ de gorra for free.

el gorrión *(plural* los gorriones*)* ■ **sparrow.**

el gorro ■ **hat: llévate el gorro de lana** take your woollen hat.

la gota
1. **drop: tienes que tomar cinco gotas de este medicamento** you have to take five drops of this medicine
2. **gout: la gota es una enfermedad muy dolorosa** gout is a very painful illness
> **ni gota** not an ounce of: **tu hermana no tiene ni gota de grasa** your sister hasn't got an ounce of fat on her
> **el gota a gota** a drip.

gotear [1] *verbo* ■ **to drip: este grifo gotea** this tap drips.

la grabación *(plural* las grabaciones*)* ■ **recording: hicieron una nueva grabación de la canción** they made a new recording of the song.

grabar [1] *verbo*
1. **to engrave: grabaron sus nombres en los anillos de boda** they engraved their names on the wedding rings
2. **to record: acaba de grabar un nuevo disco** she's just recorded a new album
3. **on video: grabé en video la fiesta de cumpleaños** I recorded the birthday party on video.

la gracia
> **hacer gracia** to amuse: **sus chistes me hacen mucha gracia** his jokes really amuse me
> **caerle en gracia a alguien** to take a liking to someone: **esta chica me cae en gracia** I've taken a liking to this girl
> **dar las gracias a alguien** to thank someone: **le dimos las gracias a Pedro por su ayuda** we thanked Pedro for his help.

gracias *interjección* ■ **thanks: ¡gracias por el regalo!** thanks for the present!
gracias —de nada thanks – you're welcome.

gracioso, sa *adjetivo* ■ **funny: contó unos chistes muy graciosos** she told some very funny jokes

⚠️ The Spanish word **gracioso** is a false friend, it does not mean "gracious".

las gradas ■ **stands: las gradas estaban llenas de espectadores** the stands were full of spectators.

el grado ■ **degree: este ángulo tiene 60 grados** this is a 60 degree angle; **estamos a cinco grados bajo cero** it's five degrees below zero.

la graduación *(plural* las graduaciones*)* ■ **graduation.**

graduado, da *adjetivo* ■ **prescription: uso gafas graduadas** I wear prescription glasses.

graduar [1] *verbo*
1. **to adjust: gradúa bien la temperatura del agua** adjust the temperature of the water carefully
2. **to calibrate: hay que graduar la balanza** we have to graduate the scales

graduarse *verbo pronominal*
1. **to graduate: me gradué el mes pasado y ya estoy trabajando** I graduated last month and I'm already working
2. **to test: tengo que graduarme la vista** I have to have my eyes tested.

la gráfica ■ **graph.**

gráfico, ca *adjetivo* ■ **graphic: es un concurso de artes gráficas** it's a graphic art competition

el gráfico ■ **table.**

la gramática ■ **grammar.**

el gramo ■ **gram, gramme** *UK.*

gran *adjetivo* ➤ **grande**

Gran is a shortened form of the word **grande**. It is used in front of a noun.

Gran Bretaña ■ **Great Britain.**

grande *adjetivo*
1. **big: su coche es demasiado grande** his car is too big; **¿cómo es de grande?** how big is it?
2. **great: es un gran hombre** he's a great man
3. **large: ha recibido una gran suma de dinero** I've received a large sum of money

▸ **a lo grande** in style: **celebró su cumpleaños a lo grande** he celebrated his birthday in style

▸ **pasárselo en grande** to have a fabulous time: **me lo pasé en grande en su fiesta** I had a fabulous time at your party.

el granero ■ barn.

granizar [10] *verbo* ■ to hail: **granizó de madrugada** it was hailing in the early morning.

el granizo ■ hail: **el granizo estropeó la cosecha** the hail ruined the crop

▸ **caer granizo** to hail: **cayó granizo sobre la ciudad** it was hailing in the city.

la granja ■ farm.

el granjero , **la granjera** ■ farmer.

el grano

1. pimple: **un grano en la nariz** she has a pimple on her nose

2. grain: **se me ha metido un grano de arena en el ojo** I got a grain of sand in my eye

▸ **ir al grano** to get to the point: **no entiendo lo que me quieres decir, ve al grano** I don't understand what you're trying to say, just get to the point

▸ **un grano de arroz** a grain of rice

▸ **un grano de café** a coffee bean.

la grapa

1. staple: **me he quedado sin grapas** I've run out of staples.

la grapadora ■ stapler.

grapar [1] *verbo* ■ to staple: **¿has grapado los folios?** have you stapled the sheets of paper?

la grasa

1. fat: **con alto contenido en grasa** high in fat

2. grease: **las manos del mecánico estaban cubiertas de grasa** the mechanic's hands were covered in grease.

gratis *adjetivo & adverbio* ■ free: **tengo dos entradas gratis para el cine** I have two free tickets to the cinema; **los menores entran gratis al concierto** children can attend the concert for free.

gratuito, ta *adjetivo*

1. free: **la entrada es gratuita los lunes** admission is free on Mondays

2. gratuitous: **su comentario fue totalmente gratuito** her comment was completely gratuitous.

grave *adjetivo*

1. serious: **éste es un problema muy grave** this is a very serious problem; **cometió un delito grave** he committed a serious crime

2. deep: **el abuelo tiene una voz muy grave** grandfather has a very deep voice

▸ **estar grave** to be seriously ill: **tuvo un accidente y está grave** he had an accident and is seriously ill.

la gravedad

1. gravity: **Newton definió las leyes de la gravedad** Newton defined the laws of gravity

2. seriousness: **no nos habíamos imaginado la gravedad del asunto** we hadn't realized the seriousness of the situation.

Grecia ■ Greece.

griego, ga

En inglés, los adjetivos que se refieren a un país o una región se escriben con mayúscula:

Greek: tiene acento griego he has a Greek accent

el griego , **la griega**

En inglés, los gentilicios se escriben con mayúscula:

Greek
los griegos the Greeks

el griego

En inglés, los idiomas se escriben con mayúscula.

Greek.

la grieta ■ crack: **hay una grieta en la pared** there is a crack in the wall.

el grifo ■ tap *UK*, faucet *US*: **el grifo del agua caliente es el de la izquierda** the tap on the left is the hot water

▸ **abrir el grifo** to turn on the tap

▸ **cerrar el grifo** to turn off the tap.

el grillo ■ cricket.

la gripe ■ flu: no he ido al colegio porque tenía gripe I didn't go to school because I had flu.

gris *adjetivo* ■ grey UK, gray US: compró unos pantalones grises she bought some grey trousers

el gris ■ grey UK, gray US: el gris es mi color favorito grey is my favourite colour.

gritar [1] *verbo* ■ to shout: un cliente le gritó a uno de los dependientes de la tienda a customer shouted at one of the shop assistants

> gritar de alegría to shout with joy: grité de alegría cuando me enteré de la noticia I shouted with joy when I heard the news

> gritar de dolor to scream with pain: gritó de dolor cuando se hizo daño en la mano he screamed with pain when he hurt his hand.

el grito ■ scream: el grito de la niña era aterrador the girl's scream was terrifying

> pegarle un grito a alguien to shout at someone: le pegó un grito al niño y éste se puso a llorar he shouted at the boy and made him cry

> a grito pelado at the top of one's voice: llamó al camarero a grito pelado he called the waiter at the the top of his voice

> el último grito the latest: el último grito en teléfonos móviles the latest in mobile phones.

la grosella ■ redcurrant.

grosero, sa *adjetivo* ■ rude: detesto su comportamiento grosero I detest his rude behaviour.

la grúa
1. crane: las grúas del puerto descargan las mercancías de los barcos the port cranes unload the ships' goods
2. tow truck
> la grúa se ha llevado el coche his car has been towed away.

grueso, sa *adjetivo* ■ thick: compré una tela gruesa para las cortinas I bought a thick cloth for the curtains; es una mujer gruesa she's a thick woman.

el gruñido
1. growl: el gruñido del perro me asustó the dog's growl scared me
2. grunt: Carlos nos contestó con un gruñido Carlos answered us with a grunt.

gruñón, gruñona *adjetivo* ■ grumpy: nos atendió un empleado gruñón a grumpy shop assistant served us; ¡no seas tan gruñona! don't be so grumpy!

el grupo ■ group: formamos un grupo de seis personas we form a group of six people
> un grupo musical a group
> el grupo sanguíneo blood group.

la gruta ■ cavern.

el guante ■ glove: se ha comprado unos guantes he's bought himself some gloves
> unos guantes de lana woollen gloves
> unos guantes de goma rubber gloves
> unos guantes de boxeo boxing gloves.

guapo, pa *adjetivo*
1. attractive: es el muchacho más guapo que conozco he's the most attractive guy I know
2. smart: iba muy guapa a la fiesta she went to the party very smart; estaba muy guapa con su vestido de seda she looked very smart in her silk dress.

el guarda
1. guard: los guardas vigilaban la costa the guards were watching the coast; el guarda de seguridad nos vio the security guard saw us
2. keeper: el guarda del museo the museum keeper; el guarda del zoo the zoo keeper.

el/la guardabosques ■ forest ranger.

el/la guardaespaldas ■ bodyguard.

el/la guardameta ■ goalkeeper: el guardameta paró el penalti the goalkeeper intercepted the penalty kick.

guardar [1] *verbo*
1. to save: guárdame un poco de cena save me some dinner; les guardamos sitio en el teatro we saved them a place at the theatre
2. to keep: guarda la entrada keep the ticket; guardo las fotos en ese cajón I keep the photos in that drawer

3. to put away: guardé la ropa en el armario I put the clothes away in the wardrobe

➤ guardar un secreto to keep a secret: no sabe guardar un secreto he can't keep a secret.

el **guardarropa** ■ cloakroom: dejamos los abrigos en el guardarropa we left the coats in the cloakroom.

la **guardería** ■ nursery (plural nurseries).

la **guardia**

1. guard: la guardia nacional está en estado de alerta the national guard is on a state of alert

2. shift: hicimos un turno de guardia nocturno we took a turn on the night shift.

el/la **guardia** ■ guard: el guardia disparó al aire the guard fired into the air

➤ un guardia civil a civil guard.

la **guarida**

1. hideout: la policía descubrió la guarida de los ladrones the police discovered the thieves' hideout

2. lair: los lobos se escondieron en su guarida the wolves hid in their lair.

Guatemala ■ Guatemala.

guatemalteco, ca adjetivo

En inglés, los adjetivos que se refieren a un país o una región se escriben con mayúscula:

Guatemalan: compré artesanías guatemaltecas I bought Guatemalan handicrafts

el **guatemalteco** , la **guatemalteca**

En inglés, los gentilicios se escriben con mayúscula:

Guatemalan: los guatemaltecos the Guatemalans.

guay adjetivo ■ cool: su último disco es muy guay his latest record is really cool.

la **guerra** ■ war: fuimos a una manifestación contra la guerra we went on a demonstration against the war; una guerra civil a civil war

➤ declarar la guerra to declare war

LA GUERRA CIVIL ESPAÑOLA

In 1936, a Spanish army division under General Franco's command staged an uprising against the republican government: this was the start of the Spanish Civil War. After three years of bitter fighting, the **nacionales** (nationalists), supported by Nazi Germany and fascist Italy, achieved victory and, in 1939, put Francisco Franco in charge of the country. Over the three years the war lasted, many artists and intellectuals, such as Federico García Lorca, were murdered. Others were forced into exile, many of them settling in France and South America, from where they condemned the horrors of war through their works, as Picasso did with his painting **Guernica**. Franco's dictatorship ended upon his death in 1975.

---

el **guerrero** , la **guerrera** ■ warrior.

el/la **guía** ■ guide: el guía nos explicó la historia de la catedral the guide explained the cathedral's history to us.

la **guía**

1. guide: sus enseñanzas son una guía para mí his teachings are a guide for me

2. guidebook: compraron una guía de la ciudad they bought a guidebook to the city

3. directory (plural **directories**): buscó la información en la guía de la universidad he looked for the information in the university directory

➤ una guía telefónica a telephone directory

guiar [7] verbo ■ to guide: José guió a sus amigos por las calles de la ciudad José guided his friends through the city's streets.

guiñar [1] verbo

➤ guiñar el ojo to wink: me guiñó el ojo mientras me hablaba he winked at me while he was talking to me.

el **guiño** ■ wink: Luis le hizo un guiño a María Luis gave a winked at María.

el **guion** (plural los guiones)

1. script: el guion de la película es excelente the film script is excellent

2. hyphen: algunas palabras compuestas se escriben con guion some compounds words are written with a hyphen.

el guisante ■ pea.

guisar [1] *verbo* ■ to cook: guisé el pollo con hierbas I cooked the chicken with herbs.

el guiso ■ stew.

la guitarra ■ guitar: Alfredo toca muy bien la guitarra Alfredo plays the guitar very well.

la guitarrista ■ guitarist.

la gula ■ gluttony.

el gusano ■ worm: hay un gusano en la manzana there's a worm in the apple
> un gusano de seda a silkworm.

gustar [1] *verbo*
1. to like: a Susana le gusta el cine Susana likes the cinema; no me gustó que me gritaran I didn't like them shouting at me; a Pedro le gusta María Pedro likes María; ¿te gusta jugar al ajedrez? do you like playing chess?
2. to be pleasing: es una música que gusta mucho it's very pleasing music.

el gusto ■ taste: el gusto es uno de los sentidos más importantes taste is one of the most important senses; esta pareja tiene gustos incompatibles this couple have incompatible tastes
> con mucho gusto with pleasure: ¿podría avisarme cuando lleguen? —con mucho gusto could you let me know when they arrive? – with pleasure
> tener buen gusto to have good taste: tienen buen gusto para la decoración they have good taste in decoration
> iré a tu fiesta con mucho gusto I'd be delighted to come to your party
> de mal gusto in bad taste, tasteless: una broma de mal gusto a tasteless joke
> tener mal gusto to have bad taste: tiene mal gusto para vestirse he has bad taste in clothes
> para mi gusto for my taste: para mi gusto está demasiado salado it's too salty for my taste
> mucho gusto it's a pleasure: le presento a mi jefe —mucho gusto en conocerlo let me introduce you to my boss – it's a pleasure to meet you.

el haba

Feminine noun that takes **un** or **el** in the singular.

bean.

haber [4] *verbo* ■ to have: ¿qué habéis comido? what have you eaten?; han ido a Santiago they have travelled to Santiago
> hay *en singular* there is: hay una sola persona en el cine there is only one person in the cinema
> hay *en plural* there are: hay 30 niños en la fiesta there are 30 children at the party
> hay que it is necessary: hay que ayudar a Matilde it is necessary to help Matilde; en la reunión habría unas 15 personas there were some 15 people at the meeting
> no hay de qué don't mention it: gracias —no hay de qué thanks – don't mention it
> ¿qué hay? how are things?: ¿qué hay? —todo bien, gracias how are things? – everything's fine, thanks.

hábil *adjetivo* ■ skilful UK, skillful US: es un carpintero muy hábil he's a very skilful carpenter.

la habilidad ■ skill: tiene una gran habilidad para las manualidades he has a great skill for handicrafts.

la habitación *(plural* las habitaciones)
1. room: este hotel tiene 30 habitaciones this hotel has 30 rooms
2. bedroom: me he pasado la tarde en mi habitación I spent the afternoon in my bedroom

> una **habitación individual** a single room
> una **habitación doble** a double room.

el/la **habitante** ■ inhabitant.

el **hábito** ■ habit: **tiene el hábito de acostarse tarde** he has the habit of going to bed late; **tiene algunos malos hábitos** he has some bad habits.

habitual *adjetivo*
1. **customary: esta no es una conducta habitual en él** this is not customary behaviour for him
2. **regular: Ana es una cliente habitual** Ana is a regular customer.

hablar [1] *verbo*
1. **to talk: el niño todavía no habla** the boy isn't talking yet; **siempre hablan de fútbol** they're always talking about football; **tengo que hablar contigo** I have tot talk to you
2. **to speak: ¿hablas español?** do you speak Spanish?; **mis amigos hablan ruso** my friends speak Russian
> **hablar hasta por los codos** to talk too much: **Juan no me gusta porque habla hasta por los codos** I don't like Juan because he talks too much
> **hablar mal** to say bad things about: **siempre habla mal de ella** he always says bad things about her

hablarse *verbo pronominal*
> **Roberto y María ya no se hablan** Roberto and María don't speak to each one any more.

hacer [43] *verbo*
1. **to make: las abejas hacen miel** bees make honey; **no hagas tanto ruido** dont' make so much noise; **voy a hacer paella** I'm going to make a paella; **¿podrías hacer la cama?** could you make the bed?
2. **to do: tienes que hacer los deberes** you have to do your homework; **los sábados hago la compra** I do the shopping on Saturday; **Mariana hace teatro** Mariana does theater; **hacen gimnasia todas las mañanas** they do gymnastics every morning
> **hace de la bruja mala** she plays the part of the evil witch
> **hace calor** it's hot

hace dos años que no tengo vacaciones I haven't been on holiday for two years.

el **hacha**

Feminine noun that takes **un** or **el** in the singular.

axe *UK*, **ax** *US*.

hacia *preposición*
1. **towards: se dirigió hacia la salida** he headed towards the exit
2. **around: hacia finales de diciembre terminan las clases** classes finish around the end of December
> **hacia arriba** up: **el globo se fue hacia arriba** the balloon went up
> **hacia abajo** down: **tiraron la piedra hacia abajo** they threw the stone down
> **hacia delante** forwards: **continuaron hacia delante** they continued forwards
> **hacia atrás** backwards: **se cayó hacia atrás** she fell backwards.

el **hada** ■

Feminine noun that takes **un** or **el** in the singular.

fairy *(plural* **fairies***)*: **un cuento de hadas** a fairy tale.

halagar [12] *verbo* ■ **to flatter: me halagan tus comentarios** your comments flatter me.

hallar [1] *verbo* ■ **to find: hallaron un tesoro escondido** they found hidden treasure

hallarse *verbo pronominal* ■ **to be: se halla de visita oficial en el Reino Unido** he's on a official visit to the United Kingdom.

la **hamaca**
1. **hammock: colgaron una hamaca entre dos árboles** they hung a hammock between two trees
2. **deckchair: se sentó en una hamaca en la playa** he sat in a deckchair on the beach.

el **hambre**

Feminine noun that takes **un** or **el** in the singular.

hunger: este niño tiene hambre this child is hungry

morirse de hambre to starve, to die of hunger: **es lamentable que todavía haya niños que se mueran de hambre** it's terrible that there are still children dying of hunger

pasar hambre to go hungry: **en el campamento pasamos hambre** at the camp we went hungry.

la **harina** ■ flour: harina de trigo wheat flour; harina integral wholemeal flour *UK*, wholewheat flour *US*.

harto, ta *adjetivo*

1. fed up: **estoy harta de estudiar** I'm fed up with studying; **¡me tienes harto!** I'm fed up with you!

2. full: **no quiero más pastel, estoy harto** I don't want any more cake, I'm full.

hasta *(preposición, adverbio & conjunción)*

■ *preposición*

1. up to: **el agua le llegaba hasta el cuello** the water came up to his neck; **llene el depósito hasta la mitad** fill the tank up half-full

2. as far as: **fueron conmigo hasta la playa** they went with me as far as the beach

3. until: **lo cuidó hasta que se curó** she took care of him until he got better

hasta luego see you later

hasta mañana see you tomorrow

hasta pronto see you soon

■ *adverbio*

even: **hasta un niño puede aprender esto** even a child can learn this

■ *conjunción*

¿hasta cuándo piensas estudiar? how long are you going to study for?

la **hazaña** ■ feat.

la **hebilla** ■ buckle.

el **hecho**

1. action: **prefiero hechos y no palabras** I prefer actions to words

2. event: **el periodista destacó los hechos más importantes de la semana** the reporter highlighted the most important events of the week

de hecho in fact: **de hecho, los resultados fueron mucho mejor de lo que esperábamos** in fact, the results were much better than we had expected

es un hombre hecho y derecho he's a real man.

la **helada** ■ frost: **se prevén heladas a partir de mañana** frost is expected from tomorrow.

helado, da *adjetivo*

1. freezing: **esta habitación está helada** this room is freezing; **estoy helado** I'm freezing

2. stunned: **nos quedamos helados con la noticia** we were stunned by the news

el **helado** ■ ice cream.

helar [14] *verbo* ■ to freeze: **el frío ha helado el lago** the cold has frozen the lake; **anoche heló** it froze last night

helarse *verbo pronominal* ■ to freeze: **este lago se hiela en invierno** this lake freezes in winter.

la **hélice** ■ propeller.

el **helicóptero** ■ helicopter.

la **hembra** ■ female: **en algunas especies las hembras son más grandes que los machos** in some species the females are bigger than the males.

el **hemisferio** ■ hemisphere.

la **hemorragia** ■ haemorrhage *UK*, hemorrhage *US*.

heredar [1] *verbo* ■ to inherit: **heredamos una gran fortuna** we inherited a large fortune; **Juan heredó el carácter del padre** Juan inherited his father's character.

la **heredera** ■ heiress.

el **heredero** ■ heir: **los herederos recibieron una fuerte suma de dinero** the heirs received a large sum of money.

hereditario, ria *adjetivo* ■ hereditary: **una enfermedad hereditaria** a hereditary illness.

la **herencia** ■ inheritance: **recibió una cuantiosa herencia de su tío** he received a substantial inheritance from his uncle.

la **herida**

1. wound: **tiene una herida profunda en la pierna** he has a deep wound on his leg

2. injury (plural **injuries**): sufrió heridas graves he was seriously injured
> una herida de bala a bullet wound.

herido, da adjetivo

1. **wounded:** fue herido en la batalla he was wounded in the battle
2. **injured:** resultó herido de gravedad he turned out to be seriously injured

el **herido** , la **herida**

1. **injured person** (plural **injured people**): hubo cuatro heridos en el accidente there were four injured people in the accident
2. **wounded person** (plural **wounded people**): hubo 100 en heridos en la batalla there were 100 wounded people in the battle.

herir [20] verbo

1. **to injure:** fue gravemente herido en la pelea he was seriously injured in the fight
2. **to wound:** la explosión hirió a varias personas the explosion wounded several people
3. **to hurt:** con su negativa lo hirió en lo más profundo with her refusal, she hurt him deeply.

la **hermana** ■ **sister:** tengo una hermana mayor I have an older sister.

la **hermanastra** ■ **stepsister.**

el **hermanastro** ■ **stepbrother.**

el **hermano** ■ **brother:** tengo un hermano menor I have a younger brother; ¿tienes hermanos? have you got any brothers or sisters?

hermoso, sa adjetivo ■ **beautiful:** ¡qué sitio más hermoso ! what a beautiful place!

el **héroe** ■ **hero** (plural **heroes**).

heroico, ca adjetivo ■ **heroic:** su comportamiento heroico me salvó la vida his heroic behaviour saved my life.

la **heroína**

1. mujer **heroine:** la heroína de la novela the novel's heroin
2. droga **heroin.**

la **herramienta** ■ **tool:** la caja de herramientas the toolbox.

la **herrumbre** ■ **rust.**

hervir [20] verbo ■ **to boil:** herví las verduras I boiled the vegetables.

hidratante adjetivo ■ **moisturizing:** una crema hidratante a moisturizing cream.

hidratar [1] verbo ■ **to moisturize:** esta crema es ideal para hidratar la piel this cream is ideal for moisturizing the skin.

la **hiedra** ■ **ivy.**

el **hielo** ■ **ice**
> romper el hielo to break the ice: rompió el hielo con un chiste he broke the ice with a joke
> un cubito de hielo an ice cube.

la **hierba**

1. **grass:** tomamos sol en la hierba we sunbathed on the grass
2. **herb:** condimenté el pollo con hierbas I seasoned the chicken with herbs.

el **hierro** ■ **iron.**

el **hígado** ■ **liver.**

la **higiene** ■ **hygiene:** es increíble la falta de higiene de este lugar this place's lack of hygiene is incredible
> la higiene corporal personal hygiene
> la higiene dental dental hygiene.

la **hija** ■ **daughter:** tienen tres hijas y un hijo they have three daughters and one son.

el **hijo**

1. **son:** tienen tres hijos they have three sons
2. **child:** van a tener un hijo they're going to have a child
> ¿cuántos hijos tienes? —dos hijos y una hija how many children have you got? – two sons and one daughter
> un hijo adoptivo an adopted child.

la **hilera**

1. **line:** los niños formaron una hilera the children formed a line
2. **row:** hay una hilera de árboles en la entrada a la casa there's a row of trees at the entrance to the house.

el **hilo**

1. **thread:** necesito hilo para coser este dobladillo I need thread in order to sew this hem

2. trickle: de su boca salía un hilo de sangre a trickle of blood came out of his mouth

3. linen: un traje de hilo a linen suit

> **perder el hilo** to lose the thread: **siempre pierde el hilo de lo que está diciendo** he always loses the thread of what he's saying.

el **himno**

1. hymn: un libro de himnos a hymn book

2. anthem: el himno nacional the national anthem.

hincharse [1] *verbo pronominal* ■ **to swell:** se le hinchó la cara después del accidente her face swelled after the accident.

el **hipo** ■ hiccup

> **tener hipo** to have the hiccups.

la **hipocresía** ■ hypocrisy.

hipócrita *adjetivo* ■ **hypocritical:** una actitud hipócrita a hypocritical attitude

/la **hipócrita** ■ hypocrite.

el **hipopótamo** ■ hippopotamus.

la **hispanidad** ■ Spanish-speaking world

EL DÍA DE LA HISPANIDAD

This day, which is celebrated throughout Spain and Latin America, commemorates the discovery of America by Christopher Columbus, the Genoese navigator who was employed by the Catholic monarchs, Ferdinand of Aragon and Isabel of Castile. On 12th October 1492, Columbus sighted what were probably the Bahamas and on the same day he landed at Guanahaní, which he renamed San Salvador. The discovery of America marked a turning point in the history of Spain.

hispano, na *adjetivo*

En inglés, los adjetivos que se refieren a un país o una región se escriben con mayúscula:

Hispanic: la población hispana the Hispanic population
los países de habla hispana the Spanish-speaking countries

el **hispano**, la **hispana**

En inglés, los gentilicios se escriben con mayúscula:

1. *latinoamericano* **Latin American**

2. *residente en EE.UU.* **Hispanic:** los hispanos de ascendencia mexicana the Hispanics of Mexican descent.

hispanoamericano, na *adjetivo* ■ **Spanish American:** la cultura hispanoamericana Spanish American culture

el **hispanoamericano**,

la **hispanoamericano** ■ Spanish American.

hispanohablante *adjetivo* ■ **Spanish-speaking**

el/la **hispanohablante** ■ Spanish speaker.

histérico, ca *adjetivo* ■ **hysterical.**

la **historia**

1. history *(plural* **histories)**: estamos estudiando la historia de la antiguas civilizaciones we're studying the history of the ancient civilizations

2. story *(plural* **stories)**: una historia de amor a love story

> **déjate de historias y di la verdad** stop beating about the bush and tell the truth.

histórico, ca *adjetivo*

1. historic: un monumento histórico a historic monument

2. historical: un personaje histórico a historical character

> **la llegada a la Luna fue un hecho histórico** the trip to the moon was a historical event.

la **historieta** ■ comic strip.

el **hobby** *(plural* los hobbies) ■ **hobby** *(plural* **hobbies)**

> **los colecciona por hobby** he collects them as a hobby.

el **hocico**

1. *de cerdo* **snout**

2. *de perro, gato* **muzzle.**

el **hockey** ■ hockey

> **hockey sobre hielo** ice hockey
> **hockey sobre hierba** field hockey
> **hockey sobre patines** roller hockey.

el **hogar** ■ home: vivió en un hogar feliz he lived in a happy home

> la gente sin hogar the homeless
> un hogar para ancianos an old people's home.

la **hoguera** ■ bonfire.

la **hoja**
1. leaf (plural leaves): las hojas de los árboles the leaves of the trees
2. sheet: escríbelo en esta hoja write it on this sheet; una hoja en blanco a blank sheet
3. page: está en la hoja siguiente it's on the next page
> una hoja de afeitar razor blade
> una hoja de cálculo spreadsheet.

hola interjección ■ hello: hola ¿qué tal? hello – how are things?

holgazán, holgazana adjetivo ■ lazy.

el **hombre** ■ man (plural men): es un hombre inteligente he's an intelligent man
> el hombre del tiempo the weatherman
> un hombre de negocios a businessman
> un hombre rana a frogman.

el **hombro** ■ shoulder: se encogió de hombros he shrugged his shoulders.

el/la **homosexual** ■ homosexual.

hondo, da adjetivo ■ deep: una piscina muy honda a very deep swimming pool
> respirar hondo to breathe deeply
> un plato hondo a soup dish.

Honduras ■ Honduras.

hondureño, ña adjetivo

En inglés, los adjetivos que se refieren a un país o una región se escriben con mayúscula:

Honduran

el **hondureño** , la **hondureño**

En inglés, los gentilicios se escriben con mayúscula:

Honduran
los hondureños the Hondurans.

la **honestidad** ■ honesty: la honestidad es su mayor virtud honesty is his greatest virtue

honesto, ta adjetivo ■ honest.

el **hongo**
1. fungus: es causada por un hongo it's caused by a fungus
2. mushroom: un hongo comestible an edible mushroom.

el **honor** ■ honour UK, honor US.

la **honradez** ■ honesty.

honrado, da adjetivo ■ honest: es un hombre honrado he's an honest man
> se sintió honrado con su visita he felt honoured by her visit.

la **hora**
1. hour: tardé dos horas en llegar I took two hours to arrive
2. time: ¿qué hora es? what time it is?; ¿tienes hora? have you got the time?; es hora de ir al colegio it's time to go to school; ¿a qué hora empieza el programa? what time does the programme start?; ¿qué haces en tus horas libres? what do you do in your free time?
3. appointment: tengo hora con el oculista I have an appointment with the eye specialist; pedí hora en la peluquería I made an appointment at the hairdresser's
> llegar a la hora to arrive on time: nunca llega a la hora he never arrives on time
> vino a la hora de almorzar he came at lunchtime
> la hora punta the rush hour
> a todas horas the whole time: David come a todas horas David eats the whole time
> a última hora at the last minute: Inés lo hace todo a última hora Inés does everything at the last minute
> por horas by the hour: me pagan por horas they pay me by the hour.

el **horario** ■ timetable UK, schedule US: según mi horario, mañana tengo inglés according to my timetable, I have English tomorrow; no sé el horario de los trenes I don't know the train timetable
> horario de atención al público opening hours
> horario de visitas visiting times.

horizontal adjetivo ■ horizontal.

el **horizonte** ■ horizon: el sol aparece por el horizonte the sun appears on the horizon.

la **hormiga** ■ ant.

el **hormigón** (plural los hormigones) ■ concrete.

el **hormigueo** ■ tingling: tengo un hormigueo en el pie I have a tingling in my foot.

el **horno** ■ oven: un horno eléctrico an electric oven
> ser un horno to be like an oven: el gimnasio es un horno the gym is like an oven
> pollo al horno roast chicken
> patatas al horno baked potatoes
> un horno microondas a microwave oven.

el **horóscopo** ■ horoscope.

la **horquilla** ■ hairgrip UK, bobby pin US: se sujetó el pelo con horquillas she secured her hair with bobby hairgrips.

horrible adjetivo ■ horrible: ¡qué lugar tan horrible! what a horrible place!; ha hecho un tiempo horrible the weather has been horrible.

el **horror** ■ horror: escuchó un grito de horror he heard a scream of horror
> ¡qué horror! how horrible!
> los horrores de la guerra the horrors of war.

horroroso, sa adjetivo
1. horrendous: ¡qué cuadro más horroroso! what a horrendous painting!
2. horrifying: tiene unas escenas horrorosas it has some horrifying scenes
> el tiempo fue horroroso the weather was awful.

la **hortaliza** ■ vegetable.

hospedarse [1] verbo pronominal ■ to stay: se hospedaron en albergues juveniles they stayed in youth hostels.

el **hospital** ■ hospital: trabaja en el hospital she works at the hospital; los llevaron al hospital they took them to hospital.

la **hospitalidad** ■ hospitality.

hospitalizar [10] verbo ■ to hospitalize

> van a tener que hospitalizarlo he'll have to be hospitalized.

el **hotel** ■ hotel.

el **hostal** ■ budget hotel.

hoy adverbio ■ today: hoy es su cumpleaños today is her birthday; el diario de hoy today's newspaper
> hoy es posible curar muchas enfermedades nowadays it's possible to cure a lot of diseases
> de hoy en adelante from now on.

el **hoyo** ■ hole: el perro hizo un hoyo en el jardín the dog made a hole in the garden.

hueco, ca adjetivo ■ hollow

el **hueco**
1. space: hay que hacer un hueco para poner este libro we have to make a space for this book
2. room: me hicieron hueco en el taxi they made room for me in the taxi
> es difícil encontrar un hueco para aparcar it's difficult finding a place to park
> está muy ocupada pero va a hacer un hueco para recibirme she's very busy but she's going to set aside some time to see me.

la **huelga** ■ strike: una huelga general a general strike; una huelga de hambre a hunger strike
> están en huelga they're on strike
> votaron para ir a la huelga they voted to go on strike
> se declararon en huelga they went on strike.

la **huella** ■ footprint: había huellas en la nieve there were footprints in the snow
> íbamos siguiendo las huellas del coche we were following the car tracks
> desaparecieron sin dejar huella they disappeared without a trace
> huellas dactilares fingerprints.

huérfano, na adjetivo ■ orphaned
> se quedó huérfano he was orphaned
> es huérfano he's an orphan
> quieren adoptar a un niño huérfano they want to adopt an orphan

el **huérfano**, la **huérfana** ■ orphan.

la **huerta**
1. *de legumbres, verduras* **vegetable garden**
2. *de árboles frutales* **orchard.**

el **huerto**
1. *de legumbres, verduras* **vegetable garden**
2. *de árboles frutales* **orchard.**

el **hueso**
1. **bone:** encontraron un hueso de dinosaurio they found a dinosaur bone
2. **stone** *UK*, **pit** *US:* el hueso del melocotón the peach stone.

el/la **huésped** ■ **guest.**

el **huevo** ■ **egg:** los huevos son muy nutritivos eggs are very nutritious
» un huevo duro a hard-boiled egg
» un huevo estrellado a fried egg
» un huevo frito a fried egg
» un huevo pasado por agua a soft-boiled egg
» un huevo de Pascua an Easter egg
» huevos revueltos scrambled eggs.

huir [36] *verbo* ■ **to escape:** varios presos huyeron de la cárcel several prisoners escaped from prison
» huyeron cuando vieron que venía la policía they fled when they saw that the police were coming
» cuando sonó la alarma salieron huyendo when the alarm went off they ran away.

la **humanidad** ■ **humanity:** fue una gran muestra de humanidad it was a great demonstration of humanity
» la humanidad humankind
» las humanidades humanities.

humanitario, ria *adjetivo* ■ **humanitarian:** la ayuda humanitaria humanitarian aid.

humano, na *adjetivo*
1. **human:** el cuerpo humano the human body
2. **humane:** recibieron un tratamiento muy humano they received very humane treatment.

la **humareda** ■ **cloud of smoke.**

la **humedad**
1. *del aire* **humidity:** el calor y la humedad eran insoportables the heat and humidity were insufferable

2. *del suelo, en las paredes* **damp:** apareció una mancha de humedad en el techo a damp patch appeared on the ceiling
» no hace mucho calor pero hay mucha humedad it's not very hot but it's very humid.

humedecer [22] *verbo* ■ **to dampen.**

húmedo, da *adjetivo*
1. *aire* **humid:** es una ciudad con un clima húmedo it's a city with a humid climate
2. *suelo, paredes* **damp:** esta ropa está húmeda these clothes are damp; la casa es muy húmeda en invierno the house is very damp in the winter.

humilde *adjetivo* ■ **humble:** debería ser un poco más humilde he should be a little more humble
» alumnos que provienen de zonas humildes students that come from poor areas.

la **humillación** *(plural las humillaciones)* ■ **humiliation.**

humillar [1] *verbo* ■ **to humiliate.**

el **humo** ■ **smoke:** el humo de un cigarrillo cigarette smoke
» el humo de los tubos de escape exhaust fumes
» bajarle los humos a alguien to take somebody down a notch
» estaba que echaba humo he was fuming.

el **humor**
1. **mood:** el profesor estaba de muy mal humor the teacher was in a very bad mood; no estaba de humor para explicar nada she wasn't in the mood to explain anything
2. **humour** *UK*, **humor** *US:* no entiendo esa clase de humor I don't understand that kind of humour
» tiene mucho sentido del humor he has a good sense of humour.

hundirse [3] *verbo pronominal*
1. **to sink:** el lugar donde se hundió el barco the place where the boat sank
2. **to collapse:** el techo se hundió con el peso de la nieve the roof collapsed with the weight of the snow.

el **huracán** *(plural los huracanes)* ■ **hurricane.**

iberoamericano, na *adjetivo* ■ Latin American

el **iberoamericano**,

la **iberoamericana** ■ Latin American.

el **icono** ■ icon: hay que hacer clic en el icono para inicializar el programa you have to click on the icon to start up the program.

la **ida** ■ outward journey: la ida la hicimos sin problemas we made the outward journey t without problems

de ida single *UK*, one-way *US*: un billete de ida a single ticket

de ida y vuelta return *UK*, round-trip *US*: un billete de ida y vuelta a return ticket

la ida sola sale más cara one-way costs more

es mejor comprar ida y vuelta it's better to buy a round trip.

la **idea** ■ idea: creo que es una buena idea I think it's a good idea

¿tienes idea de cómo funciona esto? do you have any idea how this works?

no tengo la menor idea I don't have any idea

mi idea era ir al cine my idea was to go to the cinema

cambiar de idea to change one's mind: dijo que sí, pero cambió de idea she said yes, but changed her mind.

ideal *adjetivo* ■ ideal: es el lugar ideal para un picnic it's an ideal place for a picnic

lo ideal sería salir bien temprano the ideal thing would be to leave very early

el **ideal** ■ ideal: mi ideal es tener una carrera y viajar my ideal is to have a career and travel.

idear [1] *verbo* ■ to invent: idearon un sistema diferente they invented a different system

idearon una manera de copiar las respuestas they devised a way to copy the answers.

idéntico, ca *adjetivo* ■ identical: los dos cuadros son idénticos the two paintings are identical

Idéntico a algo identical to something: tengo una falda idéntica a la tuya I have a skirt identical to yours

Pedro es idéntico a su padre Pedro's the image of his father.

la **identidad** ■ identity (plural **identities**).

la **identificación** (plural las identificaciones) ■ identification

es necesario llevar una identificación it's necessary to carry identification.

identificar [8] *verbo* ■ to identify: identificaron al agresor they identified the attacker

identificarse *verbo pronominal* ■ to identify oneself: para entrar tienes que identificarte to get in you have to identify yourself.

el **idioma** ■ language: tiene facilidad para los idiomas she has a gift for languages

 The Spanish word **idioma** is a false friend, it does not mean "idiom".

idiota *adjetivo* ■ stupid: ¿por qué eres tan idiota? why are you so stupid?

el **ídolo** ■ idol.

la **iglesia** ■ church: hemos visitado una iglesia románica we visited a Romanesque church

se casaron por la iglesia they got married in church

la Iglesia Católica the Catholic Church.

la **ignorancia** ■ ignorance.

ignorante *adjetivo* ■ **ignorant:** son muy ignorantes they are very ignorant.

ignorar [1] *verbo* ■ **not to know:** ignoraba que era cura she didn't know that he was a priest; ignoro qué va a pasar ahora I don't know what's going to happen now

▷ si te molesta, ignóralo if he bothers you, ignore him.

igual *(adjetivo & adverbio)*

■ *adjetivo*

1. **equal:** todos somos iguales ante la ley we're all equal before the law

2. **same:** estos colores son iguales these colours are the same

▷ llevaba un suéter igual al mío he was wearing a sweater similar to mine

▷ es igual a su padre he's like his father

▷ son iguales de largo they are the same length

▷ dos por tres es igual a seis two times three equals six

▷ van iguales they're even

▷ quince iguales fifteen all

■ *adverbio*

▷ the same: los trata igual a todos he treats everybody the same; camina igual que tú he walks the same as you

▷ igual vino y no estábamos maybe he came and we weren't there

▷ me da igual cualquier día whatever day is fine for me

▷ todo le da igual it's all the same to him.

la **igualdad** ■ **equality** *(plural* equalities*)*: la igualdad ante la ley equality before the law

▷ la igualdad de oportunidades equal opportunities

▷ la igualdad de sexos gender equality.

ilegal *adjetivo* ■ **illegal:** el tráfico de armas es ilegal arms dealing is illegal; un inmigrante ilegal an illegal immigrant.

ileso, sa *adjetivo* ■ **unharmed:** todos resultaron ilesos they were all unharmed; salieron ilesos del accidente they came out of the accident unharmed.

la **iluminación** *(plural* las iluminaciones*)* ■ **lighting:** piden una mejor iluminación de las calles they are requesting better street lighting.

iluminar [1] *verbo* ■ **to illuminate** *UK,* **to light** *US:* la luz que ilumina la entrada the light that illuminates the entrance

▷ esta linterna ilumina muy poco this torch doesn't give much light

▷ se le iluminó la cara cuando lo vio her face lit up when she saw him.

la **ilusión** *(plural* las ilusiones*)*

1. **hope:** empezó con mucha ilusión he began with a lot of hope

2. **dream:** su gran ilusión es ser bailarina her big dream is to be a dancer

3. **illusion:** el espejo crea la ilusión de que la sala es más grande the mirror creates the illusion that the room is bigger

▷ una ilusión óptica an optical illusion

▷ es mejor no hacerse ilusiones it's best not to get your hopes up.

ilusionar [1] *verbo*

▷ no me ilusiona mucho la idea the idea doesn't excite me much

ilusionarse *verbo pronominal* ■ **to build up one's hopes:** se había ilusionado tanto y todo salió mal he had built up his hopes so much and everything turned out badly

▷ ilusionarse con algo to get excited about something: se ilusiona fácilmente con todo he gets easily excited about everything.

la **ilustración** *(plural* las ilustraciones*)* ■ **illustration.**

la **imagen** *(plural* las imágenes*)* ■ **image:** es la imagen que la gente tiene de mí it's the image that people have of me; el grupo quiere cambiar de imagen the group wants to change its image

▷ ser la viva imagen de alguien to be the spitting image of somebody: eres la viva imagen de tu tía you're the spitting image of your aunt.

la **imaginación** *(plural* las imaginaciones*)* ■ **imagination:** no tiene imaginación para nada he doesn't have any imagination at all; los niños tienen mucha imaginación children have a lot of imagination

▷ ni se me pasó por la imaginación contárselo it didn't cross my mind to tell him

▷ son imaginaciones tuyas you're imagining things.

imaginarse [1] *verbo pronominal* ■ **to imagine**: imagínate que estás en una playa desierta imagine that you're on a deserted beach; me imagino que ya estará en la universidad I imagine that he must be at university now; no te imaginas lo furioso que estaba you can't imagine how furious he was

> me lo imaginaba más alto I imagined him to be taller

> ¿qué dijo cuando se enteró? —imagínate what did he say when he found out? – you can imagine.

el **imán** *(plural los imanes)* ■ **magnet**.

la **imitación** *(plural las imitaciones)* ■ **imitation**: aprenden por imitación they learn by imitation; hay que tener cuidado con las imitaciones you have to be careful with imitations; no es un diamante verdadero, es una imitación it's not a real diamond, it's an imitation

> le encanta hacer imitaciones he loves to do impressions.

imitar [1] *verbo*

1. **to imitate**: trata de imitar a su padre he tries to imitate his father; imita a casi todos los profesores he impersonates almost all of the teachers

2. **to impersonate**

> te imita muy bien el acento she imitates your accent very well.

impaciente *adjetivo*

1. **impatient**: no seas tan impaciente don't be so impatient

2. **anxious**: estaba impaciente por saber quién ganó he was anxious to know who won.

el **impacto** ■ **impact**: la noticia causó un gran impacto entre los asistentes te news had a great impact on those present

> recibió un impacto de bala he was hit by a bullet.

impar *adjetivo* ■ **odd**: un número impar an odd number

el **impar** ■ **odd number**: los impares están a este lado the odd numbers are on this side.

impedir [19] *verbo*

1. **to stop**: le impidieron la entrada they stopped him from entering; si quieres ir nadie te lo va a impedir if you want to go nobody will stop you

2. **to block**: no impidan el paso do not block the way

3. **to prevent**: no lo pueden impedir they can't prevent it; la enfermedad le impide ver bien the disease prevents him from seeing well

> impedirle a alguien que haga algo to prevent somebody from doing something: quisieron impedir que reclamáramos they wanted to prevent us from protesting.

el **imperio** ■ **empire**.

impermeable *adjetivo* ■ **waterproof**

el **impermeable** ■ **raincoat**.

impertinente *adjetivo* ■ **impertinent**.

imponer [47] *verbo*

1. **to impose**: le impusieron un castigo muy severo they imposed a very severe punishment on him; le impusieron una multa they imposed a fine on him

2. **to command**: el director sabe imponer respeto the director knows how to command respect

imponerse *verbo pronominal*

1. **to prevail**: es una moda que se impuso en los sesenta it's a fashion that prevailed in the sixties

2. **to assert one's authority**: la profesora no sabe imponerse the teacher doesn't know how to assert her authority.

la **importación** *(plural las importaciones)* ■ **importing**: prohibieron la importación de productos transgénicos they prohibited the importing of genetically modified products.

la **importancia** ■ **importance**: la importancia de una buena educación the importance of a good education; un acontecimiento de gran importancia an event of great importance

> darle importancia a algo to attach importance to something: le dan mucha importancia a la presentación they attach a lot of importance to presentation

tener importancia to be important: **las notas tienen mucha importancia** grades are very important

no tiene importancia si no voy it doesn't matter if I don't go

darse importancia to give oneself airs: **se da importancia porque su padre es el alcalde** he gives himself airs because his father is the mayor.

importante *adjetivo* ■ important: **sus amigos son lo más importante para él** his friends are what's most important to him; **es una persona muy importante** he's a very important person

lo importante es prepararse con tiempo the important thing is to prepare oneself ahead of time.

importar [1] *verbo*

1. to import: **tienen que importar muchos productos** they have to import a lot of products

2. to matter: **no importa si no tienes experiencia** it doesn't matter if you don't have experience; **eso es lo único que le importa** that's the only thing that matters to her

se me ha roto —no importa I've broken it – it doesn't matter

¿te importa si se lo cuento? do you mind if I tell him?

no me importa caminar hasta el colegio I don't mind walking to school.

imposible *adjetivo* ■ impossible: **es imposible estudiar con tanto ruido** it's impossible to study with so much noise

son unos niños imposibles they're impossible children

es imposible que lo sepa she can't possibly know.

la **imprenta**

1. *máquina* printing press
2. *local* printer's.

imprescindible *adjetivo* ■ essential: **llévate sólo lo imprescindible** only take what's absolutely essential.

la **impresión** *(plural* las impresiones*)* ■ impression: **le causó muy buena impresión a la profesora** he made a very good impression

on the teacher; **da la impresión de ser muy estudioso** he gives the impression of being very studious

tengo la impresión de haber estado aquí antes I have the feeling that I've been here before

me dio mucha impresión ver tanta pobreza I was shocked to see so much poverty

me ha costado recuperarme de la impresión it's been difficult for me to recover from the shock.

impresionante *adjetivo*

1. impressive: **tiene una cantidad de vídeos impresionante** he has an impressive amount of videos

2. striking: **una mujer de una belleza impresionante** a woman of striking beauty; **el parecido es impresionante** the similarity is striking.

impresionar [1] *verbo*

1. to shock: **me impresionó ver tanta pobreza** it shocked me to see so much poverty

2. to impress: **impresionó al público con sus acrobacias** he impressed the public with his acrobatics

impresiona lo rápido que aprende it's impressive how fast he learns

impresionarse *verbo pronominal* ■ to be impressed: **los niños se impresionan con mucha facilidad** children are easily impressed.

la **impresora** ■ printer.

imprevisible *adjetivo*

1. *acontecimiento* unforeseeable
2. *reacción* unpredictable.

imprimir [3] *verbo* ■ to print.

improvisar [1] *verbo* ■ to improvise.

la **imprudencia**

conducir de esa manera fue una imprudencia it was unwise to drive in such a manner

conducir y hablar por el móvil es una imprudencia it's unwise to drive and talk on the cell phone

una imprudencia del conductor reckless driving.

imprudente *adjetivo* ■ **unwise:** es imprudente salir con este tiempo it's unwise to go out with this weather; sería imprudente tomar una decisión ahora it would be unwise to make a decision now

muchos conducen de forma imprudente many people drive in a careless manner

un conductor imprudente a careless driver.

el **impuesto** ■ **tax:** todos debemos pagar impuestos we all have to pay taxes

lo compró en la tienda libre de impuestos he bought at in the duty-free shop.

impulsar [1] *verbo* ■ **to drive:** dos motores impulsan el vehículo two engines drive the vehicle; no sabe qué lo impulsó a hacerlo she doesn't know what drove him to do it.

impulsivo, va *adjetivo* ■ **impulsive.**

el **impulso** ■ **impulse:** mi primer impulso fue esconderme my first impulse was to hide; casi siempre actúa por impulso he almost always acts on impulse

hay que tomar bastante impulso antes de saltar you have to get up enough momentum before jumping.

la **impureza** ■ **impurity** (*plural* **impurities**).

inacabado, da *adjetivo* ■ **unfinished:** he entregado un trabajo inacabado I handed in an unfinished piece of work.

inaccesible *adjetivo* ■ **inaccessible:** un lugar inaccesible an inaccessible place.

inaceptable *adjetivo* ■ **unacceptable:** ese comportamiento es inaceptable that behaviour is unacceptable.

inadvertido, da *adjetivo*

pasar inadvertido to go unnoticed: el cantante trató, sin éxito, de pasar inadvertido the singer tried, without success, to go unnoticed.

inaguantable *adjetivo* ■ **unbearable:** este calor es inaguantable this heat is unbearable.

la **inauguración** (*plural* las inauguraciones) ■ **opening:** mañana es la inauguración de la biblioteca tomorrow is the opening of the library; la ceremonia de inauguración the opening ceremony.

inaugurar [1] *verbo* ■ **to inaugurate, to open:** mañana inauguran la nueva biblioteca tomorrow they're inaugurating the new library.

el/la **inca** ■ **Inca.**

incapaz (*plural* incapaces) *adjetivo* ■ **incapable:** es incapaz de hacer una cosa así he's incapable of doing something like that.

incendiar [1] *verbo* ■ **to set fire to:** quisieron incendiar el local they tried to set fire to the place

incendiarse *verbo pronominal* ■ **to catch fire:** la casa del vecino se incendió the neighbour's house caught fire.

el **incendio** ■ **fire:** no pudieron apagar el incendio they couldn't put out the fire .

creen que fue un incendio provocado they believe that it was arson.

la **incertidumbre** ■ **uncertainty** (*plural* uncertainties).

el **incidente** ■ **incident:** el partido terminó sin incidentes the match ended without incident.

la **inclinación** (*plural* las inclinaciones)

1. tilt: la inclinación de la órbita de la tierra the tilt of the earth's orbit

2. incline: debido a una inclinación del terreno due to an incline in the land.

inclinar [1] *verbo* ■ **to tilt:** inclinó el asiento y estiró las piernas he tilted the seat and stretched his legs

inclinarse *verbo pronominal*

1. to bend down: se inclinó para recoger el libro he bent down to pick up the book

2. to lean: me incliné sobre la cuna para darle un beso I leaned over the cradle to give him a kiss; inclínate hacia adelante lean forward.

incluir [36] *verbo* ■ **to include:** el premio incluye el viaje de ida y vuelta y el alojamiento the prize includes the return trip and accommodation; se me olvidó incluirlo en la lista I forgot to include him on the list.

incluso *adverbio* ■ **even:** cualquiera lo puede hacer, incluso un niño anybody can do it, even a child; incluso nos llevó hasta casa he even took us home.

incómodo, da *adjetivo*
1. **uncomfortable:** las camas son un poco incómodas the beds are a little uncomfortable
2. **inconvenient:** es muy incómodo estar sin teléfono it's very inconvenient to be without a telephone
> sentirse incómodo to feel uncomfortable: se sentía incómodo con ese traje he felt uncomfortable in that suit.

incompatible *adjetivo* ■ **incompatible.**

incompetente *adjetivo* ■ **incompetent.**

incompleto, ta *adjetivo* ■ **incomplete.**

incomprensible *adjetivo* ■ **incomprehensible.**

inconcebible *adjetivo* ■ **unthinkable.**

inconsciente *adjetivo*
1. **unconscious:** está vivo pero inconsciente he's alive but unconscious; cayó inconsciente al suelo he fell unconscious to the floor
2. **thoughtless:** ¡cómo puedes ser tan inconscientes! how can you be so thoughtless!

el **inconveniente**
1. **problem:** surgieron algunos inconvenientes some problems came up; el inconveniente es que está en el tercer piso the problem is that it's on the third floor
2. **disadvantage:** vivir aquí tiene sus ventajas y su inconvenientes living here has its advantages and disadvantages
3. **objection:** no nos pusieron muchos inconvenientes they didn't raise many objections
> ¿tienes algún inconveniente en que lo invite? do you mind if I invite him?

incorporar [1] *verbo* ■ **to incorporate:** han incorporado muchos cambios al proyecto they're incorporated a lot of changes into the project

incorporarse *verbo pronominal*
1. **to join:** nos hemos incorporado al grupo de teatro we're joined the theatre group
2. **to sit up:** incorpórate para tomar el jarabe sit up to take the syrup.

incorrecto, ta *adjetivo* ■ **incorrect:** el uso incorrecto de una palabra the incorrect usage of a word.

increíble *adjetivo* ■ **incredible:** nos pasó algo increíble something incredible happened to us.

inculto, ta *adjetivo* ■ **ignorant:** es una persona muy inculta he's a very ignorant person.

incurable *adjetivo* ■ **incurable.**

indecente *adjetivo* ■ **indecent:** un gesto indecente an indecent gesture.

indeciso, sa *adjetivo* ■ **indecisive:** siempre ha sido muy indecisa she's always been very indecisive
> está indeciso, no sabe si ir o no he can't make up his mind, he doesn't know whether to go or not.

indefenso, sa *adjetivo* ■ **defenceless** *UK,* **defenseless** *US.*

indefinido, da *adjetivo* ■ **indefinite:** tiene los ojos de un color indefinido his eyes are an indefinite colour; se lo prestó por tiempo indefinido she loaned it to him for an indefinite period of time
> el artículo indefinido the indefinite article
> un contrato indefinido an indefinite contract.

la **independencia** ■ **independence.**

la **indemnización** *(plural las indemnizaciones)* ■ **compensation.**

independiente *adjetivo* ■ **independent.**

indestructible *adjetivo* ■ **indestructible.**

indeterminado, da *adjetivo* ■ **indeterminate:** el billete es válido para un número indeterminado de viajes the ticket is valid for an indeterminate number of trips.

la **indicación** *(plural las indicaciones)*
> nos hizo una indicación para que nos sentáramos he signalled for us to sit down.

indicar [8] *verbo*

1. to indicate: el barómetro indica mal tiempo the barometer indicates bad weather
2. to show: me indicó en el mapa cómo llegar he showed me on the map how to get there
> con un gesto nos indicó que nos sentáramos with a gesture he signaled for us to sit down
> el médico me indicó que tomara tres comprimidos al día the doctor advised me to take three tablets a day.

el **indicio** ■ sign: la fiebre es un mal indicio fever is a bad sign.

el **índice**

1. index: lo busqué en el índice I looked it up in the index
2. index finger: lo señaló con el índice he pointed to it with his index finger
3. rate: el índice de mortalidad mortality rate; el índice de natalidad birth rate.

la **indiferencia** ■ indifference.

indiferente *adjetivo* ■ indifferent: son indiferentes a todo lo que pasa en el mundo they're indifferent to everything that happens in the world
> es indiferente que sea blanco o negro it makes no difference whether it's white or black
> me es indiferente coger el bus o el metro I don't mind taking the bus or the underground.

indígena *adjetivo* ■ indigenous: la cultura indígena the indigenous culture

/la **indígena** ■ native.

la **indigestión** ■ indigestion.

la **indignación** *(plural las indignaciones)* ■ indignation: siento indignación ante tanta injusticia I feel a great deal of indignation when faced with so much injustice.

indignar [1] *verbo* ■ to infuriate, to make indignant: le indigna que pongan la música tan fuerte it infuriates him that they play the music so loud

indignarse *verbo pronominal* ■ to become indignant, to get angry: se indignó cuando le dijo lo que había hecho she became

indignant when he told her what he'd done; se indigna cuando le mienten she gets angry when they lie to her.

el **indio** , la **india** ■ Indian

En los Estados Unidos se prefiere **Native Americans** para referirse a los indios de ese país.

la **indirecta** ■ hint: me lanzó una indirecta para que me fuera he dropped a hint that I should leave.

la **indiscreción** *(plural las indiscreciones)* ■ indiscretion.

indiscreto, ta *adjetivo* ■ indiscreet: fue una pregunta muy indiscreta it was a very indiscreet question
> fue muy indiscreto al hacerle esa pregunta he was very tactless to ask her that question.

indispensable *adjetivo* ■ indispensable: es indispensable tener experiencia it's indispensable to have experience
> traed sólo lo indispensable bring only the essentials.

individual *adjetivo*

1. individual: nos sirvieron porciones individuales they served us individual portions
2. single: mi casa tiene un dormitorio individual y dos dobles my house has one single bedroom and two doubles.

el **individuo**

1. individual: todo individuo tiene derecho a la vida every individual has a right to life
2. man: la policía ha detenido a dos individuos the police has arrested two men.

la **industria** ■ industry *(plural* **industries***)*: la industria del automóvil the car industry; la industria petrolera the oil industry.

industrial *adjetivo* ■ industrial
> una zona industrial an industrial area.

la **inercia** ■ inertia.

inesperado, da *adjetivo* ■ unexpected.

inestable *adjetivo*

1. unstable: esta mesa es un poco inestable this table is a little unstable

2. changeable: habrá tiempo inestable en el sur the weather will be changeable in the south.

inevitable *adjetivo* ■ inevitable.

inexperto, ta *adjetivo* ■ inexperienced.

inexplicable *adjetivo* ■ inexplicable.

el **infarto** ■ heart attack: le dio un infarto she had a heart attack.

la **infancia** ■ infancy.

infantil *adjetivo*
1. children's: un cuento infantil a children's story
2. childish: es muy infantil para su edad he's very childish for his age.

la **infección** (*plural* las infecciones) ■ infection: tiene una infección en la garganta she has a throat infection.

infectarse [1] *verbo pronominal* ■ to become infected: mi ordenador se infectó con un virus my computer became infected with a virus; se le infectó la herida his wound became infected.

infeliz (*plural* infelices) *adjetivo* ■ unhappy: tuvo una niñez muy infeliz he had a very unhappy childhood.

inferior *adjetivo*
1. lower: la parte inferior de la pantalla the lower part of the screen; el párpado inferior the lower eyelid
2. inferior: se siente inferior a su hermano he feels inferior to his brother
> productos de calidad inferior inferior-quality products
> temperaturas inferiores a lo normal lower than normal temperatures
> un número inferior a 50 a number below 50.

el **infierno** ■ hell.

la **infinidad** ■ infinity
> tengo una infinidad de cosas por hacer I have an enormous number of things to do
> lo ha repetido infinidad de veces he has repeated it countless times.

el **infinitivo** ■ infinitive.

infinito, ta *adjetivo* ■ infinite: tiene una paciencia infinita she has infinite patience

el **infinito** ■ infinity.

inflar [1] *verbo* ■ to blow up, to inflate: hay que inflar los globos you have to blow up the balloons; paramos para inflar una rueda we stopped to inflate a tyre.

inflexible *adjetivo* ■ inflexible: el profesor es muy inflexible con los alumnos the teacher is very inflexible with the students.

la **influencia** ■ influence: tiene mucha influencia sobre los alumnos she has a lot of influence over her students; mi madre siempre ha sido una gran influencia para mí my mother has always been a big influence on me
> una persona de mucha influencia a very influential person.

influir [36] *verbo* ■ to influence: eso influyó mucho en mi decisión that influenced my decision a lot; las personas que más han influido en mí the people that have influenced me most.

la **información** (*plural* las informaciones)
1. information: hay mucha información sobre becas there is a lot of information about scholarships
2. news: me leí sólo la información internacional I only read the international news
> es una información muy valiosa it's a very valuable piece of information
> preguntemos en información a qué hora llega el tren let's ask at the information desk when the train's arriving
> en información te pueden dar el número de teléfono directory enquiries can give you the phone number.

informal *adjetivo*
1. informal: un ambiente muy informal a very informal atmosphere
2. unreliable: Pepe es muy informal Pepe is very unreliable
3. casual: había gente vestida de fiesta y con ropa informal there were people dressed for a party and in casual clothes.

informar [1] *verbo* ■ to inform: nos informaron que el avión venía con retraso they informed us that the aeroplane was late

informaron de la hora de llegada por los **altavoces** they announced the time of arrival over the loudspeakers

¿me podría informar sobre el programa de becas? could you give some information about the scholarship programme?

me informaron mal they misinformed me

me informé de todo antes del viaje I enquired into everything before the trip.

la **informática** ■ computing: a Nacho le apasiona la informática Nacho loves computing; estoy estudiando informática I'm studying computing.

informático, ca *adjetivo* ■ computer: un programa informático a computer program

el **informático**, la **informática** ■ computer expert: Luis es informático Luis is a computer expert.

el **informe** ■ report: según un informe de la policía according to a police report

pidieron informes sobre su conducta they asked for references regarding his behavior.

la **infracción** *(plural* las infracciones*)* ■ offense: lo multaron por una infracción de tráfico they fined him for a traffic offense.

la **ingeniería** ■ engineering.

el **ingeniero**, la **ingeniera** ■ engineer: es ingeniero he's an engineer.

el **ingenio** ■ ingenuity: gracias al ingenio de Pepe conseguimos aprobar thanks to Pepe's ingenuity we managed to pass.

ingenioso, sa *adjetivo*

1. clever: es un muchacho muy ingenioso he's a very clever guy; siempre tiene ideas ingeniosas she always has clever ideas

2. witty: hizo un comentario muy ingenioso he made a very witty comment.

ingenuo, nua *adjetivo* ■ naïve: ¡no seas tan ingenuo! don't be so naïve!

Inglaterra ■ England.

inglés, inglesa *adjetivo*

En inglés, los adjetivos que se refieren a un país o una región se escriben con mayúscula:

English

tiene un apellido inglés he has an English surname

el **inglés**, la **inglesa** *(plural* los ingleses*)*

En inglés, los gentilicios se escriben con mayúscula:

Englishman *(plural* **Englishmen**)*, **Englishwoman** *(plural* **Englishwomen**)*

los ingleses the English

el **inglés**

En inglés, los idiomas se escriben con mayúscula:

English.

el **ingrediente** ■ ingredient.

ingresar [1] *verbo*

1. to join: ingresó en el club hace seis meses he joined the club six months ago

2. to start: el próximo año ingresa en la universidad he starts university next year

3. to pay in: he ingresado el dinero en el banco I've paid the money into the bank

4. to be admitted: ingresó ayer en el hospital he was admitted to the hospital yesterday.

los **ingresos** ■ income: tienen muy pocos ingresos they have very little income.

la **inicial** ■ initial: pon tus iniciales aquí put your initials here.

el **inicio** ■ beginning, start: desde los inicios de su carrera profesional since the beginning of his professional career; el inicio de la guerra the start of the war.

la **injusticia** ■ injustice: hay muchas injusticias en el mundo there are many injustices in the world; es una injusticia que lo hayan castigado it's an injustice that they've punished him.

injusto, ta *adjetivo* ■ unfair: han sido muy injustos con él they've been very unfair to him; es un castigo injusto it's an unfair punishment.

inmaduro, ra *adjetivo* ■ immature: es un chico muy inmaduro he's a very immature boy.

inmediato, ta *adjetivo* ■ immediate: el alivio fue inmediato the relief was immediate

de inmediato immediately: **hazlo de inmediato** do it immediately.

inmenso, sa *adjetivo* ■ **immense**: **tiene un jardín inmenso** he has an immense garden

la inmensa mayoría de los estudiantes the vast majority of the students.

la **inmigración** *(plural* las inmigraciones*)* ■ **immigration**.

el/la **inmigrante** ■ **immigrant**.

inmortal *adjetivo* ■ **immortal**.

inmóvil *adjetivo* ■ **motionless**: **se quedó inmóvil** he remained motionless.

inmune *adjetivo* ■ **immune**: **con la vacuna soy inmune al contagio** with the vaccine I am immune to the infection.

innecesario, ria *adjetivo* ■ **unnecessary**.

la **inocencia** ■ **innocence**.

la **inocentada** ■ *practical joke played on 28th December.*

inocente *adjetivo*

1. **innocent**: **un niño inocente** an innocent child
2. **naïve**: **¡no seas inocente!** don't be naïve!
> **lo declararon inocente** they found him not guilty

DÍA DE LOS INOCENTES

This is the equivalent of April Fools' Day in Spanish-speaking countries and is celebrated on December 28. On this day people play practical jokes on their friends and try to convince them of the most outrageous hoaxes.

inofensivo, va *adjetivo* ■ **inoffensive**.

inolvidable *adjetivo* ■ **unforgettable**.

inquieto, ta *adjetivo*

1. **worried**: **están inquietos porque no les ha llamado** they're worried because he hasn't call them
2. **restless**: **mi hermano menor es muy inquieto** my little brother is very restless.

el **inquilino** , la **inquilina** ■ **tenant**.

inscribirse [3] *verbo pronominal* ■ **to enrol** *UK,* **to enroll** *US:* **me inscribí en el curso de inglés** I enrolled in the English course.

la **inscripción** *(plural* las inscripciones*)*

1. **enrollment**: **mañana abren la inscripción** enrollment starts tomorrow
2. **inscription**: **en la entrada hay una inscripción con la fecha** at the entrance there is an inscription with the date.

el **insecticida** ■ **insecticide**.

el **insecto** ■ **insect**.

la **inseguridad** ■ **insecurity** *(plural* **insecurities**)*: **se esfuerza por superar su inseguridad** he makes an effort to overcome his insecurity
> **la inseguridad en el trabajo** job insecurity
> **la inseguridad ciudadana** lack of safety on the streets.

insensible *adjetivo* ■ **insensitive**: **es una persona muy insensible** he's a very insensitive person
> **el brazo derecho le quedó insensible** his right arm became numb
> **son insensibles al frío** they're not sensitive to the cold.

inseparable *adjetivo* ■ **inseparable**.

insignificante *adjetivo* ■ **insignificant**.

insinuar [1] *verbo* ■ **to hint**: **insinuó que le gustaría venir** she hinted that she would like to come
> **insinuó que yo había copiado** he insinuated that I had copied.

insípido, da *adjetivo* ■ **insipid**.

insistir [3] *verbo* ■ **to insist**: **por más que insista no le van a dar permiso** however much he insists, they are not going to give him permission
> **insistir en algo** to insist on something: **insiste en que quiere hacerlo él solo** he insists that he wants to do it by himself; **insisten en que vaya al dentista** they insist that he go to the dentist.

la **insolación** *(plural* las insolaciones*)* ■ **sunstroke**: **le dio una insolación** she got sunstroke.

insolente *adjetivo* ■ insolent.

el **insomnio** ■ insomnia.

insoportable *adjetivo* ■ unbearable.

el **inspector** , la **inspectora** ■ inspector.

la **inspiración** *(plural* las inspiraciones*)* ■ inspiration: busca inspiración en la naturaleza he looks for inspiration in nature.

inspirar [1] *verbo*

1. to inspire: inspira respeto he inspires respect; no me inspira confianza he doesn't inspire my confidence

2. to inhale: inspire por favor inhale please

inspirarse *verbo pronominal* ■ to be inspired: la película se inspira en los años veinte the film is inspired by the twenties.

la **instalación** *(plural* las instalaciones*)* ■ installation: la instalación es gratis installation is free

> las instalaciones facilities: las instalaciones deportivas son excelentes the sports facilities are excellent.

instalar [1] *verbo* ■ to install: instalaron un sistema de seguridad they installed a security system; no puede instalar el programa he can't install the program

instalarse *verbo pronominal* ■ to settle: se instalaron en casa de sus tíos they settled in their uncle's and aunt's house.

instantáneo, nea *adjetivo* ■ instantaneous: la muerte fue instantánea death was instantaneous

> café instantáneo instant coffee.

el **instante** ■ moment: en ese mismo instante sonó el teléfono at that very moment the telephone rang; hace un instante estaba aquí he was here a moment ago

> al instante immediately: llamé y Rosa contestó al instante I called and Rosa answered immediately

> a cada instante me preguntaba la hora he was constantly asking me what time it was.

el **instinto** ■ instinct: reaccionó por instinto he reacted out of instinct

> el instinto materno maternal instinct.

la **institución** *(plural* las instituciones*)* ■ institution.

el **instituto**

1. institute: un instituto de belleza a beauty institute

2. school: el instituto está cerrado durante las vacaciones the school is closed during the holidays.

las **instrucciones** ■ instructions: tiene instrucciones de no comentarlo con nadie he has instructions not to discuss it with anybody.

el **instrumento** ■ instrument: mi madre toca varios instrumentos my mother plays several instruments

> un instrumento musical a musical instrument

> un instrumento de cuerda a string instrument

> un instrumento de percusión a percussion instrument

> un instrumento de viento a wind instrument.

insuficiente *adjetivo* ■ insufficient: una cantidad de comida insuficiente an insufficient amount of food

el **insuficiente** ■ fail

> he sacado un insuficiente en matemáticas I failed maths.

insultar [1] *verbo* ■ to insult.

el **insulto** ■ insult.

intacto, ta *adjetivo* ■ intact: descubrieron un mural maya intacto they discovered an intact Mayan mural; a pesar de los siglos sigue intacto in spite of the centuries it remains intact.

intelectual *adjetivo* ■ intellectual

el/la **intelectual** ■ intellectual.

la **inteligencia** ■ intelligence

> la inteligencia artificial artificial intelligence.

inteligente *adjetivo* ■ intelligent.

la **intemperie**

> a la intemperie out in the open: en el campamento tienen que dormir a la intemperie at the camp they have to sleep out in the open.

la **intención** *(plural* las intenciones*)* ■ **intention:** mi intención no era causar problemas my intention was not to cause problems

> con la intención de hacer algo with the intention of doing something: **lo hizo con la intención de ayudar** he did it with the intention of helping; **no tenía la más mínima intención de obedecer** he didn't have the least intention of obeying

> tenía intenciones de ir mañana I intended to go tomorrow

> lo hace con buenas intenciones he does it with good intentions

> lo que vale es la intención it's the thought that counts.

intensivo, va *adjetivo* ■ **intensive:** ofrecen cursos intensivos de inglés they offer intensive English courses.

intenso, sa *adjetivo* ■ **intense.**

intentar [1] *verbo* ■ **to try:** ya lo ha intentado varias veces he's already tried it several times; **intenta que sea lo más claro posible** try to make it as clear as possible

> intentar hacer algo to try to do something: **intenta concentrarte más en clase** try to concentrate more in class.

el **intento** ■ **attempt:** aprobó el examen al segundo intento he passed the exam on the second attempt.

intercambiar [1] *verbo* ■ **to exchange:** intercambiaron direcciones they exchanged addresses.

el **intercambio** ■ **exchange.**

el **interés** *(plural* los intereses*)* ■ **interest:** tienes que poner más interés en lo que haces you have to take more of an interest in what you do; **escuchaba con interés** she was listening with interest

> poner interés en algo to show interest in something: **no muestra ningún interés en la lectura** he doesn't show any interest in reading

> sólo lo hace por interés he only does it for self-interest

> les cobran un interés muy alto they charge them very high interest.

interesante *adjetivo* ■ **interesting.**

interesar [1] *verbo* ■ **to interest:** siempre me han interesado ese tipo de cosas that type of thing has always interested me

> le interesa mucho la música she's very interested in music

> ¿te interesaría saber más del tema? would you be interested in knowing more about the subject?

interesarse *verbo pronominal* ■ **to take an interest:** siempre se interesó por la política he always took an interest in politics.

interior *adjetivo* ■ **interior:** en el bolsillo interior de la chaqueta in the interior pocket of the jacket

> la parte interior es roja the inner part is red

el **interior** ■ **interior:** el interior del país es muy árido the country's interior is very arid

> lo que ocurre en el interior de la Tierra what occurs inside the earth

> en su interior estaba muy arrepentido deep down he was very sorry.

intermedio, dia *adjetivo*

1. **intermediate:** está en el nivel intermedio he's at intermediate level

2. **medium:** un ordenador de tamaño intermedio a medium size computer

el **intermedio** ■ **interval.**

interminable *adjetivo* ■ **unending.**

internacional *adjetivo* ■ **international.**

el **internado** ■ **boarding school.**

internar [1] *verbo* ■ **to admit:** lo internaron en un campo de refugiados they interned him in a refugee camp.

Internet ■ **Internet:** lo encontré en Internet I found it on the Internet.

interno, na *adjetivo* ■ **internal:** son problemas internos del colegio they are internal problems of the school

> está interna en un colegio de monjas she's a boarder at a convent school

> si no mejora las notas lo van a poner interno if he doesn't improve his grades they're going to send him to boarding school

> los órganos internos the internal organs.

la interpretación *(plural* las interpretaciones*)*

1. interpretation: cada uno le dio una interpretación distinta each one gave her a different interpretation

2. performance: lo que más me gustó fue la interpretación del pianista what I liked most was the pianist's performance
> interpretación simultánea simultaneous translation.

interpretar [1] *verbo*

1. to interpret: lo puedes interpretar de diferentes maneras you can interpret it in different ways

2. to play: interpretó muy bien el personaje he played the character very well; interpretó una pieza al piano she played a piece on the piano

3. to perform: van a interpretar una obra de Shakespeare they're going to perform a play by Shakespeare
> me has interpretado mal you've misunderstood me.

la intérprete ■ interpreter: quiero ser intérprete I want to be an interpreter.

interrogar [7] *verbo*

1. to question: la policía lo interrogó durante tres horas the police questioned him for three hours

2. to interrogate: los secuestradores interrogaron a los rehenes the kidnappers interrogated the hostages.

interrumpir [3] *verbo*

1. to interrupt: no interrumpas cuando alguien está hablando don't interrupt when somebody is talking; no le gusta que lo interrumpan he doesn't like to be interrupted

2. to cut short: tuvieron que interrumpir las vacaciones they had to cut their holidays short

3. to block: un árbol caído interrumpía el tráfico a fallen tree was blocking the traffic; no interrumpas el paso don't block the way.

la interrupción *(plural* las interrupciones*)* ■ interruption: no ha podido estudiar con tantas interrupciones she hasn't been able to study with so many interruptions.

el interruptor ■ switch.

el intervalo ■ interval: a intervalos de diez minutos at ten minute intervals.

el intestino ■ intestine.

la intimidad ■ privacy: mis hermanos no respetan mi intimidad my brothers don't respect my privacy
> celebraron la boda en la intimidad they had a private wedding
> lo que pase en la intimidad es cosa de ellos what happens in private is their business.

íntimo, ma *adjetivo*

1. intimate: los secretos íntimos intimate secrets

2. close: son amigos íntimos they're close friends.

la intoxicación *(plural* las intoxicaciones*)* ■ poisoning: consejos para evitar intoxicaciones advice to avoid poisoning
> intoxicación por alimentos food poisoning.

intoxicarse [8] *verbo pronominal* ■ to be poisoned: se intoxicó con el humo he was poisoned by the smoke.

la introducción *(plural* las introducciones*)* ■ introduction.

introducir [22] *verbo*

1. to insert: hay que introducir una moneda en la ranura you have to insert a coin into the slot

2. to introduce: introdujeron el sistema métrico they introduced the metric system; quieren introducir algunos cambios en el horario they want to introduce some changes in the schedule

3. to enter: introdujo los datos en el ordenador he entered the data into the computer.

el intruso , **la intrusa** ■ intruder.

la intuición *(plural* las intuiciones*)* ■ intuition: la intuición me dice que no deberíamos tomar ese camino intuition tells me that we shouldn't take that path.

la inundación *(plural* las inundaciones*)* ■ flood: las últimas inundaciones obligaron a evacuar varias casas the last floods forced the evacuation of several houses.

inundar [1] *verbo* ■ to flood: el río inundó la zona más baja del pueblo the river flooded the lowest area of the town

inundarse *verbo pronominal* ■ **to be flooded:** la zona más baja del pueblo se inundó con la tormenta the lowest area of the town was flooded in the storm.

inútil *adjetivo* ■ **useless:** nuestros esfuerzos resultaron inútiles our efforts were useless; es inútil, no lo vamos a lograr it's useless, we're not going to manage it.

invadir [3] *verbo* ■ **to invade:** el ejército enemigo invadió la ciudad the enemy army invaded the city.

inválido, da *adjetivo* ■ **disabled:** su tío quedó inválido después del accidente his uncle became disabled after the accident

el **inválido** , la **inválida** ■ **invalid:** los inválidos llegaron en silla de ruedas the invalids arrived in wheelchairs.

la **invasión** *(plural* las invasiones) ■ **invasion.**

inventar [1] *verbo*
1. **to invent:** Alexander Graham Bell inventó el teléfono Alexander Graham Bell invented the telephone
2. **to make up:** le gusta inventar historias para entretener a sus hijos he likes to make up stories to entertain his children.

el **invento** ■ **invention:** el teléfono fue un invento de Alexander Graham Bell the telephone was an invention of Alexander Graham Bell.

el **inventor** , la **inventora** ■ **inventor:** el inventor del teléfono fue Alexander Graham Bell the inventor of the telephone was Alexander Graham Bell.

el **invernadero** ■ **greenhouse:** el efecto invernadero the greenhouse effect.

la **inversión** *(plural* las inversiones) ■ **investment.**

inverso, sa *adjetivo* ■ **opposite:** en sentido inverso in the opposite direction
➤ a la inversa the other way: yo lo hice así y ellos lo hicieron a la inversa I did it this way and they did it the other way.

invertir [20] *verbo*
1. **to invest:** hay varios empresarios interesados en invertir en el país there are several businessmen interested in investing in the country
2. **to reverse:** si invertimos el orden de los números, obtendremos otro resultado if we reverse the order of the numbers, we will obtain a different result
3. **to spend:** he invertido mucho tiempo en ese trabajo I've spent a lot of time on this job.

la **investigación** *(plural* las investigaciones)
1. **investigation:** al cabo de dos días de investigación policial, capturaron al ladrón at the end of two days of police investigation, they captured the thief
2. **research:** mi amigo se dedica a la investigación en biología my friend is dedicated to research in biology.

el **investigador** , la **investigadora**
1. **investigator:** los investigadores capturaron al ladrón en un par de días the investigators captured the thief in a couple of days
2. **researcher:** el investigador descubrió una nueva reacción química the researcher discovered a new chemical reaction.

investigar [12] *verbo*
1. **to investigate:** la policía investiga el caso desde hace una semana the police have been investigating the case for a week
2. **to research:** los científicos están investigando la nueva enfermedad scientists are researching the new disease.

el **invierno** ■ **winter**
➤ en invierno in winter
➤ el próximo invierno next winter
➤ el invierno pasado last winter.

invisible *adjetivo* ■ **invisible.**

la **invitación** *(plural* las invitaciones) ■ **invitation:** no aceptaron mi invitación they didn't accept my invitation.

el **invitado** , la **invitada** ■ **guest.**

invitar [1] *verbo*
1. **to invite:** me han invitado a cenar they're invited me to dinner

2. to buy: te invito a un refresco I'll buy you a drink.

la inyección (plural las inyecciones) ■ **injection:** la enfermera me puso una inyección the nurse gave me an injection.

ir [44] verbo

1. to go: el nuevo camino irá del pueblo a la ciudad the new road will go from the town to the city; **voy al parque todos los domingos** I go to the park every Sunday; **este libro va en el estante de abajo** this book goes on the bottom shelf

2. to be: la niña iba vestida de rojo the girl was dressed in red; **iba con sus primos** he was with cousins

3. to come: ¿quieres ir conmigo? do you want to come with me?

➤ **¡vamos!** come on!

➤ **voy a comprarlo** I'm going to buy it

➤ **¿cómo te va?** how's it going?

➤ **¡que te vaya bien!** take care!

➤ **¡vaya moto!** what a fantastic motorbike!

irse verbo pronominal

1. to leave: nos vamos porque ya es tarde we're leaving because it's late now; **¡vámonos!** let's go!

2. to go out: se ha ido la luz the light's gone out.

Irlanda ■ **Ireland.**

irlandés, irlandesa

En inglés, los adjetivos que se refieren a un país o una región se escriben con mayúscula:

Irish: un pub irlandés an Irish pub

el irlandés , la irlandesa (plural los irlandeses)

En inglés, los gentilicios se escriben con mayúscula:

Irishman (plural **Irishmen**), **Irishwoman** (plural **Irishwomen**)
➤ los irlandeses the Irish.

la ira ■ **anger:** tuvo un arrebato de ira he had a fit of anger.

irracional adjetivo ■ **irrational.**

irreal adjetivo ■ **unreal.**

irregular adjetivo ■ **irregular:** la casa no es segura porque está construida en un terreno irregular the house is not safe because it's constructed on an irregular piece of land.

irresistible adjetivo

1. irresistible: esos pasteles son irresistibles those cakes are irresistible

2. unbearable: el dolor de muelas es irresistible toothache is unbearable.

irresponsable adjetivo ■ **irresponsible:** ese estudiante es muy irresponsable that student is very irresponsible.

irritado, da adjetivo

1. inflamed: tiene la piel irritada his skin is inflamed

2. irritated: Juan está irritado por la mentira que le dije Juan is irritated because of the lie that I told him.

la isla ■ **island.**

Italia ■ **Italy.**

italiano, na adjetivo

En inglés, los adjetivos que se refieren a un país o una región se escriben con mayúscula:

Italian
➤ me gustan los helados italianos I like Italian ice cream

el italiano , la italiana

En inglés, los gentilicios se escriben con mayúscula:

Italian
➤ los italianos the Italian

el italiano

En inglés, los gentilicios se escriben con mayúscula:

Italian.

el itinerario ■ **itinerary** (plural **itineraries**).

la izquierda

1. left hand: escribe con la izquierda he writes with his left hand

2. left

➤ **a la izquierda** (to the) left: tienes que girar a la izquierda you have to turn left; María está sentada a la izquierda de Juan Maria is seated to the left of Juan

de la izquierda on the left: **abre esa puerta, la de la izquierda** open that door, the one on the left

la izquierda *política* the left

ser de izquierdas to be left-wing

conducir por la izquierda to drive on the left.

izquierdo, da *adjetivo* ■ left: la pierna izquierda the left leg.

el **jabón** *(plural* los jabones*)* ■ soap: **lávate las manos con jabón** wash your hands with soap

una pastilla de jabón a bar of soap.

jamás *adverbio* ■ never: **jamás te mentí** I never lied to you.

el **jamón** *(plural* los jamones*)* ■ ham: **un bocadillo de jamón** a ham sandwich

jamón cocido o de York cooked ham

jamón serrano cured ham.

Japón ■ Japan.

japonés, japonesa *adjetivo*

En inglés, los adjetivos que se refieren a un país o una región se escriben con mayúscula:

el sushi es un plato japonés sushi is a Japanese dish

el **japonés** , la **japonesa** *(plural* los japoneses*)*

En inglés, los gentilicios se escriben con mayúscula:

Japanese
los japoneses the Japanese

el **japonés**

En inglés, los idiomas se escriben con mayúscula:

Japanese.

el **jarabe** ■ syrup.

el **jardín** *(plural* los jardines*)* ■ garden
jardín botánico botanical garden.

el **jardinero** , la **jardinera** ■ gardener.

la **jarra**
1. *de agua, de leche* jug UK, pitcher US
2. *de cerveza* beer mug.

el **jarrón** *(plural* los jarrones*)* ■ vase.

la **jaula** ■ cage.

el **jefe** , la **jefa**
1. *en una oficina* boss
2. *en un departamento* head
3. *de una tribu* chief
jefe de estado head of state.

la **jeringa** ■ syringe.

el **jersey** *(plural* jerséis*)* ■ sweater UK, jumper US.

la **jirafa** ■ giraffe.

la **joroba** ■ hump: **el camello tiene dos jorobas** the camel has two humps.

el **jorobado** , la **jorobada** ■ hunchback.

joven *adjetivo* ■ young: **es una abuela muy joven** she's a very young grandmother

el/la **joven** *(plural* los/las jóvenes*)* ■ young person *(plural* **young people***)*: **los jóvenes exigen cambios en la sociedad** young people demand changes in society

un joven a young man

una joven a young woman.

la **joya** ■ jewel
> joyas falsas fake jewels.

la **joyería**
1. *oficio* jewellery UK, jewelry US
2. *tienda* jeweller's UK, jeweler's US.

la **jubilación** *(plural* las jubilaciones*)*
1. retirement: mi padre ha llegado a la edad de jubilación my father has reached retirement age
2. pension: cobra la jubilación cada mes he draws his pension every month
> la jubilación anticipada early retirement.

jubilado, da *adjetivo* ■ pensioner, retired US: mi abuelo está jubilado desde hace 15 años my grandfather has been retired for 15 years

el **jubilado**, la **jubilada** ■ retiree: muchos jubilados están pasando dificultades económicas many pensioners are going through financial difficulties.

jubilarse [1] *verbo pronominal* ■ to retire: mi tío se jubila este año my uncle is retiring this year.

la **judía** ■ bean
> la judía blanca haricot bean
> la judía verde green bean, runner bean.

judío, a *adjetivo* ■ Jewish

el **judío**, la **judía** ■ Jew.

el **judo** ■ judo.

el **juego**
1. game: tiene muchísimos juegos de ordenador he has many computer games
2. set: compré un nuevo juego de sábanas I bought a new set of sheets
> a juego matching: un bolso a juego con los zapatos a bag and matching shoes
> hacer juego to match: esa corbata hace juego con la camisa that tie matches your shirt
> un juego de mesa a board game
> un juego de palabras a word game
> un juego de azar a game of chance
> fuera de juego offside.

el **jueves** *(plural* los jueves*)*

En inglés, los días de la semana se escriben con mayúscula:

Thursday: hoy es jueves today is Thursday; **el jueves que viene** next Thursday; **el jueves pasado** last Thursday
> **el jueves** on Thursday: **te veré el jueves** I'll see you on Thursday
> **los jueves** on Thursdays: **los jueves vamos al parque** on Thursdays we go to the park.

el **juez**, la **jueza** ■ judge: cuando el juez entró en la sala todos se pusieron de pie when the judge came into the room everybody stood up

el **jugador**, la **jugadora** ■ player.

jugar [29] *verbo* ■ to play: después de la escuela, los niños juegan en el parque after school, the children play in the park; jugamos a fútbol todos los sábados we play football every Saturday; mi padre juega a la lotería desde hace años my father has been playing the lottery for years.

el **jugo** ■ juice: esta carne no tiene jugo this meat has no juice.

el **juguete** ■ toy.

la **juguetería** ■ toy shop UK, toy store US.

el **juicio** ■ trial: el acusado fue absuelto en el juicio the accused was acquitted at the trial
> muela del juicio wisdom tooth.

julio *sustantivo masculino*

En inglés, los meses del año se escriben con mayúscula:

July: en julio in July; **el próximo julio** next July; **el pasado julio** last July.

la **jungla** ■ jungle.

junio *sustantivo masculino*

En inglés, los meses del año se escriben con mayúscula:

June: en junio in June; **el próximo junio** next June; **el pasado junio** last June.

juntar [1] *verbo* ■ **to put together:** junta los pies put your feet together; **vamos a juntar las dos mesas** we're going to put the two tables together

juntarse *verbo pronominal* ■ **to get together:** nos juntamos para celebrar los 80 años del abuelo we got together to celebrate our grandfather's 80th birthday.

junto, ta *adjetivo*
1. **close together:** pon los pies juntos put your feet close together
2. **together:** Cecilia y su marido llegaron juntos a la fiesta Cecilia and her husband arrived together at the party.

junto *adverbio*
> junto con **together with:** junto con la carta, tienes que enviar una fotocopia del pasaporte you have to send a photocopy of your passport together with the letter
> junto a **next to:** como hacía frío, se sentaron junto a la chimenea since it was cold, they sat down next to the fireplace.

el **jurado**
1. **panel:** el jurado del concurso está formado por escritores famosos the competition's panel is made up of famous writers
2. **jury** *(plural* **juries):** el jurado concluyó que el acusado es culpable del asesinato the jury concluded that the accused is guilty of the murder.

jurar [1] *verbo* ■ **to swear:** es la verdad, te lo juro it's the truth, I swear it.

la **justicia** ■ **justice:** los manifestantes reclamaban justicia the demonstrators were demanding justice.

justificar [8] *verbo* ■ **to justify:** no intentes justificar tu grosería don't try to justify your rudeness.

justo, ta *(adverbio & adjetivo)*

■ *adverbio*
1. **just:** llegué justo antes de que el tren se fuera I arrived just before the train left; **esto es justo lo que necesitaba** this is just what I needed
2. **just enough:** la comida dio justo para todos the food was just enough for everybody

■ *adjetivo*
1. **fair:** tomaron una decisión justa they made a fair decision; ¡no es justo! it's not fair!
2. **tight:** esa blusa te queda demasiado justa that blouse is too tight
> aquí tienes 300 euros justos here you have exactly 300 euros.

la **juventud**
1. **youth:** la juventud es la etapa posterior a la adolescencia youth is the stage after adolescence; **en su juventud vivió en África** he lived in Africa in his youth
2. **young people:** la juventud conduce muy deprisa young people drive very fast.

el **juzgado** ■ **court.**

juzgar [12] *verbo* ■ **to judge:** no juzgues por las apariencias don't judge by appearances.

el **kárate** ■ **karate.**

el **ketchup** ■ **ketchup.**

el **kilo** ■ **kilo:** un kilo de patatas a kilo of potatoes.

el **kilogramo** ■ **kilogram.**

el **kilómetro** ■ **kilometre** *UK,* **kilometer** *US:* todavía nos faltan 20 kilómetros we're still got 20 kilometres to go; a 150 kilómetros por hora at 150 kilometres an hour.

el **kiosco** ■ **newsstand.**

el **kiwi** ■ **kiwi.**

la *(sustantivo femenino, pronombre & artículo)*

■ *sustantivo femenino*

la: "la" es la nota anterior a "si" "la" is the note before "ti"

■ *pronombre*

1. **her:** la esperé hasta las nueve de la noche I waited for her until nine o'clock at night
2. **you:** venga por aquí señora, la acompañaré hasta la salida come this way madam, I'll take you to the exit
3. **it:** esa acuarela no está seca todavía, no la toques that watercolour is not dry yet, don't touch it

■ *artículo*

the: la manzana que me comí estaba buenísima the apple I ate was really nice; la profesora compró el libro the teacher bought the book

➤ esta corbata y la de Roberto son iguales this tie and Robert's are the same

➤ se rompió la pierna he broke his leg

> Los nombres abstractos llevan artículo en español pero no en inglés.

➤ me encanta la pintura I adore painting

➤ la vida es difícil life is difficult.

el laberinto ■ maze.

el labio ■ lip.

la labor *(plural* las labores*)* ■ work: la labor de los bomberos es muy importante firefighter's work is very important

➤ ocupación: sus labores occupation: housewife.

laboral *adjetivo* ■ working: aquí la semana laboral es de cinco días here the working week is five days.

el laboratorio ■ laboratory *(plural* laboratories*)*.

lácteo, a *adjetivo* ■ dairy: los productos lácteos más comunes son la mantequilla y el queso the most common dairy products are butter and cheese.

la ladera ■ hillside.

lado *sustantivo masculino* ■ side: al otro lado de la calle on the other side of the street; me dio un golpe en el lado izquierdo he hit me on the left side; suba por el ascensor del lado derecho go up in the lift on the right side; el triángulo tiene tres lados the triangle has three sides

➤ al lado next door

➤ al lado de next to: siéntate al lado de María sit down next to María

➤ de lado a lado from one side to the other: con el terremoto, ese muro se abrió de lado a lado with the earthquake, that wall split from one side to the other

➤ de un lado para otro backwards and forwards: se pasa todo el día de un lado para otro he spends all day going backwards and forwards

➤ por ningún lado anywhere: no encuentro las llaves por ningún lado I can't find the keys anywhere

➤ por un lado..., por otro... on the one hand..., on the other hand...: por un lado me llevaría éste, pero por otro me parece demasiado caro on the one hand I would take this one, but on the other hand it seems too expensive to me

➤ ¿vamos a pasear a algún lado? are we going to go out somewhere?

ladrar [1] *verbo* ■ to bark.

el ladrido ■ bark: a lo lejos se oían los ladridos del perro the dog's barks were heard in the distance.

el ladrillo ■ brick.

el **ladrón** , la **ladrona**
1. *de objetos* **thief** *(plural* **thieves***)*
2. *de casas* **burglar**
3. *de bancos* **robber.**

el **lagarto** ■ **lizard.**

el **lago** ■ **lake.**

la **lágrima** ■ **tear.**

la **laguna** ■ **lake.**

lamentar [1] *verbo* ■ **to be sorry:** lamento lo que ha sucedido I'm sorry about what happened

lamentarse *verbo pronominal* ■ **to complain:** no sirve de nada lamentarse there's no point in complaining.

lamer [2] *verbo* ■ **to lick:** la gata lame a sus crías para lavarlas the cat licks her litter to wash them.

la **lámpara** ■ **lamp:** apaga la lámpara cuando termines de leer turn out the lamp when you finish reading
una lámpara de mesa a table lamp.

la **lana** ■ **wool:** la lana de las ovejas sheeps' wool; me he comprado un jersey de lana I've bought myself a woollen sweater
➤ pura lana virgen pure new wool.

la **lancha** ■ **boat:** siempre salen con su lancha a hacer esquí acuático they always take their boat out to go water skiing
➤ lancha de salvamento lifeboat.

la **langosta**
1. *crustáceo* **lobster**
2. *insecto* **locust.**

el **langostino** ■ **king prawn.**

el **lanzamiento** ■ **launch:** ayer fue el lanzamiento del nuevo transbordador espacial yesterday was the launch of the new space shuttle.

lanzar [10] *verbo*
1. **to throw:** lánzame la pelota throw me the ball; le lanzaron unas piedras the threw stones at him

2. **to launch:** lanzaron el cohete desde Cabo Cañaveral they launched the rocket from Cape Canaveral
3. **to let out:** los niños estaban contentos y lanzaban gritos de alegría the children were happy and were letting out shouts of happiness
4. **to bring out:** en marzo lanzan el nuevo disco in March they're bringing out a new record.

el **lápiz** *(plural* los lápices*)* ■ **pencil:** le escribió una nota a lápiz he wrote her a note in pencil
➤ lápices de colores crayons
➤ un lápiz de labios a lipstick.

largo, ga *adjetivo*
1. **long:** caminaron una distancia larga para llegar al pueblo they walked a long distance to arrive at the town
2. **lengthy:** estas conferencias siempre son largas these lectures are always lengthy
➤ a lo largo de throughout: nos encontramos varias veces a lo largo de la semana we came across each other several times throughout the week
➤ para largo a long time: la conferencia va para largo the lecture is going to be a long time

el **largo** ■ **length:** ¿cuánto mide de largo? what length is it?, how long is it?

las *artículo*
1. **the:** las manzanas son rojas the apples are red

Cuando se refiere a partes del cuerpo u objetos personales en inglés se emplea el adjetivo posesivo: **my, your, his, her, our, their:**

lávate las manos wash your hands; poneos las botas put your boots on; me duelen las rodillas my knees hurt
■ *pronombre*
1. **them:** compró dos muñecas y se las regaló a sus sobrinas she bought two dolls and gave them to her nieces
2. **you:** las esperaré en la entrada del hotel I'll wait for you at the hotel entrance.

el **láser** *(plural* los láser*)* ■ **laser.**

la **lástima** ■ **pity:** es una lástima que no hayas podido venir it's a pity that you couldn't come me da lástima que sufra tanto I feel very sorry that he suffers so much.

la lata

1. *de cola, cerveza* **can**
2. *de atún, anchoas* **tin**
   ¡qué lata! what a drag!

lateral *adjetivo* ■ **side:** coge una calle lateral take a side street.

el latido ■ **beat.**

el látigo ■ **whip.**

Latinoamérica *sustantivo femenino* ■ **Latin America.**

latinoamericano, na *adjetivo*

En inglés, los adjetivos que se refieren a un país o una región se escriben con mayúscula:

Latin American

el latinoamericano ,

la latinoamericana

En inglés, los gentilicios se escriben con mayúscula:

Latin American: los latinoamericanos Latin Americans.

latir [3] *verbo* ■ **to beat.**

el laurel ■ **laurel**

> una hoja de laurel a bay leaf.

el lavabo

1. **sink:** lávate las manos en el lavabo wash your hands in the sink
2. **toilet** *UK,* **washroom** *US:* en la planta baja hay un lavabo there's a toilet on the ground floor.

la lavadora ■ **washing machine.**

la lavandería ■ **launderette** *UK,* **Laundromat** *US.*

lavar [1] *verbo* ■ **to wash:** ¿me has lavado la camiseta? have you washed my T-shirt?; hoy tienes que lavarte el pelo today you have to wash your hair

> lavar a mano to wash by hand
> lavar en seco to dryclean

lavarse *verbo pronominal*

1. **to wash:** hoy tienes que lavarte el pelo today you have to wash your hair
2. **to brush:** ¿ya te has lavado los dientes? have you brushed your teeth yet?

el lavavajillas

1. *electrodoméstico* **dishwasher**
2. *detergente* **washing-up liquid** *UK,* **detergent** *US.*

el lazo

1. **bow:** el paquete tenía un lazo azul the package had a blue bow
2. **lasso**
> echaron el lazo al caballo they lassoed the horse

los lazos ■ **ties:** tiene lazos muy estrechos con su familia he has very close ties with his family.

le *pronombre*

1. *a él* **him,** *a ella* **her:** le dije que me esperara, pero se fue I told him to wait for me, but he left; le entregué el premio I gave her the prize
2. *a usted* **you:** le pido que me espere aquí unos minutos I'm asking you to wait for me here for a few minutes
> le duelen los pies his feet hurt.

leal *adjetivo* ■ **loyal.**

la lección *(plural* las lecciones*)* ■ **lesson:** es mejor que estudies la lección antes de ir a clase it's better for you to study the lesson before going to class

> darle una lección a alguien to teach somebody a lesson.

la leche ■ **milk**

> leche condensada condensed milk
> leche desnatada skimmed milk *UK,* skim milk *US*
> leche semidesnatada semi-skimmed milk
> leche entera whole milk
> leche en polvo powdered milk.

el lecho ■ **bed.**

la lechuga ■ **lettuce.**

la lechuza ■ **owl.**

el lector, **la lectora** ■ reader

el lector *(plural* los lectores*)* ■ **player**
- un lector de CD a CD player
- un lector de DVD a DVD player.

la lectura ■ reading: todos los días dedica dos horas a la lectura every day he devotes two hours to reading; en esa clase hacemos tres lecturas por semana in that class we do three readings a week.

leer [35] *verbo* ■ to read: ¿sabes leer? do you know how to read?

legal *adjetivo* ■ **legal.**

la legumbre ■ pulse: las habas y las lentejas son legumbres beans and lentils are pulses.

lejano, na *adjetivo* ■ distant: se fue a vivir a un país muy lejano she went to live in a very distant country.

la lejía ■ bleach.

lejos *adverbio* ■ far: podemos ir a pie, no está lejos de aquí we can walk, it's not far from here

▶ a lo lejos in the distance: a lo lejos se ve nuestro pueblo you can see our village in the distance.

la lengua

1. tongue: el médico me pidió que le mostrara la lengua the doctor asked me to show him my tongue

2. language: habla tres lenguas she speaks three languages

▶ lengua materna mother tongue

▶ lengua oficial official language

▶ lengua viva living language

LAS LENGUAS OFICIALES

Spanish, or Castilian, which originated in the former kingdom of Castile, is not the only official language in Spain. Catalán (Catalan), gallego (Galician), valenciano (Valencian) and vascuence (Basque) are the four official languages of the country. They are spoken in Catalonia, Galicia, Valencia and the Basque Country.

el lenguado ■ sole.

el lenguaje ■ language.

la lente ■ lens: los telescopios funcionan con un sistema de lentes telescopes function with a system of lenses

▶ lentes de contacto contact lenses.

la lenteja ■ lentil.

la lentitud ■ slowness: habla con una lentitud exasperante he speaks with an exasperating slowness.

lento, ta *adjetivo* ■ slow: es lento y por eso perdió la carrera he's slow and that's why he lost the race

lento *adverbio* ■ slowly: ir lento to go slowly.

la leña ■ firewood.

el león *(plural* los leones*)* ■ lion.

la leona ■ lioness.

el leopardo ■ leopard.

les *pronombre*

1. *a ellos, a ellas* them: les pedí que me esperaran aquí unos minutos I asked them to wait for me a few minutes

2. *a ustedes* you: ¿desean que les acompañe hasta la salida? do you want me to accompany you to the exit?

▶ les duelen los pies their feet hurt.

la lesión *(plural* las lesiones*)* ■ injury *(plural* injuries*)*: los accidentados se están recuperando de las lesiones the injured are recovering from their injuries.

lesionado, da *adjetivo* ■ injured.

la letra

1. letter: la "a" es la primera letra del alfabeto "a" is the first letter of the alphabet

2. handwriting: tu letra es ilegible your handwriting is illegible

3. lyrics: ¿conoces la letra de esta canción? do you know the lyrics to this song?

el letrero ■ sign.

levantar [1] *verbo*

1. to lift: el campeón de halterofilia levanta 200 kilos the weightlifting champion lifts 200 kilos

. to raise: **el que esté de acuerdo, que levante la mano** those who agree, raise your hands

levantarse *verbo pronominal* ■ **to get up: me levanto a las siete** I get up at seven o'clock **al oír el teléfono se levantó de un salto** on hearing the telephone he jumped to his feet.

leve *adjetivo* ■ **slight: tengo una lesión leve** I have a slight injury.

a ley ■ **law: todos los ciudadanos son iguales ante la ley** all citizens are equal before the law
► **la ley de la gravedad** the law of gravity
► **la ley de la oferta y la demanda** the law of supply and demand.

a leyenda ■ **legend: según la leyenda, Rómulo y Remo fundaron Roma** according to the legend, Romulus and Remus founded Rome.

liberar [1] *verbo* ■ **to free: las autoridades liberaron al acusado** the authorities freed the accused.

la libertad ■ **freedom: tienes total libertad para tomar la decisión que te parezca mejor** you have complete freedom to make the decision that seems the best to you
► **poner a alguien en libertad** to free somebody
► **libertad de culto** worship freedom
► **libertad de expresión** freedom of speech
► **libertad de prensa** freedom of the press.

la libra ■ **pound: una libra equivale aproximadamente a medio kilo** one pound equals approximately half a kilo
► **libra esterlina** pound sterling.

librarse [1] *verbo pronominal*
. to get out of: **como está enfermo, se libró de limpiar la casa** since he's ill, he got out of cleaning the house
. to get rid of: **quiero librarme de él** I want to get rid of him.

libre *adjetivo*
. free: **no aguantaba ver al pájaro en una jaula, así que lo dejé libre** I couldn't stand seeing the bird in a cage, so I set it go free
. available: **hace rato que estoy aquí y no ha pasado ni un taxi libre** I've been here for a while and not one available taxi has gone by

. vacant, free: **llegamos tarde y ya no había asientos libres** we arrived late and there weren't any more vacant seats; **¿está libre este asiento?** is this seat free?

la librería
. *tienda* **bookshop** UK, **bookstore** US
. *estantería* **bookshelf** (plural **bookshelves**)

⚠ The Spanish word **librería** is a false friend, it doesn't mean "library".

el librero , **la librera** ■ **bookseller.**

la libreta ■ **notebook.**

el libro ■ **book: un libro de viajes** a travel book
► **un libro de bolsillo** a paperback
► **un libro de texto** a textbook
► **el libro de familia** *book giving details of births, marriages and deaths*

EL DÍA DEL LIBRO

 The 23rd April was declared World Book Day in 1995. The date coincides with the deaths of William Shakespeare and Miguel de Cervantes in 1616. However, the origins of the celebration can be traced to a Catalan tradition commemorating the day of **Sant Jordi** (Saint George, the patron saint of Catalonia). Legend has it that Saint George gave a rose to the princess he had rescued from the dragon, so, on this day in Catalonia, it is traditional for men to give women a rose and the women to give them a book in return.

la licencia ■ **licence** UK, **license** US: **una licencia de armas** an arms licence
► **licencia por enfermedad** sick leave
► **una licencia de obras** planning permission.

el licenciado , **la licenciada** ■ **graduate**
► **mi hermana es licenciada en biología** my sister is a biology graduate.

la licenciatura ■ **degree: obtuvo su licenciatura en Medicina por la Universidad de Barcelona** he got his degree in medicine from Barcelona University.

el licor (*plural* **los licores**)
. *dulce* **liqueur**
. *bebida alcohólica* **spirits.**

el/la **líder** ■ leader.

la **liebre** ■ hare.

la **liga**
1. league: el campeón de la liga fue el mismo que el año pasado the champion of the league was the same as last year's
2. garter: necesito una liga para las medias I need a garter for my stockings.

ligar [12] familiar verbo
> Alejandro sólo piensa en ligar Alejandro only thinks about picking up girls.

ligero, ra adjetivo
1. light: la ropa de lino es ligera linen is light; a mediodía siempre hago una comida ligera I always have a light meal at mid-day
2. slight: tiene un ligero acento irlandés he has a slightly Irish accent
> tomarse las cosas a la ligera not to take things seriously: Sergio se lo toma todo a la ligera Sergio doesn't take things seriously.

lila adjetivo ■ lilac

el **lila** ■ lilac: el lila es mi color favorito lilac is my favorite color.

la **lima** ■ file: preciso una lima para arreglarme las uñas I need a file to fix my fingernails.

limitar [1] verbo ■ border on: España limita con Portugal y Francia Spain borders on Portugal and France

limitarse verbo pronominal ■ to limit oneself: no quiero engordar, por eso me limito a comer frutas y verduras I don't want to get fat, that's why I'm limiting myself to eating fruit and vegetables.

el **límite**
1. boundary (plural boundaries): el balón salió de los límites del campo the ball went out of the field's boundaries
2. limit: se esforzó hasta el límite para ganar he exerted himself to the limit in order to win
> el límite de velocidad the speed limit
> el límte de edad the age limit
> todo tiene un límite everything has a limit.

el **limón** (plural los limones) ■ lemon.

la **limonada** ■ lemonade.

el **limonero** ■ lemon tree.

limpiar [1] verbo
1. to clean: tú limpia la cocina y yo limpiaré el baño you clean the kitchen and I'll clean the bathroom
2. to wipe: ¿tienes un trapo para limpiar la mesa? do you have a cloth to wipe the table?

la **limpieza**
1. cleaning: hoy he tardado cuatro horas en hacer la limpieza today the cleaning took me four hours
2. cleanliness: la limpieza es primordial en los hospitales cleanliness is essential in hospitals
> limpieza en seco dry-cleaning.

limpio, a adjetivo ■ clean
> pasar a limpio to write out neatly: antes de entregarlo tengo que pasarlo a limpio before I hand it in I have to write it out neatly.

la **línea** ■ line: la distancia más corta entre dos puntos es una línea recta the shortest distance between two points is a straight line; hay varias líneas de autobús para ir al centro there are several bus lines that go to the town centre; había leído apenas diez líneas cuando tuve que salir I had scarcely read ten lines when I had to go out
> mantener la línea to maintain one's figure: Mónica no come dulces porque quiere mantener la línea Mónica doesn't eat sweet things because she wants to maintain her figure
> una línea telefónica a telephone line.

el **lino** ■ linen.

la **linterna**
1. con pilas **torch** UK, **flashlight** US
2. farolillo **lantern.**

el **lío**
1. mess: ¡qué lío hay en esta habitación! what a mess this room is!
2. row: si no limpiamos esto antes de que llegué mamá, se va a armar un lío if we don't clean this up before mum arrives, there's going to be a row

hacerse un lío to get in a muddle: me estoy haciendo un lío con tantos números I'm getting in a muddle with all these figures.

líquido ■ liquid: ese líquido blanco probablemente sea leche this white liquid is probably milk.

liso, sa *adjetivo*
1. smooth: la piel de los bebés es lisa y suave babies' skin is smooth and soft
2. plain: me gusta más esta blusa lisa que aquella de flores I like this plain blouse more than that flowery one
3. straight: Marta tiene el pelo liso Marta has straight hair.

la **lista** ■ list: ¿dónde está la lista de invitados? where's the guest list?
➤ pasar lista to take the register UK, to take roll call US: el profesor pasa lista cada día the teacher takes the register every day
➤ una lista de espera a waiting list
➤ una lista de bodas a wedding list.

listo, ta *adjetivo*
1. smart: Marcos es un niño listo, va a tener buenas notas Marcos is a smart boy, he's going to get good marks
2. ready: cuando llegué a casa de Marisa, ya estaba lista when I arrived at Marisa's house, she was already ready.

la **litera**
1. *de dormitorio* bunk bed
2. *de barco* bunk
3. *de tren* couchette.

la **literatura** ■ literature.

el **litoral** ■ coast.

el **litro** ■ litre UK, liter US.

la **llaga** ■ wound.

la **llama**
1. *de fuego* flame
2. *animal* llama.

la **llamada** ■ call: en media hora he recibido tres llamadas I've received three calls in half an hour
➤ una llamada internacional an international call.

llamar [1] *verbo*
1. to call: la mamá de Julio lo llamaba para que entrara a comer Julio's mum was calling him to come in and eat; mañana te llamo antes de pasar a buscarte tomorrow I'll call you before coming to pick you up; su nombre es Dolores, pero la llaman Lola her name is Dolores, but they call her Lola
2. to call upon: el presidente llamó a los ministros para pedirles su opinión the president called upon the ministers to ask them their opinions
3. to knock: están llamando a la puerta somebody's knocking at the door

llamarse *verbo pronominal* ■ to be called: ¿cómo se llama su último disco? what's his latest record called?
➤ ¿cómo te llamas? —me llamo Lucía what's your name? – my name is Lucía.

llamativo, va *adjetivo* ■ eye-catching: llevaba un vestido rojo muy llamativo she was wearing a very eye-catching red dress.

llano, na *adjetivo* ■ flat.

la **llave**
1. key: puedes dejar la llave debajo del felpudo you can leave the key under the doormat
2. spanner UK, wrench US: ajustaron las tuercas con una llave they adjusted the nuts with a spanner
➤ una llave inglesa a monkey wrench
➤ una llave maestra a master key.

el **llavero** ■ keyring.

la **llegada**
1. *de tren, avión* arrival
2. *meta* finish.

llegar [12] *verbo*
1. to arrive: llegaré a las 8 I'll be arriving at 8 o'clock
2. to reach: llegar a un acuerdo to reach an agreement; no llego al estante de arriba I can't reach the top shelf
3. to get to: cuando llegues a Valencia, llámame when you get to Valencia, call me
➤ ha llegado el momento de contárselo the time has come to tell him

> llegar hasta to go as far as: la carretera llega hasta la playa the road goes as far as the beach

> llegar lejos to go far: si sigues estudiando, llegarás lejos if you keep on studying, you'll go far

> llegar a ser to become: al cabo de los años, llegó a ser un gran pianista after some years, he became a great pianist

> llegar tarde to be late: llegas tarde you're late.

llenar [1] *verbo*

1. to fill: este cajón no cierra porque lo has llenado demasiado this box won't shut because you've filled it too full

2. to be filling: la paella llena mucho paella is very filling

3. to fulfil UK, to fulfill US: su trabajo no le llena he isn't fulfilled by his work

> llenar de to fill with: la noticia me llenó de esperanza the news filled me with hope

llenarse *verbo pronominal* ■ to fill up: el estadio se llenó de aficionados the stadium filled up with fans.

lleno, na *adjetivo* ■ full: el teatro está lleno, no vamos a poder entrar the theatre is full, we're not going to be able to get in; estas medias están llenas de agujeros these stockings are full of holes

> estar lleno to be full: no me sirvas más, por favor, estoy lleno don't serve me any more, please, I'm full.

llevar [1] *verbo*

1. to take: Elena llevó los platos a la mesa Elena took the plates to the table; nos llevaron a un buen restaurante they took us to a good restaurant

2. to lead: el padre llevaba al niño de la mano the father led the boy by the hand

3. to wear: lleva un vestido azul she's wearing a blue dress

4. to carry: ¿me puedes llevar la maleta? can you carry my suitcase?

5. to have: Juan lleva bigote Juan has a moustache

> los pacientes llevan una hora esperando al doctor the patients have been waiting for the doctor for an hour

> llevar en coche to drive: me llevó a casa en coche he drove me home

llevarse *verbo pronominal*

1. to get along: los tres hermanos se llevan muy bien the three brothers get along very well

2. to take away: dice que mañana se llevará todas sus cosas he says he'll take away all his things tomorrow

> llevarse una sorpresa to get a surprise

> llevarse un susto to get a shock.

llorar [1] *verbo* ■ to cry.

llover [17] *verbo* ■ to rain: está lloviendo a cántaros it's raining cats and dogs.

la **lluvia** ■ rain.

lo *(pronombre & artículo)*

■ pronombre

1. it: ¿tu libro? hace días que no lo veo your book? I haven't seen it for days

2. him: ¿a tu hermano? hace mucho que no lo veo your brother? I haven't seen him for a long time

3. you: venga conmigo, lo llevaré hasta el despacho de su esposa come with me, I'll take you to your wife's office

■ artículo

> lo bueno es que nos reconciliamos the good thing is we made up

> prefiero lo dulce I prefer sweet things

> lo que trajiste del mercado, ponlo en la nevera put what you brought from the market in the refrigerator.

el **lobo**, la **loba** ■ wolf.

local *adjetivo* ■ local: la prensa local the local press.

el **local** ■ premises: "alquilo local comercial" "commercial premises for rent".

la **localidad**

1. town: la gente de esa localidad es muy simpática the people in that town are very nice

2. ticket: ¡qué lástima! ya se han agotado las localidades what a shame! the tickets have sold out.

localizar [10] *verbo*

1. **to find:** todavía no he podido localizar los documentos que me pidió el jefe I still haven't been able to find the documents the boss asked me for

2. **to get hold of:** no la localizo en ese número I can't get hold of her on that number

3. **to locate:** han localizado a los secuestradores they've located the kidnappers.

la **loción** *(plural* las lociones*)* ▪ lotion.

loco, ca *adjetivo*

1. **mad:** se ha vuelto loco he's gone mad

2. **crazy, mad** *UK:* ¿estás loco o qué? are you crazy or what?; está loco con su nuevo ordenador he's mad about his new computer

> **estar loco por algo** to be mad about: Julia está loca por Italia Julia is mad about Italy

> **estar loco por alguien** to be mad about somebody: María está loca por tu hermano María is mad about your brother

el **loco**, la **loca** ▪ *hombre* madman, *mujer* madwoman.

la **locomotora** ▪ locomotive.

la **locución** *(plural* las locuciones*)* ▪ phrase.

la **locura** ▪ insanity: alegaba que la locura lo llevó a cometer el asesinato he claimed that insanity led him to commit the murder

> **ser una locura** to be crazy: lo que cobran por esos zapatos es una locura what they charge for those shoes is crazy.

el **locutor**, la **locutora** ▪ announcer.

el **lodo** ▪ mud.

lógico, ca *adjetivo* ▪ logical.

lograr [1] *verbo* ▪ to achieve: siempre logra lo que se propone he always achieves what he sets out to do

> no logro entender este artículo en inglés I can't seem to understand this article in English.

la **lombriz** *(plural* las lombrices*)* ▪ earthworm.

el **lomo**

1. **back:** el lomo de un caballo the back of a horse

2. *carne de cerdo* **loin**

3. *carne de vaca* **fillet**

4. **spine:** en el lomo del libro puedes ver el título lo you can read the title on the spine of the book.

la **loncha**

1. *de queso, de jamón* **slice**

2. *de beicon* **rasher.**

la **longitud**

1. **length:** la piscina tiene 50 metros de longitud the pool is 50 meters in length

2. **longitude:** la longitud se mide a partir del meridiano de Greenwich longitude is measured from the Greenwich meridian

> **de longitud** long: la cama mide dos metros de longitud the bed is two metres long.

el **loro** ▪ parrot.

los *(pronombre & artículo)*

▪ *pronombre*

1. **them:** ¿tus zapatos rojos? no, no los he visto your red shoes? no, I haven't seen them

2. **you:** vengan conmigo, los llevaré hasta el despacho del director come with me, I'll take you to the director's office

▪ *artículo*

the: los melones ya están maduros the melons are ripe now

Las partes del cuerpo llevan en español artículo pero deben traducirse al inglés con un pronombre posesivo:

lávaos los pies antes de meteros en la cama wash your feet before getting into bed

Para describir el aspecto físico de una persona se usa el artículo en español pero no en inglés:

> tiene los ojos castaños she has brown eyes.

la **lotería** ▪ lottery *(plural* lotteries*)*.

la **lucha** ▪ fight: la lucha contra el cáncer the fight against cancer

> la lucha libre wrestling.

luchar [1] *verbo*

1. **to fight:** el regimiento luchó con valentía hasta el final the regiment fought bravely to the end

2. **to struggle:** los diputados lucharon por imponer sus ideas the MPs struggled to enforce their ideas.

luego *adverbio*

1. **then:** primero arreglé el jardín y luego me senté a disfrutar del sol first I did the gardening and then sat down to enjoy the sunshine
2. **later:** el primer grupo irá a las 3 y el segundo llegará luego the first group will go at 3 and the second will arrive later
  › **desde luego** of course: ¿quieres venir con nosotros? —¡desde luego! do you want to come with us? – of course!
  › **¡hasta luego!** see you later!

el **lugar** ■ **place:** queremos comprar una casa en algún lugar con muchos árboles we want to buy a house in a place with a lot of trees; llegó en primer lugar he came first
  › **en lugar de** instead of: en lugar de llamarme me envió un mensaje he sent me a message instead of calling me
  › **en mi/tu/su lugar** in my/your/his/her/their place: ¿qué harías tú en mi lugar? what would you do in my place?
  › **fuera de lugar** inopportune: ha sido un comentario fuera de lugar it was an inopportune comment.

el **lujo** ■ **luxury:** viven rodeados de lujo they live in the lap of luxury
  › **darse el lujo de algo** to be able to afford something: no puedo darme el lujo de acompañarte en tu viaje alrededor del mundo I can't afford to go with you on your trip around the world.

la **luna**

1. **moon:** una luna llena a full moon
2. *de coche* **window**
3. *de escaparate* **glass**
  › **estar en la luna** to have your head in the clouds: ¡estás siempre en la luna! tienes que empezar a prestar más atención you always have your head in the clouds! you need to pay more attention
  › **la luna de miel** honeymoon.

el **lunar**

1. **mole:** Alicia tiene un lunar en la mejilla izquierda Alicia has a mole on her left cheek
2. **polka-dot:** ayer me compré una blusa roja con lunares I bought a red polka-dot shirt yesterday.

el **lunes**

En inglés, los días de la semana se escriben con mayúscula:

Monday: hoy es lunes today is Monday; el próximo lunes next Monday; el pasado lunes last Monday
  › **el lunes** on Monday: te veré el lunes I'll see you on Monday
  › **los lunes** on Mondays: los lunes vamos al cine on Mondays we go to the cinema.

el **luto** ■ **mourning**
  › **estar de luto** to be in mourning.

la **lupa** ■ **magnifying glass.**

la **luz**

1. **light:** por favor, apaga la luz please turn out the light
2. **electricity:** este mes ha subido la factura de la luz the electricity bill has gone up this month
  › **dar a luz** to give birth: Susana dio a luz en su casa Susana gave birth at home.

el **macarrón** *(plural* los macarrones*)* ■ **macaroni:** hemos comido macarrones con salsa de tomate we had macaroni with tomato sauce.

la **macedonia** ■ **fruit salad:** de postre tomaré macedonia I'll have fruit salad for dessert.

la **maceta** ■ **flowerpot.**

el **macho** ■ male: el macho es el pez de colores más vivos the brightly coloured fish is the male.

macizo, za *adjetivo* ■ solid: le regalaron una pulsera de oro macizo they gave her a solid gold bracelet.

la **madera** ■ wood: esa mesa es de madera maciza, por eso pesa tanto the table is made of solid wood, that's why it's so heavy

> tener madera de to have all the makings of: esa niña tiene madera de actriz that girl has all the makings of an actress.

la **madrastra** ■ stepmother.

la **madre** ■ mother: ¿cómo se llama tu madre? what's your mother's name?
> madre política mother-in-law.

Madrid ■ Madrid.

madrileño, ña *adjetivo*

En inglés, los adjetivos que se refieren a un continente o a un país se escriben con mayúscula:

Madrilenian: el cocido es un plato madrileño the "cocido" is a Madrilenian dish.

el **madrileño** , la **madrileña**

En inglés, los gentilicios se escriben con mayúscula:

Madrilenian
los madrileños the Madrilenian.

la **madrina** ■ godmother.

la **madrugada** ■ early morning: siempre se levanta de madrugada para beber agua she always gets up early in the morning to drink some water.

madrugar [12] *verbo* ■ to get up early: detesto madrugar I hate getting up early.

maduro, ra *adjetivo*
1. ripe: los melocotones maduros tienen un delicioso perfume ripe peaches have a delicious scent
2. mature: Roberto es muy maduro para su edad Roberto is very mature for his age.

el **maestro** , la **maestra** ■ teacher.

la **magia** ■ magic: me gustaría mucho aprender a hacer magia I would love to learn how to do magic.

mágico, ca *adjetivo* ■ magic.

magnético, ca *adjetivo* ■ magnetic.

magnífico, ca *adjetivo* ■ magnificent, superb.

la **magnitud** ■ magnitude.

el **mago** , la **maga** ■ magician.

el **maíz**
1. maize, corn *US:* desde aquí se ven los campos de maíz you can see the fields of corn from here
2. sweet corn: me gusta el maíz en las ensaladas I like sweet corn in salads.

majo, ja *adjetivo*
1. *simpático* nice
2. *bonito* pretty.

mal *(adjetivo & adverbio)*
■ *adjetivo*
bad: nunca entiendo sus clases, es mal profesor I don't understand his classes, he's a bad teacher
■ *adverbio*
1. bad: este pescado huele mal this fish smells bad
2. badly: mi sobrino sigue portándose mal my nephew is still behaving badly
3. ill: me encuentro bastante mal I feel quite ill; la reunión terminó mal the meeting ended badly

el **mal**
1. evil: las fuerzas del mal the forces of evil; el bien y el mal good and evil
2. harm: es incapaz de hacer mal a nadie he's incapable of doing harm to anyone
3. disease: lamentablemente todavía existen males incurables unfortunately there are still many incurable diseases.

la **maldición** *(plural* las maldiciones*)* ■ curse: la bruja les echó una maldición the witch put a curse on them.

maleducado, da *adjetivo* ■ rude: los niños de los vecinos son muy maleducados the neighbours' children are very rude.

183

el **malentendido** ■ misunderstanding.

el **malestar**

1. unease: su decisión causó un gran malestar her decision caused great unease
2. discomfort: sintió algunas molestias después de la operación he felt some discomfort after the operation
> tengo un pequeño malestar I feel slightly unwell.

la **maleta** ■ suitcase: me llevaré una maleta pequeña I'll take a small suitcase
> hacer la maleta to pack.

el **maletero** ■ boot UK, trunk US.

malo, la adjetivo

1. bad: la película es malísima the movie was really bad; es un chico malo, que siempre se está peleando con todo el mundo he's a bad boy, he's always fighting with everyone
2. nasty, mean US: ¡no seas mala! don't be nasty!
3. ill: Iván está malo Ivan is ill
4. off: el pescado estaba malo the fish was off.

maltratar [1] verbo ■ to mistreat: el niño había sido maltratado por un familiar the boy had been mistreated by a relative.

la **mamá** ■ mum UK, mom US.

mamar [1] verbo

1. to feed: el bebé recién nacido mama cada tres horas the newborn baby feeds every three hours
2. to suckle: los gatitos están mamando the kittens are suckling.

el **mamífero** ■ mammal: una característica de los mamíferos es que tienen pelo a characteristic of mammals is that they have hair.

la **manada**

1. de vacas herd
2. de lobos, perros pack.

el **manantial** ■ spring.

la **mancha**

1. stain: su blusa tenía una mancha en el cuello her blouse had a stain on the collar
2. mark: Paloma tiene una mancha roja en la mejilla Paloma has a red mark on her cheek

3. spot: los dálmatas son perros blancos con manchas negras Dalmatians are white with black spots
> una mancha de nacimiento a birthmark.

manchar [1] verbo ■ to stain: la leche no mancha milk doesn't stain

mancharse verbo pronominal ■ to stain: cuidado, no te vayas a manchar la ropa con grasa be careful not to stain your clothes with grease.

mandar [1] verbo

1. to order: el general mandó que las tropas avanzaran the general ordered the troops to advance
2. to send: mi hermana me mandó un paquete por correo my sister sent me a package through the post
3. to set: nos ha mandado deberes para mañana she's set us some homework for tomorrow.

la **mandarina** ■ tangerine.

la **mandíbula** ■ jaw.

el **mando**
> el mando a distancia the remote control.

manejar [1] verbo

1. to manage: Alberto maneja la empresa con mucha habilidad Alberto manages the business skilfully
2. to handle: maneja el tractor muy bien he handles the tractor very well.

la **manera** ■ way: Juan tiene una manera de caminar inconfundible Juan has an unmistakeable way of walking; hazlo de esta manera do it this way
> de todas maneras anyway, in any case: de todas maneras no habría podido llamarle anyway I wouldn't have been able to call you
> de ninguna manera certainly not: ¿quieres que te ayude a preparar la cena? —de ninguna manera do you want me to help you fix dinner? —certainly not
> no hay manera de... there's no way to...: no hay manera de llegar a nuestro destino antes del anochecer there's no way we'll reach our destination before nightfall.

a **manga** ■ sleeves: llevaba una camisa de manga corta he wore a short-sleeved shirt.

el **mango**

1. handle: ¡cuidado! el mango de la sartén está caliente careful! the frying pan handle is hot
2. mango: el mango es una fruta exótica the mango is an exotic fruit.

a **manguera** ■ hose.

la **manía** ■ obsession: mi hermana tiene la manía de limpiar cosntantemente my sister has an obsession with cleaning all the time

> tenerle manía a alguien to tahe a dislike to somebody: el profesor me tiene manía the teacher has taken a dislike to me.

el **manicomio** ■ mental hospital.

la **manifestación** (plural las manifestaciones)

1. demonstration: hoy habrá una manifestación contra el terrorismo there's is going to be a demonstration against terrorism today
2. show: una manifestación de solidaridad con las víctimas a show of solidarity with the victims.

manifestar [14] verbo ■ to express: los obreros manifestaron su acuerdo con la propuesta del Ministerio de Trabajo the workers expressed their agreement with the Ministry of Work's proposal

manifestarse verbo pronominal

1. to become apparent: las consecuencias de la inundación se manifestaron pocos días después the consequences of the flood became apparent a few days later
2. to demonstrate: los estudiantes se manifestaron contra la guerra the students demonstrated against the war.

el **manillar** ■ handlebars.

la **maniobra** ■ manoeuvre UK, maneuver US: es una maniobra complicada it's a complicated manoeuvre.

maniobrar [1] verbo ■ to manoeuvre UK, to maneuver US: un tractor puede maniobrar en terrenos difíciles a tractor can manoeuvre on difficult terrain.

el **maniquí** ■ mannequin.

la **mano**

1. hand: lávate las manos wash your hands
2. coat: a esta pared le falta una mano de pintura this wall needs a coat of paint

> a mano by hand: estos jerséis son caros porque se hacen a mano these sweaters are expensive because they're made by hand

> dar(se) la mano to shake hands: Jorge y Carmen se dieron la mano cuando los presentaron Jorge and Carmen shook hands when they were introduced

> echar una mano a alguien to give someone a hand: no he terminado de recoger, ¿me echas una mano? I haven't finished cleaning up —can you give me a hand?

> de segunda mano second-hand: se ha comprado un coche de segunda mano he's bought a second-hand car.

el **manojo** ■ bunch.

la **manta** ■ blanket.

el **mantel** ■ tablecloth.

mantener [52] verbo

1. to keep: me mantuvo informado de todo he kept me informed about everything
2. to support: no quiero que mi marido me mantenga I don't want my husband to have to support me

mantenerse verbo pronominal

> mantenerse en forma to keep: con una hora de ejercicio diario se mantiene en forma he keeps in shape with an hour of exercise a day.

la **mantequilla** ■ butter.

manual adjetivo ■ manual: la costura es una actividad manual sewing is a manual activity

el **manual** ■ manual: consulta el manual antes de instalar el ordenador consult the manual before installing the computer.

la **manzana**

1. apple: acabo de comerme una deliciosa manzana I've just eaten a delicious apple

2. block: fuimos a dar la vuelta a la manzana we went for a walk around the block.

mañana *adverbio* ■ tomorrow: mañana iremos a comprarte ropa we'll go to buy you some clothes tomorrow

> ¡hasta mañana! see you tomorrow!

la **mañana** ■ morning: me levanto todos los días a las 7 de la mañana I get up every day at 7 in the morning

> pasado mañana the day after tomorrow
> mañana por la mañana tomorrow morning.

el **mapa** ■ map: está en el mapa it's on the map.

el **maquillaje** ■ make-up.

maquillarse [1] *verbo pronominal* ■ to put on make-up.

la **máquina** ■ machine

> una máquina tragaperras a slot machine
> una máquina expendedora a vending machine.

el/la **mar** ■ sea: quiero ver el mar I want to see the sea

> el Mar Mediterráneo the Mediterranean Sea.

el **maratón** *(plural* los maratones*)* ■ marathon.

la **maravilla** ■ wonder: el faro de Alejandría era una de las siete maravillas del mundo antiguo the lighthouse at Alexandria was one of the seven wonders of the ancient world

> es una maravilla... it's wonderful...: es una maravilla ver lo rápido que se ha recuperado después del accidente it's wonderful to see how quickly he's recovered after the accident.

maravilloso, sa *adjetivo* ■ wonderful.

la **marca**

1. mark: hay varias marcas en la pared, ¿de qué serán? there are several marks on the wall –I wonder what they're from

2. make: en cuanto a coches, prefiero las marcas japonesas I prefer Japanese makes when it comes to cars

3. brand: ¿qué marca de detergente usas? what brand of detergent do you use?

> ropa de marca brand-name clothing.

el **marcador** ■ scoreboard.

marcar [8] *verbo*

1. to mark: he marcado mis cosas para no perderlas I've marked my things so I won't lose them

2. to dial: ¿cuál es el número de teléfono que hay que marcar? which phone number do I need to dial?

3. to score: mi equipo marcó tres goles my team scored three goals.

la **marcha**

1. course: la marcha de los acontecimientos fue inesperada the course of events was unexpected

2. walk: hicimos una marcha de dos horas we went on a two-hour walk

3. gear: tienes que aprender a cambiar las marchas you have to learn to change gears

> sobre la marcha as I/you/he/she... go along: lo decidiré sobre la marcha I'll decide as I go along
> en marcha running: no puedes bajarte una vez que el tren esté en marcha you can't get off once the train is running
> marcha atrás reverse.

marcharse [1] *verbo pronominal* ■ to leave: se marchó del pueblo hace un año he left town a year ago.

marchitarse [1] ■ to wilt: se marchitaron las flores del jarrón the flowers in the vase wilted.

el **marco**

1. frame: el marco de la puerta es de madera the door frame is made of wood

2. framework: la exposición se produjo en el marco del congreso the exhibition took place within the framework of the congress.

la **marea** ■ tide: la marea está subiendo the tide is rising

> marea alta high tide
> marea baja low tide
> marea negra oil slick.

marear [1] *verbo* ■ to make sick: el olor a gasolina me marea the smell of petrol makes me feel sick

marearse *verbo pronominal*
1. *en general* to get sick
2. *en avión* to get airsick
3. *en coche* to get carsick.

el **mareo** ■ sickness.

el **marfil** ■ ivory.

a **margarina** ■ margarine.

el **margen** *(plural* los márgenes*)* ■ margin: la maestra puso algunos comentarios en el margen the teacher wrote some comments in the margin; nuestro equipo ganó por un amplio margen our team won by a wide margin
➤ al margen on the fringes of: se mantuvo al margen de la discusión he stayed on the fringes of the discussion.

el **marido** ■ husband.

la **marina** ■ navy: entró en la marina el año pasado he joined the navy last year.

el **marinero** , la **marinera** ■ sailor.

marino, na ■ marine: Felipe estudia geología marina Felipe studies marine geology
➤ una tortuga marina a turtle
➤ el fondo marino the seabed
➤ azul marino navy blue.

la **mariposa** ■ butterfly *(plural* **butterflies***)*.

el **marisco** ■ seafood: me encanta el marisco de Galicia I love seafood from Galicia.

marítimo, ma *adjetivo* ■ maritime.

el **mármol** ■ marble.

marrón *(plural* marrones*) adjetivo* ■ brown: compré una cartera marrón I bought a brown wallet.

el **martes**

En inglés, los días de la semana se escriben con mayúscula:

Tuesday: hoy es martes today is Tuesday; el martes que viene next Tuesday; el martes pasado last Tuesday
➤ el martes on Tuesday: te veré el martes I'll see you on Tuesday
➤ los martes on Tuesdays: los martes vamos al parque on Tuesdays we go to the park

el **martillo** ■ hammer.

marzo *sustantivo masculino*

En inglés los nombres de los meses se escriben con mayúscula:

March: en marzo in March; el próximo marzo next March; el pasado marzo last March.

más *adverbio*
1. **more:** tiene más juguetes que yo he has more toys than I do; no tengo nada más que decirle I have nothing more to say to him
2. **after:** son más de las tres it's after three
3. **better:** me gusta más nadar que correr I like swimming more than running
➤ es el edificio más alto de la ciudad it's the tallest building in the city
➤ de más too much: pagué 100 euros de más I paid 100 euros too much
➤ más bien rather: no fue un accidente, más bien lo hizo a propósito it wasn't an accident, rather he did it on purpose
➤ por más que however much: por más que lo intento, no puedo con estos problemas however much I try I just can't do these exercices.

la **masa**
1. *para tartas* pastry: está preparando una masa para un pastel de manzana she is making pastry for an apple pie
2. *para pan* dough
2. *de gente* crowd: una masa enfurecida tomó las calles a crazed crowd took to the streets.

el **masaje** ■ massage: Pedro le dio un masaje a Ana en la espalda Pedro gave Ana a back massage.

la **máscara** ■ mask.

la **mascota**
1. **pet:** no se permiten mascotas en este piso pets aren't allowed in this flat
2. **mascot:** la mascota del equipo es un oso the team's mascot is a bear.

masculino, na *adjetivo*
1. **male:** la población masculina ha aumentado en esta ciudad the city's male population has increased
2. **men's:** forma parte del equipo masculino de fútbol he's in the men's football team

3. **masculine:** Carla se viste de manera masculina Carla dresses in a masculine way.

masticar [8] *verbo* ■ **to chew:** es aconsejable masticar bien la comida you should chew your food well.

el **mástil** ■ **mast.**

matar [1] *verbo* ■ **to kill:** mataron a personas inocentes they killed innocent people; me mata tener que madrugar it kills me having to get up so early

matarse *verbo pronominal*

1. **to die, to be killed:** se mató en un accidente de avión he died o he was killed in a plane crash
2. **to kill oneself:** se mató con una pistola he killed himself with a pistol.

las **matemáticas** ■ **mathematics.**

la **materia**

1. **matter:** estudia la transformación de la materia he's studying the transformation of matter
2. **subject:** la materia que más me gusta es química my favourite subject is chemistry
   > materia gris grey matter
   > materia prima raw material.

el **material**

1. **material:** trajeron los materiales para construir la casa they brought all the materials for building the house
2. **subject matter:** el material que contiene esta revista es muy interesante the subject matter in this magazine is very interesting.

materno, na *adjetivo* ■ **maternal:** mi abuelo materno era arquitecto my maternal grandfather was an architect.

la **matrícula**

1. **enrolment** *UK,* **enrollment** *US:* ya he pagado la matrícula del curso I've paid the course enrolment fee
2. *placa de coche* **number plate** *UK,* **license plate** *US*
3. *número* **registration number:** ¿qué matrícula tienes? what's your registration number?

el **matrimonio**

1. **marriage:** éste es su segundo matrimonio it's his second marriage
2. **couple:** salimos con un matrimonio de ingenieros we went out with a couple who are both engineers
   > un matrimonio civil a civil wedding
   > un matrimonio religioso a church wedding.

máximo, ma *adjetivo*

1. **maximum:** hay un plazo máximo de tres meses the maximum period is three months
2. **highest:** es el máximo goleador del campeonato he was the highest scorer in the championships.
   > como máximo

1. **at the most:** nos costará como máximo 20 euros it'll cost us 20 euros at the most
2. **at the latest:** llegaré a las 8 como máximo I'll get there by 8 o'clock at the latest.

mayo *sustantivo masculino*

En inglés los nombres de los meses se escriben con mayúscula:

May: en mayo in May; el próximo mayo next May; el pasado mayo last May.

la **mayonesa** ■ **mayonnaise.**

mayor *adjetivo (comparative & superlative of* grande)

1. **bigger:** la casa nueva tiene un tamaño mayor que la vieja the new house is bigger than the old one
2. **older:** mi hermano mayor es soltero my older brother is single
3. **elderly:** mi abuelo ya es una persona mayor my grandfather is an elderly man
4. **greatest:** es uno de los mayores músicos de su época he's one of the greatest musicians of his era
   > de mayor quiero ser médico when I grow up I want to be a doctor
   > ser mayor de edad to be of age: Francisco ya puede votar porque es mayor de edad Francisco can vote because he's of age

el/la **mayor**

1. **adult:** es una película para mayores the film is only for adults

2. eldest: es el mayor de todos los hermanos he's the eldest of the brothers; **la mayor de las hermanas es ingeniera** the eldest of the sisters is an engineer.

la **mayoría** ■ majority *(plural* **majorities***)*: la mayoría de los alumnos aprobó el curso the majority of the students passed the course; **el partido de izquierdas obtuvo la mayoría en el parlamento** the left-wing party obtained a majority in parliament.

mayúscula *adjetivo* ■ capital letter: no olvides escribir los nombres propios con letra mayúscula don't forget to write proper nouns with a capital letter

la **mayúscula** ■ capital: los nombres propios se escriben con mayúscula proper nouns are written with a capital.

el **mazapán** *(plural* los mazapanes*) sustantivo masculino* ■ marzipan.

me *pronombre*

1. me: préstame tu libro lend me your book; **me quiere mucho** she loves me a lot

2. myself: me he hecho daño I've hurt myself
> me voy a lavar las manos I'm going to wash my hands
> a mí me gusta mucho cantar I really like to sing
> me eché una buena siesta I took a good nap.

la **mecánica** ■ mechanics: estudió mecánica he studied mechanics.

el **mecánico** , la **mecánica** ■ mechanic.

el **mechero** ■ lighter.

la **medalla**

1. medallion: le regalaron una medalla de oro she was given a gold medallion

2. medal: ganó una medalla en los Juegos Olímpicos he won a medal in the Olympic Games
> medalla de bronce bronze medal
> medalla de oro gold medal
> medalla de plata silver medal.

la **media** ■ average: tienes que calcular la media entre estos números you have to work out the average of these numbers

las **medias**
1. *hasta la cintura* tights *UK*, **pantyhose** *US*
2. *hasta el muslo* **stockings**.

mediano, na *adjetivo*
1. medium: mi hermana es de mediana estatura my sister is of medium height; **esta caja es de tamaño mediano** this is a medium-sized box
2. average: es una persona de mediana inteligencia he is a person of average intelligence.

la **medianoche** ■ midnight: llegaron a medianoche they arrived at midnight.

mediante *adverbio* ■ by means of: lograron curar la enfermedad mediante un nuevo método they managed to cure the disease by means of a new method.

el **medicamento** ■ medicine.

la **medicina** ■ medicine: estudia medicina she's studying medicine; **le recetaron una nueva medicina** he was prescribed a new medicine.

el **médico** , la **médica** ■ doctor: el médico de cabecera general practitioner
> ir al médico to go to the doctor's.

la **medida**
1. measurement: el sastre tomó las medidas al cliente the tailor took his client's measurements
2. measure: la policía tomó estrictas medidas de seguridad the police took strict security measures
> a medida custom-made: se mandó hacer un traje a medida he ordered a custom-made suit
> a medida que as: a medida que me dieron los regalos fueron entrando they gave me the presents as they came in.

medio, a *adjetivo*
1. half: se tomaron media botella de vino they drank half a bottle of wine
2. average: la temperatura media es de 25 grados centígrados the average temperature is 25 degrees centigrade
> son las cuatro y media it's half past four

■ *adverbio*

half: la niña estaba medio dormida cuando llegamos the little girl was half asleep when we arrived

▶ a medias

1. **half-finished:** he dejado el trabajo a medias I left the work hal-finished

2. **half each:** hemos pagado a medias we paid half each

el **medio** ■ **middle:** hay un monumento en el medio de la plaza there is a monument in the middle of the square

▶ en medio **between:** me senté en medio de mis dos amigas I sat between my two friends

▶ el medio ambiente the environment

▶ los medios de comunicación the media

▶ un medio de transporte a means of transport.

el **mediodía**

1. **noon, mid-day:** la ceremonia empieza a las 12 del mediodía the ceremony begins at 12 noon

2. **lunchtime:** a mediodía he comido un bocadillo I had a sandwich at lunchtime

---

MEDIODÍA

In some Spanish-speaking countries **mediodía** means 12 o'clock noon, while in others it refers to "lunchtime," which can take place anywhere between noon and three o'clock in the afternoon. To avoid confusion, make sure you know what time a person means when you agree to meet them at **mediodía** .

---

medir [19] *verbo* ■ **to measure:** ¿has medido la pared? have you measured the wall?; la mesa mide más de un metro the table is more than a metre across

▶ ¿cuánto mides? how tall are you?

mediterráneo, a *adjetivo* ■ **Mediterranean**

el **Mediterráneo** ■ **the Mediterranean.**

la **mejilla** ■ **cheek.**

el **mejillón** (*plural* los mejillones) ■ **mussel.**

mejor (*adjetivo & adverbio*)

■ *adjetivo (comparative & superlative of* bueno)

1. **better:** tiene un coche mejor que el mío she has a better car than I do

2. **best:** Susana es mi mejor amiga Susana is my best friend

■ *adverbio*

better: Ricardo juega al fútbol mejor que yo Ricardo plays football better than I do

▶ ¿te encuentras mejor? are you feeling better?

el/la **mejor** ■ **the best:** es la mejor de la clase she's the best in the class.

Melilla ■ **Melilla**

melillense *adjetivo* ■ **of** o **relating to Melilla.**

el/la **melillense** ■ **inhabitant** o **native of Melilla.**

mejorar [1] *verbo* ■ **to improve:** el tiempo mejoró the weather improved

mejorarse *verbo pronominal;* ■ **to get better:** ¡que te mejores! get better soon!

el **mellizo** , la **melliza** ■ **twin.**

el **melocotón** (*plural* los melocotones) ■ **peach.**

la **melodía** ■ **melody** (*plural* **melodies**).

el **melón** (*plural* los melones) ■ **melon.**

la **memoria** ■ **memory** (*plural* **memories**): Agustín tiene una memoria increíble Agustín has an incredible memory; quiero ampliar la memoria de mi ordenador I want to expand my computer's memory

▶ de memoria **by heart:** sabe de memoria las tablas de multiplicar she knows the multiplication tables by heart.

memorizar [10] *verbo* ■ **to memorize:** memorizó un largo poema he memorized a long poem.

mencionar [1] *verbo* ■ **to mention:** mencionó que iba a llegar tarde she mentioned she would be late.

el **mendigo** , la **mendiga** ■ **beggar.**

menor *adjetivo* ■ **younger:** soy menor de lo que parezco I'm younger than I look

▶ Raúl es el hijo menor de mis tíos Raúl is my aunt and uncle's youngest son

▶ se irrita frente al menor problema she gets upset at the slightest problem no tengo la menor idea I don't have the slightest idea

la **menor** ■ youngest: el menor de los dos hermanos es ingeniero the youngest of the two brothers is an engineer; es la menor de la clase she's the youngest in the class

> está prohibida la venta de cigarrillos a menores the sale of cigarettes to minors is against the law

> menor de edad minor.

menos (preposición, adverbio & adjetivo)

■ preposición

1. minus: diez menos cinco es cinco ten minus five is five

2. except: fuimos todos menos Ricardo we all went except for Ricardo

■ adverbio

less: la película es menos interesante de lo que me esperaba the film is less interesting than I thought

■ adjetivo

1. comparativo – delante de un sustantivo singular less: gana menos dinero que tú he earns less money than you

2. comparativo – delante de un sustantivo plural fewer: había menos gente que en la primera función there were fewer people than at the first performance

3. superlativo – delante de un sustantivo singular the least: los países donde hay menos desempleo countries where there's the least unemployment

4. superlativo – delante de un sustantivo plural the fewest: la clase con menos alumnos the class with the fewest pupils

> son las once menos cinco it's five to eleven

> al menos at least: había al menos 1.000 personas there were at least 1,000 people

> de menos too little: me dieron 20 euros de menos they gave me 20 euros too little

> menos mal just as well: menos mal que dejó de llover just as well it stopped raining

> por lo menos at least: pesa por lo menos 80 kilos he weighs at least 80 kilos.

el **mensaje** ■ message: dejé el mensaje en el contestador I left a message on the answering machine.

el **mensajero** , la **mensajera** ■ messenger: trabaja de mensajero en una oficina he works as a messenger in an office.

mensual adjetivo ■ monthly: es una revista mensual it's a monthly magazine.

la **menta** ■ mint: unos caramelos de menta mints.

la **mente** ■ mind: Lucía tiene una mente brillante Lucía has a brilliant mind

> quedarse con la mente en blanco to go blank: me quedé con la mente en blanco en medio del examen my mind went blank in the middle of the exam

> tener en mente to have in mind: tengo en mente la persona ideal para el trabajo I have the perfect person in mind for the job.

mentir [20] verbo ■ to lie: no me mientas más don't lie to me anymore.

la **mentira** ■ lie: lo castigaron por decir mentiras he was punished for telling lies.

mentiroso, sa adjetivo ■ liar: es la persona más mentirosa que conozco she's the biggest liar I know

el **mentiroso** , la **mentirosa** ■ liar: detesto a los mentirosos I hate liars.

el **menú** ■ menu: el menú del día set menu; el menú desplegable drop-down menu.

menudo, da adjetivo

1. small: la carta estaba escrita con letra menuda the letter was written in small handwriting

2. finely: pica la cebolla muy menuda chop the onion very finely

> ¡menuda sorpresa! what a surprise!

> a menudo often: a menudo acompaño a mi abuela a misa I often go to mass with my grandmother.

el **meñique** ■ little finger.

el **mercado** ■ market: hicimos las compras en el mercado we did our shopping in the market

> el mercado negro the black market

> el mercado de valores the stock market.

la **mercancía** ■ **goods:** nos vendieron mercancía dañada they sold us damaged goods.

merecer [22] *verbo* ■ **to deserve:** merece que le castiguen he deserves to be punished

merecerse *verbo pronominal* ■ **to deserve:** se merece unas buenas vacaciones he deserves a good holiday.

merendar [14] *verbo* ■ **to have an afternoon snack:** merendamos en casa de unos amigos we had an afternoon snack at our friends' house.

el **merengue** ■ **meringue.**

la **merienda** ■ **afternoon snack:** tomamos la merienda en casa de unos amigos we had an afternoon snack at our friends' house.

el **mérito** ■ **merit.**

la **merluza** ■ **hake.**

la **mermelada**
1. *de cítricos* **marmalade**
2. *de otras frutas* **jam.**

el **mes** ■ **month:** el mes que más me gusta es diciembre my favorite month is December
> **estar de tres meses** to be three months pregnant: **María está justo de tres meses** María is barely three months pregnant.

la **mesa** ■ **table:** compré una mesa nueva para el comedor I bought a new table for the dining room
> **poner la mesa** to set the table: **puso la mesa antes de que llegaran los invitados** she set the table before the guests arrived
> **quitar la mesa** to clear the table: **quitó la mesa cuando los invitados se fueron** he cleared the table when the guests had left
> **¡a la mesa!** dinner is ready!

la **meseta** ■ **plateau.**

la **meta**
1. **goal:** nuestra meta es triunfar our goal is to succeed
2. **finishing line:** el deportista colombiano fue el primero en cruzar la meta the Colombian athlete was the first to cross the finishing line.

el **metal** ■ **metal:** el oro es un metal noble gold is a precious metal.

meter [2] *verbo*
1. **to put:** metió toda su ropa en una maleta he put all his clothes in a suitcase; **metieron al niño en una escuela privada** they put the boy in a private school
2. **to score:** metió el gol ganador she scored the winning goal

meterse *verbo pronominal*
1. **to go:** se metió en el cuarto equivocado she went into the wrong room
2. **to go in:** no te metas en el agua después de comer don't go in the water after eating
3. **to pry into:** no te metas en mi vida don't pry into my life
> **meterse con** to pick on: **se metieron con Luis en el recreo** they picked on Luis at playtime.

el **método** ■ **method:** inventaron un nuevo método de enseñanza de lenguas they invented a new method for teaching languages.

el **metro**
1. **metre** *UK*, **meter** *US*: José mide casi dos metros José is nearly two meters tall
2. **underground** *UK*, **subway** *US*: tomamos el metro para ir al centro de la ciudad we took the underground into the city
3. **tape measure:** necesito el metro para medir la puerta I need the tape measure to measure the door
> **un metro cuadrado** a square meter
> **un metro cúbico** a cubic metre.

México ■ **Mexico.**

mexicano, na *adjetivo*

En inglés, los adjetivos que se refieren a un continente o a un país se escriben con mayúscula:

Mexican: me interesa mucho la cultura mexicana I'm very interested in Mexican culture

el **mexicano** , la **mexicana**

En inglés los gentilicios se escriben con mayúscula:

Mexican: los mexicanos the Mexicans.

la **mezcla** ■ mixture: preparamos una mezcla de aceite y vinagre we made a mixture of oil and vinegar.

mezclar [1] *verbo* ■ to mix: mezcló los ingredientes en un bol she mixed the ingredients in a bowl

> no se mezcló con la gente del lugar he didn't mix with the locals.

mi *adjetivo* ■ my: mi casa queda en la playa my house is on the beach.

mí *pronombre* ■ me: el regalo es para mí the present is for me

> me gusta reflexionar sobre mí misma I like to think about myself.

el **micro** *(abreviatura de* micrófono*)* ■ mike.

el **microbio** ■ microbe.

el **micrófono** ■ microphone.

el **microondas** *(plural* los microondas*)* sustantivo masculino ■ microwave.

el **microscopio** ■ microscope.

el **miedo** ■ fear: está paralizado por el miedo he's paralyzed by fear

> dar miedo algo a alguien to scare someone: me da miedo volar I'm scared of flying; me dan miedo las serpientes I'm frightened of snakes

> tener miedo to be afraid, to be frightened: tiene miedo a los perros he's afraid of dog.

la **miel** ■ honey.

el **miembro**

1. limb: los miembros inferiores del ser humano son las piernas the legs are a human being's lower limbs

2. member: es miembro de un club deportivo he's a member of a sports club.

mientras *adverbio* ■ while: empezó a llover mientras caminaba it started to rain while she was walking; conserva tu trabajo mientras puedas keep your job while you can

> mientras me pondré a estudiar I'll study in the meantime

> no vayas mientras no te inviten don't go if you haven't been invited

> mientras que while, whereas: tú has ganado, mientras que yo he quedado el último you've won whereas I came last.

el **miércoles** *(plural* los miércoles*)*

En inglés, los días de la semana se escriben con mayúscula:

Wednesday: hoy es miércoles today is Wednesday; el miércoles que viene next Wednesday; el miércoles pasado last Wednesday

> el miércoles on Wednesday: te veré el miércoles I'll see you on Wednesday

> los miércoles on Wednesdays: los miércoles vamos al parque on Wednesdays we go to the park.

la **miga** ■ crumb.

mil *numeral* ■ thousand: esta tele cuesta más de mil euros this TV costs over a thousand euros; acudieron miles de personas thousands of people came.

el **milagro** ■ miracle: es un milagro que sobreviviera al accidente it's a miracle she survived the accident

> de milagro miraculously: se salvó de milagro she miraculously survived.

militar *adjetivo* ■ military: ha ingresado en la escuela militar he joined military school

el/la **militar** ■ soldier: mi abuelo era militar my grandfather was a soldier

> los militares tomaron el poder the military took power.

el **millón** *(plural* los millones*)* ■ million: gastó millones en la reforma de la casa he spent millions on alterations to the house; tengo un millón de problemas I have a million problems.

el **millonario** , la **millonaria** ■ millionaire.

mimar [1] *verbo* ■ to spoil: todos miman a la pequeña they all spoil the little girl.

la **mina**

1. mine: la mina está abandonada the mine is abandoned

2. lead: se me rompió la mina del lápiz the lead in my pencil broke.

el **mineral** ■ mineral.

el **minero** , la **minera** ■ miner: algunos mineros trabajan en condiciones inhumanas some miners work in very inhuman conditions.

mínimo, ma *adjetivo*

1. minimum: paga la tarifa mínima he pays the minimum fare
2. minute: la distancia entre las dos ciudades era mínima the distance between the two cities was minute

el **mínimo** ■ minimum: quieren reducir los gastos al mínimo they want to cut costs to the minimum; lo mínimo sería darle las gracias a Juan por su ayuda the minimum would be to thank Juan for his help.

el **ministerio** ■ ministry *(plural* **ministries***)*, department *US*
> Ministerio de Defensa Ministry of Defence, Defense Department
> Ministerio de Hacienda Treasury *UK*, Treasury Department *US*.

el **ministro** , la **ministra**

1. minister, secretary *US (plural* **secretaries***)*: Ministro de Asuntos Exteriores Foreign Minister *UK*, Secretary of State *US*; Ministro de Hacienda Chancellor of the Exchequer *UK*, Secretary of the Treasury *US*
2. minister: la ministra habló en la ceremonia religiosa the minister spoke at the religious ceremony.

la **minoría** ■ minority *(plural* **minorities***)*: una minoría de la población es analfabeta a minority of the population is illiterate
> las minorías étnicas ethnic minorities.

la **minúscula** ■ lower-case letter.

minusválido, da *adjetivo* ■ disabled: las personas minusválidas piden igualdad de oportunidades disabled people are calling for the same opportunities

el **minusválido** , la **minusválida** ■ disabled person.

el **minuto** ■ minute: espera un minuto, por favor wait a minute, please.

mío *adjetivo & pronombre* ■ mine: ese perro es mío that dog is mine; su casa es muy bonita pero la mía es más grande her house is very pretty, but mine is bigger.

miope *adjetivo* ■ short-sighted *UK*, near-sighted *US*.

la **mirada**

1. look: con una sola mirada me entendió he understood me with just one look
2. gaze: Antonio tiene una mirada penetrante Antonio has a penetrating gaze.

mirar [1] *verbo*

1. to look: miraba por la ventana she was looking out of the window; mira si tienes suficiente dinero look and see if you have enough money
2. to check: me miraron las maletas en la aduana they checked my suitcases at customs
3. to peek: miraron por un agujero they peeked through a hole
4. to watch out: ¡mira lo que haces! watch what you're doing!
> mirar hacia adelante to look in front of you: mira hacia adelante cuando camines look in front of you when you're walking
> mirar hacia arriba to look up: el niño miró hacia arriba en busca de su globo the boy looked up in search of his balloon

mirarse *verbo pronominal*

1. to look at yourself: se miró en el espejo del pasillo she looked at herself in the mirror in the corridor
2. to look at each other: se miraron con complicidad they looked at each other complicity.

la **misa** ■ mass.

la **miseria**

1. poverty: vivían en la absoluta miseria they lived in absolute poverty
2. pittance: gana una miseria she earns a pittance.

la **misión** *(plural* las misiones*)* ■ mission: el embajador tuvo la misión de continuar el proceso de paz the ambassador's mission was to further the peace process.

mismo, ma *adjetivo*

1. same: llevo la misma camisa que ayer I'm wearing the same shirt I wore yesterday

2. **myself:** yo misma lo vi I saw him myself

3. **exact:** repetí sus mismas palabras I repeated her exact words

o **mismo**, la **misma** *pronombre* ■ **same:** María ya no es la misma de antes María just isn't the same any more; **siempre dice lo mismo** he always says the same

lo mismo (...) que the same (...) as: **no es lo mismo cocinar para dos que para una familia** cooking for two is not the same as cooking for a family

mismo *adverbio* ■ **right:** aparcó delante mismo de mi casa he parked right in front of my house; **ahora mismo vuelvo** I'll be right back.

el **misterio** ■ **mystery** (plural **mysteries**).

la **mitad** ■ **half:** nos comimos la mitad del postre we ate half the dessert; **la mitad de los estudiantes ha aprobado** over half the students have passed

cortar algo por la mitad to cut something in half: **corta la cebolla por la mitad** cut the onion in half

a mitad de precio half-price

a mitad de camino half-way.

mixto, ta *adjetivo*

1. **mixed:** comí una ensalada mixta I ate a mixed salad

2. **co-educational:** es una escuela mixta it's a co-educational school.

la **mochila** ■ **rucksack.**

la **moda** ■ **fashion:** el mundo de la moda the fashion world

estar de moda to be in fashion: **ahora están de moda los pantalones anchos** wide trousers are now in fashion

ir a la moda to be fashionable: **siempre quiere ir a la moda** she always wants to be fashionable

ponerse de moda to come into fashion: **el tango se puso de moda** the tango has come into fashion.

los **modales** ■ **manners:** tiene muy buenos modales he has very nice manners.

el/la **modelo** ■ **model:** quiere ser modelo she wants to be a model

el **modelo** ■ **model:** haz un dibujo siguiendo el modelo do a drawing according to the model; **ha salido un nuevo modelo de lavadora** a new model of washing machine has come out.

moderno, na *adjetivo* ■ **modern:** vivimos en una casa moderna we live in a modern house.

modesto, ta *adjetivo* ■ **modest:** es un hombre modesto y no presume de nada he's a modest man and doesn't show off about anything; **compramos un apartamento modesto** we bought a modest apartment.

modificar [8] *verbo*

1. **to alter:** debes modificar todo el texto you have to alter the whole text

2. **to modify:** los adjetivos modifican a los sustantivos adjectives modify nouns.

el **modo**

1. **way:** tiene un modo especial de caminar he has a special way of walking

2. **manners:** la dependienta de la tienda tiene muy malos modos the shop assistant has very bad manners

3. **mood:** estuvimos practicando el modo subjuntivo en clase de español we practiced the subjunctive mood in Spanish class

de modo que so that: **explicó la situación de modo que todos la entendiéramos** he explained the situation so that we would all understand it

de todos modos anyway: **de todos modos, tu comportamiento me parece lamentable** anyway, your behaviour is deplorable

de ningún modo no way: **¿iremos a la fiesta?—¡de ningún modo!** are we going to the party?—no way!

mojar [1] *verbo*

1. **to wet:** mojé el suelo de la cocina I wet the kitchen floor

2. **to dip:** el niño mojó el pan en la sopa the boy dipped his bread in his soup

mojarse *verbo pronominal* ■ **to get wet:** nos mojamos con la lluvia we got wet in the rain.

el **molde** ■ **cake tin** *UK*, **cake pan** *US*: hice el pastel en un molde redondo I made the cake in a round cake tin.

moler [17] *verbo* ■ **to grind**: molió el grano del café he ground the coffee beans.

molestar [1] *verbo*

1. **to annoy**: me molesta la impuntualidad de la gente people who aren't punctual annoy me
2. **to bother**: no molestes a Juan mientras trabaja don't bother Juan while he's working
1. **to mind**: ¿te molesta que fume? do you mind if I smoke?
4. **to hurt**: le molestan los zapatos nuevos his new shoes hurt him

 The Spanish word **molestar** is a false friend, it does not mean "to molest".

molestarse *verbo pronominal*

1. **to get upset**: Irene se molestó con Silvia por lo que le dijo Irene got upset with Silvia because of what she said
2. **to bother**: ni se ha molestado en levantarse he didn't even bother to get up.

la **molestia**

1. **hassle**: espero no causarte ninguna molestia I don't want to cause you any hassle
2. **pain**: siento algunas molestias en la pierna I have some pains in my leg
▷ no ser ninguna molestia to be no trouble at all: no es ninguna molestia prestarte dinero it's no trouble at all to lend you some money
▷ tomarse la molestia to take the trouble: se tomó la molestia de pasar a visitarme he took the trouble to stop by and visit me.

molesto, ta *adjetivo*

1. **annoying**: el goteo del grifo es muy molesto the dripping of the tap is very annoying
2. **uncomfortable**: el paciente se siente molesto porque el dolor no cede the patient is uncomfortable because the pain hasn't receded.

el **molino** ■ **mill**
un molino de agua a watermill
un molino de viento a windmill.

el **momento**

1. **moment**: en el momento en que yo salía, ella entraba she walked in the moment I was

leaving; fueron momentos de mucha angustia they were of great distress moments
2. **minute**: estaré lista en un momento I'll be ready in just a minute
3. **opportunity** (*plural* **opportunities**): aproveché el momento para escaparme de la fiesta I took the opportunity to escape from the party
▷ de momento for the moment: de momento no necesito nada más for the moment I don't need anything else
▷ de un momento a otro any minute now: van a llegar de un momento a otro they'll be here any minute now.

la **monarquía** ■ **monarchy**.

el **monasterio** ■ **monastery** (*plural* **monasteries**).

la **moneda**

1. **coin**: necesito cambio en monedas I need some change in coins
2. **currency** (*plural* **currencies**): la moneda de la Unión Europea es el euro the currency of the European Union is the euro.

el **monedero** ■ **purse** *UK*, **change purse** *US*.

el **monitor** , la **monitora** ■ **monitor**.

la **monja** ■ **nun**.

el **monje** ■ **monk**.

mono, na *adjetivo* ■ **pretty**: tiene una habitación muy mona she has a very pretty room

el **mono** , la **mona** ■ **monkey**

el **mono** ■ **coveralls**: los mecánicos usan un mono azul the mechanics wear blue coveralls.

el **monopatín** (*plural* los monopatines) ■ **skateboard**.

monótono, na *adjetivo* ■ **monotonous**: tengo un trabajo muy monótono I have a very monotonous job.

el **monovolumen** (*plural* los monopatines) ■ **people carrier**.

el **monstruo** ■ **monster**.

la **montaña** ■ **mountain**
▷ una montaña rusa a roller coaster.

montar [1] *verbo*

1. to ride: montar en bicicleta to ride a bicycle; montamos a caballo durante las vacaciones we went horse riding during our holidays

2. to set up: montó una exposición de arte moderno he set up a modern art exhibition

3. assemble: ¿me ayudas a montar el armario? can you help me to assemble the cupboard?

el **monte**

1. mountain: los montes de la zona son de poca altura the mountains around here aren't very high

2. scrubland: el ladrón se escondió en el monte the thief hid in the scrubland.

el **montón** (*plural* los montones)

1. pile: en ese montón de fotos debe estar la que busco the picture I'm looking for must be in that pile

2. load: había montones de gente en el concierto there were loads of people at the concert

> ser del montón to be average: es un chico del montón it's just an average guy.

el **monumento** ■ monument: levantaron un monumento en honor al poeta they built a monument in honour of the poet.

el **moño** ■ bun: se recoge el pelo en un moño she puts her hair in a bun.

la **moqueta** ■ fitted carpet.

la **mora** ■ blackberry (*plural* blackberries): he hecho una mermelada de moras buenísima I've made a delicious blackberry jam.

la **moral**

1. morals, morality: es una persona de dudosa moral he's a person of questionable morals

2. morale: no hay que dejar que decaiga la moral del grupo we have to keep up the group's morale.

la **morcilla** ■ black pudding.

morder [17] *verbo* ■ to bite: el cachorro me mordió el tobillo the puppy bit me on the ankle; me mordí la lengua I bit my tongue; me muerdo las uñas I bite my nails.

el **mordisco** ■ bite: ¿me das un mordisco de tu bocadillo? can I have a bite of your sandwich?

> dar un mordisco to bite: el perro me dio un mordisco the dog bit me.

moreno, na *adjetivo*

1. tanned, brown: mi hermana tiene la piel morena por el sol my sister's skin is tanned from the sun; estás muy morena you're very brown

2. dark: Luis es de piel morena Luis has dark skin; Sara tiene el pelo moreno Sara has dark hair

> azúcar moreno brown sugar.

morir [18] *verbo* ■ to die: su tío murió en un accidente her uncle died in an accident

morirse *verbo pronominal* ■ to die: su gato se ha muerto her cat has died

> morirse de aburrimiento to die of boredom: me moría de aburrimiento en la clase I was dying of boredom in class

> morirse de frío to be freezing: cierra la ventana o me moriré de frío close the window or I'll freeze

> morirse de hambre to be starving: todavía no hemos comido y yo me muero de hambre we haven't had lunch yet and I'm starving

> morirse de miedo to be terrified: se muere de miedo cuando se queda sola en casa she's terrified when she's alone in the house

> morirse por hacer algo to be dying to do something: me muero por comer un bocadillo de atún I'm dying for a tuna sandwich

> morirse de sueño to be tired out: anoche salí y hoy me muero de sueño I went out yesterday night and today I'm tired out.

mortal *adjetivo*

1. fatal: tiene una enfermedad mortal she has a fatal disease

2. mortal: todos somos seres mortales we're all mortal

3. deadly: la película es de un aburrimiento mortal the film was deadly boring.

la **mosca** ■ fly (*plural* flies).

el **mosquito** ■ mosquito.

la **mostaza** ■ mustard.

el **mostrador**

1. *de tienda* counter
2. *de aeropuerto* check-in desk.

mostrar [16] *verbo* ■ to show: la vendedora nos mostró una camisa carísima the saleswoman showed us a very expensive shirt; un policía me mostró cómo llegar al museo a policeman showed me how to get to the museum.

el **mote** ■ nickname.

el **motivo**

1. reason: la maestra explicó el motivo de su ausencia the teacher explained the reason for her absence
2. motif: dibujó unos motivos navideños she drew some Christmas motifs
> con motivo de for: viajó a Perú con motivo de un congreso he travelled to Peru for a conference
> motivo de divorcio grounds for divorce.

la **moto** *(abreviatura de* motocicleta*)* ■ motorcycle, motorbike *UK*.

la **motocicleta** ■ motorcycle, motorbike *UK*.

el **motor** ■ engine: se rompió el motor del coche the car's engine died.

el/la **motorista** ■ motorcyclist.

mover [17] *verbo*

1. to move: movió la silla he moved the chair; te toca mover it's your turn to move
2. to handle: mueven grandes cantidades de dinero they handle large sums of money

moverse *verbo pronominal* ■ to move: muévete un poco hacia aquí move this way a little; el barco se movió durante todo el trayecto the boat swayed during the whole trip; ¡no te muevas! don't move!

el **móvil**

1. motive: se desconoce el móvil del crimen the motive of the crime is unknown
2. *UK* mobile, *US* cell: llámame al móvil esta tarde call me on my mobile this afternoon.

el **movimiento**

1. movement: hizo un movimiento con la mano he made a movement with his hand
2. activity: hay mucho movimiento en la calle there is a lot of activity in the street.

el **muchacho** , la **muchacha** ■ kid: los muchachos fueron al cine the kids went to the cinema

la **muchacha** ■ maid: mi casa está hecha un desastre porque estoy sin muchacha my house is a mess because I don't have a maid.

la **muchedumbre** ■ crowd.

mucho, cha *adjetivo & adverbio*

1. a lot of: tengo muchos lápices de colores I have a lot of colored pencils
2. much: no tuvo mucha suerte he didn't have much luck
> hoy hace mucho calor it's very hot today
> hace mucho tiempo que no lo veo it's been a long time since I've seen him

mucho *adverbio*

1. a lot: sabe mucho de filosofía he knows a lot about philosophy
2. much: soy mucho mayor que mi hermana I'm much older than my sister.

mudarse [1] *verbo pronominal* ■ to move: se mudaron a la ciudad they moved to the city.

mudo, da *adjetivo*

1. dumb, mute: se quedó muda como consecuencia de un golpe en la cabeza she went dumb after a blow to the head
2. silent: la "h" es la única letra muda del español "h" is the only silent letter in Spanish

el **mudo** , la **muda** ■ dumb person *(plural* dumb people*)*, mute: hay una escuela para mudos en el barrio there is a school for dumb people in the neighbourhood.

el **mueble** ■ piece of furniture: un mueble bonito a very nice piece of furniture; los muebles the furniture; compré muebles nuevos I bought new furniture.

la **muela** ■ tooth *(plural* teeth*)*: tengo un fuerte dolor de muelas I have a strong toothache
> una muela del juicio a wisdom tooth.

el muelle
1. *de puerto* **dock, quay:** descargaron las mercancías en el muelle they unloaded the foods at the dock
2. *de río* **wharf:** el barco atracó en el muelle the boat docked at the wharf
3. **spring:** compramos un colchón con muelles resistentes we bought a mattress with strong springs.

la muerte ■ **death:** muchas personas creen que hay vida después de la muerte many people believe there is life after death; fueron condenados a muerte they were condemned to death.

muerto, ta *adjetivo* ■ **dead:** encontramos un perro muerto en la carretera we found a dead dog on the road
➤ estar muerto de cansancio to be dead beat

el muerto , la muerta ■ **dead person:** había un muerto en la acera there was a dead person on the pavement
➤ afortunadamente no hubo muertos en el accidente fortunately no one was killed in the accident.

la muestra
1. **sample:** nos regalaron una muestra de perfume they gave us a perfume sample; le sacaron una muestra de sangre they took a blood sample from him
2. **pattern:** usaron mi vestido como muestra they used my dress as a pattern.

la mujer
1. **woman** *(plural* **women***):* las mujeres de la familia organizaron una fiesta the women in the family organized a party
2. **wife** *(plural* **wives***):* Gonzalo me presentó a su mujer Gonzalo introduced me to his wife
➤ una mujer policía a policewoman.

la muleta ■ **crutch:** hace un mes que lleva muletas he's been on crutches for a month.

la multa ■ **fine:** una multa de 150 euros a 150-euro fine
➤ poner una multa to fine.

la multiplicación *(plural* las multiplicaciones*)* ■ **multiplication:** el niño es muy bueno haciendo multiplicaciones the boy is very good at multiplication.

multiplicar [8] *verbo*
1. **to multiply:** multiplica 48 por 2 multiply 48 by 2
2. **to increase rapidly:** se ha multiplicado la pobreza en esta región poverty has increased rapidly in this region.

la multitud ■ **crowd:** una multitud de admiradores fue al concierto a crowd of fans attended the concert.

mundial *adjetivo* ■ **world:** una guerra mundial a world war
➤ el hambre es un problema de escala mundial hunger is a problem on a worldwide scale

el mundial ■ **world championships:** el mundial de Ciclismo the World Cycling Championship; el mundial de Fútbol del 2002 se jugó en Japón y Corea the 2002 World Cup took place in Japan and Korea.

el mundo ■ **world:** quieren dar la vuelta al mundo they want to go around the world; me atrae el mundo del deporte I'm attracted by the world of sports
➤ todo el mundo everybody, everyone: todo el mundo se enteró del secreto de Adriana everybody found out about Adriana's secret
➤ el tercer mundo the Third World.

municipal *adjetivo* ■ **municipal:** han construido una piscina municipal they've built a municipal swimming pool.

la muñeca
1. **wrist:** se cayó y se rompió la muñeca derecha she fell and broke her right wrist
2. **doll:** se entretiene todo el día con sus muñecas she's happy playing with her dolls all day.

la muralla ■ **wall:** están construyendo una muralla defensiva they're building a defensive wall.

Murcia ■ **Murcia.**

murciano, na *adjetivo*

En inglés, los adjetivos que se refieren a un país o una región se escriben con mayúscula:

Murcian: la costa murciana the Murcian coast

el **murciano** , la **murciana**

> En inglés, los gentilicios se escriben con mayúscula:

Murcian: los murcianos the Murcians.

el **murciélago** ■ bat.

murmurar [1] *verbo*

1. **to murmur:** se enfadó y salió de casa murmurando algo que no entendí he got angry and left the house murmuring something I didn't catch

2. **to gossip:** se pasan el tiempo murmurando sobre ella they spend all their time gossiping about her

el **muro** ■ **wall:** los muros de los castillos medievales eran de piedra the walls of medieval castles were made of stone.

el **músculo** ■ muscle.

el **museo** ■ museum
> museo de ciencias naturales natural history museum

EL MUSEO DEL PRADO

 Madrid's **Museo del Prado** (Prado Museum) is one of the world's biggest museums. Highlights of its major collections of paintings include masterpieces by Velázquez and Goya.

---

la **música** ■ **music:** me gusta la música pop I like pop music
> música clásica classical music
> música de fondo background music.

el **músico** , la **música** ■ musician.

el **muslo** ■ thigh.

el **musulmán** , la **musulmana** *(plural* los musulmanes) ■ Muslim.

mutuo, tua *adjetivo* ■ mutual.

muy *adverbio*

1. **very:** dicen que esa película es muy buena they say that film is very good; hizo el examen muy mal he did the exam very badly; juega muy mal al fútbol he plays football very well

2. **too:** este pantalón no me sirve, es muy corto para mí these trousers are no good, they're too short for me.

el **nabo** ■ turnip.

nacer [22] *verbo* ■ **to be born:** Diana nació en 1992 Diana was born in 1992.

el **nacimiento** ■ **birth:** el nacimiento del bebé llenó de alegría a la familia the birth of the baby filled the family with joy
> fecha de nacimiento date of birth: ¿cuál es tu fecha de nacimiento? what's your date of birth?

la **nación** *(plural* las naciones) ■ **nation**
> las Naciones Unidas the United Nations.

nacional *adjetivo* ■ national.

la **nacionalidad** *(plural* las nacionalidades) ■ **nationality** *(plural* **nationalities**): ¿cuál es tu nacionalidad? what is your nationality?

nada *(pronombre & adverbio)*

■ *pronombre*

1. **nothing:** vamos a almorzar fuera porque en casa no hay nada de comer we're going out for lunch because there is nothing to eat at home; ¿qué compraste? —nada what did you buy? —nothing

2. **anything:** ¿no compraste nada? didn't you buy anything?; Juan se fue sin decir nada Juan left without saying anything
> de nada you're welcome: ¡gracias! —de nada thank you! —you're welcome
> dentro de nada very soon: el curso acabará dentro de nada the course will be over very soon
> nada más

1. **anything else:** no quiero nada más I don't want anything else

2. no sooner: nada más llegar nosotros, apareció Juan no sooner had we arrived than Juan appeared

nada de nada nothing at all

■ *adverbio*

at all: estoy agotada, anoche no dormí nada I'm exhausted, I didn't get any sleep at all last night.

nadar [1] *verbo* ■ to swim.

nadie *pronombre*

1. nobody, no one: ¿ya ha llegado alguien? —no, nadie has anybody arrived yet? –no, nobody

2. anybody, anyone: ¿todavía no ha llegado nadie? has anybody arrived yet?; no obedece a nadie he doesn't obey anyone.

la **nalga** ■ buttock.

naranja *adjetivo* ■ orange: llevaba un suéter naranja he wore an orange sweater

el **naranja** ■ orange: mi color favorito es el naranja my favourite colour is orange

la **naranja** ■ orange: hice zumo de naranja para el desayuno I made orange juice for breakfast.

la **nariz** (*plural* las narices) ■ nose: suénate la nariz blow your nose.

la **narración** (*plural* las narraciones) ■ story (*plural* stories).

narrar [1] *verbo* ■ to narrate.

la **nata** ■ cream: he comprado un pastel de nata I've bought a cream cake.

la **natación** ■ swimming: me encanta la natación I love swimming.

natural *adjetivo* ■ natural.

la **naturaleza** ■ nature: pasamos los fines de semana en el campo, en contacto con la naturaleza we spend weekends in the country, in touch with nature.

el **naufragio** ■ shipwreck.

las **náuseas** ■ tiene náuseas y le duele la cabeza she feels nauseous and has a headache.

la **navaja** ■ penknife (*plural* penknives).

Navarra ■ Navarre.

navarro, rra *adjetivo*

En inglés, los adjetivos que se refieren a un país o una región se escriben con mayúscula:

Navarrese: los espárragos navarros the Navarrese asparagus

el **navarro** , la **navarra**

En inglés, los gentilicios se escriben con mayúscula:

Navarrese: los navarros the Navarrese.

la **nave** ■ ship

una nave espacial a spaceship.

el **navegador** ■ browser: ¿qué navegador tienes instalado en tu ordenador? what browser do you have on your computer?

navegar [12] *verbo*

1. to sail: salimos a navegar en su nuevo velero we went sailing on his new sailing boat

2. to surf: pasa horas y horas navegando por Internet he spends hours and hours surfing the Internet.

la **Navidad** (*plural* las Navidades) ■ Christmas: vamos a pasar las Navidades en casa de mis abuelos we're spending Christmas at my grandparents' house; en Navidad veo a todos mis primos at Christmas I see all my cousins

¡Feliz Navidad! Merry Christmas!

navideño, ña *adjetivo* ■ Christmas: las fiestas navideñas the Christmas holidays.

necesario, ria *adjetivo* ■ necessary: haremos lo que sea necesario we will do whatever is necessary.

necesitar [1] *verbo* ■ to need: si somos cuatro para la cena, necesitamos un pollo entero if there are four of us having dinner we'll need a whole chicken.

negar [25] *verbo*

1. to deny: le pregunté si había roto el cristal y lo negó I asked if he had broken the pane of glass and he denied it

2. to refuse: la abuela malcría a los nietos, nunca les niega nada grandma spoils her grandchildren, she never refuses them anything

negarse *verbo pronominal* ■ **to refuse:** Juan se negó a que lo ayudara Juan refused my help.

negativo, va *adjetivo* ■ **negative:** nos dio una respuesta negativa he gave us a negative answer; ¡no seas tan negativo! don't be so negative!

negociar [1] *verbo* ■ **to negotiate:** los presidentes se reunieron para negociar un acuerdo the presidents gathered to negotiate an agreement.

el **negocio** ■ **business:** trabaja en un negocio familiar he works in a family business; mi tío se dedica a los negocios my uncle is a businessman.

negro, gra *adjetivo* ■ **black:** hoy me voy a poner el pantalón negro con la blusa roja I'll wear the black pants with the red blouse today

el **negro** , la **negra** ■ **black person.**

el **negro** ■ **black:** el negro es mi color favorito black is my favourite colour

el **nervio** ■ **nerve:** el dentista me anestesió el nervio de la muela the dentist numbed the nerve of my tooth

los **nervios** ■ **nerves:** cálmate, no permitas que los nervios te afecten durante la prueba calm down, don't let nerves get to you during the test

➤ esa chica me pone de los nervios that girl gets on my nerves.

nervioso, sa *adjetivo* ■ **nervous:** es un niño muy nervioso que distrae a toda la clase he's a nervous boy who distracts the whole class

➤ ponerse nervioso

1. to get on one's nerves: me pone nervioso que hable de ese modo it get on my nerves when he talks like that

2. to get in a state: ¡no te pongas nervioso! don't get in a state!

el **neumático** ■ **tyre** *UK*, **tire** *US*.

neutro, tra *adjetivo* ■ **neutral.**

la **nevada** ■ **snowfall.**

nevar [14] *verbo* ■ **to snow:** hace varios días que nieva sin parar it's been snowing continuously for several days.

la **nevera** ■ **fridge** *UK*, **ice box** *US*.

ni *conjunción*

1. or: no sabe leer ni escribir he doesn't know read or write

2. nor: no vino ni me llamó he didn't come, nor did he call

➤ ni... ni neither... nor: no quiero ni pollo ni pescado I want neither chicken nor fish

➤ ni siquiera not even: ni siquiera se despidió cuando se fue he didn't even say goodbye when he left

➤ ¡ni lo sé ni me importa! I don't know and I don't care.

Nicaragua ■ **Nicaragua.**

nicaragüense *adjetivo*

En inglés, los adjetivos que se refieren a un país o una región se escriben con mayúscula:

Nicaraguan

el/la **nicaragüense**

En inglés, los gentilicios se escriben con mayúscula:

Nicaraguan

➤ los nicaragüenses the Nicaraguans.

el **nido** ■ **nest.**

la **niebla** ■ **fog.**

la **nieta** ■ **granddaughter.**

el **nieto** ■ **grandson.**

los **nietos** ■ **grandchildren.**

la **nieve** ■ **snow.**

ningún *adjetivo* ➤ ninguno

Shortened form of **ninguno** used before masculine singular nouns.

ninguno, na *(adjetivo & pronombre)*

■ *adjetivo*

any: no encontramos ninguna película interesante we couldn't find any interesting films

> por ningún lado anywhere: no vi a tu hermana por ningún lado I didn't see your sister anywhere

> ningún momento never: en ningún momento me dijo que se sentía mal she never said she felt ill

■ *pronombre*

1. none: ninguno de los niños sabía japonés none of the children knew Japanese
2. neither: ninguno de los dos sacó buena nota neither of them got a good grade.

la **niña** ■ girl: una niña pequeña a small girl.

la **niñera** ■ nanny *(plural* nannies*)*.

la **niñez** ■ childhood.

el **niño** ■ boy: un niño de cinco años a five year old boy

> esta película no es apta para niños this film isn't suitable for children.

el **nivel** ■ level: la ciudad está a mil metros sobre el nivel del mar the city is a thousand metres above the sea level; el nivel educativo aquí es muy alto the educational level here is very high

> el nivel de vida the standard of living.

no *adverbio* ■ no: ¿vienes? —no are you coming? —no; ¡he dicho que no! I said no!

> no tengo tiempo I don't have time

> es vasco, ¿no? he's Basque, isn't he?

noble *adjetivo* ■ noble.

la **noche**

1. night: llovió toda la noche it rained all night
2. dark: se nos hizo tarde, cuando llegamos ya era de noche we were running late and it was dark by the time we arrived

> ¡Buenas noches!

1. *saludo* good evening!
2. *despedida* good night!

> de la noche at night: las diez de la noche ten o'clock at night

> de noche night-time: cuando en América es de día, en Extremo Oriente es de noche when it's daytime in America it's night-time in the Far East

> por la noche at night: no es sano comer alimentos muy pesados por la noche it's not healthy to eat a heavy meal at night.

la **Nochebuena** ■ Christmas Eve.

la **Nochevieja** ■ New Year's Eve.

nocturno, na *adjetivo*

1. night: tomaremos el tren nocturno we'll take the night train
2. nocturnal: el búho es un ave nocturna owls are nocturnal birds
3. evening: hay clases nocturnas en el instituto there are evening classes at the school.

el **nombre**

1. name: no sé su nombre, pero su apellido es González I don't know his first name, but his surname is González
2. noun: palabras como "casa" y "puerta" son nombres words like "house" and "door" are nouns

> nombre de pila first name

> nombre propio the proper name

> nombre y apellidos name and surname.

el **noreste** ■ northeast.

la **norma** ■ rule: para poder cumplir las normas, hay que conocerlas you have to know the rules to follow them.

normal *adjetivo* ■ normal: es normal que extrañes a tu familia si es la primera vez que estás lejos de casa it's normal to miss your family if it's the first time you've been away from home

> normal y corriente ordinary: es un chico normal y corriente he's an ordinary guy.

el **noroeste** ■ northwest.

norte *adjetivo* ■ north: Santander está en la costa norte de España Santander is on the north coast of Spain

el **norte** ■ en el norte de la ciudad: in the north of the city en el norte de la ciudad; fuimos hacia el norte we went north

> al norte de north of: Gerona está al norte de Barcelona Gerona is north of Barcelona.

norteamericano, na *adjetivo*

En inglés, los adjetivos que se refieren a un país o una región se escriben con mayúscula:

North American

el **norteamericano** ,

la **norteamericana**

En inglés, los gentilicios se escriben con mayúscula:

North American.

nos *pronombre*

1. **us:** todavía no nos han entregado las notas they haven't given us our marks yet
2. **ourselves:** nos divertimos mucho we really enjoyed ourselves
3. **each other:** no nos conocíamos, pero mi hermano nos presentó en la fiesta we didn't know each other but my brother introduced us at the party
4. **our:** nos duelen las piernas our legs ache

nosotros *pronombre*

1. **we:** ellos quieren helado pero nosotros preferimos fruta they want ice cream but we prefer fruit
2. **us:** los abuelos vinieron al parque con nosotros our grandparents came to the park with us; ¡abre, somos nosotros! open us, it's us!

la **nota**

1. **note:** vamos a dejarle una nota con la dirección we'll leave her a note with the address; "do" es la primera nota de la escala musical "do" is the first note on the musical scale
2. **mark** *UK*, **grade:** no estoy nada contenta con mis notas este trimestre I'm not at all happy with my marks this term.

> LAS NOTAS
>
> In Spain, homework and exams are generally marked out of 10. To achieve an average mark students need to get at least a 5. The marks receive different classifications such as **sobresaliente** (outstanding), which is equivalent to an "A" and is awarded for marks between 9 and 10, or **insuficiente** (unsatisfactory), which is equivalent to a "D" and given to marks from 0 to 5.

notable *adjetivo* ■ **remarkable:** "Rayuela" es la obra más notable de Cortázar "Hopscotch" is Cortázar's most remarkable book.

notar [1] *verbo*

1. **to notice:** ¿has notado que lleva un calcetín marrón y otro verde? did you notice she's wearing one brown sock and one green?
2. **to feel:** con estos guantes no noto el frío I don't feel the cold in these gloves

notarse *verbo pronominal* ■ **to be able to tell:** se nota que ha estado llorando, tiene los ojos irritados you can tell she's been crying, her eyes are all red.

la **noticia** ■ **news:** papá escucha las noticias en la radio todas las mañanas Dad listens to the news on the radio every morning; tengo una buena noticia que darte I have some good news for you.

la **novedad**

1. **novelty:** como nunca había visto una jirafa para ella era una novedad since she'd never seen a giraffe before it was quite a novelty for her
2. **latest thing:** ahora la novedad es combinar verde con naranja the latest thing is to combine green and orange
3. **news:** al volver de viaje quiso enterarse de las novedades del país when she returned from her trip she wanted to catch up on the country's news.

noveno, na *numeral* ■ **ninth:** llegó novena en la carrera he came ninth in the race.

noventa *numeral* ■ **ninety:** tiene casi noventa años she's nearly ninety

el **noventa** ■ **ninety:** el noventa es un número par ninety is an even number.

la **novela** ■ **novel.**

la **novia**

1. **girlfriend:** ¿tienes novia? do you have a girlfriend?
2. **bride:** la novia estaba elegantísima en su boda the bride looked very elegant at the wedding.

noviembre *sustantivo masculino*

En inglés los nombres de los meses se escriben con mayúscula:

November: en noviembre in November; el próximo noviembre next November; el pasado noviembre last November.

el novio

1. boyfriend: ¿tienes novio? do you have a boyfriend?

2. groom: el novio estaba elegantísimo en su boda the groom looked very elegant at the wedding

> los novios the bride and the groom.

la nube ■ cloud.

nublado, da *adjetivo* ■ **cloudy:** hoy está muy nublado it's very cloudy today.

la nuca ■ nape of the neck.

nuclear *adjetivo* ■ **nuclear.**

el núcleo ■ **nucleus:** el núcleo de la célula contiene información genética the cell's nucleus contains genetic information

> el núcleo familiar the family unit.

el nudo ■ knot.

la nuera ■ daughter-in-law.

nuestro, tra *(adjetivo & pronombre)*

■ *adjetivo*

our: invitamos a nuestros amigos a pasar un día en el campo we invited our friends to spend a day in the country

■ *pronombre*

ours: el coche de mis primos es azul y el nuestro es rojo our cousins' car is blue and ours is red; es un amigo nuestro he's a friend of ours.

nueve *numeral* ■ **nine:** tiene nueve hijos she has nine children

> mi hermana tiene nueve años my sister is nine years old

> son las nueve it's nine o'clock

> el nueve de abril the ninth of April *UK*, April ninth *US*.

nuevo, va *adjetivo* ■ **new:** llegó en su coche nuevo she arrived in her new car

> de nuevo again; de nuevo try again.

la nuez *(plural* las nueces) ■ **walnut.**

el número

1. number: ¿cuál es tu número de la suerte? what's your lucky number?; los sustantivos en español tienen género y número in Spanish, nouns have number and gender

2. size: ¿qué número calzas? what size shoe do you take?

3. issue: quiero comprar los números atrasados de esa revista I want to buy the back issues of that magazine

> un número de fax a fax number

> un número de identificación personal a PIN

> un número de matrícula a registration number *UK*, a license number *US*

> un número de teléfono a phone number.

nunca *adverbio*

1. never: nunca me llama he never calls me

2. ever: te necesito más que nunca I need you more than ever; no había estado nunca allí I hadn't ever been there.

nutritivo, va *adjetivo* ■ **nutritious:** las frutas y verduras son muy nutritivas fruit and vegetables are very nutritious.

ñoño, ña *adjetivo* ■ **spineless.**

o *conjunción* ■ **or:** ¿cuáles prefieres: los rojos o los blancos? which ones do you prefer: the red ones or the white ones?

> o... o... either... or...: el doctor puede atenderte o mañana o la semana que viene the doctor can see you either tomorrow or next week; o te callas o nos vamos if you don't shut up we're leaving.

obedecer [22] *verbo* ■ **to obey:** este niño no obedece a nadie this child doesn't obey anybody.

obediente _adjetivo_ ■ obedient.

la **obesidad** ■ obesity.

objetivo, va _adjetivo_ ■ objective: hizo una presentación objetiva de la situación he gave an objective presentation of the situation

el **objetivo** ■ aim, objective: el objetivo de la película es mostrar cómo viven los esquimales the aim of the film is to show how Inuits live.

el **objeto** ■ object: un objeto de plástico a plastic object.

la **obligación** _(plural_ las obligaciones_)_ ■ obligation: los padres tienen la obligación de cuidar a sus hijos parents have the obligation of caring for their children.

obligar [12] _verbo_ ■ to make: a mi hermano lo obligan a estudiar inglés they make my brother study English.

obligatorio, ria _adjetivo_ ■ obligatory: una signatura obligatoria a compulsory subject.

la **obra**
1. work: en este museo hay varias obras de Velázquez there are several works by Velázquez in this museum
2. play: en ese teatro están dando una obra sensacional they're putting on a sensational play at that theatre
3. building site: con el ruido de la obra de al lado, no puedo concentrarme I can't concentrate with the noise from the neighbouring building site.

el **obrero** , la **obrera** ■ worker
➤ un obrero calificado a skilled worker
➤ un obrero de la construcción a construction worker.

el **obsequio** ■ gift.

la **observación** _(plural_ las observaciones_)_
1. observation: el paciente está en observación the patient is under observation
2. comment: la maestra anotó varias observaciones en mi trabajo the teacher wrote down several comments on my paper.

observador, ra _adjetivo_ ■ observant: es muy observadora, descubrió todas las diferencias entre las dos figuras she's very observant, she noted all the differences between the two figures.

observar [1] _verbo_
1. to observe: se dedicó a observar y estudiar a los monos en la selva he devoted himself to observing and studying monkeys in the jungle
2. to remark: este dibujo es excelente, observó la maestra this drawing is excellent, remarked the teacher.

el **obstáculo** ■ obstacle: pese a los obstáculos, Javier logró terminar su carrera in spite of the obstacles, Javier managed to finish his studies; participará en una carrera de obstáculos they took part in an obstacle race.

obtener [52] _verbo_
1. to obtain: obtuvimos los resultados que queríamos con mucho trabajo with a lot of work, we obtained the results that we wanted
2. to get: obtuvo el primer premio she got first prize.

la **ocasión** _(plural_ las ocasiones_)_
1. opportunity _(plural_ opportunities_)_: todavía no he tenido ocasión de conocerla I still haven't had the opportunity to meet her
2. occasion: me prestó el coche en varias ocasiones he lent me his car on several occasions.

el **Occidente** ■ the West.

el **océano** ■ ocean
➤ el Océano Atlántico the Atlantic Ocean
➤ el Océano Pacífico the Pacific Ocean
➤ el Océano Índico the Indian Ocean.

ochenta _numeral_ ■ eighty: tiene casi ochenta años he's nearly eighty; hay ochenta y seis alumnos there are eighty six pupils

el **ochenta** ■ eighty: el ochenta es un número par eighty is an even number.

ocho _numeral_ ■ eight: tiene ocho hijos she has eight children
➤ mi hermana tiene ocho años my sister is eight years old

son las ocho it's eight o'clock

el **ocho** ■ eight
el ocho de abril the eighth of April *UK,* April eighth *US.*

el **ocio** ■ leisure.

octavo, va *numeral* ■ eighth: llegó octavo a la meta he came eighth at the finishing line.

octubre *sustantivo masculino* ■ October: en octubre in October; el próximo octubre next October; el pasado octubre last October

En inglés los nombres de los meses se escriben con mayúscula.

ocultar [1] *verbo* ■ to hide: no me ocultes la verdad don't hide the truth from me

ocultarse *verbo pronominal* ■ to hide: se ocultaron detrás de la puerta they hid behind the door.

ocupar [1] *verbo*

1. to take up: este ropero es muy grande, ocupa toda la habitación the wardrobe is too big, it takes up the whole room
2. to occupy: ¿quién está ocupando ese asiento? who's occupying that seat?
3. to live in: nosotros ocupamos la habitación del fondo, la de enfrente está libre we live in the room at the back, the one at the front is unoccupied
4. to take control of: durante la guerra, el ejército enemigo ocupó la capital during the war, the enemy army took control of the capital

ocuparse *verbo pronominal*

1. to take care of, to look after: los abuelos se van a ocupar de los niños este fin de semana their grandparents are going to take care of the children this weekend; ahora me ocupo de la empresa de mi padre now I look after my father's company
2. to see to: yo me ocupo de eso I'll see to it.

ocurrir [3] *verbo* ■ to happen: la historia cuenta lo que ocurrió en el pasado history tells what happened in the past; ¿qué te ocurre? what's the matter with you?

ocurrirse *verbo pronominal* ■ to think of: ¿se te ocurre algo para regalarle a mamá

el día de su cumpleaños? can you think of something to give mum for her birthday?

odiar [1] *verbo* ■ to hate: ¿cuál es la verdura que más odias? what is the vegetable that you hate the most?; ¿por qué odias a tu vecina? why do you hate your neighbour?

el **odio** ■ hatred: le he cogido odio a la televisión I've developed a hatred for television.

oeste *adjetivo* ■ west: Galway está en la costa oeste de Irlanda Galway is on the west coast of Ireland

el **oeste** ■ west: el sol se oculta por el oeste the sun sets in the west; el oeste de la ciudad the west of the city; fuimos hacia el oeste we went west

> al oeste de west of: está al oeste de Madrid it's west of Madrid.

ofender [2] *verbo* ■ to offend: es muy maleducado y ofende a las personas sin darse cuenta he's very rude and he offends people without realizing it

ofenderse *verbo pronominal* ■ to be offended: se ofendió porque no la invitaron a la fiesta she was offended because they didn't invite her to the party.

la **oferta** ■ offer: recibí dos ofertas de trabajo I received two job offers

> estar de oferta to be on special offer: los plátanos están de oferta bananas are on special offer

> hay muchas ofertas de trabajo para los informáticos there are many job vacancies for computer specialists.

oficial *adjetivo* ■ official: la piscina municipal se inaugura mañana con un acto oficial the city swimming pool will be inaugurated tomorrow with an official ceremony

el/la **oficial** *(plural* los/las oficiales*)* ■ officer: el oficial de policía vino a ver qué sucedía the police officer came to see what was happening; es oficial de Marina he's an officer in the navy.

la **oficina** ■ office.

el **oficio** ■ trade: ¿qué oficio te gustaría aprender? what trade would you like to learn?

ofrecer [22] *verbo* ■ to offer: la vendedora me ofreció varios vestidos the saleswoman offered me several dresses

ofrecerse *verbo pronominal* ■ to offer to: el vecino se ofreció para ayudarnos con la mudanza the neighbour offered to help us with the move.

el **oído**

1. ear: tengo una infección en el oído derecho I have an infection in my right ear
2. hearing: el oído es uno de los cinco sentidos hearing is one of the five senses
▷ de oído by ear: toca la guitarra de oído he plays the guitar by ear.

oír [45] *verbo*

1. to hear: habla más fuerte, que no te oigo speak louder, I can't hear you; lo he oído en la radio I heard it on the radio
2. *escuchar* to listen to: oigo la radio por la mañana I listen to the radio in the morning.

el **ojal** ■ buttonhole.

ojalá *interjección*

1. I hope: ¡ojalá que pare llover! I hope it stops raining!
2. if only: ¡ojalá pudiera! if only I could!

las **ojeras** ■ circles under the eyes: ¿estás bien? tienes unas ojeras enormes are you all right? you have huge circles under your eyes.

el **ojo** ■ eye: me ha entrado algo en el ojo I've got something in my eye
▷ ¡ojo! watch out!: ¡ojo al cruzar la calle! watch out crossing the street!
▷ no pegar ojo not to get a wink of sleep: no he pegado ojo en toda la noche I didn't get a wink of sleep all night
▷ en un abrir y cerrar de ojos in a flash: preparó la cena en un abrir y cerrar de ojos he made dinner in a flash.

la **ola** ■ wave
▷ una ola de calor a heatwave.

oler [34] *verbo* ■ to smell: acércate y huele las rosas come near and smell the roses
▷ oler a to smell like: huele a perfume it smells like perfume

▷ oler bien to smell good: ese perfume huele muy bien that perfume smells very good
▷ oler mal to smell bad: aquí huele mal it smells bad in here.

las **olimpiadas** ■ the Olympics.

olímpico, ca *adjetivo* ■ Olympic: el atletismo es un deporte olímpico athletics is an Olympic sport.

el **olfato** ■ smell: el olfato es uno de los cinco sentidos smell is one of the five senses.

la **olla** ■ pan: herví el agua en una olla I boiled the water in a pan
▷ una olla a presión a pressure cooker.

el **olor** ■ smell: ¡qué olor más bueno! what a delicious smell!; me encanta el olor a café I love the smell of coffee.

olvidar [1] *verbo*

1. to forget: olvidaste llamar a tu madre you forgot to call your mother
2. to leave: olvidé el paraguas en la silla I left my umbrella on the chair.

el **ombligo** ■ navel.

la **onda** ■ wave.

la **ONG** (*abreviatura de* Organización no Gubernamental*)* ■ NGO.

la **ONU** (*abreviatura de* Organización de las Naciones Unidas*)* ■ UN.

la **opción** (*plural* las opciones) ■ option: tienes varias opciones, elige la que te parezca mejor you have several options, choose the one that seems best to you.

la **operación** (*plural* las operaciones) ■ operation: por suerte la operación de apéndice de mi hermana salió bien fortunately my sister's appendix operation came out well.

la **ópera** ■ opera.

operar [1] *verbo* ■ to operate on: el oculista la va a operar de cataratas the eye specialist is going to operate on her for cataracts

operarse *verbo pronominal* ■ to have an operation: mañana se opera de cataratas tomorrow she's having an operation for cataracts.

opinar [1] *verbo*

1. **to give one's opinion: es mejor no opinar
cuando uno no conoce el tema** it's better to
not give one's opinion when one is not familiar
with the topic
2. **to think: ¿qué opinas de los grupos ecolo-
gistas?** what do you think of ecological
groups?

la **opinión** *(plural* las opiniones*)* ■ **opinion:
¿cuál es tu opinión sobre los grupos ecolo-
gistas?** what's your opinion about ecological
groups?

oponerse [47] *verbo pronominal* ■ **to be
opposed: nuestro grupo se opone a la tala
indiscriminada en los bosques** our group is
opposed to indiscriminate tree felling in the
forests.

la **oportunidad** *(plural* las oportunidades*)*
■ **opportunity** *(plural* **opportunities***)*: **tuvo
la oportunidad de pasar todo el verano en
la playa** she had the opportunity to spend all
summer at the beach.

la **oposición** *(plural* las oposiciones*)* ■ **opposition: la iniciativa de la maestra chocó con
la oposición de los alumnos** the teacher's
plans collided with the students' opposition

las **oposiciones** ■ **competitive exams.**

optativo, va *adjetivo* ■ **optional: historia es obligatoria, pero dibujo es optativa**
history is compulsory, but drawing is optional.

la **óptica** ■ **optician's: hoy he ido a la óptica a hacerme unas gafas nuevas** today I
went to the optician's to have some new glasses made.

optimista *adjetivo* ■ **optimistic: Clara es
muy optimista** Clara is very optimistic.

opuesto, ta *adjetivo*

1. **opposing: Sara y yo tenemos opiniones
opuestas** Sara and I have opposing views
2. **opposite: vivimos en direcciones opuestas** we live in opposite directions.

la **oración** *(plural* las oraciones*)*

1. **prayer: algunas personas dicen una oración antes de la comida** some people say a
prayer before the meal

2. **sentence: analiza esta oración** analyse this
sentence.

oral *adjetivo* ■ **oral: mañana tenemos un
examen oral** tomorrow we have an oral exam
"**administrar por vía oral**" "to be taken
orally".

la **órbita** ■ **orbit: la Luna describe una órbita ovalada alrededor de la Tierra** the
moon travels in an oval orbit around the earth.

el **orden**

1. **order: poneos en fila, por orden de altura**
get in line, by order of height; **por orden alfabético** in alphabetical order
2. **to tidy up: hay que poner un poco de orden en esta oficina** we have to tidy up this
office a bit

la **orden** *(plural* las órdenes*)* ■ **order: siempre está dando órdenes** she's always giving
orders

¡a sus órdenes, capitán! yes, captain!

ordenado, da *adjetivo*

1. **arranged: estos libros están ordenados
por temas** these books are arranged by topic
2. **tidy: es muy ordenada, siempre tiene la
casa impecable** she's very tidy, she always
has her house tidy.

el **ordenador** ■ **computer.**

ordenar [1] *verbo*

1. **to arrange: hay que ordenar estos libros**
we have to arrange these books
2. **to order: el profesor nos ordenó que nos ca-
lláramos** the teacher ordered us to be quiet.

la **oreja** ■ **ear.**

orgánico, ca *adjetivo* ■ **organic: la materia orgánica se descompone naturalmente
con el paso del tiempo** organic material de-
composes naturally with the passage of time.

el **organismo** ■ **organization: un organismo internacional** an international organization.

la **organización** *(plural* las organizaciones*)*
■ **organization, organisation** *UK*: **la organización es importante para poder estudiar con eficiencia** organization is important

to be able to study efficiently; **trabaja en una organización no gubernamental** he works in a non-governmental organization.

organizar [10] *verbo* ■ **to organize, to organise** UK: **Diego y Rodrigo se encargaron de organizar la fiesta de fin de año** Diego and Rodrigo were in charge of organizing the New Year's Eve party

organizarse *verbo pronominal* ■ **to organize oneself: tienes que hacer un esfuerzo para organizarte** you have to make an effort to organize yourself.

el **órgano** ■ **organ: el corazón es el órgano principal del cuerpo humano** the heart is the main organ of the human body; **ese músico escribió varias piezas para órgano** that musician wrote several pieces for the organ.

orgulloso, sa *adjetivo* ■ **proud: está muy orgulloso de su familia** he's very proud of his family.

la **orientación** (*plural* las orientaciones)
> **no tiene sentido de la orientación** he has no sense of direction
> **¿cuál es la orientación de la casa?** which way does the house face?
> **orientación profesional** careers advice.

orientar [1] *verbo* ■ **to direct: el profesor orientó a sus alumnos en el trabajo** the teacher directed her students in their work

orientarse *verbo pronominal* ■ **to get one's bearings: deja que me oriente** let me get my bearings.

el **oriente** ■ **east: esta casa está orientada hacia oriente** this house faces east
> **el Oriente** the East.

el **origen** (*plural* los orígenes) ■ **origin: es de origen escocés** he's of Scottish origin.

original *adjetivo* ■ **original: éste es el texto original, ¿dónde están las copias?** this one is the original text, where are the copies?; **es un artista muy original** he's a very original artist.

originario, ria *adjetivo* ■ **original: ése no era el plan originario** that wasn't the original plan

> **ser originario de** to come from: **este vino es originario de la Rioja** this wine comes from la Rioja
> **sus abuelos son originarios de Francia** his grandparents come from France.

la **orilla**
1. **bank: pasearemos por la orilla del río** we'll walk along the river bank
2. **shore: me encanta dar paseos por la orilla del mar** I love to take walks on the sea shore.

la **orina** ■ **urine.**

el **oro** ■ **gold: el oro es un metal precioso** gold is a precious metal
> **de oro** gold: **¿esa sortija es de oro?** is this ring gold?
> **bañado en oro** gold-plated: **le regalamos una pulsera bañada en oro** we gave her a gold-plated bracelet
> **oro de 18 quilates** 18 carat gold: **estas alianzas son de oro de 18 quilates** these wedding rings are made of 18 carat gold.

la **orquesta** ■ **orchestra**
> **un director de orquesta** a conductor.

la **ortografía** ■ **spelling: es importante evitar las faltas de ortografía** it's important to avoid spelling mistakes.

la **oruga** ■ **caterpillar.**

os *pronombre*
1. **you: no os veo** I can't see you
2. **yourselves: ¿os habéis cortado?** did you cut yourselves?
3. **each other: ¿os queréis mucho?** do you love each other?

> Cuando se refiere a partes del cuerpo u objetos personales se emplea **your**:

lavaos las manos wash your hands.

oscurecer [22] *verbo* ■ **to get dark: en invierno, oscurece a las 5 de la tarde** in the winter, it gets dark at 5 o'clock in the afternoon.

la **oscuridad**
1. **darkness: la oscuridad de la habitación** the darkness of the room
2. **dark: ¿le tienes miedo a la oscuridad?** are you afraid of the dark?

oscuro, ra *adjetivo* ■ **dark:** aquí está muy oscuro it's very dark in here

▸ **a oscuras** in the dark; estábamos a oscuras y empezó a contarme historias de miedo we were in the dark and he began to tell me scary stories

▸ **verde oscuro** dark green.

el oso , la osa ■ **bear**

▸ un oso pardo a brown bear

▸ un oso de peluche a teddy bear

▸ un oso polar a polar bear.

la ostra ■ **oyster.**

el otoño ■ **autumn** *UK*, **fall** *US:* el próximo otoño next autumn

▸ en otoño in autumn.

otro, otra *(adjetivo & pronombre)*

■ *adjetivo*

1. **other:** me gustan más las otras clases I like the other classes more

2. **another:** quiero otro pedazo de pastel I want another piece of cake

▸ yo me refería a otra cosa I was referring to something else

▸ si no lo encuentras aquí, debe estar en otra parte if you don't find it here, it must be somewhere else

■ *pronombre*

another one: ¿puedo servirme otro? can I have another one?

▸ **el otro, la otra, los otros, las otras**

1. **the other one:** éste no me gusta, prefiero el otro I don't like this one, I prefer the other one

2. **the others:** no pedí éstos, quiero los otros I didn't order these, I want the others.

la oveja ■ **sheep** *(plural sheep).*

el ovni *(abreviatura de* objeto volador no identificado) ■ **UFO.**

oxidado, da *adjetivo* ■ **rusty:** se cortó con una lata oxidada she cut herself on a rusty tin.

oxidarse [1] *verbo pronominal* ■ **to rust:** el hierro se oxida con la humedad iron rusts with humidity.

el oxígeno ■ **oxygen.**

el ozono ■ **ozone.**

la paciencia ■ **patience**

▸ ¡ten paciencia! be patient!

el/la paciente ■ **patient:** había varios pacientes esperando al médico there were several patients waiting for the doctor.

pacífico, ca *adjetivo* ■ **peaceful:** los maestros hicieron una manifestación pacífica the teachers carried out a peaceful demonstration.

el Pacífico ■ **the Pacific.**

el pacto ■ **pact.**

padecer [22] *verbo* ■ **to suffer:** el país está padeciendo una crisis económica the country is suffering an economic crisis.

el padre ■ **father:** Juan salió a pasear con su padre Juan went out for a walk with his father; el párroco de mi iglesia es el padre Luis the parish priest of my church is Father Luis

▸ padre de familia family man

▸ mis padres my parents.

el padrino ■ **godfather.**

la paga

1. **pay:** el día 30 recibo mi paga mensual on the 30th I receive my monthly pay

2. **pocket money**

▸ paga extra salary bonus.

pagar [12] *verbo*

1. **to pay:** me dijeron que no tengo que pagar they told me that I don't have to pay

2. **to pay for:** tengo que pagar la entrada I have to pay for the ticket

▸ ¿puedo pagar con tarjeta? can I pay by card?

la **página** ■ page: id a la página 23 del libro go to page 23 of the book.

el **pago** ■ payment: el pago se hará en metálico payment will be made in cash.

el **país** *(plural* los países*)* ■ country *(plural* countries*)*.

el **paisaje** ■ landscape.

el **País Vasco** ■ the Basque Country.

la **paja** ■ straw
➤ un sombrero de paja a straw hat.

el **pájaro** ■ bird.

la **pala**
1. *de niño* spade
2. *para tierra, nieve* shovel
3. *de tenis de mesa* bat *UK*, paddle *US*
4. *de remo* blade.

la **palabra** ■ word
➤ palabra de honor word of honor.

la **palabrota** ■ swearword
➤ decir palabrotas to swear.

el **palacio** ■ palace.

el **paladar** ■ palate.

pálido, da *adjetivo* ■ pale: estaba muy pálida la última vez que la vi she was very pale the last time I saw her.

el **palillo**
1. toothpick: te olvidaste de poner los palillos en la mesa you forgot to put the toothpicks on the table
2. drumstick: perdí uno de los palillos y ahora no puedo tocar el tambor I lost one of the drumsticks and now I can't play the drum
3. chopstick: en el restaurante chino nos dieron palillos para comer at the Chinese restaurant they gave us chopsticks to eat with.

la **paliza**
1. beating: no sólo le robaron, sino que además le dieron una paliza not only did they rob him, but they also gave him a beating
1. pain: limpiar la cocina es una paliza cleaning the kitchen is a pain

➤ dar la paliza to be a pain: no me des la paliza don't be suc a pain.

la **palma** ■ palm: déjame ver las líneas en la palma de tu mano let me see the lines on the palm of your hand.

la **palmera** ■ palm tree: el camino a la playa está lleno de palmeras the road to the beach is full of palm trees.

el **palo**
1. stick: me tropecé con un palo I tripped over a stick
2. suit: los palos de la baraja española son cuatro there are four suits in Spanish pack of cards
3. club: los palos de golf golf clubs.

las **palomitas** ■ popcorn.

la **paloma** ■ pigeon.

el **pan**
1. bread: no le gusta comer mucho pan she doesn't like to eat a lot of bread
2. loaf of bread *(plural* loaves of bread*)*: pasé por la panadería y compré tres panes pequeños I went by the bakery and bought three small loaves of bread
➤ pan de molde sliced bread
➤ pan integral wholemeal bread *UK*, wholewheat bread *US*
➤ pan rallado breadcrumbs.

la **pana** ■ corduroy.

la **panadería** ■ bakery *(plural* bakeries*)*.

el **panadero** , la **panadera** ■ baker.

el **panal** ■ honeycomb.

Panamá ■ Panama.

panameño, ña *adjetivo*

En inglés, los adjetivos que se refieren a un país o una región se escriben con mayúscula:

Panamanian: los panameños the Panamanians.

el **panameño** , la **panameño**

En inglés, los gentilicios se escriben con mayúscula:

Panamanian

a **pancarta** ■ placard.

la **panda** ■ panda.

la **pandilla** ■ gang.

el **pánico** ■ panic: los ladrones sembraron el pánico en la ciudad the thieves caused panic in the city.

el **panorama**
1. view: el panorama que se ve desde aquí es muy bonito the view that you can see from here is very pretty
2. scene: el panorama político es desesperanzador the political scene is gloomy.

la **pantalla**
1. screen: limpia la pantalla del ordenador clean the computer screen
2. lampshade: compré una pantalla nueva para la lámpara I bought a new shade for the lamp

el **pantalón** (plural los pantalones) ■ trousers UK, pants US: en vez de falda ponte pantalones put on some trousers instead of a skirt
> unos pantalones vaqueros jeans.

el **pantano** ■ swamp.

la **pantera** ■ panther.

la **pantorrilla** ■ calf (plural calves): me duelen las pantorrillas my calves hurt.

el **pañal** ■ nappy (plural nappies) UK diaper US.

el **paño** ■ rag: ¿tienes un paño para limpiar la mesa? have you got a cloth to clean the table?
> un paño de cocina a dishcloth.

el **pañuelo**
1. handkerchief: estoy resfriada, ¿tienes un pañuelo? I've got a cold, have you got a handkerchief?
2. scarf (plural scarves): llevaba un pañuelo de seda alrededor del cuello she was wearing a silk scarf around her neck.

el **Papa** ■ Pope.

el **papá** ■ dad
> mis papás my mum and dad.

la **papaya** ■ papaya.

el **papel**
1. paper: estos cuadernos son de papel reciclado these notebooks are made of recycled paper
2. piece of paper: sacad un papel y escribid vuestro nombre take out a piece of paper and write your name
3. role: es el protagonista de la película, tiene el papel principal he's the star of the film, he has the main role
4. document: piden algunos papeles para hacer los trámites they're asking for some documents to carry out the transaction
> el papel higiénico toilet paper.

la **papelera** ■ wastepaper bin UK, wastepaper basket.

la **papelería** ■ stationer's.

el **paquete**
1. packet: ¿me podrías traer un paquete de galletas del supermercado? could you bring me a packet of biscuits from the supermarket?
2. parcel: tengo que ir a correos a recoger un paquete I have to go by the post office to collect a parcel.

par adjetivo ■ even: 2, 4 y 6 son números pares 2, 4 and 6 are even numbers

el **par**
1. couple: en un par de horas más termino este trabajo I'll have finished this job in another couple of hours
2. pair: necesito un par de medias verdes I need a pair of green stockings.

para preposición
1. for: es para mí it's for me; ¿para qué sirve esto? what is this for?
2. by: tiene que estar hecho para mañana it has to be done by tomorrow
3. to: me estoy preparando para correr en la maratón I'm getting ready to run in the marathon
> para siempre forever: fue a España de vacaciones y terminó quedándose para siempre she went to Spain for holiday and she ended up staying forever

> para que so that: **llama a tu madre para que no se preocupe** call your mother so that she won't be worried

> **¿para cuándo tendrá lista la traducción?** when will he have the translation ready?

el **parabrisas** *(plural* los parabrisas*)* ■ windscreen *UK*, windshield *US*.

el **paracaídas** *(plural* los paracaídas*)* ■ parachute.

el **parachoques** *(plural* los parachoques*)* ■ bumper, fender *US*.

la **parada** ■ stop: **a las dos horas hicimos una parada para descansar** after two hours we made a stop to rest

> una parada de bus a bus stop

> una parada de taxi a taxi stand.

parado, da *adjetivo*

1. **stopped: hay un tren parado en el andén, pero no sé si es el que va al centro** there's a train stopped at the platform, but I don't know if it's the one that's going to the centre

2. **unemployed: hace cinco meses que está parado** he's been unemployed for five months.

el **paraguas** *(plural* los paraguas*)* ■ umbrella.

Paraguay ■ Paraguay.

paraguayo, ya *adjetivo*

En inglés, los adjetivos que se refieren a un país o una región se escriben con mayúscula:

Paraguayan

el **paraguayo** , la **paraguaya**

En inglés, los gentilicios se escriben con mayúscula:

Paraguayan
los paraguayos the Paraguayans.

el **paraíso** ■ paradise.

paralelo, la *adjetivo* ■ parallel: **las ruedas del coche dejaron dos líneas paralelas en la arena** the car's wheels left two parallel lines in the sand.

la **parálisis** ■ paralysis.

paralítico, ca *adjetivo* ■ paralysed *UK*, paralyzed *US*

> parálisis cerebral cerebral palsy

> quedó paralítico a causa del accidente he became paralysed because of the accident

el **paralítico** , la **paralítica** ■ paralytic.

paralizar [10] *verbo* ■ to paralyse *UK*, to paralyze *US*: **un derrame le paralizó la mitad del cuerpo** a haemorrhage paralysed half of his body; **el miedo me paralizó** I was paralysed by fear.

parar [1] *verbo*

1. **to stop: paré el coche** I stopped the car; **para de hablar y come** stop talking and eat; **se le ha parado el reloj** his watch has stopped

2. **to end: la actividad para a las ocho de la noche** activity ends at eight o'clock at night; **el libro viejo fue a parar a la papelera** the old book ended up in the bin

3. **to save: el portero paró el balón** the goalkeeper saved the ball

> sin parar non-stop: lleva una semana trabajando sin parar he's been working non-stop all week

pararse *verbo pronominal* ■ to stop: **¿por qué te has parado? sigue caminando** why have you stopped? keep walking.

el **parche** ■ patch.

el **parchís** ■ ludo.

parecer [22] *verbo*

1. **to look like: por su aspecto descuidado, parece un vagabundo** because of his untidy appearance, he looks like a tramp

2. **to think: me parece que su trabajo es de pésima calidad** I think that his work is terrible

3. **to seem: no la conozco, pero parece muy inteligente** I don't know her, but she seems very intelligent

parecerse *verbo pronominal* ■ to resemble each other: **cuando eran pequeños, los dos hermanos se parecían mucho** when they were little, the two brothers resembled each other a lot.

parecido, da *adjetivo*

1. like: dicen que soy muy parecida a mi madre they say that I'm very like my mother
2. similar: he conocido un caso parecido I knew a similar case.

la **pared** ■ wall.

la **pareja**

1. couple: Virginia y Antonio hacen una buena pareja Virginia and Antonio make a nice couple
2. pair: el tenis se puede jugar en parejas tennis can be played in pairs.

el **paréntesis** *(plural* los paréntesis*)* ■ parenthesis *(plural* parentheses*)*, bracket *UK*
> entre paréntesis in brackets.

el **pariente** ■ relative: tengo un pariente en Bilbao I've got a relative in Bilbao
> un pariente cercano a close relative
> un pariente lejano a distant relative.

el **parlamento** ■ parliament.

el **paro**

1. unemployment: el mes pasado el paro bajó unemployment went down last month
2. strike: un paro de dos días a two-day strike
> estar en paro to be unemployed
> cobrar el paro to claim unemployment benefit.

parpadear [1] *verbo*

1. to blink: está nervioso y por eso parpadea tanto he's nervous and that's why he's blinking so much
2. to flicker: la luz está parpadeando, va a haber un apagón the light is flickering, there's going to be a power cut.

el **párpado** ■ eyelid.

el **parque** ■ park: jugaban en el parque they were playing in the park
> un parque de atracciones an amusement park
> un parque temático a theme park.

el **párrafo** ■ paragraph.

la **parrilla** ■ grill
> a la parrilla grilled: prefiero el pollo a la parrilla que hervido I prefer grilled chicken to boiled.

el **párroco** ■ parish priest.

la **parte**

1. portion: hay que dividir la tarta en ocho partes we have to divide the pie into eight portions
2. side: tenemos que averiguar quién está de nuestra parte we have to find out who's on our side
3. part: vivo en la parte oeste de la ciudad I live in the west part of town
> en parte partly: todo lo que ha pasado es en parte culpa tuya everything that's happened is partly your fault
> de parte de alguien from: mándale saludos a tu madre de mi parte say hello to your mum from me
> ¿de parte de quién? *on the telephone* may I ask who's speaking?

el/la **participante** ■ participant.

participar [1] *verbo* ■ to participate.

el **participio** ■ participle.

particular *adjetivo*

1. private: el hotel tiene una playa particular para los huéspedes the hotel has a private beach for the guests; clases particulares private classes
2. distinctive: tiene una forma de vestir muy particular he has a very distinctive way of dressing.

la **partida**

1. game: me ganaste dos partidas de póquer you beat me at two games of poker
2. certificate: la partida de nacimiento the birth certificate.

el **partido**

1. party *(plural* parties*)*: en política es independiente: no pertenece a ningún partido in politics he's independent: he doesn't belong to any party
2. match: espero que mi equipo gane el partido del domingo I hope that my team wins the match on Sunday.

partir [3] *verbo*

1. to divide: mamá partió el pan en cuatro trozos mum divided the bread into four pieces

2. to crack: necesito ayuda para partir este coco I need help to crack this coconut

3. to depart: la expedición partió ayer al amanecer the expedition departed yesterday at dawn

▸ a partir de starting: a partir del domingo empieza el horario de verano starting on Sunday the summer schedule begins

partirse *verbo pronominal* ■ to break in two: el jarrón se cayó de la mesa y se partió the vase fell off the table and broke in two.

la **pasa** ■ raisin.

pasado, da *adjetivo*

1. last: el verano pasado fuimos a la playa last summer we went to the seaside

2. overripe: esos plátanos deben estar pasados those bananas must be overripe.

el **pasado** ■ past: la historia estudia el pasado history studies the past.

el **pasajero** , la **pasajera** ■ passenger: vuelve a leer ese pasaje de Cervantes read that passage from Cervantes again.

el **pasaporte** ■ passport.

pasar [1] *verbo*

1. to go: ese tren pasa por varias estaciones antes de llegar al centro that train goes through several stations before arriving in the centre

2. to pass: ¿podrías pasarme el agua, por favor? could you pass me the water, please?

3. to spend: durante el verano pasamos unos días en la playa during the summer we spent a few days at the seaside

4. to happen: no sé qué pasó en la clase de ayer I don't know what happened in yesterday's class

5. to put on: ¿está Paco? —sí, te lo paso is Paco there? —yes, I'll put him on

6. to go by: pasaron 20 minutos y decidí que no esperaba más 20 minutes went by and I decided that I wasn't going to wait any more

7. to be over: cuando pasó el terremoto, muchas casas estaban destruidas when the earthquake was over, many houses were destroyed

▸ ¿qué pasa? what's the matter?

▸ ¿qué te pasa? what's the matter with you?
▸ pasarlo bien/pasarlo mal to have a good/bad time

▸ ¡paso de todo! *informal* I couldn't care less

▸ pasar por to go through: Alberto está pasando por un mal momento Alberto is going through a bad patch; esta carretera pasa por mi pueblo this road goes through my village

pasarse *verbo pronominal*

1. to go over: el atleta perdió la competición porque se pasó de la línea the athlete lost the competition because he went over the line

2. to get overripe: hay que comerse estas manzanas antes de que se pasen you have to eat these apples before they get overripe

3. to go too far: pídele perdón, te has pasado con ella apologise to her, you're gone too far.

el **pasatiempo** ■ pastime.

la **Pascua** ■ Easter

▸ ¡Felices Pascuas! Happy Christmas!

pasear [1] *verbo*

1. to take a walk: después del almuerzo, el abuelo sale a pasear por el jardín after lunch, my grandfather goes out to take a walk in the garden

2. to go for a ride: como hacía buen día, cogí la bicicleta y salí a pasear since it was a nice day, I got my bicycle and I went for a ride

3. to walk: ¿a quién le toca pasear al perro hoy? whose turn is it to walk the dog today?

el **paseo**

1. walk: después del almuerzo, el abuelo sale a dar un paseo por el jardín after lunch my grandfather goes out for a walk in the garden

2. ride: como hacía buen día, cogí la bicicleta y salí de paseo since it was a nice day, I grabbed my bicycle and went out for a ride

▸ ir de paseo to go for a walk.

el **pasillo**

1. de casa, oficina corridor

2. de avión, cine aisle.

la **pasión** *(plural* las pasiones*)* ■ passion.

el **paso**

1. step: los pasos en el tango son largos y lentos the steps are long and slow in the tango; paso a paso step by step

2. way: hay que ir por otra calle porque aquí está cerrado el paso you have to go by another street because the way is blocked here
"ceda el paso" "give way" UK, "yield" US
"prohibido el paso" "no entry"
un paso de cebra a zebra crossing.

a **pasta**
1. paste: utilicé una pasta para sellar las ventanas I used a paste to seal the windows
2. pasta: los macarrones son mi pasta preferida macaroni is my favorite pasta
3. informal **cash:** no tengo pasta para ir al cine I haven' got any cash to go to the cinema
pasta de dientes toothpaste.

el **pastel** ■ cake: a Beatriz le prepararon un pastel de chocolate para su cumpleaños they made a chocolate cake for Beatriz's birthday.

la **pastelería** ■ cake shop: en la pastelería había dos tartas que se me antojaron at the pastry shop there were two cakes that I wanted.

la **pastilla**
1. pill: el médico me recetó unas pastillas para la tos the doctor prescribed me some pills for my cough
2. bar: hay que traer seis pastillas de jabón del supermercado you have to bring six bars of soap from the supermarket.

el **pastor**
1. shepherd: el pastor cuida las ovejas the shepherd looks after the sheep
2. pastor: el pastor de mi iglesia siempre habla de la caridad the pastor in my church always talks about charity.

la **pastora** ■ shepherdess: la pastora cuida las ovejas the shepherdess looks after the sheep.

la **pata**
1. paw: el perro se clavó una espina en la pata the dog got a thorn in his paw
2. leg: no te sientes en esa silla, tiene una pata rota don't sit in that chair, it has a broken leg
tener mala pata to be unlucky
meter la pata to put one's foot in it: metí la pata al preguntarle I put my foot in it when I asked her

patas arriba upside down: tengo que arreglar la casa, está todo patas para arriba I have to tidy up the house, everything's upside down.

la **patada** ■ kick
me dio una patada he kicked me.

la **patata** ■ potato (plural **potatoes**)
patata frita chip UK, French fry US
un filete con patatas fritas steak and chips
una bolsa de patatas fritas a packet of crisps.

el **paté** ■ paté.

la **patera** ■ small boat used by immigrants to reach the Spanish coast.

la **patilla**
1. sideburn, sideboard UK: ¿te estás dejando crecer las patillas? are you letting your sideburns grow?
2. arm: se me ha roto una patilla de las gafas one of the arms on my glasses broke.

el **patín** (plural los patines)
1. de ruedas **skate, roller skate**
2. de hielo **ice skate.**

el **patinaje** ■ skating, roller skating
patinaje sobre hielo ice skating.

patinar [1] verbo
1. sobre ruedas to skate, to roller skate
2. sobre hielo to ice skate
3. un vehículo to skid.

el **patio**
1. de una casa **patio**
2. de una escuela **playground**
3. de butacas **stalls** UK, **orchestra** US.

el **patinete** ■ scooter.

el **pato** ■ duck.

la **patria** ■ homeland.

el **patrón** , la **patrona** (plural los patrones, las patronas)
1. boss: el patrón se reunió con los empleados para intentar llegar a un acuerdo the boss met with the employees to try to reach an agreement

2. **skipper:** Juan es el patrón del barco Juan is the boat's skipper

3. **patron saint:** la Merced es la patrona de Barcelona Our Lady of Mercy is the patron saint of Barcelona

el **patrón** *(plural* los patrones*)* ■ **pattern:** en esa tienda venden patrones para hacer distintos tipos de vestidos at that store they sell patterns to make different types of dresses.

la **patrulla** ■ **patrol:** una patrulla de vecinos circula por las calles cada noche a neighbourhood patrol goes throughout the streets every night.

la **pausa**

1. **pause:** después de una pausa dijo: "estoy muy cansado" after a pause he said: "I'm very tired"

2. **break:** vamos a hacer una pausa we're going to take a break.

el **pavo** ■ **turkey:** una cena de Navidad con pavo a Christmas dinner with turkey

> un pavo real a peacock.

el **payaso** , la **payasa** ■ **clown.**

la **paz** *(plural* las paces*)* ■ **peace:** no queremos la guerra, queremos vivir en paz we don't want war, we want to live in peace

> dejar a alguien en paz to leave somebody alone: deja a tu hermano en paz, que está haciendo sus deberes leave your brother alone, he's doing his homework

> hacer las paces to make up: estuvieron peleadas varios días pero al final hicieron las paces they fought for several days but in the end they made up.

el **peaje** ■ **toll:** el peaje está a un kilómetro the toll is one kilometre away.

el **peatón** *(plural* los peatones*)* ■ **pedestrian.**

peatonal *adjetivo* ■ **pedestrian:** una calle peatonal a pedestrian street.

la **peca** ■ **freckle.**

el **pecado**

1. **sin:** la pereza es uno de los siete pecados capitales laziness is one of the seven deadly sins

2. **crime:** es un pecado desperdiciar el resto del pollo it's a crime to throw away the rest of the chicken.

el **pecho**

1. *tórax* **chest:** Antonio tiene el pecho ancho y fuerte porque nada todos los días Antonio has a wide, strong chest because he swims every day; me duele el pecho my chest hurts

2. *de mujer* **breast**

> dar el pecho to breastfeed: ya es hora de darle otra vez el pecho al bebé now it's time to breastfeed the baby again.

la **pechuga** ■ **breast:** ¿qué parte del pollo prefieres: el muslo o la pechuga? what part of the chicken do you prefer: the leg or the breast?

el **pedal** ■ **pedal:** el pedal del freno the brake pedal; el pedal del acelerador the accelerator pedal.

pedalear [1] *verbo* ■ **to pedal.**

el **pedazo** ■ **piece:** sólo queda un pedazo de pan there's only one piece of bread left

> romperse en mil pedazos to smash to pieces.

el **pedido** ■ **order:** ya hice el pedido pero todavía no está listo I already placed the order but it's not ready yet.

pedir [19] *verbo*

1. **to ask:** te pedí que vinieras porque necesito ayuda I asked you to come because I need help

2. **to ask for:** he pedido otro tenedor porque éste se me ha caído al suelo I asked for another fork because I dropped this one on the floor

3. **to order:** he pedido pollo y ensalada para cinco I've ordered chicken and salad for five.

pegajoso, sa *adjetivo* ■ **sticky:** tengo las manos pegajosas, me las voy a lavar I have sticky hands, I'm going to wash them.

el **pegamento** ■ **glue.**

pegar [12] *verbo*

1. **to glue:** pegué la taza rota con pegamento especial para cerámica I glued the broken cup with special glue for ceramics

2. to give: Susana me pegó su gripe cuando fui a visitarla Susana gave me her flu when I went to visit her

3. to hit: Carlos me ha pegado Carlos hit me

4. to go with: esa camisa no pega con los pantalones verdes that shirt doesn't go with the green trousers

pegar un salto to jump: pegué un salto cuando sonó el teléfono I jumped when the telephone rang

pegar un susto a alguien to scare somebody: el gato le pegó un susto cuando saltó sobre ella the cat scared her when it jumped on her

pegarse *verbo pronominal*

1. to cling, to stick: el niño se pegó a su madre the child clung to his mother

2. to hit one another: Alejandro y Carlos se pegaron Alejandro and Carlos hit one another

pegarse un golpe con algo to bump into something.

la **pegatina** ■ sticker.

el **peinado** ■ hairstyle.

peinar [1] *verbo*

1. *con peine* to comb

2. *con cepillo* to brush

peinarse *verbo pronominal*

1. *con peine* to comb one's hair: Tomás no se peina nunca Tomás never combs his hair

2. *con cepillo* to brush one's hair.

el **peine** ■ comb.

pelar [1] *verbo*

1. *fruta* to peel

2. *nueces* to shell

hacer un frío que pela to be bitterly cold: ayer hacía un frío que pelaba yesterday it was bitterly cold

pelarse *verbo pronominal* ■ to peel: se me está pelando la nariz my nose is peeling.

el **peldaño** ■ step.

la **pelea**

1. fight: deja de pelear con tu hermana stop fighting with your sister

2. argument: Luisa tuvo otra pelea con su novio Luisa had another argument with her boyfriend.

pelear [1] *verbo*

1. to fight: los pueblos hispanoamericanos pelearon por conseguir su independencia the Hispanic Americans fought to gain their independence

2. to argue: mis hermanos pelean mucho my brothers argue a lot

pelearse *verbo pronominal*

1. to fight: Juan y Pedro se pelearon en el patio Juan and Pedro fought in the yard

2. to argue: Marta y Pablo siempre se pelean Marta and Pablo are always arguing.

la **película** ■ film *UK*, movie *US*: ¿a qué hora dan la película? what time are the showing the film?

➤ una película de dibujos animados a feature-length cartoon

➤ una película de terror a horror film

➤ una película de acción an action film

➤ una película del oeste a western

➤ una película de suspense a thriller.

el **peligro** ■ danger: el paciente está fuera de peligro the patient is out of danger

➤ correr el peligro de to run the risk of: corres el peligro de caerte si no tienes cuidado you run the risk of falling if you aren't careful.

peligroso, sa *adjetivo* ■ dangerous.

pelirrojo, ja *adjetivo* ■ red-haired

el **pelirrojo** , la **pelirroja** ■ redhead.

el **pelo** ■ hair: me lavo el pelo todos los días I wash my hair every day

➤ nos salvamos por un pelo we escaped by the skin of our teeth

➤ tomar el pelo to pull somebody's leg: ¡me estás tomando el pelo! you're pulling my leg!

la **pelota** ■ ball: jugar a la pelota to play ball

➤ hacer la pelota a alguien to suck up to somebody.

el/la **pelota** ■ creep.

la **peluca** ■ wig.

la **peluquería** ■ hairdresser's.

el **peluquero** , la **peluquera** ■ hairdresser.

la **pena**

1. **shame:** fue una pena que se muriera la tortuga de Joaquín it was a shame that Joaquín's tortoise died
2. **sentence:** el juez lo condenó a una pena de diez años the judge sentenced him to ten years in prison
> ¡qué pena! what a pity!
> dar pena to feel upset
> vale la pena it's worth it.

el **penalti** ■ penalty *(plural* **penalties***)*: Raúl falló el penalti Raúl missed the penalty.

pendiente *adjetivo* ■ **pending:** hay varios asuntos pendientes there are several matters pending.

el **pendiente** ■ earring.

la **pendiente** ■ **slope:** bajamos esquiando por la pendiente we went skiing down the slope.

el **pene** ■ penis.

la **península** ■ peninsula
> la Península Ibérica the Iberian Peninsula.

el **pensamiento** ■ **thought:** yo puedo adivinarte el pensamiento I can guess your thoughts.

pensar [14] *verbo*

1. **to think:** pensamos que es un buen candidato a la presidencia we think that he's a good candidate for the presidency
2. **to think about:** voy a pensarlo y mañana te respondo I'm going to think about it and tomorrow I'll give you an answer.

penúltimo, ma *adjetivo* ■ **next to last, penultimate:** el penúltimo corredor the next to last runner

el **penúltimo**, la **penúltima** ■ **next to last:** es el penúltimo he's next to last.

peor *adjetivo & adverbio*

1. **worse:** la película de hoy es peor que la que vimos ayer today's film is worse than the one we saw yesterday; hoy me siento peor que ayer today I feel worse than yesterday
2. **worst:** es la peor película que he visto en mi vida it's the worst firm I've ever seen.

el **pepino** ■ cucumber.

pequeño, ña *adjetivo*

1. **little:** cuando era pequeña me encantaba jugar con muñecas when I was little I loved to play with dolls
2. **small:** el paquete es pequeño the package is small

el **pequeño**, la **pequeña** ■ **child** *(plural* children*)*: los pequeños llegaron del parque cansadísimos the children arrived back from the park very tired
> de pequeño, Eduardo quería ser astronauta when he was little, Eduardo wanted to be an astronaut.

la **pera** ■ pear.

la **percha** ■ coat hanger.

perder [15] *verbo*

1. **to miss:** si no salimos ahora mismo, vas a perder el avión if we don't leave right now, you're going to miss the plane
2. **to lose:** he perdido las llaves I've lost the keys; está triste porque su equipo ha perdido he's sad because his team has lost
> perder tiempo to waste time: ponte a trabajar y no pierdas más tiempo start working and don't waste any more time

perderse *verbo pronominal* ■ **to get lost:** quiero irme antes de que oscurezca, para evitar perderme I want to go before it gets dark, to avoid getting lost.

la **pérdida** ■ **loss:** no ha logrado recuperarse de la pérdida de su madre she hasn't been able to recover from the loss of her mother; a causa de la sequía, los agricultores sufrieron pérdidas graves because of the drought, the farmers suffered severe losses
> qué pérdida de tiempo what a waste of time.

perdido, da *adjetivo* ■ **lost:** estamos perdidos we are lost
> objetos perdidos lost property *UK*, lost and found *US*.

el **perdón** *(plural* los perdones*)* ■ **forgiveness**
> pedir perdón to apologize, to apologise *UK*: nos pidió perdón por no haber venido a

visitarnos he apologized for not having come to visit us

las autoridades otorgaron el perdón al acusado the authorities pardoned the accused man

perdón, ¿me podría decir la hora? excuse me, could you tell me what time it is?

te he pisado sin querer, perdón I accidentally trod on you, I'm sorry.

perdonar [1] *verbo* ■ to forgive: lo hice sin querer, espero que me perdones I did it unintentionally, I hope that you forgive me

¡perdona! sorry!

¡perdona! te he pisado sin querer excuse me, I trod on you accidentally.

el **peregrino** , la **peregrina** ■ pilgrim.

el **perejil** ■ parsley.

la **pereza** ■ laziness.

me da pereza ponerme a estudiar I don't feel like studying.

perezoso, sa *adjetivo* ■ lazy.

la **perfección** (*plural* las perfecciones) ■ perfection: habla tres idiomas a la perfección she speaks three languages perfectly.

perfeccionar [1] *verbo* ■ to improve: tengo que perfeccionar mi nivel de inglés I have to improve my level of English.

perfecto, ta *adjetivo* ■ perfect.

el **perfil** ■ profile: los antiguos egipcios pintaban el cuerpo de frente y la cara de perfil the ancient Egyptians painted the body from the front and the face in profile.

el **perfume**

1. perfume: los perfumes franceses son apreciados en todo el mundo French perfumes are esteemed throughout the world
2. scent: me fascina el perfume de los jazmines the scent of jasmine fascinates me.

periódico, ca *adjetivo* ■ periodic: es importante hacer visitas periódicas al dentista it's important to make periodic visits to the dentist

el **periódico** ■ newspaper.

el **periodismo** ■ journalism.

el/la **periodista** ■ journalist.

el **periodo** , el **período** ■ period: el periodo de prueba dura tres meses the test period lasts three months.

perjudicar [8] *verbo*

1. to be harmful to: es mejor que no fumes, el tabaco perjudica la salud it's better that you don't smoke, tobacco is harmful to your health
2. to hurt: esta sequía va a perjudicar a los productores rurales this drought is going to hurt the rural farmers.

la **perla** ■ pearl.

permanecer [22] *verbo* ■ to stay.

permanente *adjetivo* ■ permanent.

el **permiso** ■ permission: le dieron permiso para faltar tres días they gave him permission to miss three days

con permiso excuse me: con permiso, ¿puedo pasar? excuse me, can I get by?

permitir [3] *verbo*

1. to permit: un plazo más largo nos permite trabajar con tranquilidad a later deadline permits us to work calmly
2. to allow: no les permitieron entrar porque el concierto ya había empezado they didn't allow them to enter because the concert had already started.

pero *conjunción* ■ but: el modelo de ese vestido es bonito, pero no me gusta el colour the style of that dress is pretty, but I don't like the color.

el **perro** , la **perra** ■ dog: es una perra muy tranquila she's a very quiet dog.

perseguir [32] *verbo* ■ to pursue: la policía persiguió al ladrón durante un par de horas the police pursued the thief for a couple of hours.

la **persiana** ■ blind.

la **persona** ■ person (*plural* **people**): muchas personas son partidarias del reciclaje many people are in favour of recycling

en persona in person

por persona per person.

el **personaje**

1. **character:** el personaje principal de la película the main character of the film
2. **figure:** es un personaje de la política he's a political figure.

personal *adjetivo* ■ **persona:** es un asunto personal it's a personal matter.

el **personal** ■ **staff:** nos ha ido tan bien con este restaurante que ya necesitamos más personal it's gone so well for us with this restaurant that we already need more staff.

la **personalidad**

1. **personality** *(plural* **personalities***)*: tiene una personalidad muy abierta she has a very open personality
2. **figure:** acudieron numerosas personalidades de la política a lot of political figures came.

la **perspectiva** ■ **perspective**
en perspectiva in perspective.

pertenecer [22] *verbo* ■ **to belong:** este reloj de bolsillo perteneció a mi abuelo this pocket watch belonged to my grandfather; ¿todavía perteneces al club de coleccionistas de sellos? do you still belong to the stamp collectors club?

las **pertenencias** ■ **belongings.**

perturbar [1] *verbo* ■ **to disturb:** perturba el orden público it disturbs the peace.

Perú ■ **Peru.**

peruano, na *adjetivo*

En inglés, los adjetivos que se refieren a un país o una región se escriben con mayúscula:

Peruvian

el **peruano** , la **peruana**

En inglés, los gentilicios se escriben con mayúscula:

Peruvian: los peruanos the Peruvians.

la **pesadilla** ■ **nightmare.**

pesado, da *adjetivo*

1. **heavy:** este baúl es muy pesado this trunk is very heavy; es mejor evitar comidas pe-

sadas antes de irse a dormir it's best to avoid heavy foods before going to sleep
2. **tiring:** el viaje en barco fue muy pesado the voyage was very tiring.

pesar [1] *verbo* ■ **to weigh:** el bebé pesa siete kilos the baby weighs seven kilos; por favor, ¿me podría pesar esta bolsa de naranjas? could you weigh this bag of oranges for me, please?

pesarse *verbo pronominal* ■ **to weigh oneself:** ¿te has pesado? have you weighed yourself?

la **pescadería** ■ **fish shop, fishmonger's** *UK.*

el **pescado** ■ **fish:** el pescado asado es mi plato favorito grilled fish is my favorite dish.

el **pescador** ■ **fisherman** *(plural* **fishermen***)*.

la **pescadora** ■ **fisherwoman** *(plural* **fisherwomen***)*.

pescar [8] *verbo*

1. **to go fishing:** salimos a pescar con el abuelo we went fishing with our grandfather
2. **to catch:** en un solo día pescamos 25 truchas in only one day we caught 25 trout
➤ ¡te pesqué con las manos en la masa! I caught you red-handed!

la **peseta** ■ **peseta.**

pesimista *adjetivo* ■ **pessimistic:** ¡no seas tan pesimista! don't be so pessimistic!

el **peso**

1. **weight:** ¿tiene idea del peso de esa maleta? do you have any idea what the weight of that suitcase is?
2. *moneda* **peso:** ¿a cuántos pesos chilenos equivale un peso mexicano? how many Chilean pesos equal a Mexican peso?
➤ ganar peso to put on weight: este invierno he ganado mucho peso this winter I've put on weight
➤ perder peso to lose weight: he perdido mucho peso I've lost a lot of weight.

la **pestaña** ■ **eyelash** *(plural* **eyelashes***)*.

la **peste**

1. **plague:** en Europa hubo varias pestes que diezmaron a la población in Europe there

were several plagues that decimated the population

2. stink: ¡qué peste! what a stink!

el pétalo ■ petal.

el petardo ■ banger *UK*, firecracker *US*.

la petición *(plural* las peticiones*)*

1. request: hicimos una petición al alcalde we made a request to the mayor

2. petition: entregaron una petición al gerente they handed in a petition to the manager.

el petróleo ■ oil, petroleum.

el pez *(plural* los peces*)* ■ fish *(plural* fish*)*: hay muchos peces en este río there area lot of fish in this river

> un pez de colores a goldfish

> un pez espada a swordfish.

la pezuña ■ hoof *(plural* hooves*)*.

la pianista ■ pianist.

el piano ■ piano.

la picadura

1. *de mosquito, serpiente* bite

2. *de abeja* sting.

picante *adjetivo* ■ spicy, hot: este pollo está demasiado picante para mi gusto this chicken is too spicy for my taste.

picar [8] *verbo*

1. to bite: estaba en el jardín y me picaron los mosquitos I was in the garden and the mosquitos bit me; los peces tardaron varias horas en picar the fish took several hours to bite

2. to chop: para esa sopa, hay que picar las verduras en pedazos pequeños for that soup, you have to chop the vegetables into small pieces

3. to mince *UK*, **to grind** *US*: primero tienes que picar la carne first yo have to mince the meat

4. to sting: me pican los ojos my eyes are stinging

5. to snack: no deberías picar entre horas you shouldn't snack between meals

> ten cuidado, que esta salsa pica mucho be careful, this salsa is very hot.

el picnic ■ picnic.

el pico

1. beak: la gaviota llevaba un pez en el pico the seagull was carrying a fish in its beak

2. peak: quieren llegar al pico del Aconcagua they want to get to the peak of the Aconcagua

3. pick: necesito un pico y una pala I need a pick and a shovel

> cerrar el pico to shut one's trap: me dijo que cerrara el pico he told me to shut my trap.

el picor ■ itch.

el pie

1. foot *(plural* feet*)*: a los adolescentes les crecen los pies muy rápido adolescents' feet grow very quickly

2. base: pusieron flores al pie de la estatua del héroe they put flowers at the base of the statue of the hero

> estar de pie standing

> ponerse de pie to stand

> un pie de foto a photo caption

> pies planos flat feet

> a pie on foot: como hacía buen tiempo, decidimos venir a pie since the weather was fine, we decided to come on foot.

la piedad ■ mercy.

la piedra ■ stone: Nacho me tiró una piedra Nacho threw a stone at me

> una piedra preciosa a precious stone

> de piedra stone: vive en una casa de piedra he lives in a stone house

> quedarse de piedra to be flabbergasted: me quedé de piedra cuando me enteré de la noticia I was flabbergasted when I found out the news.

la piel

1. skin: los bebés tienen la piel suave y delicada babies have soft, delicate skin; la piel de las uvas grape skin

2. leather: la piel se utiliza para fabricar zapatos leather is used to make shoes

3. fur: los abrigos de piel han pasado de moda fur coats have gone out of style

> de piel leather: este bolso es de piel this bag is leather

> tener la piel de gallina to have goose pimples.

la **pierna** ■ leg.

la **pieza** ■ piece: acabo de comprar un rompecabezas de 1.000 piezas I just bought a 1,000 piece puzzle

▸ piezas de recambio spare parts.

el **pijama** ■ pyjamas *UK*, pajamas *US*.

el **pijo** , la **pija** ■ rich kid.

la **pila**

1. battery *(plural* batteries*)*: esta radio funciona con pilas this radio runs on batteries

2. pile: una pila de libros a pile of books.

la **píldora** ■ pill.

pillar [1] *verbo*

1. to catch: creo que he pillado un resfriado I think I've caught a cold; la han pillado copiando they caught her copying

2. to hit: esta mañana casi me pilla un coche this morning I was almost hit by a car

▸ tu casa me pilla de camino your house is on my way.

pillo, lla *adjetivo*

1. *travieso* naughty

2. *astuto* streetwise

el **pillo** , la **pilla** ■ rascal.

el/la **piloto**

1. *de avión* pilot

2. *de coche* driver.

la **pimienta** ■ pepper.

el **pimiento** ■ pepper: hay pimientos de color rojo, verde y amarillo there are red, green and yellow peppers

▸ un pimiento morrón a red pepper.

el **pincel** ■ paintbrush.

pinchar [1] *verbo*

1. to puncture: los niños han pinchado la pelota the children have punctured the ball

2. to have a puncture: hemos pinchado justo al salir de casa we had a puncture just after leaving home

3. to play records: Alfredo pincha en una discoteca Alfredo plays records in a discotheque.

el **pinchazo**

1. puncture: he tenido un pinchazo en la carretera I had a puncture on the road

2. stab: sintió un pinchazo de dolor en el brazo he felt a stab of pain in his arm.

el **pingüino** ■ penguin.

el **pino** ■ pine tree.

el **pintalabios** ■ lipstick.

pintar [1] *verbo* ■ to paint: le pidieron que pintara un retrato de la familia they asked him to paint a family portrait; si quieres ahorrar dinero, podemos pintar nosotros mismos la casa if you want to save money, we can paint the house ourselves

pintarse *verbo pronominal* ■ to put one's make-up on: sólo me falta pintarme y estoy lista I just need to put my make-up on and I'll be ready.

el **pintaúñas** ■ nail polish.

el **pintor** , la **pintora** ■ painter.

la **pintura**

1. painting: Inma presentó sus primeras pinturas en una galería de la ciudad Inma showed her first paintings at a gallery in the city

2. paint: para pintar toda la casa necesitamos muchos botes de pintura in order to paint the whole house we need a lot of cans of paint

3. make-up: no he traído mis pinturas, ¿me prestas tu pintalabios? I didn't bring my make-up, could you lend me your lipstick?

la **pinza**

1. *para ropa* clothes-peg *UK*, clothespin *US*

2. *para pelo* hairgrip *UK*, bobby pin *US*

3. *de cangrejo* claw

4. tweezers: con una pinza va a ser más fácil sacarte esa espina it will be easier to get that thorn out with tweezers.

la **piña**

1. *de pino* pine cone

2. *fruta* pineapple.

el **piojo** ■ louse *(plural* lice*)*.

la **pipa**

1. pipe: fuma en pipa he smokes a pipe

2. seed: una pipa de girasol a sunflower seed.

l **piragüismo** ■ canoeing.

a **pirámide** ■ pyramid.

pirata *adjetivo* ■ pirate: el mercado de CDs y vídeos piratas aumenta día a día the pirate CD and video market grows daily; un barco pirata a pirate ship

a **pirata** ■ pirate
un pirata informático a hacker.

el **piropo** ■ compliment: Luis siempre me echa piropos Luis is always paying me compliments.

el **pis** ■ pee: el niño quiere hacer pis the little boy wants to have a pee.

a **pisada**
1. footstep: lo oigo cuando llega porque sus pisadas son muy fuertes I hear him when he arrives because his footsteps are very loud
2. footprint: en la luna ha habido pisadas humanas desde 1969 there have been human footprints on the moon since 1969.

pisar [1] *verbo* ■ to step in: mira bien por dónde caminas, no pises los charcos watch carefully where you walk, don't step in the puddles

la **piscina** ■ swimming pool.

el **piso**
1. flat: se han comprado un piso en Sevilla they've bought a flat in Seville
2. floor: vivo en un quinto piso I live on the fifth floor.

la **pista**
1. trail: la policía está detrás de la pista del asesino the police are on the trail of the murderer
2. clue: te voy a dar una pista para ayudarte a encontrar la respuesta I'm going to give you a clue to help you find the answer
> la pista de aterrizaje the runway
> la pista de atletismo the running track
> la pista de baile the dance floor
> la pista de patinaje the skating rink
> la pista de esquí the ski slope.

la **pistola** ■ pistol.

pitar [1] *verbo*
1. to blow one's whistle: el árbitro pitó el final del partido the referee blew his whistle at the end of the match
2. to blow one's horn: ese camión te ha pitado that lorry blew its horn at you.

el **pito** ■ whistle.

la **pizarra**
1. *encerado* blackboard
2. *mineral* slate.

la **pizca** ■ pinch: creo que le falta algo, agrégale una pizca de sal I think that it's lacking something, add a pinch of salt to it.

la **placa**
1. plate
2. plaque: le entregamos una placa al director we presented a plaque to the director
> la placa dental plaque
> la placa de matrículo the number plate.

el **placer** ■ pleasure.

la **plaga** ■ plague.

el **plan** ■ plan: no tenemos planes para mañana we don't have any plans for tomorrow.

la **plancha**
1. sheet: una plancha de metal a sheet of metal
2. iron: una plancha de vapor a steam iron
> a la plancha grilled: tráigame un bistec a la plancha, por favor bring me a grilled steak, please.

planchar [1] *verbo*
1. to do the ironing: detesto planchar I hate doing the ironing
2. to iron: ¿quién me va a planchar estas camisas? who is going to iron these shirts for me?

planear [1] *verbo* ■ to plan: estamos planeando una gran fiesta para fin de año we're planning a big party for New Year's Eve.

el **planeta** ■ planet.

plano, na *adjetivo* ■ flat.

el **plano**
1. *de ciudad, metro* **map**
2. *de edificio* **plan.**

la **planta**
1. **plant:** tiene tantas plantas que la casa parece una selva she has so many plants that her house looks like jungle; **hay varias plantas industriales en las afueras del pueblo** there are several industrial plants on the outskirts of town
2. **sole:** tengo una verruga en la planta del pie I've got a verruca on the sole of my foot
3. **floor:** el edificio donde trabajo tiene cuatro plantas the building where I work has four floors
> la planta baja the first floor.

plantar [1] *verbo* ■ **to plant.**

el **plástico** ■ **plastic:** una botella de plástico a plastic bottle.

la **plata** ■ **silver:** una mina de plata a silver mine; **un anillo de plata** a silver ring.

el **plátano** ■ **banana.**

el **plato**
1. **plate:** hay que poner cinco platos en la mesa we have to put five plates on the table
2. **course:** de segundo plato había pescado al horno for the second course there was baked fish
3. **dish:** su especialidad son los platos vascos Basque dishes are his speciality; **la paella es mi plato favorito** paella is my favourite dish
> el plato del día the special of the day.

la **playa** ■ **beach:** en esta playa hay que tener cuidado porque las olas son muy grandes you have to be careful because the waves are very big on this beach; **este verano nos vamos a la playa** this summer we're going to the beach.

la **plaza**
1. **square:** la abuela lleva a los nietos a la plaza todas las tardes the grandmother takes her grandchildren to the square every afternoon
2. **vacancy** *(plural* **vacancies):** ha salido una plaza de informático a vacancy for a computer programmer has come up

3. **seat:** ¿cuántas plazas tiene tu coche? how many seats has your car got?
> un coche de cuatro plazas a four-seater car
> una plaza de toros a bullring.

el **plazo** ■ **period:** el plazo para la matrícula acaba el viernes the enrolment period ends on Friday
> a plazos in instalments.

plegar [25] *verbo* ■ **to fold:** plegad las hojas y dejadlas encima de la mesa fold the sheets of paper and leave them on the table.

pleno, na *adjetivo* ■ **middle:** en plena actuación, el actor tropezó y se cayó in the middle of the performance, the actor tripped and fell
> a plena luz del día in broad daylight.

el **plomo** ■ **lead.**

la **pluma**
1. **feather:** las aves se limpian las plumas birds clean their feathers; **este bebé es más ligero que una pluma** this baby is lighter than a feather
2. **pen:** ¿me prestas una pluma para escribir una carta? can you lend me a pen to write a letter?

el **plural** ■ **plural.**

la **población** *(plural* las poblaciones) ■ **population:** la población de España ronda los 40 millones the population of España is about 40 million.

poblar [16] *verbo*
1. **to inhabit:** los árabes poblaron estas tierras hace mucho tiempo the Arabs populated this land a long time ago
2. **to populate:** a lo largo de los siglos, diferentes olas de inmigrantes poblaron América through the centuries, different waves of immigrants populated America.

pobre *adjetivo* ■ **poor:** vivíamos en un barrio pobre we used to live in a poor area; **el pobre perro tiene frío** the poor dog is cold; **el pobre Raúl vuelve a estar enfermo** poor Raúl is ill again.

pobreza ■ poverty.

poco, ca *adjetivo*

1. *con un sustantivo singular* **not much, little:** tienen poco dinero they haven't got much money o they have little money

2. *con un sustantivo plural* **not many, few:** tiene pocos amigos he hasn't got many friends o he has few friends

poco *adverbio*

1. *con un verbo* **not much:** anoche dormí muy poco I didn't sleep very much last night

2. *con un adjetivo* **not very:** la película es poco conocida the film isn't very well know

poco *pronombre* ■ **not much: come muy poco** he doesn't eat much

un poco de a little o a bit: tengo un poco de hambre I'm a bit hungry; ¿quieres un poco de pastel? do you want a bit of cake?

poder [17] *verbo*

1.

> Para expresar la posibilidad o capacidad de hacer algo se emplea **can, to be able to:**

> puedes llamarle al 223 22 55 you can call him on 223 22 55; ¿puedes ayudarme? can you help me?; ¿podrás venir a la fiesta? will you be able to come to the party?; ¿podría decirme la hora? could you tell me the time?

> **Can** se emplea en el presente y **could** en el condicional. Para el resto de tiempos verbales se emplea **to be able to.**

2.

> Para pedir y dar permiso se emplea **can, may:**

> puedes ir a la fiesta you can go to the party; ¿te puedo coger el lápiz? can I borrow your pencil?

> ¿puedo pasar? may I come in?

> **May** y **can** tienen el mismo significado en este contexto, pero **may** se emplea en el lenguaje formal

3.

> En el condicional para expresar un grado de posibilidad más remoto se usa **may, might:**

> puede que venga a veros he may come to see you

por mucho que lo intento, no puedo con las matemáticas no matter how much I try, I can't do maths

sinceramente, no puedo con Roberto frankly, I can't stand Roberto

estoy harto, no puedo más I'm fed up, I can't cope any more

puede ser maybe, perhaps: ¿crees que aceptará la invitación? —puede ser do you think he'll accept the invitation? – maybe

¿se puede? —sí, adelante may I? – yes, come in.

el **poder** ■ **power:** no me interesa el poder, sino el bienestar de mi pueblo power doesn't interest me, but rather the well-being of my people.

poderoso, sa *adjetivo* ■ **powerful.**

podrido, da *adjetivo* ■ **rotten:** había un fuerte olor a fruta podrida there was a strong smell of rotten fruit.

el **poema** ■ poem.

la **poesía**

1. **poetry:** se me hace muy difícil leer poesía I find it very difficult to read poetry

2. **poem:** Laura leyó sus poesías en la fiesta de la escuela Laura read her poems at the school party.

el/la **poeta** ■ poet.

el/la **policía**

1. *hombre* **policeman** (*plural* **policemen**)

2. *mujer* **policewoman** (*plural* **policewomen**)

la **policía** ■ **police:** pensamos que había entrado un ladrón y por eso llamamos a la policía we thought that a thief had broken in and that's why we called the police.

el **polideportivo** ■ sports centre.

político, ca *adjetivo*

1. **political:** un partido político a political party

2. **by marriage:** la esposa de mi tío es mi tía política my uncle's wife is my aunt by marriage

el **político**, la **política** ■ politician.

el **pollo** ■ chicken.

el **polo**

1. *helado* **ice lolly** (*plural* **ice lollies**) *UK*, Popsicle® *US*

2. *ropa* **polo shirt**
> **el Polo Norte** the North Pole
> **el Polo Sur** the South Pole.

la **polución** *(plural* las poluciones*)* ■ **pollution.**

el **polvo** ■ **dust: hay que limpiar este mueble porque está lleno de polvo** you have to clean this piece of furniture here because it's covered in dust.

el **polvorón** *(plural* los polvorones*)* ■ **crumbly sweet.**

la **pólvora** ■ **gunpowder.**

la **pomada** ■ **ointment.**

el **pomelo** ■ **grapefruit** *(plural* **grapefruit** o **grapefruits***)*.

el **pomo** ■ **handle: el pomo de esta puerta está pegajoso** this door's handle is sticky.

el **pómulo** ■ **cheekbone.**

poner [47] *verbo*

1. **to put: puse la silla cerca de la ventana para tener más luz** I put the chair close to the window to have more light

2. **to set: hay que poner la mesa para la cena** we have to set the table for dinner; **siempre nos ponen muchos deberes** they always set us a lot of homework; **voy a poner el despertador** I'm going to set the alarm clock

3. **to give: ¿qué nombre le van a poner al bebé?** what name are they going to give the baby?

4. **to put on: ¿pongo la televisión?** shall I put the television on?

5. **to put: queremos poner aire acondicionado** we want to put in air-conditioning

6. **to give: nos han puesto una multa** they've given us a fine

7. **to lay: las gallinas han puesto muchos huevos** the lens have laid a lot of eggs

ponerse *verbo pronominal*

1. **to put on: hace mucho frío, es mejor que te pongas el abrigo** it's very cold, it's best that you put on your coat

2. **to wear: no sé qué ponerme para la fiesta** I don't know what to wear for the party

3. **to be: Concha se puso contenta al verme** Concha was happy to see me

4. **to set: el sol se pone por el oeste** the sun sets in the west
> **ponerse a hacer algo** to get down to doing something: **creo que me voy a poner a estudiar** I think I'm going to get down to studying.

popular *adjetivo*

1. **popular: es un cantante muy popular** he's a very popular singer

2. **folk: estudia la cultura popular** he studies folk culture.

por *preposición*

1. **through: viajamos por varios países** we travelled through several countries

2. **because of: cerraron el aeropuerto por mal tiempo** they closed the airport because of bad weather

3. **times: 5 por 5 es igual a 25** 5 times 5 equals 25

4. **per: el límite de velocidad aquí es de 100 kilómetros por hora** the speed limit here is 100 kilometres per hour

5. **in: el recorrido es muy largo, hay que hacerlo por etapas** the journey is very long, we have to do it in stages

6. **at: a las 5 paso a buscarte por tu casa** at 5 o'clock I'll come pick you up at your house
> **por mí** as far as I'm concerned
> **¿por qué?** why?
> **por si** in case: **vendré esta tarde por si me necesitas** I'll come this afternoon in case you need me.

la **porcelana** ■ **china.**

el **porcentaje** ■ **percentage.**

la **porción** *(plural* las porciones*)* ■ **portion: con estos ingredientes puedes preparar hasta ocho porciones** with these ingredients you can make up eight portions with these ingredients.

porque *conjunción* ■ **because: no vino porque estaba enfermo** he didn't come because he was sick.

el **porqué** ■ **reason: quiero saber el porqué de este escándalo** I want to know the reason for this commotion.

la **porquería**

1. **junk: el desván está lleno de porquería** the attic is full of junk

2. rubbish UK, a piece of junk US: este video-juego es una porquería this video game is rubbish

3. rubbish UK, junk US: no comas tantas porquerías don't eat so much rubbish.

el **portal** ■ doorway: espérame en el portal wait for me in the doorway.

portátil adjetivo ■ portable.

el **portazo**

> dio un portazo he slammed the door
> la puerta se cerró de un portazo the door slammed shut
> desde aquí oí el portazo I heard the door slam from here.

la **portería**

1. porter's office: lo dejé en la portería I left it in the porter's office

2. goal: un saque de portería a goal kick.

el **portero** , **la** **portera**

1. goalkeeper: el portero paró el penalti the goalkeeper stopped the penalty

2. porter: le he dejado las llaves al portero I left the keys with the porter

> el portero automático the entryphone.

portorriqueño, ña adjetivo

En inglés, los adjetivos que se refieren a un país o una región se escriben con mayúscula:

Puerto Rican

el **portorriqueño** , **la** **portorriqueña**

En inglés, los gentilicios se escriben con mayúscula:

Puerto Rican: los portorriqueños the Puerto Ricans.

Portugal ■ Portugal.

portugués (plural portugueses) adjetivo

En inglés, los adjetivos que se refieren a un país o una región se escriben con mayúscula:

Portuguese

el **portugués** , **la** **portuguesa**

En inglés, los gentilicios se escriben con mayúscula:

Portuguese
los portugueses the Portuguese

el **portugués** ■ Portuguese

En inglés, los idiomas se escriben con mayúscula.

poseer [35] verbo

1. to own: sus padres poseen un chalé con piscina his parents have a holiday home with a swimming pool

2. to have: posee conocimientos de informática ha has a knowledge of computing.

posesivo, va adjetivo ■ possessive: es una persona muy posesiva he's a very possessive person

> un adjetivo posesivo a possessive adjective.

la **posibilidad**

1. possibility (plural possibilities): no había pensado en esa posibilidad I hadn't thought about that possibility

2. chance: eso le da la posibilidad de ir a la universidad that gives him the chance to go to college

> tener posibilidades de algo to have a good chance of something: tiene muchas posibilidades de llegar a la final he has a good chance of making it to the finals.

posible adjetivo ■ possible: lo siento, pero no es posible I'm sorry, but it's not possible

> ¿es posible cambiar estas entradas? is it possible to change these tickets?
> es posible que se haya perdido it's possible that he got lost
> vamos a hacer todo lo posible we're going to do everything possible
> lo antes posible as soon as possible.

la **posición** (plural las posiciones) ■ position: hay que mantenerlo en posición vertical we have to keep it in a vertical position

> ha quedado en segunda posición he came in second place.

positivo, va adjetivo ■ positive: deberías pensar en cosas positivas you ought to think about positive things; es un chico muy positivo he's a very positive guy

> el análisis dio positivo the test was positive.

posponer [47] *verbo* ■ to postpone.

la **postal** ■ postcard.

el **poste**
1. post: el balón dio en el poste derecho de la portería the ball hit the right post of the goalpost
2. pole: un poste telefónico a telegraph pole.

el **póster** *(plural* los pósters*)* ■ poster.

postizo, za *adjetivo* ■ fake.

el **postre** ■ dessert, pudding UK: ¿qué hay de postre? what is there for dessert?

la **postura** ■ position: hace dos horas que está sentado en la misma postura he's been sitting in the same position for two hours.

potable *adjetivo*
agua potable drinking water.

la **potencia** ■ power: un motor de mucha potencia a high powered engine
en potencia in the making: es un gran músico en potencia he's a great musician in the making.

potente *adjetivo* ■ powerful.

el **pozo** ■ well: un pozo de petróleo an oil well.

la **práctica** ■ practice: con la práctica aprenderás a hacerlo you'll learn how to do it with practice
en la práctica in practice: en la práctica la gente confunde esas dos palabras in practice people confuse those two words
poner algo en práctica to put something into practice: puso su idea en práctica he put his idea into practice.

las **prácticas** ■ practical training: Ana está haciendo prácticas en una editorial Ana is doing practical training at a publishing company.

practicar [8] *verbo* ■ to practise UK, to practice: necesitas practicar más tu inglés you need to practise your English more
¿practicas algún deporte? do you play a sport?

práctico, ca *adjetivo* ■ practical: es una persona muy práctica he's a very practical person.

el **prado** ■ meadow: las vacas pacen en estos prados cows graze in these meadows.

la **precaución** *(plural* las precauciones*)* ■ foresight: tuvo la precaución de dejarlo desenchufado he had the foresight to leave it unplugged
tomar precauciones to take precautions: hay que tomar precauciones cuando tomamos el sol we have to take precautions when we sunbathe.

el **precio** ■ price: van a subir los precios otra vez prices are going to go up again
¿qué precio tienen? how much are they?

precioso, sa *adjetivo* ■ beautiful.

el **precipicio** ■ cliff: cayó por un precipicio he fell off a cliff.

precipitarse [1] *verbo pronominal*
no os precipitéis y elegid con calma don't rush and choose carefully
parece que me precipité al juzgarlo it seems that I was hasty in judging him.

preciso, sa *adjetivo*
1. precise: me dio indicaciones precisas de cómo llegar he gave me precise directions for how to get there
2. accurate: un instrumento muy preciso a very accurate instrument
si es preciso, pide ayuda if necessary, ask for help
no es preciso que te lo aprendas de memoria it's not necessary for you to memorize it.

predecir [48] *verbo* ■ to predict.

la **preferencia**
1. preference: dan preferencia a los estudiantes con mejores notas they give preference to the students with better marks
2. right of way: tienen preferencia los que vienen por la izquierda the ones that come from the left have right of way
tiene preferencia por los colores brillantes she prefers bright colours.

preferir [20] *verbo* ■ to prefer: prefiere estudiar solo en su casa he prefers to study alone at home
prefiero no saberlo I'd rather not know.

el prefijo
1. *gramatical* **prefix**
2. *telefónico* **dialling code, code.**

la pregunta ■ **question:** no contestó mi pregunta he didn't answer my question
> me hicieron varias preguntas they asked me several questions.

preguntar [1] *verbo* ■ **to ask:** pregúntale a la profesora ask the teacher
> preguntarle algo a alguien to ask somebody something: le pregunté la hora I asked him what time it was
> cuando llegues allí, pregunta por Ana when you get there, ask for Ana

preguntarse *verbo pronominal* ■ **to wonder:** me pregunto por qué ha hecho eso I wonder why he did it.

el prejuicio ■ **prejudice**
> tener prejuicios to be prejudiced: no tiene prejuicios contra nadie he's not prejudiced against anybody
> prejuicios raciales racial prejudice.

premiar [1] *verbo*
1. **to give an award to:** premiaron al mejor alumno they gave an award to the best student
2. **to reward:** hay que premiar el esfuerzo we have to reward effort.

el premio
1. **prize:** ganó el primer premio she won the first prize; le dieron el Premio Nobel they gave him the Nobel Prize
2. **reward:** como premio a su buen trabajo as a reward for his good work

EL PREMIO MIGUEL DE CERVANTES

The **Premio Miguel de Cervantes** (Miguel de Cervantes Prize) was founded in 1975 and is Spain's most prestigious literary prize. Every year, it is awarded to an author writing in Spanish from any literary genre. King Juan Carlos presides over the prize-giving ceremony held on 23rd April, the date of Miguel de Cervantes's death and World Book Day. Past prizewinners include Camilo José Cela, Carlos Fuentes and Francisco Umbral.

la prenda
> prenda de vestir garment
> prendas de lana woollen garments.

prender [2] *verbo*
> prender fuego a algo to set fire to something: los ladrones prendieron fuego al coche the thieves set fire to the car.

la prensa ■ **press:** la prensa nacional the national press.

la preocupación *(plural* las preocupaciones*)*
1. **worry** *(plural* **worries***):* tienen muchas preocupaciones they have a lot of worries
2. **concern:** es un motivo de preocupación para sus padres it's a cause for concern for his parents.

preocupar [1] *verbo* ■ **to worry:** me preocupa mucho el examen de mañana tomorrow's exam worries me a lot

preocuparse *verbo pronominal* ■ **to worry:** no te preocupes don't worry
> preocuparse por algo to worry about something: mi madre se preocupa por todo my mum worries about everything
> se preocupa mucho si no llamo she gets very worried if I don't call.

la preparación *(plural* las preparaciones*)* ■ **preparation:** la preparación de los informes lleva tiempo the preparation of the reports takes time
> le falta preparación he lacks training.

preparar [1] *verbo*
1. **to prepare:** nos están preparando para el examen de admisión they're preparing us for the entrance exam
2. **to make:** prepara unos postres exquisitos he makes exquisite desserts

prepararse *verbo pronominal*
1. **to get ready:** se preparó para salir he got ready to go out
2. **to prepare:** tienen que prepararse para el examen they have to prepare for the exam
3. **to train:** se están preparando para la maratón they're training for the marathon
> prepárate para una gran sorpresa prepare yourself for a big surprise.

los **preparativos** ■ preparations.

la **preposición** (plural las preposiciones) ■ preposition.

la **presa**
1. dam: van a construir una presa they're going to build a dam
2. prey: tiburones en busca de una presa sharks in search of prey.

prescindir [3] verbo ■ prescindir de algo to do without something: hoy poca gente puede prescindir del móvil today few people can do without their mobile phones.

la **presencia** ■ presence: lo hizo en mi presencia he did it in my presence.

la **presentación** (plural las presentaciones) ■ presentation: me puso buena nota por la presentación he gave me a good mark for the presentation
   hacer las presentaciones to make the introductions: mi padre se encargó de hacer las presentaciones my father took care of making the introductions.

el **presentador** , la **presentadora**
1. presenter: la presentadora del informativo de las 8 the presenter of the 8 o'clock news
2. host: el presentador del nuevo concurso televisivo the host of the new TV quiz show.

presentar [1] verbo
1. to introduce: me presentó a su hermana she introduced me to her sister
2. to hand in: no ha presentado el trabajo he hasn't handed in his paper; el inspector presentó su dimisión the inspector handed in his resignation
3. to present: presenta el informativo de las 8 she presents the 8 o'clock news
4. to host: presenta el concurso televisivo he hosts the TV quiz show
5. to launch: va a presentar su nuevo disco he's going to launch his new album
   te presento a mi hermano let me introduce you to my brother

presentarse verbo pronominal
1. to turn up: se presentó tarde y sin los deberes he turned up late and without his homework

2. to introduce oneself: se presentó como el nuevo director he introduced himself as the new director
   no se presentó al examen he didn't take the exam.

presente adjetivo ■ present: había sólo tres alumnos presentes there were only three students present; en las presentes circunstancias under the present circumstances
   tener algo presente to bear something in mind: hay que tener presente ese aspecto del caso we have to bear in mind that aspect of the case
   ¡presente! here!

el **presente** ■ present: vive el presente sin olvidar el futuro he lives in the present without forgetting the future; dime el presente de indicativo del verbo "ser" tell me the present indicative of the verb "ser"
   los presentes those present.

el **presidente** , la **presidenta**
1. de un país, una empresa president: el presidente de los Estados Unidos the President of the United States
2. de una asociación, un jurado chairman (hombre) (plural chairmen), chairwoman (mujer) (plural chairwomen): el presidente del club de fútbol the chairman of the football club.

la **presión** (plural las presiones) ■ pressure: está sometido a una fuerte presión he's under a lot of pressure
   la presión sanguínea blood pressure
   la presión atmosférica atmospheric pressure.

preso, sa adjetivo
   está preso he's in prison
   se los llevaron presos they arrested them

el **preso** , la **presa** ■ prisoner.

el **préstamo** ■ loan: pidió un préstamo para comprarse un coche he asked for a loan to buy a car.

prestar [1] verbo ■ to lend: un amigo me prestó su bicicleta a friend lent me his bicycle
   ¿me prestas los patines? can I borrow your skates?

prestar atención to pay attention: presta más atención a lo que dice la profesora pay more attention to what the teacher says.

presumido, da *adjetivo* ■ vain.

presumir [3] *verbo* ■ to show off: lo hace sólo para presumir he only does it to show off

> Mario presume de inteligente Mario thinks he's really intelligent.

pretender [2] *verbo*

1. to expect: no pretenderán que me estudie todo esto they won't expect me to study all this; ¿pretendes que yo te crea? do you expect me to believe you?

2. to try to achieve: no sé lo que pretenden con eso I don't know what they're trying to achieve with that

3. to intend: pretenden hacernos estudiar más they intend to make us study more

> ⚠ The Spanish word **pretender** is a false friend: it does not mean "pretend".

el **pretexto** ■ excuse: era sólo un pretexto it was just an excuse.

prevenir [55] *verbo*

1. to prevent: ayuda a prevenir los resfriados it helps to prevent colds

2. to warn: mis padres me han prevenido contra los peligros de la droga my parents have warned me about the dangers of drugs

> más vale prevenir que curar prevention is better than cure.

prever [56] *verbo*

1. to anticipate: nadie lo había previsto nobody had anticipated it

2. to plan: tienen previsto finalizar las obras este año they plan to finish the building work this year

> prevén un aumento de las temperaturas a nivel mundial they foresee an increase in temperatures worldwide.

previo, via *adjetivo* ■ previous: no es necesario tener experiencia previa it's not necessary to have previous experience

> sin previo aviso without warning: llegó sin previo aviso he arrived without warning.

previsto, ta (*adjetivo & verbo*)

■ *adjetivo*

> tener previsto to plan: no tenía previsto gastar tanto he didn't plan to spend so much; la salida está prevista a las 2 the departure is planned for 2 o'clock

> un cambio que no estaba previsto an unexpected change

> todo salió como estaba previsto everything came out as expected

> tiene prevista la llegada a las 2 she's due in at 2 o'clock

■ *verbo*

> ➤ prever.

la **primaria** ■ primary school *UK*, elementary school *US*: este año termina la primaria this year he finishes primary school.

la **primavera** ■ spring: en primavera in spring.

primer *adjetivo* ➤ primero

Shortened form of **primero** used before masculine singular nouns.

primero, ra *adjetivo & pronombre* ■ first: en la primera página on the first page; el primer mes del año the first month of the year

> en primer lugar, nos dio a todos las gracias first, he thanked all of us

> se sienta en la primera fila he sits in the first row

> quiere ser la primera de la clase she wants to be at the top of the class

> fue el primero en terminar he was the first one to finish

> a primera hora de la mañana first thing in the morning

> el primer ministro the prime minister

> a primeros de enero at the beginning of January

> primeros auxilios first aid

primero *adverbio* ■ first: primero cogeremos el tren y luego el avión first we'll take the train and then the plane.

primitivo, va *adjetivo* ■ primitive.

el **primo**, la **prima** ■ cousin

> son primas hermanas they are first cousins.

la **princesa** ■ princess.

principal *adjetivo* ■ main: una de las principales causas de accidentes one of the main causes of accidents

> lo principal es ser honesto the main thing is to be honest.

el **príncipe** ■ prince.

el/la **principiante** ■ beginner.

el **principio**

1. beginning: el principio de la película es muy original the beginning of the film is very original

2. principle: se basa en un principio moral it's based on a moral principle; no tiene principios he doesn't have principles

> al principio at first: al principio dijo que no at first he said no

> en principio in principle: en principio, parecía bueno in principle, it seemed good

> desde un principio no me gustó I didn't like him from the start

> a principios de mes at the beginning of the month.

la **prisa** ■ hurry: ¿a qué viene tanta prisa? what's the hurry?

> darse prisa to hurry up: ¡date prisa! hurry up!

> correr prisa to be urgent: esto corre prisa this is urgent

> tener prisa to be in a hurry: me voy, que tengo prisa I'm going, I'm in a hurry.

la **prisión** ■ prison: fue condenado a 20 años de prisión he was sentenced to 20 years in prison.

el **prisionero** , la **prisionera** ■ prisoner.

los **prismáticos** ■ binoculars.

privado, da *adjetivo* ■ private: un colegio privado a private school; su vida privada his private life

> en privado in private: lo celebraron en privado they celebrated it in private.

el **privilegio** ■ privilege: es un gran privilegio it's a great privilege.

la **probabilidad** ■ probability (*plural* probabilities)

> no tiene ninguna probabilidad de ganar he doesn't have any chance of winning

> ¿cuáles son las probabilidades? what are the chances?

> si no estudias hay menos probabilidades de que apruebes if you don't study there's less chance that you'll pass.

probable *adjetivo* ■ likely: tal vez se perdieron —es muy probable maybe they got lost – it's very likely

> me parece muy poco probable it seems very unlikely to me

> es probable que se haya olvidado it's likely that he forgot.

el **probador** ■ fitting room, changing room *UK*.

probar [16] *verbo*

1. to prove: puedo probar que miente I can prove that he's lying

2. to test: están probando una nueva vacuna they're testing a new vaccine

3. to taste: pruébala, a ver si está bien aliñada taste it and see if it needs seasoning

4. to try: prueba esto, que te va a gustar try this, you'll like it

> me probé varias tallas I tried on several sizes.

el **problema** ■ problem: nunca pude resolver el problema I never managed to solve the problem

> tiene muchos problemas he has a lot of problems

> siempre se está metiendo en problemas he's always getting into trouble

> tiene problemas de salud he has health problems.

el **procesador** ■ processor.

el **proceso** ■ process: el proceso de paz the peace process.

la **producción** (*plural* las producciones) ■ production.

procurar [1] *verbo* ■ to try: procura llegar a tiempo try to arrive on time.

producir [23] *verbo*

1. to produce: esa región produce mucho vino this region produces a lot of wine

2. **to cause:** el accidente **produjo un gran atasco** the accident caused a major traffic jam ▪ **el polen me produce alergia** pollen gives me allergies

producirse *verbo pronominal* ▪ **to take place:** se produjo una explosión en el centro de la ciudad an explosion took place in the city centre.

el **producto** ▪ **product:** productos de belleza beauty products; productos frescos fresh produce; productos químicos chemical.

la **profesión** *(plural* las profesiones*)* ▪ **profession.**

profesional *adjetivo* ▪ **professional**

la **profesional** ▪ **professional.**

el **profesor** , la **profesora**

1. **teacher:** la profesora de inglés the English teacher

2. **instructor:** la profesora de natación the swimming instructor; el profesor de autoescuela the driving instructor

3. **professor:** es profesor universitario he's a university professor.

la **profundidad** ▪ **depth:** a una profundidad de tres metros at a depth of three metres

➤ **tiene tres metros de profundidad** it's three metres deep

➤ **en profundidad** in depth: lo estudié en profundidad I studied it in depth.

profundo, da *adjetivo* ▪ **deep:** la parte más profunda de la piscina the deepest part of the swimming pool

➤ **poco profundo** shallow: un pozo poco profundo a shallow well.

el **programa**

1. **programme** *UK*, **program** *US*: es mi programa favorito it's my favourite programme

2. **program:** un programa informático a computer program.

el **programador** , la **programadora** ▪ **programmer.**

programar [1] *verbo*

1. **to plan:** no he programado nada para las próximas vacaciones I haven't planned anything for next holidays

2. **to set:** ¿sabes cómo programar el video? do you know how to set the video recorder?

3. **to program:** primero hay que programar el ordenador first you have to program the computer.

el **progreso** ▪ **progress:** el progreso de la ciencia scientific progress; ha hecho progresos en inglés she's made progress in English.

prohibido, da *adjetivo* ▪ **forbidden:** eso está absolutamente prohibido that is absolutely forbidden

➤ **prohibido fumar** no smoking

➤ **prohibida la entrada** no entry

➤ **un medicamento prohibido en ese país** a drug banned in that country.

prohibir [60] *verbo*

1. **to prohibit:** han prohibido la publicidad del tabaco they've prohibited tobacco advertising

2. **to ban:** le prohibieron usar el móvil en clase they banned him from using his mobile phone in class

3. **to forbid:** le prohibieron los alimentos grasos they forbade him from eating fatty foods.

el **promedio** ▪ **average:** duerme un promedio de siete horas he sleeps an average of seven hours

➤ **este año he tenido un buen promedio en los estudios** this year I've had good average marks

➤ **en promedio, estudia muy poco** on average, he studies very little.

la **promesa** ▪ **promise:** siempre cumple sus promesas she always keeps her promises.

prometer [2] *verbo* ▪ **to promise:** prometiste llevarnos al cine you promised to take us to the cinema

➤ **prometió estudiar más** he promised to study more

➤ **¿me lo prometes?—te lo prometo** do you promise?—I promise.

el **pronombre** ▪ **pronoun.**

el **pronóstico** ▪ **forecast:** el pronóstico del tiempo the weather forecast.

pronto *adverbio* ▪ **soon:** va a volver pronto he's going to return soon

> ¡hasta pronto! see you soon!
> lo más pronto posible as soon as possible
> tan pronto como as soon as: llámame tan pronto como llegues call me as soon as you arrive
> de pronto oímos un grito all of a sudden we heard a scream.

pronunciar [1] *verbo*

1. to pronounce: ¿cómo se pronuncia esta palabra? how do you pronounce this word?
2. to make: el director pronunció un discurso the director made a speech.

la **propaganda**

1. advertising: hay mucha propaganda en la televisión there's a lot of advertising on television
2. junk mail: el buzón está lleno de propaganda the letter box is full of junk mail
> hacerle propaganda a algo to advertise something: le hacen mucha propaganda a ese producto they're advertising that product a lot.

la **propiedad** ■ property (plural **properties**).

el **propietario** , la **propietaria** ■ owner.

la **propina** ■ tip: ¿dejaste propina? did you leave a tip?
> le di propina la taxista I tipped the taxi driver
> ¿cuánto le diste de propina? how much did you tip him?

propio, pia *adjetivo*

1. own: tengo mi propio ordenador I have my own computer
2. *él* himself, *ella* herself: me lo dijo el propio director the director himself told me
> es muy propio de la gente de esa edad it's very typical of people of that age.

proponer [47] *verbo*

1. to suggest: nos propuso ir al cine he suggested we went to the cinema; propongo que nos vayamos I suggest that we leave
2. to nominate: lo propusieron para el premio they nominated him for the award
> le propuso matrimonio he proposed to her
> me propongo escribirles más a menudo I plan to write to them more often

> quiere proponerte algo he wants to propose something to you.

el **propósito** ■ purpose: su único propósito es ganar his only purpose is to win
> sus propósitos son buenos his intentions are good
> creo que lo hizo a propósito I think he did it on purpose
> a propósito, si lo ves dile que me llame by the way, if you see him tell him to call me.

la **propuesta** ■ proposal.

el/la **protagonista** ■ main character: al final el protagonista muere the main character dies at the end.

la **protección** (plural las protecciones) ■ protection.

proteger [11] *verbo* ■ to protect: la sombrilla nos protege del sol the sunshade protects us from the sun
> ropa para protegerse del frío clothes to protect oneself from the cold.

la **proteína** ■ protein.

la **protesta** ■ protest: se unieron a la protesta they joined the protest
> una manifestación de protesta a protest demonstration.

protestante *adjetivo* ■ Protestant: mi amigo Tomás es protestante my friend Thomas is a Protestant

el/la **protestante** ■ Protestant.

protestar [1] *verbo*

1. to complain: lo único que hace es protestar the only thing he does is complain; dejad de protestar por todo y a trabajar stop complaining about everything and get to work
2. to protest: protestan por la subida de los precios they're protesting about the increase in prices.

el **provecho**

> sacar provecho de algo to benefit from something: sacó mucho provecho de su estancia en Europa he didn't benefitted a lot from his stay in Europe
> ¡buen provecho! have a nice meal!

el proverbio ■ proverb.

la provincia ■ province.

provisional *adjetivo* ■ provisional.

provocar [8] *verbo*

1. to provoke: deja de provocar a tu hermano stop provoking your brother
2. to cause: las inundaciones han provocado el cierre de varias carreteras the floods have caused the closure of several roads
> no saben lo que provocó el incendio they don't know what started the fire.

próximo, ma *adjetivo & pronombre* ■ next: el próximo lunes tengo un examen de inglés next Monday I have an English exam; invítalo la próxima vez que lo veas invite him next time you see him
> mi casa está próxima a la playa my house is near the beach.

proyectar [1] *verbo*

1. to plan: están proyectando viajar a América they're planning to travel to America
2. to show: nos proyectaron una película they showed us a film
3. to cast: la casa proyecta su sombra en parte del jardín the house casts its shadow on part of the garden.

el proyecto

1. plan: están haciendo proyectos para las vacaciones they're making holiday plans
2. project: trabaja en un proyecto de investigación he works on a research project
> un proyecto de ley a bill.

el proyector ■ projector.

prudente *adjetivo* ■ sensible: tienes que ser más prudente you have to be more sensible
> lo más prudente es no decir nada the wisest thing is not to say anything.

la prueba

1. proof: eso es la prueba de que lo puede hacer it's proof that he can do it
2. test: le hicieron una prueba de aptitud they gave him an aptitude test; el médico me ha hecho varias pruebas the doctor has carried out several tests on me

3. event: las pruebas de atletismo the track events
> es una prueba de cariño it's a token of affection
> una prueba nuclear a nuclear test
> tienen al jugador a prueba they have the player on probation
> rímel a prueba de agua waterproof mascara
> a prueba de balas bulletproof.

el psicólogo , la psicóloga ■ psychologist.

el/la psiquiatra ■ psychiatrist.

publicar [8] *verbo* ■ to publish.

la publicidad

1. advertising: una campaña de publicidad an advertising campaign
2. publicity: le han dado mucha publicidad al asunto they've given the matter a lot of publicity; ha tenido muy mala publicidad he's had very bad publicity.

público, ca *adjetivo* ■ public: transporte público public transport; un colegio público a state school *UK*, a public school *US*

el público

1. public: todavía no está abierto al público it's still not open to the public
2. audience: el público en el cine empezó a aplaudir the audience in the movie theater began to applaud
3. spectators: el público de un estadio the stadium spectators
> hacer algo público to make something public
> hablar en público le pone nervioso speaking in public makes him nervous.

pudrirse [3] *verbo pronominal* ■ to rot.

el pueblo

1. *de pocos habitantes* village
2. *más grande* town
3. people: el pueblo se rebeló contra el dictador the people rebelled against the director
> el pueblo español the Spanish people.

el puente

1. bridge: cruzaron el puente they crossed the bridge

2. long weekend: el puente del día de la Constitución the long weekend for the Constitution day

> hacer puente to take a long weekend

> el puente aéreo the shuttle service

HACER PUENTE

When a national or religious holiday falls on a Tuesday or a Thursday, it is common practice to **hacer puente**, that is, to have a long weekend by missing work and school on the preceding Monday or the following Friday.

---

el **puerro** ■ leek.

la **puerta**

1. door: la puerta de calle estaba abierta the front door was open

2. gate: entró por la puerta del jardín he entered through the garden gate

> llamaron a la puerta they knocked at the door

> un coche de cuatro puertas a four-door car

> la puerta de embarque boarding gate.

el **puerto** ■ port

> llegar a puerto to come into port

> un puerto deportivo a marina

> un puerto de montaña a mountain pass

> un puerto marítimo a sea port

> un puerto pesquero a fishing port.

Puerto Rico ■ Puerto Rico.

puertorriqueño, ña adjetivo

En inglés, los adjetivos que se refieren a un país o una región se escriben con mayúscula:

Puerto Rican

el **puertorriqueño** ,

la **puertorriqueño**

En inglés, los gentilicios se escriben con mayúscula:

Puerto Rican: los puertorriqueños the Puerto Ricans.

pues conjunción

1. then: tengo frío —pues ponte un jersey I'm cold —then put on a pullover

2. well: ¿crees que se lo contó? —pues... no sabría decirte do you think that he told her? — well, I couldn't tell you

> ¡pues claro que me divertí! of course I had fun!

la **puesta**

> la puesta de sol the sunset

> la puesta en libertad de los rehenes the freeing of the hostages.

el **puesto**

1. place: le reservé un puesto en la mesa I saved her a place at the table

2. stall: un puesto de fruta a fruit stall

3. job: tiene un buen puesto en la universidad she has a good job at the university

> obtuvo el primer puesto he got first place.

la **pulga** ■ flea.

el **pulgar** ■ thumb.

el **pulmón** (plural los pulmones) ■ lung.

la **pulmonía** ■ pneumonia.

el **pulpo** ■ octopus.

la **pulsera** ■ bracelet: una pulsera de oro a gold bracelet.

el **pulso** ■ pulse: le tomó el pulso she took his pulse

> tiene muy buen pulso she has a very steady hand

> levantaron el piano a pulso they picked up the piano by sheer strength.

la **punta**

1. point: la punta del cuchillo the point of the knife; se ha roto la punta del lápiz the point of the pencil broke

2. tip: la punta de la lengua the tip of the tongue

3. end: la otra punta del cordel the other end of the rope; la punta de la nariz the end of the nose

> la punta de los dedos the fingertips

> este lápiz no tiene punta this pencil is not sharpened

> se recorrió España de punta a punta he travelled España from one end to the other.

la **puntería**

> tiene muy buena puntería she's a good shot.

el **punto**

1. point: ganaron por un punto they won by one point; es uno de los puntos que van a tratar it's one of the points that they're going to discuss

2. dot: el punto sobre la "i" the dot on the "i"; punto com dot com

3. stitch: le pusieron cinco puntos en la frente they gave her five stitches on her forehead

4. full stop UK, period US: hay que terminar la frase con un punto you have to end the sentence with a period

> un punto cardinal a cardinal point
> punto y coma semicolon
> dos puntos colon
> punto final full stop UK, period US
> punto y aparte full stop, new paragraph UK, period, new paragraph US
> puntos suspensivos ellipsis
> punto y seguido full stop, new sentence UK, period, new sentence US
> punto de vista point of view
> estoy a punto de terminar I'm just about to finish
> estuvo a punto de llorar he was on the verge of tears
> estuve a punto de decírselo I nearly told her
> hasta cierto punto eso es verdad in a way that's true
> son las tres en punto it's three o'clock on the dot.

la **puntuación** (plural las puntuaciones)

1. ortografía punctuation

2. examen mark UK, grade US

3. juego, partido score.

puntual adjetivo

1. punctual: Jorge es muy puntual Jorge is very punctual

2. specific: trató un par de aspectos puntuales he dealt with a couple of specific points.

el **puñado** ■ handful: un puñado de tierra a handful of soil.

el **puñal** ■ dagger.

la **puñalada** ■ stab

> le asestó una puñalada en el pecho he stabbed him in the chest.

el **puñetazo** ■ punch

> le dio un puñetazo en el ojo he punched him in the eye.

el **puño**

1. fist: luchó con los puños he fought with his fists

2. cuff: una manga con puño a sleeve with a cuff.

el **puré**

> puré de verduras vegetable purée
> puré de patatas mashed potatoes.

puro, ra adjetivo ■ pure: el aire es muy puro aquí the air is very pure here

> son puras mentiras they're all lies
> es la pura verdad it's the absolute truth
> no basta con la pura fuerza strength alone is not enough
> fue pura coincidencia it was pure coincidence
> lo hago por puro gusto I do it just for pleasure

el **puro** ■ cigar.

el **pus** ■ pus.

que (conjunción & pronombre)

■ conjunción

1. that: dijo que esperaría he said that he would wait

En inglés en el lenguaje hablado se suele omitir **that** :

decidió que no quería ir he decided he didn't want to go

2. than: tengo mejores notas que tú I have better marks than you

> **Que** no se traduce cuando va precedido de verbos que expresan deseos, ruegos etc. En tales casos en inglés se usa el infinitivo:

quiero que me ayude I want him to help me
le pedí que me llamara I asked her to call me
¡que lo pases bien! have a good time!
yo que tú no iría if I were you I wouldn't go

■ *pronombre*

1. *cuando se refiere al sujeto* **who, that: el alumno que sacó mejores notas** the student who got better marks; **el que canta es el menor** the one who's singing is the youngest; **los amigos que invité a la fiesta** the friends I invited to the party

2. *cuando de se refiere al complemento* **who, whom** *formal,* **that**

> En inglés el lenguaje hablado se suele omitir **who, whom** O **that** cuando **que** se refiere al complemento de la frase:

los amigos que invité a la fiesta the friends I invited to the party

3. **which, that: la película que ganó el Oscar** the film which won the Oscar; **la que más premios tiene** the one that has the most awards

> En inglés en el lenguaje hablado se suele omitir **which** O **that** cuando se refiere al complemento de la frase:

el disco que compré ayer the record I bought yesterday; **la clase a la que pertenezco** the class I belong to.

qué *adjetivo & pronombre*

1. **what: ¿qué día es hoy?** what day is it today?; **le voy a preguntar qué quiere hacer** I'm going to ask him what he wants to do

2. **which: ¿a qué colegio vas?** which school do you go to?; **no sé qué color elegir** I don't know which colour to choose

> **¿qué?** what?

> **¿qué tal?** how's it going?

> **¿qué tal te va en el colegio?** how's school going for you?

> **¡qué pena!** what a shame!

> **¡qué casa tan bonita!** what a beautiful house!

> **¡y qué!** so what!

quedar [1] *verbo*

1. **to suit: ese color no le queda bien** that colour doesn't suit her

2. **to be left: no queda leche** there's no milk left; **quedan dos limones** there are two lemons left

3. **to be: el colegio queda muy cerca** the school is very near

> **hemos quedado en el cine** we've arranged to meet at the cinema; **el trabajo me ha quedado muy bien** the work has turned out very well

> **queda una semana para que empiecen las vacaciones** there's one week left before the holidays start

quedarse *verbo pronominal*

1. **to stay: me quedé en el colegio estudiando** I stayed at school studying; **se quedó a dormir en mi casa** he stayed at my house to sleep

> **se quedó callado** he stayed quiet

> **me quedé dormido y llegué tarde** I overslept and arrived late

> **nos quedamos solos** we stayed by ourselves

> **se quedó calvo** he went bald

> **quedarse con algo** to keep something.

quejarse *verbo pronominal* ■ **to complain:** **¡no te quejes!** don't complain!; **se está quejando todo el día** he complains all day long; **se queja del dolor que tiene en la pierna** he's complaining about the pain in his leg.

la **quemadura** ■ **burn: tiene una quemadura en la mano** she has a burn on her hand

> **una crema para las quemaduras de sol** a cream for sunburn.

quemar [1] *verbo*

1. **to burn: quemó un montón de hojas** he burnt a lot of papers

2. **to be boiling hot: este café quema** this coffee is boiling hot

quemarse *verbo pronominal*

1. **to burn oneself:** se quemó con la estufa he burnt himself on the stove
2. **to get sunburnt:** me quemé en la piscina I got a sunburn at the pool
> me quemé la mano I burnt my hand
> se le quemó el arroz he burnt the rice
> se les quemó la casa their house burnt down.

querer [49] *verbo*

1. **to want:** ¿qué quieres? what do you want?; quiero usar el teléfono I want to use the telephone
2. **to love:** te quiero mucho I love you a lot
> ¿quieres tomar algo? would you like a drink?
> quisiera saber a qué hora sale el tren I would like to know what time the train leaves
> querer que alguien haga algo to want somebody to do something; quiere que vaya a comprar el pan he wants her to go to buy the bread
> lo hizo sin querer he didn't mean to do it
> querer decir to mean: ¿qué quiere decir esta palabra? what does this word mean?; no sé qué quiso decir con eso I don't know what he meant by that
> queriendo on purpose: me empujó queriendo he pushed me on purpose.

querido, da *adjetivo* ■ **dear:** Querido Juan... Dear Juan...

el **queso** ■ **cheese**
> queso rallado grated cheese
> queso de bola Edam
> queso fresco green cheese.

quien *pronombre*

1. *cuando se refiere al sujeto* **who, that:** la profesora fue quien me lo dijo it was the teacher who told me; fueron ellos quienes lo rompieron it was them who broke it; quien lo haya dicho no importa who said it is not important

> En inglés, el lenguaje hablado suele omitir **who** cuando se refiere al complemento de la frase:
> la persona con quien hablé the person I spoke to

2. *cuando se refiere al complemento* **who, whom** *formal,* **that.**

quién *pronombre*

1. *cuando se refiere al sujeto* **who:** ¿quién ha llamado? who called?; no sé quiénes son I don't know who they are; ¿quién es? who's there?
2. *cuando se refiere al complemento* **who, whom** *formal:* ¿a quién vas a regalar el libro? who are you going to give the book to?; ¿a quién invitaste? who did you invite?; ¿con quién fuiste? who did you go with?
> de quién whose: ¿de quién son estos zapatos? whose are these shoes?

quienquiera *pronombre* ■ **whoever:** quienquiera que sea, dile que no estoy whoever it is, tell him I'm not here.

quieto, ta *adjetivo* ■ **still**
> ¡quieto! be still!

la **química** ■ **chemistry.**

químico, ca *adjetivo* ■ **chemical**

el **químico** , la **química** ■ **chemist:** quiere ser químico he wants to be a chemist

quince *numeral* ■ **fifteen:** tiene quince primos she has fifteen cousins
> mi hermana tiene quince años my sister is fifteen years old
> el quince de abril the fifteenth of April UK, April fifteenth US.

la **quiniela** ■ **football pools.**

quinientos *numeral* ■ **five hundred:** tiene quinientas páginas it has five hundred pages.

quinto, ta *adjetivo & pronombre* ■ **fifth:** fue la quinta persona en entrar he was the fifth person to enter
> la quinta parte a fifth

el **quinto** , la **quinta** ■ **fifth:** el atleta español llegó el quinto the Spanish athlete came fifth; eres la quinta de la lista you're the fifth on the list.

el **quiosco**

1. *de periódicos* **news-stand**
2. *de flores* **flower stall**
3. *de una banda* **bandstand**
4. *de refrescos* **refreshment stall.**

el **quirófano** ■ operating theatre *UK*, operating room *US*.

quisquilloso, sa *adjetivo*

1. fussy: no es quisquilloso, se contenta con poco he's not fussy, anything satisfies him
2. touchy: está últimamente muy quisquilloso lately he's been very touchy.

quitar [1] *verbo*

1. to take away: no le quites el juguete a tu hermano don't take the toy away from your brother
2. to remove: hay que quitar esta mancha you have to remove this stain; ¿podrías quitar estas cosas de aquí? could you remove these things from here?

quitarse *verbo pronominal* ■ to take off: se quitó los zapatos she took off her shoes
> quítate de ahí get out of there
> esta mancha no se quita this stain won't come out.

quizá , quizás *adverbio* ■ maybe: quizá vaya al cine maybe I'll go to the movies.

el **rábano** ■ radish: no me gusta el rábano I don't like radish
> le importa un rábano *informal* he couldn't care less.

la **rabia**

1. rabies: lo vacunaron contra la rabia they vaccinated him against rabies

2. anger: lo hizo por rabia he did it out of anger
> me da rabia que no puedas venir it annoys me that you can't come.

el **rabo** ■ tail.

la **racha**
> están pasando por una buena racha they're going through a lucky spell
> tuvo una mala racha he went through a patch
> una racha de viento a gust of wind.

el **racimo** ■ bunch.

el **racismo** ■ racism.

racista *adjetivo* ■ racist: un comentario racista a racist comment.

racional *adjetivo* ■ rational.

el **radar** ■ radar.

radiactivo, va *adjetivo* ■ radioactive.

el **radiador** ■ radiator: enciende el radiador put the radiator on.

el **radio**

1. radius: no había nadie en un radio de cinco kilómetros there was nobody within a five-kilometres radio
2. spoke: el radio de la rueda trasera the spoke of the rear wheel.

la **radio** ■ radio: pon la radio turn on the radio; me encanta escuchar la radio I love to listen to the radio; lo oyó por la radio I heard it on the radio.

la **radiografía** ■ X-ray
> le hicieron una radiografía they gave her an X-ray.

la **raíz** *(plural* las raíces) ■ root: un árbol de raíces muy profundas a tree with very deep roots
> a raíz de as a result of
> raíz cuadrada square root.

el **rallador** ■ grater.

rallar [1] *verbo* ■ to grate.

la **rama** ■ branch: las ramas de un árbol the branches of a tree
> irse por las ramas to beat about the bush.

el ramo ■ bouquet: un ramo de rosas a bouquet of roses

➤ el ramo de la construcción the construction industry.

la rana ■ frog.

el rancho ■ ranch.

rancio, cia adjetivo ■ old.

la ranura ■ slot: introduzca la moneda en la ranura put the coin in the slot.

rápido, da adjetivo ■ fast: tu eres más rápido que yo you're faster than me

rápido adverbio ■ quickly: habla muy rápido he speaks very quickly

➤ ¡rápido! hurry up!

raptar [1] verbo ■ to abduct.

la raqueta ■ racket: una raqueta de tenis a tennis racket

➤ una raqueta de nieve a snowshoe.

raro, ra adjetivo

1. strange: me pasó algo muy raro something very strange happened to me; es un poco rara she's a bit strange

2. rare: es una pieza muy rara y valiosa it's a very rare and valuable piece

➤ ¡qué raro! how strange!

➤ es raro que llegue tan tarde it's strange for him to arrive so late

➤ tiene un sabor un poco raro it has a kind of a strange taste to it.

el rascacielos (plural los rascacielos) ■ skyscraper.

rascar [8] verbo ■ to scratch: ráscame la espalda scratch my back

➤ no te rasques don't scratch

➤ se rascó la cabeza he scratched his head.

el rasgo ■ feature: tiene los rasgos muy finos she has very delicate features

➤ lo describió a grandes rasgos he described it briefly.

el rasguño ■ scratch.

la rata ■ rat.

el rato ■ while: estuve esperando un buen rato I was waiting a good while

➤ al poco rato llegó he arrived shortly after

➤ lo hago para pasar el rato I do it to pass the time

➤ siempre le hace pasar malos ratos he always gives her a hard time

➤ el avión viene con retraso, así es que tenemos para rato the aeroplane is late so we still have some time to wait.

el ratón (plural los ratones) ■ mouse (plural mice): la casa está llena de ratones the house is full of mice

➤ haz clic con el ratón sobre este icono click on this icon with the mouse.

la raya

1. line: dibuja una raya vertical draw a vertical line

2. parting UK, part US: se peina con la raya al lado she has a side parting in her hair

3. stripe: una blusa con rayas azules y blancas a blouse with blue and white stripes

4. dash: una raya precedida de un punto a dash preceded by a dot

➤ una falda a rayas a striped skirt

➤ pasarse de la raya familiar to go too far: se pasó de la raya y lo castigaron he went too far and was punished.

rayar [1] verbo

1. to scratch: no vayas a rayar la mesa con eso don't go and scratch the table with that

2. to scrawl: rayaron toda la pared they scrawled all over the wall.

el rayo

1. lightning bolt: cayó un rayo en el campanario a lightning bolt struck the bell tower

2. ray: un rayo de luz a ray of light

➤ un rayo láser a laser beam

➤ los rayos ultravioleta ultraviolet rays

➤ los rayos X X-rays.

la raza

1. race: la raza humana the human race

2. breed: no sé de qué raza es su perro I don't know what breed her dog is

➤ es un perro de raza he's a pedigree dog.

la **razón** *(plural* las razones*)* ■ reason: no hay ninguna razón para que falte a clases there's no reason for him to miss classes

> creo que tiene razón I think he's right
> no tiene razón he's wrong
> vas a terminar por darle la razón you'll end up agreeing with him.

razonable *adjetivo* ■ reasonable.

la **reacción** *(plural* las reacciones*)* ■ reaction: tuvo una reacción alérgica she had an allergic reaction.

reaccionar [1] *verbo* ■ to react: reaccionó muy mal he reacted badly.

real *adjetivo*

1. real: vive en un mundo que no es real she lives in a world that isn't real
2. royal: la familia real the royal family
> la novela se basa en un hecho real the novel is based on a true story.

la **realidad** ■ reality: una mezcla de realidad y ficción a mix of reality and fiction

> en realidad actually, in reality: en realidad, no sé la respuesta actually, I don't know the answer
> parecen iguales pero en realidad son muy distintos they look the same but in reality they're very different
> mis deseos se hicieron realidad my dreams came true
> realidad virtual virtual reality.

realizar [10] *verbo* ■ to carry out: realizaron la operación en un hospital inglés the operation was carried out at an English hospital

> han realizado un buen trabajo they've done a good job
> quiere realizarse como persona she wants to fulfil herself
> se realizaron sus sueños his dreams came true.

la **rebaja** ■ discount: pedí que me hicieran una rebaja I asked a discount

> hacerle una rebaja a alguien to give somebody a discount: me hicieron una rebaja del diez por ciento they gave me a ten percent discount

las **rebajas** ■ sales: hoy empiezan las rebajas the sales start today.

la **rebanada** ■ slice: una rebanada de pan con mantequilla a slice of bread and butter.

el **rebaño** ■ flock

> un rebaño de ovejas a flock of sheep.

rebelde *adjetivo*

1. *persona* rebellious
2. *ejército* rebel

el/la **rebelde** ■ rebel.

rebobinar [1] *verbo* ■ to rewind.

rebotar [1] *verbo*

1. to bounce: la pelota rebotó en la pared the ball bounced against the wall
2. to ricochet: una bala rebotó en la pared a bullet ricocheted off the wall.

rebozado, da

1. *empanado* in breadcrumbs
2. *con huevo y harina* in batter.

el **recado**

1. message: le dejé un recado a la secretaria I left her a message with the secretary
2. errand: tengo que hacer unos recados I've got to run some errands.

el **recambio** ■ spare: una rueda de recambio a spare wheel.

recargar [12] *verbo*

1. to refill: tengo que recargar la pluma I have to refill the pen
2. to recharge: tengo que recargar el móvil I have to recharge my mobile phone.

la **recepción** *(plural* las recepciones*)* ■ reception.

el/la **recepcionista** ■ receptionist.

la **receta**

1. recipe: ¿me das la receta de este pastel? will you give me the recipe for this cake?
2. prescription: sólo lo venden con receta it's only available by prescription.

recetar [1] *verbo* ■ to prescribe: me recetó unas pastillas para la alergia she prescribed some pills for my allergy.

rechazar [10] *verbo*

1. **to reject: rechazaron mi idea** they rejected my idea
2. **to turn down: rechazó nuestra oferta** he turned down our offer

recibir [3] *verbo*

1. **to get: ¿has recibido mi carta?** did you get my letter?
2. **to greet: salieron a recibirme a la puerta** they came to greet me at the door
- **recibió muchos regalos** she got a lot of presents
- **todos me recibieron muy bien** they all greeted me warmly.

recién *adverbio* ■ **just: está recién pintado** it's just been painted
- **recién hecho** freshly made: **me encanta el olor del pan recién hecho** I love the smell of freshly baked bread
- **un recién nacido** a newborn baby
- **los recién casados** the newlyweds
- **"recién pintado"** "wet paint".

reciente *adjetivo* ■ **recent.**

el **recipiente** ■ **container.**

reclamar [1] *verbo*

1. **to complain: voy a reclamar al encargado** I'm going to complain to the manager
2. **to demand: reclaman una solución a sus problemas** they're demanding a solution to their problems.

recoger [21] *verbo*

1. **to pick up: recoged los papeles del suelo** pick the papers up off the floor; **recoge todo antes de irte** pick everything up before you leave; **¿a qué hora te recojo?** what time shall I pick you up?
2. **to collect: los martes recogen la basura** they collect the rubbish on Tuesdays
3. **to pick: fuimos a recoger melocotones** we went peach picking.

recomendar [1] *verbo* ■ **to recommend.**

la **recompensa** ■ **reward: ofrecen una recompensa** they're offering a reward.

reconciliarse [1] *verbo pronominal* ■ **reconciliarse con alguien** to make it up with some-

one: **se reconciliaron la cabo de tres años** they made it up with each other after three years.

reconocer [22] *verbo*

1. **to recognize, to recognise** *UK:* **no lo reconocí con la barba** I didn't recognize him with a beard.
2. **to admit: reconoció que se había equivocado** he admitted that he was wrong.

la **reconquista** ■ **reconquest**

LA RECONQUISTA

This term is used to refer to the long period during which the Christians from the Iberian Peninsula fought the Muslims who had invaded in 711. The **Reconquista** (Reconquest) ended in 1492 with the siege of Granada, which led to the definitive expulsion of the Muslims by the Catholic monarchs. The Muslims left behind them many traces of the time they spent on the Peninsula, both in the field of science, as well as in culture and particularly architecture.

el **récord** *(plural los récords)* ■ **record: el récord mundial de los 100 metros** the 100 metres world record
- **batió el récord** he broke the record
- **estableció un nuevo récord en la maratón** he set a new record for the marathon.

recordar [16] *verbo*

1. **to remember: no recuerdo su nombre** I can't remember his name; **recuerdo que te lo pedí** I remember asking you for it
2. **to remind: me recuerda a un amigo mío** he reminds me of a friend of mine; **recuérdame que lo llame** remind me to call him.

recorrer [2] *verbo*

1. **to travel round: su sueño es recorrer el mundo** his dream is to travel all round the world
2. **to cover: recorrimos esa distancia en muy poco tiempo** we quickly covered that distance
- **salieron a recorrer la ciudad** they went out to see the city.

el **recorrido** ■ **route: todos los días hace el mismo recorrido** he takes the same route every day hicieron un recorrido por toda Europa they took a trip all round Europe

un tren de largo recorrido a long-distance train.

recortar [1] *verbo* ■ to cut out: lo recorté del periódico I cut it out of the newspaper

hay que recortar los gastos we have to reduce expenses.

el **recreo** ■ break *UK*, recess *US*: tenemos el primer recreo a las diez our first recess is at ten.

la **recta** ■ straight line: dibujó una recta he drew a straight line

la recta final the home straight.

el **rectángulo** ■ rectangle.

rectificar [8] *verbo* ■ to rectify: rectificó su error he rectified his mistake.

recto, ta *adjetivo* ■ straight: una línea recta a straight line

unos pantalones rectos straight-legged trousers.

el **recuerdo**

1. memory (*plural* **memories**): tengo muy buenos recuerdos de mi primer colegio I have very good memories of my first school

2. souvenir: es un recuerdo de mi viaje it's a souvenir of my trip

lo compré de recuerdo I bought it as a souvenir

es un recuerdo de familia it's a family heirloom

dale muchos recuerdos a tu familia give my regards to your family.

recuperar [1] *verbo*

1. to get back: no pude recuperar mi dinero I couldn't get my money back

2. to make up: tenemos que recuperar las horas que perdimos we have to make up the hours we missed; tengo que recuperar el tiempo perdido I have to make up for lost time

3. to recover: ya se recuperó de la operación he's already recovered from the operation

recuperar las fuerzas to get strength back: descansamos un poco para recuperar las fuerzas we rested a while to get our strength back

recuperar el conocimiento to regain consciousness.

la **red**

1. net: una red de pesca a fishing net; la pelota tocó la red the ball touched the net

2. network: una red de carreteras a network of roads

la Red the Net.

redactar [1] *verbo* ■ to write: redactó el discurso inaugural he wrote the inaugural speech; no saben redactar they don't know how to write.

la **redacción** (*plural* las redacciones)

1. essay: tengo que hacer una redacción sobre mis vacaciones I have to write an essay about my holidays

2. editorial staff: trabaja en el equipo de redacción de la revista she works on the magazine's editorial staff.

redondo, da *adjetivo* ■ round: tiene la cara redonda she has a round face.

reducir [23] *verbo* ■ to lower: van a reducir la velocidad máxima permitida they're going to lower the speed limit.

reemplazar [10] *verbo* ■ to replace

reemplazar algo por algo to replace something with something: reemplaza esta palabra por una menos formal replace this word with a less formal one.

la **referencia** ■ reference: apuntad la referencia de este libro write down the reference for this book

hacer referencia a algo to refer to something.

referirse [20] *verbo* ■ to refer: creo que se refiere a ti I think she's referring to you; no sé a qué te refieres I don't know what you're referring to

¿a qué te refieres con eso? what do you mean by that?

reflejar [1] *verbo* ■ to reflect: la ventana reflejaba su imagen her image was reflected in the mirror.

el **reflejo** ■ reflection: el reflejo del sol en el agua the reflection of the sun in the water

reflejos ■ **reflexes**: tiene muy buenos reflejos he has very good reflexes.

reflexionar [1] *verbo* ■ **to reflect**: reflexiona bien antes de tomar una decisión reflect carefully before you make a decision; reflexionad sobre el tema reflect on the matter.

reflexivo, va *adjetivo* ■ **reflexive**: un verbo reflexivo a reflexive verb.

la reforma
1. **reform**: la reforma de la enseñanza educational reform
2. **alteration**: hicieron algunas reformas en su casa they made some alterations to the house "cerrado por reformas" "closed for alterations".

el refrán *(plural los refranes)* ■ **saying.**

refrescante *adjetivo* ■ **refreshing**: una bebida refrescante a refreshing drink.

refrescar [8] *verbo* ■ **to get cool**: por la noche siempre refresca it always gets cool at night

refrescarse *verbo pronominal* ■ **to cool off**: se tiró al agua para refrescarse she jumped into the water to cool off.

el refresco ■ **soft drink.**

el refrigerador ■ **refrigerator, fridge** UK.

el refugiado , la refugiada ■ **refugee.**

refugiarse [1] *verbo*
1. **to take shelter**: un lugar para refugiarse del frío a place to take shelter from the cold
2. **to take refuge**: se refugiaron en una iglesia they took refuge in a church.

el refugio ■ **shelter**: un refugio para las víctimas a shelter for the victims
> un refugio atómico a fallout shelter
> un refugio de montaña a mountain refuge.

la regadera ■ **watering can**: llenó la regadera de agua she filled the watering can with water.

regalar [1] *verbo*
1. **to give**: me regaló un reloj she gave me a watch; no sé qué regalarle por su cum-

pleaños I don't know what to give him for his birthday
2. **to give away**: me queda pequeño así es que lo voy a regalar it's too small for me so I'm going to give it away; estaban regalando entradas para el concierto they were giving away tickets for the concert
> me regalaron una guitarra por Navidad I was given a guitar for Christmas.

el regaliz ■ **liquorice** UK, **licorice** US.

el regalo ■ **present**: es un regalo de cumpleaños it's a birthday present
> hacerle un regalo a alguien to give somebody a present: me hizo un muy buen regalo he gave me a really good present
> una tienda de regalos a gift shop
> me lo dieron de regalo al comprar el ordenador It was free with the purchase of the computer.

regar [25] *verbo* ■ **to water**: voy a regar las plantas I'm going to water the plants.

el régimen *(plural los regímenes)*
1. **regime**: un régimen democrático a democratic regime
2. **diet**: tiene que seguir un régimen he has to follow a diet; voy a ponerme a régimen I'm going on a diet
> a régimen on a diet: estoy a régimen I'm on a diet.

la región *(plural las regiones)* ■ **region.**

registrar [1] *verbo*
1. **to search**: le registraron el equipaje they searched his luggage; registraron el edificio they searched the building
2. **to register**: los sismógrafos registraron el temblor the seismographs registered the tremor

registrarse *verbo pronominal*
1. **to check in**: nos registramos en un hotel we checked into a hotel
2. **to register**: tengo que ir a registrarme en la embajada I have to register at the embassy; se registró un fuerte terremoto en la zona a strong earthquake was registered in the zone.

la **regla**

1. **ruler:** usó una regla para medir la línea she used a ruler to measure the line
2. **rule:** ¿conoces las reglas del juego? do you know the rules of the game?
3. **period:** tener la regla to have one's period
> **en regla** in order: si quieres viajar, tienes que tener tus papeles en regla if you want to travel you'll have to put your papers in order
> **por regla general** generally: por regla general, llego al colegio temprano I generally get to school early.

el **reglamento** ■ **regulations:** el reglamento del colegio the school's regulations.

regresar [1] *verbo*

1. **to come back:** tienes que regresar temprano you have to come back early
2. **to go back:** regresaron a su país they went back to their country.

regular *adjetivo*

1. **regular:** viene a intervalos regulares he comes at regular intervals; "comer" es un verbo regular "comer" is a regular verb
2. **average:** obtuvieron unos resultados regulares they obtained average results
> me pareció una película regular it was a so-so film
> es de tamaño regular it's the regular size
> **por lo regular** usually: por lo regular, me levanto a las siete I usually get up at seven.

el/la **rehén** *(plural* los/las rehenes) ■ **hostage.**

la **reina** ■ **queen.**

el **reinado** ■ **reign.**

reinar [1] *verbo* ■ **to reign.**

el **reino** ■ **kingdom**
> el reino animal the animal kingdom
> el reino mineral the mineral kingdom
> el reino vegetal the vegetable kingdom.

el **Reino Unido** ■ **the United Kingdom.**

reír [21] *verbo* ■ **to laugh:** no me hagas reír don't make me laugh
> **echarse a reír** to burst out laughing: de pronto, se echó a reír suddenly, he burst out laughing

reírse *verbo pronominal* ■ **to laugh:** no te rías don't laugh
> se ríen de él they're laughing at him
> ¿de qué te ríes? what are you laughing at?

la **reja** ■ **grille:** había rejas en todas las ventanas there were grilles on all the windows.

la **relación** *(plural* las relaciones)

1. **relationship:** tiene una buena relación con los alumnos she has a good relationship with the students
2. **connection:** no hay ninguna relación entre los dos incidentes there's no connection between the two incidents
> **con relación a** with regard to: con relación a tu pregunta with regard to your question
> **relaciones públicas** public relations.

relacionar [1] *verbo* ■ **to relate:** tienes que relacionar unas ideas con otras you have to relate some ideas with others

relacionarse *verbo pronominal* ■ **to mix:** se relacionaron con gente de la alta sociedad they mix with high society.

relajar [1] *verbo* ■ **to relax:** el sonido del agua me relaja the sound of the water relaxes me
> tienes que aprender a relajarte you have to learn to relax.

el **relámpago** ■ **lightning:** ¿viste el relámpago? did you see the lightning?
> los relámpagos iluminaron el cielo lightning lit up the sky.

relativo, va *adjetivo*

1. **relating:** le gusta todo lo relativo a la naturaleza she likes everything relating to nature
2. **relative:** todo es relativo it's all relative
> lo hizo con relativa facilidad he did it relatively easily.

la **religión** *(plural* las religiones) ■ **religion.**

religioso, sa *adjetivo* ■ **religious:** son un pueblo muy religioso they're a very religious people

el **religioso** , la **religiosa**

1. *hombre* **monk**
2. *mujer* **nun.**

rellenar [1] *verbo*

1. **to stuff:** rellenó los tomates con carne she stuffed the tomatoes with meat

2. **to fill:** lo voy a rellenar con nata I'm going to fill it with cream; ¿con qué puedo rellenar esta grieta? what can I fill this crack with?

el **relleno**

1. **stuffing:** el relleno del pollo está delicioso the chicken's stuffing is delicious

2. **filling:** el relleno es de chocolate the filling is chocolate.

el **reloj**

1. *de pared, grande* **clock:** ese reloj está adelantado that clock is fast

2. *en la muñeca* **watch:** mi reloj se atrasa my watch is slow

   contra reloj against the clock: trabajamos contra reloj para poder terminarlo we worked against the clock to finish it

   un reloj de pared a wall clock

   un reloj despertador an alarm clock

   un reloj de pulsera wristwatch

   un reloj de sol a sundial.

remar [1] *verbo* ■ **to row.**

el **remedio** ■ **remedy** *(plural* **remedies***):* un remedio natural a natural remedy; es el mejor remedio para el acné it's the best remedy for acne

   ¡tú no tienes remedio! you're hopeless!

   esto no tiene remedio this is hopeless

   no tuve más remedio que obedecer I had no choice but to obey.

la **remitente** ■ **sender.**

el **remo**

1. **oar:** perdieron un remo they lost an oar

2. **rowing:** está en el equipo de remo he's on the rowing team.

la **remolacha** ■ **beetroot** *UK,* **beet** *US.*

el **remolino**

1. *de viento* **whirl**

2. *de agua* **whirlpool**

3. *en el pelo* **cowlick.**

el **remordimiento** ■ **remorse:** no siente el más mínimo remordimiento he doesn't feel a bit of remorse

estaba lleno de remordimientos he was full of remorse

¿no tienes remordimientos de conciencia? isn't your conscience bothering you?

remoto, ta *adjetivo* ■ **remote:** en lugares muy remotos in remote places

no tiene ni la más remota idea she doesn't have the slightest idea.

el **renacuajo** ■ **tadpole.**

rencoroso, sa *adjetivo* ■ **resentful.**

el **rendimiento** ■ **performance.**

rendir [19] *verbo*

1. **to perform well:** no está rindiendo en los estudios she's not doing very well at school

2. **to pay:** le van a rendir un homenaje they're going to pay tribute to him

   rendirse *verbo pronominal*

1. **to surrender:** se rindieron al enemigo they surrendered to the enemy

2. **to give up:** me rindo ¿cuál es la solución? I give up —what's the answer?

la **renta**

la declaración de la renta the tax return.

renunciar [1] *verbo*

1. **to give up:** renunció a su cargo de director he gave up his post as director

2. **to give up on:** renunciaron a la idea de hacer el viaje they gave up on the idea of making the trip.

reñir [61] *verbo*

1. **to quarrel:** ellos siempre están riñendo they're always quarrelling

2. **to tell off:** le riñeron por haber llegado tarde they told him off for arriving late.

el **reojo**

de reojo out of the corner of one's eye: Pablo la miró de reojo Pablo looked at her out of the corner of his eye.

la **reparación** *(plural* las reparaciones*)* ■ **repair.**

reparar [1] *verbo* ■ **to repair.**

repartir [3] *verbo*

1. **to hand out:** la profesora repartió los libros the teacher handed out the books

2. **to deliver:** reparte periódicos he delivers newspapers

3. **to deal:** ¿quién reparte las cartas? who's dealing the cards?

4. **to distribute:** repartieron los juguetes entre todos los niños they distributed the toys among all the children

▸ nos repartimos el dinero entre los cuatro we split the money four ways.

el **reparto**

1. **delivery** (plural **deliveries**)**:** no cobran por el reparto they don't charge for delivery

2. **cast:** tiene un excelente reparto it has an excellent cast

▸ reparto a domicilio delivery service.

repasar [1] verbo

1. **to revise:** están repasando para los exámenes they're revising for their exams

2. **to go over:** repasa bien las sumas go over your sums carefully.

el **repaso** ■ **check:** habrá que darle un último repaso al ordenador we'll have to give the computer a final check

▸ hacer un repaso de

1. asignatura, tema **to revise** UK, **to review** US: estamos haciendo un repaso de la materia para el examen we're revising the subject for the exam

2. **to look over:** habrá que hacer un repaso de los presupuestos we'll have to look over the budgets.

repente adverbio

▸ de repente suddenly: todo pasó tan de repente it all happened so suddenly.

repetir [19] verbo

1. **to repeat:** ¿puedes repetirme la pregunta? can you repeat the question?

2. **to do again:** tengo que repetir el trabajo I have to do the job again

3. **to have another helping:** el guiso está tan bueno que voy a repetir the stew is so good that I'm going to have another helping.

el **reportaje**

1. **report:** ayer vi un reportaje sobre la juventud actual yesterday I saw a report on today's youth

2. **article:** su reportaje salió publicado en la revista his article was published in the magazine.

el **reportero** , la **reportera** ■ reporter.

el **reposo** ■ **rest:** el médico le recomendó que hiciera reposo the doctor recommended that she had some rest.

la **representación** (plural las representaciones) ■ **performance:** hubo cien representaciones de la obra there were one hundred performances of the play

▸ en representación de as the representative of: vino el primer ministro en representación del Jefe de Estado the prime minister came as the representative of the Head of State.

el/la **representante**

1. **representative:** el representante de la empresa the company representative

2. **agent:** el representante de la cantante the singer's agent.

representar [1] verbo

1. **to represent:** representó a España en las Olimpíadas she represented Spain in the Olympics

2. **to look:** representa más edad de la que tiene he looks older than he is

3. **to perform:** esa obra es muy difícil de representar that play is very difficult to perform

4. **to depict:** vi un dibujo que representa el paisaje inglés I saw a picture depicting the English countryside

▸ no representa ningún riesgo para mí it doesn't pose any risk to me

▸ representa un 10% del coste total it represents 10% of the total cost.

reprochar [1] verbo ■ **to reproach:** siempre me reprocha mis errores he always reproaches me for my mistakes.

la **reproducción** (plural las reproducciones)

1. **reproduction:** estamos estudiando el proceso de reproducción de las plantas we're studying plant reproduction

2. **copy:** es una reproducción del cuadro original it's a copy of the original painting.

reproducir [23] *verbo* ■ **to reproduce:** han reproducido este diseño en muchos lugares they're reproduced this design in a lot of places

reproducirse *verbo pronominal* ■ **to reproduce:** los insectos se reproducen rápidamente insects reproduce quickly.

el **reptil** ■ reptile.

la **república** ■ republic.

la **República Dominicana** ■ Dominican Republic.

el **repuesto** ■ spare part: ¿venden repuestos para el coche? do you sell spare parts for the car?

la **reputación** (*plural* las reputaciones) ■ reputation: esa compañía tiene mala reputación that company has a bad reputation.

el **requisito** ■ requirement: cumple todos los requisitos para este puesto de trabajo he meets all the requirements for the job.

resbaladizo, za *adjetivo* ■ **slippery:** el suelo está muy resbaladizo the floor is very slippery.

resbalar [1] *verbo*

1. **to be slippery:** la acera resbala porque ha llovido the pavement is slippery because it has been raining

2. **to skid:** el coche resbaló con la lluvia the car skidded in the rain

resbalarse *verbo pronominal* ■ **to slip:** se resbaló en el suelo mojado he slipped on the wet floor.

el **resbalón** ■ slip

dar un resbalón to slip: dio un resbalón y se cayó he slipped and fell.

rescatar [1] *verbo* ■ **to rescue:** el socorrista rescató al nadador the lifeguard rescued the swimmer.

el **rescate** ■ rescue: fue un rescate espectacular it was a spectacular rescue.

la **reserva** ■ reservation, booking *UK:* he hecho una reserva en el restaurante I've made a booking at the restaurant.

reservar [1] *verbo* ■ **to reserve:** quisiera reservar una mesa para dos I'd like to reserve a table for two.

resfriado, da *adjetivo* ■ Juan está muy resfriado Juan has a bad cold

el **resfriado** ■ cold: me vas a pegar el resfriado you're going to give me your cold.

resfriarse [7] *verbo* ■ **to catch a cold:** te vas a resfriar you're going to catch a cold.

la **residencia** ■ residence: ¿cuál es tu lugar de residencia habitual? ¿what is your usual place of residence?

una residencia de estudiantes a hall of residence *UK*, a dormitory *US*

un permiso de residencia a residence permit una residencia de ancianos a retirement home.

los **residuos** ■ waste: el procesamiento de residuos nucleares the processing of nuclear waste.

la **resignación** (*plural* las resignaciones) ■ resignation: aceptó su castigo con resignación he accepted his punishment with resignation.

la **resina** ■ resin.

la **resistencia** ■ resistance: no ofreció ninguna resistencia she didn't put up any resistance

tiene gran resistencia física he has great stamina.

resistente *adjetivo* ■ resistant: una tela muy resistente a very resistant fabric.

resistir [3] *verbo*

1. **to resist:** tienes que resistir la tentación you have to resist temptation

2. **to stand:** no pudo resistir el frío he couldn't stand the cold

resistirse a hacer algo to refuse to do something.

la **resolución** (*plural* las resoluciones) ■ resolution: la resolución del conflicto the resolution of the conflict

una imagen de alta resolución a high-resolution image.

resolver [17] *verbo* ■ **to solve: final-mente resolvieron el problema** they finally solved the problem.

el **respaldo**
1. **back: una silla sin respaldo** a chair without a back
2. **support: expresó su respaldo a la idea** he expressed his support for the idea.

respetar [1] *verbo*
1. **to respect: respeta las opiniones de los demás** respect other people's opinions
2. **to obey: hay que respetar las reglas** you have to follow the rules.

el **respeto** ■ **respect: trata con respeto a sus mayores** he treats his elders with respect.

respetuoso, sa *adjetivo* ■ **respectful: es muy respetuoso con la naturaleza** he is very respectful of nature.

la **respiración** *(plural las respiraciones)* ■ **breathing: tiene la respiración irregular** her breathing is irregular
> **quedarse sin respiración** to become breath-less
> **aguantar la respiración** to hold one's breath
> **respiración artificial** artificial respiration.

respirar [1] *verbo* ■ **to breathe.**

responder [2] *verbo*
1. **to answer: no pudo responder a la pre-gunta de la profesora** she couldn't answer the teacher's question
2. **to reply: gracias por responder a mi co-rreo electrónico** thank you for replying to my e-mail
3. **to respond: el enfermo respondió bien al tratamiento** the patient responded well to the treatment.

la **responsabilidad** ■ **responsibility** *(plural* **responsibilities***):* **le han dado mucha responsabilidad** they've given her a lot of responsibility.

responsable *adjetivo* ■ **responsible: Ma-ría es muy responsable** María is very respon-sible
> **ser responsable de** to be responsible for: **ella es responsable del bienestar de los niños** she's responsible for the children's well-being

el/la **responsable** ■ **¿quién es el respon-sable de esto?** who is responsible for this?
> **Carla es la responsable del proyecto** Carla is in charge of the project
> **los responsables de la crisis** those responsi-ble for the crisis.

la **respuesta**
1. **answer: no sabía la respuesta a sus pregun-tas** he didn't know the answer to the questions
2. **reply** *(plural* **replies***):* **espero tu respuesta** I await your reply.

la **resta** ■ **subtraction: haz la resta y dime el resultado** do the subtraction and tell me the answer.

restar [1] *verbo* ■ **to subtract: piensa en un número y réstale cinco** think of a num-ber then subtract five from it

 The Spanish word **restar** is a false friend, it does not mean "rest".

el **restaurante** ■ **restaurant.**

restaurar [1] *verbo* ■ **to restore.**

el **resto** ■ **rest: deja el resto para mañana** leave the rest for tomorrow
> **yo me como los restos** I'll eat the leftovers.

resucitar [1] *verbo* ■ **to revive: los médicos lograron resucitarlo** the doctors managed to revive him.

el **resultado**
1. **result: el resultado del sorteo** the results of the draw
2. **score: el resultado del partido** the score of the match.

el **resumen** ■ **summary** *(plural* **summaries***):* **el resumen es demasiado largo** the sum-mary is too long
> **hacer un resumen del texto** to summarize the book
> **en resumen, me gusta más éste** in short, I prefer this one.

resumir [3] *verbo* ■ **to summarize, to summarise** *UK:* **tuvimos que resumir la película en dos párrafos** we had to summa-rize the film in two paragraphs
> **resumiendo** in short.

retirar [1] *verbo*

1. **to remove:** por favor retira los platos de la mesa please remove the plates from the table
2. **to withdraw:** fue a retirar su dinero del banco she went to withdraw her money from the bank

retirarse *verbo pronominal*

1. **to retire:** mi tío se va a retirar dentro de dos meses my uncle is going to retire in two months' time
2. **to stand down:** va a retirarse de la selección española he's going to stand down from the Spanish team
3. **to withdraw:** se han retirado las tropas the troops have been withdrawn.

el **reto** ■ **challenge:** Juan no pudo resistir el reto de Pablo Juan could not resist Pablo's challenge.

retorcer [30] *verbo* ■ **to twist:** retorció el alambre he twisted the wire.

la **retransmisión** *(plural* las retransmisiones) ■ **broadcast:** una retransmisión del partido a broadcast of the game
> una retransmisión en directo a live broadcast
> una retransmisión en diferido a recorded broadcast.

retrasado, da *adjetivo*

1. **behind:** va un poco retrasado en el colegio he's a little behind at school
2. **slow:** mi reloj va retrasado cinco minutos my watch is five minutes slow
3. **backward:** una sociedad retrasada a backward society
> ser retrasado to have learning difficulties: Julio es retrasado Julio has learning difficulties.

retrasar [1] *verbo*

1. **to postpone:** retrasaron la fiesta una semana they postponed the party for a week
2. **to delay:** la tormenta retrasó nuestro vuelo the storm delayed our flight
3. **to turn back:** este fin de semana hay que retrasar los relojes we have to put back the clocks this weekend

retrasarse *verbo pronominal* ■ **to be late:** me retrasé por el tráfico I was late because of the traffic.

el **retraso** ■ **delay:** hubo un retraso de dos horas there was a two-hour delay.

el **retrato** ■ **portrait.**

retroceder [2] *verbo*

1. **to move back:** el coche retrocedió diez metros the car moved back ten metres
2. **to retreat:** los soldados tuvieron que retroceder the soldiers had to retreat.

el **retrovisor** ■ **rear-view mirror.**

la **reunión** *(plural* las reuniones)

1. **meeting:** la reunión es a las diez the meeting is at ten
2. **reunion:** organizamos una reunión familiar el domingo pasado we organised a family reunion last Sunday.

reunir [6] *verbo*

1. **to gather:** reunió todos sus juguetes y los tiró a la basura she gathered all her toys and threw them in the trash; reunió a todos sus amigos para explicar lo que había sucedido she gathered all her friends to explain what had happened
2. **to have:** reúne todas las cualidades necesarias he has all the necessary qualities

reunirse *verbo*

1. **to get together:** se reunieron en su casa they got together at his house
2. **to gather:** los manifestantes se reunieron en la plaza del Ayuntamiento the demonstrators gathered in the town hall square
3. **to raise:** reunieron fondos para la ONG they raised funds for the NGO
4. **to meet:** la junta directiva se reúne cada tres meses the board of directors meets every three months; ¿nos reunimos a las tres? shall we meet at three?

revelar [1] *verbo*

1. **to reveal:** revelaron todos sus secretos they revealed all their secrets
2. **to develop:** llevé las fotos a revelar I took the film to be developed.

reventar [14] *verbo* ■ **to burst:** el globo reventó the balloon burst
> su actitud me revienta his attitude really bugs me.

el **revés**

1. back: el revés de la hoja de papel the back of the sheet of paper; el revés de una tela the back of a piece of material
2. backhand: tiene un revés muy poderoso she has a very powerful backhand

al revés

1. inside out: llevas los calcetines al revés you're wearing your socks inside out
2. backwards: ya no está de moda ponerse la gorra al revés it's not fashionable to wear your cap backwards anymore
3. the other way round: colócalas al revés place them the other way round
4. back to front: la foto está del revés the photo is back to front.

revisar [1] *verbo*

1. to check: el profesor revisa diariamente el trabajo de sus alumnos the teacher checks his students' work every day
2. to search: me revisaron las maletas en la aduana they searched my bags at customs.

la **revisión**

1. check: una revisión de calidad a quality check
2. service: el coche necesita una revisión the car needs a service
▸ una revisión médica a check-up.

la **revista** ■ magazine.

la **revolución** (*plural* las revoluciones) ■ revolution.

revolver [17] *verbo*

1. to stir: tu café no está revuelto your coffee hasn't been stirred
2. to turn upside down: revolvió toda la casa buscando el libro she turned the house upside down looking for the book.

el **revólver** (*plural* los revólveres) ■ revolver.

el **rey** ■ king: algún día, el príncipe llegará a ser rey one day, the prince will be king
▸ los reyes de España the King and Queen of Spain
▸ los Reyes Magos the Three Wise Men

rezar [10] *verbo* ■ to pray: siempre rezo por la paz I always pray for peace.

rico, ca *adjetivo*

1. rich: un hombre rico a rich man
2. delicious: ¡que comida más rica! what a delicious meal
▸ un país rico en petróleo a country rich in oil.

ridículo, la *adjetivo* ■ ridiculous: un ridículo sombrero con plumas a ridiculous feathered hat
▸ hacer el ridículo to make a fool of oneself.

el **riesgo** ■ risk
▸ correr el riesgo to run a risk: corres el riesgo de perderlo todo you run the risk of losing all.

el **rifle** ■ rifle.

rígido, da *adjetivo*

1. rigid: esa barra de metal es muy rígida that metal bar is very rigid
2. strict: la profesora es muy rígida y nos regaña a todos the teacher is very strict and is always scolding us.

la **rima** ■ rhyme.

el **rincón** (*plural* los rincones) ■ corner: había una telaraña en un rincón de mi habitación there was a cobweb in a corner of my room.

el **rinoceronte** ■ rhinoceros.

el **riñón** (*plural* los riñones) ■ kidney.

el **río** ■ river: en la boca del río at the mouth of the river
▸ el río Ebro the river Ebro
▸ río arriba upstream
▸ río abajo downstream.

La Rioja ■ La Rioja.

riojano, na

En inglés, los adjetivos que se refieren a un país o una región se escriben con mayúscula:

Riojan: el vino riojano Riojan wine

el riojano , la riojana

En inglés, los gentilicios se escriben con mayúscula:

Riojan
> los riojanos the Riojans.

la riqueza

1. **wealth**: la concentración de la riqueza the concentration of wealth
2. **richness**: la riqueza de la vegetación the richness of the vegetation.

la risa ■ **laugh**: tiene una risa muy contagiosa she has a very infectious laugh
> José me da risa José makes me laugh
> morirse de risa to kill oneself laughing: nos moríamos de risa con sus chistes we killed ourselves laughing at his jokes
> ¡qué risa! what a laugh!

el ritmo

1. **rhythm**: el ritmo de la música the rhythm of the music
2. **pace**: no puedo caminar a tu ritmo I can't walk at your pace.

el ritual ■ ritual.

la rival ■ rival.

rizado, da adjetivo ■ **curly**: el pelo rizado curly hair.

rizarse [10] verbo pronominal ■ **to curl**: se ha rizado el pelo she curled her hair.

el rizo ■ curl.

robar [1] verbo

1. **to rob**: intentaron robar el banco they tried to rob the bank
2. **to steal**: me robaron la cartera they stole my wallet
3. **to rip off**: si vas a esa tienda te roban you'll get ripped off if you go to that shop.

el robo

1. **robbery** (plural **robberies**): el robo de un banco a bank robbery
2. **theft**: el robo de un televisor the theft of a TV set
3. **burglary** (plural **burglaries**): el robo en una casa a burglary
4. **rip-off**: los precios en esa tienda son un robo the prices at that store are a rip-off.

el robot ■ robot.

la roca ■ rock.

la rodaja ■ **slice**: ¿me das una rodaja de tu naranja? can I have a slice of your orange?
> cebollas cortadas en rodajas sliced onions.

rodar [16] verbo ■ **to roll**: la pelota rodó por el suelo the ball rolled along the ground.

rodear [1] verbo ■ **to surround**: los admiradores del cantante lo rodearon the singer's fans surrounded him
> le gusta estar rodeado de su familia he likes to be surrounded by his family.

la rodilla ■ knee
> ponerse de rodillas to kneel down: se puso de rodillas he knelt down.

rogar [28] verbo

1. **to beg**: me rogó que no me fuera he begged me to stay
2. **to request**: se ruega a los señores pasajeros que apaguen los cigarrillos passengers are requested to put out their cigarettes
3. **to pray**: roguemos al Señor let us pray to the Lord
> "les rogamos disculpen las molestias" "we apologize for any inconvenience caused".

rojo, ja adjetivo ■ **red**: un coche rojo a red car
> se puso rojo de vergüenza he turned red with embarrassment.

el rollo ■ **roll**: un rollo de papel de cocina a roll of kitchen paper
> ser un rollo to be a bore: la clase de mates ha sido un rollo the maths class was a bore
> ¡qué rollo! what a drag!

romántico, ca adjetivo ■ romantic.

el **rombo** ▪ rhombus.

el **rompecabezas** *(plural* los rompecabezas) ▪ jigsaw puzzle.

romper [2] *verbo*

1. **to break: rompí un vaso sin querer** I accidentally broke a glass
2. **to tear: rompió el sobre en lugar de abrirlo con cuidado** he tore the envelope rather than opening it carefully
▸ **rompieron después de tres años juntos** they broke up after three years together

romperse *verbo pronominal*

1. **to break: Ana se ha roto la pierna** Ana has broken her leg; **se ha roto una taza** a cup has been broken
2. **to tear: este papel se rompe enseguida** this paper tears easily.

el **ron** ▪ rum.

roncar [8] *verbo* ▪ to snore.

ronco, ca *adjetivo*

1. **hoarse: tengo la voz ronca de tanto gritar** my voice is hoarse from shouting so much
2. **husky: Carlos tiene la voz ronca y grave** Carlos has a low, husky voice.

la **ropa** ▪ clothes: **ropa para bebés** baby clothes
▸ **la ropa de cama** bedclothes
▸ **la ropa interior** underwear
▸ **la ropa sucia** dirty laundry.

rosa *adjetivo* ▪ pink: **una blusa rosa** a pink blouse

el **rosa** ▪ pink: **el rosa se obtiene mezclando el rojo y el blanco** pink is obtained by mixing red and white

la **rosa** ▪ rose.

el **rosal** ▪ rosebush.

el **roscón** *(plural* los roscones)
▸ **el roscón de Reyes** the Epiphany ring cake.

roto, ta *adjetivo*

1. **broken: este plato está roto** this plate is broken
2. **torn: tienes la camisa rota** your shirt is ripped

3. **worn-out: lleva los zapatos rotos** he wears worn-out shoes.

rozar [10] *verbo*

1. **to brush: su beso apenas me rozó la mejilla** his kiss barely brushed my cheek
2. **to rub: los zapatos nuevos me están rozando los talones** these new shoes are rubbing against my heels
3. **to scrape: su brazo rozó contra el tronco del árbol** her arm scraped against the tree trunk.

rubio, bia *adjetivo* ▪ blond: **tiene el pelo rubio** he has blond hair

la **rueda** ▪ wheel: **ese vehículo tiene seis ruedas** that vehicle has six wheels
▸ **la rueda delantera** the front wheel
▸ **se me ha pinchado una rueda** I've had a puncture
▸ **la rueda trasera** the back wheel.

el **rugby** ▪ rugby.

el **rugido** ▪ roar: **el rugido del león** the lion's roar.

rugir [11] *verbo* ▪ to roar.

el **ruido** ▪ noise: **¿has oído ese ruido?** did you hear that noise?; **los vecinos hacen mucho ruido** the neighbours make a lot of noise.

ruidoso, sa *adjetivo* ▪ noisy.

la **ruina** ▪ ruin: **unas ruinas griegas** Greek ruins
▸ **la ciudad quedó en ruinas** the city was in ruins
▸ **ese negocio lo llevó a la ruina** that business ruined him.

la **ruleta** ▪ roulette.

el **rumbo** ▪ direction: **partió rumbo a la capital** he headed in the direction of the capital.

el **rumor**

1. **rumour** *UK,* **rumor** *US:* **he oído algunos rumores acerca de eso** I've heard some rumours about that
2. **murmur: el rumor de las olas** the murmur of the waves.

rural *adjetivo* ▪ rural.

Rusia ▪ Russia.

ruso, sa

En inglés, los adjetivos que se refieren a un país o una región se escriben con mayúscula:

Russian: Moscú es la capital rusa Moscow is the Russian capital

el **ruso**, la **rusa**

En inglés, los gentilicios se escriben con mayúscula:

Russian
los rusos the Russians

el **ruso**

En inglés, los idiomas se escriben con mayúscula.

Russian.

la **ruta** ■ route.

la **rutina** ■ routine: la rutina diaria the daily routine; un chequeo de rutina a routine check-up.

el **sábado**

En inglés, los días de la semana se escriben con mayúscula:

Saturday: hoy es sábado today is Saturday; el sábado que viene next Saturday; el sábado pasado last Saturday

> el sábado on Saturday: te veré el sábado I'll see you on Saturday

> los sábados on Saturdays: los sábados vamos al parque on Saturdays we go to the park.

la **sabana** ■ savanna, savannah.

la **sábana** ■ sheet.

saber [50] verbo

1. **to know:** ¿sabes cómo se llama? do you know his name?

2. **to know how to:** Rafael no sabe nadar Rafael doesn't know how to swim

3. **to hear:** no supe nada de él durante más de un año I didn't hear from him for over a year

4. **to taste:** esta comida sabe muy mal this food tastes awful

> saberse algo de memoria to know something by heart

el **saber** ■ knowledge.

sabio, bia adjetivo ■ wise: esas son palabras sabias those are wise words.

el **sabor**

1. **taste:** un sabor amargo a bitter taste

2. **flavour:** sabor a manzana apple flavour.

el **sacacorchos** (plural los sacacorchos) ■ corkscrew.

el **sacapuntas** (plural los sacapuntas) ■ pencil sharpener.

sacar [8] verbo

1. **to take out:** ayúdame a sacar la basura help me take out the garbage; voy a sacar a pasear al perro I'm going to take the dog out for a walk

2. **to get:** ¿pudiste sacar las entradas? were you able to get the tickets?; ha sacado buenas notas he got good marks

3. **to move:** te pedí que sacaras eso de ahí I asked you to move that out of there

4. **to release:** ha sacado un nuevo disco they've released a new record

5. en tenis **to serve**

> sácate los zapatos antes de entrar take off your shoes before you go in

> sacar una foto to take a picture

> sacar la lengua to stick out one's tongue

sacarse verbo pronominal ■ **to take off:** sácate el abrigo take off your coat.

el **saco** ■ sack: un saco de cemento a sack of cement

> un saco de dormir a sleeping bag.

el **sacrificio** ■ sacrifice.

sacudir [3] *verbo*

1. to shake: la explosión sacudió mi casa the explosion shook my house
2. to wag: el perro sacudía el rabo the dog shook its tail.

sagrado, da *adjetivo*

1. holy: La Meca es la ciudad sagrada del Islam Mecca is the holy city of Islam
2. sacred: la amistad es algo sagrado friendship is sacred.

la **sal** ■ salt.

la **sala**

1. room: es una sala muy grande it's a very big room
2. hall: sala de conciertos concert hall; sala de conferencias conference hall
3. ward UK, room US: la sala de maternidad the maternity ward

> sala de embarque departure lounge
> sala de espera waiting room
> sala de exposiciones gallery
> sala de juegos games room
> sala de profesores staffroom.

salado, da *adjetivo*

1. salty: la comida está demasiado salada the food is too salty
2. savoury UK, savory US: prefiero la comida salada I prefer savoury food.

el **salario** ■ salary (plural salaries): tiene un buen salario he has a good salary

> el salario mínimo the minimum wage.

la **salchicha** ■ sausage.

el **salchichón** (plural los salchichones) ■ a type of spicy salami.

el **saldo** ■ balance: el saldo de esta cuenta es muy bajo the balance of this account is very low.

el **salero** ■ salt cellar UK, salt shaker US.

la **salida**

1. exit: la salida está por ese pasillo a la derecha the exit is down that corridor on the right
2. departure: la hora de salida del tren es a las 3 the train's departure time is 3 o'clock
3. start: la salida de la carrera the start of the race

> nos vemos a la salida del colegio I'll see you when school finishes
> esta situación no tiene salida this situation has no solution.

salir [51] *verbo*

1. to leave: nunca salgo de mi casa sin un paraguas I never leave home without an umbrella; el avión sale a las 7 the plane leaves at 7
2. to come out: salió demasiado rápido del garaje he came out of the garage too quickly; la nueva edición sale el mes que viene the new edition comes out next month
3. to get out: ¡sal de mi casa! get out of my house!
4. to go out: como castigo no me dejaron salir durante un mes I wasn't allowed out for a month as punishment
5. to be on: salió hoy en las noticias he was on the news today

> el sol sale a las 5:30 de la mañana the sun comes up at 5:30 in the morning
> el viaje salió muy caro the trip was very expensive
> salir con alguien to go out with somebody

salirse *verbo pronominal*

1. to boil over: se ha salido la sopa the soup has boiled over
2. to come off: se salieron de la carretera they came off the road; se salió la rueda del coche the car's wheel came off.

la **saliva** ■ saliva.

el **salmón** (plural los salmones) ■ salmon.

el **salón** (plural los salones) ■ living room, lounge UK

> un salón de actos an assembly hall
> un salón de belleza a beauty salon.

salpicar [8] *verbo* ■ to splash.

a salsa ■ sauce: **la pasta venía en una salsa de vino blanco** the pasta came in a white wine sauce.

saltar [1] *verbo* ■ to jump: **no puedo saltar tan alto** I can't jump that high; **saltó por la ventana** he jumped out of the window; **los niños saltaban de alegría** the children jumped for joy; **el perro saltó la verja** the dog jumped over the fence

saltarse *verbo pronominal*

1. to skip: **no deberías saltarte ninguna comida** you shouldn't skip meals

2. to go through: **¡te has saltado un semáforo en rojo!** you've gone through a red light!

3. to ignore: **se saltó las normas** he ignored the rules

se saltó la cola she jumped the queue.

el salto

1. jump: **dio un salto enorme** he made a huge jump

2. dive: **le gusta saltar al agua** she likes diving in the water

salto de altura high jump

salto con pértiga pole vault

salto de agua waterfall

salto de longitud long jump

salto mortal somersault.

salud *interjección*

1. *al brindar* cheers!

2. *después de estornudar* bless you!

la salud ■ health: **es malo para la salud** it's bad for your health.

saludar [1] *verbo*

1. to say hello: **ni siquiera me saludó** he didn't even say hello to me

2. to wave: **lo saludé desde lejos** I waved to him from a distance

3. to greet: **me saludó con un beso** he greeted me with a kiss

4. to salute: **saludó a su capitán** he saluted his captain

Le saluda atentamente Yours sincerely *UK*, Sincerely yours *US*.

el saludo ■ regards: **os manda muchos saludos a todos** she sends her best regards to everyone

nos recibió con un cálido saludo he greeted us warmly.

salvadoreño, ña *adjetivo*

En inglés, los adjetivos que se refieren a un país o una región se escriben con mayúscula:

Salvadoran

el salvadoreño , **la salvadoreña**

En inglés, los idiomas se escriben con mayúscula.

Salvadoran: los salvadoreños the Salvadorans.

salvaje *adjetivo* ■ wild: **un animal salvaje** a wild animal.

salvar [1] *verbo* ■ to save: **le salvó la vida a su hermano** he saved his brother's life

¡te has salvado! you got out of that!

el salvavidas *(plural* los salvavidas*)*

1. *chaleco* lifejacket

1. *al brindar* lifebelt.

salvo *preposición* ■ except: **todos vinieron salvo Eduardo** everyone came except Eduardo

salvo que unless: **salvo que se especifique lo contrario** unless otherwise specified.

San *adjetivo* ■ Saint: **San Mateo** Saint Matthew

San is a shortened form of **Santo** used before the names of certain saints.

la sandalia ■ sandal.

la sandía ■ watermelon.

el sándwich *(plural* los sándwiches*)* ■ sandwich.

los sanfermines ■ *festivities of Pamplona*

LOS SANFERMINES

The fiesta de los **sanfermines** is celebrated every year in Pamplona from 6th to 14th July. Every morning, during the festivities, the **encierro** (running of the bulls) takes place. Anyone who wants to can run in front of the six bulls that will be fought in the bullring that afternoon. The route of the bull run is 800 metres long and the **encierro** usually lasts for about 3 minutes. It ends at the **corral** inside the bullring where the bullfight is going to be held.

sangrar [1] *verbo* ■ to bleed: la herida le sangraba mucho her wound was bleeding profusely.

la **sangre** ■ blood: no soporto ver sangre I can't stand the sight of blood
> reaccionó con mucha sangre fría she reacted very calmly.

la **sangría** ■ *bebida* sangría.

sano, na *adjetivo* ■ healthy: es un muchacho fuerte y sano he's a strong and healthy boy; nadar es una actividad sana swimming is a healthy activity
> sano y salvo safe and sound.

santo, ta *adjetivo* ■ holy: el santo evangelio the Holy Gospel

el **santo** , la **santa** ■ saint: tu hermano es un santo your brother is a saint.

el **santo** ■ saint's day: mañana es mi santo tomorrow is my saint's day

el **sapo** ■ toad.

el **saque** ■ serve: este tenista tiene un saque magnífico this tennis player has a magnificient serve
> un saque de banda a throw-in
> un saque de esquina a corner.

el **sarampión** (*plural* los sarampiones) ■ measles.

la **sardina** ■ sardine.

la **sartén** (*plural* las sartenes) ■ frying pan.

el **sastre** ■ tailor.

el **satélite** ■ satellite.

la **satisfacción** (*plural* las satisfacciones) ■ satisfaction: se notaba su satisfacción por el resultado you could sense his satisfaction with the outcome.

satisfecho, cha *adjetivo* ■ pleased: la profesora está muy satisfecha con sus alumnos the teacher is very pleased with her students.

la **sauna** ■ sauna.

el **saxofón** (*plural* los saxofones) ■ saxophone.

se *pronombre*

1.

> Se con sentido reflexivo se traduce por **himself, herself, itself, themselves, yourself** o **yourselves**, respectivamente:

> se hizo daño con el martillo he hurt himself with the hammer; la radio se apaga sola the radio turns itself off; se declararon ganadores they declared themselves the winners; si quiere, se puede ver en este espejo you can look at yourself in this mirror if you like

2. **each other: se quieren mucho** they love each other very much

3.

> Cuando el verbo con **se** se refiere a partes del cuerpo o ropa, el inglés usa el artículo posesivo:

> se lavó las manos he washed his hands; se ató los cordones de los zapatos he tied his shoelaces

4.

> Cuando **se** va junto a otro pronombre se traduce por **to him, to her, to them, to you**, respectivamente:

> se los presté I lent them to him

> En estos casos no se traduce cuando el nombre al que se refiere se repite en la oración:

> dáselo a tu hermano give it to your brother; es una sorpresa, no se lo cuentes a Ana it's a surprise so don't tell Ana

5.

> Cuando **se** tiene un sentido impersonal, generalmente se traduce por **you** o **it** :

> se construyó en un año it was built in a year; se puede comprar limones en el mercado you can buy lemons at the market; eso no se hace you shouldn't do that
> "se alquila" "for rent"
> se está afeitando he's shaving
> se quejó del mal servicio he complained about the bad service.

el **secador** ■ hairdryer.

la **secadora** ■ dryer: pon tu ropa en la secadora put your clothes in the dryer.

secar [8] *verbo* ■ **to dry:** ayúdame a secar los platos help me dry the dishes

secarse *verbo pronominal* ■ **to dry oneself:** se secó con la toalla he dried himself with the towel.

la **sección** *(plural* las secciones)
1. **section:** la oficina está dividida en cinco secciones the office is divided into five sections
2. **department:** trabaja en la sección de muebles he works in the furniture department.

seco, ca *adjetivo*
1. **dry:** el desierto es un lugar seco the desert is a dry place
2. **dried:** higos secos dried figs.

el **secretario** , la **secretaria** ■ **secretary** *(plural* secretaries): trabaja de secretaria en una empresa she works as a secretary in a company.

secreto, ta *adjetivo* ■ **secret:** el científico tenía una fórmula secreta the scientist had a secret formula

el **secreto** ■ **secret:** guardó el secreto durante varios años she kept the secret for a few years.

el **sector** ■ **sector.**

la **secuencia** ■ **sequence.**

secuestrar [1] *verbo*
1. **to kidnap:** secuestraron a la hija del presidente the president's daughter was kidnapped
2. **to hijack:** secuestraron el avión they hijacked the plane.

el **secuestro**
1. *de persona* **kidnapping**
2. *de avión* **hijack.**

secundario, ria *adjetivo* ■ **secondary.**

la **sed** ■ **thirst:** saciar la sed to quench one's thirst
> tengo sed I'm thirsty.

seguido, da *adjetivo* ■ **in a row:** estornudé cinco veces seguidas I sneezed five times in a row
> en seguida right away: lo haré en seguida I'll do it right away

seguido *adverbio*
> todo seguido straight ahead o straight.

seguir [32] *verbo*
1. **to follow:** sígueme a mí follow me
2. **to go along:** siga por aquí y luego dé vuelta a la derecha keep going along here then turn right
3. **to go on:** ya no puedo seguir trabajando así I can't go on working like this
> ¿sigues enfermo? are you still ill?

según *(adverbio & preposición)*
■ *adverbio*
depending on: compraré dos o tres juegos según el dinero que tenga I'll buy two or three games depending on how much money I've got
■ *preposición*
according to: según Juan, le fue bien en el examen according to Juan, he did well in the test.

segundo, da *adjetivo* ■ **second:** llegó en el segundo tren she arrived on the second train

el **segundo** , la **segunda** ■ **second:** el corredor español llegó el segundo the Spanish runner came in second

el **segundo** ■ **second:** quedan 30 segundos there are 30 seconds left.

la **seguridad**
1. **safety:** la seguridad personal personal safety
2. **security:** medidas de seguridad security measures
> le falta seguridad en sí mismo he lacks self-confidence
> lo hará con toda seguridad he'll no doubt do it
> la seguridad social social security.

seguro, ra *adjetivo*
1. **sure:** ¿estás seguro? are you sure?
2. **safe:** es bastante seguro comprar en Internet it's quite safe to buy on the Internet
3. **certain:** no es seguro que pueda jugar en el partido it's uncertain if he'll be able to play in the game

el **seguro** ■ insurance: ¿tienes seguro de vida? do you have life insurance?

seis *numeral* ■ **six:** tiene seis hijos she has six children

› mi hermana tiene seis años my sister is six years old

› son las seis it's six o'clock

› el seis de abril the sixth of April *UK*, April sixth *US*.

seiscientos *numeral* ■ **six hundred.**

la **selección** *(plural* las selecciones)*

1. selection: hay una selección de colores enorme there's a great selection of colours

2. team: participan las selecciones nacionales de varios países the national teams from several countries are participating.

seleccionar [1] *verbo* ■ **to pick:** Carmen seleccionó su vestido más nuevo para ir a la fiesta Carmen picked her newest dress to go to the party; el entrenador me ha seleccionado para jugar el sábado the trainer has picked me to play on Saturday.

el **sello**

1. stamp: un sello de correos a postage stamp

2. label: un sello discográfico a record label.

la **selva** ■ forest

› selva tropical tropical rain forest.

el **semáforo** ■ traffic light.

la **semana** ■ week: tardé dos semanas en terminarlo it took me two weeks to finish it

› fin de semana weekend: nos vemos los fines de semana we see each other on weekends

› Semana Santa Holy Week

SEMANA SANTA

📖 **Semana Santa,** or Holy Week, is the week leading up to Easter Sunday and most schools are off for this week. Thursday and Friday are holy days and many people participate in ceremonies and processions. Dried cod is a popular dish at this time.

semanal *adjetivo* ■ **weekly:** es un programa semanal de televisión it's a weekly TV show.

sembrar [14] *verbo* ■ **to sow:** sembró las semillas hace unos meses he sowed the seeds a few months ago.

semejante *adjetivo*

1. similar: descubrieron un sistema solar semejante al nuestro they discovered a solar system similar to ours

2. such: no se puede justificar semejante barbaridad you can't justify such an atrocity.

el **semestre** ■ semester.

la **semifinal** ■ semifinal.

la **semilla** ■ seed.

el **senado** ■ senate.

sencillo, lla *adjetivo*

1. simple: los deberes son bastante sencillos the homework is pretty simple; un vestido sencillo a simple dress

2. modest: Sofía es una persona muy sencilla Sofía is a modest person

el **sencillo** ■ single: el grupo tuvo éxito con ese sencillo the band had a hit with that single.

el **senderismo** ■ hiking.

el **sendero** ■ path.

la **sensación** *(plural* las sensaciones)* ■ feeling: una sensación desagradable an unpleasant feeling.

sensacional *adjetivo* ■ **sensational:** estás sensacional you look sensational.

sensato, ta *adjetivo* ■ **sensible:** parece un chico muy sensato he seems to be a very sensible boy.

sensible *adjetivo* ■ **sensitive:** crema para piel sensible cream for sensitive skin; una persona muy sensible a very sensitive person

The Spanish word **sensible** is a false friend, it doesn't mean "sensible".

sentar [14] *verbo*

1. to suit: ese peinado le sienta muy bien that haircut really suits her

2. **to do someone good: esta manzanilla te sentará bien** this camomile will do you good

sentar mal to disagree: **el pescado me ha sentado mal** the fish disagreed with me

sentarse *verbo pronominal* ■ **to sit down: siéntate ahí si quieres** sit down there if you want.

el **sentido** ■ **sense: los cinco sentidos** the five senses; **¿en qué sentido?** in which sense?; **no tiene sentido del ritmo** he has no sense of rhythm

una calle de un solo sentido a one-way street

ir en sentido contrario to go the wrong way

perder el sentido to lose consciousness

sentido común common sense

sentido del humor sense of humour.

sentimental *adjetivo* ■ **sentimental.**

el **sentimiento** ■ **feeling.**

sentir [20] *verbo*

1. **to feel: siento un aire frío** I feel a cold breeze; **no siente nada por Carlos** she doesn't feel anything for Carlos

2. **to be sorry: lo siento mucho** I'm really sorry; **siento la muerte de tu padre** I'm sorry about your father's death

3. **to hear: siento pasos** I can hear footsteps

se siente mal he doesn't feel well

se siente culpable he feels guilty.

la **seña** ■ **sign: me hizo una seña** he made a sign to me

dame tus señas give me your address.

la **señal**

1. **sign: es una señal positiva** it's a positive sign

2. **signal: la señal es muy débil** the signal is very weak

señal de tráfico traffic sign

señal de socorro distress signal

ser buena señal to be a good sign: **si la fiebre baja es una buena señal** if your temperature goes down, it's a good sign.

señalar [1] *verbo* ■ **to point: ¿puedes señalar dónde está?** can you point out where it is?

no señales a la gente con el dedo don't point at people.

el **señor**

1. **man: ese señor te está buscando** that man is looking for you

2. **Mr: el señor García** Mr García

¿puedo ayudarle, señor? can I help you, sir?

Muy señor mío… Dear Sir…

la **señora**

1. **lady** *(plural* **ladies)*: esa señora es mi profesora** that lady is my teacher

2. **Mrs: la señora García** Mrs García

3. **wife: le presento a mi señora** I'd like you to meet my wife

¿puedo ayudarla, señora? can I help you, madam?

la **señorita**

1. **young lady** *(plural* **young ladies)*: ¡tu hermana ya es una señorita!** your sister's a young lady already!

2. **Miss: todavía me llaman señorita** they still call me Miss.

separar [1] *verbo* ■ **to separate: el árbitro separó a los dos jugadores** the referee separated the two players; **separa los rojos de los azules** separate the reds from the blues

separarse *verbo pronominal* ■ **to separate: se separaron después de diez años** they separated after ten years.

septiembre , setiembre *sustantivo masculino* ■ **September: en septiembre** in September; **el próximo septiembre** next September; **el pasado septiembre** last September

En inglés los nombres de los meses se escriben con mayúscula.

séptimo, ma *numeral* ■ **seventh: Miguel llegó séptimo a la meta** Miguel reached the finishing line seventh.

ser [5] *verbo* ■ **to be: Luis es muy inteligente** Luis is very intelligent; **mi cumpleaños fue ayer** my birthday was yesterday; **es abogado** he's a lawyer; **somos veinticinco en la clase** there are twenty-five of us in the class; **soy Lucía** I'm Lucía el lápiz es para escribir the pencil is for writing

es la una y media it's half past one

esta bicicleta es de mi hermana this is my sister's bicycle

es de Blanca it's Blanca's

Rodrigo es de Guadalajara Rodrigo is from Guadalajara

las casas son de adobe the houses are made from adobe

a no ser que unless: a no ser que estudies, te va a ir mal you'll do badly unless you study

o sea so: o sea que mañana no vienes so you're not coming tomorrow

el **ser** ■ being

un ser humano a human being

los seres vivos living things.

la **serie** ■ series: fui a una serie de charlas I went to a series of talks

una serie de televisión a television series.

serio, ria adjetivo ■ serious: es una persona muy seria he's a very serious person

en serio seriously: deberías tomarte las cosas un poco más en serio you should take things more seriously.

la **serpiente** ■ snake.

el **servicio**

1. service: ofrecen un servicio muy bueno they offer very good service

2. toilet: ¿dónde está el servicio? where's the toilet?

servicio a domicilio home delivery service

servicio incluido service is included

servicio militar military service

estar de servicio to be on duty

estar fuera de servicio to be out of order.

la **servilleta** ■ napkin, serviette UK.

servir [19] verbo

1. to serve: ya han servido la cena they've already served dinner

2. to work: no tires la radio, todavía sirve don't throw away the radio, it still works

¿te sirve esta caja? can you use this box?

esto no sirve para nada this is useless

¿te sirvo más té? can I get you some more tea?

sesenta numeral ■ sixty: el sesenta es un número par sixty is an even number.

la **sesión** (plural las sesiones) ■ session: esta sesión termina a las tres this session ends at three o'clock

la última sesión the last showing.

la **seta** ■ mushroom.

setecientos numeral ■ seven hundred.

setenta numeral ■ seventy: he leído setenta páginas I've read seventy pages.

el **sexo** ■ sex.

sexto, ta numeral ■ sixth: el jugador español llegó en sexta posición the Spanish runner finished in sixth position.

sexual adjetivo ■ sexual.

si conjunción

1. if: si me lo devuelves, te perdono if you give it back to me, I'll forgive you

2. whether: pregúntale si va a venir o no ask her whether she's coming or not

como si no hubiera pasado nada as if nothing had happened.

sí (adverbio & pronombre)

■ adverbio

yes: sí, puedes salir a jugar yes, you can go out to play

a él no le gusta, pero a mí sí he doesn't like it, but I do

parece que sí so it seems

■ pronombre

1.

Sí con sentido reflexivo se traduce por **himself, herself, itself, themselves, yourself** o **yourselves**:

sabe defenderse a sí misma she knows how to defend herself; el título habla por sí mismo the title speaks for itself; debería tener más confianza en sí mismo he should have more confidence in himself; están hablando entre sí they're talking among themselves

2.

Sí con sentido impersonal se traduce por **yourself**:

es mejor decidir las cosas por sí mismo it's best to decide things for yourself

en sí in itself: **el trabajo en sí no me gusta** I don't like the work in itself.

sida *(abreviatura de síndrome de inmu-nodeficiencia adquirida)* ■ **Aids, AIDS.**

siempre *adverbio* ■ **always: esa tienda siempre está cerrada** that shop is always closed

como siempre, hace lo que quiere as usual, he does what he wants

seremos amigos para siempre we'll be friends forever

siempre y cuando provided: **sí, siempre y cuando tus notas no bajen** yes, provided your marks don't go down.

a **sierra**

1. *herramienta* **saw**

2. *cordillera* **mountain range.**

a **siesta** ■ **nap, siesta**

echarse la siesta take a nap

la hora de la siesta siesta time.

siete *numeral* ■ **seven: tiene siete hijos** she has seven children

mi hermana tiene siete años my sister is seven years old

son las siete it's seven o'clock

el siete de abril the seventh of April, April seventh *US.*

as **siglas** ■ **abbreviation.**

el **siglo** ■ **century** *(plural* **centuries): el siglo xxi** the 21st century

hace siglos que no escribe he hasn't written in ages

EL SIGLO DE ORO

The term **Siglo de Oro** (Golden Age) describes the period spanning the 16th and 17th centuries when Spain attained its zenith. Following the discovery of America, the country became the world's leading political and economic power. In the artistic realm, literature attained unparalleled prominence with authors such as Quevedo, Lope de Vega and Calderón de la Barca.

el **significado** ■ **meaning.**

significar [8] *verbo* ■ **to mean: ¿qué significa esta palabra?** what does this word mean?

¿qué significa S.A.? what does S.A. stand for?

su amistad significa mucho para mí her friendship means a lot to me.

el **signo** ■ **sign: el signo de la victoria** the V-sign

¿de qué signo eres? what sign are you?

los signos del zodíaco the signs of the zodiac.

siguiente *adjetivo* ■ **next: lo deja todo preparado para el día siguiente** she leaves everything ready for the next day; **debe venir en el siguiente vuelo** he should be on the next flight

el/la **siguiente**

¡que pase el siguiente! next!

esta calle no, la siguiente not this street, the next one.

la **sílaba** ■ **syllable.**

silbar [1] *verbo* ■ **to whistle.**

el **silbato** ■ **whistle.**

el **silbido** ■ **whistle**

llamó al perro con un silbido he called the dog with a whistle.

el **silencio** ■ **silence: necesito silencio para estudiar** I need silence when I study

¡silencio, por favor! quiet, please!

guardaron silencio en señal de respeto they remained silent as a sign of respect

en silencio silently: **escuchamos en silencio** we listened silently.

silencioso, sa *adjetivo* ■ **silent.**

la **silla** ■ **chair: se sentó en la silla** she sat in the chair

una silla de montar a saddle

una silla de ruedas a wheelchair.

el **sillón** *(plural* los sillones) ■ **armchair.**

silvestre *adjetivo* ■ **wild: moras silvestres** wild berries.

la **silueta** ■ **silhouette: al fondo vemos la silueta de la catedral** at the back we can see the silhouette of the cathedral

ejercicios para conservar la silueta exercises for keeping in shape.

el **símbolo** ■ symbol.

simpático, ca *adjetivo* ■ nice: Ana es muy simpática Ana is very nice

➤ estuvo muy simpático con nosotros he was very nice to us

➤ me cae simpático I like him

> ⚠ The Spanish word **simpático** is a false friend, it doesn't mean "sympathetic".

simple *adjetivo* ■ simple: es un ejercicio muy simple it's a very simple exercise

➤ no soy más que un simple principiante I'm a mere beginner.

simplificar [8] *verbo* ■ to simplify.

sin *preposición* ■ without: salió sin paraguas she went out without an umbrella; se fue sin despedirse he left without saying goodbye

➤ sin querer accidentally

➤ estar sin trabajo to be out of work

➤ el edificio sigue sin terminar the building remains unfinished

➤ gente sin hogar homeless people

➤ pasó la noche sin dormir she spent a sleepless night.

sincero, ra *adjetivo* ■ sincere.

el **sindicato** ■ union.

el **síndrome** ■ syndrome.

sin embargo *conjunción* ■ however: dijo que no vendría, sin embargo ahí estaba he said he wouldn't come, however there he was.

singular *adjetivo* ■ singular

el **singular** ■ singular.

sino *conjunción* ■ but: no es actriz sino bailarina she's not an actress but a dancer

➤ no sólo habla inglés, sino también dos idiomas más she not only speaks English, but also two other languages

➤ no hace sino molestar he doesn't do anything but annoy people

➤ no fue amable, sino todo lo contrario he wasn't nice, but quite the opposite.

el **sinónimo** ■ synonym.

el **síntoma** ■ symptom.

el/la **sinvergüenza** ■ crook: son todos unos sinvergüenzas they're all a bunch of crooks.

siquiera *adverbio*

➤ ni siquiera not even: no tiene ni siquiera para comprar comida he doesn't even have money to buy food: ni siquiera nos ha llamado she hasn't even called.

la **sirena**
1. *alarma* siren
2. *ser mitológico* mermaid.

el **sistema** ■ system: un nuevo sistema para enseñar inglés a new system for teaching English

➤ el sistema respiratorio the respiratory system

➤ el sistema solar the solar system

EL SISTEMA EDUCATIVO

The Spanish Educational System begins with the **educación infantil** (nursery school) for 3 to 6 year olds. Children then go on to **educación primaria** (primary education) for 6 to 12 year olds, followed by **educación secundaria obligatoria**, or **ESO** (compulsory secondary education) for 12 to 16 year olds. At this stage, students can choose between the **bachillerato general**, specialising in humanities and social sciences, and the **bachillerato tecnológico** which includes subjects such as computing and engineering. These qualifications are equivalent to A-levels in the UK and the High-School Diploma in the US, and the course lasts for two years. Students who obtain the qualification of bachillerato, can apply for a place at university. There are three types of university qualification in Spain: **diplomado** (graduate diploma), involving three years' study; **licenciado** (graduate), obtained after four, five or six years, depending on the course, and **doctorado** (doctorate), which takes six years or more.

---

el **sitio**
1. place: déjalo en su sitio leave it in its place; está en un sitio seguro it's in a safe place

2. room: no hay suficiente sitio there's not enough room; esto ocupa mucho sitio this takes up a lot of room

▷ hicieron sitio para que me sentara they made some room so I could sit down

▷ cambiaron los muebles de sitio they moved the furniture around

▷ en algún sitio debe estar it has to be around somewhere

▷ deja sus cosas en cualquier sitio he leaves his stuff everywhere

▷ no lo he visto en ningún sitio I haven't seen him anywhere

▷ un sitio web a web site.

la **situación** *(plural* las situaciones*)* ■ **situation.**

situar [6] *verbo* ■ **to locate:** ¿quién puede situarlo en el mapa? who can locate it on the map?

▷ se sitúa entre los cinco mejores tenistas del mundo she ranks among the five best tennis players in the world.

sobra *sustantivo femenino* ■ ¿alguien tiene una entrada de sobra? does anybody have a spare ticket?; sabes de sobra que a tu padre eso le molesta you know all too well that your dad hates that

▷ de sobra plenty of. tenemos tiempo de sobra we have plenty of time

as sobras ■ **leftovers:** le da las sobras al perro he gives the leftovers to the dog.

sobrar [1] *verbo* ■ **to be left over:** no sobró nada de comida there was no food left over

▷ me sobró algo de dinero I had some money left over

▷ aquí sobra una silla there's one chair too many here.

sobre *preposición*

1. on: ponlo sobre la mesa put it on the table

2. over: volamos sobre la ciudad we flew over the city

3. about: no sabe nada sobre eso he doesn't know anything about that; una película sobre cuatro adolescentes a film about four teenagers

▷ pon uno sobre otro put them one on top of the other

▷ sobre todo above all: sobre todo, apagad las luces above all, turn off the lights

▷ sobre todo specially: una película interesante, sobre todo para los jóvenes an interesting film, specially for young people

el **sobre** ■ **envelope:** un sobre aéreo an airmail envelope.

la **sobremesa** ■ **after-dinner period**

LA SOBREMESA

The time after a meal, when the dishes are cleared away and coffee and liqueurs are served, is called the **sobremesa**. People remain at the table chatting over their drinks; sometimes they play a game of cards or watch television.

sobresaliente *adjetivo* ■ **outstanding:** es un alumno sobresaliente he's an outstanding student

el **sobresaliente** *sustantivo masculino* ■ **A:** obtuvo un sobresaliente en matemáticas he got an A in maths.

sobrevivir [3] *verbo*

1. to survive: sobrevivieron todos los tripulantes all the crew survived

2. to outlive

▷ sobrevivir a algo to survive something: sobrevivieron al accidente they survived the accident

▷ sobrevivir a alguien to outlive somebody: sobrevivió a sus dos hijos he outlived his two sons.

la **sobrina** ■ **niece.**

el **sobrino** ■ **nephew:** tiene muchos sobrinos he has a lot of nieces and nephews.

sociable *adjetivo* ■ **sociable.**

social *adjetivo* ■ **social.**

la **sociedad**

1. society *(plural* societies*)*: vivimos en una sociedad multicultural we live in a multicultural society

2. company *(plural* companies*)*: formaron una sociedad para vender libros por Internet they formed a company to sell books on the Internet.

el **socio** , la **socia**
1. partner: él y mi padre son socios de la empresa he and my father are business partners
2. member: soy socio de un club de deportes I'm a member of a sports club.

el **socorro** ■ help
> oímos unos gritos pidiendo socorro we heard some cries for help
> ¡socorro! help!

el **sofá** ■ sofa: se sentó en el sofá he sat down on the sofa
> un sofá cama a sofa bed.

el **software** ■ software.

el **sol** ■ sun
> al sol in the sun: la ropa se secaba al sol the clothes dried in the sun; estaban sentados al sol they were sitting in the sun
> hace sol it's sunny
> vamos a tomar el sol we're going to sunbathe
> al salir el sol at sunrise
> al ponerse el sol at sunset.

el/la **soldado** ■ soldier.

soleado, da adjetivo ■ sunny.

la **soledad** ■ loneliness: sufren de pobreza y soledad they suffer from poverty and loneliness
> no me gusta la soledad I don't like to be alone.

soler [17] verbo
> en verano solemos ir a la playa in summer we usually go to the seaside
> suelo levantarme a las 9 I usually get up at 9 o'clock
> solíamos bañarnos en ese río we used to swim in that river.

solicitar [1] verbo
1. to apply for: voy a solicitar una beca I'm going to apply for a scholarship
2. to request: escribí solicitando información I wrote requesting information.

la **solicitud**
1. de trabajo, de beca application: rechazaron mi solicitud they rejected my application

2. de información, ayuda request
> presentar una solicitud to put in an application.

sólido, da adjetivo ■ solid.

el/la **solista** ■ soloist.

solitario, ria adjetivo ■ solitary

el **solitario** , la **solitaria** ■ loner

el **solitario** ■ patience UK, solitaire US
> le gusta jugar al solitario he likes to play patience.

solo, la adjetivo
1. alone: estaba sola she was alone
2. lonely: se siente solo he feels lonely
> quiere hablar a solas conmigo he wants to speak to me alone
> lo hizo él solo he did it on his own
> no tuve ni una sola falta I didn't have a single error
> se lo voy a decir una sola vez I'm going to tell him only once
> siempre habla solo he always talks to himself.

sólo adverbio ■ only: sólo quería un vaso de agua I only wanted a glass of water; sólo faltan tres días para mi cumpleaños there are only three days left until my birthday
> con sólo pensarlo me da rabia I get angry just thinking about it
> no sólo canta sino que también compone he not only sings but he also composes.

soltar [16] verbo
1. to let go of: no le sueltes la mano don't let go of his hand; ¡suéltame! let go of me!
2. to release: soltaron a los sospechosos they released the suspects
3. to let out: soltó al perro he let the dog out
> soltó una carcajada she burst out laughing
> se soltó el pelo she let her hair down
> los tornillos se soltaron the screws came loose.

la **soltera** ■ single woman (plural single women).

soltero, ra adjetivo ■ single: es soltero he's single
> padres solteros single parents

el **soltero** ■ bachelor.

la **solución** *(plural* las soluciones*)* ■ solution.

solucionar [1] *verbo* ■ to solve: no solucionas nada con llorar you don't solve anything by crying
> al final todo se solucionó in the end everything was resolved.

la **sombra**
1. shade: sentémonos a la sombra let's sit in the shade
2. shadow: su sombra se proyectaba en la pared her shadow was cast on the wall
> sombra de ojos eyeshadow.

el **sombrero** ■ hat.

la **sombrilla**
1. *de mano* parasol
2. *de playa, terraza* sunshade.

el **sonajero** ■ rattle.

el **sonámbulo** , la **sonámbula** ■ sleepwalker.

sonar [16] *verbo*
1. *timbre, campana* to ring: el teléfono no ha parado de sonar the telephone hasn't stopped ringing
2. *instrumento, voz* to sound: suena a música de los ochenta it sounds like eighties music
> el despertador no sonó the alarm clock didn't go off
> su cara me suena this face is familiar
> esta historia me suena this story sounds familiar
> escríbelo tal como suena write it just the way it sounds
> suénate la nariz blow your nose.

el **sonido** ■ sound.

sonreír [21] *verbo* ■ to smile: me sonrió he smiled at me.

la **sonrisa** ■ smile.

sonrojarse [1] *verbo pronominal* ■ to blush.

soñar [16] *verbo* ■ to dream: soñé que ganábamos el partido I dreamed that we were winning the game

> soñar con alguien to dream about somebody: anoche soñé con él last night I dreamt about him
> soñar con algo to dream of something: sueña con ser famoso he dreams of being famous.

la **sopa** ■ soup: sopa de cebolla onion soup.

soplar [1] *verbo* ■ to blow: está soplando un viento muy frío a very cold wind is blowing
> pide un deseo y sopla las velas blow out the candles and make a wish
> le soplaron la respuesta they whispered the answer to her.

soportar [1] *verbo*
1. to support: esta columna soporta todo el peso this column supports all the weight
2. to stand: apenas puede soportar el dolor he can barely stand the pain
> la verdad es que no la soporto the truth is that I can't stand her.

el **sorbete** ■ sorbet.

sordo, da *adjetivo* ■ deaf: es sordo he's deaf
> se quedó sordo he went deaf.

sordomudo, da *adjetivo* ■ deaf mute.

sorprendente *adjetivo* ■ surprising.

sorprender [2] *verbo* ■ to surprise: ya nada me sorprende nothing surprises me these days; no me sorprendería que lo volviera a hacer it would not surprise me if he did it again
> lo sorprendieron copiando they caught him copying
> se sorprendió al verme he was surprised to see me.

la **sorpresa** ■ surprise: quiero que sea una sorpresa I want it to be a surprise
> su pregunta me cogió por sorpresa his question took me by surprise
> le hicieron una fiesta sorpresa they gave him a surprise party.

sortear [1] *verbo*
1. to raffle: sortearon un premio estupendo they raffled a fabulous prize

2. to avoid: sortearon los obstáculos con gran habilidad they avoided the obstacles very skilfully.

el **sorteo** ■ raffle.

la **sortija** ■ ring.

soso, sa *adjetivo*
1. *persona* dull
2. *sin sabor* bland.

sospechar [1] *verbo* ■ to suspect: sospecho que mis vecinos lo hicieron I suspect that my neighbors did it

sospechar de alguien to suspect somebody: sospechan del jardinero they suspect the gardener.

sospechoso, sa *adjetivo* ■ suspicious

el **sospechoso**, la **sospechosa** ■ suspect.

el **sostén** *(plural* los sostenes*)* ■ bra.

sostener [52] *verbo*
1. to hold: sostenme la escalera, por favor hold the ladder for me, please
2. to support: estas dos vigas sostienen el techo these two beams support the roof
3. to maintain: siempre ha sostenido que él no lo hizo she's always maintained that he didn't do it

sostenerse *verbo pronominal* ■ to stand: el borracho apenas se sostenía en pie the drunk could barely stand.

el **sótano** ■ basement.

su *adjetivo*
1. *de él* his: vino con su novia he came with his girlfriend
2. *de ella* her: conozco a su marido I know her husband
3. *de una cosa, un animal* its: viene en su propia caja it comes in its own box; el perro tiene su casita the dog has its kennel
4. *de ellos, ellas, varias cosas* their: trajeron sus bicicletas they brought their bicycles; los jóvenes tienen su propio estilo young people have their own style; tiene fotos de pájaros y sus nombres he has pictures of birds and their names

5. *de usted, ustedes* your: su nombre, por favor your name, please; no olviden sus abrigos don't forget your coats.

suave *adjetivo*
1. soft: tocaban una música muy suave they were playing very soft music
2. smooth: es suave al tacto it's smooth to the touch; un aterrizaje suave a smooth landing
3. mild: tiene un clima suave it has a mild climate
4. gentle: un champú suave a gentle shampoo.

subdesarrollado, da *adjetivo* ■ underdeveloped.

la **subida**
1. rise: una subida de las temperaturas a temperature rise
2. increase: ha habido una subida de los precios there's been a price increase
3. climb: iniciaron la subida a la montaña they started the climb up the mountain.

subir [3] *verbo*
1. to go up: subimos a la colina we went up the hill; voy a subir por las escaleras I'm going to go up the stairs
2. to come up: sube que quiero decirte algo come up, I want to tell you something; ya subo I'm coming up
3. to take up: voy a subir el televisor a mi cuarto I'm going to take the television up to my room
4. to bring up: por favor, súbeme el suéter que dejé en la cocina please bring me up the sweater that I left in the kitchen
5. to rise: han subido las temperaturas the temperatures have risen; le subió la fiebre his fever rose
6. to increase: los precios han subido prices have increased
7. to climb: subió la montaña she climbed the mountain; le cuesta subir las escaleras it's hard for him to climb the stairs
8. to turn up: sube el volumen, por favor turn up the volume, please

no puedo subirme la cremallera I can't get my zip up

subirse *verbo pronominal*

subirse a algo

1. *a un coche* **to get into:** se subió a un taxi he got into a taxi
2. *un autobús, avión, bicicleta* **to get on:** nos subimos juntos al tren we got on the train together
3. *a un árbol* **to climb:** se subió al muro he climbed the wall.

el **subjuntivo** ■ subjunctive.

el **submarinismo** ■ scuba diving.

el **submarino** ■ submarine.

subrayar [1] *verbo* ■ **to underline.**

subterráneo, nea *adjetivo* ■ underground.

el **subtítulo** ■ subtitle.

suceder [2] *verbo* ■ **to happen:** ¿te ha sucedido algo? has something happened to you?

el **suceso** ■ event: el periódico explicaba el suceso con muchos detalles the newspaper reported the event in great detail.

la **suciedad** ■ dirt.

sucio, cia *adjetivo* ■ dirty: tienes la cara sucia your face is dirty.

la **sucursal** ■ branch office.

Sudamérica ■ South America.

sudamericano, na *adjetivo*

En inglés, los adjetivos que se refieren a un país o una región se escriben con mayúscula:

South American

el **sudamericano** , la **sudamericana**

En inglés, los gentilicios se escriben con mayúscula:

South American: un sudamericano a South American; los sudamericanos South Americans.

sudar [1] *verbo* ■ **to sweat.**

sudeste *adjetivo* ■ south-east

el **sudeste** ■ south-east.

sudoeste *adjetivo* ■ south-west

el **sudoeste** ■ south-east.

el **sudor** ■ sweat.

la **suegra** ■ mother-in-law (plural **mothers-in-law**).

el **suegro** ■ father-in-law (plural **fathers-in-law**): me acompañó mi suegro my father-in-law came with me

> invitó a sus suegros she invited her in-laws.

la **suela** ■ sole.

el **sueldo**

1. *mensual* salary (plural **salaries**)
2. *semanal* wages.

el **suelo**

1. *en el exterior* ground. al salir del cine me caí al suelo upon leaving the cinema I fell to the ground
2. *de una casa, edificio* floor: un suelo de madera a wooden floor.

suelto, ta *adjetivo* ■ loose: este tornillo está suelto this screw is loose; tiene una hoja suelta it has a sheet loose; el perro anda suelto the dog is loose; llevaba el pelo suelto she had her hair loose

> está prohibido vender cigarrillos sueltos it's prohibited to sell individual cigarettes

el **suelto** ■ change: ¿tienes suelto? do you have any change?

el **sueño**

1. dream: tuve un sueño muy raro I had a very strange dream
2. sleep: es falta de sueño it's lack of sleep; necesito nueve horas de sueño I need nine hours sleep
> tengo sueño I'm sleepy
> tiene el sueño muy pesado he's a heavy sleeper
> me caía de sueño I was so sleepy I could hardly stand.

la **suerte** ■ luck: deséame suerte wish me luck; ¡buena suerte! good luck!

> tener suerte to be lucky: tienes mucha suerte you're very lucky

> tuvo mala suerte he was unlucky
> por suerte luckily: por suerte todo salió bien luckily everything turned out fine.

el **suéter** ■ sweater.

suficiente *adjetivo* ■ enough: no había suficiente comida there wasn't enough food; ¿hay suficientes sillas? are there enough seats?

el **suficiente** ■ pass: obtuvo un suficiente en geografía he got a pass in geography.

sufrir [3] *verbo* ■ to suffer: ha sufrido mucho he has suffered a lot; no hagas sufrir a tu madre don't make your mother suffer
> sufre del corazón he suffers from a heart condition
> sufre de asma he suffers from asthma.

la **sugerencia** ■ suggestion.

sugerir [20] *verbo* ■ to suggest: sugiero que nos vayamos I suggest we leave.

suicidarse [1] *verbo* ■ to commit suicide.

el **suicidio** ■ suicide.

sujetar [1] *verbo*

1. to hold: tienes que sujetarlo con las dos manos you have to hold it with both hands; sujétame la escalera hold the ladder for me
2. to fix: lo sujetó a la pared con tornillos he fixed it to the wall with screws
> sujetó los papeles con un clip she fastened the papers with a clip
> sujetaba al perro con una cuerda they held on to the dog with a rope.

el **sujeto** ■ subject.

la **suma**

1. addition: están haciendo sumas they're doing addition
2. sum: la suma de los votos emitidos the sum of the votes cast
> importantes sumas de dinero significant sums of money.

sumar [1] *verbo* ■ to add: hay que sumar estas cantidades you have to add these numbers

> cuatro y cuatro suman ocho four plus four equals eight.

súper *adverbio* ■ super: lo pasé súper bien I had a super time.

superar [1] *verbo*

1. to overcome: tiene que superar su timidez he has to overcome his shyness; han superado muchos problemas they have overcome many problems
2. to surpass: los supera a todos en agilidad she surpasses them all in agility; eso supera todas las expectativas that surpasses all expectations
3. to pass: ha superado todas las pruebas he's passed all the tests
4. to exceed: ha superado el nivel permitido de alcohol he's exceeded the permitted alcohol levels
5. to break: superó la marca mundial he broke the world record
> estudia porque quiere superarse she studies because she wants to excel.

superficial *adjetivo* ■ superficial.

la **superficie**

1. surface: la superficie del lago está congelada the surface of the lake is frozen
2. area: abarca una superficie de cuatro kilómetros cuadrados it covers an area of four square kilometres.

el **supermercado** ■ supermarket.

superior *adjetivo*

1. upper: el incendio empezó en los pisos superiores the fire started on the upper floors
2. superior: es de calidad superior it's of superior quality
> superior a algo better than something: este modelo es muy superior al del año pasado this model is better than last year's
> dime un número superior a diez say me a number higher than ten; un curso de nivel superior a higher education course.

la **superstición** *(plural* las supersticiones*)* ■ superstition.

supervisar [1] *verbo* ■ to supervise.

el **superviviente** ■ survivor.

272

el suplemento
1. *cantidad extra* **extra charge**
2. *de un periódico* **supplement**.

la suplente
1. **replacement**: entró de suplente en el segundo tiempo he came in as a replacement in the second half
2. **substitute**: es el suplente del profesor de historia he's the substitute for the history teacher.

suponer [47] *verbo*
1. **to suppose**: supongo que no has hecho los deberes I suppose that you haven't done your homework; supongo que tienes razón I suppose you're right
2. **to think**: supuse que iba a cambiar de idea I thought that he was going to change his mind; supusimos que era para mañana we thought that it was for tomorrow
3. **to mean**: eso supone tener que levantarme más temprano that means I'll have to get up earlier
  ≻ supongo que sí I suppose so.

suprimir [3] *verbo* ■ **to delete**: suprimió varias frases he deleted several sentences
  ≻ van a suprimir parte de la materia del examen they're going to cut part of the material from the test.

el supuesto
  ≻ en el supuesto de que no lo supiera on the assumption that he didn't know
  ≻ por supuesto of course
  ≻ por supuesto que no of course not
  ≻ tú das por supuesto que te van a aceptar you take for granted that they're going to accept you.

sur *adjetivo* ■ **south**: Málaga está al sur de España Málaga is on the south coast of Spain

el sur ■ **south**: en el sur de la ciudad in the south of the city; fuimos hacia el sur we went south
  ≻ al sur de south of: Toledo está al sur de Madrid Toledo is south of Madrid.

el surf ■ **surfing**.

la surfista ■ **surfer**.

surgir [11] *verbo* ■ **to come up**: surgió un problema a problem came up.

suscribirse [3] *verbo* ■ **to subscribe**: me suscribí a una revista I subscribed to a magazine.

la suscripción (*plural* las suscripciones) ■ **subscription**.

suspender [2] *verbo*
1. **to cancel**: suspendieron las clases por la nieve they cancelled the classes because of the snow
2. **to stop**: suspendieron la reunión para almorzar they stopped the meeting to eat lunch
3. **to suspend**: lo suspendieron por mala conducta they suspended him for bad conduct
  ≻ suspendieron el partido a causa de la lluvia they postponed the game because of the rain.

el suspenso ■ **fail**: obtuvo un suspenso en historia he got a fail in history.

suspirar [1] *verbo* ■ **to sigh**.

el suspiro ■ **sigh**.

la sustancia ■ **substance**.

el sustantivo ■ **noun**.

sustituir [36] *verbo* ■ **to replace**: va a sustituir al director cuando se jubile she's going to replace the director when he retires; Blazek sustituyó al portero en el segundo tiempo Blazek replaced the goalkeeper in the second half
  ≻ sustituir algo por algo to substitute something with something: puedes sustituir el azúcar por sacarina you can substitute the sugar with saccharin.

el sustituto , la sustituta
1. *permanente* **replacement**
2. *temporal* **substitute**.

el susto ■ **scare**: me llevé un gran susto I had a bad scare
  ≻ ¡qué susto me has dado! what a scare you gave me!
  ≻ tener susto to be afraid.

susurrar [1] *verbo* ■ **to whisper**: le susurró algo al oído he whispered something in her ear.

suyo, ya *adjetivo & pronombre*

1. *de él* **his:** fue idea suya it was his idea; **no es asunto suyo** it's none of his business
2. *de ella* **her:** no es asunto suyo it's none of her business
3. *de usted, ustedes* **your:** ¿son estas hijas suyas? are these your daughters?
4. *de ellos, ellas* **their:** ¿es ésta su calle? —no, la suya es la próxima is this their street? – no, theirs is the next one

■ *pronombre*

1. *de él* **his:** el suyo es blanco his is white; esta no es su hija, la suya es mucho más joven this is not his daughter, his is much younger
2. *de ella* **hers:** el suyo es rojo hers is red; esta no es su hermana, la suya no ha venido this is not her sister, hers hasn't come
3. *de usted, de ustedes* **yours:** el rojo es el suyo the red one is yours; éstos no son sus asientos, ésos son los suyos these aren't your seats, those are yours
4. *de ellos, ellas* **theirs**
> **llegaron con un amigo suyo** they arrived with a friend of theirs
> **estas fotos son suyas** these photos are theirs.

el **tabaco** ■ tobacco.

la **tabla**

1. **board:** con un par de tablas hizo una mesa he made a table with a couple of boards

2. **table:** las tablas de los verbos the verb tables
> las tablas de multiplicar multiplication tables
> una tabla de picar a chopping board
> la tabla de planchar the ironing board
> una tabla de surf a surfboard.

el **tablero** ■ **board:** un tablero de ajedrez a chessboard
> el tablero de mandos the control panel.

la **tableta**

1. *de chocolate* **bar**
2. *medicamento* **tablet.**

el **taburete** ■ **stool.**

tacaño, ña *adjetivo* ■ **stingy**

el **tacaño** , la **tacaña** ■ **skinflint.**

tachar [1] *verbo* ■ **to cross:** taché su nombre de la lista I crossed her name from the list
> los tachan de machistas they accused them of being chauvinists.

el **taco**

1. *de billetes, papeles* **wad**
2. *de entradas* **book**
3. *para tornillo* **Rawlplug®** *UK,* **Rawl®** *US*
4. *en el billar* **cue**
5. *de jamón, queso* **cube**
6. *palabrota* **swearword.**

el **tacón** *(plural* los tacones*)* ■ **heel:** se le rompió el tacón her heel broke
> zapatos de tacón high-heeled shoes.

la **táctica** ■ **tactics:** van a tener que cambiar de táctica they're going to have to change tactics.

el **tacto**

1. **touch:** es suave al tacto it's soft to the touch
2. **tact:** le falta tacto she's lacking tact
> tiene mucho tacto he's very tactful.

tal *(adjetivo & adverbio)*

■ *adjetivo*

such: lo dijo de tal manera que me ofendió he said it in such a manner as to offend me
> nadie esperaba tal cantidad de público nobody expected such a large crowd
> un tal Mario preguntó por ti someone called Mario asked for you

adverbio

¿qué tal? how's it going?

¿qué tal estuvo la fiesta? how was the party?

lo hice tal como me lo explicaste I did it exactly like you explained

no todo es tal como lo vemos not everything is just as we see it

te lo presto con tal que me lo devuelvas luego I'll loan it to you provided that you return it to me later

tal vez maybe.

el **taladro** ■ drill.

el **talento** ■ talent: **tiene talento para el dibujo** he has a talent for drawing.

la **talla** ■ size: **¿qué talla usas?** what size do you take?

tallar [1] *verbo*

1. *la madera* to carve

2. *una joya, el cristal* to cut.

el **taller**

1. *de mecánico* garage

2. *de artista* studio

3. *de carpintero, electricista* workshop

> **un taller de poesía** a poetry workshop.

el **tallo** ■ stem.

el **talón** *(plural los talones)*

1. *del pie, de un calcetín* heel

2. *de un cheque, recibo* stub.

el **tamaño** ■ size: **¿qué tamaño tiene?** what size is it?; **son del mismo tamaño** they're the same size.

también *adverbio* ■ also, too, as, well: **a mí también me regalaron uno** they also gave one to me; **canta y también toca el piano** he sings and he plays the piano too; **Pepe lo sabía —y yo también** Pepe knew it — and me too; **quiero ir —nosotros también** I want to go — I do as well.

el **tambor** ■ drum.

tampoco *adverbio*

1. **either:** **yo tampoco lo sé** I don't know either; **no estudió ni tampoco hizo los deberes** he didn't study and he didn't do his homework either

2. **neither:** **no quiero ir y Pepe tampoco** I don't want to go and neither does Pepe; **no puedo hacerlo —yo tampoco** I can't do it — me neither; **no sabía que tenía un hermano —nosotros tampoco** she didn't know that he had a brother — neither did we.

el **tampón** *(plural los tampones)* ■ tampon.

tan *adverbio*

1. **so:** **no comas tan rápido** don't eat so quickly; **¡es tan divertido!** it's so entertaining!

2. **such:** **lo pasamos tan bien** we had such a good time; **nunca había visto un perro tan grande** I had never seen such a large dog

> **¡que película tan aburrida!** what a boring film!

> **lo pusiste tan arriba que no lo puedo coger** you put it so high up that I can't reach it

> **tan... como** as... as: **no es tan inteligente como su hermano** he's not as intelligent as his brother: **ven tan pronto como puedas** come as soon as you can.

el **tanque** ■ tank.

tanto, ta *adjetivo & pronombre*

El adjetivo se traduce por **so much** o **so many** según el sustantivo en inglés sea singular o plural respectivamente:

1. **so much:** **había tanta comida** there was so much food; **tengo tanto trabajo que hacer** I have so much work to do

2. **so many:** **me hizo tantas preguntas** she asked me so many questions; **nunca había visto tanta gente aquí** I had never seen so many people here; **ayer había mucha gente, pero hoy no hay tanta** yesterday there were a lot of people, but today there aren't so many

> **he traído tanto dinero como tú** I've brought as much money as you

> **ya no tiene tantos amigos como antes** now he doesn't have as many friends as before

> **no tiene tanta importancia** it's not that important

> **tiene tanta suerte** he's so lucky

> **una mujer de unos veinte y tantos años** a woman of twenty-odd years

> **Javier llegó a las tantas** Javier arrived in the early hours

> **por lo tanto** therefore

tanto *adverbio*

1. **so much: le quiere tanto** she loves him so much

2. **so often: ya no voy tanto al cine** I don't go to the cinema so often any more

> **no sé por qué tardó tanto** I don't know why he took so long

> **no debería trabajar tanto** she shouldn't work so much

> **he estudiado tanto como tú** I've studied as much as you

> **tanto Ana como José suspendieron** both Ana and José failed

el **tanto**

1. **goal: ganaron un tanto a cero** they won, one goal to zero

2. **amount: hay que pagar un tanto fijo cada mes** you have to pay a fixed amount each month

> **lo puse al tanto de todo** I fill him in on everything

> **te voy a mantener al tanto** I'll keep you informed

> **un tanto por ciento** a percentage.

la **tapa**

1. *de olla, caja* **lid**

2. *de libro, revista* **cover: su nombre estaba en la tapa del libro** his name was on the cover of the book

3. *en el bar* **bar snack**

> **un libro de tapas blandas** a paperback book

> **un libro de tapas duras** a hardback book

> ⚠ The Spanish word **tapa** is a false friend, it doesn't mean "tap".

tapar [1] *verbo*

1. **to cover: lo tapó con papel de aluminio** she covered it with aluminium foil

2. **to put the lid on: tienes que tapar la olla** you have to put the lid on the pot

3. **to fill: están tapando los agujeros en la calle** they're filling the holes in the street

> **tapa la botella** put the cap on the bottle

> **no me tapes el sol** don't block my sunlight

taparse *verbo pronominal*

1. **to cover: se tapó la boca con la mano** she covered her mouth with her hand; **la tapó con una manta** he covered her with a blanket

2. **to get blocked: se me tapa la nariz** my nose is blocked

> **tápate bien** wrap yourself up well.

el **tapón** *(plural* los tapones*)*

1. *del lavabo, fregadero* **stopper**

2. *de botella* **top**

3. *de corcho* **cork**

4. *para los oídos* **earplug.**

la **taquilla**

1. *de teatro, cine* **box office**

2. *en estación, estadio* **ticket office.**

tardar [1] *verbo*

> **tardaron dos horas en llegar** they took two hours to arrive

> **por favor, no tardes** please, don't be late

> **¿cuánto tardaste en leerlo?** how long did you take to read it?

> **están tardando en darme los resultados** they're taking a while to give me the results

> **no tardó en darse cuenta** he didn't take long to realize

> **en tren se tarda media hora** it takes half an hour by train.

tarde *adverbio* ■ **late: ya es demasiado tarde** it's too late now

> **¡date prisa, que vamos a llegar! tarde** hurry up! we're going to be late

> **más tarde** later

> **tarde o temprano** sooner or later

la **tarde**

1. **afternoon: a las cuatro de la tarde** at four o'clock in the afternoon; **buenas tardes** good

afternoon; **mañana por la tarde** tomorrow afternoon

2. **evening**: **a las 7 de la tarde** at 7 o'clock in the evening; **buenas tardes** good evening; **hoy por la tarde** this evening.

la tarifa

1. *de transporte* **fare**: **los escolares pagan tarifa reducida** schoolchildren pay a reduced fare

2. *de la luz, del agua* **rate**

3. *lista de precios* **tariff.**

la tarjeta ■ **card**: **me envió una tarjeta para mi cumpleaños** he sent me a card for my birthday

> **una tarjeta amarilla/roja** a yellow/red card
> **una tarjeta de cajero automático** a cashpoint card *UK*, an ATM card *US*
> **una tarjeta de crédito** a credit card
> **una tarjeta de embarque** a boarding pass
> **una tarjeta de Navidad** a Christmas card
> **una tarjeta de visita** a business card
> **una tarjeta de sonido** a sound card
> **una tarjeta postal** a postcard
> **una tarjeta telefónica** a telephone card.

el tarro ■ **jar**: **un tarro de mermelada** a jar of jam.

la tarta

1. *pastel* **cake**

2. *hojaldre* **pie.**

tartamudear [1] *verbo* ■ **to stammer, to stutter.**

tartamudo, da *adjetivo*

> **es tartamudo** he has a stammer.

la tasa ■ **rate**: **la tasa de mortalidad** the death rate; **la tasa de natalidad** the birth rate.

el tatuaje ■ **tattoo.**

el taxi ■ **taxi.**

la taxista ■ **taxi driver.**

el tazón (*plural* los tazones*)* ■ **bowl.**

la taza

1. **cup**: **me tomé una taza de café** I drank a cup of coffee

2. **cupful**: **agregar dos tazas de azúcar** add two cupfuls of sugar.

te *pronombre*

1. **you**: **te llamó ayer** she called you yesterday; **te lo dije** I told you

2. **yourself**: **¿te has cortado?** have you cut yourself?; **sólo si te portas bien** only if you behave yourself

> **¡no te muevas!** don't move!
> **ponte los zapatos** put your shoes on.

el té (*plural* los tés*)* ■ **tea**: **¿quieres té?** do you want some tea?

> **un té con limón** a tea with lemon.

el teatro ■ **theatre** *UK*, **theater** *US*: **fuimos al teatro** we went to the theater

> **no le pasa nada, todo es puro teatro** *informal* nothing's wrong with him, it's all an act.

el tebeo ■ **comic.**

el techo ■ **ceiling**: **dos lámparas colgaban del techo** two lights hung from the ceiling.

la tecla ■ **key**: **las teclas del piano** the piano keys; **si pulsas esta tecla se apaga el ordenador** if you press this key the computer will switch off.

el teclado ■ **keyboard**: **se me ha bloqueado el teclado** my keyboard's jammed.

la técnica ■ **technique.**

técnico, ca *adjetivo* ■ **technical**

el técnico , la técnica

1. **technician**: **es técnico dental** he's a dental technician

2. **repairman** (*plural* **repairmen**): **el técnico vino a arreglar el televisor** the repairman came to mend the television.

la tecnología ■ **technology** (*plural* **technologies**).

la teja ■ **tile.**

el tejado ■ **roof.**

tejer [2] *verbo* ■ **to sew**: **esto me lo tejió mi madre** my mother sewed this for me.

el tejido

1. *tela* **fabric**

2. *del cuerpo humano* **tissue.**

la tela ■ **cloth**: **necesitas un metro de tela** you need a metre of cloth.

la telaraña

1. *nueva* **spider's web** *UK*, **spiderweb** *US*: había un insecto atrapado en la telaraña there was an insect trapped in the spider's web
2. *vieja, con polvo* **cobweb**: el desván está lleno de telarañas the attic is full of cobwebs.

la tele ■ *informal* **TV**: lo dieron por la tele it was on TV.

el/la telefonista ■ **telephone operator**.

el teléfono

1. **telephone, phone**: no tiene teléfono he doesn't have a telephone
2. **telephone number, phone number**: ¿me das tu teléfono? will you give me your phone number?
   - está hablando por teléfono con un amigo he's talking with a friend on the telephone
   - me llamó por teléfono he called me on the telephone; un teléfono fijo a landline
   - un teléfono móvil a mobile phone *UK*, a cellphone *US*
   - un teléfono de tarjeta a card phone.

el telegrama ■ **telegram**.

la telenovela ■ **soap opera**.

el telescopio ■ **telescope**.

el telespectador , la telespectadora ■ **viewer**.

el telesilla ■ **chairlift**.

el telesquí *(plural los telesquís)* ■ **ski lift**.

la televisión ■ **television**: lo vimos por televisión we saw it on television
- la televisión digital digital television.

el televisor ■ **television set**.

el tema

1. **subject**: ¿qué opinas del tema? what's your opinion on the subject?
2. **topic**: el tema de la conferencia the topic of the lecture; el tema de mi proyecto es el medioambiente the topic of my project is the environment
3. **theme**: un tema musical a musical theme; el tema de la exposición the theme of the exhibition

- estás cambiando de tema you're changing the subject
- los temas de actualidad current affairs.

temblar [14] *verbo* ■ **to tremble**: le temblaban las manos her hands were trembling
- estaba temblando de frío he was shivering with cold
- temblaba de miedo she was trembling with fear
- la explosión hizo temblar el edificio the explosion made the building tremble.

el temblor ■ **shaking**: ¿sentiste el temblor? did you feel the shaking?
- un temblor de tierra an earth tremor.

temer [2] *verbo*

1. **to be afraid**: todos temen al director everybody's afraid of the director; no temas, no te va a pasar nada don't be afraid, nothing's going to happen to you; teme que no va ser posible he's afraid that it's not going to be possible
2. **to fear**: temen por su vida they fear for their lives
- me temo que no es tan simple como crees I'm afraid it's not as simple as you think
- temen por su vida they fear for their lives.

el temor ■ **fear**: el temor a lo desconocido the fear of unknown
- por temor a for fear of: no salen de noche por temor a los robos they don't go out at night for fear of robbery.

la temperatura ■ **temperature**: ¿qué temperatura hace hoy? what's the temperature today?; le tomó la temperatura she took his temperature.

la tempestad ■ **storm**.

templado, da *adjetivo*

1. **mild**: regiones de clima templado regions with a mild climate
2. **warm**: un aparato que mantiene la comida templada a device that keeps food warm; peces de agua templada warm water fish.

el templo ■ **temple**.

la temporada ■ **season**: la temporada de vacaciones the holiday season; ha jugado cuatro temporadas he has played for four seasons

está pasando una temporada en Estados Unidos he's spending some time in the United States
la temporada alta the high season
la temporada baja the low season
la temporada de esquí the ski season.

temporal *adjetivo* ■ temporary

temporal ■ storm.

temprano, na *adverbio* ■ early: llegué temprano I arrived early.

tenaz *adjetivo* ■ tough.

tenazas
1. *de cangrejo, escorpión* pincers
2. *de herrero, chimenea* tongs
3. *de electricista* pliers.

tendencia
1. tendency (*plural* tendencies): tiene tendencia a engordar he has a tendency to put on weight
2. trend: las últimas tendencias de la moda the latest trends in fashion; la actual tendencia hacia la globalización the current trend towards globalization.

tender [15] *verbo*
1. *la ropa* to hang out: la tendió al sol she hung it out in the sun
2. to lay out: tendió la toalla en el suelo he laid the towel out on the ground
   tender a to tend to: tiende a exagerar he tends to exaggerate
   le tendieron una trampa they set a trap for him

tenderse *verbo pronominal* ■ to stretch out: se tendió en la arena she stretched out in the sand.

el tendón (*plural* los tendones) ■ tendon
el tendón de Aquiles Achilles' heel.

el tenedor ■ fork.

tener [52] *verbo*
1. to have, to have got: tienen dos perros they have two dogs o they have got two dogs; tengo dos hermanos I have two brothers o I have got two brothers; no tengo muchos amigos I don't have many friends o I haven't got many friends; tenían una casa en la playa pero la

han vendido they had a house on the beach but they've sold it; tiene el pelo corto she has short hair o she has got short hair

2.

Cuando el verbo tener va seguido de un sustantivo que indica una sensación, el inglés usa to be seguido de un adjetivo:

to be: tenemos hambre we're hungry; tengo sed I'm thirsty; no tengas miedo don't be afraid

3. to hold: tenme la escalera hold the ladder for me; ¿me puedes tener esto un momento, por favor? can you hold this for me for a moment, please?
   tengo las manos sucias my hands are dirty
   ¿cuántos años tienes? how old are you?
   tengo muchas cosas que hacer I have a lot of things to do
   tiene que ir al dentista she has to go to the dentist
   tengo que hacer más ejercicio I have to exercise more
   tened mucho cuidado be very careful; no tengo nada que ver con esto I haven't got anything to do with this.

el/la teniente ■ lieutenant.

el tenis ■ tennis.

el/la tenista ■ tennis player.

la tensión (*plural* las tensiones)
1. tension: había mucha tensión en el ambiente there was a lot of tension in the atmosphere
2. stress: durante los exámenes pasamos por un periodo de mucha tensión during the exams we went through a period of a lot of stress
   siempre está en tensión he's always stressed out.

tenso, sa *adjetivo*
1. tense: el ambiente estaba muy tenso the atmosphere was very tense
2. taut: la cuerda no está suficientemente tensa the rope is not taut enough.

la tentación (*plural* las tentaciones) ■ temptation.

teñir [19] *verbo* ■ **to dye:** tiñó la camiseta de azul she dyed the T-shirt blue; se tiñe el pelo she dyes her hair.

la **teoría** ■ **theory** (*plural* **theories***)*: mi teoría es que copió en el examen my theory is that he copied in the exam

en teoría in theory: eso es verdad en teoría pero no en la práctica that is true in theory but not in practice.

teórico, ca *adjetivo* ■ **theoretical.**

tercer *numeral* ➤ **tercero**

Shortened form of **tercero** used before masculine singular nouns.

tercero, ra *numeral*

Tercero becomes **tercer** when it comes before a singular masculine noun:

third: lo conseguí a la tercera vez I got it the third time around; vive en el tercer piso he lives on the third floor; llegó tercero he came in third; soy el tercero de la lista I'm the third on the list

una tercera parte de los estudiantes a third of the students

el Tercer Mundo the Third World

las personas de la tercera edad senior citizens.

el **tercio** ■ **third:** un tercio de la población a third of the population.

el **terciopelo** ■ **velvet.**

terco, ca *adjetivo* ■ **stubborn.**

el **terminal** ■ *informático* **terminal**

la **terminal** ■ **terminal:** llega por la terminal dos it arrives at terminal two

la terminal de autobuses the bus station.

terminar [1] *verbo*

1. **to finish:** ya he terminado la deberes I've already finished my homework

2. **to end:** la clase no ha terminado todavía class hasn't ended yet; ¿a qué hora termina la película? what time does the film end?

3. **to end up:** terminé aceptando la invitación I ended up accepting the invitation;

todos terminamos rendidos we all ended up exhausted

los zapatos terminan en punta the shoes are pointy

terminó con su novio she broke it off with her boyfriend

hay que terminar con la indisciplina you have to stop the lack of discipline

terminarse *verbo pronominal*

se nos terminó el dinero we ran out of money

se me han terminado las vacaciones my vacations were over.

el **término** ■ **term:** es un término técnico it's a technical term

por término medio, duermo ocho horas cada noche on average, I sleep eight hours a night

en términos generales el nivel es muy bajo generally speaking the level is very low

al término at the end: al término de la conferencia, hizo varias preguntas at the end of the lecture, he asked several questions.

el **termo** ■ **thermos.**

el **termómetro** ■ **thermometer.**

la **ternera**

1. *de ternero* **veal**

2. *de buey* **beef:** una hamburguesa de ternera a beefburger.

la **ternura** ■ **tenderness.**

la **terraza**

1. *balcón* **balcony** (*plural* **balconies***)*

2. **roof terrace**

un bar con terraza a terrace bar.

el **terremoto** ■ **earthquake.**

el **terreno**

1. **land:** la casa tiene mucho terreno the house has a lot of land; es un terreno muy fértil it's very fertile land

2. **piece of land:** se compraron un terreno en la costa they bought a piece of land on the coast; son dueños de varios terrenos they're owners of several pieces of land

lo vamos a decidir sobre el terreno we're going to decide it on the spot.

terrestre *adjetivo* ■ land: transporte terrestre land transport
la superficie terrestre the Earth's surface.

terrible *adjetivo* ■ terrible: fue un accidente terrible it was a terrible accident
› tenía un calor terrible I was terribly hot
› tengo un sueño terrible I'm awfully sleepy.

el territorio ■ territory *(plural* territories).

el terrón *(plural* los terrones)
› un terrón de azúcar a sugar lump.

el terror ■ terror: el temblor causó terror en el pueblo the tremor caused terror in the village
› les tiene terror a las arañas she's terrified of spiders
› una película de terror a horror film *UK*, a horror movie *US*.

el terrorismo ■ terrorism.

terrorista *adjetivo* ■ terrorist: un atentado terrorista a terrorist attack.

la terrorista ■ terrorist.

el tesoro ■ treasure: un tesoro escondido a hidden treasure
› ¿cómo estás, tesoro? how are you darling?
› eres un tesoro you're a real gem.

el test ■ test: un test psicológico a psychological test.

el testamento ■ will
› hacer testamento to make one's will.

la testigo ■ witness
› fue testigo de la boda de mis padres he was a witness at my parents' wedding
› fuimos testigos del accidente we witnessed the accident.

la tetera
1. *para servir té* teapot
2. *eléctrica* kettle.

el texto ■ text
› un libro de texto a textbook.

ti *pronombre*
1. you: lo compré para ti I bought it for you; he estado pensando en ti I've been thinking about you

2. yourself: guárdalo para ti keep it for yourself; tienes que pensar más en ti you have to think more about yourself
› ¿y a ti qué te importa ? what's it got to do with you?

tibio, bia *adjetivo* ■ lukewarm.

el tiburón *(plural* los tiburones) ■ shark.

el tic ■ tic: es un tic nervioso it's a nervous tic.

el tiempo
1. time: ¿qué haces en tu tiempo libre? what do you do in your free time?; la mayor parte del tiempo most of the time; así ganamos tiempo that way we'll save time
2. weather: ¿cómo está el tiempo? what's the weather like?; hace buen tiempo the weather is nice; hace mal tiempo the weather is bad
3. tense: tiempo compuesto compound tense
4. half: marcaron el gol en el primer tiempo they scored the goal in the first half
› a tiempo in time: llegaste justo a tiempo para desayunar you arrived just in time to have breakfast
› llegaron al mismo tiempo they arrived at the same time
› no pierdas el tiempo don't waste time
› ¿cuánto tiempo hace que esperas? how long have you been waiting?
› hace tiempo que no viene he hasn't come for a while
› no me llevó mucho tiempo it didn't take me much time
› ¡cuánto tiempo sin verte! long time no see!
› ¿qué tiempo tiene la niña? how old is the girl?
› Ana llegó primero y al poco tiempo, Pepe Ana arrived first and Pepe soon after
› en esos tiempos la vida era más barata in those days life was less expensive
› en los últimos tiempos recently.

la tienda ■ shop *UK*, store *US*: una tienda de ropa a clothes shop
› fuimos de tiendas we went shopping
› una tienda de comestibles a grocer's shop *UK*, a grocery store *US*
› una tienda de campaña a tent.

tierno, na *adjetivo* ■ **tender**: la carne estaba muy tierna the meat was very tender; es una persona muy tierna she's a very tender person.

la **tierra**
1. **land**: cultivan la tierra they cultivate the land; un viaje por tierra a journey by land; finalmente llegaron a tierra at last they reached land
2. **soil**: aquí la tierra es muy fértil the soil is very fertile here
  extraña su tierra she misses her homeland
> la Tierra Earth.

tieso, sa *adjetivo* ■ **stiff**.

el **tigre** ■ **tiger**.

las **tijeras** ■ **scissors**: córtalo con las tijeras cut it with the scissors
> necesito unas tijeras I need a pair of scissors.

la **tila** ■ **lime-blossom tea**.

la **tilde** ■ **swung, tilde**.

el **timbre** ■ **bell**: sonó el timbre the bell rang.

tímido, da *adjetivo* ■ **shy**.

la **tinta** ■ **ink**: una mancha de tinta an ink stain.

el **tinto** ■ **red wine**: se tomó una copa de tinto she had a glass of red wine.

la **tintorería** ■ **dry cleaner's**.

la **tía**
1. **aunt**: la tía Marta Aunt Marta
2. *informal* **girl**: es una tía muy simpática she's a really nice girl.

el **tío**
1. **uncle**: el tío Juan Uncle Juan
2. *informal* **guy**: es un tío muy simpático he's a really nice guy
> un regalo de mis tíos a present from my aunt and uncle.

típico, ca *adjetivo* ■ **typical**: el típico andaluz the typical Andalusian
> eso es típico de él that's typical of him
> un baile típico del norte a traditional dance from the north of the country.

el **tipo**
1. **type**: el tipo de música preferida por los jóvenes the type of music preferred by young people
2. *informal* **guy**: ¿quién es ese tipo? who's that guy?; es un tipo muy divertido he's a really fun guy
3. **figure**: tiene muy buen tipo she has a very good figure
> va todo tipo de gente all sorts of people go.

la **tirada** ■ **throw**: sacó dos cincos a la primera tirada de dados he rolled two fives with the first throw of the dice
> de una tirada in one stretch: hicimos el viaje de una tirada we made the trip in one stretch.

el **tirano** , la **tirana** ■ **tyrant**.

tirante *adjetivo*
1. *cuerda, cable* **tight**
2. *ambiente, situación* **tense**

el **tirante** ■ **strap**: un vestido de tirantes a dress with straps

los **tirantes** ■ **braces** *UK*, **suspenders** *US*.

tirar [1] *verbo*
1. **to throw**: tírame las llaves throw me the keys; les tiraban piedras a los policías they were throwing stones at the police
2. **to throw away**: deberías tirar esto, ya no sirve you should throw this away, it's no good anymore
3. **to knock down**: van a tirar la pared they're going to knock down the wall
4. **to waste**: qué manera de tirar el dinero what a way to waste money
> voy a tirar todo esto a la basura I'm going to throw all this away with the rubbish
> me empujó y me tiró al suelo he pushed me and knocked me to the ground
> tiraron muchas bombas they dropped a lot of bombs
> tiré el florero sin querer I accidentally dropped the vase
> tiraron con fuerza de la cuerda they tugged hard at the rope
> vamos tirando we're getting by

tirarse *verbo pronominal*
- **se tiró al agua** she dived into the water
- **se tiró de cabeza** he dived in head first
- **quería tirarse por la ventana** he wanted to throw himself out of the window
- **se tiró en la cama** he lay down on the bed.

la tirita® ■ sticking plaster® *UK*, **Band-Aid®** *US*.

tiritar [1] *verbo* ■ to shiver: **tiritaba de frío** he was shivering with cold.

el tiro ■ shot: **disparó un tiro** he fired a shot
- **lo mataron de un tiro** they shot him to death
- **le salió el tiro por la culata** it backfired on him
- **tiro al blanco** target practice
- **un tiro libre**
1. *en fútbol* a free kick
2. *en baloncesto* a free throw.

el tirón *(plural los tirones)* ■ tug: **dale un buen tirón** give it a good tug
- **le dio un tirón de orejas** she reprimanded him
- **leí el libro de un tirón** I read the book straight through
- **dormí 12 horas de un tirón** I slept 12 hours straight.

el tiroteo ■ shoot-out: **hubo un tiroteo entre la policía y los asaltantes** there was a shoot-out between the police and the assailants.

el títere ■ puppet.

la titular
1. **holder:** **el titular de un pasaporte** the holder of a passport
2. **first-team player:** **juega de titular** he's a first-team player.

el titular ■ headline: **viene en todos los titulares** it's in all the headlines.

el título
1. **title:** **no me acuerdo del título de la canción** I don't remember the title of the song
2. **degree:** **acaba de recibir su título universitario** she has just received her university degree
3. **diploma:** **tenía su título colgado en la pared** he had his diploma hanging on the wall
- **tiene el título de abogado** he's a qualified lawyer.

la tiza ■ chalk
- **lo escribió con una tiza** she wrote it with a piece of chalk.

la toalla ■ towel
- **una toalla de baño** a bath towel
- **una toalla de manos** a hand towel
- **tirar la toalla** to throw in the towel.

el tobillo ■ ankle
- **me torcí el tobillo** I twisted my ankle.

el tobogán *(plural los toboganes)* ■ slide.

el tocadiscos *(plural los tocadiscos)* ■ record player.

tocar [8] *verbo*
1. **to touch:** **no toques el ordenador** don't touch the computer; **le tocó la mano** she touched his hand
2. **to play:** **¿sabes tocar la guitarra?** do you know how to play the guitar?; **toca el piano muy bien** he plays the piano very well
3. **to ring:** **tocó el timbre** the bell rang
4. **to win:** **le ha tocado la lotería** he's won the lottery
- **¿a quién le toca?** whose turn is it?
- **me toca a mí** it's my turn
- **le tocó el más grande** he got the biggest one.

el tocino ■ bacon.

todavía *adverbio*
1.

Todavía se traduce por **still** cuando se trata de oraciones afirmativas o interrogativas:

still: todavía la quiere he still loves her; **¿todavía vives en la misma casa?** do you still live in the same house?

2.

Todavía se traduce por **yet** cuando se trata de oraciones negativas:

yet: no la he visto todavía I haven't seen her yet; **todavía no ha llegado** she hasn't arrived yet

3. **even:** **ahí hace todavía más calor** it's even hotter there.

todo, da *adjetivo & pronombre*
1. **all:** **invitó a todas sus amigas** she invited all her friends; **gente de todo tipo** all sorts of

people; **el más caro de todos** the most expensive of all; **todas son grandes** they're all big

2. **every: voy todas las semanas** I go every week

3. **whole: se tomó toda la botella** she drank the whole bottle; **vino toda su familia** his whole family came; **toda la verdad** the whole truth

> **ya es todo un hombre** now he's every inch a man

> **todo el mundo lo sabe** everybody knows

■ *pronombre*

1. **everything: se lo comieron todo** they ate everything; **el dinero no lo es todo** money isn't everything

2. **everybody, everyone: todos vinieron** everybody came; **todos lo saben** everybody knows

3. **all: los vendieron todos** they sold them all; **eso es todo, por ahora** that's all, for now

> **en esa tienda venden de todo** they sell everything in that shop.

el toldo

1. *de playa* **sunshade**

2. *en tienda, patio* **awning** .

tolerar [1] *verbo* ■ **to tolerate: no voy a tolerar una cosa así** I'm not going to tolerate something like that

> **se lo toleran todo a sus hijos** they put up with everything from their children

> **no tolero a la gente mal educada** I can't stand rude people.

tomar [1] *verbo*

1. **to drink: ¿qué vas a tomar?** what are you going to drink?; **se tomaron toda la botella** they drank the whole bottle

2. **to take: tomamos un taxi** we took a taxi; **siempre tomo el mismo tren** I always take the same train; **me voy a tomar el día libre** I'm going to take the day off; **se tomó la molestia de venir hasta aquí** he took the trouble to come all the way here

3. **to have: nos tomamos un helado** we'll have an ice cream; **¿qué quieres tomar?** what do you want to drink?

> **me tomó la mano** he took my hand

> **la tomó del brazo** he took her by the arm

> **tomé apuntes en clase** I took notes in class

> **tomó nota de todo lo que dijo** he took note of everything she said

> **toma la primera calle a la izquierda** take the first street on the left

> **toma, te dejaste esto en mi mesa** here, you left this in my desk

> **le tomé cariño** I became fond of him

> **te están tomando el pelo** they're pulling your leg

> **estuvo tomando el sol** he was sunbathing

> **salió a tomar el aire** she went outside to get some fresh air

> **no te lo tomes a mal** don't take it badly

> **se lo toma todo en broma** he takes everything as a joke.

el tomate ■ **tomato** (*plural* **tomatoes**): **una ensalada de tomates** a tomato salad

> **un tomate verde** a green tomato.

el tomo ■ **volume.**

la tonelada ■ **ton.**

el tono

1. **tone: me di cuenta por el tono de su voz** I realized by the tone of his voice

2. **shade: siempre se viste con tonos claros** she always dresses in light shades

> **el tono de marcar** the dial tone

> **tonos de móvil** ring tones.

la tontería

> **estás diciendo tonterías** you're talking nonsense

> **¡no digas tonterías!** don't talk nonsense!

> **se pelearon por una tontería** they fought over nothing

> **lo que hiciste fue una tontería** what you did was foolish.

tonto, ta *adjetivo* ■ **silly: eres muy tonto** you're very silly

> **¡qué excusa más tonta!** what a stupid excuse!

el tope

1. **limit: le pusieron un tope al número de llamadas que puede hacer** they put a limit on the number of calls she can make

2. *de una puerta* **doorstop**

el estadio estaba lleno hasta los topes the stadium was completely full.

el **toque** ■ touch: sólo me falta darle los últimos toques all I have left is to give it the finishing touches

> un toque de queda a curfew.

el **tórax** ■ thorax.

torcer [30] *verbo*

1. to twist: le estás torciendo el brazo you're twisting his arm; ayer me torcí un tobillo yesterday I twisted my ankle
2. to turn: tenemos que torcer a la izquierda we have to turn left.

torear [1] *verbo* ■ to fight.

el **torero** , la **torera** ■ bullfighter.

la **tormenta** ■ storm.

el **tornillo** ■ screw.

el **toro** ■ bull

LOS TOROS

Bullfighting is very popular in Spain and South America and is a tradition dating back thousands of years. Usually, at a bullfight, three bullfighters, dressed in their suits of lights and attended by their **cuadrilla** (helpers) confront six bulls, two per toreador. The bullfight is divided into three phases: in the **tercio de varas,** the toreador fights with a red cape and brings the bull face to face with a picador who stabs the bull with his lance; in the **tercio de banderillas,** three pairs of banderillas are thrust into the bull's neck; finally, in the **tercio de espadas,** the toreador fights with the bull itself and kills it with a sword thrust known as an **estocada.** If the bullfight has been good, the matador, applauded by the public, is awarded the bulls' ears and tail as a prize.

torpe *adjetivo*

1. clumsy: no le des ninguna tarea delicada, es muy torpe don't give him a delicate task, he's very clumsy
2. awkward: el bebé todavía tiene un andar torpe baby still has an awkward walk.

la **torre** ■ tower: el campanario está en la torre más alta de la iglesia the belfry is in the church's highest tower.

la **torta**

1. *a small flat cake*
2. *familiar* **slap:** mi hermano me dio una torta my brother gave me a slap

> no entender ni torta not to understand a thing: no entiendo ni torta de física I don't understand a thing about physics.

la **tortilla** ■ omelette: la tortilla española clásica se prepara con huevos, patatas y cebolla the classic Spanish omelette is made with eggs, potatoes and onion

> una tortilla francesa a French omelette

LA TORTILLA ESPAÑOLA

A **tortilla española** is a type of thick omelette filled with fried onions and potatoes, then sliced into wedges. In some Latin American countries, this Spanish dish is commonly eaten as a "fast food".

la **tortuga**

1. *de tierra* **tortoise** *UK,* **turtle** *US*
2. *de mar* **turtle.**

la **tos** ■ cough: está resfriada y tiene mucha tos she has a cold and a bad cough.

toser [2] *verbo* ■ to cough: estuvo tosiendo toda la noche he was coughing all night.

la **tostada**

> una tostada a piece of toast

> ¿quieres tostadas? would you like some toast?

la **tostadora** ■ toaster.

tostar [16] *verbo* ■ to toast: tostamos varias rebanadas de pan y las comimos con mermelada we toasted several slices of bread and we ate them with jam

tostarse *verbo pronominal* ■ to tan: me he quedado dormida en la playa y me he tostado I fell asleep on the beach and I got a tan.

total *(adjetivo & adverbio)*

■ *adjetivo*

complete: necesitamos silencio total we need complete silence

■ *adverbio*

after all: voy contigo al supermercado, total, no tengo nada que hacer I'm going with you to the supermarket, after all, I don't have anything to do.

el **total** ■ total: el total de sumar 10 más 10 es 20 the total from adding 10 plus 10 is 20

> en total, seremos 15 there will be 15 of us in total.

tóxico, ca *adjetivo* ■ poisonous.

el **trabajador** , la **trabajadora** ■ worker

DÍA DE LOS TRABAJADORES

May 1 is Labour Day in many Spanish-speaking countries. People have the day off from work, and workers often participate in rallies organized by trade unions.

trabajar [1] *verbo* ■ to work: trabajan en una editorial they work in a publishing house

> ¿quién trabaja en esa película? who's in that film?

el **trabajo**

1. **job**: tardó sólo un par de semanas en encontrar trabajo he only took a couple of weeks to find a job

2. **work**: si quieres hablar con ella ahora, puedes llamarla al trabajo if you want to talk to her now, you can call her at work

3. **essay**: ¿cuándo tenemos que entregar el trabajo de historia? when do we have to hand in the history essay?

el **tractor** ■ tractor.

la **tradición** *(plural* las tradiciones*)* ■ tradition.

tradicional *adjetivo* ■ traditional.

la **traducción** *(plural* las traducciones*)* ■ translation.

traducir [23] *verbo* ■ to translate: hay que traducir estas frases del español al inglés you have to translate these sentences from Spanish into English.

el **traductor** , la **traductora** ■ translator.

traer [53] *verbo*

1. **to bring**: tengo frío, por favor tráeme una manta I'm cold, please bring me a blanket

2. **to have**: este diccionario trae muchos ejemplos this dictionary has a lot of examples

3. **to wear**: mi madre trae las sandalias que le regalé my mother is wearing the sandals I gave her.

el **tráfico** ■ traffic: por la mala visibilidad, hubo varios accidentes de tráfico because of the poor visibility, there were several traffic accidents.

tragar [12] *verbo* ■ to swallow.

la **tragedia** ■ tragedy *(plural* **tragedies***)*.

trágico, ca *adjetivo* ■ tragic: perdió a toda su familia en un trágico accidente he lost his whole family in a tragic accident.

el **trago**

1. **swallow**: tenía mucha sed y se bebió toda el agua de un trago she was very thirsty so she drank all the water in one swallow

2. **sip**: quiero sólo un trago, para probar I only want a sip, just to try it.

el **traje**

1. **suit**: para la entrevista de trabajo, Juan se puso un traje azul Juan put on a blue suit for the job interview

2. **costume**: mañana es el concurso de trajes típicos regionales tomorrow is the competition of typical regional costumes

> un traje de baño

1. *de hombre* swimming trunks

2. *de mujer* a swimsuit

> un traje de chaqueta a suit

> un traje de gala an evening dress

> un traje de noche evening dress

> un traje de novia a wedding dress.

la **trama** ■ plot: ¿podrías contarme la trama de la película? could you tell me the plot of that film?

el **trámite** ■ procedure: los trámites se han complicado procedures have become complicated.

el **tramo**

1. **section**: este tramo de carretera está en mal estado this section of the road is in a bad state of repair

. flight: la abuela no puede subir más de cuatro tramos de escalera our grandmother can't go up more than four flights of stairs.

a trampa ■ trap: los cazadores pusieron una trampa para el oso the hunters laid a trap for the bear

caer en la trampa to fall into the trap

hacer trampa to cheat: **siempre gana porque hace trampa** she always wins because she cheats.

el trampolín *(plural* los trampolines*)* ■ diving board.

el tramposo, sa *adjetivo* ■ cheat: **eres un tramposo y por eso siempre ganas** you're a cheat and that's why you always win.

tranquilizar [10] *verbo* ■ to calm down: **mi hermano me tranquilizó** my brother calmed me down

tranquilizarse *verbo pronominal* ■ to calm down: **¡tranquilízate, no pasa nada!** calm down!

tranquilo, la *adjetivo*

. calm: tienes que estar tranquilo para la prueba you have to be calm for the test

. quiet: vive en un pueblo tranquilo he lives in a quiet village.

transcurrir [3] *verbo*

. to take place: la historia de Drácula transcurre en Transilvania the story of Dracula takes place in Transylvania

. to pass: ya han transcurrido dos años desde que llegué a esta ciudad two years have already passed since I arrived in this city.

la transeúnte ■ passer-by.

transformar [1] *verbo*

. to change: el mago transformó al conejo en una paloma the wizard changed the rabbit into a dove

. to transform: la tecnología está transformando los métodos educativos technology is transforming educational methods

transformarse *verbo pronominal*

. to be converted: en esta presa, la fuerza del agua se transforma en energía eléctri-

ca at this dam, the force of the water is converted into electric energy

. to change: desde la última vez que estuve aquí, este país se ha transformado this country has changed since the last time I was here.

transgénico, ca *adjetivo* ■ genetically modified.

el tránsito ■ traffic.

transmitir [3] *verbo*

. to pass on: le transmitiré a mi familia tus saludos I will pass your greetings on to my family

. to broadcast: la radio acaba de transmitir la alerta the radio has just broadcast the alert.

transparente *adjetivo* ■ transparent.

la transpiración *(plural* las transpiraciones*)* ■ perspiration.

transpirar [1] *verbo* ■ to perspire.

transportar [1] *verbo* ■ to transport: transportaremos la mercancía por barco we'll transport the merchandise by boat.

el transporte ■ transport *UK,* transportation *US:* el sistema de transporte aquí es bastante bueno the transport system here is pretty good

medio de transporte means of transport *UK,* means of transportation *US*

el transporte público public transport.

el tranvía ■ tram *UK,* streetcar *US.*

el trapo ■ rag: ¿dónde hay un trapo para limpiar la mesa? where is there a rag to clean the table?

un trapo de cocina a dishcloth

un trapo del polvo a duster.

la tráquea ■ windpipe.

tras *preposición* ■ after: tras los incidentes en el estadio, todos los partidos de la temporada se suspendieron after the incidents in the stadium, all the season's games were cancelled

día tras día day after day: regó los árboles día tras día, pero la sequía terminó matándolos he watered the trees day after day, but the drought ended up killing them.

trasero, ra *adjetivo* ■ **back:** los niños deben viajar en el asiento trasero del coche children must ride in the back seat of the car

el **trasero** ■ **backside.**

trasladar [1] *verbo*

1. **to move:** hay que trasladar el equipo de música al jardín we have to move the music equipment to the garden; nos trasladamos de casa el viernes we're moving house on Friday

2. **to transfer:** me han trasladado a otra sucursal they're transferred me to another branch.

trasplantar [1] *verbo* ■ **to transplant.**

el **trasplante** ■ **transplant.**

el **trasto** ■ **junk:** el sótano está lleno de trastos the basement is full of junk.

el **tratado** ■ **treaty** (*plural* **treaties**).

el **tratamiento** ■ **treatment:** está siguiendo un tratamiento para adelgazar she's following a treatment to get thinner

un tratamiento de textos a word processing.

tratar [1] *verbo*

1. **to treat:** son excelentes anfitriones, nos trataron muy bien they are excellent hosts, they treated us very well; necesito un médico que me trate esta alergia I need a doctor to treat this allergy for me

2. **to address:** se tratan de usted they address each other as "usted"

3. **to try:** no trates de engañarme porque no tardaré en descubrir la verdad don't try to deceive me because I won't take long to discover the truth

4. **to deal with:** trataremos este tema en la clase de mañana we'll deal with this theme in tomorrow's class

5. **to deal about:** ¿de qué trata este artículo? what's this article about?

el **trato** ■ **deal:** José y Pedro hicieron un trato José and Pedro made a deal.

través *preposición*

a través de through: me enteré a través de una amiga I found out through a friend.

la **travesura** ■ **prank**
hacer travesuras to play pranks.

travieso, sa *adjetivo* ■ **naughty.**

el **trayecto**

1. **journey:** no paró de hablar en todo el trayecto he didn't stop talking the whole journey

2. **route:** dile al taxista que elija el trayecto más corto tell the taxi driver to choose the shortest route.

la **trayectoria** ■ **path:** la trayectoria del cometa Halley describe una parábola the path of Halley's comet traces a parabola.

trazar [10] *verbo* ■ **to draw.**

el **trébol**

1. *planta* **clover**
2. *carta* **club.**

tremendo, da *adjetivo* ■ **tremendous:** aquí las diferencias entre los pobres y los ricos son tremendas here the differences between the poor and the rich are tremendous.

el **tren** ■ **train:** viajar en tren to travel by train
el tren de alta velocidad the high-speed train.

la **trenza** ■ **plait** *UK*, **braid.**

trepar [1] *verbo* ■ **to climb:** algunos niños tienen miedo de trepar a los árboles some children are afraid of climbing trees.

tres *numeral* ■ **three:** tiene tres hijos she has three children
mi hermana tiene tres años my sister is three years old
son las tres it's three o'clock
el tres de abril the third of April.

el **triángulo** ■ **triangle.**

la **tribu** ■ **tribe.**

la **tribuna** ■ **stands:** toda mi familia estaba en la tribuna my whole family was in the stands.

el **tribunal**

1. **court:** terminaron yendo a un tribunal para resolver el conflicto they ended up going to court to resolve the conflict

2. **board of examiners:** el tribunal premió el trabajo dedicado a la conservación del medioambiente the board of examiners

gave an award to the work dedicated to environmental preservation.

triciclo ■ tricycle.

trigo ■ wheat.

trinar [1] *verbo* ■ to sing: cuando amaneció los pájaros empezaron a trinar when the day dawned the birds began to sing.

trimestre
1. *escolar* term
2. *periodo del año* quarter.

trineo ■ sleigh.

triple *adjetivo* ■ triple.

tripulación (*plural* las tripulaciones) ■ crew.

triste *adjetivo* ■ sad: está triste porque no lo dejaron ir al circo he's sad because they didn't let him go to the circus; me dijeron que esa película es muy triste they told me that that film is very sad.

tristeza ■ sadness
me dio mucha tristeza la muerte de mi perro the death of my dog made me very sad.

triunfar [1] *verbo*
1. to triumph: en la Segunda Guerra Mundial, los países aliados triunfaron in World War II, the Allied countries triumphed
2. to succeed: ¡espero que triunfes en la vida! I hope that you succeed in life!

triunfo ■ victory (*plural* victories): el equipo ganador celebró el triunfo durante varios días the winning team celebrated the victory for several days.

trofeo ■ trophy (*plural* trophies).

trompa
1. *de elefante* trunk
2. *instrumento musical* horn.

tronco
1. trunk: una planta trepadora se ha enroscado en el tronco de este árbol a climbing plant has wound itself around the trunk of this tree; en tu dibujo, el tronco del niño ha quedado más largo que las piernas in your drawing, the child's trunk is longer than his legs

2. log: puse varios troncos en la chimenea para avivar el fuego I put several logs on the fireplace to revive the fire
dormir como un tronco to sleep like a log: estaba tan cansada que dormí como un tronco I was so tired that I slept like a log.

tropezar [10] *verbo* ■ to stumble on: tropecé con el escalón I stumbled on the stairs

tropezarse *verbo pronominal* ■ to run into: me tropecé con Antonio al salir del cine I ran into Antonio when I was coming out of the cinema.

tropezón (*plural* los tropezones) dio un tropezón he stumbled.

tropical *adjetivo* ■ tropical.

trópico ■ tropic
el trópico de Cáncer the Tropic of Cancer
el trópico de Capricornio the Tropic of Capricorn.

trotar [1] *verbo* ■ to trot.

trote ■ trot
ir al trote to trot: mi caballo iba al trote my horse was trotting.

trozo ■ piece: cuidado, no camines descalza porque puede haber trozos de vidrio en el suelo be careful, don't walk barefoot because there might be pieces of glass on the floor.

truco ■ trick: el mago hizo unos trucos excelentes the magician did some excellent tricks.

trueno ■ thunder.

tu *adjetivo* ■ your: me gusta tu jersey I like your sweater; quiero que me presentes a tus amigas I want you to introduce me to your friends.

tú *pronombre* ■ you: haz lo que tú quieras do what you want; ella corre más rápido que tú she runs faster than you
tú mismo yourself: hazlo tú misma do it yourself.

tuberculosis ■ tuberculosis.

la **tubería** ■ pipes.

el **tubo**
1. pipe: el tubo de escape the exhaust pipe
2. tube: en el baño encontrarás un tubo de crema para las manos in the bathroom you'll find a tube of hand cream.

la **tuerca** ■ nut.

tuerto, ta adjetivo ■ one-eyed: el pirata era tuerto the pirate was one-eyed.

la **tumba**
1. grave: la tumba de mi bisabuela está en Ávila my great-grandmother's grave is in Ávila
2. tomb: las tumbas de los faraones están en pirámides the pharaohs' tombs are in the pyramids.

tumbar [1] verbo ■ to knock down: el boxeador tumbó a su rival the boxer knocked down his rival

tumbarse verbo pronominal ■ to lie down: llegó cansadísima y se tumbó en el sofá she arrived extremely tired and lay down on the sofa.

la **tuna** ■ group of student minstrels

> **LA TUNA**
>
> The **tuna** is a tradition inherited from the students of the 13th century and still exists in many Spanish universities. The word refers to a group of minstrels made up of students from the same faculty who sing traditional songs accompanied by traditional instruments, such as guitars, mandolins, lutes and tambourines. They also wear a typical costume consisting of a black cape tied with several coloured ribbons and bearing the university crest. They sing in the streets and at restaurants in return for money and are often invited to sing in other cities and even abroad.

el **túnel** ■ tunnel.

la **turbina** ■ turbine.

turbio, bia adjetivo ■ cloudy: el agua se ve muy turbia the water looks very cloudy.

la **turbulencia** ■ turbulence: si mantienes el cinturón ajustado, no correrás peligro cuando haya turbulencias if you keep your seat belt fastened, you won't be in danger when there's turbulence.

el **turismo** ■ tourism: el turismo es la principal fuente de ingresos de la región tourism is the main source of income for the region

> hacer turismo to travel around: vamos a dedicar todo el verano a hacer turismo we're going to dedicate the whole summer to travelling

> turismo rural rural tourism.

el/la **turista** ■ tourist.

turnarse [1] verbo pronominal ■ to take turns: nos turnamos para lavar los platos we took turns with the washing up.

el **turno**
1. turn: espera un poquito, todavía no es tu turno wait a little bit, it's still not your turn
2. shift: el turno de noche empieza a las 10 the night shift begins at 10 o'clock.

la **tutela** ■ guardianship: el juez le dio la tutela de mis primos a mis padres the judge gave guardianship of my cousins to my parents.

el **turrón** (plural los turrones) ■ a type of nougat traditionally eaten at Christmas.

tutearse [1] verbo pronominal
> se tutean they call one other "tú".

el **tuteo** ■ use of the familiar form "tú"

> **TUTEO**
>
> In Spanish there are two words for the second person singular: one is the informal **tú**, the other is the formal **usted**. **Tuteo** refers to the use of **tú**, which varies greatly from country to country in Latin America. Generally, children and teenagers use **tú** for others their age and **usted** for adults. However, if there is a close relationship with an adult, such as a parent, grandparent, aunt, uncle, or teacher, it is common for the informal **tú** to be used.

el **tutor** , la **tutora** ■ guardian: mis padres son los tutores de mis primos my parents are my cousins' guardians.

tuyo, ya *(adjetivo & pronombre)*

■ *adjetivo*

yours: el libro rojo es mío y el azul es tuyo the red book is mine and the blue one is yours; ¿son tuyos estos papeles? are these papers yours?; ¿esta falda es tuya? is this skirt yours?

■ *pronombre*

yours: este libro es mío, ¿dónde está el tuyo? this book is mine, where's yours?; he devuelto mis libros pero no los tuyos I've taken back my books but not yours; la tuya es la más bonita yours is prettier.

u *conjunción*

Used instead of **o** before words beginning with **o** or **ho**.

or: elige uno u otro choose one or the other.

la **UE** *(abreviatura de* Unión Europea*)* ■ **EU.**

la **úlcera** ■ **ulcer.**

último, ma *adjetivo*

1. **last:** es mi último año de estudios it's my last year of studies

2. **top:** viven en el último piso they live on the top floor

3. **back:** se sentó en la última fila she sat on the back row

el **último** , la **última** ■ **last:** el corredor alemán llegó el último the German runner came in last

> **por último** finally.

un, una *(artículo & numeral)*

■ *artículo*

1. **a, an:** tiene un coche nuevo he's got a new car; dame una taza give me a cup; ¿podrías prestarme un paraguas? could you lend me an umbrella?

2. **some:** se fue a la playa con unos amigos he went to the beach with some friends

■ *numeral*

one: tiene un hijo she has one son

> mi hermana tiene un año my sister is one year old

> es la una it's one o'clock.

undécimo, ma *adjetivo & pronombre* ■ **eleventh:** el corredor japonés quedó en undécima posición the Japanese runner finished in eleventh position.

único, ca *adjetivo*

1. **only:** es el único par de zapatos que me gusta it's the only pair of shoes that I like

2. **unique:** este pintor es originalísimo, su obra es única this painter is very original, his work is unique

el **único** , la **única** ■ **the only one:** fue el único que llegó puntual he was the only one to arrive on time.

la **unidad**

1. **unit:** la caja de 20 unidades cuesta el doble que la de 10 the box with 20 units costs twice as much as the one with 10

2. **unity:** es importante que haya unidad entre los miembros de la familia it's important for there to be unity among family members

> la unidad de cuidados intensivos the intensive care unit.

el **uniforme** ■ **uniform:** el uniforme de mi escuela es azul my school uniform is blue.

la **unión** *(plural* las uniones*)* ■ **unity:** es importante que haya unión entre los hermanos it's important for there to be unity between the brothers

> la Unión Europea the European Union.

unir [3] *verbo*

1. **to join:** esta carretera une el pueblo con la capital this road joins the town with the

capital; **si unimos estos dos tubos, obtendremos uno más largo** if we join these two tubes, we'll get a longer one

2. **to unite: ante las dificultades económicas, la familia se unió** confronted with economic difficulties, the family united.

universal *adjetivo* ■ universal: **los derechos humanos son universales** human rights are universal.

la **universidad** ■ university (*plural* universities).

universitario, ria *adjetivo* ■ university: **un estudiante universitario** a university student

➤ **después del bachillerato haré estudios universitarios** after secondary school I'm going to study at the university

el **universitario** , la **universitaria**

1. **university student: los universitarios estudian muchísimo** university students study a lot

2. **university graduate: un universitario accede a mejor salario que un obrero** a university graduate earns a better salary than a worker.

el **universo** ■ universe.

uno, una (*adjetivo & pronombre*)

■ *adjetivo*

one: sólo quiero una entrada, no dos I only want one ticket, not two

■ *pronombre*

one: no quiero dos libros, sino sólo uno I don't want two books, only one; **Pablo tiene dos hermanas y yo una** Pablo has two sisters and I've got one

el **uno**

1. **one: uno y uno son dos** one and one are two

2. **first: hoy es el uno de abril** today is the first of April *UK*, today is April first *US*

unos , **unas** (*adjetivo & pronombre*)

■ *adjetivo*

about: me ha costado unos mil euros it cost me about a thousand euros; **había unas tres mil personas** there were about three thousand people

■ *pronombre*

some: unos llegaron a las 10 y otros a las 11 some arrived at 10 and others at 11.

untar [1] *verbo* ■ to spread: **quiero mantequilla para untar en el pan** I want some butter to spread on the bread.

la **uña** ■ fingernail.

urbano, na *adjetivo* ■ urban.

la **urbe** ■ metropolis.

la **urgencia** ■ emergency (*plural* emergencies): **los médicos siempre reciben llamadas de urgencia** doctors always receive emergency calls

➤ **tenía urgencia de ir al banco y salió volando** she was in a hurry to go to the bank so she left quickly

➤ **tuvieron que llevar a su hijo a urgencias** they had to take their son to casualty.

urgente *adjetivo* ■ urgent: **he recibido una llamada urgente, tengo que salir enseguida** I've received an urgent call, I have to leave immediately.

Uruguay ■ Uruguay.

uruguayo, ya *adjetivo*

En inglés, los adjetivos que se refieren a un país o una región se escriben con mayúscula:

Uruguayan

el **uruguayo** , la **uruguaya**

En inglés, los gentilicios se escriben con mayúscula:

Uruguayan.

usado, da *adjetivo*

1. **used: un coche usado es más barato que uno nuevo** a used car is cheaper than a new one

2. **worn: estos zapatos están muy usados** these shoes are very worn.

usar [1] *verbo*

1. **to take: usa las escaleras porque el ascensor está averiado** take the stairs because the lift is out of order

2. **to use: uso una máquina de afeitar eléctrica** I use an electric shaver

3. **to wear:** ¿qué perfume usas? what perfume do you wear?

el **uso** ■ use: creo que este aparato tiene otros usos, además de abrir latas I think this appliance has other uses, besides opening tins.

usted *(plural* ustedes*) pronombre* ■ **you:** ¿cómo está usted? how are you?; ¿cómo están ustedes? how are you?

> tratar a alguien de usted to call somebody "usted".

usual *adjetivo* ■ **normal:** es usual que los adolescentes tengan problemas con sus padres it's normal for teenagers to have problems with their parents.

el **usuario** , la **usuaria** ■ **user:** los usuarios se quejaron por el aumento de tarifas the users complained about the increase in charges.

el **utensilio** ■ **utensil:** las sartenes y las cacerolas son utensilios de cocina frying pans and pots are kitchen utensils.

útil *adjetivo* ■ **useful.**

la **utilidad** ■ **usefulness:** no le veo la utilidad a esa cacerola tan grande I don't see the usefulness of this big pot.

la **utilización** *(plural* las utilizaciones*)* ■ **use:** la utilización de energía eléctrica trajo grandes progresos the use of electric energy brought great progress.

utilizar [10] *verbo* ■ **to use:** para preparar el postre utilicé huevos, leche y azúcar to make the dessert I used eggs, milk and sugar.

la **uva** ■ **grape**

LAS DOCE UVAS

On New Year's Eve, in Spain, it is traditional to eat 12 grapes in time to the 12 chimes of midnight. People who manage to eat all 12 grapes are guaranteed good luck throughout the coming year. Spaniards watch the live television broadcast of the12 chimes of midnight coming from the Puerta del Sol in Madrid, the square in the city where thousands of revellers gather to celebrate the arrival of the New Year.

la **vaca**

1. **cow:** las vacas comen hierba cows eat grass
2. **beef:** no come carne de vaca he doesn't eat beef.

la **vacaciones** ■ **holidays** *UK,* **vacation** *US:* durante las vacaciones de verano vamos a la playa during summer holidays we go to the seaside.

vaciar [7] *verbo* ■ **to empty:** hay que vaciar estos cajones para limpiarlos bien you have to empty these boxes to clean them properly.

vacío, cia *adjetivo* ■ **empty:** esta botella está vacía, ¿la tiramos? this bottle is empty, should we throw it away?

el **vacío**

1. **space:** en el vídeo vi a los astronautas flotando en el vacío on the video I saw the astronauts floating in space
2. **void:** perdió el equilibrio y cayó al vacío he lost his balance and fell into the void
> envasado al vacío vacuum-packed.

la **vacuna** ■ **vaccine:** las vacunas previenen enfermedades vaccines prevent diseases.

la **vacunación** *(plural* las vacunaciones*)* ■ **vaccination:** mañana empieza la campaña de vacunación contra la gripe tomorrow the flu vaccination campaign begins.

vacunar [1] *verbo* ■ **to vaccinate:** hay que vacunar a los perros contra la rabia you have to vaccinate dogs for rabies

vacunarse *verbo pronominal* ■ **to get vaccinated**: ¿ya han vacunado a los niños contra la poliomielitis? have the children already been vaccinated against polio?

el **vagabundo** , la **vagabunda** ■ tramp *UK*, hobo *US*: debajo de ese puente viven varios vagabundos several tramps live underneath that bridge.

vago, ga *adjetivo*
1. **lazy**: no seas vago don't be lazy
2. **vague**: las indicaciones para llegar a tu casa eran muy vagas y me perdí the directions to get to your house were very vague and I got lost.

el **vagón** *(plural* los vagones*)*
1. *de tren* **coach, carriage** *UK*, car *US*
2. *de mercancías* **wagon** *UK*, car *US*: los vagones transportaban maquinaria agrícola the wagons carried farm machinery
  > el vagón restaurante the dining car.

el **vaho** ■ **steam**: el agua hirviendo despide mucho vaho boiling water releases off a lot of steam.

la **vainilla** ■ **vanilla**
  > helado de vainilla vanilla ice cream.

la **vajilla**
1. **dishes**: entre las tres podemos lavar la vajilla en 15 minutos between the three of us we can wash the dishes in 15 minutes
2. **dinner service**: podríamos regalarles una vajilla para la boda we could give them a dinner service for their wedding.

el **vale**
1. *de regalo, de descuento* **voucher**
2. *de compra* **coupon**

  vale *interjección* ■ **Ok, all right**: ¿quieres que vayamos al cine? —¡vale! do you want to go to the cinema? – Ok!

Valencia ■ Valencia.

valenciano, na

En inglés, los adjetivos que se refieren a un país o una región se escriben con mayúscula:

Valencian: la paella valenciana the Valencian paella

el **valenciano** , la **valenciana**

En inglés, los gentilicios se escriben con mayúscula:

Valencian
  > los valencianos the Valencians

el **valenciano**

En inglés, los idiomas se escriben con mayúscula:

Valencian.

valer **[54]** *verbo*
1. **to cost**: ¿cuánto vale un kilo de peras? how much does a kilo of pears cost?
2. **to equal**: en matemáticas, dos cuartos valen lo mismo que un medio in mathematics, two fourths equal the same as one half
3. **to be valid**: la prueba no valió porque muchos copiaron the test wasn't valid because a lot of people copied
  > valer la pena to be worth it: voy a comprar las manzanas, a ese precio, vale la pena I'm going to buy the apples, at that price, it's worth it
  > más vale que te lleves el coche, está lloviendo mucho you'd better take the car, it's raining heavily
  > ¡no vale hacer trampas! you're not allowed to cheat!

  valiente *adjetivo* ■ **brave.**

  valioso, sa *adjetivo* ■ **valuable**: le robaron a mamá un anillo muy valioso they stole a very valuable ring from my mum.

la **valla** ■ **fence**
  > valla publicitaria hoarding *UK*, billboard *US*.

el **valle** ■ **valley.**

el **valor**
1. **value**: Julia tiene muchos valores, entre ellos, la honestidad Julia has many values, among them, honesty
  > esta pulsera tiene un gran valor sentimental this bracelet has great sentimental value for me
2. **importance**: las palabras del abuelo fueron de gran valor para mí the words of my grandfather were of great importance to me

3. courage: Luis se lanzó con valor para salvar al niño Luis rushed in with courage to save the child.

la **válvula** ■ valve.

vano, na *adjetivo* ■ useless: los esfuerzos por salvarlo fueron vanos the efforts to save him were useless

en vano in vain: los esfuerzos por salvarlo fueron en vano the efforts to save him were in vain.

el **vapor** ■ steam: el vapor del agua caliente empañó las ventanas the steam from the hot water fogged the windows

plancha a vapor steam iron

al vapor steamed: es muy sano comer verduras al vapor it's very healthy to eat vegetables.

vaquero, ra *adjetivo* ■ denim: una camisa vaquera a denim shirt

os **vaqueros** ■ jeans.

variable *adjetivo* ■ changeable: el clima allí es muy variable the climate there is very changeable.

variado, da *adjetivo* ■ varied: Ana se compró una falda de colores variados Ana bought a skirt of varied colours.

variar [7] *verbo* ■ to vary: en primavera, las temperaturas varían entre 15 y 20 grados in spring the temperatures vary between 15 and 20 degrees.

la **varicela** ■ chicken pox.

la **variedad** ■ variety (*plural* varieties): la variedad de tipos de sangre exige un análisis antes de la transfusión the variety of blood types requires an analysis before the transfusion.

varios, rias *adjetivo* ■ several: ¿cuánto hace que no la ves? —varios meses how long has it been since you saw her? – several months.

el **varón** (*plural* los varones) ■ man (*plural* men): es un grupo mixto: hay varones y mujeres it's a mixed group: there are men and women.

vasco, ca

En inglés, los adjetivos que se refieren a un país o una región se escriben con mayúscula:

Basque: San Sebastián es una ciudad vasca San Sebastian is a Basque city

el **vasco** , la **vasca**

En inglés, los gentilicios se escriben con mayúscula:

Basque
los vascos the Basque

el **vasco**

En inglés, los idiomas se escriben con mayúscula:

Basque.

la **vasija** ■ vessel: ese artesano hace y vende vasijas de barro that craftsman makes and sells clay vessels.

el **vaso**
1. glass: quiero un vaso de agua, por favor I want a glass of water, please
2. cup: para los niños son más prácticos los vasos de plástico plastic cups are more practical for children
3. vessel: los vasos sanguíneos forman parte del sistema circulatorio blood vessels form part of the circulatory system

⚠️ The Spanish word **vaso** is a false friend, it doesn't mean "vase".

vaya *interjección* ■ well: ¡vaya, no sabía que se había casado con ella! well I didn't know he'd married her!

el **vecindario** ■ neighbourhood *UK*, neighborhood *US*: los habitantes del vecindario organizaron una fiesta the residents of the neighbourhood organized a party.

el **vecino** , la **vecina**
1. neighbour *UK*, neighbor *US*: Susana es mi vecina Susana is my neighbour
2. resident: hace muchos años que Pedro es vecino de este pueblo Pedro has been a resident of this town for many years.

la **vegetación** *(plural las vegetaciones)* ■ vegetation: la selva tiene una vegetación exuberante the jungle has lush vegetation.

vegetal *adjetivo* ■ plant: estamos estudiando diferentes especies vegetales we're studying different plant species

el **vegetal** ■ vegetable: los vegetales necesitan agua, luz y tierra para desarrollarse plants need water, light and soil to develop.

vegetariano, na *adjetivo* ■ vegetarian: una dieta vegetariana a vegetarian diet

el **vegetariano** , la **vegetariana** ■ vegetarian: los vegetarianos no comen carne vegetarians don't eat meat.

el **vehículo** ■ vehicle: el avión, el tren y el coche son vehículos modernos the airplane, the train and the car are modern vehicles.

veinte *numeral* ■ twenty: mi hermana tiene veinte años my sister is twenty; estamos a veinte de mayo it's the twentieth of May *UK*, it's May twentieth *US*.

veintiuno, na *numeral* ■ twenty-one: tiene veintiuna faldas she's got twenty-one skirts; estamos a veintiuno de diciembre it's the twenty-first of December *UK*, it's December twenty-first *US*.

la **vejez** ■ old age: el cuidado de la salud es muy importante en la vejez healthcare is very important in old age.

la **vejiga** ■ bladder.

la **vela**
1. candle: están de moda las velas perfumadas y de colores coloured and scented candles are in fashion
2. sail: cerca de la costa se veían las velas de los barcos near the coast you could see the sails of the boats
   ▪ barco a vela sailing boat *UK,* sailboat *US*
   ▪ pasar la noche en vela to not sleep all night: el niño tuvo fiebre y los padres pasaron la noche en vela the boy had fever and the parents didn't sleep all night.

velarse [1] *verbo pronominal* ■ to blur: se han velado las fotos the photos are blurred.

el **velero** ■ sailing ship.

el **vello**
1. *en el cuerpo* hair
2. *en la cara* down.

el **velo** ■ veil.

la **velocidad**
1. speed: ¿cuál es el límite de velocidad en esta carretera? what's the speed limit on this road?
2. gear: cambiar de marcha to change gear.

veloz *adjetivo* ■ fast: la liebre es más veloz que la tortuga the hare is faster than the turtle.

la **vena** ■ vein.

el **venado**
1. *animal* deer *(plural* **deer**)
2. *carne* venison.

el **vencedor** , la **vencedora** ■ winner.

vencer [9] *verbo*
1. to defeat: el ejército nacional venció a las fuerzas extranjeras the national army defeated the foreign forces
2. to beat: el nadador chino venció a los demás en la primera prueba the Chinese swimmer beat the others in the first round
3. to overcome: estaba muy cansada y finalmente le venció el sueño she was very tired and finally sleep overcame her
4. to expire: el plazo de entrega vence mañana the delivery date expires tomorrow.

la **venda**
1. bandage: llevaba una venda en el brazo izquierdo he was wearing a bandage on his left arm
2. blindfold: los secuestradores le pusieron una venda en los ojos the kidnappers put a blindfold over his eyes.

vendar [1] *verbo*
1. to bandage: le vendaron el tobillo they bandaged his ankle
2. to blindfold: los secuestradores le vendaron los ojos the kidnappers blindfolded him.

el **vendedor** ■ salesman *(plural* **salesmen**)
▶ vendedor ambulante street seller.

la **vendedora** ■ saleswoman *(plural* **sales-women***)*.

vender [2] *verbo* ■ to sell: los vecinos venden su casa the neighbours are selling their house

"se vende" "for sale"

la casa se vendió por 300.000 euros the house sold for 300,000 euros.

el **veneno**

1. poison: con este veneno nos libraremos de las ratas with this poison we'll be free of the rats

2. venom: hay que inyectarte suero para combatir el veneno de la serpiente we have to inject you with serum to fight the snake's venom.

venenoso, sa *adjetivo* ■ poisonous.

Venezuela ■ Venezuela.

venezolano, na *adjetivo*

En inglés, los adjetivos que se refieren a un país o una región se escriben con mayúscula:

Venezuelan

el **venezolano** , la **venezolana**

En inglés, los gentilicios se escriben con mayúscula:

Venezuelan.

la **venganza** ■ vengeance: las víctimas del estafador juraron venganza the swindler's victims swore vengeance.

vengarse [12] *verbo pronominal* ■ to take revenge: las víctimas juraron que se vengarían del estafador the victims swore that they would take revenge on the swindler.

venir [55] *verbo*

1. to come: ¿vinieron en coche o en taxi? did they come by car or by taxi?; el ruido viene de la casa de al lado the noise comes from the next door

2. to be back: espérame un minuto, ya vengo wait for me just a minute, I'll be back

3. to be: la información viene en este manual the information is in this manual

que viene next: la semana que viene next week.

la **venta** ■ sale: las ventas siempre aumentan en diciembre sales always increase in December

estar en venta to be for sale.

la **ventaja** ■ advantage: tiene la ventaja de saber inglés y francés she has the advantage of knowing English and French.

la **ventana** ■ window.

la **ventanilla**

1. *de coche* window

2. *de cine, teatro, estadio* box office.

la **ventilación** *(plural* las ventilaciones*)* ■ ventilation: ¡en este cuarto me ahogo! tiene muy poca ventilación I suffocate in this room! It has very little ventilation.

el **ventilador** ■ fan: ¡cuidado! no metas los dedos en el ventilador careful! don't put your fingers in the fan.

ventilar [1] *verbo* ■ to ventilate: antes de limpiar, hay que ventilar bien la habitación before cleaning, you have to ventilate the room well.

ver [56] *verbo*

1. to see: no veo bien, necesito gafas I don't see well, I need glasses

2. to watch: no es bueno que pases todo el día viendo la tele it's not good for you to spend all day watching TV

tu respuesta no tiene nada que ver con lo que te he preguntado your answer doesn't have anything to do with what I asked you

verse *verbo pronominal*

1. to be obvious: se ve que no sabe nada de inglés it's obvious that he doesn't know any English

2. to meet: ¿nos vemos esta tarde? shall we meet this evening?

veranear [1] *verbo* ■ to spend the summer: veraneamos en la Costa Brava we spend the summer on the Costa Brava.

el **verano** ■ summer: las vacaciones de verano the summer holidays

> **en verano** in summer
> **el próximo verano** next summer.

veras *adverbio*
> **de veras** really.

veraz *adjetivo* ■ **truthful: pocos diarios dan información veraz** few newspapers give truthful information.

verbal *adjetivo* ■ **verbal: el indicativo y el imperativo son modos verbales** the indicative and the imperative are verbal moods.

el **verbo** ■ verb.

la **verdad** ■ **truth: no me gustan las mentiras, quiero la verdad** I don't like lies, I want the truth

> **de verdad** real: **me regalaron un coche, pero no es de verdad, sino de radiocontrol** they gave me a car, but it's not real, it's remote control.

verdadero, ra *adjetivo* ■ **real: le llaman Boni, pero su verdadero nombre es Eduardo** they call him Boni, but his real name is Eduardo.

verde *adjetivo*
1. **green: me puse la blusa blanca con el pantalón verde** I put on the white blouse with the green trousers
2. **unripe: no es saludable comer fruta cuando todavía está verde** it's not healthy to eat fruit when it's still unripe.

el **verde** ■ **green: mi color preferido es el verde** my favorite colour is green.

la **verdura** ■ **vegetable: las lechugas, las espinacas y las cebollas son verduras** lettuce, spinach and onions are vegetables.

la **vereda** ■ **path: por esa vereda puedes llegar al río** you can get to the river on that path.

vergonzoso, sa *adjetivo*
1. **shy: es muy vergonzosa, no se anima a hablar en público** she's very shy, she can't bring herself to speak in public
2. **disgraceful: es vergonzoso que haya niños que pasen hambre** it's disgraceful that there are children that go hungry.

la **vergüenza** ■ **disgrace: cómo le van a pegar así a un niño —¡es una vergüenza!** I can't believe they would hit a child like that – it's a disgrace!

> **me caí de la silla y me dio una vergüenza terrible** I fell off the chair and I was terribly embarrassed.

verídico, ca *adjetivo* ■ **true: la película se basa en una historia verídica** the film is based on a true story.

verosímil *adjetivo* ■ **likely: no creo ni una palabra, esa historia no tiene nada de verosímil** I don't believe a word of it he says, that story is not likely at all.

la **versión** *(plural* las versiones*)* ■ **version: el testigo dio su versión de los hechos** the witness gave her version of the facts

> **una película en versión original** a film in the original language.

el **verso** ■ **poem: sabe de memoria algunos versos de Neruda** he knows some of Neruda's poems by heart.

la **vértebra** ■ **vertebra** *(plural* **vertebrae***)*.

vertical *adjetivo* ■ **vertical: traza dos líneas verticales y dos horizontales** draw two vertical lines and two horizontal ones

> **ponlo vertical** put it vertical.

el **vértigo** ■ **vertigo: no puedo subir muy alto porque tengo vértigo** I can't go up very high because I have vertigo

> **dar vértigo** to make dizzy: **no puede subir porque la altura le da vértigo** he can't go up because heights make him dizzy.

el **vestíbulo**
1. *de casa* **hall**
2. *de teatro* **foyer**
3. *de edificio público* **lobby** *(plural* **lobbies***)*.

el **vestido** ■ **dress: me compré un precioso vestido floreado** I bought a lovely flowered dress

> **vestido de novia** wedding dress.

la **vestimenta** ■ **clothing: la vestimenta ha cambiado mucho a lo largo de la historia** clothing has changed a lot throughout history.

vestir [19] *verbo*

- to dress: Luisa y Juana se entretienen vistiendo a las muñecas Luisa and Juana entertain themselves dressing their dolls; Pedro viste muy bien Pedro dresses very well
- to wear: vestía vaqueros y una blusa she was wearing jeans and a blouse

vestirse *verbo pronominal*

- to get dressed: ¿cuánto tardas en vestirte? how long do you take to get dressed?
- to dress up: María se vistió de hada María dressed up as a fairy.

el **vestuario**

- en *piscina* locker room
- en *teatro* dressing room.

el **veterinario** , la **veterinaria** ■ veterinarian *UK*, vet *US*.

la **vez** (*plural* las veces) ■ time: ya te pedí cien veces que te callaras I've already asked you a hundred times to be quiet

- a la vez at the same time: no puedo hacerlo todo a la vez I can't do it all at once
- a veces sometimes: a veces pienso que no debería haber venido sometimes I think that I shouldn't have come
- dos veces twice: nos encontramos dos veces por semana para ir a nadar we meet twice a week to go swimming
- en vez de instead of: en vez de ir al parque, podríamos ir a la playa, ¿no? instead of going to the park, we could go to the beach, don't you think?
- otra vez again: no puedo creer que estés aquí otra vez I can't believe that you're here again
- tal vez maybe: tal vez no entiendan inglés maybe they don't understand English
- una vez once: nos vemos para tomar el té una vez por semana we meet once a week to have tea.

la **vía**

- track: las vías del tren son de hierro the railway tracks are made of iron
- platform: el tren sale por la vía tres the train leaves from platform three
- route: en los países con muchos ríos, la vía fluvial es muy utilizada in countries with a lot of rivers, river routes are often used

- por vía aérea by airmail
- por vía marítima by sea
- un país en vías de desarrollo a developing country.

el **viaducto** ■ viaduct.

viajar [1] *verbo* ■ to travel: no le gusta viajar en avión he doesn't like to travelling by plane.

el **viaje**

- trip: vamos a hacer un viaje por América del Sur we're going to take a trip through South America
- journey: está muy cansada después de un viaje tan largo she's very tired after such a long journey
- viaje de negocios business trip
- viaje de placer pleasure trip
- ¡buen viaje! have a good trip! o have a good journey!

el **viajero** , la **viajera** ■ traveller *UK*, traveler *US*: los viajeros llegaron cansados, después de muchas horas de vuelo the travellers arrived tired, after many hours aboard the plane.

la **víbora** ■ viper.

la **vibración** (*plural* las vibraciones) ■ vibration.

vibrar [1] *verbo* ■ to vibrate: los cristales de las ventanas vibran cuando estalla un trueno the glass in the windows vibrates when the thunder booms.

el **vicio** ■ vice: fumar es un vicio perjudicial para la salud smoking is a vice that's bad for your health.

la **víctima** ■ victim: la inundación produjo cien víctimas there were a hundred victims from the flood.

la **victoria** ■ victory (*plural* victories): la victoria fue para el equipo local the victory went to the local team.

la **vid** ■ vine.

la **vida** ■ life: toda su vida la pasó en un pequeño pueblo she spent all her life in a small town

- vida nocturna nightlife.

el **vídeo**

1. **video:** podríamos alquilar un vídeo para esta noche we could rent a video for tonight

2. **video cassette player:** se ha estropeado el vídeo, hay que llevarlo a arreglar the video cassette player has broken, we have to take it to be mended.

el **videoclip** (plural los videoclips) sustantivo masculino ■ video clip.

el **videojuego** ■ video game.

el **vidrio**

1. **glass:** prefiero las botellas de vidrio a las de plástico I prefer glass bottles to plastic ones

2. **window pane:** se ha roto un vidrio de mi ventana y entra frío a window pane in my room broke and the cold comes in.

la **vieja** ■ old woman (plural old women).

viejo, ja adjetivo ■ old: estos zapatos están muy viejos, tengo que comprar otros these shoes are very old, I have to buy some others; me lo ha contado un viejo amigo an old friend told me.

el **viejo** ■ old man (plural old men): un viejo estaba cruzando la calle an old man was crossing the road

▸ aquí los viejos no reciben jubilaciones dignas, viven en la miseria here the elderly don't get decent retirement pensions, they live in poverty

▸ los viejos old people, the elderly.

el **viento** ■ wind: no hace frío, pero hay mucho viento it's not cold, but there's a lot of wind.

el **vientre** ■ stomach: el fuerte dolor en el vientre resultó ser apendicitis the strong stomach pain ended up being appendicitis.

el **viernes** (plural los viernes)

En inglés, los días de la semana se escriben con mayúscula:

Friday: hoy es viernes today is Friday; el viernes que viene next Friday; el viernes pasado last Friday; el viernes on Friday; te veré el viernes I'll see you on Friday; los viernes on Fridays; los viernes vamos al parque on Fridays we go to the park.

el/la **vigilante** ■ security guard: contrataron tres vigilantes para el turno de noche they hired three security guards for the night shift.

vigilar [1] verbo

1. **to guard:** varios policías vigilaban a los presos several police officers were guarding the prisoners

2. **to keep an eye on:** hay que vigilar a los niños cuando están en la piscina you have to keep an eye on the children when they're in the pool

3. **to watch:** creo que nos vigilan, cuidado con lo que dices I think they're watching us, careful with what you say.

el **vigor** ■ vitality: los niños suelen tener mucho vigor children often have a lot of vitality.

vil adjetivo ■ vile.

la **villa**

1. **villa:** se compraron una preciosa villa, construída en un gran terreno they bought a lovely villa, built on a large piece of land

2. **small town:** pasamos el fin de semana en una villa marinera, cerca de la capital we spent the weekend in a small seaside town, near the capital.

el **villancico** ■ carol.

el **vinagre** ■ vinegar.

el **vínculo** ■ bond: tiene un vínculo muy fuerte con su familia he has a very strong bond with his family.

el **vino** ■ wine: ¿me sirves un vaso de vino? can you pour me a glass of wine?

▸ vino blanco white wine
▸ vino rosado rose wine
▸ vino tinto red wine.

la **viña** ■ vineyard.

el **viñedo** ■ vineyard.

la **violencia** ■ violence: la violencia no es la manera de resolver los conflictos violence is not the way to resolve conflicts.

violento, ta *adjetivo* ■ **violent: anoche oí una discusión muy violenta entre los vecinos** last night I heard a very violent argument between the neighbours.

violeta *adjetivo* ■ **violet: me voy a poner la blusa blanca con el pantalón violeta** I'm going to put on the white blouse with the violet trousers

el **violeta** ■ **violet: el violeta es mi color favorito** violet is my favourite colour.

la **violeta** ■ **violet.**

el **violín** *(plural los violines)* ■ **violin.**

la **violinista** ■ **violinist.**

la **violonchelista** ■ **cellist.**

el **violonchelo** ■ **cello.**

virgen *adjetivo*

1. **virgin: por el bien de todos, es importante preservar la selva virgen** for everybody's good, it's important to preserve the virgin jungle

2. **blank: una cinta de vídeo virgen** a blank videotape

> **pura lana virgen** pure new wool

la **Virgen** *(plural vírgenes)* ■ **virgin: la virgen María es la madre de Jesús** the Virgin Mary is the mother of Jesus.

viril *adjetivo* ■ **manly: tiene una voz muy viril** he has a very manly voice.

virtual *adjetivo* ■ **virtual**

> **realidad virtual** virtual reality.

la **virtud** ■ **virtue: la honestidad es una de sus virtudes** honesty is one of his virtues.

la **viruela** ■ **smallpox.**

el **virus** *(plural los virus)* ■ **virus: algunos virus provocan resfriados y gripes** some viruses cause colds and flu.

las **vísceras** ■ **entrails.**

la **visera** ■ **peak: siempre lleva la visera de la gorra hacia atrás** he always wears the peak of his cap backwards.

la **visibilidad** ■ **visibility: la neblina afecta la visibilidad en la carretera** the fog affects visibility on the road.

visible *adjetivo* ■ **visible: la cerradura tenía marcas visibles: habían tratado de forzarla** the lock had visible marks: they had tried to force it.

la **visión** *(plural las visiones)*

1. **eyesight: fue perdiendo la visión hasta quedarse ciego** he gradually lost his eyesight until he went blind

2. **seeing: la visión de aquella escena le impresionó** seeing that scene shocked him; **no hay nadie ahí, ves visiones** there's nobody there, you're seeing things

3. **view: esa es otra visión del problema** this is another view of the problem

> **no hay nadie ahí, ves visiones** there's nobody there, you're seeing things.

la **visita**

1. **visit: después de la visita de mis sobrinos, la casa es un caos** after my nieces' and nephews' visit, the house is in chaos

2. **visitor: anoche las visitas se quedaron hasta tardísimo** last night the visitors stayed until very late

> **horario de visita** visiting hours.

el/la **visitante** ■ **visitor: a los visitantes les encantan las playas de nuestro país** visitors love our country's beaches.

visitar [1] *verbo* ■ **to visit: vinieron a visitarnos nuestros primos españoles** our Spanish cousins came to visit us.

el **visor** ■ **viewfinder: miró por el visor de la cámara y sacó la foto** he looked through the camera's viewfinder and took the picture.

la **víspera** ■ **eve: la víspera del viaje no pude dormir** I couldn't sleep on the eve of the trip.

la **vista**

1. **sight: la vista es uno de los cinco sentidos** sight is one of the five senses

2. **view: compramos una preciosa casa con vistas al mar** we bought a lovely house with a view of the sea

> **conocer a alguien de vista** to know somebody by sight

> **¡hasta la vista!** see you!

por lo visto apparently: **por lo visto, Carla se ha ido de vacaciones** apparently, Carla has gone on holiday.

vistoso, sa *adjetivo* ■ **showy**: **tenía un vestido muy vistoso, rojo y amarillo** she had a very showy dress, red and yellow.

visual *adjetivo* ■ **visual**: **tiene muy buena memoria visual, siempre recuerda la cara de la gente** he has very good visual memory, he always remembers people's faces.

vital *adjetivo*
1. **vital**: **el corazón es un órgano vital** the heart is a vital organ
2. **full of vitality**: **mi abuela es muy vital** my grandmother is full of vitality.

la **vitalidad** ■ **vitality**: **la abuela tiene una vitalidad increíble, se las arregla sola para todo** my grandmother has incredible vitality, she manages on her own.

la **vitamina** ■ **vitamin**: **la naranja es una buena fuente de vitamina C** oranges are a good source of vitamin C.

la **vitrina**
1. *en casa* **glass cabinet**
2. *en tienda* **showcase**.

la **viuda** ■ **widow**: **las viudas tienen derecho a una pensión** widows have a right to a pension.

viudo, da *adjetivo* ■ **widowed**: **se quedó viuda pocos meses después de la boda** she was widowed only a few months after the wedding

el **viudo** ■ **widower**.

los **víveres** ■ **supplies**: **la lista de víveres para la excursión incluía frutas, embutidos y agua** the list of supplies for the outing included fruit, cold meats and water.

la **vivienda** ■ **dwelling**: **han construido muchas viviendas en las afueras de la ciudad** they've built a lot of dwellings on the outskirts of the city.

vivir [3] *verbo*
1. **to live**: **desde muy joven vive de su propio trabajo** from a very young age he's lived from his own work; **vive en el centro de la ciudad** she lives in the city centre
2. **to be alive**: **el perro quedó malherido, pero aún vive** the dog was badly injured, but it's still alive.

vivo, va *adjetivo*
1. **alive**: **el herido sigue vivo** the injured man is still alive; **¡no tires esa planta! está viva** don't throw that plant out! it's alive
2. **vivid**: **me gusta decorar la casa con colores vivos** I like to decorate the house with vivid colours.

el **vocablo** ■ **word**.

el **vocabulario** ■ **vocabulary**: **este libro es difícil porque tiene mucho vocabulario técnico** this book is difficult because it has a lot of technical vocabulary.

la **vocación** *(plural las vocaciones)* ■ **vocation**: **su vocación es la pintura** painting is her vocation.

vocal *adjetivo* ■ **vocal**: **no puede cantar porque tiene las cuerdas vocales inflamadas** he can't sing because his vocal cords are inflamed.

la **vocal** *(plural las vocales)* ■ **vowel**: **"a, e, i, o, u" son las cinco vocales españolas** "a, e, i, o, u" are the five vowels in Spanish.

el **volante** ■ **steering wheel**: **gira un poco el volante a la derecha** turn the steering wheel a little to the right.

volar [16] *verbo*
1. **to fly**: **los aviones vuelan a unos 10.000 metros de altura** aeroplanes fly at an altitude of about 10,000 metres
2. **to blow up**: **han volado el puente** they're blown up the bridge.

el **volcán** *(plural los volcanes)* ■ **volcano** *(plural* **volcanoes***)*.

volcánico, ca *adjetivo* ■ **volcanic**: **las erupciones son producto de la actividad volcánica** eruptions are a product of volcanic activity.

volcar [62] *verbo*

. **to dump:** el camión volcó su carga en el basurero the truck dumped its load at the rubbish dump; tienes que volcar toda la información en ese fichero you have to dump all the information onto that life

2. **to overturn:** el coche derrapó en la curva y volcó unos metros más adelante the car skidded on the bend and overturned over a few metres further along

3. **to knock over:** el gato volcó la maceta the cat knocked over the flowerpot.

la **voltereta**

1. *en el suelo* **forward roll**

2. *en el aire* **somersault.**

el **volumen** *(plural* los volúmenes) ■ **volume:** la maestra pidió que calculáramos el volumen de un cubo the teacher asked us to calculate the volume of a cube; esa novela se publicó en tres volúmenes that novel was published in three volumes; ¿podrías bajar el volumen de la radio, por favor? could you turn down the radio, please?; ¿podrías bajar el volumen, por favor? could you turn down the volume, please?; subid el volumen de la tele turn up the TV.

voluminoso, sa *adjetivo* ■ **massive:** esa mesa es tan voluminosa que no pasa por la puerta that table is so massive that it doesn't go through the door.

la **voluntad** ■ **will:** con la fuerza de voluntad que tiene puede conseguirlo todo with the will power that he has he can do anything; hizo el viaje contra su voluntad he made the trip against his will.

voluntario, ria *adjetivo* ■ **volunteer:** ese médico hace trabajo voluntario: atiende a los pacientes y no les cobra that doctor does volunteer work: he waits on patients and doesn't charge them

> Marga lo hizo de forma voluntaria Marga did it voluntarily

el **voluntario** , la **voluntaria** ■ **volunteer:** después del terremoto, muchos voluntarios se ofrecieron para ayudar after the earthquake, many volunteers offered to help.

volver [17] *verbo*

1. **to come back:** espérame un minuto que enseguida vuelvo wait for me for a minute, I'm coming right back

2. **to go back:** tengo que volver al colegio now I have to go back to school

3. **to turn:** le volvió la espalda he turned his back on her

> volver a hacer algo to do something again: dice que no volverá a fumar he say that he won't smoke again

volverse *verbo pronominal*

1. **to go back:** me vuelvo a casa, que es muy tarde I'm going home, it's late

2. **to become, to get:** se ha vuelto muy cariñoso he's become very affectionate

3. **to turn round, to turn around:** me volví para verla I turned round to see her.

vomitar [1] *verbo* ■ **to vomit.**

el **vómito** ■ **vomit.**

la **voracidad** ■ **voraciousness.**

voraz *adjetivo* ■ **voracious:** tiene un apetito voraz he has a voracious appetite.

vosotros, tras *pronombre*

1. *como sujeto* **you:** vosotros coméis mucha fruta you eat a lot of fruit; vosotras podéis venir más tarde you could come later

2. *como complemento* **you:** se han ido sin vosotros they have gone without you; vendrán con vosotras they will come with you; ¿estos juguetes son para vosotros? are these toys for you?

> entre vosotros between yourselves

> vosotros mismos yourselves.

votar [1] *verbo* ■ **to vote:** aquí se puede votar a partir de los 18 años here you can vote starting at 18 years of age; ¿a quién has votado? who did you vote for?

el **voto** ■ **vote:** en algunos países, el voto es obligatorio in some countries, voting is compulsory.

la **voz** *(plural* las voces) ■ **voice:** Antonio tiene la voz grave Antonio has a deep voice

> hablar en voz alta to talk aloud
> hablar en voz baja to speak in a low voice
> dar voces to spread the word.

el **vuelo** ■ flight: es entretenido observar el vuelo de los pájaros it's entertaining to observe birds' flight.

la **vuelta**

1. turn: este paso de baile incluye varias vueltas this dance step includes several turns
2. return: un billete de ida y vuelta a return ticket
3. lap: dieron cinco vueltas a la pista they did five laps around the track
4. change: la cajera se olvidó de darme la vuelta the checkout girl forgot to give me my change
5. walk: ¿vamos a dar una vuelta por el parque? are we going to go for a walk around the park?
6. ride: salimos a dar una vuelta en el coche nuevo de mi tío we went out for a ride in my uncle's new car

> dar la vuelta a la página to turn the page
> dar la vuelta al mundo to go round the world
> dar vueltas de campana to overturn
> darle vueltas a algo to think something over: hace días que le doy vueltas a ese asunto I've been thinking that matter over for some days
> darse la vuelta to turn round, to turn around
> estar de vuelta to be back.

vuestro, tra (adjetivo & pronombre)

■ adjetivo
your: vuestro padre os espera your father is waiting for you

■ pronombre
yours: ¿son vuestros? are they yours?

vulgar adjetivo

1. common: ¿sabes el nombre vulgar de la cefalea? do you know the common name for a migraine?
2. vulgar, coarse: siempre habla a gritos, es una chica muy vulgar she's always shouting, she's a very coarse girl.

el **walkman®** (plural los walkmans) ■ Walkman®.

el **waterpolo** ■ water polo.

la **web**

1. Internet, la Red web: voy a buscar esta información en la web I'm going to look up this information on the web
2. sitio, página website.

el **whisky** (plural los whiskys) ■ whisky.

el **windsurf** ■ windsurfing: me gusta hacer windsurf I like windsurfing.

la **xenofobia** ■ xenophobia.

el **xilófono** ■ xylophone.

y *conjunción* ■ **and: acaban de llegar Andrés y su novia** Andrés and his girlfriend just arrived; **yo soy del Betis, ¿y tú?** I support Betis, and you?

¿y qué? so what?: **el coche no funciona —¿y qué? podemos ir en taxi** the car's not working – so what? we can go by taxi

son las ocho y veinte it's twenty past eight o it's eight twenty.

ya *adverbio*

1. already: ya he terminado los deberes I've already finished my homework

2. now: he engordado y este vestido ya no me sirve I've put on weight and this dress isn't any use to me now

ya que since: **ya que vas de compras, trae algo de fruta** since you're going shopping, bring some fruit

ya no quiero más sopa I don't want any more soup

ya nos veremos mañana see you tomorrow

ya lo sé I know

y ya está and that's it: **pasa el trapo y ya está** give it a wipe with a cloth and that's it.

el yacimiento ■ **site: aquí encontraron un gran yacimiento con restos de dinosaurios** they found a huge site here with dinosaur remains.

el yate ■ yacht.

la yegua ■ mare.

la yema

1. yolk: la yema de huevo tiene una alta concentración de colesterol egg yolk has a high concentration of cholesterol

2. tip: en las yemas de los dedos están las huellas dactilares fingerprints are on the tips of the fingers.

el yerno ■ son-in-law *(plural* sons-in law).

yo *pronombre*

1. I: Rosa y yo queremos ser bailarinas Rosa and I want to be dancers

2. me: ¿quién quiere ir al parque? —¡yo! who wants to go to the park? – me!; **soy yo** it's me; **es más listo que yo** he's cleverer than me; **quiero pastel —¡yo también!** I want some cake – me too!

yo que tú if I were you.

el yogur ■ yoghurt, yogurt.

el yudo ■ judo.

la zambullida ■ **dive: su zambullida salpicó a todos los que estaban alrededor de la piscina** his dive splashed everybody that was around the pool.

zambullirse **[3]** *verbo pronominal* ■ **to dive in: si el agua está fría, es mejor zambullirse que entrar poco a poco** if the water is cold, it's better to dive in than to go in little by little.

la **zanahoria** ■ carrot.

la **zancadilla**
> le hicieron una zancadilla y casi se cayó they tripped him and he almost fell down.

la **zanja** ■ ditch: como estaba oscuro, no vio la zanja y se cayó since it was dark, he didn't see the ditch and he fell.

la **zapatería** ■ shoe shop *UK*, shoe store *US*: necesito zapatos nuevos, ¿dónde hay una zapatería? I need new shoes, where is a shoe shop?

el **zapatero** , la **zapatera** ■ shoemaker.

la **zapatilla**
1. slipper: en casa siempre llevo zapatillas I always wear slippers at home
2. trainer *UK*, sneaker *US*: hoy no puedo salir a correr porque he perdido mis zapatillas I can't go running today because I've lost my trainers
3. ballet shoes: la bailarina llevaba zapatillas de colores the ballerina was wearing coloured ballet shoes.

el **zapato** ■ shoe
> zapato plano flat shoe
> zapato de tacón high-heeled shoe.

la **zarpa** ■ claw.

zarpar [1] *verbo* ■ to set sail: el barco zarpa mañana the boat sets sail tomorrow.

la **zarzamora** ■ blackberry *(plural* black-berries*)*.

el **zigzag** ■ zigzag.

la **zona** ■ zone: la zona comercial de la ciudad está en el centro the commercial zone of the city is in the centre
> zona verde green zone
> zona industrial industrial zone.

el **zoo** ■ zoo.

la **zoología** ■ zoology.

el **zoológico** ■ zoo.

el **zorro** ■ fox.

zumbar [1] *verbo* ■ to buzz.

el **zumbido** ■ buzzing.

el **zumo** ■ juice: el zumo de naranja tiene mucha vitamina C orange juice has a lot of vitamin C.

el **zurcido** ■ darn: los calcetines están llenos de zurcidos the socks are full of darns.

zurdo, da *adjetivo*
1. left-handed: Juan es zurdo Juan is left-handed
2. left-footed: es un jugador zurdo he's a left-footed player

el **zurdo** , la **zurda** ■ left-handed person *(plural* **left-handed people***)*.

Spanish verbs

		1 amar	2 temer	3 partir	4 haber
indicativo	**presente**	amo	temo	parto	he
		amas	temes	partes	has
		ama	teme	parte	ha, hay
		amamos	tememos	partimos	hemos
		amáis	teméis	partís	habéis
		aman	temen	parten	han
	pretérito imperfecto	amaba	temía	partía	había
		amabas	temías	partías	habías
		amaba	temía	partía	había
		amábamos	temíamos	partíamos	habíamos
		amabais	temíais	partíais	habíais
		amaban	temían	partían	habían
	pretérito indefinido	amé	temí	partí	hube
		amaste	temiste	partiste	hubiste
		amó	temió	partió	hubo
		amamos	temimos	partimos	hubimos
		amasteis	temisteis	partisteis	hubisteis
		amaron	temieron	partieron	hubieron
	futuro	amaré	temeré	partiré	habré
		amarás	temerás	partirás	habrás
		amará	temerá	partirá	habrá
		amaremos	temeremos	partiremos	habremos
		amaréis	temeréis	partiréis	habréis
		amarán	temerán	partirán	habrán
	condicional	amaría	temería	partiría	habría
		amarías	temerías	partirías	habrías
		amaría	temería	partiría	habría
		amaríamos	temeríamos	partiríamos	habríamos
		amaríais	temeríais	partiríais	habríais
		amarían	temerían	partirían	habrían
subjuntivo	**presente**	ame	tema	parta	haya
		ames	temas	partas	hayas
		ame	tema	parta	haya
		amemos	temamos	partamos	hayamos
		améis	temáis	partáis	hayáis
		amen	teman	partan	hayan
	imperfecto	amara, -se	temiera, -se	partiera, -se	hubiera, -ese
		amaras, -ses	temieras, -ses	partieras, -ses	hubieras, -ses
		amara, -se	temiera, -se	partiera, -se	hubiera, -se
		amáramos, -semos	temiéramos, -semos	partiéramos, -semos	hubiéramos, -semos
		amarais, -seis	temierais, -seis	partierais, -seis	hubierais, -seis
		amaran, -sen	temieran, -sen	partieran, -sen	hubieran, -sen
	imperativo	ama (tú)	teme (tú)	parte (tú)	*no se usa*
		amad (vosotros/as)	temed (vosotros/as)	partid (vosotros/as)	
	gerundio, participio	amando, amado	temiendo, temido	partiendo, partido	habiendo, habido

I

Spanish verbs

		5 ser	**6 actuar**	**7 guiar**	**8 sacar**
indicativo	presente	soy	actúo	guío	saco
		eres	actúas	guías	sacas
		es	actúa	guía	saca
		somos	actuamos	guiamos	sacamos
		sois	actuáis	guiáis	sacáis
		son	actúan	guían	sacan
	pretérito imperfecto	era	actuaba	guiaba	sacaba
		eras	actuabas	guiabas	sacabas
		era	actuaba	guiaba	sacaba
		éramos	actuábamos	guiábamos	sacábamos
		erais	actuabais	guiabais	sacabais
		eran	actuaban	guiaban	sacaban
	pretérito indefinido	fui	actué	guié	saqué
		fuiste	actuaste	guiaste	sacaste
		fue	actuó	guió	sacó
		fuimos	actuamos	guiamos	sacamos
		fuisteis	actuasteis	guiasteis	sacasteis
		fueron	actuaron	guiaron	sacaron
	futuro	seré	actuaré	guiaré	sacaré
		serás	actuarás	guiarás	sacarás
		será	actuará	guiará	sacará
		seremos	actuaremos	guiaremos	sacaremos
		seréis	actuaréis	guiaréis	sacaréis
		serán	actuarán	guiarán	sacarán
	condicional	sería	actuaría	guiaría	sacaría
		serías	actuarías	guiarías	sacarías
		sería	actuaría	guiaría	sacaría
		seríamos	actuaríamos	guiaríamos	sacaríamos
		seríais	actuaríais	guiaríais	sacaríais
		serían	actuarían	guiarían	sacarían
subjuntivo	presente	sea	actúe	guíe	saque
		seas	actúes	guíes	saques
		sea	actúe	guíe	saque
		seamos	actuemos	guiemos	saquemos
		seáis	actuéis	guiéis	saquéis
		sean	actúen	guíen	saquen
	imperfecto	fuera, -se	actuara, -se	guiara, -se	sacara, -se
		fueras, -ses	actuaras, -ses	guiaras, -ses	sacaras, -ses
		fuera, -se	actuara, -se	guiara, -se	sacara, -se
		fuéramos, -semos	actuáramos, -semos	guiáramos, -semos	sacáramos, -semos
		fuerais, -seis	actuarais, -seis	guiarais, -seis	sacarais, -seis
		fueran, -sen	actuaran, -sen	guiaran, -sen	sacaran, -sen
	imperativo	sé (tú)	actúa (tú)	guía (tú)	saca (tú)
		sed (vosotros/as)	actuad (vosotros/as)	guiad (vosotros/as)	sacad (vosotros/as)
	gerundio, participio	siendo,	actuando,	guiando,	sacando,
		sido	actuado	guiado	sacado

9 convencer	10 cazar	11 dirigir	12 llegar	13 distinguir
convenzo	cazo	dirijo	llego	distingo
convences	cazas	diriges	llegas	distingues
convence	caza	dirige	llega	distingue
convencemos	cazamos	dirigimos	llegamos	distinguimos
convencéis	cazáis	dirigís	llegáis	distinguís
convencen	cazan	dirigen	llegan	distinguen
convencía	cazaba	dirigía	llegaba	distinguía
convencías	cazabas	dirigías	llegabas	distinguías
convencía	cazaba	dirigía	llegaba	distinguía
convencíamos	cazábamos	dirigíamos	llegábamos	distinguíamos
convencíais	cazabais	dirigíais	llegabais	distinguíais
convencían	cazaban	dirigían	llegaban	distinguían
convencí	cacé	dirigí	llegué	distinguí
convenciste	cazaste	dirigiste	llegaste	distinguiste
convenció	cazó	dirigió	llegó	distinguió
convencimos	cazamos	dirigimos	llegamos	distinguimos
convencisteis	cazasteis	dirigisteis	llegasteis	distinguisteis
convencieron	cazaron	dirigieron	llegaron	distinguieron
convenceré	cazaré	dirigiré	llegaré	distinguiré
convencerás	cazarás	dirigirás	llegarás	distinguirás
convencerá	cazará	dirigirá	llegará	distinguirá
convenceremos	cazaremos	dirigiremos	llegaremos	distinguiremos
convenceréis	cazaréis	dirigiréis	llegaréis	distinguiréis
convencerán	cazarán	dirigirán	llegarán	distinguirán
convencería	cazaría	dirigiría	llegaría	distinguiría
convencerías	cazarías	dirigirías	llegarías	distinguirías
convencería	cazaría	dirigiría	llegaría	distinguiría
convenceríamos	cazaríamos	dirigiríamos	llegaríamos	distinguiríamos
convenceríais	cazaríais	dirigiríais	llegaríais	distinguiríais
convencerían	cazarían	dirigirían	llegarían	distinguirían
convenza	cace	dirija	llegue	distinga
convenzas	caces	dirijas	llegues	distingas
convenza	cace	dirija	llegue	distinga
convenzamos	cacemos	dirijamos	lleguemos	distingamos
convenzáis	cacéis	dirijáis	lleguéis	distingáis
convenzan	cacen	dirijan	lleguen	distingan
convenciera, -se	cazara, -se	dirigiera, -se	llegara, -se	distinguiera, -se
convencieras, -ses	cazaras, -ses	dirigieras, -ses	llegaras, -ses	distinguieras, -ses
convenciera, -se	cazara, -se	dirigiera, -se	llegara, -se	distinguiera, -se
convenciéramos, -semos	cazáramos, -semos	dirigiéramos, -semos	llegáramos, -semos	distinguiéramos, -semos
convencierais, -seis	cazarais, -seis	dirigierais, -seis	llegarais, -seis	distinguierais, -seis
convencieran, -sen	cazaran, -sen	dirigieran, -sen	llegaran, -sen	distinguieran, -sen
convence (tú)	caza (tú)	dirige (tú)	llega (tú)	distingue (tú)
convenced (vosotros/as)	cazad (vosotros/as)	dirigid (vosotros/as)	llegad (vosotros/as)	distinguid (vosotros/as)
convenciendo, convencido	cazando, cazado	dirigiendo, dirigido	llegando, llegado	distinguiendo, distinguido

		14 acertar	**15** entender	**16** sonar	**17** mover
indicativo	presente	acierto	entiendo	sueno	muevo
		aciertas	entiendes	suenas	mueves
		acierta	entiende	suena	mueve
		acertamos	entendemos	sonamos	movemos
		acertáis	entendéis	sonáis	movéis
		aciertan	entienden	suenan	mueven
	pretérito imperfecto	acertaba	entendía	sonaba	movía
		acertabas	entendías	sonabas	movías
		acertaba	entendía	sonaba	movía
		acertábamos	entendíamos	sonábamos	movíamos
		acertabais	entendíais	sonabais	movíais
		acertaban	entendían	sonaban	movían
	pretérito indefinido	acerté	entendí	soné	moví
		acertaste	entendiste	sonaste	moviste
		acertó	entendió	sonó	movió
		acertamos	entendimos	sonamos	movimos
		acertasteis	entendisteis	sonasteis	movisteis
		acertaron	entendieron	sonaron	movieron
	futuro	acertaré	entenderé	sonaré	moveré
		acertarás	entenderás	sonarás	moverás
		acertará	entenderá	sonará	moverá
		acertaremos	entenderemos	sonaremos	moveremos
		acertaréis	entenderéis	sonaréis	moveréis
		acertarán	entenderán	sonarán	moverán
	condicional	acertaría	entendería	sonaría	movería
		acertarías	entenderías	sonarías	moverías
		acertaría	entendería	sonaría	movería
		acertaríamos	entenderíamos	sonaríamos	moveríamos
		acertaríais	entenderíais	sonaríais	moveríais
		acertarían	entenderían	sonarían	moverían
subjuntivo	presente	acierte	entienda	suene	mueva
		aciertes	entiendas	suenes	muevas
		acierte	entienda	suene	mueva
		acertemos	entendamos	sonemos	movamos
		acertéis	entendáis	sonéis	mováis
		acierten	entiendan	suenen	muevan
	imperfecto	acertara, -se	entendiera, -se	sonara, -se	moviera, -se
		acertaras,-ses	entendieras, -ses	sonaras, -ses	movieras, -ses
		acertara, -se	entendiera, -se	sonara, -se	moviera, -se
		acertáramos, -semos	entendiéramos, -semos	sonáramos, -semos	moviéramos, -semos
		acertarais, -seis	entendierais, -seis	sonarais, -seis	movierais, -seis
		acertaran, -sen	entendieran, -sen	sonaran, -sen	movieran, -sen
	imperativo	acierta (tú)	entiende (tú)	suena (tú)	mueve (tú)
		acertad (vosotros/as)	entended (vosotros/as)	sonad (vosotros/as)	moved (vosotros/as)
	gerundio, participio	acertando, acertado	entendiendo, entendido	sonando, sonado	moviendo, movido

18 dormir	**19** pedir	**20** sentir	**21** reír	**22** conocer
duermo	pido	siento	río	conozco
duermes	pides	sientes	ríes	conoces
duerme	pide	siente	ríe	conoce
dormimos	pedimos	sentimos	reímos	conocemos
dormís	pedís	sentís	reís	conocéis
duermen	piden	sienten	ríen	conocen
dormía	pedía	sentía	reía	conocía
dormías	pedías	sentías	reías	conocías
dormía	pedía	sentía	reía	conocía
dormíamos	pedíamos	sentíamos	reíamos	conocíamos
dormíais	pedíais	sentíais	reíais	conocíais
dormían	pedían	sentían	reían	conocían
dormí	pedí	sentí	reí	conocí
dormiste	pediste	sentiste	reíste	conociste
durmió	pidió	sintió	rió	conoció
dormimos	pedimos	sentimos	reímos	conocimos
dormisteis	pedisteis	sentisteis	reísteis	conocisteis
durmieron	pidieron	sintieron	rieron	conocieron
dormiré	pediré	sentiré	reiré	conoceré
dormirás	pedirás	sentirás	reirás	conocerás
dormirá	pedirá	sentirá	reirá	conocerá
dormiremos	pediremos	sentiremos	reiremos	conoceremos
dormiréis	pediréis	sentiréis	reiréis	conoceréis
dormirán	pedirán	sentirán	reirán	conocerán
dormiría	pediría	sentiría	reiría	conocería
dormirías	pedirías	sentirías	reirías	conocerías
dormiría	pediría	sentiría	reiría	conocería
dormiríamos	pediríamos	sentiríamos	reiríamos	conoceríamos
dormiríais	pediríais	sentiríais	reiríais	conoceríais
dormirían	pedirían	sentirían	reirían	conocerían
duerma	pida	sienta	ría	conozca
duermas	pidas	sientas	rías	conozcas
duerma	pida	sienta	ría	conozca
durmamos	pidamos	sintamos	riamos	conozcamos
durmáis	pidáis	sintáis	riáis	conozcáis
duerman	pidan	sientan	rían	conozcan
durmiera, -se	pidiera, -se	sintiera, -se	riera, -se	conociera, -se
durmieras, -ses	pidieras, -ses	sintieras, -ses	rieras, -ses	conocieras, -ses
durmiera, -se	pidiera, -se	sintiera, -se	riera, -se	conociera, -se
durmiéramos, -semos	pidiéramos, -semos	sintiéramos, -semos	riéramos, -semos	conociéramos, -semos
durmierais, -seis	pidierais, -seis	sintierais, -seis	rierais, -seis	conocierais, -seis
durmieran, -sen	pidieran, -sen	sintieran, -sen	rieran, -sen	conocieran, -sen
duerme (tú)	pide (tú)	siente (tú)	ríe (tú)	conoce (tú)
dormid (vosotros/as)	pedid (vosotros/as)	sentid (vosotros/as)	reíd (vosotros/as)	conoced (vosotros/as)
durmiendo,	pidiendo,	sintiendo,	riendo,	conociendo,
dormido	pedido	sentido	reído	conocido

		23 conducir	**24 comenzar**	**25 negar**	**26 forzar**
indicativo	presente	conduzco	comienzo	niego	fuerzo
		conduces	comienzas	niegas	fuerzas
		conduce	comienza	niega	fuerza
		conducimos	comenzamos	negamos	forzamos
		conducís	comenzáis	negáis	forzáis
		conducen	comienzan	niegan	fuerzan
	pretérito imperfecto	conducía	comenzaba	negaba	forzaba
		conducías	comenzabas	negabas	forzabas
		conducía	comenzaba	negaba	forzaba
		conducíamos	comenzábamos	negábamos	forzábamos
		conducíais	comenzabais	negabais	forzabais
		conducían	comenzaban	negaban	forzaban
	pretérito indefinido	conduje	comencé	negué	forcé
		condujiste	comenzaste	negaste	forzaste
		condujo	comenzó	negó	forzó
		condujimos	comenzamos	negamos	forzamos
		condujisteis	comenzasteis	negasteis	forzasteis
		condujeron	comenzaron	negaron	forzaron
	futuro	conduciré	comenzaré	negaré	forzaré
		conducirás	comenzarás	negarás	forzarás
		conducirá	comenzará	negará	forzará
		conduciremos	comenzaremos	negaremos	forzaremos
		conduciréis	comenzaréis	negaréis	forzaréis
		conducirán	comenzarán	negarán	forzarán
	condicional	conduciría	comenzaría	negaría	forzaría
		conducirías	comenzarías	negarías	forzarías
		conduciría	comenzaría	negaría	forzaría
		conduciríamos	comenzaríamos	negaríamos	forzaríamos
		conduciríais	comenzaríais	negaríais	forzaríais
		conducirían	comenzarían	negarían	forzarían
subjuntivo	presente	conduzca	comience	niegue	fuerce
		conduzcas	comiences	niegues	fuerces
		conduzca	comience	niegue	fuerce
		conduzcamos	comencemos	neguemos	forcemos
		conduzcáis	comencéis	neguéis	forcéis
		conduzcan	comiencen	nieguen	fuercen
	imperfecto	condujera, -ese	comenzara, -se	negara, -se	forzara, -se
		condujeras, -ses	comenzaras, -ses	negaras, -ses	forzaras, -ses
		condujera, -se	comenzara, -se	negara, -se	forzara, -se
		condujéramos, -semos	comenzáramos, -semos	negáramos, -semos	forzáramos, -semos
		condujerais, -seis	comenzarais, -seis	negarais, -seis	forzarais, -seis
		condujeran, -sen	comenzaran, -sen	negaran, -sen	forzaran, -sen
	imperativo	conduce (tú)	comienza (tú)	niega (tú)	fuerza (tú)
		conducid (vosotros/as)	comenzad (vosotros/as)	negad (vosotros/as)	forzad (vosotros/as)
	gerundio, participio	conduciendo,	comenzando,	negando,	forzando,
		conducido	comenzado	negado	forzado

27 avergonzar	28 colgar	29 jugar	30 cocer	31 corregir
avergüenzo	cuelgo	juego	cuezo	corrijo
avergüenzas	cuelgas	juegas	cueces	corriges
avergüenza	cuelga	juega	cuece	corrige
avergonzamos	colgamos	jugamos	cocemos	corregimos
avergonzáis	colgáis	jugáis	cocéis	corregís
avergüenzan	cuelgan	juegan	cuecen	corrigen
avergonzaba	colgaba	jugaba	cocía	corregía
avergonzabas	colgabas	jugabas	cocías	corregías
avergonzaba	colgaba	jugaba	cocía	corregía
avergonzábamos	colgábamos	jugábamos	cocíamos	corregíamos
avergonzabais	colgabais	jugabais	cocíais	corregíais
avergonzaban	colgaban	jugaban	cocían	corregían
avergoncé	colgué	jugué	cocí	corregí
avergonzaste	colgaste	jugaste	cociste	corregiste
avergonzó	colgó	jugó	coció	corrigió
avergonzamos	colgamos	jugamos	cocimos	corregimos
avergonzasteis	colgasteis	jugasteis	cocisteis	corregisteis
avergonzaron	colgaron	jugaron	cocieron	corrigieron
avergonzaré	colgaré	jugaré	coceré	corregiré
avergonzarás	colgarás	jugarás	cocerás	corregirás
avergonzará	colgará	jugará	cocerá	corregirá
avergonzaremos	colgaremos	jugaremos	coceremos	corregiremos
avergonzaréis	colgaréis	jugaréis	coceréis	corregiréis
avergonzarán	colgarán	jugarán	cocerán	corregirán
avergonzaría	colgaría	jugaría	cocería	corregiría
avergonzarías	colgarías	jugarías	cocerías	corregirías
avergonzaría	colgaría	jugaría	cocería	corregiría
avergonzaríamos	colgaríamos	jugaríamos	coceríamos	corregiríamos
avergonzaríais	colgaríais	jugaríais	coceríais	corregiríais
avergonzarían	colgarían	jugarían	cocerían	corregirían
avergüence	cuelgue	juegue	cueza	corrija
avergüences	cuelgues	juegues	cuezas	corrijas
avergüence	cuelgue	juegue	cueza	corrija
avergoncemos	colguemos	juguemos	cozamos	corrijamos
avergoncéis	colguéis	juguéis	cozáis	corrijáis
avergüencen	cuelguen	jueguen	cuezan	corrijan
avergonzara, -se	colgara, -se	jugara, -se	cociera, -se	corrigiera,-se
avergonzaras, -ses	colgaras, -ses	jugaras, -ses	cocieras, -ses	corrigieras, -ses
avergonzara, -se	colgara, -se	jugara, -se	cociera, -se	corrigiera, -se
avergonzáramos, -semos	colgáramos, -semos	jugáramos, -semos	cociéramos, -semos	corrigiéramos, -semos
avergonzarais, -seis	colgarais, -seis	jugarais, -seis	cocierais, -seis	corrigierais, -seis
avergonzaran, -sen	colgaran, -sen	jugaran, -sen	cocieran, -sen	corrigieran, -sen
avergüenza (tú)	cuelga (tú)	juega (tú)	cuece (tú)	corrige (tú)
avergonzad (vosotros/as)	colgad (vosotros/as)	jugad (vosotros/as)	coced (vosotros/as)	corregid (vosotros/as)
avergonzando,	colgando,	jugando,	cociendo,	corrigiendo,
avergonzado	colgado	jugado	cocido	corregido

		32 seguir	33 averiguar	34 oler	35 leer
indicativo	presente	sigo	averiguo	huelo	leo
		sigues	averiguas	hueles	lees
		sigue	averigua	huele	lee
		seguimos	averiguamos	olemos	leemos
		seguís	averiguáis	oléis	leéis
		siguen	averiguan	huelen	leen
	pretérito imperfecto	seguía	averiguaba	olía	leía
		seguías	averiguabas	olías	leías
		seguía	averiguaba	olía	leía
		seguíamos	averiguábamos	olíamos	leíamos
		seguíais	averiguabais	olíais	leíais
		seguían	averiguaban	olían	leían
	pretérito indefinido	seguí	averigüé	olí	leí
		seguiste	averiguaste	oliste	leíste
		siguió	averiguó	olió	leyó
		seguimos	averiguamos	olimos	leímos
		seguisteis	averiguasteis	olisteis	leísteis
		siguieron	averiguaron	olieron	leyeron
	futuro	seguiré	averiguaré	oleré	leeré
		seguirás	averiguarás	olerás	leerás
		seguirá	averiguará	olerá	leerá
		seguiremos	averiguaremos	oleremos	leeremos
		seguiréis	averiguaréis	oleréis	leeréis
		seguirán	averiguarán	olerán	leerán
	condicional	seguiría	averiguaría	olería	leería
		seguirías	averiguarías	olerías	leerías
		seguiría	averiguaría	olería	leería
		seguiríamos	averiguaríamos	oleríamos	leeríamos
		seguiríais	averiguaríais	oleríais	leeríais
		seguirían	averiguarían	olerían	leerían
subjuntivo	presente	siga	averigüe	huela	lea
		sigas	averigües	huelas	leas
		siga	averigüe	huela	lea
		sigamos	averigüemos	olamos	leamos
		sigáis	averigüéis	oláis	leáis
		sigan	averigüen	huelan	lean
	imperfecto	siguiera, -se	averiguara, -se	oliera, -se	leyera, -se
		siguieras, -ses	averiguaras, -ses	olieras, -ses	leyeras, -ses
		siguiera, -se	averiguara, -se	oliera, -se	leyera, -se
		siguiéramos, -semos	averiguáramos, -semos	oliéramos, -semos	leyéramos, -semos
		siguierais, -seis	averiguarais, -seis	olierais, -seis	leyerais, -seis
		siguieran, -sen	averiguaran, -sen	olieran, -sen	leyeran, -sen
	imperativo	sigue (tú)	averigua (tú)	huele (tú)	lee (tú)
		seguid (vosotros/as)	averiguad (vosotros/as)	oled (vosotros/as)	leed (vosotros/as)
	gerundio, participio	siguiendo,	averiguando,	oliendo,	leyendo,
		seguido	averiguado	olido	leído

36 huir	37 andar	38 caber	39 caer	40 dar
huyo	ando	quepo	caigo	doy
huyes	andas	cabes	caes	das
huye	anda	cabe	cae	da
huimos	andamos	cabemos	caemos	damos
huís	andáis	cabéis	caéis	dais
huyen	andan	caben	caen	dan
huía	andaba	cabía	caía	daba
huías	andabas	cabías	caías	dabas
huía	andaba	cabía	caía	daba
huíamos	andábamos	cabíamos	caíamos	dábamos
huíais	andabais	cabíais	caíais	dabais
huían	andaban	cabían	caían	daban
huí	anduve	cupe	caí	di
huiste	anduviste	cupiste	caíste	diste
huyó	anduvo	cupo	cayó	dio
huimos	anduvimos	cupimos	raímos	dimos
huisteis	anduvisteis	cupisteis	caísteis	disteis
huyeron	anduvieron	cupieron	cayeron	dieron
huiré	andaré	cabré	caeré	daré
huirás	andarás	cabrás	caerás	darás
huirá	andará	cabrá	caerá	dará
huiremos	andaremos	cabremos	caeremos	daremos
huiréis	andaréis	cabréis	caeréis	daréis
huirán	andarán	cabrán	caerán	darán
huiría	andaría	cabría	caería	daría
huirías	andarías	cabrías	caerías	darías
huiría	andaría	cabría	caería	daría
huiríamos	andaríamos	cabríamos	caeríamos	daríamos
huiríais	andaríais	cabríais	caeríais	daríais
huirían	andarían	cabrían	caerían	darían
huya	ande	quepa	caiga	dé
huyas	andes	quepas	caigas	des
huya	ande	quepa	caiga	dé
huyamos	andemos	quepamos	caigamos	demos
huyáis	andéis	quepáis	caigáis	deis
huyan	anden	quepan	caigan	den
huyera, -se	anduviera, -se	cupiera, -se	cayera, -se	diera, -se
huyeras, -ses	anduvieras, -ses	cupieras, -ses	cayeras, -ses	dieras, -ses
huyera, -se	anduviera, -se	cupiera, -se	cayera, -se	diera, -se
huyéramos,-semos	anduviéramos, -semos	cupiéramos, -semos	cayéramos, -semos	diéramos, -semos
huyerais, -seis	anduvierais, -seis	cupierais, -seis	cayerais, -seis	dierais, -seis
huyeran, -sen	anduvieran, -sen	cupieran, -sen	cayeran, -sen	dieran, -sen
huye (tú)	anda (tú)	cabe (tú)	cae (tú)	da (tú)
huid (vosotros/as)	andad (vosotros/as)	cabed (vosotros/as)	caed (vosotros/as)	dad (vosotros/as)
huyendo,	andando,	cabiendo,	cayendo,	dando,
huido	andado	cabido	caído	dado

Spanish verbs

		41 decir	**42** estar	**43** hacer	**44** ir
indicativo	presente	digo	estoy	hago	voy
		dices	estás	haces	vas
		dice	está	hace	va
		decimos	estamos	hacemos	vamos
		decís	estáis	hacéis	vais
		dicen	están	hacen	van
	pretérito imperfecto	decía	estaba	hacía	iba
		decías	estabas	hacías	ibas
		decía	estaba	hacía	iba
		decíamos	estábamos	hacíamos	íbamos
		decíais	estabais	hacíais	ibais
		decían	estaban	hacían	iban
	pretérito indefinido	dije	estuve	hice	fui
		dijiste	estuviste	hiciste	fuiste
		dijo	estuvo	hizo	fue
		dijimos	estuvimos	hicimos	fuimos
		dijisteis	estuvisteis	hicisteis	fuisteis
		dijeron	estuvieron	hicieron	fueron
	futuro	diré	estaré	haré	iré
		dirás	estarás	harás	irás
		dirá	estará	hará	irá
		diremos	estaremos	haremos	iremos
		diréis	estaréis	haréis	iréis
		dirán	estarán	harán	irán
	condicional	diría	estaría	haría	iría
		dirías	estarías	harías	irías
		diría	estaría	haría	iría
		diríamos	estaríamos	haríamos	iríamos
		diríais	estaríais	haríais	iríais
		dirían	estarían	harían	irían
subjuntivo	presente	diga	esté	haga	vaya
		digas	estés	hagas	vayas
		diga	esté	haga	vaya
		digamos	estemos	hagamos	vayamos
		digáis	estéis	hagáis	vayáis
		digan	estén	hagan	vayan
	imperfecto	dijera, -se	estuviera, -se	hiciera, -se	fuera, -se
		dijeras, -ses	estuvieras, -ses	hicieras, -ses	fueras, -ses
		dijera, -se	estuviera, -se	hiciera, -se	fuera, -se
		dijéramos, -semos	estuviéramos, -semos	hiciéramos, -semos	fuéramos, -semos
		dijerais, -seis	estuvierais, -seis	hicierais, -seis	fuerais, -seis
		dijeran, -sen	estuvieran, -sen	hicieran, -sen	fueran, -sen
	imperativo	di (tú)	está (tú)	haz (tú)	ve (tú)
		decid (vosotros/as)	estad (vosotros/as)	haced (vosotros/as)	id (vosotros/as)
	gerundio, participio	diciendo,	estando,	haciendo,	yendo,
		dicho	estado	hecho	ido

45 oír	46 poder	47 poner	48 predecir	49 querer
oigo	puedo	pongo	predigo	quiero
oyes	puedes	pones	predices	quieres
oye	puede	pone	predice	quiere
oímos	podemos	ponemos	predecimos	queremos
oís	podéis	ponéis	predecís	queréis
oyen	pueden	ponen	predicen	quieren
oía	podía	ponía	predecía	quería
oías	podías	ponías	predecías	querías
oía	podía	ponía	predecía	quería
oíamos	podíamos	poníamos	predecíamos	queríamos
oíais	podíais	poníais	predecíais	queríais
oían	podían	ponían	predecían	querían
oí	pude	puse	predije	quise
oíste	pudiste	pusiste	predijiste	quisiste
oyó	pudo	puso	predijo	quiso
oímos	pudimos	pusimos	predijimos	quisimos
oísteis	pudisteis	pusisteis	predijisteis	quisisteis
oyeron	pudieron	pusieron	predijeron	quisieron
oiré	podré	pondré	predeciré	querré
oirás	podrás	pondrás	predecirás	querrás
oirá	podrá	pondrá	predecirá	querrá
oiremos	podremos	pondremos	predeciremos	querremos
oiréis	podréis	pondréis	predeciréis	querréis
oirán	podrán	pondrán	predecirán	querrán
oiría	podría	pondría	predeciría	querría
oirías	podrías	pondrías	predecirías	querrías
oiría	podría	pondría	predeciría	querría
oiríamos	podríamos	pondríamos	predeciríamos	querríamos
oiríais	podríais	pondríais	predeciríais	querríais
oirían	podrían	pondrían	predecirían	querrían
oiga	pueda	ponga	prediga	quiera
oigas	puedas	pongas	predigas	quieras
oiga	pueda	ponga	prediga	quiera
oigamos	podamos	pongamos	predigamos	queramos
oigáis	podáis	pongáis	predigáis	queráis
oigan	puedan	pongan	predigan	quieran
oyera, -se	pudiera, -se	pusiera, -se	predijera, -se	quisiera, -se
oyeras, -ses	pudieras, -ses	pusieras, -ses	predijeras, -ses	quisieras, -ses
oyera, -se	pudiera, -se	pusiera, -se	predijera, -se	quisiera, -se
oyéramos, -semos	pudiéramos, -semos	pusiéramos, -semos	predijéramos, -semos	quisiéramos, -semos
oyerais, -seis	pudierais, -seis	pusierais, -seis	predijerais, -seis	quisierais, -seis
oyeran, -sen	pudieran, -sen	pusieran, -sen	predijeran, -sen	quisieran, -sen
oye (tú)	puede (tú)	pon (tú)	predice (tú)	quiere (tú)
oíd (vosotros/as)	poded (vosotros/as)	poned (vosotros/as)	predecid (vosotros/as)	quered (vosotros/as)
oyendo,	pudiendo,	poniendo,	prediciendo,	queriendo,
oído	podido	puesto	predicho	querido

Spanish verbs

		50 saber	**51** salir	**52** tener	**53** traer
indicativo	presente	sé	salgo	tengo	traigo
		sabes	sales	tienes	traes
		sabe	sale	tiene	trae
		sabemos	salimos	tenemos	traemos
		sabéis	salís	tenéis	traéis
		saben	salen	tienen	traen
	pretérito imperfecto	sabía	salía	tenía	traía
		sabías	salías	tenías	traías
		sabía	salía	tenía	traía
		sabíamos	salíamos	teníamos	traíamos
		sabíais	salíais	teníais	traíais
		sabían	salían	tenían	traían
	pretérito indefinido	supe	salí	tuve	traje
		supiste	saliste	tuviste	trajiste
		supo	salió	tuvo	trajo
		supimos	salimos	tuvimos	trajimos
		supisteis	salisteis	tuvisteis	trajisteis
		supieron	salieron	tuvieron	trajeron
	futuro	sabré	saldré	tendré	traeré
		sabrás	saldrás	tendrás	traerás
		sabrá	saldrá	tendrá	traerá
		sabremos	saldremos	tendremos	traeremos
		sabréis	saldréis	tendréis	traeréis
		sabrán	saldrán	tendrán	traerán
	condicional	sabría	saldría	tendría	traería
		sabrías	saldrías	tendrías	traerías
		sabría	saldría	tendría	traería
		sabríamos	saldríamos	tendríamos	traeríamos
		sabríais	saldríais	tendríais	traeríais
		sabrían	saldrían	tendrían	traerían
subjuntivo	presente	sepa	salga	tenga	traiga
		sepas	salgas	tengas	traigas
		sepa	salga	tenga	traiga
		sepamos	salgamos	tengamos	traigamos
		sepáis	salgáis	tengáis	traigáis
		sepan	salgan	tengan	traigan
	imperfecto	supiera, -se	saliera, -se	tuviera, -se	trajera, -se
		supieras, -ses	salieras, -ses	tuvieras, -ses	trajeras, -ses
		supiera, -se	saliera, -se	tuviera, -se	trajera, -se
		supiéramos, -semos	saliéramos, -semos	tuviéramos, -semos	trajéramos, -semos
		supierais, -seis	salierais, -seis	tuvierais, -seis	trajerais, -seis
		supieran, -sen	salieran, -sen	tuvieran, -sen	trajeran, -sen
	imperativo	sabe (tú)	sal (tú)	ten (tú)	trae (tú)
		sabed (vosotros/as)	salid (vosotros/as)	tened (vosotros/as)	traed (vosotros/as)
	gerundio, participio	sabiendo,	saliendo,	teniendo,	trayendo,
		sabido	salido	tenido	traído

54 valer	**55** venir	**56** ver	**57** abolir	**58** aislar
valgo	vengo	veo	*no se usa*	aíslo
vales	vienes	ves	*no se usa*	aíslas
vale	viene	ve	*no se usa*	aísla
valemos	venimos	vemos	abolimos	aislamos
valéis	venís	veis	abolís	aisláis
valen	vienen	ven	*no se usa*	aíslan
valía	venía	veía	abolía	aislaba
valías	venías	veías	abolías	aislabas
valía	venía	veía	abolía	aislaba
valíamos	veníamos	veíamos	abolíamos	aislábamos
valíais	veníais	veíais	abolíais	aislabais
valían	venían	veían	abolían	aislaban
valí	vine	vi	abolí	aislé
valiste	viniste	viste	abolimos	aislaste
valió	vino	vio	abolió	aisló
valimos	vinimos	vimos	abolimos	aislamos
vallsteis	vinisteis	visteis	abolisteis	aislasteis
valieron	vinieron	vieron	abolieron	aislaron
valdré	vendré	veré	aboliré	aislaré
valdrás	vendrás	verás	abolirás	aislarás
valdrá	vendrá	verá	abolirá	aislará
valdremos	vendremos	veremos	aboliremos	aislaremos
valdréis	vendréis	veréis	aboliréis	aislaréis
valdrán	vendrán	verán	abolirán	aislarán
valdría	vendría	vería	aboliría	aislaría
valdrías	vendrías	verías	abolirías	aislarias
valdría	vendría	vería	abolirían	aislaría
valdríamos	vendríamos	veríamos	aboliríamos	aislaríamos
valdríais	vendríais	veríais	aboliríais	aislaríais
valdrían	vendrían	verían	abolirían	aislarían
valga	venga	vea	*no se usa*	aísle
valgas	vengas	veas	*no se usa*	aísles
valga	venga	vea	*no se usa*	aísle
valgamos	vengamos	veamos	*no se usa*	aislemos
valgáis	vengáis	veáis	*no se usa*	aisléis
valgan	vengan	vean	*no se usa*	aíslen
valiera, -se	viniera, -se	viera, -se	aboliera, -se	aíslara, -se
valieras, -ses	vinieras, -ses	vieras, -ses	abolieras, -ses	aislaras, -ses
valiera, -se	viniera, -se	viera, -se	aboliera, -se	aislara, -se
valiéramos, -semos	viniéramos, -semos	viéramos, -semos	aboliéramos, -semos	aisláramos, -semos
valierais, -seis	vinierais, -seis	vierais, -seis	abolierais, -seis	aislarais, -seis
valieran, -sen	vinieran, -sen	vieran, -sen	abolieran, -sen	aislaran, -sen
vale (tú)	ven (tú)	ve (tú)	*no se usa*	aísla (tú)
valed (vosotros/as)	venid (vosotros/as)	ved (vosotros/as)	abolid (vosotros/as)	aislad (vosotros/as)
valiendo,	viniendo,	viendo,	aboliendo,	aislando,
valido	venido	visto	abolido	aislado

		59 adquirir	60 prohibir	61 reñir	62 volcar
indicativo	**presente**	adquiero	prohíbo	riño	vuelco
		adquieres	prohíbes	riñes	vuelcas
		adquiere	prohíbe	riñe	vuelca
		adquirimos	prohibimos	reñimos	volcamos
		adquirís	prohibís	reñís	volcáis
		adquieren	prohíben	riñen	vuelcan
	pretérito imperfecto	adquiría	prohibía	reñía	volcaba
		adquirías	prohibías	reñías	volcabas
		adquiría	prohibía	reñía	volcaba
		adquiríamos	prohibíamos	reñíamos	volcábamos
		adquirías	prohibíais	reñíais	volcabais
		adquirían	prohibían	reñían	volcaban
	pretérito indefinido	adquirí	prohibí	reñí	volqué
		adquiriste	prohibiste	reñiste	volcaste
		adquirió	prohibió	riñó	volcó
		adquirimos	prohibimos	reñimos	volcamos
		adquiristeis	prohibisteis	reñisteis	volcasteis
		adquirieron	prohibieron	riñeron	volcaron
	futuro	adquiriré	prohibiré	reñiré	volcaré
		adquirirás	prohibirás	reñirás	volcarás
		adquirirá	prohibirá	reñirá	volcará
		adquiriremos	prohibiremos	reñiremos	volcaremos
		adquiriréis	prohibiréis	reñiréis	volcaréis
		adquirirán	prohibirán	reñirán	volcarán
	condicional	adquiriría	prohibiría	reñiría	volcaría
		adquirirías	prohibirías	reñirías	volcarías
		adquiriría	prohibiría	reñiría	volcaría
		adquiriríamos	prohibiríamos	reñiríamos	volcaríamos
		adquiriríais	prohibiríais	reñiríais	volcaríais
		adquirirían	prohibirían	reñirían	volcarían
subjuntivo	**presente**	adquiera	prohíba	riña	vuelque
		adquieras	prohíbas	riñas	vuelques
		adquiera	prohíba	riña	vuelque
		adquiramos	prohibamos	riñamos	volquemos
		adquiráis	prohibáis	riñáis	volquéis
		adquieran	prohíban	riñan	vuelquen
	imperfecto	adquiriera, -se	prohibiera, -se	riñera, -se	volcara, -se
		adquirieras, -ses	prohibieras, -ses	riñeras, -ses	volcaras, -ses
		adquiriera, -se	prohibiera, -se	riñera, -se	volcara, -se
		adquiriéramos, -semos	prohibiéramos, -semos	riñéramos, -semos	volcáramos, -semos
		adquirierais, -seis	prohibierais, -seis	riñerais, -seis	volcarais, -seis
		adquirieran, -sen	prohibieran, -sen	riñeran, -sen	volcaran, -sen
	imperativo	adquiere (tú)	prohíbe (tú)	riñe (tú)	vuelca (tú)
		adquirid (vosotros/as)	prohibid (vosotros/as)	reñid (vosotros/as)	volcad (vosotros/as)
	gerundio, participio	adquiriendo,	prohibiendo,	riñendo,	volcando,
		adquirido	prohibido	reñido	volcado